MW00861269

NEW
TESTAMENT
THEOLOGY

NEW TESTAMENT THEOLOGY

Magnifying God in Christ

Thomas R. Schreiner

Baker Academic
a division of Baker Publishing Group
Grand Rapids, Michigan

© 2008 by Thomas R. Schreiner

Published by Baker Academic
a division of Baker Publishing Group
P.O. Box 6287, Grand Rapids, MI 49516-6287
www.bakeracademic.com

Printed in the United States of America

All rights reserved. No part of this publication may be reproduced, stored in a retrieval system, or transmitted in any form or by any means—for example, electronic, photocopy, recording—without the prior written permission of the publisher. The only exception is brief quotations in printed reviews.

Library of Congress Cataloging-in-Publication Data
Schreiner, Thomas R.
    New Testament theology : magnifying God in Christ / Thomas R. Schreiner.
        p.   cm.
    Includes bibliographical references and indexes.
    ISBN 978-0-8010-2680-5 (cloth)
    1. Bible. N. T.—Theology. I. Title.
BS2397.S47 2008
230—dc22   2007043653

Unless otherwise indicated, Scripture quotations are from The Holy Bible, English Standard Version, copyright © 2001 by Crossway Bibles, a division of Good News Publishers. Used by permission. All rights reserved.

Scripture quotations labeled HCSB are from the Holman Christian Standard Bible, copyright 1999, 2000, 2002, 2003 by Holman Bible Publishers. Used by permission.

Scripture quotations labeled KJV are from the King James Version of the Bible.

Scripture quotations labeled NASB are from the New American Standard Bible®, copyright © 1960, 1962, 1963, 1968, 1971, 1972, 1973, 1975, 1977, 1995 by The Lockman Foundation. Used by permission.

Scripture quotations labeled NIV are from the Holy Bible, New International Version®. NIV®. Copyright © 1973, 1978, 1984 by Biblica, Inc.™ Used by permission of Zondervan. All rights reserved worldwide. www.zondervan.com

Scripture quotations labeled NJB are from THE NEW JERUSALEM BIBLE, copyright © 1985 by Darton, Longman & Todd, Ltd. and Doubleday, a division of Random House, Inc. Reprinted by permission.

Scripture quotations labeled NRSV are from the New Revised Standard Version of the Bible, copyright © 1989, by the Division of Christian Education of the National Council of the Churches of Christ in the United States of America. Used by permission. All rights reserved.

Scripture quotations labeled RSV are from the Revised Standard Version of the Bible, copyright 1952 [2nd edition, 1971] by the Division of Christian Education of the National Council of the Churches of Christ in the United States of America. Used by permission. All rights reserved.

Scripture quotations labeled TNIV are from the Holy Bible, Today's New International Version®. TNIV®. Copyright © 2001, 2005 by Biblica, Inc.™ Used by permission of Zondervan. All rights reserved worldwide. www.zondervan.com

The internet addresses, email addresses, and phone numbers in this book are accurate at the time of publication. They are provided as a resource. Baker Publishing Group does not endorse them or vouch for their content or permanence.

To Bruce Ware
Beloved friend, colleague,
and inspiration

Contents

Preface

Writing this book has been both a joyful and frustrating experience. The joy has come in learning, for as I wrote, new vistas opened before me, and I saw truths that previously were hidden from me. The frustration came from the time it took to put this book in final form, along with the recognition that it could never quite match up with my hopes and desires. I wrote the first three drafts without consulting any secondary sources. Before I wrote, I carefully took notes on the entire NT, noting what NT authors discussed, so that my NT theology would be anchored by the text. I proceeded this way so that I would be compelled to work inductively from the biblical text instead of deriving my outline or general train of thought from others. Even in these three drafts, however, I am indebted to those who have taught me and whose work I have read over the years. After writing the initial drafts, I read secondary sources. Naturally, such reading led to further revisions, and I am immensely grateful to the outstanding work of many scholars who have sharpened my understanding of NT theology. My hope is that this book will function as a useful text for pastors and students. Perhaps scholars will benefit from it as well.

Thematic versus Book-by-Book Approaches

How should a NT theology be written? For readers who are interested in a more in-depth discussion of this matter historically and in terms of method, I recommend the appendix. Here I ask whether the individual contributions of each NT writer can be analyzed separately.[1] One

1. So Marshall 2004; Thielman 2005.

advantage of such an approach is that a sharper profile of the theology of each writer or book is featured. If NT theology is presented thematically, the unique contribution of particular writers may be swallowed up by the prominence of, say, Paul. Letters such as 2 Peter and Jude may be submerged or only surface occasionally. The contribution of the entire NT canon may be slighted, and hence the claim to be a NT theology called into question.

Investigating each book separately, then, opens some fresh windows in doing NT theology, and a thematic approach inevitably omits some of the distinctives uncovered in the book-by-book structure. Nevertheless, I have chosen a thematic approach in this work because a thematic structure also has some advantages. The coherence and the unity of NT theology are explained more clearly if a NT theology is presented thematically. Is a study of each individual writer truly a NT theology, or is it a theology of Matthew, Mark, Luke, Paul, and so forth? Further, if one studies Matthew first, then Mark, then Luke, and so on, the reader may grow weary of three separate studies on the Son of Man, the Son of God, and Jesus the Messiah. I am not saying, however, that a study of each book separately is illegitimate. Such an approach opens vistas onto the text that are obscured, at least in part, by a thematic approach. I reject the claim that there is one correct way to write a NT theology. The subject matter of NT theology is too vast and comprehensive to be exhausted by any single approach. Barr rightly says that "there can be no such thing as the one appropriate method for biblical theology."[2] No NT theology will ever do justice to the complexity and beauty of the NT. Each of the various approaches and perspectives can cast a different light upon the NT, and in that sense having a number of different approaches is helpful.[3] Fruitful NT theologies could be written from the standpoint of NT eschatology, the people of God, Christology, ethics, and so on.

In Defense of a Thematic Approach

I believe, however, that a thematic approach is particularly needed today, with the proviso that it is truly rooted in biblical theology. Guthrie studied the NT in terms of its major themes, but his work borders on a systematic theology.[4] Schlatter, on the other hand, explored NT theology

2. Barr 1999: 61. See also his remarks on p. 342.
3. For instance, redaction criticism is useful in detecting distinctive themes in the Gospels, though recent work on the Gospels rightly emphasizes that they were written not merely for specific communities but for all Christians. See the programmatic work of Bauckham 1998; see also Hengel 2000: 98, 106–7.
4. Guthrie 1981.

from a thematic standpoint in a creative and insightful manner.[5] Many NT scholars shy away from such an approach today, fearing that it too closely resembles systematic theology. They worry about domesticating the text by our own categories. Some scholars, perhaps even many, think that there is no such thing as a unified NT theology. For those who believe that the NT represents conflicting theologies, the whole enterprise is hopeless from the outset. I will say something in the appendix about why writing a NT theology is justified, and why we can assume that NT theology is coherent and consistent, not contradictory. Of course, those who think that there are contradictions are probably not much happier about a NT theology that focuses on individual writers and writings. After all, if the whole of the NT contains contradictions, there is no reason to think that individual writers are spared from such.

Let me return to what was noted above. A thematic approach runs the danger of domesticating the text and squeezing out the diversity of the NT. Still, it is a risk worth taking. Our Western world is worried about metanarratives, and hence much of the work in NT studies examines a small part of the NT, or even a single verse in the NT. It is safer to present one's conclusions on a single verse than it is to say what the entire NT is about. Perhaps it is saner as well! And no NT theology is helpful if the writer has not gotten dirty by studying the text inductively, piece by piece. And yet there is another side to the story. We understand each of the pieces in the NT by our understanding of the whole, by our worldview, by our own metanarrative. We can fall into the illusion that if we study a "part," then we are dealing with just the "evidence," "the hard phenomena" of the text. But our understanding of any piece of evidence is also affected by our standpoint, our worldview. We do not assess any piece of evidence from a neutral and objective standpoint. Hence, there is a dialogue between the inductive and deductive that constantly occurs. If we do not venture to consider NT theology as a whole, we are in danger of skewing the particular piece of evidence that we study. Examining the NT thematically, then, may assist us in understanding the pieces that make up the NT.

I have already noted the benefit of considering each writer individually. But there is another liability in studying each writer individually. We need to recall that none of the NT documents claims to be the "theology" of the writer in question. This is particularly obvious in the case of the epistles. The Epistles are occasional writings directed to specific situations and circumstances in the life of churches. It is somewhat distorting, then, to write a theology of, say, Jude or James. We can hardly claim that they have packaged the whole of their theology into such short

5. Schlatter 1997; 1999.

letters. Of course, Paul is different in that he wrote thirteen letters (in my view), and so we have a larger corpus from which to construct his thought.[6] But even in Paul's case we do not have a complete map of his convictions. Some holes still exist.

In the same way, more can be said about Matthew and Mark, Luke-Acts, and the Johannine writings than can be said about Jude. Useful studies of the particular emphases of these writings have been produced. We need to remember, however, the constraints under which the Gospel writers composed their works. I am assuming at this juncture that they were historians *and* theologians.[7] They were not free, in other words, to construct a theology sundered from the actual words and works of Jesus. When we compare John to the Synoptic Gospels, it is obvious that different perspectives add tremendous richness to our understanding of Jesus Christ. The differences between John and the Synoptics are obvious to the most elementary reader. Furthermore, redaction criticism has demonstrated that the Synoptics differ from one another as well. Still, I believe that the Gospels are grounded in history.[8] The diversity of perspectives indicates neither a lack of interest in history nor the presence of a freeness to compose in accord with one's desires. We have four Gospels because the depth and breadth of Jesus Christ could not be captured by a single one. Here the recent emphasis that the Gospels were intended for wider audiences is a salutary correction to the view that the Gospels were limited to specific communities.[9]

A grasp of the nature of the Gospels, grounded as they are in history, is imperative for doing NT theology. The Gospel writers focus on the work and words of Jesus before his death and resurrection and the gift of the Spirit. Therefore, the Gospels should not be misconstrued as full-orbed theologies of Matthew, Mark, Luke, and John. These authors are faithful to the history, to the events that occurred before the resurrection and the gift of the Spirit. They are not attempting to compose theological treatises that summarize their theology. I am not denying that the Gospel writers are theologians, nor am I suggesting that the Gospels are bare history.

6. In my judgment, all the letters attributed to Paul are authentic. The Pastoral Epistles are the first to be contested, but solid reasons exist to support authenticity. See Fee 1988: 23–26; W. Mounce 2000: lxvi–cxxix; Knight 1992: 21–52; Ellis 1992. For a full discussion that opts against Pauline authorship, see Marshall 1999: 57–92.

7. See Bauckham 2006, where the role of the earliest eyewitnesses is emphasized. I do not agree with all of Bauckham's conclusions. For instance, I believe that the apostle John wrote the Fourth Gospel. Still, Bauckham rightly argues that the Gospel traditions stem from eyewitness testimony.

8. See Barnett 1999. Meier (1991; 1994; 2001) takes a more skeptical approach than I do regarding the historical Jesus, yet in his outstanding and careful work he establishes a clear historical core relative to Jesus.

9. Bauckham 1998.

The Gospels are theological history, containing an interpretation of the works and words of Jesus of Nazareth. Nevertheless, they are *gospels* that bear witness to Jesus Christ and his historical work. They are located at a certain juncture in the history of salvation. When considering the theology of the Gospels, we must attend to the location of the writer on the redemptive-historical timeline. Some matters in the Gospels remain undeveloped because the promises are not realized until the death and resurrection of Christ. Hence, the Gospels conclude with the expectation and promise that the Spirit will be poured out on God's people. The blessing of the Spirit is not given, however, in the Gospels themselves. In this sense, the rest of the NT should be located in a different place in salvation history than the Gospels.

In summary, none of the NT writings contains the whole of what is taught in the NT. They are accurate but partial and fragmentary witnesses. They witness truly but not exhaustively to the gospel of Jesus Christ. Hence, a thematic approach to NT theology is invaluable because it attempts to capture the whole of what is taught by considering all twenty-seven books.

The Question of a Center

Is there a single center for NT theology? The question of a center has long been debated, and many different centers have been proposed. I think it is safe to say that no alleged center will ever become the consensus. In one sense, having several different centers is useful, as NT theology can be studied helpfully from a number of different perspectives. Since the various perspectives are interlocking and not mutually exclusive, there are a diversity of ways by which the NT can be explored. Furthermore, examining the NT from different angles allows new light to be shed upon the text. Since the subject matter of NT theology is God himself, we are not surprised to learn that none of our scholarly endeavors ever exhausts the subject matter.

It is illuminating to consider NT theology from a twofold perspective. First, God's purpose in all that he does is to bring honor to himself and to Jesus Christ. The NT is radically God-centered. We could say that the NT is about God magnifying himself in Christ through the Spirit. We could easily fail to see the supremacy of God and the centrality of Christ in the NT precisely because these themes are part of the warp and woof of the NT. Sometimes we fail to see what is most obvious, what is right before our eyes. The focus on God and Christ may be taken for granted, and we become interested in themes that are "new" to us, themes that we have not seen before. Any NT theology that does not focus on what

God has done in Christ, however, fails to see what is fundamental to and pervasive in the text of Scripture.

Second, the centrality of God in Christ leads to abstraction if it is not closely related to the history of salvation, to the fulfillment of God's promises.[10] We have in the Scriptures the story of God's saving plan (which includes judgment, of course).[11] The NT unfolds the fulfillment of the promises made in the OT. One of the striking themes in the NT is that of the "already–not yet." God has inaugurated his kingdom, but he has not consummated it. He has begun to fulfill his saving promises, but he has not yet completed all that he has started. No one can grasp the message of the NT if redemptive history is slighted. The NT does not negate the OT but fulfills it. One of the major tasks of any NT theology is to explain how this is so. Redemptive history is fundamental, then, to grasping the message of the NT. Still, God's ultimate purpose is not the fulfillment of his plan. He must have a purpose, an aim, a goal in such a plan. Here the purpose of all of salvation history emerges. God works out his saving plan so that he would be magnified in Christ, so that his name would be honored.

In most instances when citing a text from the Synoptic Gospels for which there are parallels, I cite only Matthew and then indicate that there are parallels from Mark or Luke or both. No significance should be ascribed to my citation of Matthew. I have selected it simply because it is the first Gospel listed in the canon of the NT as it has come down to us. I am not suggesting in any case that Matthew is the first Gospel. I chose to cite Matthew rather than Mark because those who did not read my preface might think that I was endorsing the two-source view of the Synoptic Problem. I am not intending any solution to the source-critical issue in citing Matthew. In any case, this book does not depend upon or promote any particular view of the Synoptic Problem. The focus is on the final form of the Gospels, not the order in which they were written.

Instead of citing numerous secondary sources, I have cited authors representatively. The body of literature in NT studies far exceeds the ability of anyone to even come close to reading all that is written. Hence, any citation of secondary sources must be selective. I hope that what I have cited is inclusive of various points of view. On controversial matters I have tried to point readers to commentaries, articles, and monographs in which the verse or issue is discussed in more detail. Given the wealth of commentaries, many different choices could have been made. I cite the commentaries that have been most helpful and insightful for me.

---

10. Hooker (2006: 75–76) maintains that what is fundamental in NT theology is what God has done in Christ.

11. Hamilton (2006a) argues that the center for all of Scripture is the glory of God in salvation through judgment.

Throughout the book I cite items from the bibliography by author and date, except for dictionary articles, which I cite according to author, dictionary, and page numbers. For bibliographic information on dictionaries, see the abbreviation list. Unless indicated otherwise, Scripture citations come from the English Standard Version.

Acknowledgments

I am grateful to Jason Meyer, who read several chapters of the book and provided insightful feedback that helped me to clarify its purpose. Also deserving special thanks is John Meade, who read the entire manuscript and pointed out a number of errors and raised pertinent questions that needed to be addressed. He also provided immense help in assembling the bibliography. Justin Taylor carefully read several chapters of the book and suggested numerous changes that improved its quality. I am grateful to Justin for his friendship and for taking time out of his busy schedule to read portions of the book. Matt Crawford also helped me with the bibliography and footnotes in the final stages and saved me from a number of errors with his time-intensive and detailed work. I am thankful for his outstanding help in such tedious work. Matthew Montonini generously compiled the name and Scripture indexes. I am extremely grateful to him for his labor of love. I also extend thanks to him for his friendship and support. Jim Kinney from Baker Academic has supported and encouraged me during the years in which this book was written. I am delighted that Baker Academic is willing to publish such a work. Further, Brian Bolger has shepherded this book through the editing process and has improved it in countless ways. The Southern Baptist Theological Seminary deserves special thanks, as I could not have finished this work without the sabbatical leave granted by the seminary. I am particularly thankful to the president, R. Albert Mohler Jr., and the vice president, Russell Moore, for their encouragement and support of scholarship. I am thankful for my wife, Diane. Her untiring love, support, and strength have been an inspiration. It is her witness that led me to see that God is dazzlingly beautiful, and that Jesus Christ deserves all honor and praise. Finally, I dedicate this book to Bruce Ware. He has been a dear friend and brother for nearly thirty years. I have learned much from him, both theologically and personally. His godly example has been a constant inspiration to me.

Abbreviations

Bible Texts and Versions

ESV	English Standard Version
HCSB	Holman Christian Standard Bible
KJV	King James Version
LXX	Septuagint
MT	Masoretic Text
NASB	New American Standard Bible
NIV	New International Version
NJB	The New Jerusalem Bible
NRSV	New Revised Standard Version
NT	New Testament
OT	Old Testament
RSV	Revised Standard Version
TNIV	Today's New International Version

Apocrypha and Septuagint

1–4 Esd.	1–4 Esdras
1–4 Macc.	1–4 Maccabees
Sir.	Sirach
Tob.	Tobit
Wis.	Wisdom of Solomon

Old Testament Pseudepigrapha

Apoc. Mos.	*Apocalypse of Moses*
2 Bar.	*2 Baruch* (*Syriac Apocalypse*)
1 En.	*1 Enoch*
4 Ezra	*4 Ezra*
Jub.	*Jubilees*
Let. Aris.	*Letter of Aristeas*
Odes Sol.	*Odes of Solomon*
Ps.-Phoc.	Pseudo-Phocylides
Pss. Sol.	*Psalms of Solomon*
Sib. Or.	*Sibylline Oracles*
T. Benj.	*Testament of Benjamin*
T. Dan	*Testament of Dan*
T. Jos.	*Testament of Joseph*
T. Jud.	*Testament of Judah*
T. Levi	*Testament of Levi*
T. Mos.	*Testament of Moses*
T. Naph.	*Testament of Naphtali*
T. Reu.	*Testament of Reuben*
T. Sim.	*Testament of Simeon*

Qumran

CD-A	*Damascus Document*[a]
CD-B	*Damascus Document*[b]
1QH[a]	*1QHodayot*[a]

1QM	*1QWar Scroll*
1QpHab	*1QPesher Habakkuk*
1QS	*1QRule of the Community*
1QSa	*1QRule of the Congregation*
1QSb	*1QRule of Benedictions*
3Q15	*3QCopper Scroll*
4Q246	*Apocryphon of Daniel*
4Q369	*4QPrayer of Enosh (?)*
4QcommGen^a	*4QCommentary on Genesis A*
4QFlor	*4QFlorilegium*
4QMMT	*4QHalakhic Letter*
4QpIsa^a	*4QIsaiah Pesher^a*
4QSM	*4QSefer ha-Milhamah*
11QMelch.	*Melchizedek*
11QT^a	*11Qtemple Scroll^a*

Rabbinic Literature

m. 'Abot	*Mishnah 'Abot*
m. Ber.	*Mishnah Berakot*
m. Sanh.	*Mishnah Sanhedrin*
m. Soṭah	*Mishnah Soṭah*
m. Sukkah	*Mishnah Sukkah*
y. Ber.	*Jerusalem Talmud Berakot*

Targumic Texts

Frg. Tg.	*Fragmentary Targum*

Apostolic Fathers

Barn.	*Epistle of Barnabas*
Did.	*Didache*
Ign. *Eph.*	Ignatius, *To the Ephesians*

Dio Chrysostom

Ven.	*Venator (Or. 7)*

Epictetus

Ench.	*Enchiridion*

Josephus

Ag. Ap.	*Against Apion*
Ant.	*Jewish Antiquities*
J.W.	*Jewish War*

Juvenal

Sat.	*Satirae*

Ovid

Am.	*Amores*

Philo

Cherubim	*On the Cherubim*
Confusion	*On the Confusion of Tongues*
Decalogue	*On the Decalogue*
Flight	*On Flight and Finding*
Hypothetica	*Hypothetica*
QG	*Questions and Answers on Genesis*
Spec. Laws	*On the Special Laws*

Plutarch

Conj. praec.	*Conjugalia praecepta*

Seneca

Ben.	*De beneficiis*
Helv.	*Ad Helviam*
Ira	*De ira*

Tacitus

Ann.	*Annales*

Periodicals, Reference Works, and Serials

AB	Anchor Bible
ABD	*Anchor Bible Dictionary,* ed. D. N. Freedman (6 vols.; New York: Doubleday, 1992)
ABRL	Anchor Bible Reference Library
AGJU	Arbeiten zur Geschichte des antiken Judentums und des Urchristentums
ALGHJ	Arbeiten zur Literatur und Geschichte des hellenistischen Judentums
AnBib	Analecta biblica
ATANT	Abhandlungen zur Theologie des Alten und Neuen Testaments
AUSDDS	Andrews University Seminary Doctoral Dissertation Series
BA	*Biblical Archaeologist*
BBB	Bonner biblische Beiträge
BBR	*Bulletin for Biblical Research*
BDAG	*Greek-English Lexicon of the New Testament and Other Early Christian Literature,* by W. Bauer, F. W. Danker, W. F. Arndt, and F. W. Gingrich (3rd ed.; Chicago: University of Chicago Press, 1999)
BECNT	Baker Exegetical Commentary on the New Testament
BETL	Bibliotheca ephemeridum theologicarum lovaniensium
BevT	Beiträge zur evangelischen Theologie
BGBE	Beiträge zur Geschichte der biblischen Exegese
Bib	*Biblica*
BIS	Biblical Interpretation Series
BJRL	*Bulletin of the John Rylands University Library of Manchester*
BNTC	Black's New Testament Commentaries
BSac	*Bibliotheca sacra*
BZ	*Biblische Zeitschrift*
BZNW	Beihefte zur Zeitschrift für die neutestamentliche Wissenschaft
CBQ	*Catholic Biblical Quarterly*
CNT	Commentaire de Nouveau Testament
ConBNT	Coniectanea biblica: New Testament Series
CTJ	*Calvin Theological Journal*
DJG	*Dictionary of Jesus and the Gospels,* ed. J. B. Green and S. McKnight (Downers Grove, IL: InterVarsity Press, 1992)
DLNT	*Dictionary of the Later New Testament and Its Developments,* ed. R. P. Martin and P. H. Davids (Downers Grove, IL: InterVarsity Press, 1997)
DPL	*Dictionary of Paul and His Letters,* ed. G. F. Hawthorne and R. P. Martin (Downers Grove,

	IL: InterVarsity Press, 1993)	IVPNTC	IVP New Testament Commentary
EBib	*Etudes bibliques*	*JBL*	*Journal of Biblical Literature*
EDNT	*Exegetical Dictionary of the New Testament,* ed. H. Balz and G. Schneider (ET; 3 vols.; Grand Rapids: Eerdmans, 1990–1993)	JBLMS	Journal of Biblical Literature Monograph Series
EKKNT	Evangelisch-katholischer Kommentar zum Neuen Testament	*JETS*	*Journal of the Evangelical Theological Society*
		JPTSup	Journal of Pentecostal Theology: Supplement Series
EvQ	*Evangelical Quarterly*	JSJSup	Supplements to the Journal for the Study of Judaism
ExAud	*Ex auditu*		
ExpTim	*Expository Times*		
FFNT	Foundations and Facets: New Testament	*JSNT*	*Journal for the Study of the New Testament*
FRLANT	Forschungen zur Religion und Literatur des Alten und Neuen Testaments	JSNTSup	Journal for the Study of the New Testament: Supplement Series
HBT	*Horizons in Biblical Theology*	JSOTSup	Journal for the Study of the Old Testament: Supplement Series
HDR	Harvard Dissertations in Religion	*JTC*	*Journal for Theology and the Church*
HNTC	Harper's New Testament Commentaries	*JTS*	*Journal of Theological Studies*
HTKNT	Herders theologischer Kommentar zum Neuen Testament	*JTT*	*Journal of Translation and Textlinguistics*
HTR	*Harvard Theological Review*	KEK	Kritisch-exegetischer Kommentar über das Neue Testament (Meyer-Kommentar)
HUT	Hermeneutische Untersuchungen zur Theologie	KSt	Kohlhammer Studienbücher
IBC	Interpretation: A Bible Commentary for Teaching and Preaching	*LS*	*Louvain Studies*
		MdB	Le monde de la Bible
IBS	*Irish Biblical Studies*	NAC	New American Commentary
ICC	International Critical Commentary	NACSBT	NAC Studies in Bible and Theology
IDB	*The Interpreter's Dictionary of the Bible,* ed. G. A. Buttrick (4 vols.; Nashville: Abingdon, 1962)	NCB	New Century Bible
		NDBT	*New Dictionary of Biblical Theology,* ed. T. D. Alexander and B. S. Rosner (Downers Grove,
Int	*Interpretation*		

	IL: InterVarsity Press, 2000)	SBJT	*Southern Baptist Journal of Theology*
Neot	*Neotestamentica*	SBLDS	Society of Biblical Literature Dissertation Series
NIBCNT	New International Biblical Commentary on the New Testament		
NICNT	New International Commentary on the New Testament	SBLMS	Society of Biblical Literature Monograph Series
NICOT	New International Commentary on the Old Testament	SBT	Studies in Biblical Theology
		SBTS	Sources for Biblical and Theological Study
NIDNTT	*New International Dictionary of New Testament Theology*, ed. C. Brown (4 vols.; Grand Rapids: Zondervan, 1975–1985)	SESJ	Suomen eksegeettisen seuran julkaisuja
		SHS	Scripture and Hermeneutics Series
		SJLA	Studies in Judaism in Late Antiquity
NIGTC	New International Greek Testament Commentary	*SJT*	*Scottish Journal of Theology*
NIVAC	NIV Application Commentary	SJTOP	Scottish Journal of Theology Occasional Papers
NovT	*Novum Testamentum*	SNT	Studien zum Neuen Testament
NovTSup	Novum Testamentum Supplements	SNTSMS	Society for New Testament Studies Monograph Series
NTAbh	Neutestamentliche Abhandlungen		
NTOA	Novum Testamentum et Orbis Antiquus	SNTSU	Studien zum Neuen Testament und seiner Umwelt
NTS	*New Testament Studies*		
NTT	New Testament Theology	SNTW	Studies of the New Testament and Its World
OTL	Old Testament Library		
PBM	Paternoster Biblical Monographs	SOTBT	Studies in Old Testament Biblical Theology
PBTM	Paternoster Biblical and Theological Monographs	SP	Sacra Pagina
		SR	*Studies in Religion*
PNTC	Pillar New Testament Commentary	StBL	Studies in Biblical Literature
PSB	*Princeton Seminary Bulletin*	TB	Theologische Bücherei: Neudrucke und Berichte aus dem 20. Jahrhundert
QD	Quaestiones disputatae		
RB	*Revue biblique*	*TBei*	*Theologische Beiträge*
RTR	*Reformed Theological Review*	*TDNT*	*Theological Dictionary of the New Testament*, ed. G. Kittel and G. Friedrich, trans. G. W. Bromiley
SBEC	Studies in the Bible and Early Christianity		

	(10 vols.; Grand Rapids: Eerdmans, 1964–1976)
TJ	*Trinity Journal*
TJT	*Toronto Journal of Theology*
TNTC	Tyndale New Testament Commentaries
TOTC	Tyndale Old Testament Commentaries
TPINTC	TPI New Testament Commentaries
TS	*Theological Studies*
TSAJ	Texte und Studien zum antiken Judentum
TUGAL	Texte und Untersuchungen zur Geschichte der altchristlichen Literatur
TynBul	*Tyndale Bulletin*
TZ	*Theologische Zeitschrift*
USQR	*Union Seminary Quarterly Review*

VCSup	Supplements to Vigiliae christianae
VT	*Vetus Testamentum*
WBC	Word Biblical Commentary
WEC	Wycliffe Exegetical Commentary
WMANT	Wissenschaftliche Monographien zum Alten und Neuen Testament
WTJ	*Westminster Theological Journal*
WUNT	Wissenschaftliche Untersuchungen zum Neuen Testament
ZNW	*Zeitschrift für die neutestamentliche Wissenschaft und die Kunde der älteren Kirche*
ZTK	*Zeitschrift für Theologie und Kirche*

Introduction

The thesis advanced in this book is that NT theology is God-focused, Christ-centered, and Spirit-saturated, but the work of the Father, Son, and Spirit must be understood along a salvation-historical timeline; that is, God's promises are already fulfilled but not yet consummated in Christ Jesus. We will see that the ministry of Jesus Christ and the work of the Spirit are fundamental for the fulfilling of God's promises. The coming of Jesus Christ and the work of the Spirit are the prime indications that God is beginning to fulfill the saving promises made to Abraham.

In the succeeding chapters we will examine in more detail the theme that God's saving promises in Christ and through the Spirit have already been fulfilled but have not yet reached their consummation.[1] In this chapter the aim is to give a kind of guided tour or small taste of the main thesis of the book, so that readers will see that the primacy of God is communicated in a story that unfolds God's saving work in history. We could say that God is central to the NT witness, but such a claim without elaboration could be viewed as abstract and removed from reality. I will argue for the centrality of God in Christ in the concrete and specific witness of the NT as it unfolds God's saving work in history. Another way to put this is that God will receive all the glory for his work in Christ by the Spirit as he works out his purpose in redemptive history. Further, redemptive history is characterized by inaugurated but not consummated eschatology, so that the glory that belongs to God has not yet reached its zenith but it will.

1. The language of "already–not yet" has rightly become a commonplace in NT theology.

The Old Testament Backdrop

Before surveying the NT witness, we need to take a cursory look at the OT. We could summarize the OT under the rubrics of creation, fall, and redemption. The centrality of God is featured in the fact that he is the creator of all. God's sovereign creation of the universe is a pervasive theme in the OT, indicating that he is Lord of the cosmos and the central actor of the OT story. He made human beings in his image so that they would display his glory, reflect his character, and rule the world for God (Gen. 1:26–27; 2:15–17). Adam and Eve rejected God's lordship and struck out on their own. God's judgment of Adam and Eve also communicates his lordship and is a preview to the pervasive theme of judgment in the OT. Every act of God's judgment demonstrates that he is sovereign and Lord. Still, the story line of the OT concludes not with judgment but with the promise of redemption. This promise of redemption informs the OT story and the NT witness as well.

We can fairly say that the OT is animated with an eschatological hope. Gen. 3:15 forecasts a day when the seed of the woman will triumph over the seed of the serpent. Subsequent history appeared to mock the promise, for the seed of the serpent ruled over human beings during the days of Noah and at the Tower of Babel. God's promise of blessing for the whole world focused upon one man, Abraham. The Lord promised Abraham and his descendants land, seed, and a blessing that would encompass the entire world (e.g., Gen. 12:1–3; 18:18; 22:17–18; 26:3–4; 28:14–15; 35:12–13). The future character of the promise is evident, for Abraham, Isaac, and Jacob did not have a multitude of children, nor did they possess the land of the promise, and worldwide blessing was far from being realized.

The promise begins to be fulfilled in the Pentateuch, for the people of Israel multiplied in accord with God's promise. Then the promise of the land of Canaan became theirs during the days of Joshua. It seemed that the nation was poised to become the vehicle for worldwide blessing, but a cycle of sin and judgment ensued in the days of the judges. David's accession as king and the everlasting covenant made with him (2 Sam. 7) demonstrated that worldwide blessing would come to pass through a Davidic descendant. But the story of the kings of Judah, not to mention the kings of Israel, sadly disappointed. The nation spiraled downward until it was carried into exile by Babylon in 586 BC. Yahweh promised through the prophets, however, the dawning of a new covenant (Jer. 31:31–34), a coming kingdom (Obad. 21), a rebuilding of David's fallen booth (Amos 9:11–15), a new day for Jerusalem and Zion (Joel 3:15–21; Zeph. 3:15–20), a pouring out of God's Spirit (Joel 2:28), a day when the Lord would give his people a new heart and Spirit so that they would obey him (Ezek. 36:26–27), a new exodus when God would liberate his people once again (e.g., Isa. 43:5–9), and even a new creation (Isa. 65:17–25; 66:22). None of these promises were fulfilled during the OT era, and so this brings us to the NT witness.

The Synoptic Gospels

When the ministry of Jesus commenced, these great promises, which would fulfill the original blessings pledged to Abraham and confirmed to David, had not yet come to pass. What we see in the NT witness, however, is that God's end-time promises reach their fulfillment in Jesus of Nazareth. The God-centeredness of the message may easily be missed, for it is the creator God who is fulfilling his promises in Jesus Christ. And Jesus the Messiah carried out his ministry in the power of the Spirit. The fulfillment takes place, though, in an unexpected way, for God's saving promises are inaugurated but not consummated. The NT expresses this truth in a variety of ways, but it is fundamental to the entire message of the NT documents, whether it be the Synoptic Gospels, John, Paul, Peter, Hebrews, or Revelation. Here I want to sketch it in God's work relative to salvation history, so that it is apparent to the reader that an inaugurated but unconsummated eschatology is pervasive in the NT.

In the next chapter I will enlarge on the Synoptic understanding of the kingdom. Here I simply observe briefly the "already–not yet" character of the kingdom in the message of Jesus. Jesus declared that God's kingdom had already arrived in his ministry, and its arrival was demonstrated in the exorcism of demons by the Spirit (Matt. 12:28).[2] Even though Jesus claimed that the kingdom had dawned in his ministry, he instructed his disciples to pray for the kingdom to come (Matt. 6:10; Luke 11:2). The saving power of the kingdom manifested itself in Jesus' ministry, but the kingdom did not come in all of its apocalyptic power. The same theme, as we will see in the next chapter, manifests itself in Jesus' parables where both the present and the future dimensions of the kingdom are featured. Moreover, Jesus declared in his ministry that the eschatological promises were realized, for he gave sight to the blind, enabled the lame to walk, cleansed lepers, opened the ears of the deaf, raised the dead, and proclaimed the good news of God's kingdom (Matt. 11:5). These promises hail from Isaiah, which proclaims the coming of a new creation where the desert blossoms, streams flow in the desert, and ravenous beasts no longer destroy (Isa. 29:17; 35). It is the day of God's salvation, when he comes to vindicate his people and rescue them

---

2. Luke (Luke 11:20) refers to the finger of God rather than the Spirit of God.

from exile. It is clear in the Gospels that Jesus' miracles and exorcisms are manifestations of the kingdom, signs that the new age has broken in. His miracles and exorcisms indicate the dawning of a new creation, and yet Jesus also taught that there is an age to come when God will judge the wicked and vindicate the righteous (e.g., Matt. 12:32; 13:39–40, 49; 24:3; 28:20; Mark 10:30; Luke 18:30; 20:35). Jewish thought regularly distinguished between "this age" and "the coming age." It seems that Jesus taught the overlap of the ages, for in his ministry the age to come penetrated this present evil age, and yet the coming age had not yet been consummated.

The promised baptism of the Holy Spirit indicated the arrival of the new age (Matt. 3:11; Mark 1:8; Luke 3:16), fulfilling the promise of the Spirit predicted in the prophets. During his ministry Jesus was the bearer of the Spirit, but after his exaltation he would become the dispenser of the Spirit. The work of the Spirit in Jesus' ministry and beyond must be interpreted against the backdrop of the OT, where the gift of the Spirit heralds God's eschatological work. We see here the trinitarian character of God's saving work, for God sent Jesus into the world so that Jesus would baptize his followers with the Holy Spirit, thereby inaugurating the fulfillment of the promise that all nations would be blessed through Abraham (Gen. 12:1–3).

There are also a number of indications in the Synoptics that the new exodus has been fulfilled in Jesus' ministry.[3] The return from Babylon predicted by Isaiah did not come to pass in all its fullness when Israel returned from exile during the days of Cyrus. The ministry of John the Baptist, some five hundred years later, commenced with the promise that God would fulfill the great promise of the new exodus (Matt. 3:3; Mark 1:2–3; Luke 3:4–6). The baptism in the Jordan River by John signaled that the people were, so to speak, entering into the land of the promise again, as they did after the first exodus when they crossed the Jordan and entered the promised land (Mark 1:5 par.). The Baptist was the new Elijah, who arrived on the scene before the coming of God's promised salvation (Matt. 11:14; 17:12; Mark 1:2, 6; Luke 1:17). The most significant and obvious indication of the fulfillment of God's promises was the coming of Jesus himself. The Gospels make it clear that he is the promised Messiah, the prophet predicted in Deut. 18:15, the Son of Man of Dan. 7, and the Son of God. And yet when Jesus came as the promised Messiah, not all of God's promises were fulfilled immediately. There is an already–not yet dimension here that is quite striking.[4]

---

3. For a fruitful exploration of the "new exodus" theme in Mark's Gospel, see Watts 2000.

4. A significant part of this book will unpack the theme of Christology, for certainly Christ himself is central to NT theology!

The transfiguration signals the already–not yet character of Jesus' life (Matt. 17:1–8 par.), for the glory and splendor of Jesus were veiled during his ministry. The transfiguration anticipated, however, the future coming of Jesus in glory, power, and majesty (cf. 2 Pet. 1:16–18). Luke emphasizes that God's covenantal promises were fulfilled in the birth of the Baptist and supremely in Jesus (Luke 1:46–55, 67–79; 2:29–32). Still, the full realization of those promises was not obtained in Jesus' ministry, for the destruction of Israel's enemies remained unfulfilled. Nevertheless, Luke clearly identifies Jesus as the fulfillment of God's covenant with Israel. This seems confirmed by the programmatic text where Jesus drew from Isa. 61 and Isa. 58 to commence his ministry (Luke 4:18–19). The eschatological promises for Israel dawned in Jesus, but, significantly, he did not cite the part from Isaiah that speaks of God's eschatological judgment, suggesting that the judgment is reserved for another and future day.

The Johannine Literature

Certainly the person who takes center stage in the Gospel of John is Jesus Christ, in whom God's promises reach a striking fulfillment. Indeed, the clarity and forthrightness of John's Christology sets it apart from the Synoptic Gospels, even though Jesus is the central character in the Synoptics as well. The Christology of John's Gospel blazes forth throughout the narrative: Jesus is the Christ, the Prophet, the Son of Man, the Son of God, and can also rightly be called God. In Jesus Christ, supremely, the promises of God are fulfilled. But John repeatedly instructs his readers that Jesus was sent by the Father and always did the Father's will. Hence, it is not as if the Father is a cipher in Johannine theology. Furthermore, Jesus promised that both he and the Father would send the Spirit to instruct and empower his disciples. The trinitarian character of this Gospel is conspicuous. Nevertheless, the Father, Son, and Spirit are not presented as loci in a systematic theology. The saving work is part of the story line of salvation.

John's Gospel is distinct from the Synoptics, for the eschatological character of the Gospel of John is expressed not by the kingdom of God but by the term "eternal life."[5] We simply note here that eternal life denotes the life of the age to come. John emphasizes that the life of the age to come already belongs to those who believe in Jesus (John 5:24), so that he stresses the present realization of end-time promises. Even though John concentrates upon realized eschatology, the "not yet"

---

5. For fuller discussion of the theme of eternal life, see chapter 2.

dimension is maintained. The resurrection of the body and final judgment are reserved for the future (John 5:28–29; 6:39–40, 44). Elsewhere John teaches that the judgment of the end time has already taken place (John 3:18–19; 9:39–41) through Jesus' death on the cross (John 12:31), so that those who keep his word will never die (John 8:52; 11:25–26). On the other hand, the whole world does not yet know about God's judgment. Hence, Jesus will declare it openly to the entire world on the last day (John 5:27–29; 12:48). In the future Jesus will return, after his death and exaltation, so that the disciples will be where he is (John 14:1–3). An eschatological tension is maintained in John. For instance, Jesus prayed that the disciples, who already believed in him, would be preserved until the last day, when they would see God's glory (John 17:11, 15, 24).

One of the most striking indications of the intrusion of the age to come in John's Gospel is his emphasis on the Holy Spirit. In the OT the Spirit was promised as an eschatological gift. In John's Gospel the gift of the Spirit is given by virtue of the exaltation of Jesus Christ. The Spirit is granted to Jesus' disciples after his glorification (John 7:39; 14:26; 15:26; 16:13), and even during Jesus' ministry the disciples know "the Spirit of truth" because he dwells with them (John 14:17).

A similar eschatological tension is found in 1 John. The light is now shining in Christ, and the darkness is passing away (1 John 2:8), just as the world is passing away (1 John 2:17). The last hour has arrived, since many antichrists are on the scene, and yet a final and definitive antichrist is still to come (1 John 2:18). On the other hand, the light now shines because Jesus has been revealed as the Christ in the flesh (1 John 2:22–23; cf. 2 John 7). He is the Son of God and the fulfillment of God's promises (1 John 5:10–12). Believers are now God's children and have passed from death to life, so that the life of the age to come, eternal life, is theirs now (1 John 3:1–2, 14; 5:12–13). And yet the day of Christ's coming and the consummation of salvation is in the future (1 John 2:28; 3:2). The gift of the Spirit testifies that the last days have come (1 John 3:24; 4:13; cf. 5:6, 8), and yet the final judgment has not yet arrived.

The Acts of the Apostles

In the book of Acts, which is a continuation of the Gospel of Luke, the most striking indication of the fulfillment of God's promises is the gift of the Spirit on Pentecost (Acts 1:5, 8; 2:1–4). The Spirit given at Pentecost becomes the signature of God's salvation and the fulfillment of his end-time promises in Acts. Here we should simply note that we have the fulfillment of God's end-time promise. The Spirit, of course, is given only after Jesus is raised and exalted to God's right hand (Acts

1:9–11; 2:33). The ministry, death, and resurrection of Jesus and now the gift of the Spirit indicate that the promise of worldwide blessing made to Abraham is now being fulfilled (Acts 3:24–26; 10:43; 13:23, 26–27, 32; 15:15–17; 17:2–3; 24:14–15; 26:22–23; 28:23). The disciples, not surprisingly, think that the gift of the Spirit is correlated with the denouement of God's kingdom (Acts 1:6), for in the OT prophecies the giving of the Spirit betokens the consummation of God's purposes. Jesus informs them that the prophecies will not be fulfilled in quite the way they expected (Acts 1:7–8). The Spirit will come, but the conclusion of salvation history will not be immediate, and God has not disclosed to human beings when history will terminate.

One of the prominent themes in Acts is the resurrection of Jesus (e.g., Acts 2:24–32; 3:15; 4:10; 5:30; 10:40–41; 13:30–37; 23:6–10; 24:15; 26:8), an event that also concludes each of the Gospels. The resurrection of Jesus should not be construed simply as an inexplicable event in history. It signified the commencement of the general resurrection—the intrusion of the new age and the new creation. Jesus now reigns as Lord and Christ (Acts 2:36). The promised Messiah and Lord has come and rules over all the world by virtue of his resurrection and exaltation. And yet in Acts God has not yet wrapped up all of history. Jesus will come again to fulfill all God's promises and to judge the living and the dead (Acts 3:19–21; 10:42; 17:31; cf. 24:25). Hence, the resurrection constitutes a clear example of the already–not yet theme.

The Pauline Literature

Looking at the introduction to the letter of the Romans, we gain a glimpse of the heart of Paul's theology (Rom. 1:1–5). God has sent his Son, Jesus Christ, to fulfill the promises made in the OT Scriptures. He is the promised Messiah, and also he now reigns as the Son of God in power since he has been exalted to God's right hand. His resurrection by the Holy Spirit signals that the age to come has dawned, and Paul as an apostle longs to bring this good news to both Jews and Gentiles. What animates Paul's mission is the glory and honor of the name of Jesus Christ. The Pauline mission, then, has a doxological purpose. I will try to demonstrate in more detail later that Paul's theology is God- and Christ-centered, and that the work of the Spirit is inseparable from the ministry, death, and resurrection of Jesus Christ. The trinitarian character of Pauline theology cannot be detached from the biblical story line. God's greatness is featured in the story of redemption unfolded in the NT.

Indeed, the already–not yet theme is so woven into Paul's theology that discussing it could easily launch a full-fledged treatment of Paul's theology. We will focus on some aspects of his view of the fulfillment of God's promises in more detail in due course. Here I want to note the pervasiveness of this theme in Paul's thought. Looking at inaugurated but not yet consummated eschatology in Paul is akin to looking into a kaleidoscope. As we shake the kaleidoscope, we get a different picture, but the same thought is expressed from a different point of view. To shift the analogy, if we consider Paul's theology from the perspective of an archaeological dig, wherever we dig a shaft, we find the already–not yet, even though the precise terms in which this theology is expressed may differ. It seems, then, that inaugurated but not yet consummated eschatology belongs to the fundamental structure of Paul's thought. Thus our purpose here is not to exposit these themes but to strike the keys so that we see how this theme pervades Paul's theology.

As we have already noted, Paul proclaims that the fulfillment of God's saving promises has occurred in Jesus Christ, for through his ministry, death, resurrection, and exaltation he has fulfilled God's word to Abraham and David (cf. Rom. 1:1–4). The saving righteousness of God revealed in Jesus Christ fulfills what the law and the prophets anticipated (Rom. 3:21–22). God's righteousness has become a reality not through the Mosaic law but through the promise made with Abraham (Rom. 4:1–25; Gal. 3:1–4:7). Paul maintains that he is righteous now by faith instead of by observing the law (Phil. 3:2–9), and yet there is an eschatological tension, for he is not yet perfect and still awaits the resurrection (Phil. 3:10–16).

Interestingly, Paul often uses the verb *katargeō* (a verb very difficult to translate—perhaps "make ineffective" or "set aside") to designate the change between the old era and the new. In Christ the body of sin has been set aside (Rom. 6:6); believers are released from the Mosaic law (Rom. 7:2, 6; 2 Cor. 3:11, 13–14; Eph. 2:15); the rulers of this age are passing away (1 Cor. 2:6); God will set aside our corruptible bodies (1 Cor. 6:13); spiritual gifts will pass away at the eschaton when Christ returns (1 Cor. 13:8, 10); when the kingdom comes in its fullness, evil angelic powers will be removed and death itself will be destroyed (1 Cor. 15:24, 26); God will destroy the lawless one (2 Thess. 2:8); God has abolished death and inaugurated life through the gospel (2 Tim. 1:10). We see, then, with this single verb *katargeō*, the inauguration of God's promises, and yet at the same time believers have not yet received the fullness that God has promised.

Another way to understand what is being said here is that all of the saving works of God in Christ are eschatological gifts. The declaration that people are righteous during the present time indicates that God's end-time verdict has now been pronounced ahead of the last day, and it will be declared to the whole world on the day of judgment (cf. Rom.

5:1; 8:33–34; Gal. 5:5). Salvation is fundamentally eschatological because it represents deliverance from God's wrath on the final day (Rom. 5:9; 1 Thess. 1:10; 5:9). And yet that salvation belongs now to those who believe in Jesus Christ (Eph. 2:8–9), so that the gift of the end time belongs to believers during the present evil age. Now is the time of salvation (2 Cor. 6:2), so that God's eschatological promises have penetrated a world that has not been transformed. So too redemption will be the portion of believers when their bodies are redeemed and made whole (Rom. 8:23; Eph. 1:14). And yet believers are now redeemed and forgiven through the blood of Christ (Eph. 1:7; Col. 1:14).

The resurrection of Jesus Christ indicates that the end-time resurrection has begun, as we noted earlier. Paul clearly shares this belief (Rom. 1:4). Further, he argues emphatically that Jesus has indeed been raised from the dead (1 Cor. 15:1–11). Still, there is an unexpected interval between the resurrection of Christ and the resurrection of believers (1 Cor. 15:20–28). The last days have commenced with the resurrection of Christ as the firstfruits, but believers still await the bodily resurrection. Death as the last enemy has not yet been abolished and destroyed. Even though Christ reigns now as the second Adam, so that God's promises are being fulfilled, there is an eschatological proviso, for all things are not yet subjected under his feet, and God is not yet seen to be all in all. Those who contend that the resurrection has already taken place have fallen prey to an overrealized eschatology (2 Tim. 2:18). On the other hand, the power of Christ's resurrection reaches into the present age. Even now believers walk in the newness of life (Rom. 6:4) and are alive to God (Rom. 6:11). They have died with Christ and been raised with him in the heavenly places (Eph. 2:6; Col. 2:12; 3:1), and yet they still await the future resurrection.[6]

Paul also argues that the new creation has dawned in Jesus Christ. Those who are in Christ Jesus are now a new creation (2 Cor. 5:17). Now that the new creation has arrived, the Mosaic covenant, which demanded circumcision, is no longer binding (Gal. 6:15). The new creation is tied to the promise of "the new self" (Eph. 4:24), and this new person represents what believers are in Christ instead of what they are in Adam (Rom. 5:12–19; 1 Cor. 15:21–22). Believers are a new creation in Christ Jesus and created by God to do good works (Eph. 2:10). The "new creation" language fits with the theme that believers have been regenerated, which is the work of the eschatological Spirit (Titus 3:5). The dawning of the new creation does not signify, however, that the present evil age is terminated (Gal. 1:4). The old age and the new creation overlap at the same time! Believers still await their full revelation as children of God.

6. See Gaffin 2006: 60–63.

The present world is still corrupted and awaits its full transformation (Rom. 8:18–25). Believers, then, are a new creation in an old world. But the reality is even more complex, for even though believers are new persons in Christ, in that the old person—the old Adam—was crucified with Christ (Rom. 6:6; Col. 3:9–10), they must still put off the old person and put on the new (Eph. 4:22–24). As Rom. 13:14 says, they must "put on the Lord Jesus Christ." Believers await not only a transformed world but also their own final transformation.

Just as Paul uses the language of the new creation, so also he adopts typical Jewish language of this age and the age to come (Eph. 1:21). This age is designated as "the present evil age" (Gal. 1:4; cf. 1 Tim. 6:17), and believers are not to be conformed to this age (Rom. 12:2), as Demas was (2 Tim. 4:10), for the world dominates the lives of unbelievers (Eph. 2:2). The era between the cross and resurrection is characterized as "the evil day" (Eph. 6:13), and hence "the days are evil" (Eph. 5:16). Indeed, believers have been granted grace to live the life of the age to come in the midst of the present evil age (Titus 2:12). The rulers of this age crucified Jesus Christ because they were unaware that he was the glorious Lord (1 Cor. 2:6, 8). The intellectual worldview that controls the mind-set of unbelievers is limited to this age (1 Cor. 1:20; 3:18), and Satan rules as the god of this age (2 Cor. 4:4). The present evil age is not the only reality, for the "ends of the ages" have now dawned in Jesus Christ (1 Cor. 10:11 NRSV), and believers by virtue of the cross of Christ are delivered from this age (Gal. 1:4), so that the cross of Christ represents the intrusion of the new age, or as Paul says in Gal. 6:14–15, the new creation. The world in its present form is passing away (1 Cor. 7:31). Jesus, therefore, reigns in the present evil age, and his rule will reach its climax in the age to come (Eph. 1:21; cf. 1 Cor. 15:24–28), so that in the coming ages all will marvel over the grace of God displayed in Jesus Christ (Eph. 2:7). The complexity of the present age is illustrated by two truths just noted. On one hand, Satan is the god of this age (2 Cor. 4:4). On the other hand, Jesus rules now as exalted Lord. Satan's dominion indicates that Jesus' reign has not reached its denouement, that the day when all things will be subjected to him has not yet arrived (1 Cor. 15:25–28).

The indicative and imperative in Pauline theology is a prime example of the already–not yet character of his theology. Believers are, so to speak, unleavened in Christ because Christ the Passover lamb has been sacrificed and has purged the evil from their lives through the forgiveness of their sins (1 Cor. 5:6–8). So believers can be described as unleavened. And yet they must also remove the leaven from their lives to be a new lump in the Lord.

Believers are God's children (Gal. 3:26), adopted into his family (Rom. 8:14–17; Gal. 4:4–7). But Paul also reserves adoption for the last day, when our bodies are redeemed (Rom. 8:23). Here we do not have an either-or but an already–not yet. Similarly, believers are heirs now in Christ (Rom. 8:17; Gal. 3:29; 4:7; Titus 3:7), but they have not yet obtained all that has been promised. Believers are God's holy ones now (e.g., Rom. 1:7; 1 Cor. 1:2) and are sanctified in Christ (1 Cor. 6:11), yet Paul can say that believers must grow in holiness (cf. Rom. 6:19–22; 2 Cor. 7:1; 1 Thess. 4:3–8). At the same time, perfect sanctification is reserved for the day when Jesus returns (Eph. 5:26; Col. 1:22–23; 1 Thess. 3:13; 5:23–24). There is apparently an already–not yet in Paul's understanding of holiness. Believers enjoy eternal life now, and yet they must run to win the prize (Phil. 3:12–14). All must exercise discipline to obtain the final reward (1 Cor. 9:24–27). On the one hand, eternal life is promised to those who belong to God, and yet on the other hand, God has fulfilled his promise in bringing Jesus Christ into the world (Titus 1:2–3), so that his grace is now realized (Titus 2:11; cf. 3:4).

As we have seen previously, the gift of the Spirit is the signature of the new age. The coming of the Spirit represents the emblem of God's saving promises, and hence the Spirit is featured in Pauline theology (cf. Rom. 8:1–17; Gal. 3:1–5, 14). The gift of the Spirit represents the eschatological tension in Paul, for the Spirit is the guarantee that God will finish what he has begun, so that believers experience the end-time resurrection (2 Cor. 1:22; 5:5; Eph. 1:13–14). The Spirit is the firstfruits, indicating that God will redeem the bodies of believers (Rom. 8:23). So too the coming of the Spirit indicates that God has fulfilled his new-covenant promises (Jer. 31:31–34; Ezek. 11:18–19; 36:26–27), promises that never came to fruition under the Mosaic law—the old covenant (2 Cor. 3:14). But now that the Spirit has come, believers are enabled to do what could never be done by the letter (*gramma*—i.e., the law without the Spirit [Rom. 2:28–29; 7:5–6; 2 Cor. 3:6]). In fulfillment of God's new-covenant promise they are enabled to observe God's law (Rom. 8:4; 2 Cor. 3:17; cf. Gal. 5:14).

The contrast between justification by faith versus justification by works of law (Rom. 3:20, 28; Gal. 2:16–21; 3:1–5, 10) must also be understood against the backdrop of Pauline eschatology and the contrast between the old covenant and the new. Hence, those under the law, like Hagar, represent the Sinai covenant, while those freed from the law are part of the eschatological Jerusalem (Gal. 4:21–31). Paul's theology resonates with eschatological polarities, or what Martyn calls apocalyptic antimonies,[7] so that the contrast between faith and works of law is eschatological, as is the opposition between the flesh and the Spirit, the old person and the new person, and the old creation and the new creation.

7. Martyn 1985.

Believers are presently citizens of heaven, and yet there is an eschatological proviso, for they await the promise of the resurrection (Phil. 3:20–21). Believers are now hidden with Christ in God, and yet they await Christ's coming and future glory (Col. 3:3–4). God's promises are fulfilled in Christ in the fullness of time, so that those who have the Spirit are God's children (Gal. 4:4–6). The focus of NT theology is the supremacy of God in Christ through the Spirit, and hence we find that God's promises are fulfilled in Christ by the Spirit.

Hebrews and James

It has been said that Hebrews is almost Platonic because it contrasts the heavenly and the earthly realms, but the vertical perspective of Hebrews must be plotted along horizontal or salvation-historical lines. The book opens with a majestic statement about Jesus Christ, declaring that he has fulfilled the prophecies of old (Heb. 1:1–4). His sitting down at the right hand of God demonstrates that he is both the Messiah and the Son of God (Ps. 110). Hence, the promises that God would reign over all the earth are beginning to be fulfilled in the reign of his Son. The trinitarian character of eschatological salvation is also evident, for the giving of the Spirit and his gifts is the signature of the commencement of the new age (Heb. 2:4). And those who belong to the new people of God have become partakers of the Spirit promised in the OT Scriptures (Heb. 6:4). Apostasy is particularly abhorrent, for it means that believers trample underfoot God's Son and despise God's gracious Spirit (Heb. 10:29).

A "not yet" intervenes, however, for believers still await the day when all the Son's enemies will be placed under his feet (Heb. 1:14; 2:5–8; 10:12–13). God's eschatological salvation has dawned, for death has been defeated through the death of Jesus Christ (Heb. 2:14–16). In the same way, God's promised rest is available for those who trust and obey God (Heb. 4:2–3), though the consummation of that rest is still to come (Heb. 4:1–11).[8] The rest is available "today" (Heb. 4:7). God's kingdom belongs to believers even now, but the day when the created things will be removed is coming, and then the consummation of God's purposes will be realized (Heb. 12:26–28). Believers have already come to the heavenly Jerusalem, the city of the living God (Heb. 12:22), but at the same time they seek the coming city (Heb. 13:14), just as Abraham and Sarah and the patriarchs did (Heb. 11:10, 13–16).

The prominence of eschatology in Hebrews is confirmed by the extensive citation of the new covenant of Jer. 31 (cf. Heb. 8:8–12; 10:16–18). The

8. So Rhee 2001: 51–52.

author argues that the new covenant has arrived through the sacrifice of Jesus on the cross. The old covenant, which is tied up with the Levitical priesthood and the Mosaic law, anticipates Jesus' Melchizedekian priesthood and a new order. The typology of Hebrews, in other words, services the eschatology of Hebrews. The temporary nature of the Levitical priesthood and the OT law are evident because they did not bring perfection or full forgiveness of sins, whereas the sacrifice of Christ brought final and definitive forgiveness of sins because he was a sinless and perfect sacrifice and a willing human victim, unlike animal sacrifices, which were brute beasts offered apart from their will (Heb. 7:11–28; 10:1–18). Even though Christ offered the perfect and definitive sacrifice "at the end of the ages" (Heb. 9:26), the end of salvation history has not yet arrived, for believers still await the final judgment, the return of Jesus Christ (Heb. 9:27–28; 10:37), and the drawing near of the final day (Heb. 10:25). Indeed, the warning passages that permeate Hebrews are set against the backdrop of its already–not yet eschatology, for in order to receive the eschatological reward, those who believe must continue to believe and obey until Jesus returns. The examples of faith in Heb. 11, therefore, focus on the eschatological character of faith, demonstrating that those who have trusted in God throughout history did not receive the promised reward during their time on earth. Heb. 11:39–40 emphasizes progress in salvation history. We have something better, so that OT saints are not perfected without us, and yet all believers look forward to the same end-time reward.

The letter of James does not emphasize the fulfillment of God's promises in the same way as does most of the rest of the NT. What James emphasizes is the final fulfillment of God's promises on the last day (James 2:12–13; 5:1–5)—the day of Christ's return (James 5:7–9). Then believers will be perfect and complete (James 1:4), exalted (James 1:9), and will receive the crown of life (James 1:12). God's salvation is fundamentally eschatological, and hence believers must do good works to be justified (James 2:14–26; 5:20). Still, there is acknowledgment that God has already given believers new life (James 1:18) and chosen them to be his children (James 2:5). It is evident that Jesus Christ and the Holy Spirit do not play a prominent role in James. Still, I will argue in due course that the lack of emphasis could be overstated, and hence the fulfillment of God's promises through the Father, Son, and Spirit is likely an assumed backdrop in James's letter.

1–2 Peter and Jude

The fulfillment of God's saving promises through the Father, Son, and Spirit is featured in 1 Pet. 1:2. The age to come has been inaugurated through the death and resurrection of Jesus Christ (1 Pet. 1:3, 11; 2:21, 24; 3:18), just as it was prophesied by the Spirit (1 Pet. 1:10–12). Hence, his death and resurrection herald the inauguration of "the last times" (1 Pet. 1:20; cf. 1:18–21). Jesus now reigns in heaven over all angelic powers (1 Pet. 3:22). The inauguration of God's end-time promises is clear, for believers are born again (1 Pet. 1:3, 23), and the promises made to Israel are fulfilled in the church as the new people of God, the new Israel (1 Pet. 2:9–10). What the temple and priesthood anticipated is fulfilled in Jesus Christ (1 Pet. 2:4–9). Still, the "not yet" looms large over the letter, for believers are suffering at the hands of the ungodly and are exiles on earth (1 Pet. 1:1, 17; 2:11; 4:1–6). The salvation promised to them is fundamentally eschatological (1 Pet. 1:5, 9), so that they will not receive an inheritance until the final day (1 Pet. 1:4). The final revelation of Jesus Christ is still in the future (1 Pet. 1:7, 13; 4:13; 5:4; cf. 4:7), and they must continue to believe in and obey him until he returns (1 Pet. 3:9–12; cf. 5:4). When the end-time judgment takes place (1 Pet. 4:5, 17), believers will be exalted and rewarded (1 Pet. 5:4, 6, 10).

The letters of 2 Peter and Jude are brief, and much of Jude is contained in 2 Pet. 2. However, Peter commences his second letter with the theme of the fulfillment of God's promises.[9] The saving righteousness of God has now been realized through Jesus Christ as God and Savior (2 Pet. 1:2). God has given to believers, in fulfillment of his promises, everything they need through the power of Jesus Christ, so that even now believers partake of God's divine nature (2 Pet. 1:3–4). The promises of salvation belong to believers, then, through knowing Jesus Christ as Lord and Savior (2 Pet. 2:20; 3:18; cf. 1:8). Despite the emphasis on knowing Jesus Christ as Lord and Savior now, eschatological reservation also character-izes 2 Peter. Believers must practice godliness to receive entrance into the kingdom on the last day (2 Pet. 1:5–11; 3:14–15). The final realization of all of God's promises has not occurred, so that believers still await the return of Jesus Christ (2 Pet. 1:16–18; 3:3–10). Those who give themselves to evil will be judged on the last day (2 Pet. 2), and therefore believers must persevere to receive the promised reward and end-time salvation (2 Pet. 3:15). The new creation—the new heavens and earth—that God promised is still coming (2 Pet. 3:13; cf. 3:7, 10).

The letter of Jude runs along the same lines. Believers enjoy a "com-mon salvation" (Jude 3) through Jesus Christ (Jude 4). The Father has set his love upon them, and they are kept by Jesus Christ (Jude 2; cf. 24–25). However, Jude emphasizes the "not yet." Those who give themselves

---

9. Most scholars today argue that 2 Peter is pseudonymous, but I depart from the main-stream view of NT scholarship here and argue that the letter is authentic (see Schreiner 2003: 255–76). Hence, in this book I will assume the authenticity of 2 Peter.

over to evil will face judgment on the last day (Jude 5–16). In the interim believers must keep themselves in God's love and not abandon the faith once delivered to them (Jude 3, 20–21).

Revelation

Revelation features the fulfillment of God's saving promises in Jesus Christ. He is the "Lion from the tribe of Judah" and "the Root of David" (Rev. 5:5), fulfilling the covenant that God established with David. Believers are now released from their sins because of his death and are established even now as a kingdom and priests (Rev. 1:5–6; 5:9–10; 7:14). We see in the vision in Rev. 1:12–20 that Jesus is the Son of Man predicted in Dan. 7. He has authority over Death and Hades, so that even now believers face death with confidence. The God who is the creator of all (Rev. 4) is also the redeemer through Christ (Rev. 5), and he sends his Spirit into the world as a result of Christ's work (Rev. 5:6; cf. 1:4). Satan has been defeated at the cross and expelled from heaven (Rev. 12:7–10), so that believers share Christ's victory over Satan because of Christ's blood (Rev. 12:11).

The already, then, is not omitted in Revelation, but certainly the focus is on the "not yet," though we must see that the "not yet" has been secured by Christ's death and resurrection, so that complete confidence in final victory is taught. Revelation looks ahead to Jesus' second coming, when he will consummate history, reward believers, and punish the disobedient. The future coming of Christ reminds readers of the necessity to persevere and to continue believing until that day arrives (Rev. 2:1–3:22). Indeed, the exhortations to perseverance and faithfulness (e.g., Rev. 13:10; 14:12) function against the backdrop of eschatology. Those addressed must keep believing in order to receive the eschatological reward on the day when Jesus returns. Judgment, of course, permeates Revelation, and this theme reminds the readers that evil will not triumph, and that those who are persecuting the church of Jesus Christ or who have allied themselves with the beast, Babylon, and the false prophet will certainly be defeated. The new creation is coming (Rev. 21:1–22:5), wherein God will make good on all the promises uttered. But the sum and substance of the promise is that God and the Lamb will reside with believers and dwell with them forever. The capstone of all biblical theology is summed up in the words "they will see his face" (Rev. 22:4).

PART 1

THE FULFILLMENT
OF GOD'S SAVING PROMISES

The Already–Not Yet

1

✦ ✦ ✦ ✦ ✦ ✦ ✦ ✦ ✦ ✦ ✦ ✦ ✦ ✦ ✦ ✦ ✦ ✦

The Kingdom of God in the Synoptic Gospels

Introduction: A Brief Recapitulation of the Old Testament Story

We begin with the kingdom of God, which certainly is of prime importance in NT theology.[1] Goldsworthy remarks, "The idea of the rule of God over creation, over all creatures, over the kingdoms of the world, and in a unique and special way, over his chosen and redeemed people, is the very heart of the message of the Hebrew scriptures."[2] In the pages of the NT it is made clear that God's promises are fulfilled, the end of the ages has come (1 Cor. 10:11), the new creation has dawned, eternal life has arrived, and the new covenant is a reality. In the first part of this book we will explore these themes, for the NT continues the narrative begun in the OT. It picks up the story of salvation from the OT, where God promised to bless the whole world through Abraham and his descendants (Gen. 3:15; 12:1–3; 13:14–17; 15:4–5; 17:4–8, 19; 18:18–19; 22:17–18; 26:3–4; 28:14–15; 35:12–13).[3] In particular, the Lord promised Abraham land, seed, and universal blessing. Genesis relates the story of the seed, or descendants, pledged to Abraham. The promises were not

1. For a brief survey of the kingdom in the OT and Jewish Second Temple literature, see Meier 1994: 243–70.
2. Goldsworthy, *NDBT* 618.
3. For two illuminating windows into OT theology from a canonical perspective, see Alexander 2002; Dempster 2003.

easily fulfilled, as both Sarah and Rebecca struggled with barrenness, and it was a long road before the birth of Isaac and Jacob and Esau. Nor were the land promises fulfilled, inasmuch as Abraham, Isaac, and Jacob were nomads in the land of promise, and Genesis concludes with Israel in Egypt.

Still, God was slowly fulfilling his promise. Jacob had twelve sons, and the promise of countless seed begins to become a reality in the book of Exodus. Indeed, so many Israelites were born that Pharaoh began to fear for the survival of his people and power. If the promise of many descendants was slowly becoming a reality, Exodus–Joshua recounts how the Lord fulfilled his promise that Israel would possess the land of Canaan. Yahweh rescued Israel from slavery in Egypt with remarkable signs and wonders, and Moses led the nation to Sinai, where God made a covenant with them and gave them his law. Still, the nation was recalcitrant and stubborn, for they made a golden calf, tested the Lord in numerous ways, and failed to believe that he would give them victory in Canaan. The Lord judged the adults of the wilderness generation, condemning them to forty years of wandering in the wilderness. Only after the death of Moses did Joshua lead Israel into the land of Canaan, and the Lord again worked in stunning and miraculous ways to help Israel conquer their enemies and take possession of the land. Two of God's promises were fulfilled: Israel was in the land and amply populated.

It is not enough, of course, that Israel resided in the land in large numbers. They had a mandate to live as the people of the Lord, to trust in God and do his will. We see in the period of the judges that Israel failed miserably. Instead of living as a holy and distinct people, they adopted Canaanite ways and turned against the Lord. The Lord judged his people by raising up other nations to oppress and subject them. When Israel cried to the Lord for deliverance, he raised up deliverers to save them from their oppressors. Unfortunately, the obedience of Israel was always short-lived, and hence they were caught up in a seemingly endless cycle of deliverance-defection-judgment-repentance.

Judges ends on a rather dour note. The behavior of the tribe of Dan in attacking a quiet and peaceful people and in hiring a priest to support their own agenda was a far cry from what the Lord commanded. The rape and murder of the Levite's concubine and then the subsequent support from the tribe of Benjamin relay the depth to which Israel had fallen. The narrator remarks that Israel had no king and the people did as they pleased (Judg. 17:6; 21:25). The degradation of Israel is apparent with the opening of 1 Samuel, for Eli's sons, Hophni and Phinehas, represent the corruption of the priesthood. The Lord raised up Samuel as a prophet and judge, but the accession of Samuel did not constitute a long-term solution, since his sons were corrupt and the nation as a whole did not truly trust in Yahweh. Israel longed for a king so that they could be like the other nations, but such a desire demonstrated a refusal to accept God's kingship. Israel did not live under God's lordship as his holy people but rather longed to be like the nations that had kings leading them into battle. Nevertheless, the Lord agreed that Israel should have a king. Though Israel's motives were stained, the king anticipated the Lord's future reign over his people.[4] As the first king, Saul recapitulated the history of Israel. Initially he was humble and pliable in the Lord's hands, but soon he forsook his trust in God and conducted the kingdom in his own way and in accord with his own wisdom. Therefore, God rejected Saul as king and refused to raise up a dynasty after him.

Instead the Lord appointed and exalted David as king. David became the model of a "man after God's own heart," showing in his refusal to avenge Saul that he trusted wholly in the Lord. Because of his reliance upon the Lord, David was granted victory by God over Israel's enemies. For the first time Israel appeared to be the people of the Lord, living under his lordship in the land. David desired to build a temple for the Lord in Jerusalem to show his devotion to the Lord and to centralize worship in accord with Deut. 17. But God forbade David to build the temple because he had spilled blood in war. David's successor and son, Solomon, a man of peace, would build the temple. However, God enacted a covenant with David in which he promised that his dynasty would last forever. David desired to build a house for God, but the Lord pledged that he would build a house for David that would last forever. Individual descendants of David would be punished and even rejected if they sinned, but the dynasty would never end. The covenant enacted with David would last forever (2 Sam. 7; Pss. 89; 132). It is clear, then, that the promises of blessing for the whole world and the hope that Israel would become a people truly obedient to the Lord would be realized through a king, a descendant of David. Often in the prophets the hope of a future king, an offspring of David, is featured. God's saving promises would be realized upon the coming of the promised king.

Despite all of David's strengths, clearly he was not the ideal king. His adultery with Bathsheba and the murder of Uriah caused Israel to spiral downward, and he came startlingly close to losing the kingship. David pointed forward to a future king, one who was more devoted to the Lord and nobler than he. The reader is poised to think that the greater

---

4. Scholars have long wrestled over the fact that Israel was wrongly motivated in desiring a king, while at the same time it seemed to be the Lord's plan that Israel have a king. A future king for Israel was not an accommodation to the nation, as if the kingship were inferior to God's original plan. The problem was Israel's motive in desiring a king, for they longed to be like the nations in having a king go before them and fight their battles (rightly D. Howard 1990).

king could be Solomon. He began his reign with a desire to rule Israel wisely, and as a man of peace he built the temple of the Lord. As time passed, however, Solomon strayed from the Lord, as he was enticed by his many wives to worship false gods. The peace and wisdom that Solomon seemed to promise would be realized by another king. The Lord judged Solomon for his defection, and after his death the kingdom was split into two: Israel in the north, Judah in the south.

Every king from the northern kingdom, Israel, was ungodly, worshiping at altars forbidden by the Torah. The nation experienced some political highs and lows, but the Lord's word of judgment was inevitable. In 722 BC the Assyrians conquered the northern kingdom and exiled the people. The southern kingdom, which preserved the line of David, was not nearly as bleak. Several of its kings were truly devoted to the Lord. And yet the overall trajectory was still downward, and Judah traced Israel's steps and rebelled against the Lord's commands. God's word of judgment was unleashed on Judah as well, and Babylon sent Judah into exile, capturing Jerusalem and burning the temple in 586 BC.

Most of the prophetic books were written during the reigns of the kings of Israel and Judah. Any brief summary of the prophets surely would be inadequate, but we can say that the prophets proclaim both judgment and salvation—what is often identified as the day of the Lord.[5] Those who turned away from God and refused to obey his word were judged. These words of judgment were fulfilled when the exile became a reality in 722 BC and 586 BC. Nevertheless, judgment was not the final word for Israel. The prophets looked forward to a day when God's saving promises would be fulfilled, his kingdom would come, the new covenant would be inaugurated, a new exodus from Babylon would be realized, the Spirit would be poured out on Israel, and Israel would keep God's law. The prophets promised a new creation, a new temple, a new covenant, and a new king. The exile would be over, and the wilderness would bloom.

The great promises in the prophets, however, were not fulfilled when the exile ended in 536 BC.[6] Israel did return from Babylon and a temple was built, yet the temple was insignificant in comparison to the Solomonic temple. Nor was the nation enjoying glorious prosperity, the kind of glory envisioned in Isa. 40–66. Israel was small, struggling, and under the oppression of former powers. Ezra, Nehemiah, Haggai, Zechariah,

5. For a helpful survey on the day of the Lord, see Beasley-Murray 1986: 11–16; see also Hiers, *ABD* 2:82–83; House 2007: 179–224.

6. For a summary of what Israel anticipated and longed for, see Bauckham 2001: 435–37. What Bauckham describes as restoration here can also be described as the fulfillment of kingdom promises. The terminology used is not decisive, since different expressions are used to denote the same reality.

and Malachi document the low spiritual state of the nation. Nor did matters improve in the four hundred years before the coming of Jesus of Nazareth. Israel was a pawn in the struggle between the Ptolemies and the Seleucids. A brief period of freedom dawned with the Hasmoneans in the second and first centuries BC, but the interlude was brief, and soon the Romans swept in and subjugated Israel, appointing the Herodians and procurators to rule the land.[7]

This all-too-brief sketch of Israel's history helps us understand the significance of Jesus' claim that the kingdom of God had drawn near (Matt. 4:17; Mark 1:15).[8] Those hearing Jesus did not ask for a definition of the kingdom. They understood him to be proclaiming the dawn of a glorious new era in which Israel would be exalted and the nations made subservient to Israel's God.[9] The Lord would reign over the whole earth, the son of David would serve as king, and the exile would be over. The new covenant would be fulfilled, God's people would keep his law, and the promised new creation would become a reality. The Lord would pour out his Spirit on all flesh, and the promise to Abraham that all nations would be blessed, to the ends of the earth, would become a reality.

Centrality of the Kingdom of God in Jesus' Teaching

The Synoptic Gospels make it immediately apparent that the kingdom of God is central to Jesus' teaching. In this regard he is not to be differentiated from John the Baptist, who likewise proclaimed the coming kingdom (Matt. 3:2). John's preaching in the desert and his baptism in the Jordan signal the promise of a new exodus for those who repent and confess their sins (Matt. 3:3–6),[10] but judgment will come for those who fail to repent (Matt. 3:7–10). The expression "kingdom of God" occurs

7. On the kingdom of God in Second Temple Judaism, see Beasley-Murray 1986: 46–51.

8. The verb *engizō* in Mark 1:15 has precipitated much discussion. Dodd (1936: 44) argues that the kingdom has come in its fullness. Others argue that the verb signifies nearness rather than arrival (e.g., Marcus 2000: 172–73). It is more likely, however, that the verb form cannot be confined to the present or the future and includes both. For this latter view, see France 2002: 92–93; Beasley-Murray 1986: 73. Meier (1994: 430–34) argues that the evidence is too ambiguous to derive a certain conclusion.

9. For the kingdom of God in the OT, see Beasley-Murray 1986: 17–25. For an apt description of what Israel expected, see *Pss. Sol.* 17–18.

10. Meier (1994: 46) says, "The desert naturally conjured up for Jews of any stripe the founding events of the exodus from Egypt, the covenant at Sinai, and the forty years of wandering in the wilderness." He goes on to say, "Likewise, the waters of the Jordan were an apt symbol not only for the washing away of sin but also for the entrance of Israel into a new and better life after its wandering in the desert of rebellion against its God."

four times in Matthew, fourteen in Mark, thirty-two in Luke, and four in John. At first glance, it might appear that Matthew does not use the phrase often, but then we notice that Matthew uses the expression "kingdom of heaven" thirty-two times.[11] Older dispensational thought distinguished between the "kingdom of God" and the "kingdom of heaven," but today very few argue for such a distinction. The usual scholarly explanation today is that the Gospel of Matthew was addressed to Jews, and the Jews often reverentially avoided using God's name.[12] The term "heaven," it is argued, was a reverential substitute for "God." It follows, on this view, that the expressions "kingdom of God" and "kingdom of heaven" refer to the same reality and should not be distinguished.

Recent work by Pennington on the term "heaven" in Matthew, however, has demonstrated the inadequacy of the scholarly consensus in Matthew.[13] It is quite unlikely that Matthew used the term "heaven" to avoid referring to God out of reverence, for he refers to God over fifty times elsewhere in the Gospel and actually uses "kingdom of God" on four occasions.[14] Moreover, Jewish evidence that the term "heaven" was used to avoid the name of God out of reverence is lacking. Hence, it is more persuasive to argue that Matthew uses the term "heaven" for a particular purpose in the narrative.

The substance of Pennington's case is as follows. When "heaven" (*ouranos*) is used in the singular without the term "earth" or its equivalent nearby, it usually refers to the sky (Matt. 16:1–3; cf. 6:26; 8:20; 13:32; 14:19; 26:64).[15] The plural "heavens" (*ouranoi*), on the other hand, typically refers to the invisible divine realm (e.g., Matt. 3:16–17; 5:12, 16; 18:10; 19:21). When the pair "heaven and earth" is used, it may denote the entirety of the universe created by God (Matt. 5:18; 11:25; 24:35; cf. Gen. 1:1). But even more common in Matthew is the use of heaven and earth to contrast life according to God's will and ways with life lived

11. Pennington (2007: 2–3) remarks, "'Kingdom of heaven' is found nowhere else in the OT, NT, or any preceding Second Temple literature. Similar phrases appear occasionally in the Apocrypha, but kingdom of heaven is found only in literature which postdates Matthew. Even these occurrences are quite infrequent (e.g., twice in the Mishnah and three times in the Gospel of Thomas)."

12. See Dodd 1936: 34; Meier 1994: 239.

13. Pennington (2007: 67–76) summarizes his thesis on heaven in Matthew with four points: (1) we see a preference for the plural form *ouranoi*; (2) we find an emphasis on the word pair "heaven and earth"; (3) Matthew regularly refers to the Father in heaven; (4) the phrase "the kingdom of heaven" is prominent in Matthew.

14. Pamment (1981) suggests a less convincing distinction. She claims that "kingdom of heaven" refers to an imminent but future coming of the kingdom, whereas "kingdom of God" refers to the kingdom already actualized in the present.

15. Matt. 23:22 seems to be an exception where the singular "heaven" appears to refer to God's realm; "the powers of the heavens" in Matt. 24:29 also seems to be an exception (see also Matt. 24:31).

according to human standards. In Matt. 6:1–21 Jesus' instructions on righteousness point to a heaven-versus-earth contrast, whether the issue is almsgiving, prayer, or fasting. The contrast between heaven and earth is illustrated by Matt. 6:19–20: "Do not lay up for yourselves treasures on earth, where moth and rust destroy and where thieves break in and steal, but lay up for yourselves treasures in heaven, where neither moth nor rust destroys and where thieves do not break in and steal" (cf. Matt. 5:34–35; 6:10; 11:23;[16] 21:25;[17] 28:18).

Matthew uses the plural "heavens" to speak of the Father in heaven on thirteen occasions, and "kingdom of heaven" thirty-two times to contrast the heavenly and earthly realm. The usage here confirms that the plural "heavens" refers to God, while the singular "heaven" refers to the sky.[18] In other words, Matthew intentionally uses heaven and earth to contrast God's ways with those of human beings. The disjunction between God's ways and ours is also evident in (1) the "heaven and earth" pairs; (2) the emphasis that the Father is in heaven (separated and exalted above human beings); and (3) the contrast between the heavenly kingdom and the kingdoms that are earthly and wicked. Hence, the expression "kingdom of heaven" focuses on the truth that God's kingdom is from above. His kingdom is not an earthly one but rather represents his sovereignty and rule over all other kingdoms and all other so-called gods. In particular, Matthew emphasizes the inbreaking of God's heavenly kingdom in Jesus.[19] The earthly and inhumane kingdoms described in Dan. 7 are giving way to the kingdom from above with the coming of Jesus Christ.

Matthew and the other Gospels do not speak only of the "kingdom of heaven" or the "kingdom of God," for the word "kingdom" occurs alone eighteen times in Matthew, four times in Mark, twelve times in Luke, and twice in John. Most of these examples refer to God's kingdom. It is very clear, then, that the kingdom of God is a central theme in the first three Gospels. John clearly moves in another direction, and we will explore John's terminology in the next chapter.

The importance of the kingdom of God in Jesus' teaching is also apparent by the location of the sayings about the kingdom. For example, both Matthew and Mark introduce Jesus' teaching ministry with pregnant sayings about the kingdom of God. "From that time Jesus began to preach, saying, 'Repent, for the kingdom of heaven is at hand'" (Matt. 4:17). "Now after John was arrested, Jesus came into Galilee, proclaiming

16. The contrast here is between heaven and Hades.
17. Here Matthew contrasts what is from heaven with what is from human beings.
18. The singular is also used in "heaven and earth" pairs, following the pattern of the LXX, regardless of the referent.
19. For a survey on the kingdom of heaven in Matthew, see Kingsbury 1975: 128–60.

the gospel of God, and saying, 'The time is fulfilled, and the kingdom of God is at hand; repent and believe in the gospel'" (Mark 1:14–15). Jesus proclaimed the imminence of the kingdom, the fulfillment of the good news that God would redeem his people. This promise of good news (*euangelion*) reaches back to Isaiah, where the good news is the new exodus from Babylon, the return from exile (Isa. 40:9; 52:7). The return from exile promised by Isaiah, however, cannot be limited merely to return from exile, since Isaiah promises that God will fulfill all of his saving promises to Israel culminating in a new creation (Isa. 65:17; 66:22).[20] Even though Israel returned from exile in 536 BC, the fullness of what was promised in Isa. 40–66 did not become a reality. The new creation did not commence, nor was the rule of evil shattered. Interestingly, the Jews did not conclude from this that Isaiah's prophecies were mistaken, but both the Qumran community (1QM IX, 19–21) and early Christians believed that Isaiah's prophesies were being fulfilled in their day. Jesus proclaimed that Israel was about to receive what God had promised. God would rule and reign over his people in a saving way. At the outset of his ministry Jesus heralds this work, calling upon Israel to repent and trust in God.

The importance of the kingdom is also attested by the summary statements that epitomize Jesus' ministry.[21] "And he went throughout all Galilee, teaching in their synagogues and proclaiming the gospel of the kingdom and healing every disease and every affliction among the people" (Matt. 4:23; cf. 9:35; 24:14; Luke 4:43). Jesus' ministry in Galilee consisted of teaching, healing, and proclaiming the good news of the kingdom. Again the conjunction of new creation and kingdom appears, for the healing of every disease means that the old order is passing away. Similar summary statements that focus on the kingdom of God in the preaching of Jesus appear in Matt. 9:35; Luke 4:43–44; 8:1; 9:11. The kingdom does not belong to the periphery of Jesus' ministry, for, as Luke informs us, after his resurrection, in the few days that he had to instruct his disciples, Jesus over the course of forty days spoke to them "about the kingdom of God" (Acts 1:3). Indeed, when Jesus commissioned his disciples to preach during his ministry, they proclaimed the kingdom

20. We see from this that the Gospel writers did not typically refer to the fulfillment of God's promises in terms of return from exile or as a new exodus. Instead, they spoke of the coming of God's kingdom. It is important to see, however, that the coming of the kingdom means the fulfillment of God's promises regarding a new exodus and return from exile. Hence, there is no need to drive a wedge between the notion of God's kingdom and new exodus and return from exile, though it is important for the sake of precision to note that the terminology typically used in the Gospels is not that of a new exodus or a return from exile but of the coming of the kingdom of God (but see Matt. 2:15, 18).

21. It should also be noted that John the Baptist anticipated the arrival of the kingdom and the coming of another (see R. Webb 1991: 55, 196–97, 261–88).

of God (Matt. 10:7; Luke 9:2). If the kingdom of God was the theme of Jesus' instruction in the days subsequent to his resurrection, it must have been a central feature of Jesus' ministry.

Understanding the Kingdom

How should we understand what Jesus meant by the "kingdom of God"? Our OT survey provides some assistance in forming a definition, for we see the emphasis on the fulfillment of God's saving promises. It is also helpful to consider some specific OT and Jewish antecedents that refer to God's kingdom. The ruling power of the Lord is demonstrated at the exodus when he destroyed the Egyptians and saved Israel (Exod. 15:18). Israel also looked forward to the day when God's rule would be established and their enemies thwarted. "And in the days of those kings the God of heaven will set up a kingdom that shall never be destroyed, nor shall this kingdom be left to another people. It shall crush all these kingdoms and bring them to an end, and it shall stand forever" (Dan. 2:44). This future kingdom would be realized under the Son of Man (Dan. 7:14, 18, 23, 27), and a descendant of David would rule in this kingdom (Isa. 9:2–7; 11). Ultimately, Israel longed for and expected the future reign of the Lord over all the earth (Isa. 24:23).[22] Zephaniah directed his eye toward the future and promised a future reign of God as king in the midst of Israel (Zeph. 3:15). Indeed, the Lord "will become king over all the earth" (Zech. 14:9 NRSV). The emphasis is on the future reign of the Lord, his triumph over Israel's enemies in coming days. Hence, when Edom is subjugated—and "Edom" probably includes a reference to all God's enemies—the Lord will reign (Obad. 21). The booth of David will be established again and the Lord will rule over the world, and the fruitfulness of this world demonstrates that it will be a new creation (Amos 9:11–15).

The expectation of a future rule of God in which he fulfills his promises to Israel and subjugates his enemies continues in Second Temple literature. For example, in the *War Scroll* from Qumran a great battle is envisioned in which the people of God will triumph. A similar expectation of a glorious future is envisioned in the *Testament of Moses*: "Then his kingdom will appear throughout the whole creation. Then the devil will have an end. Yea, sorrow will be led away with him" (*T. Mos.* 10:1;

---

22. Isa. 24:23 speaks of the Lord reigning over Mount Zion and in Jerusalem, but in the context of Isa. 24–27 this refers to the Lord's reign over the whole world, for Isa. 24–27 emphasizes the Lord's eschatological judgment and rule over the whole earth (see esp. 24:20–22; 25:6–9; 26:11–19; 27:1).

cf. *2 Bar.* 73:1–7).[23] In *Pss. Sol.* 17–18 the psalmist prays that the Lord will raise up a Davidic king, the Messiah, to cast sinners out of Jerusalem and to rule over his holy people. Gentile nations will be subservient to him, and all the earth will live in fear of the Lord. Or, we can think of what Josephus (*Ant.* 18.23–25) calls the "fourth philosophy," the sect with Judas the Galilean as their leader. They refused to capitulate to any other governing authority, convinced that only the Lord should rule over them. Scholars dispute whether this party should be called "the Zealots" at this early stage.[24] In any case, we see the roots of a way of thinking that culminated in the Jewish rebellion against Rome in AD 66–70. The Jewish longing for God's future kingdom is also expressed in the Kaddish: "May he let his kingdom rule in your lives . . . and in your days and in the lives of the whole house of Israel, very soon and in a near time."[25] Interestingly, the desire for Israel to triumph and to see surrounding nations defeated is expressed in a thoroughly Jewish way in Luke 1, indicating Luke's faithful rendering of early Jewish piety before the coming of the Messiah. If we interpret the relevant verbs as futures, Mary anticipates the judgment of evil rulers and the fulfillment of God's promises to Abraham (Luke 1:52–55).[26] With the birth of Jesus, God has begun to fulfill his promises, though the complete fulfillment, as the reader of all of Luke-Acts knows, lies in the future.[27] Similarly, Zechariah rejoiced that God had visited his people and brought in his promised redemption (Luke 1:68–75).[28] In the fulfillment of God's covenant with Abraham, Zechariah saw the realization of the promise that Israel would be liberated from its enemies.

Eschatological Kingdom in Jesus' Teaching

The brief survey of OT and Jewish teaching on the kingdom reveals that the kingdom was anticipated in the future; the focus was on the eschatological kingdom. When we turn to the teaching of Jesus, we see that he too expected a future kingdom, an end-time kingdom wherein God

---

23. All Pseudepigrapha citations are from Charlesworth 1983–1985.

24. For discussion of this matter, see Hengel (1989b), who answers in the affirmative, and Horsley and Hanson (1985), who answer in the negative.

25. Taken from Meier 1994: 297. See also Meier's (1994: 361–62n36) sound and careful discussion regarding the date of the tradition.

26. Marshall (2005: 157–62) argues that the verbs that express God's saving action on behalf of his people in Luke 1–2 point to the spiritual dimensions of Jesus' mission.

27. See Juel 1983: 21; Seccombe 1982: 76–77.

28. Indeed, Maddox (1982: 137–42, 183, 186) argues that one of the central themes in Luke-Acts is the fulfillment of God's eschatological promises. See also Bock 1987: 70–74; Kee 1990: 6–27.

would fulfill his saving promises. This is evident from the Lord's Prayer, in which believers are to pray, "Your kingdom come" (Matt. 6:10; Luke 11:2).[29] Jesus also speaks to the disciples of the day when he will come "in his kingdom" (Matt. 16:28; cf. Luke 23:51), which clearly refers to the future fulfillment of the kingdom promise. When the kingdom comes, the judgment will commence, and all will be appraised for the way they have lived (Matt. 25:31–46). The coming kingdom can be described as a great end-time feast in which the righteous will rejoice but others will be cast out into the darkness (Matt. 8:11–12; 26:29; Mark 14:25; Luke 14:15; 22:16, 18, 29–30; cf. Isa. 25:6–8).[30] The futurity of the kingdom is evident in the call to "inherit the kingdom" that has been prepared by God from the beginning (Matt. 25:34). Jesus did not believe that the kingdom had come in its fullness in his day, for he envisioned a future day when he would enjoy the messianic banquet in God's kingdom (Mark 14:25; Luke 22:18).[31] Some of the Beatitudes also promise a future reward when the kingdom arrives (see Matt. 5:3–12; Luke 6:20–23).[32] Clearly, Jesus did not teach a completely realized eschatology. He anticipated a period of time in which believers awaited the fulfillment of God's saving promises and the unleashing of his terrible judgments.

Perhaps the most remarkable feature in Jesus' teaching about the kingdom is the role that he envisions for himself. He is the king and judge, deciding both who enters the kingdom and who is excluded from it (Matt. 25:31–46). The Father will deny access to the kingdom to those who deny Jesus before others, whereas those who confess Jesus will be inducted into God's presence (Matt. 10:32–33 par.). The Son of Man saying in Matt. 26:64 indicates that Jesus saw his return as the event that commences the eschatological kingdom. When we speak of the kingdom, inevitably we are introduced to Christology, for Jesus does not merely speak abstractly about the coming kingdom. He invariably considers his own role as paramount in the eschatological kingdom. The most remarkable feature of the kingdom is the role of Jesus Christ himself.

It is when we think of Christology that the uniqueness of Jesus' view of the kingdom is clarified. The Qumran community and the Pharisees believed that if the Torah were kept more faithfully, God would fulfill his promises. Israel had been unfaithful to the Lord because it repeatedly

29. See Meier 1994: 291–301. Many commentators argue that the petition that God's name be hallowed (Matt. 6:9; Luke 11:2) is also eschatological (e.g., Fitzmyer 1985: 898; Davies and Allison 1988: 603).

30. Meier (1994: 309–17) argues that Matt. 8:11–12 and the parallel in Luke 13:28–29 are authentic and demonstrate Jesus' belief in the futurity of the kingdom.

31. See Meier 1994: 302–9.

32. For detailed discussion, see Meier 1994: 317–36.

sinned and violated his law.[33] Hence, they urged rigorous and meticulous observation of the ways of the Lord. By way of contrast, Jesus called on the people to repent and to recognize that God had sent him. The focus is not on the Torah but on Jesus himself and a right relation with him.[34] What Jesus called for was, in one sense, stunningly simple, but it was also remarkably different from the views of his contemporaries, and so opposition developed.

Nor did Jesus advocate cooperation with the Roman authorities, which seems to have been the pathway of the Sadducees and the political elite in Israel. Jesus believed that those who desired the approval of Rome had compromised with the world. The fulfillment of God's promises would not come through worldly wisdom and political machinations. He called upon people to turn to the Lord in a fresh and vital way, and to show their allegiance to the God of Israel by becoming one of his disciples.

Others in Israel opted for a political solution of a different character. Many believed that the power of Rome should be removed through guerilla warfare and violence. We think of Judas the Galilean (Acts 5:37; Josephus, *J.W.* 2.118), Theudas (Acts 5:36), and the Egyptian who tried to lead a revolt in Israel (Acts 21:38; Josephus, *J.W.* 2.261–263; *Ant.* 20.169–172). Still others could be mentioned. The end result was the Jewish war of AD 66–70 and the Bar Kokhba rebellion of AD 132–135. Both were severely crushed by the Romans. Jesus had a completely different vision of the coming of the kingdom. He repudiated any notion that the kingdom could be inaugurated through a violent program of resistance.[35] In some ways, those who opted for violence fell into the same trap that captured the Sadducees, except that they chose another form of political action. Jesus did not call for a political revolution; he trusted in the power of the word of God (Mark 4:28) and focused on the need of the nation to repent and turn to God. Jesus summoned the people not to revolt but to pay taxes to Caesar (Matt. 22:15–22 par.). Thus he deliberately downplayed what was considered to be a matter of great political importance in his day. Jesus did not focus on the structures of evil that need to be dismantled, though certainly he recognized that evil permeated society. What will change society is individuals turning from

33. Scholars have debated intensely the role of the Pharisees in Second Temple Judaism. Deines (2001) rightly argues that the Pharisees had the most influence among all the religious movements during Jesus' ministry. See also Deines 1997, a definitive work on the Pharisees.

34. For the christological focus in Jesus' view of the kingdom, see Beasley-Murray 1986: 74.

35. Some have maintained that Jesus in actuality was a supporter of violent revolution (e.g., Brandon 1967). Few, however, are convinced of this thesis, and it has been decisively refuted by the small but decisive work of Hengel 1971.

their sin and committing themselves wholly to God. Even more striking, Jesus was convinced that he would transform the world by suffering and dying instead of leading a revolt and triumphing over political enemies. Matthew indicates that Jesus did not come to lead armies into the streets and thereby quash his enemies. On the contrary, he came to heal bruised reeds and to sustain flickering wicks. The kingdom, therefore, would be attained not by militaristic machinations but by Jesus submitting to the will of God and giving his life for the sake of his people (Matt. 12:18–21). Even though the Synoptics do not often cite Isa. 53, it seems that the vision that Jesus had for his own ministry comports with the substance of that chapter, where suffering is the pathway to victory.

The Presence of the Kingdom

The kingdom of God cannot be restricted to the future in the ministry and teaching of Jesus. It is also a present reality.[36] There is a sense, of course, in which God always and invariably rules as king over all. This is illustrated by Ps. 103:19: "The Lord has established his throne in the heavens, and his kingdom rules over all." God reigns at all times and in all places over all that occurs in history. The psalmist therefore declares, "The Lord reigns" (Ps. 93:1; 97:1; 99:1). The universal lordship of God is a staple of OT piety: "God reigns over the nations; God sits on his holy throne" (Ps. 47:8). Israel longed for the coming of God's kingdom in the future but also believed that God was in control of all of history. This is expressed well in the words of Nebuchadnezzar in Dan. 4:34–35: "At the end of the days I, Nebuchadnezzar, lifted my eyes to heaven, and my reason returned to me, and I blessed the Most High, and praised and honored him who lives forever, for his dominion is an everlasting dominion, and his kingdom endures from generation to generation; all the inhabitants of the earth are accounted as nothing, and he does according to his will among the host of heaven and among the inhabitants of the earth; and none can stay his hand or say to him, 'What have you done?'" Jesus too held the notion that God rules over all, that his sovereignty extends over the whole earth. He did not depart from the OT on this matter.

It is clear, then, that when Jesus spoke of the future coming of the kingdom, he was not referring to God's sovereign reign over all of history, for God has always ruled over all that occurs. The coming of the kingdom that Jesus proclaimed designated something new, a time when God's enemies would be demonstrably defeated and the righteous would

---

36. Meier (1994: 242) rightly argues that the kingdom is present according to Jesus, and thus his teaching about the kingdom cannot be confined to existentialism.

be visibly blessed. The future coming of the kingdom relates to the re-alization of God's promises of salvation. God has always ruled over the whole world, but when Jesus arrived on the scene of history, he had not yet fulfilled the saving promises found in the OT, nor were the enemies of God now vanquished.[37] When Jesus announced the presence of the kingdom, he declared that God was about to bring about the salvation that he had always promised.

One of the unique elements of Jesus' teaching about God's kingdom is that it is both present and future.[38] When we speak of God's kingdom as present in the ministry of Jesus, we are not referring to the notion that God is sovereign over all of history. Rather, the kingdom is present in Jesus' ministry in that the saving promises of the kingdom (i.e., the saving rule of God) had dawned with his coming. In other words, the OT promises of a new covenant and a new creation and a new exodus were beginning to be fulfilled in the ministry of Jesus. How does the presence of the kingdom in Jesus' ministry fit together with the prayer for the kingdom to come? Why pray for the kingdom to come if it has already arrived in the person of Jesus? Many scholars now agree that the kingdom of God in Jesus' teaching is both present and future.[39] In other words, the kingdom is already inaugurated but not yet consum-mated.[40] We will now explore in more detail in what sense the kingdom is already present in the ministry of Jesus.

One of the most remarkable statements in the Gospels is found in Matt. 12:28, where Jesus says, "But if it is by the Spirit of God that I cast out demons, then the kingdom of God has come upon you." In the parallel saying, instead of "Spirit of God," Jesus uses the expression "finger of God" (Luke 11:20).[41] Our interest at this point is not on the difference between "Spirit" and "finger," for in either instance the emphasis is on God's power. What is remarkable is that Jesus saw in his exorcisms a sign that the kingdom of God had broken into history.[42] Some interpreters

37. See Dunn 1975b: 47.

38. This emphasis on the presence of the kingdom in Jesus' ministry with a simultaneous expectation of a future consummation is supported also by an examination of Luke-Acts alone (see Maddox 1982: 132–45; also Green 1995: 94–101).

39. Jeremias 1971: 96–108; Kümmel 1957; 1973: 33–39; Ladd 1993: 54–102. There are different nuances in the views of these scholars, but there is general agreement regarding the already–not yet character of the kingdom. For this view in Luke, see Nolland 1998; Marshall 1970: 128–36.

40. Dunn (1975b: 308–18) especially emphasizes the role of the Spirit in the already–not yet character of Jesus' ministry.

41. See the full discussion in Meier 1994: 407–23. Cf. Luke 19:11–44, which Guy (1997) argues supports both the present and the future dimensions of the kingdom.

42. The objection that the kingdom would have also arrived, given Jesus' argument, through the exorcisms of others is unsustainable. As Davies and Allison (1991: 341) note,

have maintained that the saying means only that the kingdom has drawn near; however, the natural meaning of the verb *phthanō* in this context is "arrived" or "has come."[43] Indeed, some promote such an interpretation because they assume that the kingdom is *only* future and eschatological—the same view the Pharisees likely held. Jesus proclaimed that Israel should have perceived in his victory over Satan that the salvation promised in the OT had arrived. The new creation was, in some sense, a reality, for Adam failed to cast the snake out of the garden, but Jesus succeeded in casting out Satan (Matt. 12:28).[44]

According to the Matthean version (Matt. 12:28), the eschatological Spirit promised in the OT was active in Jesus' ministry. Here we have the early evidence for the already–not yet tension that informs the NT.[45] The kingdom had already arrived in the person and ministry of Jesus, but God's enemies had not yet been entirely removed, and the people of God did not yet possess all the blessings pledged to them in the OT.

The kingdom of God was present also in Jesus' miraculous signs and preaching. A programmatic text for this point is Luke 4:16–30, for here Luke portrays the inauguration of Jesus' public ministry and almost certainly relates Jesus' customary message.[46] Jesus began by citing the OT Scriptures and claiming that they reach fulfillment in his person and ministry (cf. Isa. 61:1–2; 58:6; 29:18).[47] The claim is a stunning one, for the OT text refers to the fulfillment of God's end-time promises. Jesus claimed that he is anointed with the eschatological Spirit (cf. Isa. 44:3; Ezek. 11:18–19; 36:26–27; Joel 2:28).[48] The good news of release from exile had now been realized through him. The year of the Lord's favor

---

"Jesus accepts the miracles of others but holds his own to be of different import because of his identity. What is decisive is not the exorcisms but the exorcist." It is probably also the case that Jesus' authority over demons was qualitatively different from the authority of other exorcists.

43. See Dodd 1936: 43–45. For further discussion of this verb along with the various options, see Marshall 1978b: 476; Hagner 1993b: 343; Nolland 2005: 500–501; Fitzmyer 1985: 922. Luz (2001: 204) argues that in Matt. 12:28 the kingdom is present in miracles and exorcisms but has not come in transcendent power in its fullness.

44. So Beale 2004: 173.

45. For a convincing analysis of this verse, see Beasley-Murray 1986: 75–80.

46. See Beasley-Murray 1986: 85–91. Fitzmyer (1981a: 526) comments, "It is an important episode in the Lucan Gospel . . . foreshadowing in a way the account of the entire ministry that is to follow." See also Marshall 1978b: 176; Green 1995: 76.

47. It is likely we have a reference to the Jubilee Year (Lev. 25) here (Marshall 1978b: 184; Bock 1994: 410), but this view is contested (Tannehill 1986: 67–68).

48. Contra Conzelmann (1960: 95), who thinks that the Spirit is not the end-time gift in Luke's theology. This is linked with Conzelmann's view that Jesus' ministry is the middle of time separated from the time of the church, in which the delay of the parousia plays a significant role. For criticisms of Conzelmann's view, see Marshall 1970: 85–88, 107–11, 129–34, 144–50.

and the liberty of God's people had arrived. It does not appear here that Jesus merely states that these promises will be fulfilled at the consummation of all things. Even now, through his healing ministry, the blind were receiving sight. The gospel that he proclaimed means that the poor were hearing the glad tidings in the present. Indeed, Jesus skipped over the line in Isa. 61 that speaks of the Lord's vengeance and referred only to the time of his favor. This suggests that the present time is not a time of vengeance but the day of salvation. The day of vengeance was delayed, and yet, surprisingly enough, the day of favor and salvation had dawned in the person and ministry of Jesus.

A text that points in the same direction is Matt. 11:2–6 (par.).[49] John the Baptist voiced doubts about Jesus, presumably because he languished in prison, and his expectations regarding the kingdom were not realized.[50] We can think back to the words of his father, Zechariah, anticipating salvation "from our enemies and from the hand of all who hate us" (Luke 1:71).[51] Surely, John perceived that the political impact of Jesus' ministry was small and so began to question whether he was truly "the coming one." Jesus did not reply to John's messengers directly but pointed them to what was accomplished in his ministry: the blind seeing, the lame walking, lepers cleansed, the deaf hearing, and the dead raised. Indeed, the good news was being preached to the poor. Once again Jesus cited texts in Isaiah that related what the Lord would do when he freed his people from exile (Isa. 35:1–10; cf. 40:9; 42:6–7; 52:7). The remarkable thing about Isa. 35 is that it clearly speaks of a new creative work of God. The wilderness will become as beautiful and lush as a garden. The desert will flow with streams of water. No rapacious beast will destroy anyone, and when Israel returns to Zion with inexpressible joy, they will be blessed forever. Here we have the language of new creation and a new exodus. At the same time, God will inflict vengeance upon Israel's enemies (Isa. 35:4). What stands out is that many of the prophecies found here remained unfulfilled in Jesus' ministry. Israel did not reside in Jerusalem with everlasting joy and with freedom from fear of enemies. The Romans were still menacingly present in Jesus' day. No vengeance was meted out to Israel's enemies. The world was not transformed into

49. See Beasley-Murray 1986: 80–84; Davies and Allison 1991: 242–43; Hagner 1993b: 300–301. For the Lukan parallel, see Fitzmyer 1981a: 664–65. Fitzmyer maintains that the Baptist has to reinterpret his view of the Messiah because Jesus is not a "fiery reformer." Hagner (1993b: 301) is more precise in saying that Jesus is not fulfilling the role of the judge in the present time (so also Bock 1994: 669–70).

50. For a helpful discussion on the typological and prophetic role of the Baptist, see Evans 2002.

51. Scholars have long recognized the importance of salvation in Luke's theology. See Marshall 1970 on Lukan theology; Green 1998.

a new creation. All of these facts must have contributed to John's doubts about whether Jesus was truly the coming one.

Jesus responds by instructing John about the nature of his ministry. His work among the blind, the lame, the deaf, and the poor reveal that God is fulfilling his promises in Jesus. The new exodus and return from exile promised by Isaiah are a reality for those who respond to Jesus' message—the good news of the gospel is being proclaimed. And yet Jesus himself recognizes that the fulfillment astonishes. He says, "Blessed is the one who is not offended by me" (Matt. 11:6). The prophecies of Isaiah are beginning to be fulfilled, but they are not yet fulfilled in their totality. The kingdom really is present in Jesus' ministry, and yet all that God has promised to do has not become a reality. If John has eyes to see, he must perceive the eschatological tension. Something unexpected has arisen. The promises are not coming to pass in the way John or anyone else expected. God is working remarkably in Jesus' ministry, and yet only some of what is predicted has been realized. The kingdom has arrived, and yet Israel must await the day of vengeance and the completion of all that God promised.[52] It is telling that Jesus, when citing Isaiah, omits the day of vengeance when he proclaims the kingdom (cf. Isa. 19:20; 35:4; 61:2).[53] We should not conclude from this that Jesus rejects any notion of future punishment; rather, the day of judgment is not now—today is the day of salvation.

Jesus also taught that the kingdom had come in his person. The text in Luke 17:20–21 is particularly important. The Pharisees wanted to discuss the coming of the eschatological kingdom. How could they know when it would arrive? What signs will precede its coming? Jesus flatly rejected such speculation. The kingdom cannot be forecasted by observing and interpreting signs. The kingdom of God, Jesus declared, "is among you" (NRSV). The term used here is *entos*, and hence it is possible, as some translations render it, that Jesus says that "the kingdom of God is within you" (KJV, NIV). This interpretation is unlikely, however, for Jesus addressed the Pharisees, and it is quite implausible that he claimed that the kingdom of God was within them! Moreover, Jesus did not say elsewhere that the kingdom is within people. The Pharisees were caught up with excitement over their ability to detect the arrival of the kingdom, but Jesus announced that they were blind to its presence right in front of them.[54] The kingdom had arrived in the

---

52. Meier (1994: 439–50) also rightly argues that Mark 2:18–20 points to the presence of the kingdom.

53. See Meier 1994: 134.

54. Hence, Jesus speaks here of the presence of the kingdom, not its future coming (rightly Bock 1996: 1417–18).

person of Jesus.[55] The Pharisees did not possess any categories, however, to comprehend what Jesus was saying. If the kingdom had arrived, then how could one explain the continuing presence of the Romans and the downtrodden state of Israel? They failed to grasp that Jesus was teaching an already–not yet kingdom. The kingdom was present in the person of Jesus, but it would not be consummated until after his death and resurrection when he will return in glory. Indeed, Jesus specifically distinguished between his first and second advents in this very context (see Luke 17:20–37). Such a concept was completely mystifying to the Pharisees. We know from the Gospels that supporters, such as Jesus' disciples and John the Baptist, had difficulty understanding Jesus' conception of the kingdom. How much more was this true of those who questioned and opposed him?

Those who belong to God will inherit the kingdom in the future, and yet it is also the case that Jesus' disciples were members of God's kingdom during the present age. Those who are poor in spirit share now in the power of the kingdom (Matt. 5:3; cf. Luke 6:20). Those persecuted for Jesus' sake participate in the blessings of the kingdom even while being mistreated (Matt. 5:10). Among the most difficult statements in the Gospels are Matt. 11:12 and Luke 16:16. The meaning of these verses is intensely debated, and it is wise not to base any significant thesis about Jesus' ministry on a disputed text.[56] I understand Matt. 11:12 to say that the kingdom of God has been advancing forcefully in the world from the time that the Baptist began to preach. Jesus did not proclaim a different message from that of the Baptist.[57] He too heralded the message of the kingdom. What this verse teaches is that the kingdom is now active in a powerful way in the world. It is not merely a future power. The kingdom had arrived, particularly in the preaching and ministry of Jesus of Nazareth. Demons were being cast out, the sick healed, and the needy transformed by the good news of salvation. The last part of Matt. 11:12 probably means that only those who make a decisive commitment to be part of the kingdom

55. See the clear defense of this view in Bock 1996: 1415–17; see also Kümmel 1957: 34. Beasley-Murray (1986: 97–103) claims that the verse means that the kingdom of God is within reach of those who hear the good news being proclaimed by and in the person of Jesus. Fitzmyer (1985: 1159, 1161–62) maintains that "among you" and "in your reach" are equally possible, and the meaning is not greatly affected either way. But for a convincing argument favoring authenticity and the meaning "in your midst," see Meier 1994: 423–30.

56. See Beasley-Murray 1986: 91–96.

57. For a survey of the options for this verse, see Davies and Allison 1991: 254–55; Hagner 1993b: 306–7. Hagner understands the verse negatively, so that it speaks of the kingdom suffering violence and of violent people plundering it (see also Davies and Allison 1991: 255–56; Meier 1994: 160).

receive its blessings. The kingdom has come, but one must grasp the kingdom and give it priority to receive its blessings. Luke 16:16, then, has a similar meaning.[58] The good news of the kingdom, the gospel of the kingdom, had been proclaimed from the time of John the Baptist onward, though it obtains its supreme expression in the ministry and proclamation of Jesus. The emphasis on good news suggests that the kingdom preached fulfills the promises of return from exile prophesied in Isaiah (Isa. 40:9; 52:7).[59] Luke adds, "and everyone forces his way into it" (Luke 16:16). This saying should be interpreted similarly to what we found in Matthew. One must act decisively and give up all to enter the kingdom. The blessings of the kingdom will pass by those who put something else above the kingdom, for Jesus demanded that the kingdom be preeminent in the lives of those who claim to be people of the Lord (Matt. 6:33).

The Parables and the Kingdom

In Matt. 13:11 Jesus says that the parables reveal the "secrets" or "mysteries" of the kingdom.[60] Jesus' parables can be studied from a number of different angles. Here we want to explore what the parables tell us about the kingdom of God.[61] We saw above that the difficult sayings in Matt. 11:12 and Luke 16:16 focus on the power of the kingdom. The kingdom's power is communicated also in parables, and we begin with one that is unique to Mark (Mark 4:26–29). The kingdom is compared to seed sown on the ground. The sower sleeps, and yet the seed sprouts and grows in a way that is incomprehensible to the sower. The seed then begins to bear fruit, and finally when the fruit is ripened, the crop is harvested. Jesus emphasized that the power of the kingdom stems from the word of God. The word itself creates life and fruitfulness, and the speaker of the word is amazed at how it continues to bear fruit even when he is absent. As Beasley-Murray notes, the account "sets forth the coming reign of God as a process attributable solely to the miraculous working of God."[62] This parable also reveals

58. So Marshall 1978b: 629–30; Fitzmyer 1985: 1117. Bock (1996: 1352–54) understands the verse as imploring all to enter the kingdom. It should be noted as well that most commentators claim that the saying has a different meaning in Matthew than in Luke.

59. See Watts 2000: 96–102.

60. On the theme of parables and the kingdom, see Jeremias 1972: 115–24.

61. In a more thorough examination of the parables, Blomberg (1990a: 297–302) demonstrates that they support the notion that the kingdom is both present and future.

62. Beasley-Murray 1986: 126. See also Hooker 1991: 136; Hultgren 2000: 388; Marcus 2000: 326–28; France 2002: 214–15.

the already–not yet character of the kingdom. The kingdom even now bears fruit and accomplishes its purpose in the world. By the word of God it advances. Still, the kingdom is not consummated until the end of the age, when the judgment comes.

The parable of the four soils (Matt. 13:1–9, 18–23 par.) teaches a number of different truths. Jülicher rightly reacted against an indiscriminate allegorizing of parables, but he overcompensated by insisting that parables only have one point.[63] To say in advance that parables cannot have any allegorical features determines in advance their interpretation. Whether parables have one point or whether they contain some allegorical elements must be resolved by investigating each parable separately instead of trying to formulate a principle that embraces every parable.[64] What we are seeking here is what the parable of the four soils teaches about the kingdom of God. A striking feature of the parable is that when the kingdom is proclaimed, not all accept its message. There are four different kinds of soil, and only the last bears genuine fruit. All the other soils fail to persevere in bearing fruit, and they represent people who are unsaved on the day of judgment.[65] One of the mysteries of the kingdom communicated here is that the word of the kingdom will not immediately have overwhelming success in this world.[66] Many will reject the good news about the kingdom, but they will not be judged instantly. The Jews expected the kingdom to arrive in apocalyptic power, sweeping away all opponents. But this parable reveals that the message of the kingdom does not operate initially in this manner. In and through the preaching of Jesus the kingdom is successful only in some hearts. The whole world is not changed dramatically, and yet the kingdom is at work; it is operating in the world, transforming hearts through the message of the kingdom. Still, some people resist the message of the kingdom and refuse to believe. This parable communicates the secret of the kingdom: it is already here through the preached word, but the day of judgment is reserved for the future.[67]

63. Jülicher argued that in Jesus' teaching, parables only had one point, but the Gospel writers turned the parables into allegories (see Baird 2003: 158–59).

64. Blomberg (1990a) effectively criticizes the notion that parables must be restricted to one truth and provides his own constructive understanding of Jesus' parables. For classic works on the parables, see Dodd 1936; Jeremias 1972. For more recent work, see Hultgren 2000.

65. See Hagner 1993b: 381.

66. The surprising nature of the kingdom is captured well by Marcus 2000: 295–96.

67. The observations of Vickers (2004: 17) on this parable are helpful: "The Kingdom is not initially coming on the scene with fanfare or in a cataclysmic battle." He points out that the adverse response to Jesus' ministry in the Gospels does not contradict the promise that the kingdom has arrived, for it has not come in such a way that it overwhelms its enemies immediately.

The parable of the weeds (Matt. 13:24–30, 36–43) communicates a message that is rather similar to the parable of the four soils. The Jews expected that when the kingdom arrived, their enemies would be removed and paradise would commence. Jesus revealed one of the mysteries of the kingdom in the parable of the weeds. The word of the kingdom is spread throughout the world by the Son of Man. As expected, God's word is effective and powerful, producing "children of the kingdom" (Matt. 13:38). Still, all is not well in the world, for the devil also sows "children of the evil one" (Matt. 13:38). The arrival of the kingdom does not transform the world into a place of peace and prosperity. The world is a battleground between children of God and children of the devil. The kingdom is truly present, as is evidenced by the children of the kingdom. The kingdom of God has come in transforming power. But astonishingly, the enemies of the kingdom persist and are not removed from the scene. The world is filled with ambiguity and tension between those transformed by the kingdom and those hating the kingdom.[68] Indeed, in some instances it is difficult to discern who genuinely belongs to the kingdom and who does not. Only on the final day will we be able to discern clearly all those who genuinely were believers and those who only appeared to belong to God. Hence, the mystery of the kingdom is that an interval exists between the inauguration and the consummation of the kingdom. The day of judgment lies in the future, and when that day arrives, the Son of Man will punish those who practice evil and will reward the righteous. On the last day the prophecy of Daniel, that the righteous will shine like stars, will reach its fulfillment (Dan. 12:1–3; cf. Phil. 2:15). In the meantime, even though the kingdom is present and active in the world, the struggle with evil continues, and we are unable to discern infallibly those who are genuine believers.

The parable of the net (Matt. 13:47–50) is similar in some ways to the parable of the weeds. During the present age the kingdom is like a fishing net that gathers a variety of fish, both good and bad. So too in the present age the kingdom embraces both good and evil but without judging the evil definitively. The evil as well as the good are caught up in the power of the kingdom that sweeps through the world. Only at the end of the age will those who are evil be separated from those who are good. The punishment is not immediate but future. The kingdom is now sweeping through the world, gathering up into its net both good and evil, but the day of judgment is coming, the day when the kingdom will be consummated and evil will be judged.

---

68. Rightly Hagner 1993b: 395. Hultgren (2000: 299) concludes from this that the church is a mixed entity, consisting of both good and evil. But Luz (2001: 268–70) contends that the church is specifically excluded from purview here. Hultgren (2000: 300–301) individualizes the parable unduly in saying that good and evil also reside in each believer.

The nature of the kingdom is captured well by the parables of the mustard seed and the leaven.[69] These parables likewise present the mystery of the kingdom. Again we must remind ourselves that the Jews thought that the kingdom would demolish their enemies, arrive with overwhelming force, and be evident to all. Jesus, however, taught that the kingdom does not arrive as a massive tree that holds sway over the earth like the kingdom of Nebuchadnezzar (Dan. 4). The kingdom's coming is as inconspicuous and small as a mustard seed—the smallest seed of Jesus' day (Matt. 13:31–32 par.). It is like a small seed in a vegetable garden.[70] The coming of the kingdom is not trumpeted to the entire world for all to know that it has appeared.[71] Eventually the kingdom of God becomes a tree that dominates the entire earth. The image of the mustard seed becoming a tree probably indicates that the kingdom of God grows throughout history.[72] What started out small becomes larger.[73] Nevertheless, this should not be interpreted to mean that the kingdom will eventually rule over this world before the return of Christ and become evident to all. The kingdom grows, but even its increase does not represent an apocalyptic forcefulness that steamrolls opposition. Many observe the world and see no indication of its presence at all. Ultimately, however, the kingdom of God will rule and reign over the whole world. On the day of judgment and salvation the kingdom will be consummated. What began as a small mustard seed will end up as a towering tree ruling over all.

The parable of the leaven (Matt. 13:33 par.) should be interpreted like the parable of the mustard seed, and its placement immediately after the latter suggests that the two make basically the same point. The kingdom does not arrive manifestly and clearly but rather is nearly invisible, like leaven in flour.[74] In other words, the watching world does not perceive the presence of the kingdom. Still, Jesus maintained that the kingdom had arrived in his ministry even though it is hidden and obscured. Once again the permeation of the flour with leaven signifies a gradual growth of the kingdom, but that growth is perceptible only to the eye of faith,

---

69. See the classic exposition in Jeremias 1972: 146–53.

70. See Luz 2001: 261.

71. Stein (1981: 95) comments that what is distinctive here is not "the greatness of the kingdom of God in its final manifestation, for every Jew who heard Jesus would agree with this. . . . What was not recognized nor understood was the smallness and insignificance of its beginning."

72. So Davies and Allison 1991: 419, though they caution rightly against equating the kingdom of God with the church.

73. It may be the case, on the other hand, that this feature of the parable should not be pressed (so Jeremias 1972: 148; Hultgren 2000: 401).

74. Luz (2001: 262–63) argues that the parable emphasizes not the small amount of leaven but rather its hiddenness.

for the kingdom does not advance by crushing God's enemies. Jesus contrasted what the kingdom is like in this present age with its consummation in the age to come. Only at the end will the kingdom rule over all, and then it will be as comprehensive and complete as leaven in dough. The kingdom is already here, even if obscure and hidden as leaven, and eventually it will triumph completely.

In the midst of the parables in Matt. 13, Ps. 78 is cited to explain why Jesus spoke in parables (Matt. 13:34–35).[75] Psalm 78 reviews the history of Israel until the time of David, emphasizing Israel's hard heart and rebellion against God. Matthew interprets the psalm prophetically (cf. the use of the word "prophet" in Matt. 13:35) to demonstrate that the psalm anticipated Jesus' generation, for the Israel of Jesus' day was still rebellious. They resisted the word of the Lord proclaimed through Jesus. This fits with Matt. 13:13–15 (cf. Mark 4:11–12; Luke 8:9–10), where the prophecy of Isa. 6 is seen to be fulfilled through Jesus' teaching of parables. The parables function to harden stiff-necked and rebellious Israel.[76] The mysteries of the kingdom are closed to them, but the disciples, by God's grace, have been given insight to know the secrets of the kingdom (Matt. 13:11). They are incomparably blessed because God has revealed the nature of the kingdom to them (Matt. 13:16–17). Psalm 78, then, reveals something about the kingdom. Even Israel is not genuinely open to the message of the kingdom. The Israel of Jesus' day is like Israel throughout history, the Israel that went into exile because of its rebellion. Psalm 78 concludes, however, with God's faithfulness to his promise. He raised up David to shepherd his people. So too God had now raised up Jesus as Israel's Messiah. Those who had eyes to see perceive that in Jesus the kingdom has begun, but many in Israel failed to perceive the mystery of the kingdom.

Even though the kingdom is nearly invisible, it is incomparably precious. The value of the kingdom is communicated in the parables of the hidden treasure and the pearl of great value (Matt. 13:44–46). Both parables emphasize the hiddenness of the kingdom. The treasure and the pearl are discovered by assiduously searching for them. The kingdom is not apparent on first glance, nor is its value grasped by all. The end of the age has not yet come, when the kingdom of God will rule over all, where the righteous are blessed and the wicked punished. Currently the

---

75. On the reference to Ps. 78 here, see Carson 1984: 321–23.

76. The view proposed here fits with the claim by Watts (2000: 184–209) that Mark 4:11–12 represents Yahweh's judicial hardening of those who have consistently turned against the Lord's will. See also the perceptive exegesis in Marcus 2000: 299–301, 305–7; Evans 1988: 92–99. Matt. 13:13 emphasizes human responsibility (rightly Davies and Allison 1991: 392), but if Watts is correct, we have a different emphasis, not a different theology.

kingdom is like a hidden treasure or an obscure pearl. So the kingdom really is present in the world in the ministry of Jesus. And those who perceive the value of the kingdom joyfully give up all to enter into it. Its value is not conspicuous, however; on the day when the kingdom is consummated, all will perceive that the kingdom is exceedingly precious.[77] But in the interval between the "already" and the "not yet," only some discern the worth of the kingdom.

Jesus concluded the parables in Matt. 13 by comparing the kingdom of heaven to a scribe "who brings out of his treasure what is new and what is old" (Matt. 13:52). Jesus considered here the OT, the many prophecies about the kingdom of God. The disciple of Jesus, however, must interpret the prophecies in light of what is new, the dawning of the kingdom of God in the ministry of Jesus. The wise disciple, then, both grasps the meaning of the OT prophecy and discerns its fulfillment in Jesus. The new and the old are rightly related and correlated to one another.[78] The old is not imposed upon the new, nor does the new squelch the old. Both the new and the old have their proper place, but the old, ultimately and finally, can be grasped only by those who understand the newness present in Jesus.

Miracles and the Kingdom

The inauguration of the kingdom is manifested by signs, wonders, and healings.[79] Jesus' miracles are not just the promise of the kingdom; they are themselves the actualization, at least in part, of the kingdom.[80] We noted earlier that Jesus pointed to Isa. 35 to demonstrate to the Baptist and his disciples that he truly is the coming one. In Isa. 35 the arrival of God's kingdom is evidenced by a new work of creation in which the wilderness will bloom, streams will flow in the desert, and voracious beasts will become tame.[81] Israel will return from exile and will experience everlasting joy. Israel did return from exile, but they hardly experienced everlasting joy. Nor did the blind see, the lame walk, and the deaf hear.

77. Beasley-Murray (1986: 111) remarks, "The point is that the worth of what has come to the finders is so great that they are happy to pay whatever price is necessary to get it."

78. See Davies and Allison 1991: 446–48; Hagner 1993b: 402; Luz 2001: 287–88. The "priority" is "given to the new" because it is mentioned first (Nolland 2005: 571).

79. See the vigorous study by Kallas (1961), who overstates his point here and there. See also Tannehill (1986: 89), who focuses on the message in Luke.

80. So Twelftree 1999: 263, 268–72, 276.

81. Many scholars, of course, have doubted the reality of the miracles. But Schlatter (1997: 174–91) showed that they cannot be stripped from Jesus' message of the kingdom.

In many texts in the Synoptic Gospels the proclamation of the gospel is accompanied by physical healing and the exorcism of demons (e.g., Matt. 4:23; 9:35; 10:7–8; Luke 9:11; 10:9, 17; 11:20). Jesus' exorcisms instantiate his victory over Satan and demons, indicating that the kingdom is now present and that Jesus has triumphed over the reign of evil.[82] Furthermore, if we look at the Synoptic Gospels as a whole, we see that much attention is devoted to Jesus' healings and exorcisms. We have warrant from the summary statements themselves (Matt. 4:23; 9:35; Luke 9:2, 11) to see these as manifestations of the kingdom of God. Indeed, we have seen from Isa. 35 that such healings are indications of the presence of the kingdom, of the kingdom already exerting its power in this present evil age. Adherents of rationalistic liberalism denied the reality of the miraculous because of their Enlightenment worldview, which denied the intervention of God in the cosmos. Their problem with the miracles arose from their philosophical standpoint and cannot be derived from a study of the text. It is clear that the Gospel writers believed that the miracles truly occurred. The miracles are not merely spiritual realities that can be reduced to spiritual lessons or moral truths.[83] Indeed, there are sound reasons for believing that the miracles actually occurred in Jesus' ministry, that the stories go back to the historical Jesus.[84] Meier says about the miracles "that total fabrication by the early church is, practically speaking, impossible"; and, "the tradition of Jesus' miracles is more firmly supported by the criteria of historicity than are a number of other well-known and often readily accepted traditions about his life and ministry. . . . Put dramatically but with not too much exaggeration: if the miracle tradition from Jesus' public ministry were rejected *in toto* as unhistorical, so should every other Gospel tradition about him."[85] Indeed, Meier does not shrink back from saying that, as far as one can determine matters historically, there are solid grounds for believing that

---

82. See Twelftree 1993; 1999.

83. Indeed, the credibility of miracles increases when we consider the matter philosophically. I contend that we must presuppose the truth of the Scriptures and the biblical worldview, for no worldview can be proved ultimately, definitively, and without lingering questions. That does not mean, however, that we do not consider evidence. All other worldviews ultimately succumb to rationalism or irrationalism, or the evidence adduced for their truth fails to persuade. When we consider the biblical worldview, we also find that historical evidence confirms the worldview adopted. See Frame 1987.

84. Twelftree 1999: 281–330; Meier 1994: 509–1038. Meier does not claim that the miracles actually happened, for he maintains that the actuality of miracles lies outside the realm of historical study. Instead, Meier, with painstaking care and remarkable thoroughness, evaluates whether the claim that miracles occurred goes back to the historical Jesus. His judgments vary somewhat from miracle to miracle, but in the main he argues that the reports are credibly attributed to the historical Jesus.

85. Meier 1994: 630.

Jesus raised people from the dead.[86] Nor can the miracles be explained away with rationalistic explanations, such as the idea that Jesus was walking on the shore rather than the water, or that at the feeding of the five thousand the young boy shared his lunch, which inspired others to do the same, or that those apparently raised from the dead were not really dead. Kallas rightly says, "The kingdom meant the defeat of Satan, and the re-creation, the restoration, of the world that Satan had stolen and subjugated."[87] Nevertheless, the miracles also point to God's future kingdom, the new creation devoid of sickness, disease, and demons (see Rev. 21:1–8). The miracles, then, testify to the already–not yet character of the kingdom. They demonstrate that the kingdom has entered into this world, and yet not everyone is healed, which shows that the kingdom is not yet consummated. Death and evil still cast their long shadow over the world.

Jesus' miracles, then, are signs of the kingdom, manifestations of the new creation.[88] Restoring health to the sick or freeing the demonized from oppression signals the onset of the new age, and this is a harbinger of the new creation where sickness is absent and the impact of demons only a memory. Jesus' power over sickness and demons demonstrates that he rules over disease and the demonic. The forces of evil cannot triumph over him; he reigns over all that deforms and destroys. In the same way, the nature miracles (e.g., Matt. 14:13–33) reveal Jesus' mastery over the created world, demonstrating that he is the sovereign ruler over all creation. "Each miracle is—at least in part—the actual arrival of salvation."[89] These miracles also anticipate the new creation where the entirety of the created order reflects the order and justice intended for the world from the beginning.

If miracles point to something beyond themselves, then those observing them should perceive God's mighty work through Jesus in the wonders performed. The miracles performed by Jesus fit with two major themes of this work. First, as we have already seen, they signify the inbreaking of God's kingdom—the arrival of the age to come in the midst of this present evil age. But second, they also testify to Jesus' identity.[90] They

---

86. Meier 1994: 773–873. Meier (1994: 968) is not claiming that these accounts are actually miracles but only that what occurred was thought to be miraculous by some of Jesus' contemporaries. It is not my purpose here to examine Meier's philosophical approach, which is, I think, too limiting. My point is simply that even within the bounds of his criteria solid reasons exist to believe that Jesus performed many miracles. Incidentally, Meier (1994: 874–1038) is more skeptical about the historical reliability of the nature miracles, except for the miraculous feedings.

87. Kallas 1961: 81.

88. Beale 2004: 174.

89. Crump 2006: 43.

90. Rightly Twelftree 1999: 93–96, 181–82, 223, 225, 234–35, 275–76.

demonstrate that Jesus is the Messiah, the Son of Man, the Son of God, and the Lord of all. This is scarcely surprising, for the coming of the kingdom also signals the arrival of the king. It would be a strange state of affairs if the kingdom arrived without its king and lord!

We think here of John's distinctive vocabulary whereby he identifies Jesus' miracles as "signs" (*sēmeia*).[91] As signs, they point to something, to someone, beyond themselves. For example, the miracle at Cana anticipates the day when God will fulfill all his promises, when wine will flow down the hills (John 2:1–11; cf. Joel 3:18; Amos 9:13). The healing on the Sabbath points forward to the Sabbath rest of the eschatological day (John 5:1–18). The feeding of the five thousand signifies that Jesus is the bread of life and that he gives true life to the world, a life that transcends the eating of manna (John 6:1–59). The healing of the blind man indicates that Jesus is the true light of the world and that he removes spiritual blindness (John 8:12–9:41). The raising of Lazarus anticipates the final resurrection, which will be enjoyed by all of God's people (John 11). John does not criticize signs as inadequate or superficial, as a first glance at some texts might suggest (John 2:23–25; 4:48).[92] The stated purpose of his Gospel makes it clear that the signs *should* lead human beings to put their faith in Jesus (John 20:30–31; cf. 12:37). If the signs do not lead to faith, the fault lies not in the signs but in human beings who refuse to believe and who fail to see in the signs who Jesus is.

Even though Acts extends beyond the ministry of Jesus, we see that miracles have a similar function in Acts. The apostles proclaimed that Jesus' miracles demonstrate that he was accredited by God as the Messiah (Acts 2:22; 10:38). When Peter and John healed a lame man (Acts 3:1–10), the astonishing character of the healing provided an opportunity for Peter to preach the message of forgiveness through Jesus Christ and to explain that any healing comes exclusively through the name of Jesus (Acts 3:11–26). The signs, wonders, and miracles performed by the apostles played a vital role in the spread of the gospel (Acts 5:12–16; 9:32–43). Similarly, the signs and wonders of Stephen and Philip attested that they were speaking God's message and gave them an opportunity to proclaim the word of God both to opponents and to those interested in hearing the message (Acts 6:8–7:53; 8:5–24). Similarly, God granted Paul and Barnabas the ability to do miracles on their first missionary journey (Acts 15:12). The miracles not only opened the door for the word of the gospel but also were manifestations of the kingdom themselves. Juel observes that the miracles "offer evidence that the 'last days' have

91. Due to the subject matter addressed here, I am including Johannine material at this point.

92. For the view of the Johannine signs defended here, see M. M. Thompson 1988: 53–86.

indeed arrived and that the Spirit, poured out by the risen Jesus from his place at God's right hand, is at work."[93] They anticipate the new creation where sickness, deformity, and disease will be left behind. The signs and wonders of the apostles are manifestations of the kingdom and represent the continuation of Jesus' teaching and ministry (Acts 1:1, 3).

Other Views of the Kingdom

At this juncture we will explore all too briefly some of the views of the kingdom in the history of the church. The early church tended to equate the kingdom with the church.[94] It is more satisfying, however, to say that the kingdom works in and through the church but is not coequal with the church. The church per se cannot be identified with the ruling power of God, even though God's transforming power is manifested in the church. The church has been tempted throughout history to construct an overrealized view of the kingdom and to view itself as the full manifestation of the kingdom of God.

Liberalism collapsed the kingdom into the notion of the fatherhood of God and the fraternity of humankind.[95] In this view, the kingdom of God is basically equated with ethics. The liberal conception of the kingdom is a classic example of imposing a preferred notion of the kingdom, a culturally acceptable view of the kingdom, upon the Gospels. More than a hundred years ago Weiss demonstrated that the apocalyptic nature of the kingdom was completely ignored by liberalism.[96] Liberalism's view of the kingdom domesticated the kingdom in the teaching of Jesus and thus failed to do true biblical theology.

The apocalyptic view of the kingdom that has influenced NT study to this day was articulated, as we noted above, by Weiss. Schweitzer embraced Weiss's conclusions, using them to argue against liberalism's understanding of the kingdom. This view has sometimes been called "consistent eschatology" or "thoroughgoing eschatology."[97] In Schweitzer's view, Jesus traveled to Jerusalem to compel God to bring in the kingdom, but his noble attempt failed. In other words, Jesus' idea of the kingdom was mistaken. He incorrectly believed the kingdom was imminent, and we realize from our standpoint in history that Jesus was misguided. If Schweitzer was correct, it is difficult to know how Jesus' message of the kingdom relates to us today. It would seem that Jesus' view stands as a

---

93. Juel 1983: 62.
94. See the helpful discussion of this matter in Ladd 1993: 103–17.
95. For example, Harnack 1957.
96. Weiss 1971 (the first edition was published in 1892).
97. Schweitzer 1968: 238–69, 330–97.

monument to the delusion that God was about to bring in his kingdom and fulfill his promises. Since it did not happen, should we venerate Jesus for his aspirations while realizing that he was profoundly mistaken? On Schweitzer's terms, it seems that Jesus could only be hailed as a failed revolutionary. I will argue in due course that we do not need to embrace Schweitzer's conclusion that Jesus was mistaken, and so Jesus' conception of the kingdom still speaks to us today. Furthermore, the already–not yet character of the kingdom is not explained adequately by Schweitzer, and inaugurated eschatology solves some of the problems raised by Schweitzer.

The Bultmannian school understood the kingdom existentially. This is captured well in this statement by Bultmann: "The essential thing about the eschatological message is the idea of God that operates in it and the idea of human existence that it contains—not the belief that the end of the world is just ahead."[98] According to Bultmann, Jesus was mistaken about when the world would end, but if we demythologize his message and apply it to ourselves, it still speaks to us today. Bultmann commented similarly: "The coming of the Kingdom of God is therefore not really an event in the course of time, which is due to occur sometime and toward which man can either take a definite attitude or hold himself neutral."[99] Bultmann removed the kingdom from space-time reality and focused on the existence of human beings. We find the same theme in his disciple Conzelmann. The nearness of the kingdom "does not represent a primarily neutral statement about the length or brevity of an interval of time, but a fact which determines human existence; man has no more time left to himself. He must respond to the kingdom in the present moment."[100] But why should human beings respond if the kingdom is not a historical reality, if Jesus was mistaken about the time of the end? It seems arbitrary to claim that what Jesus taught about the kingdom is flawed and then to apply it to our lives, even if in a demythologized form. Furthermore, the existential worldview of Bultmann and his disciples is imposed upon the NT instead of being a faithful rendition of the NT kerygma.

More recently scholars have emphasized the already–not yet character of the kingdom. Dodd put his emphasis initially on realized eschatology and seemed to allow little room for future eschatology.[101] Scholars such as Jeremias, Kümmel, Goppelt, Cullmann, Ladd, and Beasley-Murray

98. Bultmann 1951: 23. See also Bultmann 1962: 27–56.
99. Bultmann 1962: 51–52.
100. Conzelmann 1969: 111.
101. Dodd 1936: 50–51. In the remainder of the book Dodd argues that parables and statements regarding the Son of Man that seem to refer to a future kingdom in their original historical context emphasized realized eschatology. Hence, according to Dodd,

have emphasized inaugurated eschatology in the teaching of Jesus.[102] They differ on details and in emphasis, but they seem to have rightly captured a main theme in the teaching of Jesus. Ladd's definition helpfully captures Jesus' notion of the kingdom: "The Kingdom of God is the redemptive reign of God dynamically active to establish his rule among human beings, and . . . this Kingdom, which will appear as an apocalyptic act at the end of the age, has already come into human history in the person and mission of Jesus to overcome evil, to deliver people from its power, and to bring them into the blessings of God's reign."[103] We can say, then, that the kingdom was inaugurated in the ministry and death and resurrection of Jesus, but the kingdom will not be consummated until he returns. The emphasis on the kingdom fits with one of the major themes of this book. As Beasley-Murray says, "Yet the sovereign action of God must by its very nature finally disclose itself in the consummate glory of the Creator-Redeemer."[104]

Fulfillment Formulae in Matthew

The coming of the kingdom means that God's promises of old are being fulfilled. This theme is evident in all four Gospels and indeed in all of the NT. The purpose here is not to trace the theme broadly but rather to investigate the particular emphasis on fulfillment in Matthew.[105] Nor will we examine the fulfillment of the law in Matthew here, for that theme is significant enough to warrant separate treatment elsewhere.

In some instances prophecy and fulfillment appear to be rather direct. For instance, Mic. 5:2 predicted that the Messiah would be born in Bethlehem, and Matthew narrates how this prophecy was fulfilled (Matt. 2:1–12). Interestingly, a fulfillment formula is not used in this text, but Matthew clearly perceives that Jesus' birth fulfilled Micah's prophecy. Perhaps some might find a problem in Micah's claim that Bethlehem is too small to be considered among the clans of Judah, whereas Matthew emphasizes that Bethlehem should not be considered as despised or too small.[106] The difference between the texts is one of perspective.

---

the theme of future eschatology was a later addition. Dodd (1953: 447n1) later signaled his agreement with Jeremias (see the next note).

102. Jeremias (1972: 230) describes his view as eschatology that is in the process of being realized. See also Kümmel 1957; Cullmann 1964; Beasley-Murray 1986; Goppelt 1981: 43–76; Ladd 1993.

103. Ladd 1993: 89–90.

104. Beasley-Murray 1986: 74.

105. For useful surveys of the theme, see France 1989: 166–205; Stanton 1988: 205–10.

106. See Davies and Allison 1988: 242–43. But see Hagner (1993b: 29), who mentions a possible reading of the Hebrew that would fit with what we find in Matthew.

Micah stresses that even though Bethlehem is insignificant, God will surprisingly raise up a ruler from it. Matthew does not contradict this truth; he simply affirms that Bethlehem, despite its size, should not be considered insignificant, since the ruler hails from it.[107]

Other texts in Matthew conceive of the fulfillment of prophecy rather differently. The OT event functions as a model or type of that which is fulfilled in Jesus. Hence, the OT text is fulfilled in a typological fashion.[108] We think of the famous fulfillment formula relative to the virgin birth in Matt. 1:22–23.[109] The virgin birth of Jesus, in which he saves his people from their sins, fulfilled the ancient prophecy of Isaiah. When we examine Isa. 7 in context, however, we see that matters become more complicated. The text addresses the period when Ahaz was king of Judah, suffering a severe threat from Rezin, the king of Syria, and Pekah, the king of Israel. These two kings had formed an alliance and intended to install upon Judah's throne another leader, Tabeel. Judah and Ahaz are terrified by the prospect, but the Lord promises that the conspiracy against Judah will not succeed. No rival will supplant the son of David as the king of Judah.

The Lord invited Ahaz to ask him for a sign to confirm the Lord's faithfulness to his promise, but Ahaz refused to ask him for a sign. His refusal was a sign not of faith but of rebellion. Nevertheless, the Lord granted him a sign anyway. The sign is that a virgin or young woman will bear a child and name him "Immanuel." He is called "Immanuel" because his birth testifies to God's presence with his people, confirming the promise that Syria and Israel would not install another king in Judah. Commentators have long debated how to interpret this sign, and space is lacking here to give a full accounting of the various proposals.[110] Here I will attempt to defend the view that seems most plausible to me. First, the notion that the prophecy is a straightforward prediction of the birth of Jesus does not explain well the features found in Isa. 7–8 itself. Immediately after the prophecy is uttered in Isa. 7:14, we are told that the boy who will be born will eat curds and honey at an age at which he grasps the difference between good and evil (Isa. 7:15). Isaiah 7:16 is even more specific. Before the child can distinguish between good and evil, both kingdoms that threaten Judah (i.e., Israel and Syria) will

107. Rightly Carson 1984: 87–88.
108. See Hagner 1993b: 20–21.
109. For a brief analysis of possible antecedents, see Davies and Allison 1988: 214–16. They conclude that there are no clear parallels or precursors to the story in either Hellenistic or Jewish literature. For a vibrant defense of the historical and theological veracity of the virgin birth, see Machen 1965.
110. Childs (2001: 60–81) ultimately understands the text messianically and relates the prophecy to Isa. 9:6–7. See also Motyer 1993: 86.

be judged. We learn from the subsequent verses that Assyria will function as the agent of judgment upon Israel and Syria. As a result of the
Assyrian invasion, the land will be devastated. All that remains will be
curds and honey (Isa. 7:22). Before the promised child is old enough to
distinguish between right and wrong, the Lord will remove Syria and
Israel by the hand of Assyria.

Who is the son spoken of in this text? A good case can be made for
Hezekiah, and that would fit nicely with the Matthean emphasis on the
birth of Jesus.[111] Hezekiah would function as the prototype of a later
king, Jesus of Nazareth. The case seems still stronger when we include
the prophecies of a coming king in Isa. 9:1–7; 11:1–10. Nevertheless, it
seems that Isa. 8 suggests that the son in view is Isaiah's son Maher-
shalal-hash-baz (Isa. 8:1).[112] Isaiah specifically notes that he had sexual
relations with the prophetess and that she conceived (Isa. 8:3). This
fits the notion that a young woman would conceive and have a child.
Furthermore, Isa. 8:4 indicates that before the boy could articulate the
words "mother" or "father," Assyria would despoil Israel and Syria. The
parallel with Isa. 7 is unmistakable, where we are informed that judgment will come upon Israel and Syria before the child can distinguish
between good and evil.

Isaiah proceeds to explain in chapter 8 that Assyria will sweep into the
land and judge Israel and Syria (Isa. 8:5–8). Assyria will sweep in like a
flood and even come up to the neck of Judah, so that it almost takes the
whole country. But as we read later in Isa. 36–37, Assyria was unable to
conquer Jerusalem itself. The repetition of "Immanuel" in Isa. 8:8 also
links chapter 8 with chapter 7. God was with his people, preserving them
from complete annihilation by Assyria (see also Isa. 8:10). The people,
therefore, were not to fear the conspiracy hatched by Syria and Israel
but only to fear the Lord (Isa. 8:11–13). The significance of Isaiah's child
is that he is a sign and portent (Isa. 8:18), strengthening the case that
he is the child spoken of in this instance. It is true that another child is
coming (Isa. 9:6–7) to whom ultimate rule will belong, but Isaiah likely
refers to his own child in chapters 7–8.[113] The fact that two names are
used for Isaiah's child, "Immanuel" and "Maher-shalal-hash-baz," is
not a problem, for the son functioned symbolically on more than one
level. The names signify two realities. The judgment from Assyria would
come quickly, and yet God would be present with his people. He will

111. R. Brown (1977: 147–49) thinks that the child is Davidic and notes that some see it
as Hezekiah (e.g., Schibler 1995: 99). Carson (1984: 79–80) emphasizes that Isa. 7:1–9:7
is a unit, culminating with the son promised in Isa. 9:6–7.

112. R. Brown (1977: 148) dismisses this view because the prophetess already had a
son. See also Motyer 1993: 86–87.

113. So Oswalt 1986: 212–13, 220, 227.

not allow the southern kingdom of Judah to fall when the devastation from Assyria comes.

This brief explication of Isa. 7–8 helps us grasp Matthew's citation of the fulfillment formula. How can Matthew use this text with reference to the virgin birth if it relates to a child begotten by a young woman? The most satisfactory answer is that Matthew reads the text typologically. What God did for his people in the past anticipates and foreshadows his work in the future. Even in the context of Isaiah the future dimension of the promise is adumbrated, for in chapter 9 Isaiah proceeds to speak of a child, a son of David, who will rule the nations (Isa. 9:2–7). The term used for "young woman" (NRSV) in Hebrew ('almâ) could refer to a virgin, and the LXX uses the word *parthenos*, which is defined as "virgin." That the woman in Matthew is a virgin is not surprising, for there is escalation between the type and the fulfillment. If the sign in the days of Ahaz was surprising, how much greater is the sign of salvation in the days of final fulfillment? If God was present with his people in saving them from Assyria, how much more is Immanuel now present in Jesus the Christ? We also see a theme that frames the entire book of Matthew. Jesus is Immanuel—God with us (Matt. 1:23)—and the book concludes with Jesus' words, "I am with you always, to the end of the age." All that the OT teaches about God being with his people is fulfilled in Jesus as Immanuel.

The fulfillment text from Hosea 11:1 is puzzling. Matthew maintains that Hosea 11:1 ("Out of Egypt I called my son") was fulfilled when Jesus returned from his sojourn in Egypt (Matt. 2:13–15). Modern readers are perplexed as to why this text was selected, for it appears not to be a prophecy but a historical reflection on Israel's exodus from Egypt, for the full verse of Hosea 11:1 reads, "When Israel was a child, I loved him, and out of Egypt I called my son." The "son" in the second half of the verse, in accord with Hebrew parallelism, clearly is "Israel." If this is the case, on what basis did Matthew see a fulfillment in Jesus leaving Egypt? Some scholars have suggested that the connection is altogether arbitrary. When we grasp, however, that Matthew thinks typologically in terms of the unfolding narrative of redemptive history, his appeal to Hosea 11:1 fits with his redemptive-historical understanding of the OT. God's son in the OT is identified as Israel (Exod. 4:22–23), and as the story line unfolds, we see that Israel as God's son was represented by the son of David (e.g., 2 Sam. 7:14). And, as will be explained later, Matthew identified Jesus as the true Israel and as the fulfillment of the promises made to David. Hence, a text that refers to Israel may legitimately be applied to Jesus because he is the true Israel.[114]

114. See Davies and Allison 1988: 263.

We still wonder, though, how Matthew seizes upon Hosea 11:1 as prophetic, since the text refers to a historical event. Upon a closer reading, however, we discern that chapter 11 of Hosea itself engages in a typological reading of Israel's history.[115] The chapter begins with the verse that we have been considering, where Hosea called to mind Israel's exodus from Egypt. Nevertheless, Israel did not respond to God's tender love by cleaving to him (Hosea 11:2–4). Instead, they turned to idols and sacrificed to the Baals despite being liberated by Yahweh and nurtured by his love. Therefore, the Lord pledged that he would send them as captives to Assyria. Their place of exile on this occasion will be not Egypt but Assyria (Hosea 11:5–7). This threat, of course, became a reality when the northern kingdom was exiled in 722 BC. Hosea 11:8–9 turns the spotlight on God's anguish. He wonders how he can give up his people, how he can hand them over to their adversaries. He pledges that he will not destroy them in the same way that he obliterated Admah and Zeboiim when Sodom and Gomorrah were pulverized. These verses do not rescind the promise that Israel will be exiled. The reference to the cities destroyed when Sodom and Gomorrah were annihilated provides the clue to the meaning of the text. Even though Israel deserved to be wiped out entirely, the Lord will have mercy on them. Assyria will capture them and deport them, but the nation will not be utterly extinguished as Admah and Zeboiim were. The Lord will preserve a remnant.

Hosea 11:10–11 promises, then, that the Lord will restore his people from exile. The Lord as a lion-king will roar, and his people will come trembling back to him. Like frail birds, they will return to their homes from Assyria and Egypt. Hosea's reference to Egypt here is fascinating and instructive, for he has already said in Hosea 11:5 that Israel will not return to Egypt but will be exiled to Assyria. Why, then, does he speak of a return from Assyria *and Egypt* if the people will not go to Egypt? We know from Hosea 11:5 that the reference to Egypt was not literal. Thus Hosea refers to a return from Egypt for typological reasons. We think back to the first verse of the chapter, which begins with the reflection that God called his son, Israel, out of Egypt. The exodus from Egypt functions as a type for what God will now do in Hosea's day.[116] Just as he freed Israel from Egyptian bondage, so he will liberate them in a new exodus from Assyria. Hosea 11:1, therefore, is not merely a historical remembrance of God's work in the past; it points forward to God's promise for Hosea's day, to a new liberating work of God. Hosea himself, then, views Israel's

115. For this view, I am dependent upon the unpublished work of my OT colleague Duane Garrett. On the typological connection, see also Hagner 1993b: 36–37; Carson 1984: 91–93; France 1989: 207–8; Luz 1989: 146.

116. Isaiah also used exodus traditions in this typological way, predicting a new exodus from Babylon (esp. in Isa. 40–66).

history typologically. If what I have suggested is correct, then Matthew used typology just as Hosea did.[117] Matthew believed that the return from exile promised in Hosea ultimately became a reality with the true son of Israel, Jesus Christ. In calling Jesus out of Egypt—in replicating the history of Israel—we see that Jesus is the true Israel, the true son of the promise, the fulfillment of God's saving purposes.

Matthew recounted Herod's slaying of children aged two years and under (Matt. 2:16–18), seeing it as a fulfillment of Jer. 31:15. Again the use of the OT seems to be eccentric, for in the OT context Jeremiah referred to Israel's exile to Babylon. Rachel wept because her children were removed from the land. Matthew, on the other hand, referred to the literal slaying of children by Herod. It is likely again that Matthew drew a typological connection between an event in Israelite history and his own day.[118] The words about Rachel weeping for her children are drawn from a context in Jeremiah that promises that God will bring back his people from exile. He will make a new covenant with his people and give them a new heart so that they will keep his law (Jer. 31:31–34). Indeed, the words that immediately follow the reference to Rachel weeping for her children pledge that God will bring her children back to the land (Jer. 31:17–26). The promise of a return from exile was fulfilled in part in Jeremiah's day, but the fullness of what was promised in Jer. 30–33 had not become a reality. The slaying of children by Herod revealed that Israel was, so to speak, still under the dominion of evil nations. The only explanation for such, according to the OT, was that Israel was still not freed from its sin. God had not yet placed the law on his people's hearts. Matthew saw Israel's freedom from sin and liberation as now occurring through Jesus Christ. The time for weeping has now ended, and the day of redemption and the fulfillment of the new covenant was at hand.

Perhaps the most puzzling fulfillment formula occurs in Matt. 2:23, where Jesus' origin from Nazareth is said to fulfill the words "He shall be called a Nazarene."[119] Nothing in the OT clearly indicates that the Messiah would be a Nazarene.[120] Most likely, Matthew engages in a play on words here, and the reference is to Isa. 11:1 where a "branch" (*nēṣer*)

---

117. The word "typology" is subject to a number of different interpretations, and some worry that it could be construed as an open door to unrestrained allegorizing. But as long as typology is rooted in the OT, it is difficult to deny that Matthew saw patterns in the OT (see France 1989: 185–86). For an insightful study of typology, see Davidson 1981.

118. Davies and Allison (1988: 267) note a number of connections between the story in Matthew and Jer. 31. For the typological use of the OT here, see Hagner 1993b: 38; Carson 1984: 95. See also Nolland 2005: 125.

119. See discussion of this issue in Luz 1989: 149–50.

120. Carson (1984: 97) thinks that the point is that Jesus fulfills the OT prophecies that the Messiah would be despised, since Nazareth was considered a lowly place.

from Jesse will bear fruit.[121] Isaiah 11:1–10 clearly referred to a son of David who would rule as Messiah by the anointing of the Spirit and introduce a new age of peace and righteousness, an age in which the wolf and the lamb will dwell peacefully together. Alternatively, perhaps a connection is made between "Nazarene" and "Nazirite." In Judg. 13:5 Samson was to be dedicated to God as a Nazirite (*nāzîr*) from his birth (see also Num. 6; Judg. 16:17; Amos 2:11–12).[122] Matthew possibly intended for readers to exploit both texts, seeing Jesus like Samson as one dedicated to God from his birth and as the one who will save his people (cf. Matt. 1:21).[123] Just as David, as the son of Jesse, was an unlikely candidate for king over Israel (see 1 Sam. 16:6–13), so also Jesus hails from an unexpected place as the Messiah of his people.

Matthew 3:15 does not, strictly speaking, have a fulfillment formula, but the verb "fulfill" (*plēroō*) is used, and so it will be discussed here. The Baptist proclaims that people should be baptized to receive forgiveness of sins (Matt. 3:6). When Jesus came to John for baptism, John protested that their roles should be reversed, presumably because Jesus did not need to be baptized for the sake of his sins but John did (Matt. 3:13–14).[124] Jesus quieted John's objections by saying that his baptism was necessary "to fulfill all righteousness" (Matt. 3:15). The word "fulfill" suggests that Jesus fulfills what is prophesied in the OT.[125] Again the Matthean account is cryptic and not replicated in the other Synoptic Gospels. We have already considered, however, that Matthew depicts Jesus as the true Israel. It is likely, then, that Jesus identified himself with Israel in this text. Furthermore, the story line of Matthew as a whole must be included to grasp the significance of the phrase—a story that culminates with Jesus' death.[126] Therefore, as the representative of his people, Jesus

---

121. Hagner 1993b: 40–41. Nolland (2005: 130) thinks both Isa. 11:1 and Isa. 42:6 are alluded to.

122. Davies and Allison (1988: 276) point out "in the LXX an interchange between *nazaraios theou* and *hagios theou* (see A and B for Judg 13.7; 16.17)." Such a connection may suggest an allusion to Isa. 4:3 in this instance.

123. In support of this view, see the detailed discussion in Davies and Allison 1988: 275–81, though they see a secondary reference to Isa. 11:1. See also R. Brown 1977: 223. But Hagner (1993b: 41) probably is right in saying that Jesus does not fit as a Nazirite, because he was accused of being a drunkard, and he touched corpses when raising them.

124. Campbell (1996: 194) argues that baptism is used with the meaning of "overwhelm," designating both the outpouring of the Spirit and the fiery wrath of God's judgment. This interpretation, Campbell argues, is borne out by Luke 12:49–50.

125. So Davies and Allison 1988: 325–27, but they are less convincing in defining this as obedience to God's will. Hagner (1993b: 56) convincingly argues that "righteousness" (*dikaiosynē*) does not invariably refer to fulfilling God's ethical demands in Matthew (contra Przybylski 1980). In this context righteousness refers not to "moral goodness but . . . the will of God in the sense of God's saving activity."

126. Contra Luz 1989: 179.

undergoes baptism, and hence his baptism forecasts his death for the sake of his people.[127]

The beginning of Jesus' ministry in Galilee is identified in Matt. 4:14–16 as a fulfillment of Scripture. Matthew hearkens back to Isaiah's words that the land of Zebulun and Naphtali, Galilee of the Gentiles, which has been shrouded in darkness, has seen a great light (Isa. 8:22–9:2). In the context of Isaiah this is followed immediately by an oracle promising victory through one who sits on the throne of David. He will rule as the "Wonderful Counselor, Mighty God, Everlasting Father, Prince of Peace" (Isa. 9:6). Since the location is Galilee, it seems that the darkness predicted is the capture of the northern kingdom by Assyria (see Isa. 7–10). But the time of judgment is followed by the dawn of salvation, the coming of a great light. Matthew finds the fulfillment of this prophecy in Jesus of Nazareth. He is the one who sits on David's throne (see Matt. 1:1–17). In Matthew's day Israel was under the shadow of Rome, but Jesus is the great light who spells the end of exile and the fulfillment of God's saving promises.

All three Synoptic Gospels relate Jesus' healing of Peter's mother-in-law and his healing of the sick and expelling of demons (Matt. 8:14–16; Mark 1:29–34; Luke 4:38–41), but only Matthew adds this comment: "This was to fulfill what was spoken by the prophet Isaiah, 'He took our illnesses and bore our diseases'" (Matt. 8:17). The citation comes from Isa. 53:4, where the Servant of the Lord suffers for the sins of Israel. We shall examine the title "Servant of the Lord" in due course, but we should note here that the Servant of the Lord is also identified as Jacob or Israel (Isa. 41:8; 44:1, 2, 21; 45:4; 48:20; 49:3). Hagner rightly comments that "Isa. 53:4 guarantees no one healing in the present age. What is guaranteed is that Christ's atoning death will in the eschaton provide healing for all. The healings through the ministry of Jesus and those experienced in our day are the first-fruits, the down payment, of the final experience of deliverance."[128]

We have another indication, then, that Jesus functions as the true Israel suffering for the sake of his people. Matthew quotes rather extensively from a Servant of the Lord text in Matt. 12:18–21. The text in this instance is from Isa. 42:1–4, and again a fulfillment of this text is assigned to Jesus' ministry.[129] The Servant is anointed with God's Spirit, but he is not a warrior who creates tumult by waging war in the streets of the cities. He does not crush the bruised reed and does not snuff out

---

127. Rightly Hagner 1993b: 57. Other scholars maintain that Jesus' baptism simply represents his obedience here and functions as an example for believers (e.g., Hartman 1997: 24–25).

128. Hagner 1993b: 211. See also Carson 1984: 205–7.

129. For these themes, see Hagner 1993b: 338–39.

the wick that barely burns. The context in which Matthew cited these words is illuminating. The Pharisees, having seen Jesus' Sabbath healings, have decided to destroy him (Matt. 12:1–14). Presumably, Jesus could have responded with force, crushing his opposition with God's help. Instead, he humbly withdrew from those who opposed him (Matt. 12:15) and refused to take the stance of a warrior. He healed the weak and refused notoriety (Matt. 12:15–16). He delivered a demonized man who was blind and mute (Matt. 12:22). Matthew emphasizes that Jesus is a servant king rather than a warrior king.

Jesus' speaking in parables (Matt. 13:35) is said to fulfill the words of the psalmist (Ps. 78:2).[130] Psalm 78 recounts the history of God's saving acts on behalf of his people and their continual failure to believe and obey. It culminates with his raising up David to shepherd his people (Ps. 78:70–72). As we noted previously, the parables disclose that God fulfills his saving promises in unexpected ways. Perhaps Matthew hints that Jesus' contemporaries were like Israel of old. They failed to see the fulfillment in Jesus, despite the truth that God was fulfilling his kingdom promises through him. Still, Jesus is the new David whom God has raised up to shepherd his people. Those who have eyes to see the meaning of the parables discern that God has not abandoned his people but has faithfully fulfilled his promises in him.

Jesus' entrance into Jerusalem on a donkey (Matt. 21:5–6) fulfilled Zech. 9:9, which prophesied that Jerusalem's humble king would arrive on a donkey. We see again the theme that Jesus is a king whose nature is contrary to the popular expectations of his day. He did not establish his kingship by winning wars. His entrance on the donkey indicated that he triumphs through suffering, as the rest of the passion narrative in Matthew clarifies. The same theme is prosecuted with fulfillment formulae when Jesus was arrested (Matt. 26:50–56). One of Jesus' disciples wielded his sword, ready for battle, and sliced off the ear of the high priest's slave. Jesus rebuked him, teaching that all who conquer by violence will meet the same fate eventually. Indeed, if this were the time for battle, Jesus could summon the assistance of twelve legions of angels. Jesus submitted to the cross in order to fulfill what the Scriptures teach (Matt. 26:54). In this way "the Scriptures of the prophets" are fulfilled (Matt. 26:56). In this instance no particular text from the OT is adduced. The testimony of the Scriptures as a whole points toward the cross.

The last text with a fulfillment formula appears in Matt. 27:9–10, where the money that Judas received for his treachery was used to buy a potter's field for a cemetery. Curiously, Matthew says that the text

---

130. For discussion on whether the reference to Ps. 78:2 is apt, see Davies and Allison 1991: 426.

fulfills Jeremiah, although the fulfillment text contains words from Zech. 11:12–13.[131] Whatever we make of Matthew's use of the OT here, it is clear that he saw the passion of Jesus, down to its very details, as fulfilling prophecy.

The fulfillment formulae in Matthew indicate that Jesus is the promised Messiah. The saving promises given to Israel, found in texts that pledge return from exile, find their terminus in him. Hence, they confirm the truth that the kingdom has dawned in Jesus. If the fulfillment formulae begin by emphasizing that Jesus is the promised one and the one through whom God's salvation for Israel will be realized—and this is the case especially in Matt. 1–4—then as the Gospel continues, the focus shifts to what kind of Messiah he is. Jesus is a servant Messiah. He has come not to win a military victory but rather to suffer for his people. His death was not an accident or a tragedy but represents the fulfillment of prophecy. Jewish readers in particular would need assurance that Jesus' suffering was God's intention, and that this intention squared with the OT. In the fulfillment formulae Matthew establishes that Jesus is the Messiah, and that he is a suffering Messiah. But the focus on Jesus' suffering and death indicates that God's saving promises have not yet been consummated, that the new creation and new exodus have not yet reached their denouement.

Conclusion

The kingdom of God is a central theme in Jesus' ministry, and the meaning of the concept must be discerned from the OT because Jesus nowhere defines it. When Jesus referred to God's kingdom, he had in mind God's saving power, the fulfillment of his saving promises. When God's saving promises become a reality, then those who are God's enemies will be judged. Still, Jesus called attention to God's saving work on behalf of his people. The surprising element in Jesus' teaching on the kingdom is its ambiguous character. The kingdom can be explained in terms of the already–not yet. The kingdom was inaugurated in Jesus' ministry but not yet consummated. It had arrived, but the full salvation and judgment promised had not yet come to pass. Finally, Matthew emphasized Jesus' role in the kingdom. The kingdom promises are fulfilled in Jesus and through his ministry and death and resurrection. As the Son of Man, he will determine who enters God's kingdom on the final day.

---

131. See discussion in Hagner 1993b: 813–15; Carson 1984: 562–66; Luz 2005: 467–68, 474–75; Nolland 2005: 1156–58. Davies and Allison (1997: 568–69) probably are right in seeing a mixed citation here.

2

⁂ ⁂ ⁂ ⁂ ⁂ ⁂ ⁂ ⁂ ⁂ ⁂ ⁂ ⁂ ⁂ ⁂ ⁂ ⁂ ⁂

Eternal Life and Eschatology in John's Theology

Is the Gospel of John History or Theology?

The differences between John's Gospel and the Synoptic Gospels have provoked many to question whether the former is genuine history.[1] Questions about the historical rootage of this Gospel have a long-standing history in Gospel criticism. Many elements found in the Synoptics are missing in John. There are no lepers, no demon exorcisms, no tax collectors, no Sadducees, and no Sermon on the Mount. The infancy narratives, the garden of Gethsemane, and the Lord's Supper are absent. John has little in the way of parables, and virtually all the Synoptic parables are lacking. The temple cleansing is not at the end of the Gospel story but at the beginning.

John also contains much material that is not in the Synoptics. We find stories about a wedding at Cana, Nicodemus, a Samaritan woman at Jacob's well, the healing of a man at the pool of Bethzatha, and the resurrection of Lazarus. Jesus appears before Annas only in John, and

---

1. For a concise discussion of some of the differences and commonalities between John and the Synoptics, see L. Johnson 2006: 97–102. Johnson's sketch is particularly useful in reminding readers that the Synoptics and John share the same perspective on a profound level.

John seems to have a distinctive date for the Passover and to extend Jesus' ministry to three or four years, whereas the Synoptics suggest only one or two years. The discourses in John are also long and leisurely and seem different in character from the sayings of Jesus in the Synoptics. The Christology is bolder and more explicit. A dualism exists between truth and error, light and darkness, above and below, Spirit and flesh that has suggested Hellenistic influence to some. The eschatology is almost completely realized instead of future.[2] Hence, many scholars who think that the Synoptics are at least basically historical doubt the historical accuracy of John, concluding that theology trumps history in the Fourth Gospel.

It is not my intention here to discuss the matter of historicity in detail. Such a venture would require a book-length treatment. Nevertheless, we can sketch in reasons why John should be taken seriously as a historian.[3] Perhaps we should note first that John's relationship to the Synoptics is controverted. Unanimous agreement does not exist as to whether John used the Synoptic Gospels as a literary source.[4] Even in texts where the same incident is recounted in the Synoptics and in John, the linguistic variation is significant enough to call into question literary dependence. And yet it also seems that John is aware of Synoptic traditions, even if he does not show an awareness of these Gospels as literary sources. Nevertheless, he intentionally chose to write his own distinctive account of the life of Jesus. It follows, then, that the failure to include events and sayings found in the Synoptics does not necessarily call into question John's historicity.

The historical quality of the Fourth Gospel, in other words, must be assessed on its own terms and cannot be dismissed merely by observing the variations from the Synoptic accounts. Direct contradictions of the Synoptics, naturally, would raise serious questions about the historicity of John or the Synoptics. One of the striking features in John's Gospel is that the writer claimed to be an eyewitness (John 1:14; 19:35; 20:8; 21:24) and insisted that his testimony is true.[5] Indeed, a very good case can still be made that the Beloved Disciple was the apostle John

---

2. See Dodd 1953: 7, 148.

3. For support of this view, see Carson 1991b: 29–94; Köstenberger 2002: 2–216; and especially the detailed defense in Blomberg 2001. See also Smalley 1978: 162–90; and the convincing article by Bauckham (2007).

4. Gardner-Smith (1938) initiated the modern discussion with his study arguing for the literary independence of John from the Synoptics. For a brief and clear survey, see Beasley-Murray 1987: xxxv–xxxvii.

5. For the fundamental role of eyewitnesses in preserving Gospel traditions, see the groundbreaking work by Bauckham (2006), and note his claim that eyewitness testimony is central in the Gospel of John (2006: 358–83), though in contrast to my view, he thinks that the author was John the elder.

himself.[6] The author was familiar with Judaism. He knew about messianic expectations, Jewish purification rites (John 2:6), Jewish views of Samaritans (John 4:9, 27), the importance of the Sabbath (John 5:10; 7:21–23; 9:14), the libation at the Feast of Tabernacles (John 7:37; 8:12), and the danger of defilement at Passover (John 18:28; 19:31–42). He also knew about Jewish history, such as the building of the temple (John 2:20), the mutual hostility between Samaritans and Jews (John 4:4–42), the contempt for the Diaspora (John 7:35), and the role of Annas and Caiaphas (John 11:49; 18:13–14, 19–24). This Gospel has been verified in terms of some concrete details—the kind of details that suggest an eyewitness and one who is concerned about history.[7] The pool in John 5:1–9 is not a figment of John's imagination. It fits with what is found in the *Copper Scroll* from Qumran and archaeological work near St. Anne's church in Jerusalem.[8] So too, the pool of Siloam (John 9:6–7) is noted by Josephus (*J.W.* 6.363) and mentioned in the *Copper Scroll* (3Q15 X, 15–16).[9] The stoa of the temple in John 10:23 accords with what we know of the temple and with Josephus (*Ant.* 15.396–402; 20.221; *J.W.* 5.184–185; cf. Acts 3:11; 5:12). The brook of Kidron that John mentions is indeed a wadi (John 18:1).[10]

Numerous minor details in the Gospel suggest eyewitness remembrance:[11] the six water pots in Cana (John 2:6), the naming of Philip and Andrew (John 6:7), the barley loaves at the feeding of the five thousand (John 6:9), the detail that the disciples rowed out twenty-five to thirty stadia (John 6:19), the odor that filled the house when Mary anointed Jesus' body for burial (John 12:3), Peter's beckoning of the Beloved Disciple (John 13:24), the reaction of soldiers at Jesus' arrest (John 18:6), the name of the high priest's servant (John 18:10), the weight of embalming spices (John 19:39), the knowledge of the disciples' reactions (John 2:11, 24; 6:15, 61; 13:1), and the catch of 153 fish (John 21:11).

6. Such a position is the minority view in NT scholarship today. For the standard critical view, see Lindars 1972: 28–34; Barrett 1978: 100–134. Hengel (1989a) argues intriguingly that the author was not John the apostle but John the elder. The evidence, however, for a second John, a John the elder who should be distinguished from the apostle John, is unconvincing. Indeed, the most likely reading of the evidence from Papias is that John the apostle and John the elder are one and the same person. Despite the critical consensus, it seems that the arguments supporting apostolic authorship are still the strongest. See especially Carson 1991b: 68–81.

7. The older study by Morris (1969a) is still invaluable. See especially his discussion of authorship (Morris 1969a: 218–92). For more recent studies that defend John's historical accuracy, see Carson 1981b; Blomberg 2001. See now the important article on historiography in John by Bauckham (2007).

8. So Meier 1994: 681, 729–30n11.

9. See Meier 1994: 696–97.

10. See Köstenberger 2004: 504.

11. See the compilation of evidence and discussion in Morris 1969a: 233–44.

These details do not prove that the author was an eyewitness, but they are consistent with such a view.

Virtually all agree that this Gospel is cast in John's own idiom. Hence, there are instances in which it is difficult to discern where John himself is speaking or Jesus (cf. John 3:16–21, 31–36). When John reports Jesus' words, he summarizes them and clothes them in his own style, but it does not follow from this that he invents or distorts the words of the historical Jesus. John writes in his own style and yet respects the historical particularity of the events that transpired. The Christology of this Gospel is more explicit, and this is evident in both the prologue (John 1:1–18) and Thomas's confession (John 20:28), leading some to think that John reflects the view of the later church. We could overemphasize, however, the high Christology of John. Nathaniel spoke better than he knew in identifying Jesus as the king of Israel and God's Son (John 1:46–51). In using the expression "Son of God," he likely did not mean that Jesus was divine but rather used the title to indicate that Jesus was the Messiah (John 1:49; cf. Matt. 16:16). Nathaniel's words, from a postresurrection perspective, have a deeper meaning than Nathaniel imagined, and hence his confession can be read at more than one level, but we know that messianic expectation was diverse and high in the day of Jesus, and so there is no reason to doubt that Nathaniel in a moment of enthusiasm could have uttered such words.

We should observe that in John's Gospel Jesus disclosed himself plainly as the Messiah only to the Samaritan woman (John 4:25–26) during his public ministry, and he does not overtly identify himself as the Messiah with regularity. Jesus often spoke cryptically so that his hearers were uncertain about what he was claiming about himself (e.g., John 10:24–25; 16:28–29). Such observations fit with the "misunderstanding" theme that is common in John. Jesus' disciples and those listening to him often fail to grasp what he says. John informs us that understanding was gained only after the resurrection (John 2:18–22; 7:37–39; 12:16; 16:12–13; 21:18–23).[12] Apparently, John does not impose postresurrection insight upon his narrative, for he specifically informs the readers on a number of occasions that the disciples could not and did not grasp Jesus' words or actions until the Spirit was given or Jesus was risen. Recording the misapprehensions of others suggests that John was interested in what actually occurred in the ministry of Jesus.

NT scholarship in previous days maintained a significant distinction between Hellenistic and Palestinian Judaism, identifying John with the former and concluding that John was not earthed in the Jewish

---

12. Carson (1982) rightly argues that this theme, so common in John, is an indication of the historical veracity of this Gospel.

milieu of Jesus' day. The discovery of the Dead Sea Scrolls and further study of Palestinian Judaism have overturned such conclusions. We now know that Palestinian Judaism was significantly influenced by Hellenism.[13] Furthermore, alleged Hellenistic features in John appear also in the Dead Sea Scrolls, such as the opposition between light and darkness, truth and error, and Spirit and flesh.[14] Scholars can no longer confidently place John in the Hellenistic category and dismiss its accuracy for that reason. Certainly, much more could and should be said about John's relationship to history, but space is lacking here to examine the issue in detail, and readers should consult other sources for a full discussion of the matter. In this study, however, I will work from the assumption that John's Gospel is both theological and historical, and that the theological depth of this Gospel does not mean that it is historically inaccurate.

Eternal Life

One of the primary themes in John's Gospel is life.[15] Life in John is not an abstract entity but rather is rooted in John's Jewish worldview. Life belongs to the age to come, which is inaugurated by the resurrection. What is remarkable in reading John is his emphasis on the gift of life now. He does not focus on the future age when the resurrection will occur. He fixes his gaze on what believers in Christ possess even now through faith in Jesus as the Christ. The gift of life in the present age is available only because Jesus is the resurrection and the life (John 11:25).[16] John anchors the believer's enjoyment of life to the resurrection of Jesus Christ in history. The life of the age to come has dawned because Jesus of Nazareth has risen from the dead (ch. 20). In the resurrection of Jesus the coming age has invaded the present age. Life has penetrated where only death reigned. Light has dawned where darkness shrouded all. Truth has arrived to conquer falsehood. John impresses upon the reader the presence of life now because the resurrection of Jesus in history shines in the darkness (John 1:5), demonstrating his victory over the ruler of the world (John 12:31) and over the power of death. Jesus, by virtue of his death, has cast out the world's ruler, Satan.

---

13. In this regard, see especially the decisive work of Hengel 1974.

14. See the sensible discussion in Carson 1991b: 33–34; Ladd 1993: 255. The commonalities between the Fourth Gospel and the Dead Sea Scrolls contributed to "the new look on the Fourth Gospel" (J. A. T. Robinson 1962: 94–106).

15. For this theme, see Dodd 1953: 144–50; Ladd 1993: 290–305.

16. See R. Brown 1966: 434; Barrett 1978: 396.

The triumph over death is achieved in Jesus' resurrection, and in John the resurrection of Jesus is rooted in history.[17] John does not hang his teaching about life upon a gnostic hope of life in some ethereal sphere. He does not conceive of life as spiritual over against the material. Life is inaugurated in the space-time sphere by the physical resurrection of Jesus from the dead. John leaves us in no doubt that Jesus' resurrection means the resurrection of the body. The account begins with Mary Magdalene fretting because Jesus' body is absent from the tomb (John 20:2). The folding up of the face cloth and the presence of the linen cloths testified to the absence of Jesus' body (John 20:6–7),[18] for grave robbers would have stolen the linen and left the tomb in disarray.[19] Subsequently, Mary Magdalene saw Jesus standing before her, and he is not merely a spirit but rather is someone who can be touched and handled (John 20:14–17). Moreover, Jesus demonstrated that he is risen by showing his hands and feet to his disciples (John 20:20), and he invited the skeptical Thomas to put his hands and fingers into his hands and side to remove any doubts that he is truly risen (John 20:25–27). The intrusion of life from the age to come cannot be relegated to a spiritual concept in John; the resurrection of Jesus testifies that the life of the coming age has invaded space-time history.

The emphasis on the present fulfillment of God's promises in John is rooted in the cross and resurrection of Jesus Christ. Hence, those who enjoy eternal life now eat Jesus' flesh and drink his blood (John 6:53–54). This language startles, and it would shock any Jew because the consumption of blood is most emphatically forbidden in the OT (Gen. 9:4). Clearly, the reference to Jesus' flesh and blood refers to his death, which is given for the life of the world (John 6:51). Life in the age to come is available only through Jesus, who possesses life in himself (John 5:26) and is the way, the truth, and the life (John 14:6). Participation in life does not stem from abstract faith in God or his goodness but rather comes by a faith that eats Jesus' flesh and drinks his blood. In other words, the life of the age to come becomes a reality as one trusts in the work of Jesus on the cross and in his resurrection. The age to come has entered history, then, through history—the gruesome death and physical resurrection of Jesus the Christ.

The crucified and risen Lord, then, has introduced life into the world, and that life shines in the darkness (John 1:4–5). He is the light of life (John 8:12) and came so that people could have life (John 10:10). The

---

17. In defense of the historical nature of the report on the resurrection in John's Gospel, see Wright 2003: 440–48, 662–79.

18. So Beasley-Murray 1987: 372.

19. R. Brown 1970: 1007; cf. Barrett 1978: 563.

life of the age to come is, therefore, radically Christ-centered. Eternal life comes by knowing Jesus Christ and by knowing the one true God (John 17:3). Jesus is the food, the bread, that must be consumed for one to enjoy eternal life (John 6:35, 48). We saw above that Jesus becomes food for people by virtue of his death on their behalf. Human beings must come to Jesus in order to enjoy life (John 5:40). Indeed, the purpose of this Gospel is enunciated in the claim that one must believe in Jesus in order to obtain eternal life (John 20:30–31).[20] We are not surprised to learn that John frequently emphasizes that those who believe enjoy life eternal (John 3:15–16, 36; 5:24; 6:47). The teaching of 1 John is similar.[21] Jesus is the life, and the life was manifested in history through the incarnation (1 John 1:1–2). The promise of eternal life is realized in him (1 John 2:25), and such life is secured by his death (1 John 3:16), in which he yielded up his life for others. Hence, all those who believe in the Son enjoy eternal life now because such life is bound up with Jesus and his self-revelation (1 John 5:11–13). As the epistle says in closing, Jesus himself "is the true God and eternal life" (1 John 5:20).

Since Jesus Christ has died and been raised as the Son of God, it follows that the age to come has penetrated the evil era. Meier rightly claims that John's eschatology is inseparable from his Christology. "Because the Word has become flesh, the last day has become the present moment."[22] First John 2:8 demonstrates that the new age has arrived, for "the darkness is passing away and the true light is already shining." The overlap between the present and future ages is evident in this verse, for the darkness and light exist concurrently. The age to come has arrived by virtue of the death and resurrection of Christ, but its arrival does not spell the immediate removal of evil and darkness. The Jews expected that when the coming age dawned, the evil age would be set aside immediately. The fulfillment of the OT promises is realized, however, in a surprising way. The light shines without instantaneously quenching the darkness. We would be mistaken, though, to conclude that light and darkness are now equivalent, as if the two balance each other with equal force. John emphasizes the defeat and doom of evil (it is passing away) and the triumph of the light (it is shining). Ultimately the light that has

---

20. Scholars dispute the purpose of John's Gospel. For a handy survey of work up until 1978, see Smalley 1978: 122–49. Some maintain that it was written for believers (e.g., R. Brown 1970: 1060; Barrett 1978: 575; Ridderbos 1997: 652). Others argue that it was written particularly for evangelistic purposes (Dodd 1953: 9; Carson 1987a; 2005). Beasley-Murray (1987: 387–88) seems to opt for both views.

21. With most scholars, I maintain that the author of the Gospel of John and 1–3 John is the same person.

22. Meier 1994: 811.

dawned in Christ will shine triumphantly over all; even now the defeat of darkness is sure.

Jesus, as the Son, has inaugurated the new age by virtue of his death and resurrection, for John accentuates the truth that believers possess the life of the coming age even now. Belief does not merely secure life in the coming age; those who believe enjoy life even now (John 3:15). As John 3:36 declares, "Whoever believes in the Son has eternal life." The text does not relegate such life to the future but rather sees it as the present possession of believers. The same theme is communicated powerfully in John 5:24–25: "Truly, truly, I say to you, whoever hears my word and believes him who sent me has eternal life. He does not come into judgment but has passed from death to life. Truly, truly, I say to you, an hour is coming, and is now here, when the dead will hear the voice of the Son of God, and those who hear will live." The final judgment is reserved for the future, and yet those who believe in the Son will never face such a judgment, for they have already entered into life.[23] They face the day of reckoning with confidence because of their trust in the Son. The same theme sounds in John 5:25, where the "dead" refers to the spiritually dead who hear the voice of God's Son in the present era ("is now here"). Since they hear God's voice even now in history, John cannot have in mind future physical resurrection.[24] Those who hear the Son's voice will live in the present age; they are transferred even now from death to life.

Interestingly, 1 John 3:14 communicates the same reality in declaring, "We know that we have passed [*metabainō*] out of death into life, because we love the brothers. Whoever does not love abides in death."[25] The same verb, *metabainō*, is used in John 5:24, again conveying the truth that believers currently possess life.[26] The great transaction has occurred so that the reign of death has ended, even though believers still await physical death. Nevertheless, they have now passed into life and abide in life, and hence the age to come is now a reality. As Jesus declares in John 10:28, "I give them eternal life." Such life is not reserved for a future time but is the present gift of the Son of God to his sheep.

Clearly, then, John emphasizes the "already" when he speaks of life. Because of this emphasis, some scholars deny that there is any "not yet" in his teaching. They claim that future eschatology is entirely collapsed into present eschatology in John's theology. Such a perspective can be maintained, however, only by denying or omitting some of the

23. So Lindars 1972: 224; Barrett 1978: 261.
24. So Barrett 1978: 262; cf. Ridderbos 1997: 198.
25. See R. Brown 1982: 445; Smalley 1984: 188.
26. The perfect tense of the verb in both John 5:24 and 1 John 3:14 signifies the completion of the action in the past, emphasizing that life has already commenced.

Johannine material. Bultmann embraces such a conclusion and supports it by identifying as a later gloss any text that includes future eschatology (e.g., John 5:28–29).[27] We must be suspicious of any scholar who domesticates the text to fit a preconceived scheme, when the text itself points us to a more complex reality. Bultmann was partially right, for John certainly underscores present eschatology, but unfortunately Bultmann failed to see that the eschatological tension present in the rest of the NT is maintained in John also, even if John places his emphasis on fulfillment in the present age.[28]

The tension between the future and the present is evident in John 10:28, a verse that we noted above. Eternal life is the present possession of the believer, and those who possess such life will never perish. The presence of life now secures the future so that believers will never die. The life that belongs to believers in this present evil age guarantees that death will never triumph, and so we can say that there is an indissoluble connection between the life that believers now possess and the future realization of life forever. Still, even though believers now enjoy eternal life and the future has been secured, the promises of the future have not yet been fully realized and obtained. Believers await the future with confidence because they have eternal life through Jesus Christ.

Several texts demonstrate that John did not surrender future eschatology and focus solely on realized eschatology. John, as we have seen, emphasizes that believers have already passed from death into life, and so they already possess the life of the new age (John 5:24–25). And yet a mere few verses later, the future physical resurrection of both believers and unbelievers is announced (John 5:28–29).[29] Those who have practiced evil will be raised for judgment, whereas those who have done what is good will experience the resurrection of life. Even though John highlights the theme that believers already possess eternal life, he does not become one-dimensional and deny a future fulfillment. The present experience of eternal life is not the consummation of God's purposes; instead, eternal life in the present age is, so to speak, the guarantee that believers will experience physical resurrection in the same way as Jesus the Christ. In the same way, John declares that unbelievers already stand under judgment in the present age (John 3:18) and God's wrath abides on them now (John 3:36), and yet there will also be final judgment on the day when unbelievers are resurrected.

27. See Bultmann 1971: 261. Bultmann (1971: 219) also argues that the references to being raised on the last day in John 6:39, 40, 44 are editorial additions.

28. Rightly Smalley 1978: 235–41.

29. Lindars 1972: 226–27; Carson 1991b: 258; Ridderbos 1997: 201. Barrett (1978: 263) wrongly restricts the resurrection and judgment to unbelievers.

The theme of final resurrection surfaces often in the "bread of life" discourse in John 6. Jesus offered life in the present to all who will trust in him, come to him, abide in him, or eat of him. Those who are believers can also be described as those given by the Father to the Son (John 6:37)—that is, those who are drawn by the Father (John 6:44). The account is punctuated with the refrain that those who are given to the Son by the Father (John 6:65) will be raised on the last day (John 6:39, 40, 44, 54). Those who come to Jesus and eat of him participate in life now, but the present experience of life does not exhaust God's promises, for he will raise physically from the dead all those who trust in Christ. The already is a preview of the not yet, containing the promise of final victory over death.

The future dimension of Johannine thought is also reflected in the promise of Jesus' return. The meaning of John 14:2–3 is disputed, but it likely refers to the future coming of Jesus, not to the promise of the Spirit after the resurrection.[30] Jesus pledged to his disciples not that he will visit them where they reside but that he will come and take them to be where he is, with the Father. Jesus will take them to be with himself in the rooms of the Father's dwelling, so that believers will live with him forever. The prayer of Jesus in John 17 runs along somewhat similar lines. He prayed that believers will be preserved and unified in his absence and that they will not fall prey to the stratagems of the evil one. The language of preservation, however, suggests a day when the work of keeping is completed, when the task has been accomplished. This interpretation is confirmed by John 17:24: "Father, I desire that they also, whom you have given me, may be with me where I am, to see my glory that you have given me because you loved me before the foundation of the world." Presently, believers are not with Jesus, but he anticipated a day when the church has been united and the work of preservation has reached its goal, and then believers will reside with Jesus and see him in all his glory and beauty. Clearly, John does not teach a fully realized eschatology but rather anticipates a day when Christ's dazzling glory will be seen.

The relation between present and future eschatology can also be discerned in 1 John. We have already looked at 1 John 2:8, where it is said that the darkness is passing away and the true light is even now shining. This text implies future eschatology inasmuch as the darkness has not yet been eclipsed in its entirety. Believers still anticipate the light streaming upon them with its full intensity and the quenching of

---

30. For a helpful survey and convincing explanation of these verses, see Beasley-Murray 1987: 250–51. Contra Gundry (1967a), who sees a reference to Jesus coming in the Spirit. Barrett (1978: 457) rather confusingly mixes the future and present together here. Lindars (1972: 471) wrongly sees a reference to Jesus coming in the resurrection.

darkness. First John 2:17 speaks in similar terms in declaring that the world and its desires "are passing away," whereas the one who does God's will remains forever. John recognizes that the world and its desires still entice believers and have not lost their allure, but a day is coming when God's ways will embrace the whole of reality, so that the desires of the present world are no more.

The truth that believers are now forgiven of their sins and know God (1 John 2:12–14), and can be assured that they are his children (1 John 3:1–3), and even be sure of eternal life (1 John 5:11–13) does not cancel out the pressures from the world. The world still exists and continues to allure believers. And yet believers now enjoy victory over the world by faith (1 John 5:4–5). The charm of the world is temporary inasmuch as it is transient. Those doing God's will can be assured that they will live forever. The joy of being God's children in the present era certifies that believers will be perfected when they see Jesus (1 John 3:1–3). John recognizes that there is a hope that has not yet been attained, and he characterizes it as hope because believers can be assured that they will be perfected. We see, then, that John's eschatology is quite similar to what we saw in the Synoptic Gospels. He accentuates the already more than the Synoptic Gospels do, yet without rejecting the future promise of the resurrection. The future resurrection, in fact, is secured by the gift of life now.

Johannine Dualism

Scholars have often discussed Johannine dualism, and some have even classified it as a species of Hellenistic thought.[31] The discovery of the Dead Sea Scrolls showed that such a theory lacked substantive evidence, for similar dualism is found in the writings of the Qumran community.[32] When we read the Dead Sea Scrolls, we see that the dualism there is not ontological but eschatological. In the same way, the dualism in John is not ontological but eschatological. Christ is the sovereign agent of creation (John 1:3, 10) in Johannine theology. Indeed, John particularly emphasizes the sovereignty and control of God over all things. Hence, there is no notion that the devil is equal in power or that he might triumph over God.

31. For the various backgrounds postulated for John's thought, see Barrett 1978: 27–41; Beasley-Murray 1987: liii–lxvi. Both Barrett and Beasley-Murray propose a diverse background that includes both Judaism and Hellenism.

32. For the view that the background to John's Gospel is fundamentally Jewish, see Carson 1991b: 58–63.

What we have in John, then, is an ethical and eschatological dualism between truth and error, light and darkness, what is above and what is below. Jesus declared to the Jewish leaders that they are from below and from this world, whereas he is from above and from heaven (John 8:23). In what sense were the Jewish leaders from below? Jesus explained that they are relegated to this world because of their sin, confirming that the dualism in view here is ethical. We understand, therefore, why Jesus demanded that Nicodemus be born from above (John 3:3, 7). As a sinner from below, he needed the work of the Spirit to enter God's kingdom.

Another way of designating those who are below is through the use of the term "world" (*kosmos*).[33] Those who are "below" are also described as those who "are of this world" (John 8:23). Sometimes John uses the term "world" to refer to that which was created—the realm in which human beings live. For instance, the world is said to be created by Jesus (John 1:10; cf. 9:32 [which speaks of the world beginning]; 13:1; 17:5). The world is also the place where human beings live, and Jesus participated in such life. We see this meaning in John 6:14: "When the people saw the sign that he [Jesus] had done, they said, 'This is indeed the prophet who is to come into the world!'" (see also John 1:10; 9:5; 10:36; 11:27; 12:46; 18:20). The term most often describes human beings, or at least what most human beings are doing: "Look, the world has gone after him" (John 12:19; cf. 7:4; 8:26). In most of these instances in John the term "world" is colored by its association with evil. Even in speaking of Jesus' coming into the world, intimations of his arrival into a sphere dominated by evil are present, since he came to be the world's Savior.

John predominantly uses "world" to designate the people of the world, but in doing so he highlights their subjection to evil, so that he announces that the entire world is under the power of the evil one (1 John 5:19). The devil is characterized as "the ruler of this world" (John 12:31; 14:30; 16:11), which signifies that human beings are in thrall to wickedness. The world failed to recognize Jesus as God's Word and the agent of salvation (John 1:10). Indeed, since the world is under Satan's rule, it hates Jesus (John 7:7) and his disciples, who have been called out of the world (John 15:18–19; 17:14–16; 1 John 3:13). Because the world does not know Jesus, it does not know his disciples either (1 John 3:1). The calling of the disciples out of the world indicates that they too were once part of the world, and hence those who are now believers were also once under the world's influence. Disciples formerly were part of the world, but now they have been rescued by Jesus from the world. Now the disciples are in the world but not "of the world" (John 17:13–16),

---

33. For a useful survey of *kosmos* in John, see Barrett 1978: 161–62. Compare the qualifications of Barrett's view in Carson 1991b: 123; Balz, *EDNT* 2:312.

since Jesus has freed disciples from the world's dominion by choosing them out of the world (John 15:19) and by overcoming the world (John 16:33). The disciples have been given by the Father to the Son (John 6:37; 13:1; 17:6, 9). Disciples overcome the world through their faith—that is, by believing that Jesus is God's Son (1 John 5:4–5)—and the subsequent verses indicate that they conquer on the basis of his death. Jesus, therefore, did not manifest himself to the world after his resurrection in the same way that he revealed himself to his disciples (John 14:22; 16:20). Nevertheless, the disciples were sent into the world to proclaim the message of salvation (John 17:18, 21), so that the world would come to believe that God sent Jesus.

The world's evil manifests itself in what it desires and its fierce pride (1 John 2:16). False prophets proclaim the world's message, and their content is celebrated by those in the world, but the message is that of the antichrist (1 John 4:1–6). The world does not have any capacity to receive the Spirit of truth (John 14:17) and does not know the Father (John 17:25), and hence people in the world are wakened out of their slumber only by the convicting work of the Spirit (John 16:8–11). The world cannot grant true peace, for peace in the midst of trouble comes only from Christ (John 14:31).

The only hope for the world, therefore, is Jesus Christ. John often emphasizes that the only deliverance for the world is Jesus Christ. The love of God for the world is not due to its attractiveness, as if God loved the world because of its loveliness; rather, God shows his love for the world by sending Christ for its salvation, even though it is remarkably evil (John 3:16; 10:36). The sin of the world can be atoned for only by Jesus Christ, who is God's lamb who removes the world's sin (John 1:29). In Samaria Jesus is acclaimed as "the Savior of the world" (John 4:42; cf. 1 John 4:14). Jesus came into the world to bear witness to the truth, even though his kingdom is not of this world (John 18:36–37). He was sent into the world so that it might live (1 John 4:9). The five thousand fed by Jesus believed that he was the prophet sent into the world (John 6:15). Jesus is God's bread that grants life to the world (John 6:33; cf. 11:27), and the life bestowed on the world is available through his death (John 6:51), so that the world lives on the basis of eating his flesh and drinking his blood. Propitiation—the satisfaction of God's wrath against the sins of the whole world—is accomplished by the death of Jesus (1 John 2:2). The only light for the world is Jesus (John 8:12; 9:5; 11:9; 12:46), for without him the world remains shrouded in darkness. These texts suggest that John often uses the term "world" to refer to the entire human race without distinction. John recognizes often that not everyone believes, and hence he is not teaching that the sins of every single person in the world are actually removed by Jesus' death. Nor when he says that

Jesus is the Savior of the world should we conclude that every single person in the world is saved by Jesus. What John emphasizes, rather, is that the whole world without distinction, both Jews and Gentiles, is the object of God's saving love in Christ.

Jesus also came to bring judgment onto the world, since those who refuse to believe him are condemned (John 9:39). What Jesus says in John 9:39 seems to contradict the claim that Jesus came not to judge the world but to save it (John 12:47), but the contradiction is superficial. Jesus' intention in coming into the world was to save it, but those who refused to believe in him were thereby judged, and so he came to judge in a secondary but not a primary sense.[34] His explicit intention in coming to the earth was to save the world, but those who refuse his salvation must come under judgment, even though salvation was Jesus' primary intention. Jesus' death spells salvation for the world, but it is also the case that Jesus by his death judges the world and evicts its ruler (John 12:31).

Therefore, John's theology of the world should also be understood eschatologically, for believers enjoy salvation in the midst of an evil world that is opposed to God and his Son. The devil rules the entire world, but Jesus has come to save his own in the world. His saving work has liberated believers from the evil of the world, and they are given strength to withstand the blandishments of the world, the false teaching of antichrists, and the work of the devil. The world and its influence are passing away (1 John 2:17), and the final victory is sure because Jesus has triumphed over the world via his cross.

The contrast between light and darkness should be understood in similar terms. Jesus himself is the light of the world (John 1:4; 8:12). The darkness hates the light and tries to conquer and understand it but is unable to do so (John 1:5).[35] Darkness represents evil that shrinks back from the penetrating and exposing gaze of the light (John 3:19–21). The corollary to hatred of the light is a love for darkness, and the light is detested because of the wickedness of human beings who flee from the uncovering of their evil. Those who do not follow Jesus live in the realm of evil (John 8:12; 11:9–10; 12:35). They continue in their blinding darkness because they insist upon their goodness and do not want to admit that they fail to live in the light (John 9:39–41). The first rays of light dawn when human beings confess their radical evil and blindness, but those in the darkness dogmatically insist on their own goodness, and

---

34. See Barrett 1978: 365, 430.

35. The verb *katalambanō* probably has a double meaning here, signifying both "overcome" and "comprehend" (so Barrett 1978: 158). Contra Lindars (1972: 87), who restricts the meaning to "overcome," and Ridderbos (1997: 39–40), who argues that only a misunderstanding is in view.

escape from darkness comes only for those who believe in Jesus (John 12:46). Once again, the eschatological character of light and darkness is present by implication, for the light is now dawning with the coming of Jesus, so that the realm of darkness is now illuminated by the radiance of his presence.

The epistle of 1 John nuances matters a bit differently but appears to travel along the same arteries. God is light, and as such he is totally good and cannot be charged with evil (1 John 1:5). Those who walk in the darkness are secessionists from the church. They have left the Johannine community and claim to be without sin (1 John 1:8). Apparently, they maintained that they had not sinned since their conversion (1 John 1:10).[36] Conversely, those who walk in the light know that they are sinners and, by confessing their sins, acknowledge before God that they have fallen short of his will and ways (1 John 1:7, 9). They look to Jesus as the righteous one, the propitiation for their sins (1 John 2:2). The wicked, then, are those who insist on their goodness; they are blinded by the darkness and fail to see that hating their brothers and sisters is a parable of their death (1 John 2:9–10). The eschatological character of the light/darkness theme in John is clarified by 1 John 2:8, a verse that we noted above. The darkness is passing away, while the light is now shining. Those who live in the darkness of evil are dominated by the one who rules over the citizens of this world (1 John 5:19), but the light shines in the lives of believers, for they are born of God, and the evil one cannot harm them (1 John 5:18). Believers can be assured that they belong to God even in the midst of this evil world (1 John 5:19). In contrast to those who are under the dominion of the evil one, they have understanding of the one true God (1 John 5:20).

The contrast between truth and falsehood also constitutes a separation between good and evil. Jesus is the revelation of God and represents perfect goodness, and so he is the truth (John 14:6). He is "full of grace and truth" (John 1:14; cf. 1:17), and the Spirit is also the Spirit of truth (John 14:17; 15:26; 16:13). The witnesses testifying about Jesus are true (John 5:31–33; 8:13–19). Since Jesus seeks God's glory, his message is true and contains no falsehood (John 7:18, 28). The truth that people need cannot be confined to the intellect, for it frees people from the dominion of sin (John 8:32–34), and Jesus claimed that true freedom from bondage comes from him (John 8:36). So-called disciples are unwilling to hear the truth from Jesus (John 8:40, 45) because they belong to the father of lies, the devil (John 8:43–44). Hence, Jesus said that all those who belong to the truth will listen to his voice (John 18:37; cf. 8:47; 10:4). Pilate's refusal to listen to Jesus demonstrated that he was dominated by

---

36. For this interpretation, see R. Brown 1982: 212, 234.

darkness (John 18:38), and his cynical question about truth (the pseudo-refuge of every person fleeing from goodness) testified to his spiritual state. Truth is found in the word of God (John 17:17), and believers will be preserved and sanctified by such truth. The truth is concretely present in Jesus himself (John 14:6). Once again, the contrast between truth and falsehood has an eschatological cast, for truth has entered history in the person of Jesus Christ. Truth for John is not an abstract entity but rather has entered history in the Word made flesh. Hence, those who live in the realm of falsehood can be freed only through the truth that is in Jesus.

Conclusion

The Synoptic Gospels emphasize the fulfillment of God's promises by speaking of the kingdom of God, but in John the focus is not on God's kingdom but on eternal life. Still, the two notions are remarkably similar. As Köstenberger says, "That the expressions 'kingdom of God' and 'eternal life' are essentially equivalent is suggested by their parallel use in Matthew 19:16, 24 pars."[37] John particularly emphasizes that this life is available now for those who believe in Jesus, while conversely those who do not put their trust in Jesus stand under God's judgment even now. Even though John focuses on present eschatology, it would be a mistake to conclude that he eliminates future eschatology. We noted a number of texts that indicate that the inauguration of eternal life in the ministry of Jesus does not rule out a future consummation. We have also observed that Johannine dualism should not be interpreted ontologically; rather, it is part and parcel of his eschatology. Those who belong to Jesus are freed from the world and its dominion. Those who are from below can belong to the realm above through faith and trust in Jesus. So too light and truth belong to those who trust in Jesus, since he is the light and the truth, whereas those who reject Jesus walk in darkness and are shrouded in error. When we perceive that John's dualism should be interpreted in light of his eschatology, it is clear that his dualism belongs on Jewish soil. It should be interpreted in light of the fulfillment of God's saving promises.

37. Köstenberger 2004: 123.

3

※ ※ ※ ※ ※ ※ ※ ※ ※ ※ ※ ※ ※ ※ ※ ※ ※ ※

Inaugurated Eschatology
Outside the Gospels

The purpose of this chapter is to show that the tension between inaugurated and consummated eschatology identified in the Synoptic Gospels
and in the Johannine literature also informs the remainder of the NT.[1]
Indeed, the prominence of the already–not yet in Paul confirms that
eschatological tension was a characteristic feature of NT theology.[2]

Jewish thought distinguished between this age and the age to come.
This age is marred by sin, disease, and death, whereas the age to come
brings life, abundance, and joy.[3] Those who belong to God should "flee
from the shadow of this age" (4 Esd. 2:36 RSV), and "those who have
departed from the shadow of this age have received glorious garments
from the Lord" (4 Esd. 2:39 RSV).[4] The author remarks that "this age
is full of sadness and infirmities" (4 Esd. 4:27 RSV). Jacob and Esau

---

1. In defense of this, see the fundamental work of Cullmann 1964.

2. In this respect, Paul's theology matches the theology of Jesus. See Kümmel (1973:
141–51), who sees continuity between Paul and Jesus. The compatibility of Paul and Jesus
has been rightly set forth in the important work of D. Wenham 1995.

3. Meier (1994: 363n43) points out that the OT typically speaks of the coming of God's
kingdom. The language of "this age" and "the age to come" belongs to later Jewish literature and cannot be traced definitely to the NT period.

4. Most scholars agree that chapter 2 derives from a later Christian hand, but we likely
see here the influence of Jewish eschatology even in the Christian redaction.

represent righteousness and evil, and so the author remarks, "Esau is the end of this age, and Jacob is the beginning of the age that follows" (4 Esd. 6:9 RSV). The coming age is clearly delineated from this present age, "But the day of judgment will be the end of this age and the beginning of the immortal age to come, in which corruption has passed away" (4 Esd. 7:113 RSV). The present age is evil and corrupt (4 Esd. 9:18–19 RSV).

The distinction between the two ages, as we have already observed, is found in the Gospels. Matthew contrasts "this age" with "the age to come" (Matt. 12:32). Mark and Luke place eternal life in the age to come (Mark 10:30; Luke 18:30). Jesus contrasts the "sons of this age" who marry with those who "attain" the coming age, where marriage is no longer practiced (Luke 20:34–35). Those who belong to "this age" are consumed with wealth (Luke 16:8), and hence Jesus speaks of the worries and concerns that animate people during this age (Matt. 13:22; Mark 4:19). Since there is an age to come, the present age is temporary and will come to an end (Matt. 13:39, 40, 49; 24:3; 28:20).

Two Ages in Paul's Letters

The term "kingdom" and the phrase "kingdom of God" are not common in Paul, and yet the instances where they do occur indicate that the already–not yet theme, so characteristic of the teaching of Jesus, is present in these Pauline texts as well (Rom. 14:17; 1 Cor. 4:20; 6:9–10; 15:24, 50; Gal. 5:21; Eph. 5:5; Col. 1:13; 4:11; 1 Thess. 2:12; 2 Thess. 1:5; 2 Tim. 4:1, 18).[5] In most instances the "kingdom of God" refers to the future kingdom that awaits believers (see esp. 1 Cor. 6:9–10; 15:24; Eph. 5:5), but in Col. 1:13 believers are now transferred to God's kingdom, and Rom. 14:17 suggests that the power of the kingdom is now at work because believers now enjoy the gift of the Spirit, and hence righteousness, joy, and peace are theirs.

Paul also believed in two ages: this present evil age and the coming age of righteousness.[6] The clearest example is found in Eph. 1:21, where he specifically differentiates between "this age" and "the one to come,"

5. For a study of kingdom in some of these texts, see Donfried 2002: 233–52. Donfried sees the already–not yet theme and maintains that continuity exists here with the teaching of Jesus.

6. For a recognition of the fundamental nature of the already–not yet tension in Paul, see Keck 2006: 112–13.

claiming that Jesus rules over all during the present age and will continue his reign in the coming era.[7]

Paul often contrasted the values and behavior of those living in this age with those of the coming one. Satan is described as the god of this age (2 Cor. 4:4), indicating that those under the dominion of the devil engage in false worship.[8] Since Satan rules as the god of this age, it follows that unbelievers live in accord with the standards of this world (Eph. 2:2).[9] The impact of the old world order displays itself in the domain of scholarship and the intellect. The rhetoricians and debaters of this age are celebrated (1 Cor. 1:20). Those endowed with rhetorical ability are deemed wise (1 Cor. 1:20; 3:18–19).[10] But Paul was unimpressed with the dazzling skills of orators because the rulers of this age, with all their so-called wisdom, crucified the glorious Lord (1 Cor. 2:6, 8), demonstrating their failure to grasp true wisdom.

Paul taught that Christians live in between the times inasmuch as the present evil age lingers, even as the new age has invaded history. "The ends of the ages have come" (1 Cor. 10:11 NRSV), signifying the fulfillment, at least in part, of God's saving promises. The cross and resurrection of Christ are the turning point in history. Believers have been set "free from the present evil age" by virtue of the death of Christ (Gal. 1:4 NRSV).[11] The form of this present world is passing away (1 Cor. 7:29–31), so that the activities of everyday life are relativized in light of the coming eschaton. Joy and sorrow, buying and selling, marriage and education must all be viewed in light of the shortness of the time—the temporary character of human history. Therefore, Paul did not criticize riches per se, but he did warn the rich in the present era not to pin their hopes on that which is fleeting (1 Tim. 6:17).

Christians live in, so to speak, the "twilight zone," for they have experienced the saving power of the age to come, and yet they still reside in the present evil age. Even now Jesus reigns, but the consummation of his rule and the destruction of every enemy have not yet occurred (Eph. 1:21; 1 Cor. 15:26–28). Because of the cross of Christ believers are a new creation (Gal. 1:4; 2 Cor. 5:17), and yet the redemption that they enjoy

---

7. The importance of eschatology in Pauline theology is rightly emphasized in Ridderbos 1975; see also Pate 1995. The thought of Beker (1980) runs along similar lines, and he posits that the apocalyptic triumph of God is the central theme in Paul.

8. For a reference to Satan here, see Garland 1999: 210–11.

9. The term used here is *aiōn* rather than *kosmos*.

10. For the view that the Corinthians estimated Paul and Apollos according to their rhetorical ability, see Litfin 1994; Winter 1997.

11. Martyn (1997: 91) rightly sees the apocalyptic nature of Paul's theology here, which he emphasizes throughout his Galatians commentary, but he mistakenly excludes salvation history, postulating a false either-or between apocalyptic and salvation history instead of seeing a both-and.

(Rom. 3:24) is not yet completed, for they endure the anguish of death and await the redemption of the body (Rom. 8:23; cf. Eph. 1:14). In the meantime, as believers inhabit the interval between inauguration and consummation, they must resist the blandishments of this world (Rom. 12:2). The world allures and captivates even those who have the firstfruits of the Spirit, but those in whom the Spirit dwells must surmount fleshly desires and live in the realm of the Spirit (Rom. 8:13).

Despite the lingering presence of the present evil age, the age to come has dawned by virtue of the death of Christ (Gal. 1:4). The death and resurrection of Christ inaugurate the age to come, and the emblem of its advent is the gift of the Spirit. The promise of the Spirit in Isa. 44:3 is tucked into a context in which Yahweh promises a new exodus in which he will deliver his people from Babylonian exile and return them to their own land: "For I will pour water on the thirsty land, and streams on the dry ground; I will pour my Spirit upon your offspring, and my blessing on your descendants."[12] Isaiah 40–66 pledges not only return from exile but also the fulfillment of all of God's promises to his people. Isaiah envisions a new creation where the wilderness will bloom and waters will flow in the desert. God will create a new heavens and new earth where joy will redound and peace will reign, even between the wolf and the lamb (Isa. 65:17–25; 66:22). The Jerusalem above (Gal. 4:26) is a reality even now for believers, though they await the eschaton.[13]

Paul alluded to the prophecy of Isa. 44:3 in Gal. 3:14, and the latter functions as the conclusion and main point of Paul's dense and crucial argument in Gal. 3:10–14. Here I quickly sum up Paul's argument. God's curse remains on all who rely on works of the law, since the law requires perfect obedience and no one keeps it without fail. The only way to be right with God is by faith in Christ, since observance of the law leads to a curse. The curse pronounced upon lawbreakers is removed by the cross of Christ, wherein Christ took the curse deserved by sinners upon himself. Therefore, Gentiles receive the promise of "the blessing of Abraham" and the "promise of the Spirit" (Gal. 3:14 NRSV) by faith. It is likely that "the blessing of Abraham" and the "promise of the Spirit" refer to the same reality in Gal. 3:14.[14] Paul contended that Gentiles did not need to receive

12. Surprisingly, Childs (2001: 341–42) says nothing about the promise of the Spirit here.

13. Rightly Lincoln 1981: 21–22, 25, 29. This fits with Phil. 3:20, where the believer's "state and constitutive government is in heaven" (so Lincoln 1981: 100), and we have a prime example of realized eschatology here, for believers are now part of a heavenly commonwealth but await (Phil. 3:21) the future resurrection (see Lincoln 1981: 101–3). See also Fee 1995: 378–80.

14. So Matera 1992: 120; Dunn 1993: 179; Longenecker 1990: 123; Martyn 1997: 321; contra H. Betz 1979: 152.

circumcision in order to belong to the people of God, for the gift of the Spirit testified that they were God's children. They received the miracle-working presence of the Spirit by faith and not by works of law (Gal. 3:1–5). The Galatians gladly and confidently called God their Father because they were his children, and that sonship was certified by the Spirit.

Galatians 3:14 mentions both "the blessing of Abraham" and "the promise of the Spirit" (NRSV), drawing us into the orbit of Isa. 44:3. In the Isaiah text the blessing and the Spirit, and indeed the water in the desert, describe the same reality with different terminology. We can conclude the same in Gal. 3:14. The end-time blessing sworn to Abraham (Gen. 12:1–3) reaches its fulfillment in the gift of the Spirit. To put it another way, the blessing of Abraham *is* the promise of the Spirit. The allusion to Isa. 44:3 also leads us to the conclusion that the promise of the Spirit is God's eschatological gift—the fulfillment of his promise to vindicate his people. Israel returned from exile to Babylon in 536 BC, but that return did not constitute a fulfillment of all that was pledged in Isa. 40–66.[15] Early Christians believed that the promises in Isaiah were being fulfilled in their days, particularly in the gift of the Spirit. Still, everything promised in Isa. 40–66 had not become a reality. The new heavens and new earth had not yet arrived. The Spirit, then, constitutes the "firstfruits" (*aparchē*) of God's work (Rom. 8:23). Just as Christ is the firstfruits of the resurrection (1 Cor. 15:20, 23), guaranteeing the physical resurrection of believers, so the gift of the Spirit ensures that God will fulfill the remainder of his saving promises. The Spirit constitutes a pledge (*arrabōn*) that God will redeem the bodies of believers by raising them from the dead on the last day (Eph. 1:14; cf. Rom. 8:23; 2 Cor. 1:22). All of this fits with the main point being argued here: the presence of the Spirit indicates that the new age has dawned, but believers have not yet obtained all that God has promised.[16]

New Creation

The eschatological granting of the Spirit portends the arrival of a new creation. We see this clearly in Isa. 32:14–18:

15. What we see here is a typological understanding of fulfillment. For a classic discussion of this theme, see Goppelt 1982a, and for an even more helpful treatment overall, see Davidson 1981.

16. If the Spirit is the gift of the new age, then the term "flesh" in Paul should be understood in terms of redemptive history. For a survey of the various understandings of the term "flesh" in Paul, along with an emphasis on salvation history in understanding Paul's distinctive use of the term "flesh," see Ridderbos 1975: 64–68, 100–107; Dunn 1998: 62–73. Russell (1993; 1995) also has argued that "flesh" in Paul must be understood in terms of redemptive history, though he underestimates the anthropological dimension of the term.

For the palace is forsaken, the populous city deserted; the hill and the watchtower will become dens forever, a joy of wild donkeys, a pasture of flocks; until the Spirit is poured upon us from on high, and the wilderness becomes a fruitful field, and the fruitful field is deemed a forest. Then justice will dwell in the wilderness, and righteousness abide in the fruitful field. And the effect of righteousness will be peace, and the result of righteousness, quietness and trust forever. My people will abide in a peaceful habitation, in secure dwellings, and in quiet resting places.

The granting of the Spirit is accompanied by the renewal of creation, so that the wilderness blossoms with fruit. In Isaiah return from exile cannot be sundered from a transformation of creation. When Israel returns from Babylon, mountains, hills, and trees will rejoice, and instead of thorns and briers there will be myrtles and cypresses (Isa. 55:12–13).

God pledges to transform the natural world as we know it: "I will open rivers on the bare heights, and fountains in the midst of the valleys. I will make the wilderness a pool of water, and the dry land springs of water. I will put in the wilderness the cedar, the acacia, the myrtle, and the olive. I will set in the desert the cypress, the plane and the pine together" (Isa. 41:18–19). Elsewhere in Isaiah God renovates the world so that it becomes a new creation (Isa. 65:17; 66:22). According to Paul, the new creation has dawned. Believers in Jesus Christ are a new creation (2 Cor. 5:17).[17] In the context of 2 Cor. 5 this new creative work of God is centered in the reconciling work of Christ on the cross, whereby transgressions are not counted against those befriended to God through Christ. Nor does the arrival of the new creation spell the consummation of all of God's promises, for in 2 Cor. 5:1–10 the resurrection of the body is reserved for the future. Paul's "new creation" theme, then, fits with the already–not yet tension observed elsewhere.

The theme of new creation surfaces in Gal. 6:15 as well.[18] The Jewish teachers insisted that Gentile converts submit to circumcision to become part of Abraham's family (Gal. 5:2–6; 6:12–13). Paul emphatically rejected

17. For a careful analysis of the verse, see Harris 2005: 430–34. Harris (2005: 432) contends that the background here is "anthropological and personal, not cosmological and eschatological." For an emphasis on the new cosmos and world order, see Barrett 1973: 173; R. Martin 1986: 152. Hubbard (2002: 11–76) argues that the Jewish background indicates that the new creation is both anthropological and cosmological. So also Garland 1999: 286–87; Furnish 1984: 314–15, 332–33.

18. The "new creation" theme, according to some, focuses not on the anthropological change inside a person but on God's new work in the world that he created (so Weima 1993: 102; Dunn 1993: 342–43). But Hubbard (2002) rightly argues that the anthropological notions are actually at the forefront here in Paul's theology, and that his new-creation theology is intimately related with the new-age work of the Spirit. Longenecker (1990: 295–96) seems to hold a view similar to Hubbard's. For the new creation in Galatians, see also Martyn 1997: 570–74.

imposing circumcision on Gentiles because it diminishes Christ's work on the cross (Gal. 1:4; 2:19–20; 3:1, 13; 4:4–5; 5:11; 6:14) and focuses on human accomplishment.[19] The only emblems needed on Paul's body are the marks (*stigmata*) of the cross (Gal. 6:17). Paul boasted only in the cross, refusing to put any credence in the standards of the world (Gal. 6:14). The cross, then, effects the new creation. Paul drew attention to the soteriological dimensions of God's creative work, excluding human works as the basis for right standing with God. Circumcision in and of itself is irrelevant—nor should anyone take pride in being uncircumcised. Boasting in uncircumcision falls prey to the same trap as boasting in circumcision, since both manifest pride in human performance. The new creation fixes our attention on the cross of Christ, where salvation has been definitively accomplished.

When we think about the term "creation" in Paul, its background must be sought in the OT, especially on God's work in creating the heavens and earth. The term "creation" features God's sovereignty and unrivaled power. As we noted, the "new creation" theme in Paul centers on the cross of Christ, where God's saving and gracious work for human beings was effected. Invariably the creation motif in Pauline writings has a soteriological cast. Satan blinds unbelievers so that they do not see the stunning beauty of God in Christ (2 Cor. 4:4). Paul compared the work of conversion to that of creation, in which the same God who summoned light out of darkness shines his light in human hearts so that they perceive God's glory in Jesus Christ (2 Cor. 4:6). Unbelievers, according to Eph. 2:1–4, live under the dominion of sin, insensitive to the things of God and lacking any desire or ability to change. God's grace, however, breaks through the hardness of human hearts and grants life, so that believers are raised and seated with Christ (Eph. 2:5–10). This gracious work of God is also said to be his creative work.[20] God's work of new creation is nothing other than the power of his grace, reflecting his sovereign work in bestowing life on those who are dead (cf. Rom. 4:17). Later in Ephesians God's gracious work is described in terms of the creation of "the new self" (*ton kainon anthrōpon* [Eph. 4:24]). The "new man" is Christ Jesus (Eph. 2:15 my translation; cf. Col. 3:11), and Jews and Gentiles form one body in Christ. In Eph. 4:24 Paul calls upon believers to be what they are in Christ, focusing again on God's gracious and redeeming work.

The inauguration of the new creation in the present age points forward to the future, for Christians anticipate with confidence and joy the life of the age to come, when they will enjoy eternal life (e.g., Rom. 2:7; 5:21;

---

19. Borgen (1980) argues that the cross functions as the replacement for circumcision in Galatians. See also Borgen 1982.

20. See Lincoln 1990: 114; Best 1998: 230; Hoehner 2002: 347–48.

6:23; Gal. 6:8; Titus 1:2). As the messianic and Davidic king (Ps. 110:1), Jesus now rules over every enemy (Eph. 1:19–23; 1 Cor. 15:26–28). But the fullness of his power will be evident on the final day of judgment and salvation. Then believers will celebrate and commemorate forever the grace bestowed on them in Christ Jesus (Eph. 2:7).

The Gift of the Spirit in Acts

The gift of the Spirit signals the arrival of the eschaton. According to the prophet Joel, God pledged to pour out his Spirit (Joel 2:28). Joel anticipated the day of the Lord, when Yahweh would reverse the fortunes of Israel by vindicating his people and punishing the nations that opposed Israel (Joel 3). Those who curse Israel would be cursed, and those who bless Israel would be blessed, in accordance with God's promise to Abraham (Gen. 12:3). Joel pointed forward to the day when Jerusalem would become holy, and the land would burst with fruitfulness as wine and milk flow in abundance and a fountain springs up from the Lord's house (Joel 3:17–18). We note again here the language of a new creation. God will avenge himself on nations that resisted him, whereas Jerusalem will become a peaceful habitation.

The signature of such promises is the dispensing of the Spirit, and in Acts Peter proclaimed that the day of fulfillment had come (Acts 2:16–21).[21] The Spirit was poured out by Jesus, the crucified and risen Lord (Acts 2:33), for at his exaltation he was crowned as Lord and Christ (Acts 2:36), and he granted the Spirit to his people. The enthronement of Jesus of Nazareth as Lord and Christ fulfilled the Davidic covenant, indicating that he reigns as the Davidic king (cf. 2 Sam. 7; 1 Chron. 17; Pss. 89; 132). As the messianic king, he confers the Spirit on his people, and the gift of the Spirit indicates that God's promises are now being fulfilled. Luke, however, did not envisage the coming of the Spirit as the completion of all of God's promises. History will reach its culmination and climax at the coming of Jesus Christ, when God will fulfill everything promised in the prophetic writings (Acts 3:20–21). Jesus now reigns, and the Spirit now indwells the hearts of believers, but in the interim before Jesus comes again, he rules from heaven. The apostles' question to Jesus about when the kingdom will be restored to Israel (Acts

21. "That the events he describes were the fulfillment of Scripture is a central part of Luke's understanding of them" (Barrett 1994: 135). Fitzmyer (1998: 252) rightly argues that Luke saw a fulfillment of the Joel prophecy here and the inbreaking of the last days. Jervell (1984: 99–104) rightly detects continuity between the OT and NT relative to the Spirit but significantly downplays the newness coincident with the gift of the Spirit in Luke-Acts.

1:6) should not be dismissed as a mistaken departure into nationalistic ideology.[22] Jesus' promise of the Spirit naturally precipitated the question, since in the OT the restoration of Israel was indissolubly joined with the promise that God would pour out his Spirit (cf. Isa. 32; 44:1–5; Ezek. 36–37). The disciples did not yet comprehend the already–not yet tension that informed Jesus' earthly ministry. Jesus answered the question by implying that the restoration of Israel and the fulfillment of all of God's promises are not coterminous with the granting of the Spirit (Acts 1:7–8). An interval exists between the gift of the Spirit and the consummation.

The Resurrection of Jesus

If we can speak of the giving of the Spirit as the arrival of the eschaton, we should note that before the coming of the Spirit, Jesus was raised from the dead.[23] The resurrection of Jesus is one of the central themes of Acts (Acts 1:22; 2:24–36; 3:13–15, 21–26; 4:2, 10–11, 33; 5:30–32; 7:37; 10:40–41; 13:30–37; 17:18, 31–32; 23:6–8; 24:15, 21; 26:8), and it cannot be sundered from his exaltation to God's right hand. We find the background for the theme of resurrection in the OT.[24] Ezekiel 37 looks forward to the day when Israel and Judah will be reunited.[25] The Lord will place his Spirit in his people (v. 14), return them from exile (v. 21), form them into a united people (v. 22), cleanse them from their sins (v. 23), and grant them the ability to keep his commands (v. 24). In other words, God will fulfill his long-standing covenantal promises to his people (vv. 26–27), so that his sanctuary will be among them, and he will be their God and they will be his people. God's saving purposes will be realized when a new David arrives (vv. 24–25) who will lead them as their prince. Ezekiel used a startling and vivid picture to describe the future union of Israel and Judah: resurrection from the dead. The restoration of Israel is portrayed in terms of the resurrection of corpses, as if the nation in its present state is nothing more than a collection of bones in a valley

22. Barrett (1994: 76–77), for example, does not clearly draw the connection between the question and the fulfillment of the OT promises. For the connection, see Polhill 1992: 84; Turner 1996: 299; Penney 1997: 69–71.

23. The crucial work on the resurrection is Wright 2003. Wright (2003: 32–84) demonstrates that in the Greco-Roman world there was no expectation of or hope for a bodily resurrection, and hence the NT hope is grounded in the OT view of the body.

24. For a fine survey of resurrection in the OT and Second Temple Judaism, see Wright 2003: 85–206. Wright (2003: 123) thinks that the hope of the resurrection began with the servant texts in Isaiah.

25. See especially Block 1998: 383–92, 399; Wright 2003: 119–21.

that needs flesh and life.[26] Such new life comes from the breath of the Spirit, who will animate all Israel and unify them, fulfilling the promises originally made to Abraham.

Space forbids us from considering all the complex issues that arise in Ezek. 37. What is clear, however, is that resurrection signifies the fulfillment of God's promises, the inauguration of the age to come—the restoration of exile and the return of Israel. We see the same emphasis in Isa. 26. The Lord will judge and destroy the human city that mistreats the poor and flows with evil. In its stead he will establish an impregnable city of salvation for the righteous, for those who trust in Yahweh. Amazingly, this future hope is not limited to the living, and Isaiah declares that the dead will rise; they will awake and sing for joy in the fulfillment of God's promises (Isa. 26:19).[27] Daniel 12 runs along the same lines, placing the resurrection of the dead at the time of the end when God will vindicate his people and judge the wicked.[28] In every instance the resurrection signals the onset of the new age, the time when God's saving promises are finally realized.

Hence, the proclamation of Jesus' resurrection in Acts—one of its most prominent themes—means nothing less than the arrival of the coming age of salvation. For Jews, resurrection could mean only one thing: the old age has passed away and the new has come. God's promise to vindicate his people and restore Israel was no longer a word about the future; the threshold had been crossed with the resurrection of Jesus of Nazareth. Incidentally, this suggests that Jesus is the true Israel (a theme that we will examine in due course). Still, the arrival of the resurrection and the new age contained a surprise inasmuch as the present evil age continued to exist and did not vanish immediately. The new and old ages coexist simultaneously now that Jesus has been raised from the dead. The new has come, but the old persists. The new certainly will triumph, but not without an interval in which death remains. Luke concentrates on the resurrection of Jesus in Acts because it is the emblem of the new age, the signature of God's promises.

We find in Paul a similar emphasis on the resurrection of Jesus, although, because of problems in the churches, he explains more clearly the interval between Jesus' resurrection and that of believers.[29] The resurrection of Jesus spells his exaltation to God's right hand as the powerful

26. Wright (2003: 124) correctly observes that restoration from exile and future resurrection are often intertwined and difficult to separate from one another.

27. Childs (2001: 191–92) rightly argues that it is a false dichotomy to ask whether the promise is for restoration of the nation or a future resurrection. See also Wright 2003: 116–18; Motyer 1993: 218–20.

28. See Wright 2003: 109–15; Baldwin 1978: 204–5.

29. For resurrection in Paul, see Wright 2003: 209–76.

Son of God (Rom. 1:4).[30] Jesus as the resurrected and exalted one now reigns over every angelic power (Eph. 1:19–23). The fundamental nature of Jesus' resurrection for Christian belief is apparent from its presence in confessional statements that briefly summarize the elements of the gospel (Rom. 4:25; 10:9; 1 Cor. 15:1–11). Those who reject the resurrection of Jesus deny the gospel, for justification and salvation are available only for those who confess that Jesus was raised from the dead. The resurrected Christ will deliver his people from God's wrath on the day of the Lord (1 Thess. 1:10).[31] The text just cited from 1 Thessalonians confirms the same eschatological tension noted in Acts. The age to come has arrived now that Jesus has been raised from the dead, but believers live between the times. They await the final day of judgment, when God will inflict his wrath on those who have not placed their trust and faith in Jesus. Jesus' resurrection testifies to the inauguration of the age of fulfillment, but God's promises are not yet consummated, for Jesus is coming again, and on that day he will spare his people from "the wrath to come."

A similar note is sounded in Rom. 8:11. The Spirit of the resurrected Jesus indwells his people. We have already seen that the indwelling Spirit signifies the gift of the new age, and here the gift of the Spirit is connected closely to the risen Christ, which is scarcely surprising since the Spirit is given when Christ is exalted. Two indications of the new age coalesce here: Christ's resurrection and the gift of the Spirit. The arrival of the age of promise, however, does not mean that the era of evil has ceased. Even though Christ has been raised and has poured out his Spirit, Christians still die—the age of evil is defeated, but it still kills Christians in its last gasp. Yet, the indwelling Spirit of the resurrected Christ guarantees that believers will be raised on the last day. Death will not have the last word for believers; it represents the last painful but ultimately ineffective attack against Christians. Believers live in the interval between Christ's resurrection and theirs with the sure confidence that they will live because Christ lives.

Understanding the interlude between the resurrection of Christ and the resurrection of believers is no trivial matter. Those who proclaim that the physical resurrection of believers has already occurred "have swerved from the truth" of the gospel (2 Tim. 2:18).[32] Those who collapse

30. The resurrection here signals the arrival of the age to come. See Schreiner 1998: 44–45.

31. See Wanamaker 1990: 88. The present tense of the participle *rhyomenon* in 1 Thess. 1:10 should not be pressed to say that Jesus is protecting believers even now (contra Best 1972: 84).

32. The opponents likely believed that the only resurrection that believers experienced was spiritual and that it occurred at baptism (so Marshall 1999: 751–54; W. Mounce 2000:

the not yet into the already have deviated from orthodoxy. Perhaps those questioning the resurrection in 1 Cor. 15 were similar to the opponents in 2 Timothy. In insisting that there is no resurrection of the dead (1 Cor. 15:12), they probably taught that a future physical resurrection was a fantasy (cf. 1 Cor. 15:35).[33] They may have believed that the only resurrection that believers receive is the spiritual resurrection in which believers are raised with Christ (Eph. 2:6; Col. 3:1), dismissing a future physical resurrection because such a notion was repulsive to the Greek mind. Conceivably, they identified themselves as spiritually exalted even now as possessors of "wisdom" (cf. 1 Cor. 1:17–2:16; 3:18–23; 4:6–7; 6:5), and their spiritual maturity is confirmed by the spiritual gifts operating in their midst, particularly speaking in tongues like the angels of heaven (1 Cor. 12:14–30; 14; see esp. 13:1).[34] They were reigning as kings, and so what need could there possibly be for a future physical resurrection (1 Cor. 4:8)? Their distorted conception of the resurrection may have contributed to their defense of sexual sin (1 Cor. 6:12–20), as some may have argued that what we do with our bodies is irrelevant.

For Paul, belief in the future resurrection of believers is nonnegotiable. Those who reject the future physical resurrection of believers also deny the physical resurrection of Christ (1 Cor. 15:13, 15–16), even if they claim to support the latter. The two are inseparable for Paul, so that one cannot trumpet the resurrection of Christ and at the same time dismiss the future resurrection of believers. Interestingly, Paul did not *argue for* the inextricable connection between the resurrection of Christ and believers; he *assumed* dogmatically that anyone who writes off the resurrection of believers cannot and does not believe in Christ's resurrection. He pressed the matter further. Those who set aside Christ's resurrection have believed in vain and have not received forgiveness of sins (1 Cor. 15:14, 17). Indeed, believers who have died will perish eternally if Christ is not risen (1 Cor. 15:18).

What is fundamental for Paul, then, is grasping the interval between Christ's physical resurrection and ours. Christ is already resurrected, but believers are not yet raised. Christ is the "firstfruits" of the resurrection (1 Cor. 15:20, 23), so that his resurrection guarantees the same for all his people. Still, the resurrection of Christ does not secure the immediate resurrection of those who believe. Christians have the Spirit and are raised spiritually with Christ, but they will not be raised physically until

---

527–28). Less likely is the idea, defended by Dibelius and Conzelmann (1972: 112), that such a view can be ascribed to Gnosticism.

33. For a summary of the discussion, see Thiselton 2000: 1169–78. Wright (2003: 316) thinks that they denied the resurrection for pagan reasons, not because they held to an overrealized eschatology.

34. So Fee 1987: 10–15.

Jesus comes again (1 Cor. 15:23). Death as the last enemy still manifests its power in this world (1 Cor. 15:26), signaling that all things are not yet subjected to Christ (1 Cor. 15:27–28). The resurrection of Christ, then, reveals that the new age has broken in, and yet the consummation of all things has not occurred, for believers will not be raised until Christ returns. Meanwhile, Christians live in the awkward time period between the inauguration and the completion of God's promise.[35]

Hebrews

At first glance, it seems that Hebrews does not share the same eschatological viewpoint evident in the rest of the NT. The linear eschatology found elsewhere in the NT appears to be replaced by a vertical contrast between what is below and what is above. Indeed, Hebrews could be interpreted along Platonic lines, with the earthly representing the heavenly, so that the latter is the archetype of the former.[36] The true tent was not the tabernacle erected by Moses (Heb. 8:2), for the earthly tent points to and represents the very presence of God in heaven (Heb. 9:24). The holy place and the inner sanctum of the temple (the holy of holies) are merely copies and anticipations of God's dwelling. The author of Hebrews drew upon Exod. 25:40, where Moses was instructed to make the tabernacle in accord with the pattern revealed to him on Mount Sinai. The earthly articles of the tabernacle (Heb. 9:1–5), it seems, mirror heavenly reality. Similarly, the sacrifices and gifts offered, along with the various regulations relating to foods and drinks and washings, relate only to the physical and symbolic sphere (Heb. 9:8–10). They must point to something greater and higher, for they cannot effect forgiveness of sins. The earthly sacrifices purify the copies of the heavenly things, but they fail to secure forgiveness in God's very presence (Heb. 9:23–24). Only the sacrifice of Christ truly and definitively achieves full atonement for sin. Just as the tabernacle and the articles in it point to a vertical reality, so also the earthly priests from the tribe of Levi anticipate a superior priesthood, a Melchizedekian one. The priests "serve a copy and shadow

35. Even in Colossians, which often is seen as advancing only a realized eschatology, we see, in Col. 3:4, eschatological reservation and the recognition that the future has not yet arrived in its fullness (rightly Lincoln 1981: 129, 131–34; see also O'Brien 1982: 168–69; Dunn 1996b: 207–8; cf. Lohse 1971: 134–35). Lincoln (1981: 165–67) likewise argues that although Ephesians emphasizes realized eschatology, future eschatology is held in tension with the present fulfillment of God's promises. Best (1998: 52–55), on the other hand, maintains that the perspective in Ephesians is incompatible with what he deems the genuine Paul.

36. The Platonism would be of the sort found in Philo's work. However, Platonic or Philonic influence has been shown by Williamson (1970) to be quite unlikely.

of the heavenly things" (Heb. 8:5; cf. 10:1). Hence, the ritual duties of the priests symbolize access into God's presence (Heb. 9:6–8). The holy of holies may be entered into only once a year by priests, signifying the unavailability of regular and unhindered admission to God.

Even though Hebrews has superficial affinities with Platonic thought, the "vertical" language of the letter should be plotted into its eschatological worldview.[37] The already–not yet tension found elsewhere in the NT permeates Hebrews as well.[38] The focus on eschatology surfaces in the opening verses of the letter, where "these last days" have arrived with the coming of God's Son (Heb. 1:2) and the fulfillment of OT prophecy (Heb. 1:5–14). Final and definitive forgiveness of sins has been accomplished by the work of Christ (Heb. 1:3; 10:12); the power of the coming age has invaded this present era (Heb. 6:5). Forgiveness of sins must be understood eschatologically along the lines of promise and fulfillment.[39] The author of Hebrews argues that forgiveness signals the fulfillment of the new covenant (Heb. 8:6–13; 10:16–18; cf. Jer. 31:31–34). Inevitably, therefore, the old covenant has become obsolete and is no longer in force for Christians. The contrast between the old and new covenants certifies that the timeline of redemptive history is crucial for the author.[40]

The eschatological cast of the author's mind is apparent in Heb. 9:26 as well. Christ "appeared once for all at the end of the ages to put away sin by the sacrifice of himself." The "end of the ages" is another way of speaking of "these last days" (Heb. 1:2). The forgiveness of sins "at the end of the ages" confirms the fulfillment of the new-covenant promises found in Jeremiah. The end of redemptive history has dawned by virtue of the work of Christ. The author fixes our attention on the work of Christ that is featured at the beginning of the letter, where after accomplishing cleansing for sins, Christ sat down at God's right hand (Heb. 1:3). The author's thought cannot be restricted to vertical categories, as it also operates horizontally on a redemptive-historical timeline. Hebrews does not dismiss OT revelation as a mistake or substandard but conceives of his-

---

37. The view that Hebrews represented the Hellenistic Judaism typified by Philo has been supported by some, especially Spicq (1952–1953: 1:39–91). This view is scrutinized carefully and rejected by Williamson (1970). For the eschatological character of Hebrews, see Peterson 1982: 131; Michel 1966: 288–89. The view of Käsemann (1984) that Hebrews is gnostic has won few adherents, for scholars, particularly in light of the Qumran manuscripts, have recognized the Jewish character of the letter. See also the careful discussion of the background of the letter, both Christian and non-Christian, in Hurst 1990. For a discussion of the socio-rhetorical perspective, see deSilva 1995.

38. See the classic argument by Barrett (1954) on eschatology in Hebrews. See also Rissi 1987: 125; Scholer 1991: 122–23, 143, 205.

39. On the significance of promise in Hebrews, with attention to its eschatological (both present and future) character, see Käsemann 1984: 26–37.

40. The newness of the new covenant in Hebrews is captured well in Lehne 1990.

tory in terms of promise and fulfillment. OT sacrifices point toward and anticipate the sacrifice of Christ. God ordained the Aaronic priesthood but never intended it to last forever. The Aaronic priesthood functions as a type of the Melchizedekian priesthood, which is superior because it is based on God's oath (Heb. 7:11–28). The old covenant prepares the way for and even prophesies the coming of the new.

The "vertical" themes in Hebrews, then, should be integrated into a redemptive-historical schema. The earthly tabernacle not only mirrors a heavenly tabernacle (God's very presence) but also became passé when Christ arrived and secured access to God. The Aaronic priesthood and regulations serve as copies and shadows of what is heavenly, and the heavenly reality manifests itself in history when Christ arrives as the Melchizedekian priest and fulfills the OT shadows and types. Hebrews 10:1 captures well the relationship between the vertical and horizontal in the letter: "The law has but a shadow of the good things to come." The substance and very image of the realities portrayed by the law is Christ himself. Still, the law points to Christ, just as a shadow represents the substance of a body. The author locates the law along the redemptive-historical timeline, in that it anticipates what is to come. The "vertical" motifs in Hebrews cannot be identified as Platonic, since they are earthed in history, being placed by the author into the stream of salvation history.

The age of fulfillment has arrived, since Jesus has accomplished purification of sins (Heb. 1:3) in fulfillment of the new-covenant promise. "For by a single offering he has perfected for all time those who are being sanctified" (Heb. 10:14). Jesus now reigns as the messianic king in fulfillment of Ps. 110:1 (Heb. 1:3, 13; 10:12). We might conclude that Hebrews swallows up the not yet into the already because it emphasizes Jesus' reign and final forgiveness of sins. Hebrews, however, maintains the same eschatological tension as is found in the rest of the NT witness. Jesus now reigns, but enemies still remain and have not yet been subjected under his feet (Heb. 1:13; 10:12–13; cf. Ps. 110:1). Christ has dealt with sin definitively once for all, and yet the day of judgment has not yet commenced, and believers await Jesus' return when he will complete the salvation already accomplished (Heb. 9:26–28). Psalm 8 reflects upon humanity's role in the universe—the high honor of ruling the entire world for God. Hebrews 2 engages in a commentary on the psalm, acknowledging that the world is not ruled by human beings the way it should be (Heb. 2:8). We know that the world has gone awry because of death (Heb. 2:14–15), and death can be traced to the wickedness of human beings. Jesus, however, succeeded where Adam and the rest of humanity failed. As the sinless one, he lived as the perfect "Adam" (Heb. 4:15; 7:26). Moreover, because of his suffering and death, he is exalted and now "crowned with glory and honor" (Heb. 2:9). The already–not yet tension infuses Heb. 2. Jesus reigns as the second Adam, but the work of his reign is incomplete. He has defeated death for believers, and yet believers are not exempted from physical death (Heb. 2:14–15).

The believing recipients of Hebrews have been forgiven; they have been sanctified once and for all by the sacrifice of Christ (Heb. 10:14), and yet the whole of Hebrews indicates an eschatological reserve. The readers are urgently warned not to forsake the salvation that they have embraced. They must not drift away from "such a great salvation" (Heb. 2:1–4). They must stoke the fires of faith and obedience, so that they do not harden their hearts and fail to enter God's rest (Heb. 3:12–4:13).[41] They must shake off lethargy and dullness so that they do not fall away and fail to obtain the promise (Heb. 5:11–6:12). They must hold fast the confession of faith and continue believing God's unseen promises, for those who fail to trust in God will experience his vengeance (Heb. 10:19–12:3). They must heed the voice of the one speaking, for God is a consuming fire (Heb. 12:25–29). Homiletical warnings permeate the letter, demonstrating that believers inhabit the period between the already and the not yet. Salvation in that sense is eschatological, and believers await its consummation, and hence they are called to believe, obey, and endure in the interval. The heavenly city and country have not yet arrived (Heb. 11:10, 13–16). Believers in Christ do not find a lasting city on this earth (Heb. 13:14). The tension between what has already been received and the final reception of salvation is reflected well in the teaching on entering God's rest. Hebrews 4:3 apparently claims that those who believe in Christ have already entered God's rest.[42] Furthermore, the use of the word "today" (Heb. 4:7) emphasizes the present realization, at least in part, of the promise. And yet Heb. 3:12–4:11 emphasizes repeatedly that the promised rest still remains for God's people (Heb. 4:1, 6). The rest is fundamentally eschatological since those who rest cease from their works as God ceased from his (Heb. 4:10). When believers enter the heavenly city, they cease activity because the day of striving has come to an end.

Soundings from the Rest of the New Testament

The already–not yet theme is not as pervasive in the rest of the NT (James, 1–2 Peter, Jude, and Revelation). The purpose and occasional nature of the documents furnish an adequate explanation. The book of

---

41. France (1996: 271–72) rightly argues that the rest here refers to heavenly rest.

42. So Attridge 1989: 126; Lincoln 1982: 210–13; Lane 1991a: 99; against this, see Scholer 1991: 202–4.

Revelation, being a prophetic-apocalyptic work, naturally focuses on the day of future judgment and salvation when God vindicates his people and condemns the wicked. During the present age the church suffers and dies for its witness to Jesus, and the beast and Babylon oppress the people of God. Still, believers should shun fear and embrace hope because the beast's hour of triumph will not endure. Satan's opportunity to persecute Christians is limited to three and one-half years (Rev. 12:14)—that is, forty-two months (Rev. 11:2; 13:5) or one thousand two hundred and sixty days (Rev. 11:3; 12:6). Scholars dispute whether the interval of time should be construed literally or whether the number is symbolic.[43] The latter seems more likely because the number "seven" symbolizes perfection and completeness, as in Rev. 1:4, where the seven spirits stand for the Holy Spirit. One half of seven denotes a time in which evil dominates and rules over the world, the time when Satan has been cast from heaven to earth after the victory accomplished by Christ at the cross (Rev. 12:7–12). He persecutes the people of God during this interval (Rev. 12:14), so that it seems that the evil period designated by half of seven years refers to the entire era between the cross of Christ and his return.[44]

Since believers suffer in the interval between the cross and resurrection, Revelation looks forward to the consummation of God's purposes, to the day when Satan, the beast, and the false prophet are consigned to the lake of fire (Rev. 19:20; 20:10), when Babylon will be overthrown (Rev. 17:1–19:5), when the blood of the saints will be avenged (Rev. 6:9–11)—the day when the kingdoms of the world become the kingdom of our Lord and his Christ (Rev. 11:15–19). At the consummation God will introduce a new heaven and earth, and he will fulfill his covenant and dwell personally with his people (Rev. 21:1–22:5).

The book of Revelation fixes our attention on the completion of God's covenantal promises, but the "already" theme is not entirely absent. Christ has delivered believers "from our sins by his blood and made us a kingdom, priests to his God and Father" (Rev. 1:5–6). The decisive battle for believers has been won. They conquer "by the blood of the Lamb" (Rev. 12:11). Their robes are glistening white by virtue of Jesus' blood as God's lamb (Rev. 7:14). Jesus has expelled Satan from heaven (Rev. 12:9) and been exalted to the right hand of God and his throne (Rev. 12:5) by virtue of his work on the cross. As God's slain lamb, he has opened the scroll with seven seals (Rev. 5:1–14), so that the definitive and irrevocable work in salvation history has been done. In the interim

---

43. Walvoord (1966: 178) takes it literally, while Osborne (2002: 414–15) thinks that it refers to a limited time near the end of history.

44. So Beale 1999b: 565–68, 669. For further discussion, see Aune 1998: 609–10.

period in which Satan attacks believers, they must endure suffering
(Rev. 3:10; 13:10; 14:12) and "conquer" (Rev. 2:7, 11, 17, 26; 3:5, 12, 21;
15:2; 21:7) to obtain the final reward. The already–not yet schema is
present in Revelation. The cross of Christ is the fulcrum of history; he
has redeemed believers from sin. Still, they must suffer and endure until
Jesus returns and recompenses their enemies.

The letters of James and 1 Peter are addressed to believers undergoing
trials and/or persecution. Again, we must recall the occasional and circumstantial character of both letters, since neither constitutes a treatise
on Christian theology. Both authors intend to strengthen believers facing
difficulties that could quench their faith. James concentrates on parenesis,
exhorting his readers to live in a way that pleases God while encounter-
ing trials.[45] He regularly considers the day of judgment as the time when
believers will be exalted and unbelievers will face judgment. The "poor"
(my translation), a term used virtually synonymously with "believer,"
will be exalted at the judgment, whereas the "rich" will perish (James
1:9–11). The one who shows mercy to others and desists from partiality,
particularly to the economically well-off, will obtain mercy on the last day
(James 2:12–13). The wealthy who oppress their workers and deny them
their wages in order to live sumptuously are storing up judgment against
themselves on the day of reckoning (James 5:1–6). The righteous should
exercise patience because the Lord will come soon, even if his delay seems
inordinately long (James 5:7–8).[46] Since ethical exhortation dominates the
letter, the lack of emphasis on realized eschatology is unremarkable.

Still, two texts seem to point toward a realized eschatology. First,
there is James 1:18: "Of his own will he brought us forth by the word
of truth, that we should be a kind of firstfruits of his creatures." Some
scholars maintain that James contemplates our physical birth as human
beings.[47] The verb "brought forth" (*apokyeō*) designates physical birth
elsewhere.[48] Further, the preceding verse speaks of God's generous gifts
to all, focusing on the creation of the sun, moon, and stars (James 1:17).
Human beings could be described as "the firstfruits" of God's creation
in that they are, according to Gen. 1, the crown of creation—the only
creatures made in God's image. Despite some good arguments supporting
a reference to physical creation, it is probable that James speaks of the
spiritual birth of his readers—their new life in Christ.[49] The goodness

45. Bauckham (1999b: 25–28) is likely correct in suggesting that James is an encyclical
letter written to the Jewish Diaspora in both the East and the West.

46. See also James 5:3 (see L. Cheung 2003: 252).

47. So Elliott-Binns 1956.

48. See the entry in BDAG.

49. Dibelius 1975: 103–7; Davids 1982: 88–90; Moo 2000: 79–80. Laws (1980: 75–78)
argues that both physical creation and new life in Christ are included.

of God is celebrated in James 1:13–18, with the emphasis that he does not tempt anyone to sin but instead lavishes his goodness on all. Writing to Christians, James climaxed his tribute to God's beneficence by reminding them that God granted them new life. An important piece of evidence tilts the scales to spiritual birth: the means used to grant new birth was "the word of truth." In Paul the phrase "word of truth" invariably refers to the gospel of Christ (2 Cor. 6:7; Eph. 1:13; Col. 1:5; 2 Tim. 2:15). Unfortunately, James did not use the expression elsewhere, but the term "word" (*logos*) appears three times in the next paragraph to denote the message that he proclaimed (James 1:21–23). For instance, in James 1:21 the "implanted word" is able to "save" their souls. Both verses of James 1:22–23 stress that the readers must not only hear the word but also put it into action. It seems likely, then, that the "word of truth" in James 1:18 refers to the gospel.[50] Even though believers await the judgment of the final day, they are spiritually the firstfruits of God's promised work in all his creation. Ultimately, he promises new heavens and a new earth (Isa. 65:17; 66:22), and the new life of believers testifies that they are the first installment of the blessing intended for all of creation. The second indication of realized eschatology is in James 2:5: even now God has chosen that the poor would be "rich in faith and heirs of the kingdom." In this present era they are God's people and trust in him, and yet they await the eschatological gift of the kingdom.

In his first letter Peter addressed suffering believers, encouraging them to persevere in their troubles because of the promise of end-time salvation.[51] Sufferings cause grief and represent God's purifying judgment of his flock, but they last briefly compared to the final inheritance that believers will receive when Jesus returns (1 Pet. 1:4–7; 4:17; 5:10). Peter emphasized the future character of salvation in describing it as an inheritance that believers will receive in the future (1 Pet. 1:4). Both husbands and wives share the same destiny as "co-heirs of the grace of life" (1 Pet. 3:7 my translation). Presently God fortifies believers so that they will obtain a salvation that will be revealed only when Jesus comes again (1 Pet. 1:5, 7). In one sense, salvation is incomplete, for believers await "the outcome of" their "faith," which is "the salvation of" their "souls" (1 Pet. 1:9), and elders shepherding the flock anticipate receiving a glorious and permanent reward when Jesus appears (1 Pet. 5:4). In speaking of loving life and seeing good days (1 Pet. 3:10), Peter likely referred to life in the eschaton—the future reward awaiting the righteous. Supporting this interpretation is the judgment

50. This is because the word that saves in James 1:21 refers to the gospel (so Laws 1980: 82; Davids 1982: 95; Moo 2000: 79–80), though Laws does not see the implication for James 1:18.

51. Dryden (2006) rightly emphasizes the inseparability of theology and ethics in 1 Peter, showing that Peter is fundamentally concerned about the virtuous lives of Christians.

awaiting the wicked according to 1 Pet. 3:12, for the Lord's face will turn against them forever on the last day.

Peter did not confine himself to future eschatology, for God has caused believers to be born again by means of the word of the gospel (1 Pet. 1:3, 23).[52] Their eschatological hope is grounded in the new life that they have already received (1 Pet. 1:3). God has ransomed believers from their vain and futile life by means of Christ's blood (1 Pet. 1:18–19). The decisive and fundamental change has already occurred in their lives, so that the redemption that they possess now anchors their future hope. The remarkable text about the OT prophets in 1 Pet. 1:10–12 verifies that believers live on the fulfillment side of the promise. The prophets searched diligently, wondering when the prophecies about the Messiah would be fulfilled. They discovered that their ministry was not intended for their own times; they prophesied for the sake of the believers of Peter's day. Clearly, the readers should appreciate that they live during the age of fulfillment, in the era when God's promises are coming to pass. The last times have arrived, and their commencement is attested by the coming of Jesus the Christ (1 Pet. 1:20).

The letters of 2 Peter and Jude responded to licentious false teachers in the churches. Both of them, therefore, emphasized the eschatological judgment of such opponents. The adversaries in 2 Peter may have collapsed the not yet entirely into the already, so that they denied the second coming of Christ (2 Pet. 3:1–13). The transfiguration functions as a proleptic anticipation of Christ's return, and his coming will commence the day of judgment, when scoffers will be destroyed. Neither Peter nor Jude said much about the already, doubtless because of the circumstances encountered in their churches in responding to teachers who denied a future judgment. Still, Jude reminded believers that they are beloved by God and kept by Jesus Christ (Jude 1). Peter taught that believers even now share in the divine nature and have escaped the world's corruption (2 Pet. 1:3–4; 2:20). Both authors proclaimed that God keeps those who are his, and that he will guard them from the onslaughts of the false teachers until the last day (2 Pet. 2:9; Jude 24–25).

Conclusion

The tension between the already and the not yet that we saw with respect to the kingdom of God in the Synoptic Gospels and regarding eternal life in John permeates the remainder of the NT as well. The authors address the theme in a variety of ways, and hence there is not

---

52. Dryden (2006: 64–89) describes God's saving work in 1 Peter in terms of the "narrative worldview" and "meta-history" that ground parenesis.

a set terminology. In some instances we have a contrast between this age and the coming one. Other texts speak of a new creation, or the word "salvation" is used to denote both the present fulfillment of God's promises and the final fulfillment. Some pieces of literature (e.g., Revelation) focus on final fulfillment, whereas others (e.g., Ephesians and Colossians) put the emphasis on realized eschatology. The variation is likely accounted for by the purpose of the author and the situation of the readers. Still, in every case we find that God has begun to fulfill his saving promises in Jesus Christ, and yet believers still await the completion of what God has promised. The promises made to Abraham have been fulfilled in a decisive way through the ministry, death, and resurrection of Jesus Christ, but the end of history has not arrived. To use an illustration from the theater, the opening curtain has risen on the play announced so long ago by the OT, but the final curtain has yet to come down on the last act.

PART 2

THE GOD
OF THE PROMISE

*The Saving Work of the Father,
Son, and Spirit*

4

※ ※ ※ ※ ※ ※ ※ ※ ※ ※ ※ ※ ※ ※ ※ ※ ※ ※ ※

The Centrality of God
in New Testament Theology

We tend to look past what constantly stands in front of us. If we see them every day, we often take for granted verdant trees, stunning sunsets, and powerful waves thundering on the beach. Similarly, in reading the NT we are prone to screen out what the NT says about God himself. God is, so to speak, shoved to the side, and we investigate other themes, such as justification, reconciliation, redemptive history, and new creation. I suggest that the centrality of God in Christ is the foundational theme for the narrative unfolded in the NT. We must beware, of course, of abstracting God himself from the story communicated in the NT. Focusing on God does not mean that we engage in systematic theology that also considers the philosophical and contemporary entailments of what the Scriptures teach about God, and some studies do not consider adequately the story line of Scripture in constructing a doctrine of God.[1] Biblical theology does not pursue the philosophical implications of the doctrine of God, for such an enterprise is distinctive of systematic theology. We may think that nothing further needs to be said about "God" in a theology of the NT because it is obvious and assumed that our theology is about God. But if we ignore what is obvious and assumed, we may overlook one of the most important themes in NT theology. We may gaze past what looms massively in front of us simply because we are accustomed to the scenery.

---

1. But for an outstanding study of God in systematic theology, see Frame 2002.

It should also be said at the outset that the grounding theme of NT theology is magnifying God in Christ. Separating the revelation of God in the NT from Christology, as if God is central and Christ is secondary, is impossible.[2] God is magnified and praised in revealing himself through Christ as God fulfills his saving promises. The coming of Christ does not diminish the centrality of God but rather enhances it. Christ does not summon attention to himself so that God is pushed off center stage. God receives praise, glory, and honor for the ministry, death, and resurrection of Christ. God planned, after all, that Christ would come and accomplish redemption for his people. The topic of Christology is so massive, however, that we must separate our study of Christ from God, at least for the sake of economy. I could try to interweave Christology into the present chapter, but it would become terribly long, and so for the purpose of analysis I need to devote quite a few chapters to what God has done in Christ. In doing so, I am faithful to the NT emphasis on Christ's work. Furthermore, the saving work of God in Christ has made possible the gift of the Holy Spirit. Therefore, in succeeding chapters we will consider what NT theology has to say about the Father, the Son, and the Holy Spirit.

It might be objected that to speak of the Father, Son, and Spirit is to fall prey to systematic theology and to later trinitarian theology. However, the argument made here is that an inductive study of the NT itself demonstrates that the Father, Son, and Spirit are foundational and central to NT theology. Moreover, our study of the Father, Son, and Spirit must be integrated with the previous chapters of this book, which focused on the fulfillment of God's saving promises—the already–not yet theme in the NT. Our study of God in the following chapters does not deviate from the redemptive-historical focus of the previous chapters. The Father fulfills his saving promises in history by sending his Son, and the Son's work is vindicated through the sending of the Spirit. In the work of the Father, Son, and Spirit our focus is directed to the God of the promise and to God's saving work in fulfilling the promises.

The Synoptic Gospels

Old Testament Backdrop

When we read the Gospels, and indeed the entire NT, we see that the view of God is grounded in the OT.[3] The NT writers build upon the foundation

---

2. Following the pattern of the NT, I usually am referring to the Father when using the term "God."

3. For reflections on the meaning of the term "God" in the OT and in Second Temple Judaism, see M. M. Thompson 2001: 22–48. See also House 1998 for an OT theology that rightly focuses on God.

laid in the OT Scriptures, where God's sovereignty, uniqueness, and mercy are explicated, and therefore he deserves and demands that all human beings give themselves unreservedly to him. Here we only have space to indicate in the briefest of ways the OT backdrop. One of the pervasive themes in the OT, from the very first verse, is that God is the creator of all that exists. Indeed, God's role as creator is woven into the fabric of nearly every piece of literature. Since God is the creator of all, he is the sovereign Lord, who demands to be worshiped above anything or anyone in the universe (Exod. 20:3), for he is the one true and living God. Creatures, by definition, should give primacy to their creator. Deuteronomy 6:4–5 was fundamental to Jewish thought, and the Shema (Deut. 6:4) was said daily by Israelites. They were reminded by these words that there is only one God, and that their supreme loyalty should be given to him alone. God is not an impersonal creator, and he has shown his mercy and love to his people by redeeming them from slavery in Egypt. M. M. Thompson summarizes well the OT portrayal of God: "God is identified, first, as the Maker and Creator of all that is. God is the life-giving God. Because God is the creator of all, God is also supreme over all other beings, whether heavenly or human. Epithets such as 'Almighty' and 'Most High' indicate God's supremacy over all other figures and underscore the extent of God's sovereignty. As Creator and Sovereign, God therefore merits worship and honor."[4]

Isaiah also emphasized repeatedly that Yahweh is the one and only God, and that idols stem from the futile imagination of human beings: "Assemble yourselves and come; draw near together, you survivors of the nations! They have no knowledge who carry about their wooden idols, and keep on praying to a god that cannot save. Declare and present your case; let them take counsel together! Who told this long ago? Who declared it of old? Was it not I, the LORD? And there is no other god besides me, a righteous God and a Savior; there is none besides me" (Isa. 45:20–21; see also Isa. 44). Yahweh is the true and living God, the first and the last, and the ruler of the kingdoms of the world. Moreover, he has entered into covenant with his people, and so Isaiah promised that he will rescue his people from exile.

In the book of Daniel the sovereignty and rule of God over all nations is expressed in a number of texts. For example, "At the end of the days I, Nebuchadnezzar, lifted my eyes to heaven, and my reason returned to me, and I blessed the Most High, and praised and honored him who lives forever, for his dominion is an everlasting dominion, and his kingdom endures from generation to generation; all the inhabitants of the earth are accounted as nothing, and he does according to his will among the

---

4. M. M. Thompson 2001: 54.

host of heaven and among the inhabitants of the earth; and none can stay his hand or say to him, 'What have you done?'" (Dan. 4:34–35). When NT writers refer to God, they refer to the true and living God revealed in the OT, the God who reigns over the nations. God's rule over all things is grounded in the fact that he is the creator of all things, the maker of heaven and earth. The NT, of course, declares that God is the creator of all things, but NT writers do not emphasize that theme to the same degree that we find in the OT, for it finds its full exposition and elaboration in the OT, and NT writers, when speaking of God as creator, draw upon and assume what is fully explicated in the OT.

The God of the Kingdom

As we consider what the Synoptic Gospels say about God, it is necessary to be selective because the material under consideration is practically endless and relates to the other themes presented in this book. The aim here is to cite representative texts so that the major themes expressed in the Synoptics are included. We begin with the kingdom of God. What the Synoptics teach about God can be embraced under three major themes: (1) God's sovereignty, (2) God's mercy, and (3) God's glory, which is the goal of human life. Interestingly, the three themes coalesce in a theme that has already been explored in some detail in chapter 1: the kingdom of God/heaven. As we noted previously, the term "heaven" emphasizes God's sovereignty and majesty. He is the one exalted far above human beings. Both "kingdom of heaven" and "kingdom of God" refer to the kingdom that belongs to God. There is no need to rehearse again here how pervasive this theme is in the Synoptics. What must be noted, however, is the fact that the kingdom is *God's*. He is the sovereign one who rules over all. In considering the fulfillment of God's promise in redemptive history, we are liable to fix our attention on the fulfillment of God's saving promises and to forget the God of the kingdom. Jesus advances God's saving promises and God's plan for the world. The God of the kingdom is the true God of the OT, the God who created the world and promised that the whole world would be blessed through Abraham.

The kingdom of God suggests God's rule and reign over all, but we have also seen that the kingdom of God in the Synoptics refers to the fulfillment of God's saving promises. The coming of the kingdom in Jesus Christ testifies that God is a promise-keeping God, and hence the coming of the kingdom spells the fulfillment of his promise to bless his people. Matthew's opening genealogy conveys that God is a promise-keeper, for Jesus is traced back to David and Abraham (Matt. 1:1–17). He fulfills the covenant to bless the whole world made to Abraham (Gen. 12:3) and the covenant of an eternal dynasty pledged to David (2 Sam. 7; 1 Chron. 17).

In the same way, the infancy narratives in Luke 1–2 emphasize that God is fulfilling his covenantal promises relating to his kingdom.

God's kingdom calls attention to both his sovereignty and his mercy, but it also communicates the goal for human existence. Human beings are to live for the sake of God's kingdom, and nothing should take precedence over the kingdom (e.g., Matt. 6:33). But this means that human beings are to give the whole of their lives over to God because the kingdom *belongs to God*. He is the great treasure that is received when the kingdom is found (see Matt. 13:44–46). To live for the sake of the kingdom is simply another way of saying that human beings live for God's sake—for his glory.[5] He is to be the sum and substance of human life and to take priority in everything.

The kingdom of God includes the three themes of God's sovereignty, God's mercy, and God's glory (the aim of human existence). It seems that these same three themes capture well what the Synoptics teach about God, and so we will investigate further what the Synoptics communicate regarding God's sovereignty, God's mercy, and the reason and goal of human existence.

God's Sovereignty

The word "sovereignty" designates God's rule and control over the world that he has made. The notion of God's sovereignty is rooted in the OT, where God is regularly described as the creator of all that exists. The one who is creator of all is also the sovereign ruler of all. God will keep his saving promises because he is the sovereign God who created everything (Matt. 19:4 par.; Mark 13:19). He bestows beauty on the lilies and clothes the grass of the field (Matt. 6:28–30 par.). He is the living God (Matt. 26:63); nothing is outside the realm of possibility for him, so that he can grant conception to a virgin (Luke 1:37) and give eternal life to human beings (Matt. 19:26 par.). The angelic words to Mary echo the words that the Lord spoke to Abraham when he and Sarah could not have a child because of old age and barrenness: "Is anything too hard for the LORD?" (Gen. 18:14). Human beings limit God because they do not know his power to raise people from the dead (Matt. 22:29 par.). If he wills, he can turn stones into the children of Abraham (Matt. 3:9 par.), and he could, if he so desired, deliver Jesus from death even when he was upon the cross (Matt. 27:43).[6]

---

5. Rightly Schlatter 1997: 160.

6. The words of Matt. 27:43, of course, come from Jesus' opponents, but they are not mistaken in thinking that God could save Jesus from death if he so desired. What Jesus' adversaries failed to understand is that God did not desire to save Jesus from death on the cross.

God declares his will authoritatively through his word (e.g., Matt. 4:4 par.; 15:6 par.; Luke 3:2; 5:1; 8:11, 21; 11:28). His authority manifests itself in his control over the course of history. He raised up David and installed him as king over Israel (Luke 1:32).[7] Angels are commissioned by God to carry out his will and purposes (e.g., Matt. 1:20, 24; 2:13, 19; 4:11 par.; Luke 1:19, 26; 2:9–14). Not even a sparrow falls apart from his will, and hence believers can be assured that he watches over and cares for them (Matt. 10:29–31 par.). The infancy narratives also relate God's sovereignty, for despite Herod's machinations, Jesus escapes from his clutches (Matt. 2). The story echoes the preservation of Moses and Israel during the time of the Pharaohs, impressing upon the reader God's sovereignty in working out his saving plan.[8] God knows the hearts of all people infallibly (Luke 16:15). He hides the revelation of himself from those who are wise and proud but discloses himself to those who are humble as children (Matt. 11:25–26 par.). The centrality of God is evident in Luke-Acts, as Rosner argues, because the power of the word in the spread of the gospel comes from God himself (cf. Luke 8:4–15; Acts 6:7; 12:24; 19:20).[9] Or, as Jervell points out, the spread of the gospel in Acts is the remarkable work of God himself (Acts 10–11; 14:27; 15:7–10, 14; 16:14).[10] He is the one who overcomes the limitations and weaknesses of his witnesses so that the gospel spreads.

God's Mercy

The Father rules over all things, but his reign over all reflects his love and mercy.[11] The birds find their daily sustenance from his hand (Matt. 6:26 par.), and he adorns flowers with their spectacular and quiet beauty (Matt. 6:28–29 par.). God's love cannot be limited to the people of God; he demonstrates his love to unbelievers in sending sunlight and rain to all (Matt. 5:45). He knows what people need even before they voice their requests in prayer, and hence frantic and superstitious repetitions

---

7. Green (1995: 37) argues that God is often "in the background of the story" in Luke, as the one who guides unfolding events (see also pp. 38–39).

8. For the importance of God's plan in Luke-Acts, see Squires 1993. Squires (1993: 37) says, "The concentration of divine activity throughout the two volumes is such that we might reasonably speak of God as the subject of the whole story." Bock (1998) also focuses on the fulfillment of God's plan and his saving promises in Acts (see also Tiede 1980: 103–18; Green 1995: 28–37, 47–49; Reasoner 1999). See also Peterson (1993), who qualifies the work of Squires so that Luke-Acts emphasizes the fulfillment of God's plan for the edification of believers rather than for apologetic reasons.

9. Rosner 1998: 221–25.

10. Jervell 1996: 22.

11. In fact, it is artificial to separate God's sovereignty from his love, for he exercises his love sovereignly. Hence, in some cases I cite verses already noted under God's sovereignty.

should be avoided (Matt. 6:7–8; Luke 12:30). We see from these texts that God's sovereignty expresses his love. God's sovereignty does not signify the harsh rule of a tyrannical and mean-spirited despot. He gives good things to those who make requests of him (Matt. 7:11), or as Luke says, he grants the Holy Spirit to those who entreat him for the Spirit (Luke 11:13). God should not be compared to a malicious father who smuggles a serpent that looks like a fish into his child's lunch (Luke 11:11).[12] When asked for an egg, he does not substitute a scorpion that is rolled up so that it appears to be an egg (Luke 11:12). His heart is generous and giving, and he is not a crabbed and penurious father. He is good (Mark 10:18 par.), and he forgives the sins of those who come to him in repentance (Mark 2:7 par.). God's beneficence is captured well in Luke 12:32: "Fear not, little flock, for it is your Father's good pleasure to give you the kingdom." The Father's tender care for his weak and needy people is represented by his giving them the kingdom. He does not give the kingdom reluctantly or grudgingly, but he joyfully bestows it on his people.

The love of God is remarkably displayed in the parables of Luke 15.[13] The lost sheep, the lost coin, and the lost sons all represent God's overflowing joy when sinners repent and turn to him. All three parables are designed to defend before the Pharisees and scribes Jesus' table fellowship with social outcasts and sinners (Luke 15:1–2). The unforgettable story of the two lost sons communicates this truth powerfully. The father in the parable does not bear a grudge against his returning younger son by recalling how he wasted his inheritance. In Palestinian culture running was considered undignified, but the father does not care about decorum.[14] Filled with compassion, he runs to greet his son and embraces him with kisses. And the father does not allow the son to finish his confession (cf. Luke 15:18–19 with 15:21). He celebrates his son's return by outfitting him with the best robe and with shoes and a ring, and by preparing a fattened calf for a celebratory feast. The younger son represents tax collectors and sinners who have wasted their lives by abandoning the ways of God (Luke 15:1–2). The older son, who supposedly was compliant and obedient ("I never disobeyed your command" [Luke 15:29]), represents the Pharisees and scribes. He returns from a hard day's work and is scandalized to discover that a party is being thrown to celebrate the return of his brother, who is a scoundrel. The father, however, is unrelenting in his love. He pleads with the older brother to join the festivities. Jesus here communicates

12. In support of the interpretation offered here on Luke 11:11–12, see Bailey 1976: 136–37.

13. For a masterful exposition, see Jeremias 1972: 124–32. See also Hultgren 2000: 70–91.

14. See Jeremias 1972: 130; Bailey 1976: 181.

God's love for Pharisees, and the parable ends with this question re-verberating in the ears of the readers: Will the Pharisees come to the party? Indeed, will the reader?

Responding to the love of God is a crucial matter, for God is also the holy one, the judge of all. He summons people to trust in him and to do his will. He shows mercy to sinners who acknowledge their sin (Luke 18:9–14) and rewards those who seek him (Matt. 6:1, 4, 6, 18). The love of God cannot be understood apart from the holiness and the judgment of God. Those who refuse to submit to his lordship will face judgment on the last day (Matt. 7:1–2; 10:15; 11:20–24; Luke 10:13–15). Trees that fail to bear good fruit will be cut down and cast into the fire (Matt. 7:19; cf. Luke 3:9). Those who do not have faith will be cast out into the darkness, where there is weeping and gnashing of teeth (Matt. 8:12; cf. Luke 13:25–30). Weeping and gnashing of teeth will also be the lot of those without a wedding garment, those who are not dressed to enter the Messianic banquet (Matt. 22:11–14). Human beings should fear God, who is able to cast them into hell (Matt. 10:28 par.). If people do not repent, they will perish (Luke 13:1–9). The failure to conquer sin will result in unquenchable fire on the last day (Mark 9:42–48), and those who refuse to forgive others will not receive forgiveness from God (Matt. 6:14–15; 18:21–35). God will punish the tenants in the vineyard who do not bear fruit (Matt. 21:40–41 par.). The rich who fail to care for the poor and do not repent will suffer forever (Luke 16:19–31). God's mercy, then, can be understood only against the background of his righteous anger against sin and the judgment to come. The day of mercy has arrived in the preaching of the kingdom, and the hand beckoning sinners to repent is extended. In the gospel of Jesus Christ and the preaching of God's kingdom the "tender mercy" of God has dawned (Luke 1:78–79).

God's Glory

Since God is the creator and the sovereign of all, he demands primacy in the lives of all people. In speaking of God's glory, the intention is not to restrict the theme to the places where the word "glory" (*doxa, doxazō*) appears. The word "glory" is used broadly to capture the supremacy of God in everything. In other words, human beings exist to obey, believe in, and praise God. For instance, Jesus did not fall prey to sentimentality with respect to his family; he maintained that those who do God's will constitute his family (Matt. 12:50 par.). God exercises an absolute claim upon the lives of all. Thus the most important thing in life is that God's name be honored and hallowed (Matt. 6:9 par.). In the Matthean ver-sion of the Lord's Prayer, hallowing God's name is carried out when his kingdom comes and when his will is done (Matt. 6:10).[15] Jesus rejected Satan's invitation to leap from the pinnacle of the temple because such an act would constitute a testing of God (Matt. 4:7 par.; cf. Deut. 6:16). Jesus drew upon Deut. 6 again when Satan tried to entice Jesus to worship him. Jesus replied that he must worship and serve God alone (Matt. 4:8–10 par.; cf. Deut. 6:13). It seems clear that sin is heinous because it constitutes a dishonoring of God and a refusal to trust in him.

God's primacy over everything animates Jesus' teaching. Money lurks as a great danger because it easily becomes one's god. Those entranced with treasures on earth lose out on the treasures in heaven (Matt. 6:19–21 par.). The parable of the rich fool illustrates the danger of earthly riches (Luke 12:16–21). The rich man is not faulted for the capital investment of building bigger barns, as if planning how to increase the profitability of one's business were blameworthy. Rather, Jesus identifies the rich man's fundamental sin as his failure to be "rich toward God" (Luke 12:21). The rich man neglected to think about God at all, so that he conceived of his life as a perpetual vacation where he could relax and enjoy his wealth. Jesus taught that God allows no competitors. Human beings cannot serve two masters (Matt. 6:24 par.), and so the kingdom of God must have first claim upon their lives (Matt. 6:33). The final reward that human beings will receive cannot be equated with earthly blessings, as if heaven were merely a supercharged version of the pleasures of this world. The greatest joy, reserved for the pure in heart, is seeing God himself (Matt. 5:8). No joy can be compared to the vision of God promised to the faithful.

God's absolute priority is expressed by Jesus' reply to the rich young ruler (Matt. 19:17; Mark 10:18; Luke 18:19). Both Mark and Luke pose the question starkly, so that Jesus queried why the rich man calls him good, whereas in Matthew the question is, "Why do you ask me about what is good?" In all three accounts Jesus declared that only God is good, calling attention to the beauty of God's moral perfection. Since God is supreme, it follows that loving God with all of one's being and strength is elevated as the most important command in the Scriptures (Matt. 22:37–40; Mark 12:28–34; cf. Luke 10:25–27). This command, of course, finds its roots in the Shema (Deut. 6:4). The scribe in Mark rightly perceived that ardent and genuine love for God is not necessarily expressed by the performance of religious duties such as sacrifices. Religious exercises may become perfunctory so that they are sundered from love for God. Jesus excoriated the religious leaders because although the

---

15. Stettler (2004: 155) rightly says that the hallowing of God's name "is a governing principle underlying Jesus' entire ministry." Marshall (1978b: 457) notes that "the establishment of God's glory is the first theme of the prayer."

temple should be dedicated to prayer, temple worship was plagued by financial corruption (Matt. 21:12–19 par.). The religious tradition practiced by the Pharisees irritated Jesus because it substituted rituals for heart devotion and elevated human traditions above God's word (Matt. 15:1–11 par.). Jesus was not satisfied with lips that mouth the correct words if the hearts of human beings stray far from God. He demanded authenticity and affection in the worship of God.

The supremacy of God over all things means that nothing is more important than glorifying God. Good works are commended not merely because they help others—though that too is important—but also because they bring glory to God (Matt. 5:13–16). When the ten lepers were cleansed, the Samaritan stood out because he praised and thanked God for his healing (Luke 17:11–19). The Samaritan, who stood outside mainstream Judaism, recognized that God deserves praise for his mercy. The nine who did not give thanks stood condemned because they failed to do what is most important in life. When Jesus raised the only son of the widow of Nain from the dead, people were amazed and glorified God (Luke 7:16). The woman disfigured by a disablement for eighteen years glorified God when Jesus healed her (Luke 13:13). Jesus' healings often and rightly stimulated people to give praise and glory to God (Matt. 15:29–31).

The Gospel of Luke begins and ends with praise of God. Mary and Zechariah magnified and blessed the Lord for fulfilling his covenantal promises (Luke 1:46–55, 68–79). The angels praised God and gave him glory at the birth of the Christ (Luke 2:13–14). And the shepherds blessed God because the Christ was revealed to them (Luke 2:20). Simeon and Anna also responded with praise and thanksgiving (Luke 2:28, 38). Luke's Gospel concludes with the disciples in the temple praising and blessing God (Luke 24:53), thereby fulfilling the true purpose for which the temple existed, in contrast to those who had turned the temple into a place of financial advantage (Luke 19:45–48).

God acts in history to fulfill his saving promises, and the fulfillment of such promises reveals how glorious and great and beautiful God is. The gift of salvation is not prized over the giver. The gift reveals the giver in all his power, love, and goodness. Hence, people responded by praising and honoring God for the salvation that they received. The heart of NT theology is the work of God in Christ in saving his people, and such saving work brings praise, honor, and glory to God.

God as Father

Clearly, the kingdom of God tells us much about the God of the Synoptic Gospels, but another theme that is remarkably prominent is the fatherhood of God.[16] M. M. Thompson argues that Jesus' emphasis on God as Father must not be severed from his mission, from the promise that an inheritance belongs to those who repent and obey God as their Father.[17] Scholars in the past emphasized the distinctiveness of Jesus' calling God "Father." Jeremias in particular called attention to the uniqueness of Jesus' use of the term "Father" in terms of his experience with God.[18] Some references to God as "Father" exist in Jewish literature previous to the time of Jesus, but the frequency with which Jesus used the term stands out.[19] Jesus distinctively and emphatically addressed God as "Father."[20] Some have concluded that the frequency and intimacy of the term indicates that "Father" is equivalent to "Abba," which is then rendered "Daddy." Surely Jesus' relationship with God was intimate and unique, and his many references to God as "Father" are distinctive. Still, it goes beyond the evidence, as Barr has demonstrated, to conclude that "Father" should be equated with "Daddy."[21] France concurs with Barr but remarks that Jeremias never intended such a conclusion to be drawn, since "Abba" "conveys the respectful intimacy of a son in a patriarchal family."[22]

Jesus' Unique Relationship with God

In the Synoptic Gospels, according to my count, Jesus used the term "my Father" or "my heavenly Father" on nineteen occasions, with the

16. For a survey of the theme of God's fatherhood in the Synoptic Gospels, see M. M. Thompson 2000: 87–115.

17. M. M. Thompson 2000: 71–86.

18. See Jeremias 1967: 11–67; 1971: 61–68. See the summary and evaluation of Jeremias's views in M. M. Thompson 2000: 21–34.

19. For a survey of OT and Second Temple literature on God as Father, see M. M. Thompson 2000: 35–55; 2001: 58–69. Thompson (2000: 54) emphasizes three themes in the literature: (1) God as Father is "the source or origin of a family or clan and provides an inheritance to his children"; (2) "a father protects and provides for his children"; (3) "a father is a figure of authority to whom obedience and honor are properly rendered."

20. Davies and Allison (1988: 601–2) criticize some excesses in Jeremias's study by pointing to evidence of calling God "Father" in Jewish circles and their reservations about rendering "Abba" as "Daddy." Still, they claim that Jesus' use of "Father" was "characteristic" and "distinctive" (see also Dunn 1975b: 21–26). And Jeremias (1971: 67) himself corrects the idea that "Abba" should be rendered as "Daddy."

21. Barr 1988. See also Vermes 1993: 152–83; Crump 2006: 97–100. But the scholarship of Jeremias is essentially vindicated in the judicious study of Lee 2005: 122–36. Less convincing is the claim of M. M. Thompson (2000: 84) that Jesus' relationship with God as Father does not signal a "new intimacy" with God but rather reflects the same trust that Israel had in God. Nor is Thompson (2000: 30–32) persuasive in casting doubts on whether Jesus' use of "Abba" reflected Jesus' experience and intimacy with God. See the evaluation of Thompson's view in Lee 2005: 132–35.

22. France 2002: 584.

majority of them occurring in the Gospel of Matthew.[23] The extraordinary boldness in Jesus' relationship with God is illustrated by his saying that humans are required to do the will of "my Father" (Matt. 7:21; 12:50; cf. 25:34), and that only those who confess Jesus will be acknowledged by "my Father" (Matt. 10:32–33).

The centrality of the Son blazes into view in Matt. 11:25–27 (cf. Luke 10:21–22).[24] The sovereignty of God in hiding revelation from the wise and disclosing it to children was celebrated by Jesus. He acknowledged that such was the Father's good pleasure. In Matt. 11:27 he made the astonishing declaration: "All things have been handed over to me by my Father." The sovereignty belonging to the Father, then, is also vouchsafed to the Son. But Jesus proceeded to say even more. The relationship shared between the Father and the Son is exclusive and mutual. Only the Father truly knows the Son, and conversely, only the Son truly knows the Father. Such statements are nowhere made in the NT about any other human being or even angels, though the language used is reminiscent of Johannine Christology. This is not to say that the Christology enunciated here contradicts the Synoptics. Indeed, as we examine the Christology of the Synoptics further in subsequent chapters, we will see that this text accords with Synoptic Christology. Jesus declared in Matt. 11:25–26 that people come to know the Father by virtue of his gracious will. In Matt. 11:27 he supplemented this truth by adding that human beings come to know the Father only if the Son wishes to disclose the Father to them. If Jesus mediates knowledge of God, and God and Jesus know each other mutually and exclusively, then it seems fair to conclude that Jesus shares divine honor. And yet only the Father knows the day when Jesus will return (Matt. 24:36; Mark 13:32).

God is also the Father of those who trust in him by faith, and yet Jesus has a distinctive and unique relationship with the Father. He also referred to what is revealed by "my Father" (Matt. 16:17); the uprooting of those not planted by "my heavenly Father" (Matt. 15:13); "the face of my Father" (Matt. 18:10); the carrying out of the prayers of the church by "my Father" (Matt. 18:19); the punishment that will be inflicted on those who refuse to forgive by "my heavenly Father" (Matt. 18:35); the places of privilege prepared in the kingdom by "my Father" (Matt. 20:23); those blessed by "my Father" (Matt. 25:34); those who will drink new wine "in my Father's kingdom" (Matt. 26:29); the assigning of the kingdom by "my Father" (Luke 22:29); the twelve legions of angels ready

23. Actually, the phrase never occurs in Mark.
24. For a good survey of scholarly opinion, along with the judgment that the substance of the saying is authentic, see Fitzmyer 1985: 865–70. For further defenses of authenticity, see Marshall 1978b: 432; Hagner 1993b: 317–18; Carson 1984: 276–77; Lee 2005: 137–42.

to be unleashed by "my Father" if Jesus so desires it (Matt. 26:53); the promise of the Spirit from "my Father" (Luke 24:49).

The most remarkable use of "Father" occurs during Jesus' sufferings in Gethsemane. The horror of his impending suffering on the cross overwhelmed him. He began to long for a way to avoid the agony that awaited him. He prayed, "Abba, Father, all things are possible for you. Remove this cup from me. Yet, not what I will, but what you will" (Mark 14:36; cf. Matt. 26:39, 42; Luke 22:42). The use of the word "Abba" represents the Aramaic word for "Father," likely reproducing the exact word used by the historical Jesus.[25] Perhaps the word is recalled because of the unforgettable poignancy of that moment. Even when Jesus cried out to be spared from horrific suffering, he called out to his Father. In that hour of agony God remained his beloved Father and Lord, to whom he subjected his life.

Jesus' special relationship to his Father is relayed in Luke 2:41–52, which tells of Jesus and his parents journeying to Jerusalem for Passover. His parents left for Nazareth, thinking that the twelve-year-old Jesus was returning home with relatives or other friends. Upon discovering his absence, they returned to Jerusalem and found him in the temple after three days of searching.[26] Jesus astonished everyone with the depth of his questions and answers. Still, his parents were distressed that he had not informed them of his whereabouts. He replied, "Why were you looking for me? Did you not know that I must be in my Father's house?" (Luke 2:49).[27] Jesus communicated to his parents that his relationship with his heavenly Father took precedence over his relationship with his earthly parents. He had a unique and final responsibility to the Father in heaven that superseded the authority of his parents.

The Father's Authority

The term "Father" in the Synoptic Gospels indicates God's authority and goodness. In this sense, it is quite similar to what is taught about God where the emphasis is on his sovereignty, mercy, and primacy. Matthew

25. Hooker (1991: 348) says, "Its retention suggests that it was remembered as Jesus' distinctive way of addressing God" (cf. Cranfield 1963: 433; Lane 1974: 517–18). Matthew (Matt. 26:39, 42) and Luke (Luke 22:42) only have the word "Father" (*pater*) and do not use the term "Abba."

26. The three days may be reckoned inclusively, so that on the first day Jesus' parents realized that he did not make the trip, on the second day they looked in vain, and on the third day they found him. See Fitzmyer 1981a: 441–42.

27. R. Brown (1977: 475–77) argues that it is most likely that with the words *en tois tou patros mou* (lit., "in the [things] of my Father"), Jesus refers to his Father's house because he makes this statement in the temple. Brown also carefully discusses other interpretive options. For a similarly careful discussion, see Fitzmyer 1981a: 443–44.

often uses the phrase "Father in heaven."[28] Outside of Matthew we find the phrase only in Mark 11:26. Identifying God as "the Father in heaven" highlights his authority and sovereignty. This is confirmed by the observation elsewhere in Matthew that heaven is God's throne (Matt. 5:34; 23:22). The Father is also designated as "Lord of heaven and earth" (Matt. 11:25; Luke 10:21). Heaven represents that which is transcendent and invisible to human beings, and so it is striking when God speaks from heaven (Matt. 3:16–17 par.). The Spirit of the Father also speaks through Jesus' disciples (Matt. 10:20), and after Jesus' ascension the promise of the Father, which is identified as the Holy Spirit, will be sent by the Father (Luke 24:49).

The authority and power of the Father are evident, for he sees what people do in secret and will reward them accordingly (Matt. 6:4, 6, 18). Nothing is hidden from his gaze, and as Father, he knows what his people need before they voice their requests (Matt. 6:8, 32 par.). Only the Father knows the day on which the Son is returning, and this date is hidden from angels and even from the Son (Matt. 24:36 par.). Since God is the sovereign Father, human beings are required to do his will and to obey what he says (Matt. 7:21; 12:50; cf. 10:32–33). Those who do the Father's bidding will shine like the sun at the close of the age, while the rest will be thrown into the fire (Matt. 13:41–43). Those who refuse to forgive others will not be forgiven by the Father on the day of judgment (Matt. 6:14–15; 18:35; Mark 11:25). Along the same lines, those who were not planted by the Father will be uprooted on the day of judgment (Matt. 15:13).

The authority of the Father is evident, for Jesus would not ask him to remove the cup of the cross unless he were convinced that God could change the oncoming circumstances in such a way that the cross would be avoided (Mark 14:36 par.). Similarly, Jesus remarked that if he were to appeal to the Father, twelve legions of angels would prevent his suffering and death (Matt. 26:53). Hence, when Jesus died, he commended his spirit to his Father (Luke 23:46). The uniqueness of God as Father is such that no human being should be accorded the title "Father" with the same significance that applies to God (Matt. 23:9). The term "Father" is part of the divine name (Matt. 28:19), and the Son of Man comes with the glory that belongs only to the Father (Matt. 16:27 par.).

The Goodness of the Father

The term "Father" not only designates God's authority and sovereignty but also communicates his goodness. He is "perfect" (Matt. 5:48), or

---

28. Matt. 5:16, 45; 6:1, 9; 7:11, 21; 10:32, 33; 12:50; 16:17; 18:10, 14, 19. The expression "heavenly Father" occurs in Matt. 5:48; 6:14, 26, 32; 15:13; 18:25; 23:9.

"merciful" in the Lukan version of the saying (Luke 6:36). His mercy is reflected in Jesus' request from the cross that the Father forgive those who crucified him (Luke 23:34). The Father has an intense love for his "little ones" (Matt. 18:10–14), and he seeks one who is lost in the same way that a shepherd pursues a lost sheep and rejoices with all his strength when the lost are restored to the fold (Luke 15:3–7). He is the Father of those who believe in him and obey him, so that they can pray to him as a kind Father (Matt. 6:9 par.; cf. Luke 11:5–8). As a gracious Father, he gives good things to his children (Matt. 7:11), and the good thing in Luke is the Holy Spirit (Luke 11:13). His kindness can never be separated from his sovereignty, for a sparrow does not fall without him (Matt. 10:29), and if he attends to sparrows in such a way, then his children can be assured of his protection and their security (Matt. 6:26 par.).

Jesus is distinctively and uniquely the Son of the Father, but God's goodness manifests itself in that believers also call upon God as Father. Believers are "sons of your Father" (Matt. 5:45); give glory to "your Father" (Matt. 5:16); are to be perfect and merciful as is "your Father" (Matt. 5:48; Luke 6:36); will be rewarded by "your Father" (Matt. 6:1, 4, 6, 18); pray to their Father (Matt. 6:6, 9; Luke 11:2), who knows what they need (Matt. 6:8, 26, 32; Luke 12:30) and who gives good gifts (Matt. 7:11; Luke 11:13).[29] The Spirit of the Father speaks through disciples (Matt. 10:20), and the righteous "will shine like the sun in the kingdom of their Father" (Matt. 13:43).

The Gospel of John

The Revelation of God

One of the noticeable features in John's Gospel is the Jewish and OT background in his references to God.[30] John does not expound the nature of God, for he assumes and builds upon the teaching of the OT. Monotheism, of course, is a nonnegotiable in the OT, and thus John teaches that there is only one true God, who has existed from the beginning (John 1:1; 17:3). No one has ever seen God, since he is invisible and his glory overwhelms human beings (John 1:18). When John says "God is spirit" (John 4:24), he means, according to Barrett, that God "is invisible and

29. The good gift is the Holy Spirit in Luke. For a helpful discussion of the significance of the reference to the Spirit, see Bock 1996: 1062–63.

30. See the survey of "Father" in the Johannine writings in M. M. Thompson 2000: 133–54. In a subsequent book Thompson (2001) argues that John's Gospel is theocentric, not merely christocentric. The focus on Christ, in other words, does not diminish God but enhances him, so that the Son reveals the Father.

unknowable,"[31] and thus imperceptible to human beings. Despite God being a spirit and invisible, John does not teach that God is unknowable, for the entire thrust of this Gospel is that God has revealed himself in his Son, and that the Father has sent the Son.[32] The God of the Gospel of John is not a silent God. He has spoken to his people through the OT Scriptures (e.g., John 5:45–47; cf. 9:29),[33] and finally and supremely in Jesus. The Scripture as God's Word cannot be nullified (John 10:35), and in Jesus the OT promise that God would teach his people has become a reality (John 6:45). God has now conveyed his final and definitive word through his Son, who has explained the Father (John 1:18; 14:9). God has not only spoken, but also he has acted. In particular, God has demonstrated his love for the world in sending his Son for its salvation (John 3:16; 20:30–31). God sent the Son to save the world, not to condemn it (John 3:17), and hence the Son is God's supreme gift to the world (John 4:10).

The God who has revealed himself to human beings is truth, and hence he is trustworthy (John 3:33). He has manifested his glory to the world in sending his Son to die as the Lamb of God for the sin of the world (John 11:4, 40; 13:31–32; 17:1, 4, 5). God's love and mercy, of course, are not all that can be said of God. John, with his realized eschatology, emphasizes that unbelievers already stand under God's judgment. Those who do not believe are condemned already, and God's wrath remains on them (John 3:18, 36), but he also teaches that there will be an end-time judgment for those who practice evil (John 5:29). Moses will stand as a witness against Jewish leaders who refused to believe (John 5:45).

John emphasizes that salvation is God's work and cannot be accomplished or effected by human beings.[34] Those who are saved have been born of God (John 1:13; 3:3, 5, 7). The new life is bestowed supernaturally by God himself. The gift character of salvation is emphasized in John. Those who come to the Son in belief are given by the Father to the Son (John 6:37). Jesus grants eternal life only to those whom the Father has given to him (John 17:2), and Jesus reveals God's name to those whom God has given him (John 17:6, 24). Jesus restricted his prayer to those

---

31. Barrett 1978: 238. Barrett (1978: 238–39) goes on to say that God has revealed through the Spirit the truth in Jesus. See also Carson 1991b: 225.

32. So also Moloney 2002: 109–11. Nor does John suggest that God is unknowable in everyday life (rightly Ridderbos 1997: 164).

33. The claim in John 9:29 that God has spoken to Moses was voiced by the Jewish leaders. John, however, does not disagree with this claim. What he objects to is their failure to see that God has spoken supremely and finally in Jesus (John 1:17–18; 5:39–40, 45–46). Rightly Carson 1991b: 374.

34. For a helpful exposition of divine sovereignty and human responsibility in the Gospel of John, see Carson 1981a.

whom the Father has given him (John 17:9), and he fulfilled the Father's will in preserving to the end all those given to him by the Father (John 6:39). He also prayed that the Father would keep and preserve them until the last day (John 17:11, 15); hence, they will never apostatize and will be raised from the dead to new life on the last day. If people are not drawn by the Father to the Son, they will be unable to come to Jesus for life (John 6:44). Conversely, those whom the Father has taught will certainly come to Jesus (John 6:45). They are part of the flock given to Jesus by the Father (John 10:29), whereas those who failed to believe were not given by the Father to the Son (John 6:64–65).

Human beings are to respond to the revelation of God in Jesus by believing in Jesus (John 14:1), and we will see more about this in due course. Here it should be noted that human beings are called upon to give glory to God in all that they do.[35] For God's "glory is to be understood as a revelation of God, or as the intervention of his power in history."[36] Hence, the man born blind to whom Jesus restored sight should glorify and praise God for his healing (John 9:24).[37] Jesus healed Lazarus (John 11:4, 40), conducted his ministry, and went to his death (John 13:31–32; 17:1, 4, 5) to bring glory to God, for God is glorified in the work of his Son.[38] The object and the aim of one's existence are to bring glory to God, and so we see that the foundational theme of NT theology—the glory of God—is central in John's Gospel as well. Peter's death, though gruesome, will bring glory to God, presumably because he will die for the sake of Jesus Christ (John 21:19). The Jews who did not believe in Jesus are indicted because rather than prizing God's glory, they lived for the approbation and respect of human beings (John 5:44; 12:43). They were not animated by love for God (John 5:42), but rather they lived to please people. The purpose of life, however, is to serve God, even though some who think that they are doing so are deceived (John 16:2). God is served when he is glorified, and, as we will see later, God is supremely glorified, according to the Gospel of John, when he is trusted. In particular, God is glorified when human beings believe that Jesus is the Christ and the Son of God (John 20:30–31)—the Lamb of God who has come to remove the world's sins (John 1:29), for the Son glorifies the Father particularly in his death (John 13:31–32; 17:1, 4, 5).

---

35. On glory in John's Gospel, see Hegermann, *EDNT* 1:347–48.

36. Aalen, *NIDNTT* 2:48.

37. The words are those of Jewish leaders who encourage the formerly blind man to give glory to God rather than to Jesus. They are right in what they affirm and wrong in what they deny.

38. For the significance of the glory of God in John's Gospel, see Moloney 2002: 116–19.

The Fatherhood of God

JESUS' SPECIAL RELATIONSHIP WITH THE FATHER

The fatherhood of God, as in the Synoptic Gospels, is central in John's Gospel. Indeed, the fatherhood of God is emphasized even more in John than in the Synoptics. What is particularly striking, however, is that John does not emphasize that God is the Father of believers. Instead, the focus is on God as the Father of Jesus.[39] Jesus' intimate relationship with God is such that he often refers to God as "my Father." In many texts the Father's relationship to Jesus is underscored: Jesus has the right to work on the Sabbath because "my Father" is also working (John 5:17); he is the true bread given from heaven by "my Father" (John 6:32); the Jews do not know "my Father" (John 8:19); Jesus' speech derives from "my Father" (John 8:38); he honors "my Father" (John 8:49). We also note the glory given to Jesus by "my Father" (John 8:54); the command given to him by "my Father" (John 10:18); the sheep given to him by "my Father" (John 10:29); the works of "my Father" done by Jesus (John 10:37); the fact that those who know Jesus also know "my Father" (John 14:7); Jesus being "in my Father" (John 14:20); those who keep Jesus' commands being loved by "my Father" (John 14:21, 23); Jesus as the vine but "my Father" as "the vinedresser" (John 15:1); "my Father" being glorified by fruit bearing (John 15:8); Jesus' communication of truths to his disciples from "my Father" (John 15:15); those who hate Jesus as those who also hate "my Father" (John 15:23–24).

The last of such references in John's Gospel is particularly noteworthy. Jesus speaks of "my Father" and "your Father," of "my God" and "your God" (John 20:17). Jesus clearly distinguished in this verse between his unique relationship with the Father and the relationship that his disciples enjoyed with the Father.[40] He did not class himself with the disciples but rather isolated his relationship with God as exceptional. Jesus is the exclusive and unique Son of the Father. The distinctive nature of Jesus' relationship with the Father manifests itself especially in the Gospel of John. The claims made about his relationship with the Father are stunning, signifying the high Christology that informs John's Gospel. Hence, Jesus defended his healing on the Sabbath because he works just as his Father works (John 5:17).[41] The

39. On this point, see M. M. Thompson 2001: 51, 69–100.

40. Rightly Barrett 1978: 566. Contra R. Brown (1970: 1016), who thinks that what we find in John is parallel to Ruth 1:16. The consistent distinction drawn by Jesus of his relationship with the Father over against the disciples weighs against Brown's view, even though it is true that Jesus also emphasizes that he and the disciples enjoy the same Father.

41. See M. M. Thompson 2000: 147.

Jewish opponents rightly deduced from this claim that Jesus was making himself equal to God (John 5:18), so that Jesus and the Father are one (John 10:30).

The Father glorifies the Son (John 8:54) and has set his seal of approval on him (John 6:27). Jesus does the works of the Father (John 10:37) and is in the Father (John 10:38; 14:10, 20). Human beings can come to the Father only through Jesus (John 14:6) and must honor the Son just as they honor the Father (John 5:23). He knows the Father just as the Father knows him (John 10:15), and they are mutually in one another (John 10:38; 17:21). Those who have known and seen Jesus have known and seen the Father (John 14:7–9; cf. 16:3). Indeed, those who hate Jesus also hate the Father (John 15:23–24). The Father uniquely loves the Son and has shown and given him everything (John 3:35; 5:20; 10:17; 13:3; 15:9; 16:15), so that the Father glorifies the Son (John 8:54; 17:5), and thereby the Son also glorifies the Father (John 17:1). Such astounding truths cannot be said of anyone else.

John also teaches, however, that the Son depends on the Father, and that the Father is greater than the Son (John 10:29; 14:28). He does only what the Father does (John 5:19, 36),[42] and he was sent by the Father,[43] and so he honors the Father (John 8:49), and his food is to do the Father's will (John 4:34), especially by answering prayer (John 14:13; 15:16). His teaching comes from the Father (John 8:28; 15:15). The Father testifies to the Son, setting his seal upon him as the one he sent (John 3:33–34; 5:32, 34, 36, 37; 6:27; 8:18). The Son's life derives from the Father (John 5:26), and he lives because of the Father (John 6:57).[44] The Father has given the Son to the world as the bread of life (John 6:32). There are texts in John that emphasize Jesus' equality with the Father and his subordination to the Father.[45] John does not work out theologically how these two fit together. Clearly, he sees Jesus as having the same honor that belongs to the Father, but he does not abandon monotheism. John

---

42. M. M. Thompson (2000: 150) emphasizes that Jesus is never said to obey the Father, but she overstates her point because John likewise never uses the verb "obey" to render the obedience of disciples to God. Compare here Jesus' keeping his Father's word or commands (John 8:55; 15:10) and his doing what the Father commanded (John 14:31).

43. I am including both the verbs *pempō* and *apostellō* here because the difference between them is, in my view, merely stylistic variation: John 3:17, 34; 4:34; 5:23, 24, 30, 36, 37, 38; 6:29, 38, 39, 44, 57; 7:16, 18, 28, 29, 33; 8:16, 18, 26, 29, 42; 9:4; 10:36; 11:42; 12:44, 45, 49; 13:20; 14:24; 15:21; 16:5; 17:3, 8, 18, 21, 23, 25; 20:21. This view of these two verbs is a consensus among commentators (see Barrett 1978: 569; Köstenberger 2004: 573–74n13).

44. And yet, as M. M. Thompson (2000: 142–43) shows, John also emphasizes that Jesus has life in himself.

45. On the relationship between equality and functional subordination, see Barrett 1982: 19–36; Carson 1981a: 146–60.

redefines monotheism by teaching that Jesus deserves the same honor as the Father without identifying him as the Father.

FATHER OF DISCIPLES

God is uniquely the Father of Jesus the Christ, but he is also the Father of Jesus' disciples (John 20:17). The Father is supreme over all and has life in himself (John 5:21). Since God is the Father of disciples, their aim and goal in life should always be to worship him (John 4:23–24). God is not pleased with just any worship, for people must worship him "in spirit and truth." Eternal life is knowing God as the one true God, though remarkably, John immediately adds that they also must know Jesus Christ, whom the Father has sent (John 17:3). The purpose of life is to honor God, though again, John insists that God cannot be honored if Jesus Christ is not honored (John 5:23). The purpose of every life is to honor God in Christ, which fits, of course, with the major thesis that I put forth in this book. The Father is glorified if people bear much fruit (John 15:8), and this fruit likely involves both Christian character and the spread of the gospel so that others receive eternal life.

Acts

God Sovereignly Works Out His Plan

The God of Acts is the sovereign God who fulfills his plans in the stream of redemptive history.[46] The time of fulfillment is in God's hands, for he has "fixed by his own authority" "times or seasons" (Acts 1:7). Stephen proclaimed God's sovereignty in his speech in Acts 7, and in doing so he reflects the worldview of the OT. God graciously appeared to Abraham with both commands and promises (Acts 7:2–8). He sustained Joseph and preserved Israel during their time in Egypt (Acts 7:9–16). He raised up Moses as a deliverer even though his contemporaries rejected him, just as Joseph's brothers had turned away from him (Acts 7:17–44). A persistent theme in Acts is that God has fulfilled prophecy in the ministry, death, and resurrection of Christ (Acts 2:17–36; 3:11–26; 4:9–12; 24:14–15; 26:6–7, 22–23; 28:23). Paul emphasized in his sermon at Antioch that God's promises fulfilled in Jesus are part and parcel of God's covenant made with Israel from the beginning, that the Davidic covenant reaches its fulfillment in Jesus (Acts 13:16–41). The saving

---

46. A focus on God's plan has been seen by many scholars in Luke-Acts. For the development of this theme and discussion with earlier scholarship on God's plan in Luke-Acts, see Squires 1993.

promises that are being realized in redemptive history are the promises of *God*; he is acting to carry out his will and purposes.

The narrative in Acts, of course, features the spread of the gospel to the Gentiles. Luke recounts again and again that the acceptance of the gospel by the Gentiles is due to the sovereignty of God.[47] Therefore, Acts supports one of the main themes of this book, for Luke focuses on the God who fulfills his saving promises. The story about Cornelius is a prime example. An angel appeared to Cornelius while he was praying and instructed him about where he could find Peter, who was miles away in Joppa at the home of Simon the tanner (Acts 10:1–8). Meanwhile, Peter had no intention of expending his energies in evangelizing Gentiles (Acts 10:9–16). He suddenly fell into a trance while praying on the rooftop, and a sheet descended from heaven containing a myriad of unclean animals. God enjoined him to kill and eat animals forbidden by Levitical regulations (Lev. 11:1–44). Peter adamantly refused to indulge because the foods were prohibited, but a divine voice told him to partake because God had declared the foods clean. Peter naturally was perplexed and confused about the nature of the vision (Acts 10:17–23a), but as he pondered it, emissaries from Cornelius arrived at Simon the tanner's house. Peter departed with them to visit Cornelius and his friends (Acts 10:23b–48), and he explained the gospel to them. He did not, however, issue a call for repentance and faith. Nevertheless, while Peter recounted the gospel, the Holy Spirit fell upon those gathered, and the Gentiles spoke in tongues, demonstrating that they had the Spirit. Peter concluded that they should be baptized because clearly they were part of God's people.

Luke reviews the story in Acts 11:1–18, setting forth Peter's defense to Jews who criticized him for eating with Gentiles. The repetition of the account indicates how crucial the Cornelius event was for Luke's theology. Peter's apologetic can be summed up rather easily. He recounted what happened and clarified that he had virtually nothing to do with the Gentiles' reception of the gospel. Clearly it was God's sovereign work from the appearance of the angel to Cornelius, the vision Peter received, and the unbidden falling of the Spirit on the Gentiles. Peter could not stand in God's way and withhold baptism from those who received the Spirit (Acts 11:17). Peter's hearers glorified and praised God, rightly concluding that he had granted the "repentance that leads to life" to the Gentiles (Acts 11:18). Thereby God acted to fulfill his saving promise to Abraham by blessing all people, both Jew and Gentile, through Jesus Christ (cf. Gen. 12:1–3).

That God sovereignly works out his plan is clear from all of Acts. The martyrdom of Stephen was a great tragedy, but it led to the scattering

---

47. See Stenschke 1999: 276–303.

of believers and the spreading of the word (Acts 8:1–4). The conversion of Paul, related three times in Acts (Acts 9:1–19; 22:1–16; 26:1–23), testified to God's sovereign work in both saving Paul and in appointing him as the missionary to bring the gospel to the Gentiles. It takes no great insight to see that Paul's transformation derives from God's intervention in his life. Luke concludes the first missionary journey of Paul and Barnabas with the explanation that God "had opened a door of faith to the Gentiles" (Acts 14:27; cf. 15:4, 12). Salvation is the Lord's work. Peter recalled at the Jerusalem Council how God determined that the Gentiles (Cornelius and his friends) would hear the gospel and believe through his visit (Acts 15:7). Paul's ministry can be summarized in terms of the things that God has done through him.[48] The priority of God's grace is quite clear from the response of the Gentiles to Paul's gospel in Acts 13:48: "And as many as were appointed to eternal life believed." Luke does not write that those who believed were appointed to eternal life, but rather that those who were appointed by God to experience eternal life subsequently believed.[49] He thereby underlines God's grace that secures the response of belief in the hearts of Gentiles.

The Jews opposed Paul in Corinth and attempted to turn the civil authorities against him, but God assured Paul that the mission would be successful, that he had many people in Corinth who would be converted through Paul's ministry (Acts 18:1–11). Hence, Paul should not depart from the city but rather remain faithful in declaring the gospel. God had appointed that Paul's missionary venture would be successful. God's promise and sovereignty are displayed in the next event, for the Jews brought charges against Paul before Gallio (Acts 18:12–17), but Gallio dismissed the charges as an internecine Jewish squabble. Paul was free to continue proclaiming the gospel, and the leader of the synagogue received a beating, which presumably is an indication that the Jewish tactic against Paul backfired. Paul's arrest in Jerusalem, appeal to Caesar, and eventual imprisonment in Rome (Acts 21–28) fulfilled God's plan as well (cf. Acts 19:21), even though all these events took place in a way unanticipated by Paul. God's plan was being worked out as Paul bore witness in Jerusalem and Rome (Acts 23:11) in order to fulfill the prophecy that he would proclaim God's name "before the Gentiles and kings and the children of Israel" (Acts 9:15). What God promises will surely come to pass, and so when an angel revealed to Paul that every single life on the ship would be spared, despite a ferocious storm, it turned out just as God said (Acts 27:13–44). Acts emphasizes that God is

48. So Squires 1993: 62.

49. So Barrett 1994: 658. Contra Conzelmann (1987: 106), who rejects the idea but provides no explanation of the verse. For a full and convincing discussion of the verse that considers alternatives, see Stenschke 1999: 283–88.

working out his saving plan for the world. He is fulfilling his covenantal promises through Jesus Christ and bringing to pass what he pledged. Acts does not portray an abstract doctrine of God; rather, it reveals a God who acts to fulfill his saving promises.

God's sovereign rule over all things does not mean that everything that occurs is intrinsically good. It was God's plan that Jesus suffer and die for the sins of his people. A common theme is that believers must be prepared to suffer as well. The death of Stephen indicates that God's plan is often worked out through the suffering of his own people. In Acts 12 Herod took action against the church and beheaded James the brother of John. Luke expresses no shock, recording the event abruptly and without detail.[50] The death of James scarcely led to the conclusion that God is not in control, for Peter was released supernaturally, probably because of the church's fervent prayers. Luke is not suggesting that the church failed to pray for James. He offers no explanation for the deliverance of Peter and the execution of James, proposing no neatly packaged answer for why some suffer and others are spared. God's rule over the world does not lend itself to formulas by which evil can be easily explained. Given Luke's worldview, he must have believed that God *could have* delivered James as well, and yet no reason for God's actions are given. The rationale for much of what happens is obscured from human vision. Still, God's control over all is conveyed powerfully by the conclusion of the story. The same Herod who executed James is struck dead by God when he fails to give God glory.[51] God rules over the kings of the earth, and the evil that they inflict is under his hand, but God himself is untainted by evil.

God's rule over all is featured supremely, as we noted earlier, in the death of Christ. Christ's death, as Acts 2:23 indicates, was due to God's predestined plan and foreknowledge. Luke does not conceive of Jesus' execution as an unfortunate accident that God attempted to forestall. God's plan from the beginning was that Christ die for the sins of his people. And yet Acts 2:23 also declares that those who put Christ to death should not have done so and are held responsible for their evil behavior.[52] This same perspective appears in Acts 4:27–28, where Herod,

50. As Barrett (1994: 569) says about this story, "Suffering and death were a real part of the experience of the early church."

51. Barrett (1994: 572) notes that Luke does not explicitly draw the conclusion that God punished Herod, but it seems fair to say that this is the point of the narrative, for the story itself leads the reader to such a conclusion. Fitzmyer (1998: 486, 491) rightly argues that Herod's death was seen by the church as a quid pro quo. So also Haenchen 1971: 387.

52. Squires (1993: 179) comments, "Luke is aware of the dilemma which his emphasis on divine providence produces; but he refrains from such an explicitly philosophical discussion of free-will and determinism." See also Haenchen 1971: 180.

Pilate, the Gentiles, and even Jewish leaders conspired against Jesus in putting him to death. Indeed, as the apostles prayed in Acts 4:23–31, they were responding to persecution inflicted on them from Jewish leaders (Acts 4:1–22). Nevertheless, what happened to Jesus was in accord with God's plan and predestined purpose (Acts 4:28). Luke emphasizes again God's sovereignty and control over all things, even the evil that occurs. Of course, Acts also emphasizes that God vindicates Christ by raising him from the dead (Acts 3:15; 4:10; 5:30; 10:40; 13:30, 37; 26:8).

One of the major themes, therefore, for Luke is that God's purpose and plan cannot be thwarted. This perspective is summarized well by the Pharisee Gamaliel, who cautioned his contemporaries from waging an all-out campaign of violence against Christians, lest they find themselves fighting a fruitless battle against God himself (Acts 5:34–39). The nature of God's purpose in Luke-Acts is often denoted by the words "it is necessary" (*dei*).[53] The death and resurrection of Jesus are necessarily part of God's plan (Luke 9:22; 13:33; 17:25; 24:7). Indeed, everything that occurs in the ministry, death, and resurrection of Jesus fulfills God's plan found in the Scriptures (Luke 22:7; 24:44). When Jesus' parents questioned his remaining in Jerusalem at twelve years of age, he declared that he must devote himself to the things of his Father (Luke 2:49). When the crowds attempted to restrain Jesus from going elsewhere, he departed anyway with the conviction that he was ordained to preach the kingdom of God in other cities (Luke 4:43). Similarly, it was God's plan that Paul suffer as he announced the message to the ends of the earth (Acts 9:16). Luke emphasizes that it was the divine plan that Paul go to Rome and testify before Caesar (Acts 19:21; 23:11; 25:10).

God's plan and purpose will be accomplished because he is the true and living God who made the world (Acts 4:24, 28). Jews and proselytes were nurtured in the teaching that God created the world and was the one and only God. Two texts in Acts are particularly interesting, for they describe Paul's preaching when he encounters pagans—those unfamiliar with OT theology. When Paul healed a lame man in Lystra, the people concluded that he and Barnabas were the gods Hermes and Zeus, respectively, and the priest of Zeus was prepared to offer sacrifice (Acts 14:8–13). Paul and Barnabas were horrified, protesting that they were mere mortals, and that people should turn from the futility of idols and worship the living God, who created all things and provided them with food (Acts 14:14–16).

Paul's proclamation of the gospel at the Areopagus, where Stoic and Epicurean philosophers congregated, sounds out similar themes (Acts

---

53. In defense of the notion that Luke-Acts should be studied as a unity, see Tannehill 1986.

17:22–31).[54] Since his hearers were ignorant of the OT Scriptures and redemptive history, Paul did not begin by proclaiming to them that Jesus fulfills God's covenantal promises. Such a declaration would have been virtually meaningless to those unacquainted with the OT narrative. Those who were present lacked knowledge of the true God and worshiped many gods. Hence, Paul commenced with the theme that God is the creator of all as the sovereign Lord of heaven and earth. God cannot be restricted to temples made by human beings, for such temples typically are built with the notion that God needs human service, as if he needs the assistance offered by human beings. Since God is the sovereign Lord and creator, however, he needs nothing from human beings. God does not need human beings, but human beings need God because he gives "life and breath and everything" (Acts 17:25). Human beings, in their ignorance of the true God, craft gods in their own image and likeness, as if God can be domesticated or represented by human ingenuity. Such an enterprise turns reality on its head. Humans should not attempt to make "God" in their likeness; rather, God made human beings in his own likeness as his offspring (cf. Gen. 1:26–27). Those with a pagan worldview need to be nurtured in the creation theology of the OT in order to understand that Jesus is the one who fulfills the promises of the creator God.

We see, then, that the God of Acts is the God of mission. He sovereignly and lovingly acts to fulfill his saving promises. He intervenes in history to carry out his purposes, whether that involves initiating the conversion of Paul, or bringing Peter to Cornelius to proclaim the gospel, or frustrating Jewish attempts to bring the ministry of Paul to an end.

God's Glory

God's glory constitutes an important theme in Acts. We have noted above the inclusion of the Gentiles in the story of Cornelius and his friends (Acts 10:1–11:18). When skeptical Jewish Christians heard Peter's explanation of God's work in bringing Gentiles to himself, they surrendered their opposition and gave glory to God for his saving work (Acts 11:18). Similarly, Paul rehearsed all that God did in and through him to win Gentiles to the "Way," and the church in Jerusalem recognized God's work and gave him glory (Acts 21:19–20). When Herod accepted the praise of the people of Tyre and Sidon who celebrated his oration as the speech of a god, God struck him dead because he arrogated glory to himself instead of giving all the glory to God (Acts 12:20–23). Silas and Paul reflected God's worth and preciousness when they sang and praised his name in a Philippian jail after being whipped as criminals (Acts 16:25).

54. Schnabel (2004b: 1392–1404) rightly emphasizes that Paul confronts the worldview of his hearers rather than accommodating it.

Paul defended himself against criminal charges, summarizing his life as a follower of the Way as one in which he worships God (Acts 24:14). We see from this brief sketch that God's saving and judging work both bring him glory and praise. The ultimate purpose for mission is the glory of God, so that his name will be magnified among all peoples.

The Pauline Literature

The centrality of God pulsates through Paul's theology.[55] We cannot do justice to the depth and complexity of this theme in Paul, and it is not my intention here to attempt a full-scale investigation of Paul's view of God.[56] Instead, the goal is to touch on some high points in order to demonstrate the centrality of God in Pauline theology. Paul stands in line with his Jewish heritage in confessing that God is one (1 Cor. 8:4, 6; Eph. 4:6; 1 Tim. 2:5). This one God is also the Father (Eph. 4:6), from whom every family on earth receives its name (Eph. 3:14–15). It is clear, therefore, that Paul, despite his high Christology, does not depart from Jewish monotheism.[57] He is a Jew nurtured in the OT and conceives of God as one and as the Lord of all.

When we open Paul's letter to the Romans, which almost all would agree is his greatest, the God-entranced vision of the writing is apparent. Most conceive of sin in terms of failing to do what is mandated, and Paul certainly agrees. Fundamentally, however, sin exists when people fail to thank and glorify God (Rom. 1:21). The root sin consists in worshiping and serving the creature rather than the creator (Rom. 1:25). People sin when they fail to acknowledge God (Rom. 1:28). All the discrete acts of sin, therefore, are a *consequence* of failing to honor and give thanks to

55. Plevnik (1989) argued that the center of Paul's theology was God's saving action in Christ, in which the focus is on Christ's death and resurrection, with the confession that he is the transcendent Son of God. Several years later Plevnik (2003: 555n6) argued that the terms "foundation" or "basis" are preferable to "center." Plevnik (2003: 562–63) continues to claim that Jesus' identity as God's Son is fundamental to the Pauline gospel, but now he also maintains, in a way that fits remarkably with the outline of this book (and I saw this essay after completing the first two drafts of my work), "that the Holy Spirit as well belongs to the center of Pauline theology," because the Spirit was involved in raising Christ and in the salvation of believers from beginning to end. Another one of Paul's "fundamental issues," according to Plevnik (2003: 564), is "belief in one God, the Father." It seems, then, that Plevnik would concur with the trinitarian focus that I employ in this book. Plevnik (2003: 567) concludes his article by saying, "All this indicates that the center or the basis of Pauline theology is not in the effects of Christ's salvific action but on a deeper level, in the underlying relationship of the Father, the Son, and the Spirit to one another and in their joint contribution to our salvation."

56. For a helpful study on God in Pauline theology, see Seifrid 2005.

57. So also Lau 1996: 270–71.

God (Rom. 1:24, 26, 28).[58] Paul indicts his fellow Jews as sinners because their actions have caused unbelievers to revile God's name (Rom. 2:24). The behavior of the Jews is heinous because it casts a stain upon God's name. The sins recorded in Rom. 3:10–18 culminate with the rationale behind them all: the failure to fear God (Rom. 3:18).

Idolatry, then, must be shunned (1 Cor. 10:14), for God brooks no competitors (1 Cor. 10:21–22) and will not tolerate those who try to serve him and yet compromise by eating in the temples of idols.[59] The purpose of life is to please God, but those who are in the flesh are unable to do so (Rom. 8:7–8). The aim of life, then, is to live with all of one's strength in giving praise to God. Paul expresses this truth in saying that he does everything for the sake of the gospel (1 Cor. 9:23). But the gospel is supremely about and from God (Rom. 1:1; 1 Tim. 1:11), and so living for the gospel is simply another way of saying that one lives for God's sake.

As creatures, then, human beings are summoned to praise God and give him glory. They glorify God by trusting him as Abraham did, for "he grew strong in his faith as he gave glory to God" (Rom. 4:20). Faith glorifies God because it looks to him as the one who can provide and act on our behalf, so Abraham trusted that God could grant life to the dead and call things into existence that did not yet exist (Rom. 4:17). Faith casts itself upon God's power instead of the intelligence and giftedness of human beings (1 Cor. 2:5). Sin boasts in human ability and strength (1 Cor. 1:29), but those who know God boast in him alone (1 Cor. 1:31). God placed Paul in life-threatening situations, so perilous that he despaired of living, so that his hope would rest in the God who raises the dead (2 Cor. 1:8–9).[60] God wills that all put their hope in him, whether the widow who lives on the margins financially (1 Tim. 5:5) or the rich who are prone to rely on their wealth instead of God (1 Tim. 6:17).

All people, even believers, are prone to forget about God. The Corinthians quarreled over the wisdom of those who ministered to them,

---

58. The importance of thanksgiving in Pauline theology is captured effectively in Pao 2002. Pao argues that thanksgiving is intimately connected with "God-centeredness." Hence, the call to thanksgiving means that God is to be praised as creator and as covenant Lord. Thanksgiving, then, is the fundamental response of the creature to the creator. Thus we are not surprised that the call to give thanks in every circumstance (Col. 3:17) represents the heart of the Pauline gospel. Indeed, Col. 3:17 shows the close tie between thanksgiving and Christ's lordship, the latter of which, Pao (2002: 116) notes, is "at the center of the Pauline gospel." On the other hand, to speak of those who love themselves (2 Tim. 3:2) is to provide "the essential definition of what it meant to live a life without God" (Pao 2002: 163).

59. Pao (2002: 153–57) demonstrates that the exhortations against idolatry in 1 Cor. 10 can be rephrased to say that God's people should not be ungrateful to God.

60. See Harris 2005: 157–58.

probably debating the rhetorical ability of Paul, Apollos, and Cephas (1 Cor. 1:11–12, 17; 2:3–4).[61] What distresses Paul most is that apparently their minds have strayed from God. God is the one who causes growth in the church, not the human minister (1 Cor. 3:7). The Corinthians do not belong to Paul, Apollos, or Cephas, for they are God's cultivated field and God's architectural masterpiece (1 Cor. 3:9). Boasting in human ministers is shallow and superficial, for the Corinthians have something infinitely better than weak human beings. Because they belong to Christ, they belong to God, and once someone belongs to God, then everything belongs to the believer—whether death or life (1 Cor. 3:21–23). In 2 Corinthians Paul's opponents engaged in boasting. They made comparisons to see if one was greater than another (2 Cor. 10:12). They bragged about the effectiveness of their own ministry, which Paul finds highly ironic because they have not planted any churches but simply horn in on Paul's labors (2 Cor. 10:13–16). Ultimately, the only boasting that counts is boasting in the Lord and what he has done, for only the commendation of the Lord matters (2 Cor. 10:17–18). Hence, Paul ministered not to flatter or please people but to please God (Gal. 1:10; 1 Thess. 2:4–6). Paul's ministry was designed to extend the grace of God to as many human beings as possible, and this extension of grace will lead to thanksgiving and glory to God (2 Cor. 4:15).

Praising God is not passionless for Paul, for those who praise him exult in him (Rom. 5:11). When believers reflect on God's saving work, they bless him (Eph. 1:3; cf. 2 Cor. 1:3). Ephesians 1:3–14 recounts in exalted language the saving work of God in Christ from his electing purpose and the forgiveness of sins to the gift of the Spirit. God's salvation is not, however, his ultimate work. Three times Paul explains that the redemptive benefits are for the praise of the glories of God's grace (Eph. 1:6, 12, 14). God chooses, redeems, and sanctifies so that he will be honored for his grace. The purpose of life can be summed up in the call to love God and know him (1 Cor. 8:3). The description of love in 1 Cor. 13:4–7 sums up God's character supremely. To live in love, Eph. 3:17–19 suggests, is to be filled with all of God's fullness.[62] The Christian life, according to Paul, means that one is God-saturated, which manifests itself in love. Those who demonstrate love to others are taught by God himself to do so (1 Thess. 4:9),[63] demonstrating his new-covenant work in the hearts of believers (cf. Isa. 54:13; Jer. 31:31–34).

61. That the issue lying behind the divisions centered on the rhetorical ability of Paul and Apollos is argued in Litfin 1994; Winter 1997.

62. See Lincoln 1990: 214–15; Best 1998: 348.

63. Wanamaker (1990: 160) suggests from Isa. 54 (esp. v. 13) that Paul thinks that being taught by God indicates that the age of salvation has arrived (cf. Bruce 1982b: 90; Beale 2003: 125). See especially Witmer 2006. Best (1972: 173) downplays the OT allusion.

Paul states the truth of God's supremacy in a myriad of different ways. Believers exist for God's sake (1 Cor. 8:6)—that is, so that the entirety of their lives reflects his beauty. This explains why Paul can say that believers are to do all things for God's glory, including eating or drinking (1 Cor. 10:31), for human beings are to eat food in gratefulness because it comes from his hands as the creator (1 Cor. 10:26). Believers may eat any food "God created" as long as they give thanks, since gifts such as food and marriage are to be celebrated as from the creator's hand, not denied as if they are tainted with evil (cf. Rom. 14:6; 1 Tim. 4:1–5). Elsewhere the same thought is expressed when Paul declares that believers ought to give thanks for all things (Eph. 5:20), and this gratefulness manifests itself when believers acknowledge God's lordship over every area of their lives (Rom. 14:7–9). The importance of gratefulness is confirmed by the thanksgiving introductions in almost every Pauline letter (see also 2 Cor. 2:14; 8:16; 1 Thess. 2:13).[64] Their repetition may dull us to their significance, for Paul frequently and regularly turns to God in thanksgiving and praise. When he thinks of the churches that he planted and their growth in grace, he lifts his voice in praise and thanksgiving to God.

Since believers are to live for God's sake, they are summoned to imitate God (Eph. 5:1). They are to live in a way that is worthy of the God who called them into his kingdom (1 Thess. 2:12). As believers, they should consider how they can live in a way that pleases God (1 Thess. 4:1). Those who grow in holiness bring glory and praise to God (Phil. 1:11). They are to live holy and sanctified lives, especially in terms of their sexual purity (1 Thess. 4:3–8). What believers do with their bodies and in their sexual practices is no small matter, for they are called to glorify God with their bodies (1 Cor. 6:20). Those who live in lust do so because they do not truly know God (1 Thess. 4:5). God hands people over to sexual sin who do not give him praise or thanks as the creator (Rom. 1:25–27). Paul prizes the state of being unmarried, which allows a person to devote his or her life entirely to pleasing God (1 Cor. 7:32–35). Supremely, believers are to praise God for his merciful and saving work in Christ (Rom. 15:8–12).

God is adored and worshiped because of who he is and what he does. God judges righteously and impartially so that his judgments are just (Rom. 2:2, 5; 1 Cor. 5:13; cf. Gal. 2:6).[65] His judgment reveals his righteousness (Rom. 3:5), both in salvation and judgment (Rom. 3:25–26). God judges the wicked in accord with what they have done, thus his

---

64. For the significance of the thanksgiving introductions in Paul, see the programmatic study of O'Brien 1977. For the importance of thanksgiving in Paul's theology, see Pao 2002.

65. For the theme of divine impartiality in Romans, see Bassler 1982.

judgment is righteous (2 Thess. 1:5–10). He will not be scorned by those
who reject his ways (Gal. 6:7).

The God and Father of the Lord Jesus Christ is not an abstract entity.[66] He has structured all of history so that it finds apex, summation,
and unification in Christ (Eph. 1:9–10).[67] He is "the King of the ages"
(1 Tim. 1:17). Lau says that in the Pastoral Epistles the emphasis is "on
the transcendent sovereignty and majesty of the eternal, invisible and
incomprehensible God."[68] God works in ways that far exceed human
expectations (Eph. 3:20). Believers owe their spiritual gifts to God's
sovereign choice, for he has arranged the members of the body according to his will (1 Cor. 12:18, 27). Even when he hardens someone like
Pharaoh, he continues to be just and righteous (Rom. 9:14–18), and he
dulls those who reject his gracious offers so that they have no capacity
to discern the truth and be saved (2 Thess. 2:11–12). He is the sovereign
Lord who rules and reigns over history, showing severity to some and
kindness to others (Rom. 11:22). When believers quarrel over which
religious days to observe and which foods can be consumed, they must
desist from passing judgment on others and must live before the God
who will judge them on the last day (Rom. 14:4, 10–12). The election of
Israel, their hardening to the gospel, the inclusion of the Gentiles, and
the end-time final salvation of Israel are all part of God's surprising and
wise plan (Rom. 9:1–11:32). God's work in history and the fulfillment of
his saving promises cause Paul's heart to well up in praise to God for his
inscrutable wisdom and unsurpassed knowledge (Rom. 11:33–35). He
confesses that God deserves all the glory because "from him and through
him and to him are all things" (Rom. 11:36). The reconciling work by
which human beings become friends with God is due to the work of God
(2 Cor. 5:18). Thanks flow to God especially for his grace (1 Cor. 1:4),
by which he saves human beings from the rule of sin and death. Hence,
when believers hear about Paul's conversion, they glorify God for his
converting work (Gal. 1:24; cf. 1:15–17; 1 Cor. 15:9–11; 1 Tim. 1:12–17;
2 Tim. 2:24–26). They do not attribute the change in Paul's life to his own
moral virtue or insight. God chose believers to salvation from the beginning (2 Thess. 2:13).[69] He has spared them from his eschatological wrath

66. On God as Father in Paul, see M. M. Thompson 2000: 116–32.
67. Lincoln (1990: 32–33) shows that the infinitive *anakephalaiōsasthai* in Eph. 1:10
indicates that all things are summed up and unified in Christ, but Hoehner (2002: 219–21)
rightly argues, in contrast to Lincoln, that there is also the idea of sovereignty here. See
also the helpful discussion in O'Brien 1999: 111–15.
68. Lau 1996: 271.
69. Wanamaker (1990: 266) argues that the textual evidence is divided, so the best
reading must be established internally. He is likely correct in seeing a reference to "from
the beginning" rather than "firstfruits." Contra Bruce 1982b: 189–90.

and appointed them to salvation (1 Thess. 5:9). Those who persevere to the end can only give credit to God, since he completes the work that he has begun in his faithfulness (Phil. 1:6; 1 Thess. 5:24).

God's grace reveals his mercy and love, which are so great that believers will never come to the end of the wonder of what God has done for them in Christ (Eph. 2:7–8).[70] God's wisdom will be on display forever for the work that he has accomplished in the church and in Christ Jesus (Eph. 3:9–11).[71] God's ultimate purpose in the church is to evoke the recognition of his glory (Eph. 3:21). Only God's grace can account for the stunning generosity of the Macedonians, since they gave unstintingly even in their poverty (2 Cor. 8:1–5), and Paul further maintains that the resources by which people help others financially come from God himself (2 Cor. 9:8). God supplies every financial need of his people as the giver of all gifts (Phil. 4:19). Paul celebrates the generosity of the Corinthians because it testifies to their trust and joy in God. Others will see their liberality and give thanks to God (2 Cor. 9:11–12). They will glorify God when they see that the Corinthians' faith has radically changed their lives (2 Cor. 9:13–14). Thereby people will be pointed to God himself, who gave Christ as his unspeakably great gift to human beings (2 Cor. 9:15).[72] Slaves should submit to masters, not simply because it is socially acceptable, but so that no one will revile God's name (1 Tim. 6:1; cf. Titus 2:1–10).

It is not as if God merely reigns over "sacred history" while the secular world takes its own course. Governmental rulers owe their position over others to God, who ordained them to serve (Rom. 13:1–2). There is also a sense, of course, in which sin and death oppose God's purposes. His rule will be ultimately and finally enacted when he puts everything under Christ's feet (1 Cor. 15:27–28). God is also the faithful God (Rom. 3:3–4), and his promises never fail (Rom. 9:6). He will fulfill his promise of life in the age to come, since he cannot lie (Titus 1:2). All of God's promises find their "yes" in Jesus Christ (2 Cor. 1:20). The title "Savior" comes to prominence in the Pastoral Epistles, where God is often designated as the Savior of his people (1 Tim. 2:3; 4:10; Titus 2:10; 3:4). Couser argues that the Pastoral Epistles have placed at crucial junctures in the letters "elaborate descriptions of God . . . to reinforce God's sovereign control

70. On the importance of this verse in Paul's argument, see Lincoln 1990: 109–11; O'Brien 1999: 172–73; Hoehner 2002: 336–39.

71. See Lincoln 1990: 185–89; Hoehner 2002: 458–64. Best (1998: 322–23) thinks that only the evil powers are in view, while Hoehner thinks that both evil and good angels may be in mind. O'Brien (1999: 246–47) suggests that both good and bad angels are in view, with a focus on the latter.

72. In support of a reference to Christ, see Harris 2005: 659–60; Garland 1999: 415; Barrett 1973: 241. R. Martin (1986: 295) thinks that the gift is likely the "universal Gospel." Furnish (1984: 452) argues that the gift is God's grace operative in generous giving.

of salvation-history."[73] God is the sovereign one, for he appoints the time of Christ's coming (1 Tim. 6:15–16). He is the "King of the ages" (1 Tim. 1:17), who rules over all.[74] He is immortal, invisible, and the only true God. The glory of God surpasses human imagination, and hence he dwells in light that cannot even be approached by human beings (1 Tim. 6:15–16). He is deathless and the king and sovereign of all. God is the "blessed" one, suggesting that his happiness cannot be obstructed by human beings or any other creature (1 Tim. 6:15). As Couser says, the God who blesses others "can become the God who is blessed."[75]

We see, then, God's supremacy in all of the Pauline letters. Paul does not propound an abstract and philosophical doctrine of God separated from everyday life. The God and Father of our Lord Jesus Christ is the Lord of history, the one who fulfills his saving promises, and the one who is to be glorified, honored, and praised in all things.

Hebrews

When examining Hebrews and the remaining pieces of literature in the NT, we must remember that we do not have the extensive corpus that we benefit from in reading Paul.[76] We must not conclude from the absence of something in these writings that the authors necessarily reject that which is emphasized by Paul or the Gospel writers. Each piece of literature is addressed to a particular circumstance and thus is crafted to speak to the situation facing the readers. The epistle to the Hebrews was written to respond to readers tempted to return to Judaism. The writer emphasizes truths particularly suited to his readers, such as God's sovereignty, God's righteous judgment of those who abandon him, and the fulfillment of God's saving promises in Christ.

God as Sovereign in Acting and Speaking

God is the sovereign creator of the entire universe (Heb. 11:3). He rested after completing his creative work (Heb. 4:4), not because he

73. Couser 2000: 205.

74. Couser (2000: 281) rightly observes that the sovereign and great God of 1 Tim. 1:17 cannot be separated from the saving action of God described in 1 Tim. 1:12–16. Hence, the two should not be segregated from one another. For discussion of the verse, see W. Mounce 2000: 59–60; Marshall 1999: 404–5, both rightly arguing that God is in view here rather than Christ.

75. Couser 2000: 279. Couser (2000: 280) goes on to argue that the connotations of aloofness in the term "blessed" "have been tempered by its association with God's redemptive acts in Christ."

76. For a brief summary of what Hebrews teaches about God, see Rissi 1987: 27–33.

was weary, but because his work was completed. The majestic opening to the letter reminds readers that the God whom they worship reveals himself authoritatively in human words. He spoke his word through the prophets in the past, but now he has spoken definitively and finally in the Son (Heb. 1:1–2). The author of Hebrews clearly believes that God has revealed himself and spoken through the OT Scriptures. The author introduces OT citations with a number of expressions that emphasize God's speech: "For to which of the angels did God ever say" (Heb. 1:5); "he says" (Heb. 1:6); "Of the angels he says" (Heb. 1:7); "But of the Son he says" (Heb. 1:8); "And to which of the angels has he ever said" (Heb. 1:13); "he has said" (Heb. 4:3); "'Today,' saying through David so long afterward, in the words already quoted" (Heb. 4:7); "Christ . . . was appointed by the one who said to him" (Heb. 5:5); "as he says also in another place" (Heb. 5:6); "this one was made a priest" by "the one who said to him" (Heb. 7:21); "he finds fault with them when he says" (Heb. 8:8); "when Christ came into the world, he said" (Heb. 10:5). The author of Hebrews clearly views God as a "talking God," one who exists (Heb. 11:6) and is not silent. He has communicated to his people through the Scriptures and now supremely and finally and definitively in Jesus Christ. Indeed, he even uttered an oath about the Melchizedekian priesthood of Jesus, granting surety to believers of the salvation that Jesus has achieved (Heb. 6:13–17). The God who has spoken cannot lie (Heb. 6:18); hence, the readers must pay heed to what has been uttered (Heb. 2:1; cf. 11:7).

God has borne witness by signs and wonders and gifts of the Spirit to revelation that supersedes the law mediated by angels (Heb. 2:1–4). The God who speaks is sovereign over history, revealing that the message of the Son represents the culmination and fulfillment of the OT. He is the God who sits on the throne (Heb. 4:16; 8:1; 12:2). A series of warning passages admonish the readers that they will face God's judgment if they return to the revelation transmitted through Moses instead of persevering in faithfulness to Christ (Heb. 2:1–4; 3:12–4:13; 5:11–6:12; 10:26–31; 12:25–29). The same God who judges apostasy will also judge those who practice sexual immorality (Heb. 13:4). His judgment is not arbitrary or unfair but rather just and righteous (Heb. 6:10). Human beings should hold God in awe and reverence because he "is a consuming fire" (Heb. 12:29). Falling into the hands of the God who inflicts his vengeance on those who abandon him is terrifying (Heb. 10:27–31). His word pierces swiftly and penetratingly, and no human being can hide from the creator God. Hence humans must continue to trust in God if they wish to avoid the sword of judgment (Heb. 4:12–13).

God Fulfills His Promises

As the creator of all things (Heb. 3:4), the living God has subjected the world to Christ (Heb. 2:8); God possesses the power to raise the dead (Heb. 11:19), just as he raised Jesus Christ (Heb. 13:20); and he has promised to establish a heavenly city in the future (Heb. 11:10, 16; 12:22). He will shake the world in the future so that his kingdom is established and the wicked are removed from the scene (Heb. 12:26–28). God's promises cannot fail, since God cannot lie, and he even certified the surety of his promise to Abraham by taking an oath (Heb. 6:13). The readers will be able to go on to maturity only if God grants permission (Heb. 6:3). Believers who are brothers and sisters of Jesus Christ were given to Christ by God himself (Heb. 2:13). Indeed, God is the one who sanctifies them, setting them apart to do his will (Heb. 2:11; cf. 10:14).

This God of salvation and judgment is the one "for whom and through whom all things exist" (Heb. 2:10). In other words, all human beings are to live to honor him.[77] They are to praise his name and do good because these are the sacrifices that bring him pleasure (Heb. 13:15–16). Human beings please God by trusting in him and believing in his existence (Heb. 11:5–6). The author of Hebrews often clarifies that trusting in God and obeying God cannot be sundered from one another, though the latter is rooted in the former (cf. Heb. 3:12, 18–19; 4:2, 6; 10:35–11:40). Those who trust in God will find him to be one who rewards such trust (Heb. 11:6). Noah found that he was spared from destruction (Heb. 11:7). Abraham and the patriarchs were promised a better country and homeland (Heb. 11:10–16). All looked forward to the fulfillment of the promise that has come in Jesus as the crucified and risen one. Those who turn away from Christ cut themselves off from the very reward that will be enjoyed by Abraham, Moses, and all the heroes of the faith whom they venerate. The Lord is a strong helper who will sustain his people in difficult times, because he will never leave or forsake his own (Heb. 13:5–6).

James

The letter of James is a letter of exhortation that hails from Jewish Christianity. In contrast to some canonical writings, much more is said about God than Christ. The parenetic style of James precludes a philosophical or abstract discussion of the character of God. James speaks of God insofar as he relates to the daily life of believers. He says nothing

---

77. Peterson (1982: 56) argues that the verse points to God's sovereignty and the truth that he acts according to his character. Compare the comments of P. Hughes 1977: 98. Indeed, it reminds us of how Paul speaks of God (e.g., Rom. 11:36 [so Michel 1966: 147]).

about God that would surprise anyone rooted in OT piety. The oneness of God is assumed (James 2:19), though James warns his readers that assent to such is scarcely sufficient, since even demons recognize this truth. In a letter that concentrates on the responsibility of believers, we expect the theme of God's judgment. He is the eschatological judge who will exalt poor believers and humiliate rich unbelievers, for the rich oppress God's people and revile God's name (James 1:9–11; 2:6–7; 5:1–5). God will show mercy as the end-time judge only to those who show mercy to those in need (James 2:12–13). Hence, if believers cast their lot with rich unbelievers, they reveal their antagonism to God. If the rich revile God's name and will be judged for their behavior, then it follows that believers are to honor God's name, particularly by their godly lifestyle. The joy of praising God as Lord and Father is intimated in James 3:9.

The churches that James addressed clearly were facing difficulties, especially in the financial realm. They were tempted to fawn on the rich and to court friendship with the world to gain economic security. James sternly warns them that God tolerates no rivals, echoing the OT prophets who warned Israel against the sin of harlotry. Those who angle to receive the commendation of the world set themselves in opposition to God. God must be supreme in their hearts. They must submit to God as Lord and draw near to him to receive strength (James 4:7–8).

In the midst of their sufferings believers apparently doubted God's beneficence. James therefore exhorts them by calling attention to God's goodness. If they need wisdom, God is the source of all wisdom, and he grants his gifts to people generously and gladly, not grudgingly (James 1:5). Perhaps James thinks particularly of God's saving love bestowed on his people. Therefore, James summons his readers to trust in God's goodness, to put their faith in his love for them (James 1:6–8).

The theme in James 1:12–18 is remarkably similar. In the midst of trials the readers apparently were inclined to think that God was tormenting and tempting them. James assures them that God does not lure human beings into sin (James 1:13). God finds evil utterly repulsive, and so he would never entice humans to sin. Sin finds its origins in the complex and twisted desires of human beings (James 1:14). Believers will not trust God in their trials unless they are convinced of his goodness and love. James teaches that "every good gift and every perfect gift is from above" (James 1:17). They can cling to God in the midst of life's pressures because he longs to bless them. His goodness is reflected in both the old creation and the new creation. He is the "Father of lights" (James 1:17). James probably alludes here to the creation of the sun, moon, and stars in Genesis, even using the term "lights" from Gen. 1:15–16.[78] The loveliness of the sun, moon, and stars testifies to God's beauty, and perhaps there is also the idea that the food that sustains us is a gift of God.

The meaning of James 1:18 is debated, but it seems that James reflects here on the new creation. The "word of truth" refers to the gospel, by which God begets believers as his children.[79] This interpretation matches with James 2:5, where God's election accounts for believers being rich in faith. James maintains, then, that the new life that believers enjoy is the result of God's gracious action on their behalf. He gave them birth, so to speak, and chose them to be his children. He has implanted his word in their hearts (James 1:21), so that the work promised in the new covenant has become a reality in their lives. Laato says, "The free grace of God never leads to a permission to libertinism, but an enablement to fulfill God's will."[80] Since James is a parenetic work, it does not elaborate on the salvation provided by God. Nevertheless, we have glimpses of the truth that God saves his people because of his mercy and grace. He has lavished his generosity upon believers, and so they should rely upon him during their stressful times. Finally, James 1:17 emphasizes that God is unalterably good. He is not changeable—one day generous and the next day stingy. His character remains the same. He does not vary from season to season or year to year.

The letter of James, then, highlights God's just judgment and his generous goodness. Both themes are included so that believers will not depart from God but instead will put their trust in him. Those who side with rich oppressors will face God's righteous anger and judgment, while those who persevere in faith and good works will enjoy God's generosity and goodness.

1 Peter

The letter of 1 Peter, like James, hardly contains a complete exposition or treatise about God, since Peter also writes with the assumption that the OT revelation about God has already been accepted by the readers.[81] Peter addresses believers suffering for their faith in Christ, encouraging them to persevere and maintain a witness by their good works in a

78. In support of this interpretation, see Laws 1980: 73; L. Johnson 1995: 196.

79. In defense of the view that James refers to creation rather than redemption, see Elliott-Binns 1956. Most commentators, however, believe that the new creation is in view. See, for example, Laato 1997: 48–49.

80. Laato 1997: 51. See also his comments on p. 52.

81. R. Martin (1994: 104–7) contends that in 1 Peter God is sovereign, Christ is the model believer, and God is the holy one who protects his own.

hostile world. His statements about God fit with the situation facing the churches in Asia Minor. He often emphasizes that God is sovereign and in control. The suffering of the churches is not pointless or beyond God's reach. It is not as if God stands idly by, frustrated by his helplessness while pagans afflict Christian believers. Instead, the suffering of those addressed accords with God's will (1 Pet. 3:17; 4:19). Peter does not offer here a full-orbed resolution of the problem of evil, but he does provide some help in considering the role of evil in the world. For instance, even though suffering is ascribed to God's will, unbelievers are still considered to be responsible for their mistreatment of believers. Therefore, they will face judgment on the last day (1 Pet. 3:16; 4:5, 18) unless they respond to God's patience and repent (1 Pet. 2:12; 3:20). They cannot exempt themselves from judgment by saying that they were instruments of God's will. The reality of human evil is affirmed, and the responsibility for it lies in the actions of human beings, so that God recompenses those who practice evil (1 Pet. 3:12). And yet the suffering of believers does not occur randomly or by chance. God rules over the world of human beings, even if a philosophical resolution of how God's sovereign rule fits with the genuine evil of human beings is not provided. Dominion and sovereignty belong to God forever (1 Pet. 5:11). He foreknew the time in salvation history when Jesus Christ would arrive (1 Pet. 1:20), and so the entire course of history is under his supervision and jurisdiction.

Believers are encouraged to place their trust (1 Pet. 4:19) and hope (1 Pet. 1:13; cf. 1:21) in God, knowing that he is sovereign over all things. They know that he is a God who lifts up the humble and debases the proud (1 Pet. 5:5), and so they can give to God all their worries and concerns (1 Pet. 5:7) because they are assured that he will vindicate them on the last day and grant them eschatological salvation (1 Pet. 1:3–9; 5:10). Believers live before a sovereign God and Father who will reward them on the last day (1 Pet. 3:10–12) and will judge them impartially (1 Pet. 1:17). God, therefore, is not to be trifled with but must be feared as the holy one (1 Pet. 1:17; 2:17). Believers must live holy lives in accord with the God who called them to himself (1 Pet. 1:15–16; 5:10). They are summoned to live for the will of God rather than the pleasures of this age (1 Pet. 4:2). They should live consciously in the presence of God in everything they do (1 Pet. 2:19).[82]

God can be trusted during suffering because of his sovereignty over all things. He foreknew from the beginning of time when Christ would come (1 Pet. 1:20). God's rule over all would not beget trust in him if he

---

82. The words of 1 Pet. 2:19 are directed to slaves, but many commentators remark that the admonitions to slaves here are paradigmatic for all readers. See, for example, Thurén 1995: 140; Brox 1986: 128.

were not also good. Tyrants may exercise absolute control, and yet they are only feared, not trusted or loved. God, on the other hand, can be trusted because he cares for believers (1 Pet. 5:7). Believers have been the recipients of his saving mercy (1 Pet. 1:3–9; 2:10), and so they know the wonders of his love. They were foreknown for salvation by God before the world was inaugurated (1 Pet. 1:1). As God chose Israel of old, so also he has elected believers to be his children, his elect sojourners in an evil world (1 Pet. 1:1). The church of Jesus Christ is the new people of God—the new Israel. They are God's "chosen race" and are his people now (1 Pet. 2:9–10). God has bestowed his grace upon them and called them to salvation (1 Pet. 5:10), and his calling has secured a response from his people. Believers have been born again through the word of the gospel (1 Pet. 1:3, 23).[83]

Peter communicates in a variety of ways that salvation is of the Lord: believers are God's elect, foreknown, chosen, and born-again. The reference to God's "mighty hand" (1 Pet. 5:6) alludes to the exodus, where God delivered his people from Egyptian bondage (e.g., Exod. 3:19; Deut. 4:34; 5:15; 6:21). The salvation given in Jesus Christ is the new exodus, to which the Egyptian liberation pointed (cf. 1 Pet. 1:10–12). Believers are guarded by God's power even now so that they will obtain eschatological salvation (1 Pet. 1:5).[84] In response, believers should bless and praise God for his extraordinary mercy and grace in their lives (1 Pet. 1:3). They should proclaim his excellencies in worship and evangelism (1 Pet. 2:9).[85] The God-centered vision of the rest of the NT is clearly present in 1 Peter as well.

2 Peter and Jude

We will examine the letters of 2 Peter and Jude together because both are brief, and the content of Jude overlaps significantly with 2 Pet. 2.[86] Both letters react to the presence of false teachers in the churches. In Jude the adversaries appear to have intruded from the outside (Jude 4),

83. Goppelt (1993: 81) remarks, "Even in anthropological perspective, the basis for being a Christian is not a decision or the appropriation of a commandment, but the second birth established in God's mercy, the manifestation of a new being."

84. Best (1971: 77) maintains that this verse implies that faith is the gift of God, for otherwise, "the reference to God's power" is "unnecessary and provides no assurance to the believer since what he doubts is his own power to cling to God in trial."

85. J. Elliott (2000: 439–40) contends that both worship and evangelism are in view. Many scholars think that Peter confines himself to worship (e.g., Michaels 1988: 100; Bechtler 1998: 158–59).

86. The literary relationship of Jude and 2 Peter is disputed. I agree with the consensus view, that 2 Peter draws upon Jude. See Schreiner 2003: 415–19.

whereas in 2 Peter they probably arose from within the congregation (2 Pet. 2:1). We lack a comprehensive description of the opponents in both instances, but it is clear that the adversaries were libertines who likely used the message of grace (perhaps distorting Pauline teaching [2 Pet. 3:15–16]) as an excuse for moral license. Therefore, one of the major themes in both letters is God's righteous judgment of sinners (Jude 4–16; 2 Pet. 2:3–16; 3:7, 10).[87] God is ever the holy one, and those who live dissolute lives will not stand in his presence on the eschatological day. The judgments on sinning angels, the flood generation, Sodom and Gomorrah, and Israel anticipate the final judgment that will be meted out by God on the false teachers and those who follow in their wake (Jude 5–7; 2 Pet. 2:4–6). The message of God's judgment, of course, is not novel; it is rooted in OT revelation where God judges those who despise him and fail to do his will. Both letters imply that God judges because he is righteous and just, so evil must be recompensed.

God's final judgment of evil cannot be separated from his sovereignty.[88] If God were not Lord, then he would lack the power to enforce his judgment. Peter particularly calls this fact to the readers' attention by reminding them of creation and the flood (2 Pet. 3:5–6). Both creation and the flood signify God's rule over the universe. He brought the world into existence initially by his word and through water. Similarly, water and the word were the means he employed to destroy the world through a cataclysm. The readers can be assured, then, that God is able to intervene in the world. Contrary to the false teachers who deny the future coming of the Lord (2 Pet. 3:4), the cosmos will not continue without interruption. The world is not independent of God but rather is subject to his will, even to his catastrophic interventions. Indeed, history will conclude with a fiery consumption of heaven and earth (2 Pet. 3:7, 10, 12) because God is the sovereign ruler of history.

Some scholars have become preoccupied with judgment in 2 Peter and Jude and have failed to see other themes, with the result that the letters too often have been seen as one-sided screeds against the false teachers. Both 2 Peter and Jude, however, feature God's grace as well. The grace of God frames Jude's letter, for he commences by reminding readers that they are called by God to be his children. God has specially set his love upon them, and they are protected and kept from the designs of the intruders by Jesus Christ himself (Jude 1). The letter concludes

---

87. So R. Martin 1994: 155–58.

88. Joubert (1998: 68) captures well the implications of God's judgment: "The actions of people, however contrary they seemed to appear to the divine will, were thus in no way outside the control of God. History has continued to run its predetermined course, in spite of various forms of evil and catastrophes. The false teachers in the midst of Jude's community will therefore also not interfere with the divine plan."

with a doxology (Jude 24–25) that returns to the theme of God's sustaining love. He is able to keep believers from succumbing to apostasy. Jude likely means by this that God *will* keep the readers from apostasy. Such a promise does not diminish the need for readers to keep themselves in God's love (Jude 21). The reference to God's love probably alludes to his saving work in calling believers to himself. Indeed, mercy, peace, and love flow into the lives of believers only from God himself (Jude 2). One of the main themes of Jude, then, is that God is the one who saves. He sets his love on believers and guards them from apostasy.

We see in 2 Peter that God speaks and declares his word in history. His voice sounded forth on the mountain when he declared his pleasure in Jesus as his beloved Son (2 Pet. 1:18). He has also spoken through the prophetic writings of the OT Scriptures (2 Pet. 1:19–21). The words of prophets were nothing less than the word of God himself. Paul's writings stem from wisdom given to him by God (2 Pet. 3:15–16), and therefore his letters are part of the inspired Scriptures. God is the creator of all (2 Pet. 3:5), and the earth was formed by his word. His spoken word is also the means by which he judged the world at the flood and will judge it by fire on the last day (2 Pet. 3:6–7). In fact, God's judgment of the ungodly emerges as one of the central themes in 2 Peter (esp. 2 Pet. 2). The judgment of the wicked reveals that God is the holy one who does not tolerate sin forever, though his patience (2 Pet. 3:9, 15) gives people the opportunity to repent and be saved. God's patience should never be interpreted as benign indifference, for just as he judged angels, the flood generation, and Sodom and Gomorrah, so also on the last day he will pass judgment against those who practice evil (2 Pet. 2:9). God's promises are sure because he never acts contrary to what he has pledged. Hence, Christ will return, and a new heavens and earth will come to pass because God has promised such (2 Pet. 3:8, 13).

God has set his favor upon Jesus as the Christ, as is evidenced by Jesus' transfiguration, where God bestowed honor and glory upon Jesus as his Son (2 Pet. 1:17). God is revealed, therefore, as the Father of the Lord Jesus Christ, and as the "Majestic Glory"—the awesome God of creation and redemption.

The theme of grace also informs 2 Peter. Those who believe do so because God has granted them the saving gift of righteousness that comes from Jesus Christ (2 Pet. 1:1). Most commentators argue that this refers to God's fairness and equity, but the term "righteousness" likely has an OT background referring to God's saving activity (e.g., Ps. 88:12; 98:2–3; Isa. 42:6; 45:8; 46:13; Mic. 6:5; 7:9).[89] Such an understanding fits with 2 Pet. 1:3–4, where everything that believers need for a godly life has been

---

89. For this view, see Schreiner 2003: 286–87.

granted to them. One of Peter's favorite words is "knowledge" (*epignosis*), and salvation is aptly described as knowledge of God (2 Pet. 1:2; cf. 1:3, 8; 2:20). God's love for his own is expressed in his election and calling of believers (2 Pet. 1:10). Election refers to God's choosing believers unto salvation, and calling likely refers to the grace that secures a believing response to the message of the gospel. God's love is also expressed in his preservation of believers. Peter introduces the example of Noah and Lot (2 Pet. 2:5–9) to underscore that God is able to preserve believers, even when they live in environments that are remarkably hostile to righteous living. He concludes, "The Lord knows how to rescue the godly from trials" (2 Pet. 2:9). The God of 2 Peter cannot be limited to thunder and lightning; he is also the loving one who sustains his people in the midst of the pressures that could cause them to turn away from the truth. God is the faithful one who will fulfill his promise regarding the coming of Christ. Prophecy comes from God, and so it is utterly reliable because God is true (2 Pet. 1:19–21). The apparent delay in the coming of Christ cannot be attributed to any change in God's plan. He reckons the passing of time differently than do human beings, since for him a day is like a thousand years, and a thousand years like a day (2 Pet. 3:8). Christ does not come immediately, giving time for those who need to repent, for God longs for all to repent so that they will not perish at the judgment (2 Pet. 3:9). The message proclaimed in 2 Peter here echoes Ezekiel. God does not take pleasure in the death of the wicked but desires that they repent and find life (Ezek. 18:23, 32). God is not only a God of judgment but also one who grants grace and peace and salvation (2 Pet. 1:2).

1 John

The letter of 1 John addresses a situation in which some have seceded from the church and apparently established a rival church (cf. 1 John 2:19). The believers remaining in the Johannine churches were troubled about the secessionists and struggled for assurance. They were plagued with doubts and wondered if those who seceded were the true church. John writes to assure and convince them that they truly know God (1 John 2:12–14; 5:13). John particularly emphasizes the goodness and love of God. The secessionists, perhaps under the influence of a kind of proto-Gnosticism, felt that they transcended any moral norms. Apparently they were convinced that sin was impossible for them (1 John 1:6–10),[90] and such a belief led to moral license and hatred for fellow believers (1 John

---

90. R. Brown (1982: 205–6, 212, 233–35) argues that 1 John 1:8 refers to the guilt of sin, and 1 John 1:10 to the claim that they have not sinned since their conversion. Smalley (1984: 28–29) is more convincing on 1 John 1:8 in saying that the secessionists claimed

2:3–6, 9–11; 3:4–10, 15–18; 4:8, 20; 5:2–3). John reminds his readers, as an antidote to the secessionists, that "God is light" (1 John 1:5). In the context of 1 John he means by this that God is holy, for John goes on to say in the same verse that there is no darkness in God. God is radiantly and beautifully good and unstained by any moral defilement. Hence, anyone who claims to know God and yet practices evil contradicts the profession of allegiance to God.

The love of God shines out as a central theme in the letter. God displayed his love supremely in the gift of his Son, Jesus Christ, who died on behalf of sinners and atoned for their sins (1 John 1:7; 2:2; 3:16; 4:9–10). John announces that "God is light" (1 John 1:5), and he also proclaims that "God is love" (1 John 4:8, 16). For John, the love of God is not an abstract attribute but is displayed in the sending of Christ and his atonement on the cross. John particularly emphasizes that believers did not take the initiative in loving God. They did not demonstrate their devotion to God with their piety and thereby merit his love. One of the characteristic themes in John's Gospel is that the Father sent the Son. The same theme is found in 1 John, and in every instance the Father sent the Son to bring salvation. God sent his Son so that human beings would enjoy new life (1 John 4:9). God sent him as an atoning sacrifice as a satisfaction for sins (1 John 4:10).

We should note here that God sent Jesus in love to appease his wrath. Theologians tend to find the notion that God's wrath is appeased as primitive and contrary to the God of love. It seems akin to pagan gods who are bloodthirsty, punitive, and vengeful. Certainly John does not communicate an arbitrary, whimsical, and quick-tempered God who lashes out in blind anger at human beings. He emphasizes that God sent his Son in love to satisfy his wrath. What we have here is a complex understanding of God. He is both loving and angry. His anger is rooted in his goodness and holiness, for "God is light" (1 John 1:5). But God in his love has sent Jesus to satisfy his own anger. We must be careful to preserve the mystery of God's person here, for we have no human analogies to one who has anger that is completely righteous and whose love satisfies his own anger. No neat equations or formulas adequately explain the reality portrayed. God's sending of his Son, however, eliminates any notion of a loving Son and a vengeful Father. It is the Father, after all, who "sent his Son to be the Savior of the world" (1 John 4:14).

Since the Father sent the Son, he has borne witness to the Son (1 John 5:9–12). He has revealed that eternal life can be gained only by believing in the Son. Hence, those who reject the Son have also rejected the

---

to be sinless or not to have a sinful disposition. Smalley (1984: 32–33) suggests also that 1 John 1:8 and 1:10 cannot be distinguished sharply from one another.

testimony and witness that comes from God himself. The message that John proclaims (1 John 1:1–5) is, after all, from God himself, so that those who reject the apostolic testimony cut themselves off from fellowship with both the Father and the Son (1 John 1:3).

Those who know God's love personally are his dear children and have experienced the wonder and joy of being the children of God (1 John 3:1–2). God poured out his love on them first, and any love that believers express toward God is a response to his love (1 John 3:16; 4:10, 19). One of the fundamental themes of 1 John is that God's love takes the initiative, so that human love is an answering love. Human love for God is always a response to God's love, which is demonstrated in the cross of Jesus Christ.

The priority of God's love is clearly communicated in texts that refer to being "born" (*gennaō*) of God. Because they are born of God, believers have stopped their previous practice of sin (1 John 3:9; 5:18). Only those who are born of God overcome the world (1 John 5:4). Those who show love to fellow believers do so because they have been born of God (1 John 4:7). Those who believe that Jesus is the Christ exercise such belief because they are born of God (1 John 5:1). The metaphor "born of God" indicates that new life from God secures right actions and beliefs. Those whom God has granted life practice righteousness, love, overcome the world, and believe in Jesus. John does not teach that people first show love and then are born of God, or that they are born of God after believing in Jesus; in every case he uses a perfect tense, so that being born of God precedes believing, loving, or overcoming the world. In this way the power of God's grace is communicated, so that every good thing performed by believers stems from God's work.

Those who do not love their brothers and sisters demonstrate that they have not experienced God's love (1 John 2:9–11; 3:13–18; 4:7–8, 20–21; 5:1–2). They are not truly in the circle of God's people, since abiding in love is an essential fruit of those who truly belong to God. Those who experience God's love are perfected in his love (1 John 2:5). Those who do not genuinely know God love the world and all that it offers rather than God (1 John 2:15).

For John, then, the Christian life means that one walks in the light and lives in love. Those who belong to God have a deep and profound love for God. He is the source of their joy and the longing of their hearts. John's theology is God-saturated and God-centered, for the new life can be characterized as fellowship with the Father (1 John 1:3). This fellowship with God can also be described as knowing the Father or knowing the one who is from the beginning (1 John 2:13–14). God is the beloved Father of those who are part of God's family. Doubtless the teaching of Jesus is reflected in saying that God is the Father of those who belong to Christ. The eternality of God and his sovereignty over all come to the forefront in the words "him who was from the beginning" (1 John 2:13). The God of light and love has always been and always will be. Knowing him and loving him is not a mere epiphenomenon of existence but rather is the portion of God's people forever.

Revelation

The book of Revelation is not a treatise on the last times, nor is it a detailed description of what will occur in the future. John addresses seven churches of his day in Asia Minor to encourage and strengthen them in the face of Roman persecution and in the temptation to compromise with their surrounding social world. The book of Revelation clearly belongs to the genre of apocalyptic literature, as is evident in the imagery, the use of symbolic numbers, and the emphasis on future vindication. John also characterizes the work as a prophecy (Rev. 1:3; 22:7, 10, 18–19). Here we lack the space to investigate the prophetic and apocalyptic dimensions of Revelation, but it probably is correct to designate the book as "prophetic-apocalyptic," so that the two categories are not separated from one another.[91] We must particularly remember that Revelation was written to the churches of John's day. The book still speaks to Christians today, but it was addressed originally to the churches in Asia Minor, and its message could be grasped by the original readers.[92]

John writes Revelation to encourage believers to persevere and conquer in the midst of their difficulties, especially the discrimination and persecution fomented by the Roman Empire (Rev. 2:7, 11, 17, 26–27; 3:5, 12, 21; 13:10; 14:12; 21:7). He also consoles the readers, assuring them that God will judge Rome and its empire—the new Babylon and the beast. They should take comfort, knowing that the joys of fellowship with God await them if they persevere (e.g., Rev. 7:15–17; 21:1–8). Revelation, then, does not depart from the rest of the NT in focusing on judgment. God's judgment of unbelievers, necessary as it is, prepares believers for the future day when they can enjoy God forever. The new heaven and earth are not described in terms of earthly joys. The language of the tabernacle finds its fulfillment in the presence of God with his people forever (Rev. 21:3). What believers will experience in the future is the radiant presence of God with them—so radiant that no other light is needed (Rev. 21:22–23; 22:5). No light or temple is needed in the heavenly city, for the temple always pointed to God's presence with

---

91. Ladd (1957) argues that there is no need to choose between prophecy and apocalyptic in NT eschatology, for the two are often conjoined. See also Beale 1999b: 37–43.

92. On the genre of Revelation, see Bauckham 1993a: 2–22; 1993b: 38–91.

his people, and even the light of the heavenly bodies anticipates the luminosity of God's presence.[93] Revelation terminates not with a word of judgment but with the fulfillment of God's covenantal promise that in the new creation he will be the God of believers and they will be his children (Rev. 21:7). Every tear and sorrow will pass away (Rev. 7:16–17; 21:4), for a new creation will be inaugurated.

We could say, then, that Revelation is radically God-centered.[94] The message of the book could be summarized in the angel's directive "Worship God" (Rev. 19:10; 22:9). Believers will serve in God's presence forever and experience the comfort of his sheltering love (Rev. 7:15). One of the prime reasons that God is worshiped and adored in Revelation is his sovereignty. John's message to a persecuted and afflicted church is that God reigns. God is designated in Revelation as the one "who is and who was and who is to come" (Rev. 1:4, 8; 4:8). In two texts he is said to be the one "who is and who was" (Rev. 11:17; 16:5). Here we have clear allusion to Exod. 3:14, where God reveals himself to Moses as "I AM WHO I AM" and with the words "I AM has sent me to you." Interpreters debate the proper translation of the Lord's revelation of himself in this verse,[95] but in any case, the reference is to Yahweh, the God who has made a special covenant with his people Israel. We see the same emphasis in Isaiah. Yahweh, in contrast to the false idols of Babylon, declares "I am he" (*egō eimi* [LXX: Isa. 41:4; 43:10, 25; 45:8, 18, 19; 46:4; 48:12; 51:12; cf. 45:22; 46:9; 48:17]). In fulfillment of his covenant he will liberate his people from Babylon and bring them back from exile.

The order of the words in the expression the one "who is and who was and who is to come" (Rev. 1:4, 8; 4:8) is significant. God is first designated as the one "who is" because he reigns now over all things, even over the beast that is the Roman Empire. He has not forgotten his covenant with his people, even though they are suffering. God is also the one "who was," for he is the everlasting God. His sovereignty is nothing new, for God has always ruled over history. Finally, we see the distinctive feature of Revelation. God is also the one "who is to come." He will fulfill his saving promises and pronounce judgment over those who resist his will. God has reigned over all of history, but that does not mean that there is no future dimension to his rule. His reign will be consummated and reach its desired goal when he comes. We noticed above that there are two texts that refer to God as the one "who is and who was" (Rev. 11:17; 16:5) but omit any reference to his coming. The context of these texts

---

93. For the theology of the temple in the entirety of Scripture and in Revelation, see Beale 2004.

94. Bauckham (1993a: 23) says, "The theology of Revelation is highly theocentric."

95. For a survey of interpretation, both ancient and modern, see Childs 1974: 50, 60–64, 85–87.

reveals the reason for the omission.[96] In both instances God's coming is now imminent. This is particularly evident in Rev. 11:17. When the seventh trumpet blows, the kingdom of the world has come to an end and the kingdom of the Lord and Christ commences (Rev. 11:15). God has "taken his great power and begun to reign" (Rev. 11:17). God's coming is no longer a future event but a compelling reality.

God is also designated as "the Alpha and Omega" (Rev. 1:8; 21:6) and "the Almighty" (Rev. 1:8; 4:8; 11:17; 15:3; 16:7, 14; 19:6, 15; 21:22). The words "Alpha and Omega" represent the first and last letters in the Greek alphabet, signifying that God reigns over all of history. This understanding is confirmed by Rev. 21:6, which immediately adds the words "the beginning and the end" to "Alpha and Omega." No segment of history elapses apart from God's rule. The term "Almighty" (*pantokratōr*) underscores God's dominion over all things as well. It may seem that Rome exercises control over history, but God is working his purposes out as the Almighty One.

The churches that John addressed likely felt small and weak and perhaps were tempted to see themselves as victims of powers beyond their control. In response, John constantly emphasizes God's supremacy over all things. Thus he regularly uses the term "throne" to designate God's power and rule (Rev. 1:4; 3:21; 4:2, 3, 4, 5, 6, 9, 10; 5:1, 6, 7, 11, 13; 6:16; 7:9, 10, 11, 15, 17; 8:3; 12:5; 14:3; 16:17; 19:4, 5; 20:11, 12; 21:3, 5; 22:1, 3).[97] Believers are motivated to persevere and are consoled about their present condition when they become convinced that their circumstances are under God's direction. He ultimately will judge their enemies and grant those who are faithful an eternal reward.

One of the key chapters in Revelation is chapter 4, where John is granted a vision of God on his throne. The God revealed to him, however, is too glorious to be seen by human eyes. His glory is compared to priceless gems that radiate with beauty (Rev. 4:3).[98] We have a clear allusion here to the vision of God in Ezek. 1:26–28, where Ezekiel sees the glory of the Lord and describes God in similar terms. Entering God's presence is fearsome because something like a massive thunderstorm blazes in his presence. The angels surrounding the throne echo the words of the seraphim in Isa. 6:3 with the words "Holy, holy, holy" (Rev. 4:8). The God on the throne is transcendent, terrible and beautiful in his holiness. The holy and sovereign one is the creator of all that is (Rev. 4:11). Indeed, he is the sovereign Lord precisely because he is the creator. The

96. Rightly Bauckham 1993a: 29. See also Caird 1966: 141; Beale 1999b: 613.

97. Bauckham (1993a: 31) sees God's throne as "one of the central symbols of the whole book."

98. God's splendor and transcendence are communicated by the vision (Bauckham 1993a: 32; Beale 1999b: 320).

one who brought all things into existence also determines the course of human history. The destruction of Babylon (which in John's context likely is Rome) by the beast and the ten kings is the work of God himself; he put it into their minds to destroy the great city (Rev. 17:16–17). For John, none of this is abstract theology, for the vision of God on his throne tears back the curtain on reality. The four living creatures and twenty-four elders fall down and worship in God's presence as he rules from his throne (Rev. 4:8–11). The worship given by the angels should be replicated by human beings. When humans see God in his holiness and recognize him as king, perceiving him in all his glory, they will be stunned into worshiping him as creator and Lord.

As we have noted already, one of the central themes of Revelation is that God should be worshiped. He deserves praise because salvation comes from him (Rev. 7:10–12). He is worshiped because he will accomplish his kingdom promises (Rev. 11:15–19), both in recompensing evil and in rewarding his servants. Revelation 12 indicates that God protects his people from Satan's attempt to destroy them (Rev. 12:13–17). Another way of describing conversion is to say that when people are saved, they give glory to God (Rev. 11:13; 14:7); they worship him as their creator and lord. Unbelievers worship the beast (Rev. 13:15), but those who know God refuse to succumb to economic pressure to bow before the emperor (Rev. 14:9–12).[99] Those who know God sing the same song of worship hymned by Moses in Exod. 15, declaring that God deserves praise for his saving deeds, his unutterable beauty, his justice, and his goodness (Rev. 15:3–4).

One of the pervasive themes in Revelation is that God judges the wicked. The God who rules over all and is the creator of all will righteously requite those who practice evil and resist his authority. Rome and the Roman Empire, depicted as the new Babylon and the beast respectively, wreak havoc upon God's people. The beast probably represents the military might of the Roman Empire, and Babylon represents its economic oppression.[100] "The harlot rides on the beast (Rev. 17:3), because the prosperity of the city of Rome at the Emperor's expense and her corrupting influence over the Empire rest on the power achieved and maintained by the imperial armies."[101] Revelation depicts the judgments that will be unleashed upon those who do not know God (Rev. 6:1–17; 8:1–9:21; 14:14–20; 15:1–16:21; 17:1–19:4; 20:11–15). The God who inflicts judgment and is the holy one is full of wrath because of the evil of human beings (Rev. 6:17; 11:18; 14:10, 19; 15:1, 7; 16:1, 19; 19:15). The holiness of God is expressed in the throne-room vision where "flashes

99. McKelvey (2003: 178) notes that what bothers John about Jezebel and her ilk is that idolatry is pervasive not only in the empire but also in the church.

100. R. Mounce 1977: 251; Bauckham 1993a: 35–36; Beale 1999b: 684–85.

101. Bauckham 1993a: 36.

of lightning, and rumblings and peals of thunder" (Rev. 4:5) emanate from God's presence. Similar language is used with the seventh seal, the seventh trumpet, and the seventh bowl (the imagery is remarkably similar to the theophany on Mount Sinai in Exod. 19:16–19):[102]

- Seventh seal: "there were peals of thunder, rumblings, flashes of lightning, and an earthquake" (Rev. 8:5)
- Seventh trumpet: "there were flashes of lightning, rumblings, peals of thunder, an earthquake, and heavy hail" (Rev. 11:19)
- Seventh bowl: "there were flashes of lightning, rumblings, peals of thunder, and a great earthquake . . . and great hailstones" (Rev. 16:18–21)

Is God an arbitrary and unjust judge? Does he pour out his judgments with a vindictive fury that is unwarranted and excessive? John emphasizes repeatedly that people deserve the judgments they receive. Human beings are judged not by an arbitrary standard but in accord with the works that they have done (Rev. 20:11–15). Before the bowl judgments are poured out, God is extolled as king because his ways are "just and true" (Rev. 15:3). The punishment meted out fits with the extent of the crime. Indeed, the judgments were designed to provoke people to repent, but people stubbornly refuse to change their ways (Rev. 9:20–21; 16:9, 11). Those who repent give glory to God, honoring his justice by admitting wrongdoing, but those who are recalcitrant reject and curse God (Rev. 16:8–11), for they hate any intrusion by him into their lives. They do not repent, because they desire to worship their idols rather than God (Rev. 9:20).

John seems sensitive to the question of whether the judgments are fair, for he interrupts the comprehensive bowl judgments with these words from an angel and from the altar: "For they shed the blood of saints and prophets, and you have given them blood to drink. It is what they deserve! . . . Yes, Lord God, the Almighty, true and just are your judgments!" (Rev. 16:6–7). Those who shed the blood of God's people now experience the sentence that they have earned. God's justice is not called into question by his judgments but rather is truly vindicated. Babylon, the "mother of harlots," has become drunk with the blood of God's holy ones (Rev. 17:6). She has raped other peoples in order to live luxuriously and sumptuously. God is merely repaying her for her sins that have reached as high as heaven (Rev. 18:5–6). Rome is judged not only for persecuting and killing believers but also for its military and economic exploitation.[103] Revelation 18:24 clarifies that Rome is held

102. Bauckham 1993a: 41–42; and see especially Bauckham 1977.
103. See Caird 1966: 223; Bauckham 1993a: 38–39.

responsible for murdering unbelievers as well: "And in her was found the blood of prophets and of saints, and of all who have been slain on earth." The judgment on Babylon culminates with an exclamation from a great multitude that God's "judgments are true and just" (Rev. 19:2), for the whore Babylon has infected the entire earth with her harlotry and shed the blood of God's people.

God's judgments, therefore, do not call into question his justice but rather express it. Therefore, the people of God respond to his judgments by praising and worshiping him. When Babylon, the wicked oppressor and corrupter of the earth, is destroyed, believers cry out "Hallelujah!" (Rev. 19:1, 3). The four living creatures and twenty-four elders, who probably are angelic beings, join the chorus with the words "Amen! Hallelujah!" (Rev. 19:4). God is worshiped for the righteous outpouring of his wrath and justice. His wrath does not diminish his glory but rather manifests it for all to see. The holy one does not tolerate evil. Those who blaspheme against God (Rev. 13:6) will not ultimately triumph. Bauckham rightly comments that Revelation can be regarded as an answer to the Lord's Prayer: "Our Father in heaven, hallowed be your name. Your kingdom come, your will be done, on earth as it is in heaven" (Matt. 6:9–10). Bauckham observes, "John and his readers lived in a world in which God's name was not hallowed, his will was not done, and evil ruled through the oppression and exploitation of the Roman system of power."[104]

Conclusion

Our survey of "God" in the NT reveals that he is foundational for NT theology. The God of the NT is not a new God; he is the God of the OT—the creator and redeemer. The promise of universal blessing given to Abraham and his descendants in the OT is fulfilled by this God. He is a God of love and mercy, so that he fulfills his saving promises to bless the whole world. He is the God who has revealed himself in Jesus Christ and offers salvation to all through the crucified and risen one. He is the sovereign God who rules over all of history, and hence the words that he has spoken are reliable and true. Because he is sovereign, he is able to fulfill his saving promises. At the same time, as the sovereign God, he judges those who practice evil, demonstrating that evil will not have the last word. All human beings are called upon to honor and worship the creator God. All their energy and strength are to be used to praise him, and God is particularly glorified when human beings trust him and therefore obey him.

104. Bauckham 1993a: 40.

5

❧ ❧

The Centrality of Christ
in the Synoptic Gospels

In the preceding chapter we explored the centrality of God in NT writings. Naturally, much of what is believed about God remains unexpressed or at least receives little elaboration, for the authors presuppose what the OT itself discloses about God. We have attempted to observe some of what is implicit and explicit in the NT discourse about God, while recognizing that no NT writer intends to provide a treatise on the subject. The God-centeredness of their vision is still apparent, even though they assume that readers are already acquainted with God as he is revealed in the OT.

The state of affairs is remarkably different when it comes to Jesus the Christ. He clearly takes center stage in almost every piece of NT literature, with the apparent exception of James. Does the pervasiveness of the Christ in the NT contradict or diminish God's supremacy? The answer is no, because Jesus is prominent as the one who fulfills God's saving and covenantal promises in the OT. Attention is fixed on Jesus in order to demonstrate that God has been faithful to what he pledged. Further, NT writers regularly teach that God sent Jesus Christ to bring glory to himself. The coming of the Christ does not diminish God's glory but rather enhances it. So the centrality of Jesus is in no conflict with the supremacy of God but instead makes it shine brighter.

The primacy of Jesus is so pervasive that even the keenest readers are likely to overlook some of what the NT says.[1] One way to consider the person of Jesus is by examining the titles ascribed to Jesus: Prophet, Messiah, Lord, Son of Man, Son of God, and so on. Each of these topics, of course, deserves a book in its own right, but clearly that is impossible here. I will not restrict this study to titles, for studies on Christology often concentrate exclusively on the titles given to Jesus and thus fail to communicate the richness and full-orbed picture of Jesus Christ in the NT.[2] This chapter is the first of many on the Christology of the NT, indicating the centrality of Jesus Christ in NT theology. And we must remember that even in these chapters we are scratching the surface, for the NT is clearly christocentric. In this chapter we will look at the centrality of Jesus in the Synoptic Gospels, but we will avoid the titles ascribed to Jesus and concentrate instead on other indications of Christ's supremacy. What D. Wenham says about Luke could be said about all the Gospels: "Luke's first and foremost theme is Jesus. This may be stating the obvious, but it is still worth saying."[3]

Debate on the Identity of Jesus

The preeminence of Jesus is so pervasively woven into the Synoptic Gospels that he is the prominent character throughout the narrative.[4] Jesus' miracles and words stirred up debate about his identity even among those who were not his disciples. Herod, plagued by fear and superstition, thought that Jesus was John the Baptist risen from the dead (Matt. 14:2 par.). Luke indicates that Herod's assessment was shared by others (Luke 9:7), indicating that public debate swirled around the identity of Jesus, for some thought that he was Elijah, Jeremiah, or even a new prophet (Matt. 16:14; Mark 6:15; 8:28; Luke 9:8, 19). Jesus' opponents, however, concluded that he was not sent from God. They identified him as Beelzebul, the ruler of demons, contending that he cast out demons by satanic means (Matt. 9:34; 12:24, 27 par.). The religious leaders probably argued from Deut. 13:1–3 that Jesus was a deceiver:[5]

1. The parables of Jesus also suggest an implicit Christology. See Blomberg 1990a: 316–23.

2. See the criticisms by Keck (1986: 368–70) of relying exclusively on titles.

3. D. Wenham 2005: 83. Wenham (2005: 84) goes on to say about Luke-Acts, "In both volumes, then, the good news of Jesus is central."

4. This is acknowledged by scholars who employ a narrative approach. For a sampling of such approaches, see Kingsbury 1983; 1986; Culpepper 1983. Culpepper's study is on the Gospel of John.

5. See C. Brown 1984: 313–14.

"If a prophet or a dreamer of dreams arises among you and gives you a sign or a wonder, and the sign or wonder that he tells you comes to pass, and if he says, 'Let us go after other gods,' which you have not known, 'and let us serve them,' you shall not listen to the words of that prophet or that dreamer of dreams. For the LORD your God is testing you, to know whether you love the LORD your God with all your heart and with all your soul." Jesus' miracles, according to the religious leaders, did not indicate that he came from God but rather were a test from God to discern whether Israel was truly faithful to him. We may add here that in John's Gospel too the Jewish leaders thought that anyone who followed Jesus was deceived and lacked an understanding of Torah (John 7:12, 47–49). After Jesus' death, he was described by the religious leaders as an "impostor" (*planos* [Matt. 27:63]). In later Jewish tradition Jesus continued to be rejected as one who aligned himself with the powers of evil and to be dismissed as a magician.[6] The standard criticism of Jesus by the religious authorities, then, was not that his miracles were phony but that they had an evil origin. No consensus, therefore, emerged on the identity of Jesus during his lifetime. We turn now, however, to the view of Jesus promulgated in the Synoptic Gospels. The goal here is not to be exhaustive but to sketch in the variegated picture of Jesus in the Gospels so that the centrality of Jesus is impressed upon the reader.

Fulfillment in Jesus

We begin with the theme of fulfillment in Matthew, but since I examined this theme in some detail earlier, the topic will be covered in a briefer form here, nor will the discussion be confined to the fulfillment formulae. We should remind ourselves at the outset that the fulfillment formulae encapsulate two major themes of this book: (1) God's saving promises are being fulfilled; (2) his promises are being fulfilled in the person of Jesus Christ.

Matthew opens with a genealogy (Matt. 1:1–17), emphasizing that Jesus is the son of David and the son of Abraham. Matthew constructs the genealogy in three segments of fourteen, probably to facilitate its memorization, since it is clear that he skipped some of the names that belong on the genealogical tree. Any Jewish reader would discern the significance of Jesus as David's son. If he is David's son, then he qualifies

---

6. See Davies and Allison 1997: 654. For further discussion of these traditions, see Meier (1991: 93–98), who maintains that they contribute no independent knowledge about Jesus of Nazareth in any case.

to be the Messiah, the anointed king promised in the OT. That Jesus is the son of David is surely the emphasis in the genealogy.[7]

Why does Matthew stress also that Jesus is Abraham's son? Abraham holds pride of place as the progenitor of the Jewish people, and the one with whom God entered into a covenant (Gen. 12:1–3; 15:9–21; 17:1–14). Matthew likely emphasizes here at the beginning of his Gospel that Jesus is the one through whom God's promise of universal blessing—a promise that will include the nations—is fulfilled.[8] This may be one of the reasons that women are included in the genealogy (Tamar, Rahab, Ruth).[9] Each of these women was not a native Israelite, and Matthew may have included them to indicate that Jesus fulfills what was anticipated in the OT: the blessing of all nations. If so, then Jesus' injunction to make disciples of all nations at the end of the Gospel (Matt. 28:19) frames the entire book. We note that this command is given because "all authority in heaven and earth has been given" to Jesus (Matt. 28:18). Clearly, God himself has delegated such authority to Jesus, and it is his intention that all peoples be blessed through him as the son of David and Abraham.

The distinctiveness of Jesus is demonstrated in his conception by the Holy Spirit, for what we have here is better described as a virginal conception than a virgin birth (Matt. 1:18, 20), though Matthew informs us that Mary remained a virgin until Jesus was born (Matt. 1:25).[10] Luke is the only other Gospel writer who speaks of the virginal conception (Luke 1:34–35), but the story there is told from Mary's perspective rather than

7. So R. Brown 1977: 85; Davies and Allison 1988: 156–57; Hagner 1993b: 9. I argued earlier that Jesus' speaking in parables (Matt. 13:35) in fulfillment of Ps. 78:2 also points to Jesus being the new David whom God raised up to shepherd his people (cf. Ps. 78:70–72).

8. Rightly Davies and Allison 1988: 158; Hagner 1993b: 9–10; Luz 1989: 113. R. Brown (1977: 68) tentatively endorses such a judgment.

9. See R. Brown 1977: 74. For a concise survey of options, see Davies and Allison 1988: 170–72; Luz 1989: 109–10; Nolland 2005: 73–77. Carson (1984: 66) rightly argues that the women may have been included for more than one reason, so that the themes of surprise, scandal, and Gentile inclusion are all in view. Hagner (1993b: 10) thinks that the women are chosen because they reflect "the abundant presence of both surprise and scandal in the Messiah's lineage." Luz (1989: 110) inclines to the view that Gentile inclusion is the purpose.

10. On the virginal conception, see R. Brown 1977: 517–33. For a critique of Brown's view, see Davies and Allison 1988: 200–201. For a vigorous defense of the virginal conception both historically and theologically, see Machen 1965. For a recent vigorous defense of a more succinct nature, see Carson 1984: 71–74. Hagner (1993b: 16) maintains that one cannot demonstrate that the virginal conception is historical, and yet it may be accepted as history for those who believe in God's interventions in history. Luz (1989: 123–27) supplies a useful history of interpretation, though he rejects the account historically.

Joseph's.[11] The significance of the son is relayed in the promise that "he will save his people from their sins" (Matt. 1:21). Matthew clearly thinks that this word is fulfilled in the death of Jesus, where his blood is poured out covenantally for the forgiveness of sins (Matt. 26:28; cf. 20:28).

The fulfillment theme in Matthew demonstrates that OT prophecy anticipated and pointed toward Jesus. He is the king of the Jews and the Messiah, for he was, as prophesied by Mic. 5:2, born in Bethlehem (Matt. 2:1–6). But he is more than a king, for he is virginally conceived, as Isaiah prophesied (Isa. 7:14), and hence he is also Immanuel, signifying that God is with his people in the person of Jesus (Matt. 1:22–23). At the same time, Jesus is the true Israel, for like Israel of old (Hosea 11:1) he was called out of Egypt (Matt. 2:13–15). Perhaps, as I argued earlier, Matthew uses this text to suggest that the new exodus promised in Hosea will be realized in Jesus of Nazareth.[12] Jesus succeeded, however, where Israel failed, for during Israel's forty years in the wilderness they succumbed to sin again and again. When Jesus was tested for forty days in the wilderness, however, he triumphed over Satan's temptations through the word of God (Matt. 4:1–11).[13]

The "new exodus" theme seems to surface again in the citation of Jer. 31:15 in Matt. 2:16–18. Herod's slaying of the children reminds the reader that Israel is still in exile, that the salvation promised in the new covenant has not yet arrived. At the same time, Matthew draws on the very chapter in which the new-covenant promise is contained (Jer. 31:31–34), indicating that hope survives, for the new-covenant promises of Jeremiah will be realized in Jesus. The promise of salvation for those shrouded in darkness sounds forth in Isa. 8:22–9:7, culminating in the son who will sit on David's throne and will defeat all enemies. Jesus is the heir to David's throne and is the great light who will dispel the darkness brought on by sin and exile (Matt. 4:14–16).

We saw earlier that the citation of Hosea 11:1 points to Jesus as the new Israel. We have a further suggestion of the same in Jesus' baptism where he submits to John's baptism "to fulfill all righteousness" (Matt. 3:15). Acceptance of John's baptism signifies Jesus' identification with his people, so that he is willing to take upon himself the judgment that Israel deserves. At the same time, Israel is often designated as the Servant of

11. That Luke relied on Mary as a source is vigorously criticized by R. Brown 1977: 35–37. For a credible response to Brown, see Carson 1984: 71.

12. Allison (1993: 195–96) maintains that Jesus' story is a story of a new exodus. Cf. Hagner 1993b: 36, 38.

13. "Thus Jesus, the embodiment of Israel and the fulfiller of all her hopes, repeats in his own experience the experience of Israel—with, of course, the one major difference, that whereas Israel failed its test in the wilderness, Jesus succeeds, demonstrating the perfection of his sonship" (Hagner 1993b: 62).

the Lord in Isaiah (Isa. 41:8–9; 44:1–2, 21; 45:4; 48:20; 49:3), and Jesus in Matthew's Gospel takes upon himself the vocation of the servant by suffering for the sake of his people (cf. Isa. 52:13–53:12). Jesus' healing ministry is cited as fulfilling the ministry of the Servant of the Lord, who bears the diseases of God's people (Matt. 8:14–17). Matthew also quotes a long citation from Isa. 42:1–4, in which Jesus as God's servant is anointed with the Spirit of the Lord and brings justice and salvation to the ends of the earth (Matt. 12:18–21). Hence, Jesus enters Jerusalem not on a war horse but meekly upon a donkey (Matt. 21:5–6; cf. Zech. 9:9), signifying that he has come to Jerusalem to die, not to wage war. To fulfill the Scriptures, Jesus submits to his arrest and forthcoming death instead of resorting to the sword (Matt. 26:50–56).

Matthew's emphasis on fulfillment indicates that Jesus is the true Israel who fulfills what God always intended when he chose Israel to be his people. He is the obedient Servant of the Lord who always does the will of the Father. He brings victory and freedom to his people not by waging war but by suffering in their place. His death is not an accident or a tragedy but fulfills the Scriptures and is the means by which God's saving plan is realized. Jesus is also the true and better David who fulfills the promises that a new David would come who would free Israel from exile and bring salvation to the ends of the earth. Jewish readers would see from Matthew's Gospel that Jesus' suffering and death as the Messiah did not contradict the Scriptures but actually fulfilled what they prophesied all along, and hence Jesus' death, instead of calling into question his messianic status, confirms it.

Jesus as the New Moses

Scholars debate whether Matthew depicts Jesus as the new Moses.[14] In my judgment, the theme is present but not particularly prominent. Still, there are some indications that Jesus is a new and superior Moses.[15] He ascends to the mount and teaches his disciples from there (Matt. 5:1), which is redolent of Moses receiving the Torah on Mount Sinai. Perhaps a Mosaic allusion is also intended at the conclusion of the Gospel where the disciples gathered on the mountain and were enjoined to make dis-

14. Allison (1993: 142) rightly argues that Jesus serving as the new Israel does not exclude the truth that he may have also been identified as the new Moses. The two are "correlative" instead of being mutually exclusive. France (1989: 186–89) rightly argues that the theme is not dominant and is usually subordinate to other themes.

15. See Longenecker 1970: 36; Hays 1996: 94–96. For a thorough examination of this theme, see Allison 1993. Space is lacking here to interact with Allison in detail, but in my view, he rightly sees the theme of Jesus as the new Moses, although he periodically over-interprets the evidence. Still, Allison's study is the indispensable resource on the topic.

ciples, but now the commands of Jesus (not the Mosaic law) should be taught to all (Matt. 28:16–20). Jesus is not just the mediator of the law but is "Immanuel" (Matt. 1:23), the one who is always with his people (Matt. 28:20). In what are often called "the antitheses," Jesus stands forth as the sovereign interpreter of the Mosaic law.[16] He authoritatively contrasts his commands with the interpretations proposed by the Pharisees and scribes ("You have heard that it was said" [Matt. 5:21, 27, 33, 38, 43] or "It was also said" [Matt. 5:31]) by declaring, "But I say to you" (Matt. 5:22, 28, 32, 34, 39, 44).[17] He sovereignly interprets the Mosaic law regarding divorce (Matt. 19:3–12; cf. Mark 10:2–12; Luke 16:18). Indeed, the law is fulfilled in Jesus himself (Matt. 5:17–20).

Just as manna was given to the people in the wilderness in Moses' day, so also Jesus miraculously provided food for the people in the feeding of the five thousand (Matt. 14:13–21; cf. Mark 6:32–44; Luke 9:10b–17) and of the four thousand (Matt. 15:32–39; cf. Mark 8:1–10).[18] Perhaps Matthew also compares and contrasts Jesus to Moses in the transfiguration scene (Matt. 17:1–9). We are told that Jesus' face shines, just as Moses' did (Exod. 34:29), and the presence of Moses and Elijah together may suggest that Jesus fulfills what the law and the prophets anticipated. Matthew emphasizes that after the transfiguration the disciples saw no one but Jesus, suggesting that he takes precedence over both Moses and Elijah (Matt. 17:8). Moses promised that a prophet would arise to replace him in the future (Deut. 18:15–22).[19] This coming prophet would speak God's word, and the people should pay heed to him.[20] We see a clear allusion to this text in the transfiguration scene, for Moses and Elijah appear and speak to Jesus, but Jesus is the focus of God's revelation. The divine voice enjoins the disciples present to listen to Jesus (*akouete autou* [Matt. 17:5; Mark 9:7; Luke 9:35]).[21] The allusion to Deut. 18:15 is clear, suggesting that Jesus is a new and better Moses.

Other parallels may exist. The Pharaoh of Moses' day and Herod the Great in Jesus' time attempted to kill children—Pharaoh every male Hebrew infant, and Herod all male children aged two and under (Exod. 1:15–16; Matt. 2:16–18).[22] Moses fled Egypt because Pharaoh desired

---

16. Allison (1993: 182) rejects the notion that we have antitheses here.

17. We will examine the antithesis again in chapter 16 on the law.

18. See Twelftree 1999: 77.

19. On the theme of Jesus as the prophet in the NT, see Cullmann 1963: 13–50; Dunn 1975b: 82–84. Wright (1996) especially emphasizes Jesus' role as a prophet.

20. Stettler (2004: 165) sees the parallel and says that Jesus' "instruction is to be seen on a level with God's commandments."

21. In Luke the word order is *autou akouete*. Most commentators agree that there is an allusion to Deut. 18:15 here (see Hagner 1995: 494; Nolland 2005: 704; France 2002: 355; Fitzmyer 1981a: 803).

22. For other possible parallels, see Allison 1993: 143–46.

to kill him (Exod. 2:15), and Jesus escaped from Israel because Herod intended to put him to death (Matt. 2:13–14). God instructed Moses to return to Egypt when those attempting to kill him had died (Exod. 4:19), and Joseph receives similar instructions about bringing Jesus back to Israel (Matt. 2:19–20). Jesus' birth, however, stands in contrast to Moses. Only Jesus is conceived by a virgin, and unlike Moses, he is "God with us" (Matt. 1:23).

Jesus is portrayed as a new and better Moses because all of God's promises are fulfilled in him. The prophet predicted by Moses (Deut. 18:15) is none other than Jesus. The law and the prophets point to Jesus. God's final and definitive word to his people is found not in the Mosaic law but in the words of Jesus Christ as the sovereign interpreter of the law.

Jesus as True Wisdom

The theme that Jesus is the true wisdom is related to his being the new Moses because, as we will see, God's wisdom manifests itself particularly in the Torah.[23] Perhaps Jesus identifies himself as the true wisdom when he invites people to come to him, promising that he will grant rest to those who do so (Matt. 11:28; cf. Sir. 6:26–28; 51:20–30). Matthew perhaps draws here on the view that wisdom is to be identified with Torah.[24] If so, Jesus is not only the true wisdom but also the true Torah, for instead of exhorting people to take up the yoke of Torah,[25] he urges them to take up his yoke, his instruction (Matt. 11:29).[26] They are to learn from him, for unlike the Torah, his "yoke is easy" and his "burden is light" (Matt. 11:30). Jesus' yoke stands in contrast to the Sabbath regulations of the Pharisees that immediately follow in the narrative (Matt. 12:1–14), which

23. Supporting the importance of wisdom Christology is Witherington 1990; 1994. Gathercole (2006: 193–209) is likely correct in saying that we should speak of wisdom motifs rather than a full-blown wisdom Christology. France (1989: 302–6) maintains that wisdom is a minor theme in Matthean theology. See Lee (2005: 37–62), who rightly argues that wisdom in the OT and in Second Temple Judaism can never be identified as a hypostasis, so that the exalted language sometimes used of wisdom is better designated as personification.

24. See the link between wisdom and Torah in the discussion on Sirach below.

25. For the notion of the yoke of Torah, see *m. 'Abot* 3:5. Sirach identifies wisdom as a yoke (Sir. 6:30; 51:26) and equates wisdom and Torah (Sir. 24:23).

26. It is common to see wisdom Christology in this text without necessarily claiming direct dependence on Sirach (see Hagner 1993b: 323; Luz 2001: 171–72). Carson (1984: 277–78), however, points out the differences between Jesus' invitation and the words of Sirach (Sir. 51:23–27). Nolland (2005: 475) sees "wisdom imagery" rather than "wisdom christology." Davies and Allison (1991: 295) argue that wisdom Christology plays a minor role in Matthew.

weigh heavily upon people. People will find rest for their souls when they come to Jesus instead of seeking it through the law.

Jesus' invitation to come to him recalls wisdom's public invitation to come to her for instruction (Prov. 1:20–33). The long invitation from wisdom in Prov. 8 is particularly important. She that was with God from the creation of the world invites human beings to come to her, to gain understanding, and to find life. She has built her house and prepared a feast to which all those who are foolish are invited (Prov. 9:1–12). Matthew's words (Matt. 11:28–30), as already noted, are also similar in some respects to Sirach's exhortation on wisdom (Sir. 6:26–28; 51:20–30). Sirach exhorts people to "come to her with all your soul" (Sir. 6:26) and "you will find the rest she gives" (*heurēseis tēn anapausin autēs* [Sir. 6:28]).[27] He explains that wisdom belongs to those who "reflect on the statutes of the Lord" (Sir. 6:37). Wisdom is a "yoke" (*zygon* [Sir. 51:26]), and people are to "draw near" (*engisate* [Sir. 51:23]) to her, for Sirach has labored little (*kopiaō*) and yet "found for myself much rest" (*heuron emautō pollēn anapausin* [Sir. 51:27 my translation]).[28]

The link between wisdom and Torah is evident in the saying "In all wisdom there is fulfillment of the law" (Sir. 19:20; cf. 21:11). Sirach 24 contains a discourse on wisdom in which, in dependence on Prov. 8:22–31, wisdom resides with God during the creation of the world. Sirach also highlights the special prerogative of Israel relative to wisdom. Of all the nations, only Israel received wisdom. We are not surprised, then, in this meditation on wisdom that wisdom and Torah are identified: "All this is the book of the covenant of the Most High God, the law which Moses commanded us as an inheritance for the congregations of Jacob" (Sir. 24:23).[29] The notion that wisdom finds its expression in Torah is rooted in the OT itself (Deut. 4:6). Already in Proverbs those who keep God's commands demonstrate their wisdom (Prov. 2:1–2; 3:1; 4:1–11; 6:20–23; 7:1–4).[30] According to Matthew, those who desire wisdom will come to Jesus. The Torah and wisdom point to Jesus, for he embodies both.[31] Those who are convinced that wisdom terminates in Torah are mistaken, for the law points to Jesus. No human being qualifies to be called a

27. Unless specified otherwise, all citations from Sirach are from the RSV.

28. Davies and Allison (1991: 293) see no dependence upon Sirach here and think that both texts "exhibit certain similarities because they both incorporate Torah and Wisdom motifs."

29. The convergence of wisdom and Torah is evident also in *m. 'Abot* 6:7.

30. The injunction to bind the father's teaching to oneself (Prov. 3:3; 6:21; 7:3) recalls the similar command regarding the Torah as a sign (Deut. 6:8; 11:18).

31. Luz (2001: 149–50 [but see his cautions]) and Hagner (1993b: 311) argue for a wisdom Christology in the saying in Matt. 11:19, but Carson (1984: 270–71) maintains that the reference is to God, and wisdom Christology cannot be read out of the text. See also Nolland (2005: 464), who perceives wisdom imagery but not wisdom Christology.

teacher, except the Christ (Matt. 23:10). He is the sovereign interpreter and fulfillment of the Torah as the Messiah. The superiority of Jesus is also reflected in his debate with the Pharisees, when he suggests that he is greater than Jonah and wiser than Solomon (Matt. 12:41–42; Luke 11:31–32).[32] The latter provides further evidence that Jesus is identified as true wisdom. That Jesus is the true wisdom is confirmed by the truth that the OT Scripture points to Jesus and is fulfilled in him. The law, the prophets, and the psalms, rightly understood, anticipate the coming of Jesus (Luke 24:44). Jesus opens the hearts of his disciples so that they understand that the Scriptures are about him (Luke 24:45).

Jesus as a Prophet

Jesus' role as a prophet[33] was acknowledged by some during his ministry and clearly was endorsed by the Synoptic writers.[34] When the people of Jesus' hometown doubted his legitimacy, he identified himself as a prophet, even though he was rejected by the very ones who should have recognized that he came from God (Matt. 13:53–58 par.). When the widow of Nain's son was raised from the dead, the people exclaimed that Jesus was a great prophet (Luke 7:11–17).[35] The crowds in Jerusalem hailed Jesus as a prophet near the end of his ministry (Matt. 21:11, 46), as did the two persons traveling to Emmaus (Luke 24:19).

Jesus displays his prophetic authority by his predictions that come to pass. He affirms the authority of his words, declaring that they will never pass away (Matt. 24:35 par.). He accurately predicts that Peter will deny him three times (Matt. 26:34 par.; John 13:38). Jesus' anticipation that Peter would deny him is remarkable, but what stands out is the specificity of the prediction, for knowing that Peter would make three separate denials cannot be attributed merely to a good knowledge of Peter's character. Identifying the exact number of denials is evidence of unusual prophetic authority. Jesus' self-claims, according to the Gospel writers, are vindicated by his resurrection from the dead, for he regularly predicted during his ministry his death and resurrection (cf. Matt. 16:21; 17:22–23; 20:17–19 par.).[36] He foresaw that as a prophet he must die in Jerusalem (Luke 13:33), and he interpreted the sign of Jonah as

32. So Hagner 1993b: 355.

33. On Jesus' status as a prophet, see Schnider, *EDNT* 3:184–85; Peisker, *NIDNTT* 3:83. Both emphasize that Jesus was a prophet but much more than a prophet.

34. Wright (1996) in particular emphasizes that Jesus was a prophet.

35. For the theme that Jesus is the prophet in Luke, see Tannehill 1986: 96–99; Fitzmyer 1981a: 213–15.

36. Luke 9:44 lacks reference to Jesus' death and resurrection.

relating to himself, discerning in it a promise of his own resurrection (Luke 11:29–30).

Jesus also demonstrated his prophetic stature in his ability to know the thoughts of others. When he declared to the paralytic that his sins were forgiven, he knew that the scribes and Pharisees were convinced that he was blaspheming (Matt. 9:2–5 par.). Simon the Pharisee was convinced that Jesus could not truly be a prophet because he allowed a sinful woman to touch him, apparently revealing that Jesus did not know her sinful character (Luke 7:39). Jesus, however, revealed that he was truly a prophet, for the parable of the two debtors that immediately follows (Luke 7:40–43) indicates that Jesus knew Simon's objection and read his mind, and hence Jesus was truly a prophet. Jesus realized the woman's sinfulness, and even more striking, he knew that Simon saw himself as righteous and hence did not think he needed forgiveness for sin. Similarly, when Jesus' opponents queried him about paying taxes to Caesar, Jesus realized that the question was inauthentic, stemming from their malice toward him (Matt. 22:18 par.). Indeed, Jesus' ability to know the thoughts of others so regularly suggests that he is more than a prophet, but certainly he is not less than a prophet.[37]

Jesus' prophetic authority is reflected particularly when he entered the temple and expelled those selling and buying, enraged that God's house had been turned into a marketplace (Matt. 21:12–13 par.).[38] Some scholars detect here a prophecy of the temple's destruction, so that this event led to the death of Jesus.[39] Others claim that the cleansing does not portend the temple's destruction. They contend that Jesus, like the prophets of old, indicted the religious authorities (and perhaps the people as well) because they violated God's will.[40] Both interpretations are compatible. Even in Israel's past history the corruption of the people contributed to the destruction of the temple, and so too here. The religious authorities took umbrage over Jesus' actions and inquired how he could exercise such authority (Matt. 21:23). The same kind of authority manifests itself in Jesus' cursing of the fig tree (Matt. 21:19–21

37. See Marcus 2000: 222; Gathercole 2006: 70–71.

38. Note that the crowds identified Jesus as a prophet immediately before the cleansing of the temple (Matt. 21:11).

39. See E. Sanders 1985: 61–76; Wright 1996: 490, 551, 644; cf. Stuhlmacher (1993: 30–31), who sees a messianic claim in the temple cleansing. Stein (2001: 215) objects that the temple cleansing is not even mentioned at Jesus' trial, so that evidence is lacking that the temple cleansing was perceived as a messianic claim or action. For a different reading of the evidence, see France 2002: 437.

40. Evans (1989) argues that Jesus' action was not a portent of the temple's destruction (see also Hooker 1991: 262–66). Davies and Allison (1997: 135–36) probably are correct in arguing that both views are compatible, for the temple will be destroyed partly because of the corruption present in it.

par.; cf. Luke 13:6–7). Clearly, the fig tree represents Israel (cf. Hosea 9:10), and Jesus curses the nation because of its lack of fruit, probably forecasting the destruction of Jerusalem in AD 70.[41] The symbolism of the cleansing of the temple and the cursing of the fig tree recall prophetic symbolism and the judgments that the prophets threatened against Israel and Judah. The prediction that Jerusalem and the temple would be destroyed within a generation (Matt. 24 par.) was highly significant, and the fulfillment of these prophecies verified Jesus' prophetic status, although, of course, by AD 70 it was clear to believers that Jesus was more than a prophet.

Jesus, then, demonstrated that he was a prophet both by his words and by his actions. He predicts the future infallibly, as did the prophets of old, knows the thoughts of his opponents, and demonstrates by his authoritative actions his prophetic stature. When we add to this the evidence noted above about Jesus serving as the new Moses, then the divine voice on the mountain sums up well the message of the Synoptic Gospels. Disciples are to listen to Jesus (Matt. 17:5; Mark 9:7; Luke 9:35; cf. Deut. 18:15) as God's final and definitive prophet.

The authority of Jesus transcends that of all the prophets who preceded him. No OT prophet called people to himself the way Jesus did. Jesus reflects his authority in saying, "Follow me, and I will make you fishers for men" (Matt. 4:19 par.; cf. Luke 5:10; Matt. 9:9). Jesus is God's final prophet, but he is more than a prophet. In the parable of the vineyard (Matt. 21:33–46 par.), he is the last in the line of God's messengers, and yet he is not merely the final prophet but is also the son of the vineyard owner.[42] Jesus takes it upon himself to declare that John is the greatest of the prophets but least in the kingdom, and that John is Elijah who will precede the coming one (Matt. 11:10–11, 14; Luke 7:27–28). But Jesus is greater than John because John merely baptized with water, whereas Jesus will baptize with the Holy Spirit, bringing in the promised age to come (Matt. 3:11 par.; cf. John 1:33).

The Revelation of Jesus in His Miracles and Exorcisms

The Synoptic Gospels feature Jesus' distinctiveness in his miracles, exorcisms, and raising of the dead. The uniqueness of Jesus' person is evident in the healing of the leper (Matt. 8:1–4 par.). Jesus does not contract uncleanness in touching a leper, unlike what we would expect

41. Rightly Hagner 1995: 605–6; Davies and Allison 1997: 151–52; Luz 2005: 23; Nolland 2005: 852. Contra Carson (1984: 445–46), who restricts the message to a cursing of hypocrites.

42. That Jesus is the son in the story is obvious (rightly France 2002: 460–61).

from reading the OT. On the contrary, his touch overcomes the un-cleanness of the leper and restores him. The uncleanness of the leper is not contagious when Jesus touches him; instead, Jesus' cleanness, so to speak, is contagious.[43] As Davies and Allison observe, Jesus does not pronounce that the healing is God's will, but that it is his.[44] In the same way, the healing ministry of Jesus highlights his distinctive-ness (Matt. 4:23–25; 8:16; 9:35; 15:30–31; 19:2; Mark 1:32–34; 3:7–12; 6:53–56; 7:37; Luke 4:40–41). The text in Matt. 15:30–31 is instructive, for Jesus' healing ministry causes people to glorify the one God, the God of Israel. Mark places the exorcism of a demon near the begin-ning of his Gospel to demonstrate Jesus' authority (Mark 1:21–28; cf. Luke 4:31–37). The demon recognizes Jesus as "the Holy One of God" (Mark 1:24 par.).

Mark presents in some detail another account of an exorcism (Mark 5:1–20 par.).[45] The text emphasizes the hopelessness of the man in question. He wandered about cemeteries and mountains, could not be restrained by fetters, used stones to self-inflict physical damage, and was beset by great misery. The reader discovers that a legion of demons inhabit the man. The drowning of two thousand pigs verifies in the story that Jesus genuinely delivered the man from a multitude of demons, for the suicidal behavior in the pigs occurred after Jesus releases the demons to enter into the pigs.[46] The account fixes atten-tion on Jesus. Indeed, a remarkable parallel between the work of God and that of Jesus concludes the narrative (Mark 5:19–20; Luke 8:39).[47] Jesus instructs the man to declare to what "the Lord has done for you," but the man spreads the good news of what "Jesus had done for him." The same juxtaposition and overlap of the work of Jesus and of God appears in the story of the healing of the ten lepers, one of whom returns to give thanks (Luke 17:11–19). The one Samaritan who was cleansed praises God, but at the same time he gives thanks to Jesus (Luke 17:15–18). Apparently, giving thanks to Jesus and praising God

43. Stettler (2004: 160n21) rightly argues that the story here is quite remarkable be-cause "in the Old Testament, only impurity and holiness are 'active' in the sense that they can expand their realms; purity and profanity are passive. They do not expand." But the holiness of Jesus is contagious, so that when he touches a leper, instead of Jesus becoming unclean, the leper is inducted into the realm of the holy (Stettler 2004: 159–61).

44. Davies and Allison 1991: 14.

45. As is typical in Matthew, the story is remarkably abbreviated. Also, Matthew recounts the exorcism of two men instead of one.

46. "The destruction of the pigs perhaps indicates the destruction of the unclean spirits and certainly underlines the cure of the demoniac" (Hooker 1991: 141). See also Marcus 2000: 351.

47. See Hooker 1991: 145–46; Marcus 2000: 354; France 2002: 233; Fitzmyer 1981a: 740.

are not in conflict.[48] Indeed, God is praised and glorified when human beings give thanks to Jesus.

The astounding work of Jesus is featured when he raised Jairus's daughter from the dead. In all three Synoptics the story of the healing of the woman who had been hemorrhaging for twelve years is juxtaposed with the raising of the young girl (Matt. 9:18–26 par.). As usual, Matthew abbreviates the story, and the fullest account is in Mark. It seems that the two accounts are intended to be interpreted together. The girl is twelve years old, and the woman has suffered from the affliction for twelve years. Both are hopeless cases, for the woman has a chronic deteriorating condition that baffles physicians, and the young girl is deceased. In both instances the person is restored by Jesus' touch, and faith in Jesus is the pathway to healing and life. The Gospel writers compel their readers to ask, Who is this person who can heal intractable diseases and raise the dead?

When a storm assailed the Sea of Galilee, Jesus exercised his authority over the recalcitrant wind and waves as well. He speaks the word, and the storm instantly subsides (Matt. 8:23–27 par.).[49] Indeed, he rebukes the storm with the same imperious authority with which he expels demons. In the OT only Yahweh triumphs over a stormy sea. When a storm threatened the lives of sailors, and they despaired of life, the Lord delivered them from the tempest (Ps. 107:23–32). "He made the storm be still, and the waves of the sea were hushed" (Ps. 107:29; cf. Job 9:8; Ps. 65:7; 77:19; Isa. 43:16; 51:9–10; Hab. 3:15).[50] The disciples recognized the numinous power of Jesus in quieting the storm and rightly exclaimed, "Who then is this, that even wind and sea obey him?" (Mark 4:41; cf. Matt. 8:27; Luke 8:25).[51] A similar miracle takes place in Jesus' walking upon the sea (Matt. 14:25; Mark 6:48; cf. John 6:19). Again this hearkens back to Yahweh, who walks upon the sea (Job 9:8 LXX; cf. Ps. 77:19; Isa. 51:9–10; Hab. 3:15), which emphasizes God's uniqueness in doing so.[52] In this instance we have a convergence of Matthew, Mark, and John, for in each account when the disciples are filled with terror, Jesus replies with the exact same words: *egō eimi, mē*

48. "The glorification of God expresses itself in gratitude to Jesus. . . . Only here in the NT is thanks expressed to Jesus; it is addressed elsewhere to God himself" (Fitzmyer 1985: 1155).

49. See Davies and Allison 1991: 75. See also the helpful discussion in Gathercole 2006: 61–63.

50. A number of parallels to the story of Jonah at sea exist as well (see Davies and Allison 1991: 70).

51. For the view that Jesus' divinity is revealed here, see Marcus 2000: 432; Hurtado 2003: 286.

52. See Davies and Allison 1991: 504; Twelftree 1999: 78; and especially the insightful discussion in Meier 1994: 914–19.

phobeisthe ("I am; do not fear" my translation). In John's Gospel the words "I am" almost certainly hearken back to Exod. 3:14 and to texts in Isaiah that refer to the one and only God (e.g., Isa. 41:10; 43:10, 45:18). Given John's Christology, it is clear that Jesus is considered to be God (John 1:1). Scholars debate whether "I am" has the same significance in the Synoptics, but it seems that the antecedents in Isaiah point us in that direction.[53] If so, then the disciples are rebuked in Mark for failing to see Jesus' divine identity.[54]

Jesus as the Culmination of God's Revelation

Redemptive history culminates with the coming of Jesus. The law and the prophets find their fulfillment in him. We see this in a debate over Sabbath regulations where Jesus notes that the priests minister in the temple on the Sabbath and do not commit an infraction (Matt. 12:5). He then justifies his healing on the Sabbath with the claim, "Something greater than the temple is here" (Matt. 12:6).[55] The significance of the claim becomes evident when we consider the prominence of the temple in Jewish life. A saying of Simeon the Just states, "By three things the world is sustained: by the Law, by the Temple-service, and by deeds of loving-kindness" (*m. 'Abot* 1:2). The Markan and Lukan accounts omit Jesus' saying about the temple (Mark 2:23–28; Luke 6:1–5), and perhaps it is included in Matthew because Matthew especially addresses Jewish concerns. Still, all the accounts say that Jesus is the Lord of the Sabbath (Matt. 12:8 par.), and only one who has divine status could function as Lord of the Sabbath.

In Jesus' controversy with the religious leaders he recounted the parable of the tenants in the vineyard (Matt. 21:33–46 par.). What is noteworthy in this account is that Jesus identifies himself as the culmination of God's revelation to his people.[56] He is the son who was sent after the slaves were summarily rejected. The parable also

53. The "I am" formula in Mark 6:50 has an absolute meaning and conveys Jesus' power over the sea, just as Yahweh is sovereign over the sea (C. Williams 2000: 214–24; Harner 1970: 34–35; Lane 1974: 237; contra France 2002: 273n71). C. Williams (2000: 219–23) sees a number of similarities between the account in Mark and Exodus traditions and Isa. 40–66. For the Johannine "I am" sayings, see chapter 7 in this book.

54. So Twelftree 1999: 78.

55. The something greater probably is Jesus (Davies and Allison 1991: 314), though Carson (1984: 282) sees it as Jesus and the kingdom that he is inaugurating. Contra Luz (2001: 181–82), who sees the greater thing as mercy. The emphasis by Hagner (1993b: 330) on the ministry of Jesus fails to put sufficient emphasis on the role of Jesus himself.

56. Hooker (1991: 276) wrongly de-emphasizes the reference to Jesus here in the original telling of the story. For a more convincing analysis, see Hagner 1995: 619–20.

suggests his ultimate vindication, for despite being rejected by the leaders, he will become the cornerstone of God's building (Matt. 21:42 par.; cf. Ps. 118:22), presumably the foundation stone of God's new temple—the new people of God. Indeed, Jesus is the stone that will crush all those opposed to him and to God (Matt. 21:44 par.).[57] The parable of the invitation to the wedding feast (Matt. 22:1–14) yields the same conclusion. The wedding feast points to the eschatological consummation of God's purposes—the messianic banquet of the last day (Isa. 25:6–8). What we should notice here is that the feast is celebrated in honor of the father's son, and in Matthew there is no doubt that this is Jesus himself. We note again that in the teaching of Jesus, the Father himself desires to have a wedding feast for his Son. The Father is not dishonored by the Son and plans to bestow honor on the Son at the eschatological banquet. Further, Jesus takes on God's prerogative and laments that he longed to gather Israel as a hen gathers her chicks under her wings (Matt. 23:37 par.), and he looks forward to the day when Israel will pronounce a blessing over his coming (Matt. 23:39 par.).

Jesus' Supremacy in Calling People to Discipleship

The stature of Jesus is indisputable in that he calls others to be his disciples, and in calling them he asserts his authority in a remarkable and distinctive way. Jesus commences his ministry by calling some to be his disciples (Matt. 4:18–22 par.). What is remarkable is that Jesus summons the disciples to follow him and does not merely say that they should be devoted to God. The available evidence indicates that rabbis did not summon others to follow them.[58] Instead, would-be disciples sought rabbis out and asked to serve as their disciples. Jesus, however, took the initiative in calling others to be his disciples, and he did not ask if they wanted to follow him. He sovereignly and authoritatively called them to do so. Further, he speaks of his own power, promising them that he would grant them the ability to fish for people. He does not envision a time, as did the disciples of the rabbis, when they would graduate and, in turn, attract their own students.[59] Disciples are called upon to follow Jesus literally and to leave their families. When would-be followers declare their intention to become Jesus' disciples, he does not reply that they should only follow God (Matt. 8:19–22; Luke 9:57–62;

---

57. This saying is not present in Mark.
58. See Meier 2001: 52–54.
59. See Meier 2001: 54–55.

14:25–33);[60] rather, he emphasizes the difficulty of following him and the cost of discipleship.

Jesus must have supremacy even over one's family—a startling message for the culture of Jesus' day, for other rabbis did not require people to leave their families.[61] Nor did others make the kind of shocking declaration that we find in Jesus' teaching: "Whoever loves father or mother more than me is not worthy of me, and whoever loves son or daughter more than me is not worthy of me" (Matt. 10:37).[62] No title is used to indicate Jesus' status here, but we do have a high Christology. The response to Jesus is the central question of all of history. Jesus also proclaims that he came not to bring peace but division. Even family members will split over their allegiance to Jesus (Matt. 10:34–36; Luke 12:51–53), and the division will not stop with families. Jesus envisions that "all nations" will hate his disciples for his sake (Matt. 24:9; Mark 13:13; Luke 21:17).

When Jesus' family sought to speak to him, he asked who his mother and brothers were (Matt. 12:46–50; Mark 3:31–35; cf. Luke 8:19–21; 11:27–28).[63] He then declared that those who do the Father's will should be counted as his brother, sister, and mother. The distinctiveness of the saying is that those who obey the Father are considered to be part of *Jesus'* family. Jesus could have said that they are reckoned to be part of the family of God, but the saying indicates Jesus' unique relationship with God and suggests that all those in a right relation with God are members of Jesus' family.

Jesus' authority is evident when he declares, "I came not to call the righteous, but sinners" (Matt. 9:13; Mark 2:17). Luke adds that Jesus came to call sinners to repent (Luke 5:32). Jesus does not merely speak in God's name; he himself summons human beings to renounce their sins, suggesting his unique role and stature as the one whom God sent. Jesus also insists that people must be willing to take up their cross and to die in following him (Matt. 10:38–39 par.). He says that those who give up their lives "for my sake" (and "for the sake of the gospel" [Mark 8:35 NRSV]) will retrieve them in the end (Matt. 10:39; 16:25; Luke 9:24). Those who will receive an eschatological reward are those who hear and do the words taught by Jesus, but those who disobey his teaching will

---

60. "Jesus . . . calls individuals to discipleship in an equally sovereign and absolute manner" (Hagner 1993b: 218). Marshall (1978b: 408) comments, "The commitment required is absolute and goes beyond that of a pupil to a rabbinic teacher." For the high Christology implied in Jesus' summons for disciples to follow him, see Hengel 1996: 3–15. On discipleship in the Greco-Roman world, Judaism, and Matthew's Gospel, see the careful historical work of Wilkins 1995.

61. See Meier 2001: 55–73.

62. See Hagner 1993b: 292.

63. "To be related to Jesus in this way is to become a family member of the kingdom, something far more significant than mere blood relationships" (Hagner 1993b: 358).

be destroyed (Matt. 7:24–26 par.). Bartimaeus, after being healed, demonstrates that he has been saved by faith and follows Jesus (Mark 10:52; cf. Matt. 20:34; Luke 18:43). Clearly, Jesus deserves the kind of devotion reserved for God himself. Jesus does not envision himself, however, as displacing God, for the one who receives Jesus receives the Father, who appointed and sent Jesus (Matt. 10:40; cf. Luke 10:16; John 13:20). The emphasis on Jesus himself is remarkable, however, for he can say that the one who receives a child "in my name welcomes me" (Matt. 18:5).[64] He does not shrink back from being invoked as "Lord, Lord" (Matt. 7:21–23), and he acknowledges that he has the authority to determine who will be included and excluded from God's kingdom.[65]

When the rich young ruler approached Jesus, he addressed Jesus as "good teacher" (Mark 10:17; Luke 18:18; but in Matt. 19:16 simply "teacher"). In Mark and Luke, Jesus asks why he calls him good, pointing him to the one God (Mark 10:18; Luke 18:19), whereas in Matthew he says, "Why do you ask me about what is good?" (Matt. 19:17). We should not see this text as undermining the high Christology that is pervasive in the Synoptic Gospels. Jesus challenges the rich man to consider God in the beauty of his moral goodness. Jesus has an extraordinarily high view of himself, but he does not think that he displaces God;[66] rather, he summons people to worship and obey the one God of Israel. Nevertheless, that worship of God involves high regard for Jesus is clear in this account, for the rich man must give up all his possessions and follow Jesus in order to inherit eternal life (Matt. 19:21; Mark 10:21; Luke 18:22; cf. Matt. 19:27 par.), for only those who have abandoned family and fortune for Jesus' sake will receive eternal life on the last day (Matt. 19:29; Mark 10:29–30; Luke 18:29–30).[67] Jesus ultimately tells the rich man what to do, thus taking a divine role in his life.[68] What is even more striking is that Jesus summons the rich man to follow him.

The Response to Jesus Determines One's Place in the Kingdom

Those who honor Jesus apparently honor God as well. He pronounces eschatological judgment on those who failed to repent upon hearing his

---

64. Mark adds here that the one who receives Jesus also receives the Father, who sent him (Mark 9:37).

65. So also France 1989: 309: "Men's ultimate destiny rests on their relationship with him."

66. See Schlatter 1997: 310–11.

67. See the helpful comments by France (2002: 402) and Lane (1974: 365–66) regarding the Markan version, and Fitzmyer (1985: 1197) for Luke. On the unique reading in Matthew, see Hagner 1995: 557; Carson 1984: 421–23.

68. See Gathercole 2006: 74.

preaching and seeing his miracles (Matt. 11:20–24 par.). Luke adds that those who respond to the preaching of the seventy are in truth responding to Jesus, and those who respond to Jesus are actually obeying the Father (Luke 10:16).[69] The demons submit to the disciples in the name of Jesus (Luke 10:17) because he has given the disciples authority over demonic powers (Luke 10:19). Those who offer a cup of water to disciples because they belong to Christ will be rewarded (Mark 9:41).[70] The presence of Jesus with the disciples supersedes the traditional practice of fasting (Matt. 9:14–15 par.).[71] He is the bridegroom, and fasting is not fitting during a time of such celebration. Moreover, he is the bridegroom who will return to receive his people (Matt. 25:1–13). Those who are unprepared will be excluded from the kingdom. We see the same truth in Matt. 25:31–46, where judgment is determined on the basis of one's response to Jesus.[72]

The disciples are blessed when they are persecuted and criticized because of their allegiance to Jesus (Matt. 5:11 par.). When the disciples are rejected, they "will be hated by all for my name's sake" (Matt. 10:22). Jesus is the "master of the house" (Matt. 10:25). Those who acknowledge Jesus before people will be acknowledged before the Father, but those who deny him will be denied by the Father (Matt. 10:32–33 par.). The disciples will be persecuted by synagogue leaders and will be imprisoned—all for the sake of Jesus (Luke 21:12).

The Synoptic Gospels also teach that Jesus will reign in God's future kingdom. James and John request to sit at Jesus' right hand and left hand when he reigns (Matt. 20:21; Mark 10:37).[73] Jesus does not deny his future reign. He says rather that the Father determines who will sit at his right or left hand (Matt. 20:23; Mark 10:40). We see again the remarkable exaltation of Jesus and at the same time the notion that the Father is the ultimate authority.[74]

69. Whether the correct reading in Luke 10:1 is "seventy" or "seventy-two" is difficult to discern, but in any case it is not crucial for the argument here (see Marshall 1978b: 414–15). See the fuller discussion of their role by Schnabel (2004a: 316–26), who accepts "seventy-two" as the more difficult reading and rejects a symbolic meaning in the number "seventy."

70. The parallel saying in Matt. 10:42 lacks any reference to Christ.

71. France (2002: 139), in his analysis of the Markan account (Mark 2:18–22), rightly says, "This central place in the drama of the new beginning suggests a messianic role for Jesus, even though the bridegroom was not, as far as we know, a current image for the Messiah. This verse may therefore properly be read as a veiled messianic claim."

72. So France 1989: 309–11.

73. In Matt. 20:21, however, it is not James and John who make this request but their mother.

74. We should note here that the Son does not know the day of his return; such knowledge is reserved for the Father only (Matt. 24:36; Mark 13:32). The ignorance of the Son

Jesus possesses a unique authority, for the Father has given the kingdom to him (Luke 22:29–30). Similarly, he will give the kingdom to his disciples, so that they will judge Israel's twelve tribes. We might conclude from the disciples' role in the kingdom that they are equivalent to Jesus, but this is a misreading of the text, for the disciples, says Jesus, will "eat and drink at *my* table in *my* kingdom" (Luke 22:30). The distinctiveness and special authority of Jesus distinguishes him from the disciples. Jesus' special role in the kingdom was acknowledged by the crucified criminal who repents, asking to be remembered when Jesus comes into his kingdom (Luke 23:42). Jesus could have disavowed any idea that the kingdom is his. Instead, Jesus declared that the man would dwell with him in paradise that very day (Luke 23:43).[75] The confidence and authority with which Jesus assures the man is striking. It is clear that one's relationship with Jesus determines whether or not one will enjoy the future blessings of the kingdom.

Jesus' New Meal and New Community

In due course we will examine Jesus' death, but we should note here Jesus' initiation of the Last Supper, so that the bread and wine are now celebrated in remembrance of *his death*. Indeed, the shedding of his blood avails for the forgiveness of sins and is the basis of the new covenant (Matt. 26:26–29; Mark 14:22–25; Luke 22:14–20).[76] The death of Jesus appears to displace sacrifices as the means by which forgiveness of sins is secured. It is quite obvious, then, that the relationship that people have with Jesus is crucial for their future destiny.

When believers gather to pray, Jesus says, he is present with them (Matt. 18:20).[77] No prophet, king, or priest in Israel ever said anything remotely similar, and this fact demonstrates the astonishingly high Christology of Matthew's Gospel. Matthew also includes references to the people of God, even calling them the "church." What should be noted here is that Jesus claims that he will build the church. Indeed, he says,

---

here is quite compatible with the incarnation (rightly Hagner 1995: 716; France 2002: 544; Carson 1984: 508).

75. On this verse, see Bock 1996: 1857–58.

76. Jesus speaks of the vicarious and soteriological nature of his sacrifice. See the full and insightful discussion in Nolland 2005: 1078–83; cf. France 2002: 569–71; Fitzmyer 1985: 1391; Hagner 1995: 773.

77. "Here as elsewhere, Jesus takes God's place" (Carson 1984: 404). "Without in any way identifying Jesus with God personally and ontologically, functionally the statement describes Jesus as acting precisely where according to biblical and Jewish belief God himself acts" (Luz 2001: 459). See also Hagner 1995: 533; Nolland 2005: 751.

"I will build *my* church" (Matt. 16:18).[78] The strangeness of the words
is apparent if we imagine any other human being saying such a thing.
Further, Jesus says that he gives the kingdom's keys to his disciples, so
that whatever they bind and loose is approved by God himself (Matt.
16:19). The distinctive relationship between the Father and Son manifests
itself in that Jesus bestows the keys of the kingdom and God implements
what Jesus' disciples do in his name. Matthew also indicates that Jesus
is the shepherd, and his disciples constitute the flock (Matt. 26:31 par.),
demonstrating again that Jesus is the leader of the new people of God.

Indications of Jesus' Divine Stature

The evidence accumulates that points to Jesus' divine stature and prerogatives in the Synoptic Gospels. Jesus' uniqueness manifests itself when
Elizabeth acknowledges that Mary "is the mother of my Lord" (Luke 1:43).[79]
Such an attribution is quite striking because Jesus was still in Mary's
womb.[80] On another occasion a centurion does not assign any particular
title to Jesus, but he recognizes that he is unworthy to receive Jesus in his
house (Matt. 8:8; Luke 7:6–7), suggesting Jesus' uniqueness.

The centrality and distinctiveness of Jesus is featured in his forgiveness
of sins. The theme that Jesus forgives sins emerges in the account of the
healing of the paralytic (Matt. 9:2–8 par.). What should be noted is Jesus'
response to the accusation that only God can forgive sins. He could have
protested that he was not forgiving sins by virtue of his own authority,
and that he was only pronouncing forgiveness in God's name, like the
prophets of old. Jesus goes out of his way, however, to demonstrate that

78. Hagner (1995: 471) notes that the pronoun "is emphatic by its position. It is the messianic community of the Messiah, and the statement is thus an implicit messianic claim."
So also Carson 1984: 369. The standard critical view is that Matt. 16:17–19 is inauthentic,
but for a defense of authenticity, see Carson 1984: 366; Meyer 1979: 187–95. For a more
nuanced view, which still sees a historical core, see Hagner 1995: 465–66.

79. Marshall (1978b: 81) tentatively suggests a reference to Jesus' messianic role. See
Luke 2:11.

80. Bock (1987: 69–70, 80–82) rightly remarks that Luke does not emphasize Jesus'
lordship here, but the use of the term "Lord" here and in Luke 2:11 foreshadows the high
Christology of Luke-Acts. Bock (1987: 80) argues that the title "Lord" is used in a restrained
way in this Gospel. Even though Jesus is addressed as "Lord" in Luke, the full meaning
of the term was not grasped by those who used the title. But "Lord" in Luke 2:11, Bock
(1987: 81) argues, "suggests that absolute sovereignty and divine relationship which Jesus
possesses in his role as salvation-bringer." Bock (1987: 80) also suggests that the term
meant "master" upon the lips of those who addressed Jesus. Still, Luke probably intended
that readers see a deeper significance in light of the whole narrative. Luke uses the term
"Lord" editorially in reference to Jesus, showing his estimate of his role (e.g., Luke 7:13,
19; 10:1, 39, 41; 11:39; 13:15; 17:5–6).

he, as the Son of Man, possesses the authority to forgive sins, which is the prerogative of God alone. He heals the paralytic in order to demonstrate that he possesses the authority to forgive sinners.[81] Jesus' healing of the paralytic and his claim to forgive represent divine actions, hearkening back to Ps. 103:3, where Yahweh is the one who forgives sins and heals diseases (cf. Isa. 33:24).[82] Furthermore, the story features Jesus' divine authority in healing, demonstrating that he is sovereignly pronouncing forgiveness (Mark 2:11–12).[83] In addition, the charge of blasphemy in Mark 2:7 is picked up later in Mark 14:61–64, where Jesus is condemned for arrogating to himself divine prerogatives, and such a charge is anticipated in this account.[84] Hence, Jesus' pronouncement of forgiveness also points to the cross as the basis of the forgiveness given.

The same sovereign freedom in forgiving sin manifests itself in Jesus' meal with Simon the Pharisee (Luke 7:36–50). The story concludes with the declaration to the sinful woman that her sins have been forgiven. Jesus' authority to forgive sins is evident in the account, for Luke concludes with the astonished query of those present, "Who is this, who even forgives sins?" (Luke 7:49).[85] The parable of the Pharisee and tax collector ends on a similar note (Luke 18:14). Jesus simply declares that the tax collector was justified rather than the Pharisee. Declaring who will be forgiven is a divine prerogative, and thereby Luke testifies to Jesus' divine status.[86]

The ending of Luke's Gospel also exalts Jesus. Forgiveness of sin for all peoples and nations should be proclaimed throughout the world in Jesus' name (Luke 24:47). After his ascension, Jesus will send "the promise of the Father"—the Spirit—to his own (Luke 24:49). The close association between Jesus and the Father manifests itself here, for the Father's promised gift is bestowed by Jesus himself. Finally, Jesus' exalted position is conveyed by his ascension to heaven and his blessing of his followers (Luke 24:50–51). Luke concludes on a remarkable note. The disciples of Jesus were monotheists well schooled in OT devotion, and yet they worship

81. See especially France 2002: 125–29. See also Stuhlmacher 1993: 19; Hooker 1991: 86–88 (though Hooker has doubts about whether the story goes back to the historical Jesus). Bousset (1970: 77) protests that the miracle is too paltry to establish claims to divinity. But see the insightful discussion by Hofius (2000: 38–56), who argues that in context there is not a divine passive here, as if Jesus merely claims that God is forgiving the paralytic's sins.

82. Hofius 2000: 43, 46–47. There is no notion, then, that one action is more difficult than the other. Both represent God's sovereign power.

83. Hofius 2000: 43, 46. Davies and Allison (1991: 92) argue that the physical healing demonstrates that Jesus is able to do the harder thing, which is to forgive sins.

84. Hofius 2000: 54.

85. Bock (1994: 706–7) convincingly argues that Jesus' words convey that he is more than a prophet, that they demonstrate his authority to forgive sins.

86. Rightly Hultgren 2000: 125.

Jesus (Luke 24:52). Such worship of Jesus, however, does not contradict their devotion to monotheism and the one God of Israel and of the world, for the next verse informs us that they blessed and praised God (Luke 24:53).[87] Apparently, the early Christians did not think that worshiping Jesus contradicted praising and worshiping the one God, and hence in some sense Jesus was divine, without excluding the deity of the Father.

Jesus informed Peter that Satan had requested to sift him and the other disciples like wheat (Luke 22:31–32). The sifting process, it appears, would destroy their faith and render them apostates. Jesus assured Peter that Satan's request would not be granted, for Jesus had prayed that Peter's faith would not lapse. The prayer of Jesus is not an uncertain affair. He knows that his request will be granted, and hence he anticipates the occasion "when" Peter returns from his denial of Christ. Not only is it clear that Jesus prayed authoritatively, but Mark 9:24 also appears to show a prayer addressed to Jesus. The man with the demonized boy cries out to Jesus, "I believe; help my unbelief!" The most natural way of understanding his prayer is that he addresses Jesus himself, asking that Jesus grant him faith. But only God is able to beget faith in others, and hence, probably instinctively and without any reflection on the significance of what he was doing, the boy's father entreats Jesus as one entreats God. Presumably, Mark includes this in his Gospel because the man's instincts were fitting and accorded with Jesus' stature.

Name Christology

In biblical thought a name often denotes the character and essence of a person (cf. Exod. 34:5–7), so that knowing God's name takes on

---

87. Scholars have considered carefully the antecedents to the Christian conception of Jesus, exploring both its continuity and discontinuity with Jewish antecedents. The literature here is enormous. For entry into the debate, see Segal 1977; Hurtado 1988; Stuckenbruck 1995. For a survey of recent work and a helpful evaluation, see Lee 2005: 1–116. Some have questioned whether it is fitting to characterize Jewish belief as monotheistic. Hurtado (2003: 32–53) demonstrates that monotheism aptly describes Judaism of the Second Temple period and early Christianity (see also Lee 2005: 21–25). Bauckham (1999a) argues that monotheism was indeed characteristic of Judaism in the Second Temple period but thinks that it is a mistake to attempt to derive some continuity between the high Christology of the NT and Jewish intermediary figures. He suggests instead that the Christology of the NT is compatible with monotheism when we recognize that there is some distinction within the unique identity of God, so that monotheism does not require "unitariness." Bauckham (1999a: 28) observes, "The key to the way in which Jewish monotheism and high Christology were compatible in the early Christian movement is not the claim that Jewish monotheism left room for ambiguous semi-divinities, but the recognition that its understanding of the unique identity of the one God left room for the inclusion of Jesus in that identity."

great significance.[88] Jacob discloses his name to the man who wrestled with him and is granted a new name, but the one who wrestled with Jacob, who is identified as God himself, does not tell Jacob his name (Gen. 32:27–30), thus demonstrating his transcendence. The revelation of God's name (Exod. 3:6–15) indicated that he was the covenant God who would fulfill his saving promises to Israel.[89] "Misuse of God's name in magic or false oaths . . . is forbidden (Exod. 20:7), for the name of Yahweh is a gift of the revelation which is not at man's disposal."[90] The reason that God's name is awesome is that "whoever knows God's name knows God—or as much of God as he has revealed."[91] Thus it is important to discern the significance of the name in relationship to Jesus in the Synoptic Gospels.

The Synoptics travel along the arteries of the OT in emphasizing that God's name must be hallowed (Matt. 6:9) and that his name is holy (Luke 1:49). It is evident, therefore, that what the Synoptics say about Jesus' name suggests his deity, for they were written within a monotheistic framework. Prophets are to prophesy not in their own name but in the name of the Lord (Jer. 11:21; 14:15; 23:25), but it is assumed that people will prophesy in Jesus' name (Matt. 7:22). This is quite significant because in Deut. 18:18–20 prophets speak in Yahweh's name, and hence speaking in Jesus' name bears the same significance as speaking in Yahweh's name.[92] Similarly, the Gentiles will put their hope in Jesus' name (Matt. 12:21), but hope and trust are to be put only in the Lord. No prophets or angels invite human beings to put their trust in them, but they always summon human beings to hope or trust in God himself. Yet Matthew envisions Gentiles putting their hope in Jesus' name. The heavenly power of Jesus' name is indisputable, for the demons are subjected in his name (Luke 10:17). We would expect that demons would submit themselves to God's name, and yet they are defeated in Jesus' name. Believers are to prophesy in Jesus' name and hope in his name, and demons are subjected in his name. Perhaps even more astonishing, forgiveness is to be offered and repentance demanded in his name (Luke 24:47).[93] Forgiveness is the prerogative of God, and yet it now comes on the basis of Jesus' name.

88. For the importance of name in NT Christology, see Longenecker 1970: 41–46; Hartman 1997; Gathercole 2006: 65–68.

89. The name of the Lord in the OT does not signify an independent hypostasis but is a personification referring to God himself (see Lee 2005: 77–84).

90. Bietenhard, *NIDNTT* 2:650.

91. Hartman, *EDNT* 2:520.

92. So Gathercole 2006: 67–68.

93. "In the OT, the phrase indicates Yahweh's authority—authority that has now been transferred to Jesus, the mediator of God's promise" (Bock 1996: 1939).

Indeed, baptism is not restricted to God's name; the names of the Son and the Spirit are also included (Matt. 28:19).

God himself should be supreme in the heart and life of every person, and yet Jesus commends those who leave everything for the sake of his name and follow him in discipleship (Matt. 19:29). Nowhere do apostles or other messengers of God summon people to leave everything for the sake of their own name, so the distinctiveness of the saying stands out. Moreover, Jesus anticipates the people of God gathering in his name (Matt. 18:20)[94] and promises his presence in such meetings. Obviously, Jesus is not guaranteeing his physical presence, and it seems to follow that the divine ability to transcend spatial limitations is promised. Mark 9:37 (cf. Matt. 18:5; Luke 9:48) is quite remarkable, for Jesus claims that those who welcome children in his name also receive him. At the same time, in welcoming Jesus, they welcome the Father who sent him. Jesus thereby articulates his extraordinary relationship with the Father. Apparently, the prominence of Jesus' name does not diminish the glory of the Father but rather enhances it.

Jesus' name is so prominent that others will claim to come in his name (Matt. 24:5 par.), and his name will exercise such influence that his disciples will be brought before secular rulers for its sake (Luke 21:12). Indeed, believers will be hated throughout the world on account of Jesus' name (Matt. 10:22; 24:9 par.).

Jesus' Preexistence in the Synoptic Gospels

The recent work of Gathercole supporting Jesus' preexistence is fresh and convincing, and the arguments that he sets forth are summarized here.[95] The preexistence of Jesus is suggested because he is a heavenly figure in the Synoptic Gospels. That Jesus belongs to heaven is clear from the transfiguration (Matt. 17:1–8 par.), for his shining face and dazzling garments indicate that he belongs to the heavenly sphere, as does the appearance of Moses and Elijah to speak with him. The appearance of Moses and Elijah demonstrates that Jesus belongs to their world, which is a heavenly one. Scholars naturally are struck by Jesus' acknowledgment of ignorance about the final day in Matt. 24:36 (par.). We must note, however, that in that text Jesus places himself in the heavenly hierarchy, not with human beings on earth. It is precisely because he is part of the heavenly council, like the angels, that it is surprising that the future day is hidden from him.

94. Cf. *m. 'Abot* 4:11, where God's people assemble for the sake of heaven's name.
95. Gathercole 2006.

Jesus' role in the heavenly council manifests itself in Luke 10:20, for he knows that the disciples' names are written in heaven. Such knowledge is reserved for a heavenly being. The same knowledge of heavenly realities is disclosed in Jesus' well-known words in Matt. 11:25–27 (par.), which we will investigate further in a later chapter. What is remarkable is that Jesus knows from whom God has hidden knowledge and to whom he has disclosed it. Further, as the Son, he knows what the Father's good pleasure is. The Son's knowledge of the Father is not limited to Jesus' ministry but transcends his ministry and indeed precedes it, for the mutual and exclusive knowledge between the Father and the Son points to the truth that the Son has been the Son of the Father forever. Furthermore, as Gathercole observes, Jesus' choosing to whom he will reveal himself in this text "places him squarely on the divine side of reality: it is difficult to conceive of anyone but a divine figure having this role."[96] In Mark 13:32 (cf. Matt. 24:36) Jesus does not know the time of the end, but he places himself with other heavenly beings, such as angels, rather than with human beings. It is somewhat remarkable that Jesus does not have knowledge of the end, since he, like the angels, belongs to the heavenly realm. We also see that Jesus is a heavenly intercessor (Luke 22:31–32), for his prayer for Simon and the other disciples secures their belief and prevents them from committing apostasy. Finally, other heavenly figures recognize Jesus, while those on earth fail to comprehend who he is. The demons and unclean spirits acknowledge that Jesus is God's holy one and his Son (Mark 1:24; 3:11–12 par.). Most significantly, the Father himself places his imprimatur on the Son, disclosing at his baptism that he is well pleased with Jesus as his Son (Matt. 3:16–17 par.).

The preexistence of Jesus is implied by his claim that he sent the prophets (Matt. 23:34–36). This verse, as Gathercole points out, is quite astonishing, for in the OT the Lord is the one who sends the prophets to his people. For Jesus to say that he sends the prophets aligns him with Yahweh rather than with other human beings.[97] No other example exists where a prophet or wisdom teacher makes this sort of self-claim.

The story in which Peter begs Jesus to depart because Peter is too sinful to be in his presence is illuminating.[98] Green points to the parallels with Isa. 6:1–10, where Isaiah was undone in the Lord's presence, and Peter has a similar reaction in Jesus' presence here.[99] The account intimates that Jesus is like Yahweh, in whose presence a sinful person

96. Gathercole 2006: 56.
97. Gathercole 2006: 71–72.
98. This text came to my attention in Gathercole 2006: 75.
99. Green 1997: 233.

cannot abide, and hence the account places Jesus with God rather than with human beings.[100]

In addition, the claim that Jesus is the "sunrise" (*anatolē*) on high (Luke 1:78) points to his preexistence. Gathercole points out four pieces of evidence in support. First, the term is associated with the Messiah in Jewish tradition (cf. Zech. 3:8; 6:12 LXX; *y. Ber.* 2:4; Philo, *Confusion* 62). Second, the sunrise or dawn will come "from on high," in contrast to what is written in Zechariah, where the branch comes from earth (Zech. 6:12 LXX). Coming from on high indicates that the sunrise hails from heaven, from God's realm (cf. Luke 24:49; 2 Sam. 22:17; Ps. 101:20 LXX [102:20 MT; 102:19 ET]). Third, the language of visitation points to deity, for in the OT God is the one who visits with judgment and salvation.[101] Fourth, the sunrise came to shed light on his people (Luke 1:79), which fits with the messianic prophecy in Isa. 9:1, 5–6.

Gathercole's study is particularly helpful in its analysis of sayings in the Synoptics that relate to Jesus' coming. The sayings can be split into three categories. First, on two occasions demons query whether Jesus has come to destroy them (Mark 1:24 par.; Matt. 8:29 [cf. Mark 5:7; Luke 8:28]). Jesus is portrayed in exalted terms on both occasions, and his heavenly origin is suggested by his being called the "Holy One of God" and the "Son of God." Jesus' coming to destroy the demons is not an ordinary visit of a human being; rather, it is the visit of one from the heavenly realm who comes to put an end to powers that also transcend the human realm.

Second, there are six sayings in which Jesus declares why he has come. He has come to preach the good news of the kingdom in Israel (Mark 1:38 par.); to call sinners instead of the righteous (Matt. 9:13 par.); to fulfill rather than abolish the law and the prophets (Matt. 5:17); to cast a fire onto the earth (Luke 12:49); to bring a sword and division rather than peace to earth (Matt. 10:34 par.); and to divide family members against one another (Matt. 10:35). Gathercole rightly argues that Luke 12:49 is the clearest in terms of preexistence. Casting fire upon the earth is a divine prerogative and is reminiscent of the brimstone and fire that the Lord rained upon Sodom and Gomorrah (Gen. 19:24). Some might argue that it is akin to the fire rained upon Elijah's opponents during his ministry (2 Kings 1:10–12). The parallel is not apt because Elijah prayed that God would cast fire upon the earth, whereas Jesus says that he himself casts fire upon the earth, which is akin to God raining down fire and brimstone upon Sodom and Gomorrah. Further, it is unlikely

---

100. Of course, the point of the story is not to say that Jesus is only divine; he is a human being as well.

101. See Beyer, *TDNT* 2:601–5.

that Jesus could cast a fire on the earth *from* the earth, so that the cosmic and transcendent character of his activity is evident. When Jesus speaks of bringing a sword to the earth (Matt. 10:34), perhaps there is an allusion to the sword wielded by the angel of the Lord (Num. 22:31; Josh. 5:13–14; 1 Chron. 21:16). If so, we have further evidence of Jesus' preexistence.

Third, there are two "Son of Man" sayings where Jesus articulates the purpose of his coming. The Son of Man came to serve others instead of to be served, and to offer his life as a ransom (Matt. 20:28 par.); and he came "to seek and to save the lost" (Luke 19:10). The seeking and saving of the lost alludes to the activity of shepherds who leave their flocks to seek their sheep. Most important, in Ezekiel it is God himself who seeks his sheep and is the shepherd of the flock (Ezek. 34:11–12), so that Jesus takes on a divine role here.

In summary, it seems that Gathercole rightly discerns the meaning of Jesus' "I have come" sayings in which there is a purpose formula. Each saying emphasizes the purpose of Jesus' coming, implying that Jesus comes from outside the human sphere for a mission upon earth, which in turn suggests that his origin hails from outside the sphere of humanity. In each instance Jesus' coming refers to the totality of his earthly ministry and is not confined to a single instance, as if he were merely describing a visit from Nazareth to Capernaum to accomplish a particular goal.

Some have maintained that what is said about Jesus is analogous to prophets, noting, for example, the words of Josephus to Vespasian (Josephus, *J.W.* 3.400).[102] Gathercole notes, however, that this text refers to only a single incident in Josephus's life, not the totality of his work. Furthermore, it is obvious that Josephus is an earthly figure. The closest parallels to Jesus' "I have come" are found in angelic visits to earth where they summarize their visit with "I have come" declarations (e.g., Dan. 9:22–23; 10:12, 14, 20; *4 Ezra* 6:30; 7:2; *2 Bar.* 71:3).[103] It seems that the most common use of the "I have come" formula is to designate the purpose of a heavenly figure's coming to earth in which the totality of the visit is explicated, whereas the same formula is not used to describe the totality of a human figure's coming. The closest parallels to Jesus' coming statements, then, can be traced not to the coming of human beings but rather to the coming of angels to earth. Such parallels suggest that Jesus' coming cannot be confined to the earthly sphere but instead points to his coming from heaven to earth.

---

102. Meier 1994: 151. Meier (1994: 151) also points to the fact that both John the Baptist and Jesus are said to come (Luke 7:33–34), which in his judgment rules out preexistence in the "I have come" sayings.

103. See Gathercole 2006: 95–99.

Conclusion

The Synoptic Gospels advance the story line of redemptive history, finding the fulfillment of God's promises in Jesus Christ. What we have seen in this chapter is how the entire story of God's plan converges on Jesus. During his ministry intense debate was generated as to who he was. The Synoptic writers inform us that he is the fulfillment of the OT Scriptures. He is the new and better Moses, and both the Torah and wisdom point to him. Indeed, he is the prophet prophesied by Moses to be raised up by God for Israel, and he is the culmination of God's revelation. His exorcisms and miracles demonstrate that he is the Holy One of God, the one in whom God's saving promises were coming to pass.

Jesus' divine stature is also clearly taught in the Synoptics, for he summoned human beings to follow him in discipleship and taught that they must even be willing to die for his sake. How people responded to him would determine whether or not they entered the kingdom of God. If they denied Jesus, they would be denied by God himself. Jesus instituted a new meal that would be repeated in his remembrance, and he gathered a new community that assembled in his name. The divine status of Jesus is evident because he forgave sins on his own authority. Further, he claimed to be part of God's heavenly council, and the "I have come" sayings point toward preexistence, specifying why he came from heaven to earth. In the same way, the emphasis on Jesus' name signifies his divine position, for what is said about Jesus' name is elsewhere attributed only to God himself.

6

The Messiah and the Son of Man in the Gospels

In the preceding chapter we focused on the centrality of Jesus in the Synoptic Gospels by considering a number of themes that highlight Jesus' supremacy. In doing so, we saw clearly that God's saving promises were fulfilled in Jesus, that redemptive history finds its consummation in him. We saw in the preceding chapter that Jesus is the main character in the narrative even if we leave out of consideration the titles that are given to him. In this chapter and the subsequent ones, however, we will consider some titles that are ascribed to Jesus, for Jesus' fulfillment of God's purposes is also explicated by his titles. In this chapter we consider two of the central titles, "Messiah" and "Son of Man." Although controversy surrounds both titles, we will see that in both instances Jesus fulfills OT prophecy and is the key agent in the working out of God's purposes in history.

Messiah

The Term "Anointed"

The term "Messiah" simply means "anointed one."[1] To call someone "Messiah," whether with the verbal or nominal form, does not mean that

1. For the use of the term historically, see Horbury 1998: 7–13.

the person so-called is actually God, as many in popular circles think. It simply designates someone who is anointed by God for a particular task. Nor does the term "anointed one" necessarily mean that one is a king. In the OT priests were anointed by God.[2] In fact, even inanimate objects could be anointed to set them apart for the holy, such as unleavened cakes (Exod. 29:2; Lev. 2:4; 7:12), the altar of burnt offering (Exod. 29:36; 40:10; Lev. 8:11), the basin and stand (Exod. 40:11), the ark, the tent of meeting, and its furniture (Exod. 30:26; 40:9; cf. Lev. 8:10; Dan. 9:24). It is not as common for prophets to be called "anointed," but the appellation does occur (1 Kings 19:15; Isa. 61:1; cf. 1 Chron. 16:22; Ps. 105:15). Kings, of course, often were anointed or designated as the Lord's anointed.[3] Designating the king as anointed did not suggest that he was divine. Indeed, even Cyrus, a pagan king who did not know Yahweh (Isa. 45:4–5), was described as Yahweh's anointed (Isa. 45:1).

Old Testament Context

Scholars have often noted that the OT says little about the coming of a future anointed one.[4] Is the NT expectation for Messiah, then, fundamentally misconceived? Does it dramatically misread the OT? If we restricted ourselves to the word "Messiah," we could legitimately say that the NT veered away from the meaning of the OT. What actually takes place, however, is quite understandable and accords with the OT. In order to grasp how by the NT period there was a general expectation of Messiah, even though the OT does not emphasize a coming Messiah (but cf. Dan. 9:25–26), we need to develop the argument as we proceed. First, it should be observed that David and his heirs are often described as anointed ones.[5] Second, David and his heirs were not merely anointed as kings individually apart from God's larger saving purposes. Yahweh made a covenant with David in which he pledged that David's dynasty would never end, that one of his sons would always rule upon the throne (2 Sam. 7:11–29; 1 Chron. 17:10–27).[6] God's covenant love with David is irrevocable, so that God will never remove his covenantal

2. Exod. 28:41; 29:7; 30:30; 40:13, 15; Lev. 4:3, 5, 16; 6:20; 7:36; 8:12; 16:32; Num. 3:3; 35:25.

3. For example, Judg. 9:8, 15; 1 Sam. 2:10; 10:1; 15:1; 16:3, 6, 12, 13; 2 Sam. 2:4, 7; 3:39; 5:3, 17; 12:7; 19:10; 1 Kings 1:34, 39; Ps. 2:2; 45:7; 89:20; 132:10.

4. For a survey of critical analyses regarding the Messiah in the OT, see Horbury 1998: 13–25. Horbury (1998: 29) argues that the canonical shaping of the OT itself points toward a messianic hope. See also Strauss (1995: 35–57), who surveys the OT and Jewish views.

5. See 1 Sam. 16:12–13; 2 Sam. 2:4, 7; 3:39; 5:3, 17; 12:7; 1 Kings 1:34, 39, 45; 5:1; Ps. 89:20, 38, 51; 132:10, 17.

6. For a study of the messianic hope in 1–2 Samuel, 1–2 Kings, and 1–2 Chronicles, see, respectively, Satterthwaite 1995; Provan 1995; B. Kelly 1995.

love from David's heirs, though he will punish any descendants on the throne who sin.

Psalm 89 reflects an understanding of the Davidic covenant after David's death. God's promise to David is based on his steadfast covenantal love (Ps. 89:2–4). His covenant consists in the promise that one of David's descendants will always rule on the throne. The covenantal promise is summarized well in Ps. 89:28–29: "My steadfast love I will keep for him forever, and my covenant will stand firm for him. I will establish his offspring forever and his throne as the days of the heavens." David's descendants will be disciplined and corrected if they sin, but God will never revoke his promised covenant to David; the kingdom established with him will not be withdrawn (Ps. 89:30–37). The psalmist is distressed, however, because when he writes, God seems to have withdrawn his favor from the Davidic king (Ps. 89:38–45). He entreats God to act in accord with his covenantal and faithful love and fulfill his promise to David (Ps. 89:49).

Psalm 132 also reaffirms God's oath to place one of David's sons on the throne (Ps. 132:11). But Ps. 132:12 suggests that the promise depends upon the obedience of David's heirs. Those who disobey will not receive the promised blessing. The psalm ends, however, with confidence that in the future the Davidic king will triumph over his enemies (Ps. 132:17–18). Perhaps the best way to resolve the tension is to acknowledge that God will so work that ultimately and finally there will be one from the Davidic line who meets the conditions, so that the promise will be fulfilled. Such a reading seems to do justice to Ps. 132, which calls attention to conditions and yet gives assurance that the promise will ultimately be fulfilled.

Such an interpretation of Ps. 132 fits with the canonical witness of the rest of the OT. Hosea 3:5 looks to the future, promising that Israel will seek Yahweh their God and David as their king. It is doubtful that Hosea refers to the literal David here, since he was long dead. Hosea envisions future salvation for Israel, but this salvation will be theirs under a Davidic king, in fulfillment of the promise originally made to David.[7] The reference to a Davidic king is particularly striking in Hosea because the prophecy is largely, though not exclusively, addressed to the northern kingdom of Israel instead of the southern kingdom of Judah. Micah 5:2 should be placed in a category similar to the Hosea text.[8] Micah does not use the name "David," but surely he has a Davidic type of king in mind,

---

7. Rightly Garrett 1997: 104.

8. Jenson (1995: 204–11), in my judgment, underestimates the fulfillment of Mic. 5:2 in Matt. 2:6.

for he speaks of a ruler coming from Judah, and the natural conclusion is that the ruler from Judah descends from David.

Isaiah 7–8 forecasts the day when the Assyrians will conquer the northern kingdom of Israel and the kingdom of Syria and will nearly conquer the southern kingdom of Judah as well.[9] Ultimately, however, Judah and its king will triumph. Isaiah 9:2–7 promises that the Lord will bring victory to his people and that they will conquer every foreign army. This victory will occur through a son, through one who will govern the people of God. The son who will triumph will sit on David's throne. He will be, in the well-known words, the "Wonderful Counselor, Mighty God, Everlasting Father, Prince of Peace" (Isa. 9:6). Since this person sits on David's throne, he surely is a descendant of David, one who fulfills the covenant made with David.[10]

The Davidic roots of the future king are clear in Isa. 11, for he is a "shoot from the stump of Jesse" (Isa. 11:1) and "the root of Jesse" (Isa. 11:10).[11] He will be endowed with the Spirit and introduce a period of peace and righteousness as ruler. The future dimension of the covenant with David is suggested by Isa. 55:3–4 as well. God's faithful mercies to David are such that he will be a "leader" and "commander."[12]

Jeremiah quite often refers to a future fulfillment of the promise made to David. Jeremiah 23:5–6 is particularly striking: "Behold, the days are coming, declares the LORD, when I will raise up for David a righteous Branch, and he shall reign as king and deal wisely, and shall execute justice and righteousness in the land. In his days Judah will be saved, and Israel will dwell securely. And this is the name by which he will be called: 'The LORD is our righteousness.'" A Davidic king is not consigned to the past but rather is the hope of the future. When the Lord raises up this ruler, Judah and Israel will flourish and prosper (cf. Jer. 30:9; 33:15, 17). He emphasizes that the covenant with David cannot be broken (Jer. 33:20–22, 25–26). A similar promise surfaces in Ezekiel: "And I will set up over them one shepherd, my servant David, and he shall feed them: he shall feed them and be their shepherd. And I, the LORD, will be their God, and my servant David shall be prince among them. I am the LORD; I have spoken" (Ezek. 34:23–24).[13] The typological nature of Ezekiel's

9. In defense of the notion that the king in Isaiah should be interpreted in messianic terms, see Schultz 1995; Schibler 1995.

10. See Childs (2001: 81), who sees the child as messianic and says, "The language is not just of a wishful thinking for a better time, but the confession of Israel's belief in a divine ruler who will replace once and for all the unfaithful reign of kings like Ahaz." See also Motyer 1993: 103–5; Oswalt 1986: 245–48.

11. See Oswalt 1986: 279, 287.

12. Childs (2001: 434) understands the phrase as an objective genitive referring to the enduring mercies to David.

13. For the Messiah in Ezekiel, see Block 1995.

language is clear, for when he speaks of "David," he intends the reader to think not of David literally but rather of a descendant of David who will sit on his throne (cf. Ezek. 37:24–25).

We have seen thus far that the Davidic king was anointed as a sovereign, and that the Davidic covenant promised that a descendant of David would always sit on the throne. Few texts explicitly promise a coming anointed one, though Dan. 9:25–26 seems to be an exception. Readers of the OT, however, naturally combined together the promises of the Davidic covenant with the fact that kings were anointed. No violence is done to the OT in saying that it promises the coming of a Messiah, for when we merge the promises of the Davidic covenant with the anointing of the Davidic king, it is legitimate to say that the OT looks forward to the coming of an anointed one in the line of David.

Second Temple Views of Messiah

This survey does not suggest that postbiblical Judaism had a unified view of the Messiah. Not surprisingly, a number of different ideas circulated, so that a diversity of perspectives is evident in terms of the messianic hope.[14] We are simply saying that the expectation for a coming anointed king from the line of David accords quite well with what the OT itself says.[15] Moreover, the notion that a Messiah from the line of David would appear in the future, destroy God's enemies, and grant peace to Israel was probably widely accepted.[16] We see this in *Psalms of Solomon*, which most scholars agree came from Pharisaic circles.[17] Affirmation of the Davidic covenant is clear in *Pss. Sol.* 17:4: "Lord, you chose David to be king over Israel, and swore to him about his descendants forever, that his kingdom should not fail before you."[18] The author laments that God's

14. Contra Horbury (1998: 86–108), the evidence does not support a clear notion of the Messiah's preexistence in Second Temple Judaism (see the judicious weighing of the evidence in Lee 2005: 99–115).

15. For a brief survey of the OT and postbiblical Jewish evidence, see Cullmann 1963: 113–17. For a helpful survey of Second Temple Judaism relative to the Messiah, see Beasley-Murray 1986: 52–62.

16. Scholars who have engaged in work on Second Temple Judaism have often emphasized the diversity of views regarding the Messiah in the literature, and the absence of the theme in a number of pieces of literature. Nevertheless, it is likely the case that messianism was more pervasive and coherent than some have suggested. For studies that accord with the claim made here, see J. J. Collins 1995; Horbury 1998. Others argue that the notion that most Jews looked for the coming of a Messiah does not fit with the sources (e.g., Charlesworth 1992; E. Sanders 1992: 295). Horbury (1998: 52–59) in particular includes a valuable section on the Apocrypha, arguing that the messianic hope is not as lacking as is often claimed.

17. On the Messiah in *Psalms of Solomon*, see J. J. Collins 1995: 49–56.

18. All Pseudepigrapha citations are from Charlesworth 1983–1985.

people have been expelled from the land because of sinners in the midst of Israel. He prays that God would "raise up for them their king, the son of David, to rule over your servant Israel" (*Pss. Sol.* 17:21). Such a king would purify Jerusalem, evict Gentiles, and remove sinful Israelites. A holy and righteous people will inhabit the land, and Gentile nations will serve him (*Pss. Sol.* 17:22–31). The ruler is identified as "the Lord Messiah" (*Pss. Sol.* 17:32). He will be endowed with the Holy Spirit (*Pss. Sol.* 17:37) and will rule Israel righteously. The psalmist goes on to pray that God would "cleanse Israel . . . for the appointed day when his Messiah will reign" (*Pss. Sol.* 18:5). Again, he is identified as "the Lord Messiah" (*Pss. Sol.* 18:7). The messianic expectation in *Psalms of Solomon* accords substantially with what we have found in the OT.[19]

Josephus's accounts of the various national deliverers fit a similar conception, though it should be observed that not all of these persons necessarily believed that they were the Messiah,[20] and perhaps the word "Messiah" should be reserved for those of Davidic origin.[21] In any case, they were convinced that the promises made to Israel would be realized through their activities. Various people rose up, such as Judas, Simon, and Athronges, who apparently believed that they were the ones to deliver Israel (*Ant.* 17.271–285).[22] Others took actions that signaled that the Jews would be freed from Roman dominion, just as they were liberated from Egypt at the exodus. Theudas promised that the Jordan River would part because of his prophetic powers, and that the people would pass over the river, though the procurator Fadus forcefully intervened and slew Theudas and many of his followers (*Ant.* 20.97–98). Similarly, the Egyptian pledged that he would overcome the Romans in Jerusalem, though it is unclear whether he pledged to do so by force (*J. W.* 2.261–263) or by divine intervention (*Ant.* 20.169–172), but again the plot came to nothing when the procurator Felix attacked the Egyptian and his allies. During the Jewish revolt of AD 66–70, it seems that Menahem, son of Judas the

19. Horbury (1998: 97–98) discerns a notion of preexistence in *Pss. Sol.* 17:42.

20. See the helpful survey in J. J. Collins 1995: 196–204. Horsley (1992) in particular emphasizes that many of these movements were initiated by prophets and maintains that there was not great interest in the coming of a Messiah during the Second Temple period. Horsley rightly cautions us against seeing a unified conception of the Messiah during the Second Temple era, and he also demonstrates that some of the so-called deliverers did not (at least according to our sources) claim to be the Messiah. Still, Horsley underestimates the desire for and the anticipation of the coming of a messianic type of deliverer in a general sense during the Second Temple period. R. Webb identifies those promising deliverance as "popular prophets" (see R. Webb 1991: 333–39). See the survey in R. Brown 1994: 1:679–93.

21. So R. Brown 1994: 1:681–82.

22. See Farmer 1957–1958. But R. Brown (1994: 1:682) points out that none of these were Davidic.

Galilean, and Simon bar Giora had royal aspirations (*J.W.* 2.433–444; 7.29–31). Even though no one succeeded in driving out the Romans and in bringing freedom to Israel, the persistence of such would-be deliverers indicates that the hope for a deliverer was deeply rooted in Jewish thinking. Even after the shock of AD 70, Simon bar Kosiba proclaimed himself king and led a revolt (AD 132–135), so deeply ingrained was the expectation of a future deliverer.[23] The Mishnah and much of Jewish literature subsequent to the Mishnah displays scant interest in the Messiah.[24] On the other hand, messianic movements and persons have cropped up regularly in the last two thousand years.[25]

When we read the Dead Sea Scrolls, we note that the messianic hope is not confined to the Davidic line.[26] Two Messiahs are expected, both a priestly and a kingly Messiah: a priestly Messiah from the tribe of Aaron, and a kingly Messiah from the tribe of Judah (1QS IX, 11; CD-A XII, 23; XIV, 19; CD-B XIX, 10–11; 20:1). It appears that the priestly Messiah takes precedence over the kingly Messiah, and the latter is dependent on the interpretation of the former (1QSa II, 12–21; 4QpIsaª III, 23–25; 4QSM 5; 4QFlor 1, I, 11; CD-A VII, 18; 11QTª LVIII, 18–19; cf. 1QM XVI, 13; XVIII, 5).[27] Still, there is significant evidence of a Davidic leader as well, so that a messianic king is not excluded (CD-A VII, 19; 4QpIsaª III, 11–25; 4QSM 5; 4QFlor 1, I, 11–13; 4QcommGenª V; 1QHª III [*bottom*], 4–5).[28] The "branch of David" would destroy the ungodly and conquer the nations (1QSb V, 20–29).

Testaments of the Twelve Patriarchs is similar in some ways to what we find in the Dead Sea Scrolls. Unraveling what these documents

23. For a survey of the revolt of bar Kosiba and the messianic spirit that accompanied it, see J. J. Collins 1995: 201–3. Interestingly, Philo shows little interest in the messianic hope. Perhaps this can be explained by his location in Alexandria. Nevertheless, a messianic hope is not entirely lacking in Philo. He foresees the coming of a man, on the basis of Num. 24:7, who will fulfill the role of a Mosaic king who will bring deliverance to Israel (so Borgen 1992). Borgen (1992: 358) says, "Philo looks for the Messiah to come in the form of 'a man' who is seen as a final commander-in-chief and emperor of the Hebrew nation as the head of nations."

24. The near silence can be interpreted variously, but it may be explained by the character and nature of the Mishnah. Some glimmers of a messianic hope persist in the Mishnah (*m. Ber.* 1:5; *m. Soṭah* 9:15). For the Messiah in the Mishnah and subsequent Jewish literature, see Neusner 1984.

25. For messianic movements within Jewish circles in the last two thousand years, see Cohn-Sherbok 1997: 43–60, 81–170.

26. Space is lacking here to enter the scholarly debate over the Messiah in the Dead Sea Scrolls. For a more in-depth discussion, see Oegema 1998.

27. This matter is debated. For helpful analyses, see J. J. Collins 1995: 74–80; Talmon 1992: 101–15.

28. For further discussion, see J. J. Collins 1995: 56–67; Horbury 1998: 59–62; Oegema 1998.

teach about Messiah is difficult because they may be originally Christian or originally Jewish with later Christian interpolations, making it challenging to discern what is Jewish or distinctively Christian. It seems, though, that the material on two Messiahs, priestly and kingly, is more likely Jewish than Christian because such an interpretation does not fit cleanly with the Christian view that there is only one Messiah, Jesus. In *Testament of Reuben* authority is granted to both Levi and Judah (*T. Reu.* 6:5–12). The "anointed priest" (*T. Reu.* 6:8) hails from Reuben. It is difficult to discern whether in the last verses sovereignty is granted to Levi or to Judah. If the former, we have evidence for the superiority of a priestly anointed one. The kingly role appears to be given to the priest in the *Testament of Levi* as well (*T. Levi* 18:2–9). In *T. Levi* 18:3 the author appears to draw on Num. 24:17 in explaining his rule.

Priestly preeminence is emphasized in the *Testament of Judah* (*T. Jud.* 21:1–4). The priesthood belongs to Levi, and kingship to Judah. And yet God "has subjected the kingship to the priesthood" (*T. Jud.* 21:2). Judah deals with earthly matters, and Levi with heavenly ones. "As heaven is superior to earth, so is God's priesthood superior to the kingdom on earth" (*T. Jud.* 21:3). Kingship and rule belong to Judah and will be restored to him (*T. Jud.* 22:2–3). Messianic themes predominate in *T. Jud.* 24, where Num. 24:17 is again alluded to, so that the same OT text is applied to the tribes of both Levi and Judah. A star of Jacob will arise as promised, "like the Sun of righteousness" (*T. Jud.* 24:1; cf. Mal. 4:2). He is God's "Shoot" (*T. Jud.* 24:4, 6), and this likely is a reference to his Davidic roots. When we take the entirety of *Testaments of the Twelve Patriarchs* into account, it appears that the priestly Messiah takes precedence over the kingly one.

In *4 Ezra* the Messiah is designated as God's son, but his reign is limited to four hundred years, and after those years have elapsed, he will die (*4 Ezra* 7:28–29). *Fourth Ezra* was written after AD 70, and so perhaps the death of the Messiah is a reaction to Christian conceptions. On the other hand, the OT itself could be interpreted to say that the Messiah would die, for we saw earlier that the OT itself does not clearly teach, or at least it was not clearly perceived to teach, that the Messiah was divine. *Fourth Ezra* pictures the Messiah as a lion, teaching also that the Messiah descends from David and that God will reveal him at the end of days. When he comes, he will judge the wicked (the eagle, which is Rome) and vindicate the righteous remnant (*4 Ezra* 12:31–34). The Messiah probably is to be identified with "the man of the sea" in *4 Ezra*, which we will examine in the next chapter. The Messiah is also a conquering leader according to *2 Baruch* (*2 Bar.*

40:1–4; 70:10; 72:2–4).[29] Collins writes, "This concept of the Davidic messiah as the warrior king who would destroy the enemies of Israel and institute an era of unending peace constitutes the common core of Jewish messianism around the turn of the era."[30] Still, the Messiah in *1 Enoch* and *4 Ezra* may also be distinguished, for in the case of *1 Enoch* the Messiah rules as the Son of Man from heaven, while in *4 Ezra* he is a warrior.[31]

Jesus as Messiah in the Gospels

The NT teaching on the Messiah flows from the Jewish and OT antecedents.[32] As the Messiah, he is the one who announces the kingdom, for the kingdom cannot be separated from its king. We have already seen that Jesus proclaimed a kingdom that upended the expectations of his contemporaries.[33] So we are not astonished that Jesus was not the Messiah whom the Jewish people had in mind. Indeed, in the Gospels Jesus' reserve in identifying himself as the Messiah is quite striking.[34] He did not publicly proclaim himself as the Messiah when his ministry commenced, nor did he regularly use the title. Instead, as we will see, he preferred to identify himself as the "Son of Man." This has led some scholars to doubt whether Jesus even believed that he was the Messiah, but such a judgment makes the same mistake (for different reasons) that Jesus' contemporaries made. When we read the Gospels (and not some scholarly reconstruction), it is quite evident that Jesus believed that he was the Messiah.[35] A turning point of his ministry occurred in

29. At this juncture we could also include *1 Enoch*, but we will delay examination of this text until we investigate "Son of Man," since that title is prominent in *1 En.* 37–71 and is linked with Messiah in *1 Enoch*.

30. J. J. Collins 1995: 68.

31. So also J. J. Collins 1995: 187. Collins, however, proceeds to identify the commonalities between the two because in each instance the Son of Man is an individual, the Messiah, and preexistent.

32. Rightly Horbury 1998: 112.

33. Strauss (1995: 261–336) connects Jesus' messianic status with the arrival of the new exodus. When we remember that the new exodus is another way of referring to the coming of the kingdom, it is evident that Strauss makes the same point being argued for here.

34. In considering the Messiah in the Gospels, I am including the Gospel of John with the Synoptics.

35. This view has been sharply contested by many scholars, but they deviate from the text itself to establish their theories. For a persuasive defense of the notion that Jesus identified himself as the Messiah, see Longenecker 1970: 62–82. Over against much of critical scholarship, Stuhlmacher (1993: 1–38) maintains that Jesus saw himself as the Messiah, and he argues that the terms "Christ," "Son of Man," and "Son of God" are all to be interpreted messianically in the ministry of Jesus. Those who deny the messianic

Caesarea Philippi (Matt. 16:13–20 par.).[36] He privately asked his disciples to identify him, for people thought he was a prophet, John the Baptist, Jeremiah, or the like. Peter responded that Jesus is the Christ, the Messiah. All the Gospel accounts clearly view Peter's identification as accurate.[37] In Matthew's Gospel Jesus traces Peter's insight to revelation from God, so that Peter could not claim that he had the wisdom to perceive who Jesus was (Matt. 16:17). Still, every account concludes with the disciples being sternly warned not to disseminate to others what they now know.

The restriction cannot be explained by saying that Jesus did not truly believe that he was the Messiah. It is historically improbable that the first disciples so badly understood or distorted their leader's teaching. Nor is it likely that the messianic secret theory of W. Wrede accounts for the evidence in a satisfactory way.[38] Jesus' hesitation to proclaim himself as the Messiah or to accept the title publicly is best explained by the explosive political implications of accepting the title. In all the Jewish traditions the Messiah reigns as king, and one of his prime tasks is to expel Gentiles from Israel. This theme especially manifests itself in *Psalms of Solomon*, but it is by no means limited to that text, as the history narrated by Josephus shows. If Jesus had identified himself as the Messiah, he would have concocted a political brew that would inevitably boil over. Most important, Jesus did not intend to fulfill the promises in the manner expected by most Jews. He would conquer not through military might and force but through suffering and death. The promises of the kingdom would come to pass through sacrificial love instead of at the point of a sword.

---

consciousness of Jesus include Bultmann 1951: 32; Conzelmann and Lindemann 1988: 323–24.

36. In Markan scholarship it is quite common to argue that Mark is correcting various wrong Christologies, but this view is effectively dismantled by Kingsbury 1983: 25–45.

37. Nevertheless, quite a few scholars have maintained that Peter's confession was mistaken. A better solution is to say that Peter's confession is "correct" but "insufficient" because he does not grasp the nature of Jesus' mission as Messiah (rightly Kingsbury 1983: 94–97).

38. Wrede (1971) argued that the messianic secret was incorporated by Mark from pre-Markan tradition. Historically, Jesus did not claim to be the Messiah, and hence the texts in which Jesus exhorted people to conceal his messianic identity are a theological construct stemming from the early church community rather than from Jesus himself. For an effective response to Wrede, see Dunn 1970b. For a review of scholarship up to 1969 and a proposal that does more justice to the evidence than Wrede's theory, see Aune 1969. Kingsbury (1983: 1–45), in a review of Markan scholarship up until 1983, demonstrates how the messianic secret and other construals of Mark's Christology are deficient in that they depart from the narrative world of Mark. I am not hereby endorsing all of Kingsbury's own conclusions regarding Markan Christology, but his work improves on that of his predecessors in that it considers Mark's Gospel as a literary whole.

The Synoptics make it plain that none of the disciples grasped Jesus' mission. They concurred with Peter that he was the Messiah. But when Jesus articulated his vocation, which included suffering and death, Peter rebuked Jesus (Matt. 16:21–23 par.). Jesus in turn called Peter's intervention and perspective satanic. If even Jesus' closest and most loyal followers could not grasp the nature of his messianic mission, we can scarcely doubt that the remainder of the people would have been completely baffled by the idea that the Messiah would suffer. Jesus could not use the title "Messiah" without imperiling his entire mission, since those whom he addressed would have concluded that he would be a conquering king. His reserve, therefore, does not indicate self-doubt about his messianic status; rather, it reflects a desire to forestall serious misconceptions on the part of his followers and the attending crowds of people.

On occasion Jesus did declare himself to be the Messiah. When the Samaritan woman announced that the Messiah will come and clarify everything, Jesus responded that he was the Messiah she sought (John 4:25–26). The reply to the Samaritan woman contrasts with the less-direct words to the Jewish leaders who demand that Jesus openly pronounce whether he is the Christ (John 10:24–26). A direct answer is not provided to their question. In response to the Jewish leaders Jesus said that his works indicate whether or not he is the Messiah. Why did Jesus tell the Samaritan woman straight out that he was the Messiah, although she did not even ask him that question, but refuse to give a direct answer to the religious leaders? It seems that the religious leaders did not ask the question as people sincerely seeking God. They desired to entrap Jesus by his own words. Perhaps Jesus felt free to speak to the Samaritan woman precisely because she was outside the mainstream of Palestinian Judaism. His claim to be the Messiah would not arouse a political movement among the Samaritans.[39]

The incident in which Nathaniel acclaimed Jesus as the king of Israel and the Son of God (John 1:49) may seem to contradict the argument here.[40] Andrew and Philip also seemed to embrace Jesus as Messiah from the outset (John 1:41, 45). Did the disciples, then, from the beginning of Jesus' ministry know that Jesus was the Messiah and God's Son?[41] We must beware of exaggerating the insight of the disciples at this early stage. For example, Nathaniel utters his words after Jesus announced that he had spied him under a fig tree. The enthusiasm of the moment gripped Nathaniel. The Gospel writer certainly concurred with Nathan-

39. So also R. Brown 1966: 172–73; Carson 1991b: 227; Köstenberger 2004: 158.
40. Dodd (1953: 229) notes the persistence of the theme in John that the Messiah is king.
41. As Beasley-Murray (1987: 27) says, "On Nathaniel's lips the two titles are virtually synonymous." See also Ridderbos 1997: 91.

iel's words, but it is likely that Nathaniel spoke better than he knew due to his enthusiasm.[42] Further, Jesus did not directly affirm his words by saying something like, "You are correct. I am the Messiah." Instead, he noted that Nathaniel would see greater things than Jesus' ability to discern where Nathaniel was located. The disciples recognized Jesus as Messiah from the beginning, but they also likely had doubts because Jesus did not fit their conception of what the Messiah would do. We should not conceive of their view of Jesus as if they wrote down the right answer on a test. Their understanding of Jesus ebbed and flowed as they traveled with him and were taught by him. Sometimes they veered toward thinking that he was the Messiah, but it seems that on other occasions they were assailed with doubts about his identity.

Jesus was hailed publicly as David's son or the king of the Jews on a few occasions (e.g., Matt. 9:27; 20:30–31; 21:9 par.).[43] Jesus seemed to accept the acclamations, but he avoided giving a direct answer. Further, the healing of the blind near Jericho and the triumphal entry came near the end of his ministry. He was recognized as David's son by the Canaanite woman (Matt. 15:22), though again he did not confirm her words directly. In any case, the event occurred outside the confines of Israel and represented the words of a Gentile. The people wondered whether Jesus was David's son (Matt. 12:23), and they were divided as to whether he could truly be the Davidic Messiah (John 7:26–27, 31, 42–43; 12:34) because confusion arose over whether Jesus fit what the Scriptures taught regarding the Messiah. When people sought to install Jesus as king, he turned his back on such a political agenda (John 6:15). Near the end of Jesus' ministry Martha confessed that Jesus was the Christ and the Son of God (John 11:27), and apparently some Jews claimed that Jesus was the Messiah and consequently were expelled from the synagogue (John 9:22).

When asked at his trial whether or not he is the Messiah, Jesus agrees that he is (Matt. 26:63–64; Mark 14:61–62; Luke 22:66–70).[44] Bock maintains that Jesus' appeal to Ps. 110:1 and Dan. 7:13 was considered to be blasphemy.[45] In claiming to ride on the clouds of heaven, Jesus claimed for himself something that was true only of God (cf. Exod. 13:21; Num.

---

42. For John, the title "Son of God" has a greater significance (see Carson 1991b: 162; Wright 2003: 672). For a careful discussion of the whole matter, see R. Brown 1966: 87–88.

43. R. Brown (1977: 505–12) argues that the notion that Jesus was genealogically descended from David is historically plausible.

44. See Marshall 1978b: 851; Hagner 1995: 709–10; Davies and Allison 1997: 528–29; France 2002: 610–11. See especially the detailed discussion in R. Brown 1994: 1:461–547.

45. See Bock's (2000: 197–209) survey of alternatives and his own assessment. For his defense of authenticity, see Bock 2000: 209–33.

10:34; Ps. 104:3; Isa. 19:1). Bock goes on to say that Jesus' claim to be the end-time judge was not blasphemy per se to the Jewish leaders (given the tradition of Enoch as Son of Man); what they objected to was Jesus' arrogation of a *divine* role, where he shares divine honor with God.[46] Bock is correct that the startling directness with which the earthly Jesus claimed such authority would scandalize the religious leaders. Honored Jewish heroes of the past might have been considered worthy of such a role, though even here, as Bock shows, some Jews were nervous about Enoch's reputed status. Assigning divine authority to Jesus, as a teacher from Galilee, was, however, unthinkable. Nolland suggests that Jesus' words would be considered blasphemous in that he claimed messianic status but his words and actions did not fit with such a claim in the eyes of the religious leaders. For someone to claim that he was the Messiah, when clearly he was a messianic pretender, could be judged as blasphemy.[47] Jesus' reply was the most direct in Mark, but the religious leaders took his answer to be an affirmation and, because he proclaimed himself as God's Son, charged him with blasphemy. In any case, it appears that Jesus was more forthright about his identity as the cross drew near. His messianic status can be discerned only in light of the cross. So it is not that Jesus ever denied that he was the Messiah, but rather that the triumphant view of Messiah so popular in Judaism vied with his own conception of his messianic mission. Had he used the title "Messiah" openly, he was certain to have been misunderstood. Hence, he felt free to use the title openly near the end of his ministry, only when his death was impending.[48]

The Gospel writers note the irony at Jesus' trial and death, for then the title "king" or "king of the Jews" was used freely in reference to Jesus. Pilate's anxiety over Jesus was provoked by the assertion that he was a rival king (Luke 23:2). When Pilate asked Jesus if he is "the king of the Jews," Jesus parried that they certainly think that he is a king because they are about to put him to death as such (Matt. 27:11; Mark 15:2; Luke 23:3; John 18:33–34, 37). Pilate flung in the face of the Jews the issue of what he should do with their king (Mark 15:9, 12; John 18:39). Pilate certainly did not think that Jesus was truly a king, but his words had a

46. So also Luz 2005: 430–32; Davies and Allison 1997: 532. See also Hooker (1967: 173), who says, "To claim for oneself a seat at the right hand of power, however, is to claim a share in the authority of God; to appropriate to oneself such authority and to bestow on oneself this unique status in the sight of God and man would almost certainly have been regarded as blasphemy."

47. Nolland 2005: 1133. Schlatter (1997: 370) argues along the same lines. The fact that Jesus could not defend himself from punishment and was about to be put to death on a cross indicated that he was blaspheming in the eyes of the religious leaders.

48. Moule (1977: 35) says that Jesus believed that he was the Messiah but reinterpreted what that meant.

deeper meaning. God speaks through him to underscore the truth that the Jews are indeed deliberating about what to do with their king and have determined to put him to death.

The drama reaches a fever pitch in John's Gospel when the religious leaders sensed that their plan to put Jesus to death could slip away, and so they remarked that Pilate would betray his loyalty to Caesar if he allowed a rival king to escape with impunity (John 19:12). Pilate knew how to play the game of political survival, and so he conceded. But he poked his finger in the eyes of the religious leaders by asking them to look upon their king (John 19:14). Little did Pilate or the religious leaders perceive that they were gazing at their king at that very moment. The leaders clamored for his crucifixion, and Pilate maliciously and impudently retorted, "Shall I crucify your king?" The Jews responded, "We have no king but Caesar" (John 19:15). Even though they were not serious about their loyalty to Caesar, their words condemned them. They preferred the political machinations of Rome to their true king. The inscription on the cross testified, ironically enough, that Jesus died as the king of the Jews (Matt. 27:37 par.; John 19:19–21). The soldiers who hailed Jesus as the "king of the Jews" failed to realize that Jesus' kingship was one that entailed suffering, and that his suffering was the pathway to his messianic exaltation (Matt. 27:29; Mark 15:18; John 19:3). Nor did the Jewish leaders and others realize when mocking him that if he were to come down from the cross, such an action would deny his kingship rather than confirm it (Matt. 27:41–42 par.).

Some have interpreted Jesus' query to the Pharisees about the Messiah as Jesus denying that the Messiah was David's son (Matt. 22:41–46 par.).[49] Jesus appealed to the first verse of Ps. 110 to point out that the Messiah was David's lord.[50] He asked the Pharisees how this fits with the Messiah also being David's son. If taken in isolation, this passage perhaps could be understood as a refutation of the Davidic lineage of the Messiah. We have already seen that Jesus accepts, even if obliquely, acclamations as David's son. Furthermore, Matthew and Luke clearly teach that Jesus is David's son and a Davidic Messiah, and in composing their Gospels they scarcely understood the account in question as a denial of such a truth. Another interpretation of what Jesus meant fits well with the narrative of the Gospels as a whole: Jesus understood the

49. So, for example, Bousset 1970: 34–35; Klausner 1929: 320. Cullmann (1963: 130–33) rejects this view, noting also that the evangelists themselves could not have understood the text in this way because elsewhere Jesus is said to be descended from David, though Cullmann maintains that in Mark the point is that Jesus did not necessarily need to be from David's line, even if in fact he is.

50. See discussion in Bock 1987: 128–32.

Messiah to be both son and lord of David. In other words, the Messiah was not less than the son of David, but certainly he was more.[51]

We have already noted that the story line of the Gospels reveals that Jesus is the Christ. Thus we are not surprised that each story ends with the resurrection, for the resurrection confirms that Jesus was truly the Messiah, because he was tried and executed as a false messiah, and his resurrection vindicated his messianic claim.[52] Here we should observe that each of the Gospel writers, using editorial references, confirms Jesus' messianic identity. Mark does not constantly repeat that Jesus is the Christ. Nonetheless, he intends for his readers to read the narrative and to draw that conclusion. This is manifestly clear from the first verse of his Gospel, which is programmatic for all that follows: "The beginning of the gospel of Jesus Christ, the Son of God" (Mark 1:1).[53] Anyone who reads Mark's story and fails to see that Jesus is the Christ misreads the account, since the reader is clued into the identity of Jesus from the first verse. Hence, when Peter said that Jesus was the Christ (Mark 8:27–30), the turning point of the Gospel has come, for from that point on Jesus instructed the disciples about the nature of his messiahship: he is a suffering Messiah.[54]

Jesus' messianic identity likewise stamps Matthew's Gospel from the first verse.[55] The genealogy commencing this Gospel (Matt. 1:1–17) begins, "The book of the genealogy of Jesus Christ, the son of David" (Matt. 1:1). Matthew could hardly be clearer, since he labels Jesus as the "Christ" and then informs us that he is David's son. Indeed, the genealogy focuses on David, for his name is repeated five times (Matt. 1:1, 6, 17), and he appears at the beginning, the middle, and the conclusion of the genealogy. The term "Christ" is not found in the middle of the genealogy, but it functions as an envelope for the whole by appearing in Matt. 1:1 and with a decided emphasis in Matt. 1:16–17. As the narrative continues, Matthew goes on to speak of the birth of "Jesus Christ" (Matt. 1:18), again identifying him for the reader. He emphasizes that Joseph was David's son (Matt. 1:20),

---

51. Horbury (1998: 150) sees a line of thought from messianism to the worship of Christ, and so he sees messianism and the worship of Christ not as polar conceptions but rather as compatible notions. But the line of argument is not clearly persuasive because evidence is lacking that Judaism believed in a preexistent Messiah.

52. So Wright 2003: 559–83.

53. Marcus (2000: 146–47) rightly says that in this text "Jesus Christ" is both an objective and a subjective genitive. The good news is both about and from Jesus Christ.

54. Jesus, then, did not disagree with Peter's confession of him as the Messiah, but he realized that his disciples did not yet grasp that he was a suffering Messiah (see Hawkin 1972).

55. For a brief survey, see France 1989: 281–86. Verseput (1987: 533–37) demonstrates that there is no criticism of the notion that Jesus is the Messiah in Matthew; rather, Matthew affirms enthusiastically that Jesus is Israel's Messiah.

and after the genealogy no reader can miss the significance of such a comment. We see Matthew's editing when John in prison hears about "the deeds of Christ" (Matt. 11:2). Matthew writes so that the Jewish reader will confess that Jesus is the Christ, the son of David.

Luke, too, affirms that Jesus is the Messiah from the outset of the Gospel.[56] When Gabriel announced the birth of Jesus, he said that Jesus will sit on David's throne (Luke 1:32). God has fulfilled his saving and covenant promises by raising "up a horn of salvation for us in the house of his servant David" (Luke 1:69). He emphasizes that Joseph descended from David (Luke 2:4), and the shepherds were told that a child born "in the city of David" is none other than "Christ the Lord" (Luke 2:11). The formulation here is strikingly close to what we saw in *Psalms of Solomon* (*Pss. Sol.* 17:32; 18:7). It was revealed to Simeon that he would not die before he saw "the Lord's Christ" (Luke 2:26). In the Lukan genealogy Jesus is identified as a son of David (Luke 3:31),[57] even though the genealogy differs from Matthew's.[58] Demons also recognized that Jesus is the Christ (Luke 4:41).

The centrality of Jesus being identified as the Messiah is clear in the Gospel of John, for John explicitly informs the readers that he wrote so that Jesus would be confessed as Messiah and the Son of God (John 20:30–31). This passage serves as the purpose statement and the conclusion of this Gospel, and it echoes the prologue, where Jesus is identified as the Messiah (John 1:17). Indeed, eternal life is defined as knowing God and Jesus as Messiah. The importance of Jesus' messianic identity in John's Gospel is patently clear.

Each of the Gospels, therefore, emphasizes that Jesus is the Messiah, the promised son of David. Jesus himself did not use the title often because it was liable to be misunderstood in the political milieu of first-century Palestinian Judaism. Jesus' followers gradually came to realize that he was the Messiah. They were baffled and confused, however, by the notion that Jesus as the Messiah would suffer and die. Only after Jesus was raised from the dead did they comprehend how suffering and death could fit with him being the Messiah. Even with his disciples Jesus did not immediately or often declare himself to be the Messiah, for they were prone to misunderstand the import of the office. Once we perceive that the title was almost invariably misunderstood by Jesus' contemporaries and

---

56. For full-scale studies that convincingly demonstrate the importance of Jesus as the Davidic Messiah in Luke-Acts, see Bock 1987; Strauss 1995. The differences between Bock and Strauss do not pertain to the thesis argued here.

57. Jesus' claim in Luke 4:18–21 that he is the bringer of salvation also points to his messianic status (see Bock 1987: 109–10).

58. See especially here the discussion in Strauss 1995: 209–15. R. Brown (1977: 503–4) argues that the problems with all harmonizations are insurmountable and thus rejects this as a likely solution. But for a plausible explanation, see Carson 1984: 64–65.

even by his closest followers, we can explain the phenomenon in which the Gospel writers from the beginning of their writings declare Jesus as Messiah, while at the same time Jesus uses the title sparingly. The clear announcement by the Gospel writers that Jesus was the Messiah does not contradict his reticence in using the title. His hesitation was due to the misunderstanding that accompanied the title, but the Gospel writers had no need to share the same reluctance, for they wrote after the death and resurrection of Jesus. That Jesus was a crucified Messiah was plain in retrospect, but prospectively such an understanding was obscure.

Son of Man

Old Testament Background

One of the most important designations for Jesus in the Gospels is "Son of Man."[59] Consequently, intense discussion over the meaning of the term has informed NT scholarship since critical study commenced. We begin with the OT use of the term. In Hebrew the expression "son of man" (*ben 'ādām*) is simply another way of saying "human being." This is clear from Hebrew parallelism in a number of texts. "God is not man, that he should lie, or a son of man, that he should change his mind" (Num. 23:19). Clearly, "man" and "son of man" here are synonymous, referring to human beings in general. The same phenomenon is evident in Ps. 8:4: "What is man that you are mindful of him, and the son of man that you care for him?" The psalmist does not have a different entity in view with the term "son of man"; it is another way of speaking about human beings. A similar use of the term is evident in a number of OT texts (cf. Job 25:6; Isa. 51:12; 56:2; Jer. 49:18, 33; 50:40; 51:43). In Ezekiel the term "son of man" is used, by my count, ninety-three times (e.g., Ezek. 2:1, 3, 6, 8). In the context of Ezekiel the emphasis is likely on Ezekiel's mortality and weakness in contrast to the glory and majesty of God.[60] He is merely human in contrast to the awesome majesty of God.

Psalm 80 rehearses God's saving acts on behalf of Israel and their present desolation and devastation at the hand of foreign nations. The psalmist

---

59. There has been intense discussion of the derivation of "Son of Man" in terms of the history of religions, with a wide range of suggestions including Iranian, Chaldean, Egyptian, Mandean, Manichean, Gnostic, and Jewish roots. It is possible that the term derives in part from other sources, since Jewish thought was not sealed off from the rest of the world, but the primary background should be sought in Judaism in regard to NT interpretation. J. J. Collins (1995: 174) remarks, "The notion that the Son of Man was a variant of a widespread myth of the Primordial Man has been laid to rest with no regrets" (see also p. 175).

60. In his commentary on Ezekiel, Block (1997; 1998) translates the phrase consistently as "human."

asks God to intervene and to restore the nation. Israel is compared to a vine that Yahweh planted and tended that now has been cut down. Yahweh is implored to take regard for "the son whom you made strong for yourself" (Ps. 80:15). Psalm 80:17 contains a similar request: "Let your hand be on the man of your right hand, the son of man whom you have made strong for yourself."[61] In this context the "son" may be Israel (cf. Exod. 4:22) represented by the image of a vine (cf. Isa. 5:1–7). Alternatively, the "son" may be the anointed king who represents Israel as a whole. In either instance, "son of man" points not to Israel's weakness or mortality but rather to its special relationship with Yahweh.

The most controversial reference to "son of man" in the OT is in Dan. 7. Here "son of man" is in Aramaic, *bar 'ĕnāš* (Dan. 7:13). Some scholars have identified the son of man in the chapter as a divine figure.[62] Others have detected a reference to the archangel Michael[63] or perhaps to one angel who represents the angelic host. The appearance of angels in human form supports this interpretation (Dan. 8:15; 10:16), and Dan. 10:16 speaks of an angel appearing as *bĕnê 'ādām*, the "sons of men" (my translation). Deciphering the meaning of "son of man" in Dan. 7 should rely on its context. In Dan. 7 four different kingdoms are depicted as bestial animals: Babylon as a lion with eagle's wings; Medo-Persia as a bear; Greece as a leopard; Rome as an indescribably ferocious beast, a terrible combination of the beastly character of all the kingdoms.[64] The kingdoms are depicted as beasts because they are like rapacious animals, brutalizing and terrorizing the peoples of the world. The kingdom of God, on the other hand, will ultimately conquer and destroy all these other kingdoms. God's kingdom is given to a "son of man." We have seen above that "son of man" in the OT is merely a way of saying that one is a human being. Such an interpretation is reflected in the NRSV's translation of Dan. 7:13: "I saw one like a human being coming with the clouds of heaven." The kingdom is given to this son of man forever, so that all other kingdoms are subjugated to the kingdom of a son of man. The reason for using the term "son of man" is to contrast his kingdom with the beastly kingdoms described earlier in the chapter. The kingdom of a son of man will be humane and beneficent instead of bringing

61. A. Anderson (1972: 586) thinks that the "son of man" here either is the king (perhaps Josiah) or designates Israel, but he rejects a messianic reading. Kidner (1975: 292) thinks that Israel is in view but claims that it finds its final fulfillment in Jesus as Son of Man.

62. Kim 1983; Caragounis 1986. In saying that the Son of Man is also the Son of God, Kim does not deny the view that the Son of Man also represents the people of God.

63. J. J. Collins 1993: 304–10.

64. Many scholars divide Medo-Persia into two entities, so that the fourth beast is identified as Greece (e.g., J. J. Collins 1993: 295–99). The resolution to this issue is not crucial for the argument being made here.

devastation as do the beastly kingdoms. His kingdom will bring peace and joy to human beings instead of death and destruction.

What is particularly fascinating is the interpretation given to Daniel regarding his vision of the four beasts and the son of man. In Dan. 7:17 the beasts are said to represent four kings. We can fairly conclude that these kings function as the representative heads of the various kingdoms. The kingdom given to a son of man in the vision is explained in terms of the kingdom being given to the saints: "But the saints of the Most High shall receive the kingdom and possess the kingdom forever, forever and ever" (Dan. 7:18). Twice more the vision is explained as the kingdom being handed over to the saints (Dan. 7:22, 27).

We noted above that some identify "son of man" with an angel or angels, but it is more likely that "the saints" here refers to the children of Israel.[65] The expression used in Dan. 7:13 is "son of man" in the singular, not "sons of men" (my translation of *běnê 'ādām*) as in Dan. 10:16.[66] The singular refers to human beings elsewhere, as we have seen, and thus we should draw the same conclusion in this instance. A reference to human beings also seems likely because Dan. 7:21 refers to the saints being conquered by the "horn." The saints who are conquered almost certainly are the Israelites who are oppressed and persecuted by this evil ruler, and not angels. Daniel 7:25 seems to validate this interpretation, for this same king will "wear out the saints" for three and one-half years. It is difficult to believe that he triumphs over angels for this period of time. Rather, he mistreats the people of God. Finally, Dan. 7:27 confirms a reference to Israel. The kingdom is given to "the people of the saints of the Most High." The word "people" (*'am*) almost certainly refers to Israel as the people of God. They are the recipients of the kingdom. Pagan nations will rule for a certain period of history, but they will not ultimately triumph. God will intervene, judge the wicked, inaugurate the kingdom, and give it to his people.

There may be an indication, however, that the corporate people of God—the saints of the Most High—are represented by one figure.[67] In Dan. 7:13–14 the focus on an individual also seems to be present:[68] "I saw in the night visions, and behold, with the clouds of heaven there

65. For this view, see Casey 1979: 24–46; Hooker 1967: 11–30; Beasley-Murray 1986: 29–32; Caragounis 1986: 45–46; Dunn 1996a: 67–75.

66. Beasley-Murray (1986: 32) rightly points out that neither Gabriel nor Michael is mentioned in Dan. 7, which confirms the supposition that they are not in view here.

67. So Beasley-Murray 1986: 31–33; Gentry 2003: 71–72. But Dunn (1996a: 67–87) dissents from this view, limits the reference to Israel, and maintains that the individual understanding of the Son of Man stemmed from early Christianity or Jesus rather than from the intention of Daniel itself. Casey (1979: 24–46) also argues strongly that "son of man" in Daniel only refers to the Jewish people, the saints, and that any wider reference is precluded.

68. Cullmann (1963: 138–40) argues similarly that "son of man" is not a title in Daniel, but the son of man does represent the saints. Given the parallel with the four kings and

came one like a son of man, and he came to the Ancient of Days and was presented before him. And to him was given dominion and glory and a kingdom, that all peoples, nations, and languages should serve him; his dominion is an everlasting dominion, which shall not pass away, and his kingdom one that shall not be destroyed." The vision is explicated so that a son of man is identified as the saints, but we have already seen that the kingdoms are interpreted to refer to four kings (Dan. 7:17). Apparently, the four kingdoms are represented by the kings who rule over them. Similarly, "son of man" may refer to Israel as the people of God, and at the same time Israel may be represented by an individual. Just as kings function as the corporate representative of nations, so also an individual could represent Israel. Moreover, there are indications of the son of man's divinity in Daniel.[69] The Aramaic verb for "serve" (*plḥ*) in Dan. 7:27 is used elsewhere of service and worship of God (Dan. 3:12, 14, 17, 18, 28; 6:17, 21; 7:14). Further, coming on the clouds of heaven in Dan. 7:13 suggests deity, for elsewhere in the OT only God rides on the clouds of heaven.[70] Indeed, the son of man in Daniel does not grasp rule through military conquest by which he brutally rules over other human beings. He is given the kingdom by God himself, and thereby he fulfills the role for which human beings were created (Ps. 8).[71]

Son of Man in Second Temple Judaism

In postbiblical Judaism "Son of Man" shows up often in *1 En.* 37–71.[72] Students of *1 Enoch* agree that it is pre-Christian, but particular debate has been engendered by *1 En.* 37–71 because those chapters are not in evidence at Qumran. Hence, scholars debate whether the chapters are pre- or post-Christian.[73] We cannot delve into that discussion here, though it seems to me that those who argue for a date before AD 70 are persuasive. Even if the chapters are post-Christian, they almost certainly represent independent tradition—perhaps in this instance a response

---

kingdoms in Dan. 7, Cullmann argues that the son of man could function representatively for the saints.

69. See Caragounis 1986: 35–81; Gentry 2003: 72–74. I differ from Caragounis in that he sees the son of man in Dan. 7 only as a heavenly figure and excludes any identification with the people of Israel.

70. Caragounis 1986: 71–73.

71. So Gentry 2003: 74–75.

72. I will capitalize "Son of Man" in *1 Enoch* because it seems to function as a title there.

73. Most date the book either before AD 70 or AD 100 (e.g., Burkett 1999: 71–72; Borsch 1992: 141; Black 1992: 161–62; Hengel 2006: 97). Such a date would suggest that the book had no influence on NT writers.

to Christian tradition, for the Son of Man is not Jesus of Nazareth but may even be Enoch himself.[74]

One of the striking features of *1 En.* 37–71 is that the term "Son of Man" is a title referring to an individual.[75] The term denotes not Israel corporately but rather a solitary person. Just as Dan. 7 predicted, this Son of Man will crush sinners, remove hostile kings, and accomplish the Lord's will (*1 En.* 46:3–6).[76] It seems that the author teaches that the Son of Man preexisted with God before the world began, seeing him as the light of the nations and the one whom all shall worship (*1 En.* 48:2–6; 62:7).[77] He is also identified as the Messiah (*1 En.* 48:10; 52:4). He is God's elect one, endowed with the Spirit as prophesied in Isa. 11:2 (*1 En.* 49:1–4; 51:3–4; 52:6; 53:6). God's chosen one sits on God's glorious throne and judges demonic powers and sinners for the Lord's sake (*1 En.* 55:4; 61:8; 62:2–3). The chosen one who sits on the throne and judges sinners is clearly the Son of Man (*1 En.* 62:7–8; 63:11; 69:29). The righteous will enjoy the eschatological feast with him (*1 En.* 62:14; cf. 70:1; 71:17). The Son of Man is even identified as Enoch (*1 En.* 60:10; 71:14), though there is also evidence that the two should be distinguished (*1 En.* 70:1). Hence, many scholars question whether Enoch is truly identified with the Son of Man as portrayed in the previous chapters.[78]

Many fascinating questions emerge in *1 En.* 37–71 that cannot be resolved here. Perhaps the reference to preexistence does not refer to actual preexistence,[79] but on balance preexistence seems to be in view (*1 En.* 48:3).[80] It seems odd that a Jewish writing would refer to the worship of the Son of Man, but perhaps this is simply a dramatic way of emphasizing exaltation. Though some see a corporate reference to Israel, it seems more likely that an individual is in view. Such an exalted view of the Son of Man indicates that the NT is not alone in discerning an exalted figure in the phrase.[81]

---

74. Burkett (1999: 97–120) argues that there is not a unified Son of Man tradition in Judaism. Instead Dan. 7 was interpreted in various ways.

75. Cullmann (1963: 140–42) says that the Son of Man in *1 Enoch* is not merely representative but rather denotes an individual who existed before creation and is considered to be the Messiah. Cullmann (1963: 142) remarks, "His divine majesty cannot be emphasized strongly enough."

76. In other words, it is clear that the Son of Man tradition in *1 Enoch* draws upon Dan. 7 (cf. *1 En.* 46:1; 47:3).

77. In support of preexistence, see J. J. Collins 1995: 143; Burkett 1999: 100–101.

78. The complexities of that issue cannot be resolved here (see J. J. Collins 1995: 178–81; Burkett 1999: 101–2). VanderKam (1992: 183) suggests that the earthly Enoch had a "supernatural double who had existed before being embodied in the person of Enoch."

79. So VanderKam 1992: 180–82.

80. So Caragounis 1986: 114; J. J. Collins 1995: 179; Horbury 1998: 103–4.

81. Horbury (1998: 107) maintains, "It is true that the superhuman and spiritual aspects of the descriptions do not abolish the humanity of the messiah; but it is also true that the

Perhaps a tradition related to the son of man is also present in *4 Ezra*. Scholars generally agree that chapters 3–14 are Jewish, whereas chapters 1–2 and 15–16 were added by a later Christian redactor.[82] *Fourth Ezra* was written after AD 70, and so we have independent Jewish tradition regarding the son of man and the Messiah, for it is likely that the son of man and Messiah are the same person. We learn from the vision that this man came from the sea, perhaps to counter the evil kingdoms that emerged from the sea in Dan. 7:2–3 (*4 Ezra* 13:3), though when the vision is explained, Ezra is told that it represents the incomprehensibility of the vision concerning this son. This man seems to be the son of man, for the allusion to Dan. 7:13 appears to exist in saying that the man "flew with the clouds of heaven" (*4 Ezra* 13:3).[83] Human beings conspired to wage war against the man from the sea, but "he carved out for himself a great mountain and flew up upon it" (*4 Ezra* 13:6). The mountain here perhaps alludes to Dan. 2:4, referring to the kingdom of God that will triumph throughout the world over the political powers opposed to God. The man of the sea will destroy his opponents with the breath of his mouth (*4 Ezra* 13:8–11; cf. Isa. 11:4) and call a peaceable people to himself (*4 Ezra* 13:12–13).

The vision that Ezra received is then explained to him. The man from the sea—"who will himself deliver his creation; and he will direct those who are left" (*4 Ezra* 13:26)—has been concealed by God for ages. The man from the sea is identified as God's son (*4 Ezra* 13:32).[84] The nations will gather to fight against him, but the son will judge and destroy them (*4 Ezra* 13:37–39). He will gather the ten tribes back to Israel and also grant peace to those within Israel (*4 Ezra* 13:40–50).[85]

Son of Man in the Synoptic Gospels

The use of the term "Son of Man" in the Synoptic Gospels has always been highly interesting to those studying the Gospels,[86] and the number of differing interpretations proposed is nothing short of

---

messiah is widely, not just exceptionally, depicted with emphasis on his superhuman and spiritual aspect." Caragounis (1986: 119) argues that the reference to worship shows that the Son of Man in *1 Enoch* is a divine figure.

82. See Metzger (1983: 517–18, 520, 522).

83. J. J. Collins (1995: 183) suggests that the original may have read "son of man."

84. But contra Caragounis (1986: 129–30), since the Messiah dies after four hundred years in *4 Ezra*, he should not be identified as divine.

85. In some texts in rabbinic literature the son of man of Dan. 7 was understood to be the Messiah. See the discussion of the texts in Burkett 1999: 114–18.

86. For a careful analysis of the term "son of man" in Jewish literature, see Fitzmyer 1979: 143–60. On the import of Son of Man in the Gospels, Longenecker 1970: 82–93 is valuable and insightful.

astonishing.[87] One of the striking features is that the title is reserved almost exclusively to the Gospels.[88] Matthew uses the expression thirty times,[89] Mark fourteen,[90] Luke twenty-five, and John thirteen. We will look at John's use of the phrase separately, given John's distinctive Christology. Outside the Gospels, the term is used with reference to Jesus only in Acts 7:56; Heb. 2:6; Rev. 1:13; 14:14. Whether the term actually refers to Jesus in Rev. 14:14 is a matter of significant debate among scholars.[91] It is also unclear whether the phrase in Heb. 2:6 draws on the same circle of tradition that we see in the Gospels. In any case, the paucity of references outside the Gospels confirms that the use of the term within the Gospels themselves is the crucial matter for our study.

The "Son of Man" sayings often are placed in three categories:[92] (1) those that refer to the Son of Man's work on earth; (2) those that refer to his suffering; (3) those that refer to the future. These categories overlap in some cases. For example, the sayings about suffering also relate to what happens on earth. Some of the sayings do not fit neatly into any category, demonstrating that the categories are imperfect. Still, the division is a useful way of analyzing the different sayings.

We will begin with what scholars typically call the earthly sayings.[93] The Son of Man is persecuted, and so he has nowhere to lay his head (Matt. 8:20; Luke 9:58); detractors accuse him of excessive eating and drinking (Matt. 11:19; Luke 7:34); the disciples are blessed if persecuted for the sake of the Son of Man (Luke 6:22); he has the authority to forgive sins (Matt. 9:6; Mark 2:10; Luke 5:24); he is Lord of the Sabbath (Matt. 12:8; Mark 2:28; Luke 6:5); those who speak a word against him can

87. The various interpretations are too numerous to explore here. For a clear and succinct survey along with an evaluation of the views proposed, see Burkett 1999; see also Caragounis 1986: 9–33.

88. Many scholars maintain that "Son of Man" is not a title (see the following discussion and cf. Hurtado 2003: 293, 296–97, 303–5). Hurtado's view is weakened in that he claims that "Son of Man" is merely a "*literary device*" rather than a title (Hurtado 2003: 297), and he downplays the allusions to Dan. 7:13–14 in the Gospels (Hurtado 2003: 298–99). Fitzmyer (1979: 14, 153–55) argues that the expression "son of man" is not a title in Dan. 7:13–14 or in any of the Aramaic literature previous to the NT era, but he maintains that "Son of Man" is a title in the NT itself, and that Dan. 7:13–14 (though not itself titular) was the impetus for the titular sense in the Gospel. It is clear that "Son of Man" is a title in the Gospels and clearly alludes to Dan. 7 (Dunn 1996a: 66).

89. For a brief and useful survey of the Matthean use of the term, see France 1989: 288–92.

90. For an insightful survey on the Son of Man in Mark, see Kingsbury 1983: 157–79.

91. For a reference to Christ, see Caird 1966: 190–91; R. Mounce 1977: 279; Beale 1999b: 770–71; Osborne 2002: 550. For a reference to an angelic being, see Aune 1998: 840–42.

92. See, for example, Fitzmyer 1979: 144; Marshall 1976: 69–72.

93. I list the Synoptic parallel passages for thoroughness in this instance.

be forgiven, but those who blaspheme the Spirit cannot (Matt. 12:32; Luke 12:10);[94] he sows the good seed of God's word (Matt. 13:37); he has come to seek and save the lost (Luke 19:10).[95] The designation "earthly" for these sayings is misleading if it is taken to mean "insignificant." The authority of the Son of Man breathes through these sayings because he forgives sins, is sovereign over the Sabbath, speaks God's word, and has a mission from God to seek and to save those who are lost. The other sayings focus on persecution and could perhaps even be placed in the category of the suffering Son of Man. The significance of the Son of Man is still highlighted because to suffer for his sake is a blessing, and those who follow him in discipleship must be willing to walk the path that he trod.

The second category of sayings relates to suffering.[96] Just as John the Baptist suffered at the hands of Herod, so the Son of Man will suffer (Matt. 17:12; Mark 9:12–13). Jesus, in the passion predictions, said that the Son of Man would be handed over to authorities by the religious leaders in Judaism, be mistreated and persecuted, put to death, and raised on the third day.[97] In most of these texts the suffering of the Son of Man overlaps with his future triumph, for he will not only suffer but also be raised from the dead (see also Matt. 17:9; Mark 9:9). So, we have another instance where the discrete categories do not quite fit. We see the same phenomenon in the saying about Jonah (Matt. 12:40; Luke 11:30). Just as Jonah was in the whale for three days, so the Son of Man will be in the grave for the same period of time. The implication is that just as Jonah was delivered from the whale, so will the Son of Man be set free from death. It is not as if Jesus will be sentenced to death inadvertently. As the Son of Man, he came to earth to serve and "to give his life as a ransom for many" (Matt. 20:28; Mark 10:45). His death was planned by God beforehand, and that this was his destiny as the Son of Man is attested by the Scriptures (Matt. 26:24; Mark 14:21; Luke 22:22; see also Luke 22:48). Not surprisingly, the sayings about the suffering Son of Man focus on the future death of Jesus. Jesus' predictions indicate

94. This could be placed in the future category because forgiveness is ultimately eschatological.

95. Tannehill (1986: 125) argues that the story of Zacchaeus plays a programmatic role in Luke, illustrating the purpose of Jesus' ministry.

96. Hooker (1967: 26–30) argues that "son of man" in Dan. 7 refers to Israel and to both Israel's suffering and its final vindication. For Mark, Hooker (1967: 181) says that the three categories of sayings refer to "an authority which is in turn proclaimed, denied, and vindicated."

97. (1) Matt. 16:21; Mark 8:31; Luke 9:22; (2) Matt. 17:22–23; Mark 9:31; Luke 9:44; (3) Matt. 20:18–19; Mark 10:33–34; Luke 18:31–33; (4) Matt. 26:2; (5) Matt. 26:45; Mark 14:41; (6) Luke 24:6–7.

that his death was not a terrible accident but rather was part of God's plan from the beginning.

The last category includes sayings about the Son of Man that relate to the future. The disciples will not finish evangelizing Israel "before the Son of Man comes" (Matt. 10:23). The Son of Man will commission his angels to remove from his kingdom all the unrighteous. The wicked will be punished and the righteous will shine in the kingdom forever (Matt. 13:41–43). The Son of Man will come in the future and repay all people according to what they have done (Matt. 16:27). On the day of judgment the Son of Man will be ashamed of those who are ashamed of Jesus (Mark 8:38; Luke 9:26). Similarly, those who acknowledge Jesus before others will be acknowledged by the Son of Man before God's angels (Luke 12:8).

Jesus asks whether people will continue to believe when the Son of Man comes (Luke 18:8). Disciples should stay vigilant to the end, praying that they will be able "to stand before the Son of Man" on the last day (Luke 21:36). Some of Jesus' disciples will not die before seeing "the Son of Man coming in his kingdom" (Matt. 16:28). In the coming world when the Son of Man sits on his throne, the twelve disciples will also sit on thrones, ruling the people of God (Matt. 19:28). In the future the disciples will desire "to see one of the days of the Son of Man" (Luke 17:22).[98] The Son of Man will come as clearly as lightning that blazes across the entire expanse of the sky (Matt. 24:27; Luke 17:24). People "will see the Son of Man coming on the clouds of heaven with power and great glory" (Matt. 24:30; Mark 13:26; Luke 21:27). People will be unprepared for the Son of Man's coming as they were unprepared for judgment during the days of Noah and Lot (Matt. 24:37–39; Luke 17:26–30). The Son of Man is coming at an hour that people do not expect (Matt. 24:44; Luke 12:40). He will come with a brilliant glory and reign on his throne (Matt. 25:31). Jesus tells the religious leaders at his trial, "You will see the Son of Man sitting at the right hand of power and coming on the clouds of heaven" (Matt. 26:64; Mark 14:62; cf. Luke 22:69).[99] The future sayings emphasize the glory of the Son of Man when he comes to the earth. He will reign and rule and determine the final destiny of those on earth.

If we put the Son of Man sayings together, it becomes clear that according to the Gospel writers, Jesus is the Son of Man. He has the authority to forgive sins, seeks those who are lost, and is the Lord of the Sabbath. At the same time, he is the suffering Son of Man. He will be rejected

98. This saying could be placed in the category of earthly sayings as well because it could be interpreted to refer to the Son of Man's life on earth.

99. Cullmann (1963: 121, 126) says that the claim to be the Son of Man is more radical than the claim to be Messiah, and that Jesus rejects the common political notions associated with Messiah, not the actual claim to be the Messiah. ·

by his contemporaries and ultimately be sentenced to death. His death should not be viewed as an accident; rather, he dies as a ransom for many. Nor will death triumph over Jesus as the Son of Man. He will be raised from the dead, and in the future he will come again with power as the Son of Man reigning at God's right hand. He will punish those who do evil and will vindicate the righteous. The high Christology in the Son of Man sayings is evident. He is clearly identified with God and takes on divine prerogatives as the one who forgives sins, is the Lord of the Sabbath, and is the judge of all on the last day.[100]

Scholars have disputed vigorously whether the Son of Man sayings are authentic, whether they can be genuinely traced back to the historical Jesus. The main task of a NT theology is not to discern authenticity but to set forth the theology contained in the Gospels. In other words, we need to explicate the theology of the Son of Man in the Gospels regardless of the question of authenticity. Nevertheless, there are good reasons to believe that the theology contained in the Gospels and the tradition about the historical Jesus is not historical fantasy (Luke 1:1–4). The Gospel writers did not write exact transcripts of what happened, but it was their intention to represent faithfully the words and works of the historical Jesus.

Some scholars have argued that all of the Son of Man sayings are inauthentic.[101] In every instance, they allege, the expression "Son of Man" comes from the Gospel writers or the church communities represented, instead of from the historical Jesus. Bultmann argues that the eschatological sayings come from Jesus himself, but he contends that the Son of Man in these instances refers not to Jesus himself but to another who will return as the Son of Man.[102] Higgins, on the other hand, thinks that only the eschatological sayings are authentic and that they refer to Jesus himself.[103] Other scholars restrict the authentic sayings to those that relate to the earthly Son of Man.[104] Most of the scholars who opt for this view maintain that "Son of Man" is not a title but an idiomatic self-reference, so that "Son of Man" is a way of saying "I" or "someone." Finally, some scholars think that sayings in all the categories are authentic.[105]

100. In other words, the Son of God is also the suffering Son of Man (so Caragounis 1986: 141–42). On the suffering son of man in Daniel, see Moule 1977: 27.
101. For example, Vielhauer 1963; Käsemann 1964b: 43–44; Perrin 1967: 164–206.
102. For example, Bultmann 1963: 112, 128, 150–52; 1951: 29–31.
103. Higgins 1964: 185–92.
104. For example, Vermes 1973: 160–91; 1983: 89–99; Casey 1979; 1985; 1987; Lindars 1983; Schweizer 1970: 166–71 (mainly earthly).
105. For example, Marshall 1976: 63–82; Cullmann 1963: 155–61; Caragounis 1986: 147–67; Kim 1983: 7–14.

The last view is the most credible. It is curious that many scholars doubt the authenticity of "Son of Man" when it clearly matches the criterion of dissimilarity. The phrase is scarcely used outside the Gospels, and so we do not have an example of a term that was a favorite in the writings of the early church. If the church placed the title on the lips of the historical Jesus, we have difficulty understanding why it is lacking elsewhere in the NT.[106] It seems that some scholars doubt the authenticity of the term on the basis of its high Christology—contrary to the very canons of criticism they embrace. If one accepts the standard solution to the Synoptic problem, then the term also fits the criterion of multiple attestation. It occurs in Mark fourteen times, in the Q material eleven times, in the special M material six times, in the special L material seven times, and in the Gospel of John thirteen times.[107] The remarkable variety of contexts in which the term occurs constitutes significant evidence supporting authenticity. Finally, the Semitic character of the term suggests authenticity. Clearly, we are not dealing with an instance of a Hellenistic way of speaking imposed on Palestinian materials. The "son of" expression is typically Palestinian and Jewish, reaching back, as we have seen, into the OT itself.

What does the term "Son of Man" mean? Some have seen it as a transcendent messianic reference. A number of scholars today, however, argue that it is an idiomatic self-reference—a way of referring to human beings or to oneself. For example, Vermes thinks that it hails from Aramaic and is a circumlocution for "I" or "me." Thus "Son of Man" is not an exalted title but rather a modest self-reference to Jesus' present activity in the world.[108] In saying this, of course, Vermes dismisses all future sayings as inauthentic. Casey's view is similar in some respects to the position defended by Vermes.[109] He maintains that "Son of Man" generally refers to human beings, and the speaker is included within the class of human beings. Thus, the statements are both general and specific at the same time. He contends that twelve of the sayings are authentic,[110] but any references alluding to Dan. 7:13–14 are judged to be inauthentic. The study by Lindars falls into the same general orbit as those of Vermes and Casey.[111] When using the term "Son of Man," the speaker refers to himself as part of a general class of persons. Lindars

106. Rightly Cullmann 1963: 155.
107. I am not necessarily endorsing the source-critical view expressed here. I am simply showing that "Son of Man" is authentic based on standard source-critical views.
108. Vermes 1973: 160–91; 1983: 89–99.
109. Casey 1979; 1985; 1987.
110. Matt. 8:20; 11:19; 12:32; Mark 2:10, 28; 8:38; 9:12; 10:45; 14:21 (twice); Luke 12:8; 22:48.
111. Lindars 1983.

thinks that the term is distinctive to Jesus' speech and that nine of the sayings are authentic.[112] According to Lindars, the Greek translation in the Gospels made the phrase look like a title and a self-reference exclusively.[113] The evangelists, therefore, misunderstood the idiom. Lindars agrees with Casey that any references to Dan. 7 are later creations and cannot be traced to the historical Jesus.

The work of Vermes, Casey, and Lindars represents careful and critical attempts to discern the meaning of the term "Son of Man" in the life of the historical Jesus. Their solutions, however, are unpersuasive for several reasons. First, Fitzmyer has pointed out that only one of Vermes's examples of a circumlocution fits,[114] but this solitary example is post-NT and hence inadmissible as evidence.[115] We have, therefore, no clear evidence of the idiom as Vermes interprets it prior to or contemporaneous with the NT.[116] Second, Burkett argues that the nontitular views have proved wanting. It has not been demonstrated that *"bar enasha* without a demonstrative pronoun could mean 'this man' (= 'I') in the same way as *hahu bar gabra."*[117] Moreover, Burkett argues that both the generic and the indefinite views produce implausible interpretations apart from a very few instances and thus cannot be accepted as legitimate.[118]

Second, the conclusions stand only if some of the sayings are excluded, particularly the eschatological ones, as authentic. We have noted, however, that there are good reasons to believe that sayings in all the categories can be attributed to the historical Jesus. If this is the case, then "Son of Man" cannot be limited to a modest self-reference but must include the coming Son of Man in glory.[119]

Third, the nontitular view stands in contrast to what we find in the Gospels themselves, for it is clear that the Gospel writers used "Son of Man" as a title.[120] It is quite unlikely that the Gospel writers misunderstood the term to refer to a title if originally it was merely a humble way of refer-

112. Matt. 8:20; 11:19; 12:32; Mark 2:10; Luke 11:30; 12:8–9; also three sayings from the passion narrative in Mark as construed by Lindars.

113. In support of the view that "Son of Man" is not a title, see also Bauckham 1985.

114. The Geniza fragment of a Targum to Gen. 4:14.

115. Fitzmyer 1979: 152–53. Fitzmyer (1979: 152) also argues, contra Vermes, that the Aramaic phrase גברא ההוא (*hahu gabra*, "that man") is not equivalent to "son of man."

116. Owen and Shepherd (2001) have also demonstrated that the linguistic solution proposed by these three scholars does not accord with the Aramaic evidence now available to us.

117. Burkett 1994: 520.

118. Burkett 1994. For further criticisms, especially of Vermes and Lindars, see Caragounis 1986: 21–33.

119. Caragounis (1986: 25–27) rightly says that even the use of "I" instead of "Son of Man" in some of the Synoptic parallels does not demonstrate that "Son of Man" means "I."

120. Burkett (1999: 93) comments, "In most sayings, the Greek expression gives the best sense when understood as a title referring to Jesus."

ring to oneself. Nor would it be persuasive to argue that they deliberately (or even inadvertently) modified the meaning of the expression so that it became a title, for if this were the case, we would expect the term to be used as a title elsewhere in the NT. What is striking, of course, is that the remainder of the NT does not use "Son of Man" as a title.

Fourth, a titular use of "Son of Man" is supported by *1 Enoch*, which was composed in a time frame adjacent to the NT. Hence, interpreting the phrase as a title would not contradict the Palestinian milieu in which it was birthed.

Fifth, the term "Son of Man" is clearly a title in the final form of the Gospels as we now have them. Much of scholarship is devoted to an understanding of the term contrary to that held by the Gospel writers themselves. At the end of the day, my task in this work is to explicate what the Gospels themselves say, and clearly the term "Son of Man" refers to Jesus himself and functions as a title.

Why did Jesus use the title "Son of Man" so often and in comparison, relatively speaking, the title "Messiah" so little? We have seen that the title "Messiah" was apt to be understood in militaristic and political terms, contrary to Jesus' mission. The term "Son of Man," on the other hand, was ambiguous.[121] Even though the term was used in the OT, there was some uncertainty about its meaning. We have seen that typically in the OT "son of man" simply means "human being." Even in Dan. 7:13–14 "son of man" represents a humane and civilizing kingdom in contrast to the bestial kingdoms that maltreat human beings. Jesus preferred "Son of Man" because he could pour his own content into it. We see from John 12:34 that Jesus' contemporaries were perplexed and puzzled by his use of the term.[122] By using this term, he did not automatically arouse suspicion and antagonism, and he could slowly teach his followers the significance and meaning of "Son of Man." Their understanding of "Son of Man" could be reoriented as Jesus' teaching and ministry progressed.

When we examine what the Gospel writers teach about "Son of Man" and we place it against the landscape of Dan. 7, we see that the main themes about the son of man in Daniel are applied to Jesus by the Gospel writers. The son of man, as we noted previously, is identified as the saints in Dan. 7 (Dan. 7:18, 22, 27). We also saw evidence that the saints in Dan. 7 could also be represented by one figure. The Gospel writers likely conceived of Jesus as the representative man—the one who embodies the people of God.[123] The kingdom given to the saints, then, is

---

121. So Cullmann 1963: 154.

122. Caragounis (1986: 138–39) argues that they were puzzled because they believed the Son of Man would live forever, while Jesus was pointing to his sufferings.

123. For this view, see Moule 1977: 14; 1995: 278. Burkett (1999: 121) rejects the corporate interpretation, but his reasons are not decisive, for the individual and the corporate

given to Jesus as the Son of Man. The twelve disciples will rule over the people of God—the twelve tribes of Israel—because of their allegiance to Jesus as the Son of Man (Matt. 19:28). Jesus has a distinctive place in the kingdom as the one who sits at God's right hand. The kingdom given to the Son of Man by the Ancient of Days in Dan. 7:13, then, is (according to the Gospel writers) given to Jesus himself.[124] He is the Son of Man who receives the kingdom.

Daniel also hints that the son of man distinctively and uniquely shares God's rule, for all peoples everywhere serve him (Dan. 7:14). He possesses the kingdom forever. NT writers see this fulfilled in the coming of the Son of Man in the future when he will reign on his throne and pass judgment on all human beings. Jesus, therefore, is the exalted Son of Man of Dan. 7. It may be the case, in addition, that the suffering Son of Man can be traced back to Dan. 7. The saints suffer and are even prevailed over by the horn (Dan. 7:21, 25). Since Jesus embodies the saints and represents them, the suffering Son of Man could be discerned in these texts. Perhaps Jesus himself saw the themes of both the Son of Man's suffering and his exaltation in Dan. 7. If so, then the Son of Man is none other than the suffering servant. In this instance both Dan. 7 and Isa. 53 speak of the suffering and exaltation of the one whom NT writers identified as Jesus the Christ.[125]

Son of Man in the Gospel of John

The Son of Man in John fits with the exalted Christology of this Gospel as a whole and bears the distinctive stamp of Johannine theology.[126] It would be a mistake, however, to drive too large of a wedge between the Son of Man in the Synoptics and in John. Borsch remarks on the overlap between the Synoptics and John relative to the Son of Man: "What is, on any explanation, so remarkable about these sets of traditions is that they say many of the same things about the Son of Man in quite distinctive language."[127] Jesus responded to Nathaniel's enthusiastic acclamation of

---

should not be played off against each other. The individual Son of Man, Jesus, represents his people.

124. Burkett (1999: 122–23) rightly sees Dan. 7:13 as the source of the title, though he suggests, contrary to what is claimed here, that it stems from the early church rather than from Jesus himself.

125. Cullmann (1963: 161) argues that a striking innovation occurred in the ministry of Jesus in that he combined the Son of Man with the Servant of the Lord of Isa. 53. In both cases, as well, the Son of Man and the Servant of the Lord have a representative function.

126. For a survey of the Johannine theme, see Dodd 1953: 241–49; Higgins 1964: 153–84. Moule (1977: 18) thinks that John distinctively teaches the Son of Man's preexistence.

127. Borsch 1992: 142.

his messiahship with the claim that he would see still greater things (John 1:50–51). The heavens would open, which is a typical way of saying that he would receive revelation, and he would see angels "descending and ascending on the Son of man." The meaning of this verse is not easy to discern. John alludes to Gen. 28:12, where Jacob dreams at Bethel and sees a ladder, probably something like a ziggurat, reaching up to heaven and angels ascending and descending upon the ladder.[128] John replaces the ladder with Jesus as the Son of Man, teaching that access to God has become a reality through Jesus.[129] The stairway indicates that Jesus "is the stairway between heaven and earth."[130] Perhaps a connection also exists between John 1:51 and John 3:13; 6:62. Jesus as the Son of Man is the one who has ascended and descended into heaven (John 3:13). Life is available to all because Jesus has come down from heaven and has returned to God's presence.

Perhaps Jesus' ascension (cf. John 6:62) evokes Dan. 7:13–14, whereby he enters the presence of the Ancient of Days to receive a kingdom. If so, we would have an example of John's inaugurated eschatology. The saying about the Son of Man in John 6:62 occurs in a context in which even some of Jesus' disciples are scandalized over his teaching. Jesus emphasizes that the Spirit alone gives life and grants the ability to grasp what he teaches (John 6:63). If some of his so-called disciples are offended by his words, how would they respond if they saw him as the Son of Man ascending to heaven (John 6:62)?[131] In Johannine theology the ascension and Jesus' glorification occur via the cross. Jesus emphasized that their sense of being offended would not be removed even if they saw him return to God's presence, for the means by which he will be exalted as the Son of Man is the suffering of the cross.

John often emphasizes that the Son of Man will be lifted up (John 3:14; 8:28; 12:34) and glorified (John 12:23; 13:31). The lifting up and the glorification both refer to the cross. The positive terms used for Jesus' death indicate that it is the pathway to his exaltation and glorification. Jesus is exalted not despite the cross but precisely because of it. If he did not die as the Son of Man, he would not be rewarded by God with the

---

128. It is possible that the angels of God were ascending and descending upon Jacob himself (so Carson 1991b: 163), but it is more natural to see a reference to the ladder because it is explicitly mentioned in context and because one would expect that the angels would ascend and descend upon the piece of equipment that reaches up to heaven (rightly Ridderbos 1997: 94).

129. See Barrett 1978: 187. Cullmann (1963: 186) observes, "The bridge between heaven and earth is no longer geographically defined, but is connected with the person of Jesus Christ."

130. Beale 2004: 196; cf. Ridderbos 1997: 94–95.

131. See Barrett 1978: 303; Carson 1991b: 301. Ridderbos (1997: 245–46) argues that we have no reference to the cross here, only Jesus' exaltation.

kingdom at his exaltation (cf. Dan. 7:13–14). God did not glorify Jesus despite the shameful suffering of the cross; rather, God grants glory to Jesus *because* of his suffering on the cross. The glory of Jesus shines in his degradation, pain, and dishonor. Jesus receives glory as the ruling Son of Man by virtue of his work on the cross. Jesus is exalted on high as the crucified one. He is displayed in all his glory as the one who died for his sheep (John 10:15). We should note also that the statement on the lifting up of the Son of Man follows the word about his ascent and descent (John 3:13–14). We have further evidence, therefore, that Jesus' descent from heaven and ascent to God occur through his suffering and death. Jesus' authority as the Son of Man is dependent on his death on a cross.

We should be careful not to minimize the distinctive contribution of Johannine theology. Nevertheless, John accords with the Synoptics in seeing a suffering and exalted Son of Man. John emphasizes the exaltation and glorification of the Son of Man *in* suffering. He teaches that suffering is the pathway to glory. But the Son of Man would not be glorious for John if death on the cross were the last word. The cross is effective only because it functions as the way to God, because it is bound up with Jesus' ascent to God, where he rules as the heavenly Son of Man. The Son of Man in John, as in the Synoptics, suffers and is exalted, though John puts more emphasis on his exaltation on earth, which fits with his emphasis on realized eschatology.

Since Jesus is the Son of Man, people must believe in him to have life. The blind man of John 9 belongs to Jesus' flock because he puts his faith in him as the Son of Man and worships him (John 9:35–38). The high Christology of John is evident here, and since Jesus is worshiped as Son of Man, the title "Son of Man" is practically equivalent with "Son of God." In Dan. 7:13–14 the son of man receives the kingdom and authority (cf. Dan. 7:18, 22, 27). John clearly identifies Jesus as this Son of Man, for he is the one who will execute end-time judgment. We see from John 5:28–29 that the judgment cannot be limited to the present age; it will be finally executed on the day of resurrection, when people will experience either life everlasting or judgment. We saw from John 9:35 that believing in Jesus as Son of Man is the means to escape judgment, even in this present evil age. As the Son of Man, Jesus grants eternal life to his own (John 6:27). Given John's emphasis on the lifting up and glorification of the Son of Man on the cross, we are not surprised to discover that one must eat the flesh and drink the blood of the Son of Man to have life (John 6:53). Eternal life and triumph over judgment come only by feeding on the death of Jesus, by relying on his mangled flesh and shed blood. In the Gospel of John "Son of Man" fits with the

Gospel's realized eschatology. Still, all the elements of the Synoptics are present; they are simply considered from a fresh angle.

Other References to Son of Man in the New Testament

Since the term "Son of Man" is scarcely used outside the Gospels in the NT, here we will look at the remaining references together. Paul never uses the title "Son of Man," though some scholars have drawn a connection by appealing to Paul's Adam Christology. In any case, a clear reference to the "Son of Man" title is lacking. The term occurs once in Acts in a context that continues to fascinate and tantalize. Stephen outraged the Jewish leaders in his speech and with his bold declaration that they have failed to please God and have consistently resisted the Holy Spirit. Luke proceeds to inform us that Stephen, "full of the Holy Spirit, gazed into heaven and saw the glory of God, and Jesus standing at the right hand of God. And he said, 'Behold, I see the heavens opened, and the Son of Man standing at the right hand of God'" (Acts 7:55–56). Stephen, animated by the Spirit, had a heavenly revelation. Jesus as the Son of Man stands at God's right hand, and hence Luke draws here on Dan. 7:13–14, where the son of man is presented before God himself. Jesus is the glorious son of man from Dan. 7 who receives the kingdom from the Ancient of Days. What is remarkable about this text, however, is that Jesus is standing rather than sitting. How do we account for this? Since the text has a judicial nature (Stephen is charged with blasphemy before the Sanhedrin), Jesus' standing should be interpreted in light of the legal character of the account. Presumably, Jesus stands as Stephen's defendant, pleading his case before God.[132] It is Stephen's way of saying to the people that God himself and the Son of Man of Dan. 7 consider him to be not a blasphemer but a true Israelite, a true son of the covenant. Conversely, Stephen's opponents are not faithful members of the covenant.

---

132. For a full discussion of the various options and a defense of a view largely compatible with what is argued here, see Bock 1987: 221–24; Crump 1992: 178–97. Fitzmyer (1998: 393) comments, "Whatever the meaning of the Son of Man's 'standing' might be, Stephen is accorded a vision of the risen Christ, who has been exalted to a position of honor next to God (2:33), and the vision confirms the accusations Stephen has expressed in his speech." Drawing on the work of T. Preiss, Cullmann (1963: 183n3) concludes that "at the moment the human judge condemns Stephen, the Son of Man as intercessor entreats God for his justification." For the view that the Son of Man functions here as an intercessor, see Higgins 1964: 145–46. He may also be standing to welcome Stephen or in judgment against the Jews. For a brief survey of the possibilities, see Conzelmann 1987: 59–60; Fitzmyer 1998: 392–93; Barrett 1994: 384–85. Barrett (1994: 385) concludes his survey by saying, "The main point is that Stephen in his dispute with the Jewish authorities is proved right by God himself."

The term "son of man" appears also in Heb. 2:6. In this instance, however, Hebrews is citing Ps. 8, and so scholars debate whether the term
here has any titular significance.[133] Perhaps here "son of man" is simply
equivalent to "human being." Still, an echo of Dan. 7:13–14 may also be
present, or possibly the themes of Ps. 8 and Dan. 7:13–14 overlap at this
juncture.[134] Psalm 8 reflects on the place of human beings in God's world,
concluding that God made them as the crown of all creation, as the ruler
of all that he has made. Hebrews picks up this theme but argues that
human beings have failed to fulfill their mandate, which reaches back
to Gen. 1:28; 2:15. Jesus functions as the representative human being,
succeeding where all other human beings have failed. Hebrews 2 goes
on to argue that those who are Jesus' brothers and sisters share his victory with him. He represents them and atones for them by his suffering
on the cross. The thematic overlap with Dan. 7 is remarkable, for that
chapter also looks forward to the day when human beings (the saints)
will rule the world. Jesus, according to Hebrews, is the representative
human being who suffers for his people but is now exalted because of
his suffering. Even if Heb. 2 does not draw on Dan. 7, it echoes the same
theology and themes.

In Rev. 1:13–14 John sees Jesus as "one like a son of man" in a vision.
The vision is stocked with OT allusions, but Rev. 1:14 clearly alludes to
Dan. 7:9, 13–14. We will explore the Christology of Revelation in more
detail later, but at this point we note John's modification of Dan. 7.
Whereas in Dan. 7:9 Yahweh has white hair like wool, as white as snow,
in Revelation the son of man is said to have hair "white like wool, as
white as snow" (Rev. 1:14). Such an adjustment should not be explained
as a mistake on the part of John, as if he did not read Daniel carefully
and inadvertently merged what was said about the son of man and the
Ancient of Days. John consistently adapts OT allusions in Revelation,
and he does so intentionally.[135] The point in this instance is that the Son
of Man, Jesus Christ, shares the same stature with the Ancient of Days.
In due course we will see the amazingly high Christology that permeates
Revelation, and so what we have in this instance is characteristic.[136] The
term "Son of Man" was not used often outside the Gospels, since it was

133. Higgins (1964: 146–47) argues that in Hebrews we have a conception of a preexistent
Son of Man similar to Johannine and Pauline Christology.

134. So Bruce 1964: 35–36; P. Hughes 1977: 85. Against any connection to Dan. 7, see
Attridge 1989: 73–74; Lane 1991a: 47.

135. See Aune 1997: 94–95; Beale 1999b: 209; Osborne 2002: 90.

136. Ignatius mistakenly appears to limit "Son of Man" to Jesus' human nature (Ign. *Eph.*
20:2), whereas in the Gospels the Son of Man shares divine glory. The same mistake is
evident in the *Epistle of Barnabas* (*Barn.* 12:10). The meaning of the term in *Odes of Solomon* is more difficult to discern (*Odes Sol.* 36:3).

ambiguous and not readily comprehensible to Gentiles. Hence, the term is limited on the whole to the Gospel tradition and is not emphasized by other writers in the NT canon.

Conclusion

The fulfillment of redemptive history and of God's saving promises centers on Jesus himself. He is the Messiah, the anointed one promised in the OT. Even though the term "Messiah" is not a technical one in the OT for a coming descendant of David, the OT often teaches that a descendant of David would rule on the throne and that a day of peace and joy would commence at his coming. NT writers, like the writer of *Psalms of Solomon*, coalesce the promise of a future son of David with the notion of an anointed one. The use of "Messiah" to refer to a descendant of David is not surprising, since the king in the OT was an anointed one. The Gospel writers, then, claim that Jesus is the promised son of David. He is the one who fulfills the covenant made with David, where God pledges that David's dynasty will remain forever. Hence, the end-time age of peace and victory over enemies has arrived with the coming of Jesus as Messiah. Jesus' messiahship fits with one of the major themes of this book in that it contains a shocking twist—an already and a not yet. Jesus taught that he would not reign as the Messiah unless he first suffered as Messiah. The path to the crown was the cross. Such an understanding of the Messiah conflicted with the worldview of Jews in the Second Temple period. A "suffering Messiah" was a contradiction in terms. Jesus' reluctance to use the title "Messiah" can be traced to the political expectations that it aroused, for the Jews would expect a leader who would rout the Romans, judge sinners in Israel, and introduce an age of peace. Since Jesus had a profoundly different conception of his messianic role, he used "Messiah" rarely so as to avoid sparking nationalistic passions. Even Jesus' disciples were discombobulated by the idea that Jesus would suffer as the Messiah. Hence, even though they believed that he was the Messiah, they did not truly grasp the nature of his messianic mission until after the resurrection. The resurrection vindicated Jesus' messianic claims, demonstrating that Jesus was now reigning as Messiah and Lord from heaven. However, the already–not yet still obtained, for even though Jesus reigned from heaven, evil was not purged from the earth. The final victory over evil awaited the return of Jesus as Messiah and king.

The misunderstanding that arose over the term "Messiah" explains why Jesus preferred the term "Son of Man." In the OT the expression "son of man" is equivalent to "human being" and could even be used to

denote the weakness and mortality of human beings, as it does in Ezekiel. Nevertheless, despite the objections of many scholars, the primary
background of the use of the title in the Gospels can be traced to Dan.
7, where the son of man represents the saints and receives the kingdom
from the Ancient of Days. His kingdom will be humane and civilizing
rather than bestial and rapacious like the rulers who preceded him.
Because the meaning of "son of man" was ambiguous, it was the ideal
term for Jesus to use with reference to himself. Jesus uses the term to
refer to his ministry on earth, his suffering, and his glorification in the
future. Even the sayings about suffering anticipate glorification, for they
promise a future resurrection. Hence, the authority and the rule of the
Son of Man form the theme that pulls together all the references to the
Son of Man. The title is not merely used to emphasize Jesus' humility.
Even as a man on earth, Jesus has the authority to forgive sins and is
Lord of the Sabbath. Hence, Jesus' use of "Son of Man" fits with what we
have seen with reference to Messiah. In both instances suffering is the
pathway to glory. The promise of a kingdom in Dan. 7 finds its fulfillment
in Jesus himself, but the means by which the kingdom comes involves
suffering for the Son of Man. Indeed, the Son of Man's suffering is the
means by which he will obtain rule over all. God's saving promises, then,
are fulfilled in Jesus, but the astonishing element is the way in which
redemptive history reaches its consummation. Jesus suffers as the Son
of Man before he is glorified as such.

7

✿ ✿ ✿ ✿ ✿ ✿ ✿ ✿ ✿ ✿ ✿ ✿ ✿ ✿ ✿ ✿ ✿ ✿ ✿ ✿

Son of God, I Am, and Logos

Scholars have long recognized the centrality of Jesus and the high Christology in John's Gospel. In chapter 5 I sought to demonstrate the centrality of Jesus in the Synoptic Gospels by attending to the variety of ways in which he is preeminent in the narrative. We also saw in chapter 5 a high Christology in the Synoptics that is easily missed by readers who attend only to titles. In chapter 6 the focus shifted to the titles "Messiah" and "Son of Man." Neither title necessarily signifies deity, but what is remarkable is the content that Jesus poured into both of them. In both instances Jesus stressed that suffering would precede glory. In this chapter we turn to titles that clearly describe Jesus' glory and splendor. The deity of Jesus clearly shines forth in the title "Son of God," the "I am" sayings, and the Johannine teaching on the Logos. There is the danger of abstracting the titles from the person, so that an artificial portrait of Jesus is formed. Jesus is depicted in a variety of ways because no single description captures the fullness of his person. Still, the focus is ultimately on Jesus himself and not on the titles ascribed to him, though in the final analysis the titles cannot, of course, be separated from who Jesus is. Furthermore, we must continue to see that the titles cannot be separated from redemptive history. Since Jesus is Son of God, I Am, and Logos, God's saving promises are fulfilled only in Jesus and in knowing Jesus as the Son of God.

Son of God

Old Testament Context

When examining the term "Son of God," we will begin with the OT and then examine the use of the term in the Synoptic Gospels and then the Gospel of John.[1] If we begin with the plural "sons of God" in the OT, we find that the expression applies particularly to angels (Gen. 6:2, 4; Deut. 32:8; Job 1:6; 2:1; 38:7; Ps. 29:1; 82:6; 89:6).[2] Of course, the interpretation of Gen. 6:1–4 is contested, and space is lacking here to discuss the many interpretations offered. Lexically, however, it seems that "sons of God" refers to angels, and this interpretation is borne out by both the NT and the Jewish tradition. In a number of texts the LXX renders "sons of God" (*běnê 'ělōhîm*) as "angels" (*angeloi*) (Deut. 32:8; Job 1:6; 2:1; 38:7). The term "sons of God," then, can refer to heavenly beings, to God's heavenly court.

The singular, "son of God," refers to Israel, signifying God's special and covenantal relationship with his people. In Exod. 4:22 Israel is designated as God's "firstborn son" (*huios prōtotokos*). The collocation of "son" and "firstborn" indicates that Israel enjoyed the privileges of primogeniture as God's son (cf. Jer. 31:9). The northern kingdom, under the appellation "Ephraim," was God's "beloved son" (*huios agapētos* [Jer. 31:20 LXX my translation]). Israel's exodus from Egypt is described as the calling out of God's "son" (Hosea 11:1). Although the terminology is not used often, God is also represented as the father of Israel (Deut. 32:6; Jer. 3:4) or with maternal imagery as the one who gave birth to his people (Deut. 32:18). The plural "sons" also denotes God's fatherly relation to Israel (Deut. 14:1; Isa. 43:6), though sometimes it emphasizes Israel's treachery as those in a unique relationship with God (Deut. 32:5; Isa. 45:11; Hosea 1:10).[3] In every instance it is likely that Yahweh's covenantal relationship with Israel is in view.

The Davidic king is also specially related to God, via the Davidic covenant, and designated as son. God relates to the Davidic king as a father to a son, and he will never withdraw his covenantal love from the king (2 Sam. 7:14–15; 1 Chron. 17:13–14; 22:10; 28:6–7). As we noted previously, Ps. 89 reflects on God's promise to David and his heirs in a situation where the covenantal promises are not being fulfilled. The psalmist celebrates God's unbreakable covenantal love to the Davidic

---

1. For the OT background along with a consideration of some Qumran evidence, see Fitzmyer 1979: 102–7. For the Jewish and Hellenistic background, see the brief and helpful summary in Cullmann 1963: 270–75.

2. Different Hebrew words for "God" are used in some of these expressions.

3. We should note that both sons and daughters are included in Deut. 32:19; Isa. 43:6, and that the LXX adds daughters in Isa. 45:11.

king, using it as a basis to plead to God for the fulfillment of his promise. The Davidic king will address God as his father and his rock. God in turn considers the king as his "firstborn [*prōtotokos*], the highest of the kings of the earth" (Ps. 89:26–27). The one who sits on David's throne and who will rule in peace and justice is a "son" (Isa. 9:6), suggesting his unique relationship to God. According to Ps. 2, the nations of the world chafe at and attempt to dislodge the rule of Yahweh's anointed. But Yahweh has designated the anointed king as his "son" and has installed him as his king (Ps. 2:6). To this son will be given the rule over all nations, even to the ends of the earth. Hence, other nations must bow in submission to this "son" or else be destroyed by him (Ps. 2:12).

Considering the OT as a canonical unit, we observe that Israel occupies a special position as God's son. And yet the Davidic king also functions as God's unique son. The king receives the same covenantal promise that Israel receives. Ultimately, he will rule the world as God's vicegerent. God's promise to the Davidic king does not contradict his promise to Israel; rather, the king represents Israel as a whole. He functions as Israel's covenantal head, through whom the promises will be secured. Israel will rule the world for God through its appointed king, who will be the son of David.

"Son of God" seems to have been a messianic title in Second Temple Judaism as well.[4] Several texts from Qumran are most naturally understood to refer to the Messiah as the Son of God (cf. 4QFlor 1 I, 10–12, citing 2 Sam. 7:12–14; 1QSa II, 11–12, which speaks of begetting the Messiah; 4Q369; 4Q246).[5] The Messiah is also God's Son in *4 Ezra* (*4 Ezra* 7:28–29; 13:32, 37, 52; 14:9).[6] Collins rightly concludes that the Son of God brings about peace and establishes the kingdom, much like the Messiah.[7] Hence, the conjunction between "Messiah" and "Son of God" in the NT is scarcely surprising. Indeed, in Jewish circles "Son of God" did not designate one as deity, though in the NT it becomes clear that Jesus is the Son of God in an even more profound way than anticipated at Qumran.

---

4. So Horbury 1998: 113. The notion that "Son of God" comes from Hellenistic circles, though widespread in the history of NT studies, is unpersuasive (rightly Evans 1998: 153).

5. For the view defended here, see J. J. Collins 1995: 154–65; Evans 1998. According to Fitzmyer (1979: 105–6), the expression "Son of God" was not used of the Davidic king in Jewish writings prior to the NT, but Collins's assessment of the evidence is more persuasive, for it seems that both Qumran and NT writings inferred that the messianic king was the Son of God because David's successor is identified as God's "son" at the inception of the Davidic covenant (2 Sam. 7:14).

6. For the Son of God in *4 Ezra*, see J. J. Collins 1995: 165–67.

7. J. J. Collins 1995: 167.

Matthew and Mark

If we open the Synoptic Gospels with the OT background in mind, the theme that Jesus is the true Son of God—the true Israel—emerges.[8] As we noted previously, Matthew sees a fulfillment of Hosea 11:1 in Jesus' return from Egypt, though in the original context Hosea refers to the exodus of Israel from Egypt. Matthew suggests from this text that Jesus is the true Israel, the Son of God. At Jesus' baptism and his transfiguration the divine voice identifies him as God's "beloved son" (*huios agapētos* [Matt. 3:17 par.; 17:5 par.]).[9] We saw earlier that in the OT Israel is acclaimed as God's beloved son. Isaac is also called the beloved son of Abraham (Gen. 22:2, 12, 16), as the son of the promise. Similarly, Jesus is the promised heir as God's beloved son.

The title "Son of God," however, is not limited to the notion that Jesus is the true Israel.[10] It also signifies that he fulfills the promises made to David.[11] He is the king of Israel, the one anointed by God to rule over his people. When Jesus calms the storm, the disciples confess that he is God's Son (Matt. 14:33).[12] Perhaps the disciples received a glimmer of Jesus' special relation to God, but they likely meant by this acclamation that Jesus was truly the Messiah, the one to whom the covenantal promises given to David pointed. The same conclusion should be drawn from Matt. 16:16, where at a crucial juncture in the Gospel Peter exclaims that Jesus is "the Christ, the Son of the living God."[13] It is doubtful that at this stage in his thinking Peter grasped that Jesus was divine.[14] The titles "Christ" and "Son of God" were synonyms, denoting that Jesus was the Messiah of Israel. Equating "Messiah" with "Son of God" is scarcely

8. We should not interpret "Son of God" in light of the alleged divine men of the Greco-Roman world (rightly Fitzmyer 1979: 106; Dunn 1996a: 16–19) or from a Hellenistic background (contra, e.g., Bultmann 1951: 128–33). Several studies have demonstrated insuperable weaknesses in the *theios anēr* theory (Holladay 1977; Brady 1992). Blackburn (1991) argues that the Markan miracle traditions do not reflect a "divine man" Christology. Holladay (1977) demonstrates that the alleged link between Hellenism and Judaism in Josephus and Philo cannot be substantiated, since a careful examination of their writings reveals that they did not think that human beings were deified.

9. In the preferred reading among the Greek texts of Luke's Gospel, God's voice refers to Jesus as "my Son, my chosen one" at the transfiguration (Luke 9:35).

10. Kingsbury (1975: 40–83) argues that "Son of God" is the central christological title in Matthew.

11. Some scholars doubt that "Son of God" raises Davidic associations, but the notion is defended well by Longenecker (1970: 93–99).

12. Cullmann (1963: 279) notes that Jesus is recognized as the Son of God in the Synoptics "only in exceptional cases" based on "special supernatural knowledge."

13. Contra Cullmann (1963: 280), Peter's confession should not be assigned to another context.

14. Peter likely understood the title "Son of God" in messianic terms, but Matthew points the reader to a deeper understanding (Carson 1984: 365–66).

surprising, given the OT background sketched above. Perhaps the same equation exists in Luke 1:32, where Jesus is promised David's throne and identified as "the Son of the Most High."[15]

We have seen that the title "Son of God" means that Jesus is the true Israel and the Messiah, the promised son of David. The Gospel writers, however, see a deeper meaning in the appellation "Son of God." Jesus also shares a unique and special relation with God.[16] He even shares the prerogatives of deity without compromising the oneness of God. Indeed, this last category is what the Gospel writers emphasize. Mark, for example, introduces his Gospel[17] with the proclamation that Jesus is the Christ, "the Son of God" (Mark 1:1).[18] The Gospel concludes with the same words on the lips of the centurion (Mark 15:39). The centurion recognized that Jesus submitted to God in his death, and so he died as God's obedient Son.[19] Significantly, the centurion identified Jesus only after his work on the cross was completed, suggesting that Jesus can be understood rightly as God's Son only in light of the cross.[20] The demons also understood who Jesus is better than did Jews living in Palestine, for the former group recognized that Jesus is God's unique Son (Mark 3:11; 5:7). The divine voice also acclaimed Jesus as the Son of God at his baptism and transfiguration (Mark 1:11; 9:7). An examination of the Markan usage as a whole shows that he does not emphasize by the title that Jesus is the true Israel or even that he is the Davidic king; rather, what comes to the forefront is Jesus' special relationship with God.[21] When in Mark's Gospel Jesus walks on the stormy waves and declares "it is I" (*egō eimi* [Mark 6:50]), the story implies that Jesus shares the identity of God.[22]

Matthew, as we noted, uses "Son" or "Son of God" in contexts where the title likely refers to the true Israel or Messiah. What must be empha-

15. Bock (1987: 67–68) rightly argues that in Luke 1 Jesus was the Messiah at birth, not adopted as such at that point.

16. See Verseput 1987, a nuanced study that France (1989: 292–98) generally endorses, though he rightly points out that Verseput underestimates Jesus' unique relation to God and his unique status as God's Son.

17. Mark 1:1 should be read as the introduction to the entire Gospel, not merely to Mark 1:1–15 (rightly Boring 1990; France 2002: 50–51; Hurtado 2003: 309; contra Lane 1974: 42; Hooker 1991: 33).

18. "Son of God" is lacking in some Greek texts but should be regarded as original (France 2002: 49).

19. So Kingsbury 1983: 131.

20. For the centrality of Jesus as the Son of God in Mark, see Kingsbury 1983: 47–55.

21. Cullmann (1963: 282–83) argues that the title designates Jesus' obedience to his Father and his special and unique relationship to God.

22. Marcus (2000: 432) says that here Mark suggests Jesus' divinity, even though not stating it outright. See also Hurtado 2003: 286.

sized, however, is that Matthew typically uses the phrase to denote Jesus' special and unique relation to God. Jesus' sonship cannot be limited to his being the true Israel or the Messiah, for he is even to be worshiped as God's Son. The distinctiveness of Jesus as God's Son emerges in Matt. 1:23, for Jesus as the Son is Immanuel—"God with us." Such language is not merely symbolic, for Matthew concludes with the promise of Jesus' permanent presence with his people (Matt. 28:20).[23] As God's Son, Jesus is God himself with his people, though this does not exclude or cancel out monotheism or the unique authority of the Father. The devil (Matt. 4:3, 6) and demons (Matt. 8:29) recognized that Jesus is God's Son. They did not merely mean that Jesus is the Messiah; they acknowledged his exclusive relation to God. The uniqueness of Jesus' relation to God is evident in Matt. 11:27:[24] "All things have been handed over to me by my Father, and no one knows the Son except the Father, and no one knows the Father except the Son and anyone to whom the Son chooses to reveal him." The Father and the Son know each other exclusively, mutually, and intimately. Only the Father truly knows the Son, and only the Son truly knows the Father. The priority of the Father is maintained because he has given to the Son all that he enjoys.[25] And yet no person can come to know the Father unless the Son desires to reveal the Father to that person. As with the "Immanuel" text, it is clear here that Jesus' sonship cannot be limited to his serving as the Messiah. He has a relationship with the Father that is inimitable and exclusive. Indeed, Matthew clearly implies Jesus' divine status here, for he and the Father have mutual knowledge, and the Son is the only one who knows the Father. Further, it is clear in this text that Jesus is part of the divine heavenly council and is thus in a separate category from all human beings.[26]

Jesus' uniqueness as God's Son stands out in the baptismal formula (Matt. 28:19). Baptism is to be applied in the name of the Father, the Son, and the Spirit. There is one name, and yet three different entities that are to be invoked during baptism. Here we are on the brink of the full trinitarian formulas of later church history, although Matthew, of course,

23. See Hagner 1993b: 21; Luz 2005: 634; Nolland 2005: 1271; contra Davies and Allison 1988: 217.

24. Hagner (1993b: 319–20) rightly argues that the use of "Son" here reflects the Christology that Jesus is uniquely and distinctively God's Son (see also Luz 2001: 164–70 [although he thinks that it is a church creation]). "The point is that Jesus thus has a unique role as the mediator of the knowledge of God to humankind. This role is directly linked with the person of Jesus, his identity as the unique representative of God" (Hagner 1993b: 320).

25. Many interpreters understand *panta* ("all things") here to refer to knowledge (e.g., Davies and Allison 1991: 279; Luz 2001: 166), but Nolland (2005: 471–72) is probably correct in seeing a general and comprehensive reference.

26. Crump (1992: 49–75) points out from the parallel in Matthew that Jesus' role in intercession and prayer here reveals a high Christology.

does not work out his statement into the notion of three persons and one divine essence. What is clear here is that the title "Son" represents divinity. He is equal in some sense with the Father. Examining Matthew's Gospel as a whole, we see that he clearly invests the title "Son of God" with divine significance. So when Jesus is identified as God's Son at his baptism and transfiguration (Matt. 3:17; 17:5), the point is that he has a unique relation to God.

In summary, in some instances persons using the title "Son of God" may have meant nothing more than "Messiah." It is difficult for us to make such distinctions, however, because Matthew and the other Gospel writers were not interested merely in the historical meaning of what was said. Peter probably grasped only that Jesus was the Messiah when he identified him as God's Son (Matt. 16:16; cf. 16:23), but he spoke better than he knew. Jesus was God's Son in a more amazing way than Peter contemplated. When the centurion acclaimed Jesus as God's Son (Matt. 27:54), his words meant more than "Jesus is the Messiah," even if he did not grasp the full dimensions of the words that he uttered.[27]

It is more difficult to discern at Jesus' trial what the high priest meant when he asked Jesus if he was the Messiah, "the Son of God" (Matt. 26:63). Was the high priest inquiring whether Jesus is in some sense divine? On the basis of OT antecedents the title "Son of God" could be equivalent to "Messiah." The Sanhedrin concluded that Jesus blasphemed, and yet claiming to be the Messiah was not blasphemous per se. Jesus links together here the Son of God and the Son of Man (Matt. 26:63–64). It seems, then, that "Son of God" means more than "Messiah" here, designating Jesus' unique relation to God and his claim to share God's power by claiming his place on the heavenly throne.[28] When Jesus was dying upon the cross, some reviled him, demanding that he prove himself as God's Son by coming down from the cross (Matt. 27:40, 43). Again, it is just possible that they meant by this that the true Messiah would never die on the cross. Certainty on these historical questions

27. It is unlikely that the centurion grasped the full import of his words, and hence he spoke better than he knew (Hagner 1995: 852–53; France 2002: 659–60). Nolland (2005: 1220) suggests that we are not meant to probe too deeply into the centurion's consciousness. Luz (2005: 569–70) rightly and strongly argues that in the Matthean context Jesus is confessed here as the divine Son. For a helpful discussion of the use of "righteous" rather than "Son of God" in Luke 23:47, see Bock 1996: 1863–64. For further discussion, see R. Brown 1994: 2:1143–52, 1160–67.

28. So Gathercole 2006: 278, 292; Evans 2001: 453–57. In *m. Sanh.* 7:5 blasphemy is defined as the pronouncing of the divine name, but both Bock (2000: 30–112) and A. Collins (2004) have demonstrated that blasphemy was defined in a broader sense during the NT era. Jesus' blasphemy, they both argue, consisted in his claiming power that belonged only to God (see also Stuhlmacher 1993: 32). See also the discussion on blasphemy in R. Brown 1994: 1:520–47.

eludes us. What does seem clear is that "Son of God" in Matthew cannot be limited to "Messiah." Matthew wants readers to see all the "Son of God" statements in light of the full revelation that has come after Jesus' death and resurrection. Jesus is not simply the Messiah; he stands in a special relationship with the Father and, like the Father, is divine.[29]

Luke

It comes as no surprise that Luke also emphasizes Jesus' unique relation to God, since many of the same texts from Mark and Matthew are included. Jesus is acclaimed at his baptism as God's beloved Son (Luke 3:22) and at his transfiguration as God's elect Son (Luke 9:35). As in Matthew, both the devil (Luke 4:3, 9) and demons (Luke 4:41; 8:28) confess that Jesus is God's Son. Jesus' unique and exclusive relationship with the Father is expressed in Luke as well (Luke 10:22; cf. Matt. 11:27). The question from Caiaphas as to whether Jesus is God's Son is also included (Luke 22:70). Jesus is also designated as God's Son because he was conceived by the Holy Spirit instead of by a human father (Luke 1:35).[30] This last text confirms that Luke understood Jesus' sonship to be unique.[31] When we examine Luke's Gospel as a whole, it becomes clear that Jesus' sonship conveys his divine status, but there is no need to cover the same ground again, since Luke's view accords with what we have seen in Matthew and Mark.

John's Gospel

The high Christology of John's Gospel is evident to all, and in the history of NT scholarship this high Christology has led many to doubt the historical veracity of John's portrait of Jesus. It is not my purpose here to defend John's accuracy in detail, since my focus is on John's theology. Nevertheless, despite the objections of many, good reasons

29. With Cullmann (1963: 289), we should also note that Jesus almost certainly is the son in the parable of the tenants (Matt. 21:33–46 par.). Cullmann (e.g., 1963: 293, 306), however, wrongly sets ontology against function. Nolland (2005: 873–74) argues that Jesus is the son here, but Christology per se is not emphasized.

30. Hence, Jesus is also superior to the Baptist, for although the Baptist's birth was remarkable, it resulted from a human father (see also R. Brown 1977: 300). R. Brown (1977: 314) also rightly argues that the birth of Jesus is not sexual in any way. Rather, the Spirit's role is analogous to the hovering of the Spirit over the waters before the first creation. Just as the world was void, so too was Mary's womb. With the virginal conception, Luke emphasizes that Jesus was always the Son of God (R. Brown 1977: 316).

31. Bock (1987: 63–67) argues, however, that in calling Jesus the Son of God, Luke emphasizes not Jesus' ontological status but rather his rule as the Davidic king. If so, then "Son of God" for Luke is basically equivalent to Jesus being hailed as the Davidic king.

exist to support the historical accuracy of John's portrait.[32] There is some evidence in John, as we saw in the Synoptics, that "Son of God" is equivalent to "Messiah." I suggested earlier that when Nathaniel exclaimed that Jesus was the "Son of God" and "the King of Israel" (John 1:49), he did not mean by "Son of God" that Jesus is divine.[33] "Son of God" in this instance is simply another way of saying that Jesus is the Messiah. We probably can draw the same conclusion from Martha's confession in John 11:27. When she said that Jesus is the "Christ" and the "Son of God," she likely used the two terms synonymously, for it is improbable at this early stage that she even considered whether Jesus was divine.[34] When Pilate was informed at Jesus' trial that Jesus called himself God's Son (John 19:7), this could be interpreted as saying that Pilate believed that Jesus claimed divinity. The rest of the passion narrative in John, however, suggests that Jesus' opponents charged Jesus with claiming to be a king—the Messiah[35]—and asserting a blasphemous unity with God but did not grasp that Jesus claimed divinity.[36]

When these statements are set against the backdrop of Johannine theology as a whole, however, the point is that all these people spoke better than they knew. Jesus is God's Son in a way they never imagined or contemplated. John's purpose in his Gospel is to persuade readers to believe that Jesus is the Christ, God's Son (John 20:31). In this purpose statement the terms "Christ" and "Son of God" are not merely equivalent. "Christ" refers to Jesus being the Messiah, but "Son of God" also indicates Jesus' special relation to God—his divinity. That Jesus' sonship implies deity is clear from a number of texts. For instance, the Father and the Son know each other intimately and exclusively (John 10:15).[37] The mutuality of the statement excludes the notion that the Son's knowledge of the Father is akin to the knowledge that human beings have of God. Jesus does not merely say here that the Father gave him knowledge, but simply that he knows the Father, showing his independence.

John's Gospel also emphasizes the priority of the Father and suggests a kind of subordination in the Son. For instance, John often emphasizes

---

32. For sources that support this view, see chapter 2, note 3.

33. See Beasley-Murray 1987: 27; Carson 1991b: 162; see also R. Brown 1966: 87–88.

34. Rightly Koester 2003: 121. Contra Morris (1971: 552), it does not seem that Martha uses the terms with "their maximum content." For the view that this stems only from John's theology, see Barrett 1978: 397.

35. Barrett (1978: 542) does not think that the Johannine account necessarily represents what happened, and so he interprets the statement to refer to equality with God. R. Brown (1970: 891) thinks that John gives a title that later expressed the conflict between church and synagogue.

36. Köstenberger (2004: 533–34) notes that here they may have simply been identifying Jesus as the Messiah. Carson (1991b: 599) detects more significance.

37. See Barrett 1978: 375–76.

that Jesus was sent by the Father into the world.[38] Jesus as the one sent by God discharges God's will and represents God to human beings. What God communicates to the world by sending his Son is the depth and intensity of his love. God sent the Son to save the world, not to condemn it, although those who do not believe in the Son are condemned even now (John 3:16–18; cf. 6:40). At the same time, the Son's coming into the world demonstrates his love for and submission to the Father. The Son works not independently but rather solely in concert with and in dependence upon the Father (John 5:19, 30; 7:16; 14:31; 15:15). He teaches what the Father teaches, commands what the Father commands, and reveals what the Father reveals. The subordination of the Son in John's theology, however, does not mean that Jesus is not divine or is a lesser deity.[39] John does not work out for readers how the Son can be dependent upon the Father and be sent by the Father while at the same time sharing deity with the Father. The philosophical and theological implications of his statements were worked out in the early church and continue to be reflected upon by theologians today. The distinctiveness of the Son is evident, for the Father uniquely loves the Son and has handed all things over to him, so that those who believe in the Son have life but those who fail to believe experience even now God's wrath (John 3:35–36; cf. 5:20; 10:17; 20:17).

The subordination of the Son is not the only story in John's Gospel, for John clearly teaches also that Jesus as the Son is equal to God, and that he is divine. For instance, Jesus declares that he as the Son grants life to whom he wishes, and the final judgment will be determined by him (John 5:21–22). Granting life to others is a divine activity, for life comes not from human beings but from God himself, and yet the Son claims that he has the ability to bestow life. The divinity of the Son is suggested in that he gives his sheep eternal life, which is a divine activity. Those to whom he grants such life will never perish, for no one can snatch them from his hand (John 10:29). John immediately proceeds to the notion that the Father and the Son are one (John 10:30), suggesting again the divine activity involved in granting and preserving life. Similarly, passing judgment on others is a divine prerogative, but the Son will assess the life of each one and determine the final reward. Even in granting life or judging others, the Son is not divided from the Father,

---

38. John 3:17, 34; 4:34; 5:23, 24, 30, 36, 37, 38; 6:29, 38, 39, 44, 57; 7:16; 8:16, 18, 26, 29, 42; 9:4; 10:36; 11:42; 12:44, 45, 49; 13:20; 14:24, 31; 15:15, 21; 16:5; 17:3, 8, 18, 21, 23, 25; 20:21.

39. As Ridderbos (1997: 192–93) has observed, Jesus does not reject the notion that he is equal with God but instead emphasizes that he is the Son. As the Son, he is fully equal with God but has not made himself equal with God.

for the Son always does the works intended by the Father (John 5:36; 10:32, 37–38).

The stature of the Son blazes forth in one of the most remarkable statements in John: the Son must be honored in the same way as the Father (John 5:23; cf. 8:19).[40] Indeed, those who fail to honor the Son also fail to honor the Father. It seems, then, that John is arguing that the Son must be worshiped in the same way as the Father, for the honor that belongs to the one and only God must also be given to the Son. In the monotheistic framework in which John writes, such honoring of the Son must mean that he is fully divine, for worshiping a creature or an angel was unthinkable in Judaism.

The stature of the Son is verified when we consider his glory.[41] Jesus uniquely manifests the glory of God as the Son of the Father (John 1:14), and his glory shines in his miracles (John 2:11). Jesus' glory is particularly revealed in the cross, and this theme will be taken up in due course. Here it should be observed that Jesus' glory suggests his deity, his absolute uniqueness as the Son of the Father. John claims that Isaiah saw Jesus' glory in his vision (John 12:41).[42] Isaiah's vision in its historical context is one in which he saw the glory of Yahweh (Isa. 6:1–13). In claiming that Isaiah saw the glory of Jesus, John clearly identifies Jesus as the holy one of Israel and places him on the same level as the Father. The Son's glory cannot be limited to this life but transcends it, for he possessed glory before the world ever came into existence (John 17:5). Nor will his glory ever end, for the Son anticipates the future when believers will see his glory forever (John 17:24). Indeed, seeing his glory is the climax and goal of the life of those who have put their trust in Jesus. The stature of the Son is also communicated by the promise that the Spirit would glorify the Son (John 16:14). Glory is not restricted to the Father but is also shared with the Son, and it is the Spirit's distinctive ministry to bring glory to the Son. We also see in John's Gospel the interplay between the Father and Son that is characteristic of John's thought. Hence, the Father is the one who glorifies the Son (John 8:54), and therefore the Son asks the Father to glorify him as the cross draws near (John 17:1, 5). The glory that the Son possesses was given to him

---

40. "So complete is the identity and function and authority between the Father and the Son that it is impossible to honour God while disregarding Jesus" (Barrett 1978: 260). See also Lincoln 2000: 75; Ridderbos 1997: 196–97.

41. On glory in John, see Barrett 1978: 166; Carson 1991b: 128.

42. For a discussion of this text, see Hurtado 2003: 379, where he remarks that the Johannine theme of Jesus' glory demonstrates "the uniqueness of the biblical God, together with an unprecedented treatment of Jesus in terms otherwise reserved for God." After all, in Isaiah (Isa. 42:8; 48:11) Yahweh categorically declares that he will not give his glory to another. Hurtado (2003: 380) suggests that the Johannine theme of God granting glory to Jesus may allude to these texts in Isaiah. See also Ridderbos 1997: 445.

by the Father (John 17:22). Indeed, the Father sent the Son to earth so he would be glorified (John 11:4; 17:1). The relationship between the Father and the Son verifies one of the major themes in this book: the Father is glorified in the Son (John 14:13). The Father and the Son are not in competition in John's Gospel, but the glory of the Son redounds to the glory of the Father.

We have seen that John maintains the priority of the Father. Jesus insists that the Father is greater than everything, even himself (John 10:29; 14:28).[43] But at the same time he also teaches that the Son and the Father are equal (John 10:30).[44] The equality in view cannot be limited to unity of purpose and aim, for the Jews took up stones to put Jesus to death for blasphemy (John 10:31–33). We think of John 5:17–18, where Jesus identified God as his Father and made himself equal to God, so that the Jews attempted to stone him for blasphemy. For John to write that Jesus was equal to God is quite astonishing, especially since he was nurtured in Jewish monotheism. Nor does he in subsequent verses of John 5 provide an explanation that nullifies the claim that Jesus is equal with God, though he does indicate that the Son is dependent on the Father. Nevertheless, Jesus is to be honored just as the Father is honored, so the full deity of the Son is clearly articulated. In John 10 as well Jesus' subsequent words about humans being gods (John 10:34–35) do not nullify the statement on the Son's deity, for Jesus is arguing from greater to lesser. If even human beings can be called gods in a derivative sense, then Jesus is not blaspheming in calling himself the Son of God, since he was consecrated by the Father as such (John 10:36).[45] Honor

43. "The Father is *fons divinitatis* in which the being of the Son has its source; the Father is God sending and commanding, the Son is God sent and obedient" (Barrett 1978: 468). For a fuller explanation that includes historical reflection in church history on the matter, see R. Brown 1970: 654–55. Ridderbos (1997: 512) argues that virtually all discussions of this verse miss the point, maintaining that there is no idea here of the relationship between the persons of the Trinity. Rather, Jesus emphasizes the inferior state for his disciples while he remains on earth.

44. Barrett (1978: 382) sees "a oneness of love and obedience even while it is a oneness of essence." Cf. Lindars 1972: 370–71; Carson 1991b: 394–95. Contra Ridderbos (1997: 371), who restricts it to unity of function in John 10:30. See Ridderbos's view in the preceding note as well.

45. See Lindars 1972: 372; Barrett 1978: 385. See Ridderbos (1997: 372–76), who rejects any argument from lesser to greater here, contending that such an argument fails to show Jesus' unique sonship. According to Ridderbos, Ps. 82 is addressed to all Israel, not just to judges or angels. Ridderbos (1997: 372–76) also claims that Jesus does not make an ontological claim here; instead, Jesus appeals to Scripture to demonstrate that he does not blaspheme in calling himself the Son of God. S. Johnson (1980: 21–37) argues that the "gods" in Ps. 82 were judges. Jesus argues typologically from the lesser to the greater, but Johnson also contends that the notion of the union of God and human beings is fundamental to the argument, and this union reaches its consummate fulfillment in Jesus Christ.

and worship are to be given to the Father and the Son, and so it is clear that the Son is divine, for in Judaism only God deserves worship. Those who hate the Son hate the Father, and vice versa (John 15:23–24). As the one who has life in himself, the Son grants life to all as a gift from the Father (John 5:25–26). To say that the Son has life in himself is to claim deity, since life belongs to God alone.[46] Jesus is the exclusive way to the Father (John 14:6). Those who have seen him and known him have seen and known the Father (John 14:7–9; 16:3).[47] The Son's works demonstrate the mutual indwelling between the Father and the Son (John 14:10–12; cf. 14:20; 16:15; 17:21).

Perhaps this is the best place to include what John's Gospel says about God's name and the name of Jesus.[48] We saw earlier, in studying the name in the Synoptics, that God's name was highly significant in the OT because it signified his presence with his people. The name theology in John's Gospel demonstrates a remarkable unity between the Father and the Son. During his ministry Jesus made known the name of the Father to his disciples (John 17:6, 26).[49] The Father's name signifies his character, and the revelation of the Father only occurs through the Son. Furthermore, Jesus kept the disciples and preserved them from apostasy in the Father's name (John 17:12), and he prays that the Father will continue to keep them in his name so that they will not stray (John 17:11). But what is truly remarkable in John 17:11–12 is the claim that God's name has been given to Jesus, for such a statement can only mean that Jesus shares divine status.[50] Jesus' prayer to the Father models what he instructs his disciples to do, for he encourages them regularly to entreat the Father in prayer in his name (John 14:13–14; 15:16; 16:23–24, 26). We know that Jesus' prayer for the preservation of disciples was answered; so also prayers offered in Jesus' name will be answered in the affirmative. Such prayers accord with the character and glory that Jesus has as the Son, and they are answered because they bring glory to the Son.

---

46. Carson (1991b: 256–57) rightly argues that this life given by the Father to the Son belongs to the Son eternally (cf. John 1:4) and thus points to the Son's deity.

47. To say that the one who has seen Jesus has seen the Father means not that the Father and Jesus are identical "but that the Son so fully embodies the Word, glory, and life of the Father that to see the Son is to see the Father" (M. M. Thompson 2001: 114).

48. Hurtado (2003: 381–92) also argues that name theology in the Gospel of John highlights the divine status of Jesus. His entire discussion bears careful reading, and I draw upon it on a number of points.

49. See Barrett 1978: 505. R. Brown (1970: 754–56) is likely correct in seeing a reference to "I Am," though what is said here cannot be restricted to such (for criticism of Brown, see Lindars 1972: 521).

50. It is likely that John refers here to the revelation of the Father given to Jesus, and hence Jesus is the unique revelation of God's character (see R. Brown 1970: 759; Beasley-Murray 1987: 299; Carson 1991b: 562).

For the disciples to ask the Father to grant their requests in Jesus' name manifests a high Christology. Prayer is directed to the Father, but it is answered on the basis of asking in Jesus' name. The uniqueness of Jesus is evident if we consider the idea of prayers being offered in the name of the Beloved Disciple or even an angel. Hurtado rightly observes how radical it is that prayers were offered in Jesus' name, given the special veneration of God's name in Jewish circles and the unheard-of idea of invoking someone else's name rather than God's in prayer.[51] Jesus' name apparently has divine power, for not only are prayers offered in his name, but also eternal life is received by believing in his name (John 1:12; 2:23; 3:18; 20:31), which suggests his divine power.[52] That Jesus belongs to the divine realm is apparent also because the Father sends the Spirit not only in his own name but also in Jesus' name (John 14:26).[53] We will explore this text further in considering the Spirit, but here we note the confluence of the Father, Son, and Spirit.

Jesus' divinity is suggested also because he knows what is in human beings (John 2:23–25), and this is verified in the succeeding story with Nicodemus, in which he informs Nicodemus of his need for new life (John 3:1–13). Moreover, Jesus is sinless. He always does what is pleasing to God (John 8:29), and no one can convict him of sin (John 8:46).[54] Because Jesus always does the Father's will, the devil has no claim on him (John 14:30–31).

The Son of God Christology in John's Gospel designates Jesus' special relation to God and emphasizes his divinity.[55] John's Christology is closely linked to his soteriology. Those who do not believe in the Son and honor him do not have eternal life. Jesus is able to grant the life of the age to come to people because he is the Son of God and because he has life in himself.

Conclusion

In the history of scholarship it has not been unusual to claim that Son of God Christology came from Hellenism, where the simple religion of

---

51. Hurtado 2003: 391.

52. Many commentators fail to note the significance of this, but Köstenberger (2004: 38–39) rightly underscores the significance of believing in Jesus' name.

53. The significance of this escapes many commentators, but see Carson 1991b: 505.

54. Cullmann (1963: 106) remarks, "With the exception of Hebrews, no other New Testament writing emphasizes so strongly as the Johannine literature the sinlessness of Jesus."

55. For this theme in John's Gospel, see Dodd 1953: 250–62. As Koester (2003: 180) notes, the theme of Jesus' preexistence demonstrates that the title "Son of God" denotes not only messiahship but also divinity.

Jesus was transmuted into another form.[56] Jewish scholars have often agreed with this assessment. Schoeps, for example, says that Paul borrowed from pagan thought and asserted that Jesus is the Son of God.[57] Bultmann insists that the notion of a dying and rising Son of God stems from mystery religions and Gnosticism, not the original kerygma.[58] Hengel demonstrates conclusively that such views lack cogency.[59] The mysteries do not know of sons of God who died or rose again, nor do devotees become children of the mystery gods. A. D. Nock points out that none of the mystery gods (e.g., Osiris) died for the sake of other human beings.[60] The real impact of mystery religions began in the second and third centuries AD, long after the writing of the NT. No evidence for such mysteries can be located in Syria in the period AD 30–50. Instead, Christianity probably exercised a strong influence on mystery religions. Others suggest that the sons of Zeus influenced the Christian development, but the dissimilarity is more striking because Zeus had countless children. The emperor was called a son of God after his death, but no claim of resurrection was made. Others have derived influence from "divine men" in Hellenism, but the alleged parallel is questionable because the existence of such figures is uncertain in the first century.[61] Most of the examples of someone claiming to be a son of God are post-Christian. Appeal to the gnostic redeemer myth is doubtful because such a myth has no evidence of being pre-Christian.[62] No pagan tradition has God sending his Son into history, nor does his Son assume human form and die. We have seen that the Son of God theme in the Gospels develops in a Jewish milieu.

The Son of God Christology in John is quite extraordinary. The disciples who hailed Jesus as the Son during his ministry probably used the term not to denote his divinity but to designate that Jesus was the Messiah. But John teaches that they spoke better than they knew. As the Son, Jesus has life in himself and will stand as the judge on the final day. He is fully divine and equal with the Father, so that those who honor the Father must honor him as well. Prayers offered in his name will be answered, and eternal life comes to those who believe in his name. At the same time, John preserves a delicate interplay between the Father and the Son. The Father indwells the Son, and the Son the Father. Jesus is the revelation of the Father and discloses his character to his disciples and to the world. Still, it was the

56. For a classic expression of this view, see Harnack 1957.
57. Schoeps 1961: 150–60.
58. Bultmann 1951: 28, 32, 50, 80.
59. Hengel 1976.
60. For Nock's view, see Hengel 1976: 26n54.
61. See note 8 in this chapter.
62. See Yamauchi 1973, a seminal study.

Father who sent the Son, and the Father always retains priority as the Father. In this sense he is greater than the Son. The Son existed with the Father before the world began and shares his glory, and disciples will enjoy the Son's glory forever in the future. And yet the Son was sent to bring glory to the Father, while at the same time the Father glorifies the Son. The Son as the sent one acts in dependence upon and in submission to his Father and constantly does what is pleasing to the Father. Christology must not be severed from soteriology, as the purpose statement of John's Gospel affirms (John 20:30–31). Life in the age to come is the portion of human beings even now if they put their trust in Jesus as the Son of God and Messiah. His name saves because his name is exalted.

The "I Am" Sayings in John

It is impossible to exhaust John's rich Christology, especially in a survey of the theology of the NT. Another dimension of his Christology stands out in the "I am" statements that are sprinkled regularly throughout the Gospel. The words "I am" (*egō eimi*) draw on God's revelation of himself to Moses when he summoned him to liberate Israel from Egypt (Exod. 3:6, 14),[63] but its closest antecedents are found in Isaiah, who regularly uses "I am" in contrasting Yahweh with the idols, assuring Israel that he will free them in a second exodus (Isa. 41:4; 43:10, 25; 45:8, 18, 19, 22; 46:4, 9; 48:12, 17; 51:12; 52:6 LXX).[64] The texts in Isaiah occur in contexts where monotheism is taught emphatically in which the creator God is contrasted with idols. "I am" is reserved for Yahweh, who ordains the end from the beginning and who will accomplish his saving purposes in the world in contrast to idols, which are powerless. As a Jew, John was well versed in OT antecedents. His use of the phrase stands as another strong piece of evidence supporting Jesus' deity, his "unique divinity and sovereignty."[65] The words "I am" in their full sense cannot and do not appear on the lips of anyone who is merely human.[66] We also notice

63. Scholars have examined parallels to the "I am" sayings in Hellenism, Gnosticism and Mandaism, and Jewish sources. For a survey of options, see Harner 1970: 26–30; Ball 1996: 24–45. Ball rightly argues that the meaning of the phrase must be explored within the literary orbit of the Fourth Gospel.

64. For this view, see Harner 1970: 6–17; Ball 1996: 264–69. For a thorough analysis of the Isaianic background, see C. Williams (2000: 23–46), who emphasizes that the phrase "I am he" serves as a divine title.

65. C. Williams 2000: 301. Williams (2000: 302, 303) argues that Jesus is presented as "the definitive revelation of God" and "the only effective agent of divine salvation."

66. "However, most striking of all is the fact that Jesus takes on himself a phrase that is reserved for Yahweh alone and thus intimately identifies himself with God's acts of creation and salvation" (Ball 1996: 203).

that the phrase occurs when Yahweh promises to liberate his people and fulfill his covenantal promises. The "I am" statements on Jesus' lips suggest, then, that in him the promises of God find their fulfillment. God's saving purposes climax in Jesus himself.

The words "I am" (*egō eimi*) do not, of course, necessarily hearken back to Exod. 3 and the use in Isaiah. In John 9:9 the man to whom Jesus restores sight identifies himself with the words "I am" (*egō eimi*), but of course he is not claiming to be divine. In Luke's Gospel Jesus confirms who he is after his resurrection because the disciples doubt his identity (Luke 24:39), but any connotations of deity seem unlikely in this context.

Interpreting some of the "I am" expressions in John is quite difficult.[67] Jesus responded to the Samaritan woman's belief in the Messiah by declaring himself to be such: "I am" (*egō eimi* [John 4:26 my translation]). Perhaps the answer is akin to John 9:9 and consists of simple identification, but given the use of the phrase elsewhere in John's Gospel, one suspects that John intends the reader to see more in the expression than would have been perceived by the Samaritan woman.[68] C. Williams argues that Jesus' wording here hails from Isa. 40–66 and cannot be restricted to one verse from the Isaiah traditions (i.e., Isa. 52:6).[69] Jesus' declaration to the woman (John 4:26) is akin to Yahweh's ability to predict the future in Isaiah (Isa. 41:22–23, 26; 43:9, 12; 48:14). Hence, Jesus' self-identification to the woman has a deeper meaning. The same question emerges when Jesus walks on water and identifies himself to the disciples in the midst of their fear (John 6:20). His declaration could be simple self-identification. Yahweh, however, is the God of the storm, and Jesus' ability to tread on water and to calm the storm suggest that the words "I am" point to his deity.[70]

Often the "I am" statements are tied to an event, so that discourse and event interpret one another.[71] After Jesus fed the five thousand (John 6:1–15), the "bread of life" discourse expounds on the event (John 6:26–59). Jesus is the new Moses giving his people bread from heaven, but he is greater than Moses, for the bread that he gives does not simply satisfy the stomach but grants eternal life. Indeed, Jesus does not merely

67. See Ball 1996: 162–76.
68. Such a view is strengthened by the suggestion that Jesus draws on Isa. 52:6 (Harner 1970: 46–47; Ball 1996: 179–81).
69. C. Williams 2000: 257–66.
70. See also Hurtado 2003: 371; Ball 1996: 74, 185. Ball sees a reference to OT epiphanies of God and traces an OT background.
71. Smalley (1978: 91–92) sets forth this view clearly in his work, but his schema at several points seems to be forced. For instance, he links the "true vine" saying (John 15:1) with the discourse in John 4. See the criticisms in Ball 1996: 147–48.

give bread from heaven; he *is* the bread of heaven. Thus he says, "I am the bread of life" (John 6:35, 48; cf. 6:41, 51, 58).[72] As the discourse unfolds, it becomes clear that the "bread" that he gives for the life of the world is his flesh (John 6:51). Here we have a clear allusion to his death on the cross. Life comes to people only from eating his flesh and drinking his blood (John 6:52–59), from believing in and trusting in Jesus as the crucified and risen Lord. Just as earthly life is sustained through the death of living things, so also eternal life is obtained only by feeding on Jesus' death, by trusting that his death is the means by which sins are forgiven.

Jesus also announces, "I am the light of the world" (John 8:12).[73] The event aligned with this declaration is almost certainly the lighting festival that occurred at the Feast of Tabernacles.[74] It also accords with the restoration of sight to the blind man in John 9. Jesus is the true revelation of God and grants spiritual sight to the blind. But those who insist that they have no need of light and refuse to admit their spiritual blindness continue to exist in darkness. The claim to be the light of the world is almost certainly a prerogative of deity. Only God can create light where there is none (Gen. 1:3, 16; Isa. 45:7; Jer. 31:35; cf. Exod. 13:21). According to the psalmist, Yahweh "is my light and my salvation" (Ps. 27:1), and Isaiah says that "the LORD will be your everlasting light" (Isa. 60:19; cf. Mic. 7:8), but John identifies Jesus as the light of the world (cf. Isa. 9:2; 42:6; 49:6).[75]

In John 10 Jesus gives the "good shepherd" discourse (10:1–30) and identifies himself as "the door" for the sheep (John 10:7, 9) and as "the good shepherd" (10:11, 14).[76] The parable is overloaded, for one cannot function both as the door for the sheepfold and as the shepherd. Such pedantic consistency is no concern to John.[77] He seizes upon various elements of the discourse to emphasize different facets of Jesus' person and ministry. The image of the door is used to convey that salvation is available only through Jesus (John 10:9). The true flock enters through that door for salvation. But Jesus is also the good shepherd for his sheep, and he lays down his life for his sheep. He stands in contrast to the

72. The word "life" ties the "I am" saying to the purpose of John's Gospel (John 1:4; 20:31).

73. Ball notes that the narrative of John 8 raises some ambiguity regarding Jesus' identity that is resolved by the conclusion of the story (1996: 82). So also C. Williams 2000: 268.

74. See *m. Sukkah* 4:1, 9–10; 5:2–4. For a summary of what occurred during the festival and its relationship to John's Gospel, see Barrett 1978: 326–27, 335; Köstenberger 2004: 239–40.

75. The reference to light also hearkens back to the prologue: John 1:4–5, 7–9 (so Ball 1996: 87).

76. Ball (1996: 93–94) notes that the narrative is set in the same context as John 9.

77. See especially Carson 1991b: 383–84.

false shepherds of Israel (Ezek. 34:1–6).[78] These bogus shepherds feed themselves instead of the sheep, exploit the sheep for their own profit, fail to care for injured or straying sheep, and dominate rather than serve them. Yahweh pledges that he will seek out and rescue his sheep (Ezek. 34:11–12). He will liberate them from exile and allow them to feed in the richness of his provision (Ezek. 34:13–14). Indeed, Yahweh promises to become their shepherd: "I myself will be the shepherd of my sheep, and I myself will make them lie down, declares the LORD God. I will seek the lost, and I will bring back the strayed, and I will bind up the injured, and I will strengthen the weak, and the fat and the strong I will destroy. I will feed them in justice" (Ezek. 34:15–16). A few verses later we are informed that a coming David will shepherd the flock: "And I will set up over them one shepherd, my servant David, and he shall feed them: he shall feed them and be their shepherd. And I, the LORD, will be their God, and my servant David shall be prince among them. I am the LORD; I have spoken" (Ezek. 34:23–24). Ezekiel's prophecy of Yahweh serving as the shepherd for the flock finds its fulfillment in Jesus as the good shepherd (cf. Ps. 23:1; Isa. 40:11).[79] Moreover, John merges the promises that the Lord and David will shepherd God's people. Both of these prophecies find their fulfillment in Jesus, for he is the Messiah and the Lord. The promises about return to exile and the covenant of peace (Ezek. 34:25) find their fulfillment in him.

Jesus also declared, "I am the resurrection and the life" (John 11:25). This declaration is followed by his raising Lazarus from the dead, so that it is closely linked with the sign performed. Since Jesus is "the resurrection and life," all who trust in him will conquer death by being resurrected (John 11:25, 27). Although realized eschatology receives the emphasis in John, future eschatology is clearly present in this text as well. Still, as is typical in John, realized eschatology comes to the forefront in the statement, "Everyone who lives and believes in me shall never die" (John 11:26). Even in the present age believers have conquered death and live with the triumphal confidence that physical death cannot remove the life that they already enjoy. The Christology behind Jesus' assertion is astonishing, for only God can raise the dead, as is evident from Ezek. 37.

Jesus also says, "I am the true vine" (John 15:1). In the OT Israel is described as the Lord's vineyard (Isa. 5:1–7; cf. Jer. 12:10), signifying that they are the elect people of the Lord.[80] Israel was the vine that the

78. For Ezek. 34 as the background, see Ball 1996: 224–26; see also Evans 1993: 28–36.
79. "Jesus identifies himself with the role which God would accomplish as the promised Good Shepherd" (Ball 1996: 225).
80. For the OT background here, see Evans 1993: 37–45.

Lord rescued from Egypt, and the psalmist prayed that the Lord would act on behalf of this vine in his day (Ps. 80:8, 14). The "son" and "son of man" in the psalm may only refer to Israel (Ps. 80:15, 17), but it is also possible that they include a reference to Israel's anointed king. If the latter is the case, then the vine in Ps. 80 may include a reference to both Israel and the Davidic king.[81] The allusions to the OT provide the necessary backdrop for interpreting John 15:1. When Jesus announced that he is the true vine, he taught that he is the true Israel. Only those branches that are connected to him and remain in him are truly members of the people of God. Whether or not one is an ethnic Israelite fades into the background, and one's relationship to Jesus is the criterion that determines membership in the people of God. That Jesus is the exclusive pathway to God is not a novel theme in John. Jesus is not the way in a general sense, but he is specifically the way to the Father. Jesus declared, "I am the way, and the truth, and the life. No one comes to the Father except through me" (John 14:6).[82] John's exclusive Christology is tied to his exclusive soteriology.

A constellation of "I am" sayings sets forth the glory of Jesus. The most striking is in John 8:58, which culminates an account beginning with Jesus' claim to be the light of the world (John 8:12). Jesus engaged in a debate with alleged disciples as to whether they were truly the children of Abraham (John 8:31–59). He asserted that only those who remain in his word are freed from the slavery of sin. His Jewish listeners were outraged at any suggestion that they were enslaved, insisting that as children of Abraham they were free. Jesus asserted that their desire to kill him proves that their father is the devil, and they countered by smearing him with charges of being a Samaritan and a demon. Jesus promised that those who keep his word will never die—an astonishing claim indeed. The Jews responded that he could not be greater than Abraham, and Abraham himself died. Jesus proclaimed that Abraham rejoiced over his coming, and then he concluded, "Truly, truly, I say to you, before Abraham was, I am" (John 8:58). The theme that membership in the people of God comes not via Abraham or being a Jew but only through Jesus emerges again. The Jesus who promised life is the ever-living one, so that as the possessor of life he can grant life to others.[83] Jesus' superiority to Abraham is evident in the discourse. The final claim is nothing short of shocking. The Jews believed that it was blasphemy, for they immediately took up stones to put him to death.[84] The "I am"

81. See chapter 6, note 61.
82. See Ball 1996: 126–28.
83. C. Williams 2000: 278.
84. Ball (1996: 92–93) rightly maintains that the narrative supports such an astonishing claim because the Jews attempt to stone Jesus. Further, the claim fits with the prologue,

statement likely draws on Exod. 3 and the texts noted in Isaiah.[85] Jesus'
statement certainly is a claim to deity, given the "I am" statement and
the assertion that he existed before Abraham lived. Indeed, the "I am"
claim indicates preexistence, that he is the everlasting one.[86]

The remaining "I am" statements should be interpreted similarly.
Jesus predicts what will happen in advance so that his disciples will
believe *egō eimi*, "I am" (John 13:19 my translation). The use of "I am"
demonstrates that such predictions are not merely the prophecies of an
ordinary prophet. Jesus demonstrates his deity by proclaiming what will
happen before it occurs. We have already noted that the "I am" formula
is common in Isa. 40–48. These same chapters often declare that Yahweh
stands apart from idols as the true God because he is able to predict the
future (Isa. 41:21–29; 42:8–9; 44:8–9; 46:9–11; 48:6). The uniqueness
of Yahweh manifests itself in his control over history. So too, Jesus is
revealed as "I am" in his ability to predict the future. The deity of Jesus
is suggested also by his words to those arresting him: "I am" (John 18:5,
6, 8 my translation).[87] The text could be read in terms of simple self-
identification, but since those who arrest Jesus fall to the ground at his
self-revelation, we should read the declaration in light of the other "I am"
statements.[88] Human beings are stunned and fall back in the presence
of the divine, so what happened here is a kind of theophany. So too the
Isaianic background is likely present when Jesus predicted the future
before it occurs, demonstrating that "I am" (John 13:19 my translation).
In Isaiah the true God differentiates himself from idols, which are powerless to predict the future, and here Jesus identified himself as divine, but
the next verse (John 13:20) indicates that he does not act independently
of the Father but rather has been sent by the Father himself, so that the
unity between the Father and the Son is emphasized.[89]

The revelation of Jesus in John can never be separated from the cross.
Jesus declared, "Unless you believe 'I am,' you shall die in your sins" (John
8:24 my translation). Those who confess Jesus as Lord and God (John
20:28) belong to God. In honoring the Son they also honor the Father
(John 5:23). Conversely, those who fail to honor the Father do not honor

---

where Jesus is the Word who was with God from the beginning. See also Harner 1970:
39–42; Carson 1991b: 358. Contra Barrett 1978: 352.

85. See Ball 1996: 197; C. Williams 2000: 276–78.

86. See Dodd 1953: 261–62. The charge of blasphemy may reflect the view that Jesus
has claimed the divine name (see R. Brown 1966: 360, 367–68; C. Williams 2000: 279–83).
Contra Ridderbos (1997: 323), who does not think that Jesus speaks of "the ontological
category of divine being."

87. We see here both Jesus' sovereignty and his submission to the way of the cross
(Ball 1996: 140).

88. So also Harner 1970: 45; Ball 1996: 141–44, 201; C. Williams 2000: 289.

89. See the full discussion in C. Williams 2000: 283–87.

the Son. Jesus also declared, "When you lift up the Son of man, you shall know that I am" (John 8:28 my translation).[90] The saying is ambiguous, and probably it has a double meaning.[91] Only those who acknowledge Jesus as the crucified one will experience life, so that those who claim to worship the one true God must also acknowledge Jesus as the one who saves.[92] On the other hand, those who refuse to acknowledge him during the present age will confess on the day of judgment that Jesus is divine. The cross is the means by which Jesus is exalted or lifted up on high as the ruler of the world.

The "I am" statements contribute significantly to Johannine Christology. They demonstrate that Jesus fulfills the OT hope for Israel. He is the way of salvation, and the cross is the means by which salvation is accomplished. Jesus is the unique revelation of God, and in addition, in Jesus God himself has been manifested among his people. The one who has seen Jesus has seen the Father (John 14:9), for he has explicated the Father to human beings (John 1:18). Jesus is the "I am" of the OT, and yet, as noted earlier, Jesus does not exhaust who God is. Jesus is not God without remainder, but he is both Lord and God, the "I am" of the OT.[93] The connection with Isa. 40–66 demonstrates that the "I am" statements are linked with soteriology, with the fulfillment of God's saving promises, with the realization of the new exodus and the new creation. God's saving promises are realized in Jesus because he is the "I am" who pledged salvation in Isa. 40–66. Hence, John does not indulge in christological speculation, for the identity of Jesus cannot be severed from his saving work.[94]

Logos

Scholars have long recognized that John's Christology is more explicit and direct than that of the Synoptic Gospels. One of his distinctive terms for Jesus is "Word" (*logos*). In considering Logos Christology, we begin with the background in Hellenism.[95] The *logos* in Hellenistic thought

90. According to Ball (1996: 90), the proximity of John 8:28 to 8:24 suggests that they should be interpreted together.

91. So also Harner 1970: 43–44; C. Williams 2000: 267–68.

92. C. Williams (2000: 266–75) rightly argues that the point here, as is clear from the OT allusions, is the identity of the one true God, and that God's identity is revealed in Jesus himself.

93. "The Son's identification with the Father is so close that he can even take words from Isaiah concerning the Lord's role as the only God, and use them of himself" (Ball 1996: 193).

94. So Ball 1996: 126–28.

95. Dodd (1953: 263–85) particularly emphasizes the word of God in the OT, wisdom, and the Logos theme in Philo. For further study of the background, see Keener 2003: 339–63

refers to both the inward thought and the expression of such thought in discourse. According to Stoicism, the *logos* rules the universe and is in the human intellect. Reason—that is, the *logos*—permeates all things. In Stoic thought the virtuous life consists in living according to nature. Living according to nature does not mean that people follow their impulses and desires. Those who live in accord with nature pattern their lives so that they live in harmony with reason. Those who conduct their lives rationally live according to nature. We must recall that the Stoic worldview is pantheistic. No personal God exists in the Stoic framework, and the course of history replicates itself again and again. In gnostic thought the *logos* functions as an intermediary being between God and human beings. Gnostic thought, however, did not influence John, since gnostic documents were composed subsequent to the writing of the NT.[96]

Since the discovery of the Dead Sea Scrolls, scholars have recognized anew John's affinity with Jewish thought.[97] In the OT God's word is effective, bringing into existence that which he says. The power of God's word is evident in Gen. 1, for whatever God says comes into existence. When God says, "Let there be light," light springs into existence (Gen. 1:3). The psalmist reflects on God's creative word: "By the word of the Lord the heavens were made, and by the breath of his mouth all their host" (Ps. 33:6). His word is not considered to be a separate entity or person in the OT, though in some cases poetic language is used that depicts the word as if it were a distinct entity. We see this in Ps. 107:20: "He sent out his word and healed them, and delivered them from their destruction." In this context God's word brings life when death threatens. A similar phenomenon is evident in Ps. 147:18, where at God's command ice, snow, and cold envelop the world, but nature is transformed when "he sends out his word and melts them; he makes his winds blow and the waters flow." The change of seasons is not due merely to the natural course of things. The fresh breezes of spring and the flowing rivers and streams stem from God's word.

(though his identifying Logos with Torah is questionable); Cullmann 1963: 251–54; Klappert and Fries, *NIDNTT* 3:1081–1117. Ridderbos (1997: 28–36) rightly argues that neither a Hellenistic background nor a fully developed wisdom Christology provides a satisfactory context for what John says about the Logos, even though wisdom motifs are present.

96. Note again the seminal work of Yamauchi 1973.

97. For a thorough exploration of the background to the Johannine prologue, see Evans 1993. Evans argues that the most convincing parallels to the prologue derive from Jewish sources, not from Gnosticism or Hermeticism. So also Dunn 1996a: 213–50; Hurtado 2003: 366. For a brief survey of the Jewish background, see Cullmann 1963: 254–58; Lee 2005: 62–77. Fossum (1995: 109–33) argues that John's Christology is rooted in biblical and postbiblical teaching on God's name and the angel of the Lord.

The natural world exists and thrives by virtue of God's sovereign power. "He sends out his command to the earth; his word runs swiftly" (Ps. 147:15). Nothing can deter God's word from taking effect, for what he declares will become reality. Hence, we read in Isa. 55:10–11, "For as the rain and the snow come down from heaven and do not return there but water the earth, making it bring forth and sprout, giving seed to the sower and bread to the eater, so shall my word be that goes out from my mouth; it shall not return to me empty, but it shall accomplish that which I purpose, and shall succeed in the thing for which I sent it." The effectiveness of God's word continues to be emphasized in postbiblical literature. God's judgments in Egypt at the time of the exodus are described as follows: "Your all-powerful word leaped from heaven, from the royal throne, into the midst of the land that was doomed, a stern warrior carrying the sharp sword of your authentic command, and stood and filled all things with death, and touched heaven while standing on the earth" (Wis. 18:15–16 NRSV). The Targumim also communicate the power of God's word. We see this in the paraphrase of Gen. 1:3: "The Word [*memra*] of the Lord said, 'Let there be light.' And there was light in his Word [*memra*]" (*Frg. Tg.* Gen. 1:3).[98] The word of God enlivens and kills; it sustains the world humans live in; it never fails in its purpose.

We have seen that the word of God plays a decisive role in the creation of the world. God's creative word, however, is also closely related to wisdom. The world was formed by God in wisdom. "The LORD possessed me at the beginning of his work, the first of his acts of old. Ages ago I was set up, at the first, before the beginning of the earth. When there were no depths I was brought forth, when there were no springs abounding with water. Before the mountains had been shaped, before the hills, I was brought forth, before he had made the earth with its fields, or the first of the dust of the world" (Prov. 8:22–26). Just as the world was created by means of God's word, it also was formed by his wisdom. In Sirach wisdom is equated with Torah, God's word to his people in the law of Moses (Sir. 24:23). God made the world by his word, and he created human beings in his wisdom. "O God of my ancestors and Lord of mercy, who have made all things by your word, and by your wisdom have formed humankind to have dominion over the creatures you have made" (Wis. 9:1–2 NRSV).

Philo uses the term *logos* more than fourteen hundred times.[99] The *logos* acts as an intermediary between God and the world. Philo establishes a synthesis of Middle Platonic and Stoic views with his Jewish

98. For the targumic parallels, see Evans 1993: 114–24.
99. So Dunn 1996a: 220. See the survey on the *logos* in Philo in Evans 1993: 100–12. See also Dodd 1953: 66–73; Segal 1977: 159–81; Kleinknecht, *TDNT* 4:77–91; Dunn 1996a: 220–30.

monotheism. According to Philo, ideas are in the mind of God, and the *logos*, contrary to the Stoics' view, is inferior to God himself, who is ultimately unknowable. *Logos* includes both the unexpressed thought and the thought that is expressed in speech. Since the *logos* functions as an intermediary, God acts on the world and creates through the *logos* (Philo, *Cherubim* 127). The *logos* is God's firstborn and his Son and is identified as the beginning (Philo, *Confusion* 146). The *logos* is described as God's image (Philo, *Flight* 101) and is even called the "second god" (Philo, *QG* 2.62), though Philo does not intend by this to say that the *logos* is a personal being or is actually divine. The *logos* is what is knowable of God. It is not a gradation of being but rather gradations in God's manifestation of himself, like the halo around the sun.[100] God is unknowable in himself, but he reaches out to the world through the *logos*. It seems that those scholars who claim that the *logos* in Philo's thought is only a personification are correct,[101] for Philo's strong monotheism rules out the idea that the *logos* is an independent being or hypostasis.

In considering the Logos in John, the echoes of *logos* in first-century culture should be borne in mind. Still, the Jewish background must be considered primary.[102] John's Gospel commences with the same words that we find in Gen. 1:1: "In the beginning" (John 1:1). In Gen. 1 all things come into existence by means of God's word, whereas in John's Gospel all of created life is ascribed to the Logos (John 1:3). John, of course, reflects on the beginning before the beginning, since the "the Word was with God" (John 1:1) before the creation of the world.[103] John also represents an advance over the OT and postbiblical Judaism because the Logos is personal and divine.[104] John slides from the Logos in John 1:1 to "this one" or "he" (*houtos*), emphasizing again the personal identity of the Logos, for the Logos is not an abstract entity. The distinctiveness of the Gospel manifests itself with his assertion that "the Word became flesh and dwelt among us" (John 1:14).[105] The personal "Word" that existed with God from all eternity took on flesh and became a human being. The Logos for John is not merely a personification but a person, not merely one who existed with God for all eternity but one who has entered his-

---

100. So Dunn 1996a: 226.

101. This is the conclusion of the survey in Dunn 1996a: 220–30. See also the careful analysis in Lee 2005: 59–75.

102. See Evans 1993. So also Cullmann 1963: 259.

103. Rightly Ridderbos (1997: 24), who also correctly argues that although John writes with the context of Gen. 1 in view, we do not have a midrash on that chapter here.

104. Rightly Dodd 1953: 275; Hurtado 2003: 367.

105. M. M. Thompson (1988: 39–52) shows that the word "flesh" means that Jesus became a human being.

tory as a human being.[106] This shocking claim sets John's Gospel apart from any other previous writing about God's word.

The Logos entered history in the person of Jesus the Christ.[107] Jesus is God's definitive and final word to human beings, expressing and revealing who God truly is. God is invisible and has never been observed by human beings (John 1:18). Jesus as God's Word has explained (*exēgeomai*) him to human beings. We should also note that the "word" in the NT is usually the gospel. John emphasizes that the gospel centers on the incarnate Word, Jesus. The human Jesus is the revelation of God, and his deity is hidden but not cancelled out by his humanity.

The progression of thought in John 1:1 reaches a climax. First, the Word existed for all eternity. There is no beginning at which he is not present. Second, "the Word was with God." The Logos and God are not equivalent, for they can be distinguished. The Word existed with God for all eternity and had fellowship with God. Third, and most stunning, John tells us that "the Word was God" (*theos ēn ho logos*). This sentence cannot be rendered as "the Word was a god." When the predicate nominative precedes the copula, the noun preceding the copula emphasizes quality. So the predicate "God" (*theos*) preceding "was" indicates that the Logos is divine.[108] He is fully God.[109] We must also remember that John was nurtured in the OT and does not tolerate polytheism. The translation "a god" would suggest polytheism, which is unthinkable for a monotheist such as John. What John teaches here is that Jesus is fully God, and yet at the same time there is only one God.[110] Could we conclude from this that John falls into modalism, so that God collapses, so to speak, into the Word? We can confidently rule out modalism, for in the preceding sentence we are told that "the Word was with God." The Word and God both existed from all eternity and enjoyed fellowship with one another. Further, John 1:2 reiterates that the Logos and God are distinct, emphasizing again that he was with God, so that the Logos cannot be God without remainder. Hence, "God" and "the Word" are separate entities in one sense. The Logos is fully divine without compromising monotheism or without falling prey to modalism. We are at the brink here of the paradox of the Trinity, in which Jesus is fully God, and God is one, and yet Jesus is not

106. Käsemann (1968) argues that the Johannine portrait of Jesus is "naively docetic." For a convincing response to Käsemann, see M. M. Thompson (1988), who shows Jesus' humanity from his origins (John 6:41; 7:2–9, 27, 41–44), his incarnation (John 1:14), his signs, and his death (John 6:51–58; 19:34–35; 20:24–29).

107. Schlatter (1999: 129) rightly emphasizes that many of our questions remain unanswered.

108. For a helpful study of the grammar here, see Wallace 1996: 256–70. See also Harris 1992: 51–71.

109. Rightly Hofius 1987: 16–17.

110. So also Hurtado 2003: 369.

God without remainder. The Father is God as well. We have the paradox of the Logos being with God and yet also being God.[111]

There is no doubt, according to the Gospel of John, that Jesus is God. The Gospel climaxes with Thomas's declaration to Jesus: "My Lord and my God" (John 20:28).[112] The disciples grasp who Jesus truly is when he is raised from the dead. The acclamation of Jesus' deity forms an inclusio with John 1:1, framing the entire Gospel. The same framing device exists in the prologue itself. The best textual reading of John 1:18 proclaims that Jesus is "the only God" (*monogenēs theos*).[113] His revelation of God is trustworthy because of his intimate relation with the Father ("who is at the Father's side") and because he is himself divine. Dunn contends that John's Gospel contains the first clear reference to the incarnation and preexistence in NT writings. He rightly sees that John is the first to move from an impersonal *logos* to the Logos becoming flesh, but we have already seen that the Synoptics teach preexistence in the "I have come" sayings and elsewhere, and we will see that Paul, the author of Hebrews, and the book of Revelation clearly taught the Son's preexistence as well (Phil. 2:6–11; Col. 1:15–20; Heb. 1:1–3; Rev. 1:17).[114] John's Christology sets forth in bold colors the divinity of Christ. He is one with the Father (John 10:30) as "the Word became flesh" (John 1:14). Yet the Father and Son are also distinguished. We noted earlier that the Father sends and the Son goes. We never read the reverse, where the Son sends and the Father goes. Clearly, a certain kind of priority belongs to the Father. The Father can be called greater than the Son without compromising the Son's deity (John 10:29; 14:28).[115] Later church history worked this out in terms of essence and function, ontology and economy.

Conclusion

One of the central questions raised by the NT is "Who is Jesus?" The Gospels teach that he is not only the Messiah but also the Son of God.

111. Cullmann (1963: 265–66) clearly articulates the paradox, but at the same time he underemphasizes the ontological nature of the Johannine statement in defense of his functional Christology.

112. "This, then, is the supreme christological pronouncement of the Fourth Gospel" (R. Brown 1970: 1047). See also Barrett 1978: 573; Carson 1991b: 658–59; Ridderbos 1997: 648. For a thorough study, see Harris 1992: 105–29.

113. Rightly Cullmann 1963: 309. Most scholars agree that this is the correct textual reading here (see Metzger 1994: 169–70; Harris 1992: 74–83; contra Büchsel, *TDNT* 4:740; Ridderbos 1997: 59). See also the full exegesis of this text in Harris 1992: 84–103.

114. Preexistence is likely taught in 1 Pet. 1:20 as well.

115. P. Anderson (1996: 260–61) rightly shows that John holds these two themes together. So also Hurtado 2003: 393–94.

The term "Son of God" designates Jesus as the true Israel and the true son of David. Hence, in some contexts those who identified Jesus as God's Son simply meant that he was the Messiah. But the title "Son of God" cannot be restricted to messiahship even in the Synoptics. The title also designates Jesus' special and intimate relationship with God. As the Son, he has a mutual and exclusive knowledge of the Father, and as the Son, he determines who knows the Father. Jesus is Immanuel—God with us—and he promises to be with his people until salvation history is consummated.

The sonship of Jesus in John's Gospel clearly sets him forth as divine. The Son is to be honored as the Father is honored, and the Father and the Son are one. The Son clearly preexisted and shared glory along with the Father before the world came into existence.[116] The Father has granted to the Son his name, so that the Son has the same dignity as the Father. The priority of the Father is maintained in John, since the Father sends and the Son obeys and acts in dependence upon the Father. At the same time the Father and the Son enjoy equal dignity. Indeed, the "I am" sayings demonstrate Jesus' deity, for the great "I am" statements regarding the Lord in Exodus and Isaiah are applied to Jesus. He existed as "I am" before Abraham was born. In the "I am" sayings we see that Jesus is the bread of life, the light of the world, the door for the sheep, the resurrection and the life, and the true vine. Indeed, Jesus is God's word and message to human beings. As God's Logos, he has existed with God from the beginning and is himself very God, so that he is the revelation of God to human beings and is confessed by Thomas as Lord and God.

The high Christology of the Gospels cannot be ascribed to Hellenism. It grew and was nurtured in Jewish circles. Those who have attempted to ascribe such Christology to Gnosticism or other Hellenistic literature have failed to make the case. The Jewish roots of Christology also indicate that we do not have ontology for ontology's sake in the Gospels. The splendor of Jesus' person means that he is the one who saves his people in accord with OT promises. The good news of God's kingdom and the promise of eternal life are secured through the one who is God's Son. Those who put their faith in the Son will be saved on the day of judgment and enjoy the life of the age to come even now. The people of God can be assured that they are saved, for their salvation has not come from one who is only a man but is the work of God himself—the Word become flesh.

---

116. Hofius (1987: 24) argues that the words "we have seen his glory" (John 1:14) indicate Jesus' deity.

8

❄ ❄ ❄ ❄ ❄ ❄ ❄ ❄ ❄ ❄ ❄ ❄ ❄ ❄ ❄ ❄ ❄ ❄

Jesus' Saving Work
in the Gospels

In the NT Christology always serves soteriology.[1] The NT writers betray no interest in Christology for its own sake. They do not spin out treatises on the nature of God and on how Jesus Christ and the Holy Spirit relate to God. Instead, they teach that God's saving promises have become a reality through the ministry, death, and resurrection of Jesus Christ, and that the dawning of the new era in Christ is signified by the sending of God's promised Spirit upon his people. In this chapter we explore the saving work of Jesus as portrayed in the Gospels. If we link this to the Christology of the Gospels, as we should, it becomes clear that the work of Jesus saves because of who he is. Jesus can accomplish what he does for his people because of who he is. The focus on the saving work of Christ in the NT reminds us of the centrality of Jesus Christ in NT theology. We begin with the Servant of the Lord, for here Jesus' work on behalf of his people is intimately related to his identity as such.

1. Keck (1986: 363) remarks, "Soteriology makes christology necessary; christology makes soteriology possible," and he goes on to say rightly that Christology cannot be reduced to soteriology.

Servant of the Lord

Old Testament Context

The decisive OT text for the Servant of the Lord is Isa. 52:13–53:12.[2] OT scholars have debated vigorously the Servant Songs in Isaiah, but our task here is to interpret them canonically, as they appear in the final form of Isaiah.[3] The servant has been identified as a king, a prophet, and a new Moses.[4] Isaiah clearly identifies Israel, the children of Abraham, as his chosen servant (Isa. 41:8–9; 44:1–2; 45:4).[5] As God's servant, Israel is blind and deaf, failing to see and hear God's word (Isa. 42:18–20; cf. 43:8–10). Israel, therefore, is a flawed and sinful servant. But Israel's sin is not the whole story. Since Israel is God's servant, their sins will be forgiven (Isa. 44:21–22) and they will be restored from exile.[6] The Lord "has redeemed his servant Jacob" and will bring them back from exile in Babylon to the land of promise (Isa. 48:20).

The servant, however, is not always coterminous with Israel. Yahweh proclaims that the servant's word about the restoration of Jerusalem and the cities of Judah will be confirmed (Isa. 44:26). The servant here is probably the prophet Isaiah, or possibly even Cyrus (Isa. 44:28). Identifying the servant in Isa. 49 is particularly difficult. At first glance, it might seem to be clear because in Isa. 49:3 the servant is called Israel. But a simple identification of the servant as Israel is precluded by further reading, for this servant also brings Jacob and Israel back to God (Isa. 49:5–6).[7] The servant cannot be restricted to Israel if he also restores Israel. There must be some distinction between the servant and Israel so that the former can liberate the latter. This servant not only will bring back Israel to Yahweh but also will function as "a light for the nations, that my salvation may reach to the end of the earth" (Isa. 49:6). Kings and princes will worship the Lord because of his servant (Isa. 49:7). Some have seen the servant here as Isaiah because he was called from the womb and his mouth is "like a sharp sword" (Isa. 49:1–2). However,

2. For a survey of Servant of the Lord in both the OT and the NT, see Dempster 2007: 128–78.

3. For a survey of various interpretations, see Hugenberger 1995: 106–19.

4. The judgment of Allison (1993: 70) that Moses served as one of several types for the Servant of the Lord in Isaiah seems more reasonable than the servant being identified as a new Moses. Contra Hugenberger 1995: 119–39.

5. Rightly Zimmerli and Jeremias 1957: 17–18.

6. The connection between return from exile and the Servant of the Lord is explicated well in Hanson 1998.

7. Zimmerli and Jeremias (1957: 25–34) argue for a reference to a prophet, suggesting that the suffering is redolent of the suffering of Jeremiah and yet goes beyond Jeremiah's sufferings.

Isaiah cannot be the exclusive reference, since salvation was not proclaimed throughout the entire world by Isaiah.[8]

Isaiah 42 does not directly identify the servant, and it might seem that the safest course is to see a reference to Israel. The servant again, however, seems to go beyond Israel in that he is endowed with the Spirit and extends justice to the nations (Isa. 42:1). The justice that he establishes will not be confined to Israel but rather reaches to the ends of the earth (Isa. 42:4). He will not create a new world order through warfare and battle and street-to-street fighting (Isa. 42:2–3). He will be "a light for the nations" (Isa. 42:6), opening blind eyes and liberating prisoners (Isa. 42:7; cf. 61:1–3).

The servant in Isa. 50 also transcends Israel. He is humble and compliant to Yahweh's instruction (Isa. 50:4). Unlike Israel, he is not rebellious (Isa. 50:5). He is persecuted and mistreated and despised by others (Isa. 50:6). Even though human beings have disgraced him, he will be vindicated by God himself so that he will not be shamed (Isa. 50:7–9). That the servant transcends Israel seems to be confirmed by Isa. 50:10, for God's people are summoned to obey the voice of his servant. If God's people need to obey the servant, then the servant cannot be entirely identified with Israel.

The Servant Songs reach their climax in Isa. 52:13–53:12. The servant cannot be coterminous with Israel in this text. He bore the griefs and sorrows of Israel, and so he must be distinguished from the nation (Isa. 53:4). The servant "was wounded for our transgressions; he was crushed for our iniquities; upon him was the chastisement that brought us peace, and with his stripes we are healed" (Isa. 53:5). Israel, of course, cannot atone for their own sins. Their iniquity is laid on him (Isa. 53:6). He was "stricken for the transgression of my people" (Isa. 53:8). The servant, on the contrary, is innocent and without transgression. He is like an innocent and silent sheep led to slaughter (Isa. 53:7). He was considered wicked, though in actuality he was free from violence and deceit (Isa. 53:9). Obviously, the servant must be distinguished from Israel because as the innocent one he atones for the sins of the people.[9]

The suffering of the servant pervades the text. His appearance is marred beyond human recognition (Isa. 52:14). He was not celebrated and acclaimed but rather despised and rejected (Isa. 53:3). He was led to death like a sacrificial lamb (Isa. 53:7). His suffering atones for the sins

---

8. Childs (2001: 383–86) argues that the servant is the prophet who himself embodies Israel. Hermisson (2006: 16, 46–47) rightly maintains that the servant transcends the prophet.

9. Some scholars dispute the atoning character of the servant's suffering. Whybray (1978: 30, 58–61, 74–76) argues that the servant, though innocent, suffers alongside and with his people, not for them.

of others and functions as a substitutionary sacrifice. Like the blood of offerings, his death will "sprinkle many nations" (Isa. 52:15). The people rightly concluded that he was "smitten by God" (Isa. 53:4), for "it was the will of the LORD to crush him" (Isa. 53:10). But they failed to grasp that he died for their sins rather than on account of his own transgressions. He bore the sins of his people sacrificially (Isa. 53:4, 11–12). He was wounded and crushed for the iniquities of his people, so that the Lord placed the sin of his people upon him (Isa. 53:5–6). Like a sacrificial lamb, he was led to death and struck down because of the transgression of Israel (Isa. 53:7–8). As a result of his suffering he will be exalted (Isa. 52:13). His days will not be snuffed out but rather prolonged (Isa. 53:10). He will see the light of life and be satisfied, and he will celebrate his victory over evil (Isa. 53:11–12).

The OT teaching regarding the Servant of the Lord is remarkably similar to what we noticed about the Son of Man. The servant is both Israel and transcends Israel. The "one and many" distinction in Isa. 53:12 verifies this, as does his being numbered with transgressors in the same verse. It seems, therefore, that Israel is represented by a particular person, one who atones for the sin of the people.[10]

Postbiblical Judaism

In postbiblical Judaism the suffering servant was not clearly identified as the suffering Messiah.[11] Actually, the Targum of Isaiah claims that the Servant of the Lord in Isa. 53 is the Messiah, but the Targum rewrites the passage dramatically.[12] The suffering of the servant is downplayed and transferred to God's enemies.[13] The servant is viewed as a triumphant figure, but it is a victory that is not preceded by a sacrifice for the sake

10. Clements (1998) emphasizes the representative role of the servant, arguing that he, like Moses, has both prophetic and kingly characteristics.

11. Rightly Cullmann 1963: 58–60. Zimmerli and Jeremias (1957: 43–78) take issue with this view, arguing that the limited evidence available indicates that Isa. 53 was understood messianically in the pre-Christian era. Zimmerli and Jeremias (1957: 93–94) locate the references in Isa. 53 to the earliest history of the church. See also the careful study by Hengel (2006), who argues that there is evidence that Isa. 53 was interpreted messianically, though evidence for vicarious suffering is sparse.

12. Sapp (1998) has carefully demonstrated that the atonement theology evident in the MT of Isa. 53 is lacking in the LXX. Hence, NT writers in drawing on Isa. 53 were most likely drawing upon the theology expressed in the MT. Michel (*NIDNTT* 3:610) says that up to AD 200, Judaism, at least according to the Targumim, had not interpreted Isa. 53 to refer to a suffering Messiah. Perhaps, Michel speculates, the notion was suppressed because of the conflict with Christianity. In support of the view that the targumic rendering of Isa. 53 was independent of Christianity, see Ådna 2006.

13. Neither is it persuasive to see reference to the Messiah as the suffering servant in Qumran (rightly J. J. Collins 1995: 123–26).

of his people. *Fourth Ezra* 7:29 says that the Messiah will die after four hundred years. There is no evidence, however, that his death plays any atoning role or that he suffers for the sake of his people. Indeed, his death in *4 Ezra* is almost casual, representing the normal cessation of life. This is a far cry from the atoning death of the servant in Isa. 53. No clear evidence exists, then, that postbiblical Judaism identified the suffering servant with the Messiah.

Synoptic Gospels

The Synoptic Gospels do not directly address the question of whether Jesus is the fulfillment of the suffering servant of Isaiah. It is clear, however, from quotations, allusions, and hints that a positive identification was made.[14] Further, we must never forget that the narrative of the Gospels culminates in the death and resurrection of Jesus, which the extended passion accounts demonstrate to be the climax of the story.[15] In the Synoptics Jesus regularly predicts his future suffering, death, and resurrection.[16] He teaches that his death and resurrection fulfill what the Scriptures predicted would happen (Matt. 26:54, 56; Mark 14:49; Luke 24:25–27, 44–46).[17] It would be difficult to discover a text that predicts death and suffering more clearly than does Isa. 52:13–53:12. As noted above, hints of a future vindication or resurrection also exist in the text. When Jesus insisted that the Scriptures predicted his suffering, death, and resurrection, a reference to Isa. 53 seems likely. In Luke 9:51 Jesus "set his face" to travel to Jerusalem and die. An allusion to Isa. 50:7

14. Hooker (1959; 1998) argues eloquently that Jesus did not conceive of his death in terms of the suffering servant of Isa. 53, and that Paul was the first writer to make such a connection. But see Stuhlmacher (2006), who convincingly argues that Jesus himself interpreted Isa. 53 in terms of his ministry and death.

15. For the importance of the narrative in Luke's account, see key articles by Moessner (1990; 1996; 2005). Strauss (1995: 325) rightly says about Luke, "It is characteristic of Luke to bring out the salvation-historical significance of Jesus through his narrative development rather than through repeated references to Old Testament prophecies fulfilled." The entire discussion by Strauss (1995: 317–33) on Jesus as the Servant in Luke-Acts is insightful and convincing.

16. Matt. 16:21; 17:22–23; 20:17–19; Mark 8:31; 9:30–31; 10:32–35; Luke 9:21–22, 44; 18:31–33. Longenecker (1970: 104–9) takes issue with Hooker's view, but his own view that the teaching on the suffering servant was muted by Hellenism and Jewish thought is doubtful. Cullmann (1963: 60–69) defends the notion that Jesus saw himself as the suffering servant.

17. Wright (1998) argues that the theology of Isa. 53 must be placed in the context of the coming of the kingdom and the story of Israel. He reminds us that Jesus' view of his own destiny and the promises of the coming of the kingdom must not be sundered from one another.

seems probable, for there the servant says that to endure suffering, "I have set my face like a flint."

A number of other details suggest that the Synoptic writers detected in Jesus' death a fulfillment of the suffering servant of Isa. 52:13–53:12. The approbation expressed in God's pleasure with Jesus at his baptism and transfiguration (Matt. 3:17; 17:5 par.) probably alludes to the Servant of the Lord in Isa. 42:1.[18] Matthew sees a fulfillment of Isa. 53:4 in Jesus' healing ministry (Matt. 8:17). The citation here is closer to the MT than the LXX. It could be objected that Jesus' healing ministry cannot be equated with his death, and hence the citation of Isa. 53 here is irrelevant. Such a judgment is too simplistic. The healing ministry of Jesus anticipates his death, in which the sorrows, diseases, and sins of his people would be atoned for.[19] Luke also cites Isa. 53, though again he does not call upon a text that directly links Jesus with the servant. Jesus anticipates his death and says to his disciples, "For I tell you that this Scripture must be fulfilled in me: 'And he was numbered with the transgressors.' For what is written about me has its fulfillment" (Luke 22:37).[20] The note of fulfillment is emphatic, for it is mentioned twice in the same verse. The OT text cited is Isa. 53:12, and again Luke's wording could be read as a literal translation of the MT, though the LXX in this instance is remarkably similar. Matthew and Mark likely allude to the same text when recounting Jesus' crucifixion in the midst of two criminals (Matt. 27:38; Mark 15:27).[21]

Isaiah 53:12 goes on to say that the servant bears the sins of many. There are good reasons to think that Luke finds Jesus to be the suffering servant of Isa. 53, and this is confirmed by Acts 8:30–35, a text that we will examine when we consider Jesus' saving work in Acts.

Perhaps we also have an allusion to Isa. 52:15 when Jesus informs the disciples that they are blessed to see what they see and to hear what they hear (Matt. 13:16). When Jesus was prosecuted at his trial, he did not engage in ardent self-defense but often remained silent when interrogated

18. So Zimmerli and Jeremias 1957: 81–82.

19. Rightly Carson 1984: 205–6.

20. See Marshall 1978b: 826; Bock 1996: 1747–48. Bock (1987: 138) thinks that Luke alludes to the whole of Isa. 53 here. The narrative that Luke composes also suggests that the servant's death is construed as atoning. See Moessner 1990; 1996; 2005. Elsewhere Marshall (1970: 172) is quite hesitant about seeing a connection between atonement in Isa. 53 and Luke. Others argue that an atonement theology cannot be read out of the Lukan use of the servant passage (Cadbury 1927: 280; Zehnle 1969: 441–42; Hooker 1959: 113–14, 149–51; O'Toole 2000). On Jesus as the servant in Luke-Acts, see Green 1990: 18–25. But he does not emphasize Jesus' sacrificial death. For example, Green (1997: 775–76) argues that in Luke 22:37 Jesus' association with sinners and the consequent hostility are in view.

21. For a lucid and brief description of typical crucifixions, see Koester 2003: 210–14. See also the longer work of Hengel 1977.

(Matt. 26:62–63; 27:12–14 par.). Such behavior fulfills Isa. 53:7, where the servant is led like a lamb to the slaughter and yet does not open his mouth in defiance or self-defense.

A crucial text for Jesus functioning as the servant is Mark 10:45: "For even the Son of Man came not to be served but to serve, and to give his life as a ransom for many" (cf. Matt. 20:28).[22] The verse does not contain a quotation from Isa. 53, though the use of the word "many" (*polloi*) alludes to the chapter that recounts the suffering and death of the servant for the "many" (Isa. 52:14–15; 53:11, 12). Further, the notion of the Son of Man coming to serve alludes to the Servant of the Lord. Finally, describing his life as a ransom for many reproduces well the notion of dying in place of and instead of others that suffuses Isa. 53,[23] and it also fits with the promise of the new exodus where Yahweh promises to redeem Israel, presumably through the work of the servant.[24] Those acquainted with the OT would likely see an allusion to Isa. 53 in the ransom saying. A similar allusion probably exists in the statement at Jesus' final passover meal: "This is my blood of the covenant, which is poured out for many" (Mark 14:24).[25] In Matthew the words "for the forgiveness of sins" are added (Matt. 26:28).[26] The use of the term "many" (*polloi*) and the notion that

22. The saying is exactly the same in Matthew except for the introductory words. Hence, Jesus merged together the Son of Man and the Servant of the Lord (so Cullmann 1963: 65). It has often been said that in Luke the theology of the cross is diminished. For instance, the Lukan parallel (Luke 22:27) does not have the ransom saying. Doble (1996: 3–4) writes, "What, precisely, is the nature of this widespread complaint against Luke? It is alleged that in Luke-Acts Jesus' death is 'played down.'" See also Creed 1930: lxxi–lxxii; Conzelmann 1960: 201; Tyson 1986: 170. For a survey of scholarship, see Herrick 1997. It is true that Luke does not bring to the forefront the soteriological significance of Jesus' death in the same way as Matthew and Mark do, but it is also true that scholars have underestimated the theology of the cross in Luke's writings. In Luke's Gospel the atoning nature of Jesus' death is supported by the allusions to the Servant of the Lord and what is said at the Last Supper (Luke 22:19–20). When we examine Acts, I will argue that the atoning significance of Jesus' death is more significant than has often been alleged. For a fuller defense of this view, see the forthcoming dissertation by John Kimbell at The Southern Baptist Theological Seminary in Louisville, Kentucky.

23. Against this view, see Hooker 1959: 77. For more detailed support, see France, 1971: 110–32; Kim 1983: 50–61; O. Betz 1998: 83–85. Head (1995: 113) observes that the term *lytron* refers to money paid as ransom for release of war prisoners or slaves. He points out that the substitutionary character of the ransom is clear also from Josephus, *Ant.* 14.107. For the substitutionary character of Jesus' death here, see also Kim 1983: 58–59.

24. For a convincing defense of an allusion to Isa. 53 in Mark 10:45, see Watts 1998; cf. Evans 2001: 120–23.

25. See especially France 1971: 121–23.

26. The authenticity of the eucharistic sayings in Luke 22:19–20 is debated. For arguments against authenticity, see Ehrman 1991. Nonetheless, the text should be accepted as authentic, and thus it supports the significance of the atonement in Lukan theology. See J. Petzer 1984; K. Petzer 1991; Walton 2000: 137–39. For the OT background for Luke, see

Jesus' death secures forgiveness of sins resonates with the themes of Isa. 53.[27] Here Jesus' death is viewed as a sacrifice that procures forgiveness, so that soteriological significance is ascribed to his death.

John's Gospel

A suggestive allusion to the servant occurs in John's notion that Jesus' death consists of his "lifting up" (*hypsoō* [John 3:14; 8:28; 12:32, 34]), for in Isa. 52:13 the servant will "be lifted up," and the LXX likewise employs the verb *hypsoō*. John shares the thought world of Isaiah remarkably, for in both accounts the exaltation of the servant becomes a reality through suffering.[28] John cites Isa. 53:1 in a significant text in which he sums up Jesus' public ministry and explains why so many Jews failed to believe in him (John 12:38). Their unbelief should not surprise, for it was predicted all along that many would not believe the proclaimed word, that the arm of the Lord would not be revealed to them. John links Isa. 53 with Isa. 6, contending that the Lord "has blinded their eyes and hardened their heart" (John 12:40).[29] All has occurred according to the divine plan so that Jesus would be put to death in accordance with the prophecy in Isa. 53. We should also note that John does not understand Isa. 53 in a fatalistic sense. He assigns responsibility to the Jews for failing to believe (John 12:43, 46–48), even if their unbelief has been predetermined. The correlation between God's hardening work and the human failure to believe is not resolved philosophically in John, but both truths stand together.[30]

The Story of Jesus' Salvation in the Synoptic Gospels

The Synoptic Gospels unpack how Jesus delivered his people as the Servant of the Lord. Hence, we will roughly trace the narrative of the Synoptics in highlighting Jesus' saving work there.

Green 1988: 187–97. Walton (2000: 108) rightly argues that the Lukan saying connotes representation and substitution. See also Walton 2000: 109–10.

27. So Farmer (1998: 265): "The expression 'pours out' is a clear echo of, if not a conscious allusion to, the language and concept of Isaiah 53." The notion that Isa. 53 is in the background is not universally shared, but is quite likely (see Stuhlmacher 1993: 50). Stuhlmacher (1993: 72) argues that the language used points to Jesus' substitutionary death for the many.

28. Seeing a double meaning in the verb is a common feature in Johannine scholarship (see Dodd 1953: 375–78; Barrett 1978: 214).

29. For further discussion of John's use of the OT here, see Evans 1988: 129–35.

30. See the helpful brief comments in Carson 1991b: 448–49 and the book-length analysis in Carson 1981a. We could say in our terms that John was a compatibilist.

As Matthew says in the birth narrative, "He will save his people from their sins" (Matt. 1:21).[31] The subsequent verses suggest that he is able to save because he is Immanuel (Matt. 1:23). Jesus, as we noted earlier, represents the true Israel in Matthew. It is clear from this Gospel, however, that as the true Israelite and the Davidic king, he is destined to suffer. He faced opposition and rejection from the outset. When the magi queried about the birthplace of the king of the Jews, Jerusalem did not pulsate with joy but rather was "troubled" (Matt. 2:3). To preserve Jesus' life his parents fled to Egypt (Matt. 2:13–18). The theme of rejection casts a shadow over the entire narrative. Jesus was not embraced but rather rejected in his hometown (Matt. 13:53–58 par.; Luke 4:16–30). Even his own family doubted his sanity, and it seems that they wanted him to cease his ministry (Mark 3:21; cf. 3:32; Luke 8:19–21).

The Pharisees hailed Jesus' healings and exorcisms not as the coming of the kingdom but rather as the work of Beelzebul (Matt. 9:34; 10:25; 12:24 par.). They were determined to destroy him because he healed on the Sabbath (Matt. 12:14 par.; Luke 13:10–17; 14:1–6) and did not follow purity regulations (Matt. 15:1–20 par.). They failed to see that Jesus' table fellowship concretely expresses the message of the kingdom and forgiveness that he offers.[32] They tragically rejected God's purpose for themselves (Luke 7:30). They were entranced with riches (Luke 16:14) and exalted themselves as moral paragons (Luke 18:9–14). The cities in which Jesus proclaimed the good news of the kingdom turned against him (Matt. 11:20–24 par.). Not only did his own reject him, but also the Samaritans spurned him, foreshadowing his death (Luke 9:51–56). The death of the Baptist also foreshadowed Jesus' fate (Matt. 14:1–12 par.).

The desire for a sign to demonstrate Jesus' authenticity stemmed from an "evil and adulterous" heart (Matt. 12:39 par.; cf. 16:1–4). Jesus warned that he came to introduce not peace but division, and that people would split over allegiance to him (Matt. 10:34–39 par.). He even admonished the Baptist not to be scandalized by him (Matt. 11:6 par.). Those who rejected him are like fickle and bored children who cannot decide which game to play (Matt. 11:16–19 par.). The religious leaders and authorities directed questions at Jesus to trap him so that they could do away with him (Matt. 19:3; 22:15–33 par.). Jesus in turn declared judgment on the Pharisees and scribes (Matt. 23:1–39 par.; cf. 16:5–12 par.).

Jesus' destiny on the cross is anticipated, therefore, throughout the Gospels. The strange event in which Jesus submits to baptism over John's protests is explained as "fitting . . . to fulfill all righteousness" (Matt.

---

31. Davies and Allison (1988: 210), though perceiving that salvation from sin is God's gift, fail to link it with Immanuel two verses later in Matthew. Hagner (1993b: 21) sees the connection.

32. See Meyer 1979: 158–62; Green 1995: 86–89.

3:15).[33] Those who plunged under the baptismal waters did so to confess their sins (Matt. 3:6), and John tried to prevent Jesus from following the same course because he recognized that such a baptism was inappropriate for the one with whom God is pleased (Matt. 3:17). Jesus consented to baptism because he identified with Israel and its sin. As the Servant of the Lord, he took upon himself the punishment that Israel deserved. He will be removed as the bridegroom for the sake of his bride (Matt. 9:15).[34] His rejection by the religious authorities, though culpable, actually fulfills God's plan. At the transfiguration Moses and Elijah discussed with Jesus his forthcoming "exodus" in Jerusalem (Luke 9:30–31). The new exodus promised in Isaiah and the new creation anticipated therein will become a reality only through Jesus' exodus at the cross. Luke also emphasized in his travel narrative (Luke 9:51–19:40) that Jesus set his face to go to Jerusalem in order to give his life in death (Luke 9:51). Jesus' purpose in coming to his people was not merely to teach them the right way but to go to the cross to secure the salvation promised in the law and the prophets.

The greatest sign in Jesus' ministry is the sign of Jonah (Matt. 12:40; 16:4 par.)—a sign that the religious leaders did not grasp. Jonah's being swallowed by the whale signified God's judgment upon the prophet for his sin. So too Jesus is judged at the cross by God—forsaken by God himself (Matt. 27:46 par.; cf. Ps. 22:1)—because he took upon himself the sin of Israel and even the sin of the world.[35] The Jewish authorities rightly concluded that Jesus' death signified God's judgment against him, but they failed to perceive that the judgment was meted out because he died as God's servant for the sake of his people, that he was saving his people from their sins. The sign of Jonah also applied to Jesus' restoration. Jonah's judgment in being swallowed by the whale was not God's

33. Only Matthew provides this explanation (cf. Mark 1:9; Luke 3:21). See Hagner 1993b: 57.

34. Most agree that "bridegroom" is not a messianic title (see Fitzmyer 1981a: 599), but some commentators are overly cautious, failing to see an allusion to Jesus' death and thereby showing that they do not read the Gospels as a whole. On the other hand, Hagner (1993b: 243) observes that we do not have an explicit passion prediction here, but in retrospect the disciples will perceive the significance of Jesus' statement (see also Nolland 2005: 390–91). See also France 2002: 140.

35. The cry of God-forsakenness should not be interpreted as one of despair and must be read in the light of the entirety of Ps. 22, which teaches that the one who trusts in God will be vindicated (rightly Stuhlmacher 1993: 54). Contra Hooker (1991: 376), Davies and Allison (1997: 625), and Luz (2005: 550–51), who reject any reference to the remainder of Ps. 22 while rightly seeing the "horror" of what occurred (see also Cranfield 1963: 458–59). Hagner (1995: 844) strikes the right balance, seeing that the whole of the psalm is in view but rightly cautioning that we must not "lessen the reality of present abandonment."

last word.[36] Jonah was delivered from judgment and vomited up on the shore. Similarly, Jesus will be restored from judgment by his resurrection from the dead, indicating that God had vindicated him as Lord and Messiah. He comprises the true Israel, and so Israelites will be saved only by believing in him.

The Synoptics do not concentrate upon explicating the significance of Jesus' death in discursive statements; rather, they unfold its meaning through the narrative.[37] In Caesarea Philippi the disciples finally grasped that Jesus is the Messiah (Matt. 16:13–20 par.). Jesus is then prepared to reveal to them what kind of Messiah he truly is, and so in each Gospel the narrative is punctuated by passion predictions (Matt. 16:21–23; 17:22–23; 20:17–19 par.; see also Matt. 26:1–2). It must be emphasized, however, that these are not merely passion predictions. Jesus also predicted his resurrection. He forecasted that the judgment and restoration of Jonah will be played out in his ministry.

Each of the Synoptic Gospels climaxes with the account of Jesus' death and resurrection, and thereby they relay both the judgment that Jesus bore on behalf of his people and God's intervention on his behalf. The opposition against Jesus reached a boiling point, and so the religious leaders plot to put him to death (Matt. 26:3–5 par.). It seems that fortune smiles on Jesus' opponents, for Judas agreed to betray him (Matt. 26:14–16 par.). We see from Judas's later regret in Matthew that his decision to betray Jesus could have gone the other way (Matt. 27:3–10), but he made the fateful decision to fulfill the prophecy that Jesus would be handed over for thirty pieces of silver (Zech. 11:13). But this is the perspective of Jesus' enemies, for God is working out his plan in the life of Jesus through the intentions of human beings, whether evil or good. Hence, Mary's anointing of Jesus was a prophetic act in that it prepared him for burial, even though in her mind the anointing was merely an act of extravagant devotion and love (Matt. 26:6–13 par.).

Jesus knew that the time appointed for him to die had arrived (Matt. 26:18). His betrayal occurred just as the Scriptures predicted, and so nothing took place by surprise, though Judas still bore responsibility for his sin (Matt. 26:24).[38] God worked in and through the actions of human

36. See Marshall 1978b: 485. The allusion to Jonah was understood retrospectively (Hagner 1993b: 354).

37. Fitzmyer (1981a: 16) recognizes that the historical and theological are bound together in Luke. We can conclude from this that Luke communicates his theology through the story.

38. Matthew is hardly suggesting that the scriptural predictions exempt Judas from moral culpability. People are held responsible for evil even when they do not comprehend why they carried out an awful deed. Hagner (1995: 815) rightly comments, "We can pity Judas, but we cannot make a hero out of him, nor alas even a believer."

beings, and so he is the one who struck down Jesus as the shepherd (Matt. 26:31 par.; cf. Zech. 13:7). The cup that Jesus received was from the Father (Matt. 26:39, 42, 44 par.). The cup in the OT represents God's wrath that is poured out upon those who have transgressed his will (Ps. 11:6; 75:8; Isa. 51:17, 22; Jer. 25:15, 17, 28; 49:12; Hab. 2:16). This cup, representing God's anger, was poured out on Jesus in accord with the Father's will. Luke particularly highlights Jesus' anguish in the garden as he sweated so profusely that his sweat fell like drops of blood to the ground and an angel had to strengthen him (Luke 22:43–44).

Jesus was assured that the Father ultimately controlled what happened to him, knowing that the Father could send legions of angels to deliver him (Matt. 26:53). All the evil actions taken against Jesus are intended to fulfill the Scriptures (Matt. 26:54, 56 par.), or as Luke says, they carry out what God has determined (Luke 22:22), but again without removing responsibility from those who conspired against him (Matt. 26:55; Luke 22:22). The Scriptures themselves forecasted that he would be considered a transgressor (Luke 22:37). Even small actions such as casting lots for his garments fulfilled scriptural predictions (Matt. 27:35 par.; cf. Ps. 22:18).

Jesus was treated as a criminal because he was reckoned as a sinner for the sake of his people (Matt. 26:55 par.). Jesus' silence and bearing of abuse indicated that he is the Servant of the Lord (Matt. 26:63, 67–68; 27:11–14 par.; cf. Isa. 53:7). The Synoptic accounts of Jesus' death must be read on more than one level, for the Scriptures are being fulfilled even though the religious authorities failed to recognize it. When Pilate queried whether Jesus is the king of the Jews, Jesus replied, "You have said so" (Matt. 27:11 par.), for upon that basis Jesus will be condemned to death (Matt. 27:37 par.). The Jews, therefore, put to death their King, Savior, and Messiah (Mark 15:32). The soldiers mocked Jesus by clothing him with a royal robe, placing a thorny crown on his head, and hailing him as the king of the Jews (Matt. 27:27–31 par.; cf. Luke 23:11). They failed to see, however, that Jesus was the suffering king, and that his suffering and crown of thorns were the pathway to his exaltation. They taunted Jesus by inviting him to come down from the cross as proof that he is truly God's Son and the king of Israel (Matt. 27:39–44 par.).[39] They failed to realize that God would deliver him after his death, and only the centurion saw that Jesus' death was the very means by which he demonstrated that he is God's Son (Matt. 27:54; Mark 15:39);[40] or as Luke portrays it, Jesus is the righteous one being put to death (Luke

---

39. Luke, however, records that one of the two criminals who were executed with Jesus repented and asked him for mercy (Luke 23:40–42).

40. See the thorough discussion in R. Brown 1994: 2:1143–52.

23:47).[41] They fulfilled by their very actions the prophecy that the Servant of the Lord would suffer. The release of Barabbas (Matt. 27:15–23 par.) also operated at a symbolic level, for hereby Jesus saved one of his people from his sins. The innocent one died on behalf of the guilty one.[42] Jesus was considered to be nothing more than a common criminal and was crucified between two others who deserved execution (Matt. 27:38 par.).

All three Synoptic Gospels emphasize Jesus' innocence. The witnesses who brought charges against Jesus were not credible and contradicted one another (Matt. 26:59–62 par.). The pagan and venal Pilate attempted to release Jesus, realizing that the charges against him were baseless and motivated by envy (Matt. 27:18 par.). Pilate's wife tried to dissuade him from condemning Jesus by relaying a dream in which she suffered, for Jesus is a "righteous man" (Matt. 27:19). Pilate attempted to ward off the crowd by protesting that Jesus had not done anything evil (Matt. 27:23 par.), and he dramatically proclaimed his own innocence by washing his hands with water before the people, with the result that the crowd accepted responsibility for Jesus' execution (Matt. 27:24–25).

Luke is even more emphatic in relaying Pilate's insistence that Jesus is innocent.[43] He declared that the charges against Jesus were groundless (Luke 23:4). Indeed, both Pilate and Herod, who hardly were seen as upholders of justice, found no guilt in Jesus (Luke 23:13–15). Pilate remonstrated with the Jewish leaders, trying to dissuade them from carrying out their intentions. He persisted in attempting to release Jesus (Luke 23:20, 22), but finally he crumbled in the face of the will of the crowd (Luke 22:23–24). The theme of Jesus' innocence accomplishes two purposes. First, Jesus was not a political criminal guilty of some terrible crime that warranted death. It was plain to see that he died on trumped-up charges. Second, and more important, he died as the innocent one, as the sinless one on behalf of others. Jesus' death on behalf of others is symbolized in his refusal to drink wine mixed with gall to mitigate the pain (Matt. 27:34 par.).[44] He would not face the pain of the cross drugged; rather, he consciously and resolutely received death at the hand of his tormentors.

41. Again see the thorough discussion in R. Brown 1994: 2:1160–67.

42. The Gospel writers were not interested in whether Barabbas truly became a believer. They detected a deeper significance in the story than was evident to Barabbas or to any who were present at his release.

43. Some scholars have thereby concluded that Luke emphasizes that Jesus is a martyr (see Dibelius 1934: 201). This view is inadequate if the atoning nature of Jesus' death is slighted.

44. See R. Brown 1994: 2:940–44.

Jesus' death opened a new way to God, symbolized by the tearing of the curtain of the temple from top to bottom (Matt. 27:51; Mark 15:38; cf. Luke 23:45), indicating that Jesus' death, not the temple, is the means of forgiveness of sins.[45] This is confirmed by reference in Matthew to those who were raised from the dead (Matt. 27:52–53), indicating that the life of the age to come had commenced now that Jesus had died and was raised.

Jesus' death alone is insufficient to save people from sins. For the sign of Jonah to be completed he must also be raised from the dead. The Synoptics take pains to show that Jesus was truly risen from the dead. His body was carefully disposed of by Joseph of Arimathea. Matthew indicates that Joseph put the body in his own new tomb; Luke adds that the tomb was unused and thus had no other corpses in it (Matt. 27:60; Luke 23:53; cf. Mark 15:42–46). The women knew the place of the tomb (Matt. 27:61 par.),[46] and a guard was even set at the tomb to secure it from theft or any other mischief (Matt. 27:62–66).

Each of the Synoptics recounts Jesus' resurrection, though the account in Mark is remarkably astringent and spare.[47] A resurrection appearance is not recorded, though it is promised (Mark 16:7). The empty tomb signaled that Jesus had risen (Mark 16:6; Matt. 28:6; Luke 24:5–7).[48] Furthermore, the resurrection "confirms the fact that Jesus' death on the cross is the decisive event of his ministry."[49] The belief of the apostles is not credible apart from the resurrection, for a crucified Messiah was a contradiction. Schlatter rightly says, "This idea [a crucified Messiah] would be one of the most curious monstrosities ever created by specula-

45. Mark probably has the curtain separating the holy place from the holy of holies in view, since this curtain has greater significance, and in the LXX the word used here (*katapetasma*) usually designates the inner curtain. The tearing of the curtain also symbolizes the future destruction of the temple and access to God through Jesus' death, so that the curtain separating the holy place from the holy of holies is in view (so Hooker 1991: 377–78; Hagner 1995: 848–49). Nolland (2005: 1212–14) and Luz (2005: 565–66) argue that the event forecasts the destruction of the temple and the dramatic and powerful action of God at the death of Jesus. France (2002: 656–57) tentatively opts for the curtain by which one passed from the courtyard to the holy place (see also Marshall 1978b: 875; Davies and Allison 1997: 629–32; Nolland 2005: 1213). For a canvass of the whole matter of the rending of the veil, see R. Brown 1994: 2:1097–1118.

46. "This note functions to certify correct knowledge concerning the specific tomb into which Jesus had been placed" (Hagner 1995: 859). For a full discussion of Jesus' tomb, see R. Brown 1994: 2:1242–83.

47. For the Markan view, see Wright (2003: 616–31), who inclines to the view that Mark intended to write beyond Mark 16:8.

48. Mark emphasizes that Jesus the Nazarene is raised (Mark 16:6), demonstrating continuity between the earthly Jesus and the risen one (so Kingsbury 1983: 134; France 2002: 680).

49. Kingsbury 1983: 134.

tive conjecture."[50] Jesus personally appeared to women first on Easter Sunday (Matt. 28:9–10). This detail is important, for women were not considered valid witnesses in court in Judaism, and no one inventing a story would make women the first witnesses of the resurrection. According to Matthew, Jesus appeared after his death to the eleven on a mountain in Galilee (Matt. 28:16–17). The stupendous nature of the event is confirmed by the admission that some doubted that Jesus was truly risen. Nevertheless, Matthew clearly teaches that Jesus himself was the one who had conquered death and commissioned the disciples.[51]

Luke records the account of Jesus' appearance to Cleopas and his companion on the road to Emmaus (Luke 24:13–35).[52] They did not recognize Jesus initially, but as they journeyed, he explained to them from the Scriptures the necessity of the Messiah's suffering before he entered into glory. Significantly, they recognize Jesus only in the breaking of bread, for Jesus is seen as he truly is only when one sees him as the crucified one. If people turn to Jesus in faith, he opens the gates of paradise, even for criminals (Luke 23:42–43).[53]

The credibility of Jesus' resurrection is emphasized in the Lukan narrative, and this anticipates Acts, where the resurrection of Jesus is featured. Jesus appeared to the disciples, and they were skeptical about whether he was really present physically (Luke 24:36–49). The risen Jesus was not spirit or ghost, for he invited the disciples to see and even to touch him to verify that he was truly among them. He proceeded to eat a piece of fish before them, for although they had doubts about Jesus, they knew that the fish existed, and spirits cannot ingest fish. Jesus then instructed them that his death and resurrection fulfilled the Scriptures and represented not a surprising turn of events but rather the outworking of God's purpose.

The story in the Synoptics, then, emphasizes that from the outset Jesus' purpose in coming to earth was to go to the cross. The Synoptics truly are passion narratives with extended introductions.[54] The cross is viewed neither as a terrible accident nor as a deranged attempt by Jesus to bring in the kingdom of God. Jesus' suffering and death were the very means by which the promises of salvation in the OT were obtained, and his resurrection from the dead indicates the securing of the promise.

---

50. Schlatter 1997: 377 (see his entire discussion, pp. 375–83).

51. For the Matthean perspective on the resurrection, see Wright 2003: 632–46.

52. For the Lukan perspective on the resurrection, see Wright 2003: 647–61.

53. Crump (1992: 88) intriguingly argues that the redeemed criminal arrives at his insight about Jesus based on Jesus' prayer for his forgiveness. For support for the authenticity of the saying, see Crump 1992: 79–85.

54. On the theme of the passion in the Gospels, see Senior 1984; 1985; 1989; see also the two-volume work of R. Brown 1994.

The resurrection, after all, signifies the arrival of the age to come—the promised age of salvation and new creation that God had pledged. The new exodus and the new creation have arrived through the suffering and resurrection of Jesus. He has taken upon himself the guilt and sin of his people so that they can enjoy freedom and joy as human beings made in God's image. I have lingered over the narrative in the Synoptics because it is crucial for the theology of each writer. Each of the Synoptics climaxes in Jesus' death and resurrection, and so the cross and resurrection are the point of the story and communicate in narrative form Jesus' saving work and the fulfillment of God's saving promises. Hence, the narrative account in the Synoptics fits with one of the major themes in this book, for it is precisely in the narrative of Jesus' life, in his cross and resurrection, that God's saving promises are realized.

Cross of Christ in John

A Sketch of John's Narrative

The narrative in John's Gospel differs in obvious ways from those of the Synoptics, and yet it must also be observed that the general pattern is similar in that Jesus' ministry of teaching and healing attracted many, but controversy also erupted over his self-claims and healing on the Sabbath. As we look at a quick sketch of the flow of the Johannine narrative, we see that the cross is foreshadowed constantly in the account.

One of the distinctive features in John is that the temple cleansing is found near the beginning of the Gospel (John 2:13–22), and so Jesus' controversy with the Jews commenced at the outset of his ministry. John often, though not invariably, used the term "the Jews" to designate the religious authorities opposed to Jesus.[55] Jesus' controversy with the Jews erupted when he healed a man on the Sabbath and told him to carry his bed (John 5:8–9, 16–18). Significantly, Jesus did not appeal to rabbinic debates to justify his behavior; instead, he declared that the Father works on the Sabbath, and thus so will he. Jesus greatly exacerbated opposition by claiming to be the bread from heaven and by insisting that people must eat his flesh and drink his blood to live (John 6:35–59). Even many of his disciples departed from him because of these assertions (John 6:60–66).

When the Feast of Tabernacles came in October of the last year of Jesus' life, "the Jews" (i.e., the religious authorities) were determined

---

55. Usually in John "the Jews" refers to the religious leaders in Judaism (see Barrett 1978: 171–72), but R. Brown (1966: lxxi) rightly notes that the term does not always refer to the religious leaders (so also Carson 1991b: 141–42).

to put him to death (John 7:1). It is clear that Jesus' healing the man on the Sabbath and instructing him to carry his bed had galvanized the religious authorities, so that they became convinced that Jesus must be put to death (John 7:21–23). The Pharisees sent officers to arrest Jesus during the feast, but the officers could not bring themselves to follow through (John 7:30, 32, 45–52), and Nicodemus urged the leaders to keep an open mind before coming to a final decision, though his words were rudely rejected. Some disciples had put their faith in Jesus, but even they were provoked by Jesus' subsequent teaching and threatened to kill him when he claimed to have existed before Abraham (John 8:58–59). Jesus was keenly aware that people desired to put him to death, and this theme threads through the discourse (John 8:37, 40, 44, 59).

The opposition to Jesus intensified when he opened the eyes of a blind man by putting mud on his eyes (John 9). Some division ensued about whether Jesus was from God, for some concluded that anyone who could open the eyes of the blind must be from God. Others were convinced that a Sabbath-breaker could not be from God (John 9:16) and was a sinner (John 9:24). Similarly, after Jesus' parable about the sheep and the good shepherd some concluded that Jesus was insane and demonic, but others questioned whether a demonized man could open the eyes of the blind (John 10:19–21; cf. 8:48). The opposition was stronger, for those who acknowledged Jesus as the Christ were expelled from the synagogue (John 9:22),[56] since the religious leaders were convinced that Jesus' self-claims constituted blasphemy (John 10:33, 36).

After Jesus claimed at the Feast of Dedication in December of his last year that he and the Father are one, the Jews were on the verge of stoning Jesus. Their attempt failed, and Jesus withdrew across the Jordan (John 10:22–42). In the spring of the year, in the last days of his life, Jesus raised Lazarus from the dead (John 11:1–44). Caiaphas and the Sanhedrin feared that Jesus' popularity would lead to a Roman invasion and a destruction of the temple, and that they would be displaced as leaders. They concluded that Jesus must be put to death for the good of the nation (John 11:45–53). So as Passover neared, the word that Jesus must be arrested was disseminated (John 11:57).

The anointing of Jesus follows, anticipating his suffering and death (John 12:1–8). Jesus did not go to Jerusalem thinking that the crowds would embrace him and overturn the decision of the ruling authorities. He was convinced that his death was imminent (John 12:27, 32–34;

---

56. It is common in Johannine scholarship to argue that expulsion from the synagogue for confessing Jesus as the Christ betrays the anachronistic character of what John wrote (see esp. Martyn 1979). Despite the popularity of this view, there are good reasons for seeing the account in John as historically credible during Jesus' ministry (see Carson 1991b: 369–72; Ridderbos 1997: 341–44; Köstenberger 2004: 288–89).

13:1–3), predicting that one of the disciples would betray him (John 13:21–30). In Jesus' final discourse (John 13–17) his future absence from his disciples dominates the account (John 13:33, 36; 16:16–24).[57] Jesus goes to prepare a place for his disciples (John 14:3), and that is why he goes now to the Father (John 14:25, 28; 16:28; 17:11, 13, 24). He gave final instructions to the disciples because his time with them was short (John 16:4–5), and he was about to send the paraclete (John 16:7).

The passion narrative in John shares many features with the Synoptics, but John presents the story with his own slant.[58] John emphasizes that everything that happens is ordained by God and fits with his plan. Jesus did not flee from his arresters but instead presented himself to them because he knew everything that was about to occur (John 18:4; cf. 13:1). The numinous quality of Jesus' person clearly terrified his arresters; they fell to the ground when Jesus identified himself (John 18:6),[59] and Jesus almost had to invite them to complete the arrest (John 18:7–8). Peter lashed out at the arresters with his sword, severing the right ear of Malchus, the high priest's servant. But Jesus rejected Peter's resort to violence, affirming that he intended to drink the cup that the Father gave to him (John 18:10–11). The cup, as in the Synoptics, represents the wrath of God.[60] Jesus committed himself to absorbing the wrath of God for the sake of his people.

Further, Jesus did not view his death as a tragedy that should have been avoided; rather, he affirmed that the cross is the Father's will—the cup that the Father had given him to drink. John also emphasizes Jesus' willingness to suffer by reporting that Jesus carried his own cross (John 19:17); the tradition that Simon of Cyrene assisted him is omitted. Similarly, John reminds the readers of Caiaphas's words about Jesus' death (John 18:14; cf. 11:49–52), and the latter were viewed as a prophecy, predicting that Jesus would die on behalf of others.

Pilate preferred that the Jews judge Jesus themselves, but his taking up the case indicates that Jesus' prediction about the manner of his death would be fulfilled (John 18:32). Nothing occurs in the passion account by happenstance or chance. God's purposes are being fulfilled. Pilate's encounter with Jesus demonstrates God's sovereignty throughout. John fills out the Synoptic encounter between Pilate and Jesus. Jesus was charged with being a rival king, but when Pilate confronted him with the

57. John 14:18–19 could refer to Jesus' coming to the disciples in the Spirit (R. Brown 1970: 645; Bultmann 1971: 617–19; Köstenberger 2004: 439), to his appearances to them after his resurrection (Carson 1991b: 501–2), or to the resurrection and the parousia as collapsed together (Barrett 1978: 463–64). I find Carson's view to be the most persuasive.

58. For the passion narrative in John, see Dodd 1953: 426–43.

59. See Beasley-Murray 1987: 322–23.

60. See Ridderbos 1997: 578; Köstenberger 2004: 509.

charge, Jesus used it as an opportunity to probe Pilate's own openness to truth (John 18:33–34). Pilate attempted to deflect the conversation away from any personal confrontation, and Jesus clarified that his kingdom is not of this world (John 18:35–36). As in the Synoptics, Jesus averred that Pilate and his accusers identified him as a king, given the charges against him (John 18:37). Even though Pilate cynically doubted that truth could be found, he realized that Jesus was innocent and attempted to release him. Still, the people asked for Barabbas in Jesus' stead (John 18:38b–40). John intimates again here that Jesus died as the innocent one in place of the guilty—Barabbas standing for the guilty. Pilate insisted again that Jesus was innocent, and that there was no basis for a guilty charge (John 19:4).

The religious authorities and the temple police called for Jesus' crucifixion, but again Pilate protested that the charges against Jesus had no basis (John 19:6). The authorities insisted that Jesus must be executed because he claimed to be God's Son. Pilate was spooked and asked Jesus about his place of origin, but when Jesus refused to answer, Pilate threatened him with imperial authority (John 19:7–10). Jesus accepted his death as the will of the Father, affirming that Pilate's authority was derived from God, and that apart from the will of God Pilate could do nothing to him (John 19:11). Pilate continued to try to release Jesus, but the Jews clamored for his death, insisting that if Pilate let off someone who claimed to be a king, then Pilate had set himself in opposition to Caesar (John 19:11–12).[61] The political consequence of the event sank in, and Pilate caved in to pressure and handed Jesus over to be crucified (John 19:13–16). The entire trial turned on whether Jesus was a political rival to Caesar, the alleged king of the Jews. The Romans and political authorities certainly treated Jesus as such (John 18:38), for they considered him dangerous enough that he should be eliminated. The soldiers mocked Jesus with a thorny crown, a purple robe, and a sarcastic acclamation (John 19:2–3), and they failed to see the irony of the events before them. Jesus' suffering and death testified that he is truly the king of the Jews, and indeed the king of all. As the suffering one, he reigned.

When Jesus wore the purple robe of kingship and the thorny crown, Pilate presented him to the crowd with the words "Behold the man" (John 19:5).[62] Pilate's words were on target, for Jesus is fully man, as

61. Scholars debate vigorously the historical details of the role of the Jews and the Romans in the death of Jesus. For a thorough survey of the entire discussion, see R. Brown 1994: 1:315–560, 665.

62. On this declaration, see in particular the insightful discussion in M. M. Thompson 1988: 107–8; see also Barrett 1978: 541; R. Brown 1994: 1:827–28 (the latter takes it to refer to Jesus' pathetic state).

the Word become flesh (John 1:14), destined to suffer and die.[63] He died between two criminals because he was judged by human beings to be the guilty one (John 19:18). And yet at the same time he died as a king, as the purple robe and crown attested. Hence, Pilate rightly declared, when he determined to execute Jesus, "Behold your King" (John 19:14).[64] The Jewish king was destined for death. Pilate's query as to whether he should crucify the king of the Jews (John 19:15) is in one sense answered in the affirmative. The Jewish authorities wanted their king to be put to death. On the other hand, the Jews also repudiated their king and affirmed that the only king they had is Caesar (John 19:15). Clearly, those who spoke such words did not mean what they said. It was "political" speech designed for the moment. Nor did Pilate believe a word that the Jews uttered, for he knew that it was all a pretext to kill Jesus. And yet by crucifying their Messiah the Jewish authorities spoke better than they knew; by rejecting the one true king they had affirmed that Caesar was their only king.[65] That Jesus was truly the king of the Jews is confirmed by the inscription that Pilate affixed to the cross (John 19:16–22). The Jews protested, asking that the inscription be amended with the words "This man said" before the inscription itself. Pilate rebuffed their request, so that the inscription stood as written. The inscription testifies, then, to the truth. Jesus is genuinely the king of the Jews.

John also sees the prophecies of Scripture as fulfilled, even down to seemingly insignificant details in the death of Jesus.[66] The dividing of Jesus' garments and his tunic by the soldiers fulfilled Scripture (John 19:23–24; cf. Ps. 22:18), as did his thirst and consumption of sour wine (John 19:28–30; cf. Ps. 69:21). John shows that Jesus even knew that he was fulfilling Scripture, emphasizing again his control over all that occurred, though we should not read this as an artificially contrived event designed to fulfill Scripture. Jesus recognized that his work was completed, and he triumphantly exclaimed, "It is finished" (John 19:30). The Jews requested that the legs of those crucified be broken, so that death would ensue more quickly and the victims could be removed from their crosses before the Sabbath to avoid defilement (John 19:31–37). The legs of the two criminals were broken, but the soldiers recognized that Jesus had already died, and so they refrained from breaking his legs. One

---

63. "The declaration *ho logos sarx egeneto* has become visible in its extremest consequence" (Bultmann 1971: 659).

64. As Barrett (1978: 546) says, "It seems likely that here he [John] has put into the mouth of Pilate an unintended truth." See also R. Brown 1994: 1:849.

65. As Bultmann (1971: 665) says, "In that moment the Jewish people surrender themselves." See also Barrett 1978: 546; R. Brown 1994: 1:849.

66. See Carson 1988: 247. Carson (1988: 249–50) notes the emphasis on typology in John's use of Scripture.

soldier pierced his side with a spear, and blood and water flowed out. Hence, two prophecies were fulfilled. First, none of Jesus' bones were broken, in accord with the specifications of the Passover lamb (Exod. 12:46; Num. 9:12). Jesus is the true Passover lamb offered for the sin of the world (cf. John 18:28; 19:14). Second, Jesus was pierced in accord with the prophecy in Zech. 12:10.

Jesus as God's Lamb

We have seen that the Johannine narrative leads to the cross of Christ, that the account from the beginning points the reader to his death. At this point we need to investigate further the Johannine theology of the death of Christ. Jesus is "the Lamb of God, who takes away the sin of the world" (John 1:29; cf. 1:36).[67] Some have understood this to refer to the warrior lamb that conquers God's enemies, since the Baptist could not have understood Jesus' atoning work.[68] The statement must be interpreted in light of this Gospel as a whole, and the narrative, as we noted above, is suffused with Jesus' death for his people.[69] Hence, the background is to be sought in the OT, where lambs were offered in sacrifice. It is more difficult to discern whether the lamb refers to the Passover lamb, the lambs offered as part of the sacrificial cultus, or the lamb of Isa. 53:7.[70] And we should not rule out that the lamb in Isa. 53:7 fulfills what we find in the Passover and the sacrificial system. In any case, it seems that later in the Gospel Jesus was sacrificed at the time that the Passover lamb was slain (John 18:28; 19:14), suggesting that Jesus is the Passover lamb, but the reference is too uncertain to determine the meaning of Lamb of God in John 1. The vagueness of the reference to the Lamb of God invites us to see a reference to

67. For the different interpretive options, see R. Brown 1966: 60–63; Barrett 1978: 176–77 (Barrett opts for a reference to the Passover lamb).

68. Dodd 1953: 230–38. Carson (1991b: 149–51) thinks that the Baptist had in mind the apocalyptic warrior lamb, but that the Baptist spoke better than he knew, so that there is also an allusion to Jesus' sacrifice. For a similar understanding, see Beasley-Murray 1987: 24–25. Köstenberger (2004: 66) rightly emphasizes the substitutionary nature of the lamb's sacrifice but thinks that the Baptist (who spoke better than he knew) thought of Jesus as a "substitutionary offering for sin that fell short of actual death" (see his entire discussion, pp. 66–68).

69. Ridderbos (1997: 72) rightly notes that the few references to the warrior lamb in Jewish literature make this a rather improbable solution; moreover, the horned lamb in Revelation suffers (Rev. 5:6) (see his entire discussion, pp. 69–75).

70. Supporting Isa. 53 are Zimmerli and Jeremias 1957: 82–83; Cullmann 1963: 71. Koester (2003: 221–23) argues that John does not conceive of Jesus' death merely as deliverance but construes the Passover imagery in such a way that Jesus' death provides atonement for sin. Koester does not limit the background to the Passover and sees allusions to the suffering servant of Isaiah and perhaps the binding of Isaac as well.

the sacrificial cultus, the Passover lamb, and the lamb in Isa. 53:7.[71] Jesus' death, in any case, displays God's love, and his sacrifice is the means by which the world is saved instead of being condemned (John 3:16–17).

Jesus' Being Lifted Up

In John's Gospel the death of Jesus is described as his being "lifted up" (*hypsoō*). In John 3:14 Jesus compared his death to the lifting up of the serpent on a pole in the wilderness (Num. 21:6–9). Just as those bitten by serpents lived if they looked upon the bronze serpent on the pole, so too those who believe in the lifted-up Jesus will have life. Paradoxically, life will be given to those who trust in one put to death. A similar paradox exists in the OT account, for serpents inflicted the wounds leading to death, and yet those who looked upon the bronze serpent that was lifted high were granted life. The use of "lift up" for the death of Jesus indicates that his death represents his exaltation, so that here John probably draws on the suffering servant who was exalted (Isa. 52:13).[72] John does not use a term that suggests humiliation but rather one that points to Jesus' glory. Jesus' death is the means by which he is exalted. Jesus' death, resurrection, and exaltation are of one piece in Johannine theology. Hence, we are not surprised that the ascension of Jesus immediately precedes his being lifted up in the narrative (John 3:13), for the two are ultimately inseparable.

In the midst of controversy Jesus declared that the Pharisees will know his true identity when he is lifted up (John 8:28). The Pharisees will recognize Jesus as the Son of Man and as "I am" only when they acknowledge him as the one lifted up by crucifixion. The cross leads to his exaltation, so that if the Pharisees do not recognize Jesus now as the Son of Man, they will do so on the day of judgment, when it becomes clear that the one who gave his life on a tree is exalted to God's right hand.[73]

71. For a background that is composite instead of pointing to only one OT text, see Bultmann 1971: 96–97 (though he wrongly excludes the idea of forgiveness coming from Jesus' death). R. Brown (1966: 60–63) thinks that both the paschal lamb and the lamb from Isa. 53:7 are in view. See also Carey 1981. However, Carey (1981: 102) too quickly rules out the sacrificial cultus (burnt offering) as a background, asserting that it was not redemptive, whereas Lev. 1:4 suggests the contrary. On the theme of expiation in John, see Grigsby 1982.

72. See Dodd 1953: 247.

73. For a similar interpretation to the one proposed here, where both salvation or judgment are envisioned, see Beasley-Murray 1987: 131–32; Carson 1991b: 345. Others see a reference only to judgment (Bultmann 1971: 349–50; R. Brown 1966: 351; Ridderbos 1997: 303–4).

In John 12:32 Jesus says, "And I, when I am lifted up from the earth, will draw all people to myself." The context must be investigated to understand this saying (John 12:20–32). Some Greeks had traveled to Jerusalem for Passover and requested to see Jesus. Jesus did not respond directly to their request but claimed that a grain of wheat must die to bear much fruit. Jesus' death, which is also described as his glorification (John 12:23, 28), brings judgment to the world. The reason that Gentiles have been excluded from salvation is that they have lived under the dominion of the world's ruler, but now that ruler will be cast out through Jesus' death. Hence, when Jesus said that he will draw all people to himself by his death, he did not speak individualistically; rather, by being lifted up on the cross he will draw both Jews and Greeks to himself.[74] The only way for the Greeks to see Jesus is to see him high and lifted up. The only access to God is through the crucified one. The crowd was stunned by what Jesus said, for they could not conceive of the necessity of the Son of Man being lifted up in death (John 12:34). What they did not see is that his death was the means by which the world (both Jews and Gentiles) would be saved.

Jesus' Going to the Father

John also alludes to the cross with two verbs for "going" (*poreuomai*, *hypagō*). The two verbs are basically synonymous and overlap in meaning. Jesus declared to the crowd that he was departing (John 7:33; 8:21), and they were puzzled, wondering if he planned to go to the dispersion (John 7:35–36) or if he was contemplating suicide (John 8:22). Even the disciples were confused about Jesus' destination, since he said that they could not depart with him (John 13:33; 14:4–5; 16:17–18). Only Jesus comprehended where he had come from and where he was going (John 8:14): he had come from God and was returning to him (John 13:3). The Jewish authorities could not go with Jesus, for he was departing to the Father (John 7:33; 14:12, 28; 16:5, 10, 17, 28). Jesus' departure was for the benefit of his disciples, because he went to prepare a place for them so that they could be with him again (John 14:2–3). He is the way by which believers can be saved (John 14:6). Hence, even though they could not follow Jesus immediately, they will enjoy his presence again (John 13:36; 16:22). How does this relate to the cross? The cross is the means by which Jesus departs to the Father. He is not reunited with his Father without undergoing death. The disciples can be united with Jesus only by his going to the Father, for his death is the basis upon which they can enjoy Jesus' presence forever. He has to prepare the way for them by giving his life so that they will have access to the Father's presence.

---

74. Rightly Carson 1991b: 444; Ridderbos 1997: 439–40. See also Barrett 1978: 427.

Jesus' Hour and Glorification

The significance of Jesus' death is conveyed also through the terms "hour" (*hōra*) and "glorify" (*doxazō*). The term "hour" conveys the fulfillment of redemptive history through Jesus (John 4:21, 23; 5:25, 28).[75] God's plan for history, however, turns upon the death of Jesus. Hence, the hour in John often represents the time of his death. When Mary asked Jesus to do something about the lack of wine at the wedding feast, Jesus responded that his hour had not yet arrived (John 2:4). Perhaps he responded in this way because the commencement of his ministry set in motion the events that would lead to his death. Jesus' death cannot occur before the time appointed by the Father. When the temple police attempted to arrest Jesus, they failed because the hour for his death had not come (John 7:30; 8:20).

Jesus' hour represents the time when he will be glorified (John 12:23).[76] His death is clearly in view, since he immediately spoke of a grain of wheat dying. He refused to ask the Father to deliver him from the hour of his death, since his death was the purpose and even "the capstone"[77] of his coming (John 12:27–28), and so he asked the Father to glorify his name. Jesus had already glorified the Father by the way he lived, but he glorified it supremely in the cross.

That Jesus' hour refers to his death is confirmed when it is defined as the time when he would depart from the world to the Father (John 13:1). As Jesus' arrest drew near, he acknowledged that the hour had come (17:1), and again the hour is defined as his glorification. According to John, Jesus' death represents not his humiliation but rather his glorification (John 13:31–32; 17:4–5), for it represents his undying love for his disciples (John 13:1).[78] What is humiliating in human eyes is beautiful in the eyes of God, for the self-giving and atoning love of Jesus displays the character of God. Jesus' death is also his glorification because it is the pathway by which he was exalted as the Son of God. John does not fix attention on the degradation of the cross but looks beyond it to the final reward granted to Jesus.

Jesus as the Bread of Life

Jesus' saving work is communicated vividly in the "bread of life" discourse (John 6:22–59). The food necessary for eternal life is Jesus

75. For "hour" in John, see Barrett 1978: 191; R. Brown 1966: 99–100; Köstenberger 2004: 95.

76. See M. M. Thompson 1988: 94–97; Barrett 1978: 166.

77. So M. M. Thompson 1988: 96.

78. Jesus' washing of the disciples' feet—the task of a slave—has no parallel in terms of a superior taking the role of a servant (Lincoln 2000: 299).

himself (John 6:27). Jesus is God's true bread, and he grants life to the world (John 6:32–33, 48). The only way one can live is by eating the bread that is Jesus (John 6:50–51). Jesus then clarified that "the bread that I will give for the life of the world is my flesh" (John 6:51). This is almost certainly a reference to Jesus' death on the cross.[79] The food that he gave for the world's life is his flesh, his death on the cross. Jesus then proceeded to speak in incredibly vivid language of the need to eat his flesh and drink his blood in order to obtain eternal life (John 6:52–59). The language would have been shocking in the extreme to the Jews, for drinking blood violated OT purity laws. The offense of the cross is thereby communicated (John 6:61). The only way human beings can have life is to feed on Jesus as the crucified one. They must put their trust in him by relying on his body and blood as the only basis by which they could enjoy eternal life.[80]

Other References to Jesus' Death

Caiaphas also prophesied about the significance of Jesus' death, though he was unaware that as God's high priest he spoke better than he knew (John 11:49–53).[81] God spoke through Caiaphas as high priest so that an official declaration about the role of Jesus' death was uttered. Caiaphas declared that Jesus would die vicariously for the sake of the people to prevent the entire nation from perishing. Jesus took the penalty upon himself that the nation deserved. John adds that the benefit of Jesus' death extends beyond Israel to include all the future children of God among the Gentiles.

We also have an allusion to Jesus' death in the washing of the disciples' feet (John 13:1–17).[82] Jesus' love to the end signified his willingness to die for his disciples (John 13:1).[83] The washing represents the cleansing effected by Jesus' death. Hence, if Peter refused to be washed, he had "no share" (*meros*) with Jesus (John 13:8); that is, he has no inheritance among God's people. Only those who are washed by Jesus enjoy forgiveness of sins.[84] Only one washing is needed because Jesus' death is efficacious (John 13:10), and the need for the disciples to be washed at this juncture of Jesus' ministry demonstrates that they still need his

---

79. Rightly M. M. Thompson 1988: 45–46; Ridderbos 1997: 238; Köstenberger 2004: 215. See also the helpful cultural background along with theological interpretation in Koester 2003: 130–34.

80. See M. M. Thompson 1988: 47.

81. "Caiaphas was made an unconscious vehicle of truth" (Barrett 1978: 407).

82. So M. M. Thompson 1988: 97–102; Barrett 1978: 436–37.

83. M. M. Thompson 1988: 99.

84. So Barrett 1978: 441; Stuhlmacher 1993: 91; M. M. Thompson 1988: 99–100.

cleansing death.[85] Jesus, of course, did not think that physical washing itself was sufficient to grant cleansing. He cleaned Judas's feet, and yet Judas was not truly clean (John 13:11). Judas did not genuinely belong among those whose sins were forgiven. Jesus' taking upon himself the role of a servant in washing the disciples' feet points forward to his servant role on the cross, where he washed his own by dying for sin and granting cleansing to those who trust in him.[86] All those who have received Jesus' gracious work and word are genuinely clean (John 15:3).[87]

Resurrection of Jesus

The resurrection of Jesus is clearly taught in John's Gospel.[88] Jesus himself promised that if the temple of his body were destroyed, he would raise it in three days (John 2:19–21). He affirmed that he had the authority to revive himself after his death (John 10:17–18). We have also seen earlier that when Jesus spoke of his being lifted up and glorified, we likely have a reference to both his death and his resurrection/exaltation.

As in the Synoptics, a woman, Mary Magdalene, traveled to the tomb first after Jesus' death, though the narrative hints that other women were with her (John 20:2). The stone was rolled away and the tomb was empty, and she dashed back to Peter and the Beloved Disciple to inform them of the state of affairs. Peter and the Beloved Disciple ran to the tomb, and they saw the linens lying there and the headcloth folded up or, perhaps better, rolled up. Grave robbers would not have left the linens behind, nor would they have folded up the headcloth.[89] The Beloved Disciple, upon seeing these things, believed that Jesus was risen (John 20:8). The empty tomb witnessed to Jesus' resurrection.

The resurrection of Jesus is not attested merely by the empty tomb. Jesus appeared to Mary Magdalene first of all (John 20:11–18). She was indisposed to believe in the resurrection because she did not even recognize Jesus when he first appeared, but she recognized him unmistakably when he uttered her name. Jesus then appeared to the disciples when they were locked in a room together (John 20:19–23). His entrance into the room demonstrated that he operated on another level, since corruptible bodies cannot enter locked rooms without some ordinary means of entrance. Jesus had a genuine body, however, because he showed the

85. M. M. Thompson 1988: 100.

86. There is also an exemplary theme in the foot washing, but this in no way cancels out the emphasis on Jesus' unique cleansing accomplished by his death (see Barrett 1978: 437; M. M. Thompson 1988: 101–2).

87. See Barrett 1978: 474.

88. See Wright 2003: 662–79.

89. Rightly Köstenberger 2004: 563–64.

disciples the wounds on his hands and feet, proving that the body once crucified was now risen.[90] Thomas was not present at this initial meeting, and Jesus appeared to him and the other disciples on the succeeding Sunday (John 20:24–29). Thomas insisted that Jesus was not risen, and that he would not believe unless he could see and touch Jesus' wounds. Jesus suddenly stood among them again through locked doors, inviting Thomas to see and touch him. Clearly, the crucified Jesus was raised from the dead, as Thomas confessed that he is Lord and God.

John 21 records a final appearance of Jesus to his disciples, while they were fishing. Jesus appeared on shore, instructed them on how to catch a great quantity of fish, and proceeded to make breakfast for them. The disciples recognized that it was Jesus, though apparently it was a bit unclear initially. Jesus then proceeded to restore Peter to ministry and summoned him to feed his sheep. The Johannine accounts teach clearly that Jesus is the risen Lord.

Conclusion

I have argued thus far in this book that God's saving promises have been fulfilled in Jesus Christ. The centrality of Jesus Christ is evident in the Gospels, as we have seen in the preceding chapters. In this chapter I have argued that Jesus' death and resurrection are the means by which God's covenantal promises are secured. The forgiveness of sins, the new creation, and the new exodus have become reality through the death and resurrection of Jesus. The reality is a complex one, however, and stands under the already–not yet motif. Even though the new age has dawned in Jesus' resurrection, the resurrection of those who belong to Jesus has been delayed. There is an unexpected interval between the resurrection of Jesus and the final resurrection. Hence, the new age is inaugurated but not consummated.

We have seen in this chapter that the shadow of the cross is forecasted throughout the story line of all four Gospels. Each one could rightly be identified as a passion narrative with an extended introduction. The Gospel writers do not explicate in great detail the significance of the cross, but we need to remind ourselves that these are narrative accounts, and so the significance of the cross is relayed through its centrality in the story as a whole. The story relays the truth that the righteous and innocent one suffered for the unrighteous. Even though the Gospels do not unpack the meaning of the cross in detail, there are indications that

---

90. Barrett (1978: 568) says that "Jesus . . . was at once sufficiently corporeal to show his wounds and sufficiently immaterial to pass through closed doors. John offers no explanation of this power, nor is it possible to supply one."

Jesus died in the place of his people to secure the forgiveness of sins. We have enough evidence to indicate that the Gospel writers identified Jesus as the Servant of the Lord from Isa. 53. He gave his life as a ransom for many to save his people from their sins. At the Lord's Supper he explained that his blood was being poured out covenantally to secure forgiveness of sins. John teaches that Jesus is the Lamb of God, who sacrificially takes away the sins of the world. His death, Caiaphas declared in a prophecy, is for the sake of the nation as a whole, so that he dies vicariously for his people. Jesus' body and blood were poured out for the life of the world. Human beings will live only if they eat Jesus' flesh and drink his blood—that is, if they put their faith in his atoning death.

Jesus' death does not save apart from the resurrection. The cross and resurrection together constitute the saving event. It is imperative to see that every Gospel narrative concludes with the resurrection, for the cross alone is insufficient to secure forgiveness of sins. John particularly emphasizes that the cross is the pathway to victory, for he describes it as a lifting up, as Jesus' glorification, and as his going to the Father. The cross, in other words, cannot be separated from Jesus' exaltation. Indeed, the cross is the very means by which Jesus is exalted and victorious over all. The cross leads to the crown.

Finally, we must put together the substance of this chapter with the preceding ones. Jesus as the crucified and risen Lord saves because of who he is. His death and resurrection save because he is the Messiah, the Son of Man, the Son of God, the great I Am, and truly God. Jesus' death is not the death of an ordinary person. Soteriology, as we noted at the start of this chapter, is indissolubly connected with Christology, and vice versa. We do violence to the NT if we separate Christology and soteriology and consider them abstractly. They are bound up together, and they are bound up with the narrative of God saving his people through Jesus Christ.

9

※ ※ ※ ※ ※ ※ ※ ※ ※ ※ ※ ※ ※ ※ ※ ※ ※

Jesus' Saving Work in Acts

The theme of this book is that the new age has dawned and God has fulfilled his covenantal promises in Jesus Christ. We have seen in the Gospels the supremacy of Jesus Christ and the centrality of Christology. We have also noted that all four Gospels are narratives that point toward Jesus' cross and resurrection—passion narratives with extended introductions. The high Christology of the Gospels reveals that Jesus saves via his work on the cross because of who he is. When we come to the book of Acts, we consider the period of time subsequent to Jesus' death and resurrection, and we observe the spread of the Christian movement. In Acts Jesus Christ and his death and resurrection are still central. Hence, it is useful to consider the Christology of Acts and God's saving work in Christ. It will become clear that Acts does not deviate from the message of the Synoptic Gospels, though it now looks back on the ministry, death, and resurrection of Jesus Christ.

Christology of Acts

When we study the Christology of Acts, it is imperative to recall that Luke and Acts were written by the same author. Examining the Christology of Luke and Acts together, then, would assist us in pulling together the strands of Luke's theology. In considering Christology, however, we examined Luke along with Matthew and Mark because the agreements among the three Synoptic Gospels are so remarkable.[1] Recalling that Luke-Acts were written by the same author, on the other hand, may forestall some interpretive missteps. In some ways the Christology of Acts seems rather undeveloped, but it is quite unlikely that the Christology of Acts should be interpreted as a step down from the Christology of Luke.[2] We saw in our study of the Synoptics that Jesus is the exalted Son of Man and the unique Son of God, and he assumes divine prerogatives. The Christology of Acts presumably will fit with what we have found in Luke, even if some of the same themes do not sound forth. In Acts, for instance, Jesus is identified as the Son of Man and the Son of God in only one text each, but the scarcity of these appellations does not yield the conclusion that Luke questions whether Jesus is the Son of Man or the Son of God.

The purpose of Acts must be recalled in any study of its Christology. Luke did not write a theological treatise, nor did he attempt to sketch out his theology. Scholars in recent years have rightly seen that Luke is a theologian, though some have unconvincingly concluded that since he is a theologian, he is not a historian.[3] It is better to say that Luke is a historian who writes history from a theological point of view.[4] All history, including that composed by Luke, is interpretive and selective. Luke did not write a neutral composition about the ministry of Jesus Christ and life in the early church. His theological slant shines through his writing. Nevertheless, contrary to the view of some, Luke did not put speeches in the mouths of Peter and Paul, nor did he construct a law-abiding Paul of his own making. What he wrote was constrained by historical events—what people truly said and did.[5] If Luke's purpose is historical as much as it is theological, it follows that we do not have anything like a complete map of Luke's theology. His theological perspective manifests itself in what he includes and how he presents the

1. A decision has to be made at precisely this point as to how to arrange NT theology. It is not as if one way is correct and others are false paths. Rather, no book can capture or exhaust the richness of NT theology, and so we profit from NT theologies that are written from a number of mutually complementary perspectives.

2. The Christology of Luke has been the subject of considerable discussion and debate in recent scholarship. For a survey of different proposals, see Buckwalter 1998: 108–12.

3. The notion that Acts does not consistently intend to relate historical events is a commonplace in critical scholarship. See, for example, Haenchen 1971: 3–132; Barrett 1998: xxxiii–liv; Pervo 1987.

4. In defense of the idea that Luke is both a historian and a theologian, see Marshall 1970.

5. In defense of this notion, see the detailed works of Gasque 1989; Hemer 1989. For the view that Acts deserves to be taken seriously as a historical document, and is substantially reliable, see Sherwin-White 1963; Hengel 1980; Palmer 1993; Gempf 1993; Fitzmyer 1998: 124–28.

material, but he does not have a free hand to twist the events to fit with his preconceptions. It is much more likely that Luke believed that history itself was guided by God's providential plan, and hence the events as they unfolded had theological significance because God stands behind and works in all of history.

Virtually all would agree that Luke's composition was informed by a theological worldview, simply on the basis of what he chose to include in his story. Where we could go astray, however, is in thinking that what Luke chose to include were necessarily the main themes in *his* theology. It is altogether possible that some topics are omitted because of the subject of his narrative. The particular angle of his work influenced what was retained and what was excluded. The danger of writing a theology on each writer of the NT is that it can communicate subtly, despite protestations, that we have something like a complete theology from that person. The advantage of writing a theology of the NT thematically is that the theology of the whole is gleaned from the perspective of twenty-seven different compositions. We have a better chance of grasping the whole of the theology of the NT era when we include a greater sampling of writings from various authors included in the canon.

Jesus as Resurrected Lord

Reading the book of Acts, we are struck with the emphasis on Jesus as the exalted and resurrected Lord.[6] Luke often includes accounts that scripturally and historically emphasize Jesus' resurrection.[7] Jesus could not be the Messiah and Lord and the one through whom people receive forgiveness of sins if he remained in the grave. Luke speaks of "many proofs" (*tekmēria*) relative to Christ's resurrection (Acts 1:3). Both Peter and Paul argued that Ps. 16 was not fulfilled in David's life, and hence the words recorded fit only with Christ's resurrection (Acts 2:24–31; 13:35–37). David decomposed in the grave, and therefore the words of Ps. 16 must point to another, one who conquered death and whose tomb was empty. The Scriptures themselves point to Christ's death and his resurrection (Acts 13:31–33; 26:22–23). Whereas the Pharisees are the primary opponents in Luke, the Sadducees come to the forefront in Acts, particularly because the apostles preached the resurrection (Acts 4:1–2; cf. 5:17). The Sadducees, of course, rejected the notion of the resurrection (Matt. 22:23; Mark 12:18; Luke 20:27; Acts 23:8).[8]

6. See especially Hurtado 2003: 179–88. Moule (1966a: 160–66) emphasizes the decisive role that the resurrection plays in the Christology of Luke-Acts.

7. Acts 1:3, 22; 2:24–32; 3:15, 26; 4:2, 10, 33; 5:30; 10:40–41; 13:30–37; 17:3, 18, 31, 32; 23:6; 24:14–15, 21; 25:19; 26:8, 23.

8. See Josephus, *J.W.* 2.165; *m. Sanh.* 10:1.

Although a crucified Messiah was a contradiction in terms for the Jews, in Athens it was Paul's preaching of the resurrection that brought derision (Acts 17:31–32).[9] Paul claimed again and again, while he was under arrest and examination for criminal actions in Jerusalem and Caesarea, that the only cause for his arrest and criminal indictment was his belief in the resurrection (Acts 23:6; 24:15, 21; 25:19; 26:6, 8, 22–23). When Paul was examined by the Sanhedrin, his affirmation of the resurrection threw the council into a dither, and the Pharisees and Sadducees began to debate the legitimacy of the resurrection (Acts 23:6–10). Paul protested before Festus and Agrippa that he stood trial simply for the fulfillment of the Pharisaic hope that there would be a resurrection (Acts 26:4–8). Resurrection is a promise of the age to come, and Jesus Christ's resurrection represents the hinge of history. The age to come in Jewish thought, as we have seen often in this book, commences with the resurrection. Hence, Jesus' resurrection signaled that the new age has come. God's saving promises are being realized.

One of the central themes in Acts, then, is that Jesus is now the exalted Lord. The crucified one has been vindicated by God. Jesus' resurrection indicates that he is "the cornerstone" of the people of God (Acts 4:11).[10] As the resurrected one, he is now "exalted" as "leader" (*archēgos*) and "savior" (Acts 5:31). Since Jesus was raised from the dead and exalted, he has been "glorified" by God himself (Acts 3:13). Paul in his speech draws on Ps. 2:7 to say that God has "begotten" Jesus by raising him from the dead (Acts 13:33). In its historical context the psalm refers to the installation of the Davidic king (Ps. 2:6–7). The installation of the Davidic king is traced to Jesus' resurrection in Acts, for as the risen one, he also ascended to heaven and sits at God's right hand (Acts 1:9–11; 2:34–35), and hence he is installed as the messianic king. In sitting at God's right hand he fulfilled the prophecy of Ps. 110:1, and therefore we note that Luke in Acts draws on the same psalm that Jesus used in his conflict with the religious leaders (Luke 20:41–44). At Jesus' resurrection God "made him both Lord and Christ" (Acts 2:36).[11] We know from the Gospel of Luke that Jesus was the Christ during his earthly ministry, and therefore this verse does not teach that Jesus "became" Lord and Christ only when raised from the dead.[12]

9. See Barrett 1998: 854, with references to primary sources on the matter.

10. Others see it as the capstone (so Conzelmann 1987: 33; Barrett 1994: 230).

11. The use of the terms "Savior" and "Lord" in reference to Jesus may have been a direct response to the imperial cult. See Brent 1999: 73–139; Cuss 1974: 53–71; Price 1984; Witherington 1998: 157–58.

12. Contra Barrett 1994: 151–52. Rightly Jones 1974: 91–93; Strauss 1995: 66–67, 144–45. Fitzmyer (1998: 260–61) argues that the term "Lord" here means that the title used of Yahweh is now applied to Jesus. Further, Jesus is now installed as the *risen* Messiah. But Strauss (1995: 143–44) cautions against reading too much into the title "Lord" here. Con-

The point of the verse is that Jesus became the exalted Lord and Christ only at his exaltation. He did not reign as Lord and Christ until he was raised from the dead and exalted to God's right hand.[13]

Buckwalter in particular shows that Jesus as the resurrected Lord is the one who pours out the Spirit on his people (Acts 2:33).[14] The use of the phrase "Spirit of Jesus" (Acts 16:7) hearkens back to the OT, where the Spirit belongs to God or the Lord. Now the Spirit is also related to Jesus, and it is this very Spirit of Jesus who guides the church of Jesus Christ in mission. Furthermore, if we consider Luke's Gospel for a moment, it is instructive that Jesus promised to give his disciples the wisdom and words to respond suitably to persecution (Luke 21:15). Such a promise fits only with one who is divine, for only one who has heavenly authority can grant such ability to disciples. The relationship between Jesus and the Spirit is quite interesting in Acts, for both Acts 2:33 and Acts 16:7 "imply that the Spirit represents, if not mediates, the exalted Jesus' presence and continued activity among his people."[15]

The lordship of Jesus is a common refrain in Acts, and we will not pause here to note all the texts (see, e.g., Acts 1:6, 21; 4:33; 15:11, 26; 19:13; 20:21). In a number of instances it is difficult to determine whether "Lord" refers to the Father or the Son, since the title is used of both. Even the ambiguity as to whether the title "Lord" refers to the Son or the Father is instructive, for it points to the truth that they share the same status. As Lord, Jesus speaks words that are authoritative (Acts 20:35; 22:18). As Jervell says, "Luke in some sense regarded Jesus as on a level with God."[16] Further, in Acts 22:18 the words come to Paul in a vision from the exalted Jesus. The exalted Jesus appeared to Paul on the road to Damascus, and such an appearance and the resulting commission suggest his divinity (Acts 9:5, 17, 27; 22:8, 10; 26:15).[17] One might object that angels appear to people and give instructions, but in Acts Jesus is designated as "Lord of all" (Acts 10:36), and such a description does not fit any angelic figure. The expression is comparable with what is said of God in Jewish tradition (Tob. 10:13; Wis. 6:7; 8:3; Sir. 36:1; 50:15, 22; 3 Macc. 5:28; *Apoc. Mos.* 35:2;

---

zelmann (1987: 21) says that the verse "has an adoptionistic ring" but cannot be construed in this way since Jesus clearly was the Messiah during his ministry.

13. In the same way, Acts 3:19–21 should not be interpreted in terms of adoptionist Christology (see Moule 1966a: 167–68).

14. Buckwalter 1998: 115–16. What follows depends on the work of Buckwalter. See also Buckwalter 1996: 180–82, 188, 195–96.

15. Buckwalter 1998: 116.

16. Jervell 1996: 29. However, Jervell (1996: 30) is mistaken in saying that Jesus was not considered to be divine in Acts.

17. Barrett (1994: 450) says about Acts 9:5, "Jesus, once dead, is now alive and more than a man."

37:4; *Jub.* 22:10, 27; 30:19; 31:13, 19).[18] In Acts 18:9–10, as Buckwalter remarks, "Jesus appears to Paul in a vision and encourages him in language reminiscent of OT theophany and prophetic calling."[19] Moreover, in Acts human beings turn to the Lord or believe in the Lord (Acts 9:35, 42; 11:21; 16:31; 18:8), and human beings are never commended for placing their trust in an angel. Paul even says that he is willing to sacrifice his life for the name of the Lord Jesus (Acts 21:13).

Further, Jesus as the exalted Lord will return on the day of the Lord (Acts 2:20, quoting Joel 2:31). This is a remarkable text, for the day of the Lord in the OT is the day of Yahweh, but the prerogative of Yahweh is now assigned to Jesus Christ at his coming.[20] Even more extraordinary, as Hurtado notes, is the announcement that "everyone who calls upon the name of the Lord shall be saved" (Acts 2:21, quoting Joel 2:32).[21] In the OT the Lord who is called upon for salvation is clearly Yahweh, but in Acts the Lord who is invoked for salvation is none other than Jesus Christ.[22] Bock rightly says, "Jesus is more than a regal Messiah, as his task and position show. He is Lord, a title which shows Jesus in his task and person to be equal with God."[23] In using the title "Lord," Luke "implies that Jesus in his risen status has been made equal with Yahweh of the OT, for 'Lord' was used by Palestinian Jews in the last pre-Christian centuries as a title for Yahweh."[24] A high Christology is also apparent in that sins are forgiven in Jesus' name.

Jesus as the Christ

As the resurrected and exalted one, but also the one who suffered for the forgiveness of sins (see below), Jesus is the Christ.[25] The word "Christ" retains its titular significance in Acts. It does not merely become a last name, as is evident in the following examples: "that he may send the

18. See Cadbury 1933: 362.

19. Buckwalter 1998: 117. Buckwalter goes on to observe that the promise of Jesus' presence suggests deity, for in the OT God promises his presence with his people (Exod. 4:12). See also Acts 23:11, where the Lord Jesus appears to Paul and predicts that his future witness in Rome will indeed take place.

20. So Hurtado 2003: 181; see also Haenchen 1971: 179; Conzelmann 1987: 20; Fitzmyer 1998: 254. Bock (1987: 163–66, 183–85) rightly argues that the use of Ps. 110 to refer to Jesus in the speech indicates that "Lord" here refers to Jesus.

21. Hurtado 2003: 181–82.

22. Hurtado (2003: 182) goes on to say, "In fact, 'Lord' clearly functions in these cases as a divine title." Hurtado (2003: 182–85) further argues that the practice of invoking Jesus as Lord was remarkably early and cannot be assigned to a later date.

23. Bock 1987: 184.

24. Fitzmyer 1998: 260. See also Fitzmyer, *EDNT* 2:328–31.

25. For a short description of the Christology in Acts, see Barrett 1998: lxxxv–lxxxvii. Jervell (1996: 27) thinks that "Christ" is the "most significant title."

Christ appointed for you, Jesus" (Acts 3:20); "they did not cease teaching and preaching Jesus as the Christ" (Acts 5:42); Paul in his preaching was "proving that Jesus was the Christ" (Acts 9:22); "This Jesus, whom I proclaim to you, is the Christ" (Acts 17:3); "Paul was testifying . . . to the Jews that the Christ was Jesus" (Acts 18:5); Apollo was "showing by the Scriptures that the Christ was Jesus" (Acts 18:28). Jesus is anointed by God as the Christ (Acts 4:27; 10:38). The messiahship of Jesus is closely intertwined with his lordship. The truth that he has been made Lord and Christ at his resurrection surfaces again here (Acts 2:36). The notion that Jesus is the Christ was, of course, already established in Luke, and Acts simply maintains what the Gospel taught. What is new in Acts is that Jesus is now the exalted Messiah by virtue of the resurrection (Acts 2:36).[26] Another way of putting it is that he is now the vindicated Messiah, for during Jesus' earthly ministry his messianic glory was veiled by his humanity, suffering, and death. Even after the resurrection, of course, not all perceive Jesus to be exalted as Messiah, but now he reigns as Messiah in glory, and his reign will be apparent to all when he returns to judge (Acts 3:20–21; 17:31).[27]

Jesus as the Servant of the Lord

The life and ministry of Jesus attest to his messiahship and lordship (Acts 2:22; 10:37–38). His miracles and good works confirm that he was anointed by God with the Holy Spirit. His death cannot be ascribed to a mistake; rather, it was God's determined plan from the beginning (Acts 2:23; 4:26–28). The Scriptures predicted all along that the Christ would suffer (Acts 3:18; 17:2–3; 26:22–23; cf. 28:23).[28] And yet those who put Jesus to death bear full responsibility for their evil deed, for Luke does not think that divine sovereignty rules out the significance of human freedom, though the solution is not worked out philosophically. In putting Jesus to death the religious leaders have crucified God's "holy" and "righteous" one (Acts 3:14; 7:52).[29] In Acts Luke clearly teaches that Jesus is the suffering servant of Isa. 53, confirming what was argued relative

---

26. Hence, there is no adoptionistic Christology here. See Bock 1987: 185–86.

27. Some have understood Acts 3:20 to teach that Jesus will become the Messiah when he returns in the future. For a refutation of this view, see Barrett 1994: 204–5; see also Fitzmyer 1998: 288.

28. Everything that has happened in Jesus' ministry has occurred in accordance with the divine plan. See Cosgrove 1984.

29. Some argue that *dikaios* ("righteous") is a messianic title (Zimmerli and Jeremias 1957: 91; Bruce 1951: 109; Conzelmann 1987: 28), but the evidence is disputed (see Barrett 1994: 196–97). Doble (1996: 70–183, 226–35) argues for a wisdom background, but this is an implausible reading of the uses in Acts. Even if it is not messianic in pre-Christian literature, it clearly has a titular force in Acts (Hurtado 2003: 189–90). Polhill (1992: 131)

to the Gospel of Luke earlier. The Ethiopian eunuch just "happened" to be reading Isa. 53 when Philip was instructed to approach his chariot (Acts 8:28–34). When the eunuch inquired about the subject of the text, Philip identified the servant as Jesus Christ. A detailed exposition of the text is not given, but the verses cited from Isaiah (Isa. 53:7–8) refer to Jesus' innocent suffering and death.[30]

The use of the word "servant" (*pais*) in Acts is disputed, but it probably hearkens back to the suffering servant of Isaiah.[31] The glorification of the servant refers to his exaltation in accord with Isa. 52:13 (Acts 3:13).[32] The reference to the servant is confirmed by the context of Acts 3, where Jesus is handed over as a criminal by his people and suffered as was prophesied (Acts 3:13–18).[33] In both Acts and Isaiah the context suggests that the glorification follows his suffering.[34] This fits with the theology of Acts, where Jesus' exaltation is subsequent to his suffering. The term "servant" is also used in Acts (4:27, 30) in a context in which the death of Jesus is implied, suggesting again an echo of Isa. 53. Nor does Luke restrict himself to the servant's suffering. The glorification of the servant implies his resurrection (Acts 3:13), and Acts 3:26 says that "God . . . raised up his servant."[35] We have an echo here of Isa. 53:11–12 (cf. Isa. 52:13) which implies the vindication of the servant after his suffering.

Acts trumpets that Jesus fulfills the OT, and such a theme makes sense because the advancement of the gospel among both Jews and Gentiles is a central theme. All the prophets looked forward to the day of fulfillment that has now come in Jesus Christ (Acts 3:24). The universal blessing promised to Abraham (Gen. 12:3) has now become a reality in Jesus Christ (Acts 3:25–26). The promise to Abraham has been fulfilled in Jesus as the "servant," suggesting that Jesus as the servant is the true offspring of Abraham. The promised blessing for Israel and all nations is funneled through him. Nor does Luke vaguely explicate Abraham's

---

suggests a link to Isa. 53:11 and the death of the righteous one. This latter view is likely correct (see Strauss 1995: 330–32; Stuhlmacher 2006: 156).

30. For a careful study of the text, see Bock 1987: 225–30.

31. Against this, see Bühner, *EDNT* 3:6; Conzelmann 1987: 28; rightly Meyer 1979: 66–67; Barrett 1994: 194; Haenchen 1971: 205–6. Zimmerli and Jeremias (1957: 80, 86, 91) argue that the use of the term *pais* in Acts 3–4 suggests that the tradition of Jesus being the servant reaches back to the earliest history of the church (cf. Stuhlmacher 2006: 156).

32. Rightly Fitzmyer 1998: 284–85. Hurtado (2003: 191) says that it communicates "a specifically Israel-oriented and royal-messianic orientation." Bühner (*EDNT* 3:6), says, "Jesus as the *pais theou* is therefore the messianic successor of the house of David and the fulfillment of Israel's messianic expectations."

33. So Bock 1987: 188.

34. See Barrett 1994: 195; Bock 1987: 189–90; Strauss 1995: 331–33.

35. Some understand this verse to refer to God bringing Jesus "on the stage of history" (so Barrett 1994: 213). Fitzmyer (1998: 291) thinks the resurrection is likely in view.

universal blessing. The blessing comes through Jesus Christ and the forgiveness of sins available through him. Thereby evil is removed from the lives of God's people.

In Acts Luke identifies Jesus as the Servant of the Lord from Isa. 53, but he does not provide a detailed or thorough explanation of how Isa. 53 relates to the death of Jesus.[36] The substitutionary character of the servant's death for the sake of his people's sins, so clear in Isa. 53, is not unpacked by Luke in Acts.[37] It is sufficient for Luke's purposes to identify Jesus as the Servant of the Lord and to emphasize that forgiveness of sins comes through his death.

Jesus' Name

Since Jesus as the Christ is the exalted Lord, Acts emphasizes the name of Jesus, signifying his authority and his divinity. Name theology is often ignored, but its significance must be grasped in order to comprehend Luke's Christology. Hurtado says that name theology "is derived directly from the Old Testament usage, where it functions as a technical expression designating prayer and sacrifice offered specifically to *Yahweh*."[38] It is quite striking, then, to see that believers are baptized in the name of Jesus Christ (Acts 2:38; 10:48). Their initiation into the people of God is based not on God's name but on the name of Jesus. Baptism is clearly associated with forgiveness of sins based on Christ's death (Acts 2:38).[39] Peter healed a lame man "in the name of Jesus Christ of Nazareth" (Acts 3:6), stressing that faith in the name of Christ is the basis of this man's healing (Acts 3:16; 4:10). When Peter heals Aenas, he says, "Jesus Christ heals you" (Acts 9:34). Healing is a divine prerogative, and such an action is ascribed to the name of Jesus Christ. The gospel proclaimed heralds "the name of Jesus Christ" (Acts 8:12). Paul and Barnabas "risked their lives for the sake of our Lord Jesus Christ" (Acts 15:26). Paul in Christ's name commanded a demon to leave a girl (Acts 16:18).[40] Most significantly, those who are saved call upon Jesus' name to experience salvation (Acts 2:21; 9:14, 21; 22:16). Indeed, his is the only name that brings salvation (Acts 4:12), and hence a divine function is clearly attributed to

---

36. Buckwalter (1996: 247–57) argues that in explicating the servant theme Luke emphasized how disciples of Jesus should serve others the way Jesus did.

37. See Bock 1987: 188–89.

38. Hurtado 2003: 197.

39. On the early Christian practice of baptizing in Jesus' name, see Hartman 1997; *ABD* 1:583–94; Hurtado 2003: 200–203.

40. Hurtado (2003: 204) observes that other figures were alleged to be responsible for exorcisms and healings in the Greco-Roman world, but Jesus should be distinguished from such persons, for his "name was invoked as uniquely efficacious." See the full discussion in Hurtado 2003: 203–6.

Jesus. As we noted earlier, the emphasis on Jesus' name is particularly striking in Acts 2:21, for in the OT context the name that is invoked for salvation is Yahweh's (Joel 2:32).[41] Hurtado concludes that such a use of name theology in Acts demonstrates that "the name of 'Jesus' itself was reverenced and functioned in the devotional life of these believers."[42] It seems that Luke's name theology points to Jesus' deity.[43]

Jesus as the Prophet and Son of God

We have already seen in Luke that Jesus is considered to be a prophet, and indeed *the* prophet.[44] Moses predicted that a new prophet would arise (Deut. 18:15–22), and Luke maintains that Jesus fulfills that prophecy (Acts 3:22–23; 7:37). The final revelation of God has been given in Jesus himself, so that he is superior to Moses. The rejection that both Joseph and Moses experienced from their contemporaries (Acts 7:9–16, 29–43) anticipated the rejection of Jesus by Stephen's contemporaries (Acts 7:52). Jesus is the Son of Man standing at God's right hand defending Stephen (Acts 7:59). He is the one who brings life into the world (*archēgos tēs zōēs*) (Acts 3:15)[45] and is God's Son (Acts 9:20).

In Acts the title "Son of God" is used only once (Acts 9:20), and so it could be equivalent to "Messiah." But the usage in Luke's Gospel suggests that "Son of God" does not only mean that Jesus is the Christ. The title "Son of God" indicates that Jesus has a unique and special relationship with God.[46] Jesus' divine stature manifests itself in Acts, for both Stephen (Acts 7:59–60) and Paul (Acts 22:19–20) prayed to Jesus, and pious Jews, of course, would voice prayers only to God.[47] Paul almost certainly prayed

41. And so it seems to follow that Jesus is "equal to Yahweh" (Buckwalter 1998: 119). Such a view rules out an adoptionistic Christology (see Buckwalter 1996: 184–91).

42. Hurtado 2003: 198–99. Hurtado (2003: 199) goes on to say that the practice is early and stems from "Jewish Christian circles."

43. See Buckwalter 1996: 182–84; 1998: 119.

44. For contemporary Jewish discussion on Deut. 18 and a prophet like Moses, see Barrett 1994: 208. See also Fitzmyer 1998: 289–90.

45. Barrett (1994: 198, 290) thinks that the point in Acts 3:15 is that Jesus brings "life into the world . . . thereby establishing a new age or reign," while in Acts 5:31 *archēgos* bears the meaning "leader" or "prince." P. Müller (*EDNT* 1:163) understands Acts 3:15 as indicating "one who leads the way into life" and not "originator," while in Acts 5:31 *archēgos* means "Leader and Savior." Fitzmyer (1998: 286) suggests "author" or "originator."

46. Contra Barrett 1994: 465. Fitzmyer (1998: 435) rightly argues that the title is not equivalent to "Messiah" (contra Haenchen 1971: 331), and even though he does not think that it bears the meaning of the term in the later creeds, the "title expressed a unique relationship of Jesus to Yahweh."

47. So Barrett 1994: 387; 1998: 1044. The prayer in Acts 1:24 is likely offered to Jesus as well. Rightly Bruce 1951: 80 (perhaps); Barrett 1994: 103; see also Peterson 1998: 386. Contra Haenchen 1971: 162; Conzelmann 1987: 12; Fitzmyer 1998: 227.

to Jesus in this text, for the divine voice said to Paul, "They will not accept your testimony about me" (Acts 22:18). The rejected witness must
refer to his proclamation of Jesus as Christ and Lord. In some texts, as
we noted earlier, it is difficult to discern whether the focus is on God or
Jesus. The Lord who appeared to Paul in a vision in Corinth was almost
surely Jesus himself (Acts 18:9–10).[48] The divine status of Jesus suggests
itself when he appeared to Paul on the road to Damascus and spoke to
him (Acts 9:4–5, 17; 22:7–10; 26:13–18).[49] The same divine authority surfaces in Jesus' encounter with Ananias. Jesus appeared to him in a vision,
summoning him to visit Paul (Acts 9:10–16). Ananias's response to the
vision accords with Isaiah's response when he saw the Lord in a vision.
Isaiah cried out, "Here am I! Send me" (Isa. 6:8). Ananias responded to
the vision by saying, "Here I am, Lord" (Acts 9:10).[50] The expression "Here
I am" (*hinnēnî*) is often used to signify humble compliance to God's will
(e.g., Gen. 22:1, 11; 31:11; 46:2; Exod. 3:4; 1 Sam. 3:4).

Luke's Christology in Acts is not as detailed as what we find in his
Gospel, but this can be ascribed to the purpose of the former work. In
Acts he emphasizes that Jesus is the resurrected Lord, and hence he is
now the exalted Lord and Christ. What Luke says about Jesus' lordship
clearly implies his divinity: he appears to Paul as the exalted Lord; human
beings put their faith in him; believers are baptized in the name of the
Lord Jesus; and Jesus is exalted as the Lord of all. Certainly only God
himself can be designated as the Lord of all. The theology of the name is
also prominent, so that Jesus takes on divine status in baptism, healing,
and salvation. Jesus' divinity is evident because he is the Son of God,
and prayers are offered to him by believers. He is clearly the Servant of
the Lord predicted in Isa. 53, the one in whom and through whom God
fulfills his promise to secure the forgiveness of sins.

The Saving Work of Christ

Since Jesus is the Christ, the exalted Lord over all, the Son of God,
the Prophet, and the Servant of the Lord, he is to be preached and proclaimed to all (Acts 5:42; 8:5, 12; 9:22; 18:5, 28; 28:31). The lordship of
Christ is not a private matter but rather is to be proclaimed throughout
the world, to both Jews and Greeks. The missionary thrust of Acts is well
known, and when linked with the lordship of Christ, it teaches that Jesus
is the universal Lord. Since Christ is Lord of all, he must be proclaimed

48. So Barrett 1998: 869; Fitzmyer 1998: 628.
49. A genuine appearance is in view here. So Wright 2003: 396.
50. The Greek in the two texts is slightly different, *idou eimi* in Isaiah and *idou egō* in
Acts, but the difference in meaning is immaterial.

to all everywhere, and all must be called upon to submit to his lordship and to confess him as Savior. The Christology of Acts, then, is tied to the mission of the church, to the mandate to witness for Christ from Jerusalem to the ends of the earth (Acts 1:8).

Because Jesus Christ is the universal Lord, salvation is available only through him.[51] The remarkable statement in Acts 4:12 could scarcely be clearer: "And there is salvation in no one else, for there is no other name under heaven given among men by which we must be saved."[52] The universal lordship of Christ entails that salvation comes exclusively and solely through him. He will judge the living and the dead on the last day (Acts 10:42; 17:31). Hence, people receive forgiveness of sins only by believing in and trusting in Jesus Christ the Lord (Acts 11:17; 16:31; 19:4; 20:21; 24:24). Repentance and faith are two sides of the same coin (cf. Acts 2:38; 3:19; 20:21), so that the one cannot be separated from the other. Luke nicely captures salvation and repentance when he says that God sent Christ "to bless you by turning every one of you from your wickedness" (Acts 3:26; cf. 5:31).

Salvation cannot be obtained through the law of Moses, but only through believing in Jesus Christ, as Paul clarifies in his speech in Antioch: "Let it be known to you therefore, brothers, that through this man forgiveness of sins is proclaimed to you, and by him everyone who believes is freed from everything from which you could not be freed by the law of Moses" (Acts 13:38–39). Since salvation is based on believing instead of doing, grace is the foundation of new life: "We believe that we will be saved through the grace of the Lord Jesus, just as they will" (Acts 15:11; cf. 11:17). If salvation were based on the law, it could be procured by human works or activity. Such a pathway to God is ruled out in Acts, for human sin rules out salvation by human works. Hence, one must proclaim the good news about Christ so that human beings can have peace with God (Acts 10:36). This good news is to be met with a response of faith.

Luke does not explain in any detail how Jesus' death and resurrection are the basis for the forgiveness of sins.[53] The connections drawn are primarily suggestive instead of didactic,[54] though scholarship generally

51. Franklin (1975: 65–67) and Zehnle (1969: 431) rightly see the importance of Jesus' exaltation for salvation but underestimate the Lukan theology of atonement.

52. "Jesus Christ is the only source and ground of salvation available for mankind" (Barrett 1994: 233).

53. In an important essay Stenschke (1998) demonstrates that Luke's anthropology was such that human beings were corrupt and thus needed forgiveness of sins. Stenschke also shows that salvation is fundamentally linked in Acts to the forgiveness of sins, even though there are other aspects to salvation. For this last point, see also Witherington 1998: 156, 160.

54. See Strauss 1995: 352.

has underestimated Luke's theology of the cross.[55] Peter proclaims that Jesus the crucified one is crowned as Lord and Christ (Acts 2:36) and then proceeds to say that forgiveness of sins is offered in Jesus' name (Acts 2:38). It appears, then, that forgiveness is based on Jesus' work as the crucified and risen Lord.[56] A similar connection emerges in Acts 3. Peter summons the people to repent for the removal of their sins (Acts 3:19) immediately after he mentions Christ's suffering (Acts 3:18). Presumably, Christ's suffering is the basis of the forgiveness offered (so also in Acts 26:18). Nor is the resurrection omitted, for the speech concludes by stressing that God raised Jesus as the Servant of the Lord from the dead, granting blessing by turning people from their wickedness (Acts 3:26). When Peter defended himself before the Sanhedrin, he reminded them that Jesus is the crucified and risen one (Acts 4:10) and then proclaimed that salvation comes only in the name of Jesus (Acts 4:12). Peter did not specifically claim here that salvation comes in Jesus' name because of his death and resurrection, but the close proximity of the themes suggests that salvation is available because Jesus had died and been raised. As the living and exalted one, who is crowned as Lord and present with his people, Jesus grants salvation.

In Acts 5:30 Peter again indicted the religious leaders for putting Jesus to death (cf. Acts 3:14–15; 4:10; 7:52; 10:39; 13:28), emphasizing that he was hung on a tree. The reference to the tree probably alludes to Deut. 21:23, so in the background we have the echo of his being cursed by God. The crucified Jesus was exalted by God himself (Acts 5:31), and hence repentance and forgiveness of sins are now available in Israel.[57] Peter intimates that Jesus took God's curse upon himself, and that forgiveness

---

55. It is common in scholarship to say that Luke-Acts lacks a soteriological view of the atonement. See, for example, Conzelmann 1960: 153; Creed 1930: lxxi–lxxii; Vielhauer 1966: 44–45; Franklin 1975: 66; Tyson 1986: 170 (Jesus' death is part of God's plan, but forgiveness is linked with Jesus' resurrection rather than his death); Barrett 1970: 59–60; Karris 1985: 115. Doble (1996: 237) says that in Luke the cross provides "no ransom and effects no forgiveness." Talbert (1976: 389) thinks that Jesus' death fulfills God's covenant but does not provide atonement for sin. Du Plessis (1994: 534–35) maintains that Jesus suffered as a martyr, but his death was not a sacrifice for sins. According to Green (1990: 8–10), salvation is gained through Jesus' exaltation, not his death. Jervell (1996: 98) says that Luke knows the theology of Jesus' sacrificial death (Luke 22:19–20; Acts 20:28) but pushes it to the sidelines. For a helpful survey on the Lukan view of the atonement, see Herrick 1997. Strauss (1995: 353) rightly emphasizes that Luke sees salvation in *"the whole Jesus event,* including the life, death, resurrection, and exaltation-enthronement."

56. Acts 26:18 suggests that forgiveness is equivalent with sanctification, being set apart in a holy sphere.

57. Bock (1987: 208–9) thinks that Luke does not argue explicitly for Jesus dying as a substitute here, but that Israel thought he was cursed by God, even though he was innocent.

is given on the basis of Jesus' work on the cross and his resurrection/
exaltation.

Peter, in summarizing the ministry of Jesus to Cornelius and his friends,
calls attention to his death and particularly his resurrection, stressing
that he appeared to chosen witnesses who ate with him (Acts 10:39–41).
The latter theme fits with Acts, where the resurrection of Jesus functions
as a central theme. Luke obviously has compressed Peter's words into
a remarkably brief and compact summary (Acts 10:37–43), assuming
that readers would fill in what was said from the remainder of Luke and
Acts. He does note that Jesus died on a tree, echoing again Deut. 21:23.
Peter concludes by teaching that forgiveness of sins is available to those
who believe in Jesus' name (Acts 10:43), implying that such forgiveness
is granted on the basis of Jesus' death and resurrection.

Paul in his speech in Pisidian Antioch declared that the Scriptures
were fulfilled in Jesus' death on a tree (Acts 13:27–29), alluding perhaps
to Deut. 21:23.[58] He proceeded to relate Jesus' resurrection, verifying it
by the appearances made to many (Acts 13:30–31). Paul excluded himself from the earliest witnesses, whereas in Acts 10:39–41 Peter included
himself among the earliest witnesses. The resurrection of Jesus was in
accord with the Scriptures, particularly Ps. 16, to which Peter also appealed in his Pentecost sermon (Acts 13:35–37; cf. 2:25–32).

Immediately after explicating the death and resurrection of Jesus,
Paul proclaimed that forgiveness of sins is available through Jesus (Acts
13:38). Indeed, he says that "therefore" (*oun*) forgiveness is now granted
through Jesus, indicating that cleansing from sin is granted on the basis
of Jesus' death and resurrection. We have a remarkably authentic Pauline touch here, for Paul says, "Through him everyone who believes is
justified from everything you could not be justified from by the law of
Moses" (Acts 13:38 NIV). Luke does not expand upon the significance
of the word "justify" (*dikaioō*) here, and yet we have a hint of what is
forthcoming in the Pauline letters. The verse should not be interpreted to
say that there were some matters for which the Mosaic law could atone
and now Christ's work fills in what could not be forgiven by the Mosaic
law.[59] Rather, Paul argues here that final forgiveness of sins and standing
in the right before God could not be accomplished by the Mosaic law.[60]
People become right with God only through believing in Jesus Christ
(Acts 4:12). Human beings are declared right before God on the basis of
Jesus' work as the crucified and risen Lord. There may be an implica-

58. See Fitzmyer 1998: 337; Barrett 1994: 642.
59. So Vielhauer 1966: 41–42. Barrett (1994: 650–51) offers some criticisms of Vielhauer
while maintaining that the latter's view is substantially correct.
60. Rightly Haenchen 1971: 412n4; Fitzmyer 1998: 518–19.

tion here, then, that Jesus' work on the cross replaces OT sacrifices. The latter pointed to him and were fulfilled in him.

There is likely an allusion to Jesus' work on the cross also in Acts 15:11, where salvation is said to be given on the basis of Christ's grace. Salvation here is equivalent to forgiveness of sins, to the cleansing of one's heart (Acts 15:9). Peter did not expatiate on the basis of the forgiveness of sins and the grace received, since he spoke to fellow believers who knew that salvation and cleansing come from Jesus as the crucified and risen Lord. He did emphasize God's grace in opposition to human works, so that the gracious and free character of salvation is underlined.

A particularly striking verse for both Christology and soteriology is Acts 20:28.[61] God obtained the church "with his own blood."[62] Harris argues that *idiou* here is a substantive and so the verse does not clearly identify Christ as God; rather, the expression refers to the blood of God's own one (i.e., Jesus).[63] Harris possibly is correct, but there is no other example of *idios* functioning as a christological title, and the expression could easily be an attributive adjective (cf. Acts 1:25), and so I incline to the interpretation that Paul slides from God to Christ because they are so intertwined in the work of salvation.[64] The reference to "God's blood" is rather startling, but it fits with what we have seen elsewhere in NT Christology, in that Jesus is both divine and human. The text also establishes that the church is saved or rescued from judgment by Christ's death. The verb *peripoieomai* signifies the saving or acquiring of God's people (cf. Isa. 43:21; Luke 17:33; cf. *peperipoiēsis* in Eph. 1:14; 1 Pet. 2:9), and this context likely refers to obtaining or acquiring because the church is said to be God's. Christ's suffering, then, secures deliverance for the people of God. This verse, then, captures one of the major themes that I trace in this book: Christology is inextricably wedded to soteriology. Christ's death secures forgiveness because his death represents the death of God himself.

61. Barrett (1998: 976–77) may be correct in arguing that Calvin reads his theology into the verse, but it also seems to be the case that Barrett underinterprets what Luke writes here.

62. Some scholars reduce the significance of the verse by claiming that we have an accommodation to Pauline theology (Franklin 1975: 66; Zehnle 1969: 440; Green 1990: 7). Ehrman (1991: 583) says that although the blood of Jesus reminds people of their guilt and thus should lead to repentance, it does not signify a theology of atonement. However, this is scarcely convincing because it fails to take seriously Luke's decision to include it in the story.

63. Harris 1992: 139–41. See also Walton 2000: 96–98.

64. The textual evidence is rather evenly divided between *ekklēsian tou kyriou* and *ekklēsian tou theou*, but the latter is more likely original (so Metzger 1994: 425–26; Harris 1992: 133–37; Walton 2000: 94–95).

Conclusion

The Christology of Acts certainly is not as developed as what we find in the Gospel of John. We must beware, however, of inferring from this that Luke had a simple Christology or that he would have rejected what we find in John's Gospel. If we take seriously Luke's task as a historian, we note that he often relays the speeches given in evangelistic settings. It is not surprising, then, that the theme that Jesus is the Christ and has been exalted as Lord and Christ at his resurrection receives prominence. The evangelistic context would also explain the emphasis on the fulfillment of prophecy and the forgiveness of sins available through Jesus. And yet there are also many indications that Jesus has divine stature, for Jesus is the Lord of all, human beings pray to Jesus, believers are baptized in his name, salvation comes through believing in and turning to the Lord Jesus, and believers call on Jesus for salvation, whereas in the OT text cited Yahweh is the one called upon (Joel 2:31). Luke does not reflect deeply on the ontological dimensions of Christology, but the material contained here fits with early Palestinian Christianity and cannot be dismissed as a low Christology.

It has often been remarked that Luke lacks an in-depth theology of the atonement, and such a judgment can be conceded if he is measured against the fuller statements found in Paul. All of Acts emphasizes that salvation comes through the Lord Jesus Christ and him alone, showing that Luke ties forgiveness of sins to the death and resurrection of Jesus Christ. Furthermore, Luke clearly teaches that human beings are saved not by observing the law but rather by believing in Jesus Christ. The gracious character of salvation is communicated, for forgiveness of sins is obtained through faith and repentance, not by living a noble life. Luke also affirms that justification comes through Jesus, not the law of Moses.[65] Justification here has a forensic flavor; believers are declared to stand in the right before God by believing instead of by keeping the law of Moses. The death of Jesus secures forgiveness of sins, and forgiveness comes only in Jesus' name. Luke does not explain in detail the basis for forgiveness of sins, but this is not surprising, since the speeches in Acts are evangelistic in nature, and they also represent compressed summaries of what was said. The fundamental point is that forgiveness is secured through the death and resurrection of Jesus Christ, and it is left to other NT writers to provide a more detailed explanation of how this is so.

---

65. It is instructive that this statement comes from the apostle Paul, and this touch suggests that Luke was a careful historian, for we would expect that a statement on justification would hail from Paul.

10

❧ ❧ ❧ ❧ ❧ ❧ ❧ ❧ ❧ ❧ ❧ ❧ ❧ ❧ ❧ ❧ ❧ ❧ ❧ ❧

The Christology of Paul

Introduction

Up to this point we have considered the Christology of the Gospels and of the Acts of the Apostles. In every instance we see in these documents Christology worked out in narrative form. As we turn to the apostle Paul, we now see Christology worked out in epistolary literature.[1] I hold the minority view that all thirteen of the letters attributed to Paul are genuine,[2] and so here his Christology will be mined from all thirteen letters. We also need to take into account where Paul stands in salvation history. The Gospels, in contrast to Paul's writings, rehearse the story of Jesus that culminates with the cross and resurrection. If the Gospels are genuine history, as I maintain in this book, then lack of clarity in some

1. Scholars have often argued that the religion of Paul departs quite radically from the historical Jesus. It is not my purpose here to respond to this issue directly. For a helpful work that demonstrates continuity between Paul and the historical Jesus, see D. Wenham 1995.

2. The first letters dismissed by some as inauthentic are the Pastoral Epistles, but for recent defenses of their authenticity, see Fee 1988: 23–26; W. Mounce 2000: lxvi–cxxix; Knight 1992: 21–52; Ellis 1992. For a full discussion that opts against Pauline authorship, see Marshall 1999: 57–92.

of their accounts of this history may be due to where the characters stood in the history of salvation. The Gospel writers do not intend to mine the full significance of Jesus' ministry, death, and resurrection but instead to recount the events leading up to and culminating in Jesus' death and resurrection. Paul, on the other hand, reflects in more detail on the significance of what Jesus accomplished, rather than writing a gospel in which he recounts the story of Jesus. The fact that he wrote letters to his churches permitted him to expound on Christology and salvation in a manner distinct from, and often fuller than, what we find in the Gospels.

The Christology of Paul is, of course, a massive topic, and here I intend only to touch on some of the main themes. In Paul's case we have the advantage of possessing thirteen letters addressed to a variety of situations, and so we are more confident of having a relatively complete picture of his Christology, though it must be added that Paul never wrote a christological treatise. In any case, Paul accords with what I have been arguing for in this book. Christ is absolutely central in the history of salvation, and God's saving promises have been fulfilled in him. The OT Scriptures point toward Jesus Christ, and the redemption pledged for God's people has come to fulfillment in him.

Centrality of Christ

Perhaps it is best to begin by noting the Christ-centeredness of Paul's theology.[3] Jesus Christ is so pervasive in Paul's letters that it is difficult to know where to begin and impossible to explore the topic to the end. We can begin with Paul's greatest letter, the Epistle to the Romans, which commences with reflection on the gospel. The gospel centers on the Son, Jesus Christ (Rom. 1:3). Or, as Paul puts it in 1 Corinthians, the gospel focuses on the cross of Christ, on Christ crucified (1 Cor. 1:17–25). God's grace has been bestowed upon his people in Christ Jesus, so that every gift that they possess is due to Christ (1 Cor. 1:4–8). Salvation can be described as "fellowship" with Jesus Christ as Lord (1 Cor. 1:9). Whether we think of justification, sanctification, reconciliation, or redemption, these are all rooted in the work of Christ on the cross. Christ "died for the ungodly" (Rom. 5:6). Christ is "our Passover" sacrifice (1 Cor. 5:7). Christ's death liberated believers from the old age of sin and evil (Gal. 1:4). The gospel is summarized in Christ's death for sinners and his

3. Fitzmyer (1989: 37–38) maintains that the gospel and Christology are central in Paul's thinking, and such a view is not far from what is being suggested here, since I am arguing that God's saving promises, which include, of course, the gospel, are fulfilled in Christ.

resurrection (1 Cor. 15:3–4). He "was delivered up for our trespasses and raised for our justification" (Rom. 4:25).

Paul's ambition as a missionary was to preach the gospel of Christ (Rom. 15:19–20), so that he could proclaim Christ where he was not known previously. The gospel can be described as "the preaching of Jesus Christ" (Rom. 16:25; cf. 2 Cor. 10:14), as the "testimony about Christ" (1 Cor. 1:6), or simply as preaching Christ (Phil. 1:15, 17–18). Paul received the gospel when Christ Jesus revealed himself to him on the road to Damascus (Gal. 1:12). Paul may have recalled that revelation when he spoke about "seeing the light of the gospel of the glory of Christ, who is the image of God" (2 Cor. 4:4).[4] The good news features the beauty and splendor of Christ, a splendor that Paul beheld when Christ appeared to him. Those who herald the gospel do not call attention to themselves or preach about themselves; they proclaim Jesus Christ as Lord (2 Cor. 4:5). Nor does focusing on Christ push God to the margins, for God's glory is maximized "in the face of Jesus Christ" (2 Cor. 4:6). The gospel can be summarized with the words "We proclaim him [Christ]" (Col. 1:28 my translation).

Since the gospel centers on Jesus Christ, when Paul says, "I do it all for the sake of the gospel" (1 Cor. 9:23), this is another way of saying that he conducted his ministry for the sake of Christ. Showing forth Jesus was his aim in all that he did. In his last letter he remarked, "Remember Jesus Christ . . . as preached in my gospel" (2 Tim. 2:8). The passion of Paul's life as a missionary was preaching the gospel, but the gospel centers on Jesus Christ, and so the heartbeat of Paul's mission was preaching Christ.

Often scholars devote attention to the titles used for Jesus Christ when setting forth Paul's Christology, and such a procedure is certainly illuminating and fitting. On the other hand, we are likely to ignore the multitude of texts where Christ is named but the focus is not on a title. Noticing such texts and themes impresses upon us in a fresh way that Paul's theology and life were Christ-saturated.

Paul's Christology identifies Jesus Christ as the second Adam. All human beings are either in Adam or in Christ. Sin came into the world through Adam, and death followed in its train (Rom. 5:12). Adam's sin brought into the world death, condemnation, and the reign of death (Rom. 5:15–19; 1 Cor. 15:21–22). By way of contrast, Christ brought the following into the world: (1) God's beneficent and lavish free gift of grace; (2) justification and life; (3) reigning in life; (4) righteousness; and (5) hope for a future resurrection (Rom. 5:15–19; 1 Cor. 15:21–22).[5]

---

4. So Kim 1982: 223–33. Harris (2005: 331) observes, "As God's *eikōn*, Christ both shares and expresses God's nature."

5. Contra Cullmann (1963: 167–70), it is scarcely clear that in 1 Cor. 15:45–47 Paul attacks the view of the two Adams (heavenly and earthly) that was similar to the view

What must be observed is that all these blessings come to believers through Jesus Christ. He is the turning point of history, the hinge upon which the life of each person depends. The only way to escape from the baleful effects of Adam's sin is by belonging to the new Adam, Jesus the Christ.

Christians are exhorted to practice certain virtues and desist from certain vices (e.g., Col. 3:5–17; Eph. 4:25–5:2). Paul can summarize what it means to put on virtues, however, by exhorting believers to "put on the Lord Jesus Christ" (Rom. 13:14). The new ethical life of believers is a Christ-centered life, a Christ-clothed life. The "new man" (Eph. 2:15 my translation) represents the new people of God, composed of both Jews and Gentiles, who are one in Christ. As Lincoln says, "Christ has created this corporate new person in himself; the new humanity is embraced in his own person."[6] This stands in contrast to the "old self" (Rom. 6:6); the old Adam, through whom people enter the world, has been crucified. The goal for believers is ultimately "knowledge of the Son of God" (Eph. 4:13), which means that the reason that believers exist is to know Jesus. And this knowledge of the Son of God finds its eschatological realization when believers become the *anēr teleios*, "perfect man" or "perfect self" (Eph. 4:13 my translation).[7] When Paul urges people to put off the "old self" (Eph. 4:22), he means the old Adam. Conversely, to put on the "new self" (Eph. 4:24) means that believers are to individually appropriate who they are in Christ.[8] In Ephesians we are quite close to where we started in Rom. 13:14: "Put on the Lord Jesus Christ."

The admonition in Rom. 13:14 fits with Colossians as well. Believers have put off the "old self"—that is, who they were in Adam when they were converted (Col. 3:9). They have put on the "new person" ("the new

---

propounded by Philo (cf. Barrett 1968: 374–75; Conzelmann [1975: 287] thinks that the attack is directed against gnostic or Philonic exegesis). Rightly Garland 2003: 736; Fee 1987: 791–93 (though Fee and Garland disagree on other features of the text's meaning). Lincoln (1981: 46) argues that here Paul refers not to the incarnation or Christ's future coming but rather to his resurrection, while Garland (2003: 736–37) argues for a reference to the parousia.

6. Lincoln 1990: 143.

7. Lincoln (1990: 257) comments, "Both the mature person and the fullness of Christ are primarily terms for the Church, yet neither can be totally separated from Christ, since for this writer the Church is always seen as incorporated in him." Best (1998: 402) sees the reference as being to "the corporate Christ . . . who is the church." Hoehner (2002: 555–56) likewise argues that the reference is to the church.

8. Hoehner (2002: 610) thinks that in Eph. 4:24 the emphasis is on the individual. O'Brien (1999: 331) sees both individual and corporate significance. Best (1998: 440) maintains that the reference cannot be to Christ directly, since it says that the new person is created. However, it seems that Best goes too far in denying that the old person refers to the old Adam, for the new creation in Ephesians is in Christ (cf. Eph. 2:10).

humanity in Christ") and are being renewed in God's image (Col. 3:10).[9]
Paul, then, reflects on Christ as the corporate head of his people. In Christ
we find Jews and Greeks, the circumcised and uncircumcised, barbarians, slaves, and even lowly Scythians. What is decisive, though, is that
"Christ is all" (Col. 3:11), words that nicely sum up the christocentric
thrust of Paul's theology.

In the bread and cup of communion, believers remember Christ's
death and they participate in Christ (1 Cor. 10:15–17; 11:23–26). The
rock that sustained Israel during its OT wanderings represents Christ
(1 Cor. 10:4).[10] All of God's promises find their affirming "yes" in Christ
(2 Cor. 1:20), and he is the only and effective mediator between God
and human beings (1 Tim. 2:5), so that he fulfills his intention to save
sinners (1 Tim. 1:15).

Paul's ethics can be described as "putting on Christ," as becoming
like Christ. He exhorts his converts to imitate him, but only insofar as
he imitates Christ (1 Cor. 11:1). Before Paul's conversion, the paradigm
and rule for his life was the Torah. Christians, however, are no longer
under the Mosaic covenant, and their rule for life is "the law of Christ"
(1 Cor. 9:21; Gal. 6:2). This means that the Torah must be interpreted
in light of the Christ event. The ultimate authority for believers is not
the law but Christ himself. He embodies the kind of life that pleases
God (Rom. 15:3).[11] The central exhortation in the letter to the Philippians appears in Phil. 1:27: "Only let your manner of life be worthy of
the gospel of Christ."[12] They are to walk worthy of the Lord (Col. 1:10).
Paul can also say that believers should live in a way that is worthy of
God (1 Thess. 2:12). It seems that living in a manner worthy of Jesus
is equivalent to living in a way that pleases God, suggesting that Jesus
shares divine status.

What believers need to know are the "ways in Christ" (1 Cor. 4:17).[13]
The new life of believers is summed up as "you learned Christ" (Eph.
4:20). The new life of believers is not primarily rules but rather a person. The meekness and gentleness of Christ are paradigmatic for Paul
(2 Cor. 10:1). Christ's love is especially manifested in his self-giving in
the cross, and believers are called to give of themselves similarly (2 Cor.
8:8–11; Eph. 5:2). In particular, husbands are to model the sacrificial
love of Christ in their relationship with their wives (Eph. 5:25), so that

9. So O'Brien 1982: 190. Contra Lohse (1971: 141–42), who understands the participles
"put off" and "put on" here as imperatives.
10. See Garland 2003: 456–58.
11. On Christ as embodying the life of believers, see Hays 1987.
12. O'Brien (1991: 145–46) argues that Phil. 1:27 is the central exhortation in Phil.
1:27–2:18. So also Fee 1995: 159–61.
13. See Thiselton 2000: 374.

they are to nourish and cherish their wives "as Christ does the church" (Eph. 5:29). Believers are exhorted to submit to one another because of reverence for Christ (Eph. 5:21). Paul does not ask wives to submit abstractly to husbands, but rather to submit "as to the Lord" (Eph. 5:22), just as the church "submits to Christ" (Eph. 5:24).

Obedience and sin, then, are intensely personal. Those who transgress sin against Christ (1 Cor. 8:12), and so believers must "take every thought captive to obey Christ" (2 Cor. 10:5).[14] We can compare this with Rom. 1:18–25, where the root sin is the failure to glorify and honor and thank God. Christ's exalted status is evident, for just as people sin against God, they also sin against Christ. Paul can even look back on Israel's sin in the wilderness and say that they tempted Christ (1 Cor. 10:9).[15] The heart and soul of sinning is personal, consisting in a failure to love the Lord (1 Cor. 16:22). Everything that one does should be carried out "in the name of the Lord Jesus," but doing such does not exclude or marginalize God, for at the same time one gives "thanks to God the Father through him" (Col. 3:17; cf. 1 Tim. 1:12).

As we noted above, believers are called to be clothed with Christ, to put him on. The fundamental reality for believers is that they are new persons now because they are joined with Christ. Believers have died with Christ in baptism (Rom. 6:3–5, 8; 7:4). They have been crucified with Christ, and the old "I" no longer lives; now Christ lives in them (Gal. 2:20). Through Christ's cross the power of the world over believers has been crucified, so that now they boast only in Christ's cross (Gal. 6:14). God has granted life to his own and raised them together with Christ (Eph. 2:5–6; Col. 3:1–3). The true life of believers is "hidden with Christ in God" (Col. 3:3). Christ is now "your life" (Col. 3:4). Baptism bears such significance because those who are "baptized into Christ have put on Christ" (Gal. 3:27). Thinking that baptism aligns one with Paul or Apollos or Peter is to veer badly off course (1 Cor. 1:12–16). Baptism matters because it is baptism into Christ.

Since believers are baptized into Christ, they are his members, his limbs, so to speak (1 Cor. 6:15). They are joined to the Lord by virtue of their conversion (1 Cor. 6:17). The physical bodies of believers are not their own (1 Cor. 6:19). The body is for the Lord (1 Cor. 6:13) and is to be used to glorify God (1 Cor. 6:20). Since Jesus Christ is Lord (more on this below), believers are to be his slaves. Slavery to Christ brings freedom to love, not bondage to sin (1 Cor. 7:22; cf. Gal. 5:13). Paul considered himself a slave of Christ (Gal. 1:10; Titus 1:1; cf. 1 Cor. 4:1).[16] Those who

14. For a detailed discussion on the meaning of the phrase, see Harris 2005: 682–84.
15. "Christ" rather than "Lord" is the better textual reading. See Thiselton 2000: 740.
16. On slavery to Christ, see Harris 1999.

live as slaves should function as an example for all believers, for they are called to serve Christ (Eph. 6:5–7; Col. 3:23–24). Timothy stands out as a believer because, unlike so many others, he seeks out not his own interests but "those of Jesus Christ," and hence he "worries" about how others are doing in their Christian life (Phil. 2:20–21). Similarly, Epaphroditus deserves honor because he endangered his life for the sake of Christ's work (Phil. 2:30). Timothy and Epaphroditus stand out, then, as Christ-centered believers.

The preeminence of Christ impresses itself upon us in a variety of ways. The church is the body of Christ (1 Cor. 12:12, 27). The gifts given to believers stem from Christ (Eph. 4:11). New life comes when Christ shines on those who reside in darkness (Eph. 5:14). Those who are separated from Christ do not belong to God and live outside the realm of God's covenantal promises (Eph. 2:12). Christ shares divine status with God, for the kingdom belongs both to God and Christ (Eph. 5:5). The coming of Christ is no mere afterthought, for God's purpose is to sum up all of redemptive history in Christ (Eph. 1:9–10), so that the fullness of his plan is manifested only in him. Indeed, Jesus is the singular offspring of Abraham (Gal. 3:16),[17] and all those who belong to Christ are members of Abraham's family (Gal. 3:29).

The church will ultimately enjoy "the fullness of Christ" (Eph. 4:13).[18] Again this expression suggests Christ's divine status, for earlier Paul refers to being "filled with all the fullness of God" (Eph. 3:19). Even in that text the fullness of God belongs to those who "know the love of Christ," a love that exceeds the capacity of human beings to plumb. The goal of Paul's life is to live so that Christ will be honored (Phil. 1:20), or as Paul puts it another way, "For to me to live is Christ, and to die is gain" (Phil. 1:21). No formal christological statement is given here, but a Jewish monotheist such as Paul can express such sentiments only because he believes that Christ is divine. Nor can the passion of his devotion to Christ be captured in abstract theological statements. His greatest desire "is to depart and be with Christ" (Phil. 1:23), and his hope is that the Philippian church will "glory in Christ Jesus" (Phil. 1:26). Those who

17. Ellis (1957: 70–73) maintains that Paul argues that Christ is the one seed of Abraham in terms of corporate solidarity (cf. Longenecker 1990: 131–32; see also the helpful discussion in Dunn 1993: 183–84). Wright (1992a: 163) suggests that the one seed is deduced from the "singularity of one *family* contrasted with the plurality of families which would result if the Torah were to be regarded the way Paul's opponents apparently regard it." J. C. Collins (2003) argues that Paul properly interpreted the sense of Gen. 22:18, which refers to one seed, namely, the Messiah. Martyn (1997: 340) claims that Paul argues for the singular from Gen. 17:8. Schoeps (1961: 234) essentially argues that what Paul does here is indefensible exegetically.

18. Hoehner (2002: 557) takes "of Christ" to be a possessive genitive here.

boast in Christ do not put their confidence in human capacities and potential (Phil. 3:3).

A changed life bearing the fruit of righteousness "comes through Jesus Christ," and yet the power of Christ displayed in believers does not compromise God's glory but rather enhances it, since the result is "to the glory and praise of God" (Phil. 1:11). An almost palpable passion for Christ suffuses Paul's writing. He looks back on his past advantages without regret "for the sake of Christ" (Phil. 3:7). He is ready to sacrifice everything else in life and even considers it all to be garbage or dung "because of the surpassing worth of knowing Christ Jesus my Lord" (Phil. 3:8) and the joy of gaining Christ. Nor does suffering diminish his desire, for suffering is the pathway to the final resurrection, where he will know Christ more intimately (Phil. 3:10–11). Those who demand circumcision to attain salvation renounce Christ, so that he no longer profits them at all (Gal. 1:6–7; 5:2). Those attempting to be justified through the law by means of circumcision have been cut off from Christ (Gal. 5:4).

The deviant philosophy in Colossae offered an alternative pathway to knowledge and wisdom. Paul identifies God's mystery as Christ himself (Col. 2:2; cf. 4:3).[19] The OT food laws are merely shadows that point to something, yes someone, greater (Col. 2:17). Everything one needs to know is in him, for "all the treasures of wisdom and knowledge" are in him (Col. 2:3). The problem with the deviant philosophy is that it is not in accord with Christ (Col. 2:8). All of God's fullness resides bodily in Christ (Col. 2:9; cf. 1:19), and so the Colossians will experience fullness only in him (Col. 2:10).

I argued earlier that God's ultimate purpose is that he be glorified in all things. Paul prays that the Thessalonian Christians would live worthily of the Lord and that their aspirations for godly lives would become a concrete reality (2 Thess. 1:11). The purpose for the petition is given in 2 Thess. 1:12: "so that the name of our Lord Jesus may be glorified in you." Apparently, in Paul's theology Jesus Christ is to be glorified just as the Father is glorified, revealing an astoundingly high Christology. The same truth is communicated in the description of Jesus' second coming. When he appears, he will be "glorified in his saints" and "be marveled at among all who have believed" (2 Thess. 1:10). Paul does not emphasize the subjective feelings of joy or the external blessings that will be the portion of believers when Jesus returns; rather, he fixes attention on Jesus Christ himself, who will be seen in all his beauty and glory so that believers will stand in awe.

19. In support of the mystery being identified as Christ himself, see O'Brien 1982: 94–95; Pokorný 1991: 107; Dunn 1996b: 131.

Christ occupies a central position in Paul's thought. He speaks of "the peace of Christ" (Col. 3:15), "the word of Christ" (Col. 3:16), Christ's patience (1 Tim. 1:16), his truth (Eph. 4:21), his power (2 Cor. 12:9), the affection of Christ (Phil. 1:8), and the "love of Christ" that "controls us" (2 Cor. 5:14). People come to salvation by putting their faith and trust in Jesus Christ (Rom. 3:22, 26; 4:24; 10:9; Gal. 2:16, 20; 3:22; Eph. 1:15; Phil. 3:9; Col. 1:4; 2:5; 2 Tim. 3:15; Philem. 5).[20] Paul is an apostle of Christ Jesus (e.g., 1 Cor. 1:1), and Epaphras is "a servant of Christ Jesus" (Col. 4:12). Paul locates the origin of his apostleship in the command of God and Christ (1 Tim. 1:1), which suggests that God and Christ are equal in stature (cf. Gal. 1:1). Paul gives commands in Christ's name (2 Thess. 3:6; cf. 1 Cor. 1:10), and Christ's command about financial support for those working in ministry is authoritative (1 Cor. 9:14).

Paul seems to equate God and Christ when he enjoins Timothy to be faithful "in the presence of God . . . and of Christ Jesus" (1 Tim. 6:13; cf. 1 Thess. 4:2).[21] When he exhorts Timothy to proclaim the gospel, he charges him "in the presence of God and of Christ Jesus" (2 Tim. 4:1). These latter two statements do not necessarily imply Christ's deity, since Paul can also give commands to Timothy "in the presence of God and of Christ Jesus and of the elect angels" (1 Tim. 5:21), though the higher status of Christ is suggested by his role in the future judgment (2 Tim. 4:1). Indeed, those who deny Christ will be denied by Christ before God on the last day (2 Tim. 2:12). The centrality of Christ is clear from five truths in the Pastoral Epistles as outlined by Lau: (1) Jesus is the end-time judge and Lord (2 Tim. 4:8); (2) Jesus and God are united in various functions (1 Tim. 1:1–2; 5:21; 6:13; 2 Tim. 1:1; 4:1; Titus 1:1, 4; 2:13); (3) the verb "save" (*sōzō*) is used of both God and Jesus (1 Tim. 1:15; 2 Tim. 1:9; 4:18); (4) thanksgiving is offered to both God and Christ (2 Tim. 1:3; 1 Tim. 1:12), and spiritual blessings come from both (1 Tim. 1:14; 2 Tim. 1:6, 18); and (5) the writer serves both God and Jesus (2 Tim. 1:3; 2:3, 15, 24; Titus 1:7).[22]

We can say that Christ is foundational for everything in Paul's thought. Christ Jesus is the foundation of the church (1 Cor. 3:11), or another way of putting the same truth is to say that he is the cornerstone (Eph. 2:20).[23] The church is based on Christ and grows

20. Many scholars maintain that many of these texts speak of the "faithfulness of Christ" rather than "faith in Christ." See chapter 15, note 74.

21. See Marshall 1999: 662 ("the pair of heavenly witnesses"); Knight 1992: 265.

22. Lau 1996: 266–67. For a survey of scholarship on the Christology of the Pastoral Epistles, see Stettler 1998: 3–22.

23. In defense of "top stone," see Lincoln 1990: 154–56. But the arguments are decisive for "cornerstone" (see O'Brien 1999: 216–18; Hoehner 2002: 404–7).

because of him (Eph. 2:21–22). Any good accomplished through Paul's ministry is by virtue of the work of Christ through him (Rom. 15:18). His boldness toward God emanates from Christ (2 Cor. 3:4; cf. 2:17). His ministry is effective because he wafts abroad the aroma of Christ (2 Cor. 2:15), even in the midst of his sufferings—or perhaps especially *because* of his sufferings. When Paul suffers, he carries about "the death of Jesus" and is "being given over to death for Jesus' sake" (2 Cor. 4:10–11), but the result is that Jesus' life shines through the suffering and mortal body of Paul. The veil of ignorance that obscures the truth of the gospel is removed only in Christ (2 Cor. 3:14). Paul's goal for believers is that Christ be formed in them (Gal. 4:19), so that they reach maturity. His aim is to present the church "as a pure virgin to Christ" (2 Cor. 11:2; cf. Eph. 5:27), since believers are to be devoted solely and entirely to Christ (2 Cor. 11:3). Maturity is obtained by beholding the glory of the Lord (2 Cor. 3:18), so that as believers gaze upon the beauty of Christ, they become more and more like him. God's glory, as Paul remarks a few verses later, is revealed "in the face of Jesus Christ" (2 Cor. 4:6). The new life of believers is portrayed as "Christ's letter," which can be read and verified by all (2 Cor. 3:3). Those who belong to Christ are masters of all and servants of none, for in Christ they have all things (1 Cor. 3:21–23). Even death and future terrors have become servants of sanctification and Christlikeness now (cf. Rom. 8:32, 37–39).

In Christ

One of the most significant elements of Paul's Christology is his teaching about being "in Christ."[24] Union with Christ or participation with Christ is surely one of the fundamental themes of his theology.[25] Believers who were in the old Adam and the old age are now members of the new age inaugurated in Christ, and they are in Christ rather than in Adam.[26] The phrase "in Christ" is used in a variety of ways and does not invari-

24. For a useful study of the "in Christ" formula in Paul, see Seifrid, *DPL* 433–36; Moule 1977: 54–63.

25. Schweitzer (1931: 219–26) argued that the mystical joining of believers in Christ was central to Pauline theology. E. Sanders (1977: 502–8), in dependence upon Schweitzer, focuses on participation in Christ. Both scholars, however, wrongly demote the importance of justification in Paul.

26. Rogerson (1970) and Porter (1990) raise objections to the way corporate personality typically is employed in NT scholarship. They rightly caution scholars against using the concept too simplistically. Still, it seems that the notion of representative headship cannot be excised from Paul. See Moule 1977: 47–96.

ably denote union with Christ, though in many instances it does focus on participation in Christ.[27]

Sometimes "in Christ" appears to be equivalent to "Christian," as in the case of Andronicus and Junia, who, Paul says, "were in Christ before me" (Rom. 16:7; cf. 16:9, 11). To say, "I know a man in Christ" (2 Cor. 12:2), where Paul speaks of himself, is to say that he is a Christian. Timothy is a "faithful child in the Lord"; that is, he is a Christian (1 Cor. 4:17; cf. Phil. 1:1; 4:21; Col. 1:2; 4:7; Philem. 23). This same notion seems to be reflected in 1 Cor. 7:39, where believers are enjoined to marry "only in the Lord." Presumably, Paul means that a believer should not marry a nonbeliever.

In other contexts the Lord seems to function as the object, as when believers are encouraged to boast in the Lord (1 Cor. 1:31; 2 Cor. 10:17; Phil. 1:26; 3:3) or are described as having confidence in the Lord (Phil. 1:14; cf. 1 Cor. 15:19; Philem. 8), trusting in Christ (Col. 1:4; 2 Tim. 3:15), or rejoicing in the Lord (Phil. 3:1; 4:4). In some of these texts there may still be the notion of one's union with Christ, so that one boasts, for example, because of one's union with Christ.

In some instances the relation specified seems to be vague (see Eph. 4:21; Phil. 4:19; 1 Thess. 5:18), as when Paul speaks of hoping and trusting in the Lord to send fellow workers (Phil. 2:19, 24; cf. Rom. 15:17; 2 Thess. 3:4), emphasizes that he speaks the truth "in Christ" (Rom. 9:1), or expresses the desire that his heart be refreshed "in Christ" (Philem. 20). In 2 Cor. 3:14 the veil is removed "in Christ" (my translation), which the ESV gives an instrumental meaning by translating the Greek as "through Christ." The Corinthians are Paul's work and the seal of his apostolic ministry "in the Lord" (1 Cor. 9:1–2). The leaders in the church "are over you in the Lord" (1 Thess. 5:12; cf. 1 Cor. 4:15). Both men and women are interdependent "in the Lord" (1 Cor. 11:11). A Christian's labor "in the Lord" is not vain (1 Cor. 15:58). Believers should be "strong in the Lord" (Eph. 6:10), receive commended emissaries "in the Lord" (Phil. 2:29; cf. Rom. 16:2), "rejoice in the Lord" (Phil. 3:1; 4:4; cf. 4:10), "stand in the Lord" (Phil. 4:1; cf. 1 Thess. 3:8), be at harmony "in the Lord" (Phil. 4:2), and obey their parents "in the Lord" (Eph. 6:1; cf. Col. 3:20).

The expression is also used instrumentally, as when Paul speaks of his belief "in the Lord" that all foods are clean (Rom. 14:14) or of someone being called "in the Lord" (1 Cor. 7:22; cf. Phil. 3:14). Believers have access to God through Christ by his blood (Eph. 2:13); so also "God in Christ forgave you" (Eph. 4:32; cf. 3:12)—that is, by means of Christ.

---

27. See the understanding of "in Christ" and mysticism in Deissmann 1927: 135–57. See also Bousset 1970: 154–63. The realistic conception of "in Christ" is not accepted by most scholars today.

God created all things by means of Christ (Col. 1:16), and the universe coheres "in him"—that is, through him (Col. 1:17). All of God's promises find their fulfillment in Christ—that is, through him (2 Cor. 1:20). The open door for mission "in the Lord" could be construed as instrumental (2 Cor. 2:12). The controversial text 2 Cor. 5:19 probably should be understood to say that "in Christ God was reconciling the world to himself."[28] God is glorified "in the church and in Christ Jesus" (Eph. 3:21), which is probably best translated instrumentally as "through the church and through Christ Jesus."

When Paul speaks of his persuasion in the Lord, the meaning could be both instrumental and also denote his union with Christ (Gal. 5:10). The same uncertainty applies to falling asleep "in Christ" (1 Cor. 15:18), for the expression could denote union with him or simply mean being a Christian. The precise meaning of the phrase is often ambiguous.[29] "You are light in the Lord" (Eph. 5:8; cf. 2 Tim. 1:1) could be instrumental but also could designate union with Christ. Colossians 3:18 is an interesting example. Wives should submit because it is "fitting in the Lord." The admonition makes sense if we understand Paul to say "fitting" as Christians or "fitting" because of one's union with Christ, or perhaps even both. The "dead in Christ" (1 Thess. 4:16) could be translated as "Christians," or perhaps it also includes the idea of union with Christ. The redemption that belongs to believers "in Christ" may be both instrumental and locative (Rom. 3:24; cf. 6:23; 1 Cor. 1:5; Eph. 3:6; Col. 1:14; 2 Tim. 2:10). Similarly, seeking "to be justified in Christ" (Gal. 2:17) could be instrumental, locative, or both.

Paul often, however, uses the "in Christ" formula in a locative sense. The fullness of deity dwells "in" Christ (Col. 1:19; 2:9). All "wisdom and knowledge" are found "in him" (Col. 2:3). The locative often designates union with Christ. As we noted earlier, people are either "in Adam" or "in Christ" (1 Cor. 1:30). If they are "in Christ," they are united with him in his death and resurrection (Rom. 6:3–5, 11; Eph. 2:5–6; Col. 2:12, 20; 3:1), so that union with Christ occurs in baptism. Christ is "all and in all" (Col. 3:11). Believers are "one body in Christ" (Rom. 12:5). The assemblies of believers in Judea are called "the churches of Judea that are in Christ" (Gal. 1:22; cf. 1 Thess. 2:14).

Because believers are in Christ, they are a new creation (2 Cor. 5:17; cf. Eph. 2:10) and "sons of God" (Gal. 3:26), and they enjoy the blessing of Abraham (Gal. 3:14). In other words, being in Christ is an eschatological reality, signifying that God's covenantal promises are theirs. Because of

28. See Harris 2005: 440–43.
29. In Phil. 1:13 "in Christ" appears to mean "for the sake of Christ," as Paul refers to his imprisonment "for Christ" (ESV).

believers' union with Christ, there is "no condemnation" (Rom. 8:1), and they are sanctified (1 Cor. 1:2). By virtue of union with Christ believers enjoy the righteousness of God (2 Cor. 5:21; cf. Phil. 3:9). They have been freed from the power of sin and death because they are united with Christ (Rom. 8:2; Gal. 2:4). Every gift is now theirs because of their participation in Christ (1 Cor. 1:4), so that believers are complete in Christ (Col. 2:10).[30] Believers are one in Christ (Gal. 3:28; cf. Eph. 2:14–16), so that neither circumcision nor uncircumcision is significant (Gal. 5:6).

Union with Christ dominates the epistle to the Ephesians.[31] Believers enjoy "every spiritual blessing" in Christ (Eph. 1:3). They are chosen "in him" and adopted "through him" (Eph. 1:4–5). Redemption is accomplished in him, as is the revelation of the mystery of his will, so that God's purpose is "to unite all things in him" (Eph. 1:7–10). Believers enjoy an inheritance in him (Eph. 1:11) and also were sealed with the Spirit in him (Eph. 1:13). In him there is one new person (Eph. 2:15). The church is God's holy temple in Christ (Eph. 2:21), and in union with him is a "dwelling place for God by the Spirit" (Eph. 2:22).

Many exhortations are also given because believers are in Christ (Eph. 4:1, 17; Col. 2:6–7; 1 Thess. 4:1; 2 Thess. 3:12). Basing commands in the union that believers have with Christ indicates that their obedience comes not from self-effort but rather is God's supernatural work. The call to unity in Philippians is grounded in the encouragement, comfort of love, participation of the Spirit, and affection that belongs to believers in Christ (Phil. 2:1–2).

The notion of union with Christ points to a high Christology, for every spiritual blessing belongs to believers because of their participation in Christ. The astonishing wonder of the blessings (new creation, redemption, election, and righteousness) suggests that Jesus Christ shares the same status with God. Otherwise, it is difficult to explain how salvation and all its attendant blessings could be secured through union with Christ. We also note again that Christology serves soteriology. Paul's theology of union with Christ reveals a remarkably high Christology, but the greatness of Christ demonstrates the richness and fullness of the salvation that believers enjoy. We should also note that union with Christ points to the fulfillment of God's eschatological promises. Those who are in Christ are no longer in the old Adam but are in the new; they are part of the new creation. In conclusion, "in Christ" fits with the centrality of Christ and the fulfillment of God's end-time promises.

30. In 2 Tim. 1:9 the gifts given to believers "in Christ" may be theirs both instrumentally and locally.

31. Many of the following texts may be instrumental as well. Lincoln (1981: 142) argues that the phrase is mainly instrumental but that an incorporative idea is present as well.

Christology of Prayer Wishes

Paul's high Christology manifests itself in his prayer wishes in the greetings of his letters.[32] He prays that believers will experience grace and peace from God the Father and the Lord Jesus Christ.[33] In 1–2 Timothy Paul adds mercy to grace and peace (1 Tim. 1:2; 2 Tim. 1:2).[34] Paul often concludes his letters with the prayer that the grace of the Lord Jesus Christ will abide with his people.[35] We have a more extended formula in Eph. 6:23–24: "Peace be to the brothers, and love with faith, from God the Father and the Lord Jesus Christ. Grace be with all who love our Lord Jesus Christ with love incorruptible." Since these prayer wishes are a commonplace, their significance may be easily overlooked. In every instance Jesus Christ shares divine status with God the Father. Paul never prays that grace might come from himself as an apostle or from an angel or any other exalted personage. Grace, mercy, or peace come only from God himself (cf. Rom. 15:30; Gal. 1:6; 2 Thess. 1:12; 1 Tim. 1:14; 2 Tim. 2:1). By putting Jesus on the same level with God the Father, Paul reveals his high Christology. This fits with other texts where God is thanked through Jesus Christ (Rom. 1:8; 7:25), peace with God is obtained through Christ (Rom. 5:1), believers rejoice in God through Christ (Rom. 5:11), grace reigns through Jesus Christ (Rom. 5:21), and God grants victory through the Lord Jesus Christ (1 Cor. 15:57). The Father is glorified in and through Jesus Christ.

Jesus as Messiah

Paul does not often speak of Jesus as David's descendant (Rom. 1:3; 15:12; 2 Tim. 2:8).[36] Some have inferred from this that the Davidic descent of Jesus was unimportant in Pauline theology. A different conclusion is preferable. In the synagogue address in Acts 13 Paul highlights that Jesus is David's offspring (Acts 13:22–23, 34–37). It seems probable that Jesus'

32. So Kammler 2003: 175. For a careful and illuminating study of the introductions to Paul's letters, see O'Brien 1977. For the closings of Paul's letters, see Weima 1994.

33. Rom. 1:7; 1 Cor. 1:3; 2 Cor. 1:2; Gal. 1:3; Eph. 1:3; Phil. 1:2; Col. 1:2; 2 Thess. 1:2; Titus 1:4; Philem. 3.

34. Allan (1963) argues that the formula in the Pastoral Epistles differs remarkably from the authentic Pauline letters, but see the response in Stettler 1998: 287–94.

35. Rom. 16:20; 1 Cor. 16:23; Gal. 6:18; Phil. 4:23; 1 Thess. 5:28; 2 Thess. 3:18; Philem. 25.

36. Lau (1996: 133–35) argues persuasively that Jesus' messianic status is not diminished by Paul, but Paul anchors the Christ event in salvation history. Nor is there an adoptionistic Christology relative to Jesus' Davidic origin (rightly Lau 1996: 136–37; Stettler 1998: 173–74).

Davidic lineage was proclaimed when Paul established the churches during his missionary preaching.[37] The messianic line of Jesus is not addressed often in the Pauline letters because they are occasional in nature, and apparently the Davidic pedigree of Jesus remained uncontroversial. Interestingly, Paul does emphasize in Romans that Jesus descends from David (Rom. 1:3; 15:12), and here Paul addresses a church that he did not establish. Furthermore, in the introduction to the letter he summarizes the common gospel confessed both by himself and the Romans (Rom. 1:1–4), suggesting that the omission of the theme elsewhere does not betray a lack of interest in Jesus' Davidic descent, which confirms that he emphasized Jesus' Davidic status when planting churches.

When Paul identifies Jesus as the Christ, presumably he assumes Jesus' Davidic background.[38] He often refers to "Jesus Christ" (eighty times) or "Christ Jesus" (eighty-nine times). It is frequently said that the term "Christ" in Paul has lost its titular sense, so that it has become a formulaic name. Such a conclusion seems unlikely, given Paul's Jewish background.[39] The title appears regularly because Jesus' messianic status was a given for Paul. He need not argue for it, since the title did not engender controversy in his churches. Perhaps "Jesus Christ" suggests that the human Jesus is the Christ, whereas "Christ Jesus" suggests that the Christ is the human Jesus, or perhaps the difference is merely stylistic. What seems highly unlikely is that a Jewish person such as Paul would use the term "Christ" without any titular associations. Though in some circles such a view has become popular orthodoxy, we should rather say that the notion that Jesus is the Messiah is a settled and uncontroversial conviction of Paul's theology.

Jesus as a Human Being

The humanity of Jesus is clear from the Synoptic Gospels, which tell of Jesus' birth and death as a human being. Some have questioned whether John's Gospel has a docetic Christology, but we saw briefly that such a view lacks credibility, and significant evidence stands against the concept.[40] The issue of Jesus' humanity is important in Paul, particularly because he wrote from a postresurrection perspective. Paul stands within the Synoptic and Johannine tradition regarding Jesus'

37. In support of the view argued here, see Hengel 1983: 73–74.

38. Hengel (1983: 65–77) sketches in the historical and theological significance of Christ in Paul.

39. Wright (1992a: 41–55) argues effectively, contrary to received opinion, that the term "Christ" in Paul has not lost its titular force. See also Hurtado 2003: 98–101.

40. See chapter 7, note 105.

humanity, for since Jesus is the Messiah descended from David, clearly he is a human being. Paul reminds the Jews that one of their greatest privileges is that Jesus was born into the world as a Jew—he is a Jewish Messiah (Rom. 9:5). Hence, because he was truly human, people may estimate him from a fleshly point of view (2 Cor. 5:16). That Jesus was human is evident also because Paul views him as the second Adam (Rom. 5:12–19). The hymn in Phil. 2 makes this clear as well. Jesus humbled himself by truly becoming a human being (Phil. 2:7). And his humanity was no charade, for he died a shameful death on a cross (Phil. 2:8). Paul's frequent references to the death of Christ plainly indicate that Jesus was genuinely human. He was the seed of Abraham (Gal. 3:16). The "one mediator" between God and humans was "the man Christ Jesus" (1 Tim. 2:5).[41] He "became poor" by taking humanity on himself (2 Cor. 8:9).[42] He was genuinely "born of woman" (Gal. 4:4). He came "in the likeness of sinful flesh" (Rom. 8:3), which means that he came into the world with a mortal body exposed to all the diseases and weaknesses shared by all human beings. Paul hammers home the physicality of Jesus' body in Col. 1:22 by using the redundant expression "his body of flesh." Jesus' death is described in the same terms in the next chapter (Col. 2:11; cf. Eph. 2:14). Paul's exalted Christology perhaps might mislead us into thinking that he denied the humanity of Jesus. However, he clearly upholds what we have seen in the Synoptic Gospels and Acts. Jesus was genuinely human. He was born into the world, had a normal human body, and suffered and died.

Jesus as Savior

The use of the term "savior" (*sōtēr*) also suggests Jesus' equality with God.[43] Lau says that "it unequivocally declares the unity of God and of Christ (the Saviour) in the enactment of the saving plan."[44] The word "Savior" appears especially often in the Pastoral Epistles, referring to God the Father on six occasions (1 Tim. 1:1; 2:3; 4:10; Titus 1:3; 2:10;

41. Jesus' humanity is emphasized here (so Knight 1992: 121). See also Marshall (1999: 430–31), who rejects other, more speculative proposals regarding the meaning.
42. Contra Dunn (1996a: 121–22), who focuses on the fellowship with God that Jesus enjoyed during his ministry that was surrendered at the cross. See the insightful discussion in Harris 2005: 579–80.
43. For the meaning of "savior" in Hellenistic, Jewish, Christian, and post-Christian literature, see Fohrer and Foerster, *TDNT* 7:1004–24. For the Jewish and Hellenistic background, in particular, see Cullmann (1963: 239–41), who argues that the OT was the primary influence on the NT.
44. Lau 1996: 122.

3:4),[45] perhaps in response to the imperial cult,[46] or its frequency in the Pastorals perhaps is explained by the false teaching of the opponents referred to there.[47] In any case, it is quite striking that the title "Savior" is applied to Christ on four occasions in the Pastorals (2 Tim. 1:10; Titus 1:4; 2:13; 3:6) and also in Philippians (Phil. 3:20) and Ephesians (Eph. 5:23).[48] The usage in Titus is especially interesting because on three different occasions Paul alternates between "God our Savior" (Titus 1:3; 2:10; 3:4) and Jesus Christ as Savior (Titus 1:4; 2:13; 3:6). We should note that in every instance almost immediately after God is identified as Savior, Christ is also said to be Savior. God and Christ have rescued believers from the peril of sin. The close equivalency between God and Christ suggests that Jesus shares the same status with God. The use of the title "Savior" emphasizes that Jesus delivered his people from sin.

Jesus as Son of God

The term "Son of God" (or simply "Son") also designates Jesus as the unique Son of the Father.[49] Paul does not use this term often—only seventeen times in all thirteen letters.[50] The gospel centers on God's Son (Rom. 1:3), and at the resurrection Jesus Christ was "appointed Son of God in power" (Rom. 1:4). The text is wrongly rendered "declared" instead of "appointed" by some versions (e.g., NASB, ESV). The verb *horizō* never means "declare," and it is likely that versions opt for this term out of concern that "appoint" suggests that Jesus was not the Son of God formerly and hence falls prey to adoptionistic Christology. But the text makes a distinction between God's Son and Jesus' appointment as Son of God "in power." God's Son preexisted before Jesus' ministry on earth, in accord with Rom. 1:3. His appointment as "Son of God in power" (Rom. 1:4 my translation) occurred at the resurrection, when he was exalted and now reigns at God's right hand as king.[51] This appoint-

45. See Fitzmyer 2002: 188–91; see also Marshall 1999: 131–32, and the survey by Dibelius and Conzelmann (1972: 100–103), who maintain that the derivation of the title cannot be specifically isolated.

46. See Baugh 1992: 335; W. Mounce 2000: cxxxiv (as a possibility).

47. Another possibility suggested by W. Mounce 2000: cxxxiv.

48. In Philippians the term may also be used over against the imperial cult (O'Brien 1991: 462n120; Fee 1995: 381).

49. Some scholars have argued that the term was borrowed from Hellenism (Bousset 1970: 91–98; 206–10; Schoeps 1961: 150–60). It has been demonstrated, however, that such a view lacks compelling evidence, and that the term derives from Jewish circles (Hengel 1976: 21–56; Hurtado 2003: 102–8).

50. This includes the use of simply "Son" and the fuller phrase "Son of God."

51. In support of preexistence, see Hengel 1976: 60, 66–76; Schreiner 1998: 38.

ment as God's Son in power expresses the same idea found in Acts 2:36, where God exalted Jesus as Lord and Christ at the resurrection.

Romans 1:9 picks up from Rom. 1:3 in speaking of "the gospel of his Son."[52] It is "the Son of God" whom Paul proclaims in his ministry of the gospel (2 Cor. 1:19). God revealed "his Son" to Paul on the road to Damascus (Gal. 1:16). God's reconciling work occurred "by the death of his Son" (Rom. 5:10). The death of Jesus for sinners took place at the initiative of God himself. He "sent" his Son as an atonement for sin and to free people from the bondage of sin (Rom. 8:3; Gal. 4:4).[53] He "did not spare his own Son but gave him up for us all" (Rom. 8:32). Those who believe put their faith and trust "in the Son of God, who loved me and gave himself for me" (Gal. 2:20). As a result of Christ's work on the cross, God "sent the Spirit of his Son" into the lives of his children (Gal. 4:6), so that they would "be conformed to the image of his Son" (Rom. 8:29). Those who have the Spirit have been "called into the fellowship of his Son" (1 Cor. 1:9). Even now they have been inducted into "the kingdom of his beloved Son" (Col. 1:13). Their aspiration and goal as believers is "knowledge of the Son of God" (Eph. 4:13), and they "wait for his Son from heaven" (1 Thess. 1:10), who will provide deliverance from God's final wrath.

We note from the foregoing texts that "Son" is often used to designate the atoning and saving work of Jesus. We see again that Christology is inextricably tied to soteriology. In addition, the word "Son" is used often where personal relations are in view, so that Paul speaks of fellowship with the Son, knowledge of the Son, and God's love in sending the Son to die. The term "Son" seems to emphasize that the relationship between Jesus and his people is one of love and fellowship and cannot be understood merely as a contractual relationship.

We saw in the Gospels that the term "Son of God" could be equivalent to "Messiah."[54] Perhaps such a notion can be detected in Jesus' appointment as Son of God in power in Rom. 1:4. Even in the Gospels, however, Jesus' sonship focuses on his unique and special relationship with God. Paul almost certainly uses the title "Son of God" to designate Jesus' unique relation to God. Indeed, we lack any clear indication that he thinks of Jesus as the Messiah or Son of David in the formula, especially since in Rom. 1:3–4 he contrasts Jesus as a descendant of David with his status as Son of God. It is also likely, given the exalted nature

52. Hengel (1976: 7–8) remarks that the term "Son of God" is especially dominant in Romans and Galatians, where Paul disputes Jewish tradition, suggesting the Jewish orbit of the term.

53. In other words, "Son of God" has a soteriological cast in Paul (so Hengel 1976: 8–9).

54. In confirmation of this, see Hurtado 2003: 103.

of the title "Son of God," that the title implies Jesus' preexistence.[55] The two texts that refer to God "sending" his Son, in particular, support a reference to preexistence (Rom. 8:3; Gal. 4:4). Sending something does not, of course, necessarily suggest preexistence. If God sends wisdom or knowledge or a spirit of confusion, no one thinks that these entities preexisted. But the sending of such abstract entities is not equivalent to the sending of a person.[56] It is hard to conceive of what Paul could possibly mean by God sending the Son if the Son only came into existence when he was born. When we speak of persons being sent, their previous existence is implied.[57]

Jesus' unique relation to the Father is also implied in a few other texts. God is "the God and Father of our Lord Jesus Christ" (Rom. 15:6; 2 Cor. 1:3; 11:31; Eph. 1:3)[58] or even "the God of our Lord Jesus Christ, the Father of glory" (Eph. 1:17). Perhaps when using the designation "God" of the Father, Paul thinks particularly of Jesus as the human Messiah. But it also seems likely that he reflects on God's priority in relation to the Son, particularly since, as we noted previously, the Son is sent by the Father into the world. In support of this, God is also identified as "the Father of our Lord Jesus Christ" (Col. 1:3). Furthermore, God is Christ's head (1 Cor. 11:3), so that the Son is under his authority and rule. The Father has an authority that is greater than the Son, for the Son will "submit" to him after the kingdom is consummated, and the Son will hand the kingdom over to the Father (1 Cor. 15:24, 28).[59] Thereby the Father will be "all in all." The priority of the Father, however, does not cancel out the truth that the Son also shares divinity. The Father is the fount and origin of all things, and the Son is the agent by which all things come to pass (1 Cor. 8:6). Paul does not work out how this fits with monotheism, which he clearly affirms. The full theological and philosophical implications were left to the later church to work out.

Jesus as Lord

The lordship of Jesus is a common feature of Pauline theology (ca. 180 times) and is communicated powerfully in the hymn in Philippians

---

55. For a defense of preexistence, see Stettler 1998: 173–80, 329–30.

56. Rightly Kammler (2003: 176). Contra Dunn 1996a: 38–45; and the hesitancy of Longenecker 1990: 170; H. Betz 1979: 206; Martyn 1997: 406–8. Matera (1992: 150) thinks that preexistence is implied in Gal. 4:4.

57. Hurtado (2003: 104) argues that the term connotes not divinity but rather Jesus' special and unique relationship to God. However, he likely separates the inseparable here.

58. In 2 Cor. 11:31 Paul says only "the Lord Jesus," not "our Lord Jesus Christ."

59. See Thiselton 2000: 1238–39.

(Phil. 2:6–11).[60] The hymn can be split into two sections, the first re-counting Jesus' humiliation (Phil. 2:6–8), and the second his exaltation (Phil. 2:9–11).[61] The stature of Jesus comes to the forefront in Phil. 2:6: he "was in the form of God." The word "form" (*morphē*) does not mean that Jesus was outwardly in the form of God but lacked the inner qualities for deity.[62] The same word occurs in Phil. 2:7, where Paul says that Jesus took "the form of a servant." The text does not mean that he appeared to be a servant but in reality was not. Jesus truly became a servant, which was manifested in the taking on of humanity. Hence, to say that Jesus "was in the form of God" is another way of saying that he was divine.[63]

60. For a survey of interpretation of the hymn that includes two prefaces from 1983 and 1997 that update the original 1967 dissertation, see the programmatic work of R. Martin 1997. The usual view is that the text is a hymn. However, the hymnic nature of the passage is contested. See Fee (1992), who rightly argues that the text must be interpreted within the context of Philippians. See also the outstanding analysis in Wright 1992a: 56–98. Nothing that I say here depends upon the passage being a hymn.

61. Reitzenstein (1978) famously ascribed Paul's theology and Christology to mystery religions. Bousset (1970: 121–52) argued that Jesus was acclaimed as Lord in Hellenistic rather than Palestinian circles. Supporting Bousset's view is Bultmann 1951: 51–52; 124–26. The problem with Bousset's solution is that the term "Lord" was used of Jesus in the earliest Jewish churches (Fitzmyer 1979: 115–42). The use of the expression *marana tha* in 1 Cor. 16:22 indicates that the lordship of Jesus belongs to the earliest period of the church (so Fitzmyer 1981b: 229; Hurtado 2003: 110–11). Bousset (1970: 129) himself appears to con-cede the weakness of his position here. Further, the notion that Palestinian Christianity can be neatly separated from Hellenistic Christianity is no longer credible. In this regard, see the definitive work of Hengel 1974. Elsewhere Hengel (1983: 33–47) trenchantly critiques scholarship subsequent to Bousset that attempts to sustain the substance of Bousset's views. For a careful analysis and rejection of Bousset's view, see Cullmann 1963: 199–215. See also the criticisms of Bousset in Longenecker 1970: 120–24. The expression *marana tha* probably should be interpreted as a prayer ("Our Lord, come") instead of as a declaration that the Lord has come or will come (so Cullmann 1963: 209–12; Longenecker 1970: 121; Fitzmyer 1979: 129), since the parallel text in Rev. 22:20 contains such a prayer.

62. Cullmann (1963: 175–78, 181–82) argues that *morphē* refers not to Jesus' divinity but rather to his existence as the heavenly man from the beginning. However, he goes on to identify Jesus as the "God-man" and equates *morphē* with John 1:1, and so it seems that he is not excluding Jesus' divinity in the term. Apparently, he thinks that Jesus' divinity was of an inferior nature until after his exaltation, for he argues that Jesus "became equal with God for the first time with his exaltation" (Cullmann 1963: 235). It would be better to say that as the Son of God, Jesus was always equal with God, and that after his exalta-tion he was equal with God *as the God-man*. Cullmann's view is also unpersuasive in that he reads "form of God" against the background of the two Adams in Philo's thought, and it is quite doubtful that Paul's thought should be outlined against this backdrop. Indeed, Cullmann's notion that Jesus preexisted as the God-man should be rejected (rightly O'Brien 1991: 265). Against the notion that Paul resorts to Adam Christology here, see Bauckham 1999a: 57; see also O'Brien 1991: 263–68.

63. O'Brien (1991: 207–11) provides a survey of the term *morphē* along with a convinc-ing conclusion emphasizing that the term "pictures the preexistent Christ as clothed in

The divinity of Jesus is confirmed by the phrase "equality with God" in Phil. 2:6, for Jesus' equality with God is another way of speaking of the "form of God."[64] Paul intended to communicate clearly to his readers here, and the phrase "equality of God" provides assistance in defining "form of God." The NRSV rightly translates the last phrase in Phil. 2:6: Jesus "did not regard equality with God as something to be exploited." The HCSB offers the same interpretation: he "did not consider equality with God as something to be used for His own advantage." This rendering of the term *harpagmos* is supported by Hoover's groundbreaking study, which has not, in my estimation, been successfully overturned.[65] We must pause here to note the significance of such a translation. Paul *assumes* that Jesus is equal with God. The verse does not teach that Jesus quit trying to attain equality with God. Rather, Paul emphasizes that Jesus did not take advantage of or exploit the equality with God that he already possessed. Furthermore, saying that Jesus emptied himself implies a self-conscious decision on his part to do so, and such a decision is possible, of course, only for one who has consciousness and existence.[66] It follows, then, that this hymn teaches the preexistence of Jesus. He shared the divine nature before he took humanity upon himself.[67]

Nor does Phil. 2:7 indicate that Jesus surrendered his deity in becoming a human being. If we attend to the Greek participles in the text, it becomes clear that Jesus emptied himself by becoming a slave, by taking on humanity.[68] The emptying consisted not in the removal of Christ's deity but rather in the addition of his humanity. Paul utilizes paradoxical language by describing Christ's emptying in terms of adding. The reference to a "servant" (*doulos*) may, given the context, allude to the suffering servant of Isa. 53,[69] but this is called into question especially by the order of the hymn, for here Paul emphasizes the incarnation and

---

the garments of divine majesty and splendour" (O'Brien 1991: 211). See also Fee 1995: 204–5; Silva 2005: 100–102.

64. So Hengel 1997: 488; O'Brien 1991: 216; Fee 1995: 207–8. See also Hurtado 2003: 121–23; Wright 1992a: 72, 75, 80–83. See discussion of the various options in R. Martin 1997: xix–xxi, 99–133.

65. This rendering of *harpagmos* is defended in Hoover 1971. See also Wright 1992a: 77–82; R. Martin 1997: xxii; O'Brien 1991: 211–16; Fee 1995: 205–7; Silva 2005: 103–4.

66. Rightly Gathercole 2006: 25. That is, Jesus *voluntarily* emptied himself, which clearly implies preexistence (so also O'Brien 1991: 217).

67. Against any notion of preexistence, see, for example, Dunn (1996a: 114–121; 1998: 292), who reduces the meaning of the text in interpreting the Christology through an Adamic framework (see also Murphy O'Connor 1976). For a convincing defense of preexistence, see Fee 1995: 203n41; R. Martin 1997: xxi; Hurtado 2003: 118–26.

68. The term *doulos* emphasizes that Jesus chose to be a slave and surrendered his rights (see O'Brien 1991: 218–23; Fee 1995: 210–14).

69. In support of an allusion to Isa. 53:12, see Zimmerli and Jeremias 1957: 97. Some doubt this view because salvation is not tied to Jesus' death here (R. Martin 1997: xxiii).

reserves Christ's death for Phil. 2:8.[70] Certainly the Philippian hymn witnesses to Jesus' humanity. The deity of Christ was veiled by his humanity and some of his divine powers were not exercised, but this is not to be equated with relinquishing his deity.

For the Son of God to become a man is to humble himself. The humiliation, as Phil. 2:8 demonstrates, did not cease with the incarnation. Presumably, Jesus could have been feted as a king and chosen not to die. Not only did he consent to become a human being, but also he was willing to undergo the agony of death for the sake of others. Not only did he consent to die, but also he subjected himself to the most degrading and humiliating and excruciatingly painful death in the Greco-Roman world—death on a cross.[71]

Philippians 2:9–11 explains that Jesus is exalted as Lord because of his humiliation.[72] The Son of God, of course, reigned with the Father eternally. But Jesus of Nazareth, the God-man, was exalted as Lord only at the resurrection. Every knee will bend and every tongue will acknowledge the lordship of Jesus. The lordship of Jesus does not diminish the Father's glory but rather enhances it because his humiliation and exaltation are "to the glory of God the Father" (Phil. 2:11).[73]

Philippians 2:9–11 clearly alludes to Isa. 45:20–25. The text in Isaiah engages in a polemic against idolatry, insisting emphatically that the God of Israel is the only true God. "And there is no other god besides me . . . there is none besides me" (Isa. 45:21; cf. 45:22). Yahweh then declares, "By myself I have sworn; from my mouth has gone out in righteousness a word that shall not return: 'To me every knee shall bow, every tongue shall swear allegiance'" (Isa. 45:23).[74] The allusion to Isaiah in Phil. 2:10–11 is evident. If we gather together the themes assembled, we see something astonishing. Paul confessed along with Isaiah that there is only one God. Yet, he applies to Jesus what Isaiah attributes to Yahweh—every knee bending and every tongue confessing. Clearly, Paul teaches

70. See O'Brien 1991: 268–71. Fee (1995: 212) suggests, however, that the Servant of the Lord may function as part of the background to this text.

71. For the conception of the cross in the Greco-Roman world and the degradation attached to it, see Hengel 1977.

72. A significant segment of scholarship maintains that no theme of imitation is present in the hymn (see, e.g., R. Martin 1997). But the notion that the text calls for an imitation of Christ is on target (see, e.g., Wright 1992a: 87; Fee 1995: 196–97, 199–201; O'Brien 1991: 203–5, 253–62; Silva 2005: 95–98). To say that believers are to imitate Christ does not lead to the conclusion that they will be exalted as Lord. The imitation is analogous.

73. The acclamation of Jesus as Lord was proclaimed in a context in which Caesar claimed to be Lord, according to Cullmann 1963: 198–99.

74. The significance of Isa. 45 for interpreting Paul's meaning is rightly emphasized and explained in O'Brien 1991: 241–43. Bauckham (1999a: 34, 51–53) argues that the divine name is given to Jesus in this passage.

that Jesus shares the same divine nature as Yahweh himself, but Paul does this without denying monotheism or the distinctions between the Father and the Son.

Another remarkable hymn to Christ is found in Col. 1:15–20.[75] This hymn likewise can be divided into two stanzas, in which Jesus is the Lord of creation (Col. 1:15–17) and the Lord of the church (Col. 1:18–20). The divine nature of Jesus is suggested by the claim that he is "the image of the invisible God" (Col. 1:15; cf. 2 Cor. 4:4).[76] Adam and Eve were created "in" God's image (Gen. 1:26–27), but Jesus *is* uniquely the image of the invisible God. The "firstborn of all creation" might suggest on first glance that Jesus is the first creature. The term "firstborn" (*prōtotokos*), however, derives from the OT, where the firstborn has the right of primogeniture. Israel is God's "firstborn" son (Exod. 4:22), receiving the same mandate given to Adam, which is to rule the world for God. The Davidic king representatively carries out this rule on behalf of God's people. Hence, we read about God's promise to David: "I will make him the firstborn, the highest of the kings of the earth" (Ps. 89:27). David was not the first Israelite king. That privilege belonged to Saul. Nor was David the oldest in his family. In fact, he was the youngest. Designating him as the "firstborn" signals his sovereignty, and this is confirmed by Hebrew parallelism. The word "firstborn" is elucidated by the phrase "the highest of the kings of the earth."

When we apply the OT meaning of the term "firstborn" to the Colossians text, it becomes clear that identifying Jesus as the firstborn does not designate him as a creature. Rather, he is the sovereign one, the ruler and Lord of all.[77] Indeed, Jesus cannot be a creature, since Col. 1:16 declares that all of creation was brought into being by Christ's agency. Not only were all things created "through him," but also they were created "for him." Jesus is the goal as well as the agent of all creation. The glory that belongs to the one true God also belongs to Jesus as creator and Lord.

The word "firstborn" probably has the notion of Jesus' temporal priority in addition to sovereignty. There is no notion, however, of his being a created being. He existed eternally before the world was created. Despite the reservations of some, this text clearly teaches preexistence.[78]

75. See the careful exposition in Wright 1992a: 99–119.

76. Kim (1982: 136–268; 2002: 165–213) argues that Paul's understanding of Christ as the image of God can be traced to his experience of Christ on the road to Damascus. On the background to the concept of the image of God, see Lohse 1971: 46–48; O'Brien 1982: 43–44; Dunn 1996a: 87–89.

77. See O'Brien 1982: 44–45. Lohse (1971: 48–49) maintains that sovereignty is in view here, not temporal priority. Pokorný (1991: 75) argues that the text is unclear on this matter. However, such unclarity is unlikely for one nurtured in Jewish monotheism.

78. Contra, for example, Dunn 1996a: xx, 187–194. Dunn sees wisdom Christology at work here but mistakenly interprets Christ through the lens of wisdom rather than seeing

Certainly, Paul draws on wisdom traditions in elucidating Christ's role in creation (Prov. 8:22–31; Wis. 7:25–27).[79] Wisdom language in the OT and in Second Temple literature does not refer to an entity or person that truly exists, and hence wisdom is personified in this literature. Even though wisdom traditions inform Christology in Colossians, the antecedents do not dictate the significance of the fulfillment. Jesus transcends wisdom because he is a person, and hence to attribute creation to him implies preexistence.[80] When Paul says that "he [Christ] is before all things" (Col. 1:17), this confessional statement refers both to Jesus' sovereignty and to his temporal priority.[81] He has always existed, and he is the Lord of the universe. Such a reading fits the Jewish background nicely because typically the oldest son in the family enjoyed the benefits of the firstborn. Jesus' lordship over creation is expressed also by the coherence of all creation in him: "in him all things hold together" (Col. 1:17). The physical world does not "run on its own" as if it has an internal mechanism by which it sustains itself. The world is sustained and upheld by Jesus Christ.

Colossians 1:18–20 explicates Jesus' lordship over the church. He is not only the Lord of the universe but also the sovereign over God's people. Identifying Jesus as "the head" (*kephalē*) of the church does not in this context mean that he is the "source" of the church's life.[82] The emphasis is on his lordship over the church, the preeminence that he has as its sovereign. The word "beginning" (*archē*) connotes that Jesus' resurrection commences the new creation and his status as the firstborn.[83] Jesus is the fountainhead and origin of the new people of God because he is "the firstborn from the dead." The word "firstborn" (*prōtotokos*), as in Col. 1:15, denotes both sovereignty and temporal priority. Jesus rules over death because he was the first to conquer death. The risen Lord is the head of the church and was raised from the dead so that he would

---

wisdom as fulfilled in Christ. Nor does the statement that Christ is the creator of all fit with Dunn's claim that *"Christ now reveals the character of the power behind the world"* (Dunn 1996a: 190). From Dunn's paraphrase we would scarcely imagine that Paul actually wrote that Christ was the agent and goal of all of creation. Lau (1996: 159, 255–56, 263–65, 269), in his study of the Pastoral Epistles, shows that the preexistence of Christ is clearly taught here as well (contra Dunn 1996a: 237–38).

79. For the view that wisdom Christology played a significant role for early Christians, see Dunn 1996a: 163–212.

80. Perhaps, then, it is best not to speak of wisdom Christology but rather of wisdom themes (see Lee 2005: 285–305).

81. Rightly Lohse 1971: 52; O'Brien 1982: 47. So also Dunn (1996a: 93–94), though he wrongly rejects the notion of personal preexistence.

82. In support of the view that *kephalē* means "authority over," see Grudem 1985; 1991; 2001; Fitzmyer 1993a.

83. Dunn 1996b: 97–98.

be "preeminent" in all things. Jesus' lordship is grounded in his divinity and his reconciling work (Col. 1:19–20). It is grounded in his divinity, for all of God's "fullness" dwelt in Jesus, just as God's glory dwelt in the tabernacle and temple (cf. Col. 2:9). In other words, Jesus is fully divine because God dwells in him completely. Further, Jesus is Lord because his reconciling work embraces the whole universe, both earthly and heavenly things. We should note again that Jesus' reconciling work is grounded in his person. He is able to reconcile all because the divine fullness dwells in him. Again we see Christology in the service of soteriology.

Jesus' lordship pervades Paul's theology, and Jesus is regularly acclaimed and proclaimed as the risen Lord (2 Cor. 4:5). God raised Jesus from the dead and seated him at his right hand (Eph. 1:20–23), and the divine session at the right hand accords with Ps. 110:1. Jesus is enthroned above all demonic powers (Eph. 1:21; cf. Col. 1:16) and rules as head over the church (Eph. 1:22; cf. 5:23; Col. 2:10, 19).[84] The church, then, expresses the fullness of Christ (Eph. 1:23). He is the ascended Lord, who has triumphed over his enemies and granted gifts to those in the church (Eph. 4:8). Jesus' ascension on high presumes his previous descent and incarnation (Eph. 4:9–10; cf. Rom. 4:24), as we saw in Phil. 2:6–11. Now, as the ascended Lord, he fills "all things" (Eph. 4:10; cf. Rom. 10:12).[85]

The Father is confessed as the one God and the creator and source of all things; Jesus Christ is confessed as Lord and as the agent by whom all things came into existence (1 Cor. 8:6).[86] One can truly and genuinely acknowledge that "Jesus is Lord" only by the work of the Holy Spirit (1 Cor. 12:3).[87] Those who have come to faith began their new life by receiving "Christ Jesus" as Lord (Col. 2:6). And only those who confess him as Lord will be saved (Rom. 10:9), for they acknowledge him as the only Lord (Eph. 4:5). Christians all over the world are characterized by a common affirmation of Jesus' lordship (1 Cor. 1:2). They live

---

84. The word "head" (*kephalē*) in Eph. 4:15 and Col. 2:19 may also have the connotation of Jesus' nurturing and feeding the church, and so it may also suggest "source" (see Lincoln 1990: 261–62; Best 1998: 408; Hoehner 2002: 567–68). But against this, see O'Brien (1999: 416n168), who thinks that such a view confuses the "referent with meaning." The notions of "source" and "authority" are not mutually exclusive but rather are compatible in Pauline theology because source fits with authority (see 1 Cor. 11:8–9). See Arnold 1994.

85. Kammler (2003: 177–78) notes that Rom. 10:12 alludes to two texts that refer to Yahweh (Ps. 85:5 LXX; Job 5:8).

86. Note how Paul links God and Christ in 1 Cor. 7:17. This text was brought to my attention by Kammler 2003: 176n48.

87. Cullmann (1963: 219–20) argues that Paul opposes emperor worship here, not spiritual enthusiasm that was untethered from the gospel. Despite the attractiveness of Cullmann's reading, it seems that Paul would have specifically rebuked the Corinthians if they were indeed acknowledging Caesar as Lord.

to please him (1 Cor. 7:32–34; cf. 6:13). They see what was hidden from "the rulers of this age": Jesus, as the crucified one, is "the Lord of glory" (1 Cor. 2:6, 8).[88]

Romans 14:1–12 is a fascinating text about Jesus' lordship. In some verses it is difficult to know whether the "Lord" referred to is God or Christ. The acknowledgment of lordship in Rom. 14:11 seems to refer to God's lordship, since Rom. 14:10 and 14:12 speak of giving an account to God on the final day. Interestingly, in Rom. 14:11 Paul cites Isa. 45:23, the same text applied to Christ in Phil. 2:10–11. In Romans, however, he applies it to the Father. The fact that Paul can apply the same OT text to God in Romans and to Christ in Philippians reveals the high stature of Christ. Even in Rom. 14:1–12 lordship is not confined to God. In Rom. 14:9 the same pattern recounted in Phil. 2:6–11 occurs. Jesus died and was raised so that he might be exalted as Lord of all. It appears, then, that the term "Lord" refers to Jesus Christ in Rom. 14:7–8.[89] These verses are highly significant, for Paul stresses that in both life and death Christians live to the Lord, so that a believer's entire life is to be devoted to the Lord. Believers, then, live the whole of their lives to please Jesus Christ as Lord. This is the sort of thing said about the Father as well, signifying the divine status of Christ. It may be that the term "Lord" in Rom. 14:4–6 refers to Christ rather than God. Unraveling the referent in these verses, however, is quite difficult. The difficulty itself is quite illuminating, for it suggests the equality of God and Christ. Perhaps our fuzziness at this point indicates that Paul himself was unconcerned to distinguish carefully between God and Christ in these verses, since they shared lordship.

Lordship and Divinity

Paul often uses the term "Lord" (*kyrios*) in his letters.[90] When he alludes to or quotes from the OT, "Lord" usually translates the divine name

88. Fitzmyer (1979: 130) concludes that the use of the term "Lord" with reference to Jesus demonstrates "that early Christians regarded Jesus as sharing in some sense in the transcendence of Yahweh, that he was somehow on a par with him." Fitzmyer goes on to note that the equality between Jesus and God does not mean that they were completely identified, and that the NT does not work out the theological implications that are later formulated at Nicea and Chalcedon.

89. Hurtado (2003: 115–16) observes that in a number of texts the lordship of Christ is combined with the theme of obedience, so that Christ's lordship manifests itself practically in the lives of his people. This is evident in Rom. 14; 16:2–20; 1 Cor. 6:12–7:40; 1 Thess. 4:2–6.

90. For this section I am dependent on Capes 1992. The next two paragraphs essentially come from Schreiner 2001 with slight revisions.

"Yahweh." Often "Lord" functions as the translation of "Yahweh" when God the Father himself is the referent (Rom. 4:7–8; 9:27–29; 11:34; 15:9–11; 1 Cor. 3:20; 2 Cor. 6:18). More significantly, in a number of texts Paul identifies the "Lord" as Jesus Christ, even though the OT allusion or quotation clearly refers to Yahweh (Rom. 10:13; 14:11; 1 Cor. 1:31; 2:16; 10:22, 26; 2 Cor. 10:17; Phil. 2:10–11; 1 Thess. 3:13; 4:6; 2 Thess. 1:7–8; 2 Tim. 2:19).[91] Some of the texts ascribed to Christ might possibly refer to God, but most of those cited clearly have Christ in view.[92] Hence, there is no doubt that texts that referred to Yahweh in the OT are applied to Jesus Christ. The significance of such a move is staggering because Paul, as a Jew and a Pharisee, was nurtured in Jewish monotheism. He knew that he was identifying Jesus himself as God in assigning Yahweh texts to him.

Capes rightly summarizes the significance of Jesus' lordship in six statements.[93] First, Jesus Christ was the object of devotion in creedal statements (Rom. 1:3–4; 10:9–10).[94] Second, believers prayed for Christ's return (1 Cor. 16:22) and identified themselves as those who "call upon the name of the Lord Jesus Christ" (1 Cor. 1:2).[95] Third, hymns focusing upon the person and work of Christ were composed (Phil. 2:6–11; Col. 1:15–20).[96] Fourth, during worship early Christians gathered in Jesus' name (1 Cor. 5:4). Fifth, new believers were baptized in Jesus' name (Rom. 6:3; Gal. 3:27). Sixth, early Christians honored Jesus by celebrating a meal called "the Lord's supper" (1 Cor. 11:20).[97] Capes is correct, then, in concluding that Jesus' lordship involved worship and necessarily implies that Paul and early Christians thought of Jesus "in the way that one thinks of God."[98] And yet God the Father is still distinct from Jesus, and Paul retains his belief in monotheism (1 Cor. 8:6).[99] Apparently, Paul did not believe that honoring and worshiping Jesus as God compromised his monotheistic belief, but neither did he collapse God and Jesus together into a kind of modalism.

91. For the texts referring to Christ, see Capes 1992: 115–60. See also Hurtado 2003: 112–13.

92. Kammler (2003: 177n56) also suggests 1 Cor. 1:31; 2 Cor. 3:16; Rom. 11:26.

93. Capes 1992: 164.

94. Reflecting on Rom. 10:9–13, Hurtado (2003: 142) notes that to "'call upon the name of the Lord' is a frequent biblical expression for the worship of *Yahweh*." See also K. Schmidt, *TDNT* 3:496–500.

95. Hurtado (2003: 116) points out that Jesus' lordship often is associated with eschatology and his return as judge.

96. See also Hurtado 2003: 146–49. We can add to this Eph. 5:19, where songs are sung *tō kyriō* (so Hengel 1983: 81). "The Lord" refers to Christ here (so O'Brien 1999: 396; Hoehner 2002: 713).

97. Hurtado (2003: 142–46) also calls attention to the significance of baptism and the Lord's Supper.

98. Capes 1992: 164.

99. So Kammler 2003: 173–75. On this text, see also Hurtado 2003: 114.

Stettler amasses significant evidence in the Pastoral Epistles for Christ's divinity: his patience (1 Tim. 1:16); the need to put faith in Jesus (1 Tim. 3:16); his glory (Titus 2:13); his kingdom (2 Tim. 4:1, 18); prayer is offered to him (2 Tim. 4:22); a doxology is offered to him (2 Tim. 4:18); like God (2 Tim. 1:3), he is thanked (1 Tim. 1:12); the saving work attributed to God in the OT is ascribed to Jesus (2 Tim. 4:17; Titus 2:14); he alone is the final judge (2 Tim. 4:1, 8).[100]

Jesus shares divine status, according to Paul, since prayers are offered to him.[101] For instance, Paul concludes 1 Corinthians with the invocation "Our Lord, come!" (1 Cor. 16:22). He does not entreat God to send Jesus but rather asks the Lord himself to return. Another example surfaces in the account about the thorn in the flesh. Three times Paul entreats "the Lord" to remove the thorn, but the Lord informs him that he will not take away the thorn, so that his power can be maximized in Paul's life (2 Cor. 12:8–9). But what is the identity of this Lord with whom Paul pleads? The context reveals that the "Lord" is Christ himself. He replies to Paul's supplication with the words "*My power* is made perfect in weakness" (2 Cor. 12:9). Paul proceeds to say that he will boast of his difficulties "so that the *power of Christ* may rest upon me" (2 Cor. 12:9). The italicized words demonstrate that the person addressed by Paul's prayer is Christ himself.[102]

Another remarkable prayer occurs in 1 Thess. 3:11–13, and it is perhaps even more remarkable because 1 Thessalonians is one of the earliest, if not the earliest, of Paul's letters.[103] The prayer is significant enough to warrant citing it in full: "Now may our God and Father himself, and our Lord Jesus, direct our way to you, and may the Lord make you increase and abound in love for one another and for all, as we do for you, so that he may establish your hearts blameless in holiness before our God and Father, at the coming of our Lord Jesus with all his saints." Both God the Father and Jesus Christ are entreated in the prayer to the end that Paul will be able to visit the Thessalonians.[104] In 1 Thess. 3:12 Christ is

---

100. Stettler 1998: 333.

101. So also Cullmann 1963: 215; Hurtado 2003: 138–40.

102. Harris (2005: 860) concurs, pointing out as well that *kyrios* in Paul typically refers to Christ, that God is addressed differently in 2 Cor. 13:7, and that other texts reflect prayers to Jesus Christ (Acts 1:24; 7:59–60; 9:10–17, 21; 22:16, 19; 1 Cor. 1:2; 16:22; Rev. 22:20). We can add to this 2 Tim. 4:22 (so Stettler 1998: 333).

103. Kammler (2003: 175) confirms this point, noting that both persons are joined together in "unerhörten weise" [an unheard of way]. Wanamaker (1990: 141) also remarks that prayer is not only addressed to God (cf. Sir. 23:1), but now Jesus is also included. See also Bruce 1982b: 71; Marshall 1983: 99–100.

104. So also Kreitzer 1987: 110. The use of the singular verb here and in 2 Thess. 2:16–17 is sometimes adduced as further evidence for the view supported here (Best 1972: 147; Morris 1959: 111). But the singular verb is used elsewhere with compound subjects

addressed as Lord, and in 1 Thess. 3:13 he is clearly distinguished from the Father. Paul prays that the Lord Jesus will grant them an increased love for one another. The divine status of Jesus is evident because only God can grant people the power to love.

The prayer in 2 Thess. 2:16–17 is remarkably similar: "Now may our Lord Jesus Christ himself, and God our Father, who loved us and gave us eternal comfort and good hope through grace, comfort your hearts and establish them in every good work and word." Again Jesus Christ and the Father are addressed together in prayer. Paul asks that they grant comfort and strengthen believers for righteous living.

The significance of such prayers should not be overlooked. As a monotheist, Paul believed that prayers should be offered only to God. Yet he clearly addresses Jesus Christ in prayer, placing him on the same level as God the Father. It is evident from this that the human Jesus was also considered to be divine.

Binitarian and Trinitarian Formulas

We should also observe some binitarian and trinitarian formulas in Paul.[105] By "trinitarian" I do not mean the fully worked out doctrinal statements of later church history. We do see, however, instances in which the Father, Jesus Christ, and the Spirit seem to be put on an equal plane. For instance, we have a binitarian statement in 1 Cor. 8:4–6. The oneness of God the Father is emphasized (1 Cor. 8:4, 6). The Father is the fount of all things, and human beings exist for his glory. Such monotheism, however, does not rule out the lordship of Jesus Christ. He is the one "through whom" God brought all things into existence, including human beings (1 Cor. 8:6). Paul retains Jewish monotheism and yet accords divine status to Jesus Christ as Lord.

The parallels between God and Christ would likely seem more astonishing if they were not so common:[106] the Holy Spirit as the Spirit of God and the Spirit of Christ (Rom. 8:9); the church as the church of God and

---

(Matt. 5:18; Mark 4:41; James 5:3). Hence, the singular verb alone does not point to the identity of God and Christ, though it does suggest that they are closely related (rightly Wanamaker 1990: 141–42).

105. Hurtado (2003: 151–53) particularly calls attention to the binitarian character of Pauline theology. Hurtado (2003: 151) observes, "Jesus is reverenced in a constellation of actions that resemble the way a god is reverenced in the Roman-era religious scene. . . . This is also not ditheism. Jesus is not reverenced as another, second god."

106. I owe these categories and references to Kammler (2003: 178–79), who provides many more examples in each category. I provide but one example for God and Christ, so that the first reference refers to God and the second to Christ, though in the case of Rom. 8:9 both examples are in one verse.

the churches of Christ (1 Cor. 1:2; Rom. 16:16); grace and love as coming from God and Christ (Rom. 5:15; 2 Cor. 8:9/Rom. 8:39; Rom. 8:35); the day of God and the day of Christ (Rom. 2:5; 1 Cor. 1:8); the judgment seat of God and the judgment seat of Christ (Rom. 14:10; 2 Cor. 5:10); faith in God and faith in Christ (Rom. 3:22; 4:24); God and Christ functioning as the end-time judge (1 Cor. 4:5; Rom. 2:16); Christians live for God but also live for Christ (Rom. 6:11; 2 Cor. 5:15); believers serve God but also serve Christ (1 Thess. 1:9; Rom. 14:18); Paul was appointed as an apostle by God and Christ (Gal. 1:15–16; Rom. 1:5). It is difficult to imagine these collocations unless Paul views Jesus Christ as divine.

A trinitarian statement emerges in the discussion of spiritual gifts. Paul observes that there is a diversity of gifts "but the same Spirit," a number of ways to serve "but the same Lord," and all different kinds of effects "but it is the same God who empowers them all in everyone" (1 Cor. 12:4–6). It is difficult to escape the conclusion that the Spirit, the Lord Jesus Christ, and God share the same status here. We see a similar phenomenon in 2 Cor. 13:14: "The grace of the Lord Jesus Christ and the love of God and the fellowship of the Holy Spirit be with you all." Grace and love, as we noted above, can come only from God himself.[107] Apparently, Jesus Christ and the Holy Spirit are divine without compromising monotheism.[108] In Eph. 4:4–6 Paul refers to "one Spirit," "one Lord," "one God and Father of all." This statement stands out because monotheism is affirmed, while at the same time the Spirit and Christ share divine status with the Father.

The trinitarian nature of Paul's theology peeps through in a variety of other texts as well. In Eph. 1:3–14 God elects and predestines in Christ and gives his Spirit as a seal and down payment. In the same way, in 2 Cor. 1:21–22 God confirms and anoints Paul and his co-workers "in Christ" and grants the Spirit as a seal and down payment.[109] In Rom. 5:5–11 God pours out his love through the Holy Spirit, and the love given through the Spirit is anchored in the self-giving love of Christ on the cross. The Spirit is identified as both the "Spirit of God" and the "Spirit of Christ" (Rom. 8:9). Further, the resurrection of Jesus is accomplished by the Father through the Spirit (Rom. 8:11). Believers are heirs of God and co-heirs with Christ, and the Spirit bears witness that believers are God's children (Rom. 8:14–17). We compare here Gal. 4:6, where "God has sent the Spirit of his Son into our hearts, crying, 'Abba! Father!'" The collocation of the Father, the Spirit, and the Son is quite

---

107. Harris (2005: 938) argues that grace comes first because both love and participation in the life of the Spirit are the result of God's love.

108. So also Harris 2005: 938.

109. Supporting the trinitarian nature of the following texts is Kammler 2003: 175n45. For the trinitarian character of 2 Cor. 1:21–22, see Harris 2005: 210.

remarkable. The verbs "sanctified" and "justified" in 1 Cor. 6:11 should be interpreted as divine passives, for God is the one who sanctifies and justifies, but he does so "in the name of the Lord Jesus Christ and by the Spirit of our God," indicating the close relationship between the Father, Son, and Spirit in the salvation of human beings.

Jesus as God

The issue of whether Jesus is specifically called "God" (*theos*) in Paul involves two texts, Rom. 9:5 and Titus 2:13.[110] In Rom. 9:4–5 Paul itemizes the blessings of the Jewish people, culminating with the truth that the Messiah comes from them. He concludes with the words "the one who is over all, God blessed for the ages, Amen" (my translation). This last phrase is the subject of ongoing controversy, for scholars debate whether Jesus or the Father is called "God" in this verse. The verse can be punctuated in various ways. If the reference is to Christ, then the options are either "Christ . . . who is over all, God blessed forever, Amen," or "Christ . . . who is God over all, blessed forever, Amen." If the reference is to God, then the phrase "who is over all" could be understood as referring to Christ, with Paul breaking off and saying with reference to the Father, "God be blessed forever, Amen." More likely if the whole phrase refers to God, then it should be translated as "God who is over all be blessed for ever, Amen" or "He who is over all, God, be blessed for ever, Amen." Several factors are adduced to support a reference to God: (1) "Blessed" (*eulogētos*) is always used with reference to God elsewhere in the NT (Mark 14:61; Luke 1:68; Rom. 1:25; 2 Cor. 1:3; 11:31; Eph. 1:3; 1 Pet. 1:3). (2) Nowhere else in the Pauline corpus does "God" (*theos*) refer to Christ, and therefore some scholars insist that Paul does not break the pattern here. (3) The unusual word order—"blessed" following "God"—can be explained by Paul's desire to highlight God's lordship over all, a typical Jewish theme (cf. Ps. 67:19–20 LXX). (4) No other doxologies to Christ exist in the indisputable Pauline letters. (5) The closest parallel text is Eph. 4:6, and there the Father is said to be "the one who is over all" (*ho epi pantōn*). (6) A closing reference to God is typical in Jewish literature. (7) The doxology in Rom. 11:33–36 refers to the Father, suggesting that the same is true in Rom. 9:5.

110. Scholars have long debated whether Paul identifies Jesus Christ as God. A thorough defense of the interpretation adopted here is presented in Harris 1992: 143–85; see also Marshall 1999: 276–78; Stettler 1998: 256–58. The discussion of Jesus as God is taken from Schreiner 2001 with minor revisions. For a careful introduction to the ascription of the term "God" to Jesus in the NT generally, see Longenecker 1970: 136–41.

The foregoing arguments, although diverse, enshrine one fundamental objection: it is thought to be quite improbable that Christ would be designated "God" (*theos*) because this is uncharacteristic of Paul elsewhere. Despite the strength of that argument, there are decisive reasons for believing that Paul departs from his normal practice and refers to Christ as "God" here:[111] (1) The phrase "according to the flesh," even though it does not require an explicit contrasting phrase, fits more smoothly if a contrasting phrase is included. The series of benefits belonging to Israel comes to a stunning conclusion, for though Christ descended from Israel ethnically, he transcends that identity because he also shares the divine nature.[112] (2) The natural antecedent to *ho ōn* ("the one who is") is "Christ," for doxologies almost always are attached to the preceding word, and asyndetic doxologies do not exist.[113] A particularly striking parallel is 2 Cor. 11:31: "The God and Father of the Lord Jesus, he who is blessed for ever, knows. . . ." The articular participle *ho ōn* ("the one who is") in this case naturally refers back to "the God and Father," and the same principle applies in Rom. 9:5 with the result that *ho hōn* refers to Christ. (3) If this were an independent doxology to God the Father, the word "blessed" would occur first as it does in every other instance in the LXX and the NT.[114] The only apparent exception is Ps. 67:19–20, but even in this instance it is doubtful that a real exception exists. (4) To break off and utter praise to God in a context in which Paul grieves over Israel fits awkwardly in the context. Ascribing blessedness to Christ after identifying him with God fits more naturally because the Messiah sharing the divine nature is the consummation of Israel's privileges. To ascribe deity to Christ heightens the profundity of Paul's grief. Not only have the Jews rejected Jesus as the Messiah, but also they are spurning one who shares the divine nature with the Father. (5) That Paul would call Christ "God" is not totally surprising, for in Phil. 2:6 Jesus is said to be "in the form of God" and "equal to God"[115] (my translation), and in Col. 1:15 he is said to be "the image of the invisible God" (see also Col. 1:19; 2:9; 1 Cor. 8:6; 2 Cor. 4:4). When we add to this the application to Christ of texts in the OT which refer to "Yahweh" (see Rom. 10:13; Phil. 2:10–11), the case becomes quite strong. Thus the idea that calling Christ "God"

111. See especially Kammler 2003.
112. So also Kammler 2003: 167.
113. See Rom. 1:25; 11:36; 2 Cor. 11:31; Gal. 1:5; Eph. 3:21; Phil. 4:20; 1 Tim. 1:17; 2 Tim. 4:18; Heb. 13:21; 1 Pet. 4:11; 2 Pet. 3:18.
114. See in the LXX Gen. 9:26; 14:20; 24:27, 31; Exod. 18:10; Ruth 4:14; 1 Sam. 25:32; 2 Sam. 6:21; 18:28; 1 Kings 1:48; 8:15, 56; 2 Chron. 2:11; 6:4; Ezra 7:27; Ps. 17:47; 27:6; 30:22; 40:14; 65:20; 67:20, 36; 71:18; 88:53; 105:48; 123:6; 143:1; Dan. 3:26; Zech. 11:5; 1 Esd. 4:40; Tob. 11:17; 13:2, 18; see in the NT Luke 1:68; 2 Cor. 1:3; Eph. 1:3; 1 Pet. 1:3.
115. Rightly Kammler 2003: 173.

is incompatible with Pauline thought should be rejected. Paul does not say that Christ is God without remainder, for the distinction between Christ and the Father must also be maintained (1 Cor. 8:6; 15:28; Phil. 2:11).[116] Nevertheless, the implication here is that Christ shares the divine nature with the Father.

The attribution in Titus 2:13 is similarly disputed, so that scholars debate whether *theos* refers to God or to Christ. The relevant part of the verse reads, *epiphaneian tēs doxēs tou megalou theou kai sōtēros hēmōn Iēsou Christou* (lit., "appearance of the glory of the great God and our Savior, Jesus Christ"). Lexically, the strongest arguments favor the claim that Jesus Christ is called "the great God." I will not reduplicate, however, the detailed arguments for this view by Harris, whom readers should consult for a thorough discussion of the possible alternatives.[117] Two reasons adduced by Harris indicate that Paul designates Jesus Christ as God here.[118] First, the phrase "God and Savior" (*theos kai sōtēr*) was a common formula in the Greco-Roman world, and it regularly refers to one deity in such formulas. There is no reason to think that Paul departs from standard practice here, and thus the most natural way to take the expression is to conclude that Paul identifies Jesus Christ as God. Second, the one article *tou* ("the") is best explained as introducing both the nouns "God" and "Savior" (*theou* and *sōtēros*).[119] If Paul had wanted to distinguish "God" and "Savior," he probably would have inserted a second definite article before the noun "Savior." By omitting the article before the second noun, Paul indicates that both nouns refer to the same person, Jesus Christ.

The main objection to this reading of the text is theological, while its primary support is grammatical. The theological objection centers on the improbability of designating Jesus as God because the attribution was rare in Pauline writings. The theological objection can be answered in a satisfying way. Paul seldom refers to Christ as God because this title could be confusing, given his monotheism. Believers could wrongly conclude that Jesus was God without remainder. Thus, Paul stresses the distinction between the Father and the Son. Paul's view, however, cannot be

---

116. Kammler (2003: 171) comments, "So identifiziert er ihn damit keineswegs mit der *Person* Gottes, des Vaters; er schreibt ihm dann als dem Sohn vielmehr jenes göttliche *Sein und Wesen* zu, das Gott, dem Vater eignet." ("So he in no way identifies him with the person of God, the Father. He attributes to him as the Son rather than divine being and essence which appertains to God the Father.")

117. See Harris 1992: 173–85; see also Lau 1996: 243–48.

118. Stettler (1998: 146–47, 331) maintains that the term *epiphaneia* presupposes Jesus' deity and reflects an incarnation theology (so also Lau 1996: 270).

119. This is the famous Granville Sharp rule. For the best contemporary explanation, see Wallace 1996: 270–90. In 1 Thess. 3:11 the addition of the second article before *kyrios* indicates that the Father and Jesus Christ are distinguished.

so neatly categorized, for he also believed that Jesus was deity, without denying monotheism. The one who accomplished salvation and inaugurated the new age is more than a human being, though certainly he is not less than human. Attributing deity to Jesus does not compromise Jewish monotheism, for Paul was not suggesting that there was more than one God. Rather, he was maintaining that there is more complexity in the identity of God than some may have thought. Scholars recently have investigated the antecedents for the theology of early Christians in Judaism and have demonstrated that the view of the early Christians did not arise in a vacuum. We do not have the space here to explore this arena in any detail, but scholars such as Alan Segal and Larry Hurtado have carefully traced traditions that posit "two powers" in heaven.[120] Antecedents clearly exist, but it cannot be denied that there is an explicit leap forward in the acclamation of Jesus the Messiah as God.

Conclusion

It is hardly controversial to say that Jesus Christ is central in Pauline theology. Nor is his centrality abstracted from everyday life, for the lordship of Christ pulsates throughout every aspect of Paul's thought, whether Paul speaks of eating or drinking or of how husbands and wives relate to one another. Paul believes that Jesus was a human being and that he was the Messiah of Israel, but he is also the Son of God, who was exalted to God's right hand at the resurrection. God's promises of rule for Israel have been fulfilled with Jesus being crowned as Lord. The new creation and new exodus and new covenant have arrived in Jesus Christ. Jesus' lordship also signals his divinity. In a multitude of ways Paul communicates that Jesus shares equal stature with God. Hence, it is not surprising that on occasion Paul also identifies Jesus Christ as God, without suggesting, however, that such an attribution cancels out the existence of the Father.

120. See Segal 1977; Hurtado 1988.

11

⚜ ⚜ ⚜ ⚜ ⚜ ⚜ ⚜ ⚜ ⚜ ⚜ ⚜ ⚜ ⚜ ⚜ ⚜ ⚜ ⚜ ⚜

The Saving Work of God
and Christ according to Paul

Paul's theology of God and Christ should not be coldly dissected, as if it can be separated from God's saving work in Christ. God and Christ are revealed so that believers will glorify and praise God for his work in delivering them from the power of sin and the degradation of death. In this chapter I will combine the saving work of God and Christ in the Pauline letters. Considering the work of God and Christ together in salvation is fitting because God saves in and through Jesus Christ. We are not surprised to encounter numerous themes in this chapter, for the work of salvation surpasses description and thus many different terms and metaphors are used to portray the wonder of what God has done in Christ.

Foreknowledge

We begin where Paul does, in Rom. 8:29. God foreknew from the beginning whom he would predestine to be like his Son, Jesus Christ. The term "foreknow" (*proginōskō*) at a minimum means that God knew from the beginning those who would belong to Jesus Christ (cf. Acts 26:5; 2 Pet. 3:17; Wis. 8:8; 18:6). It is likely, however, that the term means even more than this when attributed to God.[1] God's knowledge of his people in the OT refers to his covenantal love, by which he set his affection on his people. God "knew" or "chose" (LXX: *oida*; MT: *yd'*) Abraham as his own (Gen. 18:19). Amos 3:2 also helps us define the term. God addresses Israel, "You only have I known of all the families of the earth." God obviously knows all who live upon the earth, but he has set his covenantal affection upon Israel alone. It is the only nation upon whom God has set his saving love. We see a similar use of the word "know" in the call of Jeremiah: "Before I formed you in the womb I knew you, and before you were born I consecrated you; I appointed you a prophet to the nations" (Jer. 1:5). The Hebrew parallelism illuminates the meaning of the verb "know," in that the verbs "consecrate" and "appoint" are conjoined with it. The emphasis is on God's knowing, consecrating, and appointing work. Yahweh did not merely have knowledge that Jeremiah was in the womb; he had set his affection upon Jeremiah so that he would serve as a prophet of the Lord.

The OT background assists us in interpreting Rom. 8:29. Notice that the object of the verb "foreknew" is personal. God foreknew "those whom" (*hous*) would become like Christ. He placed his covenantal affection on certain ones according to the mystery of his grace. It seems, then, that the word "foreknow" virtually takes on the meaning "choose beforehand." Such a conclusion is supported by Rom. 11:2, where Paul discusses whether God has abandoned Israel as his people. He asserts, "God has not rejected his people whom he foreknew." The words "rejected" and "foreknew" function as antonyms in the verse. Hence, we could legitimately render the verse, "God has not rejected his people whom he chose." The word "foreknowledge" focuses on God's covenantal choice of his people—his love in choosing them to be his own.

The definition proposed here fits as well with 1 Pet. 1:20, where Christ was foreknown before the world began. This does not mean merely that God foresaw when Christ would arrive; it indicates also that God planned in his love to choose Jesus of Nazareth to be the Christ (cf. Acts 2:23; 1 Pet. 1:2). Similarly, God has foreknown from the beginning who would belong to the family of faith. In two other instances in Paul the word "know" (*ginōskō*) emphasizes the priority of God's grace. Paul refers to the conversion of the Galatian Christians in Gal. 4:9, designating it as their coming to know God.[2] But he immediately qualifies his statement, remarking that it is not fundamentally that they have come to know God, but rather that they are "known by God." Conversion is not primarily a matter of the human will choosing to know God but rather of God's

---

1. On the topic of foreknowledge, see Baugh 2000.
2. See Martyn 1997: 413.

knowing of human beings. Similarly, in 1 Cor. 8:3 we read, "If anyone loves God, he is known by God." Human love from God is an answering love, a result of God knowing human beings first.[3]

God's Love and Mercy

God's choosing or electing people to salvation is often attributed to his love. Paul draws on the OT as well here. Deuteronomy 7:6–8 is particularly important and warrants being quoted in full.

> For you are a people holy to the LORD your God. The LORD your God has chosen you to be a people for his treasured possession, out of all the peoples who are on the face of the earth. It was not because you were more in number than any other people that the LORD set his love on you and chose you, for you were the fewest of all peoples, but it is because the LORD loves you and is keeping the oath that he swore to your fathers, that the LORD has brought you out with a mighty hand and redeemed you from the house of slavery, from the hand of Pharaoh king of Egypt.

Yahweh's choosing of Israel among all the peoples of the world is equated with his setting his love on Israel. And why did Yahweh choose Israel? Not because it was a mighty nation or particularly attractive. God set his love on Israel because he loved them and because of the promise he graciously made to the patriarchs.

God's love for his people cannot be attributed to any quality in Israel or any goodness that commended the nation to him. God loved Israel because he loved them. The explanation for his choice does not and cannot go any farther back. Isaiah emphasizes the same theme. God had "chosen" Jacob, and Israel is the seed of Abraham, God's "friend." The word "friend" is too tame, for both the MT and the LXX describe Abraham as the one loved by God (LXX: *hon ēgapēsa*). Those whom God has chosen he has also loved. In Isa. 44:2 Israel is designated as the one "I have chosen." Interestingly, the LXX adds that Israel is "beloved by God" (*ho ēgapēmenos*), suggesting that the translators believed that those who were God's chosen people were the special objects of his love.

In Paul God's love is often connected to his election or calling of his people.[4] In Rom. 1:7 believers in Rome are designated as those who are called and beloved by God. Similarly, those who are elected

---

3. Hays (1997: 138) says about this verse, "The initiative in salvation comes from God, not from us. It is God who loves us first, God who elects us and delivers us from the power of sin and death."

4. So Schlatter 1999: 251.

in Thessalonica are also said to be "loved by God" (1 Thess. 1:4).[5] The message of 2 Thess. 2:13 is similar: "But we are bound to give thanks to God always for you, brethren beloved by the Lord, because God chose you from the beginning to be saved" (RSV).[6] God displays his love for the Thessalonians by choosing them to be his own. The Colossians are "God's chosen ones, holy and beloved" (Col. 3:12). The new life granted to believers when they were dead in sins is traced back to God's mercy and "the great love with which he loved us" (Eph. 2:4–5). Since God's election and love are often closely allied in Scripture, it is likely that Eph. 1:4–5 should be rendered as "in love he predestined us for adoption" instead of as "that we should be holy and blameless before him in love."[7] God's choice can be portrayed in terms of his love, as in the text "Jacob I loved, but Esau I hated" (Rom. 9:13). Paul cites Mal. 1:2–3 here, and yet it fits with his usage elsewhere and the context of Rom. 9 to define love here as electing love. So too the calling of the Gentiles in the words of Hosea 2:23 means that they are now his beloved (Rom. 9:24–25). Nor has God denied his promises to Israel: "But as regards election, they are beloved for the sake of their forefathers" (Rom. 11:28).

Just as God's election and calling are often attributed to his love, they are also ascribed to his mercy. The references to mercy are especially prominent in Rom. 9–11 and in the Pastoral Epistles. God's choice of Jacob rather than Esau, which is based solely on his will (Rom. 9:11), raises questions about God's justice (Rom. 9:14). Paul cites Exod. 33:19 to defend God's justice, for he shows mercy and compassion to whom he wishes.[8] Similarly, he shows mercy to whom he wishes and hardens whom he wishes (Rom. 9:18). Those whom God saves are "vessels of mercy" (Rom. 9:23). According to Rom. 11:30–32, God has constructed salvation history in such a way that he bestows his mercy upon both Jews and Gentiles. The pathway of history has been punctuated by surprises: the birth of Isaac as the chosen one instead of Ishmael (Rom. 9:6–9), the choice of Jacob the younger instead of Esau the elder (Rom. 9:13), the calling of the Gentiles while many of the Jews have been set aside (Rom. 9:24–29).[9] Finally, near the end of history, when all hope seems to be lost, God will save Israel (Rom. 11:23–32). The unexpected

5. For a useful summary of election in 1 Thessalonians, see Donfried 2002: 145–46.

6. In support of the reading "from the beginning" instead of "as the firstfruits," see Wanamaker 1990: 266.

7. Contra Lincoln 1990: 17; O'Brien 1999: 101; Hoehner 2002: 182–85. For the view that "in love" belongs with the participle "predestined," see Best 1998: 104, 122–23.

8. For a careful and convincing exegetical analysis of Rom. 9:1–23, see Piper 1993. For the use of the OT in Rom. 9–11 as a whole, see J. Wagner 2002: 43–305.

9. Thielman (1994b) captures well the theme of surprise in Rom. 9–11. For a more in-depth study, see Grindheim 2005.

course of history highlights the mercy of God. Salvation is not owed to any, as if God would somehow be unjust if he did not extend mercy to each individual without exception. If the latter were the case, the salvation of all would be a matter of justice, not mercy. Paul ascribes his own salvation to God's mercy, for he was the "foremost" of sinners (1 Tim. 1:13–16; cf. Titus 3:5).

Election

God's choice of some rather than others is never explained fully by Paul. Nor does he attempt a resolution to the problem of evil. The emphasis on God's mercy and love in election, however, demonstrates that the choice of any was undeserved, that the reception of salvation was a stunning gift. Sinners merit judgment and punishment, but Paul is astonished and grateful at the merciful and kind love of God that reaches out and saves some. At the same time, he asserts that those who fail to believe are fully responsible for their cold and resistant hearts. They have every reason to respond in faith and obedience but refuse to do so. Paul does not provide a philosophical resolution to what appears to be a contradiction. Perhaps we should not be too surprised, since even in science we have not resolved why electrons behave sometimes like waves and sometimes like particles, nor do we fully grasp how the human body and soul interact. The most profound realities in the universe seem to exceed our rational capacities.

The tension between divine sovereignty and human responsibility must be remembered in considering Paul's teaching on election. Paul thanks God for the faith, love, and hope of the Thessalonians, and such faith, hope, and love are finally ascribed to God's election (1 Thess. 1:2–4). God's choice of believers accounts for their trust in him and love for him. In 1 Corinthians Paul is concerned about the worldview that the Corinthians are beginning to adopt, for they are entranced with the rhetorical sophistry of speakers and are subscribing to a secular worldview. To undercut their pride he reminds them of their social status and calling (1 Cor. 1:26–31). God did not choose (*eklegomai*) intellectuals, the power brokers in society, or the social elite; rather, he chose those who were considered to be uneducated, those without influence, and the lower class. His aim was to preclude human boasting. According to 1 Cor. 1:30, people belong to Christ Jesus *ex autou* ("because of him" my translation)—that is, because of God's work. Therefore, the only boasting that is legitimate is boasting in the Lord. Paul's teaching on election has a practical aim: to nullify human pride and exalt the grace of God.

The same theme occurs in 2 Thess. 2:13. Paul rehearses in the preceding verses the deception and wickedness of the ungodly (2 Thess. 2:9–12). They perish because they delight in evil and refuse to love the truth. Should believers congratulate themselves, therefore, for responding differently? No credit belongs to believers for their change of life. Paul thanks God for his work that resulted in their salvation. God chose them "from the beginning" (RSV) for salvation. Election is introduced, then, so that believers are reminded that every good gift comes from God.

So too in Eph. 1:4, God chose believers before the world began so that they would live holy and godly lives. The theme of election is introduced as one of the blessings that believers have received (Eph. 1:3), so that they would in turn bless God. Three times Paul insists that God's redeeming work, which includes his election, should lead believers to praise God (Eph. 1:6, 12, 14). Paul introduces election not to precipitate philosophical discussions but rather to lead people to praise and honor God.[10] Some scholars argue that the election in Eph. 1:4 is corporate, referring to the church and not individuals.[11] Surely corporate election is in view, especially in Ephesians, where the focus is on the church of Jesus Christ, but on the other hand, we should not drive a wedge between the corporate and individual—both are intended.[12] It is scarcely the case that redemption, the forgiveness of sins, trust in Christ, and the sealing of the Spirit, all of which are mentioned in a very long sentence (Eph. 1:3–14), are only corporate and not individual. Nor will it do to say that the point of the verse is that God chose Christ or the church, and then human beings choose to belong to Christ or the church. The text specifically says that God chose human beings (Eph. 1:4), not Christ (true as the latter idea is theologically).[13] God chose believers "in him"; that is, the salvation that God planned is actualized in Christ.

In Col. 3:12 the election of believers and the love with which God has loved them ground the injunctions to live in humility and with kindness. Believers are exhorted to live godly lives not so that God will love them; rather, they are to live out their lives as those who know of God's election and love, as those who are secure in his grace.

Paul does not actually use the word "election" in Rom. 9, but the chapter breathes the concept. We have already noted the emphasis on God's mercy and love in choosing his people. The discussion begins

---

10. Lincoln (1990: 24) rightly emphasizes the theme of praise.

11. For a defense of this view generally in Pauline theology, see Klein 1990.

12. Rightly O'Brien 1999: 99; cf. Hoehner 2002: 176. In defense of this view on Rom. 9, see Schreiner 2000. For a critical evaluation of Schreiner, see Abasciano 2006, and for the response, see Schreiner 2006c.

13. Rightly Best 1998: 120; Hoehner 2002: 176–77. Hoehner (2002: 188–93) also demonstrates the weaknesses in M. Barth's view of election here.

with Paul's anguish over Israel's separation from God, despite the great promises that the nation enjoys (Rom. 9:1–5). The separation is no minor matter, for Paul is almost willing to be cursed and cut off from Christ on their behalf. It is clear, then, that Paul is distressed because Israel is unsaved (so also Rom. 10:1). Such a state of affairs does not nullify God's promise that he would save his people (Rom. 9:6).[14] God never pledged that every ethnic descendant of Abraham would be saved (Rom. 9:6b–9). The promise was given to Isaac, but Ishmael was excluded. The same principle is confirmed in the lives of Esau and Jacob (Rom. 9:10–13). In the mystery of his grace and mercy God chose Jacob instead of Esau. Paul excludes any notion that he selected Jacob rather than Esau because the former lived a more virtuous life. God did not scan the future and choose Jacob because of his future good works. His choice of Jacob rested on his purpose alone. God's choice of Jacob rather than Esau is not unjust, because, as we noted previously, the selection of any is due to his mercy (Rom. 9:14–18). Furthermore, God as the sovereign potter has the right to show mercy to whom he wishes (Rom. 9:19–23), so that his mercy will shine against the backdrop of his wrath.[15]

Some have argued that Paul does not have in mind election unto salvation in Rom. 9, but that he discusses the historical destiny of Israel and nations. Hence, he thinks of the place in history of the sons of Ishmael and Esau.[16] The reference to Pharaoh also demonstrates, according to many, that the destiny of nations is in view (Rom. 9:17). Paul does reflect on the destiny of peoples in these chapters, but such a destiny cannot be separated from salvation. We have already seen that Paul grieves over Israel because it is unsaved (Rom. 9:1–5; 10:1). He does not veer away from salvation and discuss historical destiny alone in the subsequent verses. All three chapters consider the salvation of Israel and the Gentiles. It is abundantly clear in Rom. 9:30–10:21 that the issue discussed is salvation. For example, Israel has not attained a righteous status with God, in that they have tried to establish righteousness by their own works, whereas those who believe are saved.

Similarly, when Paul discusses the remnant and election in Rom. 11, he argues that they are saved not on the basis of their works but by virtue of God's electing grace (Rom. 11:6).[17] Romans 11 climaxes with the promise that "all Israel will be saved" (Rom. 11:26). Paul does not

---

14. So Cranfield 1979: 473; Dunn 1988b: 539; Luz 1968: 28.

15. So Cranfield 1979: 496; Käsemann 1980: 271; Piper 1993: 214.

16. For a more detailed discussion of this view, see Schreiner 2000.

17. "Works" in this context does not refer to Jewish privilege or Israel's national prerogatives (contra Schnabel 2004b: 1315), for Paul speaks of "works" generally here, not "works of the law." Nor does Paul even include a reference to circumcision, food laws, or Sabbath in his previous discussion of the law in Rom. 9:30–10:8.

merely promise that the nation will be blessed in history, as if such a blessing could be separated from God's saving work. Furthermore, we have compelling evidence in Rom. 9:6–29 itself about how Paul thinks of salvation: (1) The promise of Abraham is restricted to those descended from Isaac (Rom. 9:6–8). (2) The contrast between "children of the flesh" and "children of God"—that is, "children of the promise" (Rom. 9:8)—separates those who are truly members of the covenant from outsiders. (3) There is a contrast between human "works" and God's "call" (Rom. 9:11); elsewhere Paul contrasts "works" and "faith," and so the very use of the term "works" indicates that salvation or the lack thereof is the issue. (4) The term "mercy" in Paul typically refers to God's saving mercy (Rom. 9:15, 16, 18, 23). (5) There is a contrast between "vessels of destruction" and "vessels of mercy" (Rom. 9:22–23); the word "destruction" (*apōleia*) is the term that Paul usually employs for eschatological ruin. (6) Paul further adds that the vessels of mercy are prepared for "glory," and glory designates the eschatological salvation awaiting believers (e.g., Rom. 2:7, 10). (7) God's calling of Jews and Gentiles is clearly a call to salvation (Rom. 9:24–26; cf. 9:11). (8) The "remnant" refers to those in Israel who are saved (Rom. 9:27). In summary, all of Rom. 9–11 relates to salvation, and the view that Paul speaks merely of historical destiny and not salvation is exegetically unpersuasive.

Another common view is that Rom. 9–11 refers to corporate but not individual election.[18] It is clear that corporate election is in view in these chapters because Paul refers to Jews and Gentiles as a whole. Nevertheless, Paul's emphasis on corporate groups does not exclude individuals. Both corporate and individual election are in view for the following reasons: (1) Singulars, not plurals, are used in Rom. 9:16, 18. (2) Israel is indicted for lack of faith in Rom. 9:30–10:21, but failure to believe cannot be limited to Israel as a corporate entity; it is also the individual fault of those who disbelieved. (3) The emphasis on the remnant indicates that there are individuals within the larger group who believed (Rom. 11:1–6). (4) Corporate groups are made up of individuals, so that the former could not exist without the latter.

Paul's theology of election should not be considered in the abstract. God's choice of a remnant guarantees that salvation is by God's grace. After Paul emphasizes that the remnant is secured by God's gracious election (Rom. 11:1–5), he remarks, "But if it is by grace, it is no longer on the basis of works; otherwise grace would no longer be grace" (Rom. 11:6). If we reify election and remove it from its soteriological context, the Pauline teaching may communicate a distant God. In Paul's view, however, election supported his teaching on the freedom of God and

18. See Schreiner 2000; 2006c.

the grace of the gospel. Election is the means by which God fulfills his saving promises.

Predestination

Predestination (*proorizō*, "predestine") is a variant way of referring to God's election, emphasizing that he predetermined beforehand what would happen.[19] We note in Rom. 8:29–30 that those whom God foreknew he predestined to be like his Son. According to 1 Cor. 2:7, God predestined his secret wisdom, which is Christ crucified, for the glory of believers. Predestination leads to salvation because God's people are predestined to be adopted as God's sons and daughters (Eph. 1:5). Indeed, everything that occurs has been predestined by God (Eph. 1:11). Nor can God's predestining work be limited to salvation, for Eph. 1:10 indicates that God has purposed to sum up everything in Christ, and this includes what happens both in heaven and on earth. God's will embraces and includes everything comprehensively.

Grace

One of the most common terms in Pauline theology is "grace" (*charis*).[20] As we noted earlier, Paul often opens and closes his letters with a prayer that God will bestow grace upon his readers. Paul is deeply conscious that his apostolic calling and ministry can be explained only by the grace of God, for he often sounds the theme that his ministry has been given to him by God (Rom. 12:3; 15:15; 1 Cor. 3:10; Gal. 2:9; Eph. 3:2, 7, 8). He recognizes that he has accomplished what he has only by God's grace (1 Cor. 15:10), and that the grace bestowed upon him is a stunning example of God's mercy (1 Cor. 15:9–10; 1 Tim. 1:12–16). Still, he claims that he has labored ardently in the ministry (1 Cor. 15:10), and that he has conducted himself in the grace of God (2 Cor. 1:12). If we cobble together what Paul says here, it appears that grace is both an undeserved gift and a power that enables Paul to carry out his ministry.

The grace of God, according to Paul's gospel, is always rooted in the work of Christ. When Paul refers to the incarnation of Christ, to his becoming poor for the sake of believers so that they might be enriched (2 Cor. 8:9), he characterizes what Christ has done as grace. God's grace has been manifested in human history in the death of Christ (Titus 2:11). Grace in Paul is often used to underline that salvation is a gift. Grace is

---

19. See Radl, *EDNT* 3:159.
20. On the power of grace, see Nolland 1986.

"given" to believers "in Christ Jesus" (1 Cor. 1:4). Hence, grace is opposed to salvation based on works.

The latter issue has become controversial in recent scholarship since the work of E. Sanders and his emphasis on covenantal nomism, in which he emphasizes that Paul did not oppose a theology of works-righteousness.[21] However, a careful look at the Pauline writings reveals the unpersuasiveness of Sanders's analysis. Titus 3:5–6 is particularly clear, since the grace given in Christ is opposed to works done "in righteousness."[22] Nothing is said here about works of law (as if he were merely opposing the imposition of Jewish ethnicity), but Paul speaks of works done in righteousness. Justification belongs to believers as a gift of God's grace (Rom. 3:24; cf. Gal. 2:16). If righteousness were attained by means of the law, then the grace of God manifested in the cross would be denied (Gal. 2:21). Grace and works are mutually exclusive as the basis of salvation. If people receive salvation on the basis of works, then salvation is deserved and even owed to them (Rom. 4:4). On the contrary, according to Paul, all people are ungodly, and hence salvation is a gift granted to those who "do not work" but rather believe in the one who pronounces the ungodly to be right in his sight (Rom. 4:5).[23]

Paul trumpets election precisely because it preserves the truth that God saves on the basis of grace instead of works (Rom. 11:6). God's calling people to salvation, before history began, is due to his grace (Gal. 1:15; 2 Tim. 1:9). If salvation were on the basis of works, it would cancel out the truth that salvation is a gift given to those who deserve punishment. Boasting would be fitting if salvation were based on works (Eph. 2:8–9). Since salvation is granted freely, apart from and in spite of what people have done, it is an undeserved gift. Grace and faith are indissolubly connected in Pauline theology (Rom. 4:13–16). If salvation is secured through human works, then the only result will be divine wrath because human beings fail to attain to the required divine standard. Salvation through faith, on the other hand, places the emphasis on the sure promise of God. Faith accords with grace because it rests on what God has accomplished in Christ (Rom. 3:21–26) rather than trusting in

21. On Judaism and Paul, see E. Sanders 1977; 1983. The new perspective is, of course, now a commonplace in Pauline scholarship. See especially Dunn 1983; 1985; 1988a; 1988b; 1990; 1992a; 1992b; 1997; Wright 1992a: 150, 240–42; 1992b: 238.

22. Many scholars maintain that Titus is post-Pauline. But even if this is the case, it still functions as a challenge to the new perspective, for then one of the earliest Pauline disciples understood the polemic against works as directed against works-righteousness. See particularly Marshall 1996; cf. W. Mounce 2000: 447–48.

23. Hofius (1989: 120–47) argues that the Pauline theology of justifying the ungodly is rooted in the OT.

the goodness of human beings. Those who attempt to be justified by the law have fallen from grace (Gal. 5:4).

The salvation that believers enjoy can be described in terms of grace. Paul says that believers "are all partakers with me of grace" (Phil. 1:7). At conversion they came to know "the grace of God in truth" (Col. 1:6). When Paul reflects on his salvation, he is reminded that God's grace overflowed into his life (1 Tim. 1:14). The lavishness of grace is a favorite theme for Paul. The saving work of God is "to the praise of his glorious grace," and forgiveness of sins testifies to "the riches of his grace" (Eph. 1:6–7). The contrast between Adam and Christ reveals the stunning abundance of the grace of Christ (Rom. 5:12–19). He not only reverses what Adam brought into the world but also carries human beings further, so that they stand in grace (Rom. 5:2). The stunning abundance of God's grace in contrast to the death and devastation wrought by Adam is highlighted.[24] Thus, Paul can say that grace abounds and grace reigns through Jesus Christ (Rom. 5:20–21).

Grace in Pauline theology is not merely a gift but also a power that transforms.[25] Paul testifies "by the grace of God I am what I am" (1 Cor. 15:10). The change in Paul's life can be ascribed only to the grace of God. Paul can bear weaknesses, insults, and difficulties because the grace of Christ is sufficient for every situation (2 Cor. 12:9). Grace not only brings forgiveness of sins but also gives new life. God's grace has made believers alive with Christ (Eph. 2:5–6; Col. 2:13), so that they are raised and seated with Christ in heaven. Grace has ordained that believers will do good works (Eph. 2:10).[26] The reign of grace in Christ (Rom. 5:21) means that believers have died to the power of sin (Rom. 6:1–11). They are no longer "under law" but rather are "under grace" (Rom. 6:14–15). Those who lived under the law lived in the old era of redemptive history, under the Sinai covenant, where sin reigned. That sin ruled under the Sinai covenant is evident from Israel's history. For Paul, living under grace does not translate into freedom to pursue one's autonomous will. Those who live in the realm of grace have become God's slaves (Rom. 6:16–23), so that now they have a desire to do God's will. Hence, the generosity of believers in contributing financially to the needs of others

24. Hofius (2001: 188–89) says of the contrast between Adam and Christ, "The overwhelming fullness and power of the grace referred to in v. 15b lies in the fact that it reverses what Adam inaugurated, overpowering the reality of sin and death and breaking their corrupting and destructive might."

25. See Berger, *EDNT* 3:458–59.

26. In this context Paul emphasizes the good works that believers *will* do, not the good works that they *must* do (see Lincoln 1990: 115–16; Hoehner 2002: 348–49). O'Brien (1999: 181) rightly sees the emphasis on divine predestination here but wrongly emphasizes *in this context* the responsibility to live in a way that pleases God.

is nothing other than the work of grace (2 Cor. 8:1, 4, 6, 7, 19). Their beneficence to others is evidence of "the surpassing grace of God upon you" and testifies to the unspeakably great gift that belongs to believers in Christ (2 Cor. 9:14–15). The gifts that believers have are due to God's grace (Rom. 12:6; Eph. 4:7). Believers seek to impart grace to others in their conversation (Eph. 4:29) and to share a word of grace with those who disbelieve (Col. 4:6).

Calling

If we resume Paul's chronology in Rom. 8:29–30, he proceeds to say that "those whom he predestined he also called" (Rom. 8:30).[27] The concept of "calling" (*kaleō*, *klēsis*, *klētos*) is a favorite of Paul's. By my count, the verb occurs thirty-three times, the noun on nine occasions, and the adjective in seven places. Several verses help us establish a definition. The gospel is proclaimed and heralded (*kēryssō*) to all, whether Jews or Greeks (1 Cor. 1:22–23), but only some among all those who hear the message are "called" (*klētos* [1 Cor. 1:24]). Indeed, in subsequent verses the term "called" is explicated in terms of those whom God "chose" (*eklegomai* [1 Cor. 1:26–28]). It seems, then, that calling occurs through the proclaimed word, and yet calling is not absolutely coterminous with the word proclaimed, since only some of those who hear the word are called. Calling, then, cannot be the same thing as being invited to be saved, for all those who hear the word preached are summoned to faith and obedience. Since calling overlaps with being chosen in this context, it seems that calling refers to God's effective work in bringing some who hear the gospel to saving faith.

The foregoing definition is confirmed in Rom. 8:30: "those whom he called he also justified."[28] We know from Rom. 5:1 that people are justified by faith, and yet Paul can say that those called are justified. It must follow, then, that calling creates faith, so that all those called are justified. The term "called" cannot mean invited and summoned to faith, for it is patently obvious that not all those invited to repent actually believe.

The power and efficacy of God's call is a repeated theme in Pauline writings. God "calls into existence things that do not exist" (Rom. 4:17).[29] In context this refers to God granting Abraham and Sarah the ability to have children. God calls life into being where no ability to produce life exists. Similarly, it was God's call that turned Paul from being a persecutor of the church to an apostle of Jesus Christ (Gal. 1:13–16). In

27. See Eckert, *EDNT* 2:242–43.
28. For further elaboration of this point, see Schreiner 1998: 450–51.
29. In defense of the interpretation proposed here, see Schreiner 1998: 236–37.

Rom. 9 God's call is closely associated with his electing work, indicating that God had effectively brought some to salvation (Rom. 9:7, 11, 24, 25, 26). Those whom God has chosen are called to faith through the proclamation of the gospel (2 Thess. 2:13–14).[30] The God who has powerfully called believers to himself will also complete his sanctifying work (1 Thess. 5:24).[31] God's call stands in contrast to works (Rom. 9:11; 2 Tim. 1:9), for human works do not and cannot save, but only the grace of God. The power of God's call is evident, for "the gifts and the calling of God are irrevocable" (Rom. 11:29).

Justification

If we continue with Paul's train of thought in Rom. 8:30, the next term is "justification," inasmuch as God justifies those whom he calls. The status of justification in Pauline theology has long been debated. Wrede identified it as a polemical doctrine in which Paul responds to his opponents and noted that it appears infrequently in nonpolemical contexts.[32] Schweitzer doubted whether justification serves as a foundation for ethics and life in the Spirit and subordinated it to Paul's "in Christ" theology, seeing justification as a "subsidiary crater" to the main crater of being in Christ.[33] Participation with Christ, rather than the juridical doctrine of justification, is trumpeted by Sanders as the center of Paul's thought.[34] Dunn maintains that Luther misunderstood Paul in formulating his view of justification.[35] It is not my purpose here to arbitrate the debate on the status of justification in Paul. It seems, however, that those who doubt its centrality overstate their case.[36] Justification in Paul means that one is vindicated in the divine tribunal at the final judgment. Such a theme exists in what is perhaps Paul's earliest letter, 1 Thessalonians, where he assures believers that they will escape God's anger at the last judgment (1 Thess. 1:10; 5:9), even though Paul does not identify such as justification. That forgiveness of sin is available through Christ's death can be traced back to the earliest elements of Pauline preaching (1 Cor.

---

30. So also Wanamaker 1990: 267.

31. Rightly Wanamaker 1990: 207.

32. Wrede 1962: 122–23. The influence of Wrede continues today. See Strecker 2000: 148–49.

33. Schweitzer 1931: 225. Grundmann (1933) contends, against Schweitzer, that mysticism and justification are not polarized in Paul but rather are integrated.

34. E. Sanders 1977: 502–8.

35. Dunn 1992b: 2. Dunn understands justification by faith to speak against pride in one's nationality, race, or culture.

36. For a defense of the cruciality of justification, see Seifrid 2000b; Fung 1981; Schrenk, *TDNT* 2: 202. Already Schlatter (1999: 239) rightly responded to objections.

15:1–5).[37] It should also be noted that the distinctive Pauline teaching on justification is included in his missionary preaching according to Acts 13:38–39. The indicative-imperative structure of Paul's thought demonstrates that the pronouncement of justification is vitally related to the new life of believers. Justification and life in the Spirit are not at loggerheads for Paul. The former is the foundation for the latter, and the joy of being right with God frees believers to obey God (Gal. 5:13–15). Nor can justification be dismissed as a legal fiction, for God's declaration creates a new reality, so that believers are rightly related to him.

Often justification is limited to God's saving righteousness, and any notion of retributive punishment is excluded. Such a view does not handle the evidence adequately, for in Rom. 3:5 righteousness refers to God's justice in judging sinners. The link between God's righteousness and wrath in Rom. 1:17–18 points in the same direction, and Rom. 2:5 specifically includes the idea of God's righteous judgment. Those who emphasize that righteousness is always relational tend to minimize the external standards to which a relationship must conform.[38]

Justification refers to God's verdict of not guilty on the day of judgment (Rom. 2:13).[39] God's eschatological verdict has now been announced in advance for those who believe in Jesus Christ.[40] Those who have been justified by the blood of Christ will be saved from God's wrath at the eschaton (Rom. 5:9). God will announce publicly to the world the verdict of not guilty on the last day, though this verdict already stands for those who belong to Christ Jesus, despite its being hidden from the eyes of the world. The forensic and legal character of the term "justify" (*dikaioō*) derives from the verbal form of *ṣdq* in the OT. Judges are to declare the righteous innocent and condemn the wicked (Deut. 25:1; cf. 2 Sam. 15:4; 1 Kings 8:31–32; 2 Chron. 6:23; Prov. 17:15; Isa. 5:23). Judges do not "make" anyone righteous. They pronounce on what is in fact the case—if they are righteous judges. In other words, the verbal form

---

37. Rightly Kim 2002: 49, 85–100. Westerholm (2004: 353–66) traces and explains well further evidence in support of the claim that the concept of justification is present in 1 Thessalonians and 1–2 Corinthians.

38. So Seifrid 2001: 419. The entire discussion by Seifrid (pp. 415–22) is a helpful corrective to the tendency to separate relationships from norms in construing righteousness.

39. Paul often uses the noun "righteousness" (*dikaiosynē*) to refer to the ethical behavior required by God (Rom. 6:13, 16, 18, 19, 20; Eph. 4:24; 5:9; Phil. 1:11; 1 Tim. 6:11; 2 Tim. 2:22). No one disputes such a usage, but the intention here is to explore the "righteousness" word group in texts that focus on God's saving work.

40. For the most satisfying explanation of the eschatological character of justification, see Gaffin 2006: 79–108. Bultmann (1964: 15) identifies the future references to justification (Rom. 5:19; Gal. 2:17; 5:5) as logical futures. For recent recognition of the future element of justification, see Rainbow (2005: 157–74), who, however, does not explicate as clearly the link between the already and the not yet in defining justification.

belongs in the forensic realm. For example, God will pass judgment on whether Paul is acquitted before the Lord on judgment day (1 Cor. 4:4). When Paul says that the doers of the law will be justified (Rom. 2:13), a declaration of righteousness is intended. God will pass judgment as to whether people are righteous—that is, whether they have done what is right and good. If they have lived righteously, according to Rom. 2:13, God will declare them to be righteous. This last example, as Westerholm has argued, is the ordinary sense of righteousness.[41] It is ordinary in the sense that it conforms with the way human judges are supposed to conduct themselves. They pass judgment against the wicked and make favorable pronouncements for the righteous.

In Paul, however, we also have what Westerholm identifies as an extraordinary meaning of righteousness.[42] In this instance God declares those who are sinners to be in the right before him if they trust in Jesus Christ for their salvation. This is extraordinary because such a verdict violates the normal and just procedure for a judge. Judges who declare the guilty to be righteous violate the standards of justice. Paul, of course, does not think that God violates any standard of justice.[43] He does teach, however, that God announces that those who believe in Jesus are in the right.

Scholars have continued to argue about the meaning of righteousness and justification in Paul.[44] A number of scholars have argued that God's righteousness should be defined as his faithfulness to the covenant.[45] The OT background plays a vital role here, for often in the OT righteousness occurs in Hebrew parallelism with God's truth, mercy, and salvation (Ps. 31:1; 36:10; 40:10; 71:2; 88:10–12; 98:2–3; 143:1; Isa. 46:13; 51:5–8). Surely God's saving actions *fulfill* his covenantal promises made to Abraham; however, evidence is lacking that righteousness should be *defined* as covenantal faithfulness.[46] The Hebrew parallelism does not establish, for example, that "mercy" means "truth," and that "salvation" and "righteousness" have precisely the same definition.[47] If every term

---

41. Westerholm 2004: 263–73.
42. Westerholm 2004: 273–84.
43. Paul unpacks why God is not unrighteous in a number of texts, such as Rom. 3:21–26; Gal. 3:10–14; 2 Cor. 5:21.
44. For a helpful entry into the discussion, see Brauch 1977: 523–42; see also Reumann 1982.
45. Wright 1995: 33–34, 39; 1997: 113–33; Dunn 1998: 340–46; S. Williams 1980: 241–90; O'Brien 1992: 75–78.
46. See the persuasive discussion in Westerholm 2004: 286–96. Note also the criticisms of Seifrid 2001, though Seifrid separates righteousness too radically from covenant and wrongly traces it only back to creation.
47. Gaffin (2006) shows that justification in Paul, though it has ecclesiological implications, is soteriological.

is assigned the same meaning as the other terms with which it appears in parallelism, then we are perilously close to saying that every word has the same meaning, which verges on saying that everything means nothing.[48]

Käsemann and Stuhlmacher have maintained that God's righteousness refers to his transforming righteousness.[49] They defend this view with a number of arguments: (1) God's righteousness is said to be "revealed" (*apokalyptetai* [Rom. 1:17]) and "manifested" (*pephanerōtai* [Rom. 3:21]). Hence, God's righteousness is an apocalyptic and effective work of God that cannot be limited to a mere declaration and includes the entire creation and not just the individual.[50] What God declares becomes a reality because he is redeemer and creator. (2) Such a view is supported by the parallelism between the "power" (Rom. 1:16), "righteousness" (Rom. 1:17), and "anger" (Rom. 1:18) of God (*theou*). All three involve genitives of source (*theou*), indicating God's activity unleashed in the world. His righteousness is not merely a static pronouncement but rather represents the unleashing of his power in an active way. In the same way, God's wrath is effective, judging people for their sin of failing to worship and praise God (Rom. 1:18–32). (3) The transformative view points to the same evidence noted above in support of covenantal faithfulness. God's righteousness in the OT is often parallel to his salvation, truth, and mercy. The background demonstrates that God's righteousness is his saving action on behalf of his people, and it should not be limited to his forensic declaration. God's gift and God's power cannot be separated from one another. (4) In Rom. 3:24 God's righteousness is "through the redemption that is in Christ Jesus." Redemption signifies the freedom and liberation of sin through Jesus Christ, finding its antecedent in God's liberation of his people from Egypt. If righteousness becomes ours through the liberation of sin effected by Jesus Christ, then righteousness must include the idea of freedom from sin. Righteousness includes, then, the notion of God's transforming power. (5) Scholars have too rigidly separated justification and sanctification. This is apparent from Rom. 6:7: "For the one who has died has been justified from sin" (my translation). Those

48. Against the view that righteousness is centrally a matter of ecclesiology rather than soteriology, Rainbow (2005: 104n22) aptly says, "We do not gain a relationship with God by being counted among his people; rather, we find a place among his people by virtue of his acceptance of us."

49. Käsemann 1969: 168–82; Stuhlmacher 1966; see also Schlatter 1999: 234–36. See also C. Müller (1964) and Kertelge (1967), who generally are in the same orbit as Käsemann and Stuhlmacher. For a summary of the various views that also details some of the differences among the various writers noted here, see Plevnik 1986: 47–52.

50. Even though Soards (1987) agrees with Käsemann's definition of righteousness, he demonstrates that the evidence for Paul utilizing a technical term from apocalyptic Judaism is lacking.

who have died with Christ have been freed from sin's power. (6) Paul speaks of grace reigning through righteousness (Rom. 5:21), of the service of righteousness (Rom. 6:18–19; 2 Cor. 3:9), and of submitting to God's righteousness (Rom. 10:3). The use of the verb "justify" (*dikaioō*) here indicates that justification cannot be limited to legal categories. God transforms those whom he declares to be in the right. The same point is evident from 2 Cor. 3:8–9. Those who benefit from the "ministry of righteousness" also enjoy the "ministry of the Spirit." The effective work of the Spirit is part and parcel of the righteousness of God.

Despite some valid insights in the notion that righteousness is transformative, the case for such a view is overstated, and righteousness and justification in Paul should be understood as forensic only.[51]

(1) We noted above that the verbal form in the OT (*ṣdq*) should be understood in terms of God's declaration.[52] The legal character of the term is apparent in a number of other OT texts as well (Job 4:17; 9:2, 14–15, 20; 13:18; Ps. 51:4; Isa. 43:9, 26).

(2) The verbal form "justify" (*dikaioō*) in Paul almost invariably refers to God's declaration and is used forensically. The forensic character of the verb is apparent from Rom. 2:13 and 1 Cor. 4:4. The law-court background of "justify" is perhaps clearest in Rom. 8:33: "Who shall bring any charge against God's elect? It is God who justifies." On the last day some may bring charges before God's chosen at the divine tribunal, but all charges will be dismissed because God has declared his people to be in the right before him. As the judge, he has declared that they are innocent of all the accusations brought against them.

(3) Paul often says that human beings are righteous by faith (e.g., Rom. 1:17; 3:22, 26; 4:3, 5, 9, 13; 9:30; 10:4; Gal. 2:16; 3:6, 11; 5:5; Phil. 3:9). In such contexts Paul contrasts righteousness by faith with righteousness by works.[53] Westerholm rightly says that in these texts Paul uses the terms "righteousness" or "justify" in an extraordinary way. Ordinarily, people are declared to be righteous in human courts on the basis of their good behavior. That is, if they did what is good, they are declared to be in the right, but if they did what is evil, they are condemned. Paul, however, maintains that it is not those who work but those who believe who are righteous before God (Rom. 4:4–5). Indeed, no one can be righteous by works before God, for all have fallen short of what he requires (Rom.

---

51. So Bultmann 1964; Cranfield 1975: 95–99; Moo 1991: 65–70, 75–86. See also the more recent contributions of Seifrid 2001; Westerholm 2004: 261–96; Rainbow 2005: 100–104.

52. Ziesler (1972) argues that the verbal form is forensic and the noun is ethical.

53. Interestingly, one of the clearest indications that righteousness is by grace rather than works is found in Titus 3:5–7. This letter is usually dismissed as post-Pauline, but the sentiment expressed here fits well with what Paul says elsewhere.

3:23). Righteousness by faith, then, must refer to the *gift* of righteousness given to human beings by God. Human beings are justified not on the basis of doing but of believing. Nor does Paul view faith as a "work" that merits the declaration of righteousness. Faith saves because it looks entirely to what God has done for believers in Christ. It rests on Christ's death for forgiveness of sins and his resurrection for the sake of their justification (Rom. 3:21–26; 4:25[54]). The righteousness given to believers, then, is alien because it is based not on anything they have done but rather on God's work in Christ. This suggests that righteousness as a gift is granted to those who believe.

(4) That righteousness is a forensic declaration is supported also by the link between righteousness and forgiveness. We have already seen the connection between righteousness and forgiveness in Rom. 4:25; 8:33. Paul slides easily from justification to forgiveness in Rom. 4:1–8. David's forgiveness of sins is nothing less than his justification—his being in the right before God (Rom. 4:6–8). The primary idea is not that David is transformed by God, even though Paul stresses the transforming power of God's grace in other contexts. The text calls attention to David's sin and his forgiveness by God, confirming the extraordinary nature of God's justice, for he forgives sinners and declares them to be in the right.

(5) The idea that righteousness is counted (*logizomai*) to believers indicates that righteousness is not native to believers, that it is granted to them by God (Rom. 3:28; 4:3–6, 8–11, 22–24; 9:8; Gal. 3:6). This argument is strengthened when we add that righteousness is counted to those who believe, not to those who work. God does not "count" sins against those who have put their faith in Christ (2 Cor. 5:19). This is a strange reckoning or counting indeed when those who have done evil are considered to be righteous. This fits with the notion, however, that believers have received "the free gift of righteousness" (Rom. 5:17).

(6) Should "the righteousness of God" also be understood as forensic (esp. Rom. 1:17; 3:21–22; 10:3; 2 Cor. 5:21)? Some scholars have maintained that Rom. 3:5, where righteousness is parallel to God's "faithfulness" and truth, supports covenantal faithfulness as the interpretation. Such an interpretation is scarcely clear in Rom. 3:1–8, for it seems that God's righteousness here refers to his judgment of sinners.[55] Romans 3:4, citing Ps. 51:4 LXX, refers to God's conquering when he judges sinners. The righteousness of God is used in a context that speaks of his wrath inflicted on the wicked and his judgment of the world on the last day (Rom. 3:5–6). Rather than referring to God's covenant faithfulness, this

54. The formula used here probably draws on Isa. 53 (Zimmerli and Jeremias 1957: 89).

55. Rightly Bultmann 1964: 13.

text refers to the ordinary definition of the word "righteousness"—that is, God judging the wicked because they have lived in an evil manner. Romans 3:5, then, does not bear on the discussion at all, for we are considering here the extraordinary definition of the word "righteousness," when Paul uses the term of God's putting sinners in the right, so that he thinks of salvation rather than judgment.

That the "righteousness of God" refers to a divine gift is clear from Phil. 3:9, where Paul speaks of "the righteousness from God" (*tēn ek theou dikaiosynēn*).[56] The righteousness is not Paul's own, deriving from his observance of the law. It is a righteousness from God himself, obtained by faith in Jesus Christ. Philippians 3:9, then, provides an important clue as to how we should interpret God's righteousness in Rom. 1:17; 3:21–22. It refers to God's saving righteousness, given as a gift to those who believe. The lack of the preposition "from" (*ek*) in the texts in Romans is not decisive, for in both instances the same subject is treated: the saving righteousness of God that is given to those who believe. It is unlikely that Paul would use a different definition of the word "righteousness" in texts that are so similar. We have seen that some argue that righteousness is transformative in Rom. 1:17 because it is parallel to God's power and wrath. It is correct to say that each of the genitives should be identified as a genitive of source. God's anger and power and righteousness all come from him. It does not follow, however, from the collocation of terms that the words all refer to a divine activity, if by that one concludes that God's righteousness must be a transforming one. The words "power," "wrath," and "righteousness" do not all have the same meaning. The phrase "righteousness of God" makes perfect sense if it designates the gift of God's righteousness.

A powerful argument supporting this view are the numerous parallels between Rom. 10:1–5 and Phil. 3:2–9. The following parallels exist: (1) a reference to God's righteousness; (2) the contrast between righteousness by law and righteousness by faith; (3) the parallel between Israel's quest to establish its own righteousness and Paul's quest to do the same; (4) in particular, Paul's emphasis on "not having a righteousness of my own that comes from the law" (Phil. 3:9) and Israel's attempt to establish its own righteousness (Rom. 10:3), a "righteousness that is based on the law" (Rom. 10:5). My point is that the parallel contexts indicate that righteousness in Rom. 10 cannot have a different definition from what we see in Phil. 3. In the latter text, righteousness clearly is a gift given to sinners—a declaration that those who have failed to keep the law but who have trusted in Jesus Christ stand in the right before God. The same gift character of righteousness, therefore, is in view in Rom. 10.

56. See Silva 2005: 160–62.

We can go further. If such is the meaning in Rom. 10, it is highly un-likely that Paul means anything different in Rom. 1:17; 3:21–22. When he speaks of God's extraordinary righteousness in declaring sinners to be in the right before him by faith in Christ, he has in mind the gift of righteousness—God's declaration of not guilty. Paul would confuse the readers if in some instances he used the term "righteousness of God" to refer to a gift of a righteous status from God and in others of a divine activity that transforms believers. He would need to explain much more clearly that he operates with such a distinction. That he refers to the gift of righteousness is also clear from 2 Cor. 5:21.[57] God made Christ to be sin, even though he was without sin, so that believers would "become the righteousness of God." The meaning of God's righteousness is expli-cated by 2 Cor. 5:19, which refers to forgiveness of sins. The verse also explains how God could grant the gift of righteousness to those who are sinners. The extraordinary gift of righteousness is secured through Christ's death on the cross. God "made him to be sin" so that those who are wicked could become righteous. An interchange between Christ and sinners is posited here.[58]

Romans 3:21–26 is a key text that is remarkably parallel to 2 Cor. 5:21.[59] This paragraph functions as the hinge for the letter to the Romans and is one of the most important, if not the most important, in the letter.[60] The placement of the text in the letter should be observed. Paul has finished arguing that all people sin and deserve judgment (Rom. 1:18–3:20). He summarizes this truth in Rom. 3:23: "For all have sinned and fall short

57. Rightly Harris 2005: 454–56. The claim by Wright (1997: 104–5) that the reference is to Paul's apostolic ministry as an incarnation of God's covenant faithfulness is quite implausible. See also the eminently clear discussion in Garland 1999: 300–302.

58. R. Martin (1986: 140, 157) thinks that the idea is that Christ was made a sin offering, drawing on Isa. 53:10. He also maintains that substitution is in view in a qualified way (pp. 143–45). Garland (1999: 300–301) argues that reference to a sin offering is unlikely, for such a view requires two different meanings for the word "sin" in the verse, and one would expect verbs such as "offer" or "present," which typically are associated with OT sacrifices (see also Bell 2002: 13–14). Garland thinks that the point is that Jesus was treated as a sinner on the cross just as he was cursed according to Gal. 3:13. In any case, Garland (1999: 301–2) also proceeds to argue that substitution is in view in the text. For the substitutionary character of Christ's sacrifice in 2 Cor. 5:21, see also Hafemann 2000: 247–48. Bell (2002: 14–16) wrongly argues that the Pauline statement that Jesus did not know sin (2 Cor. 5:21) refers only to his preexistent state.

59. Hengel (1981: 1–32) demonstrates that the offering of sacrifices to avert the wrath of the gods was common in the Greco-Roman world. Hence, Gentile readers would have no difficulty understanding the concept of a substitutionary atonement (Hengel 1981: 32). The biblical view of the atonement, of course, corrects the pagan notions present in the Greco-Roman world and thus cannot be identified with them in every respect (rightly Beckwith 1995: 106).

60. The following discussion on Rom. 3:21–26 and Gal. 3:10–14 comes substantially from Schreiner 2006b: 87–90.

of the glory of God." God demands perfect obedience, and all fall short of his standard. How, then, will people become right with God? Paul argues in Rom. 3:21–22 that a right relation with God is obtained not by keeping the law but rather through faith in Jesus Christ. All people who trust in Christ are justified by God because of the redemption accomplished by Christ Jesus (Rom. 3:24).

Romans 3:25–26 is of particular importance for our subject. God set forth Christ as a propitiatory sacrifice by virtue of Jesus' bloody death. The terms *hilastērion* and *haima* point back to the OT cultus and sacrificial system. Discussion has centered on the meaning of the term *hilastērion*, whether it should be rendered as "expiation" or "propitiation."[61] I contend that those who defend the notion of propitiation have had the better of the argument, for the term includes the sense of the averting of God's wrath—the appeasement or satisfaction of his righteousness.[62] This fits beautifully with Rom. 1:18, where the wrath of God against sin is announced, and Rom. 2:5, where the final judgment is described as the day of God's wrath. The line of argument in Rom. 1:18–3:20 provokes the reader to ask how God's wrath can be averted. The answer in Rom. 3:25 is that God's wrath has been satisfied or appeased in the death of Christ.

The words following "propitiation" substantiate the interpretation offered here. Paul explains that Christ was set forth as a mercy seat to demonstrate God's righteousness.[63] The context reveals that by "righteousness" Paul refers to God's holiness or justice, for Paul immediately refers to the sins that God passed over in previous eras. By "passing over of sins" Paul means that sins committed previously in history did not receive the full punishment deserved. Hence, God's failure to act calls into question his justice. Paul's solution is that God looked ahead to the cross of Christ, where his wrath would be appeased and justice would be satisfied. Christ as the substitute would absorb the full payment for sin.[64]

---

61. In support of expiation and the notion that judgment is merely the natural result of sin, not the expression of God's personal wrath, see Dodd 1932: 21–24; 1935: 82–95. Supporting a reference to propitiation are Morris 1965: 144–213; Nicole 1955.

62. Against the view defended here, see Hofius 1989: 33–42. Stuhlmacher (1993: 52, 56–57) rejects any notion of satisfaction, locating the death of Jesus only in the love of God. In doing so he overlooks God's holiness and justice in the cross.

63. Many scholars argue that the word *hilastērion* refers to mercy seat here (see Bell 2002: 17–19). Some of those who posit the meaning mercy seat suggest that this rules out the idea of propitiation (e.g., Bell). Such a deduction clearly is mistaken. If the proper steps were not taken on the Day of Atonement in the holy of holies, God's wrath would manifest itself (cf. Lev. 10:1–3). For the view that Paul's theology of the atonement stems from martyrological traditions, especially mediated via 4 Maccabees, see S. Williams 1975.

64. Hofius (2006) rightly sees in the letters that Christ's death functioned as a substitute for sin. He sustains his argument especially from Paul but also from 1 Peter and

The foregoing interpretation is confirmed by Rom. 3:26: "It was to show his righteousness at the present time, so that he might be just and the justifier of the one who has faith in Jesus."[65] Christ's death as a propitiation, Paul repeats, demonstrates God's holiness and justice at the present juncture of salvation history.[66] Thereby God is both "just and the justifier" of those who put their faith in Christ. God's justice is satisfied because Christ bore the full payment for sin. But God is also the justifier, because on the basis of the cross of Christ sinners receive forgiveness through faith in Jesus. In the cross of Christ the justice and mercy of God meet. God's holiness is satisfied by Christ's bearing the penalty of sin, and God's saving activity is realized in the lives of those who trust in Christ. Some object that retribution cannot be in view, since the focus is on personal relationships rather than retribution. But personal relationships and retribution are not at odds with one another. God's justice is not an attribute that can be separated from his person.

The argument of Gal. 3:10–14 is remarkably similar to Rom. 3:21–26. Galatians 3:10 teaches that God's curse stands upon all those who fail to keep God's law perfectly. How can such a curse be removed? Galatians 3:13 answers the question: "Christ redeemed us from the curse of the law by becoming a curse for [*hyper*] us—for it is written,[67] 'Cursed is everyone who is hanged on a tree.'" The curse that humans deserve was borne by Christ.[68] He died in the place of sinners.[69] The sinless one took upon himself the curse of God.

Some of the arguments supporting transformative righteousness have been answered in the course of the discussion, but we need to pause for comments on a few that have not been examined thus far.

(1) The revelation of God's saving righteousness apocalyptically in history does not establish a transformative righteousness. God's righteousness in Christ is certainly an eschatological work of God. Such a

---

Hebrews. However, Hofius argues that the NT epistles diverge from Isa. 53 in that we have "inclusive-place-taking" instead of "exclusive-place-taking." Space is lacking to interact in detail with Hofius's view, but I maintain that his interpretation fails because it is unclear that the NT epistles correct what we find in Isa. 53. It seems instead that they affirm the same teaching.

65. For further support of the interpretation offered here and interaction with the literature, see Schreiner 1998: 176–99.

66. The OT background, though keenly debated, also supports substitution. See Rodriguez 1979; G. Wenham 1995.

67. The preposition *hyper* denotes substitution here. See the discussion of this preposition in Wallace 1996: 383–89.

68. Contra Bruce 1982a: 165–66, it seems that the curse comes from God himself. Rightly Dunn 1993: 177; Morris 1965: 57–58.

69. In support of substitution, see H. Betz 1979: 151; Morris 1965: 56–59; Matera 1992: 124.

statement, however, does not necessarily establish that righteousness should be defined in terms of transformation. God's declaration about sinners is an end-time verdict that has been announced before the end has arrived. The verdict is effective in the sense that every verdict announced by God constitutes reality.

(2) The argument from redemption fails to establish the transformation view as well. Justification belongs to believers through redemption (Rom. 3:23). In some instances in Paul, however, redemption is defined primarily in terms of forgiveness of sins (Eph. 1:7; Col. 1:14). The forgiveness of sins is communicated as well in Col. 2:13–14. Paul pictures it as the erasure of debts that had accrued against believers. The definitive nature of forgiveness is portrayed in the nailing of sins to the cross, indicating that Christ has definitively and finally put away sin. The fundamental bondage of human beings can be attributed to guilt that stains them through sin. Hence, the reference to redemption does not clearly indicate that righteousness is transformative.[70]

(3) To say that those who have died with Christ "are justified of sin" (Rom. 6:7) seems at first glance to be a compelling argument for the transformative view. On the other hand, virtually all scholars agree that in the vast majority of cases the verb "justify" (*dikaioō*) is forensic. Hence, to posit a different definition here is antecedently unlikely. Furthermore, it is not as if Paul puts God's declaration of righteousness and a changed life into two discrete compartments. He believes that the two are related to one another without saying that they are precisely the same thing. God's declaration that sinners are in the right before him is the foundation for a changed life. A similar argument can be made regarding the collocation of the "ministry of righteousness" and the "ministry of the Spirit" in 2 Cor. 3:8–9. Paul never imagined that one could be righteous in God's sight without being transformed by the Spirit. And yet it still should be said that it does not follow that the transforming power of the Spirit and righteousness are precisely the same.[71] Too many of those who defend the transformative view argue for identity of meaning from parallelism of terms. Such an approach is flawed, for it collapses the meaning of words so that they become virtually indistinguishable.

Believers are justified, therefore, on the basis of Christ's work. Justification does not describe the ongoing work of the Spirit in believers. By virtue of union with Christ believers already enjoy justification in this present evil age.[72] The ground of justification is not the moral transfor-

---

70. So Piper 2002: 73–75.

71. See Harris 2005: 287–88.

72. See Gaffin 2006: 50–52. For the role of imputation in Paul's theology, see the important work of Vickers 2006.

mation of believers, even though the transforming work of the Spirit is necessary to receive eternal life.

Salvation

In Rom. 8:30 justification is followed by glorification, but I will introduce at this juncture other soteriological themes that precede final glorification, even though Paul does not mention them in Rom. 8:30. We consider here salvation, reconciliation, redemption, victory over evil powers, and sanctification.

Salvation or deliverance in Paul (*sōzō, sōtēria, rhyomai*) centers on deliverance from God's wrath on the day of judgment.[73] This is evident from what is perhaps Paul's first letter, where "Jesus . . . delivers us from the wrath to come" (1 Thess. 1:10) and "God has not destined us for wrath, but to obtain salvation through our Lord Jesus Christ" (1 Thess. 5:9). It should also be noted that salvation is fundamentally eschatological. God's wrath will be poured out on the last day. Those who are justified through Jesus' blood will be saved from God's wrath on the final day (Rom. 5:9). Similarly, those reconciled by Jesus' death "shall . . . be saved by his life" (Rom. 5:10). Believers long for final deliverance from their mortal bodies on the day of resurrection (Rom. 7:24). The eschatological character of salvation is apparent in the statement, "Salvation is nearer to us now than when we first believed" (Rom. 13:11). Salvation on the final day will belong to believers if they persevere in faith and godliness until the end (cf. 1 Tim. 2:15; 4:16; 2 Tim. 2:10). In 1 Corinthians, Paul instructs the church to discipline the man committing incest so that he would be saved on the last day (1 Cor. 5:5).

Even though salvation is an end-time gift, it is the possession of believers now. The message of the gospel brings salvation, and that salvation is the portion of believers in this present evil age. Believers are in one sense saved now before the day of judgment arrives, but such salvation casts its eyes with hope on the completion of what God has begun (Rom. 8:24). Even now believers have been saved by God's grace through faith (Eph. 2:5, 8). They have been saved not by virtue of their works but on account of God's mercy (Titus 3:5). Similarly, Paul remarks in 2 Tim. 1:9 that salvation is realized because of God's purpose and intention before history began, so that the salvation enjoyed by believers cannot be attributed to the works of believers.[74] God has "delivered" believers

73. Still there is an already–not yet theme in Paul's conception of salvation (see Radl, *EDNT* 3:320–21).

74. So Knight 1992: 374–75; W. Mounce 2000: 482–83.

from the domain of darkness and inducted them into the kingdom of his Son (Col. 1:13). Salvation is not only future and past but also has a present dimension. Believers "are being saved" because of God's power (1 Cor. 1:18). The gospel proclaimed by Paul is a fragrant aroma to those being saved (2 Cor. 2:15).

Salvation is possible only through the gospel. It is the message of the gospel that contains God's power leading to salvation (Rom. 1:16). Those who continue to believe the gospel are those who are saved on the last day (1 Cor. 15:2). The gospel focuses on what Christ has done in absorbing God's wrath, so his wrath is averted from those who put their faith in Christ (Rom. 5:9, 10; 1 Thess. 1:10; 5:9). In contexts where salvation is mentioned, Paul often refers to the message of the cross or Jesus' work on the cross and in the resurrection (1 Cor. 15:1–4).[75] It is particularly emphasized that people must believe to be saved (Rom. 10:9, 10, 13; 13:11; Eph. 1:13; 2:8; 2 Thess. 2:13; 2 Tim. 3:15).

Reconciliation and Adoption

Reconciliation presupposes a previous enmity that has been overcome.[76] Jesus admonished his disciples, before they bring an offering, to reconcile with anyone who has a complaint against them (Matt. 5:23–24). Moses, according to Stephen, attempted to reconcile two Israelites who were quarreling (Acts 7:25–26). The wife who has separated from her husband should be reconciled to him or remain unmarried (1 Cor. 7:11). The breach between human beings and God is due to human transgression (2 Cor. 5:19).[77] Human beings are God's enemies (Rom. 5:10), and the context clarifies that they are God's enemies because of their ungodliness and sin (Rom. 5:6–8). God's wrath hovers over them because of

75. Jesus' death for sins probably should be traced to Isa. 53 (Zimmerli and Jeremias 1957: 88–89), but Paul almost certainly has in mind as well the OT Scriptures as a whole (so Conzelmann 1975: 255; Fee 1987: 725; Garland 2003: 685; Thiselton 2000: 1193). Hengel (2000: 156) notes that 1 Cor. 15:1–11 demonstrates "the final unity of the primitive Christian proclamation" and issues the crucial reminder that this "passage . . . is all too easily forgotten in New Testament theology."

76. R. Martin (1989) argues that reconciliation functions as the center of Pauline theology. Though reconciliation is an important theme in Paul, it should not be viewed as central, for the saving work of God in Christ is not more central than the glory of God. Otherwise, it would be difficult to account for the role of judgment in Paul. Nor is it clear that reconciliation is clearly more central than justification.

77. The background and origin of the Pauline teaching on reconciliation have been discussed intensely. For a concise and clear survey of various proposals, see Breytenbach 1989: 5–30; Kim 2002: 215–20. Breytenbach locates the background in the language of diplomacy relating to politics and negotiations to bring about peace. He disputes any clear relation to the OT and separates reconciliation from atonement.

their unrighteousness (Rom. 5:9).[78] The same emphasis on human sins appears in Colossians. Believers are "alienated" from God and "hostile in mind" because of their "evil deeds" (Col. 1:21).

The situation in Ephesians is more complex. Gentiles are "far off" from God because they are separated from Israel (Eph. 2:11–13). Hostility exists between Jews and Gentiles because the latter are not part of the covenant. The hostility is clearly sociological in Eph. 2 inasmuch as a cultural breach exists between Jews and Gentiles. Still, the hostility cannot be accounted for solely on the basis of sociological and cultural tension. Both Jews and Gentiles also need to be reconciled to God, and Paul locates their enmity to "the law of commandments and ordinances" (Eph. 2:15), which likely refers to their failure to keep God's law. Nor is the need for repentance limited to Gentiles, for the message of peace is also proclaimed to Jews, who are "near" (Eph. 2:17).

Reconciliation between God and human beings is accomplished through the cross of Christ. The whole process of reconciliation was initiated by and carried out by God himself (2 Cor. 5:18).[79] Reconciliation is accomplished through the cross of Christ, whereby God no longer counts the sins of believers against them (2 Cor. 5:19). Their sins have been placed on Christ, whom God has made to be sin (2 Cor. 5:21). It is evident, therefore, that justification and reconciliation are closely related. Those whom God has declared to be in the right with him are also considered to be friends and beloved by him.

The close relationship between justification and reconciliation is apparent also in Romans. Those who are right with God by faith now have peace with God through our Lord Jesus Christ (Rom. 5:1).[80] It seems, therefore, that justification is the basis of reconciliation.[81] In Rom. 5:9–10 justification and reconciliation are alternate ways of describing God's work in Christ. Reconciliation has been achieved, but only at the cost of the death of Jesus Christ (Rom. 5:10). Peace and friendship with God do not come merely from God consenting to forgive human beings. Apparently, Jesus must die in place of sinners to satisfy God's justice before friendship can be restored.[82] The gift of God in Christ brings remarkable

78. Hence, we should reject the view of some (e.g., Breytenbach 1989: 154; Bell 2002: 20n102; Kim 2002: 217) who argue that the enmity is only on the side of humans.

79. For the emphasis on God's initiative in reconciliation, see Harris 2005: 436–37.

80. The indicative "we have" is to be favored over the subjunctive "let us have" in Rom. 5:1. See Schreiner 1998: 258.

81. Rightly Harris 2005: 439.

82. It is incorrect, therefore, to claim that enmity is only on the side of human beings (e.g., Hofius 1989: 36–37). Such a view relies too much on a word-study approach and fails to see that God's wrath and judgment are directed against those who are sinners.

joy to believers, and they exult in God, who has granted them the gift of reconciliation (Rom. 5:11).

In Colossians too reconciliation is rooted in the cross. Jesus made "peace by the blood of the cross" (Col. 1:20). The physicality of Jesus' death is quite emphatic in Col. 1:22, for believers are "reconciled in his body of flesh by his death." Clearly, the death of Christ is necessary to wipe out the evil deeds practiced by human beings (Col. 1:21). The reconciliation accomplished, according to Col. 1:20, is universal, including both earth and heaven. It might seem that Paul teaches a universal reconciliation, in the sense that all people will be saved. However, such a view is mistaken, for later in Colossians we see that the wrath of God will be inflicted on the disobedient on the last day (Col. 3:6). Even more striking are the words that immediately follow Col. 1:20. Paul teaches that only those who persevere until the end will be spared from God's judgment on the last day (Col. 1:21–23). It is quite unlikely, then, that Col. 1:20 promises the salvation of all. Christ's death is the means by which those who believe and repent will be saved, but it is also the means by which the entire universe is pacified and domesticated.[83] He has defeated evil powers through his death, so that they can no longer rise in rebellion against God (Col. 2:15).

Peace with God in Ephesians likewise is anchored in the cross of Christ. It is his blood that has brought Gentiles near who were far from God (Eph. 2:13). Christ establishes peace not through gestures of good will but rather "in his flesh" (Eph. 2:14–15). Reconciliation has been accomplished "through the cross" (Eph. 2:16). The proclamation of peace to both Jews and Gentiles and access to the Father through the Spirit depend on the work of Christ on the cross. Paul did not conceive of reconciliation apart from the cross, and it is intimately linked with justification. Indeed, the demand that sins be atoned for suggests that reconciliation is needed on both sides. God is hostile with human beings as well, and hence payment for sins in the cross of Christ is needed to obtain forgiveness. The difference between justification and reconciliation is that the former emphasizes that believers stand in the right before God as their judge, whereas the latter emphasizes that believers are now friends with God.

Since believers are friends with God, they are his children and adopted. Those who enjoy the gift of the Spirit are led by the same Spirit and are God's "sons" (*huioi* [Rom. 8:14]). Those who are adopted (*huiothesia*) as God's children no longer live in slavery to sin (Rom. 8:15), and this is witnessed by the fact that they love God as their dear Father. The Spirit

---

83. For a convincing defense of this view, see O'Brien 1982: 53–57. See also Pokorný 1991: 86–90; Schweizer 1982: 79–81.

confirms to believers that they are truly the "children" (*tekna*) of God (Rom. 8:16). And since believers are children now, they are assured of a future inheritance (Rom. 8:17). This future inheritance is nothing less than the completion of their adoption (Rom. 8:23)—the final redemption of the body.

In Galatians "sons of God" is a way of saying that believers have reached spiritual adulthood and spiritual maturity. Those who lived under the law were living, so to speak, in spiritual infancy. They lived in the old age of redemptive history under the tutelage of the "pedagogue" (*paidagōgos* [Gal. 3:24–25]).[84] The word "pedagogue" could be rendered "babysitter" because it delimits the period before spiritual maturity.[85] The word does not have here the connotation of "tutor" or "instructor."[86] Those who lived under the law did not receive the inheritance that God had promised, but now that Jesus Christ has come, all those who put their faith in him are God's sons (Gal. 3:26). They are spiritual adults, having received God's promise to his people. They are Abraham's true seed and thus heirs of all that God has promised (Gal. 3:29).

The argument in Gal. 4:1–7 is quite similar.[87] Paul uses an illustration to make his point. When the heir of a father's estate is a minor, he is equivalent to a slave because he is under the tutelage of guardians and managers. Life under the law is comparable to living under the supervision of guardians and managers. Those who lived under it "were enslaved" and did not enjoy the freedom that God promised (Gal. 4:3). But now a new day in redemptive history has dawned, and God has redeemed those who were under the law. They are now God's adopted children (Gal. 4:5; cf. Phil. 2:15). They are no longer minors but now are God's adult sons and daughters. The Spirit in believers gives them confidence that God is their dear Father ("Abba! Father!" [Gal. 4:6]). And since they are children, they await the promise of a future inheritance. They are children of the promise (Gal. 4:23) and of the Jerusalem above (Gal. 4:26). Hence, they are free from the slavery of sin as children of the promise and children of the free woman (Gal. 4:21–31). Those who live under the Sinai covenant cannot escape the shackles of sin, but those who have the Jerusalem above as their mother experience genuine freedom.

God's love for his children is revealed in his predestining them to be adopted (Eph. 1:5). Believers are children of the promise and thus are truly children of God in contrast to those who are children of the flesh

84. The word *paidagōgos* is rendered as "guardian" by the ESV.

85. For this understanding of "pedagogue," see Schreiner 1993a: 77–80. For further study of the pedagogue, see Longenecker 1982; N. Young 1987.

86. Rightly Martyn (1997: 362–63), who emphasizes the imprisoning nature of the pedagogue. Others understand the pedagogue positively (see Dunn 1993: 198–99; Lull 1986).

87. On adoption, see Scott 1992.

(Rom. 9:8). Those who forsake evil and remove themselves from evildo-ers are God's sons and daughters (2 Cor. 6:18). Believers are children of "light" (Eph. 5:8) and children of the light and day (1 Thess. 5:5), and hence they are to live in a new way. As God's children, believers are deeply loved by God himself (Eph. 5:1).

Redemption

Under redemption are included those terms that teach that Christ freed believers from sin (cf. *eleutheros, eleutheroō, apolytrōsis, lytroō, agorazō, exagorazō, exaireō*). Christ's work of freeing believers is fundamentally eschatological.[88] He "gave himself for our sins to deliver us from the present evil age" (Gal. 1:4). Believers have no need to receive circumci-sion, for through Christ they have been liberated from the evil cosmos. In both Eph. 1:7 and Col. 1:14 redemption is defined in terms of forgiveness of sins. As we noted earlier, the same emphasis on forgiveness of sins is likely in Rom. 3:24. Paul argues in Gal. 3:10 that every human being is under a curse because of a failure to keep God's law. Christ Jesus liber-ates from the curse those who trust him because he became a curse in their place (Gal. 3:13). The fundamental liberation needed by human beings, therefore, is forgiveness of sins.

The freedom of believers has been achieved through the cross of Christ. Those who were enslaved to sin under the law have been freed from their subjugation to sin through the death of Christ (Gal. 4:4–5). Redemption cannot be traced to anything that believers have done. It has been accomplished by Christ Jesus alone (1 Cor. 1:30). They are free from sin and now are enslaved to righteousness or, as Paul also says, to God (Rom. 6:18, 22). Slavery to righteousness is no burden, for a constant desire to do what is right is actually beautiful freedom (Gal. 5:13). Those who are in Christ no longer live under condemnation (Rom. 8:1). They are free from the penalty and guilt of sin. Freedom from sin by the power of the Spirit functions as evidence that Christ has paid the penalty for sin (Rom. 8:2–3) and has condemned sin in the flesh. We see another piece of evidence that God's justifying work in Christ is the basis for the new life of believers. The redemption accomplished by Jesus frees believers from "lawlessness" and animates them to be "zealous for good works" (Titus 2:14). The fullness of this freedom, of course, will belong to believers only on the day of final redemption (Rom. 8:21).

On occasion Paul uses the word "redemption" to refer to the consum-mation of God's work in believers. The Spirit seals believers "for the day

88. For an insightful study on redemption, see Marshall 1974. See also D. Hill 1967: 53–81.

of redemption" (Eph. 4:30). At the conclusion of history the bodies of believers will be redeemed (Rom. 8:23). God's saving work will be completed, and the fullness of redemption will then be the portion of those who have put their faith in Christ.

Do the terms used for "redemption" (*apolytrōsis, lytroō, agorazō, exagorazō*) include the cost of redemption, so that the price at which redemption is gained is also in view?[89] In some instances the price at which redemption is gained certainly is in view. Paul declares that believers "were bought with a price" (1 Cor. 6:20; 7:23). The notion of "buying" is clear in 1 Cor. 7:30: "those who buy" should live "as though they had no goods." We can conclude that the price at which believers were purchased is the death of Christ. In other texts redemption is specifically ascribed to the shedding of Christ's blood (Eph. 1:7), although the parallel text in Colossians omits the reference to Christ's blood (Col. 1:14). The omission may suggest, however, that blood is implied even though it remains unmentioned. The absence of reference to blood does not necessarily suggest that a price is excluded. Romans 3:24 is a case in point. Justification occurs "through redemption." Nothing is said about the price of redemption. Still, in this verse Paul emphasizes that justification is free, implying that it comes to believers at no cost. In the next verse Christ's blood propitiates God's anger (Rom. 3:25). The reference to "blood" in Rom. 3:25 and the freedom of his grace in Rom. 3:24 imply that redemption is procured at the cost of Christ's blood.

Other texts are less clear.[90] Nothing is said about the price of redemption in Gal. 3:13 or Gal. 4:5. Still, it is obvious in context that the death of Christ is the means by which people are freed from the curse and the enslavement that exists under law. In 1 Cor. 1:30 Paul affirms, among other things, that Christ Jesus is "our . . . redemption." One could even argue that nothing is said about the cross in this verse. Such a claim would fail, however, to consult the surrounding context, where Christ crucified represents the wisdom and power of God (1 Cor. 1:17–25; 2:2, 6, 8). Clearly wisdom, righteousness, sanctification, and redemption (1 Cor. 1:30) are given to believers by virtue of Christ's work on the cross. Titus 2:14 is quite similar in this respect: Christ "gave himself for us to redeem us from all lawlessness and to purify for himself a people for his own possession who are zealous for good works." The text fails to mention the blood of Christ as the cost of redemption, and yet the cost is implicit in his self-giving, in the life that he gave on behalf of others.[91]

89. So Warfield 1950: 429–75; Morris 1965: 16–55.
90. A balanced perspective on whether the cost of redemption is invariably in view is found in Marshall 1974.
91. See Marshall 1999: 284.

The two texts that speak of the consummation of redemption (Rom. 8:23; Eph. 4:30) are silent about the price of redemption, and they do not even mention the death of Christ. We could easily draw unwarranted conclusions from the absence of certain themes in these texts. Paul fixes attention on the completion of God's redeeming work, and he did not feel the need to explicate every dimension of redemption each time he uses the term. He assumes that the readers are well acquainted with the saving work of Christ from what he has said earlier in Romans and Ephesians.

To conclude, redemption in Paul refers to the liberation from sin that has come by means of the work of Christ. Fundamentally, this liberation belongs to believers by means of the forgiveness of their sins. Those who are redeemed, however, now have the power to live a new life that is marked by holiness and godliness. In every instance redemption focuses on the deliverance accomplished by God in Christ for believers. It also seems likely that the price of such redemption is implicit, even when it remains unstated, for the redemption that believers enjoy has come at the cost of Jesus' life and the shedding of his blood.

Triumph over Evil Powers[92]

Christ's work on the cross not only broke the power of sin but also spelled the defeat of evil and demonic powers.[93] The notion of God triumphing in battle recalls the exodus, in which Yahweh the warrior vanquished the Egyptians (Exod. 15:3). And the prophets often proclaim the day of the Lord, in which all of Yahweh's enemies will be defeated and his reign of peace will arrive for Israel (e.g., Isa. 13:6, 9; Ezek. 30:3; Joel 2:1, 11, 31; 3:14; Amos 5:18, 20; Obad. 15; Zeph. 1:7, 14; Mal. 4:5). The prophets warn, however, that Israel will not participate in this day of victory unless they renounce evil and commit themselves to righteousness.

Triumph over evil powers could be put under the theme of redemption in that both themes focus on liberation. A discrete category is fitting because redemption focuses on liberation from sin, whereas the emphasis here is on victory over evil powers. It must also be said at the outset that the dominion of evil powers is precisely because of sin. For example, the authority of Satan over unbelievers in Eph. 2:2 is intertwined with their subservience to sin and to the course of this world (Eph. 2:1–3). Victory over Satan and his demonic agents does not come from some sort of

92. This section is taken from Schreiner 2001 with some revisions.
93. For this theme in Paul and in the Scriptures generally, see Longman and Reid 1995.

mystical experience in Ephesians; rather, such triumph comes through the infusion of the resurrection life of Christ, which is granted on the basis of the work of Jesus Christ (Eph. 2:4–10). Believers are made alive with Christ, raised with Christ, and seated with Christ. Not only was Christ raised from the dead, but also he was seated at God's right hand. By definition this means that he now rules over all demonic powers (Eph. 1:21). It follows, therefore, that "he put all things under his feet" (Eph. 1:22). This statement, based on and rooted in Ps. 110:1, identifies Jesus as the Lord, the second Adam, who now exercises his rule over all creation.

Some scholars think that Ephesians is not authentically Pauline because no eschatological proviso is present here.[94] Even though Ephesians emphasizes the "already," the "not yet" theme still informs the letter. The "coming ages" have not yet arrived (Eph. 2:7), and the redemption of the body still lies in the future (Eph. 1:14). The realization of the "unity of the faith" and "mature manhood" (Eph. 4:13) will occur on the last day, when the church is presented as holy and blameless (Eph. 5:26–27). The day of eschatological reward has not yet arrived (Eph. 6:8). Most important for our discussion here, despite Christ's victory over evil powers, believers still must resist their influence (Eph. 6:10–17). A conflict between believers and these powers continues until the day of redemption.

Christ's victory over evil powers and the subjection of all things under his feet are trumpeted also in 1 Cor. 15:24–28. Here the end and the consummation of the kingdom are the time when evil powers will be vanquished (1 Cor. 15:24). The fulfillment of Ps. 110:1, therefore, will occur when he places all enemies under his feet. The battle will cease when death, the last enemy, is conquered. What is remarkable in comparing this text to Ephesians is that here the not yet is in the forefront. This difference does not constitute a contradiction, for even in 1 Cor. 15 (as in Eph. 1) the resurrection of Christ is featured. The not yet is prominent in 1 Corinthians, however, because Paul counters the overrealized eschatology of some Corinthians.[95]

Perhaps the most important text on Christ's victory over evil powers is Col. 2:15. However the details of this verse are interpreted, the subjugation of these enemies was accomplished in the cross and resurrection of Christ (Col. 2:11–15). Believers share in Christ's triumph because their sins have been forgiven, their certificate of debt has been erased, and their sins have been decisively and finally nailed to the cross. Paul refers to the triumph over demonic powers at the cross and resurrection

---

94. But see Lincoln 1990: lxxxix–xc; Best 1998: 52–55; Hoehner 2002: 56–58.
95. So Thiselton 1977–1978. It is possible, however, that the Corinthian view does not stem from an overrealized eschatology (so Hays 1997: 70–71, 252–53).

of Christ. Examining Col. 2:15 at a general level, we clearly see that the demonic powers were decisively defeated at the cross. But what does the verse specifically say? Some commentators think that the middle participle *apekdysamenos* indicates that Christ stripped off from himself demonic powers like a garment at his death, for in being subject to the power of sin at the cross and in solidarity with sinful human beings Jesus was "made subject to the demands, accusations, and schemes of the powers of evil."[96] This certainly is a possible reading, but it is also possible that the verse teaches that at the cross God stripped the rulers and authorities of their power.[97] He publicly exposed them and humiliated them (*edeigmatisen en parrēsia*). Lastly, God has "led the demons in triumphal procession [*thriambeusas*]" (my translation) in Christ. The triumphal procession was a ceremonial parade through the streets of Rome in which some captive leaders and their wares were displayed.[98] The march concluded with the execution of those conquered. It seems likely that all three metaphors should be interpreted in similar terms. The powers have lost their authority due to the cross of Christ. They have been stripped, humiliated, and led to execution. They no longer exercise any control over those in Christ. In the context Christ's triumph over evil powers is linked with forgiveness of sins, indicating that in receiving the forgiveness of sins believers have received everything that they need.[99]

Sanctification

The term "sanctification" derives from the cultic sphere (*hagiazō*, *hagiasmos*), signifying that which is set aside for the realm of the holy.[100] Several examples in Paul assist us in defining the term. In 1 Tim. 4:1–5 Paul warns Timothy about ascetic false teachers. They prohibit marriage and require abstinence from certain foods—perhaps foods that are considered unclean in accordance with the OT. Asceticism, however, contradicts the doctrine of creation, for everything that God created is good because it comes from his hand. No foods are "off limits" as long as they are received with thanksgiving. They are "sanctified" (NRSV) by

96. Longman and Reid 1995: 149 (see their entire discussion, pp. 146–49); cf. Dunn 1996b: 167–68.

97. For the view preferred here, see Lohse 1971: 111–12; O'Brien 1982: 127–28; Pokorný 1991: 140–41.

98. On Roman triumphal processions, see Hafemann 1986: 18–39.

99. Lohse (1971: 107) comments, "On the cross of Christ the certificate of indebtedness is erased; on the cross of Christ the powers and principalities are disempowered. Consequently, where there is forgiveness of sins, there is freedom from the 'powers' and 'principalities,' there is life and salvation!"

100. See Procksch, *TDNT* 1:111–13.

God's word and prayer. Food, in other words, is set apart in the realm of the holy by the creational word of God in which he declared that everything he made "was very good" (Gen. 1:31). A prayer of thanksgiving, which Paul almost certainly learned from his Jewish upbringing, also sanctifies such food, showing that it is not impure but rather belongs to the sphere of the sacred.

It appears that the Corinthians hesitated to remain in marriages with unbelievers (1 Cor. 7:12–16) because they feared defilement from engaging in sexual relations with those who did not belong to the Lord. Paul urges them not to divorce their unbelieving spouses. A divorce is permissible only if the unbeliever insists on such a course of action. The question of defilement is answered in 1 Cor. 7:14. The unbelieving spouse is sanctified and made holy by virtue of the relationship with the believing spouse. What Paul teaches here is rather startling, for the common Jewish view was that the unclean would defile the clean. Paul reverses the pattern by asserting that the pure overpowers what is unclean and inducts it into the realm of the holy. Hence, unbelieving spouses and children from such a union are considered to be holy. In this context, however, belonging to the realm of the holy is not equivalent with salvation, as Paul clarifies in 1 Cor. 7:16. The believing spouse cannot have assurance that the unbelieving spouse will be saved. Perhaps being in the realm of the holy suggests that the unbeliever enjoys the possibility of salvation.

Paul uses cultic terms to describe his ministry in Rom. 15:16. He is a "minister" (*leitourgos*) of Christ, and his ministry is a priestly one. By means of his apostolic ministry he offers, so to speak, the Gentiles on the altar before God. He prays that the conversion of the Gentiles would "be acceptable, sanctified by the Holy Spirit." Clearly, sanctification here indicates that which is acceptable as a sacrifice before God. Paul uses another example from everyday life in 2 Tim. 2:20–21. Houses contain a variety of vessels, some that are for common, everyday use and others—silver and gold—that are set aside for special occasions.[101] Paul compares this to the responsibility of believers to live holy lives. If they "cleanse themselves" from evil, they will be considered honorable vessels—"set apart as holy." Beautiful vessels of silver and gold are set apart for special occasions. Paul applies this to believers, exhorting them to live in a way that pleases God, so that they are set apart from the dishonorable behavior that was typical in their society.

Often sanctification is understood only in terms of progressive growth in the Christian life, whereas Paul typically indicates God's definitive

101. This passage has complexities that are not probed here (see Marshall 1999: 759–63).

setting aside work at conversion.[102] This is apparent from 1 Cor. 1:2, where the Corinthians are said to be "sanctified in Christ Jesus."[103] Paul could scarcely be referring to their notable progress in holiness, given the remainder of the letter, which describes a church wracked by divisions, engaging in lawsuits, indulging in sexual immorality, quarreling over food offered to idols and over spiritual gifts, and doubting the truth of the resurrection. Nevertheless, the Corinthians were sanctified by virtue of their conversion. Since they are in Christ, they belong to the realm of the holy. They are sanctified definitively or positionally, even though they are not sanctified in terms of personal behavior. We see a similar idea in Col. 3:12, where the church is said to be "holy." This statement is framed by God's election of his beloved people, and hence the Colossians are holy because they have been inducted by Christ into the holy sphere.

We should interpret 1 Cor. 6:11 within the same frame of reference: "You were washed, you were sanctified, you were justified in the name of the Lord Jesus Christ and in the Spirit of our God." The order of the verbs is remarkable here. If sanctification referred to progressive growth in the Christian life, Paul almost certainly would have placed sanctification after justification. Placing sanctification before justification indicates that definitive sanctification is in view, the sanctification that belongs to believers because they are in Christ and in the Spirit.[104] Indeed, the three verbs here do not represent any temporal order, for washing, sanctification, and justification in this text all occur at the same time, at conversion. Those who have put their faith in Christ have had their sins washed away in baptism, have been placed in the realm of the holy, and stand in the right before God their judge.

Perhaps 2 Thess. 2:13 also refers to definitive sanctification, although it is more difficult to determine whether this is the case.[105] Those whom God has chosen are saved "through sanctification by the Spirit and belief in the truth." These words certainly could fit with the notion that the Spirit slowly makes believers more and more Christlike. Still, it seems more probable that he thinks of their initial conversion, when they were inducted into the realm of the holy. What tips us in this direction is the reference to believing in the truth, which refers to belief in the gospel at conversion. Those whom God has chosen respond in faith to the gospel

102. See Peterson (1995), who rightly emphasizes the importance and prominence of definitive sanctification.

103. So Fee 1987: 32; Thiselton 2000: 76.

104. So Fee 1987: 246; Thiselton 2000: 454; Garland 2003: 216–17.

105. Wanamaker (1990: 266–67) sees the process of sanctification in view here. But for contrary arguments that seem convincing, see Beale 2003: 228.

of Christ, and the Spirit sets them apart into the realm of the holy, so that they stand before God as holy ones.

Perhaps this is the place to insert a reference to "washing," since this term likewise derives from the cult. We saw in 1 Cor. 6:11 that those who are in Christ have been washed. This almost certainly refers to baptism as the occasion when sins were cleansed on the basis of Christ's death (Rom. 6:3–4).[106] In Titus 3:5 salvation is attributed to "the washing of regeneration and renewal of the Holy Spirit." Paul reflects on the regeneration and renewal accomplished for believers by the Holy Spirit, but he designates this as a washing and a cleansing. Such cleansing is portrayed in baptism, where the sins of believers are washed away.

In Eph. 5:25–27 sanctification and washing appear together and seem to refer to the same reality with different pictures. Christ died for the church to sanctify it. Sanctification here could indicate the ongoing work of holiness in the lives of believers. Or perhaps the verse refers to the whole process of sanctification, which belongs definitively to believers at conversion and reaches its goal on the day of redemption. On the other hand, perhaps we should slightly favor a reference to the setting apart that occurs at conversion because sanctification is explained in terms of the cleansing that comes from the washing by water.[107] The reference to washing suggests that the cleansing and forgiveness that belongs to believers at baptism is in view. Hence, sanctification may indicate the definitive work that occurs at conversion. Whatever we make of Eph. 5:26, the next verse refers to the eschatological outcome of Christ's sanctifying and cleansing. Ultimately, Christ will present the church to himself without wrinkle or blemish. The church will be perfectly holy on the last day on the basis of Christ's work on the cross.

The eschatological presentation of the church is attributed to Christ's work on the cross in Col. 1:22 as well. On the last day he will "present you holy and blameless and above reproach before him" (cf. 1 Thess. 3:13). Paul is not claiming that Christians will reach moral perfection in their everyday lives before the eschaton. Believers are already in the realm of the holy, but on the last day they will be transformed so that they are without sin. Paul does not explain how this transformation will occur, though it seems that it will take place when Christ returns. It is interesting at this juncture to think of 1 John, for John says that believers will become like Christ when they see him (1 John 3:2), suggesting that the vision of Christ will be transforming. The eschatological securing of holiness is taught in 1 Thess. 5:23, so that the Thessalonians will be blameless when Christ returns. A tension emerges in Paul's thought.

106. So Hays 1997: 97.
107. So Lincoln 1990: 375; O'Brien 1999: 421.

On the one hand, it seems that the eschatological completion of holiness cannot be sundered from progress in holiness during this life; on the other hand, Paul recognizes that the work of holiness will not be accomplished in this life. He uses a future tense to assure them that God will sanctify them completely (1 Thess. 5:24). The already–not yet dimension of Paul's eschatology provides the most satisfactory solution. Believers are in the process of sanctification now, but they are not yet perfect. They long for the day when God's promise of perfecting them in holiness will be consummated.

We have seen thus far that believers are definitively placed into the sphere of the holy at conversion, and that they will be sanctified entirely on the last day. Paul also emphasizes that believers must live in a way that pleases God in the interval between their conversion and the consummation. Here we could include virtually all the parenesis in Paul's letters in which he exhorts believers to live worthily of their calling (cf. Eph. 4:1; Phil. 1:27). At this juncture, however, we will simply note some texts in which sanctification and holiness refer to the ongoing process of being conformed to God's Son. Those who have been liberated from slavery to sin and have become slaves of righteousness should live in a holy way (Rom. 6:19, 22). The metaphors of washing and holiness converge in 2 Cor. 7:1, where believers are exhorted to "cleanse [themselves] from every defilement of body and spirit, bringing holiness to completion in the fear of God." Clearly, Paul expects believers to live in a new way, indicating that they are truly consecrated to God.

In 1 Thess. 4:3–8 sanctification is expressly said to be God's will.[108] In context the focus is on abstention from sexual sin. Believers should control their own bodies (or possibly acquire spouses) in sanctification and honor. God has called believers to holy lives, so that they are not besmirched by impurity. If believers do not live in a holy fashion, they will not be saved at the eschaton (cf. 1 Tim. 2:15). Obviously, Paul does not mean that believers must live perfect lives to be saved. The Corinthian letters alone are enough to disprove that notion. Still, those who belong to Christ reveal that they are his by their changed, though imperfect, lives.

For Paul, then, sanctification usually refers to the definitive work by which God has set apart believers in the realm of the holy in Christ Jesus. This eschatological work is accomplished at conversion, so that believers can be said to be holy or sanctified in God's presence. Still, Paul recognizes the need for growth in holiness and that transformation is a process (cf. 2 Cor. 3:18), since complete sanctification and holiness

---

108. Wanamaker (1990: 150–51) says that the process of sanctification or the outcome of that process may be in Paul's view here and slightly prefers the former.

will not be granted until Christ returns.[109] Believers are already holy in Christ, and yet the fullness of that holiness will not be theirs until the day of redemption.

Inheritance, Glorification, and Resurrection

The final reward of believers can be designated by the terms "inheritance," "glorification," and "resurrection." All three refer to the end-time reward that believers will receive as beneficiaries of salvation.

The term "inheritance" (*klēronomia*; cf. *klēronomos, synklēronomos*) refers most often to the future reward promised to believers.[110] Paul warns that those who continue to practice sin will not receive the eschatological inheritance (Eph. 5:5). Conversely, slaves who serve Christ will receive an inheritance on the last day (Col. 3:24). In Galatians Paul emphasizes that the inheritance is received by grace rather than being secured through the law (cf. Gal. 3:18, 29; 4:7; see also Titus 3:7). The inheritance, then, is obtained not through doing but rather by believing. It is a promise received, not the result of something earned. It is tied irretrievably to justification by faith (Titus 3:7), and hence it is a gift of grace and a certain reward for believers. Those who belong to Christ are co-heirs with Christ (Rom. 8:17). In other words, all those who are God's children will certainly receive an inheritance (Rom. 8:17; Gal. 4:7). The gift of the Spirit, which clearly is the result of God's gracious work in Eph. 1:3–14, guarantees that believers will receive the final inheritance and be freed from their mortal bodies (Eph. 1:14). The inheritance promised to Abraham is nothing less than possession of the entire world (Rom. 4:13).[111] In other words, the future prospects before believers are nothing short of stunning and beyond any conception.

Does the emphasis on avoiding sin to receive the inheritance in Eph. 5:5 contradict the graciousness of the inheritance emphasized in the other texts that we have examined?[112] We must recall that Ephesians also teaches that salvation is received by faith, not by works (Eph. 2:8–9). It is not as if Ephesians betrays a legalistic theology in contrast to the so-called genuine Pauline letters. Indeed, Eph. 2:10 teaches that God has prepared in advance the good works believers will do. Hence, those

109. So Harris 2005: 315–17; see also R. Martin 1986: 72; Barrett 1973: 125; Garland 1999: 200–202.

110. On inheritance in the OT, Jewish tradition, and the NT, see Hester (1968), who notes that the inheritance theme fits within the already–not yet schema in Paul's theology.

111. As Hester (1968: 77–78) notes, Paul does not restrict the promise to the land of Canaan but rather widens it to include the entire world, and such a universal inheritance is tied to the work of Christ.

112. See Hoehner 2002: 662.

who are truly God's children will do the good works demanded, not in order to earn or merit salvation but as a result of God's saving power in their lives.

The eschatological glorification of believers is the hope that animates them in their everyday lives as they live in the interval between the already and the not yet (Rom. 5:2; Col. 1:27; cf. 2 Tim. 2:10), in that it gives them confidence that God will complete the salvation he has begun in them (cf. Phil. 1:6). The glorification of believers will occur when Christ returns in his glory (Col. 3:4; cf. Rom. 8:17). Glorification is not some abstract process that occurs—believers will be transformed when they see Christ in all his beauty. The hope of glory animates believers because what awaits them is incomparably beautiful and far exceeds what they can imagine (Rom. 8:18). Paul contrasts the "eternal weight of glory" destined for believers (2 Cor. 4:17–18) with what is now visible and observable. The glory promised to believers, in other words, belongs to the unseen realm and thus cannot be calculated by those living in the present evil age. Still, the promise that awaits believers is glorious freedom (Rom. 8:21), which in the context of Romans means liberation from the groaning of the sinful body (cf. Rom. 8:23) and the sighing that marks life in the mortal body (cf. Rom. 2:7). Glory will belong to believers with the coming of the new creation (Rom. 8:18–25). The body that is now marked by weakness and corruptibility will be powerful and glorious (1 Cor. 15:43; cf. Phil. 3:21). Of course, the body is dying because of the presence of sin, and so the freedom envisioned is freedom from sin with all baleful effects.

Believers receive great comfort because the hope of glory is not merely a desire without certainty that the future will be happy. The hope of glory represents a sure confidence that God will complete the saving work that he has begun. This is supported by Rom. 8:30, where the verb "glorified" summarizes God's saving work from foreknowledge to glorification. Glorification, of course, is a future event, but Paul here uses the aorist tense to designate the certainty of future glorification. All those whom God has foreknown, predestined, called, and justified will certainly be glorified. This same theme is sounded in Rom. 9:23 in a context that emphasizes God's predestinating work. God has planned beforehand that believers will enjoy the richness of his glory. God predestined before history began that Christ crucified would secure future glory for believers (1 Cor. 2:7). He has effectually called believers to inherit the kingdom and to glory (1 Thess. 2:12; 2 Thess. 2:14).

The resurrection of Jesus Christ is a fundamental element in Pauline theology (Gal. 1:1; 2 Tim. 2:8). Justification in Pauline theology is not based solely on the death of Christ. Forgiveness of sins and a right relation with God are based on both the death and the resurrection of Jesus

Christ (Rom. 4:25; cf. 1 Thess. 1:10). Salvation is secured by the crucified
and risen Lord, who sits at God's right hand and intercedes for believers
based on his work on the cross (Rom. 8:34). Christ's resurrection verifies
that he rules over every power in this age and in the age to come (Eph.
1:20–23). The resurrection of believers is anchored in the resurrection
of Jesus Christ (1 Thess. 4:14). If Christ did not conquer death, hope
would be extinguished for all deceased believers (Rom. 8:11; 1 Cor. 6:14;
2 Cor. 4:14; 5:15). The gospel that Paul proclaims centers on the crucified
and risen Lord, and both his death and resurrection are rooted in the
Scriptures (1 Cor. 15:1–4). Nor does Paul vaguely speak of a resurrection hope, as if it were some kind of ethereal future promised to God's
people. He emphasizes that Jesus Christ, after his death, appeared to a
number of people, so that they could verify that he was truly risen (1 Cor.
15:5–8).[113] On one occasion he appeared to over five hundred people at
one time, and it is difficult to believe that all five hundred suffered from
hallucinations. Nor is the resurrection the private belief of Paul alone,
for proclamation of the resurrected Lord is the message sounded out
by all the apostles (1 Cor. 15:11).

Paul clarifies in 1 Cor. 15:12–19 that the resurrection is not peripheral
or irrelevant to the gospel. Here he counteracts the notion that there is
no future resurrection for believers. Such a view is tantamount to denying the resurrection of Christ. Those who deny a future resurrection are
not genuine believers (2 Tim. 2:18). One must confess the risen Christ,
as Paul says in Romans, to be saved (Rom. 10:9). If Christ is not risen,
then Paul's preaching is vain and false (1 Cor. 15:14–15). Indeed, the faith
of the Corinthians lacks a foundation, and hence they would still stand
condemned before God as sinners (1 Cor. 15:17). Dead believers would
have no hope of a future life, but would face future judgment (1 Cor.
15:18). Risking death and suffering is beside the point if the resurrection is a myth; it would be saner to enjoy life on this earth while one
can (1 Cor. 15:30–32).

The resurrection, as we noted previously, is an indication that the life
of the age to come has arrived. Christ's resurrection indicates that the
new age has indeed dawned (Rom. 1:4). The age to come has penetrated
the present evil age (Rom. 6:4–5, 9) since Jesus has conquered both death
and sin by virtue of his resurrection from the dead. The age to come
has arrived, however, in a surprising fashion. Jesus is the "firstfruits"
(1 Cor. 15:20). He has reversed the death and degradation introduced
into the world by Adam (1 Cor. 15:21–22; Rom. 5:12–19). Contrary to
what might be expected, there is an interval between Christ's resurrec-

113. See Garland 2003: 687–90.

tion and the submission of everything in the universe to the will of God (1 Cor. 15:23–28).

Conclusion

Paul celebrates the saving work of God and Christ with a variety of metaphors and expressions, presumably because the fullness of salvation cannot be captured by one dimension of God's saving work. If there is a central theme in Paul that summarizes his soteriology, it is that salvation is of the Lord. God foreknew, elected, predestined, and called believers to himself. His grace is so powerful that it conquers sin and inducts believers into the sphere of salvation. Those whom God has chosen will receive the final inheritance promised and will be raised from the dead on the last day. Paul emphasizes that God's saving work is effective in and through Christ. Whether one thinks of justification, reconciliation, redemption, propitiation, salvation, or sanctification, each represents the saving action of God in Christ. Victory over evil powers has come about in and through Christ. Believers praise God in Christ, for Christ has won the victory, reconciled them, and placed them in a right relation to God. Paul's soteriology also matches another central theme in this book, in that it fits with the already–not yet character of Paul's theology. Believers are now justified, reconciled, redeemed, adopted, and sanctified, and yet in one sense the fullness of these gifts has not yet been experienced. A tension exists between the present possession of such gifts and their final realization. The final realization is assured because the God who has made believers his people will never forsake them and will empower them until the end. And if God in Christ saves, then believers give thanks and praise forever for the salvation that rescued them. They glorify God in Christ, for the gift is never exalted above the giver.

12

❧ ❧ ❧ ❧ ❧ ❧ ❧ ❧ ❧ ❧ ❧ ❧ ❧ ❧ ❧ ❧ ❧ ❧

The Christology of Hebrews–Revelation

In the remaining books of the NT we consider both who Jesus is and what he has accomplished for believers. When considering the Gospels and Paul, we separated who Christ is from his saving work because the quantity of material made it impractical to combine the two in one section. Still, the danger exists, and perhaps has not been avoided, of abstracting who Jesus is from what he has accomplished for his people. In Hebrews–Revelation the brevity of the material will assist us in joining Christology very closely to soteriology. Thereby the practical and salvific character of the writings will be highlighted.

Hebrews

Jesus Greater Than David

The Christology of Hebrews is richly textured and is an essential theme in the letter. The letter commences with one of the most beautiful and exalted christological texts in the NT (Heb. 1:1–4). God has spoken definitively and finally in the last days in his Son (Heb. 1:2). Here the author emphasizes that Jesus is the son of David, the messianic king. The Son is described as "the heir of all things" (Heb. 1:2), which is a clear allusion to the inheritance promised to the Davidic king in Ps.

2:8.[1] Indeed, the name "Son" is part of the inheritance granted to Jesus, by which he has become greater than the angels (Heb. 1:4).

Such an idea seems to be confirmed by the citation of Ps. 2:7 in Heb. 1:5. We should note at the outset that the author draws upon Ps. 2. In its historical context the psalmist warns the rulers of the world to submit to Israel's anointed king. The rulers of the world chafed against the Davidic king appointed by God. Still, this king had been installed as such by Yahweh himself. Yahweh had "begotten" him—that is, appointed him to be king and to rule the world on God's behalf. All the nations that resisted his sovereignty would be destroyed, and so they must submit to his rule to find refuge. The author of Hebrews applies this psalm to Jesus himself as David's son. He is the Son who will rule "the ends of the earth" (Ps. 2:8). In other words, Jesus is the one who will fulfill the promises made to Abraham, which will lead to blessing for the whole world. The begetting of the Son (Heb. 1:5) refers to Jesus' installation as the messianic king at his resurrection (cf. Heb. 5:5; Acts 13:33).[2] Jesus is greater than the angels, then, because by virtue of his death and resurrection he has been crowned as the messianic king.

After citing Ps. 2 in Heb. 1:5, the author also quotes from 2 Sam. 7:14. Chapter 7 of 2 Samuel, of course, recounts the inauguration of the Davidic covenant, so Hebrews identifies Jesus, as is common in the NT, as the fulfillment of the covenant made with David. Jesus is God's Son, and Yahweh is his Father. This sonship of Jesus, however, does not only begin at the resurrection. Jesus was the messianic king while he was still on earth, even though his status as the anointed one of Yahweh was hidden from the eyes of most human beings. What Hebrews emphasizes, however, is Jesus' exaltation—his reign over angels and the whole universe that began at his resurrection and ascension. He is God's "firstborn" (*prōtotokos*) Son, and as the Davidic heir exercises sovereignty over the people of God (Heb. 1:6).[3] Angels never received the privilege of ruling "the world to come" (Heb. 2:5). The task of ruling the world for God belongs to human beings, beginning with Adam.

1. Rightly Meier 1985a: 176–78.
2. So Meier 1985b: 505–6; Peterson 1982: 85; Lane 1991a: 25–26; P. Hughes 1977: 54; Rissi 1987: 52. Attridge (1989: 54–55) discusses the issue of whether preexistence Christology is contradicted by what is said here and sets forth various solutions. Probably the most satisfying view is that the Son of God is eternal, but at the resurrection the God-man was exalted as the messianic king and God's Son to rule over human beings.
3. For a helpful discussion of the OT background of *prōtotokos* and whether the background should be traced to Ps. 89:27 or Deut. 6; 11, see Lane 1991a: 26–27.

Jesus Greater Than Adam

Psalm 8, quoted in Heb. 2, considers the majesty of God and the wonders of the created world. What role do apparently insignificant human beings have in a world so vast and magnificent? The psalmist answers, as he reflects on the creation account in Gen. 1–2, that God appointed human beings to rule the world for God. Even though they are now lower than angels, the whole world is destined to be subject to human beings.[4] The author of Hebrews quotes this psalm (Heb. 2:6–8) and then comments on it. He acknowledges that presently the world is not under the control of human beings. The sway of death over all demonstrates that human beings suffer under the dominion of hostile powers (Heb. 2:14–15). Human beings have failed, beginning with Adam and Eve, in their quest to domesticate the world for God's praise. The world has become a wreck instead of a blessing.

The failure of human beings is not the end of the story. Jesus is the representative human being. He succeeded where the rest of the human race has failed. In that sense, he is the true human being, the only one who has genuinely lived the kind of life that humans were intended to live under God. Hebrews emphasizes in the strongest possible terms the true humanness of Jesus, both as the son of Adam (humanity) and as the son of David. As a human being, Jesus was temporarily lower than angels (Heb. 2:9). Even though the world is not yet subjected to him entirely, he is now "crowned with glory and honor" (Heb. 2:9). Jesus now sits at God's right hand as the exalted man (Heb. 1:3, 13) since he has fully atoned for sin and his work is completed.[5] The rule always promised to human beings has commenced with Jesus' exaltation.

We should note at this juncture that Hebrews operates with a schema of promise and fulfillment in which Jesus fulfills what is adumbrated in the OT. Jesus is the true human being succeeding where Adam failed. He is the fulfillment of all the promises, as argued previously, made to David, so that the rule promised to the Davidic king reaches its consummation in him.

Jesus Greater Than Moses and Joshua

Just as Jesus is the faithful son, fulfilling the task at which Adam failed and fulfilling the promises made to David, so too Jesus, like Moses, is God's faithful servant (Heb. 3:2, 5). When reading the word "servant" we are apt to

4. The author of Hebrews uses the term "son of man" here from Ps. 8, but it is debated whether the term is a messianic title (against this, see Lindars 1991: 39). See chapter 6, notes 133, 134.

5. Hengel (1983: 86) suggests that we have a fusion of Ps. 8 and Ps. 110 in early Christian tradition. For a study of Ps. 110 in Jewish and early Christian tradition, see Hay 1973.

diminish Moses' role, but to function as God's "servant" in the OT indicates both humility and one's exalted role. God's servants are those specially appointed by him to carry out his will and proclaim his message.

The OT background alluded to in Heb. 3 is vital. Miriam and Aaron were rebuked and Miriam was temporarily struck with leprosy because they complained against Moses (Num. 12:1–16). Yahweh speaks to prophets in visions and dreams, but Moses has a more exalted role as God's "servant," as God's "faithful" one (Num. 12:6–7). God spoke to Moses "mouth to mouth, clearly, and not in riddles, and he beholds the form of the LORD. Why then were you not afraid to speak against my servant Moses?" (Num. 12:8). God's relationship with Moses was unique in that Moses saw God's "form" and God spoke to him directly. Despite this exalted position, Jesus is greater than Moses, for he is not merely God's faithful servant but God's faithful Son (Heb. 3:6). One of the characteristics of Hebrews' Christology bleeds through here. Not only is Jesus a faithful Son as a human being, but also he shares the divine nature and is himself God. Much more will be said about this latter theme shortly.

Both David and Moses point toward and anticipate the coming of Jesus. Similarly, the rest given by Joshua during the days of conquest cannot be the final rest given by God, for Ps. 95, written long after the days of Joshua, speaks of a rest that God's people may still inherit (Heb. 3:12–4:11). We should notice here that in Greek "Joshua" and "Jesus" are the same name. So when Greek readers see the name "Joshua" (*Iēsous*) in Heb. 4:8, they would also think of "Jesus."[6] An allusion to Jesus fits the argument made here because Jesus functions as the greater Joshua, the one who truly brings complete and final rest to God's people.

Jesus as a Melchizedekian Priest

Hebrews maintains that Jesus is the true human being—the true Adam.[7] He is greater than Moses as the faithful Son, and greater than Joshua because he grants eschatological rest. He is the fulfillment of the promises made to David and therefore rules now as the messianic king. Hebrews emphasizes as well, however, that Jesus rules as a *priest*-king. As we commence with this theme, we are reminded that Christology serves soteriology. As a priest-king, Jesus accomplishes salvation and procures full forgiveness of sins for his people.[8]

6. Rightly Attridge 1989: 130; Bruce 1964: 76–77.
7. For the light that the Qumran scrolls shed on Hebrews' use of Melchizedek traditions, see Fitzmyer 1967; 2000; Longenecker 1978.
8. Rooke (2000) emphasizes that the priesthood of Melchizedek is both royal and priestly, and that the former often has been obscured.

We should particularly note at the outset that the one who served as a priest was invariably a human being. The high priest in Israel was a man "chosen from among men" to represent human beings before God (Heb. 5:1).[9] According to the OT, high priests were not chosen by popular vote or by acclamation of the people. One had to be appointed by God to serve as high priest (Heb. 5:4). The author of Hebrews conceives of the high priesthood in Israel typologically. It too points toward Jesus and is fulfilled in him (Heb. 5:5). According to Hebrews, however, Jesus is not an ordinary high priest. Indeed, he could not function as a high priest according to the OT law because the high priest hails from the tribe of Levi, whereas Jesus comes from the tribe of Judah (Heb. 7:13–14). Jesus has a priesthood that is more exalted and greater than the Levitical priesthood because he is a Melchizedekian priest (Heb. 5:6, 10).

The author goes to great lengths to demonstrate that the Melchizedekian priesthood is superior to the Levitical one.[10] He maintains that Melchizedek is greater than Levi because Melchizedek blessed Abraham, and the one who blesses is greater than the one who receives the blessing (Heb. 7:1, 6–7).[11] Furthermore, Abraham acknowledged Melchizedek's superiority in paying him tithes (Heb. 7:2, 4, 6, 8). In a sense, Hebrews argues, Levi paid tithes to Melchizedek, since Levi was a descendant of Abraham (Heb. 7:9–10). In other words, it was always God's intention that the Melchizedekian priesthood replace the Levitical one. The Levitical priesthood was never intended to remain in place forever. A prophecy about a Melchizedekian priesthood would never have arisen if perfection could be obtained through Levitical priesthood (Heb. 7:11–12).

The prophecy in Ps. 110:4 is foundational for the argument: "You are a priest forever, after the order of Melchizedek" (Heb. 5:6; 7:17; cf. 7:21). It has also long been recognized that Ps. 110 is perhaps the most important OT text for the author of Hebrews, since it refers to one who is both priest and king. Jesus himself appealed to Ps. 110 in his earthly ministry (Matt. 22:41–46 par.). Psalm 110:1 indicates that David's son will also be his lord, and this one will sit at God's right hand until God conquers his enemies. The author of Hebrews, in accord with Jesus' exegesis, sees Jesus as the fulfillment of the psalm. He has been exalted

9. On Jesus as the high priest in Hebrews, see Rissi 1987: 55–70.

10. Lindars (1991: 1) maintains that Hebrews is innovative and distinctive in that it is the only book in the NT in which Jesus is identified as a Melchizedekian priest, and the Day of Atonement is used to explicate Jesus' sacrifice. For the high priesthood of Jesus in NT theology, see Cullmann 1963: 83–107.

11. For a history of interpretation of Heb. 7:1–10, see Demarest 1976.

to God's right hand at the resurrection and reigns supreme over angels (Heb. 1:13).[12]

In Heb. 5:5 (cf. 7:17, 21) the author seizes upon the word "forever" from Ps. 110:4 to contrast the Melchizedekian priesthood with the Levitical one. Jesus qualifies as a Melchizedekian priest by virtue of his resurrection. His life is "indestructible" (Heb. 7:16).[13] He has no "end of life" (Heb. 7:3).[14] The Levitical priests could not retain their priestly office because they are mortal and die, but Jesus is a permanent priest "because he continues forever" (Heb. 7:23–24). "He always lives" (Heb. 7:25; 13:20–21). The superiority of Jesus' priesthood is evident, for Jesus is the only priest who has conquered death, and doubtless a living priesthood has preeminence over one that presides over death.

The superiority of Jesus' priesthood is confirmed also because the Melchizedekian priesthood is ratified by an oath, whereas the Levitical priesthood lacks one (Heb. 7:20–21). The Levitical priesthood was instituted by God, but it never received a divine oath that it would remain forever like the Melchizedekian priesthood of Jesus. For God to take an oath is highly unusual because his word alone is truth. An oath is added with respect to the Melchizedekian priesthood to underline its perpetuity and superiority.

If Jesus' priesthood is superior to the Levitical priesthood, we are not surprised to learn that Jesus' sacrifice is better than Levitical sacrifices, and in particular the sacrifices offered on the Day of Atonement, because his sacrifice accomplishes forgiveness of sins once for all. Indeed, Jesus did not need to offer sacrifice for his own sins, for he is without sin (Heb. 4:15; 7:26). The high priests bring offerings for their own sins and those of the people (Heb. 5:3; 7:27), but Jesus, as the sinless one, offers himself up as the one definitive sacrifice forever (Heb. 7:27; cf. 4:15). The new covenant, inaugurated and mediated through the death of Jesus, surpasses the old one because atonement has been secured under this covenant (Heb. 8:7–13; 10:15–18; 12:24).[15] Jesus' priestly sacrifice accomplished "eternal redemption" (Heb. 9:12) and cleanses the conscience from sin (Heb. 9:14). He did not merely secure access to God's presence in the

12. The notion that the author of Hebrews is influenced by conceptions of Melchizedek current in the Qumran community (see 11QMelch.) is not borne out by the evidence (see Hurst 1990: 58–60; Rooke 2000: 84; Attridge 1989: 192–95; Lane 1991a: 160–63). Instead, the author confines himself to the two OT texts that refer to Melchizedek (Gen. 14; Ps. 110:4).

13. The focus here is not on Christ's eternal nature but on his resurrection (so Peterson 1982: 110–11; Bruce 1964: 148; Lane 1991a: 184).

14. Lindars (1991: 37) is technically correct that the resurrection is mentioned specifically only in Heb. 13, but he fails to see that the concept of resurrection is found elsewhere in the letter.

15. On the new covenant in Hebrews, see Lehne 1990.

tabernacle by his death; he has entered God's presence in heaven in accomplishing forgiveness (Heb. 9:12, 24). OT sacrifices, such as on the Day of Atonement, were offered repeatedly or at least yearly, but Jesus obtained final forgiveness of sins with one sacrifice (Heb. 9:25–28).

The incarnation of Jesus is intimated by Heb. 10:5–10, where his intention in coming into the world was to offer himself (the author using the language of Ps. 40:6–8). He was God's "apostle" (Heb. 3:1)—that is, the one sent by God into the world to accomplish the divine will. Psalm 110 again plays a vital role in his argument, for the psalm refers to a king who sits at God's right hand, reigning forever (Ps. 110:1), and to a Melchizedekian priest who serves as a priest forever (Ps. 110:4). Jesus fulfills both the kingly and priestly roles. Indeed, Hebrews clarifies how both roles fit together. He reigns now as the exalted king, sitting at God's right hand *because* he has secured forgiveness of sins once for all by his death (Heb. 1:3, 13; 8:1; 10:12; 12:2). His kingly work and priestly work are inextricably intertwined. The rule over the world intended for human beings, traced in Ps. 8, could not become a reality as long as human beings were defiled by sin.

The tabernacle erected by Moses always pointed forward to something greater and more perfect: the very dwelling place of God in heaven (Heb. 8:2, 5; 9:11–12, 24). The sacrifices offered under the old covenant could not and did not secure forgiveness of sins. Even the yearly sacrifices offered on the Day of Atonement (Lev. 16) did not bring final forgiveness. Indeed, the various compartments of the tabernacle, and the fact that the high priest could enter the holy of holies only on the Day of Atonement, signified that free access to God was not yet granted (Heb. 9:8). It is evident that the furniture and offerings under the old covenant dealt with external matters that anticipated something better (Heb. 9:9–10). Jesus secured forgiveness not by offering the blood of animals but by offering his own blood in God's very presence (Heb. 9:11–14).[16] The covenant instituted by Moses (Exod. 24) indicated that blood had to be shed for sin to be forgiven (Heb. 9:15–22). The sacrifice of Christ fulfills what was adumbrated under the old covenant, as he offered his own blood to accomplish forgiveness of sins once for all.

The author of Hebrews emphasizes the imperfection of the old covenant priesthood and sacrifices (Heb. 7:11, 18–19). The law was only a shadow, not the substance, and hence the sacrifices offered could not bring perfection and true cleansing of the conscience (Heb. 10:1–4). If the sacrifices of animals truly achieved forgiveness, there would be no

16. The greater and more perfect tent refers here not to Jesus' body but to the heavenly tabernacle. See Peterson 1982: 140–44; see also Lane 1991b: 236–38; Attridge 1989: 246–47.

need to offer them repeatedly. The repetition of such sacrifices verifies that forgiveness was not obtained through the old covenant, for if forgiveness was granted, then the sacrifices could cease. Furthermore, the sacrifices of animals (Heb. 10:4) can never be comparable to the sacrifice of a willing and human victim (Heb. 10:5–10). Animals are constrained by others to offer their blood and have no realization of the purpose of their death. The death of Jesus, on the other hand, was the death of a human being, and the very purpose for which he entered into the world was to give his life as a sacrifice for others. No one could possibly think that the sacrifice of animals could be comparable to the propitiatory (Heb. 2:17) and willing work of Jesus as high priest.[17]

The high priests, under the old covenant, stand repeatedly offering sacrifices for sins, but Jesus sits at God's right hand because his work is finished forever (Heb. 10:11–18). The priests continue to offer sacrifices day after day, signaling that final forgiveness has not been achieved, but Jesus secured complete and final forgiveness of sins with one sacrifice: "For by a single offering he has perfected for all time those who are being sanctified" (Heb. 10:14).[18] Jesus' sacrifice fulfills what is promised in the new covenant (Jer. 31:34): complete forgiveness of sins. The sacrifices under the old covenant do not bring such forgiveness, since they are offered repeatedly.

Jesus, according to Hebrews, established for human beings the rule over creation that was shipwrecked with Adam's sin. To accomplish this victory, however, he himself as God's priest-king had to be a human being. Since human beings are flesh and blood, he had to partake of the same (Heb. 2:14). Or, as Heb. 2:17 puts it, "He had to be made like his brothers in every respect." He experienced the full range of temptations that beset human beings so that he sympathizes with the human condition (Heb. 2:18; 4:15). Indeed, Jesus had to suffer in order to be perfected (Heb. 2:10).[19] "He learned obedience through what he suffered" and thereby became "perfect" (Heb. 5:8–9; 7:28). The notion that Jesus became perfect implies imperfection, which seems rather strange, given the exalted view of Jesus explicated in Hebrews.[20] Jesus was not imperfect in the sense that he was stained by sin. Hebrews clearly

17. Jesus' high priesthood cannot be confined only to the heavenly sphere; it also includes his sacrificial work on earth (see Peterson 1982: 191–95).

18. The present participle *hagiazomenous* does not denote ongoing action here (see Bruce 1964: 241; Peterson 1982: 150; contra Attridge 1989: 281).

19. The suffering in Heb. 2:10 refers to the whole of Jesus' suffering in his ministry and should not be limited to his suffering on the cross (rightly Peterson 1982: 69), though the cross is the climax of his sufferings.

20. My understanding of perfection in Hebrews is shaped especially by the monograph by Peterson (1982), who summarizes previous research and offers the most satisfying explanation of perfection. But for a different view, see Scholer 1991: 185–200.

teaches that Jesus was a perfect and sinless sacrifice (Heb. 4:15; 7:26).[21] A careful examination of Hebrews clearly reveals that his "perfection" is obtained through suffering as a human being. Jesus had to live his life as a man in order to learn obedience in the rough and tumble of human life. As Lindars remarks, "Perfection in Hebrews means the completion of God's plan of salvation."[22] But this perfection, as Michel says, includes "his proving in temptation, his fulfillment of the priestly requirements and his exaltation as Redeemer of the heavenly world."[23] The perfection of Jesus includes the notions of human development and being proved through sufferings. His moral perfection is inextricably linked to his salvific and high priestly work by which he accomplishes redemption, so that through the cross and ascension he obtains forgiveness of sins.[24]

If we engage in a thought experiment, it might help us understand the theology of Hebrews. Could Jesus have atoned for our sins as a ten-year-old? Naturally, this is a question never asked specifically in Hebrews! Still, it seems evident that the answer is no. Jesus would have lacked the maturity and experience as a human being to suffer for the sake of his people at such a tender age. He had to experience the full range of temptation and resist allurements to sin to qualify as an atoning sacrifice (Heb. 4:15). The depth of pain in human existence had to be his, so that he knew what it was to offer up "prayers and supplications, with loud cries and tears" (Heb. 5:7).[25] Furthermore, it was necessary for Jesus to obey his Father in every painful

21. Most scholars agree with this assessment. For a defense of the comprehensive sinlessness of Jesus, see Peterson 1982: 188–90; Attridge 1989: 140–41; Lane 1991a: 114–15. Cullmann (1963: 92–95) also rightly emphasizes that Jesus is conceived of as morally perfect in Hebrews.

22. Lindars 1991: 44. Silva (1976) emphasizes the eschatological character of perfection, but Peterson (1982: 226n130) rightly objects that Silva wrongly excludes any "moral progression in Jesus' character" so that his view does not "do justice to the full scope of our writer's presentation."

23. "Seine Bewährung in der Versuchung, seine Erfüllung der priesterlichen Voraussetzungen und seine Erhöhung zum Erlöser der himmlischen Welt" (Michel 1966: 224). I owe this reference and translation to Peterson 1982: 71. Peterson (1982: 73) says, "That perfecting involved a whole sequence of events: his proving in suffering, his redemptive death to fulfil the divine requirements for the perfect expiation of sins and his exaltation to glory and honour."

24. Rightly Peterson 1982: 96–103.

25. This probably should be identified with Gethsemane (so Cullmann 1963: 96; P. Hughes 1977: 182; Peterson 1982: 86–88). See the careful discussion in R. Brown 1994: 1:227–33. Others say that Gethsemane is the most remarkable illustration of Jesus' agony but the text also reflects on his whole ministry (Bruce 1964: 98–100; Scholer 1991: 87–88). Attridge (1989: 148–49) finds any clear reference to Gethsemane less convincing (see also Lane 1991a: 119–20).

circumstance to qualify as one who could atone for the sins of others. It is not enough that Jesus never sinned as a child. It was necessary for him to demonstrate his faithfulness to God as he was tried in the crucible of sufferings. He could not become a perfect sacrifice apart from enduring the cross (Heb. 12:2). His obedience to God was demonstrated even when sinners responded to him with implacable hostility (Heb. 12:3).[26]

By learning obedience through suffering and undergoing temptation, Jesus qualified as a perfect sacrifice, as "a merciful and faithful high priest" (Heb. 2:17). Human beings had to be set free from the devil, who possesses "the power of death" (Heb. 2:14). Only through the death of a perfect human being would such freedom be effected. All those who belong to Jesus are his brothers and sisters (Heb. 2:11–13). He shares in humanity with them, so that they can participate in the victory over death with him.

Thus far we have emphasized Jesus' humanity. As a human being, he endured the pressures and sorrows that are the lot of all human beings. Further, he uniquely suffered as the sinless one on the cross for the sake of others. Jesus is greater than Moses because he is the Son rather than a servant. He is greater than Joshua because he grants eschatological rest to God's people. He is the son of David who reigns at the right hand of God. I have bracketed out of the discussion, quite artificially, the notion that Jesus is also God. Jesus is not only a human priest-king; Hebrews also trumpets him as the divine priest-king.

Jesus as Divine Son and Priest-King

The deity of Christ is clearly taught in the first chapter of Hebrews.[27] The author declares that God has spoken in his Son, and that he is the messianic king because he is "the heir of all things" (Heb. 1:2). The next line, however, reveals that Jesus is also divine, for he is also described as the agent of creation (Heb. 1:2). Here we likely have another example of wisdom tradition informing Christology (Prov. 8:22–31; Sir. 24:1–12; Wis. 7:12–8:4). In any case, Jesus is more than a human being, for only a divine being could be the agent of creation. It is also evident that he preexisted, for the world could not come into being through the Son

26. The process of learning obedience in suffering is helpfully explained in Peterson 1982: 94–96.

27. Hurst (1987) argues valiantly that Heb. 1 refers exclusively to the humanity, not the divinity, of Jesus. It seems that Hurst's argument is reductionistic in that he implies that the importance of Jesus' humanity in Heb. 2 is diminished if chapter 1 focuses on his divinity. Such a worldview, however, does not cohere with the stance of NT writers who did not neatly separate Jesus' divinity from his humanity.

if he did not exist when the world came into being.[28] Some argue that preexistence is unnecessary because wisdom did not exist as a discrete being at creation. This argument fails to convince because Jesus clearly is a person in contrast to wisdom.[29] It is difficult to conceive how he could be the agent of creation if he did not even exist. The very point of NT writers is that Jesus transcends wisdom.

When analyzing the introduction to Hebrews (Heb. 1:2–4),[30] we notice a clear example of a chiasm.

> A (God spoke to us) by his Son,
>> B whom he appointed the heir of all things,
>>> C through whom he also created the world.
>>>> D He is the radiance of the glory of God,
>>>> D′ and the exact imprint of his nature,
>>> C′ and he upholds all things by the word of his power.
>> B′ After making purification for sins,
>> he sat down at the right hand of the Majesty on high,
> A′ having become as much superior to angels as the name he has inherited is more excellent than theirs.[31]

The frame of the chiasm, A and A′, presents Jesus as the exalted Son. B and B′ emphasize his lordship over the created world as God's priest-king. C and C′ stress Jesus' role as the agent and sustainer of creation. The middle section of the chiasm, D and D′, focuses on Jesus' nature. He radiates and shines forth the glory of God.[32] Indeed, Jesus is in the

---

28. Rightly Peterson 1982: 119; cf. Lane 1991a: 12; Attridge 1989: 40. Lindars (1991: 34, 41–42) contends that the Son of God preexisted but not the man Jesus. Such an observation is formally correct, though Lindars appears to introduce too much of a disjunction between the Son of God and Jesus. Rissi (1987: 46) seems to downplay preexistence in saying that it does not concern the author.

29. Dunn (1996a: 206–9) denies that Hebrews teaches the personal preexistence of Christ, arguing that we have here wisdom Christology, and the author of Hebrews sees personified wisdom as now embodied in Jesus Christ. But against Dunn, it is difficult to give credence to the idea that the Son who created the world and whom God addresses as divine is merely an ideal Son and not the real Son who died and was exalted (see Meier 1985b: 531–33). Dunn has to insist that the author of Hebrews distinguishes between the real Son and the ideal Son, but such a thesis seems strained and artificial.

30. Many authors have posited hymnic or creedal material in Heb. 1:1–4, but this hypothesis is questionable (see Meier 1985b: 524–28). Meier (1985a: 168–76) himself proposes a different structure.

31. Meier (1985b: 523–24) argues that the OT citations in Heb. 1:5–14 generally follow the same pattern that we see in the Christology of Heb. 1:2–4.

32. The meaning of the word *apaugasma* is difficult. It may mean "radiance" or "outshining," as translated here, or "reflection." For a careful discussion of the possibilities, see Attridge 1989: 42–43.

very nature of God, representing to human beings precisely what God is like.[33]

When we consider the Christology of Hebrews, we see that the author forcefully emphasizes that Jesus is both human and divine. The two themes adjoin one another and complement each other. The author moves from humanity to divinity and from divinity to humanity easily and without calling attention to such transitions. It seems from this that Jesus' sacrifice for sins as the priest-king is effective because he is both human and divine. Both his divinity and his humanity are necessary for Jesus to accomplish God's saving purposes.

Indeed, Jesus' divinity resounds in the remainder of Heb. 1. The author of Hebrews, drawing from the LXX of Deut. 32:43, enjoins the angels to worship the Son (Heb. 1:6).[34] In the LXX the one who deserves worship is none other than God himself. Hebrews applies this text to the Son, obviously implying that he is divine.[35] Furthermore, the action demanded of angels is worship, but anyone familiar with the OT, as the author of Hebrews obviously is, knows that worship is reserved only for the one true God.[36] What we have seen elsewhere in the NT appears here as well. Jesus shares the same status with God, and so he deserves worship. However, Jesus is not all there is to God. The Father is still the Father, and the Son is distinct from him.

Angels are created by God and serve his will (Heb. 1:7), but the Son is God himself (Heb. 1:8–9). In Heb. 1:8–9 the author cites Ps. 45:6–7. In its original context the psalm is a wedding song celebrating the king's marriage.[37] Hebrews applies the text to Jesus Christ because he fulfills the promise of the Davidic covenant that a king would reign forever. What

---

33. Meier says that the present tense of the participle *ōn* points to Christ's eternal pre-existence (1985a: 179–80). "Amid this string of discrete past actions, the present stative participle *ōn* stands out like a metaphysical diamond against the black crepe of narrative" (Meier 1985a: 180). Meier proceeds to remark that in texts like these, authors transcend "purely historical modes of conception and narration and . . . probe the speculative, philosophical implications of their tremendous affirmations about God, Christ, and humanity" (Meier 1985a: 180).

34. Jesus' superiority over angels is part and parcel of the author's argument that Jesus takes precedence over the Mosaic law because the law was mediated by angels (Heb. 2:2) (rightly Meier 1985b: 520–22; Hurst 1987: 156; Lindars 1991: 38). Meier surveys other options that have been suggested, from angel worship such as we see in Colossians, to the veneration of angelic intercessors, or even the notion that there were a number of intermediaries between humans and God.

35. The attempt by Hurst (1987: 158–59) to deny that the angels worship Jesus seems quite strained. For more convincing exegesis, see Attridge 1989: 57; Lane 1991a: 28.

36. Scholars differ as to when this worship occurs, so that some see a reference to the incarnation (P. Hughes 1977: 60; Attridge 1989: 55–56), others to Jesus' exaltation (Meier 1985b: 507–11; Lane 1991a: 27–28), and others to the second coming (Rissi 1987: 91).

37. For an analysis of the phrase in the context of Ps. 45, see Harris 1992: 187–204.

is most striking is that the Son directly receives the attribution "God" in Heb. 1:8: "But of the Son, he says, 'Your throne, O God, is forever and ever.'" Even if one were to say that in the OT the reference is to Yahweh, the author of Hebrews clarifies in the introductory formula that he applies the verse to the Son. Nor does any other plausible translation exist for this line. Some have suggested that the Greek could be translated, "God is your throne," but such a rendering makes little sense.[38] The word "God" (*ho theos*) here should be understood as a vocative, and this fits with the meaning of the Hebrew text of Ps. 45:6 as well.

The citation does not only focus on the Son's divinity; it is also apparent that the Son is a human being. The emphasis on both Jesus' deity and humanity that we see elsewhere in Hebrews manifests itself in the quotation from Ps. 45. The humanity of Jesus is suggested by the Son's reign, for his scepter signals that he is the messianic king (Heb. 1:8). He is "anointed" with sovereignty because he has renounced evil and embraced goodness. When Heb. 1:9 refers to the God who has "anointed" the Son "beyond your companions," "God" here refers to the Father, who has exalted the Son above the angels as the exalted Lord. Thus the Christology of Heb. 1:8–9 is rather complex. The Son is addressed as God, and yet he is also human and the messianic king. He is God, and yet "God" anointed him as the exalted Lord. Obviously, Jesus is not God without remainder. Hebrews does not untangle all the christological themes packed into these verses in the way they were worked out in church history. The raw materials for such reflection, however, are earthed in verses like these.

Psalm 102:25–27 is another text utilized in the author's christological argument in Heb. 1. In the OT context the psalmist celebrates Yahweh's work of creation in contrast to the created order, which wears down over time. Yahweh is eternal and the same, but creation is temporary and will pass away. Hebrews applies a text that refers to Yahweh to Jesus Christ (Heb. 1:10–12).[39] Once again it is evident that the Son has the same status as the Father, without canceling out the latter's existence. The Son should be praised as the creator and the eternal one.[40] Of course, only God creates and is eternal. Jesus remains the same from generation to generation. We naturally think here of the

38. Rightly Meier 1985b: 514–15; Attridge 1989: 58–59; Lane 1991a: 29; Bruce 1964: 19–20. For a full discussion of the various options and a defense of the view accepted here, see Harris 1992: 205–27.

39. See the careful discussion in Meier 1985b: 517–18. See also Lane 1991a: 30–31; Attridge 1989: 60; Rissi 1987: 54.

40. Once again Hurst (1987: 160–62) maintains that the language used here fits with what the Messiah could do as a human being. Contra Hurst, in Jewish circles creation is a work of God, nor does Wis. 9:1–4 indicate that human beings played a role in creation.

famous words in Heb: 13:8: "Jesus Christ is the same yesterday and today and forever."

Jesus as the Son of God

When the author of Hebrews uses the term "Son" or "Son of God," it is difficult to restrict the term to either Jesus' humanity or his deity. In some contexts the focus surely is on Jesus' humanity, since he suffered as God's Son, is the Davidic king, and has been exalted to God's right hand (Heb. 1:5; 5:5, 8). Some verses emphasize that as the Son Jesus is both human and divine (Heb. 1:8–9). Hence, any attempt to distinguish clearly between humanity and divinity in the title "Son" or "Son of God" seems doomed to fail. The human Jesus is God's priest-king, now exalted to God's right hand. He has sat down at God's right hand because full atonement for sins has been accomplished. Still, we cannot neatly carve out the distinction between Jesus' deity and humanity. Jesus is also God-himself, though not God without remainder. As the God-man, the priest-king, he is the exalted "Son of God" (Heb. 4:14). Jesus is not made like Melchizedek, but Melchizedek resembles him (Heb. 7:3), so that Jesus is the prototype, and Melchizedek is, so to speak, the copy.[41] Jesus is the Son who has now been perfected forever (Heb. 7:28).[42] God has spoken definitively and finally and completely in his Son (Heb. 1:2). No further explication of God's purposes is needed. The Son reigns as Lord over God's house—that is, over the people of God (Heb. 3:6). Those who crucify the Son of God by apostasy will never repent (Heb. 6:4–6). Anyone who spurns him and his sacrifice by reverting to Judaism will face God's vengeance (Heb. 10:29–30). The Christology of Hebrews is complex indeed, emphasizing both Jesus' humanity and his deity, his suffering and his exaltation, and his weakness and his sinlessness. The sacrifice that he offered is definitive and complete because it was offered by God's priest-king, the one who is both God and man.

Further Reflections on Jesus' Saving Work in Hebrews

SALVATION

The work of Jesus is described in various ways in Hebrews, and we have already touched on many of these themes. What Jesus accomplished is portrayed as salvation, redemption, forgiveness and cleansing,

41. See Peterson 1982: 106.
42. Again I cite the conclusion of Peterson (1982: 118), where Jesus' perfection consists in *"his proving in temptation, his death as a sacrifice for sins and his heavenly exaltation."*

and sanctification. The word "salvation" (*sōtēria*; verb: *sōzō*) means "deliverance."[43] For example, Noah delivered or saved his own by building an ark (Heb. 11:7). The physical deliverance of Noah in this instance involves at the same time escape from God's judgment. In the remaining instances in Hebrews, salvation refers to deliverance from God's judgment on the final day. Hebrews was written to forestall apostasy in the lives of the readers, so that they would avert the judgment of the last day and be saved from God's fierce wrath (Heb. 10:26–31). The author does not want the readers to fall into the hands of the living God, who is a consuming fire (see also Heb. 6:4–8; 12:25–29). Salvation, then, is eschatological. The readers will inherit salvation on the last day (Heb. 1:14), when Jesus returns to complete his saving work (Heb. 9:28).

Jesus' high priestly work, sketched in earlier, is the basis of salvation. Through his suffering he is the "founder" (*archēgos*) of salvation (Heb. 2:10), and has become "the source of eternal salvation" (Heb. 5:9). The meaning of the word *archēgos* is disputed. Peterson's discussion is the most satisfying, for he argues that the word conveys the sense of both "leader" and "initiator."[44] Peterson rightly maintains that the word should not be limited to Christ's example, for in Heb. 2 Jesus died on behalf of others (Heb. 2:9), and his death shattered the power of the devil (Heb. 2:14).[45] Furthermore, the truth that Christ accomplishes salvation (he is "the founder of their salvation") indicates that the term *archēgos* should not be limited to Christ functioning as a leader or example in this context.

The warning passages that punctuate the letter were written so that the readers would persevere and be saved on the last day (Heb. 2:1–4; 3:12–4:13; 5:11–6:12; 10:26–31; 12:26–29). Those who drift away will not escape if they neglect the great salvation brought about in Christ (Heb. 2:3). Those who continue to trust God will experience the reward of eternal life (Heb. 10:35), but those who turn away will experience eschatological destruction (*apōleia* [Heb. 10:39]). Those who persevere in faith will "preserve their souls" and escape from God's wrath (Heb. 10:39).[46]

43. For the eschatological character of salvation in Hebrews, see McKnight 1992: 55–58.

44. Peterson 1982: 57–58. See the discussion of the term by Attridge (1989: 87–88), who focuses on the meaning "leader." Lane (1991a: 56–57) argues that the term should be rendered "champion." Croy (1998: 176), reflecting on Heb. 12:2, argues that Jesus was the first person obtaining the goal of faith who also brought faith to its goal and realization.

45. In Heb. 12:2, however, Peterson (1982: 171–72) thinks that the emphasis is on Jesus as the exemplar of faith, so that faith has reached its expression in the life of Jesus (cf. Bruce 1964: 351–52; Attridge 1989: 356–57). Delling (*TDNT* 8:86–87), however, slightly inclines to the view that Jesus brings the faith of believers to completion.

46. Eschatological judgment and life are in view here (so Lane 1991b: 307; Attridge 1989: 304).

The author does not think that the readers will apostatize. He is persuaded that they will heed his warnings and be saved on the last day (Heb. 6:9). Jesus' work is "a sure and steadfast anchor of the soul" that grants assurance of final victory (Heb. 6:19).[47] The author does not intend to sow doubt in the minds of the readers regarding their future salvation. The warnings point them back to Christ, who "is able to save to the uttermost those who draw near to God through him, since he always lives to make intercession for them" (Heb. 7:25).[48] The only thing that could lead to destruction is if the readers fail to put their trust in Christ, whose high priestly work saves. The author is confident, however, that through his letter his readers will continue to cling to what Christ has accomplished on the cross.

REDEMPTION AND PROPITIATION

The word "redemption" falls under the same orbit as "salvation." In Heb. 11:35 it means "deliverance" (my translation of *apolytrōsis* [ESV: "release"]), referring to those who were tortured to death and were not delivered from martyrdom but looked forward to a future resurrection. Christ, by his high priestly work, secured "eternal redemption" (*aiōnios lytrōsis* [Heb. 9:12]). Here the term "redemption" clearly has the meaning of "ransom," because redemption was achieved, as the author explicitly says, with Christ's blood. The redemption is eternal in contrast to the OT cult, which never achieved forgiveness of sins. Indeed, Hebrews emphasizes that redemption brings forgiveness of sins. Hence, the root defect with human beings is traced to sin, which in turn brings guilt. The new-covenant death of Jesus frees human beings from transgressions that remained unforgiven under the old covenant (Heb. 9:15). The sacrifice of animals, therefore, never really brought forgiveness of sins. They always pointed forward to the death of Christ, which is the only genuine basis for forgiveness (Heb. 10:4).

Here we should note that Jesus, as the high priest's offering for sins, propitiated the sins of the people (Heb. 2:17).[49] The only other place in

---

47. See P. Hughes 1977: 235.

48. Christ's intercession is based on his final and definitive sacrifice and should not be construed as a continuation of his sacrificial work in God's presence, for such a view would contradict the finality of Christ's sacrifice, which is such a prominent theme in Hebrews (so also Peterson 1982: 115). Crump (1992: 18) says that there is an implication that "the content of Christ's heavenly prayers concern the effective application of the benefits of his atonement to all those who come to God through him."

49. Peterson (1982: 64) rightly notes that the sacrifices that bring expiation also functioned to appease God's anger, so we should not drive a wedge here between expiation and propitiation. Some scholars focus on propitiation only (P. Hughes 1977: 120–23; Lane 1991a: 66). For the view that propitiation is not in view but only expiation, see Attridge 1989: 96n192. See also Büchsel, *TDNT* 3:315–16.

Hebrews where the language of propitiation is used is the reference to the OT "mercy seat" (*hilastērion*) in Heb. 9:5.[50] The mercy seat is the place where once a year, on the Day of Atonement, blood was placed to provide atonement for Israel's transgressions (Lev. 16:14–17). True propitiation, however, is secured only by the work of Jesus Christ. God was appeased on the Day of Atonement with the blood brought into his presence, but this blood pointed forward to Christ's blood, which functions as the true satisfaction for sins.

Forgiveness of Sins

Forgiveness of sins is communicated with both noncultic and cultic terms, but especially the latter. The former is found only in two texts (Heb. 9:22; 10:18). What is striking is that in both cases we have a covenantal context. The author draws on Exod. 24:3–8, where the covenant was ratified with blood to demonstrate that the shedding of blood is necessary for the forgiveness of sins (Heb. 9:22). In Heb. 10 forgiveness is grounded in the new-covenant promise, stated in Jer. 31:34, that God will no longer remember the sins of his people (Heb. 10:18). The same text from Jeremiah is quoted in Heb. 8:12.

The commentary on the citation from Jeremiah is highly significant: "Where there is forgiveness of these, there is no longer any offering for sin" (Heb. 10:18). The author's entire discussion of the OT cult and Christ's sacrifice in Heb. 9:11–10:18 leads to this ringing conclusion. The blood spilled to inaugurate the old covenant was absolutely necessary for the covenantal arrangement, but only the sacrifice of Christ truly secures forgiveness of sins.[51] The former always anticipated and pointed toward the latter. Since Christ has achieved complete forgiveness, further sacrifices are unnecessary. And not only are they unnecessary, but also they constitute a spurning of God's Son and a profaning of his blood (Heb. 10:29). A return to the old arrangement crucifies the Son again and holds him up to contempt (Heb. 6:6). We can easily see how this is so. Those who revert to animal sacrifices clearly think that such are necessary for forgiveness, but if the sacrifice of animals is necessary for forgiveness, then Christ's sacrifice becomes superfluous. This explains why the author can say that "there no longer remains a sacrifice for sins" (Heb. 10:26) if one repudiates Christ's sacrifice by returning to OT sacrifices. Since Christ's death alone fully and finally forgives sins, those who turn from

50. For the theological significance of the term, see P. Hughes 1977: 316–17.

51. Lindars (1991: 14) argues that the author writes so that the readers will feel in their conscience that their sins truly are forgiven. The readers are not experiencing in their everyday lives what it means to be forgiven of their sins, and hence they are drawn to the Levitical cult. The author wants to impress upon the minds and hearts of the readers the reality of God's forgiveness in Christ.

it cannot be forgiven.[52] Conversely, those who rest on Christ's sacrifice alone for the forgiveness of sins find that no other offering is needed. He has secured forgiveness once for all.

The author of Hebrews prefers to use the language of cleansing and purification to denote the forgiveness of sins (*katharizō, katharismos, rhantizō, rhantismos*). This is hardly surprising, since the readers were tempted to flee to the OT cult for forgiveness. Cleansing and purification are obtained through blood (*haima*). The author uses the word "blood" to compare and contrast sacrifices offered under the old dispensation with the sacrifice of Christ (Heb. 9:7, 12, 13, 14, 18, 19, 20, 21, 22, 25; 10:4, 19, 29; 11:28; 12:24; 13:11, 12, 20). Both covenants required blood, but the blood of Christ is effective and final because it achieves forgiveness of sins. The use of the word "blood" indicates that it is the death of Christ that brings forgiveness of sins.[53] The shedding of blood does not signify the release of life, as it has sometimes been explained, unless by "release of life" we mean that the person who has shed blood has died. When, under the old covenant, the blood of animals was sprinkled on the altar, the point was that the animals had died. Similarly, the shedding of Jesus' blood indicates his death. The link between "blood" and "death" is clearly communicated in Heb. 9:15–18. The will or covenant is established on the basis of blood, but that means that the one making the will or covenant has died.[54]

Since Jesus shed his blood, he has accomplished purification for sins once for all (Heb. 1:3).[55] His sitting at God's right hand (cf. Ps. 110:1) testifies that the work has been completed (Heb. 1:3, 13; 8:1; 10:12; 12:2). His blood truly cleanses from sin because we have the sacrifice of a human being who gave himself "through the eternal Spirit" (Heb. 9:13–14). The blood of animals merely cleanses the flesh; that is, they are pictures of the true washing that comes through Jesus Christ. Under the old covenant the blood was sprinkled on the tabernacle and its utensils,

52. As P. Hughes (1977: 419) says, "To reject this sacrifice is to be left with no sacrifice at all." See also Lane 1991b: 293; Attridge 1989: 293.

53. Rightly Attridge 1989: 248; Bruce 1964: 204–5n91.

54. Whether Hebrews here refers to a covenant or a will does not affect the conclusion drawn. Even if the author refers to a will, he applies what is true of wills analogously to covenants. Many commentators think that a will is in view in Heb. 9:16–17 (Attridge 1989: 255–56; Bruce 1964: 210–13; P. Hughes 1977: 368–73). In defense of a covenant, see Lane 1991b: 242–43; J. Hughes 1979.

55. Lindars (1991: 36–37) surprisingly says that Jesus' sacrificial death is muted in the opening of Hebrews, so as not to put off the readers at the outset. On the contrary, the reference to forgiveness represents the climax and the culmination of the author's argument. Meier (1985a: 183) says of this text that the author "moves immediately to what concerns him most about the earthly Jesus: his sacrifice." See also Lane (1991a: 9), who sees this as "the center" of the author's argument.

so that blood functioned as purifying agent for these external articles (Heb. 9:21–22). By contrast, Christ's blood cleanses the conscience from "dead works"—that is, works that lead to death (Heb. 9:14). Jesus' sacrifice accomplishes an interior work, furnishing the complete assurance that sins are forgiven and access to God is secured (Heb. 10:19–22). Those who are cleansed through Christ can be assured that their sins have truly been forgotten (Heb. 10:2). Hence, his cleansing is effective in God's very presence—that is, heaven itself (Heb. 9:23). The imagery used to denote this forgiveness is striking: "our hearts sprinkled clean from an evil conscience and our bodies washed with pure water" (Heb. 10:22). The washing of bodies indicates that the whole person, not merely the physical body, is cleansed by the blood of Christ.[56] The sprinkling of Christ's blood speaks better than Abel's (Heb. 12:24) because although Abel's blood testified to his faith and his walk with God in contrast to Cain (Heb. 11:4), only Christ's blood brings cleansing from sin.

SANCTIFICATION

The language of sanctification is closely related to cleansing, purification, and blood. To sanctify is to set apart in the realm of the holy. Hebrews emphasizes that Jesus Christ is the one who sanctifies and sets apart his own (Heb. 2:11). Sanctification in Hebrews typically is used to denote not progressive growth as a Christian but rather the definitive, once-for-all setting-apart work of Christ.[57] Hence, "We have been sanctified through the offering of the body of Jesus Christ once for all" (Heb. 10:10). The sanctifying work, then, was accomplished at the cross. The thought of Heb. 10:14 is similar: "For by a single offering he has perfected for all time those who are being sanctified." The death of Jesus Christ has brought perfection to believers, in contrast to the imperfection of the law and its sacrifices (Heb. 7:11, 19; 9:9; 10:1; cf. 11:40).[58] The Son, who has been perfected through suffering, offers a perfect sacrifice (Heb. 2:10; 5:9; 7:28; cf. 12:23). There is also the recognition in Heb. 2:10 that sanctification is ongoing, in that believers are in the process of sanctification. Yet the death of Christ ensures that this sanctifying work will be completed: "Jesus also suffered outside the gate in order to sanctify the people through his own blood" (Heb. 13:12). The setting apart into the realm of the holy has been achieved through Jesus' death on the cross.

56. The reference is to baptism, which portrays the cleansing of forgiveness (Lane 1991b: 287).

57. For the emphasis on definitive sanctification in Hebrews, see Peterson 1995: 33–40.

58. Perfection in Heb. 10:14 is definitive and located in the past, though it is enjoyed in the present and consummated in the future (Peterson 1982: 152–53; Attridge 1989: 281; Lane 1991b: 267).

Believers are now inducted into God's holy presence by the death of Jesus instead of by animal sacrifices. The latter only sanctify outwardly and purify the flesh (Heb. 9:13–14), whereas Jesus purifies the conscience with his sacrifice. The definitive work of Jesus in sanctification does not preclude the need to pursue holiness. Those who fail to be holy will not see the Lord (Heb. 12:14). In the light of the whole of Hebrews we can say that those who commit apostasy will not receive the final inheritance. Having been inducted into God's awesome and consuming presence by the sacrifice of Christ, no one who denies the efficacy of that sacrifice can remain in the realm of the holy.

CHRIST'S RESURRECTION

Some have said that the resurrection is relatively unimportant to the author of Hebrews,[59] but such a comment fails to see that the resurrection is taught in a number of texts. The reference to the resurrection is obvious in Heb. 13:20, where Jesus' resurrection is rooted in his work on the cross, where he shed his blood as an atonement for sin. We have already noted that the begetting of Jesus (Ps. 2:7) also refers to his resurrection (Heb. 1:5; 5:5), to his installation as the messianic king. Jesus' resurrection is also implied in the texts that refer to his reign at God's right hand (Heb. 1:13; 2:7; 10:12–13; 12:2) or his passing through the heavens to enter God's presence (Heb. 4:14; 9:11–12), for such would be impossible if he were not the resurrected Lord. For a limited period of time Jesus was lower than angels, but now he is crowned with glory and honor (Heb. 2:9–10), and this glory and honor clearly follow his death in Heb. 2.

Jesus conquered death by virtue of his own death (Heb. 2:14–15), and it is difficult to see how this could be accomplished without his resurrection. That Jesus is the resurrected Lord accords with the prophecy of Ps. 110:4 that he would be a priest "forever" (cf. Heb. 7:17, 21). Indeed, the author of Hebrews is quite emphatic that Jesus' resurrection qualifies him to serve as high priest. Jesus is superior to Levitical priests because of his "indestructible life" (Heb. 7:16), which suggests his resurrection. The Levitical priests were numerous because of death; no one priest could continue serving (Heb. 7:23). Jesus, however, functions as priest "permanently, because he continues forever" (Heb. 7:24). His life was not concluded by death; rather, "he always lives to make intercession" for his people (Heb. 7:25). The resurrection of Jesus is vital to the author's argument, for if Jesus were not raised from the dead, then he could not serve as high priest. His high priesthood would have ended with his death. Indeed, for the author of Hebrews, Jesus' resurrection demonstrates that

---

59. See, for example, Lindars 1991: 37.

he is a Melchizedekian priest. Since Jesus is not from the tribe of Levi, he does not qualify as a Levitical priest, but his resurrection from the dead testifies that he fulfills the role of a Melchizedekian priest.

Conclusion

Christology and soteriology are inseparably wedded in Hebrews. They serve the author's homiletic purpose, whereby he warns his readers about the folly of apostasy. They would thereby reject the one who is greater than Moses, David, and the Levitical priesthood. They would turn away from the one who has fulfilled the promises of the new covenant. They would repudiate the one who as a divine priest-king has secured final and definitive forgiveness of sins. Both Jesus' divinity and his humanity point to the effectiveness of his sacrifice and to his superiority to all that came before. Hence, the readers are summoned to put all their confidence in Jesus as the prophet greater than Moses, the king greater than David, the Melchizedekian priest, and the true man and the true God.

James

The Christology of James is not detailed, but neither is it as negligible as many scholars have alleged. Some have even argued that the references to Jesus in James 1:1; 2:1 were interpolated later, concluding that the letter is not even Christian but rather is general Jewish parenesis.[60] There is no plausible reason to accept such a theory, for the text should be accepted as is unless compelling grounds exist to posit interpolations. The scarcity of references to Jesus Christ can be explained by the purpose of the letter. James addresses a specific situation in which he encourages his readers to live godly lives while facing trials and difficulties. We should avoid thinking that this small letter contains the whole of James's theology or even reflects the most important themes of his theology. The Jewish character of the writing is also evident, showing that it was written in a Jewish milieu.

Even though James rarely refers explicitly to Jesus Christ, the book opens with such a reference: "James, a servant of God and of the Lord Jesus Christ" (James 1:1). James does not provide an exposition of the statement, but the opening is suggestive and points toward a high Christology.[61] James is a *doulos* ("slave" my translation) of both God and Jesus Christ, and this implies that God and Jesus Christ share the same status. The equivalency posited by James is highly significant because his

---

60. For an illuminating discussion on this matter, see L. Johnson 1995: 48–53.
61. See Dibelius 1975: 66, 126–28.

letter has a Jewish character and explicitly affirms monotheism (James 2:19). James does not work out the implications of the shared status of God and Christ, but given the Jewish flavor of the letter, the fact that he considers himself a slave of both demonstrates that Jesus Christ in some sense has the same dignity as God himself.

We should also note that in both James 1:1 and James 2:1 Jesus is identified as the Christ. It is hardly convincing to say that the title "Christ" here is analogous to using a last name, so that the titular significance of the term has evaporated.[62] The Jewish milieu in which the letter was birthed speaks strongly against such a notion. Since James is a Jew, it is quite improbable that he would use the title "Christ" without thinking that Jesus fulfilled the messianic hope from the OT. Jesus, then, is the promised Davidic king, the fulfillment of the promises found in the Davidic covenant.

James also identifies Jesus the Messiah as "Lord" (James 1:1; 2:1). His stature as Lord is confirmed by the appellation "glorious Lord" (James 2:1 my translation; cf. 2:7).[63] The Greek here is quite difficult (*tou kyriou hēmōn Iēsou Christou tēs doxēs*), but it seems most likely that the phrase should be translated "our glorious Lord Jesus Christ" (cf. 1 Cor. 2:8).[64] In any case, the glory typically associated with God is ascribed here to Jesus Christ (cf. Exod. 16:7, 10; 24:17; Lev. 9:6; see also Ps. 24:8, 10). Such language, as Davids points out, suggests Jesus' exaltation and his role as the final judge and thus points to his exalted status.[65] Elsewhere in the letter the Father is called "Lord" (James 1:7; 3:9; 4:10, 15; 5:4, 10, 11). Some of these texts are uncertain, so that in some instances references to Jesus are possible as well. On the other hand, James likely has Jesus Christ in view as Lord in some verses (James 5:7, 8, 14, 15).[66] Bauckham remarks, "The changing reference of 'the Lord' (*ho kyrios*) within the space of a few sentences in 5:7–11 reflects a high Christology in which Jesus shares the divine throne in heaven and is coming to execute the eschatological judgment of God."[67] The phrase "the coming of the Lord"

---

62. Contra Laws 1980: 47; Davids 1982: 63.

63. L. Johnson (2002: 214) says that "James acknowledges Jesus as the powerful risen one." Bauckham (1999b: 138–39) maintains that we have here "a combination of 'Jesus Christ' and 'the Lord of glory'" and suggests that it derives "from Christological exegesis of Psalm 24." Hence, he rightly rejects the view that we have adoptionistic Christology in James that is Ebionite in character.

64. See the discussion of the various options in L. Johnson 1995: 220–21; Davids 1982: 106–7; and the careful weighing of options in Dibelius 1975: 127–28; L. Cheung 2003: 246. Laws (1980: 95–97) understands "the glory" as appositional.

65. Davids 1982: 107; cf. Bauckham 1999b: 138; Edgar 2001: 61.

66. So L. Johnson 1995: 50.

67. Bauckham 1999b: 138; cf. L. Cheung 2003: 250. Bauckham also sees an allusion to Hosea 6:3 in James 5:7, indicating that the coming of Yahweh in the OT is now related

(James 5:7, 8) refers to the return of Jesus Christ in his role as the end-time judge, and this fits with the notion that he is the glorious Lord, since he will return as the sovereign one.[68]

The lordship of Christ seems to be in view also in James 5:14–15. The sick are anointed in the Lord's name and are raised up by the Lord. Anointing people in the Lord's name probably refers to Jesus Christ, so that Jesus as Lord raises up the sick (James 5:14–15).[69] The parallels in the Synoptic Gospels and Acts also suggest that here Jesus Christ is the one who heals and in whose name the sick were anointed (cf. Matt. 7:22; Mark 6:7; Luke 10:17; Acts 3:6–8, 16; 4:9–12). The name that is invoked over believers in James 2:7 is likely that of Jesus Christ.[70] Being called by the Lord's name in the OT clearly refers to Yahweh (cf. Deut. 28:10; Isa. 43:7; Jer. 14:9; Amos 9:12), and hence the reference to Jesus here points to his deity. We see from both these texts that the divine authority of Jesus is evident, for healing is sought in his name, and he has sovereign authority to heal the sick. Further, his divine status is suggested by his name being invoked by believers. The centrality of Jesus is also indicated by his being the object of faith (James 2:1).[71] When James speaks on the important topic of faith and works (James 2:14–26), presumably faith in Christ is in view. To say in a Jewish context that Christ is the object of faith suggests a high, though implicit, Christology.

James lacks the developed Christology of Paul, Hebrews, John, and even the Synoptic Gospels.[72] Still, we must beware of expecting too much from an occasional letter and reading off it the complete worldview of James. Even with the limited references to Jesus Christ, there are indications of a high Christology. Jesus is the Messiah of Israel and the glorious Lord. He apparently shares the same stature as God as Lord of all, as the one who is coming again to judge the world. Only those who put their faith in him and live out that faith in daily life will be saved on the last day.

---

to the parousia of Jesus Christ. More cautious about these references is Edgar 2001: 62. Chester (1994: 43–44) underestimates what we can say about James's Christology.

68. Rightly emphasized in Davids 1982: 182; Bauckham 1999b: 139. See also Laws 1980: 208–9.

69. See L. Johnson 1995: 331–33; cf. Dibelius 1975: 253; Laws 1980: 227–29; L. Cheung 2003: 250. The analysis of these texts by L. Johnson (2002: 214) is compatible with mine, even when he draws slightly different conclusions.

70. So Laws 1980: 105; Dibelius 1975: 140–41; L. Johnson 1995: 226; Bauckham 1999b: 139. Less certain are Davids 1982: 113; Moo 2000: 109.

71. The Greek (*tēn pistin tou kyriou hēmōn Iēsou Christou*) here should be read as an objective genitive: "faith in our Lord Jesus Christ." Contra L. Johnson 1995: 220. Rightly Moo 2000: 100–101; Davids 1982: 107; Laws 1980: 94; Dibelius 1975: 127–28.

72. Still, James is closer to Paul's Christology than is often alleged (see Bauckham 1999b: 139).

1 Peter

Jesus Is the Christ

The Christology in 1 Peter is shaped by practical and soteriological interests. We do not have the kind of christological exposition that occurs in John 1:1–18; Phil. 2:6–11; Col. 1:15–20; Heb. 1:1–3. Still, Peter's Christology shines through, at least in part, in this letter addressed to a variety of churches. Jesus' suffering and exaltation, which will be discussed soon below, is rooted in the OT Scriptures. The title "Christ," then, in 1 Peter is not superfluous. Whether Peter uses "Jesus Christ" (1 Pet. 1:1, 2, 3, 7, 13; 2:5; 3:21; 4:11), "Christ" (1 Pet. 1:11, 19; 2:21; 3:15, 16, 18; 4:1, 13, 14; 5:1, 10, 14), or "Spirit of Christ" (1 Pet. 1:11), the title "Christ," meaning "Messiah," retains its significance. Jesus, according to Peter, is the Messiah promised in the OT—the fulfillment of the Davidic covenant. The term "Christ" is used in some instances when Peter focuses on the fulfillment of OT prophecy (1 Pet. 1:11, 19; 2:21), or when he emphasizes Christ's sufferings and glory (1 Pet. 3:18; 4:1, 13, 14; 5:1, 10, 14), which is closely associated with the fulfillment of prophecy as well. Peter uses the phrases "in Christ" (1 Pet. 3:16; 5:10, 14), "in the name of Christ" (1 Pet. 4:14), and "in that name" (1 Pet. 4:16 my translation); however, when using the preposition "through," he always says "through Jesus Christ" (1 Pet. 2:5; 4:11). The "in Christ" language in 1 Peter seems equivalent to "Christian" rather than denoting union with Christ as in Paul, though 1 Pet. 5:10 is closer to the Pauline usage. We can sum up the fulfillment of prophecy regarding Christ with the words of 1 Pet. 1:20: "He was foreknown before the foundation of the world but was made manifest in the last times for your sake." The last days have dawned in Jesus Christ, and the age of fulfillment has arrived. That he would come to bring prophecy to completion was "foreknown." God destined what would happen before history began. Does the statement about Christ being foreknown imply preexistence? The verse is brief, and so it is difficult to say, though on balance the foreknowing of "the Christ" probably implies preexistence, for the language of manifestation suggests such.[73]

Jesus as Lord

Since Jesus is the exalted Lord, believers are to "sanctify Christ as Lord" (1 Pet. 3:15). He functions as the "Shepherd and Overseer" or the "Chief Shepherd" of God's people (1 Pet. 2:25; 5:4). Peter is a sent one, an "apostle of Jesus Christ" (1 Pet. 1:1), so that his authority is derived

---

73. Rightly Michaels 1988: 67; Schelke 1980: 50; Schreiner 2003: 88n144. Contra Dunn 1996a: 236–37.

and does not stem from his own will. Christians "believe in" and "love" Jesus Christ as their Lord (1 Pet. 1:8), and their "spiritual sacrifices" are "acceptable to God through Jesus Christ" only (1 Pet. 2:5). As we noted earlier, belief in Christ suggests a high Christology because only God should be the object of faith. As the exalted one, the Lord Jesus will be revealed again in the future (1 Pet. 1:7, 13; 5:4). He will reward his people and bring history to its appointed consummation. Peter also applies an OT text to Jesus Christ that refers to Yahweh.[74] The psalmist implores his readers to "taste and see that the LORD is good" (Ps. 34:8). Clearly, 1 Pet. 2:3 applies this text to Jesus Christ, and the continuation of the argument in 1 Pet. 2:4 leaves no doubt about this conclusion. Jesus Christ, then, shares the same status as Yahweh. On the other hand, as in Paul, God is designated as "the God and Father of our Lord Jesus Christ" (1 Pet. 1:3). The priority of the Father seems to be maintained as well. We see that Peter holds the common NT view that Jesus shares the same status as Yahweh, without compromising monotheism. Nor does the preeminence of Christ diminish the Father, for the work of Christ brings glory to the Father (1 Pet. 4:11). God's saving work in Christ is the means by which the Father is glorified.

Jesus' Suffering and Glory

Peter addresses churches suffering for the faith, and hence he also calls attention to Jesus' suffering and subsequent glory (1 Pet. 1:11). The suffering that Jesus endured for the sake of his people is often noted in the letter, especially if we include references to Jesus' death (1 Pet. 1:2, 11, 18–19, 21; 2:21–24; 3:18; 4:1, 13; 5:1). Jesus obviously was a human being, since he suffered and experienced death. The sufferings and glories were predicted by the prophets (1 Pet. 1:10–12), and therefore Jesus fulfills what was destined for the Christ all along. The OT sacrifices of lambs pointed toward a greater sacrifice to come (1 Pet. 1:19). The reference to a lamb here cannot be restricted to the Passover lamb, regular Levitical sacrifices with lambs, or the lamb of Isa. 53:7. Peter broadly draws on the OT background about lambs to teach that Jesus is God's spotless and precious lamb whose blood ransomed people from a futile life (1 Pet. 1:18–19).[75] The reference to an unblemished and spotless lamb suggests that Jesus was without sin, that he was a perfect sacrifice. Peter explicitly declares that Jesus "committed no sin, neither was deceit found in his mouth" (1 Pet. 2:22). He is "the righteous" one who suffered and died "for the unrighteous" (1 Pet. 3:18).[76] Jesus was

---

74. So Michaels 1988: 90; McCartney 1989: 73; J. Elliott 2000: 403; Brox 1986: 93.

75. See the discussion in Schreiner 2003: 86–87.

76. Perhaps there is an allusion here to Isa. 53:11 (Zimmerli and Jeremias 1957: 91).

truly human, and yet he stands apart from all other human beings in that he lived without sin.

The sprinkling of blood in the OT (Num. 19:4, 18–19, 21; cf. Exod. 24:6–8) anticipated the sprinkling of Christ's blood, by which forgiveness of sins is obtained (1 Pet. 1:2). Again we see that Jesus fulfilled what the OT typified. The most dramatic and significant example of the fulfillment of OT prophecy is Jesus' role as the Servant of the Lord.[77] Peter leaves no doubt that Isa. 53 points forward to Jesus. Jesus' freedom from sin and lack of deceit (1 Pet. 2:22) fulfills Isa. 53:9. The bearing of the sins of his people (1 Pet. 2:24) reaches back to Isa. 53:4, 9. The healing that comes through his wounds (1 Pet. 2:24) finds its antecedent in Isa. 53:5. The wandering of his people like sheep (1 Pet. 2:25) hearkens back to Isa. 53:6. The sufferings destined for the Christ are adumbrated in OT sacrifices and in the Servant of the Lord text. Forgiveness of sins is obtained through the spilling of Christ's blood, by his dying as a substitute for his people. His death as "the righteous for the unrighteous" is the means by which sinners are brought into God's presence (1 Pet. 3:18). In 1 Peter Christ's death is substitutionary. He dies in place of the unrighteous, and as the Servant of the Lord he dies to atone for their sins, so that the punishment that they deserve is placed on him. Jesus' death is also viewed as a ransom (1 Pet. 1:18–19). He freed believers from their sins by his blood; hence the price of the ransom is explicitly indicated.[78] In the OT a futile way of life is associated with the idolatry of paganism (e.g., Lev. 17:7; 1 Kings 16:2; 2 Kings 17:15; Ps. 23:4[79]). Through Christ's death believers have been liberated from service to false gods to serve the true and living God.

Prophecy is fulfilled not only in the sufferings of Christ but also in the glory that belongs to him now that he is exalted. Peter likely mentions the pattern of suffering and then glory to encourage those distressed in the present that they too will experience glory after suffering (1 Pet. 1:6–7; 4:12–14; 5:6, 10–11; cf. 5:1–4).[80] The hope that strengthens believers is rooted in Christ's resurrection (1 Pet. 1:3; 3:21), and his resurrection demonstrated to all that God had vindicated him and crowned him as Lord. We likely have an allusion to Ps. 110:1 in the claim that he now sits at God's right hand and that all angelic powers are subject to him (1 Pet. 3:22). The one whom God raised from the dead has also been given "glory" (1 Pet. 1:21), and 1 Pet. 3:22 suggests that the glory he now has consists of his rule at God's right hand. Peter also alludes to

77. See Cullmann 1963: 75.

78. For a helpful analysis of redemption in the NT, see Marshall 1974.

79. The allusion is clear in the LXX of each of these texts with the use of the word *mataios*.

80. For an illuminating study of this theme in 1 Peter, see Bechtler 1998.

Jesus' resurrection in the "stone" prophecies. When he identifies Jesus as "a living stone" (1 Pet. 2:4), the word "living" probably points to his resurrection. The claim that Jesus is "the cornerstone" also suggests his resurrection and exaltation (1 Pet. 2:6–7; cf. Ps. 118:22; Isa. 28:16).[81] As we noted earlier, Jesus himself appealed to Ps. 118 to intimate his future vindication (Matt. 21:42 par.). In Acts Peter appeals to the same text to say that the crucified and rejected Jesus has been raised from the dead and established as the cornerstone (Acts 4:10–11). The letter of 1 Peter moves along the same arteries. Jesus, who suffered and was rejected by his people, has now been honored and vindicated as the cornerstone. The image used points to Jesus' resurrection and exaltation.

In summary, 1 Peter highlights the fulfillment of prophecy in his Christology, and the letter follows the NT pattern in linking closely together Christology and soteriology. Peter is not interested in abstract christological theorizing. Jesus is the Christ and the Servant of the Lord, and his suffering and death secure redemption and forgiveness for believers. He fulfills OT prophecy as the son of David and as a spotless lamb sacrificed for his people. The one who suffered is also glorified and reigns in heaven as Lord. He will return in glory in the future. Indeed, Peter even applies to Jesus an OT text that refers to Yahweh, suggesting that the Father and Jesus Christ share the same status. But even here Peter reminds readers that they have tasted the goodness of Jesus as Lord. His suffering and glory are significant because they forecast glory for believers after suffering. Jesus' death is precious to Peter because it redeems from a futile life, and hence the high Christology of Peter undergirds the call to trust in Christ for eschatological salvation.

2 Peter

We could examine the Christology of 1 Peter and 2 Peter together because, in contrast to the view of many NT scholars, a good case can be made for Petrine authorship of both letters.[82] Since 1 Peter and 2 Peter address different concerns, and Jude and 2 Peter share similar content, I have decided to examine 2 Peter and then Jude. As I have emphasized in regard to other NT writings that we have examined up to this point, we should not expect these two letters to contain full christological expositions, for both have a limited purpose in their composition. Both were

81. Some argue that the reference is to the coping stone (Longenecker 1970: 51–52), but it is more likely that the cornerstone is in view (see McKelvey 1961–1962; Michaels 1988: 103; J. Elliott 2000: 425; Schreiner 2003: 109).
82. This is a minority opinion in scholarship now. For a defense of authenticity that interacts with recent scholarship, see Schreiner 2003: 21–36, 255–76.

written in response to false teachers who were troubling the churches. It appears that neither author had the leisure to write a full exposition of the gospel (cf. Jude 3).

Jesus as Messiah and Lord

Given the brevity of 2 Peter and its circumscribed purpose, we might expect little by way of Christology. Though the letter is brief, the Christology is remarkably weighty.[83] We note first of all Peter's assumption that Jesus is the Messiah. He often refers to "Jesus Christ" in the letter (2 Pet. 1:1, 8, 11, 14, 16; 2:20; 3:18). Peter does not expound on the significance of the title "Christ," but the repeated use of the term indicates that Jesus' messianic status was a given for Peter. Jesus' lordship is also prominent in the letter. One of Peter's favorite expressions is "Lord Jesus Christ" (2 Pet. 1:8, 11, 14, 16; 2:20; 3:18; cf. 3:2), though we will see shortly that he adds "Savior" to this title in some texts. Jesus is also described as "the Master who bought" people by his death (2 Pet. 2:1). Jesus is the sovereign Lord, the one exalted by God as Messiah and Master. Because Jesus is Lord, Peter is his slave and apostle (2 Pet. 1:1). The "eternal kingdom" belongs to Jesus Christ as Lord (2 Pet. 1:11). In some texts the title "Lord" is applied to God (2 Pet. 2:9, 11; 3:8–10, 15), though in the texts from 2 Pet. 3 one could argue that the reference is to Christ. Since the term "Lord" fluctuates between "God" and "Christ," it reveals the high status of Jesus Christ in this letter.[84]

Jesus as Son

Even more compelling evidence attests to Jesus' exalted status. As Lord, Jesus Christ will return with power (2 Pet. 1:16). The Father bestowed "honor" and "glory" upon him at the transfiguration, witnessing that Jesus is his "beloved Son, with whom I am well pleased" (2 Pet. 1:17). As we noted when examining this expression in the Gospels, the sonship of Jesus indicates that he is both the true Israel and the unique Son of God. God's pleasure in Jesus hearkens back to the Servant of the Lord in Isaiah (Isa. 42:1). Peter appeals to the transfiguration because it anticipates and functions as a prelude to the future coming of Christ. The transfiguration testifies to Jesus' lordship over the future, the glory and honor that will be his forever. The vision of Jesus' "majesty" (*megaleiotēs*) points to his deity. The word *megaleiotēs* here does not necessarily denote deity (cf.

83. For a thorough examination of the Christology of 2 Peter, see Callan 2001.
84. For example, the "day of the Lord" may refer to Christ's coming in 2 Pet. 3:10, whereas we have a reference to the "day of God" in 2 Pet. 3:12. Starr (2000: 30) thinks that the evidence here supports Christ's divinity.

1 Esd. 1:4; 4:40; Jer. 40:9 LXX), though it is used of God as well (Luke 9:43). Peter likely uses the term to denote Jesus' lordship and deity at his future coming. He is the lovely "morning star" that will come on the last day (2 Pet. 1:19).

Jesus as God

If some of the foregoing evidence appears ambiguous, Peter identifies Jesus as "God" in the very first verse of the letter, where he speaks of "the righteousness of our God and Savior Jesus Christ" (2 Pet. 1:1).[85] Those reading English translations might naturally think that two different persons are intended, so that God and Jesus are distinguished. In the Greek text, however, both "God" and "Savior" are included under the same article (*tou theou hēmōn kai sōtēros Iēsou Christou*). The Granville Sharp rule, which has been vindicated by recent research,[86] demonstrates that when two singular nouns are joined by *kai* and governed by the same article, they refer to the same entity. The rule applies only to common nouns, not proper nouns. Readers of the English translations could easily be misled at this point, for neither "God" nor "Savior" are proper nouns in Greek. The grammar, then, could hardly be clearer. Jesus is identified as both God and Savior in this verse.[87] The remarkably high Christology of 2 Peter shines through.

Nowhere in 1 Peter do we find such a clear assertion of Christ's deity. In the first letter Peter emphasizes Christ's sufferings and consequent glory, for sufferings are also the pathway to glory for believers who are facing trials and being oppressed by unbelievers. Why does 2 Peter, on the other hand, emphasize Christ's deity? Perhaps the reason can be located in the denial of the future coming of Christ by the false teachers. In response, Peter highlights Jesus' honor, glory, and majesty. Indeed, Jesus is fully divine and thus is the sovereign Lord of history who will fulfill all his promises.

The divinity of Christ may also be indicated by 2 Pet. 1:3–4, which refers to "his divine power" and to believers sharing in "the divine nature."[88] Interpreters debate whether the references here are to God or Christ. A decision is remarkably difficult, though on balance it seems that Peter refers to Christ. Even if this judgment is incorrect, the very ambiguity

85. Callan (2001: 253) comments, "In the first verse of the letter, the author of 2 Peter calls Jesus God." He maintains that this view is vindicated by grammar. In support of this view, see Bauckham 1983: 168–69; Starr 2000: 29; Paulsen 1992: 104–5.

86. For a thorough and convincing study, see Wallace 1996: 270–91, particularly the comments on 2 Pet. 1:1 (pp. 276–77).

87. In support of this conclusion, see the careful work in Harris 1992: 229–38.

88. So Callan 2001: 253–54.

of the text shows that Peter did not carefully distinguish between the deity of God and of Christ, so that readers are uncertain about the referent. Starr rightly observes, "Where 2 Peter could easily have specified Christ's agency in 1:3–4, then, he is content to imply it, leaving open the possibility of understanding God as the agent. This is not especially surprising, since 2 Peter would have assumed that behind Christ stands God as the one who prompts the Christ event."[89]

Other evidence supports the equality of Jesus Christ with God. "Grace and peace" become the portion of believers "in the knowledge of God and of Jesus our Lord" (2 Pet. 1:2). At first glance, we might think that this is another example of the Granville Sharp rule because "God" and "Jesus" are singular nouns joined by *kai* and standing under the same article (*tou theou kai Iēsou tou kyriou hēmōn*). The rule does not apply in this case, however, because "Jesus" is a proper noun. Hence, "God" and "Jesus" are two different referents. Nevertheless, the text places God and Jesus on the same plane, for grace and peace are maximized in the lives of believers through them. The final verse of the letter, summing up the whole of Peter's instructions, bids readers to "grow in the grace and knowledge of our Lord and Savior Jesus Christ" (2 Pet. 3:18). Peter immediately adds, "To him be the glory both now and to the day of eternity." Since Jesus is the immediate antecedent, Peter ascribes all glory to him.[90] Glory, however, belongs only to God, and therefore we see that Jesus is given the same stature and honor as God himself (cf. 2 Pet. 1:17).[91] Further, it is clear that even though Jesus is divine, "God and Jesus are clearly distinguished in 2 Peter."[92]

Jesus as Savior

Peter is not interested in an abstract discussion of Jesus Christ's divinity.[93] His stature as Messiah, Lord, and God are so important because he is the Savior. God's saving righteousness has been given to believers through the "Savior Jesus Christ" (2 Pet. 1:1, 11; cf. 3:2). Most scholars understand "righteousness" (*dikaiosynē*) in 2 Pet. 1:1 to refer to Christ's equity, so that salvation equally belongs to Jews and Gentiles or equally

---

89. Starr 2000: 34.

90. Callan (2001: 255) notes that "2 Peter praises Jesus with the kind of doxology usually restricted for God."

91. Callan 2001: 255; Caulley 1982: 116; Fuchs and Reymond 1980: 69.

92. Callan 2003: 256. Callan (2003: 259) goes on to say, "Jesus is God in the sense that he was revealed as son of God at his transfiguration. He is distinct from God because he is the son, not God himself." Callan (2003: 263) concludes that the author of 2 Peter does not provide a systematic solution as to how Jesus could be God and yet distinct from God, while it is clear that the notion of more than one God is rejected.

93. See R. Martin 1994: 158–60.

belongs to the readers and the apostles. Here, however, Peter uses language that hails from the OT. Christians have received by lot (*lachousin*) the gift of faith, and "righteousness" should be explained from its OT background as well. Hence, righteousness here refers to Christ's saving work on behalf of his people.[94] This fits with the emphasis in the verse on Jesus Christ as Savior. It is difficult to know whether the one with divine power in 2 Pet. 1:3–4 is God or Christ, though the latter seems slightly preferable. In any case, the verses emphasize the gift character of salvation. Christ has given believers all that they need for life in the age to come and to live in a way that pleases God. He has "called" (*kalesantos* [2 Pet. 1:3]) believers by his effective grace to a new life. Believers have received promises of participation in the divine nature. Peter does not refer here to the deification of believers, as if they become "little gods." Sharing the divine nature means that they become morally like God.[95] Even in this present evil age believers have become like God because they have escaped from the world's corruption (cf. 2 Pet. 2:20), but moral perfection will be theirs in its fullness only when Jesus Christ returns. The work of Christ is also described in terms of his "buying" (*agorazō*) believers from sin (2 Pet. 2:1). In other words, believers are redeemed and liberated by Christ from the thrall of sin. His death is the means by which new life has been purchased for those who know God and Christ.

Salvation comes through knowing the Lord Jesus (2 Pet. 1:2–3, 8). Peter often emphasizes the personal dimensions of new life in Christ. Not only are believers freed from sin, but also they know God and Jesus Christ. Those who live godly lives will enter the kingdom of the Savior (2 Pet. 1:11). Those who have come to know him as Savior but then renounce him will be damned (2 Pet. 2:20). Genuine salvation cannot be limited to initial decisions to follow Jesus as Lord, for those who obtain eschatological salvation persevere until the end. Such eschatological salvation is obtained by growing "in the grace and knowledge" of Jesus as Lord and Savior (2 Pet. 3:18). The grace of Christ secures the salvation of his own until the day he returns. The Lord knows how to preserve believers (2 Pet. 2:9) so that they do not apostatize.

The letter of 2 Peter emphasizes that Jesus is the Messiah, and hence he fulfills the covenantal promises made to David. Peter does not probe into such a fulfillment deeply but assumes it in his writing. He also emphasizes that Jesus is Lord and even God. The lordship and deity of Christ support his future coming in glory, which was a matter of controversy because the false teachers doubted Christ's return. Further,

---

94. In support of this interpretation, see Schreiner 2003: 286.

95. For support of this view, see Starr (2000), who carefully explores parallels to other literature.

Peter particularly emphasizes that Jesus is the Savior of his people. Such salvation is experienced through knowing God and Jesus Christ. In this way, God's saving promises are being fulfilled (2 Pet. 1:4), and Peter particularly stresses the need for perseverance to obtain the reward that God has promised.

Jude

Jesus as Lord

Despite the brevity of Jude, the Christology of the letter is remarkable.[96] In the OT Moses and others are described as servants of Yahweh. Jude begins by identifying himself as "a servant [*doulos*] of Jesus Christ" (Jude 1). If Jude is Christ's servant, then Jesus is his Master and Lord. The lordship of Jesus is clearly a central feature of Jude's Christology, for the intruders "deny our only Master and Lord, Jesus Christ" (Jude 4). Nothing in Jude indicates a denial of any particular doctrines about the lordship of Christ. Rather, the infiltrators deny Christ's lordship by the way they live—their libertine lifestyles turn the message of grace into a platform for license.[97] The phrase "apostles of our Lord Jesus Christ" (Jude 17) suggests that those so authorized transmit their teaching under Christ's direction. Only those who are the beneficiaries of the Lord's mercies will receive eternal life on the last day (Jude 21). Indeed, those who persevere to the end do so because they are "kept by" or "kept for" Jesus Christ (Jude 1). I have argued elsewhere that the former is slightly probable.[98] If this interpretation is correct, then Jesus strengthens his people so that they avoid apostasy. On the other reading, Jesus is the eschatological destiny for God's people. The glory and honor that belong to God are his "through Jesus Christ our Lord" (Jude 25). God receives glory not despite or apart from Christ but rather through him.

As the exalted Lord, Jesus will come in the future and inflict judgment on the ungodly (Jude 14–15). Jude cites *1 En.* 9 here. In *1 Enoch* the prophecy clearly referred to God. In applying a text that referred to God's judgment to Christ, Jude follows the precedent of other NT writers (cf. 1 Thess. 3:13; 2 Thess. 1:7; Rev. 19:13, 15; 22:12).[99] The verb *ēlthen* in Jude 14 is aorist, but it is rightly translated by the NJB as a future

96. Bauckham (1990: 312–13) maintains that, according to Jude, "Jesus is the eschatological agent of God's salvation and judgment," and he is the Messiah.

97. So Bauckham 1990: 303.

98. See Schreiner 2003: 430–31.

99. The following sentences in this paragraph are from Schreiner 2003, with some revisions.

("will come") and is equivalent to a "prophetic perfect."[100] Jude speaks here of the second coming of Christ. The "holy ones" with whom he will come are his angels. The coming of Christ is patterned after God's theophany on Sinai, where he came with "myriads of holy ones" (Deut. 33:2 NRSV).[101] Zechariah looks forward to the day when "the LORD my God will come, and all the holy ones with him" (Zech. 14:5). That angels would accompany Jesus at his coming is clearly taught elsewhere in the NT as well (Matt. 16:27; 25:31; Mark 8:38; Luke 9:26; 1 Thess. 3:13; 2 Thess. 1:7). The attendance of the angels at his coming indicates that the event will be stunning and majestic.[102]

Jesus as the Christ

We should note in closing that Jude relatively often speaks of Jesus as the Christ (Jude 1, 4, 17, 21, 25). The title "Christ" in Jude almost certainly is significant, for there are a number of indications that Jude hails from Palestinian Jewish circles. He cites traditions from the *Testament of Moses* (Jude 9) and *1 Enoch* (Jude 14–15). OT tradition suffuses the letter (Jude 5–7, 11), and even when he refers to the OT, as in the story about angels sinning (Jude 6), the OT story (Gen. 6:1–4) is also the subject of Jewish traditions. Therefore, when Jude identifies Jesus as the Christ, the title retains its significance, indicating that Jesus is the promised son of David.

1–3 John

The Epistles of John are closely related to the Gospel of John. Despite the reservations of some, the similarity of style points to the same author. Christology plays a major role in 1–2 John, for it is evident from the letters that opponents offered an alternate Christology. It appears that they proposed a docetic Christology that maintained that Jesus as the Christ was not truly and fully human. Perhaps they derived this view from a distinctive reading of the Gospel of John, though such a reading seems singularly unconvincing in a Gospel that announces that "the Word became flesh" (John 1:14) and concludes with his death and resurrection. The situation is different with 3 John, which is responding to a different controversy. In fact, Jesus is not even mentioned in that letter. In any

100. So Porter 1994: 37; Bauckham 1983: 93–94.
101. So Charles 1990: 111–12; cf. Bauckham 1990: 288. For the OT antecedents to Enoch's prophesy, see VanderKam 1973; Bauckham 1983: 288–302.
102. It is also possible that Jude 5 refers to Jesus rather than Lord (in reference to the Father). If so, we have a strong argument for preexistence because it speaks of Jesus saving Israel from Egypt (so Fossum 1987; Gathercole 2006: 35–41).

case, it is clear from the Johannine letters that Christology is wedded to soteriology. Those who do not believe that Jesus is the Christ come in the flesh do not have eternal life.

Jesus as the Christ

Since the secessionists in 1 John denied that Jesus was truly human, John fixes attention on the Jesus of history, without denying that he was fully God. The first verse of the letter recalls the past, with John remembering what he heard, saw, and touched (1 John 1:1). The subject of these reflections is "the word of life"—that is, Jesus himself.[103] We should note how the verbs in the first verse climax with touching, so that with each verb the historical actuality of Jesus is emphasized even more. We can hear but not see someone, and we can see but not touch someone, so John begins with hearing, proceeds to seeing, and climaxes with touching. John certifies the space-time nature of the events that transpired by reminding his readers that Jesus was no phantom: John heard, saw, and touched him. Indeed, John repeats in 1 John 1:2–3 the truth that he saw and heard Jesus. The coming of Jesus into history, the incarnation declared in John 1:14, is no illusion. As John declares twice in 1 John 1:2, "the life was made manifest." The collocation of "word of life" and "made manifest" suggests that this is simply another way of saying "the Word became flesh" (John 1:14).[104] The message that John proclaims is not ethereal, nor does it contain universal principles per se; it concerns what happened in history.

The flesh-and-blood advent of Jesus finds expression elsewhere in 1 John. Forgiveness of sin comes from the shedding of Jesus' blood (1 John 1:7), which is a vivid way of portraying his death. He surrendered his life for the sake of his people (1 John 3:16). He came at a certain time in history in that "he appeared to take away sins" (1 John 3:5), and he "appeared . . . to destroy the works of the devil" (1 John 3:8). We saw in the Gospel of John that the Father is often described as "sending" the Son. The same terminology appears in John's first letter: "God sent his only Son into the world" (1 John 4:9); he "sent his Son to be the propitiation for our sins" (1 John 4:10); "the Father has sent his Son to be the Savior of the world" (1 John 4:14). The same idea is expressed when John

103. Most scholars think that the "word of life" refers to the gospel message (see the survey and discussion in R. Brown 1982: 164–65). Smalley (1984: 5–6), though, rightly argues that a wedge should not be driven between the message and the messenger. The gospel message that is proclaimed focuses on Jesus himself.

104. It seems that the Word here refers to both the message and Jesus Christ, and hence preexistence is in view here. Contra Dunn (1996a: 245–46), who says that the text speaks of the message proclaimed rather than of Christ himself.

says that "the Son of God has come" (1 John 5:20). If we sum up these texts, we see that John focuses on the incarnation and death of God's Son. Further, it seems that the statements on God sending his Son and the coming of the Son of God imply Jesus' preexistence.[105] Jesus, who is the Christ in the flesh, is also the Son of God, who was with the Father from the beginning (1 John 1:1–2).

Those who reject the truth that the historical Jesus is the Christ are identified as antichrists (1 John 2:22).[106] Nor does such a denial merely affect their relationship with the Christ. When they deny that the human Jesus is the Christ, they also deny the Father. If they reject Jesus as God's true Son, this is tantamount, whether they realize it or not, to denying the Father as well (1 John 2:23). Only those who acknowledge that Jesus is God's Son belong to the Father. Refusal to acknowledge Jesus as the Christ is no trivial error or simply a temporary lapse of judgment; anyone who separates the Christ from the historical Jesus is an antichrist.

John circles back to the same idea in 1 John 4: "Every spirit that confesses that Jesus Christ has come in the flesh is from God" (1 John 4:2). Those who argue to the contrary manifest the spirit of the antichrist (1 John 4:3). Hence, those who claim that their utterances are from God need to be tested. The mere claim that one speaks from God does not validate the prophecy uttered. The spoken prophecies must accord with the truth that the historical Jesus is the Christ.[107] The historical actuality of the incarnation is expressed vividly in 1 John 5:6–8. Jesus as the Christ came into the world both "by the water and the blood." Water here indicates not the physical birth of Jesus but rather his baptism.[108] Blood, of course, as in 1 John 1:7, refers to Jesus' death.[109] It is insufficient to claim Jesus as the Christ only at his baptism. One must also acknowledge that Jesus is the Christ at his death, when his blood was shed for sinners. Perhaps Irenaeus accurately captures the opponents' teaching

105. So R. Brown 1982: 76.
106. See Marshall 1978a: 157–58. See the careful discussion by Smalley (1984: 110–14), who questions the Cerinthian nature of the heresy and argues that John's words here could be directed against a docetic Christology or may simply respond to the Jewish objection that Jesus of Nazareth was not the Christ. Smalley inclines to the view that we have an antidocetic statement here. See also the full discussion of the issue by R. Brown (1982: 52–54, 73–79, 352), who proposes a variant of docetic Christology by the secessionists.
107. See Marshall 1978a: 205. Smalley (1984: 222–23) thinks John attacks Docetism and those who denied Jesus' preexistence. R. Brown (1982: 492–94) maintains that John does not speak against those who deny the incarnation specifically but against those who deny "Jesus Christ come in the flesh."
108. So Marshall 1978a: 231–35; Smalley 1984: 277–80 (though he rejects Marshall's view that Cerinthianism is the problem here). Contra R. Brown (1982: 573–78), who says that both water and blood emphasize Jesus' death.
109. So Smalley 1984: 277–80.

in recounting John's opposition to Cerinthus.[110] Cerinthus taught that Jesus was anointed as the Christ at his baptism, but the Christ left him before his death. Even if John does not respond directly to Cerinthian teaching, we can infer from his letter that a Cerinthian kind of Christology hails from the antichrist. John emphasizes that Jesus was the Christ at both his baptism and his death.

Apparently, the opponents in 2 John threatened the church with faulty Christology.[111] John identifies those who propound this new teaching as "deceivers," warning that "many" itinerants have spread such an error. The nature of their error is clarified precisely: they "do not confess the coming of Jesus Christ in the flesh" (2 John 7). They likely embraced the coming of the Christ, and they probably even identified Jesus as the Christ; what they did not tolerate is any notion that Jesus was truly human.[112] The one who separates the historical Jesus from the Christ is again identified as the antichrist (2 John 7). Those who think that they are "progressing" (*ho proagōn*) in their theology but do not persevere in the orthodox teaching have separated themselves from God (2 John 9). John repeats what we saw in 1 John 2:23: only those who embrace Jesus as the Christ belong to "both the Father and the Son" (2 John 9). John brooks no opposition on this matter, insisting that those who deny that the historical Jesus is the Christ do not belong to God at all. They do not have a saving relationship with God. In summary, it is clear that John emphasizes that Christians must embrace Jesus as the Christ. That Jesus is the Messiah is fundamental to Johannine theology, as is summed up nicely in 1 John 5:1: "Everyone who believes that Jesus is the Christ has been born of God" (cf. 1 John 3:23). Conversely, those who deny that the historical Jesus is the Messiah do not belong to God.

Jesus as the Son of God

John does not restrict his teaching to the claim that the human Jesus is the Messiah; he also emphasizes that Jesus is the Son of God. Jesus is the unique Son of the Father (1 John 1:3, 7; 3:8, 23; 4:15; 2 John 3). As we noted previously, only those who confess the Son also belong to the Father (1 John 2:22–24; 2 John 9). Jesus is the unique (*monogenēs*)

110. Both R. Brown (1982: 65–68) and Smalley (1984: 111–14) raise significant objections to the Cerinthian influence. For arguments in favor of the view, see Marshall 1978a: 17–22, 70–71, 232–33.

111. Identifying the opponents in 1–2 John is quite difficult. For a thorough survey of options, see R. Brown 1982: 47–68.

112. Marshall (1978a: 70–71) contends that they denied both the incarnation and the notion that Jesus remained in the flesh. Smalley (1984: 328–29) maintains that what John says includes those who deny Jesus' humanity or divinity. R. Brown (1982: 669–70) again argues that the point is "Jesus-Christ-come-in-the-flesh."

Son of the Father (1 John 4:9; cf. John 1:14, 18; 3:16, 18), sent by the Father into the world (1 John 4:9–10, 14).[113] The faith that overcomes the world confesses that Jesus is God's Son (1 John 5:4–5). God himself has testified that eternal life is available only for those who believe in his Son (1 John 5:9–13). Nor can we divide the Son of God from the Christ, for "the Son of God has come" (1 John 5:20; cf. 3:23); he has entered human history. John's usage of the expression "Son of God" in his Gospel should inform our understanding of the title in the Johannine Epistles. Jesus as God's Son is the unique Son of the Father, standing in a special relationship to him.

Indeed, in Johannine theology it is clear that the Son of God is himself divine. The first verse of 1 John hearkens back to the first verse of John's Gospel. When John writes, "That which was from the beginning," he intends the reader to reflect on the Gospel: "In the beginning was the Word, and the Word was with God, and the Word was God" (John 1:1). Nor do the words "that which" signal an impersonal subject in 1 John, for the subsequent context reveals that the word of life "was made manifest" (1 John 1:2)—Jesus himself. Given the affinities with the prologue of John's Gospel, "the word of life" echoes what the Gospel says about "the Word." Just as the "Word" is divine in the Gospel, so too here. The words "that which was from the beginning" indicate that the Word is eternal, just as in the Gospel. The one whom the Father "sent" (1 John 4:9–10, 14) existed with the Father before he was sent as God's eternal Word.

And just as in the Gospel of John Jesus is identified as divine, so too near the end of 1 John Jesus is explicitly called "God." John remarks, "We are in him who is true, in his Son Jesus Christ. He is the true God and eternal life" (1 John 5:20). The word immediately following "Jesus Christ" is "this one" (*houtos*). The natural antecedent is the noun that immediately precedes, "Jesus Christ." Further, the words "true God" after the phrase "we are in him who is true" are more significant if the reference is to Christ, indicating that he shares the same divine status as the Father. The Johannine churches should shun idols (1 John 5:21), though it is not idolatry but rather true worship to venerate Jesus Christ as God, as the unique Son of the Father. We must note here that as God, Jesus is still the Son of the Father.[114] Hence, Jesus is not all there is to God. He remains the Son, and the Father remains the Father, and yet there is only one God.

---

113. The term *monogenēs* probably does not mean "only begotten" but rather indicates the unique Son of the Father (so R. Brown 1982: 516–17; Smalley 1984: 241–42; Marshall 1978a: 214n8). Büchsel (*TDNT* 4:737–41) argues that both meanings are in view.

114. The interpretation of 1 John 5:20 proposed here is debated. For support, see Cullmann 1963: 310; Marshall 1978a: 254–55; R. Brown 1982: 625–26. Contra Smalley 1984: 307–8; Harris 1992: 239–53.

Jesus as Truth and Light

John may also use the word "truth" as a way of referring to Jesus Christ. In the Gospel of John truth is centered on Jesus Christ; he "is the way, and the truth, and the life" (John 14:6; cf. 1:17).[115] The personal use of the word "truth" in the letters seems to support a reference to Jesus.[116] The "truth" is not in those who fail to keep God's commands (1 John 2:4). Knowing the truth is inseparable from confessing Jesus as the Messiah and God's Son (1 John 2:22–24). Those who give financial help to those who proclaim the gospel are "fellow workers for the truth" (3 John 8). Demetrius's life has received verification "from the truth itself" (3 John 12). Believers love one another "in truth" (2 John 1; 3 John 1), which perhaps is analogous to Paul's "in Christ." John also speaks of loving and knowing the truth and of the truth abiding in believers (2 John 2). Elsewhere he refers to abiding in Christ (e.g., John 15:4–6; 1 John 2:6, 24, 27–28; 3:6), knowing him (John 10:14; 14:7, 9; 17:3; 1 John 2:3–4; 3:1, 6), and loving him (John 8:42; 14:15, 21, 23–24, 28; 21:15–16; 1 John 5:1). Christians walk in the truth (2 John 4; 3 John 3–4). John says that the truth "will be with us forever" (2 John 2), suggesting that the truth is not merely an abstract quality but rather is none other than Jesus Christ himself.

Perhaps the reference to light is also an indirect allusion to Jesus Christ.[117] We know from John's Gospel that Jesus is the light of the world (John 8:12). In 1 John we are told that "God is light" (1 John 1:5). Still, the "true light" that is now shining is likely a reference to Jesus Christ, who gave the new command to love one another (1 John 2:7–8). John contrasts being "in the light" with being "in the darkness" (1 John 2:9–11) and even speaks of "abiding" in the light (1 John 2:10). Abiding in the light and living in the light could include the ideas of abiding in Christ and living in him.

The Uniqueness and Centrality of Jesus Christ

The uniqueness of Jesus Christ is expressed in other terms by John. Jesus is designated as "the righteous" one (1 John 2:1, 29; 3:7), the one who is "pure" (1 John 3:3), and the one in whom is no sin (1 John 3:5). As the righteous one, he qualifies to serve as an "advocate" (*paraklētos*)

---

115. Note also the claim that "the truth will set you free" (8:32), which is explained a few verses later as "if the Son sets you free" (John 8:36).

116. Though others may be correct in seeing a reference to "the Spirit of truth" (John 14:15–17) instead (Marshall 1978a: 62–63; Smalley 1984: 319–20; see also R. Brown 1982: 657–58).

117. See Marshall 1978a: 129–30; Smalley 1984: 58. R. Brown (1982: 268–69) argues that the light refers to Jesus and the salvation that he has accomplished.

with the Father, so that his death provides full forgiveness of sins.[118] His death provides satisfaction or propitiation for the sins of the entire world (1 John 2:2; 4:10). He is, therefore, "the Savior of the world" (1 John 4:14; cf. John 4:42). He grants understanding so that believers will have eternal life (1 John 5:20). Jesus also will manifest himself in the future (1 John 2:28). When he appears, believers will be transformed into his likeness (1 John 3:2).

The centrality of Jesus Christ is expressed in a number of other ways. The Son hears and answers the prayers of his people (1 John 5:14–15), which surely is a divine prerogative. He keeps believers, who have new life by his power (1 John 5:18), and such preservation surely is the work of God. The saving fellowship with God is described as "fellowship with the Father and with his Son Jesus Christ" (1 John 1:3), so that Jesus Christ is placed on the same plane as the Father in his saving work. The Gospel of John often refers to believing in Jesus' name or prayer in his name (see John 1:12; 2:23; 3:18; 14:13, 14, 26; 15:16, 21; 16:23, 24, 26; 20:31). Similarly, we see in John's first letter that "sins are forgiven for his name's sake" (1 John 2:12). The context suggests a reference here to Jesus Christ. What we must take note of is that sins are cleansed for the sake of Jesus himself. What is accomplished is done for his sake, in the same way that things are done for God's sake. Characteristically, faith is to be placed into Jesus' name (1 John 3:23; 5:13). Those who travel and disseminate the gospel do so "for the sake of the name" (3 John 7). As we have noted previously, name theology in Jewish circles points to divinity. Those who persevere in the gospel "abide in the Son and the Father" (1 John 2:24). We note again the equivalency posited between the Father and the Son. However, the Father and the Son are not identified in every respect. The Father sends and the Son goes (1 John 4:9–10, 14); the Father is the begetter and the Son is the begotten (1 John 5:1).

The centrality of the Son is evident because of the response demanded from human beings. God abides only in those who confess Jesus as God's Son (1 John 4:15). Those who believe that Jesus is the Messiah have received new life from God, and those who believe in Jesus also love him (1 John 5:1). God himself has borne witness concerning his Son, and human beings honor that testimony by believing in the Son (1 John 5:9–13). Those who reject the Son also reject eternal life, for everlasting life is in the Son. Those who turn against the testimony in effect call the Father a liar. The fundamental purpose of life is to see him (1 John 3:6), to know him (1 John 2:3–4; 3:6), to be "in him" (1 John 2:5). True believers abide in him until the last day (1 John 2:6, 28; 3:6, 24).

118. R. Brown (1982: 216–17) suggests that here Jesus is portrayed both as advocate and intercessor. See also Marshall 1978a: 116; Smalley 1984: 36–37.

Jesus' Saving Work

At this juncture we focus on Jesus' saving work on the cross in 1 John. The blood of Jesus cleanses from all sin (1 John 1:7; cf. 5:6). Perhaps John alludes to John 13:1–17, where Jesus' washing of the disciples' feet symbolizes the cleansing of sin about to be accomplished by Jesus' death. Forgiveness and cleansing of sin are available to those who confess their sins (1 John 1:9; cf. 2:12). The basis upon which forgiveness is granted is that Jesus Christ is the "advocate" (*paraklētos*) for those who agree that they are sinners. Furthermore, God is "just" (*dikaios* [1 John 1:9]) to forgive sins because Jesus Christ is the righteous one (*dikaios* [1 John 2:1]). God's justice is satisfied in the cross of Jesus, for Jesus is the "propitiation" (*hilasmos*) for the sins of all (1 John 2:2).[119] The love of God is demonstrated supremely in his sending Jesus to be the "propitiation" for sins (1 John 4:10). The genuineness of Jesus' love is shown in his laying down his life for believers (1 John 3:16). The implication is that believers need forgiveness of sins to be right with God. Jesus appeared on earth to take away their sin (1 John 3:5) and to destroy the devil's works (1 John 3:8), which he accomplishes by his death on the cross. Jesus, on the basis of his atoning work, is the Savior of the entire world (1 John 4:14). Characteristically, John says that believers are born of God (1 John 3:9; 4:7; 5:1, 4, 18). On one occasion, however, he ascribes being born again to Jesus Christ (1 John 2:29). We see again that the Father and the Son are linked together in their saving work, for granting new life is a divine work.

John emphasizes that the Christ cannot be separated from the human Jesus, whose blood atones for sin. Forgiveness of sins and eternal life are obtained not only by a divine Savior but also by one who was genuinely human and by the Christ who genuinely appeared in the flesh. What we see in the Johannine letters is an emphasis on both Jesus' deity and his humanity. God sent his Son to conquer sin and as a propitiation for sin. The one who was with God from the beginning as his Word has manifested himself in space-time history. The faith that saves, therefore, is in Jesus the Christ. Jesus is also the true God and eternal life. John is convinced that salvation is earthed in history, in the actual suffering and death of Jesus as the Son of God. At the same time, salvation would not be effective if Jesus were not the Son of God. John strives to preserve a full-orbed Christology for the sake of his soteriology.

119. In support of propitiation and expiation, see Marshall 1978a: 117–18; Smalley 1984: 38–40; cf. R. Brown 1982: 217–24.

Revelation

Centrality of Christ

One of the most astonishing, though often neglected, Christologies in the NT is in the book of Revelation. The book commences with the words "The revelation of Jesus Christ" (Rev. 1:1). The Greek genitive behind "of Jesus Christ" (*Iēsou Christou*) probably is both subjective and objective.[120] The book is given by Jesus Christ and is about Jesus Christ. Revelation discloses and unveils the truth about Jesus Christ, and hence the first verse captures one of the central themes of the book. Similarly, the phrases "testimony of Jesus Christ" (Rev. 1:2) and "testimony of Jesus" (Rev. 1:9; 12:17; 19:10; 20:4) fix our attention on Jesus Christ. In this case, again, the Greek genitive construction probably is both objective and subjective, so that it is the testimony about and given by Jesus.[121] So too the martyrs are put to death for their testimony of Jesus (Rev. 20:4). The testimony of and about Jesus can be described as the proclamation of God's word, in that the word heralded centers on Jesus Christ (Rev. 1:2, 9).

The centrality of Jesus is evident also in the mysterious and quite difficult sentence "The testimony of Jesus is the spirit of prophecy" (Rev. 19:10).[122] I suggest that the verse is teaching that testimony about Jesus is what constitutes Spirit-inspired prophecy. If prophecy is not Christ-centered, then it has veered away from the gospel.

Titles

Even clearer are some of the titles used for Jesus Christ. On three occasions in Revelation he declares, "I am the first and the last" (Rev. 1:17; 2:8; 22:13), emphasizing especially his sovereignty over death. What stands out, however, is that the same expression is used of Yahweh in the OT (Isa. 41:4; 44:6; 48:12). Nor would John be ignorant of the OT background, since Revelation is stocked with allusions to and echoes of the OT.[123] We see the same phenomenon with the phrases

---

120. The genitive could be objective or subjective (Aune 1997: 12; Osborne 2002: 52). Beale (1999b: 183) suggests that it is both.

121. For a genitive of source, see R. Mounce 1977: 247; Aune 1997: 19; Osborne 2002: 56–57. Beale (1999b: 183–84, 679) thinks that both notions are in view.

122. The meaning of the verse is quite uncertain. R. Mounce (1977: 342) says that "the message attested by Jesus is the essence of prophetic proclamation" (cf. Ladd 1972: 251). Still others maintain that the reference is to the Holy Spirit, who inspires prophecy (Caird 1966: 238). Bauckham (1993a: 161) says "that the witness Jesus bore is the content of Spirit-inspired prophecy." Beale (1999b: 947–48) thinks that the reference is to prophetic spirits who give testimony to Jesus.

123. Rightly Hofius 2000: 227. For the use of the OT in Revelation, see Beale 1984; Moyise 1995.

"Alpha and Omega" and "the beginning and the end." God himself announces that he is "the Alpha and Omega" at the commencement (Rev. 1:8) and conclusion (Rev. 21:6) of Revelation. Similarly, he affirms that he is "the beginning and the end" (Rev. 21:6). In the latter instance, there may be an echo of Isa. 46:10, where God declares "the end from the beginning." Both "Alpha and Omega" and "beginning and end" point to God's sovereignty over history. Since history commences and concludes with him, no part of history spins out of his control. He rules over the entire expanse of history so that his purposes will not be frustrated. Hence, the significance of Jesus saying, "I am the Alpha and the Omega . . . the beginning and the end" is not lost on the reader (Rev. 22:13). The sovereignty over history exercised by God belongs also to Jesus Christ.[124] The functions of deity are carried out by him. Jesus is "the beginning [*archē*] of God's creation" (Rev. 3:14). This does not mean that Jesus is part of the created order, for that would blatantly contradict his being the Alpha and the Omega. It means all things have their origin in Christ (cf. NRSV: "the origin of God's creation").[125] As Bauckham says, the "titles he [Christ] shares with God indicate that he shared the eternal being of God from before creation."[126]

Worship of Christ

Another set of remarkable texts should be noted in which God and Jesus Christ receive the same honor and glory. For instance, Rev. 4 is programmatic for the entire book. John has a vision of God reigning on his throne as creator, and the angelic hosts bow down and worship him as Lord of all. The focus shifts in Rev. 5 from God as creator to Jesus Christ as redeemer, the one who is both the lion who rules and the lamb who was slain. In Rev. 4:11 the angels worship God, confessing that he is worthy to be worshiped as creator. In Rev. 5:9–10 the angels ascribe worthiness to the Lamb, acknowledging that he deserves worship as redeemer. On the one hand, God is "worthy" of "glory and honor and power" (Rev. 4:11); on the other hand, Christ is "worthy" of "power and wealth and wisdom and might and honor and glory and blessing" (Rev. 5:12). Obviously, Jesus Christ as the Lamb of God deserves the same honor and glory that belongs to God. Indeed,

124. Furthermore, Revelation often speaks of Jesus' coming, but his coming cannot be separated from the coming of God himself (Hofius 2000: 225).

125. So also Bauckham 1993a: 56; Osborne 2002: 204–5; Hofius 2000: 230n42. Beale (1999b: 298) argues that the point here is that Jesus is "the *inauguration* of and *sovereign* over the new creation."

126. Bauckham 1993a: 58. See the fuller discussion in Bauckham 1993b: 118–49.

God and Jesus Christ are worshiped together at the conclusion of Rev. 5: "To him who sits on the throne and to the Lamb be blessing and honor and glory and might forever and ever!" (Rev. 5:13).[127] The twenty-four elders and four living beings then bow down and worship (Rev. 5:14).

The worship of the Lamb, Jesus Christ, along with God cannot be ascribed to a dilution of monotheism.[128] Twice John is so overcome by the glory of the angelic messenger that he bows down to worship the angel (Rev. 19:10; 22:8–9). In both instances the angel admonishes John that only God should be worshiped, and he forbids John from worshiping an angel. By way of contrast, we notice the oft-repeated collocation of God and Christ in Revelation, so that they receive equal esteem. When judgment is inflicted on the disobedient, they cry out in terror, asking that mountains and rocks would fall on them to conceal them "from the face of him who is seated on the throne, and from the wrath of the Lamb" (Rev. 6:16). This Lamb is not merely the suffering one who atones for sin; he also judges in anger those who resist his rule. Hence, John can speak of the anger of both God and the Lamb: "the great day of *their* wrath has come" (Rev. 6:17 [italics added]).

By way of contrast, the redeemed from every cultural and ethnic background stand before God and praise him. They do not merely stand, however, in God's presence; they stand "before the throne and before the Lamb" (Rev. 7:9), suggesting again the Lamb's equality with God. Indeed, they praise God for the salvation that they have received, and yet they place the Lamb on the same plane with God: "Salvation belongs to our God who sits on the throne, and to the Lamb!" (Rev. 7:10). The kingdom belongs to the "Lord and . . . his Christ" (Rev. 11:15). Similarly, we read that "the salvation and the power and the kingdom of our God and the authority of his Christ have come" (Rev. 12:10). Elsewhere those who have been redeemed are described as "firstfruits for God and the Lamb" (Rev. 14:4). They have both the name of the Lamb and the Father's name on their foreheads (Rev. 14:1). Those who conquer the second death and reign forever are not merely priests of God; they serve as "priests of God and Christ" (Rev. 20:6). The temple

127. Hengel (1983: 82) observes that "the veneration received by the Christ is not inferior to the praise and honour which are due to God himself" (see also Hofius 2000: 232). Such praise is even more striking when we consider the possible OT background: Exod. 20:11; Neh. 9:6; Ps. 146:6 (so Beale 1999b: 365–66).

128. Bauckham (1993a: 58) concludes that Jesus is not designated as "a second god" but rather is included "in the eternal being of the one God of Israel who is the only source and goal of all things." Bauckham (1993a: 60) further observes, "It seems rather that the worship of Jesus must be understood as indicating the inclusion of Jesus in the being of the one God defined by monotheistic worship."

in the new heavens and new earth is no longer a building. The earthly temple always pointed to something, or we should say "someone," greater, so that the "temple is the Lord God the Almighty and the Lamb" (Rev. 21:22). Nor does the heavenly city need created light, whether of the sun, moon, or stars, "for the glory of God gives it light" (Rev. 21:23). Characteristically, John does not leave out Jesus Christ, for he immediately adds "and its lamp is the Lamb" (Rev. 21:23).[129] Finally, God's throne, symbolizing his sovereignty and rule, is erected in the new Jerusalem. And yet Rev. 22:3 clarifies that the throne does not belong to God alone: it is "the throne of God and of the Lamb" (Rev. 22:3; cf. 22:1). The Lamb reigns equally with the Father. This astonishing and frequent collocation of God and Christ indicates that Jesus was considered to be divine in John's theology, that both God and the Lamb are to be worshiped and adored.

Priority of the Father

The language and symbolism of Revelation differs from the Gospel of John and the Johannine Epistles, but the Christology is the same. Jesus is divine.[130] He is to be worshiped as God is to be worshiped. Those who fail to worship the Lamb do not truly worship God. The sovereignty of God speaks also of the universal rule of the Lamb, the one who ordains all of history. And yet there are also indications of the priority of the Father. The authority that Jesus enjoys is a gift from the Father (Rev. 2:27).[131] If believers are faithful, Jesus will acknowledge them "before my Father and before his angels" (Rev. 3:5). After Jesus conquered, he "sat down" with the Father "on his throne" (Rev. 3:21). This latter text likely refers to Jesus' exaltation (Rev. 12:5) after his death. Even more striking, Jesus identifies the Father as "my God" (Rev. 3:12). Revelation harmonizes with what we have seen consistently in the NT. Jesus is divine and shares divine status, and yet God and Jesus are distinguished, and there is a sense in which the Father retains priority. As we found in the rest of the NT, John does not work out in any detail the philosophical and theological implications of his Christology for monotheism.

129. On the significance of the Lamb being associated with God here, see Hofius 2000: 234.

130. The fact that Jesus is worshiped should not be understood to say that the Christology of Revelation is only functional. John also speaks of Jesus ontologically (Bauckham 1993a: 63).

131. "There is a chain of authority from the Father to the Son to the conqueror" (Osborne 2002: 167).

Son of God and Word of God

John uses other titles to feature the glory of Jesus. He is "the Son of God" (Rev. 2:18). In contrast to its regular appearance in the Gospel of John, the title is used just this once in Revelation. When we consider the high Christology of the remainder of Revelation, we have good grounds for concluding that "Son of God" bears the same meaning as in the Gospel.[132] Jesus is the unique Son of the Father, having a special relationship with God. When Jesus masses his armies and prepares to come to judge the world, he is identified as the "Word of God" (Rev. 19:13) who carries out the divine judgment (cf. Wis. 18:15–16).[133] Elsewhere in Revelation the "word of God" refers to the message that John proclaims (Rev. 1:2, 9; 6:9; 20:4). We noted earlier that the message proclaimed in the word is inseparable from the testimony of Jesus (Rev. 1:2, 9; 20:4). Interestingly, the claim that "the testimony of Jesus is the spirit of prophecy" (Rev. 19:10) immediately follows the admonition to worship God. We could say that genuine prophecy exalts Jesus, and only those who exalt Jesus truly worship God. The reference to the "Word of God" (Rev. 19:13) suggests again that John draws on both the Gospel of John (John 1:1, 14) and 1 John (1 John 1:2), where Jesus is identified as the Word. He is God's message to human beings—the fulfillment of all prophecy and preaching.

Son of Man

Revelation also features Jesus as the Son of Man. As we noted when studying the Gospels, references to Jesus as the Son of Man are scarce outside the Gospels. An allusion to the "son of man" of Dan. 7:13 crops up early in Revelation: "Behold, he is coming with the clouds" (Rev. 1:7). In Dan. 7 the son of man comes with the clouds and appears before God himself, "the Ancient of Days" (Dan. 7:13). John follows NT tradition and applies this to Jesus' coming to the earth when he returns to consummate the kingdom. Perhaps we are justified in inferring that every reference to Jesus' future coming alludes indirectly to the prophecy in Dan. 7 (cf. Rev. 1:3; 2:5, 16, 25; 3:3, 11, 20; 16:15; 22:7, 10, 12, 20).[134] In any case, it is instructive to see that God himself can also be described

---

132. See Osborne 2002: 153. Roman emperors at times saw themselves as sons of God (see Aune 1997: 201–2). Beale (1999b: 259–60) argues that Jesus as Son of Man is also Son of God.

133. Caird (1966: 244) sees continuity with the Word in John 1:1 when the different purposes of the Gospel and Revelation are taken into account. R. Mounce (1977: 345–46) stresses the efficacy of God's word. See also Beale 1999b: 957–59; Osborne 2002: 683.

134. Some of these texts may refer to a coming in history before the final coming to set up his kingdom.

as the coming one (Rev. 1:4, 8; 4:8). Again we see the overlap between God and Jesus.

Jesus is explicitly recognized as the Son of Man in John's vision in Rev. 1:13–16. In the vision John sees not the historical Jesus but rather the exalted Christ. The robe that reaches to Christ's feet probably signifies his priestly authority (Rev. 1:13). Remarkably, his hair is like white wool and is "white as snow" (Rev. 1:14). The description is remarkable because in Dan. 7 Yahweh's clothing is "white as snow" and his hair is "like pure wool" (Dan. 7:9). John has not erred in his memory of the biblical account. He modifies the OT account to teach that the Son of Man deserves the same honor and glory as the Ancient of Days.[135] He is to be venerated and worshiped in the same way God is. Like God, his eyes flame with fire, searching all things so that nothing is hidden from his gaze (Rev. 1:14; 2:18, 23; 19:12). Those who secretly practice evil cannot avoid his penetrating gaze, and they will face judgment.

The Son of Man has feet of bronze refined in a furnace (Rev. 1:15). In the ancient world warfare conducted without good footwear for soldiers spelled disaster.[136] Armies that engaged in long marches could lose battles because the soldiers were incapacitated by damage done to their feet by the long journey. Jesus as the divine warrior does not suffer from the same malady. His bronze feet overcome any obstacles with ease (Rev. 2:18). He is prepared to crush any who oppose him (Rev. 2:26–27). As the divine warrior on a white horse, he is prepared to lead the armies of heaven into the last battle (Rev. 19:11–21).[137] He wields a sharp, two-edged sword in his mouth (Rev. 1:16). The double-edged sword symbolizes Jesus' word (Rev. 2:12, 16; 19:15), by which he defeats his enemies without any assistance from his army.

The voice of the Son of Man resounds like a cataract of waters (Rev. 1:15; cf. 14:2; 19:6). Ezekiel compares the sound of many waters to "the sound of the Almighty" (Ezek. 1:24).[138] The glory and brilliance of God's arrival is compared to the cascading of many waters (Ezek. 43:2). The Son of Man's face shines with a brilliance like the brightness of the sun (Rev. 1:16). Such glory on one's face is not necessarily a sign of deity, for mighty angels shine like the sun as well (Rev. 10:1). The glow from Jesus' face reminds one of the transfiguration (Matt. 17:2 par.). John faints in the presence of such glory (Rev. 1:17), just as Ezekiel was cast to the ground when he saw the glory of Yahweh (Ezek. 1:26–28). Falling

---

135. See Aune 1997: 94–95; Beale 1999b: 209; Osborne 2002: 90; Hofius 2000: 226.

136. Some see a reference to moral purity (Beale 1999b: 209–10). For the background, see Aune 1997: 95–96.

137. In the OT Yahweh is a divine warrior who triumphs in battle (Exod. 15:3). On this theme, see Longman and Reid 1995.

138. See Osborne 2002: 91.

to the ground in weakness and awe does not necessarily indicate that Jesus is divine. Daniel fainted in the presence of a glorious angel (Dan. 8:18). But when Jesus says, "I am the first and the last," it is evident that he is not merely an angel.

Whether the "one like a son of man" in Rev. 14:14 refers to Jesus is debated, and resolving the identity of the one mentioned here is not crucial for constructing the Christology of Revelation.[139] Most likely, however, the title refers to Jesus as the Son of Man, for the one spoken of here reaps the earth in judgment (Rev. 14:14–16). The main objection to identifying the "one like a son of man" as Jesus here is that this figure obeys a command issued by an angel. The subjection of the Son of Man to an angel would be odd, so we cannot be certain that Jesus himself is in view. Perhaps the best answer is that in the apocalyptic genre the angel's command simply mediates the will of God.[140]

Sovereign and Living One

Revelation is addressed to churches in Asia Minor suffering from discrimination and persecution. In response, John highlights Jesus' sovereignty over all. As the Lamb, Jesus is "King of kings" (Rev. 17:14; 19:16). The same verses affirm that he is "Lord of lords." Paul applies both titles to God in the Pastoral Epistles (1 Tim. 6:15), and in the OT Yahweh is hailed as "Lord of lords" (Deut. 10:17; Ps. 136:3), and in Second Temple literature as "King of kings" (2 Macc. 13:4; 3 Macc. 5:35).[141] Jesus rules over the kings of the earth (Rev. 1:5); it may appear that the political leaders of this world exercise control, but they serve under the authority of Jesus himself. Further, in Rev. 1:5–6 there is a doxology to Jesus, but doxologies belong to God alone.[142] Jesus is crowned with diadems symbolizing his rule over all, and the fact that no one knows his name demonstrates that no one exercises control over him (Rev. 19:12). In Hebrew culture naming signifies authority over what is named, just as Adam exercises his authority in naming the animals in the garden (Gen. 2:19).

Jesus is "the faithful witness" (Rev. 1:5; cf. 3:14; 19:11), thereby summoning suffering believers to imitate their Lord. Jesus' faithfulness is not the end of the story. He is also "the firstborn of the dead" (Rev. 1:5).[143] The promised resurrection of the age to come (i.e., the

---

139. For a reference to Christ, see Caird 1966: 190–91; R. Mounce 1977: 279; Beale 1999b: 770–71; Osborne 2002: 550. For a reference to an angelic being, see Aune 1998: 840–42.
140. So Beale 1999b: 772; Osborne 2002: 550.
141. See Hofius 2000: 224.
142. Rightly Hofius 2000: 224.
143. See especially Beale 1999b: 190–91; see also Osborne 2002: 63.

new creation) has dawned in Christ's resurrection. His resurrection is the first in history and also signals his sovereignty over death, so that the word "firstborn" indicates both temporal priority and sovereignty. He once was dead, but he has conquered death and is now "the living one" who has triumphed over death forever (Rev. 1:18). Designating Jesus as the living one is significant, for in the OT the Lord is regularly called "the living God."[144] Jesus has not merely conquered death personally; he also holds "the keys of Death and Hades" (Rev. 1:18). Death has not prevailed over Jesus, but rather Jesus has overcome death, so that it is now subjugated to him. Believers can face death with confidence, even if Rome itself stands against them, for Jesus is sovereign over death.

In a striking image, Jesus as God's Lamb is also the shepherd of God's people (Rev. 7:17).[145] We again have an echo of John's Gospel, where Jesus describes himself as the good shepherd (John 10:11, 14). Jesus' role as the shepherd points to his deity, for in the OT the Lord shepherds his people (Ps. 23:1; 28:9; 80:1; Isa. 40:11; Ezek. 34:12, 15; Mic. 7:14) and leads them to watering places (Ps. 23:2). Of course, in some texts the shepherd is a messianic figure (Ezek. 34:23; 37:24; Mic. 5:4).

Since Jesus is the living one, as the risen Christ he continues to speak to churches (Rev. 2:1, 8, 12, 18; 3:1, 7, 14). The state of the churches is not hidden from him. He knows intimately the spiritual state of each one (Rev. 2:2, 9, 13, 19; 3:1, 8, 15), and he authoritatively gives commands to the various churches. He holds the seven stars in his hand, representing the angels of the churches, and he knows the condition of the churches because he walks among the lampstands (Rev. 1:20; 2:1). Jesus' authority as the risen one is indicated by the verbs used to designate his activity (or potential activity) in the letters to the churches: he will "come" (Rev. 2:5, 16; 3:3; cf. 3:10); "remove" (Rev. 2:5); "grant" (Rev. 2:7; 3:21); "give" (Rev. 2:17, 23, 26, 28); "throw" (Rev. 2:22); "strike" (Rev. 2:23); "never blot" (Rev. 3:5); "confess" (Rev. 3:5); "make" (Rev. 3:9, 12); "keep" (Rev. 3:10); "write" (Rev. 3:12); "spit" (Rev. 3:16); "come in" (Rev. 3:20); "eat" (Rev. 3:20). Some present-tense verbs with Jesus as the subject include: "I am he who searches" (Rev. 2:23); "I do not lay on" (Rev. 2:24); "I am coming" (Rev. 3:11); "I counsel" (Rev. 3:18); "I love" (Rev. 3:19); "I reprove" (Rev. 3:19); "I discipline" (Rev. 3:19); "I stand" (Rev. 3:20). These verbs represent Jesus' authority, power, and stature.

144. Hofius 2000: 227–28.
145. See the excellent discussion in Osborne 2002: 331–32; see also Beale 1999b: 442–43.

Messiah

Revelation clearly portrays Jesus as divine, but John also teaches that Jesus is the Messiah (Rev. 1:1–2, 5; 11:15; 12:10; 20:4, 6).[146] The kingdom belongs not merely to God but also to "his Christ" (Rev. 11:15). As the Christ, Jesus has authority over all (Rev. 12:10). Those who conquer will reign with him for one thousand years (Rev. 20:4–6). He has made believers to be priests and a kingdom (Rev. 1:6; cf. 20:6). The covenant pledge that David's dynasty would persist forever is fulfilled in Jesus, for he holds "the key of David" (Rev. 3:7). Jesus is "the Lion of the tribe of Judah, the Root of David" (Rev. 5:5). At the conclusion of the book Jesus declares, "I am the root and the descendant of David, the bright morning star" (Rev. 22:16). Jesus as Lion of Judah echoes Gen. 49:9, and possibly even Num. 23:24; 24:9.[147] The lion symbolizes the strength, dignity, and royalty of Jesus. The term "root" (*rhiza*) hearkens back to Isa. 11, where a root from Jesse is promised (Isa. 11:1, 10). He will be endowed with the Spirit, judge righteously, destroy the wicked, and inaugurate peace and righteousness.

Jesus is the descendant of the people of God (Rev. 12:1–5), whom Satan desired to destroy. He has been exalted to the right hand of God, and the messianic promise of Ps. 2, that he would rule the nations with an iron rod (Ps. 2:8–9), belongs to Jesus (Rev. 12:5). The rulers of this world gather in an attempt to defeat Jesus and free themselves forever from his dominion (Rev. 19:19; cf. Ps. 2:2–3). Jesus, however, will rule them with an iron rod and destroy them (Rev. 2:26–27; 19:15). He will arrive on a white horse with the armies of heaven and vanquish his enemies by the word of his mouth (Rev. 19:11–21).[148] Those who wage war with the Lamb will not triumph, for he is sovereign over all as "Lord of lords and King of kings" (Rev. 17:14). Those who overcome will sit with Jesus on his throne forever (Rev. 3:21), whereas those who throw their lot in with the beast and yield to economic pressure to survive will face torment before the Lamb and angels (Rev. 14:10). True disciples, on the other hand, are committed to Jesus. They endure for the sake of his name (Rev. 2:3), following "the Lamb wherever he goes" (Rev. 14:4). They are willing to become martyrs because of their allegiance to Jesus (Rev. 17:6). Those who persevere under and through suffering will enjoy the marriage of the Lamb and the supper of the Lamb (Rev. 19:7, 9). Dwelling in the new Jerusalem, the bride of the Lamb, they will rejoice in his presence forever (Rev. 21:9).[149]

146. So also Bauckham 1993a: 68–69.
147. For the OT and Jewish background, see Beale 1999b: 349; Osborne 2002: 253.
148. Bauckham (1993a: 69–70) emphasizes that Jesus as the Messiah wins victory through war.
149. The centrality of the Lamb is indicated by the twelve apostles being designated as the Lamb's apostles (Rev. 21:14).

Jesus' Death

Even though Revelation emphasizes the sovereignty and glory of Christ, his death is the fulcrum of all history. He demonstrated his love to believers by freeing them from their sins by his death on the cross (Rev. 1:5).[150] Despite the threat from the Roman Empire, the fundamental need of believers is freedom from the guilt of sin. Revelation 5 is perhaps the most important chapter in the entire book, for no one is worthy to open the scroll bound with seven seals—no one, that is, except for one. John is informed that "the Lion of the tribe of Judah, the Root of David" can open the sealed book (Rev. 5:5). And yet when John actually looks to see the conqueror, he sees not a mighty lion but rather a slain lamb (Rev. 5:6).[151] The key to all history and the outworking of God's promises is the death of the Lamb. Victory over evil comes not through a military triumph but rather through the suffering of the Lamb. However, the slain Lamb is also the one who achieves victory and conquers, and so here John merges the Jewish traditions of the slain lamb and the conquering lamb.[152] As Bauckham argues, the juxtaposition of the images of the lion and the lamb signifies that Jesus as the Messiah conquers through his death.[153] By his blood he ransomed people from every ethnic and linguistic background (Rev. 5:9). Clean white robes signify access into God's presence, and robes are whitened only "in the blood of the Lamb" (Rev. 7:14).[154]

Those whose names are written in the book of life are enrolled because the Lamb has been slain on their behalf (Rev. 13:8; 21:27). The 144,000 are sealed (Rev. 7:1–8) only because they belong to the Lamb. His death is the source of their life. They sing a new song of salvation and have the name of the Father and the Lamb on their foreheads because they have been redeemed by the Lamb (Rev. 14:1–5). Similarly, believers conquer evil through Christ's blood and their willingness to face death (Rev. 12:11).[155] The healing of the nations comes from the tree of life (Rev. 22:2).

150. See Osborne 2002: 64.

151. The lamb here may include the Passover lamb and the suffering servant of Isa. 53 (so Bauckham 1993a: 70–71; Beale 1999b: 351). For an in-depth discussion of the background, see Aune 1997: 367–73.

152. For the conquering lamb in Judaism, see *1 En.* 90:9–12; *T. Jos.* 19:8; *T. Benj.* 3:8. See Osborne 2002; Beale 1999b: 351, though Beale thinks that the conquering image also derives from Daniel.

153. Bauckham 1993b: 179–85.

154. The robe dipped in blood in Rev. 19:13 probably refers to Jesus' judgment on God's enemies. Such an interpretation is supported by Isa. 63:1–6, which functions as the background (so Beale 1999b: 958–60; Osborne 2002: 682–83). Other options are that the reference is to the blood of the martyrs (Caird 1966: 243–44) or to Christ's atoning sacrifice (Morris 1969b: 230).

155. Bauckham (1993b: 228–29) understands the blood of the Lamb to refer to martyrdom, but more likely it refers to Christ's atoning work (rightly Osborne 2002: 476).

However, only those who wash their robes have access to that tree (Rev. 22:14), and we noted in Rev. 7:14 that the robes are washed and whitened only in the Lamb's blood.[156] On the basis of Christ's death, then, all are invited to take freely of the water of life (Rev. 22:17). Even though the death of Christ is noted in only a few texts in Revelation, the placement of such is fundamental for the entire book. Believers must overcome and persevere to receive a reward, but the foundation for access to the tree of life is the blood of the Lamb.

Even though Revelation is an apocalyptic work, the Christology is astonishingly explicit and high. Indeed, the Christology is analogous to that in the Gospel of John. Jesus as the Lamb is on the same plane as God and is worshiped as a divine being. He is the Messiah of Israel and the Son of God. He is the glorious Son of Man and the ruler of the kings of the earth. He is King of kings and Lord of lords. Just as God is praised, so too Jesus is praised. Just as God is the Alpha and Omega and the first and the last, so too Jesus is the Alpha and Omega and the first and the last. And it is this Jesus whose death frees believers from their sins and who makes their robes white by his blood. Revelation coheres with the main theme of this chapter: an exalted Christology secures salvation.

---

156. Bauckham (1993b: 226–27) argues that the whiteness of the saints' robes focuses on the perseverance of believers, but the metaphor of whitening with the Lamb's blood more likely points to Christ's death (rightly Beale 1999b: 436–38; Osborne 2002: 325–26).

13

❦ ❦ ❦ ❦ ❦ ❦ ❦ ❦ ❦ ❦ ❦ ❦ ❦ ❦ ❦ ❦ ❦ ❦

The Holy Spirit

Introduction

I have argued thus far in this book that the age of salvation has dawned with the coming of Jesus Christ. God's covenantal and saving promises are being fulfilled in Christ, though there is an already–not yet tension present. The fulfillment of such promises brings glory to God, who saves his people in Christ. Further, the story line of the NT is that God is magnified *in Christ*. We have seen in previous chapters that Jesus Christ fulfills God's promises and saves his people because of who he is.

What is also remarkable about the NT witness, however, is the role of the Spirit in God's saving work in Christ. The Spirit is the eschatological sign that the new age has arrived, that the new creation has become a reality. The saving work of God in Christ is implemented through the work of the Spirit. Indeed, one of the notable features of NT theology is its trinitarian cast. The later formulation of the Trinity was not merely an imposition of Greek philosophy on the NT; it arose out of an attempt to reckon seriously with the trinitarian salvation proclaimed in the NT. This is not to say, of course, that the NT itself formulates the doctrine of the Trinity. But, as we will see in this chapter, the great saving events that commenced with the coming of Jesus Christ signaled that the age of the Spirit had arrived.

Old Testament Background

Before considering the Spirit in the NT, we must touch on the OT background because it is fundamental for understanding the NT.[1] The Spirit plays a vital role in creation (cf. Ps. 33:6). Genesis suggests that the Spirit tended over creation (Gen. 1:2), so that the entire created order depends on the Spirit for life (Ps. 104:30). No one, therefore, can escape from God's Spirit, for he fills the entire earth (Ps. 139:7). Nor can any human being comprehend the wisdom of God's Spirit, since it is immeasurable (Isa. 40:13–14).

The largest category for the Spirit in the OT relates to ministry, especially the speaking forth of the word of God. The Spirit filled Bezalel so that he had the requisite wisdom and skill to build the tabernacle (Exod. 31:3; 35:31). Joshua was a suitable replacement for Moses because God's Spirit indwelt him (Num. 27:18). The Lord took some of the Spirit indwelling Moses and gave it to the seventy elders. When the Spirit came, they prophesied (Num. 11:24–25). Although Joshua expressed concern about those who did not leave the camp and yet received the Spirit, Moses voiced the desire that all the Lord's people would receive the Spirit (Num. 11:26–29). Moses' desire anticipated the age of fulfillment, the dawning of the new covenant, when all God's people would enjoy the Holy Spirit.

In the book of Judges the Spirit rushed upon those who were called "judges," equipping them to speak God's word and to win victories over enemies in the name of the Lord (Judg. 3:10; 6:34; 11:29; 13:25; 14:6, 19; 15:14). In addition, those who were anointed as kings received the Spirit. For instance, after Saul was anointed as king, the Spirit descended upon him and he prophesied (1 Sam. 10:6, 10). That same Spirit rushed upon Saul, empowering him to lead Israel into battle (1 Sam. 11:6, 11). When David was anointed as king, the Spirit came upon him, and since Saul was rejected as the anointed, the Spirit, tragically, departed from him (1 Sam. 16:13–14). When David sinned grievously, he prayed that the Lord would not remove the Spirit from him as he did from Saul (Ps. 51:11).

The Spirit of God enabled people to prophesy and speak forth his word. The ministry of the prophets in which they warned Israel about the consequences of their sin is attributed to the work of God's Spirit (Neh. 9:30; Zech. 7:12). Even the pagan Balaam, who refused to submit to Yahweh, experienced the Spirit coming upon him, and as a result he declared God's word (Num. 24:2; cf. 1 Kings 22:24). When Saul sent

---

1. For a helpful survey of the role of the Spirit in the OT, see Hamilton 2006b: 25–55.

messengers to arrest David, they were seized by the Spirit and prophesied (1 Sam. 19:20–21). The same Spirit fell upon Saul when he came to Ramah to lay his hands on David (1 Sam. 19:22–24). The Spirit spoke through David (2 Sam. 23:2) and the utterances of the prophets (1 Kings 22:24; 1 Chron. 12:18; 2 Chron. 15:1; 20:14; 24:20). The Spirit entered into Ezekiel and carried him about, and God's word was spoken through him (Ezek. 2:2; 3:12, 14, 24; 11:1, 5; 37:1; 43:5; cf. 1 Kings 18:12; 2 Kings 2:16). Daniel's ability to interpret visions and other phenomena was attributed by pagans to "the spirit of the holy gods" in him (Dan. 4:8–9, 18; 5:11, 12, 14). Micah, as a prophet, was filled with the Lord's Spirit, and so he was emboldened to declare God's word of judgment to Israel (Mic. 3:8).

As Nehemiah rehearsed the history of Israel and its unfaithfulness, he reminded them that God granted them his Spirit to instruct them (Neh. 9:20). God led his people by means of his Spirit (Ps. 143:10). Israel failed, however, to trust in the Lord and do his will. They formed an alliance with Egypt to win protection for themselves, but that covenant was not in accord with God's Spirit (Isa. 30:15). Israel rebelled against God and grieved his Holy Spirit, and so he sent them into exile (Isa. 63:10). The Lord promised, however, that his saving work in Israel would continue. He would not abandon his people. The Spirit granted rest to God's people in the past (Isa. 63:14), and Israel prayed that he would act again for the sake of his great name. Upon the return from exile, God's Spirit continued to abide with his people (Hag. 2:5). The Lord instructed them that his work would be accomplished by means of his Spirit (Zech. 4:6), not the strength or wisdom of human beings.

In any case, the promises of universal blessing given to Abraham were not realized in Israel's history. Israel looked forward to the day when a new descendant from David would arise (Isa. 11:1–10). The Spirit will rest upon him, and he will rule with wisdom and discretion. Justice will become a reality on the earth, and an age of peace and wholeness will be established in which the world will exist as God intended. This age of justice will not be established by a warrior who routs his enemies with his military exploits. Instead, the Servant of the Lord will introduce this age of peace by means of the Spirit that God has given him (Isa. 42:1–4). The Lord will anoint him with the Spirit to proclaim God's good news of return from exile and to announce the realization of all of God's promises (Isa. 61:1–4).

This future age of blessedness and peace can be designated as the age of the Spirit. The time of judgment and woe will give place to an era of justice and security (Isa. 32:16–20). The new age will dawn when "the Spirit is poured upon us from on high" (Isa. 32:15). Isaiah 40–48 is dominated by Israel's exile to Babylon because of sin and by the promise of a glorious return. The return will be possible because God will send his Spirit. "For I will pour water on the thirsty land, and streams on the dry ground; I will pour my Spirit upon your offspring, and my blessing on your descendants" (Isa. 44:3). The blessing promised to the Lord's people is the Spirit. He will refresh and sustain them as water rejuvenates a dehydrated traveler.

The same promise of the Spirit occurs in Joel 2:28–32. Israel faced judgment because they had turned away from Yahweh. Joel promised that in the latter days God would pour his Spirit out on all his people, including every social class, age group, and both males and females. The prophecy of Joel resonates with Moses' wish that all of God's people would function as prophets (Num. 11:29), for it pledges that all God's people will prophesy. When the Spirit descends, the age of salvation will also arrive, so that those who call upon the Lord will be saved.

Ezekiel could almost be called "the prophet of the Spirit." His prophecy is also dominated by the issue of exile and return. The glory of Yahweh departing from the temple represented the nadir of Israel's history. Nor does the glory depart for an unaccountable reason, as if it is a mystery. Israel violated the covenant with Yahweh and treacherously worshiped and served other gods. The problem with Israel was that its heart was like stone, impervious to the Lord's demands and resistant to his will. Israel lacked any inclination to be submissive to the will of Yahweh. The situation appeared to be hopeless, but the Lord himself pledged to help his people. In one of the most significant texts in the OT he says, "I will give them one heart, and put a new spirit within them; I will remove the heart of stone from their flesh and give them a heart of flesh, that they may walk in my statutes and keep my rules and obey them. And they shall be my people, and I will be their God" (Ezek. 11:19–20).[2] The promise is repeated in similar terms in Ezek. 36:25–26, with the additional explanation "I will put my Spirit within you, and cause you to walk in my statutes and be careful to obey my rules" (Ezek. 36:27). The Lord punished Israel with exile because of failure to obey the law. Now he pledges that he himself will solve the problem of Israel's intransigence, for his Spirit will soften their hearts so that his people will keep his commands. Israel will prosper in the land as the Lord's obedient people: "I will put my Spirit within you, and you shall live, and I will place you in your own land" (Ezek. 37:14). The coming of the Spirit is the hope of the Lord's people, for when the Spirit is sent, God's people will keep his law and reside in the land (Ezek. 39:29).

2. Block (1997: 353) drives too big a wedge between Ezek. 36:26–27, where he sees an emphasis on God's Spirit, and Ezek. 11:19–20, where he sees the focus on the human spirit.

Even though the new-covenant promise in Jeremiah does not specifically mention the Spirit, the promise given accords with what we have seen in Ezekiel. The promise is so important for the NT that it warrants an extensive citation.

> Behold, the days are coming, declares the LORD, when I will make a new covenant with the house of Israel and the house of Judah, not like the covenant that I made with their fathers on the day when I took them by the hand to bring them out of the land of Egypt, my covenant that they broke, though I was their husband, declares the LORD. But this is the covenant that I will make with the house of Israel after those days, declares the LORD: I will put my law within them, and I will write it on their hearts. And I will be their God, and they shall be my people. And no longer shall each one teach his neighbor and teach his brother, saying, "Know the LORD," for they shall all know me, from the least of them to the greatest, declares the LORD. For I will forgive their iniquity, and I will remember their sin no more. (Jer. 31:31–34)

Israel's problem under the old covenant was their failure to keep the law. The failure to abide by covenantal stipulations led to their expulsion from the land. The Lord will remedy the defect by placing the law on Israel's heart and accomplishing final forgiveness of sins. If we compare this prophecy with what was just cited from Ezekiel, we reach the conclusion that the two promises are complementary. The law will be imprinted on the heart when the Spirit is given universally to the people of God.

The Spirit in the New Testament

The Spirit in Matthew and Mark

As we noted above, the NT witness on the Spirit must be interpreted in light of the OT failure of Israel and the promise of blessing in the future. We immediately face a decision, for a good case can be made for consulting the three Synoptic Gospels together in setting forth what the NT says about the Spirit. On the other hand, Luke and Acts were composed to be read together, and this two-volume work says much about the Spirit. It seems best, then, to isolate Luke from the other Synoptics so that we can include it with Acts in studying the Spirit. As a consequence, there will be some overlap from Matthew and Mark when the teaching of Luke is explained.

The references to the Spirit in Matthew and Mark may be split into four different categories: (1) the Spirit and prophecy; (2) Jesus as the one anointed by the Spirit; (3) the promise of the baptism of the Spirit;

(4) trinitarian texts on the Spirit. We should note at the outset that the first three categories fall in line with the brief survey conducted of the OT. The Spirit is the Spirit of prophecy through whom people speak the word of God. The OT anticipates a son of David who will be anointed with the Spirit of the Lord. And finally, we noted that the OT looked forward to the day when God would pour out his Spirit on his people.

SPIRIT AND PROPHECY

We begin with the Spirit and prophecy where the Spirit works so that people speak forth God's word. Two examples stand out: Jesus introduces Ps. 110:1 into the debate about the identity of the Christ, suggesting that the Messiah is both David's Lord and his son (Mark 12:35–37; Matt. 22:41–46); Jesus prefaced his remarks with the observation that David spoke these words "in the Holy Spirit" (Mark 12:36).[3] David's words were not merely his own private opinion; they were the result of the Spirit's work, so the words that he composed are the word of God. The prophetic Spirit will also come to the aid of the disciples. Jesus envisioned the day when his disciples would be arrested, beaten, and brought to trial. He instructed them to desist from worry or even preparation before the trial occurred, for the Holy Spirit will grant them the words that they need at their defense (Matt. 10:19; Mark 13:11).[4] The prophetic Spirit should not be limited to these two texts, for the categories proposed here overlap. Certainly the Spirit that rested upon Jesus is the same Spirit of prophecy, anointing him to proclaim the word of God. Still, we establish a new category here because of Jesus' unique relation to the Spirit.

JESUS' ANOINTING WITH THE SPIRIT

Broadly speaking, Jesus' relation to the Spirit can be designated as one of anointing in that the Spirit anointed Jesus for ministry. The relationship of Jesus to the Spirit, according to Matthew, began with his conception.[5] Matthew explains that Jesus' conception did not transpire in the normal way, for Mary was a virgin when Jesus was conceived (Matt. 1:18–23).[6] Jesus' conception in Mary's womb was the product of the work of the Holy Spirit, not of sexual relations between Joseph and Mary. Matthew provides no rationale or explanation for why such a conception is important—apart from the fact that it fulfills the prophecy

3. Matthew has "in the Spirit" (Matt. 22:43). See France 2002: 487.
4. France (2002: 517–18) thinks what is said about the Spirit here is similar to the paraclete concept in John.
5. In due course we will consider what Luke says about the virginal conception.
6. On the birth narratives in Matthew, see R. Brown 1977. On the virgin birth, see Machen 1965.

of Isa. 7:14. Perhaps it is fair to conclude, at the very least, that this one conceived by the Spirit will be mightily endowed with the Spirit.

Perhaps the most important text is Jesus' anointing with the Spirit that occurs at his baptism (Matt. 3:16; Mark 1:10; cf. Luke 3:22).[7] Previously we considered the divine words of approval spoken to Jesus (Matt. 3:17 par.). Here we note the descent of the Spirit at Jesus' baptism. The significance of the Spirit's coming must be grasped. It cannot be the case that Jesus previously lacked God's approval, for the Father communicates his pleasure with his Son (Matt. 3:17 par.). Nor is it the case that Jesus is now adopted as God's Son, for his sonship (Mark 1:1; Luke 1:35) and unique status (Immanuel [Matt. 1:23]) are already attested in all the Gospels.[8] The descent of the Spirit, then, must signify Jesus' anointing for ministry. His public ministry will now commence, and God clothed him with the Spirit to empower him to carry out his task. The Spirit descended on him as a dove. It is difficult to discern why the Spirit descended as a dove, and this issue has perplexed commentators throughout history. The descent of the dove upon Jesus may suggest the inauguration of the new creation.[9] The same Spirit that hovered over the old creation (Gen. 1:2) now rested upon Jesus, signifying the new creation work of God. This may be confirmed by the release of the dove after the flood (Gen. 8:11), signifying a new beginning after judgment.

As the Spirit-anointed Messiah and Son of God, Jesus was led by the Spirit into the wilderness to be tempted by the devil (Matt. 4:1). Mark depicts the same event with the more vivid verb "drove out" (*ekballei* [Mark 1:12]). The encounter with Satan was not accidental, for the Spirit "led" Jesus into the wilderness. Israel failed to trust and obey God during its forty years in the wilderness, but Jesus as God's Son and the true Israel—the one endowed with the Spirit—trusted and obeyed him completely, resisting Satan's blandishments with the word of God.

When examining the OT above, we noted that the Servant of the Lord is anointed by the Spirit. Matthew cites a Servant of the Lord text from Isa. 42:1–3 and applies it to Jesus (Matt. 12:17–21). The Spirit that is given to

7. Jesus is anointed with the Spirit (cf. Isa. 42:1; 61:1) in commencing his public ministry (see Hagner 1993b: 57–58; France 2002: 77).

8. Menzies (1994: 132–56) rightly sees the emphasis is on anointing for ministry, but such a view need not exclude an emphasis on the commencement of the new creation.

9. For a discussion of the many options with a defense of the notion of a new creation, see Davies and Allison 1988: 331–34; Beale 2004: 171; Hagner 1993b: 58. R. Brown (1977: 66n7) thinks that such a view is possible. France (2002: 79) registers some doubts. Nolland (2005: 156) thinks that "the messenger role of the dove" is in view. Lane (1974: 50, 53–58) thinks that the dove marks out Jesus as the new Israel, and Campbell (1996: 206–8) sees a link to Israel's suffering and Jesus' call to suffer and die (Ps. 74:19; Isa. 38:14; Jer. 48:28) for Israel.

Jesus is a gentle Spirit.[10] Even though the Pharisees conspired to kill Jesus (Matt. 12:14), Jesus did not vanquish them as a warrior but rather withdrew and encouraged people not to spread the word about his healings (Matt. 12:15–16). The Spirit was given to Jesus so that he would straighten bruised reeds and fan smoldering wicks into flame. He did not come to bring war into the streets of Rome so that the Gentiles would be destroyed; instead, he came to bring hope to the Gentiles. The Spirit empowered him to bring in the kingdom by suffering instead of through violence.

The opposition to Jesus intensified as his ministry continued. After Jesus expelled a demon from a man who was blind and mute, enabling the man to see and speak (Matt. 12:22–32), the Pharisees concluded that Jesus exorcised the demon with the assistance of Beelzebul. With penetrating logic Jesus demonstrated the fallaciousness of the Pharisees' contention. Indeed, they inverted reality, for actually the exorcism indicated that Jesus expelled demons by God's Spirit, showing that the kingdom of God had arrived (Matt. 12:28).[11] We see again that Jesus was anointed by the Spirit to bring about salvation. He did not destroy his enemies; he rescued severely bruised reeds such as the demonized man. The Spirit was given to Jesus to accomplish salvation, not judgment. The text concludes with the difficult word that those who revile the Spirit will never be forgiven, although those who speak against Jesus as the Son of Man still have the opportunity for forgiveness (Matt. 12:31–32; cf. Mark 3:28–30).[12] The meaning of this saying has challenged interpreters over the centuries. The context should have the most weight in determining what the text means. The Pharisees blasphemed against the Spirit when they claimed that Jesus' exorcism and healing was demonic. If human beings see good accomplished and attribute that good to demons, they turn against God's Spirit. They will never be forgiven because they have a distorted perspective on reality in that they identify what is good and beautiful as evil.

The promise of the baptism of the Spirit is found in only one verse each in Matthew and Mark (Matt. 3:11; Mark 1:8; cf. Luke 3:16). The promise should be interpreted in light of the previously noted OT texts that pledged a great outpouring of the Spirit in the last days. The word "baptism" signifies a great immersion into the Spirit.[13] In the OT God's

---

10. So Hagner 1993b: 338.

11. Luke says that the demons were expelled "by the finger of God" (Luke 11:20).

12. Hooker (1991: 117) says about the blasphemy of the Spirit, "Mark has interpreted this as the deliberate refusal to acknowledge the activity of God's Spirit in Jesus' ministry; it is the attitude which makes a man attribute the work of God to Satan and confuse goodness and evil, truth and falsehood." Cf. Hagner 1993b: 347. For the history of interpretation, see Luz 2001: 206–8.

13. Contra Turner (1996: 180–87), who thinks that the verse promises cleansing rather than an outpouring.

people experienced the curses of the covenant because they consistently failed to do his will. When human beings receive the baptism of the Spirit, a new reality will intervene. Jesus will immerse them with the Spirit so that the hearts of his people will be purified. Mark says only that Jesus will baptize with the Spirit, but Matthew says, "He will baptize you with the Holy Spirit and with fire" (Matt. 3:11). "Fire" here may have two effects, referring first to Jesus' cleansing and purifying work by which a remnant is created (Isa. 4:2–6). At the same time, others may experience this fire as one of judgment. The theme of judgment is clear from the subsequent verse in Matthew (Matt. 3:12; cf. Luke 3:17), which declares that Jesus will clean up the threshing floor with his winnowing fork and burn the chaff with an unending fire.[14] The age of salvation arrived when Jesus baptized with the Spirit, but those who turn against him will face judgment.

Trinitarian Texts

Lastly, we should observe that a few texts have a trinitarian reference. In saying "trinitarian," I do not intend to indicate the full-fledged doctrine of the Trinity as it was articulated in later church history. The NT does not explore the theological and philosophical implications of what I am calling "trinitarian" references. Perhaps they should be identified as adumbrations of the Trinity, since the different "persons" are mentioned without any attempt to formulate how such fit with monotheism. We can say with certainty that NT writers did not for an instant think they were denying or compromising monotheism. Perhaps they even considered their teaching to be a further definition or explication of monotheism.

The first "trinitarian" reference occurs at Jesus' baptism (Matt. 3:16–17; Mark 1:10–11; cf. Luke 3:22).[15] Three different entities are involved at the same time: (1) the Father speaks from heaven, declaring that Jesus is his Son, in whom he finds pleasure; (2) the Spirit appears in the form of a dove and rests upon Jesus; (3) Jesus is baptized by John. The text is suggestive rather than determinative, but the collocation of the Father

14. Dunn (1970a: 10–14) maintains that there is one baptism, and that this purifying work of judgment would fall upon both those who repented and those who refused to repent. For the former there would be blessing, but the latter would experience destruction. R. Webb (1991: 289–95) argues that the baptism has two aspects, conferring a new spirit of holiness and purification upon the righteous, and judging and destroying the unrighteous. Menzies (1994: 123–31), to the contrary, argues that there is no reference to the purification or moral change of the righteous here. Rather, the point of the saying is that the righteous will be separated from the wicked, and this will occur as the church proclaims the gospel in the power of the Spirit.

15. It is remarkable how many commentators completely omit any comment on the role of the Father, Son, and Spirit, which perhaps reveals their theological filters. But see Davies and Allison 1988: 340.

and the Son with the Spirit is significant, particularly because the three are distinguished from one another and yet are also united in the action of Jesus' anointing. The citation of Isa. 42:1 in Matt. 12:18 also has trinitarian implications. The words "I will put my Spirit upon him" refer to the Father as the one bestowing the Spirit, the Spirit as the gift given, and the Son as the recipient of the Spirit. Clearly, no one in Isaiah's day understood him to posit a distinction between the Father and the Spirit in terms of different persons, and yet given what we have seen in Matt. 3:16 and the conclusion of Matthew's Gospel (which we will examine shortly), such a view may represent Matthew's understanding of the text in light of the coming of Jesus the Christ.

We must beware of pressing Matt. 12:32 (cf. Mark 3:29) too far, and yet it is fascinating to note that the Father, Son, and Spirit are mentioned here as well. Jesus cast out demons. He did so by the power of the Spirit, and the exorcism of demons signaled the arrival of the kingdom of God. Perhaps nothing should be made of the collocation of the three here, and yet what we find here fits, at the very least, the conclusion of Matthew's Gospel.

The most striking text, of course, comes from the risen Lord at the close of Matthew's Gospel. He charged his disciples, "Make disciples of all nations, baptizing them in the name of the Father and of the Son and of the Holy Spirit" (Matt. 28:19).[16] Initiation into the fellowship of believers commences with baptism in water. Such baptism is to be administered in one name, signifying that there is only one God. Matthew commends baptism not in the *names* of the Father, Son, and Spirit but rather in the *one name*. The one name, however, includes diversity: the threefold Father, Son, and Spirit. Baptism in the name of the Father, Son, and an angel or Peter is not permitted. Angels or Peter are excluded because baptism is administered in the divine name, indicating that the Father, the Son, and the Spirit are all divine. Matthew does not give way here to tritheism, for the one name indicates that there is only one God. And yet the Godhead is marked by diversity—the Father, the Son, and the Spirit.

The Spirit in Luke-Acts

Luke could be described as a theologian of the Holy Spirit because he frequently refers to the Spirit in his two-volume work.[17] Naturally, some overlap between Luke and the other Synoptics exists, and I will

16. See especially Carson 1984: 598. See also Hagner 1995: 887–88.
17. For excellent surveys of scholarship relative to the Holy Spirit with a focus on Luke-Acts, see Menzies 1994: 17–45; Turner 1996: 20–79. For brief summaries, see Kee 1990: 28–41; Green 1995: 41–47 (focusing on Luke).

abbreviate the exposition where it touches on the same events found in Matthew and Mark.

JESUS AS THE BEARER OF THE SPIRIT

Jesus' role as the bearer of the Spirit, which is another way of saying that he is anointed by the Spirit, begins in Luke, as in Matthew, with the virginal conception. Yet Luke draws on different traditions in the birth narratives. Luke alternates in the birth narratives between John the Baptist and Jesus. An angel appeared and announced the birth of the Baptist (Luke 1:5–25) and Jesus (Luke 1:26–38). Then the births of both John (Luke 1:57–80) and Jesus (Luke 2:1–38) are recorded. In both instances the events surrounding Jesus' birth far surpass what happened with the Baptist, demonstrating Jesus' superiority. John's conception was remarkable, for the angel Gabriel appeared to Zechariah in the temple, promising that his barren and elderly wife would have a son, and struck Zechariah mute for disbelieving (Luke 1:5–25). The conception of Jesus was even more stunning. The OT contains other accounts of elderly and barren parents giving birth to children, such as the birth of Isaac to Abraham and Sarah (Gen. 21:1–7), and Samuel to Elkanah and Hannah (1 Sam. 1:1–28). No precedent exists, however, for a virgin having a child. Mary conceived a child not through sexual relations but, miraculously, when the Holy Spirit overshadowed her (Luke 1:35). Like Matthew, Luke portrays Jesus as one who experienced the Spirit's work from his conception. He is the unique bearer of the Spirit as the one conceived by the Spirit.[18] Similarly, when the Baptist was born, Zechariah received the ability to speak again and prophesied (Luke 1:57–80). But the birth of Jesus was revealed to shepherds by an army of angels, Simeon recognized him as the Christ in the temple, and Anna praised God for the redemption of Jerusalem (Luke 2:1–38).

As noted in Matthew and Mark, Jesus was anointed by the Spirit at his baptism (Luke 3:22). Luke emphasizes that the Spirit descended in bodily form. Luke shares with the other Synoptics the leading of Jesus into the wilderness by the Spirit (Luke 4:1). His use of the verb "lead" (*agō*) conforms more closely to the Matthean than the Markan account. Distinctively, Luke remarks that Jesus returned from his time of testing in the wilderness "in the power of the Spirit" (Luke 4:14). His time of preparation and testing was now finished. He had succeeded in the wilderness where Israel had failed. He was God's obedient Son in contrast to Adam. He commenced his public ministry full of the Spirit's

---

18. See R. Brown 1977: 299–301; Fitzmyer 1981a: 337–38; Turner 1996: 156–58. Against Menzies (1994: 111–16), who thinks that Luke actually minimizes the creative role of the Spirit here.

power, equipped by the Spirit to carry out the will of God. Luke indicates thereby that the whole of Jesus' ministry was conducted in the power of the Spirit. Such a view fits with the summary of Jesus' ministry given by Peter to Cornelius and his cohorts (Acts 10:37–41). The works of Jesus are characterized as "doing good and healing all who were oppressed by the devil" (Acts 10:38). Such healings and exorcisms occurred because "God anointed Jesus of Nazareth with the Holy Spirit and with power" (Acts 10:38).[19] We note again the close association of the Spirit and power, as in Luke 4:14. The effectiveness of Jesus' ministry, his miracles and healings, flowed not from himself but from the power of the Spirit.

The same theme is impressed upon the reader by the first event recorded in Jesus' ministry in Luke (Luke 4:16–30). The story recorded here contains many of the themes in both Luke and Acts, and so the account is programmatic and fundamental for Luke's two-volume work. Our goal here is not to identify all these themes but rather to note the role of the Spirit. Jesus returned to his hometown of Nazareth. He selected the Isaiah scroll and read Isa. 61:1–2, claiming that the text was fulfilled in his person and his ministry. The text begins with the words "The Spirit of the Lord is upon me, because he has anointed me to bring good news to the poor" (Luke 4:18).[20] The text proceeds to say that Jesus was sent to free the imprisoned, to grant sight to the blind, to free the oppressed, and to herald the grace of God (Luke 4:18–19). Such a gracious ministry is due to the work of the Spirit in Jesus' life. It flows from the Spirit's anointing. We should also observe that Jesus described the whole of his ministry here, so that every dimension of his work depended upon the anointing power of the Spirit. Every good work detailed in Luke stems from the Spirit himself. Jesus truly was the bearer of the Spirit, the man marked out by the Spirit, the man uniquely strengthened by the Spirit.

The Prophetic Spirit

Another broad category for the Spirit in Luke-Acts is what is designated here "the prophetic Spirit."[21] The Spirit comes upon people so that they speak the word of God, both in spoken prophetic utterances and in the written scriptural word. In Luke the prophetic word relates

19. Barrett (1994: 524) probably is right in suggesting that Jesus was anointed with the Spirit at his baptism. See also Shelton 1991: 46–56.

20. Again the anointing of Jesus probably refers to his baptism (Fitzmyer 1981a: 529).

21. For this theme in Acts, see Turner 1998: 333–37. Jervell (1984: 107–16) underestimates the extent to which the Spirit is tied to words uttered in prophecy and hence he sunders the Spirit from the gospel.

to the fulfillment of salvation history.[22] God's redemptive plan is being worked out, and it is advanced by the prophetic words that come from the Spirit. Often in Luke-Acts the Spirit leads his people, especially in terms of mission—the spread of the gospel to the ends of the earth.

When the Spirit comes, people speak forth God's word.[23] When Mary visited Elizabeth, the latter was suddenly filled with the Spirit and spoke loudly an oracle from God (Luke 1:40–45). Under the inspiration of the Spirit Elizabeth recognized that Mary was carrying the Lord in her womb, and that Mary was the object of the Lord's special favor. The Baptist in Elizabeth's womb leaped for joy, presumably recognizing the fulfillment of the Lord's saving promise.[24] Indeed, earlier Gabriel announced that John would "be filled with the Holy Spirit, even from his mother's womb" (Luke 1:15). Such a filling testifies that John is a prophet of the Lord—indeed, the greatest prophet until the coming of the Christ (Luke 7:26–28). We should notice that Elizabeth's filling with the Spirit was not an ordinary event in her life. She spoke forth God's word to the mother of the Messiah.

Similarly, Zechariah was filled with the Spirit and prophesied, praising God that he is about to fulfill his covenantal promises by causing a son of David to sit on the throne (Luke 1:67–79).[25] The Baptist will prepare people for the coming of the Lord and the great salvation that God has promised. We see again that the prophetic word of the Spirit relates to the fulfillment of redemptive history—the outworking of God's saving promises.[26] The words of Simeon should be interpreted similarly (Luke 2:25–35). Luke informs the reader that the "Holy Spirit was upon him" (Luke 2:25), and that "he came in the Spirit into the temple" (Luke 2:27). Luke does not mean by this that previously Simeon was living in the flesh. The point is that the prophetic Spirit was upon Simeon so that he was enabled to speak forth the word of God. The Spirit had "revealed to him" previously that his life would not end before he saw the Christ

22. Turner (2005) reviews scholarship relative to the Spirit in Luke-Acts and argues that the Spirit given for empowerment and the soteriological gift of the Spirit are inseparable.

23. Menzies (1994: 107–10) and Shelton (1991: 15–32) also argue that the Spirit works prophetically in the infancy narratives with the result that those who speak bear witness to Jesus. For qualifications of their views, see Turner 1996: 140–65. Shelton rightly sees the continuity between the prophetic words uttered in Luke and those spoken in Acts, though he also underestimates the redemptive historical shift that occurred at Pentecost.

24. Fitzmyer (1981a: 357) says that "the child in Elizabeth's womb leaps prophetically."

25. "It refers here to the prophetic presence of God to Zechariah, manifest in the canticle that is to be uttered" (Fitzmyer 1981a: 382).

26. Menzies (1994: 120) rightly says that the work of the prophetic Spirit in Luke 1–2 signals that God's promises are now being fulfilled.

(Luke 2:26). The reference to revelation confirms the prophetic work of the Spirit in the declaration of God's word here. Simeon did not testify about his personal life. He confirmed that Jesus is God's agent of salvation, both for Jews and Gentiles. He also foreshadowed what is to come in Luke's Gospel, remarking that many will oppose the child Jesus. Even though the term "Spirit" is not used with reference to Anna, the Spirit's work probably is implied (Luke 2:36–38). She is called a "prophetess," and she proclaimed God's redemption.

If we take stock of the foregoing texts, we observe a close connection between the "filling" (*pimplēmi*) of the Spirit and prophecy. John the Baptist was a prophet of the Lord and filled with the Spirit from his mother's womb (Luke 1:15). Both Elizabeth and Zechariah were filled with the Spirit and prophesied (Luke 1:41, 67). The same pattern continues in Acts. When the 120 believers on the day of Pentecost were filled with the Spirit, they spoke in tongues (Acts 2:4).[27] They proclaimed "the mighty works of God" (Acts 2:11). Perhaps it is significant that the verb "fill" is not used on any other occasion when people speak in tongues in Acts. This is the only occasion in Acts in which those who speak in tongues are understood by the hearers, so that God's word is proclaimed in a comprehensible manner.

Later in the narrative the apostles were seized by the Sanhedrin and questioned about their activities. Peter defended their actions and was filled with the Spirit. He queried why they were under arrest for healing a man who was lame (Acts 4:8–9), testifying that Jesus is the crucified and risen Lord, the only Savior (Acts 4:10–12). Peter's spontaneous defense before the religious leaders represented a fulfillment of Jesus' promise that the Spirit would teach his disciples how to respond when they were prosecuted (Luke 12:11–12).[28] After Peter's defense, the religious leaders threateningly warned the disciples not to continue spreading the message about Jesus. The disciples gathered together and prayed. After prayer "they were all filled with the Holy Spirit and continued to speak the word of God with boldness" (Acts 4:31). Again, the filling of the Spirit leads to the proclamation of God's word, to testifying about what God has done in Christ. At Paul's conversion Ananias laid his hands on Paul, and the latter was filled with the Spirit (Acts 9:17). In the story line of Acts Paul's being filled with the Spirit led to the dissemination of the gospel to the ends of the earth. On the first missionary journey Elymas opposed the preaching of Paul and Barnabas. Paul, filled with the Spirit, struck Elymas blind and spoke the word of the Lord against him (Acts

27. The promise of the baptism of the Spirit in Acts 1:5 is fulfilled here (see Barrett 1994: 115). For the significance of Pentecost in general, see Dunn 1970a: 38–54. Pao (2000: 130–31) argues that the Jews gathered in Acts 2 represent the return of the exiles.

28. So also Barrett 1994: 226; Fitzmyer 1998: 300.

13:9–11). The filling of the Spirit immediately leads to an oracle of the Lord. In every instance the filling of the Spirit is related to bearing witness and speaking out the prophetic word.

The prophetic work of the Spirit is not limited to the verb "fill." We find a dramatic example in the ministry of Jesus. Jesus rejoiced in the Holy Spirit, giving thanks to God for his sovereignty and for the salvation of his disciples (Luke 10:21).[29] Luke emphasizes in particular here the work of the Spirit in Jesus' words. Since the Spirit is closely linked with the word in Luke-Acts, we are not surprised to see the Spirit's role in Scripture highlighted. For instance, the treachery of Judas was predicted by the OT Scripture, which the Spirit spoke through David (Acts 1:16–20; cf. Ps. 69:25; 109:8). In addition, the opposition faced by the church fulfills what the Spirit said through David (Acts 4:25–27; cf. Ps. 2:1–2). The words of Isaiah speak to the Jews of Paul's generation, and Paul attributed Isaiah's words to the Spirit (Acts 28:25–27; cf. Isa. 6:9–10).[30] The Holy Spirit's role in the writing of Scripture is one example of the alliance between the Spirit and the word. The Spirit speaks through the written word of Scripture, and the human authors of Scripture spoke their words under the aegis of the Holy Spirit.

The prophetic Spirit led the church as it spread the good news about Jesus Christ throughout the world. Luke often calls attention to the direction the Spirit gave his messengers as the gospel progressed from Jerusalem to the ends of the earth. The Spirit summoned Philip to go and address the Ethiopian eunuch while the latter was riding in his chariot and returning to Ethiopia (Acts 8:29). The incident is the means by which the Ethiopian heard the gospel and by which the saving message reached Ethiopia. Immediately the Spirit seized Philip, and from Azotus to Caesarea he proclaimed the good news about Jesus Christ (Acts 8:39–40). We note again that the Spirit's carrying Philip away is the means by which the gospel is proclaimed in new areas.

Luke considers the story of Cornelius to be one of the most significant accounts in the spread of the gospel, for Luke tells the story twice, taking up valuable space to communicate this account (Acts 10:1–48; 11:1–18). When the men from Cornelius appeared at the house of Simon the Tanner, the Spirit instructed Peter to go with the men and to visit Cornelius and those gathered with him (Acts 10:19–20; 11:12). The Spirit's speaking to Peter should not be construed as a private existential experience. The Spirit directed Peter because he was the means by which the Gentiles would hear the gospel. The point of the story is not the Spirit's private

29. Bock (1996: 1009) sees also a reference to the fulfillment of God's saving promises.

30. "Belief in the inspiration of the OT is plainly expressed. The words were given *through* Isaiah but the actual speaker was the Holy Spirit" (Barrett 1998: 1244).

revelation to Peter. The Spirit speaks to Peter so that he will bring the gospel to the nations. The first missionary journey of Paul and Barnabas commenced when the Holy Spirit summoned Paul and Barnabas to leave Antioch and to travel about proclaiming the gospel to Gentiles (Acts 13:2).[31] When we consider these three texts, an interesting pattern emerges. In every case the Spirit spoke to his messengers so that they brought the gospel into a new arena. The proclamation of the gospel to the Ethiopian eunuch expands the preaching of the gospel beyond the confines of the Jews, for he likely was a God-fearer. Peter spoke the good news to Cornelius and his friends, who were uncircumcised (Acts 11:3; cf. 10:28). Paul and Barnabas planned the first intentional mission to the Gentiles. Clearly, the Spirit directed his people in the fulfillment of redemptive history, in the extension of the gospel beyond the confines of the Jewish people.

On two occasions the Spirit hindered the speaking of the gospel. As Paul, Silas, and Timothy traveled through Phrygia and Galatia, the Spirit restrained them from preaching the gospel (Acts 16:6). Similarly, they tried to go to Bithynia to spread the word, but the Spirit prevented them from doing so (Acts 16:7). Both of these texts are rather mysterious, and more information about the Spirit's restraining and hindering would be illuminating. In the story line of Acts, however, this restraint becomes the means by which the gospel entered Europe. Immediately after these events Paul has his "Macedonian vision," from which his traveling band concluded that God called them to cross the Aegean Sea (Acts 16:9–10). Paul and his companions traveled to Europe, and the European mission became a stage by which Paul would ultimately end up in Rome (cf. Acts 19:21; 28:11–31). Even the Spirit's hindering work, therefore, becomes the means by which the Spirit directs his messengers to specific localities.

Agabus, as a prophet of the Lord, proclaimed God's word to the church. The Spirit revealed to him a coming famine, and he shared that word with the church in Antioch (Acts 11:27–30). This Spirit-given word was communicated so that the church could send assistance to the poor in Judea. Perhaps Luke emphasizes here that God used the famine as a means of binding together the hearts of Jewish believers and the newly converted Gentiles in Antioch. Paul likely has in mind the Holy Spirit in the constraint that he felt to travel to Jerusalem, even though the Spirit had revealed to him that sufferings awaited him wherever he traveled (Acts 20:22–23). Paul's visit to Jerusalem was related to his mission, and his ultimate destination was Rome (Acts 19:21). Furthermore, the

---

31. As Barrett (1994: 605) says, the Spirit speaks "presumably through one of the prophets."

spread of the gospel through Paul was bound up with his suffering (Acts 9:15–16). The suffering that he endured was one of the means that God used to spread the good news to the ends of the earth. Hence, the Spirit's direction is again related to the proclamation of the word and to mission.

Interestingly, some encouraged Paul not to go to Jerusalem, anticipating the sufferings that he would encounter (Acts 21:4). Luke adds that they said this "through the Spirit." Agabus prophesied that the Jews would bind Paul and hand him over to the Gentiles (Acts 21:11). Clearly, Agabus spoke as a prophet of the Lord on this occasion. He used prophetic symbolism in binding his own hands and feet, imitating here the kind of prophetic symbolism that we find in the OT (e.g., Isa. 20:1–6; Jer. 13:1–11; Ezek. 4:1–5:17).[32] Furthermore, the words of Agabus reflect a prophetic formula: "Thus says the Holy Spirit" (Acts 21:11). The word *tade* ("these things") is used repeatedly in the OT to introduce the word of the Lord (cf. also Rev. 2:1, 8, 12, 18; 3:1, 7, 14).[33] Some have suggested that Agabus was mistaken, for the Jews did not literally bind Paul and hand him over (*paradōsousin* [Acts 21:11]) to the Romans.[34] Such a judgment demands too literal a fulfillment of prophetic words. In the Lukan perspective the prophecy is fulfilled, for Paul used some of the words of Agabus in describing his own arrest: "I was delivered [*paredothēn*] as a prisoner from Jerusalem into the hands of the Romans" (Acts 28:17). A difficult problem arose in that Paul was urged by some "through the Spirit" (though Agabus is not named specifically) to desist from traveling to Jerusalem (Acts 21:4), whereas Paul felt constrained by the Spirit to go to Jerusalem (Acts 20:22–23) and ignored their advice (Acts 21:12–14). No easy solution to these two apparently contrary words from the Spirit is available. In each case the Spirit said that Paul would suffer. At least two different solutions are possible. First, it could be claimed that Paul wrongly ignored the advice not to travel to Jerusalem. Or second, perhaps the admonition that Paul should not go to Jerusalem was not truly from the Spirit. A variant of the latter solution seems to be the most promising. The prophecy that Paul would face suffering in Jerusalem was accurate and Spirit-inspired. However, the conclusion that people drew from the prophecy, that therefore Paul should not travel to Jerusalem, was mistaken and did not derive from the Spirit.[35] Nor should we fail to see that the Spirit's direction here still fits with the story line

---

32. So also Haenchen 1971: 602; Barrett 1998: 995; Fitzmyer 1998: 689.

33. So Haenchen 1971: 602.

34. So Grudem 1988a: 96–102; Barrett 1998: 995–96 (Barrett argues that such accuracy was of little concern to Luke).

35. Note here the judgment of Barrett (1998: 990): "Luke does not express himself clearly. His words taken strictly would mean either that Paul was deliberately disobedient to the

of Acts. Paul's imprisonment in Jerusalem fulfilled the promise that he would proclaim the gospel before kings, Israel, and the Gentiles (Acts 9:15). As a result of his arrest, Paul proclaimed the gospel near the temple (Acts 22:1–21), in the Sanhedrin (Acts 22:30–23:9), before the governor Felix (Acts 24), and in the presence of both the governor Felix and King Agrippa (Acts 25:1–26:32). In addition, he gained the opportunity of proclaiming the gospel to some Jews in Rome (Acts 28:17–31).

The prophetic Spirit also led the church to consolidate the mission to which it was called. In one of Luke's summary statements he observes that the church in the regions of Judea, Galilee, and Samaria was "walking . . . in the comfort of the Holy Spirit" (Acts 9:31). Such living in the consolation of the Spirit is linked with the expansion of the church in the areas noted. The gospel was taking hold in these regions, fulfilling Jesus' words in Acts 1:8. When the church met in Jerusalem to consider whether circumcision would be required of Gentiles, Peter reminded them of what happened to Cornelius and his friends. God gave them the Spirit without the distinctive badge of covenant identity (Acts 15:8). Hence, the final decision not to impose circumcision on Gentiles reflected the leading of the Spirit himself (Acts 15:28).[36] Certainly the decision on circumcision enhanced the spread of the gospel to the Gentiles, securing the truth that the gospel was one of grace. Finally, the appointment of leaders in the church was under the aegis of the Spirit. Or, more precisely, the Spirit himself designated those who would serve as overseers in the Ephesian church (Acts 20:28).[37] The way the church was ordered and structured also was under the Spirit's direction.

LIVING IN THE SPIRIT

Luke also refers to those who live a life in accord with the Spirit. The adjective "full" (*plērēs*) denotes someone who is characterized by life in the Spirit.[38] People can be "full" of other qualities besides the Spirit, and in every instance what they are "full" of characterizes their lives. The seven men chosen to assist in the matter of Hellenistic widows were full of the Spirit and wisdom (Acts 6:3). Stephen particularly stands out, and he is said to be full of the Spirit, faith, grace, and power (Acts 6:5, 8; 7:55). Perhaps such a designation is linked to Stephen's powerful proclamation

---

will of God or that the Spirit was mistaken in the guidance given. It is unthinkable that Luke intended either of these." Barrett goes on to propose the solution offered above.

36. Barrett (1998: 744) remarks, "In view of the importance of the decision this must be regarded as the outstanding example of Luke's insistence that all developments in the church's life were directed by the Spirit."

37. See Barrett 1998: 974–75.

38. On the use of the terms *plērēs*, *plēroō*, and *pimplēmi* in Luke-Acts, see Turner 1996: 165–69.

of the gospel.[39] Barnabas is described as being full of the Holy Spirit and faith (Acts 11:24), and such a life cannot be separated from his exhortation.[40] Similarly, Dorcas was full of good works and mercy for the poor (Acts 9:36). Conversely, Elymas was "full of all deceit and villainy" (Acts 13:10). We saw that the verb "fill" (*pimplēmi*) is used when people are filled with the Spirit and speak out God's word. But the term "full" (*plērēs*) is used less specifically, denoting those whose lives were dominated by the Spirit—those who lived in a way that was pleasing to God by the power of the Spirit and those who spoke forth God's word as well.[41] Similarly, another verb with the meaning "fill" (*plēroō*) falls under the same semantic range as the noun. Hence, Luke observes that the disciples were "filled" (*plēroō*) with joy and the Holy Spirit (Acts 13:52). On the other hand, the heart of Ananias was filled by Satan (Acts 5:3). We see the same usage of the verb *plēroō* by Paul: people are filled with qualities such as goodness, joy, peace, and righteousness or wickedness (cf. Rom. 1:29; 15:13–14; 2 Cor. 7:4; Phil. 1:11; Col. 1:9; 2 Tim. 1:4).

Others resisted the Spirit and failed to heed his instruction. Both Ananias and Sapphira tested the Holy Spirit by lying about how much they contributed to the church (Acts 5:1–11). Luke emphasizes that they personally sinned against the Spirit. Ananias lied "to the Holy Spirit" (Acts 5:3),[42] and both husband and wife "agreed together to test the Spirit of the Lord" (Acts 5:9). Stephen's opponents "could not withstand the wisdom and the Spirit with which he was speaking" (Acts 6:10). Stephen claimed that his accusers resisted the Holy Spirit, replicating the history of Israel (Acts 7:51). We should put the blasphemy against the Spirit (Luke 12:10) in the same category. As we noted in examining Matthew and Mark, the blasphemy represents an obstinate refusal to acknowledge goodness in the works of Jesus.

DISPENSATION OF THE SPIRIT

Jesus was the bearer of the Spirit, but he is also the one who dispenses the Spirit. He is the one who pours out the Spirit upon his people. Luke 11:13 says that the Father will "give the Holy Spirit to those who ask him," but we know from the rest of Luke-Acts that the Spirit will be given by the Father *through* Jesus. Only when Jesus was exalted to the right hand of the Father would the Spirit be poured out. The conclusion of Luke implies that the gift of the Spirit is vitally connected with Jesus' suffering,

---

39. So Shelton 1991: 137–38.

40. Shelton 1991: 138.

41. As Turner (1996: 408–12) observes, such texts indicate that the Spirit in Acts not only empowers but also plays a role in the ethical transformation of believers.

42. See the comments by Barrett (1994: 266) on the deity of the Spirit. So also Fitzmyer 1998: 323.

death, and resurrection (Luke 24:46–49).[43] The message of repentance in Jesus' name is to be proclaimed to all nations, but the disciples must not leave Jerusalem until Jesus sends "the promise of my Father upon you." Only then will they be "clothed with power from on high" (Luke 24:49) and receive the strength needed to bear witness throughout the world. Acts resumes where the Gospel of Luke left off, and Jesus admonished his disciples not to leave Jerusalem until they receive "the promise of the Father,"[44] which is identified as the baptism of the Holy Spirit (Acts 1:4–5). The receiving of the Spirit, as at the conclusion of Luke, is necessary for proclaiming the gospel to the ends of the earth (Acts 1:8). Before the Spirit is poured out, however, Jesus must ascend into heaven (Acts 1:9–11). The Spirit can be given only when Jesus is exalted as Lord and Christ (Acts 2:36), sitting at the right hand of the Father on the throne of David (Acts 2:30, 34–35). Jesus, as the one exalted to God's right hand, received the Spirit from the Father and in turn poured out this same Spirit on his disciples (Acts 2:33). The Spirit was given only after Jesus was exalted, so that Jesus would be prized as Lord and Christ by all nations.[45] Luke does not focus on a diffuse and general testimony to the truth about God through the Spirit. Rather, the Spirit's being given after Jesus' exaltation and ministry always points people to Jesus as the crucified, risen, and exalted Lord. Forgiveness of sins and the gift of the Spirit come only in the name of Jesus (Luke 24:47; Acts 2:38), for there is salvation in no other name (Acts 4:12).

Jesus' gift of the Spirit is described with different verbs in Acts.[46] We have noted already that those who spoke in tongues in Acts 2:4 are said to have been "filled" (*pimplēmi*) with the Spirit. Various other verbs are used to denote the dispensing of the Spirit, including "receive" (*lambanō*), "pour out" (*ekcheō* or *ekchynnō*), "give" (*didōmi*), "come upon" (*ercho-*

43. Menzies (1994: 159–61), to the contrary, argues that Jesus promises ongoing experiences of the prophetic Spirit, not a once-for-all gift.

44. Menzies (1994: 168–72) thinks that the reference is to the prophetic Spirit, who empowers for witness per Joel 2:28. However, the promise here refers to the giving of the Spirit, not the restoration of Israel (contra Penney 1997: 71).

45. It does not follow from this that the Spirit was not present with the disciples at all before Pentecost. Nor is it necessarily the case that the disciples who were called by Jesus first became believers at Pentecost. The disciples lived in the shadowy period when God's promises were beginning to be fulfilled, but the end-time gift of the Spirit had not yet been poured out in its fullness (see Turner 1996: 318–47). Turner (1996: 353), however, is not convinced that Pentecost denotes the coming of the time of salvation "at least for the disciples." It seems to me that epochal significance of Pentecost is maintained when we recognize some degree of fuzziness for the disciples of Jesus who lived on the cusp of fulfillment before Pentecost arrived.

46. See Hamilton 2006b: 183–203.

mai/eperchomai), "fall upon" (*epipiptō*), and "baptize" (*baptizō*). We will examine each of these verbs in order.[47]

We begin with the verb "receive" (*lambanō*). Jesus promised his disciples that they "will receive power when the Holy Spirit has come upon you" (Acts 1:8). In this context the emphasis is on the power to spread the gospel to the ends of the earth.[48] The promise that Jesus gave here clearly was fulfilled on the day of Pentecost when the disciples received the Spirit. Jesus himself received the Spirit, which in turn he poured out on his disciples (Acts 2:33). On the day of Pentecost Peter proclaimed the gospel, concluding with a call for repentance and baptism. Those who turn to Jesus "will receive the gift of the Holy Spirit" (Acts 2:38).[49] Peter and John prayed for the Samaritans so that they "might receive the Holy Spirit" (Acts 8:15), and as a result they received the Spirit (Acts 8:17). This text is unusual, for the Samaritans had already believed in Jesus Christ and yet had not received the Holy Spirit. No other example exists in which people put their faith in Jesus Christ and yet failed to receive the Spirit. Peter observed that Cornelius and those gathered at his house had received the Spirit in the same way as the early disciples (Acts 10:47). Finally, Paul asked the Ephesian twelve if they received the Spirit when they first believed (Acts 19:2). Obviously they had not, since they responded that they did not know about Paul's teaching about the Spirit.

The Holy Spirit is also said to be "poured out" (*ekcheō* or *ekchynnō*). On the day of Pentecost Peter quoted Joel 2:28–32. The prophecy that the Spirit would be poured out on all without distinction, Peter claimed, was being fulfilled (Acts 2:17–18). Certainly, Peter referred to the events that just transpired with the 120 believers on the day of Pentecost, which attracted the crowd that he addressed. Later in the same account Peter maintained that the Spirit whom Jesus received from the Father had now been poured out on his followers (Acts 2:33). The pouring out of the Spirit is undeniable because of what those in Jerusalem see and hear (Acts 2:33). Again, the pouring out of the Spirit refers to the events that occurred on Pentecost. The Spirit was also poured out on Cornelius

---

47. Pao (2000: 132–33) argues that the times of refreshing in Acts 3:20 also refer to the gift of the Spirit, and Isa. 32:15 functions as the text Luke draws upon.

48. Pao (2000: 94) is likely correct that "the ends of the earth" focuses on the inclusion of Gentiles, though such a view does not rule out geographical extension as well.

49. The claim by Menzies (1994: 203–4) that Acts 2:38 refers to the prophetic Spirit rather than the soteriological gift of the Spirit is incorrect. It demonstrates that he is forcing his theory, that the Spirit always refers to the prophetic role of the Spirit, onto the text. Indeed, Turner correctly argues that Acts 2:38 presents the norm for receiving the Spirit at conversion (1996: 358–59).

and his friends, and this is attested by their speaking in tongues (Acts 10:45–46).

God also "gives" (*didōmi*) the Spirit to his people. The Father's heart is full of kindness, and he gives the Holy Spirit to those who entreat him (Luke 11:13). The Spirit was given to the Samaritans by means of the laying on of the apostles' hands, and Simon, motivated by a desire for power, asked if he could bestow the same gift if he paid the requisite price to the apostles (Acts 8:18–19). Peter defended eating with and baptizing Cornelius and his comrades because God gave them the same gift of the Spirit that he had given the disciples on Pentecost (Acts 11:17). The terms of entrance for Gentiles were the subject of considerable controversy at the Jerusalem Council. Peter played a major role in the final decision made, for he recalled what happened when he preached the gospel to Cornelius and his friends. God gave Cornelius and his friends the Spirit without requiring circumcision and on the basis of faith alone (Acts 15:7–11). Hence, salvation is a gift of God's grace alone.

The Holy Spirit is portrayed as "coming upon" (*erchomai/eperchomai*) people. For instance, the Spirit came upon Mary, so that she conceived a child without having had sexual relations (Luke 1:35). Jesus assured the disciples that the Holy Spirit would come upon them, and that they would disseminate the gospel to the ends of the earth (Acts 1:8). Jesus' words about the Spirit's coming reached their fulfillment on the day of Pentecost when the Spirit was dispensed to those gathered in the upper room in Jerusalem. The Spirit came upon the Ephesian twelve when Paul laid his hands on them, and as a consequence they spoke in tongues and prophesied (Acts 19:6).

The Holy Spirit is said to "fall upon" (*epipiptō*) disciples. As Peter preached the word, suddenly the Holy Spirit fell on Cornelius and those gathered with him (Acts 10:44). Peter reflected on the event in Jerusalem when he responded to those who criticized him for eating with Gentiles. He remarked that the Spirit fell on them as he delivered the word, just as the Spirit fell on the disciples on the day of Pentecost (Acts 11:15).

Jesus also baptized (*baptizō*) his disciples with the Holy Spirit. John the Baptist declared that he baptized only with water, but Jesus "will baptize you with the Holy Spirit and fire" (Luke 3:16). Jesus reflected on the same reality after his resurrection (Acts 1:4–5), maintaining that the promise of the Father is to be identified with the baptism of the Spirit. Though the subject of the verb for "baptize" is not specified here, presumably Jesus is still the one who baptizes with the Spirit, as in Luke 3:16. Further, it is obvious that this promise was fulfilled at Pentecost in Acts 2 when 120 believers received the Spirit, even though the verb "baptize" is not repeated in that narrative.[50] Peter considered the same promise of the baptism of the Spirit in Acts 11 when he defended himself against charges of eating with the uncircumcised. When the Spirit fell on Cornelius and his cohorts, Peter recalled the Lord's promise that his disciples would be baptized with the Spirit (Acts 11:16). Just as Jesus baptized the 120 believers with the Spirit on Pentecost, so too he baptized Gentiles such as Cornelius with the Spirit, and this is evident because the latter spoke in tongues.

If we examine the verbs related to the dispensing of the Spirit, we see that they are mainly used with reference to four main events:[51] the giving of the Spirit at Pentecost (Luke 3:16; Acts 1:5, 8; 2:17–18, 33; 11:15–16), to the Samaritans (Acts 8:15–19), to Cornelius and his friends (Acts 10:44–45, 47; 11:15–17; 15:8), and to the Ephesian twelve (Acts 19:6–7). Another way of summarizing the evidence is to note which verbs are used with these four events: (1) "receive" (*lambanō*): Pentecost (Acts 1:8; 2:33); Samaria (Acts 8:15, 17, 19); Cornelius (Acts 10:47); the Ephesian twelve (Acts 19:2); (2) "pour out" (*ekcheō* or *ekchynnō*): Pentecost (Acts 2:17–18, 33); Cornelius (Acts 10:45); (3) "give" (*didōmi*): Pentecost (Acts 11:17; 15:8);[52] Samaria (Acts 8:18); Cornelius (Acts 11:17; 15:8); (4) "come upon" (*erchomai/eperchomai*): Pentecost (Acts 1:8); the Ephesian twelve (Acts 19:6); (5) "fall upon" (*epipiptō*): Pentecost (Acts 11:15); Cornelius (Acts 10:44; 11:15); (6) "baptize" (*baptizō*): Pentecost (Acts 1:5; 11:16); Cornelius (Acts 11:16). The verbs overlap in meaning, and so the omission of a verb with one of the events is not necessarily significant. We see the greatest variety of verbs with reference to Pentecost and the Cornelius event, but this is explained by the relative length of the narrative of these two events. The account of the Ephesian twelve has the fewest verbs, but this is reasonable because it is the shortest narrative among the four.

What is the significance of these four events for Luke's theology of the Holy Spirit? Some have argued that Luke's theology of the Spirit is tied to the charismatic gift of the Spirit that empowers for ministry.[53]

50. See Barrett 1994: 78–79, 115. The reference to "tongues as of fire" in Acts 2 signifies a theophany (Beale 2004: 204–8).

51. The exceptions are: Jesus receiving the Spirit at his exaltation (Acts 2:33); the promise that those who repent will receive the Spirit (Acts 2:38); the Spirit coming upon Mary for her virginal conception (Luke 1:35); the Spirit being given to those who ask the Father (Luke 11:13). The last text clearly fits within the paradigm of the four events discussed here. Jesus receives the Spirit when he is exalted, so he can pour it out on his people, and so that fits nicely with the pattern established here as well.

52. Since Peter says that God gave them the same gift as he gave to those on Pentecost, he teaches that the Spirit was given at Pentecost as well.

53. For a defense of this view, which makes the case from intertestamental Jewish literature and from Luke-Acts, see Menzies (1994), who argues that the emphasis on the

We saw in the discussion of the prophetic Spirit that such a conception of the Spirit certainly plays a major role in Luke-Acts. Even in the four accounts that we have just examined the notion that the Spirit equips for ministry is present. When the Spirit comes at Pentecost, the disciples will receive power to bear witness to the ends of the earth (Acts 1:8; cf. Luke 24:49). Furthermore, the Pentecost account includes one verb that I omitted in the foregoing analysis. When Jesus baptized the disciples with the Spirit, they were "filled" with the Spirit and spoke in tongues (Acts 2:4). Their "filling" and tongue-speaking were for the purpose of ministry, since a crowd gathered and Peter proclaimed the gospel. We noted above that the use of the verb "fill" (*pimplēmi*) in virtually every case is for the purpose of speaking forth God's word.

The Lukan account does not suggest a rigid separation between the Spirit's empowering and regenerating ministry in these four accounts.[54] The Pentecost narrative and the use of the verb "fill" indicate that empowerment for ministry cannot be washed out of the story. Still, it seems that the main theme in these four events, particularly in the last three accounts, is that those described are inducted into the people of God. The coming of the Spirit in Acts 8; 10; 19 was not primarily to denote empowering for charismatic ministry but rather to signify that those who received the Spirit belonged to the people of God. The emblem of their membership was their reception of the Spirit. A piece of evidence that supports the case being made here is that the verb "fill" is used only with the Pentecost account and does not appear in the stories about Samaria, Cornelius, and the Ephesian twelve. In the Pentecost story we have an overlap between the themes of empowerment for ministry and induction into the people of God. The remaining three accounts emphasize that various groups of people truly belong to the church of Jesus Christ.

The Pentecost account, then, is not only about receiving charismatic power;[55] it also represents the inception of the Spirit-endowed people of God.[56] Baptism represents initiation language, so that Jesus baptizing

---

soteriological Spirit comes from Paul. See also Stronstad 1984; Shelton 1991: 125–56 (he argues that in some instances the categories are blurred, but the emphasis is on empowerment). But against Menzies, Turner (1996: 82–138) convincingly shows that the Spirit in Judaism cannot be confined to the prophetic Spirit; the Spirit energizes works of power and produces ethical change. So also Penney (1997: 53–54), who argues as well that the Spirit is the agent of miracles.

54. See Turner 1998: 337–47. Barrett (1994: 115) argues that Luke's view of the Spirit is such that it is difficult to see any consistent pattern.

55. Menzies (1994: 173–201) is correct in claiming that the Spirit empowers for witness at Pentecost, but he wrongly posits an either-or here, so that he eliminates any reference to the soteriological work of the Spirit.

56. This is particularly emphasized in Dunn 1970a: 38–54; Barrett 1994: 108; Fitzmyer 1998: 233.

with the Spirit (Acts 1:5) indicates the commencement of the new age of the Spirit (Acts 2:17–18, 33; cf. Joel 2:28). God gave the Spirit to the believers at Pentecost for the first time (Acts 11:17; 15:8), so that Peter saw continuity between the giving of the Spirit at Pentecost and the gift of the Spirit given to Cornelius and his friends. Both groups were baptized into the new age of the Spirit.

Cornelius and his friends received the message by which they were saved from sin and judgment (Acts 11:14). Their reception of the Spirit did not involve ministry to others, though doubtless that followed.[57] What Luke highlights here, however, is their inclusion into the people of God. Circumcised Jews avoided eating with these Gentiles because they were not part of God's people and did not observe purity laws (Acts 11:2–3). Peter's vision about eating unclean animals, then, relates directly to the main point in the account (Acts 10:9–16).[58] With the coming of the Spirit and the new age, the food laws of the OT were no longer required for God's people. God had now declared these foods clean (Acts 10:15). What is decisive for entrance into the people of God is the presence of the Spirit. Luke is emphatic about the coming of the Spirit on Cornelius and his friends. The Spirit "fell on" them without any summons to repentance and faith (Acts 10:44; 11:15) by Peter. It was evident that the Spirit was "poured out" on these Gentiles (Acts 10:45).

Peter, in defending his conduct to those who questioned how he ate with the uncircumcised, acknowledged that it was not his intention to invite Cornelius to be a member of the church without circumcision. God "gave" them the Spirit, unbidden by Peter (Acts 11:17; 15:8). Clearly, Jesus had baptized them with the Spirit, just as he had the 120 believers on the day of Pentecost (Acts 11:16). Cornelius and his friends had received the Spirit in the same manner as those present on Pentecost (Acts 10:47). Hence, Peter concluded that the initiation rite of water baptism should be given to them because the presence of the Spirit indicated that they were genuinely believers (Acts 10:47–48). The presence of the Spirit, not baptism, is the decisive mark that one belongs to the church, for Peter applied baptism to those who clearly had received the Spirit. The evidence in Acts that Cornelius and his friends had received

---

57. Rightly Dunn 1970a: 70–82; Turner 1996: 378–87. Contra Menzies (1994: 215–18), who obfuscates the issue by discussing whether receiving the Spirit precedes repentance, or whether cleansing of the heart is equivalent to the gift of the Spirit, or whether the Spirit is the means or evidence of conversion. These are interesting questions, but one could agree with Menzies on every point and the main truth of the text still stands: the fact that Cornelius and his friends received the Spirit demonstrates that they are Christians, not that they are now empowered to bear witness. In any case, however, Menzies wrongly downplays the Spirit's role in conversion (see Turner 1996: 424–27, 435–37).

58. On the significance of Acts 10:1–11:18 relative to the law, see Seifrid 1987: 41–44.

the Spirit is that they spoke in tongues the same way the 120 believers did on Pentecost (Acts 10:46; cf. 11:15–16). The function of speaking in tongues at Pentecost was to bear witness to God's great works (Acts 2:11) and to provide a bridgehead for the proclamation of the gospel. It also functioned as a reversal of the confusion of languages at Babel (Gen. 11:1–9), anticipating the consummation of the age when all will understand one another.[59] In the case of Cornelius and his comrades, tongue-speaking did not furnish an opportunity for witness and ministry; rather, it confirmed to Peter and the other Jews present that these Gentiles had truly received the Spirit.[60] The Jews were hesitant to allow Gentiles to become members of God's people without circumcision, but the events accompanying Peter's visit to Cornelius verified that circumcision was not required for entrance into the people of God.

The account of the Ephesian twelve (Acts 19:1–7) bears some similarities with the Cornelius account. These twelve disciples were still living, so to speak, under the old covenant. They had not yet received the Holy Spirit (Acts 19:2)—the mark of living in the new age of redemption.[61] They were living in the transitional period of redemptive history because they had only received John's baptism. Acts 19:4 suggests that they had not yet believed in the one to whom the Baptist directed people, Jesus Christ. The pentecostal Spirit had not yet been poured out on them. Upon hearing the good news about Jesus Christ, they put their faith in him and were baptized. Their baptism signified their induction into the people of God. The baptism with water was accompanied by the coming of the Holy Spirit at the laying on of Paul's hands. They spoke in tongues and prophesied to verify that they had received the pentecostal Spirit. The narrative emphasizes that the outpoured Spirit comes only to those who put their faith in Jesus as the exalted Lord. Perhaps Luke also emphasizes that Jesus is superior to the Baptist, just as he did in the birth narratives (Luke 1:1–2:52). John's baptism with water cannot compare with the blessings introduced by Jesus' baptism with the Spirit (Luke 3:16).

The fourth incident is quite unusual. The Samaritans believed in the Lord Jesus, received water baptism, and yet they failed to receive the Spirit (Acts 8:9–13). This phenomenon may be interpreted in various ways.[62]

---

59. So Seccombe 1998: 352; Beale 2004: 201–3; contra Haenchen 1971: 174–75.

60. So Polhill 1992: 263–64; Barrett 1994: 529; Fitzmyer 1998: 467.

61. See especially Dunn 1970a: 83–89; cf. Turner 1996: 388–97. Hartman (1997: 138) maintains that they were not truly disciples because they had not received or known the Spirit (cf. Marshall 1980a: 306–7). For the contrary view, see Menzies 1994: 218–25; Fitzmyer 1998: 642–43. Barrett (1998: 894) argues that they had not heard at their baptism that the Spirit would also be bequeathed, and so they believed that they would receive nothing further than forgiveness of sins.

62. For a survey of options, see Turner 1996: 360–75.

(1) One might derive from this a two-stage experience in the Christian faith,[63] or one might say that this demonstrates that the Spirit in Luke-Acts empowers for mission and is not fundamentally an evidence of salvation.[64] First, people believe in Jesus Christ and are baptized with water. Second, they receive the Holy Spirit.[65]

(2) Another possibility is that the faith of the Samaritans was not initially genuine.[66] Their faith could be compared to the faith of Simon, which, as the narrative unfolds, is shown to be fraudulent (Acts 8:13–24). The Samaritans only truly believed when they received the Holy Spirit. Still, this view is unlikely.[67]

(3) The account could be interpreted as an exceptional incident that is recounted precisely because it is unique.[68] This suggestion seems to be the most convincing. Luke's comment in Acts 8:16 indicates that what occurred in Samaria was anomalous.[69] The verb "receive" (*lambanō*) is used three times with reference to the Holy Spirit (Acts 8:15, 17, 19), and the verb "fall upon" (*epipiptō*) once (Acts 8:16). Since Luke uses the verb "receive" here, there are no grounds for thinking that the Samaritans already had the Spirit when they first believed, and that they merely lacked the power of the Spirit. The gift of the Spirit is received at conversion, as Peter clarified in his sermon on Pentecost (Acts 2:38). The text clearly teaches that the Samaritans received the Spirit only when the apostles laid hands on them,[70] and that the Spirit was not in them at all before the laying on of apostolic hands. Further, it is difficult to believe that the account intends to teach a distinction between believing and a later reception of the Spirit with the laying on of hands. No other example of such an interval exists in Acts. In every other instance the Spirit is received when people repent and believe (Acts 2:38; 10:44–48; 11:15–18; 15:7–11; 19:4–7).[71] Indeed, nowhere else in the NT is the gift of the Spirit separated from believing in Christ by some interval.

---

63. So Ervin 1984: 25–40.

64. So Menzies 1994: 204–13.

65. For the weaknesses in this view, see Turner 1996: 371–73.

66. Dunn 1970a: 55–72.

67. Rightly Menzies 1994: 207–10; Turner 1996: 362–67 (though I disagree with them regarding the authenticity of Simon's faith).

68. See Polhill 1992: 217–18.

69. So Turner 1996: 360. See also Turner 1996: 373–75 (though Turner is hesitant to provide an explanation for the anomaly).

70. Luke does not teach that laying on of hands is a prerequisite to receiving the Spirit, for in Acts 10:44 the Spirit is given without the laying on of hands. As Barrett (1994: 412) says, we probably have a unique case here.

71. Jervell (1996: 45) says, "The idea of the Spirit as the distinguishing mark of the people of God permeates the whole of Acts." However, Jervell (1996: 45–46) de-emphasizes the newness of the gift of the Spirit in Acts and hence flattens the difference between the OT and the NT.

The key to the narrative is the requirement that Peter and John come and lay hands on the Samaritans before they can receive the Spirit (Acts 8:14–17). Philip, one of the seven (Acts 6:5) and a different person than the apostle Philip (cf. Acts 8:2), could not dispense the Spirit because he was not one of the apostles. Why must the Samaritans receive the Spirit as it is mediated through the apostolic laying on of hands? The laying on of hands is not required in every instance, for the Spirit fell on Cornelius and his friends without the imposition of hands (Acts 10:44–48). The most satisfying answer is that the apostles were needed to mediate the Spirit, so that the Samaritan church would not branch off from the Jerusalem church.[72] The church was one church, and God did not give the Samaritans the Spirit apart from the apostles, so that they would not form their own "denomination." The Samaritans had a long history in which they were separate from the Jews, worshiping, for example, on Mount Gerizim instead of in Jerusalem, and prizing the Pentateuch instead of the entirety of the OT. John Hyrcanus destroyed their temple on Mount Gerizim during his reign (134–104 BC). The tension between the Jews and the Samaritans is evident also in the NT (Luke 9:51–56; 10:33; 17:16; John 4:9; 8:48; cf. Acts 1:8; 9:31).

Since the Spirit is always given when people believe, the Lukan narrative would naturally provoke questions in the minds of readers, for it is unheard of for people to believe and not receive the Spirit. How can such a phenomenon be explained? The best answer is that God withheld the Spirit on this one occasion to prevent a breach between the Jews and Samaritans, granting the Spirit only through the hands of the apostles, so that the Samaritan church would not split off from Jerusalem.[73] The other possibility, as noted, is that the belief of the Samaritans was originally inauthentic. There are good grounds in the text, of course, to think that Simon's faith was not genuine, and it is possible that the Samaritans should be estimated similarly. The view fails to convince, however, for the point of the account is that the rest of the Samaritans are to be distinguished from Simon. Nor is there any clear evidence that the initial belief of the Samaritans was a sham. Rather, Luke informs us that they "had received the word of God" (Acts 8:14) and had "been baptized" with water in Jesus' name (Acts 8:16). Hence, the best solution seems to be that God uniquely separated the giving of the Spirit from belief.

I conclude, then, that the primary purpose for the granting of the Spirit at Pentecost, to the Samaritans, to Cornelius and his friends, and

72. So, for example, Pao 2000: 129; Schnabel 2004a: 680. Barrett (1994: 410) thinks that this answer is a possibility but not a certainty.
73. So Seccombe 1998: 359.

to the Ephesian twelve is to testify that those who receive the Spirit are members of the people of God. The pouring out of the Spirit signifies that the new age has commenced, and the giving of the Spirit fits with the missionary character of Luke-Acts. Membership in the people of God is not confined to the Jews; it includes Samaritans and Gentiles. Luke sees in the dispensation of the Spirit the widening mission of the church and the spread of the gospel of Jesus Christ, for in every case the gift of the Spirit is tied to the message of Jesus Christ as the crucified and risen Lord. I am not arguing that a ministry dimension is completely lacking in these four events, for the disciples at Pentecost also bore witness to the gospel of Christ. Still, it seems that the primary purpose was to certify that those who received the Spirit belonged to God's people.

TRINITARIAN TRACES

When we consider Luke-Acts, we see some significant indications that the being of God is complex and must be understood in terms of three-ness and oneness. Indeed, Rowe claims that "the question of the identity of God in the narrative of Luke-Acts compels us to speak in trinitarian terms."[74] He proceeds to say, "The necessity of speaking of the one God in a threefold way is the response to the pressure exerted upon the reader by the biblical narrative itself."[75] Luke has no texts regarding the Trinity that are as explicit as the baptismal formula in Matt. 28:19. We do see the same text about Jesus' baptism, the descent of the Spirit as a dove, and the Father's voice that was noted in Matthew and Mark (see Luke 3:22).[76] In the birth narrative the Spirit plays a key role in Jesus' conception, and yet he also is distinct from God.[77] Luke also depicts the Spirit in personal ways. Often we are told that the Spirit "spoke" through prophecy or in Scripture or in directing those who proclaimed the gospel.[78] God is also said to have spoken (Luke 1:45), and Jesus gave directions to Paul (Acts 22:17–19), suggesting that the Spirit performs actions carried out by the Father and the Son.

---

74. Rowe 2003: 5.

75. Rowe 2003: 6. Rowe (2003: 17–19) also argues that the ambiguity regarding the word "Lord" in Luke 1:76; 3:4 and elsewhere in Luke-Acts functions as evidence that Jesus and God were not clearly distinguished as to their status. As Rowe observes, a number of studies in Luke-Acts admit that ambiguity between God and Christ is common (Fitzmyer 1981a: 385; Jones 1974: 91; Cadbury 1933: 359). Against Fitzmyer, Rowe (2003: 20–22) argues that it is mistaken to wedge a separation between God's lordship and his name.

76. F. Spencer (2005: 116–17) points out the centrality of God, Christ, and the Spirit in Luke-Acts.

77. Rowe 2003: 14–15. Rowe (2003: 15n40) says, "It is not that the Holy Spirit is God and yet distinct from *God*, but rather that the Holy Spirit is God and distinct *within* God."

78. See the section on "The Prophetic Spirit" above.

The personal and/or divine character of the Spirit is hinted at by other bits of evidence as well. Ananias lied to the Spirit (Acts 5:3), but this is equated with lying to God (Acts 5:4). Ananias and Sapphira were indicted for testing the Spirit (Acts 5:9), but elsewhere Peter warned against testing God (Acts 15:10).[79] We compare this to Stephen's charge that Israel had consistently resisted the Spirit (Acts 7:51). The blasphemy against the Spirit also implies that the Spirit is personal (Luke 12:10). The personality of the Spirit is communicated by the letter composed by the Jerusalem Council, which claims that the decision "seemed good to the Holy Spirit and to us" (Acts 15:28).[80] Similarly, "the Holy Spirit has made you overseers" (Acts 20:28 my translation; cf. 1:8; 13:47). Only a person can appoint someone to an office. Moreover, in this same verse we see a reference to "the church of God" and apparently God's own blood, which certainly refers to the blood of Jesus. Hence, Fitzmyer rightly says about this text, "In any case, one should not miss the triadic nuance of this verse: the explicit mention of 'God,' 'the Spirit,' and the 'blood,' which implies the Son. It is a trinitarian dimension that Luke associates with the Christian community and its governance."[81]

The Spirit forbade Paul to speak in Asia and hindered the attempt to preach in Bithynia (Acts 16:6–8). Paul and his companions concluded instead from the Macedonian vision that "God had called" them to proclaim the gospel in Europe (Acts 16:10). No definite or irrefutable connection between "the Spirit" and "God" can be drawn in this text, and yet it seems that the Spirit and God work in concert, and that the guidance in either case can be said to be from God. Another text, Acts 1:4–5, witnesses to the Father, Son, and Spirit, though in an indirect way. The promise of the Spirit is from the Father, and presumably the one who baptizes with the Spirit is the Son (Luke 3:16). Similarly, Jesus is exalted to God's right hand and as a consequence pours out the Spirit (Acts 2:33). The "trinitarian" references in Luke-Acts are not prominent, nor are they emphasized. Still, the trinitarian character of what Luke writes is undeniable.

The Spirit in John

John's theology of the Spirit overlaps in some respects with what we see in Matthew and Mark and Luke-Acts, but as we would expect, there are also distinctive themes and emphases in the Johannine teaching

79. See Barrett 1994: 270.
80. Barrett (1998: 744) says that "this must be regarded as the outstanding example of Luke's insistence that all developments in the church's life were directed by the Spirit."
81. Fitzmyer 1998: 680.

on the Spirit.[82] In the new age of salvation that has arrived through
Jesus Christ all those who truly worship God, who is himself Spirit, will
worship him in Spirit and truth (John 4:23–24).[83] In the old covenant
God was worshiped at the tabernacle or temple, and Jesus affirmed the
validity and rightness of such worship. The Samaritans were dramati-
cally off kilter, for "salvation is from the Jews" (John 4:22). In the day of
fulfillment, however, the place of worship has now become irrelevant.
True worship is grounded in the work of God's Spirit and in the truth.
Since Jesus is the truth (John 14:6), any genuine worship honors the
Son (John 5:23), and those who fail to honor the Son do not honor the
Father, and hence they fail to worship truly.

ANOINTING JESUS

The Baptist's role as a witness is featured by John. The baptism of Jesus
by John is omitted in the Gospel, but John bore witness to Jesus' anointing with the Spirit. He testified that he saw the Spirit come down from
heaven like a dove and remain on Jesus (John 1:32),[84] and he reiterated
that the Spirit has descended and remained upon Jesus (John 1:34).[85]
John's teaching here does not differ dramatically from the Synoptics.
The Spirit's descent as a dove signifies that Jesus has been anointed for
his messianic ministry, and perhaps the dove also signals the arrival of
the new creation in Jesus' ministry (Gen. 1:2). The Spirit remaining on
Jesus testifies that once anointed, Jesus is never abandoned by the Spirit.
He continued to be the anointed one throughout his ministry. For John,
the anointing of Jesus by the Spirit serves the interest of Christology.
Jesus "is the Son of God" (John 1:34).

The other text on Jesus' anointing for ministry is also related to the
Baptist's ministry (John 3:22–30). Jesus, as the one sent by God, speaks
God's words; he is God's messenger (John 3:34). The latter part of John
3:34 explains why Jesus speaks God's word: God has given Jesus "the
Spirit without measure."[86] Jesus is God's chosen one because God has
poured out his Spirit upon him. The Father has demonstrated his unique
love for the Son by giving him everything (John 3:35). Failure to believe
in and obey the Son represents rejection of the one anointed by the Spirit
at the Father's behest. Jesus accomplished what he did in his ministry
by virtue of the Spirit's work within him.

82. See Dodd 1953: 213–27; Burge 1987; M. M. Thompson 2001: 145–88.
83. See Barrett 1978: 238–39.
84. Bennema (2003) argues that Spirit baptism in John's Gospel signifies the cleansing
of Israel (not a gift given to Israel) and the revelation of who Jesus is.
85. "The Spirit abides permanently upon Jesus; the Baptism was not a passing moment
of inspiration" (Barrett 1978: 178). Cf. Lindars 1972: 110.
86. Rightly M. M. Thompson 2001: 171.

THE SPIRIT OF LIFE

The Spirit in the Gospel of John is the Spirit of life—that is, the Spirit that grants eternal life, the life of the age to come.[87] The Spirit that gives life cannot be separated from the person and ministry of Jesus. Jesus, after all, is the one who will baptize his followers with the Spirit (John 1:34). He will introduce them to the age to come by giving of the Spirit. The language of baptism introduces the "water" motif in John's Gospel. John associates rather frequently water with the work of the Spirit.[88] We see antecedents for such a conception in the OT, where "water" and "streams" seem to designate the Spirit (Isa. 44:3; Ezek. 36:25–27; cf. Isa. 12:3; 32:2; 35:7; 41:17–18; 43:20; 49:10; 55:1). Jesus, as the one who baptizes with the Spirit, is the one who immerses his followers with the Spirit.

The water motif and the giving of life by the Spirit are central in Jesus' conversation with Nicodemus in John 3. Jesus brushed aside Nicodemus's commendation of his ministry, maintaining that one must be born from above and again to enter God's kingdom.[89] Nicodemus was perplexed and misunderstood Jesus, thinking that the call to be born again required reentering a mother's womb. Jesus clarified that one must be "born of water and the Spirit" to enter the kingdom (John 3:5).[90] A few have seen a reference to physical birth (breaking of water) and spiritual birth (the work of the Spirit) here. It is doubtful, however, that Jesus would bother to state the obvious fact that one must be born physically before one can be born spiritually. Clearly, only those who exist can receive new life from the Spirit! Furthermore, both "water and Spirit" follow a single preposition (*ex*), indicating that water and Spirit refer not to two different notions but rather to the same spiritual reality. Most commentators have concluded that John refers to Christian baptism.[91] This interpretation makes much better sense because Christian baptism is often associated with new life in the NT. Whether John refers to baptism in his Gospel is a matter of significant debate among commentators. Some detect the sacraments everywhere, while others think that John omits any reference to them. We cannot enter

87. "The life-giving work of the Spirit underlies every passage concerning the Spirit in John" (M. M. Thompson 2001: 186).

88. So Dunn 1970a: 186–93.

89. As is common in Johannine idiom, the word *anōthen* has the dual meaning of "above" and "again" here (Barrett 1978: 205–6; Carson 1991b: 189). Lindars (1972: 150–51) argues for "from above," and Bultmann (1971: 135–36n4) for "again."

90. For the interpretation proposed here, see the convincing study of Belleville 1980.

91. See Lindars 1972: 152; Barrett 1978: 209; Bultmann (1971: 138–39n3) thinks that it refers to baptism but argues that it is an ecclesiastical addition. For further discussion, see R. Brown 1966: 141–44.

into a detailed investigation of that matter here, though it seems to me that John does not call attention to the sacraments. In any case, if we are persuaded that the dialogue with Nicodemus is historical, then the likelihood of a reference to Christian baptism diminishes because Nicodemus could not have grasped something that did not even exist yet, and Jesus insisted that Nicodemus, being a teacher, should grasp what Jesus is saying (John 3:10).[92] Others see a reference to John's baptism, and yet it seems unlikely that the necessity of John's baptism would be emphasized in John's Gospel, especially when we consider the Johannine theme that John is merely a witness and not the true light.[93] If anything, the role of the Baptist is subordinated to Jesus in John's Gospel, and so it is quite unlikely that his baptism would be considered necessary to be part of the people of God.

Since Jesus expected Nicodemus to comprehend his insistence on the new birth, the OT furnishes the most likely background to his words. The importance of new birth by the water and the Spirit finds its antecedent in Ezek. 36:25–27: "I will sprinkle clean water on you, and you shall be clean from all your uncleannesses, and from all your idols I will cleanse you. And I will give you a new heart, and a new spirit I will put within you. And I will remove the heart of stone from your flesh and give you a heart of flesh. And I will put my Spirit within you, and cause you to walk in my statutes and be careful to obey my rules." Both water and the Spirit are prominent in Ezekiel. The water signifies cleansing and purification of sins, and God will give the Spirit so that human beings desire to obey him. Jesus instructed Nicodemus that people need forgiveness of sins and new life to enter God's kingdom. Only the Spirit of God, as Jesus explained in John 3:7, can grant new life. The flesh produces only flesh. A supernatural work of God's Spirit is required to enter God's kingdom. The work of God's Spirit is also a sovereign work, for it is compared to wind that blows mysteriously and apart from human control (John 3:8). The Spirit grants new life sovereignly and unexpectedly, producing new life where humans least expect it to occur. New life comes not from human effort or human accomplishment but from the miraculous work of God's Spirit.

The relationship between water and the Spirit is illustrated in John 7:37–39 as well. One of the great attractions of the Feast of Tabernacles was the water-pouring rite that occurred daily.[94] Jesus stood up on the last day of the feast and claimed that the ritual practiced, if understood

---

92. So Carson 1991b: 198.

93. Indeed, some have argued that there is a polemic against devotion to the Baptist in John's Gospel (Bultmann 1971: 49–52; cautiously Barrett 1978: 160).

94. See *m. Sukkah* 4:1, 9–10; 5:2–4. See also Barrett 1978: 326–27, 335; Köstenberger 2004: 239–40; Koester 2003: 197.

rightly, pointed to him. Those who thirsted should come to him and drink. The syntax of John 7:38 is greatly disputed. The Greek reads more naturally if the rivers of living water flow from believers rather than from Christ.[95] Even if one adopts the interpretation proposed here, there is no suggestion that believers autonomously produce streams of water. John 7:39 explains that these rivers of living water refer to the Spirit himself. The life-giving water that streams from believers should be traced back to the Spirit. Nor is the Spirit separable from Christ, for only those who put their trust in Jesus receive the Spirit that furnishes such refreshing waters. John clarifies that this life-giving Spirit is not yet available. He will be given only when Jesus is "glorified." Jesus must be exalted on high before the Spirit will be dispensed to his people. As we will see shortly, Jesus unpacked in his last discourse with his disciples the theme that he must depart for the Spirit to be given.

The link between the water and the Spirit adduced in the foregoing texts suggests that the water refers to the Spirit in John 4:13–14, where Jesus addressed the Samaritan woman:[96] "Everyone who drinks of this water will be thirsty again, but whoever drinks of the water that I will give him will never be thirsty forever. The water that I will give him will become in him a spring of water welling up to eternal life." The water that Jesus promises likely represents the Spirit, given the identification between the Spirit and living waters in John 7:39. The Spirit quenches human thirst forever and will spring up to life eternal, bringing to believers the life of the age to come. This is another way of saying that the Spirit grants life, since human beings depend on water for survival. The Spirit himself satisfies the thirst of the human soul, so that believers slake their thirst by drinking of him.

The Spirit's role in granting life is also expressed in John 6:63. Many in the crowd and even from Jesus' own disciples departed from him after he taught that he is the bread from heaven and that people must eat his flesh and drink his blood to have life. Jesus commented on the scandal that he created (John 6:61–62), indicating that their offense pierced to the very heart of the matter. Their taking umbrage over him would only be exacerbated, not quelled, if they saw him ascending to the Father, for he will go to the Father via the cross.[97] Hence, the flesh cannot beget life; only the Spirit can do so (John 6:63). The flesh cannot see that life comes only through Jesus' flesh and blood. Only the Spirit opens

95. So Lindars 1972: 298–300; Barrett 1978: 326–28; Carson 1991b: 322–29; Ridderbos 1997: 273–74; contra R. Brown 1966: 320–24; Beasley-Murray 1987: 114–17; Burge 1987: 88–93; Beale 2004: 197.

96. So Carson 1991b: 220; Köstenberger 2004: 150. Burge (1987: 96–104) sees a reference to the Spirit and the word.

97. See Barrett 1978: 303.

eyes so that people perceive the source of life. Jesus' words "are spirit and life" (John 6:63) because life comes only from the flesh and blood of Jesus—his death on behalf of the world (John 6:51). The life-giving Spirit, then, grants life on the basis of Jesus' death. The Spirit does not work apart from Jesus or in spite of him but rather on the basis of what he has accomplished.

We have noted that the Spirit can be given only after Jesus' death. Some see a reference to the gift of the Spirit in John 19:30.[98] Jesus declared, "It is finished," and then he died. The next phrase could be interpreted to say that he "gave up his spirit." If this is the reading, then John simply describes the death of Jesus. The Greek literally says, "He handed over the Spirit." Hence, it is possible that John refers to the gift of the Spirit that will be given to the disciples now that Jesus has died, though this reading is scarcely clear, and it is preferable to see a reference to Jesus' death alone.[99] Others see a reference to the Spirit being given in the water that poured from Jesus' side when the spear was thrust into him (John 19:34). The blood symbolized his death, upon which basis the water (the Spirit) flowed from him.[100] Again, however, John probably speaks here only of Jesus' death.[101]

John 20:22

Another difficult text is John 20:22. Jesus commissioned his disciples for mission, sending them just as the Father has sent him (John 20:21). He then breathes on them and says, "Receive the Holy Spirit" (John 20:22). Three main interpretations have been suggested.[102] (1) The disciples received the Spirit when Jesus breathed on them, and so John describes the moment of their regeneration. The day of Pentecost in Acts 2 represents the occasion when the disciples were clothed with power. A neat distinction between regeneration and empowering, however, cannot be sustained in John, and so trying to distinguish between the two events in such a way here is unpersuasive. (2) John 20:22 is the Johannine Pentecost. John does not describe Pentecost elsewhere, and so he inserts it here.[103] If we do canonical biblical theology, this solution is

---

98. Cautiously R. Brown 1970: 931. For a history of interpretation, see R. Brown 1994: 2:1178–82.

99. So Lindars 1972: 582–83; Barrett 1978: 554; Beasley-Murray 1987: 353.

100. See Burge 1987: 94–95. Koester (2003: 201–3, 227–28) thinks that the gift of the Spirit here is proleptic. On this text, see also Dodd 1953: 428.

101. Ridderbos 1997: 619–20.

102. For a helpful review of the interpretive issues and options here, see Dunn 1970a: 173–82; Beasley-Murray 1987: 380–82.

103. Lindars 1972: 612; Barrett 1978: 570 (John cannot be harmonized with Acts); Beasley-Murray 1987: 381–82 (the event is the same as the Lukan Pentecost, but John did not specify chronology [see also R. Brown 1970: 1030]); Burge 1987: 114–49.

unsatisfying. Pentecost plainly comes fifty days after Jesus' resurrection, but John locates this event on the day of resurrection. Furthermore, John 21 suggests that the disciples were not yet clothed with power, and thus the alleged infusion of the Spirit does not seem to grant much confidence or boldness. (3) Although none of the various interpretations is completely satisfying, the best solution seems to be that the event is symbolic of the future reception of the Spirit.[104] We have just noted evidence that the disciples did not receive the Spirit on the first Easter evening, for the subsequent chapter in John does not present them as bold witnesses of the gospel.[105] If we accept Acts as historically reliable, then John knew about Pentecost because he experienced it. Furthermore, if we date John in the last decade of the first century, it is likely that the churches that he addressed knew about Pentecost as well. Taking the account as symbolic also makes sense in the Johannine context because when Jesus breathed on them, he is not yet exalted, and so the Spirit cannot be given (cf. John 7:39). The action itself also suggests that symbolism is at work. Jesus breathed on them, signifying that he will grant them the Spirit after he has departed.

Revelatory Work of the Spirit

Only John identifies the Holy Spirit as a "paraclete" (*paraklētos*). Scholars have intensely discussed the significance of this designation.[106] Some have focused on the legal background of the term, contending that "advocate" summarizes well the meaning of the term. Others have suggested "helper" or "counselor." Attempts to define the word in terms of its background have come to an impasse, and no consensus has been reached in trying to find one term that embraces every usage. The way forward is to investigate the texts in which "paraclete" is used.[107] One of the primary themes in John 13–17 is Jesus' future absence from his disciples. He informed them that he was leaving and going to the Father. They were filled with sorrow, and so he explained why his absence is for their benefit. Jesus will request that the Father send them "another

---

104. Carson 1991b: 649–55; Köstenberger 2004: 574–75.

105. The fact that the disciples were not bold witnesses stands against the view of Ridderbos (1997: 643–44) that they were equipped for mission here.

106. For a helpful survey of the various backgrounds postulated, see Hamilton 2006b: 63–72; Burge 1987: 10–31. See also R. Brown 1970: 1135–44; Lindars 1972: 478–79 (sees a wide range of meaning); Bultmann 1971: 566–72 (defines it as "helper" in John in dependence upon Gnosticism); Barrett 1978: 462–63; Köstenberger 2004: 436n70 (sees "helping presence" as the unifying idea); Ridderbos 1997: 499–504 (argues that the term does not mean "advocate" in John's Gospel, that no true parallels have been found, that the usage in John is decisive for meaning, and that the "dominant idea is of someone who offers assistance in a situation in which help is needed" [Ridderbos 1997: 503]).

107. So Köstenberger 2004: 436n70.

paraclete" (*allos paraklētos*) to be with them forever (John 14:16). Jesus, in other words, is a paraclete whose personal presence has strengthened disciples and "kept" them (John 17:12). That Jesus is a paraclete is confirmed by 1 John 2:1, in that he functions as an advocate for disciples on the basis of his death. Burge rightly detects parallels between the ministry of Jesus and the paraclete: (1) Jesus reveals the Father (John 14:9), and the paraclete manifests Jesus (John 14:15–17); (2) Jesus is dependent on the Father for all things (John 5:19–20; 8:28), and the Spirit is dependent on Jesus (John 16:13); (3) Jesus glorifies the Father (John 17:4), while the Spirit glorifies Jesus (John 16:14).[108] The Spirit is also a paraclete whose presence will strengthen the disciples in an even greater way. He is with the disciples even now, but he will reside in them in the future (John 14:17).[109] Thereby they will be enabled to persevere in suffering and to bear witness to Jesus, for the Spirit given to them is the "Spirit of truth" (John 14:17; 15:26; 16:13). But M. M. Thompson rightly adds that the Spirit also performs many of the same functions as the Father: testifying (John 5:37; 8:18; 1 John 5:9; cf. John 15:26–27); glorifying Jesus (John 5:44; 8:54; 12:23, 28; 13:31–32; 17:1, 5; cf. 16:14); being with the disciples (John 14:23; 17:11, 15, 26; cf. 14:17); teaching (John 6:45; 1 John 2:26–27; cf. John 14:26; 16:13).[110]

Whether the coming of Jesus refers to his coming in the Spirit or his personal manifestation to them in his resurrection in John 14:18–20 is debated. Since Jesus said, "You will see me" (John 14:19), it seems that the reference cannot be to the coming of the Spirit but refers instead to his resurrection.[111] In any case, a reference to the Spirit seems intended in John 14:23, where the Father will make his home (*monē*) with those who do his will. He will dwell with his people by means of his Spirit. Translations such as "helper" or "counselor" for *paraklētos* are not far off, given the emphasis on his personal indwelling and presence. Perhaps a reference to the Spirit is implied in John 14:27–28, particularly if Jesus' coming to them in the latter verse is his coming by the Spirit. If there is a reference to the Spirit here, then John suggests that the Spirit is

---

108. Burge 1987: 140.

109. A textual problem emerges here because some texts read "is in you." The better reading is likely "will be in you." Even the present-tense reading would not rule out the future fulfillment of the promise, since the present tense does not necessarily denote present time (see Barrett 1978: 463; Beasley-Murray 1987: 243; Carson 1991b: 509–10). John 7:39 indicates that the Spirit will not come until Jesus is glorified, and so it seems that the fulfillment must be future.

110. M. M. Thompson 2001: 183.

111. Rightly Lindars 1972: 480–81; Beasley-Murray 1987: 258; Carson 1991b: 501–2; Ridderbos 1997: 505–6. Others see a reference to the coming of the Spirit (R. Brown 1970: 645–46; Köstenberger 2004: 439). Barrett (1978: 464) thinks that here John may have merged references to the parousia and the resurrection.

the Spirit who grants peace. Jesus grants his followers peace in that he gives them the Spirit.

Jesus reminded his disciples that his time with them was limited (John 14:25–26), but he comforted them with the promise of the coming of the paraclete—the Holy Spirit. In John 14:16 the Father will send the paraclete, but here the Father will send the paraclete in Jesus' name, suggesting that the Spirit is given as Jesus' alter ego, that he will honor Jesus' name. Interestingly, the paraclete is not identified as the "Spirit of truth" in this text, and yet his role in witnessing to the truth is prominent. He will "teach" the disciples "all things" (John 14:26), so that the apostles will faithfully pass on the truth about Jesus to their followers.[112] They will be preserved from error by the teaching ministry of the Spirit. Not only will the Spirit teach the apostles, but also he will "bring to your remembrance all that I have said to you" (John 14:26). The Spirit does not provide an independent access to truth to the disciples. He does not summon them to learn mysteries that are gleaned through some special channel of private revelation. He witnesses to the words of Jesus and reminds them of his words and teaching. They will recall everything that is necessary and crucial from Jesus' teaching, but not in their own capacity.

What is said about the paraclete here fits with John 15:26–27 as well. Jesus had just warned his disciples that while he is absent hatred will rise against them, and that such hatred is rooted in a detestation of Jesus himself (John 15:18–25). Jesus promised them that the paraclete is coming. In this instance he did not say that the Father will send the paraclete, but rather that he himself will send the paraclete "from the Father" (John 15:26). The paraclete is Jesus' gift to his disciples. Still, Jesus emphasized that the Spirit is also the Father's gift, for he goes on to speak of "the Spirit of truth who proceeds from the Father" (John 15:26). This "Spirit of truth" does not convey truth to human beings apart from Jesus, as if he operates as an independent truth-revealer to the world at large. He teaches the truth in that he witnesses to Jesus (John 15:26). He calls attention to Jesus as the Son of God, the Christ, the one who died so that humans might live. The witness of the disciples, then, must be rooted in the testimony about Jesus borne by the Spirit (John 15:27). Since the paraclete witnesses to Jesus and teaches about Jesus, the titles "advocate" and "teacher" fit with the designation as well, supporting the notion that no single term comprehends the significance of the term "paraclete."

---

112. "The promise of John 14:26 has in view the Spirit's role to the first generation of disciples, not to all subsequent Christians" (Carson 1991b: 505). Cf. Ridderbos 1997: 511.

In the next reference to the paraclete Jesus again anticipated his departure (John 16:4–5). He instructed his disciples that it is advantageous for him to depart because thereby the paraclete will come to them (John 16:7). Again, he taught that he himself will send the paraclete to them—in this case with no reference to the Father. Of course, this should not be read to deny that both the Father and the Son send the paraclete to the disciples. The paraclete's role as advocate and witness takes center stage in the coming verses. We see the paraclete's work in the world (John 16:8–11) and his work in the disciples (John 16:12–14). The meaning of John 16:8–11 is notoriously difficult.[113] We should begin by focusing on what is clear in the text. The Spirit's witness before the world is again tied inextricably to Jesus' person and work. The Spirit does not convince the world of truth apart from Jesus the Christ; he convinces the world regarding the truth in Jesus. The Spirit functions as the prosecuting attorney, persuading the world that it is guilty in terms of its stance toward Jesus. It seems, then, that the witness of the disciples will be made effective by virtue of the Spirit's witness through them (cf. John 15:26–27).

We consider now the specifics of John 16:9–11. The Spirit will convince the world about sin, righteousness, and judgment. The sin of the world centers on the failure to believe in Jesus. The world wants to do the works of God, as if it could somehow measure up to his standard (John 6:28). Jesus says that only one work is necessary: believing in the one whom the Father sent (John 6:29). Similarly, the world considers failure to believe in Jesus as a trivial thing, comparable to failing to believe, say, that Augustus was the greatest of the Caesars. The Spirit will convince the world, however, that the failure to believe in Jesus is the fundamental sin—the root of all other sin. The failure to believe in Jesus led to his execution, for no one can take a neutral stand regarding Jesus. One either believes him or hates him (John 15:18–25). One either embraces him as the Christ or puts him to death as a messianic pretender and a threat to the well-being of the nation (John 11:48–50).

What is most difficult is determining what is meant by the Spirit convicting the world about righteousness. Does he convict the world of its lack of righteousness or about the righteousness of Jesus? If the conclusions suggested above about failing to believe in Jesus are correct, then perhaps both of these matters are included. The world radically misconstrues what righteousness is in that it condemned Jesus to death as an evil impostor and blasphemer. It does not realize

113. For the various proposals on the meaning of these verses, see R. Brown 1970: 711–14; Lindars 1972: 500–504; Barrett 1978: 487–88; Beasley-Murray 1987: 280–81; Carson 1979; 1991b: 534–38; Burge 1987: 208–10; Ridderbos 1997: 531–35; Köstenberger 2004: 471–72; Lincoln 2000: 117–20.

that Jesus went "to the Father" by way of the cross for the sin of the world, not because of his own sins. The world has no conception of righteousness because it does not see who Jesus is. At the same time, then, the Spirit, who has come now that Jesus is raised and exalted, convinces the world of its lack of righteousness. Since the world condemned Jesus to death, and failure to believe in Jesus is the fundamental sin, the crucifixion of Jesus testifies to the unrighteousness of the world. The world does not see Jesus as he truly is—the Christ, the Son of God, who has come to give life. The Spirit will convince them that Jesus is the righteous one of God, and as a consequence the world is unrighteous.

Finally, the Spirit will convince the world about judgment because "the ruler of this world is judged" (John 16:11). Obviously, the "ruler of this world" is Satan (cf. John 12:31; 14:30). The world looks at Jesus' execution and concludes that he cannot be the Messiah and the Son of God. His "judgment" must have indicated that he displeased God as a messianic pretender. No one, the world reasons, could be the Christ and end up on a cross. The Spirit convinces people that the legal decision made by the Roman authorities was misguided and that the Jewish authorities did not interpret his death accurately. The cross signifies not Jesus' defeat but rather his victory over and judgment of Satan. Jesus expelled the ruler of the world by being lifted up high on the cross (John 12:31–32). The interpretation proposed here supports the suggestion that righteousness in John 16:10 has a twofold reference, referring both to the righteousness of Jesus and the lack of righteousness of the people. For here the misconceptions of judgment are also twofold. First, the Spirit will convince the world of its error about Jesus being judged and rejected by God on the cross. Second, those convicted will see that the cross accomplishes the judgment of Satan and Christ's triumph over him. What appears to human beings to be the defeat of Jesus and his rejection by God is actually the means by which he defeats the greatest enemy of the human race, Satan, and pronounces a definitive judgment against him. The witness of the Spirit, referred to here, does not take place in a vacuum; it occurs through the witness of the disciples, so that the paraclete, as Jesus' advocate, convicts the world of its guilt and Jesus' righteousness as the disciples bear witness to the gospel.

The Spirit's ministry is not limited to the world (John 16:8–11); it is also intended for believers (John 16:12–14). The teaching ministry of the Spirit is again highlighted in these verses. The disciples could not grasp all that Jesus would like to say before the cross and resurrection have taken place. They could not grasp the fullness of redemptive history until Jesus had died and was risen and the Spirit was given. Even then, they needed the Spirit to comprehend the truth. Jesus promised them again that the Spirit of truth will come to them. He will come as a teacher who "will guide" the disciples "into all the truth" (John 16:13). In other words, the Spirit will enable Jesus' disciples to comprehend the things that the historical Jesus desired to speak to them. He will guide them into the truth about Jesus because Jesus is the truth (John 14:6). The Spirit will not draw attention to himself or exalt himself, as if he speaks on his own authority. He is the one sent by the Father and the Son. He is sent by the Father in the name of the Son to bear witness to the Son. Hence, he will speak "whatever he hears" (John 16:13) from the Father and the Son. He will bear witness to both the Father and the Son because the Father and the Son share all things in common (John 16:15). In saying that the Spirit will announce the coming things (John 16:13), we should not restrict this to matters of eschatology.[114] It likely embraces all the truths that the church needs to know in the future. One of the most astonishing and illuminating statements about the Spirit appears in John 16:14. Jesus says, "He will glorify me, for he will take what is mine and declare it to you." The Spirit's role is to call attention not to himself but to the Son. Further, it seems in this context that he glorifies himself by explicating the teaching of Jesus, unfolding it in light of the cross and resurrection.[115] The Spirit's work in the world is not autonomous but rather is dependent upon Jesus. Indeed, one can discern the work of the Spirit only after Jesus is glorified. Only when Jesus is glorified as the Son of God and Messiah, the Word made flesh, is the Spirit truly at work, for the Spirit always calls attention to the Son.

The "paraclete" texts in John indicate that a number of different definitions are fitting for the term. The Spirit is a counselor, helper, advocate, and teacher. Jesus also clarifies that the Spirit will be given only after his departure. The Spirit will come only after Jesus' glorification, after he has been lifted up on the cross and returned to the Father. The "paraclete" texts also emphasize that the Spirit works in concert with and in support of Jesus. He does not operate independently; he is Jesus' alter ego. Hence, no true work of the Spirit exists apart from his witness to the Son—his ministry, death, and resurrection. The Spirit is sent by the Father and the Son to glorify Jesus—to convict people of their sin relative to Jesus and to teach and remind the disciples of the truths that they need in Jesus' absence.

114. Carson (1991b: 540) says that the phrase "refers to all that transpires *in consequence* of the pivotal revelation bound up with Jesus' person, ministry, death, resurrection and exaltation" (see also Ridderbos 1997: 536). Others take it to refer to the future (Lindars 1972: 505; Barrett 1978: 490).

115. Rightly Carson 1991b: 542; Köstenberger 2004: 474n57.

TRINITARIAN IMPULSES

We noted in the Synoptic Gospels the trinitarian dimensions of Jesus' baptism, and yet the same cannot be said of the parallel text in John (John 1:32–34). John, of course, does not include a reference to Jesus' baptism per se, though he does emphasize that the Spirit descended as a dove upon him. No reference to God's voice accompanies the story, and so the trinitarian flavor of the Synoptic accounts is lacking in John. And yet John contains a text (John 3:34–35) that suggests the same theology found in the Synoptic baptismal accounts. We are told that God gives his Spirit without measure to the Son. Anyone who has read the Synoptics immediately thinks of Jesus' baptism, where the Father anointed him with the Spirit. John 3:35 emphasizes the Father's unique love for the Son and his entrusting all things to his Son. All of this is said in a context in which the Father has also given the Spirit to the Son. Clearly, no developed trinitarian theology exists here. We have hints rather than anything definitive, and yet we still note a fascinating collocation of the Father, Son, and Spirit in this text.

The trinitarian impulses in John burst into the open in Jesus' final discourse to his disciples (John 13–17), where he promised them that the paraclete will come to them when he departs. Jesus is a paraclete, but the Spirit is "another paraclete" (John 14:16) sent by the Father who will abide with believers forever. He is seen and known by believers and will dwell in them (John 14:17). The Spirit cannot be an impersonal force, for he is seen and known.[116] Since he is "another paraclete," the implication is that he is seen and known as Jesus was seen and known by the disciples. Just as Jesus is in the disciples (John 14:20), so too the Spirit resides in them. Of course, one could conclude from this that the Spirit and Jesus should not be distinguished in any way, so that no difference remains between them. But then we run up against the stubborn fact that the Spirit is "another paraclete," so that he is to be distinguished from Jesus. If John 14:23 refers to the Spirit, as argued above, then the Father and the Son express their love to believers by dwelling with them. And yet they dwell with believers by means of the Spirit—the same Spirit sent by the Father and the Son.

We see a similar pattern in John 14:26. The Father will send the paraclete to the disciples. The Spirit is not merely a force or impulse, for he will teach the disciples and assist them so that they remember what Jesus taught them. Nor is the paraclete fully identical with the Father or the Son. He will be sent by the Father, and he will come in Jesus' name. The Spirit, then, is identified with the Father and the Son and yet is distinct from them. He teaches and helps disciples remember;

116. Contra Johnston 1970: 31–32. But see M. M. Thompson 2001: 149.

he is the paraclete that Jesus promised his followers. John 15:26 verifies what we have seen in John 14:26. In John 15:26 the Spirit is sent by the Son and proceeds from the Father. Again, he is not to be identified fully with either of them. Further, he witnesses to Jesus, so that the Father, the Son, and the Spirit again work in harmony in attesting to Jesus' ministry.

The separation of the Father, Son, and Spirit from one another seems clear from John 16:5–11. Jesus is going to the Father via the cross and his resurrection. The Spirit and the Son cannot be identified absolutely, for Jesus explicitly said that he is departing, and when he leaves, he will send the paraclete. The personal character of the Spirit is also clear, for he will convince the world about sin, righteousness, and judgment. It is difficult to conceive of how an abstract entity or force could fulfill these functions. Indeed, Jesus proceeded to say that the Spirit will direct the disciples into all truth and will speak not on his own authority but on the basis of what he hears (John 16:13). Guiding and speaking, however, are personal activities, indicating that the Spirit shares a personal relation with Jesus and with the disciples. Furthermore, the Spirit will announce the coming things, and such declarations are also the province of persons (John 16:13–14). Brown points out that the declaration of coming things echoes Isa. 44:7, where Yahweh thereby distinguishes himself from idols, and the paraclete's declaration of coming things reveals his deity, "for in so declaring the Paraclete is performing a function peculiar to God alone."[117] Indeed, the Father, Son, and Spirit are again revealed to be working in harmony with one another (John 16:15). What belongs to the Father also belongs to the Son, and yet what belongs to the Son also belongs to the Spirit, for he takes what belongs to the Son and discloses it to the disciples.

John's Gospel does not articulate the formal doctrine of the Trinity, nor are the relations between the Father, Son, and Spirit explicated in detail. For instance, the Spirit is nowhere called "God." On the other hand, in a number of texts the Spirit is placed together with the Father and Son and clearly works in harmony with them. He cannot be identified absolutely with them, for the Father and Son send the Spirit, and Jesus teaches that he will send the Spirit after he has departed to be with the Father. Nor can the Spirit be identified as a force or an impulse. He witnesses, teaches, speaks, convicts, and declares. He is seen and known by disciples. The church considered the Johannine witness in later formulating the doctrine of the Trinity, noting his personal and divine qualities.

117. R. Brown 1970: 708.

The Spirit in 1 John

SPIRIT AND ASSURANCE

The theology of the Spirit in 1 John does not replicate the teaching of John's Gospel, and yet the thought moves in the same orbit, and hence it is fitting that it should be considered here. The theology of the Spirit in this letter can be considered under the headings of assurance and witness, though the teaching on witness also functions to grant assurance. The primacy of assurance fits with the character of 1 John as a whole, for John wrote to assure the readers that they truly had eternal life (1 John 5:13; cf. 2:12–14), in contrast to those who had left the church (1 John 2:19). John weaves several themes together in addressing the issue of assurance. Those who truly belong to God keep his commands, love fellow believers, and believe that Jesus is the Christ (1 John 3:23–24). Believers also know that Jesus abides in them because he has given them the Spirit (1 John 3:24).[118] John communicates a similar truth in 1 John 4:13 in the midst of his exposition of God's love: "By this we know that we abide in him and he in us, because he has given us of his Spirit." Believers have assurance that they abide in Christ and he abides in them because of the Spirit within them.

John is not suggesting that assurance comes from the Spirit for those who refuse to love others or who do not keep God's commands or who deny that Jesus is the Christ. The Spirit is not an independent witness, as if people could claim to belong to God solely on the basis of the Spirit's witness. The strands of love, obedience, and orthodox Christology must be woven together with the Spirit's witness for an accurate grasp of John's theology of assurance. And yet the Spirit's witness cannot be collapsed into love, obedience, and Christology, so that it plays no distinguishing role. John likely refers to an internal work of the Spirit by which he communicates to the heart that one is truly a child of God. In that sense, the Spirit's work is mysterious and inaccessible to others, for the believer has an internal confirmation of the Spirit that he or she belongs to God. It is a supernatural and ineffable work that transcends ordinary human discourse or experience.

118. Marshall (1978a: 202–3) rightly connects the presence of the Spirit here with assurance in the hearts of believers. Smalley (1984: 211–12) rightly adds that a sacramental notion of the Spirit's presence should not be read out of the text here. See also R. Brown (1982: 465–66, 483–84), who thinks it unlikely, given the presence of the secessionists, that John refers to an inner experience of the Spirit here, so he relates it to confessing Jesus as the Christ (1 John 4:2). Brown rightly sees that the Spirit cannot grant assurance apart from confessing Jesus as the Christ and obedience to the gospel, but he minimizes the experiential nature of the Spirit's work in believers. It seems that John countered opponents by insisting on both the objective evidence of new life and the subjective experience of the Spirit.

THE SPIRIT AS WITNESS

The Spirit in 1 John also functions as a witness. False prophets with deviant spirits exist, and they must be discerned and rejected (1 John 4:1–6). The witness of the Spirit "confesses that Jesus Christ has come in the flesh" (1 John 4:2). The spirit that rejects Jesus as the Christ is not God's Spirit but rather is "the spirit of the antichrist" (1 John 4:3). The Spirit that testifies to the truth ratifies such an apostolic confession (1 John 4:6).

As in John's Gospel, the Spirit does not witness independently to the truth. He witnesses to Jesus, affirming that the historical Jesus is the Christ. The Spirit does not witness to truth subjectively, in the sense that one can claim a private revelation of the Spirit that contradicts the public affirmation that Jesus is the Christ. Perhaps some of the secessionists claimed an anointing of the Spirit and denied that Jesus was the Christ. The anointing that all true believers have received is likely an anointing from the word and the Spirit (1 John 2:21, 27).[119] The anointing that they received at conversion needs no supplement or addition. It accords with the tradition vouchsafed to believers at the beginning, explaining why believers need no further teaching. John does not mean by this that all instruction is superfluous. The point is that any teaching that demands "improvement" upon what they were originally taught is unnecessary. The teaching handed down from the beginning is that Jesus is the Christ come in the flesh (1 John 2:22–23). The Spirit, then, witnesses to the truth that Jesus is the Christ. The Spirit's witness is not a diffuse or general witness; rather, it confirms the historical message of the gospel communicated by apostolic messengers. The Spirit's witness invariably centers on Jesus himself.

The same theme is confirmed in 1 John 5:6–12. John directs his readers to Jesus' baptism and death—his coming by water and blood—emphasizing again that Jesus is the Christ come in the flesh. He adds that the Spirit witnesses to such a reality as the Spirit of truth (1 John 5:6).[120] Indeed, the Spirit, water, and blood form an alliance as a threefold witness to the truth of Jesus' person. The Spirit's work, then, affirms historical truths, not private judgments about spiritual realities. The Spirit's witness is inevitably tied to the work of Jesus Christ in redemptive history. John knows of no witness of the Spirit sundered from Jesus Christ. Although

---

119. See the excellent discussion in Marshall 1978a: 153–55. Dunn (1970a: 197) thinks that the priority is on the Spirit, "albeit the Spirit working in conjunction with, or even through the Word" (see also Smalley 1984: 105–7). R. Brown (1982: 342–47) inclines to an anointing with the Spirit only.

120. Marshall (1978a: 234–35) argues that as the Spirit speaks through the word, the truth is confirmed in believers. Smalley (1984: 280) locates the witness of the Spirit in preaching, prophecy, the sacraments, and his internal work in believers.

1 John does not explicitly say that the Spirit came to glorify Jesus, it is obvious that the same line of thought obtains inasmuch as the Spirit's witness is always directed to the Son of God.

TRINITARIAN IMPULSES

The first Johannine letter does not explicitly speak of the Trinity. Such a teaching was inserted into some manuscripts at 1 John 5:7 by scribes, probably in the midst of trinitarian controversies. The insertion obviously is later and by no means can be accepted as part of the original text. What we observe in 1 John is actually rather similar to the teaching of John's Gospel. If the anointing refers to the Spirit (1 John 2:20, 27), the Spirit works in harmony with the Father and the Son, testifying that Jesus is the Christ come in the flesh (1 John 2:22–23). The anointing "abides" in disciples and "teaches" them. The function of teaching fits with the Spirit's ministry in John's Gospel, where he instructs disciples. Moreover, Jesus abides in believers by his Spirit (1 John 3:24). John tends to revisit the same themes often, exploring them from different angles to enrich the understanding of his readers.

We see that the Father, Son, and Spirit work in concert, as in the Gospel. The Spirit testifies that the Father has sent Jesus in the flesh (1 John 4:1–6), confirming that he is the Savior of the world (1 John 4:14). The witness of the Spirit to Jesus at his baptism and death (1 John 5:6–8) is nothing less than the witness of God himself (1 John 5:9). Those who reject the Spirit's witness about Jesus reject God's assessment of Jesus (1 John 5:10–11). John moves easily from the Spirit to God without any awkwardness. One might argue that what we see in 1 John is a form of modalism. Against this, the Father, the Son, and the Spirit are presented as distinct from one another as well. Furthermore, evidence for distinctions is even clearer in John's Gospel, which gives every indication of being written by the same author. Nor does 1 John deny the oneness of God. The letter concludes with a warning against idolatry (1 John 5:21). The warning is rooted in the OT Scriptures, where idolatry and polytheism are contrary to the faith of Israel. Again we see adumbrations of the Trinity without a full explication of such teaching.

The Spirit in Paul's Letters

THE INAUGURATION OF THE AGE TO COME
AND THE SPIRIT IN CONVERSION

The Holy Spirit in the Pauline writings is an eschatological gift, fulfilling God's promise of the coming of the new covenant. Jesus' resurrection from the dead and his appointment as the Son of God in power in accordance with the Spirit of holiness constitute the inbreaking of the age to come (Rom. 1:4). The "Spirit of holiness" likely refers to the Holy Spirit, and a reference to the Spirit is also suggested by the contrast between the flesh and the Spirit (Rom. 1:3–4).[121] Now that Jesus has been raised from the dead and appointed as the Son of God in power in accordance with the Spirit, the day of fulfillment has arrived. Three features in the verse point to the inbreaking of the new age: (1) Jesus is now enthroned in power as the Son of God; (2) the promised resurrection of the dead has come; (3) Jesus' appointment as God's Son is in accord with the Holy Spirit. Jesus' vindication by the Spirit (1 Tim. 3:16) probably refers to his resurrection and exaltation as well.[122] We see the flesh-Spirit contrast in 1 Tim. 3:16, for Jesus "was manifested in the flesh" and "vindicated by the Spirit." When Jesus' ministry in the flesh was completed, including his death, the Spirit vindicated him by raising him from the dead.

The end-time gift of the Spirit has been granted to believers by Jesus Christ. Jesus gave the life-giving Spirit to his followers (1 Cor. 15:45), presumably at his exaltation.[123] This same Spirit guarantees the resurrection of believers, their reception of bodies animated by the Holy Spirit (1 Cor. 15:42–44). Upon conversion the Spirit is given to them as "firstfruits" (Rom. 8:23). In the OT the firstfruits function as the anticipation and pledge of the remainder of the harvest. Similarly, the gift of the Spirit guarantees that God will complete the work of redemption and raise believers from the dead. We noted in Rom. 1:4 the Spirit's role in Jesus' enthronement and resurrection. This same Spirit that raised Jesus will raise believers from the dead, for he dwells in them (Rom. 8:11). The Spirit given to believers is both a seal and a down payment (2 Cor. 1:22; Eph. 1:13–14). The Spirit given is the Spirit promised in accord with OT prophecies. The sealing of the Spirit signifies the authenticating work of the Spirit. Believers truly belong to God on account of the Spirit's work. Further, the Spirit secures the promised inheritance of the resurrection, being himself the guarantee and down payment of such an inheritance (Eph. 1:14). The eschaton has arrived with the gift of the Spirit, but it has not come in all its fullness. Believers await their final inheritance, but the gift of the Spirit assures them that final redemption is certain.

The blessing pledged to Abraham (Gen. 12:3) is nothing less than the promise of the Spirit (Isa. 44:3), and this blessing now belongs to believers (Gal. 3:14), indicating that the last days have begun. God has sent the Spirit of his Son into the hearts of believers (Gal. 4:6). By no means

---

121. See Schreiner 1998: 39–44.

122. See Stettler 1998: 97–98; cf. Dibelius and Conzelmann 1972: 62; Marshall 1999: 525–26.

123. In an important study Gaffin (1988) unpacks the eschatological force of Paul's theology. See also Conzelmann 1975: 287; Fee 1987: 789.

do the Galatians need to submit to circumcision to become part of the people of God, for they already have the end-time gift of the Spirit (Gal. 3:2, 5). God granted them the Spirit not on the basis of "works of the law" but rather because they put their trust in the good news of Christ crucified and risen. The power of the kingdom operates already in the lives of believers because they enjoy "righteousness and peace and joy in the Holy Spirit" (Rom. 14:17). Righteousness, peace, and joy are gifts of the age to come, and they have become the possession of believers even now through the Holy Spirit. Clearly, Paul did not think that the kingdom has been consummated, but the presence of the Spirit indicates that it has been inaugurated.

The gift of the Spirit is the mark of the new age and is fundamental for being a Christian. We noted that the Galatians are genuine believers because they had received the Spirit (Gal. 3:2, 5) and thus truly were God's children (Gal. 4:6). Believers know that they are God's children because they have "received the Spirit of adoption" and acknowledge God as "Abba! Father!" (Rom. 8:15). The indwelling of the Spirit is the nonnegotiable indication that one is truly a believer (Rom. 8:9). Those who do not have God's Spirit still live in the realm of the flesh; that is, they are unconverted and under the dominion of the present evil age. "Anyone who does not have the Spirit of Christ does not belong to him" (Rom. 8:9).

Believers are still mortal because of the presence of sin (Rom. 8:10), but the Spirit in them is life, a life that they enjoy because the righteousness of God is now theirs. The physical body of believers is the temple of the Holy Spirit because he indwells them, and therefore sexual sin is unthinkable (1 Cor. 6:19). Just as the Spirit indwells each believer individually, he also dwells in the church corporately (1 Cor. 3:16). The people of God cannot be limited to the Jews. Both Jews and Gentiles together, through the work of Christ Jesus, are the new temple, indwelt by God's Spirit (Eph. 2:22). Access to the Father is available to all through the Holy Spirit (Eph. 2:18). No church is genuine unless the Spirit lives in its members.

Since the Spirit is the sine qua non for believers, they can be simply described as "spiritual" (1 Cor. 3:1; Gal. 6:1). There is no notion here of some believers who are a cut above others, who constitute a spiritual elite.[124] If believers continue to live in accordance with the flesh (1 Cor. 3:1–4), they bring into question whether they are genuinely Christians, for believers are marked out by the Spirit. Believers have "received . . . the Spirit who is from God" (1 Cor. 2:12) and thus are spiritual. The

124. In Galatians, rightly Longenecker 1990: 273; Martyn 1997: 546. On 1 Cor. 3, see Fee 1987: 121–25; see also Garland 2003: 106–9.

unbeliever, on the other hand, is bereft of the Spirit. He or she is a "natural [*pyschikos*] person" (1 Cor. 2:14). Hence, they cannot welcome the things of the Spirit, for only a person of the Spirit can discern the things of the Spirit (1 Cor. 2:14–15). Paul does not imply that there are different classes of Christians. His point is that all believers have the Spirit, and therefore they are spiritual. Only those who are not indwelt by the Spirit fail to grasp the things of the Spirit. Their failure results not from inferior intelligence but from a spiritual incapacity. Those who have the Spirit grasp spiritual reality because their understanding comes from the Spirit himself, since only God's Spirit knows the mind of God (1 Cor. 2:10–12).[125] Spiritual understanding comes only from God. No one, therefore, can boast about possessing such, since the Spirit grants it as a gift.

Since the mark of new life is the presence of the Spirit, the Spirit himself witnesses with the spirits of Christians, assuring them that they are truly believers (Rom. 8:16). Believers, from conversion, know that they belong to God because God's love has been poured out into their hearts through the Holy Spirit (Rom. 5:5; cf. 15:30). One indication that the letter to Titus is genuinely Pauline is the claim that the Spirit is not given on the basis of works. God saved not because of the righteous works that believers performed but rather "by the washing of rebirth and renewal of the Holy Spirit" (Titus 3:5). It seems likely that the nouns "rebirth" and "renewal" both modify washing.[126] One argument favoring this is that the terms overlap in meaning and refer to the same reality. The word "rebirth" points to God's creative work in which a person is radically changed, and the word "renewal" signifies the beginning of the new life and the end of the old.[127] The washing is one that signifies new birth and new life. Both the new life and the new birth signified by the washing come from the Holy Spirit. He is the one who grants new life to believers and cleanses them from sin. Believers are born by the Spirit (Gal. 4:29), so their new life is a miraculous spiritual work. Baptism with water and baptism with the Spirit are closely associated in Paul's mind because both occur at the initiation of the Christian life. At conversion every believer is baptized in or immersed with the Holy

---

125. See the important essay on 1 Cor. 2:6–16 by Stuhlmacher (1987).

126. See Marshall 1999: 316–17. Some argue that the text teaches that salvation comes through the washing of regeneration *and* through the renewal of the Holy Spirit (Knight 1992: 341–44; W. Mounce 2000: 441–43). It seems more likely to me that regeneration and renewal are parallel. Hence, Paul teaches that believers are saved "through the washing of regeneration and renewal that comes from the Holy Spirit" (see Beasley-Murray 1962: 210–11; Oepke, *TDNT* 4:304).

127. So Lau 1996: 166–67.

Spirit (1 Cor. 12:13).[128] Each one drinks of the Spirit at the inception of the Christian life. Paul did not conceive of a Christian who does not have the indwelling Spirit. Such a notion is a contradiction in terms, for the presence of the Spirit is the mark that one is a believer. Often the word "sanctification" is associated with ongoing progress in the Christian life, but the term actually is used regularly for God's definitive work of setting apart believers at conversion. The latter usage seems to be in view in 2 Thess. 2:13. God saved believers "through sanctification by the Spirit and belief in the truth." Paul reflects on the initial salvation of the Thessalonians, noting God's saving work, their belief in the gospel, and the consecrating work of the Spirit by which he inducted them into the sphere of the holy. The Spirit's role in conversion is communicated also in 1 Cor. 6:11. The conversion of believers is set forth with different metaphors: washing, sanctification, and justification. The inception of the Christian life is in view here. Believers are washed in baptism, set apart as holy ones, and declared to be righteous before the divine judge. All of this is accomplished "in the name of the Lord Jesus Christ and by the Spirit of our God." The saving work accomplished is attributed to the Son and the Spirit.[129] That salvation is the Spirit's work is affirmed also in 1 Cor. 12:3. Those who curse Jesus are not moved by the Spirit, whereas those who affirm Jesus' lordship can do so only by the work of the Spirit. The Spirit moves the heart so that it truly and gladly confesses that Jesus is Lord of all. What is remarkable is that the Spirit is *given* to believers (1 Thess. 4:8). Since the Spirit bestowed is holy, no believer should be involved in sexual sin; those who do so will face God's just vengeance (1 Thess. 4:3–6).

THE SPIRIT OF POWER

The Spirit in Pauline theology is a Spirit of power. He transforms God's people. We see this clearly in Paul's letter-Spirit contrast that is noted on three different occasions (Rom. 2:29; 7:6; 2 Cor. 3:6). The letter-Spirit contrast should not be construed as a hermeneutical contrast but rather

128. O'Donnell (1999) argues that the verse most likely indicates that the Spirit is the agent of baptism rather than the element in which believers are baptized. O'Donnell demonstrates that his view is a possibility, and it seems to me that his best argument is that the prepositional phrase precedes in 1 Cor. 12:13, in contrast to Matt. 3:11; Mark 1:8; Luke 3:16; John 1:33; Acts 1:5; 11:16. He has not convincingly shown, however, that his grammatical study is determinative, for the evidence is more ambiguous than his study suggests, and it seems more likely that the reference to the baptism of the Spirit would be understood similarly in all of these texts. Since Jesus clearly is the baptizer in the other verses, that likely is the case here as well.

129. Fee (1987: 247) observes that the Spirit is "the means whereby God in the new age effects the work of Christ in the believer's life."

in terms of redemptive history.[130] Transformation of human beings did not occur in the old era under the Mosaic law, but it has been effected by the power of the Spirit in the new age. The true Jew and true circumcision are the work of God's Spirit, not the letter (Rom. 2:29). Here "the letter" refers to the OT law, and in context it almost certainly refers to the commands contained in the law (Rom. 2:17–29). The commands of the law, though good, do not provide human beings with the power to put them into practice. Mere possession of the law is useless if people do not keep it. Paul argues here that Gentiles are considered to be true Jews and enjoy the circumcision of the heart if they have the Holy Spirit. The Holy Spirit, unlike the law, grants people the ability to keep what the law commands (Rom. 2:26–27). The keeping of the law by Gentiles here is not merely hypothetical, for it is grounded in the transforming work of the Spirit.

We also see the letter-Spirit contrast in Rom. 7:6. Once again the inadequacy of the Mosaic law is the subject of discussion. The Jews typically believed that the Torah was the means by which people would be saved and sanctified, claiming that more Torah meant more life (*m. 'Abot* 2:7). Paul argues, however, that the law was given to increase transgression, not diminish it (Rom. 5:20). The prohibition against coveting exacerbated coveting (Rom. 7:7–11). Those who live in the flesh—that is, as sons and daughters of Adam—are not freed by the law (Rom. 7:5). Instead, sinful passions are stimulated by the law. Those who are in Christ live a new way. They do not serve under the letter of the law, for those who simply receive the commands of the law die. Believers serve in the power of the Spirit (Rom. 7:6). The life of the Spirit gives them the desire and the ability to keep God's commands.

The last instance of the letter-Spirit contrast occurs in 2 Cor. 3:6. Paul defends the adequacy of his ministry, appealing to the work of the Spirit in his life. His ministry is superior to the ministry of Moses, for Moses ministered under the old covenant. The old covenant contains commands written on tablets of stone (2 Cor. 3:3). This represents the "letter" of the law (2 Cor. 3:6). Paul does not criticize the content of the law, nor does the term "letter" indicate legalism or works-righteousness. The problem with the letter is that it "kills" (2 Cor. 3:6). The Mosaic covenant is described as a "ministry of death, carved in letters on stone" (2 Cor. 3:7), as a "ministry of condemnation" (2 Cor. 3:9), and a covenant that is ending (2 Cor. 3:11). The letter is rejected because it lacks transforming power. That the letter kills is supported by the failure of the Jews to keep

---

130. Contra Hays 1989: 123–53. For a survey of others who offer a hermeneutical reading, see Hafemann 1995: 16–29. But against this reading, see Hafemann 1995: 156–86, 452–58.

the law under the Mosaic covenant, as witnessed by the Assyrian and Babylonian exiles in the OT. The Spirit, on the other hand, grants life (2 Cor. 3:6). The Corinthians are Christ's letter written "with the Spirit of the living God" (2 Cor. 3:3). The new covenant is a ministry of glory, righteousness, and permanence (2 Cor. 3:8–11). The Spirit of the Lord grants freedom, and in context this likely means that the Spirit grants believers power to do God's will (2 Cor. 3:17).[131] They are free to do what God commands, whereas those who were under the law lived in slavery. Paul does not envision perfect conformity to God's will in this life. Those who have God's Spirit are progressively transformed "from one degree of glory to another" (2 Cor. 3:18). They are not changed immediately; the Spirit is slowly but surely transforming them.

The transforming work of the Spirit is particularly emphasized in Rom. 8 and Gal. 5. In both contexts Paul contrasts the power of the Spirit with the ineffectiveness of the law. The law fails because of human weakness (Rom. 8:3), not because of defects in the content of the law (Rom. 7:12). The Spirit sets believers free "from the law of sin and of death" (Rom. 8:2). Here the word "law" probably should be defined as "principle" or "rule" instead of being seen as a literal reference to the OT law.[132] The liberating work of the Spirit is anchored in the work of Jesus Christ on the cross (Rom. 8:3). Paul never contemplated the Spirit's transforming work occurring apart from Christ's work, for Christ's redemptive work is the basis of the Spirit's transformation. Paul has already explained in Rom. 7 that freedom from the law comes only through the death of Christ (Rom. 7:4, 24–25). Those who have not been forgiven of their sins by means of the death of Christ cannot do God's will, but those who walk in the Spirit fulfill the requirement of God's law (Rom. 8:4). The singular for the word "requirement" (*dikaiōma*) probably denotes the love command because it summarizes the contents of the law.[133]

Obviously, believers do not keep the injunction to love perfectly, as the letters Paul addresses to the various churches clearly show. And yet a new principle of life empowers believers. Those who are in the old Adam, the flesh, inevitably think on the things of the flesh, but those who have the Spirit think on matters of the Spirit (Rom. 8:5). The mind-set of the

131. For this view, see Hafemann 1995: 401–7. Harris (2005: 312–13) argues, against Hays, that the freedom is not hermeneutical, and he may be correct in claiming that freedom should be construed in a broad sense, including freedom from the veil of ignorance, freedom to speak boldly, freedom from the old covenant and the law, free access to God, and freedom to behold him so that one is conformed to him, though contrary to Harris, it seems that Christ is in view here rather than the Father.

132. So Cranfield 1975: 375–76; Moo 1991: 505–7. Contra Wilckens 1980: 122–23; Dunn 1988a: 416–17.

133. See R. Thompson 1986.

flesh results in death, but the mind-set of the Spirit "is life and peace" (Rom. 8:6). These verses do not contain commands for believers; rather, they describe the lives of those who have the Spirit.[134] Those who are of the flesh cannot keep God's law or please God (Rom. 8:7–8). By way of contrast, those who have God's Spirit please God and are enabled to do his will. They are free from the dominion of the flesh (Rom. 8:12).

Since believers have been set free through the Spirit, Paul exhorts them to "put to death the deeds of the body . . . by the Spirit" (Rom. 8:13). Desires for sin still crop up in believers, but now believers can slay these desires and actions by means of the indwelling Spirit. Those who are "led by the Spirit of God are sons of God" (Rom. 8:14). The evidence that people have the Spirit is that they are led by the Spirit. Paul means by this the new quality of life that believers live, not the private guidance that they receive in their daily lives.[135] Those who are in the flesh are slaves (Rom. 8:15), but those who have God as their Father are empowered by the Spirit himself. Believers are exhorted to "boil" in the Spirit as they serve the Lord (Rom. 12:11). Here "Spirit" could refer to the human spirit, and perhaps we have a both/and in this instance. The human spirit burns with fervor as the Holy Spirit works powerfully within. Similarly, hope is a gift of the Spirit (Rom. 15:13). Indeed, because of the Spirit's work believers can "abound in hope." Genuine hope, then, is the result not of human optimism or human accomplishment but of the work of God's Spirit.

Paul's explanation in Galatians is quite similar to what we find in Romans. The Jewish teachers advocate circumcision for righteousness, but such a proposal amounts to a denial of God's grace in Christ (Gal. 5:2–4). The eschatological hope of righteousness is secured not through the law but "through the Spirit, by faith" (Gal. 5:5). Those who rely on the Spirit and trust in God will live a new quality of life because faith expresses itself in love (Gal. 5:6). Believers could misuse their newly found freedom and cave in to the flesh. True freedom expresses itself in servant love for others (Gal. 5:13–14). The desires of the flesh rise up and try to captivate believers, but the flesh can be overcome if believers "walk by the Spirit" (Gal. 5:16). Walking by the Spirit means that believers put their trust in the Spirit as they take each step. They do not begin in the Spirit and then complete their Christian lives in the flesh (Gal. 3:3). They continue in the same way they began, by relying on the Spirit.

Paul acknowledged the fierce struggle waged in believers between the Spirit and the flesh (Gal. 5:17). Life in the Spirit is not somnolent

---

134. In support of the view argued for here, see Fee 1994: 539–40; Moo 1991: 518–19. Contra Dunn 1988a: 425; Cranfield 1975: 385.

135. So Moo 1991: 533; Fee 1994: 563.

or a constant experience of spiritual ecstasy. Still, Paul is fundamentally optimistic. He does not conceive of life in the Spirit as constant frustration. Those who "are led by the Spirit . . . are not under the law" (Gal. 5:18).[136] Those who yield to the Spirit are free from the law. For Paul, being under law is equivalent to being under the power of sin (cf. Rom. 6:14–15). His point is not that those who live in the Spirit are free from all moral norms or moral constraints, as if those who live in the Spirit enjoy unbridled freedom. Instead, those who yield to the Spirit conquer sin and live in love. Those who are still subject to the law end up producing the works of the flesh (Gal. 5:19–21). Those who are led by and walk in the Spirit produce the fruit of the Spirit (Gal. 5:22–23). Their lives are marked by qualities such as love, peace, and joy. Hence, Paul encourages those who have life in the Spirit to march in step with the Spirit (Gal. 5:25). They are to sow to the Spirit rather than to the flesh (Gal. 6:8).

Paul teaches elsewhere that believers need the power of the Spirit. He prays in Ephesians that believers will be "strengthened with power through his Spirit in your inner being" (Eph. 3:16). A life pleasing to the Lord will be attained only by those who are filled with the Spirit (Eph. 5:18),[137] and the result of such filling will be remarkable joy and gladness (Eph. 5:19–20).[138] The weapon that Christians wield as they live each day is "the sword of the Spirit" (Eph. 6:17). Genuine prayer is "in the Spirit" (Eph. 6:18). The role of the Spirit in prayer is explicated also in Rom. 8:26–27.[139] During the present evil age believers are beset

136. In support of the view that Paul is optimistic here rather than teaching that believers are constantly frustrated by sin, see Matera 1992: 206–7.

137. O'Brien (1999: 391–92) argues that *pneumati* is instrumental rather than denoting content, so that Paul emphasizes the means by which one is fulfilled rather than stating that one is actually filled with or by the Spirit (so also Hoehner 2002: 703–4). It is more likely, however, that both means and content are in view (Lincoln 1990: 344; cf. Fee 1994: 721–22). Best (1998: 508) rightly argues against the notion that the human spirit is in view here. The injunction to refrain from drunkenness with wine is instructive in this regard, for wine is both the means by which one becomes drunk and the content that fills one who is drunk. Gombis (2002) argues that the context of Ephesians points to a corporate filling of the Spirit rather than an individualistic filling, and that the participles should be understood as means rather than result. The corporate emphasis surely is present, though Gombis goes too far by also excluding the individual. Often in Paul both the corporate and the individual dimension are in view.

138. The parallel from Colossians demonstrates that those who are filled with the Spirit are also filled with the word, so that word and Spirit must not be segregated from one another. As Rosner (1995: 22) says, "To pit the Spirit against the Word as if they represent alternative approaches to ethics does not ring true for Paul. The Spirit does not replace but cooperates with the word."

139. For a more detailed exposition, see Schreiner 1998: 442–47. See also O'Brien 1987b.

with weakness, for often they lack certainty about what God's will is. Hence, they are unsure about what to pray for. The Spirit comes to the aid of believers, interceding for believers as they groan. Believers groan because they long for final redemption and because they live in a cosmos and in bodies corrupted by evil. The Spirit grants extraordinary assistance, however, by praying for believers in accord with God's will. The inarticulate sighs of believers do not merely spell frustration, for the Spirit prays for the saints in the midst of all the pressures and distresses of this present evil age. Indeed, the Spirit prays in accord with God's will, and thus the Father always answers the prayers voiced by the Spirit, for any prayer that matches God's will is answered in the affirmative.

The salvation that Paul hoped for in Phil. 1:19 was not merely release from prison but rather was eschatological salvation as elsewhere in his letters.[140] Such salvation could not be gained autonomously. Paul coveted the prayers of the Philippians, and he needed the provision of the Spirit to persevere until the last day. Genuine worship is not a matter of observing the law or practicing circumcision (Phil. 3:2). It is a work of God's Spirit in which people forswear boasting except in Christ Jesus (Phil. 3:3).

The letter to the Colossians reminds us that the Pauline letters are occasional rather than being treatises sent to every church. The Holy Spirit is mentioned only once. The love that the Colossians have is the result of the Spirit's work (Col. 1:8). The Pauline view that the Spirit is one of power, producing fruit in believers, is evident. The Spirit produces joy, even when believers face affliction (1 Thess. 1:6). In saying that believers are given "power and love and self-control" (2 Tim. 1:7), Paul probably also thinks of the Holy Spirit strengthening the human spirit.[141]

THE SPIRIT AND MINISTRY

The Holy Spirit plays a vital role in ministry. The proclamation of the gospel was based not on human wisdom, by which Paul means Greco-Roman rhetoric, but rather was a "demonstration of the Spirit and of power" (1 Cor. 2:4). Indeed, Paul's ministry is characterized by the Holy Spirit (2 Cor. 6:6). The proclamation of the gospel from Jerusalem to Illyricum is the result of the Spirit's power (Rom. 15:19), and so the signs and wonders in the Pauline mission derive from the Spirit. In the context of 2 Corinthians he maintains that his new-covenant ministry derives from the work of the Spirit. Similarly, the gospel that Paul proclaimed

140. So O'Brien 1991: 109–10; Fee 1995: 130–32; Silva 2005: 69–72.
141. For the definition "self-control" for *sōphronismos*, see Marshall 1999: 182–84, 698.

in Thessalonica was effective not because of Paul's words but because the Holy Spirit was powerfully present (1 Thess. 1:5). Conversions in ministry cannot be attributed to human artifice or powerful speech; they are the work of the Holy Spirit. Messengers of the gospel are called to be faithful and to "guard the good deposit" entrusted to them (2 Tim. 1:14). The "deposit" here is another way of referring to the gospel that was handed down to Timothy and others.[142] Those who minister, however, cannot preserve the gospel in their own strength; they need the indwelling Spirit to fortify them to guard the gospel.

Paul's instructions about marriage and the advisability of celibacy have provoked considerable debate. He closes the discussion by claiming that he has the Spirit of God (1 Cor. 7:40). In other words, the words that he speaks here are not merely human words, even if they are his opinion (1 Cor. 7:12, 25). They are the inspired words of one who has a gift of prophecy.[143] The insight that Jews and Gentiles are one body in Christ, not two separate peoples, was revealed to the apostles and prophets by the Holy Spirit (Eph. 3:5). Indeed, the unity of Jews and Gentiles in the church comes from the Holy Spirit himself, and believers should strive to maintain and preserve the unity that already exists (Eph. 4:3). Paul's grief and anguish over Israel's separation from Christ is the sober truth (Rom. 9:2). He affirms his truthfulness by stating that his conscience provides verification of the same through the Holy Spirit. The Spirit attests to his longing for the salvation of his kin. The apostasy of many was specifically announced beforehand through the Spirit (1 Tim. 4:1), perhaps through a prophetic word.

The Spirit grants spiritual gifts to believers for the edification of the church. Even though there are a multitude of gifts, there is one Spirit that stands behind the gifts given (1 Cor. 12:4). Paul emphasizes in the strongest possible terms that the Spirit is the one who gives wisdom, knowledge, faith, or healing (1 Cor. 12:9–10). Gifts are not the manifestation of human skill and ability and talent; they are "the manifestation of the Spirit" for the strengthening of the church (1 Cor. 12:7). Hence, the gifts exercised can be ascribed only to the work of the Holy Spirit, to his sovereign will (1 Cor. 12:11). Christians should beware of quenching the Spirit (1 Thess. 5:19), which can happen in the rejection of

---

142. The deposit is the traditional teaching that has been handed down (so Dibelius and Conzelmann 1972: 105). Knight (1992: 379–81) argues that 2 Tim. 1:12 refers to what Paul has committed to God (his life), but in 2 Tim. 1:14 Timothy is to guard the faithful teaching (so also W. Mounce 2000: 487–88, 490). Marshall (1999: 709–11) argues, after surveying a number of possibilities, that the deposit in 2 Tim. 1:12 refers to what Paul entrusts to his successors with the confidence that God will sustain the gospel handed down. In 2 Tim. 1:14 Timothy is enjoined to guard the gospel as a deposit (Marshall 1999: 714–15).

143. Rightly Garland 2003: 285; Thiselton 2000: 525–26.

all prophetic utterances.[144] Of course, Paul also warns against grieving the Spirit generally (Eph. 4:30), and in the latter context the Spirit is quenched when believers cave in to sins of bitterness, anger, and other moral failings.

The Spirit, Christ, and the Trinity

One of the major themes in Paul is the Spirit's witness to Jesus Christ. We have already noted these texts, but here we focus on the Christ-centeredness of the Spirit's ministry. The resurrection of Christ is the Spirit's work (Rom. 1:4; 1 Tim. 3:16); hence, the Spirit raised Christ so that he would be exalted and glorified. God's love is given to believers at conversion (Rom. 5:5), but the love of God granted through the Spirit is not a diffuse and general love. God's love is anchored in the death of Christ, who died for the weak, the ungodly, sinners, and his enemies (Rom. 5:6–10). Believers now serve God in newness of life through the Spirit, but this new life in the Spirit finds its basis in the work of Christ on the cross, in which the old Adam was put to death (Rom. 7:6). Similarly, in Rom. 8 Paul celebrates the freedom to keep God's commands, which is the result of the Spirit's work (Rom. 8:1–8). This liberty is secured again in the cross of Christ, who took upon himself the condemnation that humans deserved (Rom. 8:3). Believers are God's children and adopted sons and daughters because of the work of Jesus Christ (Rom. 8:14–17).

In Galatians the gift of the Spirit is *the* badge of new life, demonstrating that the Galatians should not yield to circumcision (Gal. 3:3, 5). But the Spirit was given because the Galatians put their trust in Jesus Christ as the crucified one (Gal. 3:2; cf. Titus 3:5). They have received the promise of the Spirit (Gal. 3:14) only because Christ has removed the curse of the law by becoming a curse for believers (Gal. 3:13). The Galatians did not receive the Spirit in general; they received "the Spirit of his Son" (Gal. 4:6). Further, Gal. 4:4–5 indicates that the Spirit was given on the basis of Christ's redeeming work, so that believers truly become God's children. The exhortations to walk in, be led by, march in step with, and sow to the Spirit (Gal. 5:16, 18, 25; 6:8) are rooted in the redemption that Christ achieved in the cross. Even in the parenetic section the new life in the Spirit is grounded in having crucified the flesh as members of Christ (Gal. 5:24; cf. 2:20). Living in the Spirit cannot be construed as an independent ethic.

Access to God for both Jews and Gentiles is by one Spirit (Eph. 2:18), and both Jews and Gentiles are God's new temple as the church of Jesus Christ (Eph. 2:22). What we must observe here is that this unity was

---

144. Wanamaker (1990: 202) maintains that Paul thinks of charismatic utterances generally, so that restraining both prophecies and tongue-speaking are included.

established by the blood of Christ (Eph. 2:13). He has brought the Gentiles near who were far off from God. He has broken down the barrier between Jews and Gentiles through the suffering of the cross. The blessing of the Spirit, then, cannot be severed from the death of Christ.

Washing, sanctification, and justification are ascribed to the Spirit (1 Cor. 6:11), but at the same time they occurred "in the name of the Lord Jesus Christ." Is there an implicit trinitarianism at work here? The subject of the verbs is likely God himself. He is the one who washes, sanctifies, and justifies. The entire discussion of spiritual gifts commences with the claim that no one speaking by the Spirit can invoke a curse upon Jesus; conversely, the one speaking by the Spirit confesses Jesus' lordship (1 Cor. 12:3). The discussion of the gifts of the Spirit that follows, then, is subsumed under the banner of the lordship of Christ. The fundamental criterion for determining the work of the Spirit is whether Christ is confessed and embraced as Lord. Interestingly, a trinitarian formula follows in 1 Cor. 12:4–6 in a discussion on spiritual gifts. There is "the same Spirit" (1 Cor. 12:4), "the same Lord" (1 Cor. 12:5), and "the same God" (1 Cor. 12:6). This formula is primitive, but at the same time it is suggestive of an equal relationship between the Father, Son, and Spirit. All believers are baptized in the Spirit (1 Cor. 12:13), and this is the only text in the Pauline letters that speaks of the baptism in the Spirit. If it follows the pattern in the Gospels and Luke-Acts (Matt. 3:11; Mark 1:8; Luke 3:16; John 1:33; Acts 1:5; 11:16), Jesus is the one who baptizes in or with the Spirit. The great work of the Spirit, then, is not independent of Jesus but is produced by Jesus. Indeed, as the exalted Lord, he pours out the life-giving Spirit (1 Cor. 15:45).

God has sealed believers with the Spirit and given the Spirit as a down payment of final redemption (2 Cor. 1:21–22). These gifts flow from the proclamation of God's Son in the gospel (2 Cor. 1:19). The sealing and guarantee of the Spirit are part of the fulfillment of all of God's promises in Jesus Christ (2 Cor. 1:20; cf. 1:21). The new-covenant work in the hearts of believers may be written with the ink of God's Spirit, but the letter itself is written by Christ (2 Cor. 3:3). The ministry of the Spirit, which brings freedom, as elaborated in the remainder of 2 Cor. 3, is inseparable from Christ's ministry. The veil over the eyes of those reading the old covenant is removed only in Christ (2 Cor. 3:14). When one turns to the Lord, the veil is removed (2 Cor. 3:16).[145] Paul equates Jesus Christ and the Spirit in 2 Cor. 3:17: "Now the Lord is the Spirit." It is unlikely that the statement should be interpreted to affirm absolute identity between

---

145. In the OT context the Lord clearly is Yahweh, but in the context of 2 Cor. 3 it seems more likely that the Lord is the same person mentioned in 2 Cor. 3:14, Christ (see Kim 1982: 231; Barrett 1973: 122). Contra Dunn 1970c; Furnish 1984: 211–12; Hafemann 1995: 389–92; Garland 1999: 195; Harris 2005: 308, who see a reference to Yahweh.

Jesus and the Spirit, so that no distinction exists at all between them.[146] Such a conclusion would contradict the many places in Pauline theology where they are distinguished. And yet the close association between the Spirit and Christ here demonstrates that the Spirit cannot be severed from Jesus Christ. The Spirit that believers receive is "the Spirit of Jesus Christ" (Phil. 1:19). In the same context Paul can speak of "encouragement in Christ" and "participation in the Spirit" (Phil. 2:1). Those who worship in the Spirit indicate that they do so by trusting in Christ Jesus instead of boasting in themselves (Phil. 3:3).

The close affinity between the Spirit and Christ is apparent in Rom. 8:9–11. The Spirit indwells believers, but the Spirit is identified as "the Spirit of Christ" (Rom. 8:9) and "the Spirit of him who raised Jesus from the dead" (Rom. 8:11). Paul switches from the Spirit to Christ, stating that "Christ is in you" (Rom. 8:10). It is unlikely that Paul collapses the Spirit and Christ together as if they are coterminous in every respect, given the distinctions between the two that permeate his writing. What is emphasized by the variation between Christ and the Spirit is that the Spirit does not operate outside of Christ's realm or apart from Christ's work. We see a similar alternation in Ephesians. Paul prays that believers will receive strength from the Spirit within (Eph. 3:16), but the next verse refers to Christ dwelling within the heart (Eph. 3:17), and this is closely related to experiencing Christ's love (Eph. 3:19). Believers who have the indwelling Spirit and Christ are filled with God's fullness. In this instance we have a text that is remarkably trinitarian. The Spirit, Christ, and the Father are all said to indwell believers.

And yet the Father is distinct from the Son and the Spirit. The Father elects and predestines (Eph. 1:4–5) people and reveals the purpose of his will (Eph. 1:9). Jesus redeems believers with his blood and is the agent through whom the Father works (Eph. 1:7).[147] The Spirit is the seal of God's promise, the guarantee of final redemption (Eph. 1:13–14).[148] The three are not collapsed together; they are distinguished from one another. Paul continues, however, to affirm that there is only one God (Eph. 4:6). He does not compromise monotheism. And yet in the very context in which he reaffirms monotheism we also find a trinitarian formula with the references to the "one Spirit" (Eph. 4:4), "one Lord" (Eph. 4:5), and "one God and Father of all" (Eph. 4:6). Obviously, Paul does not work

146. As Harris (2005: 310–11) points out, most commentators who see the Lord as Jesus do not argue for an ontological identification of the Lord and the Spirit here but instead see a dynamic or functional notion in this verse, so that through the Spirit the risen Lord is communicated to the people of God.

147. We noted earlier the refrain "in him" or a variant thereof in Eph. 1:3–14.

148. There is also a trinitarian structure to Titus 3:4–7, as Stettler (1998: 332) observes.

out the theological ramifications of the formula. In any case, the Spirit seems to be put on the same level with the Father and the Son. We see a similar phenomenon in 2 Cor. 13:14: "The grace of the Lord Jesus Christ, the love of God, and the fellowship of the Holy Spirit be with all of you." Jesus Christ, the Father, and the Spirit are associated together here in a remarkable way.[149] Grace flows from the Lord Jesus and love from the Father, and believers have fellowship with the Spirit.[150] In other texts, of course, grace flows from the Father, and love is given through the Spirit (Rom. 5:5). Apparently the Father, Son, and Spirit all share divine functions, but the theological implications of the statement are not pursued in detail. Barrett rightly observes that full "trinitarian orthodoxy" is not worked out here, but we have "a starting-point for such speculative thinking and for its creedal formulation. Christ, God, and the Spirit, appearing in balanced clauses in one sentence, must stand on one divine level." As Barrett remarks, what Paul writes here makes "trinitarian theology, given the setting of Christianity in the following four centuries, inevitable, yet does so unconsciously."[151]

The Spirit's work in ministry and revealing truth is centered on Christ. Paul conducts his ministry by the Spirit's power with signs and wonders, but such spiritual power is in the service of the gospel of Christ, so that the gospel is preached where Christ is not yet named (Rom. 15:19–21). Similarly, Paul claims that his proclamation was not marked by the artistic rhetoric so common among the itinerant speakers of Paul's day; rather, he spoke "in demonstration of the Spirit and of power" (1 Cor. 2:4). Paul may allude here to the signs and wonders that accompanied his preaching. Still, the work of the Spirit calls attention only to Christ crucified (1 Cor. 2:2), to the foolish message of the cross (1 Cor. 1:18). The powerful work of the Spirit is always in the service of the gospel and is never separated from the message of Christ crucified and risen. The Spirit does not do mighty works to call attention to himself; the Spirit demonstrates his power by glorifying the gospel of Christ (1 Thess. 1:5). The setting apart of God's people at conversion is the work of the Spirit (2 Thess. 2:13), but the Spirit does not work mystically and ineffably apart from the truth of the gospel. Such sanctification takes place in and through belief in the gospel. Believers receive strength through

149. In the Greek text "Jesus Christ" and "God" represent subjective genitives, but the "Holy Spirit" may be subjective or objective (see R. Martin 1986: 495–96, 504–5). Garland (1999: 556) suggests that both objective and subjective genitives may be in view.

150. In support of this interpretation, see Harris 2005: 937–41. Harris is likely correct that the order here reflects the experience of believers. Grace is given to them through Jesus Christ, and hence they experience God's love for them, and as a result they enjoy fellowship with the Holy Spirit.

151. Barrett 1973: 345. See also R. Martin 1986: 496–97.

the Holy Spirit to guard the gospel (2 Tim. 1:14). The Spirit does not merely strengthen ministers in general; he strengthens them to guard the gospel.

We have seen in 1 Cor. 2:9–16 that the Spirit reveals wisdom to God's people. When Paul speaks of wisdom for the mature, he does not have in mind a gnostic wisdom reserved for elite Christians. The wisdom granted by the Spirit is demonstrated in the cross of Christ (1 Cor. 2:6, 8), a wisdom that the rulers of the world failed to comprehend because they "crucified the Lord of glory." The wisdom revealed by the Spirit, then, centers on the cross. It does not deviate from the gospel that Paul preaches publicly and everywhere but rather is displayed in that gospel. We find in Paul, then, the same message taught in John's Gospel: the Spirit has come to glorify Jesus.

Conclusion

The Pauline theology of the Spirit has many dimensions. The gift of the Spirit represents the inauguration of the age to come, and hence when human beings have the Spirit, there is no doubt that they belong to God. The mark of conversion is the gift of the Spirit. Paul also emphasizes that the Christian life is lived in the power of the Spirit. Here Gal. 3:3 could be taken as the banner verse. The Christian life is not merely begun by the Spirit; it is also continued in the Spirit. Believers do not commence their new lives in the Spirit and complete them in the flesh. The Spirit grants power so that believers are freed to do God's will. The new obedience is not perfect, of course, but it is observable and substantial. The fruit of ministry is also the work of the Spirit. The Spirit empowers those who preach the gospel, so that the work is effective. Signs and wonders from the Spirit, for instance, may attend the proclamation of the word. Finally, we noted that the Spirit is never sundered from Christ or his gospel. The new life given to believers and the power to live lives pleasing to God are always rooted in the gospel of Jesus Christ crucified and risen. The Spirit does not float free from Christ and minister in a vacuum. His work is always tied to the redemptive work of Christ. Similarly, the Spirit's work through those who proclaim the gospel is always in service to the gospel proclaimed, so that the Spirit's power is always anchored to the kerygma. We also noted a number of trinitarian formulas in the Pauline writings. The relation between the Father, Son, and Spirit remains undeveloped in these texts, and yet there is the clear implication that the three share divine functions. Paul continues at the same time to affirm monotheism vigorously. How these two streams of thought fit together is not resolved by Paul, but apparently he saw no contradiction.

The Spirit in Hebrews

Hebrews does not refer often to the Holy Spirit. What stands out is the role of the Spirit in the history of salvation, in the fulfillment of the OT that has now dawned in Jesus Christ. This theme fits with the purpose of Hebrews as a whole, for the writer worries that his readers will abandon new-covenant realities and revert to the old covenant. One of the most provocative references to the Spirit occurs with reference to Jesus' atoning sacrifice. Jesus "through the eternal Spirit offered himself without blemish to God" (Heb. 9:14). Some commentators argue that the author points to Christ's own spirit, while others see a reference to the Holy Spirit.[152] Interestingly, the Spirit is described as "eternal," suggesting the divine character of the Spirit and thus a reference to the Holy Spirit. Of particular importance is the salvation historical context of the statement. The sacrifice of Christ secured "eternal redemption" because it was offered "through the eternal Spirit" (Heb. 9:12, 14). Animal sacrifices only purify outwardly and symbolically, restricting themselves to the earthly tabernacle. Christ's death cleanses the conscience because he is a sinless and willing sacrifice and enters into the very presence of God with his blood. Hebrews contrasts the flesh and Spirit (Heb. 9:13–14). The fleshly sacrifices of animals point toward something greater: the sacrifice of Christ offered through the Spirit. The work of the Spirit, then, is emphasized at the key turning point in redemptive history. The fulfillment of God's promises are obtained through the cross of Jesus Christ. It is this "spiritual" sacrifice that truly cleanses people from sin, so that any return to old-covenant sacrifices reverts to an old era that is no longer effective.

The Spirit's role in the fulfillment of God's promises is also evident in Heb. 6:4. The author chronicles the blessings belonging to the people of God, and perhaps the chief one is that they share (*metochous*) in the Holy Spirit. Despite the reservations of some commentators, the sharing in the Spirit signifies genuine conversion, for the same root is used of partaking of (*metechōn*) milk (Heb. 5:13). The partaking of milk does not designate an incomplete or partial digestion of milk. Similarly, sharing in the Spirit is *the* mark of new life, the prime indication that believers are Christians. The Spirit is the gift of the new age, and this is confirmed by Heb. 6:5, which says that Christians enjoy "the powers of the age to come." The various blessings of believers in Heb. 6:4–5 overlap and mutually interpret one another. The Holy Spirit, then, represents one of the blessings of the age to come, indicating that the new age has arrived.

---

152. In support of human spirit, see P. Hughes 1977: 358–60; Attridge 1989: 250–51. In support of the Holy Spirit, see Bruce 1964: 205; Lane 1991b: 240.

Hebrews 2:4 occupies the same world of discourse. The message proclaimed to the Hebrews is superior to the Mosaic law mediated by angels (Heb. 2:1–4). The salvation accomplished by Jesus is superior, attested by the fact that he has sat down at God's right hand (Heb. 1:3, 13) since the final cleansing for sins has been accomplished. God has verified that he has spoken definitively and finally in his Son and his great work on the cross (Heb. 1:1), in that he has granted apportionments of the Spirit to believers, as well as signs and wonders and miracles (Heb. 2:4). The gifts of the Spirit, then, signify that the fulfillment of salvation history has arrived. Being made partakers of the Spirit (Heb. 6:4) and receiving the gifts of the Spirit (Heb. 2:4) are both tied to the work of Christ.

The great privilege and blessing belonging to believers in Christ explains the severity of the warning in Heb. 10:26–31. Since the work of Christ fulfills what was anticipated in the Mosaic covenant, those who regress to old-covenant sacrifices cannot be forgiven their sins. They have "spurned the Son of God," "profaned the blood of the covenant," and "outraged the Spirit of grace" (Heb. 10:29). The "grace" given by the Spirit is anchored in Christ's new-covenant work on the cross. If the Hebrews relapse to animal sacrifices, they insult the Spirit by denying the effectiveness of Christ's death on their behalf. The Spirit's grace, then, is poured out on people as a result of Christ's death, his securing of the forgiveness of sins. The close link between the work of Christ and the Spirit demonstrates that the Spirit is insulted when Christ is "spurned" and his blood "profaned." The Spirit does not work apart from Christ but rather testifies to him.

On three occasions in Hebrews the author refers to the Holy Spirit's speaking or revealing, and in each case the Spirit speaks through the OT Scriptures or institutions. For instance, in Heb. 10:15–17 the author cites the new-covenant text in Jer. 31:33–34, introducing it with the words, "And the Holy Spirit also testifies to us, for after saying" (Heb. 10:15). Interestingly, the Spirit is viewed as the one speaking and bearing witness in Scripture. Further, the Spirit bears witness to the arrival of the new covenant and the passing away of the old one. The sacrifice of Jesus has accomplished complete forgiveness of sins, so that animal sacrifices are passé. The Spirit speaks through Scripture, but what Hebrews emphasizes is the Spirit's voice in terms of the passing away of the old covenant and the inauguration of the new one.

Hebrews 9:8 makes an argument along the same lines. In Heb. 9:1–5 the author chronicles the items in the tabernacle and then proceeds to describe the priestly work in the tabernacle (Heb. 9:6–7). He perceives special significance in the fact that the high priest is allowed to enter the holy of holies only once a year, on the Day of Atonement (see Lev. 16:1–34). He remarks that the Spirit himself speaks through this arrangement, revealing that free and full access to God was unavailable as long as the tabernacle or temple worship was still in force (Heb. 9:8). Once again the Spirit indicates the inadequacy of the old covenant, demonstrating that the final and definitive sacrifice was not offered until the Son of God came.

Finally, the Holy Spirit also speaks through Ps. 95. The author's long citation from the psalm commences with the introductory formula "Therefore, as the Holy Spirit says" (Heb. 3:7). The author of Hebrews proceeds to argue that the message of the psalm still applies to the readers of his day, so that they should be earnest about entering God's rest while opportunity still avails (Heb. 3:7–4:13). The link to new-covenant realities is not quite as direct in the OT citation, and yet in the flow of the argument we see that the rest given under Joshua pointed to the final and definitive rest given by Jesus Christ.

The Spirit in Hebrews is the eschatological Spirit. He testifies to the fulfillment of God's redemptive promises in Jesus Christ. He is given to believers as a result of Christ's saving work on the cross. The Spirit speaks to believers through Scripture and in the institutions of the old covenant about God's final work in Christ. We have consistently seen in the NT that the Spirit bears witness to Jesus Christ, that he calls attention to the saving work on the cross accomplished by Christ. We should also note the personal nature of the Spirit in Hebrews. He speaks and testifies through the word of God (Heb. 3:7; 10:15), and he reveals his will through OT institutions (Heb. 9:8). This is highly significant, for elsewhere "God" is said to speak in Scripture, and in Hebrews this speaking is attributed to the Spirit (cf. Heb. 1:6–8; 5:5–6; 7:21; 8:8). Hebrews 8:8 is particularly interesting, for here God speaks in the new-covenant text from Jer. 31:31–34, but this same text is later attributed to the Holy Spirit (Heb. 10:15). It appears from this that "God" and the "Holy Spirit" are placed on the same plane; both speak in the Scripture. Furthermore, just as Jesus can be "spurned" as God's Son, the Spirit can be "outraged" or "insulted" (Heb. 10:29). The Spirit is not merely a force in Hebrews but rather is God's personal Spirit.[153]

Hebrews does not reflect on or develop a doctrine of the Trinity. Still, there are three texts in which there are adumbrations of what was later developed into trinitarian doctrine. The author reflects on the great salvation that has been revealed in the Son (Heb. 2:1–4), warning the readers not to drift away. And God himself has borne witness to this salvation by signs and wonders and gifts of the Spirit (Heb. 2:4). Perhaps the

153. Lindars (1991: 57) rightly observes, however, that we do not have the later dogmatic formulation on the personality of the Spirit, though he may underestimate the personal character of the Spirit in Hebrews.

most interesting reference to God, the Son, and the Spirit in Hebrews is found in Heb. 9:14 (though whether the Holy Spirit is in view is debated), where the author remarks, "How much more will the blood of Christ, who through the eternal Spirit offered himself without blemish to God, purify our conscience from dead works to worship the living God." Here we have a reference to Christ's blood, the work of the Spirit in Christ's life, and the offering made to God. The author does not reflect on God, the Son, and the Spirit ontologically, but what we find here is suggestive. A more indirect reference occurs in Heb. 10:29, for God is not explicitly mentioned. Still, he is the one who inflicts punishment on those who spurn God's Son and insult the Spirit of grace. It is remarkable here that both the Son and the Spirit are depicted as the objects of insult, and in remarkably personal and provocative terms. Clearly, the author of Hebrews does not develop a doctrine of the Trinity, but some of the clues in the letter are tantalizing and suggestive.

The Spirit in 1 Peter

Categorizing the references to the Spirit in 1 Peter is quite difficult.[154] Most noticeable, perhaps, is the Spirit's relationship to the work of Christ. Since the different uses are not easily grouped into discrete topics, we will consider the texts in the order in which Peter presents them. The first reference to the Spirit is 1 Pet. 1:2, where Peter addresses the recipients of the letter and notes "the sanctification of the Spirit." Some think that the sanctification has to do with ongoing progress and growth in the Christian life. Certainly the noun and verb bear this meaning in some contexts (e.g., Rom. 6:19, 22; 1 Thess. 4:3; 5:23; 2 Tim. 2:21; Heb. 12:14). It is more likely in this instance, however, that definitive sanctification is in view.[155] In other words, Peter speaks of the sanctification that Christians receive at conversion. Supporting this is the context of the greeting, for the election and the obedience of the readers signify that they are members of God's people, indicating that they truly belong to the church of Jesus Christ. Peter calls attention here to the grace of God. The definitive setting apart in the realm of salvation cannot be credited to the nobility of human beings. It is the work of the Holy Spirit.

In 1 Pet. 1:10–12 Peter celebrates the special privilege that believers in Jesus Christ enjoy. Unlike the prophets, they live on the other side of the cross. Hence, they understand the significance of the prophecies uttered under the old covenant, and they live in the era in which God's eschatological salvation has penetrated this present evil age. Peter remarks that the prophecies uttered and recorded by the prophets were

154. See R. Martin 1994: 117–20.
155. See Michaels 1988: 11; Schreiner 2003: 54.

under the aegis of "the Spirit of Christ." What Peter says here echoes the prophetic Spirit of Luke-Acts. Prophetic words and those preserved in the Scriptures are the result of the Spirit's work. Significantly, the Spirit is identified here as "the Spirit of Christ." Peter goes on to say that they "predicted the sufferings of Christ and the subsequent glory" (1 Pet. 1:11). The "Spirit of Christ" bears witness to and testifies of the Christ. In particular, the Spirit predicted Christ's sufferings (his work on the cross for the salvation of his people [1 Pet. 1:18–19; 2:21–25; 3:18]) and his glories (his resurrection and exaltation to the right hand of God [1 Pet. 1:21; 2:7; 3:18–22]). The Spirit's witness, then, is focused particularly on Jesus Christ as the crucified and risen one.

Peter proceeds to say that the prophets ministered ultimately for the church of Jesus Christ, since the subject of their prophecy, Jesus Christ himself, has now come (1 Pet. 1:12). Those who proclaimed the good news of the gospel to the Petrine Christians did so "by the Holy Spirit sent from heaven" (1 Pet. 1:12). Both the OT prophets and those who herald the good news of Christ on this side of the cross speak by means of the Holy Spirit. In both instances, Peter emphasizes, they center on the gospel of Christ. The prophets anticipated the gospel by looking forward to the fulfillment of their prophecies about the Messiah as the crucified and risen Lord. Those who now proclaim the gospel announce the fulfillment of the prophetic word in the life, ministry, death, resurrection, and exaltation of Jesus Christ. In both instances the ministry of the Spirit centers on Jesus Christ. What Peter says here is remarkably similar to what we noted in the Johannine literature. The Spirit witnesses to Jesus Christ. Those who claim a witness of the Spirit but exclude or ignore Jesus Christ deviate from the Petrine view of the ministry of the Spirit, for both the OT prophets and those who proclaim the message of the gospel always call attention to the person and work of Jesus Christ. The reference to the Spirit as the one "sent from heaven" in a context that features the sufferings and glories of Christ suggests that the Spirit is given because of Jesus' exaltation. The Spirit is the gift granted by Jesus after his triumph over all his enemies and his seating at God's right hand (1 Pet. 3:22).

The church of Jesus Christ is "a spiritual house" and offers "spiritual sacrifices" (1 Pet. 2:5). The word "spiritual" here could merely denote that the church of Jesus Christ differs from the literal temple in Jerusalem and does not offer animal sacrifices. Naturally, such an idea is implied. Peter's main point, however, is likely that the church is a "spiritual house" because it is indwelt by the Holy Spirit (cf. 1 Cor. 6:19).[156] Similarly, the

156. In support of a reference to the Holy Spirit, see J. Elliott 1966: 153–54; Best 1969: 292–93.

sacrifices offered are "spiritual" because they are animated by the Holy Spirit. Since redemptive history is fulfilled in Jesus Christ, the shadows have given way to the substance, the types have reached their fulfillment. The Jerusalem temple pointed to the church of Jesus Christ indwelt by the Holy Spirit. The temple offerings point to the good works animated by the Spirit for believers (cf. Heb. 13:15–16).

Two texts appear to refer to the resurrection. The interpretation of the datives in 1 Pet. 3:18 is the subject of considerable controversy. I suggest that the first dative is locative and the second is a dative of agency, so that we should translate thus: "Christ was put to death in the flesh, but made alive by the Spirit."[157] The use of two datives antithetically does not require that both datives have the same grammatical function. The new age commenced with the resurrection of Jesus Christ, and the Spirit is a gift of the new age. In a context that features Christ's victory and rule over demonic powers (1 Pet. 3:18–22) Peter ascribes his resurrection and the beginning of his reign to the work of the Spirit. The Spirit's role in Christ's resurrection is taught elsewhere (Rom. 8:11; cf. 1 Tim. 3:16) and thus is not restricted to Peter.

The precise significance of the flesh-spirit contrast in 1 Pet. 4:6 is debated. Suffering believers are reminded that the opposition and discrimination that they face is short-lived because it is confined to this life. Believers die, and hence they receive a judgment according to the flesh, but they are promised physical resurrection by the same Spirit that raised Jesus from the dead.[158] In the eyes of unbelievers the death of believers constitutes judgment. Peter encourages the church with the promise that their final destiny is resurrection—a resurrection that is the Spirit's work.

The final use of the word "Spirit" is in 1 Pet. 4:14. Peter comforts suffering believers, reminding them that they participate in Christ's sufferings, and that their sufferings, as in the case of Christ, are a prelude to glory (1 Pet. 4:13). The suffering that believers encounter is (or should be) because of their allegiance to Christ. Those who suffer for Christ's name are blessed. To suffer as a Christian is not a matter of shame but rather represents an opportunity to glorify God (1 Pet. 4:16), and in this instance such suffering is in accordance with God's will (1 Pet. 4:19). The association between the sufferings of Christ and the sufferings of believers hearkens back to the Jesus tradition (e.g., Matt. 5:10–12). The opposition that Jesus experienced in his life is now meted out to his followers. When believers suffer, however, God's Spirit rests on them (1 Pet. 4:14). The OT background is illuminating here, for we have an

---

157. For a fuller defense of this interpretation, see Schreiner 2003: 183.
158. For further discussion on this verse, see Schreiner 2003: 208–10.

allusion to Isa. 11:2, where the Davidic Messiah is endowed with the Spirit of the Lord. Peter implies here that the Spirit that rested on Jesus also rests upon the disciples. Jesus as the Spirit-anointed Messiah pours out the same Spirit on his disciples, and their endowment with the Spirit is particularly evident when they suffer.

If we reflect on the Spirit in 1 Peter, what stands out is the Spirit's role with reference to Jesus Christ. The new age in redemptive history has dawned, and the Spirit witnesses to Jesus Christ. The age of fulfill-ment has commenced with Christ's resurrection, which was the result of the Spirit's work (1 Pet. 3:18). The same Spirit that raised Christ will also raise believers on the last day (1 Pet. 4:6). Believers are cleansed from their sins by the blood of Christ, and the Spirit sets them apart at conversion (1 Pet. 1:2). The Spirit spoke through the prophets and de-clares his word through those proclaiming the gospel, and in both cases the Spirit testifies to Jesus Christ as the crucified and risen Lord (1 Pet. 1:10–12). The Spirit has been given to believers—sent from heaven—now that Jesus Christ is exalted. Jesus, as the Spirit-anointed Messiah, sends the same Spirit upon believers that rested upon him (1 Pet. 4:14). Now that the new age of redemptive history has dawned, believers are God's new temple animated by the Spirit, and they offer "spiritual sacrifices," which means that their sacrifices are offered through the Holy Spirit. Peter knows of no work of the Spirit apart from Jesus Christ, and the Spirit's work becomes prominent after Christ's death and resurrection precisely because he came to bear witness to Jesus.

We should also note that we have a trinitarian formula in 1 Pet. 1:2. God foreknows believers, so that they are "elect exiles." The Spirit sancti-fies them, and Jesus sprinkles them with his blood.[159] The formula sug-gests the divine function of Father, Spirit, and Son. Only God foreknows the future, only a divine person can sanctify, and obedience ultimately should be directed to God himself. The threefold reference gains special prominence because it opens the letter, signifying from the outset that the saving work is accomplished by the Father, the Spirit, and Jesus Christ.

Two other texts are suggestive, though less clear than 1 Pet. 1:2. Peter refers to Christ's suffering and his being raised by the Spirit (1 Pet. 3:18). Though God is not mentioned, it is probably implied that God raised Christ by the Spirit. Further, in 1 Pet. 4:14 the Spirit of glory and of God is said to rest upon Christ. Peter alludes here to Isa. 11:1–2, where God causes his Spirit to rest upon a shoot from Jesse. Both of these texts,

---

159. L. Johnson (2002: 221) remarks, "To speak about 'God' in 1 Peter therefore demands speaking as well about Jesus Christ and about the Spirit. Although the language needed to clarify these relations is still three centuries away, it is obvious how 1 Peter both enables and demands that sort of ontological analysis."

then, are suggestive instead of definitive, but they fit nicely with the trinitarian formula in 1 Pet. 1:2.

The Spirit in James, Jude, and 2 Peter

James, Jude, and 2 Peter are included together here because these letters say little about the Spirit. Again we must recall that such a state of affairs does not indicate a lack of interest in the Spirit or a rejection of what other NT writers say about the Spirit. There is no reference to the Spirit in 2–3 John, but it is clear that the author of 1 John and the Gospel of John had a keen interest in the Spirit. All the writings under consideration here are occasional and remarkably brief. James may not mention the Holy Spirit at all. The only direct reference may be in James 4:5, which happens to be one of the most disputed verses in the entire letter. If the reference is to the Holy Spirit, the Spirit's dwelling in believers is noted.

It may be that James uses wisdom where other writers speak of the Spirit.[160] In the OT and Jewish literature the Spirit grants wisdom to God's people. It is also clear that James is infused with the Jesus tradition, whether oral or written, and some of the wisdom texts in James reflect statements about the Spirit in the Gospels. For instance, James exhorts his readers who are bereft of wisdom to ask God. He gives generously and gladly to those who request such a gift (James 1:5). The admonition is similar to what we find in Luke 11:13, where Jesus assures his disciples that God gives "good gifts" to his children; indeed, God will "give the Holy Spirit to those who ask him." Both James and Luke emphasize God's goodness in granting gifts to those who request them. Faith, according to both Luke and James, believes that God is one who desires to bless and benefit his children.

Wisdom in James 3:13–18 manifests itself by its fruit. Those who are dominated by jealousy and selfish pride reveal their folly. Indeed, they indicate that they do not belong to God at all but rather are "soulish" (my translation of *psychikē*) and "demonic" (James 3:15). Wisdom should not be equated with intellectual giftedness, for the wise person lives a righteous life and is characterized by purity, peace, gentleness, mercy, sincerity, and impartiality. What is striking here is that the evidence of true wisdom is comparable to the fruit of the Spirit (Gal. 5:22–23). The overlap between wisdom and the Spirit is suggestive, not definite. In any case, James does not specifically point his readers to the Holy Spirit, but the reference to wisdom is not remarkably far from such a conception.

---

160. So Davids 1982: 51–56. But against this, see L. Cheung 2003: 147–50.

Jude is remarkably brief, and yet we have two references to the Spirit. The first instance reminds us of James 3:15 and is perhaps one indication (among a number of others) that both Jude and James hail from Palestinian Christian circles. The interlopers in Jude have disturbed the church with their libertinism. Jude upbraids them for causing "divisions" and for being "worldly" (my translation of *psychikoi*) and "devoid of the Spirit" (Jude 19). Being "worldly" and "devoid of the Spirit" are two different ways of describing the same reality (cf. 1 Cor. 2:14; Rom. 8:9). These intruders did not share the fundamental mark of authentic Christian faith, for they lacked the Holy Spirit. They lived entirely and wholly on a natural plane.

In Jude 20–21 readers are exhorted to keep themselves in God's love. With three participles Jude explains how they are to do so: (1) by building themselves up with Christian doctrine; (2) by praying in the Holy Spirit; (3) by awaiting eagerly the return of Jesus Christ, which is the day when he will show his mercy. Our focus here is on the second item listed. Some scholars have seen a reference to praying in tongues, but this is unlikely because what Jude commands here is expected of all Christians.[161] Only some believers pray in tongues. Jude refers to the prayer animated by the Spirit, and such prayer should be woven into the fabric of the everyday Christian lives of believers.

Interestingly enough, these two verses in Jude contain a trinitarian formula. Believers are to keep themselves in the love of God, and this plainly refers to the Father. They are to pray in the Holy Spirit and await the mercy of the Lord Jesus Christ. In these two verses, then, Jude refers to the Father, the Spirit, and the Son. The reference to the Trinity is primitive, and certainly no ontological reflection is included. Yet we can hardly deny that the threefold reference is suggestive, and it seems to place the Spirit on the same level as the Father and Jesus Christ.

Only one reference to the Holy Spirit occurs in 2 Peter.[162] The text, 2 Pet. 1:21, is famous, for Peter speaks of the Holy Spirit carrying along the writers of Scripture. Human beings spoke the word, and yet ultimately the inscripturated word is the result of the Spirit's work. Human beings clearly chose to write the words deposited in Scripture, and yet Peter insists that the human will was not ultimate, for the biblical word is finally attributed to the will of God and the work of his Spirit in moving people to write the word of God. What Peter says here is hardly novel, for we have seen elsewhere, particularly in Luke-Acts and Hebrews, that the Scriptures are the work of the Holy Spirit. Perhaps there is even a

---

161. See Schreiner 2003: 483. Contra Bauckham 1983: 113; Dunn 1975b: 239–42.

162. Some think, however, that the reference to the divine nature in 2 Pet. 1:4 refers to the Holy Spirit (see Bigg 1901: 256).

trinitarian cast to 2 Pet. 1:19–21. We are reminded that prophets spoke from God as they were inspired by the Holy Spirit, but the subject of the Spirit's inspiration is the "morning star" of 2 Pet. 1:19, which surely is Jesus Christ.

The Spirit in Revelation

The Spirit in Revelation is the Spirit that speaks and prophecies and witnesses to Jesus Christ. The message that John proclaims is inspired by the Spirit. On four different occasions John emphasizes that he was "in the Spirit" (Rev. 1:10; 4:2; 17:3; 21:10).[163] At the outset of the book he remarks, "I was in the Spirit on the Lord's day" (Rev. 1:10), and he proceeded to see a vision of the Son of Man and to hear his message to the churches in Rev. 1:10–3:21. He emphasizes from the inception of the book that what he writes is the word of the Lord, that he was inspired by the Spirit to write this prophecy (Rev. 1:3).[164] The scene shifts in Rev. 4, and John is brought up to heaven into God's throne room, and further visions are given to him. He comments in Rev. 4:2, "At once I was in the Spirit," noting that the Spirit of prophecy had seized him as he beheld the visions. Similarly, an angel carried "him away in the Spirit into a wilderness" to see the great harlot, Babylon (Rev. 17:3). Again, an angel carried him "away in the Spirit" to a mountain to see the new Jerusalem (Rev. 21:10). In both instances the Spirit ensures that what John saw and recorded was the word of God. The references to John being in the Spirit occur at decisive places in the book: at the inception of the book and John's vision of heaven, and also in the contrast between the two cities, Babylon and the new Jerusalem.[165]

The Spirit also speaks to the churches in the seven letters sent to the churches of Asia Minor. Each letter is intended for a specific church—Ephesus, Smyrna, Pergamum, and so forth. Nevertheless, the individual letters also apply to all the churches. Each letter closes with the exhortation, "He who has an ear, let him hear what the Spirit is saying to the churches" (Rev. 2:7, 11, 17, 29; 3:6, 13, 22). The content of each of the seven letters represents the words of the Spirit addressed to the churches. Remarkably enough, each of the letters also claims to come from the Son of Man, for the introduction of each letter has "the words of . . ." (Rev. 2:1, 8, 12, 18; 3:1, 7, 14), in each case referring to words from Jesus Christ. The words of the risen Christ, the Son of God, therefore, are also

163. On this phrase, see Bauckham 1993b: 150–59.
164. See Beale 1999b: 203. Contra Aune (1997: 83), who sees a reference to the human spirit rather than the Holy Spirit.
165. So Bauckham 1993a: 116.

the words of the Holy Spirit.[166] John emphasizes that the Spirit speaks to the people of God, and yet the message of the Spirit is also the message of the Son of Man.

That the Spirit speaks is affirmed also in Rev. 14:13. A voice from heaven, perhaps an angel's, declares that those who die in the Lord henceforth are blessed. The Spirit concurs, pronouncing a blessing and rest for those who have labored. The Spirit also joins with the bride of Christ in issuing an invitation to come for those who desire to satisfy their thirst (Rev. 22:17). They should come to Christ for salvation. The Spirit's voice, then, summons people to come to Jesus Christ. This fits with the difficult expression in Rev. 19:10, where "the testimony of Jesus is the spirit of prophecy." This likely means that Spirit-inspired prophecy focuses on and exalts Jesus.[167]

A striking text on the Holy Spirit occurs in the grace benediction in Rev. 1:4–5. Grace and peace issue from the Father, "who is and who was and who is to come." They also come from Jesus Christ, who is described as a "faithful witness." Tucked in between the Father and the Son is a reference to "the seven spirits who are before his throne." We noted previously that grace and peace never come from an angel or an apostle; they always come from God or Jesus Christ. Hence, the seven spirits here cannot be angelic. The referent is almost certainly the Holy Spirit.[168] The number "seven" is used to denote the fullness and perfection of the Spirit, since it is typical for apocalyptic literature to use numbers symbolically. The significance of the number "seven" is apparent from the beginning of the Scripture in the creation of the world (Gen. 1:1–2:3). We have seen that Revelation emphasizes the prophetic role of the Spirit, the speaking forth of God's word. In this verse, however, we have a trinitarian formula, for grace and peace come from the Father, the Spirit, and the Son. Apparently, the Spirit shares divine prerogatives with the Father and the Son, and yet no explanation of how the Father, Son, and Spirit relate to one another is provided in Revelation.

Jesus is also said to have the seven spirits of God (Rev. 3:1). It is likely that the first usage of seven spirits in Rev. 1:4 functions as the interpretive lens by which the seven spirits should be understood here.[169] If so, then the point is likely that Jesus is the one endowed by the Spirit. Perhaps

---

166. So also Bauckham 1993a: 117.

167. Bauckham 1993a: 119. Bauckham (1993b: 161) says, "This difficult statement must mean that the witness Jesus bore is the content of Spirit-inspired prophecy."

168. Aune (1997: 33–35) thinks that the seven spirits refer to the seven archangels of Rev. 8:2 (cf. Rev. 3:1; 4:5; 5:6). However, the reference is almost certainly to the Holy Spirit (so Caird 1966: 15; Beale 1999b: 189–90; Osborne 2002: 61, 74–75).

169. As Osborne (2002: 173) observes, the power of the Spirit is given to the readers through Jesus.

there is an allusion here to Isa. 11:2, where seven different qualities are related to the Spirit, and the one upon whom the Spirit rests is none other than the descendant of Jesse—the messianic king.

God sits on his throne in Rev. 4, and his glory is stunningly beautiful. Before God's throne are "seven torches of fire, which are the seven spirits of God" (Rev. 4:5).[170] The seven "torches" (*lampades*) allude to the golden lampstand with seven lamps in Zechariah (Zech. 4:2). The lampstand in Zechariah is filled by the two olive trees, Joshua and Zerubbabel. The power for Joshua and Zerubbabel to build the temple, however, comes from the Spirit. Hence, God declares, "Not by might, nor by power, but by my Spirit says the LORD of hosts" (Zech. 4:6). Perhaps here is also an allusion to Isa. 4:4, which speaks of "a spirit of judgment" and "a spirit of burning" by which Israel is cleansed. The seven spirits burning before God's throne may refer to God's power and holiness, which make approaching God's throne a fearful thing. If this analysis is correct, then the Spirit is associated with God himself in his power and holiness.

The last reference to the seven spirits of God occurs in Rev. 5, where the Lamb is worshiped. The Lamb has seven horns and seven eyes, and John remarks that these "are the seven spirits of God sent out into all the earth" (Rev. 5:6). The seven horns and seven eyes indicate that the Lamb is all-powerful and all-knowing.[171] Nothing can conquer him, nor does anything escape his searching gaze (cf. Rev. 1:14; 2:18; 19:12). We could argue that the reference to the seven spirits continues to refer to Jesus Christ, and no reference to the Holy Spirit is in view. On the other hand, we have seen evidence that Jesus is endowed with the Spirit (Rev. 3:1). Further, the style of apocalyptic is fluid and suggestive, so that a reference to Jesus does not eliminate a reference to the Holy Spirit as well. The Lamb stands out in the vision as the one who was slain, obviously referring to Jesus' death. The sending out of the seven spirits suggests a commonplace in NT theology.[172] The Spirit is sent out to human beings as a consequence of Jesus' death and his victory over evil. The crucified and exalted Jesus gives his people the gift of the Holy Spirit. Perhaps Bauckham is correct as well in claiming that John argues here that the witness of the church in the world is accomplished by the Spirit.[173]

---

170. Osborne (2002: 231) comments, "The perfect Spirit is the means by which God will oversee and judge his creation."

171. Bauckham (1993b: 164) remarks, "It is important to realize that the eyes of Yahweh in the Old Testament indicate not only his ability to see what happens throughout the world, but also his ability to act powerfully whenever he chooses."

172. So also Bauckham (1993a: 113), who also observes that "the seven Spirits are God's presence and power on earth, bringing about God's kingdom by implementing the Lamb's victory throughout the world." See also Beale 1999b: 355; Osborne 2002: 257.

173. Bauckham 1993b: 165.

Another possible reference to the Spirit is the "breath of life" that enters the two witnesses after their deaths, so that they come back to life and join God in heaven (Rev. 11:11–12).[174] The meaning of this text cannot be separated from the interpretation of the chapter as a whole. Commentators have long disputed the identity of the two witnesses. Space is lacking to defend the view proposed here that the two witnesses, alluding to Zech. 4, refer to the Christian church.[175] Their deaths, then, signify the deaths received by God's people at the hand of the beast (Rev. 13:7, 15; cf. 16:6; 17:6; 19:2; 20:4). The breath of life alludes to Ezek. 37, where God's breath grants life to dead bones (see Ezek. 37:5, 10). The resurrection in Ezek. 37 is the work of God's Spirit: "And I will put my Spirit within you, and you shall live" (Ezek. 37:14). Hence, Rev. 11 seems to attribute the resurrection of the church of Jesus Christ to the work of the Holy Spirit.

In Revelation John stresses that the Spirit is the Spirit of prophecy. John speaks to his contemporaries by the Spirit. The Spirit speaks to the churches of Asia Minor in the letters to the seven churches and invites all to come to Jesus for life (Rev. 22:17). The Spirit authoritatively pronounces that those who die in the Lord are blessed and now enjoy rest from their labors (Rev. 14:13). The Spirit of God is closely related to Jesus Christ. The messages from the Spirit to the churches, as we noted above, also are the words of the Son of Man. Jesus is the one endowed with the Spirit (Rev. 3:1), and the Spirit is given to believers as a result of his death (Rev. 5:6). That the Spirit comes when Jesus is glorified is a central theme in the Gospel of John (see John 7:39; 16:7–15; cf. 14:16–17, 25–26; 15:26; 20:22). The Spirit is placed on the same plane as the Father and the Son, for grace and peace come from him (Rev. 1:4–5). He is the holy and powerful Spirit that resides with God (Rev. 4:5). He grants resurrection life to believers (Rev. 11:11), vindicating those who suffered for Jesus. John has no interest in ontological speculation about the Holy Spirit, but clearly the Spirit is personal, for he speaks and issues invitations. Further, he performs divine functions such as granting life and giving grace and peace. The trinitarian character of Revelation is striking, for, as we have noted previously, grace benedictions come only from God. We have a trinitarian wish for grace and peace from the Father, the Spirit, and Jesus Christ in Rev. 1:4–5.[176] Evidently, the Father, the Spirit, and the

174. So Osborne 2002: 430.

175. So Beale (1999b: 572–76), who also notes other interpretations. Bauckham (1993a: 113–14) also proposes that the allusion to Zech. 4 suggests an anointing with the oil of God's Spirit, so that the Spirit animates the prophetic ministry of the church.

176. Revelation closes in the same way as do many of Paul's letters: "The grace of the Lord Jesus be with all. Amen" (Rev. 22:21). Grace and peace come only from God, and therefore these texts signal the divine status of Jesus Christ.

Son belong on the same level, for only God can grant grace and peace. What we find here, then, is quite astonishing, even though Revelation does not pursue the ontological ramifications of the benediction.

Conclusion

The gift of the Spirit is prophesied in the OT and given in the NT, and so the Spirit is the signature and mark of the commencement of the new age. The Spirit testifies that the new creation and new exodus have arrived, that the day of fulfillment has come. Such fulfillment, of course, centers on Jesus Christ. The Gospel writers emphasize that Jesus was uniquely anointed with the Spirit beginning with his baptism, so that his entire ministry was carried out in the Spirit's strength. Jesus is not only the bearer of the Spirit but also the one who gives the Spirit to his people. In Acts the gift of the Spirit signifies that one belongs to the people of God. Such theology is not limited to Acts, of course, for Paul insists that the Galatians have no need of circumcision to belong to the people of God because the powerful work of the Spirit is evident among them and in them (Gal. 3:1–5).

The Spirit is also the Spirit of prophecy. Often in the NT those who speak for God are said to be animated by the Spirit, and in many of these texts the focus is on the fulfillment of God's saving promises. The blessing that God has promised to the whole world has arrived with the gift of the Spirit. But the giving of the Holy Spirit is tied to the ministry, death, resurrection, and exaltation of Jesus Christ. NT writers do not conceive of a ministry of the Spirit apart from the work of Jesus Christ as the crucified and risen one. The spread of the word to all nations in Acts and the Pauline letters is empowered by the Spirit, so that the Spirit is the means by which the mission goes forth, but the gift of the Spirit is conveyed through the preached word of the gospel. There is no diffuse and general work of the Spirit apart from Jesus Christ. The revelation and teaching ministry of the Spirit emphasized in John's Gospel is anchored in the work of the historical Jesus. The Spirit has come to glorify Christ and to instruct believers further regarding his death and resurrection.

The Spirit grants power for ministry but also strengthens believers so that they live lives that are pleasing to God. This too signals the arrival of the new age, for the law was unable to transform human beings, but the Spirit energizes human beings to obey God in contrast to the inability and weakness of the law. The Spirit's work in granting life is linked to the assurance granted to believers by the same Spirit, for those who have experienced God's love are assured by the witness of the Spirit in their hearts. Finally, although no formal doctrine of the Trinity is worked out or explicated in the NT, there are numerous indications of a trinitarian framework in the NT documents. Quite a few trinitarian formulas are found in the NT, and in a number of texts the Father, Son, and Spirit work together in accomplishing salvation for believers. It is difficult to believe that the Father and the Son are personal in these instances while the Spirit is subpersonal or conceived of as a force. The saving work of God becomes a reality through the Father, the Son, and the Spirit. If the saving promises of God bring glory to God through Christ, it is also the case that the Holy Spirit plays a central role in this whole process and, in particular, calls attention to Jesus Christ.

PART 3

EXPERIENCING THE PROMISE

Believing and Obeying

14

❧ ❧ ❧ ❧ ❧ ❧ ❧ ❧ ❧ ❧ ❧ ❧ ❧ ❧ ❧ ❧ ❧ ❧

The Problem of Sin

We have seen thus far that the promises of salvation were fulfilled with the coming of Jesus Christ and the work of the Holy Spirit. The new age and new creation and new covenant had indeed dawned. God deserves praise and honor, for salvation is the work of the Father, the Son, and the Spirit. NT writers do not reflect philosophically on the relationship of the Father, Son, and Spirit, and a formal doctrine of the Trinity is not enunciated. They focus on the work of salvation that is accomplished by Father, Son, and Spirit. God's promises of salvation have been accomplished through the cross of Jesus Christ and the saving work of the Holy Spirit. But why is the saving work of the Father, Son, and Spirit needed? The saving work of God presupposes that human beings need to be rescued from sin. At this juncture, therefore, we will back up to investigate the plight from which human beings need to be rescued.

The Synoptic Gospels

The Synoptic Gospels presuppose that the people of God, Israel, need a saving work of God. The story line of the OT is assumed as a backdrop, so that readers have difficulty grasping the worldview of the Synoptics without at least a rudimentary grasp of the OT. For example, Matthew opens his Gospel by referring to Israel's exile to Babylon in 586 BC

(Matt. 1:11–12, 17).[1] Anyone acquainted with the OT would be reminded that Israel was exiled because of its sin. Since the exile is prominent in Matthew's genealogy—a genealogy promising a king who would save Israel—Matthew seems to suggest that the promises that the Lord made to Israel have not been fulfilled because of Israel's sin. This is confirmed by the promise that Jesus would come and save the people Israel from their sin (Matt. 1:21).

None of the Gospel writers emphasize that Israel is still in exile, though the genealogy in Matthew refers to it three times.[2] Yet there are hints that Israel is still in exile or, perhaps better because the Gospel writers do not specifically speak of God's people being in exile, that the saving promises of God have not come to fulfillment. The proclamation of the Baptist in the wilderness (Matt. 3:3 par.) and baptism in the Jordan suggests that Israel was, so to speak, on the wrong side of the Jordan.[3] They needed to confess their sins (Matt. 3:6) in order to receive forgiveness of sins, so that God's covenant promises to Israel would be realized. They were not protected from God's wrath simply because Abraham was their father (Matt. 3:9 par.). A genealogical connection to the progenitor of the Jewish people does not ensure that one will be a recipient of God's salvation. Repentance is evidenced by good works showing that one has truly changed. The Baptist identified the common people (Luke 3:7–8) and the Pharisees and Sadducees (Matt. 3:7) as a "brood of vipers." They were, therefore, the seed not of Abraham but of the serpent (Gen. 3:15). Unless they repented, they would not enjoy God's saving work for Israel but would be judged in the same way as the Gentiles.

The Synoptics emphasize, therefore, that sin is a deeply rooted disease in Israel. Human beings are fundamentally deserving of wrath from God, lacking the godliness demanded. Their sin should provoke mourning and a hunger and thirst for the righteousness that they lack (Matt. 5:4, 6). Human beings are vividly described as rotten trees (Matt. 7:17–19; 12:33; Luke 6:43–44).[4] The evil that besets human beings is not limited to evil actions that need reformation and correction. The "tree" itself has

1. Davies and Allison (1988: 187) note that a number of Jewish works (Daniel, *1 Enoch, 2 Baruch*) "are at one in placing the epoch of the exile immediately before the epoch of redemption."

2. For the theme of exile, see Wright 1992b. Whether it is fitting to say that Israel considered itself still to be in exile is the subject of intense discussion in scholarship. For a survey of the theme, see Scott 1997. For sharp criticisms of Wright's view, see Seifrid 1994: 86–92; Bryan 2002: 12–20.

3. For an unpacking of this theme in Mark's Gospel with reference to the new exodus, see Watts 2000.

4. On the Lukan view of Gentiles previous to faith in Christ, see Stenschke 1999. Stenschke's careful and comprehensive study demonstrates that in both Luke and Acts we find an anthropology that emphasizes that Gentiles are sinners in need of God's saving work.

a deep-seated pollution requiring a new good tree in place of the rotten one. Jesus announced that human beings are not "righteous" but are "sinners." He uses the metaphor of sickness to depict what ails people (Matt. 9:12–13 par.). Unfortunately, many, especially the religious leaders, refused to admit that they were afflicted by a disease, insisting that they were righteous and in no need of a physician.[5] Human pride refuses to acknowledge spiritual poverty and the radical need for renewal.

The evil of human beings does not mean that human beings are as wicked as they can possibly be. Jesus said that human beings are "evil," but at the same time he acknowledged that parents bestow good gifts upon their children (Matt. 7:11; Luke 11:13). Human beings may have a deep affection for their children, treat their neighbors with civility, and even practice virtue in the public square and still be polluted by evil. The most serious problem among human beings is the failure to recognize the evil within and the impact of such evil on others. Therefore, Jesus commended the centurion because he recognized his unworthiness (Matt. 8:8–10 par.), for the centurion was keenly aware that he fell short of God's requirements. Those who truly know God know him in the midst of their misery because they constantly see the log of sin that blights their vision (Matt. 7:3, 5 par.).

Jesus often castigated the sin of the religious leaders, particularly the Pharisees.[6] Such strong indictments have raised the issue of anti-Semitism, especially when we consider the history of Christian mistreatment of the Jews. NT writers, however, never intended these indictments to provide a platform for the maltreatment of others. The religious leaders represented the tendency of all human beings when they rise to the top of a religious or social structure.[7] Hence, what Jesus said to the religious leaders serves as an indictment of all who fail to repent and reveals what is naturally in the heart of every human being, whether Jew or Gentile.[8]

The Pharisees and scribes are criticized because although they acknowledged the worship of God with their lips, their hearts swerved in another direction (Matt. 15:8–9 par.). The true and living God was distant from them, and their professed love lacked reality. Jesus catalogued their

His study functions as a helpful contrast and corrective to those who see an optimistic anthropology in the Lukan writings.

5. Rightly Hagner 1993b: 240.

6. The literature on the Pharisees is immense. See especially the history of research in Deines 1997. See also Neusner 1971; Rivkin 1978; E. Sanders 1990: 380–451; Silva 1986. For Neusner's response to the view of Sanders, see Neusner 1991.

7. The notion that not all Pharisees were alike is indicated by the seven different types of Pharisees. See Montefiore and Loewe 1974: 487–89.

8. Fitzmyer (1985: 1185) captures reality well in saying that "there remains in everyone more than a little of the Pharisee."

sins in Matt. 23 (cf. Mark 12:38–40; Luke 11:37–52; 20:46).[9] They failed to practice what they preached, teaching one thing and doing another. They engaged in religious observance so that others would notice them and be duly impressed by their behavior. They coveted places of honor at feasts and greetings in public because the praise of people was their god. They neglected what is weighty and clear in the law and became preoccupied with what is secondary. On the outside they appeared to be righteous and pure, but inside they were stained by deep corruption, so that they were comparable to whitewashed tombs. Their evil culminated in the execution of God's messengers, showing that they were not the seed of Abraham at all but were a "brood of vipers"—the seed of the serpent.

What is said about the leaders cannot be restricted to them. By nature the hearts of all people are dull and insensitive to the things of God, nor are people genuinely interested in hearing and seeing what God has to say to them (Matt. 13:15). Mark emphasizes that the same malady afflicts the disciples. They suffered from hard hearts that resisted the revelation of God in Jesus (Mark 6:52; 8:17, 21).[10] They failed to grasp the significance of Jesus' teaching, and their failure cannot be attributed merely to intellectual incapacity. At bottom they were also idolaters, and so they quarreled about which of them was the greatest and would receive the highest rewards in the kingdom (Mark 9:33–37; 10:35–45; Luke 9:46–48; 22:24–27).

Judgment will be meted out to those who are lawbreakers and cause others to sin (Matt. 13:41, 49). The problem with the Pharisees and Sadducees, though it is not limited to them, was that they were "evil" and "an adulterous generation" (Matt. 16:4). Their devotion was not genuinely directed to the true and living God, even though they claimed that they lived in service to him. Indeed, Israel as a whole is "faithless" and "twisted" (Matt. 17:17 par.). This is the same complaint voiced by the Lord about Israel of old (Deut. 32:5). Though they were redeemed by the Lord from Egypt, they did not truly love or obey him. Israel claimed to love the Lord, but Jesus maintained that they had always killed the prophets and rejected God's messengers, culminating in the rejection of Jesus as God's Son (Matt. 21:33–46 par.).[11] Israel had no real interest in the messianic wedding celebration and was fundamentally bored with what God offered (Matt. 22:5). Even when in attendance, Israel does not wear proper garb for a wedding (Matt. 22:11–13). Israel knew what God

9. For an intensive analysis of Matt. 23, see Garland 1979.

10. For the disciples' hardness of heart and incomprehension in Mark, see Hawkin 1972; Watts 2000: 228–36.

11. Schlatter (1997: 149) rightly says, "Jesus did not seek to shame a person through the exposure of his sin. Where sin is recognized, love remains silent."

required, for it is enshrined in the OT (Deut. 6:4–9). It is evident, though, that the nation and its leaders failed to love the Lord with everything in them (Matt. 22:37–40 par.).

What was required of Israel, therefore, is repentance (Matt. 3:2 par.). Jesus did not write off Israel and its leaders; he offered them an opportunity to turn from their sins and receive forgiveness (Matt. 4:17; Mark 1:14–15). Those who failed to repent would perish (Luke 13:3, 5).[12] The disciples and the tax collectors and sinners were not fundamentally better than the Pharisees or religious leaders. Jesus did not engage in class warfare in which he exalted the peasantry over the elite and rich. The poor can be just as petty, vain, and selfish as the rich (cf. Matt. 11:20–24). Tax collectors and sinners were differentiated from the religious leaders because they repented, not because of their nobility (Matt. 9:10 par.).[13]

Peter, as the leader of the Twelve, represented the faults and self-absorption of Jesus' disciples. He was distinguished from the religious leaders because he admitted that he was not a "good tree": "Depart from me, for I am a sinful man, O Lord" (Luke 5:8). The same distinction appears in the parable of the two lost sons, representing tax collectors and sinners and the Pharisees respectively (Luke 15:11–32). Both sons were selfish and wicked. The younger son, however, recognized what he had become. He realized what he deserved: "Father, I have sinned against heaven and before you. I am no longer worthy to be called your son. Treat me as one of your hired servants" (Luke 15:18–19). Those who sin despise God. They are dead and separated from life and are lost instead of being found (Luke 15:24, 32). The lostness of human beings is captured by the aphorism "the Son of Man came to seek and to save the lost" (Luke 19:10). The older son, however, continued to insist on his goodness, claiming to have obeyed his father perfectly (Luke 15:29). He despised the younger son and castigated him for his immorality, all the while failing to see his own evil (Luke 15:30). The father entreated the older son to repent and to join in the celebration of the younger son's return. The critique of religious leaders is not an evidence of anti-Semitism but rather functions as a warning to all. No one is free from evil. All must repent and turn away from their evil and toward God. It is not enough merely to say that one will carry out God's will; what counts is if one ultimately repents and does what God commands (Matt. 21:28–32).[14] Too many of the Pharisees congratulated themselves on their righteousness,

---

12. In Lukan scholarship some have argued that salvation is not linked to forgiveness of sins, and that repentance is not demanded. For a vigorous and convincing critique of such views, see Stenschke 1998; Witherington 1998.

13. Contra E. Sanders (1985: 203–11), who thinks that the call to repentance is a Lukan redaction. Rightly Meier 1994: 212n154.

14. See Schlatter 1997: 150.

contrasting themselves with tax collectors, who were notoriously evil (Luke 18:9–14).[15] The tax collector, on the other hand, had a true vision of himself. He realized what true repentance is, and so he exclaimed, "God, be merciful to me, a sinner" (Luke 18:13).

That sin disrupts the relation between believers and God is evident from the texts that speak of forgiveness of sins (Matt. 9:2 par.; 26:28; Luke 1:77). Even believers need to pray regularly for forgiveness of sins (Matt. 6:12 par.). What is striking about the teaching on forgiveness of sins is its "democratic" leveling, for all are corrupted and guilty because of sin, and so all need to live in repentance.

The sinfulness of human beings is perhaps most evident in their rejection of Jesus and God. Those who fail to acknowledge Jesus will be denied by him (Matt. 10:32–33 par.). Those who are scandalized by Jesus stand in opposition to God himself (Matt. 11:6 par.). The blasphemy against the Holy Spirit occurs when the miracles of Jesus are classed as the work of Beelzebul (Matt. 12:24 par.). People need to repent now that Jesus has come, for he is greater than Jonah (Matt. 12:41). The rejection of Jesus in his very own hometown signified that they were far from God (Matt. 13:53–58 par.). The so-called goodness of the rich ruler was revealed to be false because he refused to follow Jesus in discipleship (Matt. 19:21 par.). It is revealed thereby that his money was his idol, that he failed to obey both the first and the tenth commandments, for he served another god and coveted possessions (cf. Luke 12:15; 16:14–15).[16]

In the story line of the Gospels, the sin of Israel culminated in the betrayal and crucifixion of Jesus the Messiah. When he appeared in Israel's midst, God's chosen one was not embraced but was murdered. Obviously, the Romans were complicit in the events, but the Gospel accounts, despite the work of modern revisionists, are clear. The Jewish leaders took the lead in condemning Jesus to death. Indeed, the Gospels also teach that Israel as a whole failed to embrace Jesus. Such a historical truth could and has led to anti-Semitism. Anti-Semitism is, of course, a horrible evil and functions as an example of twisted logic by any who embrace it. Indeed, those who engage in it actually replicate the evil perpetrated by the Jews who condemned Jesus, revealing the irony and depth of sin. The Gospel writers never intended the execution of Jesus by the Jews to become a pretext for anti-Semitism, since from a theological standpoint

15. For a helpful exposition of the parable, see Bailey 1980: 142–56. Jesus here clearly criticizes the legalistic mind-set of the Pharisee (rightly Marshall 1978b: 681; Fitzmyer 1985: 1184–85), and as Fitzmyer notes, we have the roots here of Paul's teaching on justification.

16. "For the fact that the man goes away with darkened countenance is the sign that he has made his riches into an idol, from which it is too hard to part" (Cranfield 1963: 330).

the evangelists consistently view *all* people as evil. The very point of the story is that if the leaders of God's people, who knew the OT promises of salvation from reading the Scriptures, executed Jesus, then there is no people group anywhere at any time that would have done otherwise. The searchlight that shines on the disciples' sins and hard-heartedness indicates that they would have done the same apart from God's grace. Hence, those who use the narrative as a pretext to discriminate against Jews reveal how profoundly they have failed to grasp the meaning of the account, and how they themselves have, irony of ironies, become modern-day Pharisees. We also need to recognize that we have an internecine Jewish squabble here about truth and righteousness. The indictment of Israel was akin to the searing indictments brought by the prophets in the OT, whose words against God's people are not an evidence of hatred but rather represent a call and an opportunity for repentance.[17]

In the Synoptic Gospels sin is described colorfully. All people are stained by sin and selfish wills, even the religious leaders. The "tree" is rotten and needs to be made good. A stubborn and evil heart displays itself in a life of evil, one where God is not prized and where people are corrupted by pride. Hence, all are called upon to repent, and this repentance reveals itself in hearing and heeding the kingdom message proclaimed by Jesus.

The Gospel of John and the Johannine Letters

Sin is never analyzed abstractly in the Johannine literature, nor do we see there anything like a full-scale treatment of the topic.[18] The OT story line and revelation of God are presupposed and function as the background for understanding sin. Perhaps we can also say that sin does not receive an "objective" treatment, since all human beings have experienced it. They recognize its presence in their hearts and in the lives of fellow human beings.

The sin of human beings is portrayed by John with striking images. For instance, those who sin live in the realm of darkness. Walking in the darkness is not accidental, nor is it some cruel trick of fate. People "love" the darkness because they love practicing evil (John 3:19–20).[19]

17. See especially the essays in Evans and Hagner 1993, which argue that NT writers were not guilty of anti-Semitism. What we find is a polemic within Judaism akin to the critiques that we find in the OT prophets.

18. Here I have combined the Gospel and Epistles of John in discussing sin because the portrait of sin in both is substantially the same.

19. See Köstenberger 2004: 131. Lindars (1972: 161) mistakenly reduces the impact of sin by separating it from one's emotions.

They flee from the light because the light exposes the evil motives of the heart and evil deeds (John 3:21). The only escape from darkness is through faith in and obedience to Jesus, for he is the light of the world (John 8:12; 12:35, 46) and is the one who conquers darkness (John 1:5). Those who live in hate dwell in darkness, revealing that they belong to the old age in which darkness reigns, instead of the new era in which the light is dawning (1 John 2:8–11). The "night" functions symbolically for John. Nicodemus visited Jesus at night, revealing Nicodemus's spiritual state (John 3:2; cf. 9:4; 11:10).[20] He commended Jesus as a teacher because of the signs that he performed, but Jesus was not gratified by praise from this member of the religious elite. Nicodemus dwelt in the darkness and did not grasp Jesus' identity. He needed to be born from above (John 3:3, 5, 7) to enter the realm of light. After Judas betrayed Jesus (John 13:30), John observed that "it was night," for the betrayal of Jesus and his death is the apex of evil.[21]

John also uses a spatial metaphor to delineate those who live in the realm of darkness. They "are from below," while Jesus is "from above" (John 8:23). Another way of saying this is that they are restricted to this world, which is dominated by evil. In some instances "world" (*kosmos*) is used rather neutrally in John's Gospel: Jesus was with the Father before the creation of the world (John 17:5, 24); the world cannot contain everything that Jesus said or did (John 21:25); the world refers to human beings (John 12:19). But John typically uses the term to refer to the world of human beings that oppose God and his will.[22] Even though Jesus "was in the world" and made the world, the world of human beings did not know him or embrace him as the Son of God (John 1:10). The world neither knows nor loves the Father (John 17:25). Jesus came to the world and God demonstrated his love for the world by sending Jesus so that the world would be saved (John 3:16–17), revealing that the world's natural state is one of condemnation and judgment. John often emphasizes that Jesus' mission was to give life to the world through his death.[23] Hence, it follows that the world resides in death and darkness. The love of God for the world, therefore, calls attention at least implicitly to the dark side of the world, to the evil in the world that needs healing.

The world hates Jesus because he reproves its evil and exposes it (John 7:7; 8:26). It rejoices mightily over Jesus' death (John 16:20). In

20. Carson 1991b: 186; Barrett 1978: 204–5 (cautiously). Contra Köstenberger 2004: 120.

21. Rightly Barrett 1978: 448–49.

22. See Barrett 1978: 161–62. Carson (1991b: 122–23) argues that the term focuses on the rebellion of the created order.

23. John 1:29; 3:16–17; 4:42; 6:33, 51; 8:12; 9:5; 10:36; 11:9, 27; 12:46–47; 16:21; 18:20, 37; 1 John 2:2; 4:9, 14.

one sense, therefore, Jesus came to judge the world (John 9:39). Satan is the world's ruler (John 12:31; 14:30; 16:11), and hence all unbelievers live under his dominion (1 John 5:19), and they pay heed to the world's wisdom (1 John 4:5; 2 John 7). Jesus' kingdom is not of this world or of the present evil age (John 18:36). But Jesus has overcome Satan and the world, so that his disciples can rejoice even in this world of adversity (John 16:33). Believers overcome the world because they have been born again and because of their faith in Jesus as the Son of God (1 John 5:4–5). The world cannot and will not on its own receive the Spirit, who witnesses to the truth (John 14:17). The world believes the lies of the antichrist instead of receiving the witness to the truth (1 John 4:1, 3, 5). Those who love the world do not belong to God (1 John 2:15–17). Because the world is devoted to evil, it will not receive a revelation of Jesus' identity (John 14:19, 22) unless the Spirit convicts the world of its sin (John 16:8). And yet those who belong to Jesus have been called out of this world and are now part of his flock, though originally they too belonged to the world (John 13:1; 15:19; 17:6). Hence, their deliverance from the world can only be explained by God's grace.

There is not an absolute dualism between Jesus' flock and the world, as if the former know nothing of evil. The disciples too knew evil all too well, but they have been liberated by the work of the Lamb of God, who atoned for their sins (John 1:29). The world, on the other hand, hates Jesus' disciples because they belong to Jesus, so that the hatred of Jesus' disciples indicates that they hate Jesus himself (John 15:18–19; 17:14; 1 John 3:13; cf. 1 John 3:1). Hence, Jesus prayed especially for his disciples, who continued to reside in a world opposed to him and to the truth (John 17:9, 11). He prayed that they would be preserved from the evil one who rules over the world, and that their separation from the world of evil would continue (John 17:15–16). Nor are the lines between good and evil fixed, with only the disciples standing against the world. They are sent into the world to rescue those under the dominion of evil, knowing that some, like themselves, will be saved and acknowledge Jesus as the one sent by the Father (John 17:18, 21, 23).[24]

John squarely faces the power of evil in his writings. Even the Jews, God's chosen people, did not recognize or receive Jesus (John 1:11). Often John's portrait of the Jews is judged to be anti-Semitic because he regularly paints "the Jews" as opposing Jesus. The term "the Jews" (*hoi Ioudaioi*) in John's Gospel regularly refers to the religious leaders in

24. See Köstenberger 2004: 492.

Judaism,[25] but the term can also be used to designate Jewish practices.[26] Jesus himself is identified as a "Jew," and Jews are distinguished from Samaritans (John 4:9). Jesus himself proclaimed that "salvation is from the Jews" (John 4:22). In some contexts it is unclear whether "the Jews" refers only to religious leaders or whether it has a wider referent.[27] For instance, the Jews who believed in Jesus but then subsequently wanted to put him to death probably cannot be restricted to religious leaders (John 8:31, 48, 52, 57). Those who accuse John of anti-Semitism read him superficially and fail to grasp his message.[28] John's point is that if the people of the promise rejected Jesus, then the tentacles of evil are more powerful than anticipated. They reach out and clutch all. No one is exempted. John, after all, was a Jew himself, and he does not exempt himself or any of the disciples from evil. Their deliverance can only be explained by the love of God in sending his Son to save them from deserved condemnation. Insofar as the church has fallen prey to anti-Semitism, it too betrays subjugation to evil. But it is not anti-Semitism to say that Jesus is the Savior of the world, and that apart from Jesus all are snared by evil.

Jesus unflinchingly teaches that those who refuse to believe in him will die in their sins (John 8:21, 24). Only those who abide in his teaching will be liberated from slavery to sin (John 8:31, 34). Hence, those who do not believe in Jesus have the devil as their father (John 8:44); they are children neither of God nor of Abraham (John 8:39–40, 42, 47). They desired to kill Jesus, even if they denied that such was their intention (John 8:37, 40; cf. 8:59; 10:31). Because they were enslaved to wickedness and refused to trust in Jesus, they lived under God's wrath (John 3:18, 36). Those who practice wickedness will be raised to judgment on the last day (John 5:29). John defines sin as lawlessness (1 John 3:4), which means a refusal to do the will of God and to keep his commandments. Lawlessness, then, cannot be restricted to failure to observe God's commands. Lawlessness signifies rebellion against God and a calculated refusal to submit to him.[29]

Another way of describing the power of sin is to say that those who are born into this world are spiritually blind. If human beings would humble

25. For the view that the term most often refers to Jewish leaders, but with a sensitivity to other uses, see Carson 1991b: 141–42. See also Barrett 1978: 171–72. For references, see John 1:19; 2:18, 20; 5:10, 15, 16, 18; 7:1; 8:22; 9:18, 22; 10:19, 24, 31, 33; 11:8, 54; 13:33; 18:12, 14, 31, 36, 38; 19:7, 12, 14, 21, 31, 38.

26. John 2:6, 13; 5:1; 6:4; 7:2, 11, 13, 15; 11:55; 19:40, 42; 20:19.

27. John 6:41, 52; 7:35; 11:19, 31, 33, 36, 45; 12:9, 11; 18:20, 33, 39; 19:3, 19, 20, 21.

28. See Carson 1991b: 142.

29. Marshall (1978a: 176–77) rightly argues that sin here is not merely the failure to observe the law but rather constitutes rebellion against God. See also Smalley 1984: 154–55; R. Brown 1982: 399–400.

themselves and admit that they are blind, then they would truly see (John 9:39–41).[30] But pride and stubbornness invade the human heart so that people fail to admit that they walk in darkness. If they were willing to carry out God's will, they would realize that Jesus came from God (John 7:17). They refused to come to Jesus for life (John 5:40) or receive him in the Father's name (John 5:43). Such rejection of Jesus stems from a lust for human approval and the glory and honor that comes from peers (John 5:44).[31] People refused to believe in Jesus because they did not want to face expulsion from the synagogue (John 9:22; 12:42–43), for "they loved the glory that comes from man more than the glory that comes from God" (John 12:43). The purpose of human life is to live to the glory and praise of God. It is not surprising, then, that sin at its foundation lives for the glory and praise of human beings instead of living to please the one and only true God.

John starkly portrays human sin. The world is opposed to the things of God. Even the Jewish people, who were God's chosen ones, rejected Jesus the Messiah. Human beings live under the rule of Satan; they reside in the darkness rather than in the light; they are from below instead of from above; they love lies instead of clinging to the truth; they hate the light because the darkness seems beautiful to them. The supreme manifestation of sin is the refusal to believe in Jesus. Human beings prefer praise and glory from other humans over the love of God. Sin, then, is lawlessness, for it represents the refusal to believe in Jesus as the Christ; it is a fierce rebellion that refuses to submit to Jesus as Lord.

Acts

Acts does not reflect deeply on human sin, though this is hardly surprising, given the genre of the literature. We should also remember that what Luke says about sin (see discussion of the Synoptics above) should be added to what is found in Acts. In Peter's sermon on Pentecost he exhorted his hearers to save themselves "from this crooked generation" (Acts 2:40).[32] The wording hearkens back to Deut. 32:5 and Moses' song about Israel, where Israel is faulted for having a heart far from God. The allusion to Deuteronomy is important, for it reveals the power and influence of sin even over those who received God's revelation and were the objects of his saving work. Stephen also reached back to Israel's history

---

30. "In fact till now they were *all* blind; for v. 41 shows that the 'seeing' were only those who imagined they could see, while the 'blind' were those who knew they were blind" (Bultmann 1971: 341).

31. See Barrett 1978: 269; Lincoln 2000: 80.

32. See Barrett 1994: 157.

and found the same sins present in his day as in former generations. The people were "stiff-necked" and "uncircumcised in heart and ears" (Acts 7:51). Israel's apostasy at the incident of the golden calf revealed that the people were "stiff-necked" (Acts 7:39–41; cf. Exod. 33:3, 5; 34:9; Deut. 9:6, 13).[33] Israel's uncircumcised heart indicates that the people are unregenerate (Lev. 26:41; cf. Deut. 10:16; Jer. 4:4; 9:25–26). In the history of Israel those who were stiff-necked and resistant to God failed to do God's will as revealed in Torah. Because of their disobedience, they went into exile to both Assyria (722 BC) and Babylon (586 BC). Stephen argued that idolatry was characteristic of Israel's history (Acts 7:42–43).[34] The Jews of his day had fallen prey to the same sin; they claimed to treasure God's law but failed to observe it (Acts 6:11, 13–14; 7:39, 53).

The inability to keep God's law is also featured in Peter's comments at the Jerusalem Council (Acts 15:10–11).[35] The Pharisees among the Christian believers demanded that Gentile converts practice circumcision in order to be saved (Acts 15:1, 5). Peter remarked that the yoke of the Torah had been observed neither by the fathers nor by the people of his own generation. Hence, the only way people can be saved is through grace because human obedience has not secured (and indeed cannot secure) the promised blessing. Peter did not merely indict other people for sin; he admitted that Israel itself had been unable to keep the law. Acts 13:38–39 should be interpreted along similar lines. Instead of freeing people from sin, the Mosaic law exposes the sins that people have committed, showing that all fall short of God's favor.

The evil that pervades human life came to a climax in the crucifixion of the Lord and Messiah, Jesus of Nazareth. Stephen declared that Israel regularly persecuted and killed the prophets (Acts 7:52), and now his generation had betrayed and murdered the "Righteous One" (Acts 7:52). The apostles boldly preached to the Jews that they had sinned egregiously in crucifying the Messiah (Acts 2:23; 3:13, 17; 4:10–11; 5:30; 13:28). The Jews' persecution of the messengers of the gospel also signaled their rejection of God's salvation: the Sanhedrin threatened Peter and John for proclaiming the resurrection (Acts 4:1–22); the apostles were imprisoned, interrogated, and beaten for proclaiming the gospel (Acts 5:17–42); Stephen was seized, brought before the Sanhedrin, and stoned to death (Acts 6:8–7:53); Paul persecuted believers in various areas

33. On the significance of the incident of the golden calf and Exod. 32–34, see Hafemann 1995: 189–254.

34. They "were idolaters all the time that they were in the desert" (Lake and Cadbury 1979: 79).

35. Nolland (1980) argues that Acts 15:10 teaches the inability of people to observe the law, though not the oppressiveness of the law. See also Fitzmyer 1998: 548; Haenchen 1971: 446–47; Barrett 1998: 718–19.

before his conversion (Acts 8:3; 9:1–2, 13–14, 21); Jews plotted to kill Paul after his conversion (Acts 9:23–25); they expanded their persecution after Stephen's death (Acts 11:19); Herod put James the brother of John to death and apparently intended to kill Peter to please the Jews (Acts 12:1–19); the Jews were jealous in Antioch and spoke against the gospel and persecuted Paul and Barnabas (Acts 13:45, 50). Gentiles also mistreated believers: the magistrates in Philippi flogged Paul and Silas (Acts 16:19–24); Demetrius and his co-workers incited a riot in Ephesus (Acts 19:23–41).

Some have maintained that the polemic against the Jews in Luke-Acts represents anti-Semitism.[36] Such a judgment is understandable, given the sins committed by Christians against Jews throughout history, but it is misguided.[37] If we accept that Luke was a reliable historian, he records events in which Jews mistreated Christians. No example is given in which Christians in turn persecuted Jews, nor is there any indication that such a turn of events would be welcomed. Stephen prayed not for vengeance but for forgiveness for those who put him to death (Acts 7:60), imitating the example of Jesus (Luke 23:34). Nor are persecutors demonized and thereby a platform erected to justify hatred. The former persecutor Paul was saved and became a herald of the gospel, demonstrating that the earliest Christians did not view themselves as exempt from sin. Presumably, the hope of conversion was held out for all those who turned against believers. Moreover, as we noted above, Gentiles occasionally harmed believers as well. Such instances demonstrate that opposition to the gospel was a human problem, not the particular province of the Jews. It is not surprising that attention is focused, however, on Jewish rejection. Jesus was Jewish, as were the first Christians. They believed that their message was the fulfillment of the Hebrew Scriptures. Hence, the rejection by the Jews was particularly painful and remarkable.

The sinful condition of all becomes evident in the call to repentance and faith, which we will investigate below. The Gentile world vainly served idols rather than the creator God, who is true and living (Acts 14:15). In the past God allowed them "to walk in their own ways" (Acts 14:16), but he now summoned them to repentance. Paul did not view the idols in Athens dispassionately, remarking on the beautiful artistry evident in the numerous idols. Instead, he was provoked and irritated by their idolatry (Acts 17:16). He found a point of contact with the Athenians when addressing them (Acts 17:22–23), but clearly he believed that they had wrong notions of God that needed to be corrected (Acts 17:23–28).

36. See the thorough explication of this thesis in J. Sanders 1987.
37. See the essay by Tiede (1993), who argues that Luke should not be designated as anti-Semitic.

Their worship of God can be summarized as "ignorance" (Acts 17:30), recalling the OT view of the idolatry of pagan nations (cf. 1 Pet. 1:14). Hence, the Athenians were not saved through their gods and were challenged to repent (Acts 17:30).

The need for repentance is insisted upon for all people. The righteousness that God demanded for the coming judgment was proclaimed to Felix, making him feel distinctly uncomfortable (Acts 24:25). Paul entreated King Agrippa and all those present at his trial to become Christians (Acts 26:27–29). Those who fail to repent reside in darkness and in the realm of Satan (Acts 26:18). If they failed to believe, they would face judgment on the last day (Acts 17:31; cf. 2:40; 3:23; 4:12; 13:40–41).

Luke in Acts argues that sin characterized Israel's history. Indeed, Israel always failed to observe the law, showing that a selfish will dominated their lives. Such selfishness, however, is not restricted to the Jews, for it represents the human condition generally. Sin reached its apex in the crucifixion of Jesus Christ, the agent of God's salvation. Hence, all are called upon to repent and to put their trust in Jesus Christ in order to escape the coming judgment.

The Pauline Literature

Paul wrote thirteen letters to diverse situations, and so it is not surprising that the sin of human beings receives its most profound and extensive treatment in his writings. Hence, we concentrate especially on Paul in providing a portrait of human sin.

The fundamental sin, according to Paul, is not the failure to keep God's law—as serious as such infractions are. The root sin is the failure to praise and worship and thank God, to glorify him as God (Rom. 1:21).[38] All human beings know God because he has revealed himself through the created world. They recognize that he is truly God and that he is the almighty God, the all-powerful one. Such recognition of God's existence is not the product of philosophical reasoning or sophisticated arguments that demonstrate God's existence. All human beings, even those with a very limited capacity to reason, discern God's being and power as they perceive the created world. But they also reject God's lordship over them, for they turn to the worship of idols instead of the one true and living God (Rom. 1:23). They embrace the lie of human glory and autonomy, and hence they worship the creature rather than the creator (Rom. 1:25). Nor does Paul contemplate exceptions here, for his indictment of human beings occurs in a section that demonstrates

38. See Moxnes 1988: 213.

that no one is exempted from the power of sin, that sin embraces all of humanity (Rom. 1:18–3:20). Paul also argues that sins flow from sin. Three times he says, "God gave them up" (Rom. 1:24, 26, 28), referring to the sins that human beings commit as a consequence of their rejection of God as God. Since God is not worshiped as God, he hands human beings over to sins by which their lives and society are degraded. The idea that idolatry is the root of all other sins is not unique to Paul. Many scholars have noted influence from Wisdom of Solomon in this section: "For the worship of idols not to be named is the source and cause and end of every evil" (Wis. 14:27 NRSV).

Refusing to honor God as God and to give him glory, to worship and adore him, constitutes sin according to Paul. He therefore identifies covetousness as idolatry (Eph. 5:5; Col. 3:5). The prohibition against coveting is the tenth commandment in the Decalogue, and we see from Paul's commentary that the tenth and first commandments address the same reality. Whatever a person covets has become an idol, and hence coveting places the object of desire above God himself. Interestingly, when Paul speaks of the law's role in stimulating sin, he selects the prohibition against coveting (Rom. 7:7).[39] Whether Paul speaks of himself, Adam, or Israel in this text continues to be debated. I have argued elsewhere that Paul refers to himself, but in the last analysis the identity of the person in view is not of great importance, for even if Paul refers to himself, he mirrors the experience of Adam and Israel and exemplifies the experience of everyone who has tried to observe the law.[40] The command to refrain from coveting produced all kinds of illicit desires, so that the command that intended to bring life ended up producing death (Rom. 7:8–11). We cannot limit the prohibition against coveting to sexual lust, as if Paul reflects on entering puberty.[41] The object of coveting, unlike in the Decalogue, remains unstated, so that all coveting is included. The injunction not to covet, therefore, reveals that human beings prize their desires over the will of God, demonstrating that the true God is not their treasure, that another god rules in their lives.

The inclination to idolatry is manifested in human boasting. Paul does not condemn all boasting, for boasting in the Lord is the expression of true praise (Rom. 5:11; 1 Cor. 1:31; 2 Cor. 10:17). The boasting of sinful human beings, however, is precluded (Col. 2:18). The division

39. Here, coveting cannot be identified as the desire to keep the law (Bultmann 1955: 247–48; Käsemann 1980: 194; Hübner 1984a: 72); clearly, it refers to the transgression of the law (Räisänen 1992: 95–111; Wilckens 1980: 76, 239). Nor can coveting here be reduced to sexual lust (contra Gundry 1980). See the helpful study of Ziesler 1988.

40. The identity of the "I" in Rom. 7:7–12 is quite controversial. See Schreiner 1998: 359–65.

41. Contra Gundry 1980.

in Corinth over the wisdom of the ministers (1 Cor. 1:10–4:21) troubled Paul because the root problem was pride. The Corinthians contrasted and compared Paul and Apollos, assessing their effectiveness in terms of speaking ability (1 Cor. 1:17–18; 2:4), as to whether they used Greek rhetoric brilliantly.[42] Their evaluations led them to become puffed up (1 Cor. 4:6). Arrogance seized them to such an extent that the kingdom of God was subverted (1 Cor. 4:18–21). They had forgotten the foolish message of the cross, a message that had categorically been rejected by the wise and sophisticated of this world (1 Cor. 1:18–31). God chose the foolish, weak, and ignoble to preclude human boasting (1 Cor. 1:27–29). Human boasting contradicts the very message of the cross. It lifts up human potential, human wisdom, and human strength instead of focusing on what God has done in Christ. It is Exhibit A of idolatry.

The same concern animates Paul in addressing the "knowers" in 1 Cor. 8:1–11:1. They despised the weak who thought they were defiled in eating idol food. Loving God and being known by God had been forgotten, and the knowers had become entranced by their theological understanding. They lacked the humility that confesses that before God no one knows anything.[43] Indeed, their arrogance led them onto the precipice, for Paul warned them that they were flirting with idolatry (1 Cor. 10:1–22). Such is scarcely surprising, for pride exalts self as God instead of worshiping and honoring the one true God.

Pride lurks behind every corner and manifests itself in unexpected ways. The Corinthians were also prone to boast in the gifts that they exercised, particularly those who had the flashy and spontaneous gift of speaking in other tongues (1 Cor. 12:1–14:40). Arrogance about the gift exercised, however, must be stamped out because it is contrary to the way of love. Love never brags or puts its own foot forward (1 Cor. 13:4). Those who find their chief delight in their gifts have squeezed out the giver and exalted themselves.

The heart of sin is the self-worship that exalts the self over the one and only true God. The rejection of God's lordship manifests itself in sin, and Paul also emphasizes that sin manifests itself in relation to the law. Of course, sin exists without the law as well. As we noted above, all people, even if they have not heard the law, know the one true God but refuse to honor him as God (Rom. 1:18–21). Sin is unbelief, for faith gives glory to God in everything and trusts his promises (Rom. 4:20), but whatever human beings do apart from faith is sin (Rom. 14:23), for faith looks to God as the one who will meet every need. God repays each

42. Supporting the thesis that the issue concerns Greek rhetoric are Litfin 1994; Winter 1997. See also Hays 1997: 22, 27, 29–30, 36.

43. It is well known, however, that humility was not prized as a virtue in the Greco-Roman world. See Grundmann, *TDNT* 8:1–26.

person according to his or her works (Rom. 2:6). Those who do what is evil, whether or not they have been taught God's law, will face God's wrath on the day of judgment (Rom. 2:8–9). Those who sin without having the law are not therefore guiltless; they will perish because they have violated their consciences, which attest that the law has been written on their hearts (Rom. 2:12–15).

Jews who were taught the law from their earliest years tended to view the possession of the law as an indication of their favored status. But they themselves were condemned because they failed to do what the law demands; they practiced "the very same things" that they condemned in Gentiles (Rom. 2:1; cf. 2:3). Mere possession of the law does not stave off judgment. Those "who have sinned under the law will be judged by the law" (Rom. 2:12). Both Jews and Gentiles will be judged impartially by God (Rom. 2:11).[44] Those who do good will be rewarded with life and peace, whereas every one who does evil will face God's judgment (Rom. 2:6–10).

Paul did not deny that there is privilege in being a recipient of the law (Rom. 2:17–20) and in circumcision (Rom. 2:25), for circumcision is the sign of entrance into covenant with God.[45] But none of this is of any avail unless the Jews themselves observe the law (Rom. 2:21–22, 25).[46] It is of little consequence to preach against stealing, adultery, and idolatry if one falls prey to the same evils being denounced. Indeed, Jewish disobedience of God dishonors his name, so that even Gentiles reviled God's name because of their failure to do what God required (Rom. 2:23–24). Paul addressed Jews here who have not repented, who have "hard and impenitent" hearts (Rom. 2:5). Because of their stubbornness they have refused to believe the gospel that he proclaims. They are "stiff-necked" like the generation of the golden calf (cf. Exod. 32:9; 33:3, 5; 34:9; Deut. 9:6, 13). The same disobedience and failure to repent landed the nation in exile (cf. Isa. 40:2; 42:24–25; 43:22–28; 50:1; cf. Ezra 9:5–9). Wright in particular has popularized the notion that the Israel of Paul's day was still in "exile" because of its sins. Whether the term "exile" is the best term to describe Israel's state remains the subject of debate.[47] Perhaps agreement may be found in saying that the promises given to Israel in

44. On the importance of the theme of impartiality in Paul, see Bassler 1982.

45. Räisänen (1983) argues that the Pauline view of the law is rife with contradictions. For a convincing rebuttal of Räisänen, see Weima 1990.

46. The meaning of the word *nomos* in Paul is helpfully and convincingly sorted out by Moo (1983) and Westerholm (1986; 2004: 341–97), both of whom argue that the referent is usually the Mosaic law.

47. Some scholars argue that the Pauline view of God's fulfillment of his promises should be described as a return from exile. See Wright 1992a; Scott 1993a: 645–65; W. Webb 1993. For further examination of the exile theme, see Scott 1997. Seifrid (1994; 2000a) maintains that the exile theme is not authentically Pauline. The cautions raised by Seifrid

the OT remained unfulfilled, and most in Israel would agree that such was the case because of Israel's sin.

All people have sinned. Paul did not open a crack in the door by suggesting that some have responded positively to the revelation of God evident through the created world. The wrath of God is visited upon all people (Rom. 1:18), and all are without excuse (Rom. 1:20). Everyone is a liar in contrast to the truth of God (Rom. 3:4). Jews are not superior to Gentiles, for "all" are "under sin" (Rom. 3:9). The OT catena in Rom. 3:10–18 pounds home the conclusion. Not even one person is righteous. No person seeks God; all flee from him and violate his will. "All have turned aside . . . no one does good, not even one" (Rom. 3:12). The root of all sin is traced to lack of fear of God (Rom. 3:18).[48] "All have sinned and fall short of the glory of God" (Rom. 3:23).[49] Forgiveness cannot be obtained under the old covenant and the sacrificial cult; it is available only in Jesus Christ.

No one can be righteous before God or receive the Spirit by "works of the law," for all fail to do what is required by the law (Rom. 3:20, 28; Gal. 2:16; 3:2, 5, 10). The term "works of the law" has been the subject of considerable debate, especially with the onset of the "new perspective" on Paul.[50] Various interpretations of "works of the law" have been proposed. Bultmann argues that the very desire to do what the law requires is sin.[51] Fuller thinks that "works of the law" is shorthand for legalism; hence, those who try to bribe God with the works required by the law are trying to merit favor in his sight.[52] Dunn, representing the new perspective, claims that the works of the law focus on the identity markers of the law, those parts of the law that separate Jews from Gentiles, such as circumcision, purity laws, and Sabbath.[53] Paul, according

---

are salutary. What must be recognized is that regardless of terminology, Paul sees the promises recounted in Isaiah (esp. Isa. 40–66) as being fulfilled in Christ.

48. It has occasionally been observed that the contexts from which the OT catena is drawn posit a distinction between the righteous and the wicked (so G. Davies 1990: 80–104). Hence, Paul cannot be claiming that all people, without exception, are sinners. Such an objection fails to see the depth of Paul's argument, for his point is that people become righteous only by acknowledging that they are sinners and by putting their faith in Jesus Christ for the forgiveness of sins. See especially Dunn (1988a: 147–48, 150–51), who argues that Paul now turns against the Jews the very texts that they used to defend their righteousness (see also Moo 1991: 205).

49. The OT itself regularly teaches that all sin and need forgiveness (1 Kings 8:46; Ps. 143:2; Prov. 20:9; Eccles. 7:29).

50. For an excellent survey of both historic and more recent views of Paul relative to the law, see Westerholm 2004: 3–258.

51. Bultmann 1951: 264.

52. Fuller 1975.

53. Dunn 1983; 1985; 1992a; 1992b; 1998: 354–71. For a variant of Dunn's view with regard to Galatians, see Wisdom 2001.

to Dunn and others, criticizes nationalism not activism, ethnocentricism not legalism, exclusivism not works-righteousness. None of these views is compelling. Paul never criticized anyone for the desire to keep God's law; rather, he found fault in the failure to keep it. Even though legalism existed in Judaism in Paul's day, the phrase "works of the law" should not be defined as legalism. The phrase refers to the commands of the law and does not inherently refer to legalism. Nor is it clear that works of the law concentrate on the badges of the law, such as circumcision and dietary restrictions.[54] In Galatians works of the law became an issue because of circumcision and food laws, but Paul widened the discussion to include the law as a whole (Gal. 2:16, 19, 21; 3:10). Comparable phrases in Jewish literature most likely refer to the entirety of the law (4QFlor I, 7; 1QS V, 21; VI, 18; 4QMMT; cf. 2 Bar. 4:9; 57:2).[55] The argument of Rom. 1:18–3:20 also supports the notion that "works of the law" refers to the actions or deeds required by the law.[56] Paul did not criticize the Jews for attempting to impose boundary markers on Gentiles. He found them guilty before God because they failed to keep God's commands (cf. Rom. 2:21–22), focusing on general moral requirements.[57] Paul slides easily and without comment from "works of the law" (Rom. 3:20, 28) to "works" in general (Rom. 4:2, 4, 6). The phrase "works of the law" is inapposite in reference to Abraham because he did not live under the law. In Rom. 9:11–12 Paul defines "works" as doing something good or bad. Since Paul moves straightforwardly from "works of the law" to "works" and defines "works" as the performance of something good or bad, "works of the law" refers to doing all that the law requires.

The same conclusion should be drawn in regard to Gal. 3:10: "For all who rely on works of the law are under a curse; for it is written, 'Cursed be everyone who does not abide by all things written in the Book of the Law, and do them.'" The most natural way of interpreting this verse is to supply the proposition that no one keeps everything the law requires.[58] As we noted above, such a conclusion would not be surprising, for the

54. So Cranfield 1991; Schreiner 1991.

55. Fitzmyer (1993b: 18–35) concludes from texts in the Qumran literature (see 1QpHab VII, 11; VIII, 1; XII, 4; 11QTᵃ LVI, 3; 4QMMT) that "works of the law" in Paul designates the law in its entirety. See also Yeung 2002: 239–49. For a contrary view, see Dunn 1997.

56. For further support of this view, see Kim 2002: 66. See also Watson 2004: 68–69n77, 74.

57. Westerholm (2004: 315) argues that for Paul, "works of the law" and "law" are complementary, "because he sees the very essence of the law in its requirement of works."

58. So Hofius 1989: 53–54. Paul does not merely threaten that those who fail to do the law will be cursed (contra Stanley 1990; Braswell 1991; F. Young 1998); he pronounces a curse on all who violate the law (so Das 2001: 145–70). For a penetrating critique of Stanley and Young, see Kim 2002: 135.

OT itself testifies that all people sin.[59] The Jews are not cursed because they frowned upon including Gentiles in the covenant if the latter remained uncircumcised; rather, the curse stands upon them for failing to do what the law requires.[60] Interestingly, the later Pauline letters confirm this interpretation. For scholars who do not accept these later letters as Pauline, the same conclusion obtains anyway because in this case the earliest Pauline interpreters understood Paul to refer to works in general, not boundary markers.[61] For instance, in Eph. 2:9 Paul says that salvation is not by works, and hence human boasting is excluded. Nothing is said here about "works of the law" or circumcision. Works in general are clearly in view, and they do not contribute to salvation, for otherwise grace is ruled out and human boasting is allowed.[62]

Titus 3:5 points in the same direction: God "saved us, not because of any works of righteousness that we had done, but according to his mercy, through the water of rebirth and renewal by the Holy Spirit." The explanation of works is quite striking here in that the works are those "done in righteousness" (NASB). One could be pardoned for thinking that Luther himself might have composed the verse! In any case, there is no warrant for limiting the verse to circumcision, Sabbath, and food laws. Paul thinks of the law comprehensively (cf. 2 Tim. 1:9). Since these later texts generalize the Pauline teaching on works of the law and apply them to works in general, we have good reason to conclude that "works of the law" refers to the law in general. Paul argues that works and works of the law do not and cannot save, for all have sinned. All fall short of God's standard. Even Abraham was ungodly (Rom. 4:5).

Legalism

Is there any polemic against legalism relative to the law? Since the Reformation, scholars have been nearly unanimous in seeing such a polemic. The issue exploded into prominence with the publication of

59. Paul's reading of Deut. 27:26 in Gal. 3:10 seems to be verified by the OT context (Deut. 27:15–26), where the text emphasizes sins committed in secret that evade human eyes and yet are seen and judged by God himself (so Weinfeld 1972: 276–78; Bellefontaine 1993: 58).

60. Wright (1992a: 137–56) and Scott (1993b) argue that Paul refers here to the curse of exile for Israel's failure to keep the law (see also Watson 2004: 433). This view also suffers from lack of evidence. See especially the pointed comments in Kim 2002: 136–40; Das 2001: 148–55. Kim (2002: 141–43) demonstrates that the interpretation defended here is the most convincing.

61. See Marshall 1996; Westerholm 2004: 404–6.

62. Rightly Lincoln 1990: 112–13; Best 1998: 227; O'Brien 1999: 176–77; Hoehner 2002: 344–45.

E. Sanders's *Paul and Palestinian Judaism* in 1977.[63] Sanders forcefully argues that Judaism was not legalistic. Judaism espoused not meritorious righteousness but covenantal nomism. Jews did not teach that one must weigh merits to obtain salvation; rather, all Jews are inducted into the covenant by election, by the grace of God. They must maintain their place in the covenant by keeping the law, but their entrance into the covenant was due to God's covenantal mercy, not their law-keeping. The observance of the law was a response to God's grace, not an attempt to gain his grace. Sanders's work had an immediate impact and is a salutary correction of those who caricatured Judaism and failed to see anything but legalism in it. Still, it seems that Sanders overemphasized his own insight. Significant challenges to Sanders's paradigm have demonstrated that his view does not account for all the evidence in a satisfactory way. Elliott maintains that Judaism during the Second Temple period typically forecasted the salvation not of all of Israel but only of those who kept the Torah.[64] Avemarie has demonstrated that the two themes of election and works stand in an uneasy tension in Tannaitic literature, so that one cannot merely say that works are always subordinate to election.[65] Gathercole has come to similar conclusions in his study of Jewish literature during the Second Temple period, showing that works played a significant role in gaining salvation.[66] A study of nomism in Jewish literature indicates as well that the Judaism of Paul's day was diverse, and there were streams in Jewish thinking that do not accord with Sanders's conclusions.[67]

63. Both Moore (1921) and Montefiore (1914) preceded Sanders and protested that Judaism was not legalistic, and that such a view of Judaism was a distortion of Jewish documentary sources.

64. M. Elliott 2000. Watson (2004: 9), against E. Sanders, remarks about the law and the covenant in Judaism, "If it is possible to generalize about these texts, there seems to be broad agreement that Israel's observance or non-observance of the law is fundamental to the covenant itself." See the more detailed discussion in Watson 2004: 6–13.

65. Avemarie 1996; 1999.

66. Gathercole (2003) maintains that Jewish soteriology before AD 70 held that final salvation depended on divine election (the covenant) and obedience to Torah. See also Das 2001: 12–69.

67. Of course, Sanders himself agrees that there were exceptions to his paradigm, but he failed to see the extent to which his paradigm does not account for the evidence. See especially the essays on variegated nomism in Carson, O'Brien, and Seifrid 2001. This collection of essays, taken as a whole, argues that Sanders's view on covenantal nomism should be qualified. The Judaism of the Second Temple period is truly "variegated." Sometimes the emphasis is on God's grace, while in other instances the focus is on obedience to the law. Explaining the relationship between "covenant" and "nomism" is often difficult because the Jewish authors themselves did not explain systematically how these two strands should be explicated. Some of the writings lean in a more legalistic direction (e.g., Josephus, *2 Enoch, 4 Ezra, 2 Baruch*), while others emphasize God's grace (e.g., Wisdom of Solomon, Sirach, penitential psalms and prayers, *1 Enoch*).

When we examine the Pauline writings, it seems that there are indications that he engaged in a polemic against legalism. Legalism is defined here as the view that one's works are the basis of a right relation with God, so that one can boast in what one has accomplished. In Rom. 3:27 Paul asks whether boasting is excluded, after having clarified that salvation is granted through the atoning work of Christ and is received by faith (Rom. 3:21–26). The word "law" (*nomos*) here could refer to the Mosaic law, and a decision on this point is quite difficult. It seems more probable that here Paul uses *nomos* in terms of "principle," "rule," or "order."[68] For in this context it would be quite confusing for Paul to say that the Mosaic law is a law of faith, since he consistently opposes faith and law in this context (see also Rom. 4:13–16). The principle that rules out boasting, then, is not works, for works are the very platform for boasting. Those who do the required works can boast that they have fulfilled what was demanded. Faith, on the contrary, excludes any human boasting because it is directed to what God has done in Christ (Rom. 3:21–26). It receives righteousness from God through Christ instead of showing God how righteous one is. Hence, justification comes by faith, apart from the works required in the law. Righteousness before God is obtained by believing, not by doing.

The line of argument in Rom. 4:1–8 is similar, though here Paul takes up the case of Abraham because he is the progenitor of the Jewish people. Indeed, many Jewish traditions venerated Abraham because of his works. Paul inquires, then, on what basis Abraham stood in the right before God. If Abraham did the required works, he could legitimately boast. Paul adds, however, that Abraham could not boast "before God" (Rom. 4:2). The point of the verse is not that Abraham was in fact a godly man, but that God still rejected his works, even though he was godly. The condition is a real one. If Abraham did the works God required, he could truly boast before God, and such boasting would not be sin, for Abraham would have fulfilled what God demanded. Such an interpretation of Rom. 4:2 is confirmed by Rom. 4:4, where an example is adduced from everyday life. If employees do what is required, their paycheck is not a gift but is something they deserve. So too, if Abraham actually did what God demanded, his boasting would be fitting. But Abraham had no grounds to boast before God, since he failed to do the required works. He was, as Rom. 4:5 indicates, "ungodly." Paul alludes here to Josh. 24:2, which indicates that Abraham once served foreign gods. Abraham, then, did not

---

68. Many scholars contend that the Mosaic law is in view. See Friedrich 1954; Rhyne 1981: 67–71; Das 2001: 192–200; 2003: 155–65. On the other hand, "rule" or "principle" also has strong support (Cranfield 1975: 361–62; Räisänen 1986: 119–47; Moo 1991: 487). The issue is difficult, and I have changed my mind more than once!

stand in the right before God on the basis of works, for he failed to do what God commanded. Abraham too "sinned and [fell] short of the glory of God" (Rom. 3:23). Abraham was counted as righteous before God, as Gen. 15:6 verifies, because he trusted in God, not because he worked for God. It is not those who work for God but rather those who trust in the God who "justifies the ungodly" (Rom. 4:5) who are counted as righteous.[69]

The interpretation offered here is confirmed by Rom. 4:6–8. David also witnesses to righteousness by faith in the words of Ps. 32:1–2. This righteousness is "apart from works" (Rom. 4:6). Hence, those whose sins are forgiven, covered, and not reckoned receive a blessing from God. These verses clarify that the works that David failed to do constitute moral failures. David certainly was circumcised and presumably observed purity laws and the Sabbath. Nor is he indicted for excluding Gentiles from the promise. He needed forgiveness because of his moral infractions.[70] The example of David supports the interpretation offered relative to Abraham. Both of them were ungodly, in that both failed to observe what God commanded. Their only hope of a right relation with God, then, was on the basis of the forgiveness granted.

The same polarity between doing and believing informs Rom. 4:13–16. The inheritance promised to Abraham is not given because of observance of the law; the inheritance is received by faith. If the reception of the inheritance depends on doing the law, then faith is excluded, and the graciousness of God's promise is removed. Observing the law cannot secure the inheritance because human sin intervenes and, as a consequence, brings God's wrath. Faith, on the other hand, operates on a different principle. Faith is fundamentally receptive, so that it looks to God's promise (not human performance) for receiving the inheritance. Works direct attention to human beings and their ability to carry out what is required, whereas faith rests on God's grace and promise, recognizing that human beings are sinners.

Paul's polemic against works as the basis of salvation must be directed against those who believed that works qualified them to receive the inheritance. Otherwise, Paul's remarks are merely theoretical and address a problem that he did not face in his ministry. It is much more probable that Paul addresses a real problem that people faced. Apparently, some

69. Yeung (2002: 249–50) argues that Sir. 44:19–21 departs from the meaning of Gen. 15:6 because now Abraham's faithfulness is the "cause" of his righteousness, so that Abraham's obedience becomes meritorious in Sirach. For further discussion of Jewish interpretations of Gen. 15:6 that supports the notion that Paul interpreted the text in a radically different way, see Yeung 2002: 237–71.

70. Hofius (1989: 131) says that Paul certainly has in mind David's adultery with Bathsheba and murder of Uriah the Hittite.

believed that their works were the basis of their right relationship with God, and Paul counters that claim.

Nor is the polemic against works reserved for only a few texts. Works of the law are contrasted with faith in Jesus Christ in Gal. 2:16. Indeed, in this single verse Paul places works of the law and faith in Christ against each other three times. Doing and believing are contrasted also in Gal. 3:10–12. Those who think that they can be justified by works of law are cursed because all fail to do what God requires. On the contrary, as Hab. 2:4 affirms, righteousness with God is obtained not by doing but by faith. Indeed, righteousness by doing the law and by trusting in God are specifically contrasted with one another in Gal. 3:12.[71] The law demands works to obtain eschatological life, but faith operates a different principle: looking to Christ for the removal of the curse (Gal. 3:13–14).[72] Hence, if the inheritance were received on the basis of keeping the law, then God's promise and faith are ruled out as the basis of God's gift (Gal. 3:18). Since the inheritance is given by virtue of God's promise, it surely will be realized, and it is received by those who trust God instead of by those who work for God.[73]

Paul's argument in Rom. 9:30–10:13 follows the same lines.[74] Gentiles who have trusted in Christ are righteous in God's sight even though they were not pursuing a right relation with God. Israel, on the other hand, pursued the law to obtain a right relation with God. Such an attempt failed, however, presumably because of Israel's disobedience and because Israel pursued the law by works instead of faith. Instead of trusting Christ for righteousness, who is both the goal and end (*telos* [Rom. 10:4]) of the law, they tried to establish their own righteousness. Nothing is said in this context about exclusion of Gentiles or identity markers such as circumcision, and so establishing their own righteousness relates to works in general and cannot be restricted to boundary markers. The righteousness of the law is based on doing (Rom. 10:5),[75] but true righteousness comes by faith and looks to God, who has raised Christ from the dead. Faith looks away from self and human performance to what

71. Silva (1990) argues that Paul resists the notion that the law functioned as a source of life.

72. OT sacrifices no longer atone now that Christ has offered himself as a sacrifice (see Das 2001: 113–44), for OT sacrifices point forward to the sacrifice of Christ.

73. Westerholm (2004: 307–8) points out that Paul contrasts law and grace, and that such a contrast would have been rejected by Paul's non-Christian Jewish contemporaries. For the contrast, see, for example, Rom. 4:13–16; 11:5–6; Gal. 5:2–4. Watson (2004), in his understanding of Paul, also sees a strong contrast between law and faith, arguing that such a construal arises out of Paul's reading of the OT.

74. For an exegesis of Rom. 9:30–33, see Hofius 1989: 155–66.

75. For a defense of the Pauline reading of Lev. 18:5, see Watson 2004: 315–36 (though, contrary to Watson, I think that perfect obedience is demanded).

God has done in Christ for salvation. Again, Paul's polemic makes sense only if there were some Jews attempting to be righteous before God on the basis of their works. Otherwise, his comments are superfluous.

Does Paul fall prey, therefore, to anti-Semitism? Philippians 3:2–9 assists us in answering that question. Paul rehearses his own history in warning the Philippians about those who would want to impose circumcision and the law on the church. His observance of the law was extraordinary. He was circumcised on the eighth day in accordance with the law (cf. Lev. 12:3). He was a genuine Israelite and knew the tribe from which he hailed. Indeed, the tribe of Benjamin was one of the two tribes that remained loyal to David, and Paul (Hebrew name "Saul") probably was named after the first king of Israel. When Paul says that he was "a Hebrew of Hebrews," he probably means that he spoke Aramaic (or possibly Hebrew).[76] He was from the sect of the Pharisees, which was particularly rigorous in its observance of the law. His zeal manifested itself in his persecution of the church, and he considered himself blameless in his observance of the law. All these qualifications placed him above those who were trying to impose circumcision on the Philippians. Paul realized, however, that his accomplishments under the law were not genuinely pleasing to God. It was nothing less than "confidence in the flesh" (Phil. 3:4)—reliance upon who human beings are in Adam.[77] His so-called blamelessness in legal righteousness was not true righteousness before God (Phil. 3:6).[78] Paul had thought that he was blameless before God, but in actuality he was guilty of profound sin. In persecuting the church he was convinced that he was pleasing God, but in fact he was opposing God and Christ Jesus. As Paul looked back on his life, he never ceased to be amazed about God's grace, since his sin in persecuting the church was so grievous (1 Cor. 15:9; Eph. 3:8; 1 Tim. 1:13–14). The righteousness that Paul had before his conversion, then, was his "own" rather than the righteousness that "comes through faith in Christ" (Phil. 3:9). It is clear that it was a righteousness based on doing instead of believing. Faith stands in contrast to works as the pathway to salvation. The opponents who trumpeted observance of circumcision and the law, therefore, had fallen into the same trap that

---

76. See Hengel 1991: 25.

77. Hence, the view that Paul does not oppose legalism here is strained (contra E. Sanders 1983: Liebers 1989: 58–60; rightly Gundry 1985: 13; O'Brien 1991: 356, 362, 364, 394–96; Fee 1995: 296–97).

78. Stendahl (1976: 78–96) argues from this verse, among others, that the notion that Paul was plagued in conscience before his conversion is mistaken. On this matter Stendahl is quite right, but other dimensions in his portrayal of Paul need correction (see Espy 1985). See also O'Brien 1991: 378–81; Westerholm 2006.

previously ensnared Paul. They were not depending on the Spirit or boasting in Christ; they were relying on themselves.

When Paul criticized Jews for self-righteousness, he indicted his former life. Nor can he be faulted for anti-Semitism, for the inclination to trust in works is fundamentally not a Jewish problem but rather a human problem. If it were limited to the Jews, Paul would scarcely need to warn Gentiles about the danger of relying on one's works. A polemic against relying on works continues in the later Pauline letters. Faith is opposed to works, for the latter leads to boasting, while the former exalts grace and God's gift (Eph. 2:8–9; see also 2 Tim. 1:9; Titus 3:5). The new perspective on Paul rightly sees that he is concerned about the exclusion of the Gentiles from the promise (Rom. 4:9–12). Salvation is open to all without distinction, both Jews and Gentiles, by faith in Christ Jesus (Rom. 1:16; 2:6–11; 3:9, 22–23, 29–30; 4:9–12, 16; Gal. 3:7–9, 14; Eph. 2:11–22). But Paul also engages in a polemic against works as the basis of salvation, for those who trust in their own works trust themselves and their own goodness rather than the grace of God.

Bondage to Sin

Human beings do not merely commit sins. They are in bondage to sin, so that sin rules over them. Paul remarks that "sin reigned in death" (Rom. 5:21). Death here refers to both spiritual death—separation from God—and physical death.[79] Sin as a power rules over those who live in the realm of death. Before people become believers, they are slaves to sin (Rom. 6:6, 16–18, 20, 22) and cannot escape its grasp on their own. Those who live under the Sinai covenant are enslaved to sin (Gal. 4:24–25). The subjugation of humans under sin is expressed in the "under" (*hypo*) sayings in Paul. Unbelievers are "under a curse" (Gal. 3:10), "under sin" (Gal. 3:22), "under law" (Rom. 6:14–15; Gal. 3:23), "under a pedagogue" (Gal. 3:25 my translation),[80] "sold under sin" (Rom. 7:14), and "under the elements of the world" (Gal. 4:3 my translation).[81] For Paul, to be "under law" is equivalent to being under the old age of redemptive history, so that being under law and being under sin are equivalent realities (Gal. 5:18). The law functioned as a pedagogue or "babysitter" (Gal. 3:23, 25), supervising people until the time of the promise, until the coming of

79. Rightly Beker 1980: 224. Contra those who emphasize only physical death (e.g., Murray 1959: 181–82; Ziesler 1989: 145).

80. It is quite unlikely, then, contrary to Lull (1986), that Paul teaches in Galatians that the law's purpose was to restrain sin. See Schreiner 1993a: 74–81.

81. The interpretation of *stoicheia* has been a matter of debate, with scholars proposing that it refers to the Torah, the principles of religion and morality, the four physical elements, and angelic powers, among other interpretations. For a survey and defense of the last option, see Arnold 1996.

Christ. Those who live under the law are in bondage to sin (Rom. 7:14–25) and cannot carry out the requirements of God's law.[82] They inevitably set their minds on the things of the flesh (Rom. 8:5). Since they still live in the realm of the flesh, they cannot observe God's law, nor do they have any ability to please God (Rom. 8:7–8). Their hostility to God cannot be removed merely through willpower.

Because human beings are enslaved to sin, "the power of sin is the law" (1 Cor. 15:56).[83] Paul's statement here functions as an epigrammatic summary of Rom. 7:7–25. The law itself is holy and good (Rom. 7:12), but sin has wrapped its tentacles so tightly around human beings that it brings the law under the orbit of its influence.[84] The law has not led to the restraint of sin; it has formed an unholy alliance with sin, so that sin has increased all the more (Rom. 5:20;[85] 7:13). All of this testifies to the impotence of human beings in Adam.[86] Paul's contrast between the letter and the Spirit points to the same truth (Rom. 2:29; 7:6; 2 Cor. 3:6). The letter refers to the commands of the law. Unfortunately, the letter of the law leads to death because human beings lack the ability to practice what the law enjoins.[87] Only those who have the Spirit can obey God. This accords with the OT where the gift of the Spirit is the means by which God's people will be transformed (Isa. 44:3; Jer. 31:31–34; Ezek. 11:18–19; 36:26–27; Joel 2:28).[88]

The impotence of human beings with regard to spiritual reality is communicated in a variety of ways by Paul. The natural person—that is, the person without the Spirit—does not welcome the truths of the Spirit

82. A long-standing debate exists over whether Rom. 7:13–25 denotes pre-Christian (so Kümmel 1974: 57–73, 97–138; Ridderbos 1975: 126–30; Beker 1980: 237–43; Moo 1991: 468–96; Stuhlmacher 1994: 114–16) or Christian experience (Cranfield 1975: 341–47, 355–70; Dunn 1975a; Laato 1991: 137–82; Garlington 1994: 110–43). To ask whether Paul speaks of Christian or pre-Christian experience veers away from the main point of the text, for Paul considers the capability of human beings to keep God's law. His answer is that the flesh has no ability to do what the law demands. Insofar as believers still battle the flesh, as they wait for the fulfillment of God's promises, they experience, at least partially, what Paul describes in Rom. 7. For this view, see Schreiner 1998: 371–96.

83. On this verse, see Fee 1987: 806.

84. Contra Bultmann (1960: 147–57), the sin of Rom. 7 is not the desire to keep the law but rather the failure to observe it.

85. Hofius (2001: 200) says that in Rom. 5:20 we find "both a quantitative and a qualitative enhancement of sin."

86. Laato (1991: 83–97) demonstrates that Paul's view of human impotence diverges from Judaism where human beings were thought to be able to keep the law by exercising their free will. For some texts in Judaism that celebrate the power of free will, see Sir. 15:11–22; Pss. Sol. 9:4–5; 2 Bar. 54:15, 19; 85:5; m. 'Abot 3:16.

87. For this theme, see Hofius 1989: 84–85.

88. As noted earlier, Jer. 31:31–34 does not refer to the Holy Spirit, but its content accords with other texts where the Spirit is promised.

and indeed has no capacity for such understanding (1 Cor. 2:14). The unregenerate push the truth of the gospel away from themselves, for they find their pleasure in evil rather than in embracing the truth (2 Thess. 2:10–12). Unbeknownst to them, Satan is their god, and he has spun a veil over the minds of unbelievers so that they fail to see the beauty of Christ (2 Cor. 4:3–4; cf. 3:14). They have been snared by the devil, and he holds them as prisoners, so they invariably do his will (2 Tim. 2:26) even as they trumpet their own freedom. The state of unbelievers is spiritual death, and the consequence of that death is sin (Eph. 2:1, 5; cf. Rom. 5:12).[89] Unbelievers live under the thrall of the world, the devil, and the flesh (Eph. 2:1–3). We could say that the captivity is sociological, spiritual, and psychological. It is sociological in that unbelievers follow the dictates and fashions of the world. It is spiritual in that the devil works in their hearts to bring about disobedience. It is psychological in that the unregenerate follow the desires of the flesh. Unbelievers, whenever possible, follow the desires of their hearts, and yet this so-called freedom to indulge in desires is nothing other than slavery.

All are born into the world as "children of wrath" (Eph. 2:3),[90] destined for destruction. Those who do not belong to Jesus will face the coming wrath (1 Thess. 1:10; 5:9). They live in spiritual darkness (Eph. 5:8; Col. 1:13; 1 Thess. 5:4–5), oblivious to the truth that shines in Christ (Eph. 4:17). Their thinking about reality is twisted (Eph. 4:17), so that they have become fools instead of wise (Rom. 1:21–23). Their intellectual dullness is due to their being cut off from the life of God, and the consequence is lives given over to evil (Eph. 4:18–19). They serve idols rather than believing in and obeying the true and living God (1 Thess. 1:9), so that they are enslaved to false gods (Gal. 4:8). Paul does not envision anyone inhabiting a neutral place. One is aligned with righteousness or lawlessness, light or darkness, Christ or Satan, God's temple or idols (2 Cor. 6:14–16). Gentiles who do not trust in Christ are separated from Israel and have no portion in God's covenant promises. Since they do not know Christ, they are without hope and separated from God (Eph. 2:12).

The alienation of human beings from God is often expressed by Paul with the term "flesh" (*sarx*).[91] The word "flesh" is used in a variety of

89. Best (1981: 15) argues that Eph. 2:1 should not be limited to Gentiles but rather refers to all of pre-Christian humanity. Best (1981: 16) goes on to say that the death in view is "a realized eschatological conception of death." Cf. Lincoln 1990: 91–93; O'Brien 1999: 156–57.

90. See the perceptive comments by Lincoln (1990: 98–99), who rightly argues that the verse speaks of what human beings are by birth and fits with a notion of original sin. Cf. O'Brien 1999: 162–63; Hoehner 2002: 323. See also Best 1998: 210–12.

91. See the analyses in Ridderbos 1975: 64–68, 100–107; Dunn 1998: 62–73; Barclay 1988: 178–215. The eschatological dimension of the flesh is recognized increasingly in NT scholarship.

ways by Paul. It denotes human beings (e.g., Rom. 3:20; Gal. 2:16) and life in the body (e.g., 1 Cor. 15:39; Gal. 2:20; Phil. 1:22, 24) or focuses on descent, kinship, and earthly relationships (Rom. 1:3; 9:5; Eph. 6:5). The term is used distinctively and often by Paul to refer to what people are in Adam. Those who are spiritually dead are "in the flesh." "Flesh" should be understood in redemptive-historical categories instead of ontologically.[92] Unbelievers are in the flesh because they are in Adam (Rom. 5:12–19), and hence they belong to the present evil age (Gal. 1:4) instead of the one to come. The eschatological contrast between the flesh and the Spirit is evident in the OT (Isa. 44:3; Ezek. 11:18–19; 36:26–27; Joel 2:28). Those who are transformed by the Spirit are part of the new creation (2 Cor. 5:17), but those who are of the flesh estimate everything in accordance with the values and opinions of the flesh—even Jesus Christ (2 Cor. 5:16).

The wisdom of the flesh is impressed with the rhetorical abilities of those who proclaim the gospel and is entranced with secular wisdom rather than Christ crucified (1 Cor. 1:20, 26; 3:18–20). False teachers boast in the flesh and war according to the flesh (2 Cor. 10:3; 11:18), but Paul, in contrast, does not make promises according to the flesh (2 Cor. 1:17). Similarly, the opponents in Colossae exalt themselves because of their fleshly way of thinking (Col. 2:18), but their ascetic regime offers no help in restraining the flesh and its evil inclinations (Col. 2:23). The flesh can put on a dazzling show and seem to offer righteousness, so that people boast in its contribution (Gal. 6:12–13; Phil. 3:3–4). Such a fleshly approach stands in contradiction to the cross of Christ and exalts human beings rather than God.

Unbelievers live "in the flesh" (Rom. 7:5), and in this context Paul does not mean merely that they live in the body. Living in the flesh stands in contrast to the life in the Spirit, so that it refers to those who are spiritually dead and under the dominion of Satan as the god of this world. The same reality is designated as "the uncircumcision of your flesh" (Col. 2:13; cf. Eph. 2:11). To be uncircumcised is to be separated from the covenant people of God and thus to stand condemned before God. Those who are in the realm of the flesh, which means that they are not indwelt by the Spirit, do not and cannot keep God's law (Rom. 8:5–13). The "works of the flesh" disqualify people from entrance into the kingdom of God (Gal. 5:19–21). The works of the flesh cannot be restricted to sexual sin and drunkenness. Social sins are also prominent, such as anger, jealousy, strife, dissension, covetousness, and pride (Rom. 13:14; 2 Cor. 11:18; Gal. 5:19–21; 6:12–13; Phil. 3:3–4).[93] Those who practice

92. Flesh must not be identified with matter in Paul (rightly Schlatter 1999: 209–11).
93. For the prominence of social sins in Galatians, see Barclay 1988: 152–54, 207–9.

such works reveal that they belong to the old age instead of the age to come. Those who provide an opportunity for the flesh and sow to the flesh will experience eschatological destruction (Gal. 5:13; 6:8–9), and therefore stern warnings are given to believers about submitting to the flesh (e.g., Rom. 8:13).

The Old Adam

All people enter the world as sinners because they are sons and daughters of Adam. The influence of Adam (and Eve) is attested in Jewish tradition: "O Adam, what have you done? For though it was you who sinned, the fall was not yours alone, but ours also who are your descendants" (4 Esd. 7:118). "O Adam, what did you do to all who were born after you? And what will be said of the first Eve who obeyed the serpent, so that this whole multitude is going to corruption?" (2 Bar. 48:42–43). "Adam is, therefore, not the cause, except only for himself, but each of us has become our own Adam" (2 Bar. 54:18). "But through the devil's envy death entered the world, and those who belong to his company experience it" (Wis. 2:24). "From a woman sin had its beginning, and because of her we all die" (Sir. 25:24).

Paul puts the emphasis on Adam rather than Eve in tracing the impact of sin on the whole of humanity. The two central characters in the human history are Adam and Christ. Sin entered the world through Adam, and as a consequence of sin death reigned over all (Rom. 5:12).[94] The consequences of Adam's sin are relayed with five statements in Rom. 5:15–19: (1) death entered the world through his one trespass; (2) his one sin brought condemnation; (3) his one sin inaugurated the reign of death; (4) his one trespass resulted in condemnation for all people; (5) his disobedience led to the many becoming sinners. The consequences of Adam's sin were death, sin, and condemnation. Paul does not specifically explain how Adam's sin led to these consequences for all. It seems most likely that he views Adam as the covenantal head for humanity, just as Christ is the covenantal head for the new humanity. In any case, human beings do not enter the world suspended neutrally between good and evil. As sons and daughters of Adam, they are spring-loaded to do evil. This is confirmed by 1 Cor. 15:21–22. The sway of death over all of humanity can be traced to Adam's sin. Whether human beings like it or not, we are one community. The fountainhead of the human race affects all who come after him.[95]

94. For an exegesis of Rom. 5:12–14, see Schreiner 1998: 270–81. On the important construction *eph' hō* in Rom. 5:12, see Fitzmyer 1993c.

95. Hofius (2001: 186n135) rightly says that although Augustine misconstrued Rom. 5:12, "it is still the case that the doctrine of original sin does appropriately represent what Rom. 5:12 has to say about the fateful character of sin and death."

Conclusion

Paul's theology of sin is multifaceted and profound. The root sin is the failure to thank and glorify God for his goodness, the worship of the creature rather than the creator. The sinfulness of human beings manifests itself in coveting and in boasting: in coveting because whatever human beings desire most is their god, and in boasting because human beings take incredible pride in what they have accomplished. Sin can also be measured objectively and is universal. In other words, all human beings everywhere fail to do what God requires. They violate his written law or the law inscribed upon their hearts. The "works of the law" cannot bring salvation, for no one carries out what the law demands. Instead of curbing sin, the law reveals sin. Indeed, the remarkable subtlety of sin comes to the forefront in that sinners who fail to keep God's law become proud of their so-called morality and obedience and think it to be sufficient to merit salvation from God. The problem with human beings is not superficial, for the human race is enslaved to sin, and both sin and death rule over all. Human beings, after all, were born into the world as sons and daughters of Adam, and by virtue of their union with Adam they are under the reign of sin and death and are condemned before God.

Hebrews

When we examine the General or Catholic Epistles and Revelation, we do not find an in-depth discussion on human sin, nor do any of the writers contemplate intensely the state of human beings before salvation. This is not surprising, given the occasion that prompted each writing. All of them are written to believers in Jesus Christ, and most address churches facing false teachers or persecution. The letter to the Hebrews, for instance, warns *believers* against falling into sin and disobedience. The relationship between faith, obedience, and perseverance in Hebrews will be explored in the next chapter. It is obvious from Hebrews, of course, that sin consists in unbelief and disobedience (e.g., Heb. 3:12, 18; 4:2–3, 6, 11). The apostasy that the author warns the readers against is described in the following ways: hardening of the heart (Heb. 3:8), testing God (Heb. 3:9), going astray (Heb. 3:10), dullness of hearing (Heb. 5:11; 6:12), falling away (Heb. 6:6), deliberate sin (Heb. 10:26), spurning God's Son, profaning the blood of the covenant, and outraging the Spirit of grace (Heb. 10:29), and refusing and rejecting what God says (Heb. 12:25).

Sin is nothing less than turning away from the living God, of failing to put faith and hope in him, with the result that people turn to evil.

Even though such warnings are addressed to believers, it is clear that the sin of unbelievers consists in the failure to trust and obey God in Jesus Christ. The author speaks of the "dead works" of unbelievers (Heb. 6:1; 9:14). This expression refers to the evil deeds of unbelievers that lead to death. The emphasis on the cleansing and purification of sins through the death of Jesus Christ (e.g., Heb. 1:3; 9:14, 26, 28; 10:12, 18) demonstrates that sin needs to be forgiven. The evil of human beings needs to be atoned for if they are to escape God's judgment on the last day (Heb. 9:27). The author of Hebrews, drawing on the OT, believes that human beings suffer from guilt because of sin and need to be forgiven. The author also teaches that Jesus frees believers from slavery to and fear of death (Heb. 2:14–15). Death, then, appears to be a consequence of sin, and Jesus' high priestly ministry serves as the propitiation for sins that bring death (Heb. 2:14–18).

James

James is replete with exhortations against sin, but the author does not reflect specifically on why believers need the saving work of God. He almost certainly presumes that his readers already know why such saving work is needed, and he presses home the particular concerns that called forth his letter. James 1:13–15 opens an interesting window on sin. No one can blame God for sin, as if God actually seduces people so that they sin. Sin finds its origin in human desires that lure and entice people to wrongdoing. Human beings have various desires, and some of these desires are wrong. If they capitulate to evil desires, they sin, and sin in turn leads to death. The reference to death indicates that salvation is needed for those who fall into sin. And sin is the portion of all people, without exception, for "we all stumble in many ways" (James 3:2). The "we all" in this context includes believers, even those who teach and lead the church, so that James clearly teaches here that sin continues to afflict believers "in many ways."[96] In particular, as James immediately remarks, human beings stumble and sin in their speech. Even a single sin marks one out as a transgressor (James 2:10).[97] Here he sounds remarkably similar to Paul. No one can claim to be righteous if he or she has refrained from adultery while at the same time violating another commandment. Any infraction identifies one as a lawbreaker.

Although James does not explicitly draw the conclusion that only Christ can atone for sin, it seems that he operates with a framework

---

96. So Davids 1982: 137; Dibelius 1975: 183–84.

97. See the discussion of parallels and influences in Dibelius 1975: 144–46; Moo 2000: 114; Laws 1980: 111–12.

similar to Paul's. Even one sin brings death, and hence human beings need new life from God (cf. James 1:18; 2:5). James also describes sin as spiritual adultery (James 4:4),[98] drawing on the OT where Israel's forsaking of God is nothing less than spiritual harlotry. Sin, in other words, is treachery in that people long for the favor and approbation of the world rather than the friendship with God. Sin is not merely the doing of evil; it is fundamentally personal, involving the rejection of God's lordship over one's life.

1 Peter

Even though 1 Peter is relatively brief and addressed to churches facing persecution, the reason why people need salvation is communicated in quite a few different ways in the letter. For instance, Peter twice says that believers have been born again (1 Pet. 1:3, 23). The metaphor "born again" implies that human beings need new life to escape punishment and judgment. They are, so to speak, "dead" before they were born anew. Similarly, believers are those who will be saved on the last day (1 Pet. 1:5, 9), indicating that they were headed for destruction before hearing and believing in the gospel.

Most commentators agree that Peter addressed Gentiles instead of Jews, who enjoyed a covenantal relation with God. The unbelief of these unconverted Gentiles is designated as "ignorance" (1 Pet. 1:14). Such ignorance is not restricted to the intellectual realm; it manifests itself in evil behavior that finds its roots in desires that are contrary to God's will. Their lives were characterized by "futile ways inherited from your forefathers" (1 Pet. 1:18).[99] Peter likely has in view the idolatry that was typical among Gentiles, passed on from generation to generation. Such idolatry did not lead to life, nor is Gentile tradition venerated here. Their idolatry was futile and vain in that it separated people from the true and living God. The Gentile past of the readers is also communicated in 1 Pet. 4:2–4. Those who do not know God live for human passions and desires. They indulge in sexual sin, drunken parties, and reprehensible idolatry. They live for human pleasure rather than the will of God. Peter can say to his readers, therefore, that formerly they were not part of the people of God (1 Pet. 2:10). They were outside the realm of God's covenant people, confined to "darkness" (1 Pet. 2:9). Unbelievers are those who refuse to obey the call of the gospel (1 Pet. 2:8; 4:17; cf. 3:20). They are lost and thus need to be won to faith in Christ (1 Pet. 3:1). They

---

98. James literally calls them "adulteresses" (so the NASB; see Laws 1980: 174; Dibelius 1975: 219–20; L. Johnson 1995: 278).
99. See van Unnik 1969; Schreiner 2003: 84–85.

need forgiveness of sins through the death of Jesus Christ (1 Pet. 2:24). Another way of putting it is that all people are born into the world sick, and thus they need the healing work that comes from the forgiveness of their sins. Before people hear the gospel, they are straying from God and wandering from the truth (1 Pet. 2:25; cf. Isa. 53:6). They are unrighteous and separated from God, and the only way they can be brought to God is through the death of Jesus Christ (1 Pet. 3:18). Their consciences are stained by their evil behavior, but they are cleansed in baptism, which symbolizes Jesus' death for their sins (1 Pet. 3:21).

Jude and 2 Peter

Jude wrote to counteract intruders who have entered the church (or churches), encouraging and warning believers to resist their influence. Even though the letter is brief, sin plays a large role because condemnation of the interlopers takes center stage. Jude emphasizes throughout that sin leads to final judgment. He uses the term "ungodly" (*asebeia* word group) to depict the sin of the false teachers who have had such an adverse influence (Jude 4, 15, 18). The term indicates a refusal to submit to God's lordship, and it manifests itself in Jude in a libertine lifestyle, particularly in terms of sexual sin (Jude 4, 6–8). The spiritual state of these people is clarified in Jude 19: they are "devoid of the Spirit." In other words, they are not genuine Christians. They are merely worldly people (Jude 19) who think that they belong to the people of God. The term "worldly people" (*psychikoi*) recalls 1 Cor. 2:14, where Paul says that the natural person does not and cannot welcome the teaching of the Spirit because he or she lacks the Spirit. So too, here in Jude the intruders are separated from God and live within the realm of this world because they are bereft of the Spirit.

In many respects, 2 Peter is similar to Jude because it too is written in response to false teachers, though in this case the false teachers seem to have come from within the community (2 Pet. 2:1). Peter, like Jude, emphasizes the wickedness of the false teachers and their certain judgment (see esp. 2 Pet. 2). Perhaps they interpreted the Pauline gospel so that it became a platform for libertinism (2 Pet. 3:15–16; cf. 2:2, 7, 10, 12–14, 18–19). Human beings have sinned before God, and so they need to be cleansed of such sin to receive forgiveness (2 Pet. 1:9). Peter says nothing more about forgiveness of sins and never mentions the cross of Christ, but such omissions are explained by the circumstantial nature of the letter. The natural state of human beings is expressed in the phrase "the corruption that is in the world because of sinful desire" (2 Pet. 1:4). Believers have escaped the "corruption" (2 Pet. 1:4) or "defilements" (2 Pet.

2:20) of the world in coming to know Jesus Christ. Such corruption or defilement is rooted in a desire for what is evil. Human beings naturally incline toward and choose to carry out actions that are wicked. The use of the word "escape" (*apopheugō* [2 Pet. 1:4; 2:20]) implies that formerly believers were held captive by corruption and sin. This is confirmed by 2 Pet. 2:19, where unbelievers are said to be "slaves of corruption." They trumpet their freedom with great fanfare, but apart from Jesus Christ they cannot escape the clutches of sin. Sin is also intensely personal in that it manifests itself in the denial of Jesus Christ as Master and Lord (2 Pet. 2:1). Such a denial applies especially to those who claim to be believers and who participate in the Christian community.

Revelation

Revelation often proclaims God's judgment against those who sin and fail to repent (e.g., Rev. 2:5, 16, 21; 3:3; 9:20–21; 16:8–9). Human beings will face God's fierce wrath unless they turn from their evil ways. The author obviously is not sanguine about human goodness, nor is he blind to the corruption that is endemic to human society and governmental structures. Human beings are sinners, and they need to be freed from their sin to enter the heavenly city (Rev. 1:5; 14:4). This freedom comes through the blood of Christ. The kinds of sin that destroy human beings (unless they are denounced and turned away from) and land them in the lake of fire are recorded in Rev. 21:8, including cowardice, murder, sexual sin, idolatry, and lying. Sin is portrayed as a filth that defiles and destroys human beings (Rev. 22:11). The unclean person and the one who does what is detestable will not be delivered (Rev. 21:27) unless they wash their robes. God will judge people on the last day according to their works (Rev. 20:11–15; 22:12, 15). Those who indulge in falsehood and idolatry and plunge into sin will be condemned (Rev. 22:15).

According to Revelation, the fundamental evil of human beings is idolatry. Human beings do not want to admit that they are poor, blind, and naked (Rev. 3:17), and the context here indicates that even believers are tempted to indulge in illusion about their own goodness or lack thereof. Unbelievers cling to their idols and evil deeds even when judgment strikes (Rev. 9:20–21), even cursing God when judgment comes because of their passionate attachment to other gods (Rev. 16:9). They blaspheme and revile God because they hate him (Rev. 13:6). They give their allegiance instead to the beast—the Roman emperor and empire with all its glory and promise of financial prosperity. Hence, they worship the beast instead of the one true and living God (Rev. 13:8, 12, 15). They curse God because his judgments intervene and prevent the carrying out of their own schemes (Rev. 16:11). They demonstrate their hostility to God by making war with the Lamb (17:14; 19:11–21). Hence, they slay believers, who belong to the Lamb (Rev. 16:6; 17:6; 19:2). They long for the riches of Rome and are grieved when Rome is judged (Rev. 18:7, 9, 11–15, 19). They neither give glory to God (Rev. 16:11) nor worship him (Rev. 14:7). Apart from Christ, people are headed for death and Hades (Rev. 1:18). Those with soiled garments will not be enrolled in the book of life and will face the second death (Rev. 3:4–5).

Conclusion

When we consider the entirety of the NT, we see that sin is described in a variety of ways, communicating thereby the complexity and fullness of what is involved. Sin often is defined as the failure to keep what God has commanded, particularly in the Mosaic law. This is a particular focus of Paul, though we see the same sentiment in Acts and James. Both Paul and James maintain that only complete and perfect obedience constitutes true obedience. Any infraction marks one out as a lawbreaker. John sums up the message of the NT when he says that "sin is lawlessness" (1 John 3:4). Those who sin stand guilty before God and are deserving of his judgment. Indeed, God's wrath is poured out on those who are disobedient and guilty before him.

Sin is not summed up in defining it as disobedience. The heart of sin is the failure to worship, praise, and thank God (Rom. 1:21). It involves the worship of the creature rather than the creator. John describes the same reality as loving the honor and praise of human beings more than the honor and praise of God (John 5:44). The root sin is idolatry, and idolatry manifests itself in human boasting and pride. Legalism is another species of this same sin, for religious persons think that they are pleasing to God because of their virtue (even though they are not nearly as virtuous as they think). Hence, religion becomes the vehicle for self-congratulation and self-absorption rather than the worship of God. Faith pleases God because it counts him as powerful and looks to him to satisfy every need. Depending on one's own works is folly, for it looks to the capability of human beings.

All human beings enter into the world as sinners and condemned because they are sons and daughters of Adam (Rom. 5:12–19). Sin blinds human beings to their own wickedness and tricks people into thinking that they are righteous. Sin is not merely a matter of peccadillos or mistakes. Human beings are fiercely rebellious and stubborn, which is captured in the metaphor of being stiff-necked. The sin of human beings is manifested supremely in history in the crucifixion of Jesus of

Nazareth—the Son of God and the Son of Man—the Messiah of Israel. All enter into the world spiritually dead toward God and heading toward physical death and judgment. By nature, humans are children of wrath and are rotten trees. By birth, they are under the dominion of the old age of the flesh instead of the new age of the Spirit. They are a brood of vipers instead of children of God.

The power and depth of sin function as the backdrop to God's saving promises, for such promises represent astonishing good news, given the devastation that sin inflicts on human beings. With the coming of Jesus Christ the era of salvation and deliverance has dawned, so that with the death and resurrection of Jesus the reign of sin and death has ended. Even though Christ has triumphed over sin and death, Christians must wait patiently until the whole universe is transformed into a new creation. In the meantime, God calls for trust and obedience from all people everywhere.

15

✿ ✿ ✿ ✿ ✿ ✿ ✿ ✿ ✿ ✿ ✿ ✿ ✿ ✿ ✿ ✿ ✿ ✿

Faith and Obedience

In the previous chapter we saw that human beings as sons and daughters of Adam refuse to esteem God as God and to give him thanks and praise. They long for autonomy rather than theonomy. They belong to the present evil age and are destined to death, apart from the saving work of God in Christ. In this chapter we consider what human beings need to do to be delivered from this age of sin and death. The response expected of human beings can be summarized under the terms "faith" and "obedience." What NT writers mean by these terms will be investigated in this chapter. Even though there are some advantages in studying Luke and Acts together, I will combine the Synoptic Gospels because they share so much common material. John and the Johannine Epistles will be examined together, for the Johannine view of faith and obedience gains a sharper profile when his letters are integrated with his Gospel.

The Synoptic Gospels

The Priority of Faith

In order to be saved, believers must recognize their desperate need for God and his righteousness. Those who are aware of their poverty in spirit receive the blessing of the kingdom (Matt. 5:3).[1] Those who thirst for righteousness will be satisfied with the righteousness that comes from God himself (Matt. 5:6).[2] Luke seems to place the emphasis on physical poverty and hunger (Luke 6:20–21). Still, he does not conclude that those who are materially deprived by definition trust in God. The term "poor" in Luke derives from the OT where the poor are those who are completely dependent upon Yahweh.[3] According to Luke, those who suffer financially are more likely to depend upon God and place their hope in him. Moreover, there would be no need to long for righteousness if human beings already enjoyed it. Faith recognizes that human beings are spiritually sick and need a physician for healing; that is, human beings lack righteousness, and such righteousness will come only from God himself (Matt. 9:12–13; Mark 2:17; Luke 5:31–32).[4] Faith seeks God as its prime good, and such seeking of God is not a one-time event but rather a lifetime pattern of asking, seeking, and knocking (Matt. 7:7–8; Luke 11:9–10).

Faith is illustrated in the account of the centurion. He was convinced of the power of Jesus' word to effect a new reality. The centurion's faith exceeded what Jesus had found in Israel (Matt. 8:10; Luke 7:9). Nor can this faith be limited merely to physical healing, for Jesus, according to Matthew, proceeds to say that Gentiles will enjoy the kingdom banquet, while many of those from Israel will be excluded (Matt. 8:11–12). Hence, the faith that brought healing was also evidence of saving faith in Jesus. The woman suffering from a hemorrhage for twelve years was convinced that touching the hem of Jesus' robe would bring healing. Jesus affirmed that her "faith has saved" her (Matt. 9:22 par. my translation). Again, this faith is not restricted to physical healing, though certainly it is the case that faith brought healing. The Synoptics use the term "saved" because physical healing here functions as an emblem for spiritual healing.[5]

---

1. Jeremias (1954–1955: 369) points out that this saying is conceptually similar to Paul's claim that it is the ungodly who are justified (Rom. 4:5). See also Davies and Allison 1988: 442–44. See also Bryan (2002: 46–83), who argues that Jesus proclaimed the final judgment on apostate Israel, but at the same time he announced God's free and undeserved grace to those who were considered to be sinners.

2. The focus by Hagner (1993b: 93) on literal hunger and thirst veers away from what the verse actually says.

3. Marshall (1978b: 249) says, "It is not poverty as such which qualifies a person for salvation; the beatitudes are addressed to disciples, to those who are ready to be persecuted for the sake of the Son of Man."

4. Rightly Lane 1974: 105; contra France 2002: 135.

5. See Hagner 1993b: 250–51; Luz 2001: 42. Contrast France (2002: 238), who suggests that the woman's faith has elements of superstition. Twelftree (1999: 156–57, 163, 173) rightly argues that "save" in Luke often points to both physical healing and spiritual salvation. See the detailed study by Yeung (2002: 53–195), who defends the authenticity

Hence, both Mark and Luke immediately add the words "Go in peace," signifying a new relation to God.

The link between physical healing and eschatological salvation should not be pressed in every case. The story of the healing of the paralytic, however, illustrates that such a theme is present here as well (Matt. 9:2–8 par.). Jesus healed when he saw the faith of those who took so much trouble to bring the paralytic to Jesus. The healing, however, becomes an emblem for the forgiveness of sins, and it seems that such forgiveness is given in response to faith.[6] The link between healing and repentance and faith is confirmed by Jesus' limited ability to do miracles in his hometown (Matt. 13:53–58; Mark 6:1–6). The few miracles are ascribed to unbelief, indicating that people in these localities were resistant to Jesus more generally. Their refusal to believe in his healing power indicated that they also rejected his saving power, for the former pointed toward the latter.

The healing of the blind should be interpreted along the same lines. In Matthew's Gospel Jesus healed the blind men on account of their faith, for they believed that Jesus could perform the miracle (Matt. 9:28–30). Matthew records another healing of two blind men and in this instance does not emphasize their faith (Matt. 20:29–34). Nevertheless, their faith is implied, for they hailed Jesus as "Son of David," suggesting that they believed him to be the Messiah of Israel. The same account in Mark and Luke contains the healing of one man, Bartimaeus (Mark 10:46–52; Luke 18:35–43). Jesus was acclaimed as David's son, but the words "Your faith has saved you" are added (Mark 10:52 my translation; Luke 18:42), pointing to a deeper reality than the recovery of physical sight. Jesus was also recognized as the Messiah. The blind man (or "men" according to Matthew) perceived who Jesus is. Each account also emphasizes that the healing was not merely physical. The blind man followed Jesus to Jerusalem. He was a disciple who is willing to follow Jesus as Jesus goes to the cross.[7] The words "Your faith has saved you" point beyond physical healing to the salvation that Jesus grants to those who trust in him. The same theme is evident in the account of the ten lepers who were healed by Jesus (Luke 17:11–19).[8] Only the Samaritan returned and voiced thanks and praise

of the "faith has saved you sayings" and marshals convincing evidence for the position that both physical and spiritual salvation are in view.

6. Jesus heals in response to the faith of the four men who carried the paralytic, but we should not exclude the paralytic's own faith (Davies and Allison 1991: 88; Hagner 1993b: 232; contra France 2002: 124).

7. "Bartimaeus, now set free from his blindness, represents all those who have found enlightenment and follow the Master" (France 2002: 425).

8. Witherington (1998: 150) limits Jesus' words to physical healing here, but the parallel that he cites in Luke 7:50 suggests a deeper meaning.

to God, and he also worshiped Jesus. His physical healing, the praise in his heart, and his worship of Jesus point to a greater reality. Thus Jesus declared, "Your faith has saved you" (Luke 17:19 my translation).[9]

The fundamental requirement given to Jesus' followers is faith. This is summarized in his words to Jairus: "Do not fear, only believe" (Mark 5:36 par.). What astonished Jesus in Nazareth was that those in his own hometown lacked faith (Matt. 13:53–58 par.). Jesus reproached the Jews because they were unbelieving (Matt. 17:17 par.). The demon was expelled from the Syrophoenician woman's daughter because of the woman's persistent faith in Jesus (Matt. 15:22–29 par.). The faith of the sinful woman who intruded upon the feast at Simon's house is emphasized by Luke (Luke 7:36–50). She manifested her love for Jesus by washing his feet, drying his feet with her hair, and anointing them with ointment. Her love for Jesus flowed from the recognition that her sins had been forgiven. Some have argued on the basis of Luke 7:47 that she was forgiven *because* of her love. But the parable of the two debtors suggests otherwise, since it is the one who was forgiven a great debt who loved much, indicating that love is the consequence of forgiveness.[10] The story concludes with Jesus saying, "Your faith has saved you; go in peace" (Luke 7:50). The woman was not saved on the basis of her love; she was saved because she trusted in Jesus for the forgiveness of her sins, and as a result of that forgiveness she overflowed in love for Jesus.

The story of the Pharisee and tax collector should be interpreted similarly, even though the word "faith" does not appear in the account (Luke 18:9–14).[11] The Pharisee clearly thinks that he is "justified" (Luke 18:14) before God because of his devotion to righteousness, for he refrains from theft and sexual sin and lives justly.[12] Moreover, he goes beyond the call of duty by fasting and paying tithes on items that are not even required by the law.[13] The tax collector, on the other hand, puts his trust

9. The translation "your faith has made you well" (NRSV, ESV) instead of "your faith has saved you" obscures the connection articulated between faith and salvation toward which the miracles point. Luke in particular weaves into his narrative the truth that "your faith has saved you." The English versions aptly translate this saying in Luke 7:50, but by translating it as "your faith has made you well" in Luke 8:48; 17:19; 18:42, they fail to portray the whole of what Luke intended. For further discussion of this issue, see Witherington 1998.

10. So Jeremias 1972: 127; Fitzmyer 1981a: 687, 692; Marshall 1978b: 306, 313.

11. Marshall (1978b: 681) remarks, "Jesus' lesson is precisely that the attitude of the heart is ultimately what matters, and justification depends on the mercy of God to the penitent rather than upon the works which might be thought to earn God's favour."

12. "One achieves uprightness before God not by one's own activity but by a contrite recognition of one's own sinfulness before him" (Fitzmyer 1985: 1185).

13. The Pharisee does thank God for his righteousness, but such words should not be overinterpreted in the parable. We see from Luke's editorial comments in Luke 18:9, 14

in God for forgiveness, imploring for mercy from God. This account is remarkable because it clearly demonstrates that Jesus spoke against the notion that human beings could gain God's forgiveness on the basis of their works. It also suggests that some in Judaism believed that righteousness could be secured through works. Otherwise, the parable would address the problem of relying on works, with which no one struggled! Further, the Pauline teaching on justification is anticipated in this text, for Luke clearly implies that the tax collector is right with God because of his faith in God.[14]

The Synoptic accounts honestly portray the struggles that Jesus' disciples had in believing, though faith as small as a mustard seed (Luke 17:6) has a great effect.[15] Jesus reproached Peter for his little faith when he doubted in the midst of walking on the water (Matt. 14:31). All the disciples were indicted for their lack of faith during the storm (Luke 8:25). Mark in particular calls attention to Jesus' upbraiding of the disciples for their hard hearts (Mark 6:52; 8:14–21) and their spiritual obtuseness. Despite their dullness and lack of faith, they confessed that Jesus is God's Christ (Matt. 16:16; Mark 8:29; Luke 9:20).[16]

The deficiency of their faith is illustrated in the two-stage healing in Mark (Mark 8:22–26). The placement of the account is crucial because it occurs right before Peter acclaimed Jesus as the Christ (Mark 8:27–30) and Jesus' subsequent clarification that he would suffer and die as the Messiah (Mark 8:31–38). The two-stage healing does not indicate that Jesus lacked the ability to heal instantaneously, for nowhere else is a process of healing needed. The two stages in the healing symbolize the faith of the disciples.[17] They grasped that Jesus is the Messiah but failed to see that he is a suffering Messiah. Hence, growth in faith was needed so that they would not merely acclaim Jesus as Messiah, but also grasp that he is the Messiah who suffers and dies to atone for sin. Furthermore, the account of the healing of the epileptic boy (Mark 9:14–29 par.) suggests that faith is imperfect in this life and needs to grow. The father confessed his belief but solicited Jesus to help his unbelief (Mark 9:24).[18] Such a request implicitly represents an acknowledgment of Jesus'

that the Pharisee trusted in himself, not in God. Hence, his thanksgiving to God was not genuine. It did not spring from the heart but rather was a verbal tip of the hat.

14. For this view see Jeremias (1954–1955: 369–70; 1972: 139–44), who argues that the Semitisms in Luke 18:14 demonstrate that the saying is authentic.

15. See Bock 1996: 1390–91.

16. Peter speaks for all the disciples here.

17. Rightly Best 1970a: 325–26; Hays 1996: 77; France 2002: 322–23.

18. A few commentators think that this refers to Jesus' faith, but the faith of the father is more likely in view (Twelftree 1999: 87). For a brief survey of scholarly options, see Meier 1994: 655, 669–70n37.

deity, for only God can increase one's faith. It also reflects the truth that human faith is inherently weak and unstable, needing assistance from God to grow.

New Obedience

In the Synoptic Gospels saving faith is a living faith.[19] It is not an abstract acceptance of truths about Jesus. Hence, faith can never be separated from a new way of life—a new obedience in the lives of Jesus' followers. This is illustrated in Mark 1:15: "Repent and believe in the gospel." Genuine belief does not exist without repentance (cf. Matt. 4:17), and indeed all repentance flows from faith. Repentance means that people turn back to the Lord and the way of goodness (Luke 1:16–17).[20] The relationship between faith and repentance is illustrated well in Jesus' insistence that people turn and become like children (Matt. 18:3–4; cf. 19:14).[21] Those who humble themselves like children demonstrate their trust in God, which explains why only those who humble themselves will be exalted (Matt. 23:12). Conversely, those who exalt themselves will be humiliated on the last day because they view themselves, despite their evil, as qualified to inherit salvation.

Each of the Synoptic Gospels often stresses the new kind of life that is necessary to enter the kingdom. Such statements, however, do not contradict the truth that faith saves rather than works. The changed life of disciples is a fruit of faith and the result of faith. Those who follow Jesus in discipleship do so because they trust in him. The obedience of believers should never be construed as if it were independent of faith. On the other hand, it is unthinkable that the new relationship to Jesus would be anything less than transforming.

NEW OBEDIENCE IN MATTHEW

Matthew's emphasis on obedience illustrates the point being made. Those who do God's will are part of the family of God (Matt. 12:46–50). In the parable of the soils only those who bear fruit truly belong to God

19. Since Matthew and Luke emphasize at some length the new life in disciples, I have decided for the purpose of clarity to discuss the new obedience in each of the Synoptic Gospels separately.

20. Stuhlmacher (1993: 17) says that repentance "means turning away from the old way of life in injustice and alienation from God, and turning toward the one God and Father, to whom Jesus himself belongs. Second, it means complying with the will of this God by acts of love and righteousness."

21. See Hagner 1995: 517–18. For a good survey of possible interpretations, see Jeremias 1972: 190–91; Luz 2001: 426–29 (who emphasizes the low social status of children in the Jewish culture of Jesus' day [so also Davies and Allison 1991: 757]).

(Matt. 13:18–23).[22] Those who receive the word of the kingdom with joy but do not endure will not enter the kingdom. Nor will the person receive an inheritance who initially responds to the gospel of the kingdom but then allows the desire for the kingdom to be slowly squeezed out by the enticing pleasures of this world. The parables of the treasure in the field and the pearl of greatest value teach that the kingdom must be the consuming passion of one's life—more precious than anything else (Matt. 13:44–46).[23] The rich ruler would be saved only if he gave up all his possessions and followed Jesus in discipleship (Matt. 19:21). Those who refuse to take up their cross and follow Jesus but instead try to preserve their own lives will be ruined (Matt. 16:24–26). Only those who follow Jesus in radical discipleship will be saved on the last day. They must be willing to sacrifice comfortable homes and cut family ties for the sake of following Jesus (Matt. 8:18–22). Those who love family members more than Jesus are unworthy of him, for those who become Jesus' disciples must be prepared to die for his sake (Matt. 10:37–39).

Only good trees that produce good fruit will be spared on the day of judgment, for people will be judged by every word uttered (Matt. 12:33–37). Those who obstinately refuse to forgive others will not be forgiven by God on the day of judgment (Matt. 6:14–15; 18:21–35).[24] Jeremias says, "But the deepest secret of this love which characterizes realized discipleship is that they have learnt how to forgive. They extend to others the divine forgiveness which they have experienced, a forgiveness which passes all understanding."[25] Anything that causes people to stumble or fall away must be removed from their lives. Jesus uses hyperbolic language of cutting off a foot or hand or gouging out an eye (Matt. 5:29–30; 18:8–9) to portray the radical steps that must be taken to avoid apostasy. Both anger (Matt. 5:21–26) and lust (Matt. 5:27–28) must be conquered by believers, and they cannot be allowed to take root in the hearts of Jesus' disciples.[26] Jesus' true disciples are not those who

22. Rightly Hagner 1993b: 380–81. See also the comments by Hooker (1991: 131–32) on the Markan parallel.

23. So Hagner 1993b: 396–97; Nolland 2005: 564–66.

24. Hultgren rightly says forgiveness is not "a prerequisite or means for obtaining God's forgiveness" (2000: 29). He seems to undercut the necessity, however, of forgiveness in his comments here as well, and Crump wrongly says forgiveness is "not the condition but the evidence of being forgiven" (2006: 139). Crump fails to see that conditions do not rule out grace. Belief is a condition for salvation, but such a condition does not lead to the conclusion that grace is compromised. Further, we must see that in the NT continuing to forgive is another way of describing continued belief in the gospel.

25. Jeremias 1972: 210. See the entire exposition in Jeremias 1972: 210–14.

26. Hays (1996: 98–99) argues that Matthew sees character as flowing out of what is in the heart, though such righteous behavior is also due to training and discipleship in the ways of righteousness.

profess to do the Father's will (i.e., the Pharisees) but rather those who actually carry out the Father's will by repenting (i.e., tax collectors and prostitutes). Faithful slaves do what the master commands and will be duly rewarded, but unfaithful slaves will be excluded from the kingdom and will weep and gnash their teeth (Matt. 24:45–51).

Obedience, according to Matthew, is not an extra that brings a reward above and beyond eternal life.[27] Those who fail to do God's will are excluded from the kingdom. The parables in Matt. 25 hammer home the same theme. The five virgins excluded from the wedding banquet failed to bring the necessary oil (Matt. 25:1–13). The failure to bring oil cannot be classified merely as absentmindedness; it signifies failure to be prepared for Jesus' return.[28] In the parable of the talents those who did the master's bidding were rewarded, but the one who out of laziness did nothing and hid his talent was thrown into the outer darkness where there is "weeping and gnashing of the teeth" (Matt. 25:14–30). Jesus' judgment of the sheep and the goats is in accordance with what they have done, whether they have shown mercy and love to believers ("one of the least of these" [Matt. 25:45]).[29] Again, the issue is not merely a matter of rewards disconnected from eternal life, for the unrighteous "will go away into eternal punishment, but the righteous into eternal life" (Matt. 25:46).

Jesus' radical call to his disciples is evident throughout Matthew.[30] Those who give alms, pray, and fast (Matt. 6:1–18) in order to obtain praise from people have received the only reward they will ever get. Only those who do such things *coram Deo* will receive an eschatological reward. Similarly, treasures in heaven are reserved only for those whose treasure is God himself (Matt. 6:19–21). If the "eye" of people (i.e., the desires of their hearts) is captivated by riches, then they reveal that they serve another master: wealth rather than God (Matt. 6:22–24).[31] On the final day people must enter the narrow gate to be saved (Matt. 7:13–14). The narrow gate for Matthew clearly refers to obedience—the changed life demanded of Jesus'

27. For a discussion on obedience and reward in Matthew's theology that interacts with Matthean scholarship, see France 1989: 265–70.

28. Hagner (1995: 728–30) cautions against overreading the reference to oil so that it is identified as living an ethical life.

29. For a defense of the idea that believers are in view, see Carson 1984: 519–20; see also Hagner 1995: 744–45; Luz 1995: 129–30. Contra Jeremias (1972: 207); Hultgren (2000: 318–25), and Davies and Allison (1997: 428–29), who think that all people are in view here, not just disciples. Luz (2005: 267–74) documents that the interpretation favored here was the most common until the nineteenth and twentieth centuries.

30. For a brief sketch on discipleship in Matthew, see France 1989: 261–65.

31. These verses are quite difficult to interpret and thus controversial. For a thorough discussion, see Davies and Allison 1988: 635–41. For criticism of some aspects of their interpretation, see Hagner 1993b: 158–59.

disciples.[32] The false prophets will not receive a reward, for they are not good trees (Matt. 7:15–20). Instead of producing good fruit, their lives are wicked and fail to conform to God's will. Simply calling on Jesus as Lord does not qualify one for the kingdom (Matt. 7:21–23). People may even do miracles, exorcise demons, and utter prophecies and still be excluded from the kingdom because of their failure to do God's will. Only those who build securely on the foundation will survive the storm of the final judgment (Matt. 7:24–27). Building on the foundation, in this context in Matthew, clearly means to hear and do Jesus' words.

Jesus denounces the Pharisees and scribes for their failure to do God's will. His fundamental indictment was not that they were legalists. He criticized those who "do not practice what they teach" (Matt. 23:3 NRSV).[33] They lived for the praise of others instead of the honor and praise that comes from the one and only true God (Matt. 23:5–12).[34] They excluded others from entering the kingdom because their converts were formed in their image and thus practiced evil (Matt. 23:13–15). They engaged in casuistry to avoid keeping oaths that were taken in God's presence (Matt. 23:16–22). They concentrated on observing the minutiae of the law but overlooked what is truly crucial: "justice and mercy and faith" (Matt. 23:23 NRSV). They "strain out a gnat but swallow a camel" (Matt. 23:24 NRSV). On the outside they appeared to be righteous because they were devoted to the regulations of the Torah, and yet on the inside evil spread like a cancerous tumor (Matt. 23:25–28). They showed themselves to be vipers—the seed of the serpent (Matt. 23:33; cf. Gen. 3:15), for they followed their ancestors' footsteps in slaying God's prophets and messengers, which culminated in the crucifixion of God's Son. Twice in Matthew Jesus emphasizes, when speaking to the Pharisees, that God desires mercy instead of sacrifice (Matt. 9:10–13; 12:5–7).[35] The "weightier matters of the law" are justice, mercy, and faith (Matt. 23:23). The entirety of the law should be interpreted in light of the commands to love God and to love one's neighbor (Matt. 22:34–40).

Some conclude that Matthew's emphasis on obedience contradicts the Pauline gospel, where righteousness is obtained by faith rather than through works.[36] Matthew certainly emphasizes the new life of obedience

32. Davies and Allison (1988: 696–701) demonstrate the eschatological character of the passage. See also Hagner 1993b: 178–80.
33. Silva (1986:113–21) argues that the fundamental critique of the religious leaders was their failure to do the will of God, their toning down what God required.
34. For a careful study of Matt. 23, see Garland 1979.
35. See the insightful discussion in Hays 1996: 99–101.
36. For example, Mohrlang 1984: 42–43. Luz (1995: 146–53) sees a helpful tension. Still, Luz (1995: 59) seems to admit that ultimately they do contradict, and he sees neither as having the last word.

that is required to enter the kingdom of heaven. Still, we could exagger-ate the polarity between Matthew and Paul. Matthew recognizes that human beings are poor in spirit (Matt. 5:3); only those who recognize such will receive the power of the kingdom. In other words, people need the power of the kingdom to live in the new way demanded by Jesus. The new life that is needed is possible only with God and cannot be conjured up through human effort (Matt. 19:26). The call to obedience is nothing less than radical commitment to Jesus, so that disciples are willing to follow him and to prize him above everything. The call to follow Jesus and to obedience should not be interpreted as if perfection were necessary to obtain the final reward. God demands perfection (Matt. 5:48), but forgiveness is the last word for those who repent. The prayer that Jesus taught his disciples recognizes the need to ask for forgive-ness of sins (Matt. 6:12), presumably every day. The ultimate basis for the forgiveness of sins is the death of Jesus, which inaugurates the new covenant (Matt. 26:28).[37] Obedience is required to enter the kingdom, and Matthew thinks of continuing to follow Jesus to the end: "But the one who endures to the end will be saved" (Matt. 10:22; 24:13). Those who acknowledge Jesus will be acknowledged before God, but those who deny him will be rejected (Matt. 10:32–33). The obedience demanded in Matthew reveals whether one treasures Jesus above all else. Further, such obedience is the fruit of faith. It is not the case that obedience is conceived of as the basis for entrance into the kingdom; Jesus' death is the only basis for the forgiveness of sins, but those who trust Jesus demonstrate such faith by a new way of life.

New Obedience in Mark

The Matthean theme of obedience also exists in Mark's Gospel, though in less detail, given the comparative brevity of Mark. Our look at Mark will also be abbreviated because I will not reproduce in any detail texts examined under Matthew. The proclamation of the kingdom involves a call to repentance (Mark 1:4, 15). Only those who receive the kingdom like children will enter it (Mark 10:15). Those who do God's will comprise the family of Jesus (Mark 3:31–35). Those who refuse to forgive others will not be forgiven by God (Mark 11:25). The parable of the soils, as in Matthew, indicates that only those who persevere to the end and bear fruit will be saved (Mark 4:13–20). The story of the rich man reveals that nothing can take precedence over Jesus, and the man's commitment to God will be measured by his willingness to follow Jesus and give up his wealth (Mark 10:17–22).

---

37. Jeremias (1972: 209) states that only those who obey and forgive will be vindicated at the last judgment, and yet such vindication is still a matter of mercy, not recompense.

Mark nicely ties together Jesus' own destiny, in which he is called to go to the cross, with the call to discipleship. On three occasions Jesus predicts that he will suffer and then be raised from the dead (Mark 8:31–33; 9:30–32; 10:32–34). Each incident is followed with instruction about the call to discipleship (Mark 8:34–38; 9:33–37; 10:35–45).[38] The disciples need to realize that Jesus' call to suffer is also paradigmatic for their own lives. Peter betrayed a satanic mind-set in saying that the cross could not be the will of God for Jesus (Mark 8:32–33). Similarly, only the one who takes the path of self-denial and bears a cross to follow Jesus will enter the kingdom (Mark 8:34). The disciples must be willing to "lose their life for my sake, and for the sake of the gospel" (Mark 8:35 NRSV). Otherwise, they will be destroyed when the judgment arrives. After Jesus' second passion prediction the disciples argued about which of them was greatest (Mark 9:33–37). Jesus placed a child in their midst and swept the child into his arms. Children were to be seen and not heard in the ancient world, but his disciples must welcome children in Jesus' name, for disciples live to serve others, not to advance their own egos. Finally, James and John asked to be seated at Jesus' side in his kingdom (Mark 10:35–45). The other disciples showed their irritation, demonstrating that the standards of privilege and honor in contemporary culture animated them. Jesus rejected the status-seeking that permeated the Gentile world. Disciples are to imitate Jesus by serving others instead of seeking to be served (Mark 10:45). The pattern of Jesus' life is the pattern for disciples.

New Obedience in Luke

The Lukan teaching on repentance and discipleship contains the same themes observed in Matthew and Mark.[39] Only those who endure to the end will gain their lives (Luke 21:19), so that only those who bear fruit until the end will be preserved from judgment (Luke 8:11–15). Jesus' family consists of those who do God's will (Luke 8:19–21), and those who fail to do what Jesus says build on a foundation that will collapse (Luke 6:46–49). The narrow door that must be entered to be saved is the practice of righteousness (Luke 13:24–30), so that only those who take up their cross and follow Jesus will save their lives (Luke 9:21–27). Faithful slaves will be rewarded for doing God's will (Luke 12:35–48). Jesus must be first in one's life, hence the rich man must sell all and follow Jesus (Luke 18:22). Repentance manifests itself in reconciliation in families and a renewed commitment to righteous living (Luke 1:17). Those who are wealthy should share with those less fortunate (Luke

---

38. This motif is commonly recognized. See Best 1970a: 328–37.
39. Hence, these themes are presented in a cursory fashion here.

3:10–11). Tax collectors were not asked to abandon their jobs, but they should carry out their duties justly and without extortion (Luke 3:12–13). Similarly, soldiers were not required to resign their office, but they must desist from extorting money from others and be content with their pay (Luke 3:14).

Luke is particularly interested in how believers use their money as a fruit of repentance, and we will examine this theme in more detail later.[40] It should simply be noted here that those who find their treasures in riches instead of God will be excluded from the kingdom (e.g., Luke 6:20–26; 12:13–21, 32–34; 16:1–13, 19–31). Those who truly belong to the people of God show mercy to others in need (Luke 10:25–37).[41] The call to discipleship in Luke takes precedence over everything else in life. Family relations, home, and any other concern must take a back seat to the kingdom of God (Luke 9:57–62). Jesus even called on his people to "hate" father and mother, spouse and children, and brothers and sisters in order to become his disciples (Luke 14:26). The word "hate" here clearly is hyperbolic, for Jesus proceeded to include one's own life in what must be hated. The point is that no person or thing can take precedence over Jesus. He must reign supreme.[42] People must count the cost and be willing to give up all their possessions for Jesus' sake (Luke 14:27–33).[43]

Luke could be interpreted as teaching that obedience secures entrance into the kingdom of God. However, such a reading fails to account for all that Luke writes. As noted in the first section of this chapter, Luke often and clearly teaches that the basis of one's new life is the forgiveness of sins. The life of obedience is always rooted in faith—a faith that finds Jesus to be the joy and treasure of one's heart. Obedience is always tied to faith in and love for Jesus. Obedience is necessary for entrance into the kingdom, but such obedience expresses one's faith. Nor does Luke think of perfect obedience, for he too recognizes that believers must pray daily, "Forgive us our sins" (Luke 11:4).

Summary of the Synoptics

In examining the Synoptic Gospels we have seen that they emphasize both faith and obedience. The latter can never qualify for entrance into the kingdom because all are, as Matthew teaches, poor in spirit (Matt. 5:3). A common refrain in the Synoptics is "your faith has saved you." It is those who come to Jesus in humility as children who are saved,

40. See the discussion in chapter 18.
41. See the classic exposition in Jeremias 1972: 202–6.
42. See Marshall 1978b: 592.
43. So Seccombe 1982: 115–16.

those who, like the tax collector, recognize that they need forgiveness from God to enter his presence (Luke 18:13–14). And yet in the Synoptics faith is a living reality that follows Jesus in discipleship. It issues in a life of obedience where the will of God is done. A new tree always bears good fruit.

The Johannine Literature

The Centrality of Believing in John's Gospel

The Gospel of John uses the verb "believe" (*pisteuō*) ninety-eight times, indicating the centrality of the theme.[44] Interestingly, John never uses the noun "faith" (*pistis*) in the Gospel, but only the verb "believe."[45] The significance of the use of the verb rather than the noun certainly could be exaggerated. Perhaps the verbal use places the emphasis on believing as an action, excluding any notion of a passive faith. Even if the verb "believe" occurred rarely, its importance is indicated by the purpose of the Gospel as stated in John 20:31. John wrote so that readers would believe that Jesus is the Christ, and so that they would thereby obtain eternal life.[46] Such a concluding statement hardly surprises, for often in the Gospel John emphasizes that those who believe in Jesus receive eternal life (John 3:15–16, 18, 36; 6:40, 47), and that those who put their trust in Jesus will never die (John 11:25–26). Conversely, those who fail to believe in him will face death because of their sins (John 8:24).

A verbal form of "believe" is often followed by the preposition "in" (*eis*) with the accusative object (e.g., John 1:12; 2:11; 3:15, 16, 18, 36; 4:39; 6:29, 40).[47] It might seem that the use of the preposition *eis* would suggest a more active and dynamic faith than the use of the verb "believe" followed by the dative case. Such a theory does not appear to be borne out by the evidence, for the dative case does not signal a less robust faith in Jesus (John 5:38, 46; 10:38; 14:11).[48] A dative case is indeed used for those who have a deficient faith (John 8:31), but later in the chapter Jesus uses the dative in reproving them for failing to believe (John 8:45–46), and certainly he does not intend to say, "You should at least have a weak

44. In 1 John the verb appears nine times, and the noun *pistis* once (1 John 5:4).

45. On the significance of *pisteuō* in John, see Barth, *EDNT* 3:95–96; Bultmann, *TDNT* 6:222–28.

46. The purpose of John's Gospel is the subject of debate. For a defense of the notion that this Gospel is fundamentally evangelistic, see Carson 1987a; 2005. For further discussion, see Barrett 1978: 134–44.

47. I count thirty-four occurrences of the verb *pisteuō* plus *eis* designating faith in Jesus. In one instance, light is the object, but the light clearly refers to Jesus (John 12:36).

48. See the convincing appraisal of the evidence in Bultmann 1971: 252n2; Carson 1991b: 346–47.

faith in me"! John clearly prefers the verb *pisteuō* with the preposition *eis*, but it appears that this is a stylistic preference.

John's use of "believe" indicates that human beings receive eternal life by believing instead of working. I argued earlier that John depicts human beings as living in the realm of darkness, so that they are cut off from the light of life. They live under the dominion of the ruler of this world, and thus they practice evil, so that they hate rather than love. Human beings are spiritually blind, and so they cannot perceive the truth or understand Jesus. Eternal life is not obtained, however, by working; human beings cannot "atone" for their evil. Jesus Christ has come into the world as the Lamb of God to remove sin (John 1:29). The "work" that God requires, then, is contrary to human expectations. "This is the work of God, that you believe in him who he has sent" (John 6:29). One work suffices for human beings, and this can be defined as trusting in Jesus. Nor is this contrary to the OT, for those who believed what Moses wrote would put their faith in Jesus because Moses' writings testify to Jesus (John 5:46–47).

The Content of Belief in John's Gospel

In John belief is not a vague entity, as if a vague, amorphous faith qualifies one for eternal life. Saving faith is radically Christ-centered. One must believe in Jesus' name (John 1:12) and trust that God's love has been manifested in the giving of Jesus for eternal life (John 3:16–18). Alternatively, John can say that one must believe in the Father (John 5:24), but it is precisely the Father who sent Jesus (John 5:38; 12:44). Those who believe in God must also believe in Jesus (John 14:1);[49] it is not genuine faith in God if one does not have faith in Jesus as well. One must believe that Jesus has come from God (John 16:27, 30; 17:8, 21). There is specific content to the faith of those who belong to God. They acknowledge Jesus as "the Holy One of God" (John 6:69). Those who refuse to confess Jesus as "I am" will perish in sin (John 8:24; cf. 13:19). A blind man put his faith in Jesus as the "Son of Man" (John 9:35). Jesus did the works to demonstrate that the "Father is in me and I am in the Father" (John 10:37–38; cf. 14:10). Genuine disciples confess with Martha, "I believe that you are the Christ, the Son of God, the one coming into the world" (John 11:27). The content of saving faith is captured best by the purpose statement in John's Gospel, which affirms that Jesus did his signs so that people would acknowledge him as the Messiah and the Son of God, and as a result enjoy eternal life (John 20:31).

---

49. Both instances of *pisteuete* in this verse should be taken as imperatives. For a discussion of the options and a preference for imperatives, see Barrett 1978: 456.

Believing in 1 John

The centrality of faith in Jesus is evident also in 1 John. God's command is "that we believe in the name of his Son Jesus Christ" (1 John 3:23). Those who have been born of God believe "that Jesus is the Christ" (1 John 5:1). Those who believe "that Jesus is the Son of God" overcome the world (1 John 5:5; cf. 5:4). If one fails to believe that Jesus is God's Son, then one dismisses God's testimony as a lie (1 John 5:10). The purpose statement of John's first letter is remarkably similar to the purpose statement in the Gospel: "I write these things to you who believe in the name of the Son of God that you may know that you have eternal life" (1 John 5:13).[50] For John, the faith that saves is faith in Jesus as the Son of God, as the Messiah who has come in the flesh (1 John 2:22–23).

The Dynamism of Faith in John's Gospel

The dynamism of faith is expressed through many other terms in John, so that it is clear that faith is living and active.[51] Faith receives, obeys, drinks, hears, comes, beholds, eats, abides, goes, knows, sees, follows, enters, hates, loves, and more. We will briefly investigate these various terms here. Before commencing, however, we should note something about the meaning of "believe" in John 20:31. Scholars have long debated whether John's purpose in writing was to bring nonbelievers to initial faith or to encourage believers to continue in their faith. The difference of opinion is reflected in the NRSV. John wrote "so that you may come to believe that Jesus is the Messiah, the Son of God" (John 20:31). The alternative reading, in the footnote, says that John wrote "so that you may continue to believe that Jesus is the Messiah, the Son of God." The former accepts the aorist subjunctive of "believe" as the better reading, while the latter opts for the present subjunctive. Recent studies of verbal tenses, however, call into question whether the aorist can be limited to the initial coming to faith, for it could very well designate the call to faith in one's life as a whole.[52] The dynamic quality of faith in John suggests that what John writes should not be restricted to the initial decision to believe. For John, saving belief includes the notion of continuing to believe, and hence both the commencement of faith and the ongoing life of faith are in view here.

Several sensory metaphors convey what it means to believe in Jesus—for example, hearing, seeing, drinking, and eating. Hearing Jesus' voice

---

50. See Marshall 1978a: 243; Smalley 1984: 289–91. R. Brown (1982: 608) rightly suggests that the purpose of the entire letter is in view.

51. Barth (*EDNT* 3:96) notes this same truth and lists some of these expressions as well.

52. See the fundamental work on verbal syntax in Porter 1989.

does not automatically convey life. All those in tombs will hear his voice, but some will rise to be judged (John 5:28–29). One must both hear and believe in order to enjoy eternal life (John 5:24). In some contexts, however, the word "hear" (*akouō*) refers to an "effective" hearing, so that the one who hears lives. Those who are spiritually dead and "hear the voice of the Son of God . . . will live" (John 5:25).[53] Not all "hear" Jesus' voice in this way, for this kind of hearing is a believing hearing. Similarly, John 6:45 cites the promise of Isa. 54:13, which states that the children who return from exile will be taught by the Lord, and God will establish a new creation in his covenant of peace (cf. Isa. 54:10; Jer. 31:33–34). Those who have "heard and learned from the Father," therefore, certainly will come to Jesus (John 6:45). Such hearing in this instance inevitably leads to "coming" and believing in Jesus, whereas those who do not belong to Jesus cannot "hear" (*akouō*) his difficult teaching (John 6:60; 8:43). Jesus declares, "Whoever is of God hears the words of God. The reason why you do not hear them is that you are not of God" (John 8:47). The Johannine teaching on grace surfaces again here. Only those who are the recipients of God's saving work can hear God's words. Jesus' sheep hear his voice because they belong to his flock, and they flee from the voice of strangers (John 10:3, 5, 8, 27). Gentiles, who are not from the Jewish fold, will also hear Jesus' voice, and Jesus will make them part of his flock (John 10:16). Jesus came to witness to the truth, and "everyone who is of the truth listens to my voice" (John 18:37). Faith "hears" Jesus' words and believes, but such ability to hear comes from God himself, who grants his flock the ability to hear his words.

Faith can also be described as "seeing" Jesus, as perceiving him for who he really is. The one who "sees" (*theōreō*) Jesus also "sees" the Father, who sent him (John 12:45). Probably the verb "seeing" in John 6:40 is synonymous with "believing," so that genuine faith entails seeing who Jesus is. The account of the blind man in John 9 plays off on the idea that those who believe see who Jesus truly is. The one who was blind saw that Jesus is the Son of Man, but the Pharisees who claimed to have spiritual sight and were unwilling to admit to their blindness were enveloped in darkness (John 9:35–41). Indeed, God blinded the eyes of those who disbelieved, so that sight was impossible for them (John 12:40).

The vitality of faith is communicated through the sensory actions of drinking and eating. Drinking physical water will never quench the spiritual thirst of human beings (John 4:13). Those who drink the water given by Jesus, on the other hand, will slake their thirst forever. Those who believe in Jesus will find that their thirst is satisfied (John 6:35). Anyone who is parched should come to Jesus and drink freely (John

---

53. It is clear in context that the "hearing" is effective here (Bultmann 1971: 259).

7:37–38). Indeed, people must drink Jesus' blood to obtain life (John 6:54, 56); that is, people must believe in Jesus as the crucified Lord to gain life. The image of drinking blood would be especially scandalous to Jews, given the OT prohibition against consuming blood. It emphasizes that the death of Jesus must be embraced wholly and without reservation by those who are saved.

The same truth is conveyed by the metaphor of eating. The verbs *esthiō* and *trōgō* are used to signify eating Jesus' flesh (John 6:50, 53, 54, 56, 57, 58). Some have maintained that the latter term calls attention to the act of eating as a crunching activity, but since John often uses synonyms for the sake of variety, we probably should not press the differences between the two words.[54] All the references to eating are found in John 6, where Jesus declares that he is the bread of life. He emphasizes repeatedly that one must believe in him as the bread of life in order to enjoy eternal life (John 6:29, 35, 36, 40, 47, 64, 69). The image of eating is another way to describe the faith that leads to life. One must eat of Jesus as the bread of heaven in order to escape death (John 6:50). Just as people must consume food to live physically, so too people must eat of Jesus to "live forever" (John 6:51). John particularly emphasizes that people must "eat" Jesus' flesh to live. Jesus gives his own "flesh" for the life of the world (John 6:51), which is a clear reference to the cross. Hence, Jesus emphasizes that one must eat his flesh and drink his blood in order to enjoy eternal life (John 6:53–54, 56–58). Faith is not a mere acceptance of the notion that Jesus died; it is the active ingesting of that truth, so that believing in Jesus' death is one's food and drink. Those who believe feed on Jesus' death as the very source of their life.

The active nature of faith is conveyed by the verb "receive" (*lambanō*). The Jews did not "receive" (*paralambanō*) Jesus, but those who "receive" (*lambanō*) become God's children (John 1:11–12).[55] The religious leaders did not receive Jesus, even though he came in the name of the Father (John 5:43). Conversely, those who received Jesus also received the Father (John 13:20). The disciples' reception of Jesus is evident in that they have received and welcomed his words (John 17:8).

Coming to faith is also described as coming to know God and Jesus Christ. Knowing is conveyed by the verbs *oida* and, especially, *ginōskō*. Some scholars have maintained that the former focuses on intellectual comprehension, and the latter on personal knowing. The disjunction between the two, however, remains unconvincing, for John never conceived of personal knowing as separated from knowledge about God

---

54. See Carson 1991b: 346–48; Barrett 1978: 299.

55. Bultmann (1971: 57n2) notes that the two verbs are interchangeable. See also Barrett 1978: 163.

and Christ.[56] The use of both verbs reflects John's love for synonyms. The centrality of knowing is expressed clearly in John 17:3: "And this is eternal life, that they may know you, the only true God, and Jesus Christ whom you have sent." Believers "know" Jesus as God's holy one (John 6:69). They "know that this is indeed the Savior of the world" (John 4:42). Those who are willing to do the Father's bidding will know whether Jesus is truly from God (John 7:17; cf. 17:8, 25). The world is condemned for not knowing Jesus (John 1:10) or the Father (John 7:28; 8:19). Knowing the truth is what liberates human beings, and it is the Son himself who is the truth that sets people free (John 8:32, 36). Jesus' sheep know him and follow him (John 10:14) because they know his voice (John 10:4–5). Those who know Jesus also know the Father (John 14:7), but those who persecute believers reveal that they have not known the Son or the Father (John 8:55; 16:3; cf. 17:25).

Those who believe in Jesus "come" (*erchomai*) to him for life. Unbelief is manifested in the refusal to come to Jesus to receive life (John 5:40). Those who practice evil shrink from the light and refuse to come to it in order to spare themselves humiliation, whereas those who practice truth "come to the light" so that it is evident that the good work done in them is from God (John 3:20–21). The correlation between "coming" and "believing" is evident in John 6:35, for those who "come" to Jesus will satisfy their hunger, and those who "believe" in Jesus will slake their thirst. Jesus invites all who thirst to come to him (John 7:37). Coming to Jesus is essential because Jesus teaches in no uncertain terms that "no one comes to the Father" except through him, for he is "the way and the truth and the life" (John 14:6). Coming to Jesus portrays the action of those who believe, but such coming can be ascribed only to the grace of God because all those whom the Father has granted to the Son certainly will come to Jesus (John 6:37). Indeed, those who are not drawn by the Father cannot come to Jesus (John 6:44), whereas those who have been taught by God will come (John 6:45). It is not as if they desire to come but God prevents them from doing so; rather, unless one is drawn by the Father, one has no inclination to come to Jesus for life. Hence, Jesus says, "No one can come to me unless it is granted him by the Father" (John 6:65). Such coming to Jesus is alternatively described as being "drawn" (*helkō*) by the Father to Jesus (John 6:44; 12:32).

Genuine faith moves toward Jesus. This is evident also in John 6. Many of Jesus' disciples took offense at his teaching and ceased to follow him (John 6:66–69). Jesus asked the disciples if they wished to depart from him as well. Peter replied, "Lord, to whom shall we go? You have

56. So also Barrett 1978: 162–63. For the close relationship between knowing and believing, see Bultmann 1971: 55n6.

the words of eternal life" (John 6:68). Peter and the other disciples have
"gone" (*aperchomai*) to find life. Faith "enters" (*eiserchomai*) into the
pastures of salvation and trusts in Jesus as the good shepherd (John
10:9). Faith "follows" (*akoloutheō*) Jesus just as sheep follow their shepherd (John 10:4, 27), but Jesus' disciples run from strangers and refuse
to follow false shepherds (John 10:5). Because Jesus is the light of the
world, those who "follow" him will escape the darkness and enjoy "the
light of life" (John 8:12). Disciples of Jesus must be willing to give up
their entire lives to him and lose their lives in order to gain them for
eternal life (John 12:25). This kind of surrender is what it means to
"follow" Jesus (John 12:26). Jesus summons disciples to "follow" him
at both the beginning and the end of John's Gospel (John 1:43 [cf. 1:37];
21:19, 22), so that the call to follow Jesus functions as bookends for the
material within.

Those who believe in Jesus "abide" (*menō*) in him.[57] "Eating" and
"drinking" are vivid ways of saying that one "believes" in Jesus, and those
who eat Jesus' flesh and drink his blood "abide" in him (John 6:56). Those
who "remain" (*menō*) in his word are genuine disciples. Genuine faith
is clearly persevering faith—a faith in which one continues to trust in
Jesus. In John 15 remaining in Jesus is compared to abiding in a vine,
so that just as one cannot bear fruit apart from staying connected to a
vine, neither can disciples bear fruit unless they remain in Jesus (John
15:4–6). As in John 8:31, remaining in Jesus means that disciples continue in his teaching (John 15:7). Those who do not continue to abide
will be destroyed forever because they will be severed from the vine
(John 15:6). Remaining in Jesus is expressed concretely by obeying his
commands (John 15:10; cf. 15:16).

The converse of believing in the Son is to "disobey" (*apeitheō*) him
(John 3:36). Only those who "hate" their lives will save them on the last
day (John 12:25). Genuine love for Jesus is expressed in keeping his
word and obeying his commands (John 14:15, 21, 23–24). Jesus declares
that his disciples have kept his word (John 17:6). Those who keep Jesus'
words will conquer death (John 8:51). Jesus' supreme command is that
disciples love one another (John 13:34–35; 15:12–17), and this love is
to be patterned after Jesus' self-giving love for the disciples, his laying
down of his life for his sheep.

According to John, mere belief does not save. Many put their faith in
Jesus because of the remarkable signs that he was doing (John 2:23).
However, Jesus did not entrust himself to such people, for he knew what
was in their hearts, discerning that they did not truly grasp that his signs
pointed to the necessity of faith in him (John 2:24–25). Jesus knows what

---

57. For the significance of *menō* in John, see Hübner, *EDNT* 2:407–8.

is "in man" (*en tō anthrōpō* [John 2:25]), and John immediately glides over to "Now there was a man of the Pharisees" (John 3:1). Nicodemus illustrates the problem with human beings. He was impressed by Jesus' signs and thus has a sort of faith in him, but he needed to be born from above (John 3:3, 5, 7).

John observes that many "believed" in Jesus during the Feast of Tabernacles (John 8:30). As the narrative unfolds, however, it becomes clear that their purported faith in Jesus was not an abiding faith.[58] Jesus exhorted them that they must continue in his word in order to become free from sin (John 8:31–36), but they took umbrage at the suggestion that sin had dominion over them, claiming Abraham as their father. Jesus insisted that they were not Abraham's children, for they desired to kill him (John 8:37–42). They could not accept Jesus' message, for the devil is their father, and they, like the devil, are murderers and liars (John 8:43–46). Their rejection of Jesus' words revealed that they were not from God (John 8:47). They became enraged, insulting Jesus by calling him a Samaritan and a demoniac (John 8:48–52). When Jesus claimed to have existed prior to Abraham, they tried to stone him (John 8:53–59), confirming Jesus' claim that they desired to kill him. This brief recap of the story confirms that the "belief" in John 8:30 was not a saving belief, for genuine belief in Jesus keeps his word and does not conspire to put him to death!

The same kind of inadequate belief is reflected in John 12:42–43. Many of the authorities "believed in" Jesus, and yet they refused to acknowledge him openly because they did not want to face the wrath of the Pharisees and be expelled from the synagogues. John remarks that "they loved the glory that comes from man more than the glory that comes from God" (John 12:43). Clearly, such "faith" is not saving faith, since it does not publicly embrace Jesus, and since those who hide their faith "save" their lives instead of "losing" them for Jesus' sake (John 12:25).[59] Indeed, those who refuse to acknowledge Jesus are, in the end, comparable to the Pharisees. Jesus indicted them for failing to believe, arguing that they could not believe because they "receive glory from one another and do not seek the glory that comes from the only God" (John 5:44). The lust for human approval robbed the Pharisees of belief, and apparently the rulers fell victim to the same desire for human esteem. Genuine faith, according to John, abides in Jesus, follows him, keeps his word, shows love for him by keeping his commands, hears him, receives him, follows him, comes to him, and eats his flesh and drinks his blood.

58. So Barrett 1978: 344. See also Lincoln 2000: 90–96; Ridderbos 1997: 307–8.
59. Bultmann (1971: 454) observes that "their faith is not a genuine faith." So also Lincoln 2000: 107–8.

Transforming Faith in 1–3 John

The importance of belief in 1 John was explained earlier. The Johannine Epistles repeat many of the themes noted in John's Gospel, indicating that saving faith is a transforming faith, not a mere passive belief. Those who claim, therefore, to have "fellowship" with God—that is, to be members of his people (1 John 1:3, 6–7)—but who live evil lives contradict their profession. Only those who live in the light—that is, live in a way that pleases God—truly belong to him. God's children are those who "[walk] in the truth" (2 John 4; 3 John 3–4). Those who claim to "know" Christ but who fail to obey his commands reveal that they do not truly know him (1 John 2:3–6). Genuine believers live the way that Jesus lived. We might think that John advocates perfectionism, but he clarifies that it is those who claim to be without sin altogether who are outside the circle of God's people (1 John 1:8, 10). It appears that the secessionists from the church were convinced that they were completely free from sin (1 John 1:8). Their claim, apparently, was not that they had never sinned throughout their whole lives, but rather that they had not sinned since becoming Christians (1 John 1:10).[60] Perhaps such a stance was rooted in a proto-Gnosticism. Since John emphasizes that believers practice righteousness, the secessionists may have lived licentiously and believed that sin was impossible for them.[61] The rationale for their position is lost to us because John does not bother to explicate it in his letter, presumably because his readers knew their position all too well. The secessionists, then, claimed to have reached perfection even though they lived lives of blatant evil. John is scarcely saying, then, that believers live perfect lives but rather that their lives have been transformed. They are devoted to goodness rather than to evil, and when they sin, they freely acknowledge it (1 John 1:9).

The change in the lives of believers is evident because they love brothers and sisters in the community of faith (1 John 2:7–11). Those who fail to show such love are still in the darkness, indicating that they are not believers. The kind of hatred that Cain demonstrated for Abel shows that he did not belong to God (1 John 3:11–15). The evidence that new life has commenced, that believers "have passed out of death to life," is love for fellow believers (1 John 3:14). Such love is not an ethereal quality or a warm glow in the heart but instead expresses itself concretely in meeting the needs for food and shelter that other believers have (1 John 3:17–18). It seems that the secessionists hated believers (1 John 2:11;

---

60. So R. Brown 1982: 212, 234–35.

61. Marshall (1978a: 14–16) argues there is no clear evidence of libertinism. See the discussion by R. Brown (1982: 80–83, 234–35), who argues that the opponents were not Gnostics but were indifferent to whether or not they sinned.

4:20), but genuine love for brothers and sisters in Christ indicates that one has been born of God (1 John 4:7–8). Christ's self-giving love on the cross is the pattern for believers (1 John 3:16; 4:9–11), showing that "God is love" (1 John 4:8, 16). Nor can anyone claim genuine love for God without keeping his commands (1 John 5:3). Again, John is not suggesting that believers keep God's commands perfectly. It seems that the secessionists threw off all moral restraints, claiming that sin was now impossible for those who had reached such spiritual heights.

John regularly refers to those who are born of God and the consequences of this new life. Those who are truly born of God live righteous lives (1 John 2:29). John declares, "Those who have been born of God do not sin" (1 John 3:9);[62] "We know that those who are born of God do not sin" (1 John 5:18); "No one who abides in him sins" (1 John 3:6); "Everyone who does what is right is righteous" (1 John 3:7); "Everyone who commits sin is a child of the devil" (1 John 3:8); "All who do not do what is right are not from God" (1 John 3:10). These statements have been interpreted in various ways.[63] (1) John teaches Christians are perfect, but it is incorrect to say that John teaches that Christians can live perfect lives, for he has already stated that it is those who are convinced that they are without sin who are deceived (1 John 1:8, 10). It is also difficult to believe that John, having forgotten what he wrote in the first chapter, contradicts himself. (2) Others have suggested that John refers to an elite group of Christians who have reached a special status in which they no longer sin. However, such a reading would seem to fit with the theology of the secessionists, who claimed to be a cut above the believers in the Johannine churches. Moreover, the text does not restrict godly living to a special group of Christians but rather claims that all believers without exception—anyone born of God—do not sin. Hence, a spiritual elite cannot be in view here. (3) Others suggest that only willful and deliberate sins are intended, but there is no evidence in the text that only a special category of sins is in view. (4) An intriguing suggestion is that John refers to the sin unto death (1 John 5:16–17). Believers, therefore, are spared from the sin that leads to apostasy. Despite the truth in this viewpoint, we lack evidence that John confines himself only to apostasy. He appears to refer to sin in general.

(5) Another view is that believers do not sin as long as they are abiding in Christ. This solution might work if the verse on abiding were the only one, but it hardly explains the claim that those who are born of God do not sin. The text does not say that those who have new life only

62. The citations in this paragraph are from the NRSV.
63. For a discussion of the survey of options that includes others that are not presented here, see Marshall 1978a: 178–84; R. Brown 1982: 412–16; Smalley 1984: 159–64.

desist from sinning when they are abiding; it insists that freedom from sin marks out all those who are regenerated. (6) It has also been suggested that John refers to an ideal that is not always realized, but such a view seems to undermine John's argument, for then the secessionists could be placed in the category of those who do not always attain the ideal. John, however, excludes them from new life because of their disobedience. (7) The best solution, therefore, is that John speaks of the pattern and direction of one's life. The lives of believers are marked out by an orientation toward goodness and obedience. Many scholars have defended this view by noting the present tense of the verbs in 1 John 3:4–10, though scholarship has questioned whether such weight can be assigned to the verbal tense. Even if the present tense does not establish this view, placing these verses in the entire context of 1 John assists us in understanding John's meaning. John circles back to the same themes repeatedly, and so a consideration of the entirety of his letter is crucial in interpreting a particular part. In 1 John 1:5–2:2 he indicates that perfection is impossible for believers. Hence, in 1 John 3 he is speaking not of perfection but rather of a new direction and way of life. Genuine believers do not lead antinomian lives; they reveal their new life by their new behavior. Nevertheless, John is not suggesting that their behavior will be without any moral blemish at all, for otherwise there would be no need to confess one's sins (1 John 1:9).

As we noted earlier, John teaches that those who confess Jesus as God's Son and who have his Spirit "abide" (*menō*) in God (1 John 3:24; 4:13, 15). And yet the one who truly "abides in God" also "abides in love" (1 John 4:16; cf. 2:10; 4:12) and keeps his commands (1 John 3:24; cf. 2:6; 3:6), which means helping believers who need food, clothing, and shelter (1 John 3:17). Believers must abide in him until the end in order to be spared humiliation on the day of judgment (1 John 2:28). They must remain in the teaching they initially received and not depart from it (1 John 2:24, 27). Those who have left the community reveal that they have loved the world more than God, and that they do not truly belong to him (1 John 2:15–17). For John, perseverance is the mark of genuine faith and authenticity. What he says in 1 John 2:19 coheres well with the discourse in John 8:30–59. John says of the secessionists, "They went out from us, but they were not of us; for if they had been of us, they would have continued with us. But they went out, that it might become plain that they all are not of us" (1 John 2:19). John does not think that those who have left the church were genuine believers; he argues that their secession demonstrates that they were never authentic.

In 2 John the church is warned not to be deceived by those who deny that Jesus came in the flesh (cf. 1 John 2:22–23; 4:1–3; 5:1, 5–7). The antichrist spirit must be resisted, for those who depart from the teaching will lose the reward of eternal life (2 John 8).[64] That the reward in view is eternal life is clear from 2 John 9, for those who do not remain in the orthodox teaching about the Christ do "not have God." For John, therefore, saving faith is one that continues to trust in Jesus until the end, and it manifests that trust in love for fellow believers, obedience to Jesus' commands, and fidelity to the teaching that Jesus is the Messiah come in the flesh.

Conclusion

For John, salvation is obtained by believing. This theme is prominent in both his Gospel and in 1 John. Still, believing is not passive; it is dynamic and transforming. The work that God requires is to believe that Jesus is the one sent by God (John 6:29), and hence eternal life comes from belief alone. Still, believing cannot be separated from coming to Jesus, following him, hearing him, eating and drinking him, keeping his commands, and loving brothers and sisters. The belief that saves is one that perseveres and manifests itself in practical and concrete ways. The belief that saves confesses that Jesus is the Christ and the Son of God. It looks to him for the forgiveness of sins and for eternal life.

Acts

Faith and obedience are two sides of the same coin in Acts, just as they are in the Gospel of Luke.[65] Peter summoned those listening to him on the day of Pentecost to repent and be baptized in order to receive forgiveness of sins (Acts 2:38). Remarkably, Luke says nothing here about believing. Acts 3:19 is similar: "Repent therefore, and turn again, so that your sins may be blotted out." Once again repentance is required in order to receive forgiveness from God. The message of John the Baptist is summarized as "a baptism of repentance" (Acts 13:24; cf. 10:37). Paul proclaimed to the Athenians that God "commands all people everywhere to repent" (Acts 17:30). Again, in these texts Luke records nothing about the need to exercise faith. When Paul summarized the gospel for King Agrippa, he said that human beings "should repent and turn to God, performing deeds in keeping with their repentance" (Acts 26:20). When Peter responded to accusations from the Sanhedrin, he spoke of God granting "repentance to Israel and forgiveness of sins" (Acts

---

64. Marshall (1978a: 72) hesitates regarding the meaning. Rightly Smalley 1984: 330–32; R. Brown 1982: 672. Contra Stott (1964: 210), who thinks that a specific reward is in view rather than eternal life.

65. For more detailed support for the view argued for here, see Stein 2007.

5:31), suggesting that the latter becomes a reality through the former. The gift of the Spirit is given to those who "obey" God (Acts 5:32). The Gentiles who were converted are described at the Jerusalem Council as those "who turn to God" (Acts 15:19), with the word "turn" functioning synonymously with repentance. Paul rehearsed his conversion by remembering the injunction of Ananias to "be baptized, and wash away your sins, calling on his name" (Acts 22:16). Here baptism and "calling on his name" are mentioned rather than repentance or faith.

These citations might suggest that repentance is important for Luke rather than faith. In other texts, however, faith is required, and nothing is said about repentance. The Samaritans responded to the proclamation of Philip by believing and being baptized (Acts 8:12). Repentance and baptism appeared together in some of the texts noted above (Acts 2:38; cf. 13:24), whereas here faith and baptism are placed together. Peter declared to Cornelius and his friends that belief in Jesus brings forgiveness of sins, arguing that this is the message of the prophets (Acts 10:43). When Peter recalled the Cornelius event later at the Jerusalem Council, he summed it up as the Gentiles hearing the message of the gospel and responding with faith and trust in what was proclaimed (Acts 15:7). God did not require circumcision or any other part of the law but rather "[cleansed] their hearts by faith" (Acts 15:9). The proconsul of Cyprus, Sergius Paulus, was converted when he believed the teaching of the Lord (Acts 13:12). In Pisidian Antioch believing in Jesus to receive forgiveness of sins is contrasted with doing the law of Moses (Acts 13:38–39). Forgiveness is based not on doing but on believing; it comes from trusting in Jesus rather than observing the law.

The grace of God in salvation is apparent in Acts 13:48, for those who "were appointed to eternal life believed" (my translation). God's appointment preceded believing, and so faith is understood as God's gift.[66] Similarly, when the first missionary journey of Paul and Barnabas was completed, Luke recounts the report given upon their return to Syrian Antioch. Paul and Barnabas explained that God "had opened a door of faith to the Gentiles" (Acts 14:27; cf. 16:14). When the Philippian jailer asked what he must do to be saved, Paul and Barnabas did not summon him to repent. They replied, "Believe in the Lord Jesus, and you will be saved, you and your household" (Acts 16:31). Many responded to the preaching of Paul and Silas in Berea by believing (Acts 17:12), whereas in Athens some believed when Paul proclaimed the gospel (Acts 17:34).

---

66. "The present verse is as unqualified a statement of absolute predestination—'the eternal purpose of God' (Calvin 1961: 393)—as is found anywhere in the NT" (Barrett 1994: 658). Contrast Marshall 1980b: 231.

In Corinth Crispus and his household became believers, and many others in Corinth believed and were baptized (Acts 18:8).

The emphasis in some texts on believing and in others on repenting may seem puzzling, even contradictory. The apparent difficulty is resolved when we realize that faith and repentance are ultimately inseparable for Luke. The close relationship between these two is apparent from a number of texts. For instance, we noted that Paul summoned the Athenians to repent (Acts 17:30), but subsequently those who responded are identified as those who believed (Acts 17:34), suggesting the close linkage between the two. Another instructive example surfaces in Acts 9. When Peter healed the bedridden Aenas, Lydda and Sharon "turned to the Lord" (Acts 9:35). When he raised Tabitha from the dead, "many believed in the Lord" (Acts 9:42). The two miracle stories conclude with similar responses. Luke did not intend for readers to draw a radical disjunction between turning to the Lord in repentance and believing in him. These are simply two different ways of describing conversion.

We noted above how Peter emphasizes that Cornelius and his friends were saved because they believed (Acts 10:43; 15:7, 9). But in Acts 11:18 the Jews in Jerusalem described the conversion of Cornelius and his friends in terms of God granting them repentance. Apparently, Luke did not find belief and repentance to be mutually exclusive; they conjointly describe conversion. The vital relationship between belief and repentance is evident in Acts 11:21: "A great number who believed turned to the Lord." The same collocation appears in Acts 20:21, where Paul summarized to the Ephesian elders his ministry as one that calls for "repentance toward God" and "faith in our Lord Jesus Christ." Luke does not explain the logical or temporal relationship between faith and repentance, but he does see them as inseparably joined in God's saving work.

The indissoluble relationship between faith and repentance is confirmed by the need for persevering faith. Initial decisions of faith do not guarantee final forgiveness of sins.[67] One must continue in the faith and not apostatize. When Gentiles responded positively to the gospel in Antioch, Barnabas "exhorted them all to remain faithful to the Lord with steadfast purpose" (Acts 11:23). Those who have begun their new lives by trusting God must continue to trust him. The message to new converts on the first missionary journey of Paul and Barnabas is remarkably similar, for they were "strengthening the souls of the disciples, encouraging them to continue in the faith, and saying that through many tribulations we must enter the kingdom of God" (Acts 14:22). The words of Paul and Barnabas here likely reflect the regular admonition given to new converts. The exhortation to persist in the faith also appears after Paul and

---

67. See the survey of these texts in Stenschke 1999: 347–60.

Barnabas proclaimed the gospel in Pisidian Antioch. After Paul's address in the synagogue, they encouraged those who received the gospel "to continue in the grace of God" (Acts 13:43). Perseverance in faith means that one continues to live in God's grace, relying on his strength instead of abandoning God and relying on one's own resources.

Luke also provides some examples in Acts of those who "believed" but failed to continue in the faith. Ananias and Sapphira appeared to be genuine members of the church, but they desired to be known as generous benefactors and were also ensnared by a love for money (Acts 5:1–11). Hence, they claimed to give all the proceeds from the sale of a field, but secretly they reserved some of the profit for themselves. They did not sin in failing to give all the money to the church, for such generosity was not required. Their sin was in pretending to give all the proceeds of the sale to the church.[68] God struck down both of them so that they suddenly died for lying to the Holy Spirit. The story of Ananias and Sapphira echoes the account of Achan in the OT (Josh. 7), who, unbeknownst to others, sinned by taking some of the banned goods in Jericho. Hence, Achan himself was placed under the ban and stoned to death along with his family. Similarly, the sin of Ananias and Sapphira indicates that some within the community were not genuine believers.[69]

Paul even recognizes that those who are destined for destruction will actually appear among the leadership of the churches. He warns the Ephesian elders, "I know that after my departure fierce wolves will come in among you, not sparing the flock; and from your own selves will arise men speaking twisted things, to draw away disciples after them" (Acts 20:29–30). The false teachers will not be limited to outsiders, for some men from among the elders will swerve from the truth and have a deleterious impact on others. Perhaps the most notable example of such a departure was Simon, though he was not yet a leader in the church (Acts 8:9–24). Before embracing the gospel, Simon practiced magic and was venerated in Samaria as one who had God's power. When Philip proclaimed the gospel, Simon believed and was baptized. But when Peter and John arrived and bestowed the Spirit with the imposition of hands, Simon offered money to them if they would grant him the same ability. Peter perceived the state of Simon's heart and identified him as an unbeliever: "You have no part or share in this, for your heart is not right before God" (Acts 8:21 NRSV). The words "part" (*meris*) and "share" (*klēros*) reflect the language of inheritance, demonstrating that Simon

---

68. Rightly Barrett 1994: 262, 267; Fitzmyer 1998: 316, 323.
69. It is possible, on the other hand, that Ananias and Sapphira were genuine believers who experienced a temporary lack of faith.

had no inheritance among God's people.[70] Instead, he is "in the gall of bitterness and in the bond of iniquity" (Acts 8:23). It appears from the narrative that Simon's initial belief was not genuine but rather was a subterfuge, since he was impressed by the miracles Philip did.[71] This is not to say that the faith of the rest of the Samaritans was of the same nature. The inadequacy of Simon's faith is uncovered in the flow of the narrative and is not immediately apparent to the reader. Hence, Luke indicates that genuine faith endures. It produces works "in keeping with repentance" (Acts 26:20).

We can summarize Luke in Acts, then, as emphasizing the indissoluble nature of faith and repentance. They are two sides of the same coin. What Luke teaches in Acts fits with what we saw in his Gospel. There we saw the refrain "Your faith has saved you," but Luke also emphasizes strongly that true disciples follow Jesus. Both the Gospel of Luke and Acts underscore that faith and repentance are necessary for salvation.

The Pauline Literature

The human response of faith is fundamental, according to the Pauline gospel.[72] Human beings are "justified by faith" (Rom. 5:1), which means that people stand in the right before God through faith. When Paul gives thanks and praise for God's work in the lives of his converts, he often mentions their faith (Rom. 1:8; Eph. 1:15–16; Col. 1:3–4; 1 Thess. 1:2–3; 2 Thess. 1:3; 2 Tim. 1:3–5; Philem. 4–5). Paul preached so that the Corinthians would put their faith in God's power and not in the artistry with which he presents his message (1 Cor. 2:5; cf. Col. 2:12). For Paul, faith is not a vague and slippery entity; it is always directed to what God has done in Christ. Hence, faith trusts in the forgiveness of sins achieved through Christ on the cross. Human beings are to put their faith in God, who sent Jesus as the crucified and risen one (Rom. 4:24–25).

---

70. So Barrett 1994: 414. Peter is not threatening Simon with the prospect of perdition here (so Fitzmyer 1998: 406–7), nor is this, strictly speaking, an excommunication (so Haenchen 1971: 305), though that is closer to the truth. Rather, as Polhill (1992: 220) observes, it is likely "more a statement of nonmembership. His behavior betrayed that he had no real portion in God's people."

71. Acts 8:24 could be interpreted as Simon's repentance (Barrett 1994: 417–18; Fitzmyer 1998: 407). But against this, see Polhill 1992: 220.

72. Hofius (1989: 158–74) argues that faith is not a condition, for such a view would contradict the Pauline teaching that faith is a gift created by God's word. Hofius is correct in maintaining that faith is a gift of God. However, he creates a false disjunction when he insists that faith is not a condition. It is a condition in the sense that people will not be saved unless they believe. This condition does not preclude the truth that faith is God's gift.

Paul emphasizes that human beings are justified by faith (Rom. 1:17; Gal. 3:11), seeing in Hab. 2:4 a grounding for this claim.[73] A right relation with God is obtained "through faith in Jesus Christ for all who believe" (Rom. 3:22; cf. 3:25–26). In Gal. 2:16 Paul places "works of the law" in opposition to faith in Jesus Christ, stating three times that justification comes not through works of law but only through faith in Jesus Christ. Similarly, the Spirit is received through faith rather than the works of the law (Gal. 3:2, 5). We see in Rom. 3:28 that "a person is justified by faith apart from the works prescribed by the law." In Phil. 3:9 righteousness based on law is contrasted with righteousness that comes through faith in Christ.

Many scholars, however, read the foregoing texts in a remarkably different way, claiming that the verses refer to "the faithfulness *of* Christ" rather than "faith *in* Christ."[74] In the construction *pistis Christou*, the noun *Christou* is in the genitive,[75] so that both "faithfulness of Christ" and "faith in Christ" are grammatically feasible. A number of arguments are presented in support of "faithfulness of Christ." (1) In Rom. 3:3 *tēn pistin tou theou* clearly refers to the faithfulness of God. (2) In Rom. 4:12 *pisteōs . . . Abraam* means "the faith of Abraham." (3) It is argued that the genitive in such constructions is most naturally understood as subjective. (4) If one takes the genitive as objective, then faith in Christ is superfluous because in the key texts (e.g., Rom. 3:22; Gal. 2:16; Phil. 3:9) Paul already mentions the need to trust in Christ. (5) The "faithfulness of Jesus" is another way of referring to Jesus' obedience, which achieved salvation (Rom. 5:19; Phil. 2:8). (6) The coming of "faith" refers to redemptive history (Gal. 3:23, 25), designating the faithfulness of Christ at this time in salvation history. (7) The focus in Paul's theology is the work of God in Christ, not the human response of faith.

Despite the arguments supporting a subjective genitive, there are good reasons to prefer an objective genitive, so that Paul refers to "faith *in* Christ."[76] (1) The genitive object with "faith" is clear in some instances

73. For an intriguing explanation of Paul's hermeneutical approach to Hab. 2:4, see Watson 2004: 112–63. For the view that Paul interpreted Hab. 2:4 in accord with its historical context, see the illuminating study in Yeung 2002: 196–212. Yeung (2002: 212–25) goes on to maintain that Paul's understanding of Hab. 2:4 was influenced not only by the OT and Jewish tradition but also by Jesus tradition.

74. See, for example, L. Johnson 1982a; S. Williams 1987; Hays 1991; 2001; Wallis 1995.

75. The genitive after *pistis* varies: *Iēsou Christou* (Rom. 3:22; Gal. 2:16; 3:22), *Christou* (Gal. 2:16; Phil. 3:9), *Iēsou* (Rom. 3:26). For the sake of simplicity I will restrict it to *pistis Christou*.

76. See, for example, Hofius 1989: 154–56; Dunn 1991; Matlock 2000; Silva 2004.

(Mark 11:22; James 2:1).[77] (2) A genitive object with other verbal nouns shows that an objective genitive with the noun "faith" is quite normal grammatically—for example, "knowledge of Christ Jesus" (*tēs gnōseōs Christou Iēsou* [Phil. 3:8 my translation]). (3) Hence, those who claim that the genitive must be subjective fail to convince. (4) The texts that use the verb "believe" in a verbal construction and the noun "faith" with the genitive are not superfluous but rather emphatic, stressing the importance of faith to be right with God. Readers hearing the letter read would naturally hear the emphasis on faith in Christ, and thus this interpretation is to be preferred as the simpler of the two options. (5) In his theology Paul often contrasts works and human faith. Hence, seeing a polarity between works of law and faith in Christ, both of which are human activities, fits with what Paul does elsewhere. (6) On the other hand, nowhere else does Paul, in speaking of Jesus Christ, use the word "faith" to describe his "obedience." (7) The salvation-historical argument fails to persuade as well. Certainly, Gal. 3:23, 25 refer to the coming of faith at a certain time in redemptive history. But such an observation hardly excludes faith in Christ, for faith in Christ becomes a reality when he arrives and fulfills God's promises. We should not pit redemptive history against anthropology. (8) Nor is the emphasis on faith in Christ somehow Pelagian, as if it somehow detracts from God's work in salvation. A human response of faith does not undercut the truth that God saves, particularly if God grants faith to his own (Eph. 2:8–9).

What is the significance of the reading "faith in Christ"?[78] Some of those who defend the reading "faithfulness of Christ" say that the subjective-genitive interpretation includes both faith *in* Christ from other texts and the faithfulness *of* Christ in the *pistis Christou* texts. Hence, they claim that believing in Christ for justification is not surrendered in the subjective-genitive interpretation. The point may be granted, but it needs to be qualified, for the emphasis on believing *in* Christ for justification is lost, for only in Gal. 2:16 among the texts where *pistis Christou* occurs does Paul use a verbal form that expresses the need for faith *in* Christ. If *pistis Christou* reflects an objective genitive, then Paul highlights the importance of faith in Christ for justification. We should linger on this point for a moment. Paul often calls attention to the importance of faith, but this expression goes beyond saying that people need to believe. Now

77. For this reading of Mark 11:22, see France (2002: 448), who remarks that a subjective reading "is surely forced." Contra L. Johnson 1995: 220. Rightly Moo 2000: 100–101; Davids 1982: 107; Laws 1980: 94; Dibelius 1975: 127–28; L. Cheung 2003: 247–48.

78. A few scholars have argued for a genitive of source (e.g., Seifrid 2000b: 139–46; Watson [including the objective genitive as well] 2004: 74–76). Such a reading is possible, but it is a less likely reading and has won few adherents (see the recent discussion of the matter in Silva 2004: 218–20, 227–36).

that Jesus Christ has come and accomplished atonement, human beings need to put their faith *in* Christ to be saved. The christological focus of faith is stressed.

The polarity between faith in Christ and works of law also clarifies that human beings become right with God by believing instead of by doing. I argued earlier that works of law refers to all that the law demands, so that "works of the law" functions as a subset of works in general.[79] Paul insists in a number of texts that righteousness is obtained not by works or works of law but rather through faith. He develops this theme at some length in Rom. 3:19–4:25, 9:30–10:13; Gal. 2:16–3:14; Phil. 3:2–9. These texts teach that no one can be righteous by works of law or any other works, for all people fall short of what God demands. People can be righteous by works only if they have done all that God requires (Rom. 3:9–20; Gal. 3:10), and no one has obeyed to that extent. Even Abraham and David are classified among the ungodly because of their sins (Rom. 4:5–8).[80] The only hope for right standing with God, then, is to trust what God has done in Christ rather than depending on one's attainments. Human boasting is ruled out because human beings rest on what Christ has done to save them (Rom. 3:27–28; 4:1–3). Faith calls attention to the power of God, who justifies the ungodly (Rom. 4:5). A new reality is called into existence by the death and resurrection of Christ, so that a new relation with God is established through faith in Christ (Rom. 4:17–25).

Paul often argues that right standing with God is available for all, both Jews and Gentiles (Rom. 3:22–23). Circumcision or observance of any of the boundary markers of Judaism are not required (Rom. 3:29–30; Gal. 2:11–21). God does not justify Jews and Gentiles by a different standard; the only requirement for both is faith. That faith is the only requirement is borne out by the father of the Jewish people, Abraham (Rom. 4:9–12). Abraham was right with God *before* he was circumcised (Rom. 4:9–12), and therefore his circumcision was merely the sign and seal of righteousness that he enjoyed before circumcision. Abraham is the father both of Gentile believers who are uncircumcised and of Jewish believers who are circumcised. In both cases, however, it is only those who have the faith of Abraham who are the children of Abraham (Gal. 3:6–9). Paul placed Gen. 12 with Gen. 15 in contrast to Jewish tradition that read Gen. 15 in light of Gen. 17 and Gen. 22. It follows, then, that Abraham was right with God by virtue of his believing and trusting and not on the basis of his obedience.

79. See the discussion on works of law in chapter 14.
80. See Das 2001: 201–13.

Paul carefully followed the prescriptions of the law before his conversion (Phil. 3:2–11), but all his devotion amounted to nothing, for he did not gain Christ.[81] The only thing that he attained was his own righteousness (Phil. 3:9), and it was hardly genuine righteousness, for he had persecuted the church. Indeed, Paul looked back and saw in the persecution of the church an indication of the profundity of his sin (1 Cor. 15:9; 1 Tim. 1:13–15). Both Jews and Gentiles can be right before God only by believing in Christ instead of doing the law. Therefore, any boasting in the flesh is excluded, and believers boast only in Christ Jesus (Phil. 3:3–4). Those who seek to establish their own righteousness by observing the law are doomed to failure because they do not submit to God's righteousness in Christ (Rom. 10:3). The law points to Christ, so that he is both the goal and end (*telos*) of the law for all those who put their faith in him (Rom. 10:4). The law summons people to performance, asking them what they have done for God (Rom. 10:5). Faith, however, lifts people out of themselves and points to the crucified and risen Christ and the salvation that he has achieved (Rom. 10:6–8).[82] Those who observe the law deserve payment for following its stipulations, but faith recognizes sin, which rules out righteousness by law, and trusts in God to effect a new reality in which the ungodly are put into the right by God's grace (Rom. 4:4–5). If righteousness can be obtained by human obedience, then it rules out grace (Rom. 11:6). No gift is needed if human beings have the capacity to gain righteousness on their own. Grace, on the other hand, excludes works as the basis of a right relation with God. No one keeps God's stipulations, and therefore the only hope for justification is to trust what God has done in Christ.

Faith is fundamental to the Pauline gospel because it is always allied with grace, for faith rests on and believes in what God has accomplished through the crucified and risen Lord. Hays points out that the call to obedience in Paul's writings is rooted in the believer's union with Christ, the liberating work of God in Christ, and the work of the Holy Spirit.[83] If righteousness can be achieved through adherence to the law, then the death of Christ becomes superfluous (Gal. 2:21). The coming of Christ is an utter waste of time if the OT cult and law provide for salvation. According to Paul, however, the curse of the law can be removed only through Christ's death (Gal. 3:13), and believers are freed from the law's curse not by doing what the law requires but rather by trusting in what Christ has accomplished (Gal. 3:11–12). Paul contrasts law-obedience with faith (Rom. 10:5–8; Gal. 3:12), for the two represent two alternate

---

81. Stendahl (1976: 7) argued that Paul was called rather than converted. However, this view clearly misreads the evidence. See Segal 1990; O'Brien 2004.

82. For a helpful discussion of this text, see Seifrid 1985.

83. Hays 1996: 39.

and incompatible ways of salvation. Salvation by law is out of the question because of human disobedience, and thus the only hope for righteousness is to trust God in Christ. If righteousness were based on human obedience, then faith and the promise of God would be excluded (Rom. 4:14). Righteousness cannot be obtained by law, since human beings have transgressed (Rom. 4:15). Faith, then, cannot be equated with keeping the law. Faith comes to God empty of every claim, acknowledging that the obedience required by God is lacking. Faith rests on God's promise to save, trusting in the atonement provided in Jesus Christ for the forgiveness of sins. Law-obedience focuses on human performance and ability, whereas faith trusts what God has done in Christ. Faith and grace belong together, just as obedience and reward belong together. Faith is allied with grace because it does not depend upon what human beings accomplish but rather receives what God has done in Christ.

Faith glorifies God because it looks to him for every good gift and blessing, acknowledging that all comes from him. This helps explain why Paul can say that "whatever does not proceed from faith is sin" (Rom. 14:23).[84] Whatever people trust in is their god, and faith honors God because it confesses that he is the treasure and joy of their hearts. Abraham's faith was not merely a passive acknowledgment of God's existence. He believed in a God who raises the dead and calls into existence that which does not yet exist (Rom. 4:17). Specifically, Abraham believed that God could enliven his dead body and Sarah's dead womb and grant them a son (Rom. 4:19). Abraham put his faith in God's promise that he would be the father of many nations (Rom. 4:18, 22). As he trusted in God, "he gave glory to God" (Rom. 4:20). We see that faith gives God glory because it honors him as trustworthy, confessing that his promises will be realized. Lack of faith dishonors him because it says that God's promise to deliver his people is a lie. The faith of believers, of course, rests on the death and resurrection of Christ (Rom. 4:23–25). It is this faith that has now invaded history (Gal. 3:22–25).

The faith that saves confesses Jesus as Lord (Rom. 10:9), but his lordship is acknowledged only if he is acknowledged as the risen one who now rules over all. Salvation is open to all, both Jews and Gentiles, if they put their faith in Jesus Christ and acknowledge him as Lord (Rom. 10:11–13). All who call upon him in faith will be delivered from God's wrath on the last day. Even Gentiles may be God's children in Christ through faith (Gal. 3:26). The Spirit is working in a saving manner among those who confess Jesus as Lord (1 Cor. 12:3), so that such a confession is the work of God's Spirit. Only those who enjoy the Spirit's work recognize that the crucified one is actually the Lord of glory (1 Cor. 2:6–10).

---

84. See the more detailed discussion of this verse in Schreiner 1998: 738–39.

The Spirit is given not to those who observe the Mosaic law but rather to those who believe (Gal. 3:2, 5, 14). This is a crucial point in Pauline theology, for Paul was not an antinomian who delighted in unrighteousness. What Paul insists on is that no human works are the basis of righteousness or salvation (Eph. 2:8–9). Salvation is an undeserved gift that is received by faith alone, and thus there is no room for human beings to brag about their goodness. Those who put their trust in Christ, however, receive the Spirit. The Spirit transforms their lives so that they live in a different manner. Life in the Spirit is not the ground of justification but rather the result of justification. Good works in the lives of believers follow but do not precede their right standing with God.[85] What Paul emphasizes, therefore, is that the Spirit is given freely to those who believe and rest on what God has done for them in Christ.

Paul does not understand faith to be a momentary feeling that vanishes. Saving faith is a persevering faith. Those who "received" (*paralambanō*) the message of the gospel belong to God (1 Cor. 15:1–2), but they have believed "in vain" if they do not continue to cling to the faith that they embraced. People are converted when they turn to the Lord (2 Cor. 3:16) and forsake false gods to serve the living and true God (1 Thess. 1:9). Conversion can also be described as reconciliation (2 Cor. 5:20), so that those who previously were God's enemies have become his friends. Human beings accept the gospel proclaimed by Paul as God's message; they place their faith in the truth of the gospel (2 Thess. 2:13). Faith alone saves (cf. 1 Tim. 1:16), but genuine faith produces fruit and leads to a change in one's life. Paul speaks of a "work of faith" (1 Thess. 1:3), and here "of faith" (*pisteōs*) should be understood as a genitive of source.[86] Faith in God is dynamic and produces fruit, and if the fruit is lacking, it calls into question whether faith is genuine. The emphasis on perseverance and fruit in Paul does not contradict his teaching that justification is through faith and not works. Good works are always understood as the fruit of faith, and they function as evidence that faith is genuine. They never stand independently of faith, as if works alone can justify. Those who are a new creation in Christ Jesus do good works that are ordained for them (Eph. 2:10), but these works are the result of the new creation.

Warnings abound in the Pauline letters instructing his readers to continue in the faith in order to escape eschatological destruction.[87] Those who have fallen from the faith experience God's "severity," and

---

85. Rainbow (2005: 79–84) rightly points out Paul never speaks of good works negatively but always positively. When Paul rules out works in terms of justification, he refers to works of law or works but never uses the phrase "good works." See also Schlatter 1999: 284–86.

86. Wanamaker (1990: 75) identifies it as a subjective genitive.

87. Schnabel (1995) captures well the motivations and norms for Pauline ethics.

believers must "continue in [God's] kindness" or they "will be cut off" as well (Rom. 11:22). God's severity here refers to eschatological judgment, for in the context of Rom. 9–11 the fate of unbelieving Jews is considered. Believers who cave into the desires of the flesh will die—they will not experience eternal life (Rom. 8:13)—but those who rely on the Spirit and slay fleshly desires will enjoy life forever. The line of thought in Col. 3:5–6 is quite similar. Believers must put to death evil desires and actions because God will pour his wrath out on those who disobey on the last day. God's children are identified as those who are led by—that is, yield to—the Holy Spirit (Rom. 8:14). Those who are indwelt by the Spirit no longer live in slavery to sin (Rom. 8:15).

Paul was worried about the Corinthians for a variety of reasons. In 1 Cor. 6:1–8 he expressed astonishment that they engaged in lawsuits with fellow believers and called in unbelievers to adjudicate the cases. He indicted them for wronging (*adikeite*) fellow believers (1 Cor. 6:8). He then warned those who do wrong that "wrongdoers [*adikoi*] will not inherit the kingdom of God" (1 Cor. 6:9 NRSV).[88] Paul then itemizes various sins that exclude people from the kingdom and remarks that a life of evil is incompatible with the saving work of God that they have experienced (1 Cor. 6:9–11). Paul did not assure the Corinthians that they will be saved on the last day regardless of what they did. Lives of wickedness will disqualify them from the kingdom. Nor should we exaggerate the threat given here, as if Paul claims that anyone who commits these sins on any occasion is thereby excluded from God's kingdom. The warning addresses those who fall prey to such sins and fail to turn from them in repentance.

Uncertainty regarding the future salvation of one claiming to be a believer finds expression in the discipline of the man in the Corinthian church who was committing incest (1 Cor. 5). The church was called to judge and excommunicate this man because he continued in the sin and refused to repent. The expulsion of the man is described as handing him "over to Satan for the destruction of the flesh, so that his spirit may be saved in the day of the Lord" (1 Cor. 5:5). The saving of his spirit likely refers to eschatological salvation, deliverance from God's wrath on the day of judgment.[89] Paul did not promise that the man would be saved. He hoped that the action taken would result in his repentance and restoration and thus his salvation. Whether such will be the result depended on his response to the discipline imposed.

When Paul declares that "the wages of sin is death" (Rom. 6:23), he addressed believers and warned them about the consequences of

---

88. Fee (1987: 242) defends the link between the two verses.
89. For a helpful discussion of the issues involved, see Garland 2003: 169–77.

sin. The consequence is not merely physical death, for here death is contrasted with "eternal life." Death refers to the final judgment of the wicked. Those who turn their lives over to wickedness so that they become slaves of sin will experience death (Rom. 6:15–23). Such counsel is not given to those who are neutrally poised between death and life, as if Paul had no certainty about the direction of their lives. Believers have been transformed so that now they "have become obedient from the heart" (Rom. 6:17). They have "been set free from sin" (Rom. 6:18). The imperative is grounded in the indicative of God's work of grace in Christ. The imperative becomes a reality because of the indicative.[90]

Nor does Paul reserve his warnings only for weak Christians. All believers need to be admonished about the need to continue walking in God's ways. Paul lived in such a way that he might share in the saving blessings of the gospel (1 Cor. 9:23). The image of the race and receiving a reward in 1 Cor. 9:24–27 illustrates the need of perseverance to obtain end-time salvation.[91] The context, as we will see shortly, eliminates the idea that a reward above and beyond eternal life is in view. The Christian life is comparable to a race, and believers must run to win the prize. They must live in a disciplined way, as athletes do in training. They must conduct their lives purposefully, as boxers do when they strike opponents. They must rule over sinful desires and conquer them so that they will not be "disqualified" (*adokimos*) at the final judgment.[92] Such a warning does not fill Paul with terror and uncertainty causing him to begin to doubt whether he would receive the reward. The warning played a salutary role in his life, calling him afresh to put his faith in Jesus Christ for final salvation.

Paul uses the image of a race also in Phil. 3:12–14. This text immediately follows Phil. 3:2–11, where righteousness by faith instead of works is emphasized. Hence, the need to run the race in Phil. 3:12–14 does not contradict the claim that righteousness is by faith rather than by works. The need to run the race to the end, in Paul's mind, does not revert to works-righteousness. The life of faith is expressed in running the race to receive the eschatological prize. Nor does Paul lose sight of the indicative here. He strains to grasp the prize because he has already been grasped by Jesus Christ.

90. For two important essays on the indicative and imperative in Paul, see Bultmann 1995; Parsons 1995.

91. Rightly Barrett 1968: 218; Fee 1987: 440; Garland 2003: 444. Contra Gundry Volf 1990: 237; Thiselton 2000: 716–17.

92. Paul consistently uses the word *adokimos* to refer to those who are disqualified from receiving an eschatological reward, to those who will be damned forever (Rom. 1:28; 1 Cor. 9:27; 2 Cor. 13:5, 6, 7; 2 Tim. 3:8; Titus 1:16).

We return to 1 Corinthians and Paul's warning to the Corinthians in 1 Cor. 10, which immediately follows the call to run the race to the end (1 Cor. 9:24–27). Paul particularly addressed the "knowers" in these verses. The knowers had no compunctions about eating food offered to idols, and they even celebrated feasts in the temple of idols. They reasoned that since there is only one God and idols are an illusion, food could not damage them, for there is no such thing as defiled food because God is the creator of all. Paul actually agreed substantially with the theology of the knowers. Nevertheless, he differed in some respects and worried about their presumptuousness. Apparently, they believed that their participation in Christ spared them from any concern about future judgment. The recollection of Israel's history (1 Cor. 10:1–13) casts some light on the stance of the knowers.[93] The Corinthians should not deceive themselves, as if sharing in the sacraments magically protected them from any harm (cf. 1 Cor. 10:14–22). Israel too enjoyed a baptism of sorts when they were baptized into Moses at the Red Sea. The manna and water from the rock symbolize the Lord's Supper, so that Israel too, in a manner of speaking, enjoyed sacramental blessings. Such sacramental blessings and liberation from Egypt did not spare them from judgment. Most of them were destroyed in the wilderness, and this destruction functions as a type of the last judgment. The sins of Israel in the wilderness stand as a warning to believers, so that they will avoid the same fate. Those who presume to stand at the last judgment regardless of their behavior need to be awakened from their slumber, for those who disregard warnings are liable to fall. Paul's word, of course, is not only one of warning. He comforts believers with God's faithfulness, reminding them that God will sustain them so that they will be able to endure the troubles that beset them (1 Cor. 10:13).

Nevertheless, the Corinthians must flee idolatry and refrain from eating in idols' temples, for God will brook no opposition and will not tolerate anyone competing with his supremacy (1 Cor. 10:14–22). It is sometimes difficult to discern the line between apostasy and significant sin. Believers who had blatantly sinned during the Lord's Supper were disciplined with sickness and even death (1 Cor. 11:17–34). Such judgments of the Lord spared believers from final condemnation (1 Cor. 11:32). On the other hand, the factions present in the congregation clarified who was approved or "genuine" (*dokimoi* [1 Cor. 11:19]) in the church.[94] It seems,

93. For a fine survey of interpretation on the matter of perseverance and apostasy in this text, see Oropeza 2000: 1–34.

94. The divisions in the church will reveal who truly belongs to Christ (so Fee 1987: 538–39; Hays 1997: 195; Thiselton: 2000: 858–59). Contra Garland (2003: 538–39), who thinks that the approved are the elite members of the community sociologically.

then, that those who fall away were never genuine believers. Their apostasy confirms their inauthenticity.

Believers must examine themselves to see if their faith is genuine (2 Cor. 13:5). If they persist in sin (2 Cor. 12:20), they call into question their salvation. Believers must remain vigilant lest they accept God's grace in vain (2 Cor. 6:1). They must not become "mismatched with unbelievers" (2 Cor. 6:14 NRSV) but rather must "come out from them and be separate from them," and then God will welcome them as sons and daughters (2 Cor. 6:17–18 NRSV). Those who are deceived by the false teachers fall short of the purity needed to be vindicated on the day of judgment (2 Cor. 11:2–3). Some might label this as justification on the basis of works, but such a conclusion is mistaken.[95] Those who capitulate to the false teachers stray from a life of faith and trust.

That perseverance is rooted in faith is clear from the letter to the Galatians. Paul rejects works of law as the basis or means of salvation and insists that justification is by faith alone. Nonetheless, the centrality of faith does not preclude the need for stern warnings. Those who receive circumcision receive no benefit from Christ (Gal. 5:2–4). They must observe the entire law to be justified, but such perfect obedience is impossible and therefore futile.[96] Those who accept circumcision and attempt to be righteous by law are severed from Christ and have fallen from grace. Clearly, for Paul, the faith that saves is a persevering faith. It is a living faith that embraces a new reality, for genuine faith expresses itself in love (Gal. 5:6). Those who practice the works of the flesh will be excluded from the kingdom (Gal. 5:21), for the failure to manifest the fruit of the Spirit demonstrates that they have abandoned the pathway of faith (Gal. 5:22–23).[97] Those who sow to the flesh will harvest corruption, whereas those who sow to the Spirit will harvest eternal life (Gal. 6:8). The contrast demonstrates that sowing to the flesh will result in eschatological judgment.[98] Such a stern saying may seem surprising in Galatians, the letter of faith, freedom, and life in the Spirit. What it shows, however, is that faith and life in the Spirit lead to a new way of life, a way of life in which faith produces the fruit of the Spirit.

---

95. The work by Rainbow (2005) on the role of works in justification is an important contribution, and he rightly argues that good works are necessary for final justification. In some instances he uses unfortunate language. Rainbow (2005: 83) speaks of works as "the ground" for approval on the last day, and some could read this to say (contrary to Rainbow's view, I think) that good works are the ultimate ground for justification.

96. Contra G. Howard (1979: 16) and Bruce (1982a: 231). For an interpretation similar to the one argued for here, see Matera 1992: 181–82.

97. For Jewish antecedents to the theme of judgment according to works and for a discussion of Paul's own contribution, see Yinger 1999.

98. Rightly Matera 1992: 216; Dunn 1993: 330–31.

Those who stand in faith until the end will receive the reward God promised (Eph. 6:11–14). Believers will be presented "holy and blameless and above reproach" only if they continue in faith until the end (Col. 1:22–23). Paul does not promise that believers will be vindicated on the last day regardless of their actions. Those who deny Jesus will be denied by him on the last day (2 Tim. 2:12). Not all sin, of course, constitutes a denial of Jesus. Believers may act in a faithless manner and sin without committing apostasy (2 Tim. 2:13).[99] God is faithful to believers in such instances and will not reject them as his own. Some, however, claim to know God, but the way they live denies that they truly know him (Titus 1:16).[100] Only those who turn from wickedness will be residents in the Lord's house in the end; those who veer away from the truth never truly belonged to God (2 Tim. 2:18–19).[101] Paul will receive the final reward because he "finished the race" and "kept the faith" (2 Tim. 4:7–8, 18). Those who give their lives over to the love of money will be destroyed (1 Tim. 6:9–10). Only those who continue in the good teaching will be saved (1 Tim. 4:16).[102]

Paul teaches justification by faith and judgment according to works. Romans 3:28 is rightly interpreted to say that believers are justified by faith alone, and yet faith always produces good works, so that the faith that saves is a persevering faith. Works and faith are inseparable in Paul, for good works are always the fruit of faith. Faith looks outside itself to Jesus Christ as the crucified and risen Lord for salvation. It anchors itself to the God who gives life where there is death, trusting that God will raise believers from the dead on the last day. Hence, the call to good works in Paul's writings does not focus on the inherent power of human beings to do what is good and right and true. Every good thing is the fruit of faith and the power of God. Perseverance cannot be equated with perfection; it is nothing less than continuing to trust in God's grace until the final

99. So Dibelius and Conzelmann 1972: 109; Knight 1992: 406–7; Lau 1996: 142; W. Mounce 2000: 517–18. Contra Stettler 1998: 190–92. Marshall (1999: 741–42) takes it that the Lord is faithful to the gospel and to those who suffer for his sake, but this ignores the import of the other texts where God is said to be faithful by keeping his own to the end.

100. It is common to see the emphasis on good works in the Pastoral Epistles as a departure from the authentic Paul, but the discussion here demonstrates that it fits with the other Pauline letters. Rightly Lau 1996: 143–44; W. Mounce 2000: lxxviii–lxxx; cf. Knight 1992: 137–38.

101. Rightly W. Mounce 2000: 528–29. Contra Marshall (1999: 755–56), who limits the reference to the church. A reference to the church is included, provided that a distinction is made between those who are elect and those who fall away and prove thereby that they were not elect (so Knight 1992: 415–16).

102. The verb sōzō refers to eschatological salvation here, as is typical in the Pastoral Epistles and Paul (so Knight 1992: 211–12; Marshall 1999: 571; W. Mounce 2000: 264–65).

day. In considering Paul's teaching, we see that his emphasis on faith and works is quite compatible with the rest of the NT. Scholars of the NT have rightly emphasized the polarity that Paul draws between faith and works, whereby Paul denies that human beings can be justified by works. However, scholars often have failed to see that he also stresses the necessity of good works for justification. No contradiction exists in Paul's theology here, for such good works are the fruit of faith. Indeed, it seems that Paul and James, though they emphasize different truths, are compatible after all.

Hebrews

The issue of faith and obedience in Hebrews will be explored initially by exploring the warning passages in Hebrews.[103] The letter of Hebrews as a whole is a homily (Heb. 13:22) in which the author exhorts the readers not to depart from the Christian faith by relapsing back into Judaism and the sacrifices offered under the old covenant.[104] Many attempts have been made to identify the situation of the readers more precisely, but unfortunately the details elude us.[105] Hebrews is not a treatise in which the author beautifully but abstractly considers the Melchizedekian priesthood of Christ. The author portrays Christ as the Melchizedekian priest in order to urge his readers to remain faithful to the end. The theology of the book, in other words, points to and serves the warnings. The call to faith and obedience is the purpose for which the letter was written.

Identifying the precise parameters of the warnings in Hebrews is difficult. If one includes the exhortation to faith, the warnings include Heb. 2:1–4; 3:7–4:13; 5:11–6:12; 10:19–12:29. Most scholars do not take Heb. 10:19–12:29 as one warning, and the warnings could be limited in this section to Heb. 10:26–31 and Heb. 12:25–29. In any case, the warnings permeate the text of the letter and constitute its purpose. McKnight helpfully argues that the warnings in the letter must be interpreted together or synoptically.[106] One warning should not be isolated from the other in

---

103. For a fine summary on the importance of faith in Hebrews, see Rissi 1987: 104–13.

104. Whether the readers were tempted to turn back to Judaism is disputed in scholarship. It is, however, the majority view. See Bruce 1964: xxiii–xxx; Lane 1991a: li–lxii; Lindars 1991: 11. For a survey of possibilities, see Attridge 1989: 9–13. I am assuming with this observation that Hebrews was written before AD 70, although this too is disputed.

105. The contrast between Christ's sacrifice and the sacrifices under the old covenant suggests that the readers found the OT sacrifices offered in the temple attractive. In support of this view, see Bruce 1964: xxvi; Lindars 1991: 19–21.

106. McKnight 1992.

our attempt to understand them, for the admonitions in the letter are intended to produce one single effect or response in the readers.

If we consider all the warnings, we see that various expressions are used to implore the readers to remain faithful to Christ and the gospel. The readers should not "drift away" from the gospel proclaimed to them (Heb. 2:1).[107] They must not harden their hearts (Heb. 3:8, 15; 4:7) and "be hardened by the deceitfulness of sin" (Heb. 3:13), for it is an "evil, unbelieving heart leading you to fall away from the living God" (Heb. 3:12). The wilderness generation failed to enter God's rest because of disobedience (Heb. 3:18; 4:6, 11), and the author entreats his readers to avoid the same fate. Such disobedience, however, stems from unbelief—the failure to believe in God's promises (Heb. 3:19). The wilderness generation failed to put their trust in the good news proclaimed to them, and only believers enter into God's rest (Heb. 4:2–3). The oscillation between faith and obedience in Heb. 3:7–4:13 indicates the inseparable relationship between them. The admonitions should be interpreted not as a call to moralism or a rigorous perfectionism but rather as a call to faith. Hebrews 3:12 suggests that an unbelieving heart is the root, and turning away from God is the fruit. The fundamental reason for falling away, then, is the failure to believe and to trust in God's promises.

Hebrews 3:12–4:13 also suggests that the drifting away in Heb. 2:1–4 should be interpreted as apostasy.[108] The wilderness generation failed to enter God's rest. The rest in Canaan functions as a type of God's heavenly rest—that is, entering the presence of God himself on the last day. The author of Hebrews exhorts his readers so that they will certainly enter God's rest. Those who fail to enter his rest will experience the final judgment of God. They are outside his blessing and thus will experience God's curse. The hardening of the heart, the evil heart of unbelief, and disobedience suggest that the sin of apostasy is in view—that is, a definite departure from the gospel that they initially confessed. Believers must strive "to enter" God's rest (Heb. 4:11). They must hold fast to the faith until the end to be saved on the last day (Heb. 3:14; 4:14; 10:23).

The next major warning passage is Heb. 5:11–6:12. The admonition to "go on toward perfection" (Heb. 6:1 NRSV) should not be understood as promising perfection in this life. Perfection (*teleiotēs*) is another way of describing the heavenly rest of believers, but in this instance it denotes the eschatological perfection that awaits believers when Jesus

107. As Rissi (1987: 104) points out, faith is bound up with the word of the gospel in Hebrews and is unthinkable apart from the proclaimed word.

108. Lindars (1991: 68–69) wisely remarks that the author refers not to each and every kind of sin but to apostasy. Most commentators agree that the danger in view in Hebrews is apostasy.

returns (Heb. 9:28).[109] The readers are warned that those who have once experienced numerous blessings from God cannot repent if they fall away (Heb. 6:4–6). Some interpreters understand the participle "falling away" (*parapesontas*) in Heb. 6:6 to denote some in the church who have already fallen away. This interpretation seems to be supported by the NRSV: "and then have fallen away." When we consider the other warning passages in Hebrews, however, it is more likely that the participle should be understood as a warning, not as an accomplished fact in the lives of some. This is represented well by the ESV: "if they then fall away." In Heb. 6 the author is not commenting or reflecting on those who have fallen away but rather is admonishing and encouraging his readers not to turn away from the gospel that they have embraced.[110] This seems to be confirmed by Heb. 6:11, where the readers are urged "to show the same earnestness to have the full assurance of hope to the end" and thereby inherit the eschatological promises (Heb. 6:12).

We also see further evidence that the warning here relates to apostasy and not merely to lack of fruitfulness in the Christian life. Those who fall away cannot repent again (Heb. 6:4), and such repentance almost certainly refers to the initial turning to God in faith upon conversion. A radical defection seems to be in view, for it is described as "crucifying once again the Son of God . . . and holding him up to contempt" (Heb. 6:6). Some have understood the illustration from the ground that receives rain from heaven to support the notion that the final judgment is not intended, but rather only a general lack of fruitfulness and fulfillment in the Christian life.[111] This interpretation is unconvincing. The ground that yields thorns and thistles is labeled "worthless" (*adokimos*). This term is regularly used to denote those who will face final judgment as unbelievers (Rom. 1:28; 1 Cor. 9:27; 2 Cor. 13:5, 6, 7; 2 Tim. 3:8; Titus 1:16). To say that they are "near to being cursed" does not mean that they will escape the curse, and that they were only close to being cursed. They are near to being cursed temporally—the curse is impending—so the NRSV catches the sense well in saying they are "on the verge of being cursed."[112] Finally, the text makes it clear that the ground itself will be burned if good fruit is not produced, and the ground represents human beings, not merely the fruit or lack thereof. Another question

109. Attridge (1989: 162–63) rightly sees a realized and a future component to perfection here.

110. In support of the notion that we have a warning here, see Attridge 1989: 166. Attridge (1989: 171) remarks, "Our author does not accuse his addressees of being in this condition. . . . It is a warning that should remind them of the seriousness of their situation and the importance of renewing their commitment." Cf. Lane 1991a: 142, 145.

111. See, for example, Gleason 2002.

112. See Attridge 1989: 173; P. Hughes 1977: 223–24.

that arises is whether the descriptions of those admonished here refers to Christians, but we postpone that question until we have examined all the warning passages.

The call to endurance should be interpreted as a summons to faith and hope.[113] Those who diligently continue in the faith do so because they have the assurance that comes from hope (Heb. 6:11).[114] They will enjoy the promises of God's salvation because of their "faith and patience" (Heb. 6:12; cf. 6:16).[115] If someone falls away, it is because he or she has ceased believing and hoping in God. Such a person has ceased to find Christ's purification of sins (Heb. 1:3; 7:1–10:18) as the ground of hope and assurance.

The author's rather full development of Christ's Melchizedekian priesthood and the inauguration of the new covenant through his death (Heb. 7:1–10:18) leads us to the next warning, which is against "sinning deliberately" (Heb. 10:26). The sin is described as a spurning of God's Son, profaning the blood of Christ that inaugurated the new covenant, and outraging God's gracious Spirit (Heb. 10:29). By way of contrast, the readers should not forsake their confidence in Christ and lose the reward (Heb. 10:35). In other words, they are to continue to endure in doing the will of God (Heb. 10:36) instead of shrinking back (Heb. 10:38–39). Those who shrink back reveal that they do not believe in God or trust his promises. We see again that failure to endure flows from lack of faith, and that believing and obeying are two sides of the same coin, and this will be elaborated shortly in investigating the contribution of Heb. 11.[116]

The warning in Heb. 10:26–39 supports the claim that the sin in view is apostasy.[117] Willful persistence in sin refers to deliberate sin, which is identified in the OT as sin "with a high hand," for which there is no forgiveness (cf. Lev. 4:2, 22, 27; Num. 15:30; Deut. 17:12; Ps. 19:13). For those who sin willfully "there no longer remains a sacrifice for sins"

113. For the pastoral character of the warnings, see the helpful observations in Emmrich 2003: 88–89. He observes that the author's intent is not to ask or answer the question of whether true believers can fall away. The readers are identified as believers as long as they continue as God's pilgrims. The author does not adopt a "divine perspective" on the destiny of his readers. He writes pastorally to encourage them to endure and persevere.

114. Käsemann (1984: 39) rightly notes the close association between faith and hope in Hebrews.

115. Lindars (1991: 71) beautifully captures the three metaphors that the author uses to convey assurance in Heb. 6: "It is like a place of refuge for those in need. It is like an anchor in rough seas. It is like admission beyond the veil of the sanctuary which is the place of the presence of God himself."

116. France (1996: 257) rightly argues that Heb. 10:32–12:3 forms one argument, and so Heb. 11 cannot be separated from the exhortation in Heb. 10.

117. Peterson (1982: 169) cautions, however, that not all sin is apostasy, but apostasy is the final expression of sin.

(Heb. 10:26). In other words, if the readers turn away from the cross of Christ for the cleansing of their sins and consciences, no other sacrifice will avail.[118] Reverting to the OT cult will not offer any help, for animal sacrifices cannot take away sins (Heb. 10:4). If the readers rely on such sacrifices for forgiveness, they deny the efficacy of Christ's atonement and thus cut themselves off from the only means by which sins can be forgiven. The threat of judgment, fire, vengeance, and recompense points to the final judgment inflicted by God upon unbelievers (Heb. 10:27, 30). Nor can anyone be considered a genuine believer who tramples on (*katapatēsas*) Jesus as God's Son, treats Jesus' blood as if it were defiled and unclean instead of precious, and outrages (*enybrisas*) the Spirit that gives grace (Heb. 10:29). The reference to the Lord's judging of "his people" does not suggest that they still remain his people if they undergo judgment, for they claimed to be his people but denied him by their works.[119]

The "reward" that the Hebrews are in danger of casting away, then, is life eternal (Heb. 10:35), not merely some extra reward in heaven apart from eternal life. Endurance is necessary to receive the life God promised (Heb. 10:36). Those whom God "has no pleasure in" (Heb. 10:38) will be excluded from his presence forever. Hebrews 10:39 reveals clearly that final destruction or salvation is at stake. Those who "shrink back . . . are destroyed" (*apōleian*), but those who trust God "are saved" (lit., "possession of soul" [*peripoiēsin psychēs*]).[120] The word for "destroyed" (*apōleia*) is used regularly in the NT to denote those who will be ruined and destroyed forever in the final judgment. The previous texts have already suggested that the warning relates to obtaining final salvation, but Heb. 10:26–39 is the clearest of all and provides help in interpreting the other warning passages. It will hardly do to say that the warning texts caution not against final destruction but only against loss of fruitfulness on earth or a higher status in heaven. The warning passages should be interpreted together, and they alert readers to the deadly peril that they face if they deny the efficacy of Christ's sacrifice.

When we turn to Heb. 11, we realize that the warning texts call upon the readers to trust in the gospel. Warnings are a summons to faith, a call to trust God until the end.[121] A description of faith is provided in Heb. 11:1: "Now faith is the assurance of things hoped for, the conviction of things not seen." Faith looks toward the future and is assured that

118. Lindars (1991: 69) aptly remarks, "Paradoxically they are turning away from the means of reconciliation in the endeavor to find it."

119. See P. Hughes 1977: 425.

120. Rightly Rissi 1987: 94.

121. Peterson (1982: 168) rightly argues that faith is the "underlying theme" in Heb. 11, and that faith expresses itself in "endurance."

God will fulfill his promises, particularly the promises of eschatological blessing that are not experienced or seen now.[122] To say that faith looks forward to the future does not deny that faith is also anchored in the past.[123] Faith can rely on God's future promises only because it is grounded in the work of Christ on the cross that has secured complete cleansing from sin (Heb. 7:1–10:18). For the author of Hebrews, failure to trust God for the future demonstrates that one has lost confidence in what Christ has achieved in the past through his cross and resurrection. Those who rest in the cross of Christ will not turn away from the atonement that he provided and revert to the sacrifices offered under the OT cult. Hebrews emphasizes faith in what God has promised, for the gospel calls each person to keep believing in what Christ has achieved through the cross. Genuine faith believes that God "exists and that he rewards those who seek him" (Heb. 11:6), but for the author of Hebrews, this future reward is not a mere belief in God's existence and his reward. Faith rests on what Christ has done in securing forgiveness of sins and in inaugurating the new covenant.[124]

Hebrews 11 also supports remarkably the inseparable relationship between faith and obedience, and at the same time it verifies that faith precedes obedience, so that all obedience derives from faith and is rooted in faith.[125] The connection between faith and activity is evident in the following phrases: "By faith Abel offered" (Heb. 11:4); "By faith Noah . . . constructed an ark" (Heb. 11:7); "By faith Abraham obeyed" (Heb. 11:8); "By faith he went to live in the land of promise" (Heb. 11:9); "By faith Abraham . . . offered up Isaac" (Heb. 11:17); "By faith Isaac invoked future blessings" (Heb. 11:20); "By faith Jacob . . . blessed each of the sons of Joseph" (Heb. 11:21); "By faith Joseph . . . made mention of the exodus of the Israelites and gave directions concerning his bones" (Heb. 11:22); "By faith . . . Moses was hidden for three months" (Heb. 11:23); "By faith Moses . . . refused to be called a son of Pharaoh's daughter" (Heb. 11:24); "By faith he left Egypt" (Heb. 11:27); "By faith he kept the Passover" (Heb. 11:28); "By faith the people crossed the Red Sea" (Heb. 11:29); the author speaks of the people "who through faith conquered kingdoms, administered justice . . . became mighty in war, put foreign armies to flight" (Heb. 11:33–34 NRSV). Others by faith received strength to suffer, to be killed, or to wander outside their homelands

---

122. Lindars (1991: 111) rightly sees that in Hebrews faith has a future orientation.

123. On the future and present character of faith in Hebrews, see Rhee 2001: 186–221.

124. Rhee (2001) demonstrates through a careful analysis of the entire letter that in Hebrews faith has Christ as its object and its model.

125. For the inseparable relation between faith and obedience in Hebrews, see Käsemann 1984: 38; Rhee 2001: 96–99.

(Heb. 11:36–38). The supreme exemplar of faith is Jesus, "who for the joy that was set before him endured the cross" (Heb. 12:2).[126] The dynamism of faith is evident. Faith acts, obeys, and endures. The author of Hebrews does not fall prey to moral rigorism that demands perfection of his readers. He summons them to believe in God's promises secured in the death of Christ, to trust in the cross until the end. Faith is not a mere passive acceptance of the gospel; rather, it reaches into the very soul and transforms one's life. According to Hebrews, such active faith saves, and it is those who believe who will avoid destruction at the last judgment.

It is faith that the "people of old" exercised that gained them approval from God (Heb. 11:2). Hence, Enoch was taken into God's very presence forever because of his faith (Heb. 11:5). Noah's faith delivered him from the raging floodwaters, so that he was considered righteous before God (Heb. 11:7). Faith looks to the future, trusting that God will fulfill his promises even if they are not fulfilled in the present. Hence, Abraham, Isaac, and Jacob, even though they dwelt in tents and lived as exiles and foreigners, looked forward to the day when God would give them a heavenly city and country (Heb. 11:8–16). Abraham believed that God's promises were inviolable, and so he was convinced that God would raise Isaac from the dead if needed (Heb. 11:17–19). Isaac, Jacob, and Joseph cast their eyes forward to the days when God would fulfill his promises to his people (Heb. 11:20–22). Moses cast his lot with Israel, being willing to suffer with the people of God in the present and forsaking the riches of Egypt, for he anticipated the future reward (Heb. 11:24–26). Those who circled the walls of Jericho trusted in God's promise that the walls would fall (Heb. 11:30). The author emphasizes those who suffered while waiting for God's promises to be realized (Heb. 11:35–38). All of these OT saints looked forward to the fulfillment of God's promise that has now come to pass through Jesus (Heb. 11:39–40). Of course, Jesus is the supreme example of one who was willing to suffer to receive the reward of reigning at God's right hand (Heb. 12:2). The message to the readers is clear. They are to consider those who have gone before them in the fight of faith (Heb. 12:1). They are to throw off anything that encumbers them in the race that they are running. By faith they are to persevere to the end. Even though God's promises in Christ have been inaugurated, they too await the heavenly city. They too are exiles and foreigners in a world that does not understand them. They too await the final fulfillment of God's promises. They too may suffer mistreatment, torture, and death before the final reward comes. The author encourages them to

---

126. Croy (1998: 177) rightly argues that joy is prospective here.

keep trusting in God until the promise is a reality; they should take heart from those who preceded them and not flag in running the race.

It should be clear, then, that Heb. 11 cannot be detached from the larger epistolary context of Hebrews. Only those who trust God and do not shrink back (Heb. 10:38–39) will enter the heavenly city. Ongoing faith is not encouraged because it brings happiness in the present or makes life more fruitful in the here and now. Faith is necessary to receive the inheritance promised, for faith rests on the priestly work of Christ for salvation.

The difficulties that believers face on their journeys is compared to the discipline that parents administer to their children (Heb. 12:5–11). So too, the stresses and pressures that believers face are to be endured because God, as a loving Father, is disciplining them for their holiness. Endurance is portrayed as the lifting of their failing hands and the enabling of their collapsing knees (Heb. 12:12). They are to walk in straight paths instead of turning back to Judaism. Holiness is not optional; it is necessary in order to see the Lord on the last day (Heb. 12:14).[127] Conversely, a bitter spirit can pollute many (Heb. 12:15). Esau is held up as an example of a person who surrendered his birthright and lost his inheritance forever (Heb. 12:16–17). His life functions as a warning to the community.

The author proceeds to another stern warning in Heb. 12:25–29. The readers must not reject the words of God that address them. It seems again that the judgment threatened refers to eternal destruction. The warning this time comes not merely from earth, as it did under the Sinai covenant, but from heaven. "God is a consuming fire" who will destroy those who do not trust and obey him. The ethical exhortations in Heb. 13 flesh out the life of faith. This is confirmed by Heb. 13:7, where the readers are exhorted to "imitate" the "faith" of their leaders. Therefore, the readers are not to be entranced and won over by the regulations and rituals of the old covenant (Heb. 13:9–12). The rites practiced did not yield notable results in any case, and believers are strengthened by God's grace, for they eat at a better altar because of the atonement achieved by Jesus. Just as Jesus suffered outside the gate of Jerusalem, so the author encourages the readers a final time not to depart from Jesus (Heb. 13:13–14). They should go outside the camp of Judaism, where there is acceptance and comfort, and they should endure abuse, for the eternal city to come belongs to them.

Scholars have also discussed whether those who receive the warnings are Christians. The debate centers on Heb. 6:4–6. Are those who

127. Peterson (1982: 151) rightly maintains that holiness is "the proper response to God's grace." Cf. Lane 1991b: 450–51.

have "been enlightened," "tasted the heavenly gift," "shared in the Holy Spirit," and "tasted the goodness of the word of God and the powers of the age to come" Christians? Some have argued that they are "almost Christians."[128] That is, they have come remarkably close to Christian faith without actually becoming members of the people of God. They have been enlightened in the sense that they know a significant amount about the Christian faith, and yet this knowledge has not led them to salvation. They have tasted and sampled the heavenly gift, but they have not ingested it and made it their own. They have had experiences of the Holy Spirit and spiritual gifts, but the Spirit did not indwell them. They have even experienced the delight of the word of God without ever embracing it truly. Such an interpretation explains how such could fall away (Heb. 6:6). They fell away because they never were Christians. Similarly, according to their view, in Heb. 10:29 those who are said to be "sanctified" enjoy an outward cleansing (cf. Heb. 9:13–14). They were not truly set apart for the things of God. Those warned came close to accepting the Christian faith, but they repudiated it after initial positive experiences.

The proposed interpretation has its attractions, but it fails to convince.[129] The most natural way of reading the description of the addressees is to identify them as believers. In Heb. 10:32 the word "enlightened" (*phōtizō*) is repeated from Heb. 6:4, and clearly it refers to the time of the readers' conversion. After their enlightenment they joyfully endured all kinds of sufferings and indignities. Determining precisely what it means to taste the heavenly gift is difficult. The metaphor of tasting is also used of their experience of God's word. In each case tasting does not mean that the readers merely sampled the heavenly gift and God's word and the powers of the coming age. The verb "taste" (*geuomai*) is used of Jesus' tasting death in Heb. 2:9. Surely the author does not mean that Jesus did not experience death fully. Tasting indicates that Jesus underwent death in all its fullness. Similarly, the author addresses readers who have ingested the heavenly gift and have experienced the powers of the age to come and the joy of God's word. Most important, the author says that the readers "shared in the Holy Spirit" (Heb. 6:4). The word "shared" (*metochos*) does not denote an inferior experience with the Spirit. Just a few verses earlier a verbal form (*metexchōn*) is used of ingesting milk (Heb. 5:13). There is no suggestion that the illustration points to only a sipping of milk or a slight ingestion of it. So too, the most natural way to read the verses is to understand the author to be saying that the readers

128. See Nicole 1975; Grudem 2000. Mathewson (1999), relying on the OT background, concludes that the readers were not true believers.
129. Most commentators think that the addressees are Christians.

have received the Holy Spirit. The reception of the Holy Spirit is the hallmark of being a Christian. The presence of the Spirit indicates that the Galatians do not need to be circumcised (Gal. 3:1–5). Similarly, Peter concludes that Cornelius and his friends should be baptized because they had received the Holy Spirit (Acts 10:44–48; 11:15–17). By saying that the readers were partakers of the Spirit, the author identifies them as Christians. The same argument applies to Heb. 10:29, where those addressed are said to be "sanctified" "by the blood of the covenant." It will not do to say that the sanctification here is merely outward or ceremonial, for the blood in view here is the blood of Jesus. OT sacrifices only purify externally and outwardly, but the blood of Christ cleanses the conscience and is effective, in contrast to the sacrifices offered under the old covenant. The author does not give any indication that he addresses those who are "almost Christians."

An even more decisive argument can be introduced to support a reference to Christians. We have noted that all the warning passages must be interpreted together. They cannot be sheared off from one another so that Heb. 6 is interpreted in isolation from the other warning texts. All the warnings together make one point: do not turn away from Jesus and his atonement, or you will be destroyed; keep trusting in God until the end. It is very clear from the first warning that the author addresses both himself and his readers. He declares (with my italics added for emphasis) that "*we* must pay much closer attention to what *we* have heard, lest *we* drift away from it" (Heb. 2:1); he asks, "How shall *we* escape if *we* neglect such a great salvation?" (Heb. 2:3). Clearly, the warning is addressed to all the readers, not just some of them. It is difficult to believe that Heb. 6:4–6 should be interpreted differently. The same can be said about the warning in Heb. 3:12–4:13, for the writer addresses the readers directly: "If you hear his voice, do not harden your hearts" (Heb. 3:7–8; cf. 3:15; 4:7). The warning is personally addressed to the readers in Heb. 3:12: "Take care, brothers, lest there be in any of you an evil, unbelieving heart, leading you to fall away from the living God." The word "brothers" addresses believers directly. The author broadens out the warning to include himself in Heb. 3:14, saying that "we share in Christ, if indeed we hold our original confidence firm to the end." The "if" clause has an implicit condition, and the author applies it to himself and the entire church. The first-person plural also commences Heb. 4:1, "let us fear" (NIV), although the author switches to the second-person plural ("any of you") by the end of the verse. The warning concludes with a first-person plural as well: "Let us therefore strive to enter that rest" (Heb. 4:11). Since the warning is clearly addressed to the entire community in Heb. 2:1–4 and Heb. 3:12–4:13, it is improbable that Heb. 5:11–6:12 should be interpreted differently. The remaining warning texts also contain first-person plurals: "let us hold fast the confession of our hope without wavering" (Heb. 10:23); "if we go on sinning deliberately" (Heb. 10:26 [cf. 12:1]); "let us go to him outside the camp" (Heb. 13:13). The exhortations also seem to be addressed to the church as a whole in the second-person plural (Heb. 10:35; 12:7, 12–13, 25; 13:9). The warnings in Heb. 6 address the entire church, including the author himself, so that it functions in the same way as the other warning passages in Hebrews.

The warning passages are controversial in another respect in the history of the church. Do they teach that genuine believers can be irretrievably lost so that they are condemned in the final judgment? In early church history some understood any serious postbaptismal sin (e.g., murder and adultery) as disqualifying one from future entrance into the kingdom. This interpretation fails to see that the sin that leads to irrevocable judgment, according to Hebrews, is apostasy, by which the atonement provided by Christ is abandoned. Still, it is clear that the earliest interpreters believed that apostasy was possible. Most scholarly work on Hebrews agrees, arguing that the author threatens the readers with eschatological judgment if they depart from the gospel.[130] The threat, it is argued, would be otiose if such apostasy were impossible, and in addition there must have been examples in the author's mind of those who had committed such apostasy, such as the wilderness generation of Israel (Heb. 3:7–4:13) or Esau (Heb. 12:16–17).

A few have maintained that believers are addressed in these verses, but that the punishment threatened relates to loss of rewards and not to eschatological destruction. I have argued above that the threats are of such a nature that the punishment described cannot be limited to loss of rewards. Still others, as we noted previously, argue that those who are warned are "almost Christians." Hence, those who fall away were not genuine believers but only appeared to be Christians. The problem with this view, as is often noted, is that there is no evidence, as we have seen, that the readers are described as "almost Christians." We cannot segregate the warnings in Heb. 6 from the rest of the letter, and elsewhere the readers certainly are addressed as believers.

I suggest a different answer to the controversy.[131] The author of Hebrews writes to warn those in the church not to fall away. His purpose is not to answer the question, "Were those who have fallen away genuine Christians?" He does not look back retrospectively and assess the state of those who have departed from the Christian faith. The intent of the

130. See, for example, Attridge 1989: 167; Lane 1991a: 146.
131. For a fuller exposition of the solution proposed here, see Schreiner and Caneday 2001.

letter is quite different. The author addresses those in the church who were tempted to revert to Judaism in order to avoid discrimination and persecution. He does not cast a glance backward, contemplate the state of those who have lapsed, and ask whether they were ever genuine believers. He is walking forward, urging his readers to adhere to the gospel and continue in the faith until the return of Jesus Christ. The warnings are *prospective*, designed to prevent the readers from drifting away from the gospel that they embraced. Certainly, the author hopes that his warnings will function as one of the means by which the readers will be impeded from apostasy. The author does not say that any of his readers have actually committed apostasy. He writes so that they will not turn away from the good news that they initially believed. We misread Hebrews when we ask the question, "Can genuine Christians apostatize?" Asking the wrong question can frame the discussion so that a wrong perspective on what the author says is given. The author does not specifically address the question of whether Christians are capable of committing apostasy; rather, he writes stern warnings so that they will avoid apostasy. But surely, one could object, the writer was aware of those who had departed from the Christian faith. Under the old covenant he mentions Israel in the wilderness (Heb. 3:7–4:13) and the defection of Esau (Heb. 12:16–17).[132] There is no doubt that the writer was familiar with some who had departed from the Christian faith. However, the point here is that he does not address that question specifically. There are some indications that believers have a certain hope that is irrevocable (e.g., Heb. 6:13–20; 10:14). The author functions as pastor, warning his readers not to depart from Jesus Christ and the atonement that he has provided.[133] But he also is optimistic that his warnings will succeed (Heb. 6:9–12), for he also knows that God's promises are sure, like an anchor, providing a hope that reaches inside the veil (Heb. 6:13–20). Hence, it seems that he believes that the warnings will actually be a means by which his readers will persevere and be assured of their salvation.

The importance of obedience and perseverance is woven throughout the letter to the Hebrews, for the readers were tempted to relapse to Jewish practices to avoid discrimination and persecution. Returning to Judaism is no light matter for the author, for he views it as a repudiation of the cross and a denial of the gospel. Those who fail to endure in the Christian faith and revert to Judaism will face eternal destruction. Some in the history of interpretation have interpreted Hebrews more rigorously

132. The defection of Israel and Esau do not function as a precise parallel, for it is unclear in both instances that those who defected were recipients of transforming grace before the defection.

133. Peterson (1982: 183) argues that some who seemed to be believers will be shown to be false if they apostatize.

than the author intends. He does not threaten judgment for any significant postbaptismal sin. We should not read him to say that those who
murder or commit adultery after conversion are necessarily damned, as
serious as those sins are.[134] God's wrath is reserved for those who deny
the gospel of Christ, for they no longer rely on the death of Jesus for the
forgiveness of their sins. There is no atonement for sin for those who
turn aside from the only basis for atonement. The call to perseverance,
as the whole of Hebrews clarifies, is a call to faith. Those who endure
to the end put their faith in the death of Jesus Christ for the forgiveness
of their sins. They profess that their only hope on the day of judgment
is the purification accomplished by Christ as the Melchizedekian priest.
Only those who continue to trust God in the future by remaining within
the Christian church reveal that they have found in Jesus Christ final
forgiveness of sins.

James

James clearly emphasizes that good works are necessary to avert
final judgment. In the introduction of the letter he calls on believers to
endure while experiencing difficulties (James 1:2–4). Such endurance
will ultimately lead to moral perfection—"that you may be perfect and
complete, lacking in nothing" (James 1:4).[135] Such moral perfection
cannot be obtained in this life, and indeed James notes that "we all
stumble in many ways" (James 3:2 NIV). Here "stumble" (*ptaiō*) should
be defined as "sin," as the use of the same term in James 2:10 confirms.
Hence, the moral perfection promised by James must be eschatological,
and yet the verses also suggest that believers grow progressively in godliness during this life. Enduring trials in a way that pleases God is not
optional for James, for those who do so "will receive the crown of life"
(James 1:12). The "crown of life" refers to eternal life itself; the genitive
is appositional, so that James refers to the crown which is life.[136] Hence,
James does not refer to a reward that is above or beyond eternal life.
Only those who persevere in the difficulties that life brings will receive
eschatological life on the last day.

134. For a brief history of interpretation along with parallels in literature contemporary
with Hebrews, see Attridge 1989: 168–69.

135. In support of the notion that *teleioi* here refers to moral perfection, see Moo 2000:
56. Moo points out that the final outcome of the process of trials is in view, suggesting
that the maturity is nothing short of perfection (cf. Matt. 5:48). See also L. Johnson 1995:
178–79. Less satisfying is the discussion in Laws 1980: 53–54.

136. Rightly Laws 1980: 68; Davids 1982: 80. Moo (2000: 70–71) takes the genitive as
appositional, but in his discussion he wrongly seems to suggest that the reward is something beyond eternal life itself.

Similarly, "doing the word" is necessary to receive eschatological blessing (cf. James 1:25), just as enduring is a condition for obtaining this blessing (cf. James 1:12). Those who do not practice the word of the gospel "deceive themselves" (James 1:22 NRSV), which presumably means that they deceive themselves about being Christians. It is the one who "perseveres" (*parameinas* [James 1:25]) who will find blessing on the last day. The word of the gospel that is "implanted" in the heart must be obeyed if one is to be saved on the last day (James 1:21).[137] If the speech of believers spews out evil, it calls into question whether they are a fresh spring or a tree that bears the right kind of fruit (James 3:11–12). The illustration of the tree echoes Jesus' teaching about being a good tree (Matt. 12:33 par.), showing that the fundamental issue is not good works but what kind of tree one is. The evidence of true wisdom is not intellectual ability; rather, wisdom manifests itself in behavior that is righteous and good (James 3:13–18). Those who are full of envy and rivalry and self-promotion lack wisdom, whereas those who are gentle, peaceable, kind, and merciful are wise. James suggests that those who lack wisdom are not genuinely believers; they are "earthly, unspiritual, demonic" (*epigeios, psychikē, daimoniōdēs* [James 3:15]). Good fruit functions as the evidence of spiritual life.

Believers must humble themselves before God (James 4:6, 10), submit themselves to his rule and flee from the devil (James 4:7). They are to draw near to God and purify themselves from sin (James 4:8). They should desist from judging one another (James 4:11–12) and patiently await the return of the Lord (James 5:7–10). Partiality toward the rich does not accord with the love that should be the mark of believers in Jesus Christ (James 2:1–13). James is quite concerned that believers will fawn over the rich to ensure their own security and comfort. For James, the term "rich" (*plousios*) is basically equivalent with "unbeliever."[138] The rich mistreat believers, haul them into court, and revile the name of Jesus (James 2:6–7), whereas God has "chosen those who are poor in the world to be rich in faith" (James 2:5). James does not teach that the poor automatically belong to the people of God. They must be "rich in faith" (James 2:5), and presumably those who are economically well off could also belong to the people of God if their money is spent for the sake of the kingdom. It is

137. Rightly Davids 1982: 95; Moo 2000: 88. Laato (1997: 53) denies this because he thinks that it suggests works-righteousness, but he dissolves the tension between the indicative and imperative and fails to see that even though the former secures the latter, biblical writers still insist on the necessity of realizing the imperative. Laato does rightly conclude that the failure to do good works shows that the new creation has not occurred after all.

138. For this view, see R. Martin 1988: 25–26; Davids 1982: 76–77; Laws 1980: 62–64. Moo (2000: 66–67) seems to lean slightly toward seeing the rich as believers, while L. Johnson (1995: 190–91) inclines toward seeing them as unbelievers.

the poor "brother" (*adelphos*) who will be exalted with life in the age to come (James 1:9). James does not use the word "brother" when he turns to the rich. Instead he uses irony, declaring that they should boast in their eschatological humiliation. James is not merely speaking of the loss of their riches, as if their humiliation is limited to the stripping away of the wealth of this age. He concludes by saying that the rich themselves "will fade away" (James 1:11). Those who are rich and do not trust God will face eschatological judgment and destruction, just as the sun scorches the beautiful flowers that bloom in the fields. The rich will be judged on the last day for oppressing their laborers (James 5:1–6), and the pleasures and treasures of this life will be of no avail at the judgment. Nor is there any place for a false confidence in one's financial future, which leads to confident assertions about future profit (James 4:13–17). Any financial success is dependent on the Lord's will, and human life is a wisp that vanishes with the blowing of the wind.

Partiality should not be afforded to the rich, for those who show partiality will face judgment if they fail to show mercy to the poor and pander to the rich (James 2:13). When James says that "mercy triumphs over judgment" (James 2:13), he does not mean in context that God's mercy to human beings, despite their sinfulness, triumphs over judgment so that they will escape judgment even though they deserve it. Rather, his point is that if believers show mercy to others, especially the poor and downtrodden, then they will escape God's judgment on the last day.[139] This is James's version of Jesus' claim that one must be merciful to obtain mercy (Matt. 5:7) and be forgiving to receive forgiveness (Matt. 6:14–15 par.; 18:21–35). We see again that James insists that one must obey God in order to receive an eschatological reward.

The necessity of obedience brings us to James's famous discussion of faith and works in James 2:14–26.[140] Many scholars affirm that James contradicts the Pauline view of justification by faith apart from works.[141] The arguments supporting a contradiction are quite impressive:[142] (1) James specifically denies that justification is by faith alone (James 2:24), whereas Paul clearly implies that believers are justified by faith alone (Rom. 3:28);[143] (2) Paul claims that Abraham was justified by faith, but James

---

139. Rightly Moo 2000: 118; Davids 1982: 119; Laws 1980: 117–18 (though, contra Laws, there is no notion of merit here).

140. For a short history of interpretation, see R. Martin 1988: 82–84.

141. Representative of this view is Hengel 1987.

142. Chester (1994: 20–28, 46–53) does not claim that there is a contradiction, but he is reluctant to propose any solution and says that we must be content with tension.

143. Luther rightly argued that Rom. 3:28 teaches that justification is by faith alone. Fitzmyer (1993d: 360–62), one of the preeminent Roman Catholic biblical scholars of our time, concurs that Rom. 3:28 implies that righteousness is by faith alone.

asserts that he was justified by works in sacrificing Isaac (Rom. 4:1–8; Gal. 3:6–9; James 2:21); (3) Paul appeals to Gen. 15:6 to support Abraham being justified by faith apart from works (Rom. 4:3; Gal. 3:6), but James cites the same verse from Genesis to substantiate justification by works (James 2:23). The arguments that favor a contradiction between Paul and James certainly are striking, but I will argue below that James is more likely responding to a distortion of Pauline teaching in which an antinomian lifestyle was defended by twisting what Paul taught about justification.[144]

Various solutions have been suggested to reconcile the discrepancy between Paul and James. One possibility is that James and Paul mean something different by the word "works" (*erga*). Historically, Roman Catholic interpreters have suggested that Paul excludes ceremonial works as playing a role in justification, whereas James refers here to moral works.[145] The Reformers, of course, strenuously disagreed with the Roman Catholic interpretation, maintaining that in Paul works could not be limited to ceremonies such as circumcision or the observance of days. Interestingly, the new perspective on Paul typically identifies the works that Paul rules out for justification as those that erect barriers between Jews and Gentiles, so that the focus is on circumcision, food laws, and Sabbath. Obviously, those who endorse the new perspective are coming from a different place than Roman Catholic scholarship of the sixteenth century, and yet the interpretations share a fascinating convergence at this particular point. The new perspective solution fails, as I argued earlier, for it is not evident that Paul restricts "works of the law" or "works" to ceremonial works or those laws that divide Jews from Gentiles. Hence, it is not evident that Paul and James use the term "works" in a different sense.[146] Rainbow suggests that Paul rules out works done before conversion, whereas James focuses on postconversion works.[147] This does not imply, however, that postconversion works are perfect or that in themselves they warrant justification before God, since James freely acknowledges that even as believers, we all sin in many ways (James 3:2).

144. Rightly Laws 1980: 15–18, 131–32; L. Johnson 1995: 64. Contra Davids 1982: 20–21. Or Bauckham (1999b: 119, 131–35) may be right in suggesting that we have no response to Paul at all because matters such as purity laws and circumcision are unmentioned.

145. Jeremias (1954–1955: 370) adopts a variant of this view, though clearly he does not subscribe to Roman Catholic views. L. Johnson (1995: 62) promotes this view, arguing that in Paul works of law refers to circumcision and ritual law. So also Davids 1982: 50–51. Davids (1982: 50) says (wrongly, in my view) that works in Paul "are never moral prescriptions, but rather ceremonial rites added to the work of Christ."

146. For the notion that James thinks of works in a broad sense, see Moo 2000: 122–23.

147. Rainbow 2005: 216–17.

What is likely, however, is that Paul and James use the term "justify" (*dikaioō*) with a different nuance.[148] I argued earlier, following Westerholm, that Paul uses the word *dikaioō* to refer to extraordinary righteousness—a righteousness given to the ungodly. Paul shockingly insists that it is the ungodly who are declared to be righteous by virtue of the righteousness of Christ. James, on the other hand, uses the verb *dikaioō* to refer to ordinary righteousness; that is, God declares those who do good works to be in the right before him. Hence, Davids and others fail to convince when they maintain that in James *dikaioō* means "proved to be righteous" or "shown to be righteous."[149] In James the term means "declare righteous," but in contrast to Paul, the word is used in its ordinary sense, in that God declares those who obey to be righteous.

Often the view of the Reformers is understood to say that human beings are shown to be righteous (cf. Matt. 11:19b; Luke 7:35) before other people by their works, but they are not declared to be righteous before God by their works.[150] This solution is quite attractive, and it resolves satisfactorily the alleged contradiction between Paul and James. Nevertheless, it is doubtful that such a view handles the evidence satisfactorily. As I argued previously, it is correct to say that Paul uses the term *dikaioō* to mean "declared righteous." What is less convincing is to claim that James uses the term to mean "proved righteous" or "shown to be righteous." The term *dikaioō* may have this meaning in Luke 7:35, but such a definition would be quite unusual. Further, in a context that discusses faith, works, and justification we need good contextual evidence in order to assign a different meaning to the word "justify." Assigning to the word "justify" the meaning "declare righteous" fits with its typical meaning, and it makes good sense in the context of James.

It seems that both James and Paul use the word "justify" soteriologically, but Paul uses the word in an unusual sense in that he thinks of God declaring those who are unrighteous to be righteous. James, on the other hand, emphasizes that God declares those who are righteous to be righteous, although, as I will argue shortly, it still does not follow that James and Paul ultimately contradict one another. The soteriological context in James is evident, for he asks if a faith without works can "save" (*sōzō* [James 2:14]). The word "save" almost certainly refers to deliverance

---

148. Jeremias (1954–1955: 370–71) argues that in Paul *dikaioō* is normally synthetic, in that God adds something to the ungodly that they do not enjoy—righteousness. In James, on the other hand, *dikaioō* is analytic, so that at the last judgment God recognizes the righteousness that now exists.

149. Davids 1982: 51, 127. Against this view, see Moo 2000: 134–35.

150. Sproul 1995: 166. See also the quote from Calvin to this effect in Sproul 1995: 167. I would maintain that even though Calvin is off-kilter on this particular point, his reading of James substantially matches what is argued for here.

from God's wrath on the day when the Lord returns (cf. James 5:7–9), which is the same meaning that it often has in Paul.[151] Both "save" and "justify," then, relate to one's standing before God, not the opinion of human beings. James appeals to Genesis to support the need for works (James 2:21), and there is no suggestion in that chapter that the sacrifice of Isaac was commanded so that other people would commend Abraham. In Genesis God asserts that he now knows that Abraham fears him because of Abraham's willingness to sacrifice his son (Gen. 22:12), and God confirms the blessing given to Abraham because of the latter's obedience (Gen. 22:18). To see a reference to righteousness in the eyes of human beings does not account well for James or Gen. 22.[152]

If James uses *dikaioō* to refer to a declaration of righteousness by virtue of works, whereas Paul uses the term *dikaioō* in an unusual way to refer to the gift of righteousness granted to the ungodly, then do James and Paul contradict one another? Another proposed solution is that James differs from Paul because he uses the term to refer to eschatological justification—the pronouncement that will be made on the last day.[153] Such a reading gets us closer to resolving the differences between Paul and James, but it still does not quite succeed. The term "justify" is eschatological in Paul, in that it refers to the final judgment that has been announced ahead of time. Paul, of course, emphasizes that believers are *now* justified by faith (Rom. 5:1). The final verdict already belongs to believers who are in Christ Jesus (Rom. 8:1). It is important to add at this point that James likely uses the word "save" to refer to eschatological deliverance (James 1:21; 2:14; 4:12; 5:20).[154] Paul often uses the verb "save," as I argued earlier, to refer to end-time deliverance as well. Evidence is lacking, however, that James and Paul use the verb "justify" (*dikaioō*) differently in this sense. We can agree that "justify" is eschatological in that it represents God's verdict pronounced on the judgment day. James, however, emphasizes that this verdict has already been pronounced in history, just as Paul does. The most natural way to read James 2:21 is to

151. The eschatological nature of salvation is noted in Laato 1997: 65.

152. An even more unlikely solution is proposed by Radmacher (1990). He argues that James is not referring to a faith that saves from God's eschatological wrath, nor does justification refer to standing in the right before God. Instead, James refers to a faith that gives one a happy and fruitful life on earth, and hence the faith that has works as its fruit is entirely unnecessary for salvation on the last day. The problem with Radmacher's view is that he has to posit definitions for *sōzō* and *dikaioō* that do not fit with the remainder of the NT, nor does it square with the rest of James.

153. So Rainbow 2005: 217. Moo (2000: 138–39) argues that the time of justification is not resolved by James in James 2:23, where the noun *dikaiosynē* is used, but Moo (2000: 134–35, 141–42) maintains that the verb *dikaioō* (James 2:21, 24, 25) relates only to the last judgment.

154. Perhaps James 5:15 should be put in this category as well.

conclude that Abraham was "justified by works *when* he offered his son Isaac on the altar" (italics added).[155] One could argue that the participle should be translated as causal, but even so, the aorist passive "he was justified" (*edikaiōthē*) seems to point to a justification that belonged to Abraham *in history*. In the same way, Rahab was declared to be righteous by works "when she received the messengers and sent them out by another way" (James 2:25). In addition, Abraham's being reckoned as righteous seems to be connected to the offering of Isaac (James 2:21–23) and is not reserved for the day of judgment alone. James appears to use the word "justify" within the same time frame as Paul, referring to the final verdict of God that has already been announced in advance.

I have argued that James and Paul use the term *dikaioō* with a different nuance—James to refer to the ordinary declaration of righteousness pronounced by virtue of the works performed, and Paul to the extraordinary verdict by God that the ungodly who trust in Christ are righteous. Still, it does not follow that James and Paul ultimately contradict one another. We must recognize that they address different situations and circumstances, and those situations must be taken into account in understanding the stances of Paul and James relative to justification. Indeed, we are on the way to resolving the tension between James and Paul in seeing how they both use the term "faith" (*pistis*).[156] When James says that faith alone does not justify, faith here refers to mere intellectual assent. For instance, demons affirm monotheism, but such "faith" is not wholehearted and glad-hearted assent that leads demons to embrace Jesus Christ as Lord and Savior. Instead, the faith of demons is theologically orthodox but leads them to shudder because they fear judgment (James 2:19).[157] The faith that saves, according to Paul, embraces Jesus Christ as Savior and Lord, placing one's life entirely in his hands. James criticizes a "faith" that notionally concurs with the gospel but does not grip the whole person.[158]

155. See the critique of Moo in Gathercole 2003: 117.

156. Most commentators agree on this point. See, for example, Jeremias 1954–1955: 370. See also Moo 2000: 130–31.

157. Rainbow (2005: 221) argues against what is said here, but he fails to note that the demons, though they believe, fail to do the good works necessary, so that the problem that James finds with those whom he criticizes is the same problem that the demons have: notional belief without consequent actions. Surprisingly, Rainbow (2005: 218–23) fails to see the vital link between faith and works in James, and so he rejects what is argued for here, even though the solution that I propose seems to fit what he argues for elsewhere in his book. Indeed, some of Rainbow's comments, even in the pages noted, indicate that the works in view in James are the result of faith. See the helpful formulations in Rainbow 2005: 226–27. Note especially: "Works are indeed the evidence of faith (Jas. 2:18b), not in the sense that they are dispensable outward signs of an inward reality which could exist without them, but in the sense that the inward and outward together constitute reality. Without being acted out, faith alone shows itself to be incomplete or unreal" (Rainbow 2005: 226).

158. Rightly Davids 1982: 50.

In other words, James does not disagree with Paul's contention that faith alone justifies, but he defines carefully the kind of faith that justifies. The faith that truly justifies can never be separated from works. Works will inevitably flow as the fruit of such faith. Faith that merely accepts doctrines intellectually but does not lead to a transformed life is "dead" (James 2:17, 26) and "useless" (James 2:20). Such faith does not "profit" (*ophelos* [James 2:14, 16 RSV]) in the sense that it does not spare one from judgment on the last day. Those who have dead and barren faith will not escape judgment. True faith is demonstrated by works (James 2:18). James does not deny that faith alone saves, but it is faith that produces (*synergeō*) works and is completed (*teleioō*) by works (James 2:22). The faith that saves is living, active, and dynamic. It must produce works, just as compassion for the poor inevitably means that one cares practically for their physical needs (James 2:15–16).[159]

James and Paul do not actually contradict one another on the role of faith and works in justification. James affirms as well that faith is the root and works are the fruit.[160] James addresses a situation different from that of Paul, for the latter denies that works can function as the basis of a right relation with God. A right relation with God is obtained by faith alone. Paul responds to those who tried to establish a right relation with God on the basis of works. Paul argues that God shockingly declares those who lack any righteousness to be in the right, if they put their faith in Christ for salvation. James counters those who think that a right relation with God is genuine if there is faith without any subsequent works. James looks at God's pronouncement of righteousness from another angle: not as the fundamental basis of one's relation to God but rather as the result of faith. James responds to antinomianism, whereas Paul reacts to legalism.[161]

The foregoing comments, of course, need qualification. As I argued above, in some contexts Paul also emphasizes that good works are the fruit of faith[162] and are needed for justification (e.g., Rom. 2:13; 4:17–22).[163] The purpose of James as a whole, as is evident from this entire

159. Gathercole (2003: 117–18) argues that James 2:24 indicates that works are also the means of justification.

160. For this observation, see also Laato (1997: 87), who argues that James differs from Judaism in rejecting the native ability of the human will and emphasizes instead God's work. Laato (1997: 69) remarks, "Good works subsequently brought into effect the living nature of faith." Laato (1997: 70) also notes that faith "*only subsequently* (but nevertheless inevitably) will yield fruit." See also the helpful reflections in Bauckham 1999b: 120–27. Contra Mussner (1964: 151), who argues that the works make the faith living.

161. Jeremias (1954–1955: 370) rightly observes that James fights on a different "field of battle."

162. So also Laato 1997: 72.

163. On the role of Rom. 4:17–22, see Laato 1997: 76.

discussion, is to emphasize that good works are necessary for salvation. His letter apparently responds to a situation where moral laxity was countenanced. Nevertheless, James should not be interpreted to teach that believers can gain salvation on the basis of good works. Righteous deeds are the fruit of faith.[164] James recognizes that all believers sin in numerous ways (James 3:2), and that even one sin makes a lawbreaker of the one who commits it (James 2:10–11). Being sinners, humans lack the capacity to do the works required to merit justification. They are saved by the grace of God, for in his goodness and generosity he granted believers new life (James 1:18). Even faith is a gift of God, for God chose some to "be rich in faith and heirs of the kingdom" (James 2:5). What James hammers home is that such faith must always manifest itself in good works if it is genuine faith, but such good works are a far cry from perfection, as James 3:2 clarifies. Kierkegaard captures memorably the intention of James: "It is like a child's giving his parents a present, purchased, however, with what the child has received from his parents; all the pretentiousness that otherwise is associated with giving a present disappears since the child received from the parents the gift that he gives to the parents."[165] It seems, then, that Paul and James do not contradict one another, even though they address different circumstances. Both affirm the priority of faith in justification, and both also affirm that good works are the fruit of faith but are not the basis of justification. Hence, what James teaches fits with Paul's teaching and with what we have seen elsewhere in the NT.

1 Peter

Peter writes to churches facing suffering, encouraging them to "stand firm" in God's grace (1 Pet. 5:12).[166] Many scholars think that this admonition sums up the message of the entire letter.[167] On the one hand, believers are exhorted to stand and remain faithful to the gospel; on the other hand, only God's grace grants them the ability to stand and endure to the end. Ethical admonition permeates the letter. Believers are to set their hope on the grace that will be theirs when Christ returns (1 Pet. 1:13),

---

164. Laato (1997: 71) rightly speaks of "the priority of faith."

165. Quoted in Bauckham 1999b: 164.

166. The suffering in 1 Peter reflects sporadic persecution, not an empire-wide policy against Christians. Nor does it seem that believers are being put to death (see Schreiner 2003: 28–31). Bechtler (1998: 93–94) rightly says, "That the letter assumes that Christians have already been condemned to death, however, whether on the charge of murder or on the charge of being a Christian, seems highly unlikely. It is simply inconceivable that so grave a situation would not have been more clearly reflected in the letter."

167. See, for example, Wendland 2000: 25–26; Horrell 2002.

live holy lives (1 Pet. 1:15–16), love one another (1 Pet. 1:22; 4:8) and turn from anything that contradicts such love (1 Pet. 2:1–3), and abstain from fleshly desires (1 Pet. 2:11). Believers are to submit to governing authorities (1 Pet. 2:13–17), slaves to masters (1 Pet. 2:18–25), and wives to husbands (1 Pet. 3:1–6). Husbands are to show tender love for their wives (1 Pet. 3:7), and all believers are to prepare themselves to suffer if it is God's will (1 Pet. 4:1–6, 12–19). Elders are to lead the flock in a way that pleases God (1 Pet. 5:1–4), and the entire community should live in humility (1 Pet. 5:6–7).

Conversion is described as "obedience to Jesus Christ" (1 Pet. 1:2) or as the purification of "your souls by your obedience to the truth" (1 Pet. 1:22).[168] In these contexts Peter does not think of ongoing obedience in the Christian life as in 1 Pet. 1:15–16. The context of the opening (1 Pet. 1:1–2) indicates that conversion is in view: being chosen by God for salvation, set apart by the Spirit for salvation, and sprinkled by Jesus' blood for the forgiveness of sins. The admonition to love one another (1 Pet. 1:22) is bounded by two references to conversion: the purification of one's soul when one obeys the truth (1 Pet. 1:22), and being born again by means of God's word (1 Pet. 1:23). Conversion occurs when human beings submit their lives to God when hearing the gospel of Jesus Christ. The emphasis on obedience does not cancel out the centrality of faith. Those who believe in Jesus will escape eschatological humiliation on the last day (1 Pet. 2:6–7). Faith is also described as coming to Jesus, the living stone (1 Pet. 2:4). Peter also uses the metaphor of tasting (1 Pet. 2:3), drawing on Ps. 34:8. Those who believe taste the goodness and kindness of the Lord. The image of tasting the Lord's kindness captures the richness of faith, for faith embraces Jesus as Lord, finding him to be satisfying and fulfilling. It "comes" to him and submits to him as Lord.

If the message of Peter can be summed up as "stand firm" in grace (1 Pet. 5:12), it seems that the same theme appears in the admonition to "resist" the devil "firm in your faith" (1 Pet. 5:9). Perseverance and endurance are rooted in faith, in placing one's trust in what God has done in Christ on the cross. The ongoing role of faith is clear because God guards his people, ensuring that they will enjoy end-time salvation "through faith" (1 Pet. 1:5). Peter also teaches that believers will enjoy a final reward if they obey (1 Pet. 2:19–20). Those who long to inherit the eschatological blessing and to enjoy good days must live in a godly fashion (1 Pet. 3:10–12). Even though the citation from Ps. 34 in 1 Pet. 3:10–12 relates to life in this world, Peter, as is typical for NT writers, considers entrance into the land typologically so that it forecasts posses-

168. In defense of the view adopted here, see Schreiner 2003: 92–93.

sion of the heavenly inheritance.[169] Such an inheritance will be given only to those who refrain from evil and seek peace. Those who practice evil will experience God's judgment. What we have in 1 Peter is characteristic of the NT. Saving faith always leads to a changed life, so that there is a new obedience. Such obedience is necessary for an eschatological inheritance, but it is still conceived of as a fruit of faith. Peter's emphasis on the cross indicates that Christ's work is still foundational for the forgiveness of sins (1 Pet. 1:18–19; 2:21, 24–25; 3:18). Good works are not the basis for receiving salvation, but they are the necessary fruit of faith for life eternal.

2 Peter and Jude

Both 2 Peter and Jude are addressed to churches in which false teachers with antinomian lifestyles and agendas are threatening the church. Both writers, therefore, naturally emphasize the need for perseverance and obedience. Jude reminds his readers that God has always judged those who turn to evil, whether Israel in the wilderness, the angels who sinned, or Sodom and Gomorrah (Jude 5–7). Similarly, Cain, Balaam, and Korah function as three models of those who sinned and were judged by God. The assurance that God will judge the ungodly (Jude 14–16) should motivate the church to "keep [themselves] in the love of God" (Jude 21). The whole letter is written to secure such perseverance, though Jude places the emphasis, as we noted earlier, at the beginning and conclusion of the book on God's keeping of believers by his grace (Jude 1, 24–25). Though Jude says nothing about faith, the emphasis on God's grace indicates that enduring to the end cannot be attributed ultimately to the work of believers.

Peter likewise emphasizes the judgment of the false teachers, repeating many of the themes found in Jude (2 Pet. 2). The role of faith in receiving God's saving righteousness is stated in the introduction to the letter.[170] Nevertheless, the need for perseverance is the major theme sounded in the letter, although, as I argued earlier, at the inception of the letter God's grace in securing salvation for his people is underscored (2 Pet. 1:1–4). Hence, Peter, contrary to the view of some, does not fall prey to works-

169. So most commentators (e.g., Schelke 1980: 95; Achtemeier 1996: 226; Michaels 1988: 180; Piper 1980: 226–27). Contra Grudem (1988b: 148–49) who thinks the verses refer to blessings in this life.

170. Most scholars do not see a reference to the saving righteousness of God here but rather understand the author to be referring to God's fairness in distributing salvation to all. In defense of the view suggested here, see Schreiner 2003: 286.

righteousness or moralism.[171] In 2 Pet. 1:5–7 he exhorts his readers to pursue godly virtues, for God has given them all they need to live godly lives (2 Pet. 1:3–4). It should also be noted that faith is mentioned first, suggesting that a life of godliness flows from faith.[172] Peter is not merely interested in moral improvement in and of itself. He counters opponents who likely misinterpreted Pauline writings as a platform for libertinism (2 Pet. 3:15–16). A life of goodness is the fruit of faith, and it can never be separated from authentic faith.

Peter argues, then, that those who live in an ungodly way are "ineffective or unfruitful in the knowledge of our Lord Jesus Christ" (2 Pet. 1:8).[173] To be forgetful of the forgiveness of sins is not a trifling matter for Peter (2 Pet. 1:9), for the godly qualities called for in 2 Pet. 1:5–7 are necessary "to confirm" one's "call and election" (2 Pet. 1:10 NRSV). Those who lack such qualities, therefore, will not enjoy eschatological salvation. On the other hand, those who practice such qualities "will never fall" (2 Pet. 1:10), which means that they will never commit apostasy.[174] Some interpreters understand 2 Pet. 1:11 to be referring to an eschatological reward that is distinct from entering into the kingdom, so that it refers to an extra bonus or reward given to those who are already guaranteed of salvation.[175] But such an interpretation does not fit with 2 Pet. 1:10, where people are to confirm their call and election to salvation, not to some reward beyond salvation. Nor does it accord with the remainder of the letter, for the opponents still claimed to be Christians, but Peter asserts that their lack of perseverance demonstrates that they are not truly believers.

Peter threatens, as did Jude, judgment for those who disobey (2 Pet. 2:4–10a), but he adds the theme that God is able to preserve those who belong to him, adducing the examples of Noah and Lot. The authenticity of the faith of Noah and Lot was demonstrated by their perseverance in the midst of societies that were utterly corrupt. If God could preserve them in the midst of such evil cultures, then surely he will guard the believers in the Petrine communities. The examples of Noah and Lot also illustrate the necessity of perseverance to obtain the eschatological reward. The example of Lot is interesting for another reason. Peter

171. Rightly Charles 1997: 161.

172. On the priority of faith, see Fuchs and Reymond 1980: 56; Charles 1997: 162.

173. In 2 Peter the word *epignōsis* (2 Pet. 1:2, 3, 8; 2:20) probably refers to conversion (Picirilli 1975; Bauckham 1983: 169–70; Fornberg 1977).

174. Most commentators agree that apostasy is in view. See Bauckham 1983: 191; Fuchs and Reymond 1980: 60.

175. Fornberg (1977: 96) rightly remarks, "The author regarded good deeds as essential for salvation," but he argues that such a perspective does not necessarily contradict the Pauline view that good works are a fruit of salvation.

clearly is not calling for some kind of perfection. Some interpreters even wonder how Peter could call Lot righteous at all, given some of his actions in Genesis. Peter, however, does no violence to Genesis, for the narrator of the story finds Lot's deliverance from Sodom to be an answer to Abraham's prayer that the righteous might not perish along with the wicked (Gen. 18:24; 19:29). Furthermore, Lot's hospitality to the angelic visitors (although he was unaware that they were angels) stood in vivid contrast to the "welcome" offered by the residents of Sodom (Gen. 19:1–11). Peter does not cite Noah and Lot because they were perfect; they failed in many ways. They serve as examples because they persevered in trusting God and lived in a way that was different from the society surrounding them, despite their foibles.

In this regard Noah and Lot should be contrasted with the false teachers. The false teachers had been part of the church. Peter says that they denied "the Master who bought them" (2 Pet. 2:1). They had escaped the world through their knowledge of Christ, but subsequently they denied him, presumably by the way they lived (2 Pet. 2:20–21). Peter wrote to the church so that they would not follow the same pattern as the false teachers, who professed to believe in Christ but then departed from the holy commandment (2 Pet. 2:21), which likely refers to the gospel. The mark of genuine Christians, according to Peter, is perseverance. Those who defect from the faith demonstrate that they are dogs and pigs—that is, unclean animals that do not truly belong to the holy community (2 Pet. 2:22).[176]

The fundamental message of Peter, then, is to warn believers not to be swept away by the libertinism of the false teachers so that they depart from the gospel (2 Pet. 3:17). Instead, they are to continue growing in grace and in the knowledge of Jesus Christ (2 Pet. 3:18). They are to "be diligent to be found by him without spot and blemish, and at peace" (2 Pet. 3:14). The word "found" (heuriskō [cf. 2 Pet. 3:10]) refers to the judicial decision made by God on the final day.[177] Believers must be diligent to be blameless before him, so that they will enter into their eschatological reward. Such blamelessness involves repudiating the false teachers and staying true to the gospel until the end. Nevertheless, we are reminded from 2 Pet. 1:5 that godly living is the result of faith, and hence the call to perseverance should be interpreted as a summons to a life of faith.

176. Most commentators argue that Peter teaches here that genuine believers can apostatize. For further discussion of and defense for the view propounded here, see Schreiner 2003: 362–65.

177. The verse is notoriously difficult. Especially helpful is D. Wenham 1987. For a discussion of the various options, see Schreiner 2003: 385–87.

Revelation

The book of Revelation is in some ways remarkably similar to Hebrews. John writes to churches in Asia Minor that were facing discrimination and persecution in their newfound faith. The readers were enticed by the culture of their day. If they participated in emperor worship *and* showed devotion to Jesus, life would be much easier (Rev. 13:1–18).[178] They would stifle questions about their loyalty to the political structure in which they lived, and they would fit in with the cultural ethos of the day, in which people worshiped many gods and found them useful for a variety of purposes. John does not tolerate any compromise with Rome, nor does he countenance emperor worship. Those who worship the beast, which almost certainly is a designation of the Roman emperor, do not have their names inscribed in the book of life (Rev. 13:8). He threatens those who worship the beast with eternal torment and the fierce wrath of God (Rev. 14:9–11).[179]

Most commentators agree that Babylon represents the city of Rome (Rev. 17:18), the commercial center of the Roman Empire. Believers would find Rome alluring because it was a glorious jewel holding out the promise of economic prosperity. John, however, identifies it as a "whore" (Rev. 17:1 NRSV), and those who compromise with Rome have committed fornication (Rev. 17:2; 18:3, 9).[180] They have gotten in bed with Rome and pandered to its power to secure their own future. They have joined hands with a city that has spilled the blood of God's holy ones (Rev. 17:6; 18:24; 19:2). For John, fornication here is not literal but rather denotes worship of this world and the financial security that it brings versus worship of the one and only true God. The temptation to compromise with the current world order is apparent in the letter to the churches. Pergamum was a center of emperor worship identified as the place where Satan's throne was erected (Rev. 2:13), and Antipas was slain there, presumably because he refused to submit to emperor worship.[181] Others participated in feasts in the temples, eating foods

178. On the role of emperor worship in Revelation, see Beale 1999b: 5–12; Osborne 2002: 6–7.

179. Revelation, therefore, cannot be characterized as being a book solely of comfort and consolation for suffering believers. The text also warns believers of the severe consequences of compromise with and subservience to Rome (so Bauckham 1993a: 15–16).

180. Bauckham (1993a: 17–18) strikingly captures John's vision: "At first glance, she [Babylon] might seem to be the goddess Roma, in all her glory, a stunning personification of the civilization of Rome, as she was worshipped in many a temple in the cities of Asia. But as John sees here, she is a Roman prostitute, a seductive whore and a scheming witch, and her wealth and splendour represent the profits of her disreputable trade."

181. Caird (1966: 38) thinks that Antipas may have been slain by mob violence. Aune (1997: 182–84) argues that evidence is lacking that the imperial cult is in view here, or that

offered to idols, and practicing sexual sin (Rev. 2:14, 20–23). Participation in such events ensured that believers would be part and parcel of society and would play a continuing role in trade guilds.

John emphasizes that believers must come out of Babylon (Rev. 18:4). Otherwise, they will face the same judgment that will be inflicted upon Rome. John does not exhort believers to leave the city of Rome literally. They must give glory to God by worshiping him alone (Rev. 14:7; 15:4), and their relationship to Rome and the Roman Empire demonstrates the object of worship, so that for John, worship is not abstractly separated from everyday life. Only those who are willing to "be faithful until death" will receive "the crown of life" (Rev. 2:10).

The situation of the letter explains why John emphasizes perseverance and endurance. Believers must conquer and overcome (*nikaō*) to the end in order to receive eternal life.[182] In each of the letters to the seven churches he exhorts the readers to conquer (Rev. 2:7, 11, 17, 26; 3:5, 12, 21), by which he means that they must heed the admonitions in the letters in order to obtain the final reward on the last day. Such conquering is not optional. "To the one who conquers I will grant to eat of the tree of life, which is in the paradise of God" (Rev. 2:7). The "tree of life" alludes to the tree of life in Genesis (Gen. 2:9; 3:22) and refers to eternal life. That conquering is required for obtaining an eschatological inheritance is even clearer in Rev. 2:11: "The one who conquers will not be hurt by the second death." We know from later in Revelation that the second death is the lake of fire, and that those whose names are not recorded in the book of life are cast into the lake of fire (Rev. 20:14–15; cf. 21:8). Only those who walk with Jesus in white will receive a reward (Rev. 3:4). Those who conquer will be adorned with white robes, and their names will not be removed from the book of life (Rev. 3:5). Jesus will confess their names before the Father and the angels. The threat is clearly stated: those who fail to conquer will not remain in the book of life. The statement about Jesus confessing the conquerors' names before the Father and the angels alludes to the Synoptic saying about confessing and denying Jesus (Matt. 10:32–33 par.). The Synoptic statement includes what is implied here: those who deny Jesus will be denied by him on the last day.

The other "conquering" passages should be interpreted by means of those that are clearest. The one who conquers will receive "hidden manna" and a "white stone" (Rev. 2:17). The hidden manna and white

---

it was much of a problem according to the book of Revelation. See his thorough canvassing of the options. For a reference to the imperial cult, see Osborne 2002: 141.

182. For John, "there are clearly only two options: to conquer and inherit the eschatological promises, or to suffer the second death in the lake of fire (21:8)" (Bauckham 1993a: 92).

stone are pictures of eternal life.[183] The white stone may designate what is needed to enter the "heavenly banquet," for stones were used for "admission to public occasions."[184] Those who conquer will also rule with Jesus over the nations (Rev. 2:26–28; 3:21), and such rule is not limited to specially faithful Christians but rather is the portion of all believers. Those who conquer will be made pillars in God's temple, and the name of God and of the new Jerusalem will be written on them (Rev. 3:12). In other words, they will belong in the new Jerusalem and will be part of the people of God. Bauckham rightly says, "In a sense the whole book is about the way the Christians of the seven churches may, by being victorious with the specific situations of their own churches, enter the new Jerusalem."[185] No temple actually exists in the new Jerusalem in any case, for God and the Lamb are the temple (Rev. 21:22). Hence, saying that believers are pillars in the temple indicates that they belong to the people of God, that they will live in God's presence forever.

The "conquering" theme occurs in two other places in Revelation. Believers conquer the devil "by the blood of the lamb and by the word of their testimony, for they loved not their lives even unto death" (Rev. 12:11). The conquering by believers is grounded in the work of Christ, who gave his blood to redeem them from sin. And yet believers will not ultimately conquer unless they are willing to give their lives for the gospel. That conquering involves eternal life is clear from the last reference in Rev. 21:7. In this section the promised new heavens and earth have arrived (Rev. 21:1–8). The new Jerusalem has become a reality, and God now dwells with his people, wiping every tear from their eyes. The water of life is free to all who are thirsty (Rev. 21:6). The freeness of the gift offered does not contradict the need to conquer. Only those who conquer will inherit life and serve as God's children (Rev. 21:7). Those who do not conquer are cowards, unfaithful, murderers, those who commit sexual sin, engage in idolatry, and practice lying. They will face the second death, which is the lake of fire (Rev. 21:8). It is clear, then, that conquering is necessary to avoid the second death—the lake of fire itself.

The necessity of believers overcoming can also be described as repentance (Rev. 2:5, 16, 21–22; 3:3, 19). If believers fail to repent, Jesus will remove their lampstand (Rev. 2:5). The sharp sword of judgment will be wielded against those who refuse to repent (Rev. 2:16). Those

183. See Beale 1999b: 252.

184. Caird 1966: 42. For a helpful survey of the background, see Aune 1997: 189–91. Aune also maintains that eternal life is what is promised with these illustrations. See also Osborne 2002: 147–49, although his view that it relates to the present as well as the future is doubtful because in every letter the promise for conquerors relates to the eschatological future.

185. Bauckham 1993a: 14.

who stubbornly persist in sexual sin and do not repent will experience distress and even death (Rev. 2:21–23). Jesus will come like a thief and will judge those who resist repentance (Rev. 3:3). Earnest repentance is demanded, for Jesus will spit out of his mouth those who are lukewarm (Rev. 3:16, 19). The Christian life cannot merely be an initial moment of repentance; only those who continue to repent will receive the final reward. Believers must be faithful to death in order to obtain the crown of life (Rev. 2:10). If they are to avoid judgment, they must "hold fast" their faith until Jesus comes (Rev. 2:25). Only those who do not defile their garments will walk with Jesus in white clothing (Rev. 3:4). Genuine believers do not deny Jesus' name (Rev. 3:8), and they endure and hold fast what they have been taught (Rev. 3:10–11).

If believers must repent, it comes as no surprise that unbelievers too must repent and turn to God. Indeed, the judgments that God poured out on the world are intended to bring human beings to repentance, so that they turn to God when they see the consequences of evil. Many, however, do not humble themselves when God's judgments fall. They continue to worship their idols and do not turn from evil (Rev. 9:20–21). Instead of repenting and turning to God in faith, they become enraged against him because of their own pain and curse him (Rev. 16:9–11). The judgments are intended to bring them to repentance so that they would glorify God (Rev. 16:9). We can conclude from this that God is glorified when human beings repent and turn to him. And there is some evidence that God's judgments have a positive result, shaking some out of their doldrums, so that they glorify God by putting their faith in him (Rev. 11:13; cf. 14:7; 15:4).

In Revelation John emphasizes the concrete expression of faith in daily life. He addresses a situation in which believers faced persecution from Rome and were being enticed to compromise. John focuses not on the faith that produces obedience but rather on the obedience that is required to receive the final reward. If Revelation was written by the same John who wrote the Fourth Gospel, it is clear that elsewhere John places emphasis on believing as the sum and substance of what God demands of human beings. The only work that God requires is believing in the one whom he sent (John 6:29). In Revelation, on the other hand, we see the same kaleidoscope from a different perspective. Genuine faith cannot be isolated from the whole of life, as if it were simply a private and subjective experience. The whole of the NT clarifies that faith works, that it has a transforming effect. Hence, John writes to summon believers to endure even if they are destined for imprisonment or death (Rev. 13:9–10). Those who endure must keep God's commands and continue in "their faith in Jesus" (Rev. 14:12). The last phrase, *pistin Iēsou*, should be translated "faith in Jesus" (so the ESV), so that faith in

Jesus is inseparable from obedience.[186] Those who belong to the Lamb are "faithful" (Rev. 17:14). They are willing to give their lives for the sake of their devotion to Jesus (Rev. 20:4).

The 144,000 symbolically represent the whole people of God, both Jews and Gentiles.[187] John draws on the OT in saying that they are "virgins" and undefiled with women (Rev. 14:4). He does not mean that they are literally virgins, nor does John teach here that sexual relations automatically defile. The OT often compares idolatry to harlotry, and John's words must be placed against this backdrop.[188] Saying that the 144,000 are virgins and undefiled means that they faithfully worship the Lamb. They have not compromised with Rome and capitulated to pressure by adoring the beast. They are "blameless" (Rev. 14:5) not because they are sinless, but because they have remained devoted to the true God. Bauckham also suggests that virginity alludes to the demand for purity for those waging war (cf. Deut. 23:9–14; 1 Sam. 21:5; 2 Sam. 11:9–13), and hence God's people are dedicated to the Lord in the battle with the beast,[189] but they win the battle by enduring in faith and obedience to the end, not by attacking their foes physically. They wear "bright and pure" linen, and this linen represents their righteous actions (Rev. 19:8, 14). Conversely, those who are unclean are excluded from the heavenly city (Rev. 21:27), particularly those who engage in falsehood and do what is abominable. Only those with washed robes can enter the heavenly city (Rev. 22:14). "Outside are the dogs and sorcerers and the sexually immoral and murderers and idolaters and everyone who loves and practices falsehood" (Rev. 22:15).

Final judgment, then, is according to works. The context of the seven letters, as I argued above, exhorts believers to persevere until the end in order to receive salvation. Hence, the judgment and reward according to works relates to eternal life (Rev. 2:23). Blessing is reserved for those who keep the words of John's prophecy (Rev. 1:3; 22:7). When Jesus comes and passes judgment from the white throne, he will repay each one in accord with his or her works (Rev. 20:11–15; 22:12).[190] The judgment according to works should not be set in opposition to those whose names

---

186. Osborne (2002: 541–42) shows that faith in Jesus is inseparably linked with faithfulness to him. A reference to faith in terms of doctrinal content (so Beale 1999b: 766–67) does not fit as naturally with the emphasis on perseverance here, though Beale does not rule out other possibilities. Aune (1997: 837–38) identifies the phrase as an objective genitive: faithfulness to Jesus.

187. So Beale 1999b: 412–13, 416–23.

188. See the programmatic work of Ortlund 2002.

189. Bauckham 1993a: 78.

190. For the notion that both the righteous and the unrighteous are judged according to their works, see Osborne 2002: 721–22; Beale 1999b: 1032–33; R. Mounce 1977: 365–66.

are inscribed in the book of life, for those whose names are in the book of life have practiced what is good and true.

Some might read Revelation as if it excludes the necessity of faith. However, we must remind ourselves of the specific purpose of the book. John writes to exhort believers to persevere and obey in order to receive a final reward. The threat that believers face impels John to emphasize the necessity of faithfulness, and so he focuses on the result of faith rather than on the faith that produces such obedience. John emphasizes that only those who do God's will and keep his commands will receive the final reward on the last day. Those who fail to worship God and the Lamb and give their devotion to the beast will face judgment forever.

Conclusion

The variety of situations addressed in the NT literature and the diverse purposes of the writings mean that various themes are emphasized. In some instances faith is trumpeted as the only means by which the blessing of eternal life is received, whereas in other cases the necessity of obedience and discipleship takes center stage. I have argued in this chapter that there is a fundamental unity of approach throughout the NT. Faith is fundamental and primary for a right relation with God or for receiving eternal life. Human beings cannot obtain an eternal reward on the basis of their works, for human sin intervenes and rules out works as the pathway for blessing. Faith receives from God the salvation accomplished through Jesus Christ. Faith looks away from itself and gives glory to God as the one who delivers human beings from sin and death. Indeed, faith specifically casts its hope upon Jesus Christ as the crucified and risen Lord. Saving faith finds its roots in the cross of Jesus Christ, and so faith looks outward to what God has done in Christ instead of gazing inward upon the ability of the human subject.

The faith that saves, however, is not an abstraction, and it cannot be separated from repentance and the transformation of one's life. The NT writers never imagined a passive faith that could be sundered from a life of discipleship. Paul himself, the champion of faith, insists that true faith manifests itself in love, that only persevering faith is saving faith. Those who do not do good works will not inherit God's kingdom. Virtually all the NT writers emphasize that one must persevere to the end in order to be saved on the eschatological day. Only those who overcome will receive the final reward. Those who fall away from the living God will face him as a consuming fire. Believers confirm their calling and election by their good works, or, as James says, the faith that saves must be accompanied by good works. The priority of faith in the NT rules out legalism, but it also eliminates antinomianism. Those who have truly come to know Jesus Christ keep his commandments and show by their love for fellow believers that they are truly born again. Only those who enter through the narrow gate of obedience will be saved. Purported believers may do signs, wonders, and exorcisms, but if they do not bear good fruit, they will show that Jesus never knew them as his own.

The remarkable emphasis on the need for a transformed life does not cancel out the priority of faith. Instead, it helps readers discern the authenticity of faith so that genuine faith can be distinguished from mere notional faith—faith that resides in the intellect but has not penetrated the heart and life. All good works flow from faith and thus do not become an occasion for human boasting. The changed lives of believers simply reveal the object of their trust. It demonstrates whether they are a rotten tree or a healthy one. The NT writers do not call on dead trees to produce fruit; they call for a new tree and a new creation. Such newness is the work, as we have seen, of the Father, the Son, and the Spirit. It has already burst on the scene with the death and resurrection of Christ, and yet believers await the final act in the drama: the coming of Jesus Christ to complete the saving work that has been inaugurated.

16

❧ ❧ ❧ ❧ ❧ ❧ ❧ ❧ ❧ ❧ ❧ ❧ ❧ ❧ ❧ ❧ ❧ ❧

The Law and Salvation History

Introduction

We saw in the preceding chapter that the life of believers can be described in terms of faith and obedience. Obedience in the NT should never be separated from faith, for all obedience that is pleasing to God flows from faith. Hence, when we speak of the moral life of believers we must not abstract it from faith, as if faith sits in one compartment tightly sealed off from obedience in another. In considering the life of believers, we must investigate the role of the law, for the NT view of the OT law demonstrates both continuity and discontinuity with the OT.

The fulfillment of God's promises in Christ did not merely lead NT believers to ratify and maintain everything contained in the OT law. We see in the NT both continuity and discontinuity with the OT law. There is continuity in that the coming of Christ brings to fruition the OT promises of salvation and the righteousness demanded by God; there is discontinuity in that the covenant under which the Jewish believers lived is no longer in force, and believers are not members of ethnic Israel. The role of the OT law in the NT is one of the most complicated and controversial issues in NT theology. The goal here is to trace out the theology of NT writers on this matter. Since the role of the law is a matter of particular debate in Matthew and Luke-Acts, we will examine Mark first and then

Matthew and Luke-Acts. Then we will take up the Johannine literature, the Pauline view, and the remainder of the NT.

Mark

Isolating Mark from Matthew and Luke will lead to some repetition, but it is necessary in this instance because the Matthean and Lukan views of the law require a more detailed examination. The Markan view of the law must be set against the backdrop of the coming of the kingdom and the already–not yet fulfillment in Christ. We could fall into the trap of considering the texts in isolation and thus fail to see that the role of the law must fit into the story line of the fulfillment of God's promises in Jesus Christ. The law, in other words, must be understood in light of the gospel—the story of Christ's ministry, death, and resurrection that we find in Mark's Gospel. The plotline of Mark's Gospel informs the readers that the law always pointed toward Jesus Christ. The promises of the kingdom come to their fulfillment in him, and so the Markan account of the Lord's Supper suggests that the Passover meal points toward Jesus' death (Mark 14:12–25).[1] His death fulfilled God's covenantal promises to deliver his people. Hence, all the individual texts that we examine fit into the larger plotline of the Gospel and cannot be separated from the fulfillment of God's kingdom promises and the coming of the Christ, which I have elaborated on earlier in this book.

Some texts emphasize Jesus' sovereign freedom and authority over the OT law. For example, the OT law teaches that one who touches a leper becomes unclean (cf. Lev. 13:45–46; 22:4–6; Num. 5:2). When Jesus touched the leper, however, he did not contract uncleanness (Mark 1:40–45). Jesus' touch had a transforming and purifying power, so that rather than becoming unclean himself, he cleansed the leper and freed him from his leprosy.[2] In the OT that which is unclean defiles what is clean, but in this instance Jesus, as the clean one, purifies what is unclean by his transforming touch. Jesus' action does not invalidate the OT law, nor does he teach here that the law regarding leprosy is passé. Nevertheless, Jesus' transformation of the leper by touching him suggests a new stance toward the OT law. The law of leprosy must be interpreted in light of the coming of Jesus instead of understanding Jesus in terms of the requirements laid down for leprosy.

---

1. On the Passover meal as a pointer to Jesus' death, see Bolt 2004: 103–6; France 2002: 567–71.

2. See France 2002: 118. Westerholm (1978: 67–71) rightly argues that Jesus was unconcerned about ritual impurity.

Several disputes about the law are found in Jesus' controversies with the Pharisees (Mark 2:1–3:6). Jesus' eating with tax collectors and sinners is also suggestive in regard to his stance relative to the law (Mark 2:15–17).[3] We have no indication here that Jesus disregarded OT regulations with respect to food. The religious leaders complained not about the food that Jesus ate but rather about the company he kept when eating. The concern seems to be that their impurity would defile Jesus. Once again Jesus' view counters the cultural consensus. He saw himself as a doctor who could heal and purify those who were unclean. Sinners do not defile him. On the contrary, he cleanses and transforms sinners.

Another controversy broke out over fasting (Mark 2:18–22). Jesus' disciples did not fast, but the disciples both of John and of the Pharisees fasted regularly. The OT law did not mandate fasting, except on the Day of Atonement (Lev. 16:29, 31; 23:27, 32; Num. 29:27), though other fasts were added as time passed (Esther 9:31; Zech. 8:19). Nevertheless, Jesus' response to the demand for fasting is again suggestive of his view of the OT law.[4] Jesus did not engage in a halakic debate over whether fasting was required. He avoided a technical legal discussion. Instead, he identified himself as the bridegroom and contended that fasting is out of the question during a wedding. His coming led to a radical reevaluation of previous religious practices. To require fasting now that he had arrived as the bridegroom is like patching a new piece of cloth onto an old garment. The new cloth must not be patched over the old rules and regulations; rather, the old must give way to the new. New wine cannot be stored in old wineskins, for the newly fermented wine will burst the old wineskins. The reference to new wine signifies that the eschaton has arrived in Jesus and his ministry, the days when the mountains would drip with wine (Amos 9:13–14). The new wine being consumed in Jesus' ministry bespeaks the dawning of the new creation.[5] Hence, the newness of Jesus' coming means a radical reevaluation of religious customs and practices. They must be interpreted in light of his coming.

Two Sabbath controversies (Mark 2:23–3:6) are also instructive in discerning Jesus' view of the OT law.[6] The first concerns the disciples plucking heads of grain while walking through grainfields (Mark 2:23–28). Luke adds that they rubbed the grains in their hands before eating them (Luke 6:1). The Pharisees protested because these actions occurred on the Sabbath. Jesus again refused to enter into a debate over halakah. Presumably, he could have argued from Deut. 23:25 that what the disciples were doing did not constitute work, and therefore the charges

---

3. See Lane 1974: 103–4.
4. Here, however, the issue of the OT is not directly addressed.
5. Rightly Bolt 2004: 25–26.
6. On Jesus' view of the Sabbath, see Westerholm 1978: 92–103.

could be set aside as fallacious. Instead, he appealed to the story of David eating the bread of the presence and giving it to his companions (1 Sam. 21:1–6). What David did was not legal but nevertheless was justified because he was God's anointed. Jesus appealed to human need, saying that the law was created for the sake of human beings, not vice versa. Nonetheless, the main point is that Jesus, as the Son of Man, "is lord even of the Sabbath" (Mark 2:28). The focus should be not on what the Sabbath required but rather on Jesus as the Son of Man, suggesting that the law points forward to Jesus as Lord and must be interpreted in the light of his coming. The healing of the man with a withered hand runs along similar lines (Mark 3:1–6), even if the Christology is not as direct as what we find in Mark 2:23–28. Jesus voiced the principle that it is always fitting to do good on the Sabbath. Jesus could have selected a different day to perform his healings and thus avoid controversy. By healing on the Sabbath, however, he indicated that the Sabbath must be interpreted as pointing forward to him and his work. The Sabbath must be interpreted eschatologically and christologically as well, for it too points to the final rest that the Lord will grant to his people.[7]

The Markan text on divorce suggests a new perspective on the OT law (Mark 10:2–12). Jesus acknowledged the Mosaic permission to divorce (Deut. 24:1–4) but relativized it. God's intention for marriage can be traced back to creation, where one man and one woman become one flesh in marriage (Gen. 1:27; 2:24). Divorce and remarriage, therefore, constitute adultery. Nor did Jesus in this text maintain that the Pharisees misinterpreted the text in Deuteronomy, though he may have believed that they did (see the discussion on Matthew below). In this instance he appealed to a creational norm rather than founding his judgment on the Mosaic law. It seems, therefore, that the binding nature of Mosaic legislation is relaxed.[8]

The most fascinating and complex text on the role of the OT law is Mark 7:1–23. The Pharisees and some of their scribes complained that Jesus' disciples did not wash their hands before eating, so that contrary to Pharisaic tradition ("the tradition of the elders" [Mark 7:5]) they ate with hands that were defiled. The modern reader must realize that the debate concerned not hygiene but rather purity requirements. Jesus rejected their criticism and turned the tables on the Pharisees, arguing that their practices were human traditions rather than divine requirements. Their traditions did not bring them closer to God, for although they praised him with their lips, their hearts were cold and distant from God. Moreover, their traditions actually displaced God's command to

7. So Bolt 2004: 26.
8. See France 2002: 388.

honor one's parents, which clearly involved financial support. Instead, Pharisaic tradition encouraged children to declare "Corban" (dedicated to God) financial gifts that should have helped parents in need of material assistance. Their tradition, in other words, trumped the word of God and his commands. Jesus clearly distinguished between the OT law (the word of God) and human traditions. The former is authoritative, the latter is not.

The story, however, does not end here. Jesus proceeded to tell the people that they cannot be defiled by what enters into them but only by what proceeds out of them. He explained further, when speaking privately to his disciples, that food does not defile, for it enters into the stomach, passes through one's system, and ends up in the sewer. Mark adds his own parenthetical comment to the account: "Thus he declared all foods clean" (Mark 7:19). Human beings are rendered unclean not by foods but rather by evil thoughts and actions, such as sexual sin, pride, stealing, and murder. Mark clearly understood Jesus to say that the food laws in the OT (Lev. 11:1–44; Deut. 14:3–21) were no longer normative.[9] Here we have the clearest indication in Mark that the OT law does not function in the same way with the coming of the kingdom and Jesus the Messiah.[10] The prescriptions of the OT law are not necessarily binding now that Jesus has arrived. They must be interpreted in light of his coming.[11]

This account is quite interesting because on the one hand, Jesus accepted the OT as the word of God that sits in judgment over human traditions, while on the other hand, he argued that the food laws in the OT are not binding upon believers. Is this a contradiction? It is unlikely that such a blatant contradiction would exist in the very same text. The solution perhaps lies in considering the Markan narrative as a whole and the theme that the OT points toward Jesus Christ. He is the sovereign Lord and interpreter of the OT. Mark does not work out in any detail the implications of what we find in Mark 7:1–23, but it seems that we are on the way to the notion of the law of Christ. Jesus' teaching, which Mark mentions quite often (Mark 1:21–22, 27; 2:13; 4:1–2; 6:2, 30, 34; 8:31; 9:31; 10:1; 11:17–18; 12:35, 38; 14:49), and his interpretation of the OT now function as authoritative for believers. If this is the case, then we learn from Mark 7:1–23 that the law of Christ includes the admoni-

9. Rightly Moo 1984: 14–15; France 2002: 277–79. Cf. Marcus 2000: 457–58, though he thinks that Mark transcends the historical Jesus here. Banks (1975: 144–45) wrongly limits Jesus' saying so that it only grants freedom to eat food defiled by idols.

10. Westerholm (1978: 82) rightly notes, however, that it took the church time to grasp the full implications of what Jesus said here.

11. For a fascinating attempt to work out purity issues relative to the historical Jesus, see Bryan 2002: 130–88.

tion to honor parents, while at the same time purity laws are no longer in force.

Jesus' challenge to the rich man fits with what I have suggested here. When the man inquired about what was necessary for eternal life, Jesus reminded him of commands from the OT law, focusing on directives from the Decalogue (Mark 10:17–19). Such commands, apart from the Sabbath, were still considered authoritative for the people of God, even after the coming of Christ. Nevertheless, the OT law must now be interpreted in light of the coming of Jesus Christ. The rich man could not be saved unless he gave up all and followed Jesus in discipleship (Mark 10:21). The OT law does not stand on its own and must be read in light of the story line of Scripture, which finds its climax in Jesus Christ. The message of the OT law was summarized from OT texts well known to every Jewish person (Mark 12:28–34). People must love the Lord with all of their beings and love their neighbors as themselves. These commands are of more importance than sacrifices and offerings.[12] Still, this text in Mark's Gospel cannot be abstracted from the narrative as a whole. If human beings truly love God, they will follow Jesus in discipleship. They will give their entire lives to him. Even the command to love God and neighbor must be interpreted in terms of the coming of Jesus Christ, for he is the one who fulfills the OT promise.

If we consider Mark from a wider angle, we see that readers are summoned to follow Jesus in discipleship. His death and suffering form the paradigm for the lives of believers. Hence, each one of the passion predictions is followed with instructions on the life of discipleship (Mark 8:31–9:1; 9:30–37; 10:32–45). Those who refuse to give up their lives for the sake of Jesus and the gospel will not be saved (Mark 8:35). Those who desire to be great in the kingdom must become the servants of all (Mark 9:32–37). Those who aspire to greatness must abandon secular grasping after greatness (Mark 10:35–45). Anything that functions as an obstacle for entering the kingdom must be removed from the lives of disciples (Mark 9:42–49).

Mark does not work out in detail any view of the OT law, but we have some indications that the prescriptions in the OT law are not necessarily binding upon Jesus' disciples.[13] The law must be interpreted in light of the coming of Jesus Christ. The OT law points to Christ and is fulfilled in him, and so the law must be interpreted in light of Christ, not vice versa.

---

12. France (2002: 478) remarks that what is said here "could not but hasten the Christian abandonment of the ritual elements of the Torah."

13. Schlatter (1997: 140) rightly cautions that Jesus did not offer a comprehensive and abstract ethical system, and his ethical teaching must not be segregated from the call to repentance (cf. Schlatter 1999: 69).

Matthew

Matthew's material on the law is more extensive than what we find in Mark.[14] The more comprehensive discussion of Matthew could be explained by his Gospel being longer than Mark's. It is also likely, however, that we find more material on the law because Matthew was addressed to Jewish Christians, who would have had a keen interest in what Jesus taught about the OT law. Matthew's view of the OT law must be integrated with the narrative framework and theology of the Gospel. The kingdom has been inaugurated in Jesus Christ, and he is the promised Messiah, the Lord, the Son of Man, and the Son of God. What the OT promised, therefore, is fulfilled in him. Any theology of the law must not be severed from the story line of the Gospel, which culminates in Jesus' death and resurrection. We noted earlier the importance of the fulfillment formulae in Matthew.[15] They have a particular significance in assessing the Matthean conception of the law, for they clearly teach that Jesus fulfilled the promises made in the OT. We expect Matthew, then, to teach that Jesus fulfills what is found in the OT. Indeed, Jesus' sovereign authority as the interpreter of the law reveals that the law is subordinate to him, and that the law, rightly interpreted, supports a high Christology.[16]

In many respects, of course, Matthew's perspective on the law is shared with Mark. Many of the same accounts are contained in Matthew, and often the differences between the stories are quite minimal. Redaction criticism has helpfully isolated the differences among the Synoptic Gospels, but in some instances scholars have gone to the extreme of reading significance out of virtually every difference among the accounts.[17] The cleansing of the leper suggests a new stance toward the OT law because Jesus is not defiled by the leper, but rather his touch purifies the unclean one (Matt. 8:1–4). As in Mark, Jesus defends eating with tax collectors and sinners (Matt. 9:9–13). The controversy unfolds in a context in which Matthew follows Jesus in discipleship. Jesus, rather than the law, takes center stage. The Matthean account adds to the story from Hosea 6:6, "Go and learn what this means, 'I desire mercy, and not sacrifice'" (Matt. 9:13). The separation from tax collectors and sinners practiced by the Pharisees actually contravenes the OT, which calls for mercy and compassion. We should not underestimate, on the other hand, the newness of Jesus' gospel. Jesus is the bridegroom, and

14. For study on Matthew's view of the law, see McConnell 1969; Snodgrass 1988: 536–54; Meier 1976; Banks 1975; Hübner 1973; Barth 1963; Suggs 1970: 99–127; Broer 1986.

15. See the discussion in chapter 1.

16. So Meier 1994: 1046.

17. For example, Gundry 1994.

Jewish religious practices cannot be imposed on the new order that he brings (Matt. 9:14–17). The new wine of the gospel must be put into new wineskins, for the age in which the new wine of the eschaton is flowing has dawned (Amos 9:11–15; Joel 3:18).

In comparing the Matthean texts on the law to Mark, we find that Matthew emphasizes more than Mark the continuity between the OT and Jesus' teaching and practice. Such an emphasis is not startling, for Matthew was addressing Jewish Christians. The Pharisaic teaching did not free people but rather burdened them, whereas Jesus gives rest (Matt. 11:28–30): "My yoke is easy, and my burden is light" (Matt. 11:30). Jesus' pronouncement here appears to stand in contrast with the requirements that the Pharisees imposed on the Sabbath, for the two accounts about the Sabbath follow the declaration that Jesus' yoke is easy (Matt. 12:1–14). We should note further the centrality of Christology that envelops the accounts about the Sabbath.[18] The Father has handed all things over to the Son, and the Son and the Father have exclusive and mutual knowledge of one another (Matt. 11:27). Those who long for rest must come to Jesus (Matt. 11:28). Jesus is God's chosen servant, and he will include the Gentiles in his saving plan. He will not, in contrast to the Pharisees, crush the bruised reed or "quench a smoldering wick" (Matt. 12:20 NRSV). As we saw in Mark, therefore, the Sabbath controversies in Matthew (Matt. 12:1–14) should be interpreted in light of the Christology of the Gospel. Jesus is the new David and the Son of Man who is Lord of the Sabbath (Matt. 12:1–8). He is the one who is greater than the temple, and thus he has the prerogative to do what he wills on the Sabbath (Matt. 12:5–6).[19] Matthew again adds the logion from Hosea 6:6 indicting the leaders for being bereft of mercy and compassion. We should note again that Jesus did not venture into a detailed halakic debate with the Pharisees but rather appealed to his sovereign authority. The account of the man with the withered hand (Matt. 12:9–14) is generally similar to the Markan account. However, Matthew includes Jesus' defense of the lawfulness of his healing. If the Pharisees liberated a sheep from a pit on the Sabbath, then healing a man on the Sabbath was permissible (Matt. 12:11–12). Both Mark and Matthew emphasize that the law must be interpreted in reference to Jesus, but Matthew explains to his Jewish audience how Jesus' healings accord with the OT law.

The account of the rich man in Matthew is quite similar to Mark's (Matt. 19:16–30). Jesus enjoined him to keep the commands from the Decalogue, but he must follow Jesus and give up all in order to receive

18. Rightly Thielman 1999: 63–66.
19. Beale (2004: 179) argues that even the destruction of the temple may point to Jesus as the new temple.

eternal life. The entire law is summed up, as in Mark, with the injunctions to love God and one's neighbor (Matt. 22:34–40).[20] The law is also summed up in the golden rule (Matt. 7:12): do to others what you wish them to do to you.

Some scholars understand Matthew as endorsing a very conservative view of the OT law. Matthew often sets forth the continuity between Jesus' teaching and the OT law.[21] We have seen above that Matthew occasionally provides OT justification for Jesus' controversial actions from the OT—explanations that are lacking in Mark.[22] Only Matthew includes that those in distress from the siege of Jerusalem should pray that their flight might not occur on the Sabbath (Matt. 24:20) and mentions offering sacrifices in the temple (Matt. 5:24). Believers are even enjoined to do whatever the Pharisees teach (Matt. 23:2–3), which is quite astonishing in light of the sharp criticisms of the Pharisees that permeate this Gospel.[23] Justice, mercy, and faith are exalted above tithing, but tithing is still commended and does not appear to be abolished (Matt. 23:23–24).[24]

It might appear from the foregoing texts that Matthew only argues for continuity in his view of the OT law.[25] Certainly, Matthew focuses on the fulfillment of the law in Christ (Matt. 5:17–20), but this fulfillment also involves some discontinuity. The new wine must be placed into new wineskins (Matt. 9:14–17). Jesus did not clearly abolish the Sabbath, and yet he is the sovereign Lord and interpreter of the Sabbath (Matt. 12:1–14). The wise scribe in the kingdom is like the householder who rightly assembles both new and old and relates the old to the new (Matt. 13:52) insofar as it relates to the kingdom of God.[26] The wise scribe, in other words, does not merely repeat the old but rather explains how the old relates to the new and is fulfilled in the new, so that the old does not retain precisely the same status now that the new has arrived. The age of fulfillment prophesied in the OT has commenced with the coming of John the Baptist (Matt. 11:13).

20. Davies and Allison (1988: 508–9) demonstrate that love goes beyond written commands. See also Mohrlang 1984: 21.

21. For the view that the historical Jesus upheld the OT law, see Vermes 1993: 11–45.

22. E. Sanders (1985: 245–69) argues that the historical Jesus was essentially conservative with respect to the law, though he did not see the Torah as the final word or as binding forever.

23. Luz (1995: 122) probably is right in saying that the language is hyperbolic. So also Davies and Allison 1997: 269–70 (with a helpful survey of various interpretations).

24. But contra Mohrlang (1984: 12–14), scribal tradition is not in force for Matthew.

25. See Mohrlang 1984: 42–43; Luz 1995: 14–15.

26. See Hagner 1993b: 402.

We could overstate the element of continuity in Jesus' teaching in Matthew. Warning about the dangers of flight during the Sabbath (Matt. 24:20) should not be understood as necessarily ratifying the ongoing validity of the Sabbath for all. Jews living in Israel would find travel difficult on the Sabbath in any case.[27] Similarly, Jesus' words about offerings (Matt. 5:24) and tithing (Matt. 23:23–24), if taken seriously as words of the historical Jesus, addressed Jews who lived under the OT law. They do not, therefore, necessarily endorse sacrifices and tithing in perpetuity.[28] Jesus spoke to Jews about the religious practices of their day. Jesus himself, of course, observed the same regulations, but we would go too far to conclude that his words constitute a ratification of such commands in the future.

We must balance carefully the elements of continuity and discontinuity in the Matthean view of the law. Hengel argued that Jesus' command to "leave the dead to bury their own dead" (Matt. 8:22) contravenes the law, demonstrating a radical abrogation of the law.[29] Bockmuehl has carefully sifted the evidence and demonstrated that Hengel's view is unpersuasive.[30] Hengel relies on evidence from the third century AD and later to support his conclusion. Moreover, even the Tannaitic evidence marshaled by Hengel does not clearly point to an abrogation of the law. Hence, Matt. 8:22 (cf. Luke 9:62) does not clearly support the nullification of the law. Bockmuehl's own solution, that the saying may reflect Nazirite motifs, is intriguing but cannot be established from the existing evidence.[31] On the other hand, we have already seen that some texts point toward discontinuity. The whole of the law finds its fulfillment in Christ, but the time of fulfillment means that believers are not under the prescriptions of the law in the same way as before.[32] Matthew, like Mark, includes the account about the tradition of the elders and Jesus' saying that only what comes out of a person defiles. Matthew, unlike Mark, does not add the comment that Jesus thereby cleansed all foods (cf. Mark 7:19).[33] Some have

27. Contra Davies and Allison 1997: 349–50. Cf. Carson 1984: 501. Hagner (1995: 702) argues, on the other hand, that the issue being considered here is the difficulty of observing the Sabbath during such days.

28. See the pointed comments in Carson 1984: 481.

29. Hengel (1996: 3–15) propounded this view in a celebrated essay.

30. Bockmuehl 2000: 23–48.

31. Supporting Bockmuehl's assessment of Hengel is Fletcher-Louis 2003. Fletcher-Louis rightly argues, however, that Bockmuehl's own proposal regarding a Nazirite background is not compelling, and that the point of the saying is that those who do not follow Jesus are spiritually dead and hence his followers have no responsibility to bury them.

32. See France 1989: 191–97. Stettler (2004: 166–69) points out that Jesus emphasizes ethical rather than ritual purity.

33. Bryan (2002: 165) maintains that the issue here is second-degree impurity (i.e., foods that were defiled by contact with other things that were impure rather than unclean

concluded from this that Matthew sustains a more conservative view of the law.[34] Such a conclusion is difficult to sustain, for the declaration that foods entering the mouth do not defile clearly sets aside OT prescriptions (Matt. 15:11, 17–18), even if Matthew does not add the same comment found in Mark.[35]

A clear indication of discontinuity in Matthew relates to the temple tax required of every Israelite (Exod. 30:11–16).[36] Jesus sovereignly declared to Peter that the sons are free from paying the tax (Matt. 17:24–27).[37] Peter paid, not because it was required but only to avoid giving offense. Matthew does not state why this regulation is no longer in force, but if we consider the narrative outline of his Gospel, we receive a clue. The temple tax was required for the ransom of each Israelite. In Matthew, however, Jesus' death provides the ransom for each one (Matt. 20:28). Further, Jesus predicts the destruction of the temple, signifying God's judgment on the old order. In Jesus the new has arrived, and his coming means that the old must be interpreted in light of the coming of the kingdom and salvation in Jesus.[38]

The most extensive discussion on the law in Matthew appears in Matt. 5:17–20.[39] Jesus emphasizes that he has come to fulfill rather than abolish the law, so that even the least of the commandments should not be relaxed but rather enforced. This statement could be understood as

---

foods per se). But Stettler (2004: 169) rightly argues that it is much more likely that Jesus refers to unclean foods themselves here, for "it is much more difficult to imagine that the church would have taken a saying of Jesus which referred merely to human rules (namely the washing of hands) and turned it into a refutation of important commandments of the Torah." See the entire discussion in Stettler 2004: 168–71. See also Wright 1996: 397.

34. So Snodgrass 1988: 552–53; Barth 1963: 89–91; Mohrlang 1984: 11–12; Davies and Allison 1991: 535.

35. Rightly Carson 1984: 351–52; Thielman 1999: 66–68; France 2002: 279; contra Mohrlang 1984: 11–12.

36. In defense of a reference to the temple tax rather than a tax from Rome, see Davies and Allison 1991: 738–41.

37. See Schlatter 1997: 211; Stettler 2004: 174. Banks (1975: 92), on the other hand, maintains that this passage does not clearly set aside the law. But Bryan (2002: 225–29) shows that the law is abrogated here.

38. Stettler (2004: 177) comments, "We need to understand that Jesus, as the Holy One of God, fulfills the Torah in its deepest sense. His coming, his actions, and his death ultimately sanctify his people. Therefore, there is no longer any need for the literal keeping of the purity Torah."

39. Meier (1976: 80) argues that the focus is on the predictive function of the law. Banks (1975: 210) says that the law is fulfilled and transcended in Jesus. Carson (1984: 142–44) maintains that the law finds its eschatological fulfillment in Jesus. Davies and Allison (1988: 485–87) suggest that the law is eschatological, that it points to Jesus, and that a new law is established. Snodgrass (1988: 547) rightly remarks that the notion of accomplishing or doing the law must be included here. For a survey of the issue, see McConnell 1969: 14–29.

saying that every single law of the OT must be observed by Christians. We must recall, however, that the word "fulfill" (*plēroō*) is regularly used in fulfillment formulae in Matthew, and that OT prophecies find their goal in Jesus Christ. Furthermore, we have already observed that the entirety of the OT law is not binding for Matthew. Otherwise, the temple tax would continue to be an obligation. Hence, Jesus likely means that the OT law continues to be authoritative for believers, but only insofar as it is fulfilled in Jesus Christ. Such a fulfillment means that there are elements of continuity and discontinuity.[40] Moreover, the subsequent verses (Matt. 5:21–48) reveal that Jesus is the sovereign interpreter of the law. The contrast between "You have heard that it was said" (Matt. 5:21, 27, 33, 38, 43)[41] and "But I say to you" (Matt. 5:22, 28, 32, 34, 39, 44) indicates that the law points to, is fulfilled by, and interpreted by Jesus.

It seems that Jesus often counters a misinterpretation of the law by his contemporaries in this section.[42] The prohibition against murder cannot be restricted merely to avoidance of murder; it also includes unrighteous anger (Matt. 5:21–26). Those who allow anger free reign in their lives are liable to judgment in hell unless, by confessing their sins, they reconcile with those whom they have injured. The Pharisees and scribes limited the prohibition against adultery to the physical act (Matt. 5:27–32), but Jesus located adultery in the heart, contending that those who desire women in their hearts are guilty of adultery. Those who want to conquer illicit sexual desires must deal severely with errant sexual thoughts and must, so to speak, gouge out the eye and cut off the hand. Similarly, those who divorce their wives and marry others are guilty of adultery unless their spouses are guilty of sexual sin (*porneia* [Matt. 5:31–32; 19:3–12]).[43] It is unclear that Jesus actually abolished here the OT law about divorce in Deut. 24:1–4. The text in Deut. 24, in any case, does not commend divorce but simply permits it.[44] It seems that some of the interpreters of Jesus' day misinterpreted Deuteronomy, so that some concluded that divorce was permissible for virtually any reason. Some have suggested that the permission to

40. Davies and Allison (1988: 490) remark that circumcision is excluded because it was understood to be unnecessary.

41. Matt. 5:31 reads, "It was also said."

42. Contra L. Cheung 2003: 112. Thielman (1999: 49–58) defends well the view that Jesus actually abolishes elements of the OT law here, but I will argue that the text points in another direction. Mohrlang (1984: 12–14, 47) wrongly argues that even scribal tradition is authoritative for Matthew, concluding that the Pauline view of the law is "more fully thought-out and consistent than Matthew's."

43. I will reserve for chapter 18 a fuller discussion of divorce in the NT.

44. Rightly Mohrlang 1984: 12; Snodgrass 1988: 552; Moo 1984: 19–21. Contra McConnell 1969: 51, 62; Westerholm 1978: 114–25.

divorce for reason of *porneia* is a Matthean redactional addition so as to modify Jesus' strict teaching.[45] This view seems to have some plausibility because the exception is lacking in the other Synoptics. Nevertheless, the hypothesis should be rejected. We have no evidence elsewhere that Matthew modifies or lessens the radical nature of Jesus' teaching. The requirements for righteousness in Matthew are not less strict when compared to the other Gospels.[46] It is Matthew who insists that the righteousness of those of the kingdom must exceed that of the scribes and Pharisees (Matt. 5:20; cf. 5:48). In this case, then, Jesus did not nullify the OT law per se, but he argued that it must be interpreted in light of God's creational intention.

We seem to have a clear abrogation of the OT law when Jesus forbade his disciples to take oaths (Matt. 5:33–37). But a closer look suggests that he responded to an abuse of oath-taking practiced in his day. When we consult Matt. 23:16–22, we learn that some Jews engaged in casuistry in oath-taking.[47] Swearing by the gold of the sanctuary or the gift on the altar obligated one to fulfill the oath, whereas swearing by the temple or the altar itself was nonbinding. The text also suggests that swearing by heaven made an oath optional (Matt. 5:34; 23:22). Hence, Jesus did not literally forbid the taking of oaths but hyperbolically emphasized that human beings must tell the truth, so that a simple yes or no should suffice.[48] Westerholm rightly argues that Jesus did not intend to formulate a new rule here that forbade oath-taking; rather, Jesus was concerned with a heart that pleased God, and so his moral instruction should not be viewed as a comprehensive new law.[49] When Jesus was on trial, he responded to the high priest who demanded that he speak under oath (Matt. 26:63–64). If we consider the matter canonically, we see that Paul invoked oath formulas (Rom. 1:9; 9:1; 2 Cor. 1:23; Gal. 1:20), and he seems to be familiar with the tradition found in the Sermon on the Mount. Finally, according to Heb. 6:14–20, God himself takes an oath to comfort his own with the surety of his promise.

45. Stein, *DJG* 197.

46. Davies and Allison (1988: 531) suggest that the exception in Matthew may have been implied in Mark 10:9–10 and Luke 16:18.

47. See Westerholm 1978: 105–6.

48. That Jesus spoke hyperbolically is acknowledged by others (so Davies and Allison 1988: 535–36; Stein 1988: 11–12). Hence, Jesus reminded his hearers of the original intention of the law (so Snodgrass 1988: 551; contra Banks 1975: 194; McConnell 1969: 63–65; Moo 1984: 21). Westerholm (1978: 108) goes beyond the evidence in detecting an opposition to statutes per se in this episode.

49. Westerholm 1978: 104–13.

Jesus appeared to cancel the OT law in overturning the prescription "an eye for an eye and a tooth for a tooth" (Matt. 5:38).[50] Instead, he enjoined his disciples to nonresistance and to doing positive good to those who mistreat them (Matt. 5:38–42). It seems, however, that Jesus countered a misinterpretation of the OT law instead of abolishing it.[51] The principle of "an eye for an eye and a tooth for a tooth" reaches back to judicial contexts in the OT (Exod. 21:22–27; Lev. 24:17–22; Deut. 19:15–21). The punishment should be proportional to the crime, so that it fits the crime. Hence, cruelty that inflicts excessive penalties on the one committing the infraction must be avoided. Similarly, lax sentences given out of partiality to the defendant are prohibited as well. What Jesus spoke against here is the practice of applying the judicial principle that the punishment should fit the crime to the *personal* sphere. Individually, disciples are to forgive and do good to those who oppress them. Disciples should not take upon themselves the task of righting the wrongs of the world, as if they should personally dispense justice. Such a stance opens up the door to a desire for personal revenge. Governmental authorities, on the other hand, still assign penalties on the basis of just compensation. If the punishment is not proportional to the crime, then the basis for all justice is removed. Hence, Jesus does not abolish the OT law but rather corrects a wrong interpretation.

Nor did Jesus abolish the OT law when he said that disciples should love their enemies (Matt. 5:43–48). He again reacted to a misinterpretation of the OT that justified hating one's enemies. Love of neighbor extends to all without discrimination (Lev. 19:17–18). If Israelites saw an ox or donkey of an enemy wandering, they were to return it (Exod. 23:4). If they saw the donkey of one who hated them needing help from a burden, they were to render assistance (Exod. 23:5). It seems, therefore, that Jesus corrected a misapprehension of the OT law.

In summary, the Matthean view of the law is complex. The law points to and is fulfilled in Jesus. The law finds its climax in the arrival of the kingdom and the coming of Jesus as the Messiah, the Lord, the Son of Man, and the Son of God. He is the sovereign interpreter and Lord of the Mosaic law. In some instances Jesus corrects a wrong interpretation of the OT law. Now that the Christ has come, there is both discontinuity and continuity with regard to the law. Some of the norms of the law continue to be in force with the arrival of the kingdom and the coming

50. So Meier 1976: 157; Barth 1963: 94.
51. Davies and Allison (1988: 542) rightly comment, "While in the Pentateuch the *lex talionis* belongs to the judiciary process, this is not the sphere of application in Matthew. Jesus, to repeat, does not overthrow the principle of equivalent compensation on an institutional level—that question is just not addressed—but declares it illegitimate for his followers to apply it to their private disputes." See also Hagner 1993b: 131.

of Jesus. Other prescriptions of the law are no longer in force. The entire law must be interpreted in light of the coming of Jesus the Christ.

Luke-Acts

From one perspective, Luke seems to endorse the ongoing validity of the law. Zechariah and Elizabeth are commended for living blamelessly in accordance with the commands of the law (Luke 1:6). Joseph and Mary circumcised Jesus on the eighth day as the law specifies, and they offered the sacrifices for purification designated in the Mosaic law (Luke 2:21–24). Jesus' parents, as the OT enjoins, traveled every year to Jerusalem for Passover, and Jesus traveled with them when he reached the age of twelve (Luke 2:41–52). It could be argued that Jesus did not do anything on the Sabbath to violate its prescriptions (Luke 6:1–11; 13:10–17; 14:1–6). Those who love God and neighbor will obtain eternal life (Luke 10:25–28). When the rich ruler asked about gaining eternal life, Jesus pointed him to the commands from the Decalogue (Luke 18:18–20). Jesus said that the law and prophets were in force until the coming of the Baptist and the kingdom (Luke 16:16). Such a statement might imply that the law was no longer in force with the coming of Jesus, but Luke follows up immediately with Jesus' insistence that not even one stroke of the law will pass away (Luke 16:17).[52] After Jesus' death, the women did not anoint his body until they had rested on the Sabbath, and Luke adds that they did so in accordance with what the law enjoins (Luke 23:56).

An emphasis on keeping the prescriptions of the law can be observed also in Acts. Peter and John continued to worship in the temple, and they came to the temple at a time when the burnt offering was sacrificed (Acts 3:1).[53] The accusations that Stephen violated the law are dismissed as false (Acts 6:13–14). Stephen turned the tables on his opponents, contending that they failed to observe the law (Acts 7:53). The regulations that James expected both Jews and Gentiles to observe stem from OT regulations (Acts 15:19–20, 29; 21:25). After reading Galatians, we might expect that Paul would refuse to circumcise Timothy, but he did so (Acts 16:3). Apparently, Paul took a Nazirite vow and was traveling to Jerusalem to offer the sacrifices specified by the vow (Acts 18:18). When Paul arrived in Jerusalem, he paid for the purification of four men who had

52. Still, the law remains in force insofar as it points to and proclaims the kingdom (so Thielman 1999: 151–52). Luke does not think of the law casuistically here, according to Fitzmyer (1985: 1116), but teaches that the kingdom fulfills the OT Scriptures.
53. For details, see Fitzmyer 1998: 277.

taken a vow (Acts 21:20–26; cf. Num. 6:14–15).[54] He did so to avoid any suggestion that he taught Jews to abandon the law, or that he himself violated what it enjoins. Such a purificatory rite would also involve the offering of sacrifices, which Paul apparently did not frown upon. When Paul described his conversion to a Jewish audience, he commended Ananias as being "devout . . . according to the law" (Acts 22:12).

The previous texts might suggest that Luke advocates a remarkably conservative stance toward the OT law.[55] When we consider all the evidence in Luke-Acts, however, a distinctly different picture emerges.[56] Luke emphasizes that the prophetic Scriptures find their fulfillment in Jesus of Nazareth, particularly in his death and resurrection (Luke 24:25–27, 44–47; Acts 24:14; 26:22–23; 28:23).[57] The OT, therefore, is interpreted rightly only if it is seen to climax in the ministry, death, and resurrection of Jesus of Nazareth. The law and the prophets point toward the kingdom of God (Luke 16:16). Hence, every letter of the law finds its fulfillment in the ministry of Jesus Christ (Luke 16:17).[58] The prohibition of divorce and remarriage that immediately succeeds this saying is instructive (Luke 16:18), for the law is now interpreted by Jesus Christ.[59] Jesus did not center on the law; the law centers on Jesus.

The evidence that Luke shares in common with the other Synoptics is significant as well. The cleansing of the leper suggests that Jesus transcends the laws of leprosy (Luke 5:12–15). Jesus as the Son of Man is Lord of the Sabbath (Luke 6:1–5). Doing good on the Sabbath fits the purpose for which it was instituted (Luke 6:6–11; 14:1–6), for Jesus was not required to heal on the Sabbath (Luke 13:10–17). One of the synagogue leaders, probably representing a typical Pharisaic point of view, reproached Jesus because healings could be performed on other days. Jesus, on the other hand, believed the Sabbath was a day on which healings *should* be performed. The Sabbath was intended to feature his messianic ministry, and Jesus intentionally healed on the Sabbath be-

---

54. For a discussion of the ambiguity in the text, see Fitzmyer 1998: 694.

55. Jervell (1972: 133–51) argues that the view of the law in Luke-Acts is the most conservative in the entire NT. See also Juel 1983: 103–9.

56. Wilson (1983) argues, on the other hand, that Luke's view of the law is ambiguous and not clearly defined because Luke is indifferent about the role of the law.

57. Blomberg (1984), in an important article, argues that the law must be interpreted christologically and in terms of salvation history in Luke (see also Blomberg 1998). When the flow of the book is considered, it is clear that the OT law is no longer normative for believers, and that the law finds its fulfillment in Christ.

58. Seifrid (1989) supports the case argued here, contending that the Lukan view of the law can be characterized as messianic.

59. Thielman (1999: 152) says that Luke 16:18 functions "as an example of kingdom ethics."

cause the Sabbath points toward the eschatological rest God promised his people.

The inauguration of the kingdom through Jesus means that what the law proclaims is fulfilled in him. Such fulfillment does not mean that every aspect of the law is replaced with new content. The command to love God and neighbor remains in force (Luke 10:25–28), but even this command cannot be abstracted from Luke's Gospel as a whole. Jesus reminded the rich ruler of the commands of the Decalogue when the latter inquired about gaining eternal life (Luke 18:18–22). Nevertheless, the rich man would not enjoy eternal life unless he followed Jesus in discipleship.[60] The injunction to "leave the dead to bury their own dead" (Luke 9:60) does not directly abrogate the law. It does confirm, however, that following Jesus is God's supreme demand.

Luke does not think that all the requirements of the law are binding now that Christ is exalted and the Spirit is poured out. For instance, Stephen was charged with speaking against the law and the temple (Acts 6:11–14). Luke informs us that the charges are false. Some scholars have exaggerated Stephen's words in Acts 7:1–53, seeing in them a radical rejection of the temple.[61] The pure and simple worship of the movable sanctuary (the tabernacle), according to this view, was displaced by the temple, and God did not endorse the building of the temple. Such a view misreads the content of Stephen's speech. Stephen did not actually criticize temple worship, nor did he reject it as if it were contrary to the will of God. What Stephen did was *relativize* temple worship. He reminded his hearers that Abraham never enjoyed even a foot of space in the promised land (Acts 7:5). God is not confined to sacred spaces in working out his purposes. Similarly, Joseph was rejected by his brothers and exiled to Egypt, and yet God preserved both him and Israel there (Acts 7:9–16). The rejection of both Joseph and Moses by their contemporaries forecasted the repudiation of Jesus in Stephen's day. Stephen did not exalt tabernacle worship over the building of the temple. He reminded his hearers that God is not beholden to a temple, and that he worked in Israelite history before a temple was erected. God transcends the temple, for as sovereign Lord of the universe, he cannot

60. In chapter 18 we will consider the Lukan teaching on riches.
61. For example, Kilgallen 1976: 89–94; Maddox 1982: 53; Kee 1990: 45. For a critique of this very common interpretation, see C. Hill 1992: 41–101; see also Peterson 1998: 378; Schnabel 2004a: 667. I do not share, however, Hill's skepticism about the historical reliability of the events narrated, and it also seems that he overstates his thesis. Still, his work demonstrates that many scholars in the past appealed to Stephen for a radical critique of the law and read more into the text than was present.

be contained by a building.[62] Stephen did not reject temple worship per se but rather implied that temple worship cannot be construed as the capstone of God's work with his people. Stephen's critique of the law, then, was rather subtle. He suggested a change in the status of the temple in light of the fulfillment of salvation history with the coming of Jesus, but he did not explicitly argue that the law and temple were no longer in force.[63] In sum, Stephen's speech suggests that the law does not play the central role that it did formerly.

Peter's experience with Cornelius and his friends confirms that the commands of the law are not required. Peter's vision on the roof is particularly important (Acts 10:9–16). He saw a variety of animals in a sheet lowered from heaven. Some of the animals in the sheet were prohibited according to the OT food laws (Lev. 11:1–44; Deut. 14:3–21). We know that forbidden foods were included because God enjoined Peter to slay and eat the animals in the sheet, and Peter protested because he would not eat any food that was unclean, indicating that at least some of the animals in the vision were unclean. God replied, "What God has made clean, do not call common" (Acts 10:15). Peter saw the vision three times, clarifying that the vision was not an illusion.

The significance of the vision must be explained carefully. Luke does not deny that the OT prohibited unclean foods, nor is he suggesting that such commands were wrongheaded before the coming of Christ. His point is that these commands are no longer in force at this stage in salvation history. The relaxation of food laws is connected in the narrative with the gospel extending to the Gentiles (Acts 10:1–11:18).[64] Peter naturally was puzzled about God nullifying what previously was a commandment (Acts 10:17). But he began to see that the purification of unclean foods was connected to the Gentile mission (Acts 10:28).[65] The Gentiles received the Spirit without being circumcised, nor did they conform to Jewish purity requirements (Acts 10:44–48; 15:7–11). The spread of the gospel

62. Many think that the criticism is sharper than this (see Haenchen 1971: 290; Barrett 1994: 374–75).

63. Barrett (1994: 338) overstates his case in saying that the speech criticizes the temple but affirms the law, for the criticism of the former inevitably involves the latter.

64. The text does not state directly that food laws are no longer obligatory, but the link between unclean foods and unclean Gentiles is clearly implied in the text (Wilson 1983: 174). Further, as Seifrid (1987: 43) notes, "Contact with Gentiles was thought to bring defilement because they did not keep the purity laws." Moreover, Seifrid (1987: 43) also rightly concludes that in any case, "Peter's vision unmistakably annuls Mosaic demands." See also Turner 1982: 116; Maddox 1982: 36–37. Contra Barrett (1994: 509) and Fitzmyer (1998: 455), it is quite unlikely that Luke suggests that the foods in view have always been clean. They miss out on the salvation historical character of Luke here.

65. Some have argued that Luke downplays the significance of Peter's vision, but this objection is successfully answered by Thielman (1999: 155–56).

to all peoples is linked with the dissolution of the purity requirements of the Mosaic law. The Gentiles did not have to conform to the OT law in order to be part of the people of God. By the time of the apostolic council in Acts 15, Peter saw the implications of the Cornelius event clearly (Acts 15:7–11). The yoke of the law should not be imposed upon the Gentiles. The only entrance requirement is faith in Jesus Christ, and the gift of the Spirit confirms that they are part of the people of God. Paul's words in Acts 13:38–39 are quite similar.[66] Justification comes not through the law of Moses but rather by believing in Jesus Christ.[67] In the new era of salvation history forgiveness of sins belongs to those who trust in Jesus Christ instead of those who observe the law.[68]

Gentiles were streaming into the church after the first missionary venture of Paul and Barnabas (Acts 13:1–14:28). Paul and Barnabas had not required circumcision of those who converted. A controversy arose over whether circumcision should be required, especially from the Pharisaic faction of believers (Acts 15:1, 5). Some maintained that circumcision was necessary for salvation because the OT clearly demanded that those who enter into covenant with the Lord be circumcised (Gen. 17:9–14). Historical, textual, and theological issues join together to make Acts 15:1–35 complex and controversial. For our purposes here, however, the text as it stands is quite clear. The decision of the council was that circumcision would not be required for salvation. The Gentiles would be considered members of the church through their faith in the Lord Jesus Christ and the reception of the Holy Spirit. Again, Luke does not argue that circumcision was a mistake from the beginning, nor does he denigrate the OT requirement. His purpose is to relay that the initiation rite is no longer required at this stage in salvation history.[69] A new era has dawned with the ministry, death, and resurrection of Jesus Christ. Because he is exalted to God's right hand, the Spirit is poured out on all those who believe. The requirements of the Torah are no longer in

66. I do not follow Barrett (1994: 650–51) and others who think that here Luke did not represent accurately Pauline theology.

67. The christological focus of the speech is brought out convincingly by Kilgallen (1988).

68. The weakness of the position of Jervell (1972: 146) manifests itself at this point, for he assigns Acts 13:38–39; 15:10–11 to tradition rather than redaction. Such a conclusion, even if it is correct, fails to answer a crucial question: why would Luke include it as traditional material if it differed from his overall view? Jervell (1996: 60) argues in a later work that circumcision was not required by the OT law for Gentiles, but this runs counter to the clear requirement in the OT that one must be circumcised in order to belong to Israel (cf. Gen. 17:9–14). It is astonishing that Jervell misses this, for he insists quite strongly that Gentiles belong to restored Israel.

69. In defense of this reading of the decree, see Seifrid 1987: 44–47.

force now that God's promises are being fulfilled and the good news is going out to the Gentiles.

It is clear, then, that Luke does not propose an extremely conservative view of the law. He teaches that justification and forgiveness of sins come not through the law but rather by the grace of the Lord Jesus Christ. Food laws and circumcision, which are normative in the Mosaic law, are no longer necessary for the people of God. The fulfillment of God's promises signals a shift in redemptive history. The so-called conservative texts relating to the law in Luke should be explained within the framework of salvation history. Jesus' parents circumcised him and followed the required purification rites after his birth (Luke 2:21–24) because they lived in the period before the death and resurrection of Jesus and the descent of the Spirit. Nor does Luke have any problem with Jews observing such customs in accord with Jewish culture and history. We should not read these texts, however, as if they suggest that such practices were normative for all believers. Clearly, Luke does not think all believers should be circumcised. The observance of the Passover by Jesus and his parents (Luke 2:41–52) should be interpreted within this same framework. They lived under the law and thus observed Jewish feasts. The same could be said about the women resting on the Sabbath (Luke 23:56), though we see some indications in Luke that Jesus transcended Sabbath regulations.

Freedom from the OT law does not mean that Jews were *required* to ignore it. Peter and John participated in temple worship (Acts 3:1), presumably because of their Jewish background and perhaps also as a means of reaching their Jewish contemporaries with the gospel. Paul's circumcision of Timothy (Acts 16:1–5) has been a matter of particular controversy, especially since, according to Gal. 2:3–5, he refused to circumcise Titus.[70] If we follow the story line of Acts, we see that the apostles and the church had just determined that circumcision was unnecessary for salvation (Acts 15:1–35). The circumcision of Timothy, after this event, seems rather astonishing. Luke explains, however, that Timothy's father was a Gentile, whereas his mother was Jewish. Since Timothy's mother was Jewish, the Jews would have identified him as a Jew. Paul did not circumcise Timothy so that he would be saved; rather, he performed the circumcision so that he could bring Timothy with him when he preached the gospel in Jewish synagogues. By circumcising Timothy he avoided unnecessary controversy. Under no circumstances would Paul tolerate the circumcision of Titus (Gal. 2:3–5), for Titus was a Gentile, and such an operation would suggest that Gentiles had to be circumcised to be

---

70. On the circumcision of Timothy in Acts 16, see Schreiner, *DPL* 137–39.

saved. The case of Timothy was quite different. Paul circumcised him for cultural reasons and to advance his mission among the Jews.

Paul's taking of a vow and paying for the sacrifices of others who took a vow should be understood similarly (Acts 18:18; 21:21–26). James and the other Jewish believers encouraged Paul to conform to the law in order to demonstrate to the Jews that he did not mandate them to forsake the Jewish law or customs. Paul had no problem with Jews observing the law, and he himself was quite content to keep the prescriptions of the law when enjoying fellowship with Jews. What Paul opposed was the imposition of regulations of the law on Gentiles. Hence, Paul's taking of a vow, paying for sacrifices, and circumcising Timothy all fit within the same perspective. The law was not mandatory with the coming of Jesus Christ. Still, Paul was not an extremist. Even if circumcision was not binding for salvation, Paul had no problem with Jews practicing it and other ordinances of the law in accord with Jewish custom.

Does the so-called apostolic decree contradict what I am saying here?[71] The council determined that circumcision was unnecessary for salvation but then proceeded to say that Gentiles must "abstain only from things polluted by idols and from fornication and from whatever has been strangled and from blood" (Acts 15:20 NRSV; cf. 15:29; 21:25). The significance and meaning of the decree has long been debated. The Western text omits the things strangled and appears to turn the decree into moral requirements, so that idolatry, sexual sin, and murder are prohibited, and a negative form of the golden rule is added. Such a solution is attractive, but the textual evidence favors including the prohibition of things strangled.[72] Many scholars have maintained that the prohibitions hearken back to Lev. 17–18. Gentiles were to refrain from eating food that was improperly slaughtered, from consuming food with the blood in it, from marrying within the confines prohibited by Lev. 18:6–18, and from eating food offered to idols.[73] Bauckham argues that the clue is found in the words "in your/their midst" in Lev. 17:8, 10, 12, 13; 18:26.[74] The four commandments are what Lev. 17–18 demanded of Gentiles, who lived

71. For a survey of the various views, see Schnabel 2004a: 1015–20.

72. Rightly Bruce 1954: 311–12, 315–16; Marshall 1980b: 246–47, 253; Barrett 1998: 735–36.

73. Haenchen 1971: 449, 468–72; Turner 1982: 117–18; Conzelmann 1987: 118–19; Polhill 1992: 330–31; Fitzmyer 1998: 556–58. See the analysis of the decree in Seifrid 1987: 47–51. Seifrid (1987: 50) notes that the decree contained both ethical and ritual requirements, though the focus throughout is on the latter. Contrary to Seifrid, the reference to Moses (Acts 15:21) is not intended to contrast preaching Moses to preaching Christ. Rather, Luke simply explains why it is culturally appropriate for Gentiles to accommodate Jewish ritual concerns, without implying that they function as a law for Gentile converts (contra Catchpole 1977: 429).

74. See Bauckham 1995: 459–80.

as Gentiles but dwelt in the midst of Israel.[75] He rejects the idea that we
have a pragmatic compromise solution here; rather, these are the laws
required for Gentiles who lived among Israel. This view of the decree,
as Bauckham demonstrates, seems to be reflected in other parts of the
NT and later church history. The problem arises with Paul. According
to Bauckham, Paul initially accepted the decree but later disagreed with
some aspects of it.[76] Despite the freshness of Bauckham's view, it is unclear that the decree is mandated as part of the OT law. Barrett suggests
that what is prohibited is idolatry, fornication, and murder along with
nonparticipation in kosher foods.[77] It seems to me as well that the decree
mixes together moral and ritual requirements. But unlike Barrett, I think
that the only moral prohibition relates to sexual sin. In other words, it
is difficult to see that the immorality in view hearkens back to the regulations regarding sexual sin in Lev. 18; rather, the reference is to sexual
sin in general, for Gentiles had to be taught that sexual sin did not match
their newfound faith in Christ. The other requirements related to prohibition of nonkosher foods, including foods from which the blood was
not drained properly. The latter requirements were included to facilitate
fellowship between Christian Jews and Gentiles.

Did James introduce extra requirements for salvation after agreeing
that circumcision would not be mandated? Many scholars contend
that Paul was not present when the decree was passed, and that he
would never have agreed with its provisions. Such a reconstruction,
of course, deviates from the text of Acts as it has been preserved and
handed down to us. Reconstructions of this sort are typically a testimony to the creativity of scholars proposing them or to a one-sided
reading of the evidence. The decree fits with the narrative of Acts as a
whole and the decision of the council not to impose circumcision if it
were required for salvation. The decree was not requisite for salvation,
for such a decision would cancel out what was decided with respect
to circumcision. James addressed a common Gentile sin, sexual immorality, in order to remind them of what God required. In addition,
he addressed the matter of Jewish sensibilities and requested that
Gentiles tolerate Jewish customs for the sake of fellowship.[78] Gentiles

75. Remarkably similar here is the view of Jervell (1996: 59).

76. On the other hand, if one accepts the view of A. Cheung (1999) on food offered to
idols, then Paul never deviated from the decree, for Paul, according to Cheung, believed
that it was always wrong to eat food offered to idols. But Cheung's explanation is itself
unpersuasive.

77. See the entire discussion in Barrett 1998: 730–36.

78. The decree, then, does not mandate the observance of the Mosaic law but rather
represents a compromise to promote fellowship between Jews and Gentiles (so Thielman
1999: 156–58).

would be quite aware of Jewish concerns because the law of Moses was publicly read in synagogues throughout the cities in the Greco-Roman world (Acts 15:21). The advice that James gave to Paul should be interpreted similarly (Acts 21:21–26). He asked Paul to observe the law when he was with other Jewish Christians, but the reference to the decree was added to clarify that James did not expect Gentiles to keep the law. Instead, Gentiles agreed to observe what the decree specified to accommodate the Jews, so as to avoid giving offense to Jewish believers. The decree, then, was not mandated for salvation but rather was proposed as a *via media* to regulate fellowship between Jews and Gentiles in areas particularly sensitive to the Jews. Further, the inclusion of sexual immorality does not compromise the gospel either. We see, then, that salvation by grace does not eliminate basic moral requirements, and kosher laws would be observed to facilitate fellowship between Jews and Gentiles.

The Lukan view of the law is quite complex. The key to untangling it, I suggest, is to interpret it in light of salvation history. The law pointed to and is fulfilled in Jesus Christ. He is the fulfillment of what was prophesied in the OT. The Lukan view of the law, then, has elements of both continuity and discontinuity. There is continuity in that the law points toward Jesus Christ and is fulfilled in him. Some of the moral norms of the law seem to carry over without any changes. On the other hand, discontinuity exists as well. Circumcision and food laws were no longer required of the people of God. Gentiles were not required to conform to the Jewish Torah in order to belong to the people of God.

The Johannine Literature

The Gospel of John

In the Gospel of John the perspective on the law must be understood within the framework of Johannine theology, and particularly the high Christology that permeates the entire book. The whole of the OT anticipates the coming of Jesus Christ and finds its fulfillment in him. Those who study the Scriptures find that they are about Jesus Christ because they testify about him (John 5:39). People do not truly grasp what Moses wrote if they do not put their faith in Jesus, for Moses wrote about Jesus (John 5:45–47). Abraham was filled with joy because he saw long ago the day when Jesus would come (John 8:56). Isaiah, when he saw the glory of the Lord in the temple vision (Isa. 6:1–8), actually saw the glory of Jesus Christ (John 12:41).

Since the entirety of the OT is about Jesus Christ, we are not astonished to find that Jesus replaces the temple in Jerusalem (John 2:19–22).[79] He is the true temple, and thus only those who worship him do so in Spirit and truth (John 4:21–24).[80] The manna that sustained Israel in the wilderness is not the true bread of God (John 6:32–33, 41, 49–50). Manna did not grant eternal life, for those who consumed it suffered death. Jesus, on the other hand, is the true manna because he does not merely sustain physical life but rather confers life that never ends. Those who read the account of the manna in the desert should perceive that it points toward someone who comes from heaven who will bestow life. Jesus also fulfills the Feast of Tabernacles (John 7–9).[81] We noted earlier that he fulfills the water-pouring and light rituals during the feast (see *m. Sukkah* 4:9–10; 5:2–4). The thirst that people have can be satisfied only by Jesus, for he gives "rivers of living water" (John 7:37–38). The ritual of light during the feast anticipates the coming of Jesus, for he is "the light of the world" (John 8:12), and he grants sight to those who live in darkness and are spiritually blind (John 9). The promise that Yahweh will shepherd his people (Ps. 23:1; Ezek. 34:11–16, 23–24) is fulfilled in Jesus as the good shepherd (John 10:11, 14). In the OT the people of God are described as a vineyard (Isa. 5:1–7), but the true Israel, the true vine of the Lord, is Jesus himself (John 15:1). So too the Passover sacrifice finds its fulfillment in the lifting up and glorification of Jesus on the cross (John 18:28, 39; 19:14).

The water pots of purification used by the Jews give way now to the new wine of Jesus' ministry (John 2:1–11).[82] His glory eclipses the glory present in the old covenant (John 1:14; cf. Exod. 33:18–19, 22; 34:6–7). As we observed in the Synoptics, Jesus deliberately healed on the Sabbath (John 5:1–9), for the Sabbath anticipates the eschatological rest for God's people. Jesus' actions on the Sabbath inevitably led to conflict with the Jewish leaders. He instructed the man healed by the pool to pick up his mat, and the Jewish leaders responded with irritation, for in their eyes the carrying of the mat was equivalent to work (John 5:10–11). Jesus could have avoided the conflict by reminding the man not to carry his mat because that day was the Sabbath. Indeed, he could have waited until the next day to perform the healing. Similarly, when Jesus granted sight to the blind man, he did so on the Sabbath (John 9:1–17). Nor did he heal him only with a word; he took actions that

79. Contra M. M. Thompson 2001: 212.
80. See Thielman 1999: 94–96; Hamilton 2006b: 147–54.
81. So most commentators and Thielman 1999: 100–102.
82. Jesus turning the water into wine (John 2:1–11) also shows that OT purity regulations point to him and find their fulfillment in him. See Dodd 1953: 297; Carson 1991b: 173, 175; Thielman 1999: 92–94.

could be construed as work because he spat on the ground, shaped the mud, and placed it on the man's eyes. Surely Jesus could have healed the man with a word only, for he raised Lazarus from the dead without using any physical props and summoned him from the tomb with only his word (John 11:38–44).

The Jewish leaders were disturbed that Jesus had performed such actions on the Sabbath, and John informs his readers that they persecuted Jesus (John 5:12–16). As we observed in the Synoptics, Jesus did not engage the Jewish leaders at a halakic level. Presumably, he could have retorted that simply carrying a mat on the Sabbath did not constitute work, and he could have said the same about applying mud to the eyes of the blind man. Instead, Jesus replied with shocking words in John 5:17. He claimed that it was legitimate for him to work on the Sabbath because the Father was working as well. Jesus, then, implicitly conceded the point of the Jewish leaders. He was indeed working on the Sabbath, but such actions are legitimate, for as the Son, he does only what the Father does (John 5:19–23).[83] This is John's way of saying that Jesus is the Lord of the Sabbath. The Sabbath law no longer has the same stature now that the Son of the Father has arrived. He works with sovereign freedom on the Sabbath to heal and to cure because the Sabbath is the day on which healings should occur. By releasing human beings from their burdens and diseases, Jesus grants the rest that the Sabbath signified.

As the controversy continued over Jesus' observance (or more precisely, lack of observance) of the Sabbath, Jesus defended his actions by appealing to the Mosaic law itself (John 7:19–24). He remarked that those who criticized him did not observe the law that they claimed to treasure. Furthermore, healing on the Sabbath could not be indicted from the law itself, for circumcision was practiced on the Sabbath. If the injunction to circumcise takes precedence over the Sabbath, Jesus argued, so does healing. In this instance, then, Jesus seemed to join the debate at the halakic level, though elsewhere in John's Gospel his authority over the Sabbath and the Mosaic law is stressed.

Clearly, the Mosaic law no longer occupies the central place now that the Son has arrived. Jewish purification laws, the Sabbath, and the Passover are subordinate to Jesus and must be interpreted in light of him, rather than vice versa.[84] John's programmatic statement about

83. Thielman (1999: 83) remarks, "Jesus is not subject to the command to avoid work on the sabbath because he is equal to God. Since God is exempt from sabbath rest . . . Jesus is also." See also Carson 1991b: 247–48; Köstenberger 2004: 183–84.

84. Hays (1996: 138) says, "The law of Moses plays no explicit role in John's moral vision; it is read as prefiguring Jesus, and its meaning is seemingly absorbed into his person." M. M. Thompson (2001: 219–20) worries that the language of replacement cancels out the continuity between the old and new, and so she prefers to speak of "anticipation" or of the

the law is found in John 1:17: "The law indeed was given through Moses; grace and truth came through Jesus Christ." The significance of this verse must be read in light of what we have seen elsewhere in this Gospel about the relationship between the law and the gospel of Jesus Christ.[85] The prologue is programmatic, but its meaning is unfolded by the remainder of the book. John does not denigrate the law. Indeed, the fullness that believers have received is "grace instead of grace" (John 1:16 my translation). Contrary to what we find in most English translations and commentaries, the preposition *anti* in this verse should not be rendered "upon." What John communicates is that God poured out his grace in giving the OT law, but the grace of the law is now surpassed by the grace of the gospel.[86] The grace of the law is akin to the brightness of the moon, but now it has been eclipsed by the grace given through the sun—the gospel of Jesus Christ. We are reminded afresh of the replacement theme prominent in John's Gospel: the physical temple points toward Christ as the true temple; literal manna anticipates Jesus as the true bread from heaven; the water and light rites from the Feast of Tabernacles are redolent of Christ as the one who gives living water and is the light of the world; and the Passover sacrifice symbolizes the coming sacrifice of Christ. The grace and truth prophesied in the law are realized in Jesus Christ.[87] What the law demands, Jesus fulfills, and thus his grace is poured out in the hearts of his people.

John does emphasize the importance of observing commandments, but the commandments are not identified with the OT law. Jesus gives his disciples a new commandment: they should love others as he has loved them (John 13:34). The newness of the commandment cannot be traced to the command to show love for others, for the command to love others is rooted in the OT. What makes the command new is that Jesus' self-giving love for his disciples, manifested in his giving up his life for his sheep, becomes the paradigm for love (John 10:11, 15; 15:13).[88] Love cannot be measured simply by the observance of rules, though moral

old being "taken up" into the new. Still, the language of replacement seems fitting as long as we do not erase the particularity and significance of what is transcended.

85. Dumbrell (1986) interprets the verse in light of Exod. 34.

86. For convincing support of this interpretation, see Edwards 1988.

87. John highlights the theme that the OT Scriptures are fulfilled in the life and death of Jesus Christ (see Pancaro 1975: 492–546; Carson 1988: 245–64).

88. "The commandment is new, however, in that it corresponds to the command that regulates the regulation between Jesus and the Father . . . ; the love of the disciples for one another is not merely edifying, it reveals the Father and Son" (Barrett 1978: 452). Barrett (1978: 452) goes on to reject the criticism that John excludes love for the world, for in John's Gospel the Father's love for the world is evident in the giving of the Son.

norms are not jettisoned. Genuine love is sacrificial, consisting of giving up one's life for others.

Those who love Jesus demonstrate that love by keeping his commands and his word (John 14:15, 23–24). John does not specify what commands he has in mind, but the emphasis lies on observing the commands and words given by Jesus.[89] The content of the commands presumably includes what we find elsewhere in John's Gospel. In John 15 keeping Jesus' commands means that disciples love one another within the Christian community (John 15:10, 12–17). This love is defined in terms of yielding up one's life for a friend.[90] The sacrificial dimension of self-giving love is at the forefront for John. John points his readers not to the commands in the OT law but rather to the commands and word of Jesus himself.

1–2 John

In 1–2 John we also find an emphasis on obeying commandments. Again, the focus is on keeping the commands given by Jesus instead of the OT Torah (1 John 2:3–6). The commands of Jesus can also be designated as his word (*logos* [1 John 2:5]), which may be a reference to the gospel as a whole.[91] John gives us a clue about the content of Jesus' commands when he remarks that believers should "walk in the same way in which he walked" (1 John 2:6). Jesus himself becomes the paradigm for the lives of believers. The righteousness of Jesus functions as the standard for believers (1 John 2:29). Jesus' purity is the hope of every believer (1 John 3:3). As the sinless one, he came to destroy the works of the devil and free believers from the dominion of sin (1 John 3:4–10). Jesus' love in giving his life for the salvation of believers functions as the model and measure of genuine love (1 John 3:16). He gave his life to meet the greatest need of believers, which is life itself (1 John 4:9).

When John reminds believers of the old command that they had from the beginning, he does not reflect on the OT law (1 John 2:7–11). The old command is Jesus' injunction to love one another, a command that he gave, as we saw in John's Gospel, during his earthly ministry.[92]

---

89. "John never permits love to devolve into a sentiment or an emotion. Its expression is always moral and is revealed in obedience" (Barrett 1978: 461). Bultmann (1971: 614) slides away from the main point here in saying that the obedience demanded is faith. Even though John envisioned obedience as the fruit of faith, here he concentrates on the result of faith.

90. "It does not claim that love for friends is better than love for enemies; only that there is nothing greater you can do for your friends than die for them" (Barrett 1978: 476–77).

91. R. Brown (1982: 252, 254, 265) suggests that the oscillation between *entolē* and *logos* in John suggests that commandment and word are closely related.

92. So R. Brown 1982: 265.

The command is also new in the sense that it has become a reality in Jesus with the passing away of the old age and the coming of the new. The command to love, which finds its exemplar in Jesus' self-giving to death, must be observed among the people of God. Those who fail to love reside in darkness, demonstrating that they do not belong to God at all. Those who refuse to love are like Cain, who murdered his brother (1 John 3:11–18). Those who turn from a life of love reveal that they have not passed from death to life (1 John 3:14). Murderers do not enjoy eternal life, for instead of living like Christ to give life to others, they live only to benefit themselves and thus stamp out the lives of others to advance their own agenda. The life of love is not abstract for John; it manifests itself in caring for those who are needy—in concrete words and actions (1 John 3:17–18).

A life of love is a life inspired by God, for God himself is love (1 John 4:7–21). Again the sending of Jesus to grant life to the world is the emblem of love (1 John 4:9). The love of God is so remarkable because it takes the initiative, displaying love to those who hate him. Human love never has priority. Love for God always echoes the love that God has for us; it always responds to the love of God in Jesus Christ. Experiencing God's love means that the fear of judgment—a judgment that is well deserved apart from Christ—is removed. For John, then, a genuine experience of this love means that believers show the same kind of love for others. No one can love God and show hatred for brothers and sisters in the family of God. The sign that believers have experienced God's love is that they display this love to other Christians. Those who have drunk deeply at the well of God's love in Christ long to pass on that same love to others. Such love in their lives is an indication that God indeed dwells in them, for the mark of God's presence is the impulse to love. Hence, anyone who claims to love God but fails to love fellow believers is living in unreality. Their protestations of love toward God are contradicted by their everyday lives and their failure to love fellow Christians.

Believers are required to keep God's commands and do what pleases him (1 John 3:22). But John does not clearly hearken back to the OT law in specifying what these commands are. Indeed, in the immediately succeeding verses the commands are boiled down to believing Jesus is the Christ, loving one another, and obeying his commandments (1 John 3:23–24). Presumably, the command to love has specific features that can be filled in, such as caring for the poor (1 John 3:17). John does not, however, linger on what these features might be. People can know they are God's children if they love God and obey his commands (1 John 5:2). Then in 1 John 5:3 love for God seems to be equated with keeping his commands. This last word reminds us of John's Gospel, where genuine love for Jesus is inseparable from obedience to his commands (John 14:15, 23–24).

The message of 2 John seems quite similar. God's command is that believers walk in the truth of the gospel (2 John 4). As we saw in 1 John, the command to love one another is not new but rather represents the word that Jesus taught his disciples from the beginning (2 John 5). Love is then defined as walking in his commands (2 John 6). It is somewhat difficult to discern from this verse alone if love and the commands are coterminous. It certainly seems to be the case that love is the supreme command given by Jesus, although it also seems to be the case that such love necessarily had to manifest itself in certain concrete ways.

We see in the Gospel of John and in 1–2 John that the law points to Jesus and is fulfilled in him. The christological focus of the law fits with the centrality of Christology in John's thought. John does not focus on specific OT commands; Jesus himself becomes the exemplar and paradigm of love, especially as he displayed that love in his self-giving on the cross.

Revelation

Perhaps we can include Revelation as part of Johannine tradition here, particularly since very little is said about the Mosaic law. Believers are those who obey God's commands and the testimony of Jesus or the faith of Jesus (Rev. 12:17; 14:12). John's focus here is not on any particular commandments from the OT law but rather on the need to persevere in the midst of persecution. Believers are to adhere to the message of the gospel of Jesus Christ and not depart from him, even when Rome threatens to snuff out their lives. Perhaps John has in mind Jesus' own faithfulness unto death, so that Jesus functions as the model of godly perseverance for believers.

In terms of specific commandments, some of the churches are indicted for sexual sin and eating food offered to idols (Rev. 2:14, 20–22). The fornication of Rome consists in false worship and in compromise in order to enjoy the economic fruits of the oppressing power (Rev. 18). John says that the lake of fire will be inhabited by "the cowardly, the faithless, the detestable, . . . the murderers, the sexually immoral, sorcerers, idolaters, and all liars (Rev. 21:8; cf. 21:27). We see something quite similar in Rev. 22:15, where "dogs and sorcerers and the sexually immoral and murderers and idolaters" and liars are outside the holy city. Revelation does not address in detail the moral life of believers, for it was written to encourage believers to stay faithful to Jesus and not compromise their faith by succumbing to Roman pressure. Still, there are some moral norms mentioned because allegiance to Jesus cannot be separated from a life of moral beauty.

The Pauline Literature

Paul clearly teaches that the Mosaic covenant has come to an end,[93] and believers are no longer under it as a covenantal structure.[94] In Gal. 3:15–25 Paul distinguishes the Sinai covenant from the covenant enacted with Abraham.[95] The Abrahamic covenant is foundational, for it was given first before any provisions were added from the Sinai covenant. A covenant that was enacted 430 years after the first cannot nullify the provisions of the covenant made with Abraham. Significantly, the covenant with Abraham is designated as "promise" in contrast to the covenant enacted at Sinai. In Gal. 3:18 Paul contrasts the promissory nature of the Abrahamic covenant with receiving the inheritance on the basis of the law. The covenant with Abraham is established on the basis of God's promise. Hence, the inheritance is guaranteed because it depends not on human performance but rather on the word of God.

The law was intended to be in force only until the seed, Jesus Christ, arrived (Gal. 3:19). The problem is not the content of the law but rather that human beings were unable to obey what the law demanded and found themselves imprisoned under the power of sin (Gal. 3:21–22). The law, therefore, was intended to be in force for only a certain period of time. It functioned as pedagogue (*paidagōgos* [Gal. 3:24–25]) until salvation history reached its climax with the coming of Jesus Christ.[96] Now that Jesus Christ has come, believers no longer live under the tutelage of the Mosaic covenant.[97] The law was a "babysitter" or custodian

93. Some have argued that Paul's view of the law developed (Drane 1975; Hübner 1984a; Wilckens 1982). This view should be rejected. Because Paul was trained as a Pharisee, it is almost certain that he began to think through his view of the law from the time of his conversion (so Hengel 1991: 40–53, 70–71, esp. 79–86; Hengel and Schwemer 1997: 98–101; Stuhlmacher 1986: 69–71, 124, 134–154; Kim 2002: 1–84). Räisänen (1983: 9) observes that one of the fundamental weaknesses with the developmental view is that the tensions (contradictions, in Räisänen's view) exist within the same letters.

94. For an explication of Paul's view of the law that is quite similar to what is argued here, see Thielman 1995.

95. Paul does not merely speak against the misuse of law, as some have suggested (Cranfield 1979: 853, 857–61; D. Fuller 1980: 65–120, 199–204). Rightly Hofius 1989: 55.

96. For useful surveys on the meaning of *paidagōgos*, see Longenecker 1982; Belleville 1986: 59–63; N. Young 1987; Gordon 1989. Schneider (*EDNT* 3:2) remarks, "Paul not only characterizes the negative aspect of the law, its enslaving function; he is also able to make clear the temporary nature of its task."

97. It is unclear whether Judaism taught the law would be superseded with the arrival of the messianic age (contra Schweitzer 1968: 187–92; Schoeps 1961: 171–75). For a careful

designed for the period of infancy that has ended with the coming of Jesus Christ.

We could easily misconstrue Paul's argument here. He is not suggesting that believers are free from all moral norms, as if life in Christ is free from any moral requirements. His purpose is to argue that the old era of redemptive history under the Mosaic covenant has come to an end. Israel's tutelage under the law demonstrated that the law could not transform the hearts of God's people. Only the power of the Spirit, given because of the death and resurrection and exaltation of Jesus Christ, grants people the ability to keep God's commands. Israel, on the other hand, lived under bondage because the era of the Sinai covenant was a period not of freedom but of slavery. Such slavery, as Paul labors to clarify in Rom. 7:7–25, cannot be ascribed to the law and the Mosaic covenant per se; it results from the power of sin.

The difference between the covenants is clarified by Gal. 4:1–7. Those who lived under the Sinai covenant were like minors who had not yet received the promised inheritance. The inheritance was promised in the Abrahamic covenant, but Israel lived in the period before the promise was realized. They waited in anticipation for the fulfillment, but in the interval before the promise came to pass Israel lived in slavery under "the elements of the world" (Gal. 4:3 my translation). Hence, the law did not restrain sin in Israel but rather contributed to its bondage.[98] But a new era of redemptive history has dawned with the coming of Jesus Christ. He lived under the law to liberate those who lived under the law (Gal. 4:4–5). Those who are redeemed by Christ are no longer minors; they have reached full adulthood. They no longer live under the provisional rules of the Mosaic law that functioned as "guardians and trustees until the date set by the father" (Gal. 4:2 NRSV). They now enjoy the fulfillment of what God has promised, for they have received the Holy Spirit. Now that the new age has dawned and the Sinai covenant is passé, believers are no longer slaves but are spiritual adults.[99]

Now that Jesus Christ has come, believers are no longer "under law" (Gal. 3:23; 4:21). Again, we should not read this to say that believers are liberated from all moral norms, as if Paul were endorsing situation ethics or a morality that floats free of any absolutes. The phrase "under

---

analysis of the evidence, see W. Davies 1952. For the view that such an argument cannot be established, see Schäfer 1974.

98. Contrary to the view of Lull (1986), who maintains that according to Gal. 3–4, the law restrained sin.

99. Some scholars have maintained that the first-person plural pronouns refer to Jewish Christians, and the second-person plural pronouns to Gentile Christians. Das (2003: 120–28) demonstrates, however, that such a theory is unworkable and would actually make the letter remarkably confusing.

law" refers to the old era in salvation history—the time when the Sinai covenant was in force. Hence, for Paul, to be "under law" is equivalent to being "under the pedagogue" (Gal. 3:25). Those who are under the law are imprisoned under the power of sin (Rom. 6:14–15), for grace and law stand in contrast to one another in the history of salvation. It is not the case that grace was lacking under the Sinai covenant, for God graciously freed Israel from Egyptian bondage, and the salvation won at the exodus became a type of the salvation accomplished by Jesus Christ. Still, Israel as a whole, with the exception of the remnant, did not receive the ability to keep God's law, and thus they lived under the dominion of sin. This explains why Paul contrasts living under the law with living under grace.

Those who live under grace have died with Christ in baptism and thus have died to sin (Rom. 6:1–11). The slavery to sin that existed before baptism has been broken in their lives. They are no longer under sin's tyranny and bondage. To be under grace means that a new master has been established in the hearts of human beings. The rule of sin has been dethroned by the death and resurrection of Christ, so that believers now "walk in newness of life" (Rom. 6:4). God has performed radical heart surgery, so that those who previously lived in slavery to sin now have a desire to obey God from the heart (Rom. 6:17). The promise of the new covenant has become a reality (cf. Jer. 31:31–34). God has written the law on the heart, so that believers keep his commands. They have been "taught by God to love one another" (1 Thess. 4:9).[100] The Sinai covenant failed at this very point, for it taught people what God required but did not give them the desire to do what was commanded. Therefore, those who are "under law" are also "under a curse" (Gal. 3:10) and "imprisoned under sin" (Gal. 3:22). Paul insists, then, that he is not under the law (1 Cor. 9:20), even though he is willing to live under the prescriptions of the law in order to facilitate his mission to the Jews, so that they might place their faith in Jesus Christ. When he ministers to Gentiles, he lives apart from the law so that they understand that the Sinai covenant and its regulations are not normative for Christians (1 Cor. 9:21; Gal. 4:12). All those who have received the promised gift of the Spirit no longer live under the law (Gal. 5:18). They are freed from the Mosaic covenant because it is part of a former era.

Romans 6 declares that believers have been freed from the power of sin, and Rom. 7:1–6 looks at the same truth from another angle. Believers have been freed from the law through the death of Christ. Paul

---

100. Paul likely refers here to the work of the Holy Spirit. So Schnabel (1995: 278), who also notes an allusion to Isa. 54:13. On Isa. 54:13, see Witmer 2006. See also Bruce 1982b: 90; Marshall 1983: 115; Wanamaker 1990: 161.

contrasts living under the law, where the flesh uses the law to produce sin, with life under the Spirit, where believers are freed from slavery. The Spirit works in their hearts to give them a desire to do the will of God. Life under the law leads to death because sin has free reign. Those who have died to the law through the death of Christ have been freed by the Spirit so that they do the will of God because they are united with Christ. Returning to the law, then, is to rebuild what has been torn down with the coming of Christ (Gal. 2:18). Hence, reversion to the law can only mean the return of sin and transgression. Believers died to the law by dying with Christ (Gal. 2:19–20). They live new lives by trusting in Jesus as God's Son, and to return to the law would be a denial of God's grace in Jesus Christ (Gal. 2:21). Accepting the Sinai covenant would deny the fulfillment of the promise, so that the net effect would be that Jesus would have died for nothing.

Other Pauline texts confirm that the Mosaic covenant was an interim one that passed away with the coming of Jesus Christ. In 2 Cor. 3 the new covenant is contrasted with the old covenant (2 Cor. 3:6, 14).[101] The use of the terms "new covenant" and "old covenant" implies that the latter was no longer in force.[102] Paul contrasts the old covenant with the new: the former led to death and condemnation, the latter to life in the Spirit and righteousness. Most significant for our purposes here, the old covenant is said to be "brought to an end," while the new is "permanent" (2 Cor. 3:11).[103] The glory that was "brought to an end" on Moses' face (2 Cor. 3:13) symbolized the temporary nature of the Mosaic covenant. Christ is both the goal and the end of the law for all who believe (Rom. 10:4).[104] The prescriptions of the law have come to an end through the

101. Paul's use of the OT, particularly Exod. 34, has long been the subject of discussion. For OT antecedents and Jewish traditions that may inform Paul's discussion, see Stockhausen 1989: 42–86, 97–109, 135–50; Belleville 1991: 24–79; Hafemann 1995: 221–54. Hafemann argues that Paul interprets Exod. 34 in accord with its original meaning, and that Moses wore the veil in order to display both God's mercy and judgment. The veil represented judgment because the Lord could not manifest his glory fully to the people without destroying them. But it also represented God's mercy, for the glory on Moses' face demonstrates that the Lord had not abandoned his people, and that he would not destroy them utterly.

102. Rightly Hofius 1989: 81. Harris (2005: 302–3) says that Paul also implies here the superiority of the new covenant. But the meaning is not that the law is abolished in a legalistic sense (contra Barrett 1973: 121); rather, Paul refers to the abolition of the old covenant in salvation historical terms.

103. In support of the view that the verb *katargeō* has the notion of "passing away" here, see Watson 2004: 293–95.

104. So Harris 2005: 299–300. This verse is, of course, hotly contested. For an ardent defense supporting only "end," see Hofius 1989: 64–65. For a full-length monograph supporting only "goal," see Badenas 1985. Harris (2005: 299) is likely correct that *eis to telos* in 2 Cor. 3:13 means "until the end." See also Barrett 1973: 119; Furnish 1984:

work of Christ on the cross (Eph. 2:15), so that the long hostility between Jews and Gentiles has been cancelled through the cross. The creation of a new humanity in Christ replaces the Mosaic law.[105]

Because Paul believed that the Sinai covenant had come to an end, we are not surprised to learn that he taught that certain commands in the law were no longer required for believers. The false teachers in Galatia insisted that the Galatian Gentiles who believed in Christ had to receive circumcision in order to be saved. Paul dogmatically and forcefully resisted these teachers. Conceivably, Paul could have disagreed but tolerated a different point of view on a controversial matter, but he rejected any compromise on the matter. It is likely that the opponents promulgated circumcision on the basis of Gen. 17:9–14, arguing that it was an eternal covenant sign that was to be applied to all covenant members. According to Paul, however, receiving circumcision to be saved was a denial of the truth of the gospel (Gal. 2:3–5). Those who submitted to circumcision would lose any benefit gained from knowing Christ (Gal. 5:2–6). They would sever themselves from Christ and fall entirely from the grace of the gospel. Instead of relying on the cross of Christ and the work of the Spirit for salvation, they would place their trust in circumcision and the Sinai covenant. Such a stance denies the fulfillment that has arrived in Christ. It removes the offense of the cross and substitutes a human cutting instead of relying on the cross (Gal. 5:11–12), and thus Paul compares the OT requirement of circumcision to pagan castration. The desire to impose circumcision stems from the flesh, which loves the praise and approval of others (Gal. 6:12–17). Believers should boast only in the cross of Jesus Christ and the new creation that has become a reality through his work. The marks of circumcision, according to Paul, are akin to paganism if one trusts in them for salvation. The only marks that matter are those that believers bear because of reliance upon the cross.[106]

Paul was not opposed to circumcision per se. If circumcision is not required for salvation, it is insignificant (1 Cor. 7:19; Gal. 5:6; 6:15). People may receive circumcision for health reasons or cultural reasons. Nor should people take pride in being uncircumcised.

207. R. Martin (1986: 57, 67–68) opts for "significance." In support of "result" or "goal" in 2 Cor. 3:13, see Hafemann 1995: 357; Garland 1999: 183–90 (who follows Hafemann's detailed exegesis).

105. Scholars have proposed a number of different explanations of Eph. 2:15, seeing the abolition of the ceremonial law, the legalistic use of the law, or even the divisive function of the law. Contrary to all these explanations, Paul argues here for the setting aside of the law and its regulations. In defense of this view, see Dahl 1986: 36; Lincoln 1987: 611–12; 1990: 141–43; O'Brien 1999: 196–99; Hoehner 2002: 374–77.

106. Borgen (1980; 1982) rightly argues that the cross (not baptism) replaces circumcision in Galatians. See also the similar Pauline argument in Col. 2:11–12.

What matters is not whether people have such physical marks on their bodies. What matters is whether people are trusting God, so that love is manifested as the fruit of faith (Gal. 5:6). What matters is whether the power of the new creation is at work in one's life (Gal. 6:15). What matters is whether one keeps the commandments of God (1 Cor. 7:19).

This last verse is significant, and we will return to it. Here we want to note that keeping God's commands is exalted and set over against circumcision. We find the same phenomenon in Rom. 2:26, where Paul refers to the uncircumcised who keep the requirements of the law. What is remarkable in both of these texts is that Paul contemplates keeping God's commands and yet at the same time excludes circumcision. Jews who were nurtured in the OT law would think that such a statement was contradictory. Circumcision, after all, was one of the commandments. Two conclusions can be drawn from these Pauline statements. First, Paul assumes that circumcision is no longer required for Christians, for he speaks of it as being irrelevant. We have further evidence that the Mosaic law is no longer normative for believers. Second, Paul apparently thinks that some commands are still normative for believers. We will return to this second matter in due course.

Freedom from the requirement of circumcision is a regular theme in Paul. It appears that the opponents in Phil. 3:2–11 desired to impose circumcision on believers. Paul dismisses their insistence on circumcision and describes circumcision in pagan terms as "mutilation" (Phil. 3:2 my translation).[107] True circumcision is the work of the Spirit, so that people boast in Christ Jesus rather than focusing on their own adherence to the law (Phil. 3:3). One cannot appeal to the life of Abraham to defend the necessity of circumcision (Rom. 4:9–12), for Abraham was righteous by faith (Gen. 15) before he received circumcision (Gen. 17). Abraham received circumcision subsequently as a sign and seal of the righteousness that he enjoyed by faith. Faith, but not circumcision, is essential for membership in the church of Jesus Christ. Circumcision was instituted so that Abraham could function as the father of the Jewish people, and it was never God's intention that everyone would receive it, but rather that both Jews and Gentiles would become Abraham's children through faith.

The temporary nature of the Mosaic covenant is also apparent in Paul's view of food laws. As part of the OT law they were considered to be normative for the people of God (Lev. 11:1–44; Deut. 14:3–21). Paul, however, clearly thinks that they are not required for Christians. He implicitly endorses the strong in Rome because they have the faith

107. See Lightfoot 1953: 144; O'Brien 1991: 356–57; Fee 1995: 296.

to eat everything (Rom. 14:2).[108] Those who limit themselves to eating vegetables, on the other hand, are described as "weak." Paul grants freedom to those who abstain from certain foods, as long as they voice thanks to God (Rom. 14:6). Still, his theological convictions are aligned with the strong. "I know and am persuaded in the Lord Jesus that nothing is unclean in itself" (Rom. 14:14). The same sentiment is expressed in Rom. 14:20: "Everything is indeed clean." Paul asked the strong to refrain from eating or drinking if it caused the weak to stumble in their faith (Rom. 14:13–23). Nevertheless, he undermines the theology of the weak because he believed that all foods are clean. The claim of the Mosaic law that some foods are unclean is overturned.

The same conviction emerges in 1 Cor. 8–10 in the discussion of food offered to idols. The weak are devastated in their consciences if they consume such food, for they cannot separate the consumption of such food from their past association with idols. Despite the extremes of the "knowers" and Paul's Jewish theological background, he is theologically closer to them than to the weak. He agrees that idols do not truly exist and that there is only one God, the Father, and one Lord, Jesus Christ (1 Cor. 8:4–6). Hence, food does not present believers to God (1 Cor. 8:8). No damage is done if believers eat food offered to idols, though the "knowers" should also realize that their freedom to eat does not indicate their spiritual superiority. Paul warns the "knowers" about abusing their rights and inflicting damage upon the weak, but he concurs that eating such food is "lawful" (1 Cor. 10:23). There is nothing intrinsically wrong with eating food offered to idols, though it seems that consumption in the temple is forbidden because there believers traffic with demons (1 Cor. 10:19–22).[109] Believers may feel free to eat any food because of the doctrine of creation (1 Cor. 10:25–26). Everything that God created comes from his gracious hand and is appropriate for human consumption.

The same perspective on foods emerges in Col. 2:16–23. Those who legislate what believers should eat or drink focus on shadows rather than substance, which is Christ himself. They are moving backward in salvation history instead of living in the age of fulfillment. Such rules may have stemmed from the so-called visions of those who considered themselves the spiritual elite, but their wisdom is in name only. Those who belong to Christ have died to regulations about food and drink. Asceticism seems to promote spiritual health, but actually it panders

108. Barclay (1996) demonstrates that Paul's discussion here relativizes and ultimately undermines the continuing validity of OT food laws.

109. It is difficult to discern how Paul's advice in 1 Cor. 8–10 coheres. In my judgment, the best solution is proposed by Fee (1980), whose view is followed here. For other readings, see Fisk 1989; Horrell 1997; Hays 1997: 134–81. For other illuminating studies on food offered to idols, see Gooch 1993; A. Cheung 1999.

to human pride and severs people from Christ. Paul's view that purity laws are no longer binding probably alludes to Jesus' teaching on this matter (Mark 7:18–19).

Nor does Paul think that the observance of days or special festivals are required for believers. Along with foods in Col. 2:16–19, Paul includes festivals, new moons, and Sabbaths (cf. Gal. 4:10). These too are shadows that point to Christ. The inclusion of the Sabbath is particularly noteworthy because it was a regular feature of Jewish life and often commented on by Gentile writers in the Greco-Roman world. Sabbath observance distinguished Jews from their neighbors and was one of the boundary markers of Judaism. For Paul, however, the Sabbath is a shadow that points to Christ. Keeping the Sabbath is not prohibited. If some consider it to be a day of special significance, then they should feel free to observe it (Rom. 14:5), but they must not impose their own private judgment on others. Paul clearly sides with those who consider every day to be the same (Rom. 14:5), but even those who have such a conviction should not despise those who prize one day above another. In the same way, observing the Passover is no longer binding for Christians, but such a conclusion does not cancel out the significance of the Passover, for Christ fulfills the Passover sacrifice by his death on the cross (1 Cor. 5:7). Similarly, the command to remove leaven from houses is not mandatory for believers (1 Cor. 5:6–8). It does not follow from this that the command about leaven is irrelevant for believers, for it symbolizes the need to expunge evil from their midst and to live with sincerity and truth.

What I have said about Passover and leaven suggests the complexity of Paul's view on the Mosaic law. On the one hand, the Sinai covenant and law have passed away; on the other hand, the law is fulfilled in Christ. Because the law has passed away, believers are not obligated to keep the Sabbath, observe food laws, and be circumcised. And yet all these laws are shadows that point to Christ and are fulfilled in him. Hence, circumcision points to the circumcision of the heart accomplished by the cross of Christ (Col. 2:11–12) and by the work of the Spirit (Rom. 2:28–29; Phil. 3:3; cf. Deut. 10:16; 30:6; Jer. 4:4). Just as the Passover points to the death of Christ, so too OT sacrifices in general anticipate and reach their fulfillment in Christ's death on the cross (Rom. 3:24–26; Gal. 3:13). Jesus' death fulfills the sin offering found in the OT, and the words *peri hamartias* in Greek (Rom. 8:3; cf. Lev. 5:6–7; 9:2 LXX) refer to the sin offering (see also 2 Cor. 5:21).[110] The blood of Christ hearkens

110. So Wright 1980. Harris (2005: 452–54), however, is likely correct in arguing that the language in 2 Cor. 5:21 does not merely denote a sin offering per se. "In a sense beyond human comprehension, God treated Christ as 'sin,' aligning him so totally with sin and its

back to the blood spilled in sacrifices in the OT (Rom. 3:25; 5:9; 1 Cor. 11:25; Eph. 1:7; 2:13; Col. 1:20). The temple was considered one of the three pillars of Judaism, but Paul shows no interest in the physical temple. Believers are now the temple of the Holy Spirit (1 Cor. 3:16; 6:19; 2 Cor. 6:16). The language of uncleanness is now applied to the ethical sphere. Believers are to separate themselves from evil and live in holiness (2 Cor. 6:17; 7:1). In the OT those who committed certain blatant sins were put to death (Deut. 13:5; 17:7, 12; 21:21; 22:21). Paul does not require, however, that the man committing incest be put to death (1 Cor. 5:13). Still, the OT requirement finds a new fulfillment in Christ. The unrepentant member of the church is to be excommunicated for his sin and failure to repent (1 Cor. 5:1–13).

Despite the change of dispensation from the old covenant to the new, Paul does not criticize the content of the law. He considers God's commands to be holy, right, and good (Rom. 7:12). Moreover, the change of covenants does not mean that all of the moral norms of the OT have passed away for Christians.[111] Paul seems to carry over some of the moral norms of the law for Christians.[112] The command to honor fathers and mothers still applies to believers (Eph. 6:2). Those who live in love will keep the prohibitions against adultery, murder, stealing, and coveting and will abide by any other such commandment (Rom. 13:8–10; cf. 2:21–22; 7:7–8).[113] Those who live according to the Spirit will fulfill the ordinance of the law (Rom. 8:4),[114] or, as he says in Rom. 2:26, they will keep the precepts of the law. In this latter text as well such obedience is the result of the Spirit's work (Rom. 2:28–29).[115] The prohibition against idolatry still obtains, though Paul does not cite any particular OT text (1 Cor. 5:10–11; 6:9; 10:7, 14; 2 Cor. 6:16; Gal. 5:20; Eph. 5:5; Col. 3:5).[116]

---

dire consequences that from God's viewpoint he became indistinguishable from sin itself" (Harris 2005: 454). See also Garland 1999: 300–301.

111. Much of the material on Paul in the next couple of paragraphs stems from Schreiner 2007, though there are some changes here.

112. Harnack (1995: 27–49) wrongly argues that the OT plays virtually no role in the Pauline ethic. Rightly Gaffin 2006: 31–32.

113. Thielman (1999: 33) rightly argues that Paul thinks Christians "are obligated . . . to live by Jesus' own reshaping of the Mosaic law."

114. On the meaning of this verse, see Thielman 1999: 27–28.

115. It has been argued that the claim in Rom. 2 that Gentiles can keep the law contradicts the assertion in the whole of Rom. 1–3 that no one can keep the law (Räisänen 1983: 98–101, 106–8). The claim that the chapter is contradictory has been answered persuasively (see, e.g., Cranfield 1990; Laato 1991: 98–119; Carras 1992).

116. For the view that the OT functioned as the basis for Paul's ethics even in texts that at first glance do not seem to resort to the OT law, see Rosner 1994. See also Holtz's 1981 essay, translated in Holtz 1995: 51–71. In 1928 Harnack wrote a formative essay denying that the OT functioned as an important ethical norm in Pauline churches (see Harnack 1995: 27–49).

Paul believes that some of the standards in the OT law are normative, though he does not necessarily specify that they derive from the law: honoring and obeying parents (Rom. 1:30; Eph. 6:1–3; Col. 3:20; 1 Tim. 1:9; 2 Tim. 3:2); murder (Rom. 1:29; 13:9; 1 Tim. 1:10); adultery (Rom. 2:22; 7:3; 13:9; 1 Cor. 6:9; cf. 1 Tim. 1:10); stealing (Rom. 1:29–30; 1 Cor. 6:9–10; Eph. 4:28); lying (Col. 3:9; 1 Tim. 1:10; 4:2; Titus 1:12); coveting (Rom. 1:29; 7:7–8; Eph. 5:3, 5; Col. 3:5).[117]

How do we account for the fact that Paul proclaims the obsolescence of the Mosaic law and yet cites commands from the law as authoritative? Perhaps we can say that the commands are not normative merely because they are Mosaic. Some of the laws in the OT are included in the law of Christ (1 Cor. 9:21; Gal. 6:2).[118] But the law of Christ should not be restricted to the moral norms of the law; nor does the law of Christ call attention primarily to the Mosaic law but rather to the fulfillment of the law in and by Jesus Christ. The self-giving life of Jesus manifested particularly in his death on the cross becomes the paradigm for the lives of believers.[119] In giving exhortations to his churches, Paul does not cite the OT law often. The heart and soul of his ethic is summed up in the command to love one another (e.g., Rom. 12:9; 13:8–10; 1 Cor. 8:1–3; 13:1–13; 14:1; Gal. 5:13–15; Eph. 5:2; Col. 3:15; 1 Tim. 1:5), and many have rightly seen the injunction to love as the center of the law of Christ (cf. John 13:34–35).[120]

Love, however, cannot be separated from moral norms. We learn from 1 Thess. 4:2 that specific concrete directives were given to the churches orally. Paul gives specific and concrete parenesis to people in his churches, instructing them not to get divorced (1 Cor. 7:10–16) and to refrain from

117. It should be noted that the OT prophets do not often appeal explicitly to the moral norms of the law in declaring judgment on Israel, and yet it is clear that they believed that Israel had violated the norms of the covenant, and there are many allusions to the Sinai law in the prophetic writings.

118. For a view that is generally compatible with what is argued here, see Thielman 1999. See also Schnabel 1995: 272–73, 294–95.

119. For this understanding of the law of Christ, see Schürmann 1974; Hays 1987; Hofius 1989: 70–74; Thielman 1999: 18–19, though I differ from Hays on the meaning of *pistis Iēsou Christou*. Hofius separates the law of Christ too radically from the love command. Das (2003: 166–86) rightly argues that the law of Christ is not entirely separate from the Mosaic law, but that it is reinterpreted in the light of Christ's coming.

120. Hence, the law of Christ does not fundamentally consist of the sayings of the earthly Jesus (contra W. Davies 1948: 136–46), though such an observation does not exclude the sayings of Jesus from the law of Christ. When Paul refers to the sayings of the earthly Jesus (e.g., 1 Cor. 7:10–11), they are considered to be authoritative. The point is that Paul does not define the law of Christ exclusively or even mainly in terms of the sayings of the historical Jesus. Nonetheless, there is convincing evidence that Paul employed Jesus tradition. See M. Thompson 1991; Stuhlmacher 1983; Allison 1982; Kim 2002: 259–92; contra Neirynck 1986.

sexual immorality (1 Cor. 6:12–20; 1 Thess. 4:3–8).[121] He admonishes the idle to get to work (2 Thess. 3:6–13). A man committing incest must be disciplined (1 Cor. 5:1–13). For Paul, love does not float free of ethical norms but rather is expressed by such norms. In some ways Paul's ethic is rather general, for he does not give specific guidance for each situation. He realizes that in many situations wisdom is needed to determine the prudent and godly course of action (Eph. 5:10; Phil. 1:9–11; Col. 1:9–11). Paul does not have a casuistic ethic that prescribes the course of action for every conceivable situation, but neither does he simply appeal to the Spirit and freedom without describing how life in the Spirit expresses itself. The notion that Paul appeals to the Spirit for ethics without any ethical norms is contradicted by his parenesis. Nor should the Pauline theme of obedience be identified as legalism, for the new obedience is the work of the Spirit in those who are the new creation work of Christ. Nor does it diminish the work of the cross, for the cross is the basis and foundation for the transforming work of the Spirit in believers.

Paul's exhortations do not fall prey to legalism, for they are rooted in his gospel and the promises of God. Another way of saying this is that the imperative (God's command) is rooted in the indicative (what God has done for believers in Christ).[122] Believers are saved, redeemed, reconciled, and justified even now, and yet we have seen that each of these blessings is fundamentally eschatological. Believers are already redeemed, and yet they await final redemption. Justification belongs to believers by faith, and yet they await the hope of righteousness on the last day (Gal. 5:5). Believers would not need any ethical exhortations if they were already perfected. But in the interval between the "already" and the "not yet," ethical exhortation is needed. If the priority of the indicative is lost, then the grace of the Pauline gospel is undermined. The imperative must always flow from the indicative. On the other hand, the indicative must not swallow up the imperative so that the latter disappears. The imperatives do not compromise Paul's gospel. They should not be construed as law opposed to gospel. The imperatives are part and parcel of the gospel as long as they are woven into the story line of the Pauline gospel and flow from the indicative of what God has accomplished for us in Christ.

The tension between the indicative and imperative is evident in 1 Cor. 5:6–8. The man committing incest must be expelled from the church.

121. See especially the detailed studies of Schrage 1981; Deidun 1981. See also Schrage 1995. Schrage and Deidun serve as a valuable corrective to scholars who so emphasize love and the Spirit that they diminish the role of specific commands. Those who make this mistake include Bruce 1975; Belleville 1986: 70–71; Westerholm 1988: 198–218.

122. For an explication of this tension, see Bultmann 1995: 195–216 and especially Parsons 1995: 217–47. See also Gaffin 2006: 68–75.

The toleration of sin in the body corrupts the entire church. The church is exhorted to "cleanse out the old leaven" (1 Cor. 5:7). Here the imperative leaps into view, as the church is instructed to remove the man who is practicing incest. They are to remove the old leaven "that you may be a new lump" (1 Cor. 5:7). The incestuous man needs to be excommunicated so that the Corinthians will become pure and holy again. It seems at this point as if the imperative is almost stamping out the indicative. But Paul then adds the words "as you really are unleavened" (1 Cor. 5:7). They are unleavened because Christ as the Passover sacrifice has effectively removed the impure leaven from their lives. The indicative, then, is the fundamental reality of their lives. As believers in Christ they are free from the leaven of evil. And yet there is a tension in the interval between the already and the not yet. Even though they are unleavened in Christ, they must remove the old leaven from their lives and their church. The indicative does not cancel out the imperative; rather, it provides the foundation for carrying it out.

Another vivid example is found in Phil. 2:12–13. Paul admonishes believers to "work out your own salvation with fear and trembling" (Phil. 2:12). Such an admonition in Paul is nothing short of astonishing, for the command can be paraphrased as "accomplish your own salvation."[123] This word comes from the same Paul who regularly insists that God alone saves and that human works cannot attain salvation. Now he instructs believers to accomplish their own salvation. We must not squelch the call to obedience that surfaces in this verse. The imperative reveals that obedience is necessary for salvation on the last day. Nevertheless, if we stopped here we would badly misconstrue Paul's gospel. The imperative is grounded in the indicative. "For it is God who works in you, both to will and to work for his good pleasure" (Phil. 2:13). Any good that believers do is accomplished by God himself. Their obedience is not autonomous but rather is energized by God. He gives his people the desire and ability to obey him. Hence, this call to accomplish salvation does not fall prey to works-righteousness, nor does it commend human autonomy. All human obedience testifies to God's power and grace in the lives of his people.

The same pattern emerges in Rom. 6:1–14. Some, probably Jewish opponents, are concerned that the Pauline gospel of grace will lead to more sin, especially because he teaches that where sin abounds, grace superabounds and conquers sin (Rom. 5:20–21).[124] Paul staves off the criticism by reminding his readers that those who died with Christ in

---

123. See Fee (1995: 232–37), who overemphasizes the corporate dimension of the admonition. O'Brien (1991: 276–80) is on surer footing here. See also Silva 2005: 119–22.

124. For this view of the situation, see Schreiner 1998: 303–4.

baptism have died to the power of sin. The image "died to sin" suggests at first glance that sin is impossible for Christians, for corpses do not and cannot sin. When we look at Rom. 6 more carefully, we see that Paul emphasizes that the tyranny and dominion of sin have been dethroned for those who have died with Christ. Those who formerly were slaves to sin have been liberated from its hold on them. Such liberation, however, does not cancel out the need for exhortation. Even though believers are freed from sin's dominion, Paul exhorts them not to let sin rule or reign over them (Rom. 6:12–13). The promise that sin will not reign over them (Rom. 6:14) provides the foundation for the imperative that sin should not rule in their lives. They are not exhorted to gain freedom over sin for the first time in their lives. Since they have become obedient from the heart to the teaching that God has handed them over to (Rom. 6:17), they are to give themselves wholly to the new freedom that they enjoy.

Believers have died with Christ to the elements of the world (Col. 2:20), and therefore they are to put to death evil actions and attitudes (Col. 3:5). The old person, which represents who human beings are in Adam, has died with Christ (Rom. 6:6). Believers must remove from their lives evil attitudes, anger, and evil speech (Col. 3:8–9). They are enjoined to do so on the basis of the indicative, for they have put off the old person who they were in Adam and put on the new person who they are in Christ. Believers are clothed with Christ at baptism (Gal. 3:27). Even though believers have already put on Christ, they must also put on Christ and not make any provision for fleshly desires (Rom. 13:14). Believers have already put on the new self and removed the old, and yet Paul exhorts them in Eph. 4:22–24 to put off the old person and clothe themselves with the new person. Again, the tension between the indicative and the imperative surfaces, but there is no doubt that the indicative grounds the imperative.

Paul's letters are stocked with exhortations and commands that do not hail directly from the OT law. It seems that all these commands are embraced under the exhortation to mutual love. Hence, the Pauline ethic can be described in terms of the law of Christ. The centrality of love is evident in a variety of texts. When Paul sums up the commands of the law, the injunction to love one's neighbor as oneself comprises the message of the law (Rom. 13:8–10; Gal. 5:13–15). Those who murder someone or steal from another violate the law of love. The primacy of love is evident also in the introductions to various letters where Paul offers thanks or prayers for the congregations over which he had oversight, for he often thanks God for the faith, hope, and love of believers (Eph. 1:15; Col. 1:3–5, 8; 1 Thess. 1:3; 2 Thess. 1:3).[125] When Paul prays

125. Eph. 1:15 and 2 Thess. 1:3 omit any mention of hope.

for the Philippians, he prays that their love will grow with knowledge and discernment (Phil. 1:9–11). The virtue that binds all the others into a unity is love (Col. 3:14). The self-giving of Christ on the cross functions as the paradigm and model of love, demonstrating that love consists in giving rather than getting (Eph. 5:2, 25, 28–29), and that the life of Christ, particularly his death, exemplifies how God desires believers to live. It is also noteworthy that love is the first virtue mentioned in the fruit of the Spirit (Gal. 5:22–23) and in the exhortations in Rom. 12:9–21. The remaining virtues in these lists certainly fit under the rubric of love. When the Corinthians are plagued by self-promotion in estimating some gifts over others and in exalting themselves because of the gifts that they possessed and displayed, they are summoned in 1 Cor. 13 back to the primacy of love. Again, love is defined or expressed by a number of other virtues, such as kindness, courtesy, and patience, suggesting that love is fundamental and all-inclusive. The root problem between the weak and "the knowers" in Corinth (1 Cor. 8:1–11:1) and the weak and the strong in Rome (Rom. 14:1–15:13) is lack of love. If we stand back and consider the exhortations given to various churches, it seems evident that correction is needed because of failure to love. The trivial lawsuits plaguing the Corinthian church testify to a selfish grasping spirit that refuses to surrender its rights (1 Cor. 6:1–8). Trampling over the needs of the poor so that they have insufficient nourishment at the Lord's Supper evidences lack of love (1 Cor. 11:17–34). Sexual lust insists on satisfying one's own bodily desires without any consideration of the damage that might be inflicted on others (1 Thess. 4:3–8). Those who apply for divorce do so to advance their own comfort or station in life instead of bearing with those who are difficult to live with (1 Cor. 7:10–16).

Nor does Paul think that Christians have arrived, so that they no longer need exhortations. In Rom. 12:1–2 he admonishes believers to give their lives entirely to God as living sacrifices. They still face the danger of conformity to the world and need the continual renewal of the mind to discern God's will. God's will, then, is not instantly recognizable to believers. It takes a process of sifting (Eph. 5:10) and growth to discern what is most pleasing to God (Phil. 1:9–11; Col. 1:9–11). Even spiritual people need instruction and exhortations (Gal. 6:1), for they too can be enticed and carried away by sin. No one reaches the state in this life in which they are exempt from the lure of sin. Paul is pleased with the growth and advancement of the Thessalonians (1 Thess. 4:1–2), but he does not conclude that they have reached the pinnacle. They can increase and abound in love even more (1 Thess. 3:12). Nor does Paul exempt himself, as if he has attained heights that no one else can scale. He realizes that he has not yet gained perfection (Phil. 3:12–16). He too must run the race to the end, with the realization that perfection will be his portion only on the day of resurrection. Those who think that they stand must be on guard lest they fall (1 Cor. 10:12). Those who have died to the tyranny and dominion of sin must not let it rule over their lives (Rom. 6:1–14). Even those who "have been taught by God to love one another" (1 Thess. 4:9) profit from receiving an external word containing moral instruction.[126] Paul gives them specific admonitions to steer their course in their lives with one another (1 Thess. 5:12–22). Paul does not merely say that the Spirit and love will certainly and inevitably direct believers to the right course of action. He gives specific admonitions so that they will not be deceived about the nature of love (Rom. 12:9–21; Eph. 4:25–5:6; Col. 3:5–17). He sends Timothy to remind the Corinthians of all his ways in Christ (1 Cor. 4:17).

In reading the Pauline letters, we must always keep in mind that they are directed to specific situations. Paul does not write a theoretical treatise on ethics. He addresses problems that arise in churches over which he has pastoral oversight. Paul probably would not have included in a treatise that people should not get drunk at the Lord's Supper (1 Cor. 11:21). Nor would the issue of marriage and celibacy have been treated at such length apart from the Corinthians' questions (1 Cor. 7:1–40). The circumstantial nature of the Pauline advice must be taken into account, and yet such a perspective could be misinterpreted, as if Paul only gave situational instructions. Paul's exhortations also flow from a theological worldview and certain convictions that he had about ethical living. Further, in some passages we have general ethical exhortations that likely represent what Paul taught to all churches and believers (cf. Rom. 12:9–21; Eph. 4:25–5:6; Col. 3:5–17). The Pauline writings contain many vice and virtue lists that detail evil and exemplary behavior (Rom. 1:29–31; 13:13; 1 Cor. 5:10–11; 6:9–10; 2 Cor. 6:6; 12:20–21; Gal. 5:19–23; Eph. 4:31–32; 5:3–5; Phil. 4:8; Col. 3:5, 8, 12; 1 Tim. 1:9–10; 4:12; 6:4–5; 2 Tim. 2:22; 3:2–4; Titus 3:3).[127] Some of these lists probably are shaped to address issues that have arisen in the churches, so that they are crafted for the situations in the churches. On the whole, however, the lists reflect what Paul would regularly teach when proclaiming new life in the Spirit.

The moral map of Paul's world cannot be confined to Jewish and scriptural influence. Some of the moral norms are shared with the wider Greco-Roman world (Rom. 1:32; 2:14–15). Scholars have detected Stoic

126. See Wanamaker 1990: 161.
127. The literature on this matter is immense. Scholars have attempted to discern the origin of the vice and virtue lists, seeing them as deriving from Hellenism, Hellenistic Judaism, or even from the OT. See, for example, Easton 1932; McEleney 1974; Kruse, *DPL* 962–63; Schweizer 1979; Borgen 1988; Hartman 1995.

influence in some of Paul's admonitions (e.g., Phil. 4:8).[128] The emphasis on humility, on the other hand, swerves sharply away from what was accepted in the Greco-Roman context. Most Gentiles despised humility as subservient weakness.[129] Similarly, Paul rejected homosexuality (Rom. 1:26–27; 1 Cor. 6:9; 1 Tim. 1:10), even though some Greek writers accepted it. Paul embraces the unanimous Jewish tradition in renouncing homosexuality (e.g., Gen. 19:1–28; Lev. 18:22; 20:13; Wis. 14:26; T. Levi 17:11; T. Naph. 3:3–4; Sib. Or. 3:596–600; Josephus, Ag. Ap. 2.24, 37; Philo, Spec. Laws 3.7). Homosexuality is indicted because it is contrary to nature—that is, God's intention in creating human beings as male and female. The proscription of homosexuality by Paul has become sharply controversial today. Some have suggested that in the Pauline cultural context pederasty is condemned but not all homosexuality.[130] Such a view fails to convince, for Paul specifically refers to men committing homosexual acts with other men (Rom. 1:27), not men with boys. Furthermore, there is no evidence that older women victimized younger girls (Rom. 1:26), and so this theory does not account for the indictment of female same-sex relations. Others have suggested that those who are naturally heterosexual should not engage in homosexual relations, whereas those who are born with homosexual desires are not condemned. Such a view imposes a modern psychological view of nature onto the biblical text. Paul uses the term "nature" (physis) to refer to God's intention in creating human beings, not to describe the psychological condition and drives of human beings.[131]

In summary, the law in Paul's thought must be interpreted in light of redemptive history. The Mosaic covenant and its prescriptions are no longer in force for believers now that Jesus Christ has come. The new age of salvation history has ushered out the old age, which set boundaries between Jews and Gentiles with laws requiring circumcision, Sabbath observance, and purity. The coming of the new age does not mean that Paul has no moral norms. The law of Christ now functions as the norm for believers, and Christ's self-giving sacrifice functions as the paradigm of this law. At the same time, the law of Christ may be described as the law of love. To say that love is the heart and soul of Paul's ethic does not imply that there are no moral norms that inform the law of Christ. Indeed, some of the commands in the OT law are part of the law of Christ, for adultery, stealing, murder, and the like are forbidden because they

128. See O'Brien 1991: 500–503; Fee 1995: 415–19.
129. See O'Brien 1991: 180; Fee 1995: 187–88.
130. Scroggs 1983: 109–18.
131. For a fuller discussion on this issue, see Hays 1996: 379–406. For a comprehensive discussion of virtually every aspect of homosexuality, see Gagnon 2001. See also Schreiner 2006a.

contradict the law of love. Paul teaches that believers are free from the OT law in Christ, but he does not mean freedom from "ought." Still, all Pauline ethical exhortations are rooted in the tension between the indicative and imperative, with the indicative always functioning as the basis for the imperative. So too the only means by which believers can fulfill the law of Christ is the power of the Holy Spirit. Keeping the law of Christ is possible only because the new age has been inaugurated in Christ and because the Spirit has been poured out into the lives of believers.

James

The letter of James[132] provides an interesting window into the role of the law in early Christianity.[133] James probably was written by the brother of Jesus, and he represents the most conservative wing of the Christian church (see Acts 15:13–21; 21:18–25; 1 Cor. 15:7; Gal. 1:19; 2:9, 12; Jude 1). James is a parenetic letter, teaching that genuine faith must express itself in works. Those who do not practice good works will not be justified on the last day (James 2:14–26).[134] True wisdom manifests itself in godly behavior (James 3:13–18). James identifies the law as "the law of liberty" (James 1:25; 2:12), "the perfect law" (James 1:25), and "the royal law" (James 2:8).[135] The law is royal because it is the law of Christ the King.[136] The law in James surely includes the OT, for in James 2:9–11 transgressing the law is connected with failing to keep the commands prohibiting murder and adultery. The "law" for James is also closely related to the "word." Believers are granted new life "by the word of truth" (James 1:18), and thus this word must refer to the gospel of Christ.[137] James proceeds to

132. In this chapter I consider James immediately after Paul because the two authors are often seen to be contradictory, but it seems in this instance that they are actually quite similar in their views of the law of Christ.

133. On the law in James, see Frankemölle 1986. See also the discussion in Dibelius 1975: 116–20, where the background in Judaism and Hellenism is investigated.

134. Laato (1997: 66) notes that in James 2:14–26 James selects two individuals, Abraham and Rahab, who did good works but did not live under the law.

135. Laato (1997: 59–60) argues that the law of freedom represents the power of the new covenant in believers, while the royal law points to the law as God's highest command. Davids (1982: 100, 114) thinks that the perfect law is the law transformed and interpreted by Jesus, and this fits with the view of Bauckham (1999b: 143) that James's view of the law conforms to "the law interpreted by Jesus in his preaching of the kingdom, the law as expressing God's will for his people in the dawning of his eschatological rule." See also Moo 2000: 94, 112. Laws (1980: 87) thinks that James is too brief to help us determine what he means.

136. The reference may be to Christ here rather than God (L. Cheung 2003: 99, 133). See also Bauckham (1999b: 142), who sees a reference to God.

137. Rightly Laato 1997: 52–53; L. Cheung 2003: 87.

speak of "doing the word" and not just hearing it (James 1:22–23 NRSV), and such doing of the word can also be described as "doing" the law of liberty, the perfect law (James 1:25).[138]

The foregoing evidence suggests a close relationship between the "law" and the "gospel," if we can put it that way. Remarkably, James enjoins his readers to "receive with meekness the implanted [*emphytos*] word, which is able to save your souls" (James 1:21). The "implanted word" suggests the new-covenant work of God in which the law is written on the heart (see Jer. 31:31–34; cf. 1 Thess. 4:9).[139] An allusion to the new covenant would explain the relationship between the "word" of the gospel ("the word of truth" [James 1:18]) and the OT law in James, for when the new covenant commences, the law will be written on the heart through the gospel.[140] Another way of putting it is to say that this is James's way of speaking of the law of Christ, and it seems that for James the law of Christ also contains the moral norms of the OT law. It is particularly interesting that James, as a conservative Jewish Christian, says nothing about boundary markers, such as Sabbath, circumcision, or purity laws.[141] The silence on these matters could be interpreted variously, but the keeping of the law in James appears to be rather similar to the Pauline view of the fulfillment of the law.[142]

Most of the exhortations in James fit well with OT piety. Genuine religious practice involves care for the poor and widows (James 1:27; cf. 2:15–16), and such injunctions are prominent, of course, in the OT itself. Partiality to the rich is to be avoided, as already noted, because it violates the law of love (James 2:1–13).[143] The rich are to use their money to help others instead of oppressing the poor (James 5:1–6) or bragging about

138. See Bauckham 1999b: 146. L. Cheung (2003: 93, 96) thinks that the perfect law is linked with that which is able to save souls (James 1:21).

139. So Mitton 1966: 72; Laato 1997: 53; Bauckham 1999b: 146; Moo 2000: 94. But see Jackson-McCabe (2001), who detects the influence of Stoicism here. See also L. Cheung 2003: 88–91.

140. The "word" of the gospel and the law are closely aligned in James (see L. Johnson 1995: 214, 235).

141. For this point, see Dibelius 1975: 18, 146; Davids 1982: 47. Hengel (1983: 174n152) suggests that James distinguishes moral norms from ritual law and especially exalts the law of love. Bauckham (1999b: 147–48) argues that ritual laws are not central to James, but he expected that the Jews of his day would keep such laws, and even Paul himself normally expected Jewish Christians to observe the law, except in certain cases that would impinge upon Gentile freedom. L. Cheung (2003: 123–24) maintains that we cannot know James's stance toward cultic law.

142. Adamson (1989: 200–203) and Laws (1980: 109–10) understand the law in James to refer to the law of love. Dibelius (1975: 142) questions this view. Dibelius (1975: 120) remarks that James conceived of the law as the "perfect moral law."

143. The impact of Lev. 19:11–18 on James is well noted (e.g., Laato 1997: 57–58; L. Johnson 1982b; Bauckham 1999b: 143–44; L. Cheung 2003: 100–104).

their own financial prospects (James 4:13–16). Believers are to use their tongues to benefit others instead of poisoning and tearing down others with their speech (James 1:26; 3:1–12). Anyone familiar with Proverbs would find the admonitions regarding the tongue to be quite familiar. Quarreling with one another and friendship with the world are contrary to how God has called his people to live (James 4:1–6). Genuine wisdom consists not in intellectual virtuosity but rather in character qualities such as gentleness, winsomeness, mercy, and impartiality (James 3:13–18). Those who are full of selfish ambition and envy produce disputes and confusion wherever they land.

James also seems to draw on the Jesus tradition quite often, perhaps supporting the notion that the law is mediated through the teaching of Jesus himself.[144] The prohibition of oaths in James hearkens back to Jesus' instructions about oaths (James 5:12; cf. Matt. 5:33–37). Perhaps the command to love one's neighbor as oneself echoes Matt. 22:39 (par.) and quotes Lev. 19:18. The injunction to ask God for wisdom (James 1:5) reminds readers that disciples should ask, seek, and knock (Matt. 7:7–8 par.). Similarly, the call to ask in faith and not doubt also reminds us of Jesus' words (Matt. 21:21 par.). Every good gift comes from the Father above (James 1:17), just as Jesus taught his disciples (Matt. 7:11 par.). The call to hear and do the word is characteristic of Jesus' teaching (James 1:22–25; cf. Matt. 7:21 par.; Luke 12:47). Visiting orphans and widows reflects OT piety, but it also represents Jesus' teaching (James 1:27; cf. Matt. 25:35–45). God's choosing of the poor (James 2:5) reminds us of the blessing that belongs to the poor (Luke 6:20). To say that judgment is merciless to those who do not show mercy to others (James 2:12–13) is at least conceptually parallel with Jesus' parable on the unforgiving servant (Matt. 18:21–35). The claim to have faith without works (James 2:14–26) reminds us of those who profess Jesus as Lord but do not do his will (Matt. 7:21–23 par.).

There may be at least an echo of Jesus' teaching in the defiling impact of the tongue (James 3:6; cf. Matt. 15:18 par.). The fruit of the lips depends on the tree that produces the fruit (James 3:12), reminding us of Jesus' teaching that we should make the tree good to have pleasing fruit (Matt. 7:16–19 par.). The mourning of the wicked and the call to humility (James 4:6; 5:1) seem to have clear echoes in Jesus' teaching (Luke 6:25; 14:11). Similarly, the prohibition against judging reflects Jesus' own words (James 4:11–12; cf. Matt. 7:1–5 par.). The foolish confidence of those who think that they will make a financial killing in the

144. On this matter, see Adamson 1989: 169–94; W. Davies 1964: 402–5; Davids 1982: 47–48, 100; Dibelius 1975: 28–29; R. Martin 1988: 67–68, 71; Bauckham 1999b: 93–108; Edgar 2001: 63–94.

future (James 4:13–16) reminds us of the naïveté of the rich man in Luke 12:15–21, who thought he would live to enjoy his amassed wealth. The rotting of riches finds a parallel in Jesus' teaching (James 5:2; Matt. 6:19). There may also be a parallel in the language of the end being near, even at the door (James 5:9; Matt. 24:33 par.). Anointing the sick with oil was also practiced by Jesus' disciples (James 5:14; cf. Mark 6:13). It is difficult to know if James consciously drew on the Jesus tradition in all these parallels, but there seems to be enough evidence that he did so to conclude that the ethical teaching of Jesus played a significant role in James's ethics. Hence, we have some further evidence that the OT law is mediated through the law of Christ.

In summary, James does not offer a thoroughgoing explanation of the place of the OT law. Nevertheless, it is striking that circumcision, Sabbath, and purity laws play no role in the letter. Further, it seems that the commands of the law that are mentioned must be understood in light of the word of the gospel and the new law or royal law of Christ. Indeed, this law of Christ is a law of liberty, presumably because the word has been implanted on the soul. It seems legitimate to speak of the law of Christ, given the many allusions to the teaching of Jesus in the letter as well.

Hebrews

When we consider the NT as a whole, we clearly see that the canonical writers believed that the Mosaic covenant was temporary and that believers are no longer obligated to fulfill its stipulations.[145] The author of Hebrews engages in a sustained argument against reverting to the Aaronic priesthood and the Levitical sacrificial cultus.[146] He does not claim that the Mosaic covenant was somehow a mistake from its inception; instead, he hangs his argument on salvation-historical realities.[147] Now that Christ has arrived as the Melchizedekian priest, a return to the Levitical priesthood would constitute a denial of Christ's sacrifice. The Aaronic priests and the OT sacrifices are not rejected wholesale; they are viewed typologically. The OT priesthood and sacrifices pointed to and anticipated the sacrifice of Christ. They are the shadows, but he

145. When I speak of the Mosaic covenant or the law being temporary or obsolete, one should not conclude from this that the OT law is irrelevant for believers today, for the NT writers also emphasize that the law is fulfilled in Christ. Moreover, the OT law continues to be part of sacred Scripture for believers.

146. The letter to the Hebrews is likely directed to believers who were tempted to return to the Levitical cult.

147. For a lucid exposition of the law in Hebrews, see Thielman 1999: 111–34.

is the substance. OT sacrifices cannot forgive, since brute beasts are offered, but Christ's sacrifice is atoning, since he is a willing and sinless victim. The repetition of OT sacrifices reveals that they do not actually forgive sin, whereas the once-for-all sacrifice of Christ definitively and finally atones for sin.

The author of Hebrews maintains that a change of priesthood also constitutes a change of law (Heb. 7:11–12). Indeed, he claims that the law did not bring perfection and was weak and useless (Heb. 7:18–19).[148] In context it is clear that his point is that the law does not provide a full and final atonement for sin. Indeed, he proceeds to argue that the promise of a new covenant indicates that the Sinai covenant is now obsolete (Heb. 8:7–13). Once again, the focus is on the failure of the law to provide final forgiveness. A regular feature in Hebrews is the contrasting of the stipulations and/or punishments of the Sinai covenant over against what is required now for those belonging to Christ (Heb. 2:1–4; 9:6–10, 15–24; 10:26–31; 12:25–29; 13:9–12). Indeed, the very first verses of the letter contrast the definitive revelation given in the last days in the Son with the partial preliminary revelation given under the old covenant (Heb. 1:1–3). The contrast between Moses and Christ articulated in Heb. 3:1–6 is similar in this regard.

It seems quite evident that the author of Hebrews believes that the new covenant has displaced or, perhaps better, "fulfilled" what was promised in the old. Now that the end of the ages has arrived, a return to the old covenant would lead to final destruction. The author is strikingly severe and dogmatic. Those who return to the regulations and sacrifices of the old covenant will be damned, for to do so is to reject the work of Christ on the cross (cf. Heb. 6:4–8; 10:26–31; 12:25–29). Hence, he can say that no sacrifice for sins remains for those who turn away from Christ's sacrifice (Heb. 10:26). This is another way of saying that those who turn back to the Levitical cult have shut themselves off from any possibility of forgiveness. Literal animal sacrifices have passed away, and yet believers do offer to God spiritual sacrifices when they praise God's name and when they share financially with those who are in need (Heb. 13:15–16).

The author of Hebrews does not charge the Mosaic covenant with legalism, nor does he find fault with the specific prescriptions in the law per se. Rather, the Mosaic covenant and law had a typological and salvation-historical function. The tabernacle points to the true tabernacle in heaven, where God dwells (cf. Heb. 8:1–6; 9:1–10). The OT sacrifices and regulations anticipate the sacrifice of Christ and the era that has

---

148. Attridge (1989: 204) says that in Hebrews the law does not produce perfection, whereas in Paul's writings it does not grant life.

dawned in the new covenant (Heb. 9:11–14, 23–28; 10:1–18). OT sacrifices also point to the need to share with others and to praise God (Heb. 13:15–16). The promises of land and rest in the OT forecast the heavenly city and the Sabbath rest prepared for the people of God in the age to come (Heb. 3:7–4:13; 11:9–10, 13–16; 12:22; 13:14).

Is there any continuity between the OT law and the NT fulfillment of the law in Christ in Hebrews? The author cites the new-covenant promise of Jer. 31:31–34, where the law will be written on the hearts of believers (Heb. 8:7–13).[149] The author does not work out what the law written on the heart would mean in terms of giving specific prescriptions from the law. He clearly believes that there is a place for commands and injunctions, as we learn from the parenesis in Heb. 13. What he emphasizes, however, is that cleansing of sins has been achieved once for all through the death of Christ.

The author of Hebrews writes mainly to forestall his readers from apostasy, and thus he does not concentrate on specific ethical issues. The readers are commended for showing compassion and solidarity with fellow believers in prison (Heb. 10:34) and are exhorted to continue to show mercy to imprisoned believers (Heb. 13:3). Hospitality to strangers is encouraged by appealing to the examples of Abraham and Lot, who provided lodging and food to angels without knowing that they were angels (Heb. 13:2). A number of the exhortations indicate that the church is situated on the margin, both socially and financially. This fits with Heb. 11, which describes how the heroes of faith were often discriminated against and even persecuted. Hence, they must visit those who are in prison and provide hospitality to visiting believers. Similarly, they must not be captivated by the love of money but rather must trust that God will provide for their needs (Heb. 13:5–6). A community under social and financial pressure may crack and fall into disarray and division. Therefore, they are exhorted to live at peace with one another (Heb. 12:14). They must not let bitterness flourish, for it would lead to the defilement of many (Heb. 12:15). Sexual sin must also be avoided, so that marriage is kept pure and undefiled (Heb. 13:4). Sexual purity, hospitality, and caring for those who are in need all fit with OT morality.

To conclude, Hebrews emphasizes that the new covenant has dawned in Jesus Christ. A new priesthood means that there is a new law, which fulfills what was promised in the old. Now that the new has arrived, believers should not return to the shadows of the old. They live in the age of the fulfillment of what God has promised and have received definitive

---

149. "On the other hand, 'better' is a characteristic word for our writer and *supersession* is argued: the New Covenant has better and more effective gifts and institutions than the corresponding gifts and institutions of the Old" (Peterson 1982: 109).

forgiveness of sins. Going back to the old would be foolish and fatal. Still, believers are called upon to live in a way that pleases God, for God's law is now written on their hearts.

1 Peter

The letter of 1 Peter does not specifically engage the issue of the role of the OT law in the lives of believers. As we noted earlier, Peter certainly sees the promises of the OT fulfilled in Christ (1 Pet. 1:10–12). The blood of Jesus fulfills OT sacrifices (1 Pet. 1:2, 18–19), so that the true ransom is not the exodus from Egypt but rather the liberation from sin that comes through Jesus' blood. Jesus fulfills what was anticipated by the sacrifice of lambs in the OT (1 Pet. 1:18–19). He is the true Lamb of God and Servant of the Lord (1 Pet. 2:21–25; cf. Isa. 52:13–53:12). The temple in Jerusalem no longer plays a central role in the lives of believers. Jesus is the cornerstone of the new temple, which consists of believers in Jesus Christ (1 Pet. 2:4–8). The OT sacrifices and priesthood are now fulfilled in the church of Jesus Christ (1 Pet. 2:5, 9). All believers are priests (cf. Exod. 19:6). As priests, they do not offer animal sacrifices but rather present spiritual sacrifices through Jesus Christ (1 Pet. 2:5). The church of Jesus Christ, which includes both Jews and Gentiles, is the true Israel (1 Pet. 2:9–10; cf. Exod. 19:5–6). They are God's "chosen race" and "holy nation." They, not ethnic Israel, are the true people of God.

Although Peter does not say so explicitly, he seems to operate with the notion that believers live under a new covenant in which OT sacrifices and practices are no longer normative. Peter's call to holiness in 1 Pet. 1:14–16 confirms this judgment. Peter cites from Leviticus the injunction to be holy. It is likely that Peter does not cite the verse from any particular text in Leviticus but rather draws upon Lev. 11:44–45; 19:2; 20:7, 26. In Leviticus the call to be holy is bound up with observing the food laws (Lev. 11:1–44). Peter commands believers to be holy, but he gives no indication that holiness relates at all to foods that are consumed. Holiness relates to the ethical sphere. Although Peter does not explicitly say so, we can conclude that he sees the old covenant as being fulfilled in Jesus Christ. Hence, the regulations of the old dispensation are not normative per se for believers.

Scholars debate the extent of the Jesus tradition in the Petrine letters. Gundry thinks that it is pervasive, whereas Best sees only limited references to it.[150] The truth probably is somewhere between the views of these two scholars. When Peter speaks of being begotten by God, it

---

150. See Gundry 1967b; 1974; Best 1970b; see also Maier 1984.

is unlikely that he alludes to the Jesus tradition about being born again (cf. John 3:3, 7). The image of rebirth is rather common, suggesting that dependence is less likely. Similarly, when Peter says that the readers love Jesus though they have not seen him, it is unlikely that he is alluding to John 20:29, where Jesus commends those who believe without seeing, for Peter refers to *loving* without seeing, whereas Jesus speaks of *believing* without seeing. Nor does it seem evident that Peter recalls the Jesus tradition in his admonition to love (1 Pet. 1:22; 4:8; cf. John 13:34–35; 15:12). The call to love one another is a staple of NT parenesis and thus cannot be clearly traced to the Jesus tradition, though certainly Jesus emphasized such love. Finally, the call to live as free citizens under the government (1 Pet. 2:16), though conceptually related, is too distant from Matt. 17:26–27 to function as an allusion to Jesus' teaching.

Despite the unlikelihood of seeing a reference to the Jesus tradition in the aforementioned texts, its presence is quite clear in other instances. The call to "gird up your minds" (1 Pet. 1:13 RSV) probably echoes Luke 12:35. The citation of Ps. 118:22 in 1 Pet. 2:7 probably was mediated through the Jesus tradition as well (cf. Matt. 21:33–46 par.). The call to live a life of good conduct so that the Gentiles would glorify God (1 Pet. 2:12) almost certainly recalls the tradition in Matt. 5:16, where Jesus exhorted his disciples to let their good works shine so that people would glorify the heavenly Father. The promise that those who endure suffering while practicing goodness will receive a reward (1 Pet. 2:19) recalls Jesus' promise that those who do good to their enemies will be rewarded (Luke 6:32–35). Similarly, Peter's call to nonretaliation probably reflects Jesus' teaching (1 Pet. 3:9; cf. Matt. 5:38–42). Elders are not to lord their station over the flock (1 Pet. 5:3), and here Peter likely draws on Jesus' admonition to the apostles not to lord it over others when in a position of authority (Matt. 20:25 par.). These examples suggest that the words of Jesus played a significant role in Peter's ethical formation, especially when we consider the brevity of the epistle as a whole and the specific circumstances that evoked the letter.

In considering ethical exhortation in Peter, we should note that the imperatives are clearly grounded in the indicative. Peter begins the letter by celebrating the saving work of God in Christ by the Spirit (1 Pet. 1:1–12). The first imperative appears in 1 Pet. 1:13 after the grace of God has been set forth as the foundation for an obedient life. Even in this case the imperative is the call to continue to live in hope, looking forward to the consummation of the salvation that has been inaugurated. Peter then summons the readers to a holy obedience (1 Pet. 1:14–16), to lives of ethical beauty and goodness. One of Peter's favorite terms for the lives of believers is "conduct" (*anastrophē* [1 Pet. 1:15, 18; 2:12; 3:1, 2, 16]). Believers are to be holy in their conduct (1 Pet. 1:15) in contrast

to the futile and pagan conduct that was passed down from generation to generation (1 Pet. 1:18). The call to live a life of good works is
summarized in terms of conduct that is pleasing to God (1 Pet. 2:12).
The pure behavior of wives is summarized with the same term (1 Pet.
3:1–2), and such godly conduct should mark out Christians when they
are maligned by unbelievers (1 Pet. 3:16).

If we were to summarize Peter's ethical demand, it would be the call
to love (1 Pet. 1:22). Such love is incompatible with malice, guile, insin-
cerity, envy, and slander (1 Pet. 2:1). Peter's summons to live righteously
as members of society, whether as slaves, wives and husbands, or elders
(1 Pet. 2:13–3:7; 5:1–4), will be explored shortly.[151] We could legitimately
say, however, that in every instance the specific directives given simply
summarize the pathway and beauty of love in human relationships.
Those who live lives of love refrain from factions and quarreling (1 Pet.
3:8). They show concern for the lives of others and do not focus arro-
gantly on their own accomplishments and desires. The power of love is
displayed in the refusal to repay evil for evil (1 Pet. 3:9). The life of love
manifests itself in gracious speech, so that others are not trampled with
vicious words (1 Pet. 3:10). Similarly, loving speech does not deceive or
flatter. Those who please God seek peace with all and turn away from
a life of evil.

When Peter contemplates the end of all things, he reminds believers
that their first priority is to love, and that love covers the sins of others
(1 Pet. 4:8). Love reveals itself in hospitality and in using one's gifts to
serve and edify others (1 Pet. 4:9–11). The new life of believers displays
a dramatic difference from preconversion days (1 Pet. 4:2–4). They now
turn away from sexual sin, drunkenness, wild parties, and idolatry. The
life of love is incompatible with murder, stealing, maleficence, or even
being an annoying busybody (1 Pet. 4:15). We notice that murder and
stealing hail from the Mosaic law, though Peter does not emphasize the
source of such commands. The evil of such actions is obvious to all who
have made love the banner of their lives. In any case, some of the moral
norms of the OT fit under the rubric of love.

Peter does not reflect specifically on the role of the OT law, but he
clearly teaches that the OT points forward to Christ and finds its fulfillment in him, so that the OT must be read in light of redemptive history.
The OT law is not the center of Peter's ethical worldview; rather, he
focuses on a life of love and includes quite a few allusions to the teachings of Jesus. Jesus himself, we could say (1 Pet. 2:21–25), functions as
the model and pattern of love, for he displayed his love by giving his

151. See chapter 18.

life for the sake of others.[152] Nor does Peter fall prey to moralism, for his ethical injunctions (imperatives) are rooted in the indicative of God's saving work in Christ.

Jude and 2 Peter

Jude and 2 Peter are occasional letters that do not specifically address the issue of the OT law and its status for Christians. Both letters, however, address the moral lives of believers, for false teachers have promoted a libertine lifestyle, perhaps by distorting Pauline teaching on grace (2 Pet. 3:15–16). We have already seen in both letters that the focus is on obedience, and that such obedience is the necessary consequence of knowing God. The purpose here is to identify the moral norms found in both letters. Both writers indict the false teachers for sexual sin, and homosexuality seems to be included in their indictment (2 Pet. 2:2, 6, 13–14; Jude 6–8, 16). The criticisms of the opponents contain general denunciations, and thus it is difficult to pin down the malfeasance of the opponents. Like Korah of old, they repudiate authority (2 Pet. 2:10–12; Jude 8, 12). They deceitfully insinuate themselves into the church for the sake of financial advantage (2 Pet. 2:3, 14; Jude 12). They complain incessantly about their discontent with life but speak confidently about their own abilities (2 Pet. 2:18; Jude 16). Peter also positively commends moral qualities in the lives of his readers, seeing goodness, knowledge, self-control, endurance, godliness, mutual affection, and love (2 Pet. 1:5–7) to be the fruit of faith. Some of the qualities listed were prized in the Greco-Roman world of Peter's day. Neither letter considers the role of the OT life, for both were written to forestall apostasy and were circumscribed by their limited purpose. It does seem, however, that in both letters the new life of believers flows from God's saving and keeping work, so that again the imperative is rooted in the indicative.

Conclusion

In considering the place of the OT or Mosaic law as it relates to redemptive history, we see the diversity of the NT witness. Letters such as 2 Peter and Jude or the book of Revelation scarcely reflect on the issue at all. Many pieces of literature include no direct discussion of

---

152. See the excellent discussion by Dryden (2006: 177–89), who argues that Jesus' suffering is exemplary in 1 Peter. Dryden contends that although Jesus' suffering functions as an example throughout 1 Peter, it is also the case that Jesus' suffering, in its unique atoning work, must be distinguished from the suffering of believers.

the matter, or what is lacking is a comprehensive treatment of the question. Paul, of course, includes the most thorough analysis of the role of the OT law. Nevertheless, what is striking is the centrality of salvation history in relationship to the law. The NT writings consistently teach that the Mosaic covenant is no longer in force for believers, or at least they fail to bind their churches with practices that distinguished Jews from Gentiles, such as circumcision, Sabbath, or purity laws. Another regular feature is that the law is seen to be fulfilled in Jesus Christ and points toward his death and resurrection. Such a standpoint is reflected whether we consider Matthew, Luke-Acts, Paul, Hebrews, and so on. The NT writers do not merely argue that the Mosaic covenant is set aside in Jesus Christ; they also teach that the law finds its terminus and goal in him, so that he fulfills what is adumbrated in the OT law. Even though the phrase "law of Christ" is found only in Paul, it seems that such a phrase sums up nicely the NT witness regarding the law. The OT law is reinterpreted in light of the Christ event. The central norm of the law is love, and Jesus Christ's giving of himself on the cross is paradigmatic of the love expected of disciples. Such love, of course, is filled in by other moral content, so that love does not become a plastic thing, defined in an arbitrary way. Indeed, some of the commands from the OT are included in the definition of love (such as prohibitions against adultery, stealing, murder, and sexual sin). Still, all the norms of the law are related to Jesus Christ, and so we find in the NT letters numerous allusions to the teaching of Jesus in parenesis. Further, the call to live a new life (the imperative) is always rooted in the indicative of God's saving work in Christ. In addition, the new life is possible only by the work of the Holy Spirit. Hence, when we consider the law, the major themes of this work come together. The OT law must be interpreted in terms of salvation history, and the law is realized only through the saving work of Christ and the empowerment of the Holy Spirit.

PART 4

THE PEOPLE
OF THE PROMISE
AND THE FUTURE
OF THE PROMISE

17

✿ ✿ ✿ ✿ ✿ ✿ ✿ ✿ ✿ ✿ ✿ ✿ ✿ ✿ ✿ ✿ ✿

The People of the Promise

Introduction

God's promises are not mere abstractions. God designed to form a people who would bring him honor and glory. He called Adam and Eve as those who were made in his image to rule the world for him and to cultivate it and nourish it so that his name would be magnified (Gen. 1:26–27; 2:15). Sin disrupted the relationship between God and human beings, but God pledged to win victory through the offspring of the woman, though conflict would continue between the offspring of the serpent and the offspring of the woman (Gen. 3:15). We have seen previously that the blessing for the whole world would come through the offspring of Abraham.[1] Abraham figures largely in the NT because he was the progenitor of a new people. The children of Israel traced their origin to Abraham, and God promised that he would make a great nation from Abraham's descendants. We see in the NT how in the church of Jesus Christ God fulfilled the promise made to Abraham.

1. The promise of worldwide blessing through Abraham raises the question of mission in the OT. Some argue that the OT consciously advocates a mission to the Gentiles. A more persuasive reading of the evidence, however, is that neither in the OT nor in Judaism was there a focus on a centrifugal mission to the Gentiles. What we find in the OT is nicely summarized in the expression "Come and see," while what we find in the NT is "Go and tell." For a thorough and convincing discussion of the whole question, see Schnabel 2004a: 55–172.

Matthew and Mark

We begin by considering Matthew's vision of the people of God, and I will include a very abbreviated discussion of Mark because most of what Mark says is included in Matthew. Luke-Acts will be considered separately because the church plays such a significant role in the Lukan writings.

The notion that the church fulfills the promise to Abraham raises an intriguing question in Matthew, for it has often been observed that we find there the themes of particularism and universalism.[2] By "particularism" we mean that Matthew emphasizes that Jesus has come to fulfill his promises to ethnic Israel, while "universalism" focuses on the inclusion of the Gentiles into the people of God. A focus on Israel in Matthew is hardly astonishing, given the Jewish character of this Gospel. Matthew begins with a genealogy (Matt. 1:1–17), testifying that Jesus is the son of Abraham and the son of David.[3] Jesus is an Israelite, and not only is he an Israelite, but also he descended from David, and thus he is Israel's Messiah and king. He has come to serve as "king of the Jews" (Matt. 2:2), whose mission "is to shepherd my people Israel" (Matt. 2:6). Jesus conducted his ministry almost exclusively in Israel, focusing especially on Galilee but also on Judea and Jerusalem. He did not engage in missionary journeys to the Diaspora or commission his disciples to proclaim the kingdom to Gentiles during his ministry. Indeed, he forbade his disciples to preach to Gentiles or the Samaritans when he sent them out for ministry (Matt. 10:5). They were to limit themselves "to the lost sheep of the house of Israel" (Matt. 10:6).[4] The same emphasis emerges in the encounter with the Canaanite woman in one of Jesus' few trips outside the land (Matt. 15:21–28). The woman implored Jesus to have mercy on her demonized daughter. Finally, Jesus responded by healing the woman's child, but he also emphasized the distinctiveness of his mission.[5] He

2. Bosch (1991: 60) notes the standard critical view in saying that these two themes reflect different views of mission.

3. But the reference to Abraham also signals the fulfillment of the promise that all nations would be blessed through Abraham (so Köstenberger and O'Brien 2001: 88).

4. Particularly helpful is the discussion of this text in Hagner 1993b: 270–71 (see also Davies and Allison 1991: 167–68). Hagner emphasizes the temporary and salvation-historical character of the admonition while at the same time underscoring that Matthew includes this saying to indicate the Lord's faithfulness to his promises made to Israel. Contra Luz (2001: 74–75), who suggests a cancellation of the mission to Israel in Matt. 28:19–20.

5. For a massive and outstanding study of mission in early Christianity, see Schnabel 2004a; 2004b. For a survey of Jesus' mission, see Schnabel 2004a: 207–62.

was "sent only to the lost sheep of the house of Israel" (Matt. 15:24).[6]
The mission to Israel was urgent because the Son of Man is coming
soon, and the disciples will not complete their mission before he comes
(Matt. 10:23). The meaning of Matt. 10:23 is, of course, controversial.[7]
The coming of the Son of Man here could refer to the parousia, and
thus a mission to Israel is envisioned that lasts until the second coming.[8]
Others see a reference to Jesus' resurrection, the descent of the Spirit,
or even the success of the Gentile mission. Hagner thinks that the most
likely meaning in this context is the judgment of Jerusalem in AD 70.
On this view, the destruction of Jerusalem functioned as a type of the
final judgment and symbolized the shift from Jews to Gentiles in the
history of salvation.[9]

On the one hand, the people of God are identified as the Jews, and
yet remarkably enough Matthew also emphasizes the inclusion of the
Gentiles. The inclusion of the Gentiles surfaces in the genealogy (Matt.
1:1–17). Four women are included: Tamar, Rahab, Ruth, and the wife
of Uriah (Bathsheba). These women are mentioned probably for more
than one reason. Their inclusion indicates that God has worked in
surprising ways in redemptive history, and thus the birth of Jesus via
Mary is no exception. Still, the main purpose seems to be the inclusion
of Gentiles. Tamar and Rahab were notorious Gentile women, and yet
as Gentile women they were in the line that led to the birth of the Messiah. The canonical shape of Ruth emphasizes the genealogy that leads
up to David, the forerunner of the Messiah (Ruth 4:13–22). It seems
that the emphasis on Gentiles is confirmed by a reference to "the wife
of Uriah" (Matt. 1:6). Matthew could have easily mentioned the name
"Bathsheba," but it seems that Uriah is named instead of Bathsheba
because he was a Gentile.[10] What stands out, therefore, in the naming
of the women is their Gentile origin, which foreshadows the mission
to the Gentiles.

Matthew actually signals in a variety of ways that the universal
promise of blessing for all nations is about to be fulfilled. For instance,
Matthew declares that Jesus came to "save his people from their sins"
(Matt. 1:21), and the people in view, given the scope of the Gospel as a

---

6. Stettler (2004: 158) argues that Jesus' ministry to Galilee fulfills prophecy (Ezek.
37:15–28; Jer. 30:1–31:40; Hos. 11:8–9) in that Galilee represents the northern kingdom
and Judah the southern kingdom, and Jesus in his ministry reunites Israel.

7. For the options, see Davies and Allison 1991: 190; Hagner 1993b: 278–80; Schnabel
2004a: 303–5; Luz 2001: 91–94 (who argues that the prophecy did not come true).

8. Davies and Allison 1991: 190–92; Nolland 2005: 427–29.

9. Hagner 1993b: 280.

10. So also Luz 1995: 26.

whole (cf. Matt. 21:43; 28:19), includes both Jews and Gentiles.[11] The folding in of the Gentiles manifests itself also in the story of the magi from the east (Matt. 2:1–12).[12] These men saw the star of Bethlehem and concluded that the king of the Jews had been born. They came to give homage to this newborn king, whereas Herod was determined to destroy him, and both Herod and the elite in Jerusalem, instead of rejoicing at the birth of the messianic king, were troubled at hearing the news (Matt. 2:3). The account forecasts Jewish rejection of the good news of the kingdom and of Jesus as the Messiah. We have already seen that the mission to the Jews is prominent in Matthew, but the Jews are also summoned to repentance (Matt. 3:2; 4:17). The Sadducees and Pharisees must not count on their Jewish ancestry, as if a pure heritage would guarantee salvation (Matt. 3:7–10). The Baptist reminds them that God can turn stones into Abraham's children. Perhaps the inclusion of the Gentiles is also suggested by "Galilee of the Gentiles" (Matt. 4:15), though the phrase may refer to the influence of Gentiles in Galilee.[13]

The story of the centurion testifies that belonging to the people of God is not restricted to the Jews (Matt. 8:5–13). Jesus remarks that he had not seen in Israel faith such as the centurion had. Jesus then declared that many Gentiles from around the world would enjoy the messianic feast on the last day (cf. Isa. 25:6–8),[14] whereas many Jews will be expelled from the kingdom and dwell in darkness and experience agonizing misery. Jesus declared elsewhere that Jews who were privileged to hear the good news of the kingdom and rejected it bear unique responsibility (Matt. 11:20–24). Jesus, as the Servant of the Lord, "will proclaim justice to the Gentiles" (Matt. 12:18), and "in his name the Gentiles will hope" (Matt. 12:21). The good seed are sown throughout the whole world (Matt. 13:37–38) and cannot be restricted to Israel. The feeding of the four thousand most likely occurred in Gentile territory

11. Luz restricts the reference to Israel, but most commentators see a reference to both Jews and Gentiles (Davies and Allison 1988: 210; Hagner 1993b: 19–20).

12. Davies and Allison (1988: 227–32) rightly argue that the magi represent Gentiles, that they functioned as, so to speak, "Balaam's successors" who have seen the fulfillment of Num. 24:17, and that they fulfilled other OT prophecies (Isa. 60:3–6; cf. Ps. 72:10–11). See also Luz 1989: 34–35; Hagner 1993b: 26–27; R. Brown 1977: 182.

13. The point is not that Jesus ministered especially to Gentiles in Galilee, but rather it anticipates the good news of the kingdom spreading also to Gentiles, who also were inhabitants of Galilee (see Davies and Allison 1988: 383–85; Luz 1989: 195; Hagner 1993b: 73). Nolland (2005: 74), however, argues that the reference to the Gentiles is negative here, reminding the readers of the eighth-century exile.

14. Isaiah 25:6 specifies that the feast is "for all peoples," and hence the universal dimensions of the feast are emphasized. See Childs (2001: 184–85), who also points out that the promise here accords with Isaiah's emphasis on the new heavens and new earth.

(Matt. 15:32–39).[15] In the parable of the laborers in the vineyard the eleventh-hour workers may represent Gentiles (Matt. 20:1–16).[16] Even if the Gentiles are not in view in some of these texts, it is clear in Matthew that God's blessing enveloped Gentiles, who were not originally part of God's covenant with Israel.

The cleansing of the temple symbolizes the future judgment of Israel and the destruction of the temple in AD 70 (Matt. 21:9–17). Similarly, the cursing of the fig tree represents the cursing of Israel because of its failure to repent and believe (Matt. 21:18–22 par.).[17] God's judgment of Israel comes to a climax in the parable of the wicked tenants, where Jesus pronounces that the kingdom will be taken from Israel and be given to a nation that yields good fruit (Matt. 21:43); the nation that produces good fruit almost certainly refers to the church.[18] Some have interpreted these statements as indicating that the judgment upon Israel is irrevocable. The context, however, focuses upon the religious leaders of Jesus' day. Certainly there is a judgment upon all Israel, for the nation as a whole failed to embrace Jesus as the Messiah. Nevertheless, the disciples were to continue to proclaim the kingdom in Israel until the coming of the Son of Man (Matt. 10:23). The harvest from Israel was singularly disappointing, but it does not follow that there will be no future harvest in Israel, or that all of Israel is excluded from God's saving purposes. Matthew's point is that others besides the Jews are to be invited to share in God's kingdom blessings (Matt. 22:8–10). The gospel is to be proclaimed throughout the whole world (Matt. 24:14), but this includes both Jews and Gentiles. Jesus commissions his disciples after his resurrection to "make disciples of all nations" (Matt. 28:19).[19] There are good reasons to think that Jews are included among the nations that

15. Contra Davies and Allison 1991: 569–70. Rightly Schnabel (2004a: 339) regarding the parallel text in Mark: "There is no doubt that the account of Mk 8:1–10 is located in pagan territory." See also the perceptive comments of France (2002: 305–6) on the differences between the feeding of the five thousand and the feeding of the four thousand.

16. So Carson 1984: 428. Hagner (1995: 573) sees this reading as a possibility. Davies and Allison (1997: 67–68) argue that the parable is confined to an admonition against boasting. Against the Gentile view, see also Nolland 2005: 813.

17. See France 2002: 439–41; Hagner 1995: 605–6. Contra Carson (1984: 445), who limits the lesson to hypocrisy. Evans (2001: 160) focuses on destruction of the temple, but such destruction cannot be disentangled from the fate of Israel.

18. The meaning of this verse is quite controversial. For a defense of the interpretation adopted here, see Hagner 1995: 623. See also France 1989: 227–32. Nolland (2005: 879) rightly adds that this does not involve the exclusion of all Jews but rather includes all "who now respond to the message of the kingdom." Luz (2005: 42–43) thinks that the statement does not refer to the church but is more general.

19. For an excellent analysis and commentary, see Schnabel 2004a: 348–67.

are to be evangelized.[20] The people of God, according to Matthew, will be composed of both Jews and Gentiles. The gospel of the kingdom is to be proclaimed to all without exception.

Does Matthew contradict himself in that in some texts the disciples were to restrict their mission to Israel (Matt. 10:5–6) but elsewhere they were instructed to make disciples from every nation (Matt. 28:19)? No contradiction exists if we take Matthew seriously as history and consider the redemptive-historical character of the book. During Jesus' ministry he focused on Israel. The children of Israel, after all, were descended from Abraham and were the people of the promise. The fulfillment of God's promises was declared to them first because they had a special covenant with Yahweh. During Jesus' ministry, however, Israel on the whole (but not without exception) rejected the good news proclaimed to them by failing to repent and put their trust in Jesus as God's prophet and Messiah. After Jesus' death and resurrection, the focus shifted. The good news continued to be proclaimed in Israel, but a new wrinkle was introduced. The message of the kingdom was now to be circulated to the entire world. The different emphasis should be explained in redemptive-historical terms. During Jesus' ministry the focus was on Israel as the children of the promise. After his death and resurrection both Israel and the nations were included as recipients of the saving message. We see a remarkable salvation-historical shift here. In the OT the emphasis was not on going and proclaiming the good news; instead, the nations were invited to come and behold what God was doing in Israel. However, Jesus, after his resurrection, commissioned his disciples to go to the ends of the earth in making disciples.[21] Further, the particularist emphasis reminds the reader that God has not forsaken Israel, that he is faithful to his saving promises.

Jesus follows the OT in teaching that the people of God consists of the remnant. The remnant is limited to those who believe in Jesus and repent upon hearing the message of the kingdom. He calls disciples who will function as fishers of people in inviting others to participate in kingdom blessings (Matt. 4:18–22). There are no convincing parallels to the expression "fishers of people," suggesting that Jesus himself coined it.[22] The appointment of the Twelve as apostles would resonate with any Jew familiar with the OT (Matt. 10:1–4). Just as there were twelve patriarchs and twelve tribes of Israel representing the people of God, so too Jesus appointed twelve men as apostles who functioned as

---

20. See Meier 1977; Carson 1984: 596; France 1989: 235–37; Hagner 1995: 887; Davies and Allison 1997: 684; Nolland 2005: 1265–66; Luz 2005: 628–31. Contra Hare and Harrington 1975.

21. See Bosch 1991: 17, 19.

22. So Schnabel 2004a: 275–77.

the leaders of the remnant of Israel—the true Israel within ethnic Israel. Even without the use of the word "church" (*ekklēsia*), we have here the notion of a new community gathered in Jesus' name.[23] Only those who listen to and obey the message of the kingdom that the Twelve proclaim will be spared judgment (Matt. 10:5–15). The message that the Twelve proclaim centers on Jesus, so that families in Israel reveal whether they truly belong to God by their response to Jesus and his messengers (Matt. 10:32–39). Indeed, Jesus teaches that families will be divided over their response to him, demonstrating that the remnant comprises those who show allegiance to Jesus. Those who welcome the apostles and their message indicate that they also welcome Jesus (Matt. 10:40). Those who do the Father's will belong to Jesus' family (Matt. 12:46–50), so that the people of God are redefined in terms of relationship with Jesus. Further, Jesus teaches that when the new world commences, the apostles "will also sit on twelve thrones, judging the twelve tribes of Israel" (Matt. 19:28; cf. Luke 22:29–30).[24] In Daniel the saints from Israel will receive the kingdom and enjoy authority (Dan. 7:22, 27), but now the authority to judge Israel is given to the twelve apostles.[25]

Given that Jesus defined the new community in terms of its relationship with him, it is not astonishing that Jesus spoke of the "church" (*ekklēsia*). Indeed, he refers to "my church" (Matt. 16:18), indicating that the true remnant within Israel belongs to and is governed by him.[26] The declaration "I will build my church" is given in response to Peter's confession that Jesus is the Christ and Son of God (Matt. 16:13–18). Intense debate has centered on the words "You are Peter, and on this rock I will build my church" (Matt. 16:18). Protestant exegesis has traditionally understood the rock to represent Peter's confession of Jesus as Christ, so that Jesus' messianic status functions as the foundation of the church. Roman Catholic exegesis has defended the view that the rock is Peter himself, finding evidence here to support papal supremacy in the church of Jesus Christ. Neither view as traditionally defended is credible. Reading a doctrine of papal supremacy into the text is an anachronism. Protestants have sometimes defended their view by noting the difference between the two Greek words for rock: *petros* for Peter's name, and *petra*

23. The selection of the Twelve signifies the restoration of Israel (Meier 2001: 128–63; E. Sanders 1985: 98–106; Meyer 1979: 153–54; Schnabel 2002a: 45).

24. The Twelve represent the new Israel and will sit in judgment over unbelieving Israel (Hagner 1995: 565; see also Jervell 1996: 81). But Fitzmyer (1985: 1419) argues that the Lukan saying focuses on ruling rather than judgment. It seems difficult, however, to separate ruling from exercising judgment.

25. Schnabel 2002a: 45.

26. In defense of the authenticity of Matt. 16:17–19, see Meyer 1979: 185–97; Carson 1984: 366; France 1989: 211. Davies and Allison (1991: 604–15) tentatively opt for authenticity. For the contrary perspective, see Luz 2001: 357–60.

for the rock upon which the church is built. The difference between the two Greek words, however, is insignificant. *Petros* is masculine because it designates Peter's name, and *petra* ("rock") is a feminine noun that most likely renders the Aramaic term *kēfaʾ*. Furthermore, if Jesus spoke these words in Aramaic, then the difference between the gender of the two terms that is evident in Greek vanishes.[27] What we have here, then, is a play on words, so that it is most natural to read the text to say that the church would be built upon Peter as the rock.[28] Davies and Allison suggest a background in Isa. 51:1–2, where Abraham is considered as the rock or foundation of the people of God, and here Peter fulfills that founding role.[29] As the head of the Twelve, Peter represents the new community of Jesus. Jesus' new assembly, then, is built upon the apostles. Peter, as the first among equals and representative of the Twelve, has the keys of the kingdom.[30] Jesus promised that death will not conquer the church, but rather the church will triumph over the power of evil.[31] Jesus has given them authority to govern, so that they bind and loose on earth what is bound or loosed in heaven (Matt. 16:19).[32] What they permit or forbid, in other words, is what God endorses or condemns.[33]

27. Even though the masculine *petros* for "rock," according to Nolland (2005: 669), "eventually fell into disuse," he thinks that there is some significance in the change to the feminine *petra* and argues that Peter is the rock "in the act of confessing Jesus as the Christ."

28. For views that generally fit with what is argued here, see Davies and Allison 1991: 623–27; Wilkins 1995: 189–94; Carson 1984: 368; Hagner 1995: 470.

29. Davies and Allison 1991: 624.

30. For a balanced discussion of Peter's role, see France 1989: 244–46. On the one hand, Peter played a unique role in redemptive history as the apostle who was first among equals. On the other hand, he is portrayed as fallible and sinful like all other disciples. Luz (2001: 370–75) summarizes the history of interpretation, showing that a papal interpretation is not original but rather commenced in the third century.

31. For the history of interpretation of "the gates of hell," see Davies and Allison 1991: 630–34. They opt for the view that demonic powers will not conquer the church, but the OT background connects the "gates of Sheol" with death (cf. Job 17:16; 38:17; Ps. 9:13; 107:18; Isa. 38:10; Jon. 2:2; see also Wis. 16:13; 3 Macc. 5:51; Sir. 51:9; Rev. 1:18; 6:8; 20:13–14), so the focus probably is on death, though some connection with the view proposed by Davies and Allison is possible because death and demonic rule are intertwined.

32. Binding and loosing in Matthew should be interpreted widely to include behavior that is permitted or forbidden, teaching that is legitimate or false, and by implication forgiveness of sins or the refusal to grant such (see Hagner 1995: 472–74). Others restrict it to entrance or dismissal from the kingdom (Carson 1984: 373–74; Wilkins 1995: 194–97). Davies and Allison (1991: 635–41) survey various interpretations and argue that the teaching authority, particularly of Peter, is in view.

33. France (1989: 247n11) argues that the future-perfect verb tenses indicate that the church binds and looses what has already been determined in heaven, so as to preclude any notion that the church arbitrarily or automatically reflects the will of God. But Nolland (2005: 681) claims that this presses the tenses too far, so that it signifies that what is bound on earth is at the same time bound in heaven. Davies and Allison (1991: 638–39)

Obviously, this should not be taken to teach that the apostles were infallible in every particular, as if every arbitrary thing that they might have done received God's blessing.

The other text that refers to the church is Matt. 18:15–20. This text addresses the matter of disciplining a brother or sister who has sinned within the church.[34] Those who sin and fail to repent are to be corrected first by the person who is sinned against or who discovers the sin. If the one who committed the infraction repents, the matter should be forgotten. If one persists in the sin, then two or three brothers or sisters from the community should confront the person in question. If he or she repents, then, again, the matter should be forgotten. However, if the person becomes recalcitrant and still refuses to turn away from sin, then the matter must be brought to the entire church. If the person heeds the admonition of the church and repents, then he or she is restored to fellowship in the community. If, on the other hand, the counsel of the church is repudiated, then the unrepentant brother or sister must be expelled from the church and reckoned as an unbeliever. The sayings about binding and loosing and agreeing on earth are rooted in a disciplinary context. Jesus gave instructions to preserve the purity and vitality of the new remnant. Insofar as the church truly gathers in Jesus' name in exercising discipline, they carry out Jesus' will.[35] Jesus did not grant the church unrestricted authority to carry out every whim. When the church is gathered in Jesus' name, then its binding and loosing fulfill his will. The following parable (Matt. 18:21–35) indicates that the church is to be a forgiving and loving community. Reproof and correction are always to be carried out in the spirit of love and kindness and for the benefit of the one disciplined.

When we compare Mark to Matthew, we see that the former says little about the new community gathered around Jesus. Jesus does call disciples to fish for people, so that they would participate in the summons to Israel to repent (Mark 1:16–20). Those who belong to Jesus' family are those who do the Father's will (Mark 3:31–35). Jesus also appoints the Twelve as apostles (Mark 3:13–19). As in Matthew, the Twelve represent the new nucleus of the people of God. They are the true Israel, and those

---

maintain that God's decision is subsequent to what the church determines, for the parallel in Matt. 18:18 shows that God concurs with what is already decided upon on earth (cf. the perfect periphrastics in Isa. 8:17; Heb. 2:13). The tenses alone do not resolve the issue, but Matthew does not grant unrestricted authority to the Twelve. He assumes that the binding and the loosing is authoritative insofar as it corresponds with the divine will.

34. See Hagner 1995: 531–33. France (1989: 248–49) underestimates the disciplinary function of the church here.

35. Luz (1995: 105) notes that the church, not leaders or some ecclesiastical court, disciplines the recalcitrant.

who listen to the message proclaimed by Jesus and the Twelve become members of the new Israel.[36]

Matthew emphasizes, then, that the message of salvation was sent first to the Jews as the people of the promise. Both the Baptist and Jesus called upon Israel to repent to receive the promised blessings. Such repentance was necessary to be part of the new community that was formed by Jesus himself. The leaders of this new community, this new remnant, were the twelve apostles, who signified restored Israel. Those who repented and responded positively to Jesus' ministry were considered to be part of restored Israel. Unfortunately, many in Israel failed to respond to the kingdom message of Jesus and thus were destined for judgment. At the same time, there are indications here and there in Jesus' ministry that the people of God will not be confined to Israel. Gentiles who repent and believe will also belong to the people of God. Indeed, after his resurrection Jesus specifically enjoins his disciples to go and make disciples of all nations (Matt. 28:18–19), so that the people of God will embrace all peoples everywhere who submit to Jesus' teaching and join the people of God by baptism.[37] By the conclusion of Matthew's Gospel we have a conscious mission to all peoples. The participle "going" (*poreuthentes*) clearly has an imperatival sense, and this is verified by parallel texts in Matthew (Matt. 2:8; 9:13; 11:4; 17:27; 28:7). Nor is the commission complete with initial evangelization, for the command to make disciples includes teaching all that Jesus has commanded the disciples, which surely includes the teaching found in Matthew's Gospel. Of course, the requirement for initial entry into the people of God is also relayed in the insistence upon baptism. The threefold baptismal formula is unique to Matthew.[38] Matthew also includes instructions on discipline in the people of God, for the purity of the restored Israel must be maintained so that others would see the good works done and glorify God as well (Matt. 5:16). The church, as a community that does good, calls attention to God's beauty. Its light is to shine for the sake of unbelievers, so that they confess that God is glorious. When Jesus said that the disciples are the world's salt and must not lose their saltiness (Matt. 5:13), he probably did not mean that they

---

36. Meier (2001: 148–54), considering the issue more broadly, rightly says that Jesus' choosing of the Twelve symbolizes the regathering of Israel's twelve tribes.

37. It is a common view that Christian baptism derives from the practice of John the Baptist (so Hartman 1997: 9, 31–32). More controversial is whether the Baptist's practice was influenced by proselyte baptism, since the date of the latter is uncertain. For support of such a view, see Beasley-Murray 1962: 18–31; for the contrary position, see McKnight 1991: 82–85.

38. Most critical scholars claim that the formula is inauthentic (see Hartman 1997: 147), but see Hagner 1995: 883.

are to act as a preservative. Instead, salt points to the distinctiveness of the church.[39] The church must stand forth as distinct from the world in the way it lives as disciples of Jesus. This view of salt seems to be confirmed from Luke 14:34, where salt that loses its ability to season is worthless. The point here does not seem to be the preservative nature of salt but rather the distinctive tang and taste that it provides. Such a view fits with the context because Jesus' disciples, as the light of the world, stand out in a dark world (Matt. 5:14–16). Such a view also fits the wider context of Matt. 5–7. Disciples have a distinct profile over against the world. They admit that they are poor in spirit, are peacemakers and merciful, endure persecution, do not hate those who mistreat them, are not marked by lust and abuse of women, love their enemies, do not practice religion for the praise of others, trust God for their physical needs, and do not judge others. Believers who live in such a way are salt and light. They communicate their difference from the world and shine as witnesses in a dark world.

Luke-Acts

Luke-Acts play a crucial part in our understanding of the nature and mission of the people of God.[40] The book of Acts in particular casts light upon the mission of the church. I will also include in this section Luke's particular emphasis on prayer because it plays a central role in the Lukan writings in the fulfillment of God's saving promises and in the mission of the church.

Mission to Jews and Gentiles

Luke-Acts opens with the promise that the Lord will fulfill the covenantal promises he has made to his people (Luke 1:17).[41] The promises made to Abraham will be realized for Israel (Luke 1:54–55, 72–75). He will redeem his people by establishing a Davidic king who will save Israel

---

39. This idea was first suggested to me by one of my students, Jonathan Leeman, who in 2004 wrote a paper titled "Matthew's Beatitudes in Biblical Theological Context." He also pointed me to a sermon by Phillip D. Jenson, "The High Price of Salt," given at Capitol Baptist Church in Washington, DC, on May 14, 2000.

40. For an excellent survey of mission in Luke-Acts, see Köstenberger and O'Brien 2001: 111–59.

41. Jervell (1996: 34) argues that Luke's favorite term for the church is "people" (*laos*), and that the term is reserved for Israel. However, Jervell (1996: 40) minimizes the place of Gentiles as God's people in Acts, although he rightly says that Gentiles have come to share in what belongs to Israel. But the call to go to the ends of the earth in Acts 1:8 (contra Jervell 1996: 41–42) refers also to the inclusion of Gentiles.

from their enemies (Luke 1:68–71). At first glance, it appears that the fulfillment of God's promises to Israel will occur in a straightforward way, so that Israel will finally enjoy political and religious supremacy. Rome and any other competitor to the throne will be defeated, and Israel will thrive under God's favor. Simeon predicts, however, that the coming Davidic king will be opposed by some within Israel, and that Mary will suffer grief (Luke 2:34–35).[42] Some ambiguity arises, therefore, as to how the promise will be fulfilled.

The Baptist proclaimed repentance to Israel, maintaining that the promise of return from exile in Isaiah would not be fulfilled unless the people turned to God to receive forgiveness of sins (Luke 3:3–6).[43] The people could not comfort themselves with their heritage, thinking that their biological descent from Abraham would spare them from God's wrath (Luke 3:7–9). God is able to raise up children of Abraham from stones, and thus only those who manifest the fruits of repentance truly qualify as Abraham's children. One of the primary themes of Luke-Acts emerges here: the promise of salvation belongs only to repentant Israel and thus is not guaranteed to every ethnic Jew.

Luke 4:25–30 forecasts a prominent theme in Luke-Acts: Jewish rejection[44] of the gospel and Gentile acceptance.[45] The rejection of Jesus manifested itself in his being rebuffed by the religious leaders of the day. They bore special responsibility as leaders for the spiritual welfare of the nation. The Jewish leaders identified Jesus with Beelzebul (Luke 11:15), and Jesus in turn denounced them for their evil (Luke 11:37–52), but he also lamented and grieved over Jerusalem because of its coming judgment (Luke 13:34–35; 19:41–44). Jesus' conflict with the leaders reached its climax at his trial and crucifixion, but Jesus prayed that those who condemned him to death would be forgiven (Luke 23:34).[46] The call to love one's enemies is part of the Lukan Gospel as well (Luke 6:27–36).[47]

42. See Fitzmyer 1981a: 422–23.

43. So also R. Webb 1991: 181–82, 364; Hartman 1997: 13, 15.

44. Some have seen this as an evidence of anti-Semitism (so J. Sanders 1987). For a better assessment, see Juel 1983: 30–31. The view of Jervell (1972: 41–74) of the function of Israel serves as a counter to Sanders, even though his argument is taken too far (see also Tiede 1980). The same charge has been raised against Matthew. See the balanced assessment of the evidence in France 1989: 238–41.

45. So Tannehill (1986: 71), who emphasizes that the Gentile mission is forecasted. Jervell (1972: 42–74) mistakenly downplays this theme, but he also rightly stresses that there is not a wholesale rejection of Israel.

46. This verse is textually disputed. For a summary of the discussion and an argument supporting inclusion and authenticity, see Bock 1996: 1868–69.

47. For an in-depth and helpful study of this theme, see Piper 1979.

The faith of the centurion was not matched by anyone in Israel (Luke 7:9). Here we have a surprising reversal of what was expected. Gentiles put their faith in Jesus and repented, whereas many of the Jews (Luke 7:31–35; 10:13–16), and particularly their leaders, refused to respond to the message of the kingdom. The parable of the great dinner testifies to the same truth (Luke 14:15–24), for the Jews who were invited to the banquet refused to come and so the Gentiles were invited to the supper.[48] The healing of the ten lepers is emblematic of the story line in Luke (Luke 17:11–19). Of the ten healed, only the Samaritan returned to give thanks, while the Jews who were healed failed to return and praise God. Luke does not concentrate on Jewish culpability because of hatred for the Jews; rather, he focuses on it because they were the people of the promise, those for whom Jesus' message of salvation was particularly intended. Hence, it was all the more astonishing that they turned away from the words that would bring them life.

The pattern of Jewish rejection continues in Acts. In Acts the Sadducees come to the forefront as the opponents of the Christian faith, whereas in the Gospels the Pharisees stood out as adversaries. The Sadducees objected strenuously to the new sect because believers in Jesus trumpeted his resurrection and because the apostles indicted the religious leaders for putting Jesus to death (Acts 2:22–23; 3:14; 4:10; 5:30). A careful reading of these texts suggests that the apostles did not restrict guilt for Jesus' death to Jewish leaders. In some sense the whole nation bore responsibility for putting him to death. Hence, all must repent and turn to God in order to be saved (Acts 3:19–20). If Israel repented, it would receive the blessings God promised throughout the Scriptures (Acts 3:19–26).

One of the prominent themes in Luke-Acts, therefore, is the Jewish rejection of the gospel. Luke calls it to his readers' attention again and again. It does not follow from this, however, that Luke is anti-Semitic or anti-Jewish. We are reminded that the people of the promise did not receive the message particularly intended for them. The conclusion of Acts (Acts 28:17–31) should not be interpreted to say that Christians should no longer proclaim the good news to the Jews and restrict themselves only to Gentiles.[49] Luke's point is that the majority of Israel did not respond to the gospel. It is not as if the church is composed only of Gentiles. In the Lukan scheme the church is the *true* Israel and is composed of both

---

48. See Fitzmyer (1985: 1053), who also emphasizes that the text teaches that some of the Jews responded positively to Jesus' message.

49. Witherington (1998: 162) points out, contrary to J. Sanders, that the response of the Jews, even at the conclusion of Acts, is mixed. It is not the case that all the Jews reject the message proclaimed.

Jews and Gentiles.[50] Jesus calls his disciples to become fishers of people (Luke 5:1–11). The twelve apostles function as the nucleus for restored Israel, representing the twelve tribes of Israel (Luke 6:12–16). Hence, for Luke it is important that a twelfth apostle be added to replace Judas before the Spirit is poured out on Pentecost (Acts 1:15–26).[51] The nucleus of the people of God must be established before the new work of God on Pentecost commences. The true Israel is represented by the apostles;[52] those who respond to their message belong to the people of God.[53]

Luke, like all the Gospel writers, focuses on Jewish rejection because most refused to believe in the gospel. The negative response of the majority does not mean that God has washed his hands of Israel or that believers should no longer proclaim the gospel to the Jews. There was a remnant in Israel that responded positively to the gospel proclaimed by Jesus and his disciples. Many tax collectors and sinners believed in Jesus' message of salvation (Luke 5:29; 7:29, 36–50; 8:36–49; 10:21–22; 15:1–2; 19:1–10), so that the remnant in Israel came from quite an unexpected source. Mary and Martha represented the remnant within Israel that believed in Jesus (Luke 10:38–42). As we will see later, in Luke it is the poor who put their trust in Jesus in contrast to the rich. The people of God are those who humbly and with childlike devotion put their trust in Jesus (Luke 18:15–17).

Even though Acts centers on Jewish rejection of the gospel, Luke also indicates positive Jewish responses to the gospel and the spread of the gospel to the ends of the earth. God's promise that the whole world would be blessed through Abraham (Gen. 12:3) began to be fulfilled as the gospel spread throughout the world. Three thousand responded in repentance and were baptized on the day of Pentecost (Acts 2:41). Soon thereafter the number of believers grew to five thousand (Acts 4:4), all from Jewish circles. The church continued to grow, and the increase came from Jewish men and women (Acts 5:14). We might think from the remainder of Luke that all of the religious leaders rejected the gospel, but such a judgment would be too simplistic. Luke naturally concentrates on the rejection by leaders because they served in an official capacity.

---

50. Jervell (1972: 53) is right (even though he disagrees with the phrase "true Israel") in saying that Gentiles now participate in Israel's blessings, but this does not mean that Israel has been replaced or that the promises given to Israel have been transferred to Gentiles. I am not endorsing Jervell's entire scheme of the relationship between Jews and Gentiles, for the true Israel is composed of Jews and Gentiles.

51. See L. Johnson 1977: 174–83. For an excellent exposition of the role of the apostles in Luke-Acts, with attention being drawn to the parallels drawn between Peter and Paul's ministries, see Clark 1998.

52. So Seccombe 1998: 351.

53. But compare here Jervell (1972: 41–74), who argues that the true Israel consists only of Jews who have repented and believed.

Still, he writes in Acts 6:7 that the number of disciples (clearly Jewish) in Jerusalem increased remarkably. Not only did the number of Jewish believers continue to grow, but also "a great many priests became obedient to the faith" (Acts 6:7).[54] The majority of the leaders did not believe in the gospel preached by the apostles, and yet a large number of priests did believe. Israel was not entirely bereft of the gospel (see also Acts 9:31; 13:43–44; 14:1–4; 17:4, 11–12; 21:20; 28:24–25).

Luke does not believe that the Jewish people are categorically and completely cut off from salvation, and yet he particularly emphasizes Gentile inclusion and mission. Those who were not literal sons and daughters of Abraham were becoming members of the people of God through faith in Jesus Christ. The angels declared that the good news of a Savior from the line of David is "for all the people" (Luke 2:10), which may include Gentiles as well as Jews, given Luke's story line.[55] Simeon clearly included the Gentiles in the circle of blessing, for Jesus was not only the glory of Israel but also "a light for revelation to the Gentiles" (Luke 2:32). When the way of the Lord is prepared in the wilderness, "all flesh shall see the salvation of God" (Luke 3:6).[56] The fulfillment of God's promises means that the promise of universal blessing given to Abraham (Gen. 12:3) was becoming a reality. Jesus' programmatic sermon in Nazareth highlighted the inclusion of the Gentiles. Elijah, he reminded them, was sent to a Sidonian widow instead of to widows in Israel, and Elisha healed Namaan the Syrian from leprosy rather than lepers in Israel (Luke 4:25–27). God works out his saving purposes in unexpected and unanticipated ways. The calling of Peter and the other disciples is associated with a great catch of fish, symbolizing the worldwide mission to which they are summoned.[57] The parable of the good Samaritan indicates that the Samaritans are not outside the circle of God's saving love (Luke 10:25–37; see also 17:10–19). The parable of the great dinner also points to the inclusion of Gentiles (Luke 14:15–24). The vineyard being given to others probably signifies that it is given to Gentiles rather than the Jewish leaders (Luke 20:16).[58] Finally, Luke's Gospel ends with the call to preach forgiveness of sins and repentance "to all nations" (Luke 24:47), which means that both Jews and Gentiles

---

54. Schnabel (2004a: 425) suggests that Essenes are more likely in view because few Sadducees would believe, although Luke leaves the matter unclear.

55. Contra Marshall 1978b: 109; Fitzmyer 1981a: 409.

56. See Marshall 1978b: 137.

57. Tannehill (1986: 204) remarks that the catch of fish in Luke 5:1–11 forecasts the "expanding mission in which Jesus is already engaged."

58. See Fitzmyer 1985: 1281. Marshall (1978b: 731) is hesitant about seeing an application to the Gentiles, but it seems that he fails to read the verse in light of Luke-Acts as a whole.

are to be reached with God's salvation. Luke focuses on the mission of the church to spread the gospel to all people groups everywhere, and this mission is carried out only after Jesus' death and resurrection, for it is in his name that salvation is extended to all peoples (cf. Acts 4:12).

Acts picks up where the Gospel of Luke leaves off. The Holy Spirit will enable the disciples to witness to Jesus not only within Israel but also "to the ends of the earth" (Acts 1:8),[59] and the latter certainly includes Gentiles. The theme of Acts is the spread of the gospel by the power of the Spirit. Hengel rightly puts his finger on the pulse of the theology of Luke-Acts in saying, "In short, the history and theology of earliest Christianity are 'mission history' and 'mission theology.' A church and theology which forgets or denies the missionary sending of believers as messengers of salvation in a world threatened by disaster surrenders its very foundation and in doing so surrenders itself."[60] Acts relates the account of the gospel's progress from Jerusalem, Judea, Galilee, and Samaria to the Gentile world. The gospel's origin from Jerusalem probably fulfills the promise that the word of the Lord would go out from Jerusalem to the whole world (see Isa. 2:1–4).[61] Paul planted churches in major cities, and these centers functioned as a base from which the gospel was disseminated to outlying areas.[62] Nor should we think that Paul's arrival in Rome constituted the gospel reaching the ends of the earth.[63] The gospel taking root in Rome was an indication that Jesus' promise was being fulfilled, but there was still much work to be done, and the Spirit would continue to enable the church as he strengthened Paul and others to bring the gospel to all nations.

In Acts the mission is accomplished through the word of God. At crucial points in the narrative where Luke summarizes the story, the inherent power of the word is featured.[64] The word is portrayed as a plant that grows (Acts 6:7; 12:24; 19:20). Its intrinsic power is such that it multiplies wherever it goes (Acts 12:24), so that not even a king such as Herod Agrippa I (Acts 12:1–23) can prevent its growth, despite his attempt to squelch the word by putting to death messengers such as

59. So Shelton 1991: 125–27. For the missionary character of Luke's view of the Spirit, see Penney 1997. For the same theme in Acts, see Kee 1990: 30–35.
60. Hengel 1983: 64.
61. So Penney 1997: 73.
62. Hengel (1983: 49–50) says that Paul concentrated on the provincial capitals in the Roman Empire. He maintained contact with co-workers and assistants who brought the gospel to the hinterlands. See also Hofius 2002: 2–4; Bosch 1991: 130.
63. Hengel (1983: 101) maintains that reaching Rome did not equal the ends of the earth; rather, it was but one goal along the way, for it was known in Paul's day that there were other geographical areas where the gospel had not yet been proclaimed. So also Rosner 1998: 218; Schnabel 2004a: 373–76.
64. See Pao 2000: 147–80.

James the brother of John. The word triumphs over all opposition, so that it shows its strength (*ischyō* [Acts 19:20]) and conquers all demonic competitors (Acts 19:1–19). It is not surprising, therefore, that the gospel can be described as the speaking of the word (Acts 4:31; 8:25; 11:19; 13:46; 14:25; 16:6, 32), the spreading of the good news of the word (Acts 8:4; 15:35), proclaiming the word (Acts 13:5; 15:36; 17:13), and teaching the word (Acts 18:11). The apostles particularly devoted themselves to this powerful word (Acts 6:2, 4; cf. 18:5), and this word centers on Jesus Christ (Acts 10:36), for the word focuses on what is central in the gospel—Jesus Christ himself. Hence, in Acts the word cannot be separated from the kerygma or apostolic sermons that punctuate the narrative. The word has such power that it brings the Spirit (Acts 10:44) and pushes forward like the wind in its force and effectiveness (Acts 13:49). The word is able to build up believers and give them an eschatological inheritance (Acts 20:32).

The word and the Spirit, of course, belong together, for as we just noted, the word brings the Spirit. One of the promises in Acts is that the Spirit will be poured out not only upon Israel but also upon "all flesh" (Acts 2:17), so that everyone from every ethnic background who calls upon the Lord in faith will be saved (Acts 2:21).[65] The promise of the blessing of Abraham is given to the Jews first (Acts 3:25–26), but it is intended ultimately for all peoples everywhere (Gen. 12:3). The fulfillment of God's promises was always intended to lead to salvation not just for Jews but rather for the whole world. The story line of Acts unpacks how the good news was spread from Jerusalem to the ends of the earth. The expulsion of Philip from Jerusalem led him to an Ethiopian eunuch who embraced the gospel as explicated from Isa. 53 (Acts 8:26–40).[66] The conversion of Paul propels the Gentile mission forward, for God chose him to proclaim his name among the Gentiles (Acts 9:15).

The inclusion of and mission to the Gentiles took a major step forward with the conversion of Cornelius and his friends (Acts 10:1–11:18). Cornelius was an uncircumcised Gentile and can be designated as a

---

65. See Polhill 1992: 109; Fitzmyer 1998: 252. But see Barrett 1994: 136.

66. Barrett (1994: 420–21) argues that the Ethiopian, being a eunuch, could not have been a proselyte, but his conversion is distinguished from Cornelius and his friends in that he is a solitary individual. But Schnabel (2004a: 684–85) suggests that the term "eunuch" is not necessarily literal, and that it is more probable that the eunuch was a court official who was a proselyte. Polhill (1992: 219–20) argues that the official was an actual eunuch because the text says that he was a eunuch *and* an official; hence, Polhill maintains that the eunuch was a God-fearer rather than a proselyte. Fitzmyer (1998: 410, 412), on the other hand, argues that in the Lukan story line Peter opens the door to the Gentiles (Acts 15:7). Hence, the eunuch was either Jewish or a Jewish proselyte (cf. Isa. 56:3–4).

God-fearer who was attracted to Jewish monotheism and morality.[67] As Peter explained the gospel, the Spirit fell on Cornelius and his cohorts, demonstrating that they were part of the people of God. The inclusion of the Gentiles clearly was a work of God ("Then to the Gentiles also God has granted repentance that leads to life" [Acts 11:18]). Furthermore, even persecution led to the spread of the church. The persecution that began with the death of Stephen propelled some Jews to Antioch, and they announced the good news to Gentiles who embraced the gospel, so that many Gentiles became part of the church of Jesus Christ in Antioch (Acts 11:19–26).[68] The expansion of the church continued to be driven by the missionary ventures of Paul and his various colleagues in the remainder of Acts.

Leadership and the Church

We noted earlier that the people of God are represented by the twelve apostles. The true Israel comes not from the twelve tribes of Israel but rather from those who heed the message proclaimed by the twelve apostles. The Twelve accompanied Jesus during his earthly ministry and were witnesses of his resurrection (Acts 1:21–22). They were specially commissioned to serve as apostles by Jesus Christ (Luke 6:12–16; Acts 1:2, 23–26). The teaching of the apostles functioned as authoritative tradition for the church (Acts 2:42).[69] The apostles had a special responsibility for teaching and prayer, and so they appointed others to care for the physical needs of the church (Acts 6:1–6). The apostles performed signs and wonders both to validate their teaching and also as a sign of the kingdom's presence (Acts 2:43; 4:33; 5:12). The authority of the apostles is evident when problems arose in the church. They decided how to resolve the problem in the church with the Hellenistic widows who were overlooked in the daily distribution of food (Acts 6:1–6). The Samaritans did not receive the Holy Spirit until the apostles laid hands on them, guaranteeing that the Samaritans would not establish a separate church apart from apostolic authority (Acts 8:14–17).[70] The controversy over whether

67. Barrett (1994: 499–501) notes in a careful discussion that the term "God-fearer" is not invariably a technical one, but also argues that Cornelius essentially fits such a category (see also Fitzmyer 1998: 449–50; Polhill 1992: 252n71). Schnabel (2004a: 712) suggests that Cornelius may have been a God-fearer, but not openly so.

68. Luke does not necessarily intend to say that the events recorded here were subsequent to the Cornelius event, since he does not specify the chronology of events here (so Barrett 1994: 546). Hengel (1983: 63) argues that the first mission to non-Jews was precipitated by Hellenistic Jews.

69. See Schnabel 2004a: 409–11.

70. So Carson 1987b: 144–45. Barrett (1994: 410) maintains that the reason for sending Peter and John cannot be discerned. Fitzmyer (1998: 400–401) claims that the Spirit

circumcision would be required for Gentiles was brought to Jerusalem for the apostles to resolve (Acts 15:2, 4, 6, 22–23; 16:4). There is some ambiguity in the Lukan portrait of the apostles, for typically he restricts the term "apostle" to the Twelve, but in one instance he includes Paul and Barnabas (Acts 14:4, 14).

Nor is the leadership of the church restricted to the apostles. It is interesting to note that in Acts 15 the elders of the churches in Jerusalem, in addition to the apostles, played a role in the controversy over circumcision (Acts 15:2, 4, 6, 22–23; 16:4).[71] The term "elders" derives from the OT and apparently was used by the Jews for leaders in the community (see Acts 4:5, 8, 23; 6:12; 23:14; 24:1; 25:15).[72] The word "elders" is also used for the leaders of the church in Jerusalem in Acts 11:30. Apparently, appointing leaders as elders was not restricted to the church of Jerusalem. Paul and Barnabas selected elders for every church planted on their first missionary journey (Acts 14:23).[73] This text also indicates that each church had a plurality of elders, since Luke specifically says that elders were appointed for every church. Another interesting use of the term "elders" for church leaders is found in Acts 20:17, where the leaders of the church (or possibly churches) in Ephesus are so designated. A few verses later in the same speech, however, the same men are called "overseers" (*episkopoi*), and their position as overseers is ascribed to the Holy Spirit (Acts 20:28). It seems safe to conclude, therefore, that elders and overseers are two different designations for the same office.[74] Perhaps the term "elder" emphasizes the stature of the office, and "overseer" the function. Some of the functions of elders and overseers are also clarified in this text (Acts 20:17–35). Overseers are to shepherd the church and to be on guard because false teachers will arise from within the elders themselves to draw believers away from the truth. Hence, elders must carefully teach the whole counsel of God.

---

is conveyed through the apostles or those sent by them, and here the splintering of the Samaritan church is precluded. Polhill (1992: 217) wrongly maintains that Peter and John are viewed here as participants who visited to offer encouragement and support. Such a view does not adequately explain why the Spirit came only through the laying on of their hands.

71. On elders in Acts, see Barrett 1994: 566; on elders in general, see Merkle 2003.

72. For some OT texts, see Exod. 3:16; Lev. 4:15; Num. 11:25; Deut. 5:23; Josh. 20:4; Judg. 8:16; Ruth 4:2; 1 Sam. 8:4; 1 Kings 8:1; 1 Chron. 11:3; Ezra 5:9; Ps. 107:32; Prov. 31:23; Jer. 19:1; Lam. 2:10; Ezek. 8:1; Joel 1:14.

73. For a defense of the reliability of the account, see Merkle 2003: 126–29. Conversely, see Haenchen 1971: 436; Barrett 1994: 688.

74. So Merkle 2003: 130; Fitzmyer 1998: 678–79. Barrett (1998: 975–76) helpfully argues that although the terms refer to the same persons, it does not follow from this that the terms are synonymous in meaning.

Paul also functions as an example for the elders in his public and private teaching, in enduring trials, and in his financial integrity.

No other offices are clearly mentioned in Acts. Many have seen the institution of deacons in the appointment of the seven to care for Hellenistic widows (Acts 6:1–6).[75] It may be that these seven functioned as deacons, though Acts never uses the term "deacons" (*diakonoi*) to describe them. In Acts 6:1–2 the care that they express for the widows is called "ministry" (*diakonia*), and their work is "to serve tables" (*diakonein trapezais*). If this is a diaconal ministry, the focus is on meeting the financial and physical needs of those in the church. If the seven had titles, Luke fails to convey them.

The Church and the Way

One of the striking features in Acts is the focus on the church. The decision over whether circumcision should be imposed on Gentiles was not restricted to the apostles and elders alone but also was agreed upon by the church in Jerusalem (Acts 15:22).[76] The term "church" (*ekklēsia*) reaches back to the OT term *qāhāl*, denoting Israel as God's assembly.[77] Acts 7:38 refers to this assembly of God's people in the wilderness with Moses. The term *ekklēsia* may also be used of secular assemblies. The riot in Ephesus is designated as an assembly (Acts 19:32, 39, 40) in which people gathered to express their opinion.

In Acts the term "church" typically refers to local churches. Interestingly, these local assemblies are not said to be part of the church but are themselves designated as the church.[78] There are references to the church in Jerusalem (Acts 5:11; 8:1, 3; 11:22; 12:1, 5; 15:4), Antioch (Acts 11:26; 13:1; 14:27; 15:3), Caesarea (Acts 18:22), Ephesus (Acts 20:17, 28),[79] the churches planted on Paul's missionary journeys (Acts 14:23), and the churches in Syria and Cilicia (Acts 15:41). On the other hand, perhaps Acts 9:31 refers to the universal church—"So the church throughout all Judea, Galilee, and Samaria had peace and was being built up"—though

---

75. We cannot be certain that these appointees were deacons (see Fitzmyer 2004: 592). Barrett (1994: 304) insists that it was not the intention here to relay the origin of deacons.

76. The scanty evidence of the text makes it difficult to determine the precise role that the church played (see Barrett 1998: 738; Fitzmyer 1998: 564).

77. See Barrett 1998: lxxxviii. But this is debated, and thus Roloff (*EDNT* 1:411–12) locates the term in apocalyptic Judaism rather than in the LXX. See also Fitzmyer 1998: 325.

78. See Roloff, *EDNT* 1:413.

79. Acts 20:28 could be read as a reference to the universal church, but the context in which Paul addresses the Ephesian elders may indicate a reference to the local church or churches in Ephesus.

it may also refer to local churches in the various regions.[80] Nor did each church live in isolation from other churches. They were under apostolic oversight, and when the issue of circumcision arose, a meeting was called in Jerusalem that included members from the church in Antioch (Acts 15:1–35). When the church in Jerusalem heard about Gentile converts in Antioch and the growth of the church there, they sent Barnabas to encourage them in the faith (Acts 11:19–24). Maintaining the unity of the church of Jesus Christ probably was one of their aims. The importance of unity is suggested also by the visit of Peter and John to Samaria, in which the Spirit was given only through the apostles (Acts 8:14–17). The church in Samaria was thereby preserved from taking off on its own and was established on an apostolic basis. When Paul returned to Jerusalem, James encouraged him to pay for the purification of some men who had taken a vow for the sake of the unity of the church there (Acts 21:17–26). So, on the one hand, the church in various places is the church, not merely part of the church; on the other hand, there is also the sense in which the church is one throughout the world whose unity must be preserved.

The new movement is also called "the Way" (*hē hodos*) in Acts.[81] The meaning of the term can be gleaned from several texts in Acts. Even though the woman who had a spirit of divination was rebuked by Paul and the spirit exorcised, she rightly identified Paul's message as the "way of salvation" (Acts 16:17). Apollos was "instructed in the way of the Lord" (Acts 18:25), but Priscilla and Aquila take Apollos aside to sharpen and increase his understanding in "the way of God" (Acts 18:26). The "way" designates both the God-honoring lifestyle required of God's people and the claim that Jesus is the way to God. The Way was called a "sect" by opponents (Acts 24:14), and the term is used in contexts in which the church was persecuted for its witness. Paul persecuted the Way and thus traveled to Damascus to try to stamp it out (Acts 9:2; 22:4). Many in Ephesus criticized the Way, so Paul departed from the synagogue and set up his base of operations in Tyrannus's lecture hall (Acts 19:9). Controversy over the Way precipitated the riot in Ephesus (Acts 19:23). Paul's appearance before Felix functions as another example of persecution of the Way (Acts 24:14). Pao notes that the term "Way" is often used in contexts where the true people of God, believers in Christ, are

---

80. See Roloff, *EDNT* 1:414. Barrett (1994: 473) says that in Acts the term typically refers to local churches, but he is noncommittal here. But perhaps the reference is to the "local church represented in these different regions" (Fitzmyer 1998: 440). So also Polhill 1992: 244.

81. The most striking parallels are found in the Qumran literature (see Barrett 1994: 448), from which Fitzmyer (1998: 423–24) thinks the term was borrowed.

distinguished from opponents. Hence, the Way designates believers in Christ as the true Israel.[82]

Baptism

The initiation rite for the church was baptism. Luke emphasizes in Acts that people were baptized almost immediately after expressing faith and repentance.[83] The three thousand who repented and believed on the day of Pentecost were baptized on that same day (Acts 2:38, 41).[84] When the Samaritans believed in Jesus Christ, Philip baptized them (Acts 8:12). The story of the Ethiopian eunuch is particularly noteworthy in this regard, for Philip baptized him on the spot as they were traveling after the eunuch put his faith in the gospel (Acts 8:36, 38). Similarly, Paul received baptism almost immediately subsequent to his conversion (Acts 9:18; 22:16). When the Spirit fell suddenly on Cornelius and his friends, Peter concluded that they should be baptized because they now belonged to the people of God (Acts 10:47–48). Similarly, Lydia was baptized after she received the word spoken by Paul (Acts 16:14–15). The story of the Philippian jailer confirms the importance of baptism as an initiation rite, for he and his family were baptized immediately on the very night they believed in the gospel (Acts 16:33). Finally, when the Corinthians believed, they were also baptized (Acts 18:8).

In Acts baptism is done in the name of Jesus Christ (Acts 2:38; 8:12; 10:48) or in the name of the Lord Jesus (Acts 8:16; 19:5).[85] The threefold baptismal formula of Matt. 28:19 clearly is missing.[86] Some argue that the difference is significant, indicating that another baptismal practice was observed early and that the Matthean formula was added later. It is equally possible, however, that the expression used in Acts reflects the

82. See Pao (2000: 51–69), who traces this theme to the new-exodus theme in Isaiah.

83. For this theme in Acts, see Stein 2007.

84. Hartman (1997: 130) says that "baptism becomes, so to speak, the external side of their acceptance of the message and its impact."

85. Luke uses various pronouns here, but Hartman (1997: 37) says, "Luke, when writing Acts, hardly thought that there was any difference in the meaning of the different formulae." Scholars also debate the significance of the formula. Some have seen an analogy with banking terminology, whereby the one baptized becomes the property of the Lord. Others argue for a Hebraic or Aramaic background but come to the same conclusion, that the baptized one becomes Jesus' property. Hartman argues that the background is Jewish-rabbinic, and that the formula has a generalized meaning "with regard to" or "having in mind." For a survey of the various views and Hartman's own proposal, see Hartman 1997: 37–50.

86. The preposition *eis* here probably denotes ownership, signifying that believers are slaves of God, Christ, and the Spirit (Harris 1999: 109–10).

Lukan focus on the role of Jesus Christ in baptism.[87] Baptism into the Christian church centers on the work of Jesus Christ, and thus we find the emphasis on being baptized in Jesus' name. The initiatory role of baptism is clear because it is received "for the forgiveness of your sins" (Acts 2:38).[88] In Acts 22:16 baptism is associated with washing one's sins away. Furthermore, in virtually every text in Acts baptism follows repentance and faith, demonstrating that it is the rite of entrance into the Christian community. The question of whether one could be saved apart from baptism was not asked by early Christians, for unbaptized Christians were unheard of and an anomaly. All Christians received baptism upon believing in Jesus Christ and repenting of their sins.[89] As we observed above, people were baptized almost immediately after believing in Jesus as the Christ. In the story of Cornelius the Spirit is given before baptism (Acts 10:44–48), suggesting that baptism itself does not save in a quasi-sacramental way.

Acts 2:42: Life of the Church

Acts 2:42 sketches in the life of the church in Jerusalem: "They devoted themselves to the apostles' teaching and fellowship, to the breaking of bread and the prayers." This verse functions well as an outline for the nature of the church in Acts, so we will look at teaching, fellowship, the breaking of bread, and, in more depth in a separate section below, prayer. We need no elaborate detail on teaching here because I have sketched in earlier the apostolic kerygma in Acts. We simply need to remind ourselves from the speeches in Acts that the apostolic teaching focused on the ministry, death, and resurrection of Jesus Christ. He fulfilled OT prophecies about the Messiah, and forgiveness of sins comes only through him. All teaching in Acts is measured by whether it accords with what the apostles teach. Often Luke focuses on the teaching of Paul and the apostles (Acts 4:2, 18; 5:21, 25, 28, 42; 13:12; 15:35; 17:19; 18:11; 20:20; 21:28; 28:31). Such teaching focuses on the proclamation of the gospel (*euangelizō* [Acts 5:42; 8:4, 12, 25, 35, 40; 11:20; 13:32; 14:7, 15, 21; 15:35; 16:10; 17:18] or *katangellō* [see Acts 3:24; 4:2; 13:5, 38; 15:36; 16:17; 17:3, 13, 23; 26:23]). The teaching of Jesus is continued in the book of Acts (Acts 1:1).

87. Hartman (1997: 166–68) argues that eschatology and a relationship to Christ are fundamental in Christian baptism, and since eschatology is central, the Spirit as an eschatological gift is also conveyed in baptism.

88. Polhill (1992: 117) strays from the text in attempting to distance baptism from forgiveness of sins. For a better explanation, see Stein 2007.

89. Hartman (1997: 134) rightly notes that baptism is associated in Acts with repentance, being saved, forgiveness of sins, reception by God, the gift of the Spirit, belief in Jesus, and proclamation of the gospel. See also Stein 2007.

Teaching focuses on the transmission of tradition, and in Acts it focuses particularly on proclamation and instruction about the good news
of Jesus Christ. Prophecy, on the other hand, refers to the spontaneous
work of the Spirit by which people speak the word of the Lord.[90] The
speaking in tongues on Pentecost (Acts 2:1–4), in which those present
were speaking about "the mighty works of God" (Acts 2:11), fulfills
the word of Joel that when the Spirit is poured out, God's people will
prophesy (Acts 2:17–18). Presumably, then, every instance in which
tongue-speaking is comprehensible is equivalent to prophesy. This
seems to be confirmed by Acts 19:6, where the Ephesian twelve spoke
in tongues and prophesied, suggesting that the two are inseparable in
this instance.[91] The most notable prophet in Acts is Agabus. The Spirit
revealed to him that a famine would occur in the Greco-Roman world
during the reign of Claudius, and the church responded by providing
for the needs of saints in Jerusalem (Acts 11:27–30). Agabus also took
Paul's belt, tied up his own feet, and declared through the Holy Spirit
that the Jews in Jerusalem would bind Paul and give him up to the
Gentiles (Acts 21:10–11). Agabus's actions echo the symbolic acts of
OT prophets. Furthermore, the phrase "thus says the Holy Spirit" represents a prophetic formula.[92] Some argue that Agabus was mistaken,
for in Acts 22 the Jews did not literally bind Paul and hand him over
to the Romans.[93] Instead, they attempted to beat him to death, and the
Romans rescued him from the Jews in Jerusalem. Such a view makes
the mistake of interpreting Agabus's prophecy too literally. Paul himself
echoes Agabus's very words when he says to the Jews in Jerusalem, "I
was arrested in Jerusalem and handed over to the Romans" (Acts 28:17
NRSV). Prophecy is not limited to men, for women prophesy as well
(Acts 2:18). Furthermore, Philip's four daughters functioned as prophets
(Acts 21:9), though no record of their prophecies is included. In Acts
13:1–3 both prophets and teachers were worshiping the Lord in Syrian
Antioch. The Lord told those gathered that Barnabas and Paul should

90. Fitzmyer (1998: 481) thinks that prophets, in Luke's eyes, may have been "inspired
or gifted preachers." Haenchen (1971: 373) sees an emphasis on prediction but notes that
Acts 15:32 may point in a different direction. See also the balanced assessment in Polhill
1992: 274n129. Best (1972: 239) argues that the prophets were not the same as preachers.
Dunn (1975b: 170–76, 186–87, 228, 230, 237, 280–84) says that prophecy and teaching are
closely related because both include interpretation, but prophecy relates to interpreting
new revelations, whereas teaching interprets tradition.

91. So Conzelmann 1987: 159–60, but Barrett (1994: 137) distinguishes them.

92. So Haenchen 1971: 602; Barrett 1998: 995; Fitzmyer 1998: 689.

93. See the discussion of prophecy in Grudem 1982: 58–67. Barrett (1998: 995–96)
remarks that Agabus's words were not "strictly accurate," and that Luke is unconcerned
about exact details in the fulfillment of prophecies, and that the wording may reflect what
happened to Jesus.

be set aside for mission. It seems quite likely that the command came from a prophetic word in which the Spirit revealed his will to one of the prophets present.[94]

The second item mentioned in Acts 2:42 is the fellowship that marked the church. The fellowship of the church is portrayed beautifully in the concern for the material needs of others. The church's unity was not merely an abstract and ethereal sense of oneness. Those who had financial needs were provided for by others who had prospered economically (Acts 2:44–47; 4:32–37).[95] The hypocrisy of Ananias and Sapphira, who sinned by pretending to give more than they did, shows that the early church was not perfect (Acts 5:1–11).[96] Feelings of being overlooked and slighted were not absent from the early church, for the Hellenistic widows (probably the Greek-speaking widows) were not receiving the food that they needed for sustenance (Acts 6:1–6). Still, the apostles reacted quickly to the practical problem, appointing seven Hellenistic Jews to see that food was properly distributed, for the witness of the church would be severely compromised if the needs of any in the church were unmet.

Third, the church is characterized by the breaking of bread (Acts 2:42).[97] The breaking of bread likely refers to the Lord's Supper, which was celebrated at the end of meals.[98] Since church members devoted themselves to the breaking of bread, it appears that the Lord's Supper was celebrated quite often (Acts 2:46). Luke probably refers not to family meals but rather to meals at homes in which the church gathered. The frequency of the Lord's Supper is indicated by the reference to breaking bread "on the first day of the week" in Troas (Acts 20:7).[99] The collocation of breaking bread and the time in which it was held (Sunday) suggest that no ordinary meal is in view here.

94. So Barrett 1994: 605.

95. Barrett (1994: 168) does not get it quite right for Acts 2 when he says that "communal rather than private ownership of wealth" was "being practiced." It seems that believers still owned their wealth privately but voluntarily contributed it to help others. Fitzmyer (1998: 272), on the other hand, thinks that it is unclear whether communal life was voluntary or obligatory. But as Polhill (1992: 120–21) points out, the regular selling of property points to private ownership in which necessities were shared.

96. Rightly Barrett (1994: 262), though he wrongly thinks that this contradicts Acts 4:34, since the giving described there is also voluntary.

97. For a discussion of the various views, see Barrett 1994: 164–65. The reference to broken bread and the distinction from the meals shared in common in Acts 2:46 suggest that the Lord's Supper is in view here (so Fitzmyer 1998: 270–72; Polhill 1992: 119).

98. Though it has been disputed by some, the Lord's Supper should be understood as a Passover meal (so Marshall 1980a; Stuhlmacher 1993: 65–69).

99. Barrett (1998: xcii–xciii) sees reference to a common meal but is skeptical that it refers to a eucharistic meal. For a reference to the Lord's Supper, see Polhill 1992: 418; Fitzmyer 1998: 669.

Prayer

Here we will look more in depth at the fourth characteristic of church life described in Acts 2:42. The early church was marked by prayer.[100] Prayer is a major theme in Luke-Acts and is central to the expansion of the church's mission. Hence, we must consult both Luke and Acts to discern its centrality. When an angel appeared to Zechariah at the altar of incense, he assured Zechariah that his prayer had been heard (Luke 1:13). It is difficult to know whether the prayer related to the fulfillment of God's covenantal promises to Israel or to the desire for a son. Perhaps both are in view here.[101]

Prayer plays a central role at key points in Jesus' ministry.[102] Only Luke tells us that Jesus was praying when he was baptized and anointed for ministry (Luke 3:21), presumably so that he would be empowered for ministry.[103] During the rush and crush of ministry Jesus would withdraw alone and find time to pray (Luke 5:16), and Crump is likely correct in maintaining that prayer played an integral role in the fulfilling of Jesus' mission.[104] One of the most important decisions in Jesus' life was the choosing of the Twelve, and thus it is significant that he spent an entire night in prayer before selecting the nucleus of restored Israel (Luke 6:12).[105] A defining event in the Gospels occurred at Caesarea Philippi when Jesus asked the disciples about his identity (Luke 9:18–20). Luke informs us that Jesus asked the question after he had prayed alone (Luke 9:18). Presumably, he prayed that God would grant the disciples the correct understanding of his person.[106] Jesus' transfiguration revealed to the three disciples who were with him the glory and majesty of Jesus, and Luke indicates that Jesus was transfigured while praying (Luke 9:28–29).[107] The Lord's Prayer is the one prayer recorded that Jesus taught his disciples (Luke 11:2–4), and interestingly, the request for such instruction came when the disciples saw him praying (Luke

100. The specific nature of the prayers is difficult to determine from this text (Barrett 1994: 166).

101. Marshall (1978b: 56) thinks that Zechariah was praying for the coming of the Messiah but not a son. Fitzmyer (1981a: 325) suggests that he was praying both for a son and for redemption for Israel. Bock (1994: 82–83) argues that he prayed for redemption, but this was answered in terms of past prayers for a son.

102. That prayer occurs at crucial points in the history of salvation is supported by Smalley. In particular, Smalley (1973) argues that Spirit, kingdom, and prayer are intimately connected in Luke.

103. Crump 1992: 109–16.

104. Crump 1992: 142–44.

105. So also Crump 1992: 145.

106. See Crump 1992: 21–34.

107. Crump (1992: 42–48) thinks that Jesus' prayer played a revelatory role in the transfiguration.

11:1). Jesus informed Simon and all the disciples that he had prayed for them, and that their faith would not fail in the impending trial (Luke 22:31–32).[108] Jesus was confident that his prayer would be answered, for he told Peter to strengthen his brothers after his repentance. Jesus also instructed his disciples to pray that they would not enter a time of trial (Luke 22:40, 46).[109] He probably means by this that disciples were to pray that they would not face trials that would overwhelm and conquer them. Jesus did not give instructions to his disciples that he failed to apply to himself. He prayed that the Father would remove the cup of wrath from himself, feeling as a human being that it was too much for him (Luke 22:42). Ultimately, however, he resigned himself to God's will in the matter. Jesus modeled for his disciples what it means to love one's enemies. When he hung upon the cross as the victim of monstrous injustice, he prayed that the Father would forgive those who took his life (Luke 23:34).[110] And at the hour of his death he put his trust in God, commending his life into God's hands (Luke 23:46). Surely, this prayer was answered in his resurrection.[111]

Jesus also instructed his disciples in prayer, and some of these texts we have already noted. He exhorted his followers to pray for those who mistreat them (Luke 6:28). The Lord's Prayer functions as the model for all prayer (Luke 11:2–4), and it is well known that we have an abbreviated version of what we find in Matthew. What is striking is the God-centeredness of the prayer.[112] Believers are to begin prayer by focusing on the Father, asking that his name will be honored and esteemed. The fundamental request in prayer is that God would be prized as God in the world. Prayer runs off course unless it is God-focused, Christ-centered, and Spirit-motivated, for otherwise it becomes a means of pandering to human desires.[113] Then, believers are to pray for the coming of God's kingdom, which in Luke-Acts fits nicely with the spread of the gospel throughout the world.[114] In the second part of the prayer believers pray for their own needs. First, they ask that God would supply the need for food every day, so that it is acknowledged that every good gift comes from God. Second, believers ask God for forgiveness, and those who truly seek forgiveness also do not hold onto grudges against others. Finally,

108. See Crump 1992: 154–62. Crump (1992: 173) also suggests that Jesus did not pray against Judas, but neither did he pray for him (in contrast to his praying for Peter).

109. Crump (1992: 171) intriguingly suggests that the disciples' faith failed temporarily because they did not heed Jesus' admonition.

110. In defense of the originality of the prayer, see Bock 1996: 1867–68.

111. See Bock 1996: 1862.

112. Marshall (1978b: 457) says that "the establishment of God's glory is the first theme of the prayer."

113. See Schlatter 1997: 194.

114. See Cullmann 1995.

believers pray that God will spare them from any temptation or trial that would lead them to apostasy.[115] God knows the strength of each one, and thus believers pray that God will not lead them in paths beyond their ability to endure. This last petition is essentially repeated in Luke 21:36, which comes near the close of Jesus' eschatological discourse, where he predicts the destruction of Jerusalem and the coming of the end. Jesus concludes by saying, "But stay awake at all times, praying that you may have strength to escape all these things that are going to take place, and to stand before the Son of Man." The strength that believers pray for here is that they will be enabled to avoid apostasy, so that they will stand vindicated and righteous before the Son of Man on the last day.[116] The prayer that believers would "not enter into temptation" (Luke 22:40, 46) should be interpreted similarly. Believers should pray that God will keep them from anything that would overwhelm them to the extent that they would outlive their love for him.

Luke contains fascinating parables in which Jesus gave instructions on prayer. We consider first the parable of the friend arriving at midnight (Luke 11:5–8). In this parable a visitor arrives at the home of a friend at midnight, but the host has no food to give to the visitor, which is unthinkable in Middle Eastern culture.[117] So the host goes to another friend's house and asks for three loaves of bread so that he can satisfy the needs of his guest. The potential donor of the bread protests that the hour is late, the house is secure, and the children are already asleep. We should think here of homes where everyone slept in the same room, so that with any disturbance the whole house awakes.[118] All parents know the consequences of waking young children at night! Nevertheless, the host succeeds in getting food from his friend because of his "persistence" (Luke 11:8 NRSV). The word used here is *anaideia*, and some translate it as "shamelessness," relating it to the person who is reluctant to provide the requested food.[119] According to this interpretation, he relents and gives the needed food because he does not want the bad reputation acquired by those who refuse to share with someone in need. This interpetation is attractive but unconvincing. The context suggests that the shameless

---

115. For a reference to apostasy, see Fitzmyer 1985: 906–7. Bock (1996: 1055–56) argues that the reference is to all sin, including apostasy.

116. See Marshall 1978b: 783.

117. So Jeremias 1972: 157; Fitzmyer 1985: 911; Bailey 1976: 119–23.

118. Rightly Jeremias 1972: 157–58.

119. So Bailey 1976: 125–34; Marshall 1978b: 465. Against this, see Fitzmyer 1985: 912. Bock (1996: 1059–60) thinks that the focus is on the boldness, not the persistence, of the petitioner. The interpretation of the parable that follows focuses on boldness and persistence. Jeremias (1972: 159) wrongly divides the theme of persistence from the original meaning of the parable, given God's longing to give good gifts to his children. Jeremias separates here what should be kept together.

persistence of the person who is attempting to get food for his guest is in view.[120] The verses that immediately follow emphasize the necessity of asking, seeking, and knocking to receive God's blessing. The three terms indicate the need for persistence, perseverance, and boldness in prayer. It is the one who continues to seek and knock who finds.

Does the parable teach, then, that God is like the man who is asked for bread? Is God reluctant to give what his people need, but, if bothered incessantly by them, he will finally relent and provide for them? Certainly not! God is *contrasted* with the person in the house, for he delights to give to his children. This is confirmed by Luke 11:11–13. If a child asks for a fish, is there any father who would give his child a snake? Of if a child desires an egg, would an earthly father give him a scorpion?[121] Human fathers, evil as they are, long to give what is good to their children. How much more, then, will the heavenly Father, who is perfectly good and kind, grant what his children need? And their greatest need is for the Holy Spirit. What Luke 11:5–13 teaches, therefore, is that God's people are to persevere in prayer not because God is reluctant to give to them, but precisely because God longs to give to them what they need. Persistence in prayer is grounded in the goodness of God, so that believers continue to come to him because they know he desires to bless them.

Jesus' other dramatic parable on prayer focuses on the unjust judge and the needy widow (Luke 18:2–5). The judge did not care what people thought, nor did he fear God. Hence, he kept ignoring the claim for justice brought to him by the widow, who lacked political leverage. Finally, however, he relented because the widow kept bothering him, so that he tired of putting her off.[122] Some think that the verb "beat me down" (*hypōpiazō*) refers to the judge's fear of losing his reputation in the community.[123] But this interpretation is unlikely because the parable already stated that the judge did not care what others thought of him. Nor is it probable that a widow, who lacked legal and political power, could destroy the judge's reputation. Hence, the point of the parable again is persistence in prayer. The woman obtained her request because she was relentless in asking for justice.

120. Crump (2006: 65–72) rightly sees that the word *anaideia* means "shameless," but he declines to link this meaning with the context of the parable and thus misinterprets *anaideia* as referring to the person in bed with his family.

121. We know, of course, that some fathers are evil enough to do such things, but Jesus remarks on what is ordinarily the case: fathers love their children and desire to give them what they need.

122. Bock (1996: 1449–50) rightly says that the judge fears being emotionally drained.

123. Marshall 1978b: 673.

That the parable is about persistence in prayer is confirmed by the Lukan comment made even before the parable, informing the reader about the meaning of the parable: "And he told them a parable to the effect that they ought always to pray and not lose heart" (Luke 18:1).[124] The parable is designed, therefore, to encourage believers to persevere in prayer.

The parable raises yet another question. Is God like the unjust judge and reluctant to grant justice to his children? Once again it is obvious that the parable works by way of contrast. If even an unjust judge grants justice to someone who is inconsequential to him, how much more will God vindicate his children? The lesson that Jesus draws from the parable in Luke 18:7–8 demonstrates that God will provide justice for his elect. Not only so, but he will give them justice quickly (*en tachei*). Still, there is a built-in tension in the story, for if justice is granted quickly, why would believers be prone to lose heart in their prayers (Luke 18:1)? The widow has to persist for a long time before she gets the justice that she deserves from the judge (Luke 18:2–5). Believers are to cry out to God in prayer "day and night" (Luke 18:7). Furthermore, Jesus closes the parable by asking if faith will still exist on earth when the Son of Man comes (Luke 18:8). If justice were granted quickly, it would seem that there would be no question of faith flourishing on earth. The best solution to this tension seems to be that the fulfillment of God's purposes are soon according to his timetable, whereas such fulfillment may seem agonizingly slow to human beings.[125] Hence, they are tempted to give up and cease praying. Jesus encouraged his disciples to persist in prayer with the sure confidence that God would soon vindicate them.

When we examine the second part of Luke's two-volume work, we see that prayer was woven into the warp and woof of the everyday life of the church. As Acts 2:42 says, "They devoted themselves to . . . the prayers." The apostles in particular were obligated to "devote [themselves] to prayer and to the ministry of the word" (Acts 6:4). Before the Spirit was poured out on Pentecost, the 120 believers gathered in an upper room and devoted themselves to prayer (Acts 1:12–14). When it came time to select the twelfth and final apostle, the early church did not rely on its own wisdom but rather asked God to direct them through prayer (Acts 1:24–25). Similarly, the apostles laid their hands on and prayed for the seven who were appointed to deal with the problem of the Hellenistic widows (Acts 6:6). The Sanhedrin threatened the apostles for preaching Jesus as the crucified and risen Lord, and the apostles returned from

124. For the emphasis on persistence, see Jeremias 1972: 154–56.
125. The parable raises the question of the delay of the parousia. For an excellent discussion of this matter in relation to Luke 18:1–18, see Bock 1996: 1453–56.

that meeting and prayed that the Sovereign Lord, the Lord of history, who determined all that happened to Jesus Christ in Jerusalem, would grant them boldness to continue to proclaim the gospel (Acts 4:23–31). They prayed that God would confirm his message through signs and wonders. The prayer is clearly portrayed as being answered in the shaking of the building, the filling of the Spirit, and the bold witness to God's word (Acts 4:31).

The Spirit was not received by the Samaritans until Peter and John prayed for such to happen (Acts 8:15). Similarly, Saul was praying when God instructed Ananias to go to him and to lay hands on him so that he would receive the Spirit (Acts 9:10–18). After Peter prayed, Dorcas was raised from death to life (Acts 9:40). We have seen that one of the programmatic texts in Acts is the conversion of Cornelius and his friends. Cornelius was commended as a man of regular prayer (Acts 10:2), and it seems fair to conclude that an angel appeared to him while he was praying (Acts 10:3). Furthermore, God granted Peter the vision of animals in a sheet lowered to the earth while he was praying (Acts 10:9). Through this vision God communicated his will to Peter about unclean foods and the mission to the Gentiles. Peter's liberation from prison was due to the sovereign work of God, and yet we are also told that the church was praying fervently (Acts 12:5, 12). The commissioning of Barnabas and Paul for the first intentional mission to the Gentiles occurred in a context of worship, fasting, and prayer (Acts 13:2–3). After Paul and Barnabas had planted new churches on the first missionary journey, they appointed elders in the churches, and with prayer they commended them to the Lord (Acts 14:23). Paul and Silas were unjustly flogged in Philippi, and yet they prayed and praised God in prison (Acts 16:25), and God used subsequent events to bring the Philippian jailer to faith. After Paul's address to the Ephesian elders, he prayed with them (Acts 20:36). In the region of Tyre Paul prayed with others while kneeling on the beach (Acts 21:5). Paul received the vision instructing him to go to the Gentiles while praying in the temple (Acts 22:17). Finally, Paul's healings on the island of Malta were accompanied by prayer (Acts 28:8).

Conclusion

Acts emphasizes that important events in the history of salvation were accompanied by prayer, whether the choosing of the twelfth apostle, the descent of the Spirit, the visit to Cornelius, or the first intentional Gentile mission. Prayer in Acts, in particular, focuses on the mission of the church to bring the good news to the ends of the earth. Further, the regular mention of prayer and the emphasis on being devoted to prayer illustrate the prominent place that prayer held in the life of the early church. Thereby the church indicated its reliance on God for the accomplishment of every good thing.

The church plays a major role in the theology of Luke-Acts. God's covenantal promises were fulfilled in Jesus of Nazareth, so that the saving message was first proclaimed in Israel. Many Jews, however, rejected the good news proclaimed by Jesus Christ, and Jesus himself appointed twelve apostles as the true and restored Israel. The continuing rejection by the majority of Israel of the message of salvation is related in Acts, while at the same time the message of salvation expands to include the Gentiles in the story line of Acts. Jesus, who in Luke is the bearer of the Spirit, is the one in Acts who pours out the Spirit so that his disciples are empowered to bring the saving message to all peoples everywhere. The church is established on the basis of the teaching of the apostles, the fellowship and generosity of the new community, baptism of new converts, the breaking of bread in the Lord's Supper, and prayer. By emphasizing these different elements, Luke sketches in the nature of life in the early church.

The Gospel and Epistles of John

Both the Gospel and Epistles of John focus on the individual's relationship to God rather than the church as a corporate community. We should not conclude from this that John had no interest in the corporate life of the church. The limited purposes of his writing should caution us against making confident statements about his lack of interest in the church. In one sense, John shows intense concern about the corporate life of believers. He constantly emphasizes the love that should mark the Christian community. Believers are to love one another just as Jesus loved them in giving his life for their sakes (John 13:34–35; 1 John 3:11–18). In loving one another corporately in the community, Christians demonstrate to the world that God is love (1 John 4:7–21). Love constitutes the distinctive command that Jesus gave to his disciples (1 John 2:7–11; cf. 2 John 5–6), and he calls his disciples to love one another and thereby to distinguish themselves from the world, which hates them (John 15:12–16:4). Love serves and assists the one who is in need, and thus Jesus models sacrificial and humble love in washing the disciples' feet (John 13:12–17). The new community is marked by mutual fellowship (1 John 1:7), and this fellowship expresses itself supremely in love for one another. It is striking that John emphasizes love for one another rather than for the world.[126] This should not be interpreted as rejection

---

126. The world is not excluded, but it will be drawn to the quality of the love among disciples (Bultmann 1971: 528). See also Barrett 1978: 452.

of love for the world, as if John lacks any concern for the plight of the world; rather, what demonstrates to the world the authenticity of the gospel is the love that believers express to one another (John 13:34–35). Such love certifies the reality of the truth that Jesus proclaimed and removes it from abstraction. The vitality and energy of love, both its beauty and winsomeness, are compelling and attractive.

Nor should we conclude that John lacks a theology of mission. Indeed, the focal point of mission in John's Gospel is Jesus himself, for as we have seen earlier, Jesus is sent by the Father for the salvation of the world.[127] Furthermore, just as Jesus was sent by the Father, so also he sends out his disciples for the sake of the world (cf. John 15:27; 17:18; 20:21). As Köstenberger and O'Brien remark, "John describes the mission of the disciples in terms of 'harvesting' (4:38), 'fruitbearing' (15:8, 16), and 'witnessing' (15:27). All of these terms place the disciples in the humble position of extending the mission of another, Jesus."[128] The disciples are sent out to continue Jesus' mission through the work of the Spirit, so that they bear witness to Jesus. Thereby they continue the harvest that Jesus began. They bear fruit by bringing to others the message of Jesus. The purpose of John's Gospel, after all, centers on mission (John 20:30–31), and that mission does not terminate with Jesus' glorification but rather continues in the ministry of the disciples and all those who put their faith in Jesus as the Son of God.

Hence, Jesus prays for the unity and oneness of the church (John 17:20–26) for the sake of the world.[129] The unity of the church expresses itself in the unity and beauty of love. The unity cannot be confined to the horizontal sphere. Believers are united because the Father and Son indwell them, and Jesus has given them the glory that the Father gave him. Those who see the glory and magnificence of the Son will be united in the truth that the Father sent the Son. The unity that Jesus prays for here is unity in the splendor of the truth, the truth that the Father has sent Jesus as his Son. Believers are united in the experience and the realization of knowing God's name. The same love that the Father has for the Son has been vouchsafed to the believers. Indeed, the Son himself indwells believers, so that their unity is grounded in the experience of God's love in their hearts, so that the confession that the Father sent the Son is not merely an intellectual recognition. The unity of believers is grounded in both truth and love, and a community grounded in truth and love witnesses to the world about the truth of the gospel.

127. Köstenberger 1998: 45–52; Köstenberger and O'Brien 2001: 204–9.
128. Köstenberger and O'Brien 2001: 210. See further Köstenberger 1998; Köstenberger and O'Brien 2001: 203–26.
129. See Carson 1991b: 568.

That the people of God function as a community is also evident in John 10, where Jesus' disciples are his sheep and flock. Jesus is the shepherd of the sheep, and the sheep listen to his voice and follow him (John 10:3–4). But Jesus' flock is not limited to the Jews; he also declares that he has sheep from other folds, and that they will listen to the shepherd's voice and become one flock (John 10:16). The reference here certainly is to the inclusion of the Gentiles into the people of God.[130] Nor will the Jews and Gentiles constitute two different flocks. There will be one united flock that finds its concord in submitting to the voice of Jesus as the good shepherd. Jesus did not die merely for the sake of the Jewish people; he died also to gather the scattered children of God (i.e., both Jews and Gentiles) into one united people of God (John 11:51–52). John does not exclude Jews from God's saving purposes, but at the same time he heralds the participation of Gentiles. Greeks arrive at Jesus' last Passover and long to see and meet him (John 12:20–21). Jesus apparently did not introduce himself to them at this time; instead, he focused on his impending death, for this is the means by which he will draw all to himself (John 12:32)—that is, both Jews and Gentiles. God's people enter into a saving relationship with God and a profound love for one another by virtue of the saving work of Jesus on their behalf. Jesus as the true vine is the true Israel (John 15:1)—the leader of the new people of God. Hence, anyone who desires to be part of the people of God must be connected to the vine.

In 2 John the church is portrayed as an "elect lady" (2 John 1, 5).[131] The image of the church being a woman hearkens back to the OT, where Israel is described as Yahweh's wife, and he is her bridegroom (e.g., Isa. 50:1; 54:6; Jer. 3:1, 8–9, 20; 5:7; Ezek. 16:32; Hosea 3:1). Paul similarly describes the church as the bride of Christ (Eph. 5:22–33). In Revelation the people of God are the bride of the Lamb and await the messianic marriage supper (Rev. 19:7–9). In 2 John the elect lady represents the specific church to which John addresses his letter. Conversely, the church from which he writes sends its greetings: "The children of your elect sister greet you" (2 John 13). The unity of the church is conveyed by the warm greetings and affection that exist between the two churches. The elect lady does not refer to a particular woman, even though John speaks of her children (2 John 1, 4, 13). The children and the elect lady are the same entities viewed from a different perspective. The elect lady designates the church as a whole, while the children refer to the members of the church, whom John rejoices in insofar as they are walking in the truth.[132]

---

130. So Barrett 1978: 376; Ridderbos 1997: 363.
131. So Stott 1964: 200–202; R. Brown 1982: 651–55; Smalley 1984: 318.
132. Marshall 1978a: 60–61; Smalley 1984: 318–19; R. Brown 1982: 655.

Leaders

John says little about the leadership of the church. He likely assumes that the readers know about the calling of the apostles, and brief accounts are given about the calling of some of those who served as apostles (see John 1:35–51), though John himself never uses the term "apostle." Still, he clearly knows about and recognizes the apostleship, for he writes naturally and without explanation about "the twelve" (John 6:67). Jesus chose the Twelve (John 6:70), and Judas, the betrayer, was one of them (John 6:71), as was Thomas, who initially doubted the resurrection (John 20:24). The primacy of the eyewitnesses is demonstrated by 1 John 1:1–4. The "we" in these verses probably relates to John as an apostle, for the date and destination of 1 John are such that only an apostle qualifies as one who heard, saw, and touched Jesus.[133] Jesus entered history at a particular point in time, and he "was made manifest to us" (1 John 1:2)—that is, the apostles.[134] Hence, John as an eyewitness announced the saving message to those who heard him. He declared the message so that people "may have fellowship with us" (1 John 1:3)—that is, the original apostolic eyewitnesses. We might expect John to say immediately that he proclaimed the good news so that people would have fellowship with the Father and the Son, but fellowship with John as an apostle precedes fellowship with the Father and the Son. The Son was manifested in history to the apostles, and thus the readers have fellowship with the Son and the Father only if they heed and accept the message conveyed by the original eyewitnesses. Fellowship with the apostolic eyewitnesses is a precondition to fellowship with God. Hence, John can say later that those who repudiate the message transmitted by him as an eyewitness do not listen to God (1 John 4:6).[135] Jesus chose the Twelve (John 6:70), then, to exercise authority over the church of Jesus Christ. The three letters of John represent that authority in action, for he decisively pronounces on matters of life and teaching that affect the churches addressed.

133. The writer belongs to the circle of eyewitnesses (rightly Stott 1964: 61–63; Marshall 1978a: 106–7; Bauckham 2006: 373–75 [though he thinks that the author is John the elder]). Smalley (1984: 8) understands the first-person plural to refer generally to the guardians of orthodoxy. R. Brown (1982: 158–61) defends a version of the "Johannine school" interpretation.

134. Even though John does not use the word "apostle" here, the notion of apostolic authority is present conceptually.

135. So Stott 1964: 157–58. Perhaps John has in view here the whole of the church with its teachers (see Marshall 1978a: 209; Smalley 1984: 229). For an excellent discussion of the alternatives with preference for a nondistinctive use of the first-person plural, see R. Brown 1982: 499.

John, of course, does not grant the Twelve unrestricted privilege to rule in arbitrary ways. They must themselves serve the gospel of Jesus Christ and faithfully transmit "the teaching of Christ" (2 John 9).[136] Anyone, including a so-called apostle, who deviates from such teaching does not belong to God (2 John 9). Tyranny and despotism in leaders must be avoided at all costs. Diotrephes is criticized because he loved preeminence and refused to countenance apostolic authority (3 John 9–10). He forbade the acceptance of traveling missionaries (3 John 10; cf. 5–8) into his own church and excommunicated from the church those who desired to receive them. Such abuses of authority are condemned, for positions of authority are not platforms for selfishness but rather represent a call for faithful service to the gospel. Authority can be wielded only for the sake of the gospel, never for private and personal advancement. Apostolic authority, in other words, is always subservient to the word. Jesus restored Peter after his threefold denial with a threefold call to "feed my lambs," "tend my sheep," and "feed my sheep" (John 21:15–17). Peter was not given the privilege of leadership but rather its responsibility, and he was called upon to strengthen the flock by feeding and tending it. This background helps us to explain Jesus' claim that sins are forgiven and retained at the prerogative of the apostles (John 20:23).[137] Here Jesus hardly grants the Twelve a whimsical and arbitrary authority to pronounce whatever they wish to people. Forgiveness or the lack thereof is declared on the basis of the gospel that the apostles proclaim. Forgiveness is tied to the atoning death of Jesus Christ. The apostles pronounced forgiveness upon those who put their faith in the Son as the one who grants eternal life. This saying on the forgiveness of sins cannot be sundered from the remainder of John's Gospel so that it stands out as a foreign element. Instead, it must be interpreted in light of the theme of the Gospel as a whole. Eternal life is granted to those who believe in Jesus' name (John 20:30–31), and the apostles announced God's forgiveness to those who put their trust in Jesus.

Baptism and Communion

Scholars have long debated whether John's Gospel refers to baptism or communion.[138] Many scholars have seen a reference to baptism in the

---

136. Bauckham (2006: 372–73) rightly argues that the first-person plurals in 3 John 9–12 designate the writer as an eyewitness.

137. For a thorough discussion of the possibilities, see R. Brown 1970: 1039–45. For defense of the view suggested here, see Carson 1991b: 655–56.

138. For a survey of the issue, see Burge 1987: 150–97.

need to be born of water and the Spirit (John 3:5).[139] I argued previously that this is not a reference to Christian baptism but rather alludes to Ezek. 11:18–19; 36:26–27.[140] Indeed, there does not seem to be a direct reference to Christian baptism anywhere in John's Gospel, though some have seen a reference to baptism in almost every mention of water in this Gospel. Similarly, it seems that John intentionally omits any reference to the Lord's Supper. The institution that is so prominent in the passion narratives in the Synoptic Gospels is missing in John's Gospel. Some scholars, of course, detect a reference to the Lord's Supper in the "bread of life" discourse.[141] A direct reference to the Lord's Supper, however, seems unlikely.[142] It does not fit Johannine theology to say that one must partake of the Lord's Supper in order to have eternal life, but Jesus in the discourse clearly says that one must eat his flesh and drink his blood to enjoy eternal life (John 6:53). If we take the historical context seriously, it is difficult to see how this could be construed literally, for Jesus was present with his disciples. Indeed, the misunderstanding of the people fits with other misunderstandings in John. Those hearing Jesus took him literally and were perplexed and scandalized (John 6:52, 60). Similarly, Nicodemus took Jesus literally when he said that one must be born again (John 3:4). The Samaritan woman believed that Jesus was speaking literally about water in promising her living water (John 4:11–12). The parallels suggest, then, that Jesus was not speaking literally about eating his flesh and drinking his blood. The reference is to his death on behalf of his people and to the need to put one's faith in the atonement provided. The language of eating Jesus' flesh and drinking his blood vividly communicates the vitality of faith. The work that God requires is believing in the one whom he sent (John 6:29). The hunger of anyone who comes to Jesus will be satisfied; the thirst of anyone who believes in Jesus will be quenched (John 6:35). Augustine caught the meaning of what John wrote: "Believe, and you have eaten."[143]

139. For example, Lindars 1972: 152; Barrett 1978: 209. For a discussion of the various options, see R. Brown 1966: 141–44. Bultmann (1971: 138–39n3) maintains that the reference to water was added by an ecclesiastical redactor.

140. So Belleville 1980.

141. For example, Stuhlmacher 1993: 88–99. For the history of interpretation, see R. Brown 1966: 272. Bultmann (1971: 234–37) thinks that the reference to the Lord's Supper (John 6:51b–58) was added by the redactor. The view of R. Brown (1966: 272–74, 284–93) seems to be an adaptation of Bultmann's.

142. Lindars (1972: 251) thinks that the eucharistic interpretation is latent. See also Barrett 1978: 284, 297. Carson (1991b: 277–80) argues that the supper points to Jesus himself and is not the focus of the text.

143. Koester (2003: 103), reflecting the words of Augustine, says "'To eat' is 'to believe.'"

We could go too far in the other direction. We should not read John as if he were antisacramental. The cleansing in water may not refer directly to Christian baptism (e.g., John 3:5; 13:1–10),[144] but the cleansing with water points to the forgiveness received in the washing away of sins in baptism. Similarly, the "bread of life" discourse does not refer directly to the Eucharist, and yet John likely intended a secondary reference to the Lord's Supper. When believers break the bread and drink the wine, they feed on the work of Jesus in giving his flesh and shedding his blood on their behalf. The "bread of life" discourse points in a secondary way to the Lord's Supper.[145] Perhaps John does not focus on the sacraments because he wants belief in Jesus Christ for salvation to take center stage. Baptism and the Lord's Supper do not provide some kind of magical or automatic communication with God. Faith rests in the work of Jesus Christ alone. It feeds on him in his death and resurrection.

Conclusion

We do not have any full-orbed theology of the church in John. Nothing is said about the structure or leaders of the church, though it is clear that the apostles were authoritative witnesses. Nor does John provide direct teaching on baptism or the Lord's Supper, though his teaching on the salvation that Jesus accomplished points to both of these secondarily. John does emphasize the love that should be the mark of true disciples, pointing to Jesus' self-sacrifice as the paradigm of love.

The Pauline Literature

The term that Paul typically uses to designate the communities that he established is *ekklēsia* ("church").[146] The word *ekklēsia* derives from the OT, where the people of Israel were the *qĕhal yhwh* (e.g., Num. 16:3; 20:4; Deut. 23:1, 8; 1 Chron. 28:8) or *qĕhal yiśrā'ēl* (e.g., Exod. 12:6; Lev. 16:17; Num. 14:5). The former was usually translated in the LXX as *ekklēsia kyriou*. Paul often uses the phrase "church of God" (1 Cor. 1:2; 10:32; 11:22; 15:9; 2 Cor. 1:1; Gal. 1:13; 1 Tim. 3:5; cf. 1 Cor. 11:16; 1 Thess. 2:14; 2 Thess. 1:4; 1 Tim. 3:15). The use of this expression with reference to Paul's converts demonstrates that he conceived of the church as the true Israel, the new people of God, and the fulfillment of what

144. For baptism in John, see Hartman 1997: 155–59.

145. Against the view that the discourse refers to the Eucharist, see Dunn 1971. Koester speaks of "echoes" (2003: 103).

146. This section draws upon Schreiner 2001: 331–410. Often I use the exact wording, but the material here is abbreviated, revised, and in some instances expanded.

God intended with Israel. This does not necessarily mean that there is no role or future for ethnic Israel (as I will argue in chapter 19).

Paul often refers to local assemblies and gatherings as churches (Rom. 16:5, 23; 1 Cor. 1:2; 16:19; 2 Cor. 1:1; Col. 4:15, 16; 1 Thess. 1:1; 2 Thess. 1:1; Philem. 2). Most scholars believe that at least four or five house churches existed in Rome (Rom. 16:5, 10–11, 14–15).[147] Sometimes Paul uses the plural "churches," but a locality is given, suggesting a number of local churches in a certain geographical setting: "the churches of Galatia" (1 Cor. 16:1; Gal. 1:2); "the churches of Asia" (1 Cor. 16:19); "the churches of Macedonia" (2 Cor. 8:1); "the churches of Judea" (Gal. 1:22).

Paul also uses the plural "churches" of the various local assemblies (Rom. 16:4, 16; 1 Cor. 11:16; 14:33, 34; 16:1, 19; 2 Cor. 8:1, 18–19; 11:8, 28; 12:13; Gal. 1:2, 22; 1 Thess. 2:14; 2 Thess. 1:4). This does not detract from the authenticity of local assemblies, but the plural does emphasize the interrelationship and unity among various churches. Paul also appeals to the plurality of churches when he feels that a particular church is misled. He reminds the Corinthians that the other churches follow the custom regarding the veiling of women (1 Cor. 11:16), and that in all other assemblies women keep silent (1 Cor. 14:33–34). His instructions about remaining in one's calling are not unique to Corinth but rather represent what he says "in all the churches" (1 Cor. 7:17). The responsibility for mutual care moves Paul to remind the Corinthians of the plurality of the churches when he asks and exhorts them to contribute to the collection (1 Cor. 16:1; 2 Cor. 8:1, 18, 19, 23; 11:8; 12:13).

Scholars who dispute the Pauline authorship of Colossians and Ephesians often doubt that Paul ever referred to the universal church. But O'Brien is likely correct in arguing that the church should be thought of as a heavenly assembly.[148] Those who believe in Christ already belong to God's assembly located in the heavens. Even in the letters commonly acknowledged as Pauline, Paul occasionally refers to church as a whole without restricting it to a single locality (e.g., 1 Cor. 12:28).[149] The emphasis on the universal church (or the heavenly assembly) is most evident in Colossians and Ephesians.[150] As we noted previously, local churches are mentioned in Colossians (Col. 4:15–16). But references to the universal church are also found. Christ is said to be "the head of the body, the church" (Col. 1:18; cf. 1:24). One might restrict these sayings to the local church, but the phrase "the body, the church" suggests the heavenly assembly. And yet we must admit that the fluidity of usage continues,

147. See Schreiner 1998: 797–98.
148. O'Brien 1987a: 88–119, esp. 93–98.
149. Contra the reading of this text in Dunn 1998: 578–79. Perhaps a wider reference is in view in 1 Cor. 15:9; Gal. 1:13; Phil. 3:6 as well.
150. See Roloff, *EDNT* 1:414–15.

for no disjunction between the universal and local church is intended, even if the emphasis is on the heavenly assembly.

The focus on the universal church is most evident in Ephesians. Perhaps this is due to the letter being an encyclical. Jesus is the head of the church (Eph. 1:22). Through the church God's wisdom is disclosed to angelic powers (Eph. 3:10). Glory redounds to God in the church (Eph. 3:21). The parallel between husbands and wives and Christ and the church receives extended attention in Eph. 5:22–33 (see esp. Eph. 5:32). Christ is the head of the church (Eph. 5:23), and the church is subject to Christ (Eph. 5:24). Christ demonstrated his love for the church through his death (Eph. 5:25). Though the focus is on the universal church, the boundary lines between the universal and local church remain somewhat indistinct. Still, Paul concentrates his discussion on the church as a whole.

The Body and the Unity of the Church

The best-known metaphor for the church in Pauline writings is the body of Christ. Scholars have been fascinated as to the origin of the metaphor.[151] No theory can be proved, and in the end where Paul got the idea is less important than how he used it. The former can never be more than a hypothesis, but the latter can be explored from Paul's letters.

In Paul's earlier letters the body metaphor is used to emphasize the unity of the church. In 1 Cor. 10:16–17 an analogy between the one loaf shared at the Lord's Supper and the body of Christ is forged. Sharing the cup involves sharing in the benefits of Christ's blood, and sharing the loaf involves sharing in the benefits of Christ's death (1 Cor. 10:16).[152] Paul detects significance in the fact that there is "one bread" (1 Cor. 10:17). The unity of the loaf demonstrates that believers are one body—that is, united in Christ.[153] The unity stems from the source of their life because all believers partake of the same bread. The life of believers derives from their feeding upon the crucified and resurrected Lord.

An extended discussion on the church as a body ensues in 1 Cor. 12. Divisions over spiritual gifts created havoc in Corinth (1 Cor. 12–14). Paul attempts to provide perspective without quenching the use of such gifts in the community. His main theme is unity in diversity (see also Rom. 12:4–5). Paul reminds the Corinthians that diversity does not cancel out unity but is instead an expression of it. The metaphor of the body dominates 1 Cor. 12:12–27. The body is one and yet has many different members; the variety of members does not nullify the fact that there is

---

151. For a survey of the discussion, see Dunn 1998: 549–551.
152. So Fee 1987: 467–69; Barrett 1968: 232.
153. See Stuhlmacher 1993: 83–84.

one body. The unity of the body is realized at baptism, where believers are baptized into one body (1 Cor. 12:13).[154] By definition, the one body is also characterized by diversity (1 Cor. 12:14), for bodies are made up of many members. No member of the body should feel inferior or superior (1 Cor. 12:15–24), for every member is needed. The unity of the body manifests itself in mutual care, so that all participate in another's joy or sorrow (1 Cor. 12:25–26).

Some scholars doubt that Paul wrote Ephesians and Colossians, citing in support of this view, among other reasons, that the metaphor of the body changes. Here Paul speaks of Christ as being the *head* of the body (Eph. 1:22–23; 4:16; 5:23; Col. 1:18; 2:19) instead of using the term "head" as he did in Corinthians to denote a member of the body.[155] Doubting Pauline authorship on this basis is unpersuasive. Understanding the church as Christ's body is a metaphor, and it is common to change a metaphor to make a different point. Those who object to such a shift construe metaphors too rigidly. Paul here emphasizes Christ's lordship over the church.

Unity is also a theme in Ephesians and Colossians. Believers must let Christ's peace have dominion in their corporate life, for they were called to such harmony as the body of Christ (Col. 3:15). In Eph. 2:11–3:13 Paul emphasizes the unity of Jews and Gentiles in Christ. By virtue of the work of Christ on the cross, Jews and Gentiles are no longer estranged from one another, nor are they estranged from God. They have both been "reconcile[d] . . . to God in one body through the cross" (Eph. 2:16). The inclusion of Gentiles is highlighted because formerly they were cut off from the covenant people and separated from the promises of Israel. Christ has come and broken down the barrier that separated Jews and Gentiles. The peace established between Jews and Gentiles, expressed in the "one body" that they now share, is rooted in the gospel, the message of the crucified and risen Lord (Eph. 2:17–18). It is this gospel that proclaims peace to those who are near and far. It is on the basis of this gospel that both Jews and Gentiles have access to God through the Spirit. Paul exults in the fact that Gentiles are no longer strangers and aliens but rather are fellow citizens with Israel and members of God's household. Again, the theme that the church is the true Israel emerges.[156] The mystery revealed to Paul is that Gentiles are "fellow heirs, members of

154. The baptism is performed by Jesus in the Spirit rather than by the Spirit (contra Dunn 1970a: 127–28; O'Donnell 1999: 311–36).

155. Modern representatives of those who doubt Pauline authorship include Best 1998: 6–40; Lincoln 1990: lix–lxxiii. For convincing defenses of Pauline authorship, see Hoehner 2002: 2–61; O'Brien 1999: 4–47.

156. Lincoln (1987: 608–17) argues that the incorporation of Gentiles into the people of God should not be construed as if Gentiles become part of Israel. Instead, the church

the same body [*syssōma*], and partakers of the promise in Christ Jesus through the gospel" (Eph. 3:6).[157]

Since the church is so extraordinary, we are not surprised to learn later that it is "through the church that the manifold wisdom of God" is displayed (Eph. 3:10). The church enshrined God's plan for history, revealing to all creation the wisdom and depth of God's saving plan. The church is the locus of God's glory, the theater in which he displays his grace and love. The church features God's wisdom, declaring to the whole universe that the outworking of history is not arbitrary but rather fulfills God's plan. Since the church is at the center of God's purposes, Paul summons it to live up to its calling (Eph. 4:1–3). When the church follows its Lord, it brings honor to God and to the Lord Jesus Christ. The church fulfills its calling in particular when it maintains "the unity of the Spirit in the bond of peace" (Eph. 4:3). We have already seen from Eph. 2:11–3:13 that the unity of the church was established through the blood of Christ. The church is called upon not to create unity but rather to preserve the unity that already exists. The basis of this unity is proclaimed again in Eph. 4:4–6.

The unity of the body continues to be a theme in the discussion of spiritual gifts (Eph. 4:7–16). Various gifts are given to the church so that the body will be edified (Eph. 4:12). This edification is defined further as "unity of the faith" (Eph. 4:13). Such unity is realized when believers come to the knowledge of God's Son, when they grow up into maturity and reach the full stature of Christ (Eph. 4:13). This vision for the church will not be fulfilled perfectly until the day of redemption, but Paul expects that it will be attained in some measure in this age. The church will be stabilized so that it will not be rocked by every new and devious teaching (Eph. 4:14). The unity that Paul envisions, therefore, cannot be described merely as feelings of harmony and love, as important as the expression of love is. The unity demanded is rooted in truth and is jeopardized by deviant teaching. Unity will be realized only if the church is faithful to the truth of the gospel and avoids teachings contrary to this gospel. Hence, according to Eph. 4:15, the church will grow up into its head only through the proclamation of the truth of the gospel. This verse is not simply saying that believers should speak the truth in love, but that the truth of the gospel should be heralded with love, for the context

---

is conceived of as a new entity, a new creation, so that the church is a "third race," so to speak. Others speak of the church as "re-created Israel" (Grindheim 2003: 537).

157. Grindheim (2003: 533) argues that the mystery "is the fulfillment of something that is planned by God, something that was previously unknown, but now proclaimed." Grindheim (2003: 531–53) rightly maintains that the future salvation of Gentiles was promised in the OT, so that the newness consists not in the promise of salvation but rather in the inclusion of Gentiles in God's people apart from the Mosaic law.

focuses on the gifts that Christ has given to the church for speaking the word and warns against the danger of false teaching.[158]

The theme of the unity of the church is so pervasive that we must survey some texts briefly. In Romans, for instance, Paul writes to rally the Roman churches around his gospel so that they will support his venture to Spain. The section on the weak and the strong (Rom. 14:1–15:13) indicates that the church was polarized over unclean food and the observance of days. Paul could hardly convince the church to support the furtherance of the gospel if they were quarrelling over various matters. Paul's aim was to work toward harmony between Jews and Gentiles, so "that together you may with one voice glorify the God and Father of our Lord Jesus Christ" (Rom. 15:6). The Corinthian church also experienced divisions over food (1 Cor. 8:1–11:1). The text differs in a number of respects from Rom. 14:1–15:13, but the desire for unity is parallel to Rom. 14–15.

The Corinthians also were divided over their estimation of church leaders (1 Cor. 1:10–4:21), so that some followed Paul, others Apollos, others Cephas, and apparently others said that they followed Christ. Paul was intensely troubled by their factions because personality cults nullify the cross of Christ. He wanted the church to unite on the basis of the cross, which undercuts human pride. Factions existed not because Paul and Apollos had different theologies (otherwise Paul would scarcely encourage Apollos to visit Corinth [1 Cor. 16:12]) but rather because attaching themselves to one leader versus another pandered to the ego of the Corinthians. Significant evidence exists that the Philippian church was plagued by disunity.[159] Paul specifically exhorts Euodia and Syntyche to come to peace (Phil. 4:2–3), asking other believers to help them do so. The sustained exhortation to unity (Phil. 1:27–2:4) suggests that a serious problem needed to be remedied in the church.

The Church as Temple and People

Paul does not often call the church God's temple (*naos*). Yet the fact that he does so at all (1 Cor. 3:16–17; 2 Cor. 6:16; Eph. 2:21) is significant because the temple was fundamental to Judaism, one of the pillars upon which Judaism rested.[160] For Paul, by contrast, the Jerusalem temple no longer plays a central role. Nor is there any reference to priests serving as cultic functionaries, nor were any sacrifices recommended, since the one definitive sacrifice was that of Christ. To have a "religion" without a temple, priests, or sacrifices would have seemed quite strange in the

---

158. See Lincoln 1990: 259–60; Best 1998: 406–8; O'Brien 1999: 310–11. Hoehner (2002: 564–65), conversely, takes the phrase to mean that we are to live truthfully in love.

159. See Peterlin 1995, though he overemphasizes his insight.

160. For the theme of the church as the new temple in Paul, see Beale 2004: 245–68.

Greco-Roman world. The newness of the gospel emerges at this very point. God's new building cannot be confined to a physical structure but is the church (1 Cor. 3:9)—that is, the people of God is his dwelling place. The foundation of this building is Jesus Christ, and the Spirit dwells in believers, not in the temple in Jerusalem (1 Cor. 3:16).

In 2 Cor. 6:16 Paul clarifies that the temple imagery of the OT is fulfilled in God's dwelling in his people corporately. Uncleanness is contracted not through unclean food or by violating other Levitical regulations but rather through sin (2 Cor. 7:1). Temple imagery is also found in the word "access" (*prosagōgē*). Access to God is available not through some cultic process but rather through faith in Christ (Rom. 5:2). Believers now have access to God not through the sacrificial system and the temple in Jerusalem but rather in the Spirit on the basis of the cross of Christ (Eph. 2:18). Since Gentiles are now part of God's temple, they are members of his household (*oikeioi* [Eph. 2:19]). In the temple the court of the Gentiles was segregated from the court of the Israelites, and a famous sign posted there proclaimed that any Gentile who entered forbidden precincts in the temple would be slain.[161] In God's new temple Jews and Gentiles are no longer alienated from one another but are equal members of the same house.

In Ephesians the church is said to be built upon the foundation of the apostles and prophets instead of Christ (Eph. 2:20). At first glance, this seems to contradict 1 Cor. 3:10–11, where the foundation of the house is restricted to Jesus Christ. But we must avoid reading metaphors too rigidly, expecting that Paul will always use the same metaphor for the same purpose. In actuality, the Ephesians text makes the same point as 1 Cor. 3:10–11. Jesus Christ is the cornerstone of the building (Eph. 2:20); that is, he is the crucial element in the whole building.[162] The entire building takes its shape and structure from him.[163] Such a statement communicates the same truth articulated in 1 Cor. 3:10–11, where Jesus Christ is announced as the only foundation for the church. To say that the apostles and prophets are the foundation of the church is not a genuine contradiction, for the teaching of the apostles and prophets must adhere to the gospel of Jesus Christ in order to be authoritative.

Believers are God's temple in Christ and are "built together into a dwelling place for God by the Spirit" (Eph. 2:22). The theology here is

161. "No man of another race is to enter within the fence and enclosure around the Temple. Whoever is caught will have only himself to thank for the death which follows" (cited in Lincoln 1990: 141).

162. For Christ as the cornerstone, see Hoehner 2002: 404–7. Contra Lincoln (1990: 154–56), who sees Christ as the capstone here.

163. Schlatter (1999: 188) captures the truth that Paul did not see himself as a hero, nor did he teach that believers should look to him or his greatness. Instead, he exalted God and Christ.

similar to what we have seen in 1 Cor. 3:16 and 2 Cor. 6:16: the church is God's temple. Ephesians does not represent an advance over the Corinthian letters in this respect. Nor do the Pastoral Epistles deviate from genuine Pauline teaching in saying that the church is "the household of God" (1 Tim. 3:15).[164] Temple imagery probably is present here, but there is also the idea that the church is structured after the household (cf. 1 Tim. 3:4–5, 12; 5:4).

The OT often refers to Israel as God's "people" (*laos*). It is somewhat surprising how little Paul employs this term to refer to the church of Jesus Christ (Rom. 9:25–26; 2 Cor. 6:16; Titus 2:14).[165] The use of the term indicates, however, that the blessings of Israel are now fulfilled in the church of Christ, since in Rom. 9 Paul picks up the language of Hosea 1:9; 2:23 and applies it to the church.

Spiritual Gifts

Reading 1 Cor. 12–14, we see that contention over spiritual gifts divided the Corinthian church. The following table represents the spiritual gifts listed by Paul.

1 Cor. 12:8–10	1 Cor. 12:28–30	Rom. 12:6–8	Eph. 4:11
Word of wisdom	Apostles	Prophecy	Apostles
Word of knowledge	Prophets	Serving	Prophets
Faith	Teachers	Teaching	Evangelists
Healing	Miracles	Exhortation	Pastors-teachers
Miracles	Healings	Giving	
Prophecy	Helps	Leading	
Distinguishing of spirits	Administration	Mercy	
Tongues	Tongues		
Interpretation of tongues	Interpretation of tongues		

The emphasis on *charisma* and the Spirit relative to gifts brings to the forefront an important Pauline theme.[166] Gifts are not an indication of greater spirituality. The Corinthians apparently were inclined to

164. Some (e.g., Marshall 1999: 507–8) think that we do not have temple imagery here but rather an illustration from the secular household (cf. 1 Tim. 3:4–5). But there is no need for an either-or here, since the language of pillar and support also suggests reference to a building (Knight 1992: 179–80; W. Mounce 2000: 220–21).

165. Marshall (1999: 285–86) argues that the use of the term *laos* in Titus 2:14 shows that OT language for God's people is now applied to the church of Jesus Christ. The OT texts alluded to (cf. Exod. 19:5; Deut. 7:6; 14:2; 26:18) point to this conclusion (see Knight 1992: 328; W. Mounce 2000: 431–32).

166. On spiritual gifts in Paul, see the careful study of Dunn 1975b: 199–258.

believe that a gift such as tongues demonstrated the Spirit's presence in a more remarkable way.[167] Paul utterly rejects any such idea. Any ability that one has derives from God and is the result of his grace. No human boasting is permitted. "All these things are empowered by one and the same Spirit, who apportions to each one individually as he wills" (1 Cor. 12:11). The gift that one has is attributed to the sovereignty of the Spirit and cannot be ascribed to one's own spirituality.

Since gifts are the result of God's grace and sovereignty, it follows that all gifts are exercised under the lordship of Christ. Paul begins his discussion of spiritual gifts in 1 Cor. 12:1–3 by affirming that no one acknowledges that "Jesus is Lord" except through the work of the Holy Spirit (1 Cor. 12:3). The banner over all gifts is the acclamation of the lordship of Christ, and the inspiration for all gifts comes from the Holy Spirit. It is God's intention, therefore, that a diversity (*diairesis*) of gifts exists (1 Cor. 12:4–6). Any notion that all believers would exercise the same gift is rejected (1 Cor. 12:27–30). Nor *should* all believers exercise the same gift. It would be a strange body indeed if everyone were an eye or an ear (1 Cor. 12:17). A body, by definition, is composed of diverse members (1 Cor. 12:12, 14; Rom. 12:4–5).

Gifts were not given for narcissistic purposes but rather "for the common good" (1 Cor. 12:7). Therefore, no schism should injure the body; instead, members should care for one another (1 Cor. 12:25–26). Paul labors in 1 Cor. 14 to communicate that gifts are intended to edify others. He has no use for uninterpreted tongues in the assembly, for they fail to build up others (1 Cor. 14:1–5). Prophecy is preferable to tongues because others will be edified, encouraged, and consoled (1 Cor. 14:3). Edification and understanding are indissolubly connected for Paul (1 Cor. 14:26).

In Eph. 4 the purpose of granting gifted persons to the church is "to equip the saints for the work of the ministry, for building up the body of Christ" (Eph. 4:12). Unity in the faith—the doctrinal truth of the gospel—indicates that edification is a reality (Eph. 4:13). The focus on understanding is remarkable. Being carried away by new and dangerous teaching is evidence of immaturity (Eph. 4:14). Mature believers, on the other hand, receive the truth about Christ and thereby they grow. Edification becomes a reality through proper teaching and comprehension (Eph. 4:15–16). The emphasis on learning is not surprising when the gifted people listed are apostles, prophets, evangelists, and pastors and teachers (Eph. 4:11). This is not to say that only some Christians play a role in building up the body of Christ. The body grows through the contribution of each and every individual part (Eph. 4:16: *en metrō henos hekastou merous*).

---

167. So Fee 1987: 571–73; Garland 2003: 558–59.

Perhaps the most important perspective on spiritual gifts appears in 1 Cor. 13. This chapter is inserted intentionally in the midst of the discussion on spiritual gifts. It must not be explained as a digression or extraneous to the main purpose of 1 Cor. 12–14, as if it were unrelated to the content of the two chapters that surround it on either side. Showing love for one another is vastly more important than exercising any gift. Exalting gifts over love places primacy on the temporal instead of the eternal, the superficial and partial over against what is lasting and complete (1 Cor. 13:8–13).

We have been examining gifts in general, but the specific gifts identified by Paul have not been defined. Most scholars agree that the lists are not exhaustive but rather representative, though any additional gifts probably could be placed under one of the categories found in Rom. 12:6–8. Space precludes defining all the gifts here, so that the focus will be on those that are controversial or specially important. As in 1 Pet. 4:10–11, the gifts listed can be placed under the headings of serving and teaching, and they are all intended for the growth of the church.

Teaching is mentioned specifically in Rom. 12:7; 1 Cor. 12:28. The same gift is also likely in view when Paul refers to "pastors and teachers" in Eph. 4:11. Teaching differs from prophecy in that it is rooted in and dependent upon previously transmitted tradition.[168] It does not involve a spontaneous word but rather an explication of a word already given. Paul emphasizes on more than one occasion that the churches are to conform to handed-down traditions (Rom. 6:17; 16:17; 2 Thess. 2:15; 1 Tim. 4:11; 6:2; 2 Tim. 2:2; Titus 1:11). Such traditions would need to be taught and explained.

The most difficult gifts to define probably are prophecy, tongues, and apostleship. Prophecy can be defined as communicating revelations from God in a spontaneous utterance.[169] In 1 Cor. 14:6, for example, the words "revelation" and "prophecy" probably are overlapping terms (cf. 1 Cor. 14:26). The close relationship between prophecy and revelation is cemented by 1 Cor. 14:29–33a. Especially instructive is 1 Cor. 14:30, which describes prophecy in terms of a revelation granted suddenly to one who is sitting down.

The most controversial gift that Paul discusses is that of tongues. Apparently, the Corinthians believed that speaking in tongues was a mark of greater spirituality, and perhaps the Corinthians supported their overrealized eschatology by referring to their ability to speak in tongues,

---

168. See Greeven 1952–1953: 19–23; Ridderbos 1975: 453; Rengstorf, *TDNT* 2:147; Aune 1983: 217.

169. For similar understandings of prophecy, see Aune 1983: Grudem 1982; Turner 1996: 185–220; Hays 1997: 234, 242; Forbes 1995: 218–21, but Forbes distinguishes in some respects the Lukan and Pauline conceptions.

and thus Paul had to place this gift in proper perspective. Tongues are a gift from God and should not be despised or forbidden (1 Cor. 14:39), and yet they should not be confused with entrance into a heavenly existence. Tongues, prophecy, and knowledge belong to what is partial, and they will cease when the perfect arrives at the second coming of Christ (1 Cor. 13:8–12).

Tongues without a corresponding interpretation are unedifying (1 Cor. 14:1–19) because no one understands what is being said, and Paul's overriding concern in his discussion of tongues and prophecy is the edification of the church. Confusion reigned in the church at Corinth, so he limited tongue-speaking to two or three people (1 Cor. 14:27–28). If an interpreter is lacking, the one speaking in tongues should be silent. Paul rejects the idea that the gift takes over believers so that they lose control. The "spiritual gifts of the prophets are subject to the prophets" (1 Cor. 14:32 my translation). Believers can and must control what they are doing.

For Paul, does tongue-speaking involve foreign languages, or is some kind of ecstatic utterance involved?[170] In Acts 2 the gift seems to be in human languages because people from all over the world hear the apostles "speaking in the native language of each" (Acts 2:6 NRSV), "each of us in our own language in which we were born" (Acts 2:8 my translation), "in our own languages" (Acts 2:11 NRSV). Nor is there any evidence elsewhere in Acts that speaking in tongues is different in character (Acts 10:44–48; 19:6). It seems unlikely that a different kind of tongues is intended in subsequent chapters in Acts, since Luke gives no indication of a variance from the first occurrence.

Most scholars, however, believe that Paul differs from Luke, and certainly this is possible. It is unlikely, however, that tongues are simply an ecstatic utterance without any underlying code at all, for Paul also includes the gift of interpretation.[171] Interpretation of tongues cannot occur unless tongues have some kind of decipherable code. The word "tongue" (*glōssa*) suggests some kind of language, some kind of code. Some scholars contend that the tongues in view are the languages of angels (see 1 Cor. 13:1). In this instance the tongue would qualify as a language, and yet the code of the language would be indiscernible to human beings.[172] The reference to the tongues of angels, however, could just as easily be a rhetorical flourish on Paul's part. Certainly, he engages

---

170. On the nature of tongue-speaking, see the convincing arguments in Forbes 1995: 44–74, 92–102; see also Gundry 1966. The mainstream view is defended in Garland 2003: 583–86; Fee 1987: 598. And see especially the incredibly detailed and highly illuminating discussion in Thiselton 2000: 970–88.

171. For an alternate view, see Thiselton 1979. For a convincing refutation of Thiselton, see Forbes 1995: 65–72.

172. For this view, see Fee 1987: 597–98, 630–31; Carson 1987b: 77–88.

in hyperbole in 1 Cor. 13:2 when he speaks of a gift of prophecy that grasps "all mysteries" and "all knowledge." Similarly, adding "tongues of angels" to "human tongues" (1 Cor. 13:1 NRSV) may be hyperbolic.

The strongest argument for tongues being some kind of ecstatic prayer language is found in 1 Cor. 14:2. Those who speak in tongues "speak not to people but to God; for no one understands, but he speaks mysteries by [or 'in'] the Spirit" (my translation). In Acts 2, on the other hand, those who speak in tongues proclaim to people "the mighty works of God" (Acts 2:11) and those present do understand what is being said. Thus, 1 Cor. 14 describes a tongue that is incomprehensible and addressed only to God, whereas Acts 2 involves a tongue that people understand and that speaks about God.

Despite the fact that most interpreters now seem to favor ecstatic utterances, I remain unconvinced, for both passages must be read in context, not as isolated proof texts. In 1 Cor. 14:1–5 Paul argues that prophecy is superior to tongues because it is comprehensible. Interpreted tongues, on the other hand, are equivalent to prophecy because people can understand what is said. Paul's comment about tongues in 1 Cor. 14:2 must be understood carefully. The reference here is to uninterpreted tongues. If no interpreter is present, then no one can understand what the tongue-speaker says. The speaker utters mysteries that are incomprehensible to all who are present and speaks "to God" in the sense that only God understands what is said. Such a statement about tongues does not contradict Acts 2. The tongues are comprehensible in Acts 2 only because those who understood the languages spoken were present. The tongue-speakers themselves were speaking mysteries, for presumably they had no idea about the meaning of their utterances. Even in 1 Cor. 14:1–5 Paul agrees that tongue-speaking is no longer a mystery if an interpreter can translate what is said. There is no compelling evidence, therefore, to say that Acts and 1 Corinthians refer to two different gifts of tongues. In both instances languages with a discernible code are in view. This idea is not countered by 1 Cor. 14:2, for here Paul simply describes the nature of tongues without an interpreter. In such a case no one but God understands what is being said. However, if an interpreter is present, then the tongue is no longer mysterious.

Paul refers to those gifted as apostles in 1 Cor. 12:28–29 and Eph. 4:11.[173] Paul typically uses the word *apostolos* of his own authoritative ministry, but we should not conclude from this that the term is invariably technical. For instance, in 2 Cor. 8:23 and Phil. 2:25 it is best defined

---

173. Garland (2003: 599) argues that the apostles in 1 Cor. 12:28 "appear to be a closed circle." So also Thiselton (2000: 1015), who argues that in 1 Cor. 12:28 "eschatological apostles" are in view who "had no successors."

as "messenger," with no suggestion of special authority (see also Rom. 16:7). It is probable that the term "apostles" in both 1 Cor. 12:28–29 and Eph. 2:20; 3:5; 4:11 is used in a technical sense. It appears that Paul did not expect any apostles to appear after him, for he claims that he is the last of the apostles (1 Cor. 15:7–8). The distinctiveness of the apostles emerges in the affirmation that the church is built on the foundation of the apostles and prophets (Eph. 2:20). Once the foundation has been laid, such authoritative apostles and prophets are superfluous.[174] Indeed, God's revelation as to the nature of the church (Eph. 3:5) has been uniquely revealed to the apostles and prophets. Thus, when Paul says in 1 Cor. 12:28 that first there are apostles and then prophets, the thought is similar to Eph. 2:20, where the distinctive foundational role of the apostles and prophets is taught.

Mission

Many theologies of Paul and NT theologies say nothing about mission, but Paul was a missionary-theologian and a missionary pastor to his churches. We see from Acts and his letters that he traveled constantly to plant churches to further his mission. Paul's theology drove his mission. Bosch rightly says that Paul believed that human beings outside Christ were "utterly lost, en route to perdition."[175] When Paul thinks of Gentiles who did not believe in Christ and were outside of Israel, he identifies them as being without Christ and without God (Eph. 2:11–12). Those who do not hear the gospel will be judged, and thus it is imperative that the word be proclaimed to the ends of the earth (Rom. 10:14–17). Paul does not envision salvation as occurring through the revelation from nature (Rom. 1:18–32) or conscience (Rom. 2:14–15), for he argues that those who know God through the created order are without excuse, that they suppress the revelation that they receive. So too, those who know God's moral norms, whether through the Mosaic law or a kind of built-in natural law, will perish because of their disobedience (Rom. 2:12). We need to recall that what Paul says about the human response to revelation through nature or conscience is tucked into a section that concludes with the universality of sin, where all are condemned for their sin (Rom. 3:9–20). Hence, salvation comes only through faith in Jesus Christ. Paul's theology, then, drove him to proclaim the gospel to both Jews and Gentiles.

Paul desired to proclaim the gospel in virgin areas, so that Christ would be praised where he was previously unknown (Rom. 15:20–24; 2 Cor. 10:13–16). His apostolic sufferings were one of the primary means by

174. See Hoehner 2002: 398–99.
175. Bosch 1991: 134.

which the word of the gospel was proclaimed in new areas (Col. 1:24–29). His sufferings were a corollary of Christ's sufferings, in that his suffering was the means by which the good news was extended to the Gentiles.

Scott argues that Paul was convinced from the OT (Ezek. 5:5; 38:12) that Jerusalem was the center or "navel" of the world.[176] His mission to the Gentiles began in Jerusalem and from there extended to the nations of the world. What Scott emphasizes is that Paul was influenced by the table of nations in Gen. 10, so that his distinctive mission was to reach the Japhethites. Indeed, Scott thinks that Paul longed to travel to Spain because the people there were the last portion of the Japhethites who had to believe in order for the fullness of the Gentiles to be completed (Rom. 11:25). Schnabel rightly raises a number of problems with this view, though here I enumerate only a few.[177] First, clear evidence that Paul relied on the table of nations is lacking, for he never mentions it in his writings. Second, Paul's reliance on divine direction calls into question whether he followed the table of nations. Would there be a need for guidance if Paul simply followed the table of nations? Third, Scott has to argue that Paul's plan to reach the Japhethites commenced in AD 48, so that the first fifteen or so years of his missionary work fall outside the scheme. If Scott is correct, what caused Paul to adopt a new pattern in AD 48? Fourth, certain areas that belonged to the Japhethites were not reached by Paul (Bithynia, Media, and parts of Europe where Japhethites resided). It is difficult to see why Paul did not concentrate on reaching these peoples if he relied on the table of nations. Fifth, if Paul preached in Asia outside of Ephesus, and if he proclaimed the gospel in Crete (Titus), then he labored among peoples who were not Japhethites. It seems, then, that Scott's intriguing suggestion lacks sufficient evidence to be accepted.

Did Paul encourage the churches that he planted to engage in evangelism?[178] Surprisingly, the evidence that he did so is rather meager.[179] Nonetheless, enough evidence exists to conclude that Paul desired his churches to evangelize others.[180] For instance, in Phil. 1:12–18 we read that the majority of believers were speaking the word more boldly because of Paul's imprisonment. Further, it is likely in Phil. 2:16 that he exhorts the church to hold forth the word of life,[181] demonstrating that

176. Scott 1995.
177. Schnabel 2004a: 498–99; 2004b: 1298–99.
178. For a helpful survey of scholarship on this matter, see Plummer 2006: 1–42.
179. See, for example, Bowers 1991.
180. See Plummer 2006: 71–105; Schnabel 2004b: 1459–67; Köstenberger and O'Brien 2001: 191–98.
181. The ESV translates the word *epechontes* as "holding fast," but "holding forth" is preferable according to Plummer 2006: 74–77. Perhaps Paul intended a double meaning here.

they were to proclaim the gospel to outsiders. Indeed, Paul alludes to Dan. 12:3 in Phil. 2:15, and the believers in Daniel shine brightly and "turn many to righteousness." In the same way, when the Philippians shine brightly, they would extend the word of life to others. Readiness to proclaim the gospel is most likely in view in Eph. 6:15, with an allusion to Isa. 52:7 standing in the background. Further, "the sword of the Spirit," which is "the word of God" (Eph. 6:17), refers to the word of the gospel. Since the sword is an offensive weapon, it likely signifies the advance of the gospel in the world through missionary proclamation. Paul's call to imitate him (1 Cor. 4:16; 11:1) suggests that the Corinthians were encouraged to spread the gospel, particularly since 1 Cor. 11:1 occurs in a context where Paul explicates his desire to live in such a way that both Jews and Gentiles, the strong and weak, are won for the gospel (1 Cor. 9:19–23).[182]

Plummer argues that the missionary character of the church is implied by the very nature of the gospel.[183] It is a powerful word that brings salvation (Rom. 1:16). The word of the cross, though foolish in the eyes of human beings, has saving power (1 Cor. 1:17–25). The word of the gospel came with the power of the Spirit (1 Thess. 1:5). Indeed, the word cannot be bound, for it has inherent power (2 Tim. 2:9). Wherever the word travels, it bears fruit and grows (Col. 1:5–6), suggesting an irrepressible force. This saving word works effectively in all believers (1 Thess. 2:13). The word reverberates out from the Thessalonians (1 Thess. 1:8), and thus believers are to pray for its diffusion (2 Thess. 3:1).

Baptism

No extended discussion or defense of baptism occurs in Paul's writings. Presumably, he received the tradition of baptism from believers who preceded him, and he practiced it accordingly. Some scholars have attributed Pauline baptism to the mystery religions.[184] Few scholars would espouse such a theory today.[185] Our knowledge of the rites of mystery cults is frustratingly vague, and there is no decisive evidence that some kind of washing was a requirement for initiation. We should not be surprised, actually, if many different religious cults employed some kind of washing ritual for entrance, since cleansing with water is an obvious way to depict the beginning of a new life. Such parallels, however, do

---

182. Also pointing to the evangelistic activity of churches are 1 Cor. 7:12–16; 14:23–25 (see Plummer 2006: 93–96). See also Titus 2:1–10 and the excellent discussion in Plummer 2006: 98–105.

183. See the full discussion in Plummer 2006: 50–64.

184. So Reitzenstein 1978: 78–79; Bousset 1970: 188–94.

185. Cf. G. Wagner 1967; Wedderburn 1987; Agersnap 1999: 52–98.

not establish dependence of one movement upon another. In any case, clear parallels are lacking in regard to Paul and mystery religions.

For Paul, baptism is linked with a whole complex of initiation events: receiving the Spirit, confessing Christ as Lord, believing in Christ, being justified, and so on.[186] We would be mistaken, however, to read baptism into all of these texts, even though Paul never conceived of a believer having the Spirit without being baptized. Even though those who were anointed and sealed with the Spirit (2 Cor. 1:21–22; Eph. 1:13) received such a seal or anointing at baptism (i.e., conversion), we would transcend the evidence to identify these metaphors with baptism.

Perhaps the best place to begin is with Paul's assertion that there is "one baptism" (Eph. 4:5). Some query whether Spirit or water baptism is intended. Certainly Paul associated the reception of the Spirit with baptism (1 Cor. 12:13; Titus 3:5), so that he never envisaged people being baptized who had not received the Spirit. Nevertheless, water baptism probably was at the forefront of his mind here, for baptism in water, as we see in Acts, was invariably the rite of entrance into the new community.[187] Water baptism signaled that one had joined the Christian church. Paul appeals to baptism as a mark of unity in Eph. 4:5 because it was a given that all his converts were baptized at conversion. No debate existed on the necessity of baptism, for it was unheard of for any believer to refuse baptism. It is quite likely that baptism was by immersion in the NT era,[188] and thus the picture is one of submersion under water where death would occur apart from emersion.

The common experience of baptism is communicated in 1 Cor. 12:13: "For in the one Spirit we were all baptized into one body—Jews or Greeks, slaves or free—and we all were made to drink of one Spirit." The antecedent for Paul's statement here, as Dunn maintains, is the tradition stemming from John the Baptist: "I have baptized you in water, but he will baptize you with the Holy Spirit" (Mark 1:8; cf. Matt. 3:11; Luke 3:16; John 1:33; Acts 1:5; 11:16). The word *en* in 1 Cor. 12:13 should be translated not "by" but rather "in," for elsewhere in the NT the agent of baptism is regularly designated by *hypo* (e.g., Matt. 3:6, 13, 14; Mark

---

186. Cf. Stein 1988: 116–26.

187. See especially Cross 2002; also Cross 1999: 185–87. Contra Knight 1992: 341–42; W. Mounce 2000: 448. Marshall (1999: 318) leans in the same direction as Mounce.

188. Marshall (2002) argues that the mode may have been pouring rather than immersion. Köstenberger (2007: 18n21) maintains that immersion is in view, since "Marshall fails to note that *baptizō*, as an intensive form of *baptō*, which clearly means 'to dip,' most likely also refers to immersion. He also fails to note passages in the LXX where *baptizō* indisputably conveys the notion of immersion (e.g., Naaman's 'dipping himself' seven times in the Jordan, 2 Kings 5:14: *ebaptisanto*) and does not consider the references to Jesus' 'coming up out of the water' in Matt. 3:16 par. Mark 1:10, which also strongly suggest immersion (see also *Barn.* 11:11; cf. *Did.* 7)."

1:5; Luke 3:7; 7:30), and the element with which they are baptized by *en* (Matt. 3:6, 11; Mark 1:8; Luke 3:16; John 1:26, 31, 33; Acts 1:5; 11:16). Baptism in 1 Cor. 12:13 is linked especially with incorporation into the body of Christ, so that baptism involves induction into the people of God. Here we see the close association between baptism and the Spirit, demonstrating that the reception of water baptism and reception of the Spirit occur at the same time.[189]

The initiatory nature of baptism is confirmed by 1 Cor. 6:11 and Eph. 5:26. In the former Paul says, "You were washed . . . in the name of the Lord Jesus Christ and by the Spirit of our God," and in the latter that Christ died to sanctify the church, "having cleansed her by the washing of water by the word." Titus 3:5 is comparable: "He saved us . . . by the washing of regeneration and renewal of the Holy Spirit." None of these verses specifically mentions baptism, but the terms "washing" and "cleansing" are obvious references to the practice.[190] Some scholars downplay any reference to water baptism, maintaining that the focus in these texts is only on the Spirit.[191] Such an interpretation is a case of "either-or" exegesis, whereas a "both-and" solution fits better. The focus on the Spirit is evident in Titus 3:5 and 1 Cor. 6:11. The background to these verses probably is Ezek. 36:25–27. Here the sprinkling of clean water is coterminous with receiving a new heart and a new S/spirit.[192]

In Titus 3:5 the words "regeneration" (*palingenesia*) and "renewal" (*anakainōsis*) both modify "washing" (*loutron*) and function as parallel terms.[193] The washing is one that involves regeneration and renewal. It does not follow from this that the washing is understood mechanically, as if the water magically transforms people. Both the "regeneration" and "renewal" come from the Holy Spirit. The Spirit is fundamental in Paul's theology, for the reception of the Spirit preceded baptism in water. Still, Paul linked washing with water and the washing with the Spirit. Both occurred at conversion. The two ideas can be conceptually distinguished, but Paul often merges them together in his writings, and we do Paul a disservice if we segregate them in such a way that any reference to water baptism is deleted from the aforementioned texts.

189. For this emphasis, see Beasley-Murray 1962: 168–69.

190. Some also see a reference to baptism in sealing (2 Cor. 1:22; Eph. 1:13), but the language is too vague to form a clear connection (Hartman 1997: 53; see also Garland 1999: 107n126). Harris (2005: 210) carefully argues that there is no direct reference to baptism, but what is said here is "evocative of baptism."

191. For example, Dunn 1970a: 121.

192. Some scholars see an allusion to the bridal bath of Ezek. 16:8–14 rather than baptism in Eph. 5:26 (e.g., O'Brien 1999: 422–23; Hoehner 2002: 753–54; Dunn 1970a: 162–65). But there is no need to posit an either-or here (rightly Hartman 1997: 106; Lincoln 1990: 375–76; Beasley-Murray 1962: 201; Bruce 1984: 386–88).

193. See chapter 13, note 126.

Baptism designates conversion another way, in that it is associated with being plunged into or immersed in Christ. In Gal. 3:26 Paul affirms that believers are God's children in Christ Jesus through faith. The ground for this assertion (*gar*) is that all believers were clothed with Christ when they were baptized into Christ: "For as many of you as were baptized into Christ have put on Christ" (Gal. 3:27). The fundamental reality for believers is not their ethnicity (Jew or Greek), gender (male or female), or class (slave or free). What is fundamental is whether they are in Christ, for all those in Christ are Abraham's seed (Gal. 3:28–29). One becomes part of Abraham's family not through circumcision but rather through faith. In baptism they have been transferred from the first Adam to the second, from the old era of redemptive history to the new.

Romans 6 also emphasizes that in baptism believers are incorporated into Christ. Baptism in Rom. 6:3 is explained as being plunged into Christ Jesus, being immersed into him as the second Adam. Those who are baptized into Christ have shared in his death (Rom. 6:3–4). Debate exists over whether Rom. 6:3–5 also communicates sharing in Christ's resurrection. If so, baptism pictures being plunged underneath the water with Christ (dead and buried) and then rising again from the waters.[194] Paul does not explicitly portray resurrection with emergence from the baptismal waters, though such an idea seems to be implied in Rom. 6:4–5. Death is defeated by being united with Christ in his death and resurrection. It is at baptism that the old Adam died with Christ: "our old self was crucified with [Christ]" (Rom. 6:6).

That believers have died and been raised with Christ in baptism is suggested by Col. 2:12, where Paul tells the Colossians that they were "buried with [Christ] in baptism, in which you were also raised with him through faith in the powerful working of God who raised him from the dead" (my translation). Paul affirms that believers have been buried together with Christ in baptism. If "in which" (*en hō*) refers to baptism—and baptism is the immediate antecedent—then he also asserts that believers were also raised with Christ via baptism.[195] We must notice again that baptism is not understood mechanically. It is inevitably linked with faith (Col. 2:12). Paul uses water baptism as a shorthand for conversion, for a whole complex of events is associated with baptism: trust in Christ, reception of the Spirit, confessing Christ as Lord, justification, adoption, and so on.

The importance of baptism for early Christians is communicated by 1 Cor. 15:29, which indicates that at least some Corinthians were being baptized on behalf of the dead. The details of the practice are obscure.

194. See Schreiner 1998: 308–9.
195. For the view defended here, see Beasley-Murray 1962: 153–54.

Scholars cannot identify with certainty why the Corinthians were conducting baptisms for the dead.[196] Perhaps, on occasion, a believer died in the interval between coming to faith and receiving baptism. Baptism was considered so important by the Corinthians that they went ahead and conducted a baptism on behalf of the person who died.[197] We gather from 1 Cor. 10 that some understood baptism and the Lord's Supper in a magical sense, thinking that they were preserved from any harm, so that they could sin with impunity. A foreshadowing of baptism is detected in Israel's escape from Egypt, and thus baptism does not automatically shield one from God's wrath (1 Cor. 10:1–12). Paul never separates baptism from the rest of the Christian life, so that it alone props up believers.

Also instructive in discerning Paul's view of baptism is 1 Cor. 1:10–17. The Corinthians had split into different factions, some adhering to Paul, others to Apollos, others to Peter, and others to Christ. Paul's mission was not "to baptize but to preach the gospel" (1 Cor. 1:17). This text is misinterpreted if understood as a denial of baptism. Certainly, all Pauline converts were baptized, but it was inconsequential to Paul if he personally baptized them. We should not conclude from this that he saw baptism itself as immaterial. Still, baptism is clearly subordinated here to the preaching of the gospel. We receive a hint that baptism could be unduly exalted and function in opposition to the gospel that Paul preached. Baptism was important for Paul. It must be understood, however, in light of the gospel, so that the gospel, not baptism, receives priority.[198]

The Lord's Supper

One of the remarkable features of the Lord's Supper in Paul's writings is that, were it not for 1 Corinthians, we would not even know that it was practiced in Pauline communities. This serves as a reminder that the Pauline letters are occasional letters addressed to specific situations. The Lord's Supper was part of the tradition that was passed on and accepted in the churches (cf. Matt. 26:28; Mark 14:22–25; Luke 22:19–20; Acts 2:42, 46; 20:7). It is likely that Paul communicated the tradition about the Lord's Supper when he established the various churches. The Lord's Supper probably was observed regularly in his churches, and in most cases no definite problems emerged, and so nothing is said about it except in 1 Corinthians. As in the case of baptism, some scholars have argued that the Lord's Supper is dependent upon mystery religions.

196. For a survey of options, see Schnackenburg 1964: 95–102; Thiselton 2000: 1240–49.

197. So Wright 2003: 338.

198. See Schnabel 2004b: 1442.

But the same objections leveled against baptism being derived from the mystery religions apply here. We have little knowledge of the rites of mystery religions, and although meals are a common feature in religious cults, analogy does not prove dependence. It is much more likely that Paul's understanding comes from the historical Jesus, per his own explanation in 1 Cor. 11:23–26. When we compare Paul's wording with the accounts in the Synoptic Gospels, it is immediately evident that the Pauline account is closest to what we find in Luke 22:19–20.

In 1 Cor. 10:14–22 Paul draws an analogy between participating in the Lord's Supper and idolatrous meals so that he might convince the readers to eschew the latter. Those who drink of the cup are partaking of the benefits of Christ's death on their behalf. Similarly, those who consume the broken bread share in the benefits of Christ's body. The broken bread symbolizes the body of Christ given for his people in his death. The cup symbolizes Christ's blood shed for his people. All believers share the one bread, and it follows from this that there is one body— that is, one church.

The second text in which the Lord's Supper is addressed is 1 Cor. 11:17–34. Identifying the precise problem in the church is difficult, but the general nature of the situation is clear enough. Paul is dismayed because divisions among the members surfaced when they gathered for the Lord's Supper. The divisions in this instance are not theological but social. The Lord's Supper in Paul's day was celebrated as part of a regular meal. Apparently, rich members in the community were eating and drinking sumptuously during these meals, while the poor were not even getting enough to eat. It seems most likely that a full meal occurred between the cup rite and the bread rite.[199] One view posits that the rich came to the supper before the poor and were eating and drinking the food before (*prolambanō*) the poor arrived.[200] By the time the poor arrived, they had little or nothing to eat. By treating the poor in this way, the rich were preserving class distinctions characteristic of secular society. According to this view, Paul counsels the community, therefore, to wait for one another (*ekdechesthe*) when eating (1 Cor. 11:33). But this view stumbles on 1 Cor. 11:21, for the words "each one" (*hekastos*) and the phrase "when the time comes to eat" (*en tō phagein*) more plausibly refer to communal eating by the entire congregation.[201] Moreover, the words "one goes hungry, another gets drunk" (1 Cor. 11:21) refer to the eating described in the same verse and thus relate to the entire congregation. Another scenario is more likely.[202] The rich were bringing their own food

199. In support of this view, see Hofius 1993: 77–88.
200. Stuhlmacher 1993: 86–87.
201. For the argument here, see Hofius 1993: 90.
202. See the important analysis in Hofius 1993: 88–96.

to the meal and consuming it, while the poor did not have a sufficient amount.[203] Both rich and poor were gathered together at the same time and in the same place, and the rich were feasting sumptuously, while the poor were consuming mere scraps. The imperative *ekdechesthe* in 1 Cor. 11:33 does not mean "wait for one another" (NRSV), as it is rendered in virtually every English version. Rather, the term means to "receive, accept, welcome" one another—that is, demonstrate hospitality to one another by sharing in table fellowship (note the TNIV: "you should all eat together").[204]

Paul was incensed that such a callous disregard of poorer brothers and sisters in Christ occurred at the Lord's Supper. Indeed, the behavior exhibited indicates that what was being celebrated was not truly the Lord's Supper (1 Cor. 11:20). To say that they were meeting in honor of the Lord while at the same time the poor were being despised and some of the rich were getting drunk is a contradiction. Such behavior amounts to a despising of God's church and humiliation of the poor (1 Cor. 11:21). Those who treat fellow believers poorly fail to understand that the Lord's Supper signifies Christ giving his life for the sake of others. They fail to discern the significance of Christ's death, for by his death he created one people, and thus those who mistreat fellow believers at the Lord's Supper reveal that they have little or no understanding of why Christ died.[205]

Paul emphasizes in 1 Cor. 11:23–26 that in the Lord's Supper they commemorate Christ's self-giving on behalf of his people. The rich Corinthians were scarcely remembering his death if they oppressed the poor at the very time the supper was being celebrated. Genuinely remembering the Lord's death makes a difference in one's everyday life.[206] Paul has no place for "sacramental devotion" that coexists with social oppression. Proclaiming the Lord's death (1 Cor. 11:26) in the supper must be matched by the self-giving characteristic of the Lord Jesus. The Lord's Supper is genuinely in honor of the Lord only when the members share

---

203. The verb *prolambanō*, as Hofius (1993: 90–92) shows, can also be translated "take" and does not necessarily mean "take before." See also the convincing and clear discussion in Garland 2003: 540–41. See also Hays 1997: 196–97, 202–3; Thiselton 2000: 863. Fee (1987: 542) is quite ambivalent about the meaning and inclines to the position that a temporal meaning is not in view.

204. So Hofius 1993: 93–94.

205. It is likely that the saying about discerning the body in 1 Cor. 11:29 stands for the body of Christ (so Hofius 1993: 114n223; Garland 2003: 552–53; Thiselton 2000: 891–94) rather than the church as Christ's body (e.g., Fee 1987: 563–64).

206. The call to remember hearkens back to the Passover, where Israel is called upon to remember God's saving acts on behalf of his people. Of course, the remembrance centers on Jesus' death for his people and the fulfillment of God's promises (Stuhlmacher 1993: 85–86). See also Garland 2003: 547–48 and the full discussion of remembrance in Thiselton 2000: 878–82.

the meal together and the poor are not ignored. If some protested in defense of their behavior, then they should stay home (1 Cor. 11:33–34). Paul does not advise believers to satisfy selfish desires at home, as if they can live for themselves at home but not when the community is gathered; rather, he reproves them for not living according to the cross, insisting that they should not gather with the people of God if they insist on living selfishly.[207]

This text reminds us that Paul does not separate the theological and the social. Those who eat the Lord's Supper in an unworthy manner—in this context, by mistreating the poor—are guilty of sinning against "the body and blood of the Lord" (1 Cor. 11:27). They contradict the very essence of the Lord's Supper by using it as an occasion to pander to their selfish interests. Paul calls on believers to "test" (*dokimazō* [1 Cor. 11:28]) themselves before partaking of the bread and cup, for those who are oppressing the poor and doing no self-examination bring judgment upon themselves. Indeed, Paul suggests that some in the community are not "genuine" (*dokimos* [1 Cor. 11:19]), meaning that they are not truly believers. The judgment that afflicts those in the community in 1 Cor. 11:29, however, is not the same thing as the judgment inflicted upon those who are not genuine believers. In 1 Cor. 11:30 the judgments fall short of eternal punishment. The Lord disciplined some through sickness and illness, and others were even dying. Paul views such judgments as merciful, for they prevent sinning believers from receiving the condemnation that the world experiences at the last judgment (1 Cor. 11:31–32).

The words "I received" (*paralambanō*) and "I delivered" (*paradidōmi*) suggest that Paul received the tradition of the Lord's Supper from believers who preceded him (1 Cor. 11:23).[208] We have already noted that the Pauline tradition is closest to the Lukan form. For Paul, the Lord's Supper is a commemoration of the heart of the gospel. The bread represents Christ's body, broken in death for sinners. The remembrance of such is not merely a mental act; it involves the transformation of one's life because Paul links it with genuine concern for poorer members in the community. Further, the remembrance occurs with the proclamation of Jesus as the crucified and risen Lord.[209] Those who have truly experienced God's grace as mediated in Christ's death long to bless others, just as they themselves have received the blessing of forgiveness through Christ's self-giving on their behalf. Remembering is not merely

---

207. Rightly Garland 2003: 555.

208. See Barrett 1968: 264–65; Conzelmann 1975: 195–96. Even clearer is Fee 1987: 548.

209. See Hofius 1993: 106–8. But contra Hofius, it is unclear to me that the remembering occurred in the prayers spoken over the bread and cup, though this is possible. It is just as likely that the remembering occurred in the proclamation of the gospel and in prayers.

a mental act; it determines one's existence.[210] The cup represents the inauguration of the new covenant promised in Jeremiah (Jer. 31:31–34). The shedding of Christ's blood inaugurates a new era when the new covenant becomes a reality. The new covenant provides both forgiveness of sins and the indwelling Spirit (Ezek. 11:18–19; 36:26–27). Paul also adds a forward-looking word about the Lord's Supper. Those who share in it proclaim the death of the Lord until he comes again (1 Cor. 11:26). Perhaps Paul reflects here on Jesus' saying that he will eat the Passover meal again in the kingdom of God (Luke 22:16). The Lord's Supper also communicates the already–not yet character of Paul's theology. The new covenant has arrived, but it is not yet completely fulfilled.[211] It will reach its consummation when the Lord returns, when the kingdom is consummated.

Students of church history know that interpreting the Lord's Supper has been a matter of much controversy. Most of the debate has centered on what the text means when Jesus says of the bread, "This is my body" (1 Cor. 11:24). Luther and Zwingli argued ardently over the meaning of the word "is" (*estin*) here, coming, unfortunately, to no agreement. How literally should we take it? We have another clue that is often overlooked. In 1 Cor. 11:25 Paul reports Jesus saying, "This cup is the new covenant in my blood." Obviously, the word "is" cannot be taken literally here, for clearly the cup itself is not actually the new covenant. Paul means, rather, that the cup represents the new covenant inaugurated by Christ's blood.[212] Similarly, when Jesus says that the bread "is my body," it likely means that it represents what Christ has done on behalf of the church through his sacrifice.

Church Leaders

In regard to church offices and leaders in the church, we should note at the outset that scholars often have posed the "authentic" and "charismatic" Paul against the "inauthentic" and "structured" Paul.[213] For example, Käsemann says, "For we may assert without hesitation that the Pauline community had no presbytery during the Apostle's lifetime."[214] According to this view, the genuine Pauline churches were spontaneous, open, free, and Spirit-directed, whereas the post-Pauline churches

210. Hofius 1993: 109.
211. Scholars often read too much into Paul's comment here. Rightly Garland 2003: 549–50.
212. See Garland 2003: 546; Fee 1987: 550. Contra Conzelmann (1975: 197–98), who interprets the text sacramentally.
213. For example, Käsemann 1964a; Dunn 1977: 109–16.
214. Käsemann 1964a: 86.

became institutional, rigid, and leadership-oriented so that the freedom of the Spirit was no longer the norm. This portrait in which the "charismatic" Paul is posed against the "structured" Paul is deeply flawed.[215] The Pauline churches were charismatic, but they were also structured. Charisma and structure are not mutually exclusive.[216] Dependence upon the Spirit does not exclude order.

When we read the Pauline letters carefully, we see that leaders and teachers were present in the community from the beginning. The terminology used for such leaders varies, showing that normative titles were not in place from the beginning. However, we cannot, on the basis of the diverse nomenclature, argue that structured leadership was nonexistent. The early letters, of course, do not contain any sustained discussion on church leadership. But it does not follow from this that such leadership was unimportant or nonexistent. Since Pauline letters are occasional, we should not expect every topic to be covered in his letters, and thus it is not surprising that leadership was more of an issue in some letters—the Pastoral Epistles—than in others. Perhaps Paul expressed himself more fully on this subject in the Pastoral Epistles because he recognized that he was near the end of his life.

The presence of church leaders is evident from early Pauline letters. In 1 Thess. 5:12 believers are charged to respect those who labor among them, lead them, and admonish them.[217] The combination of these three functions and the exhortation to regard such people in love "because of their work" (1 Thess. 5:13) indicates that leaders in the community are in view.

We also see an indication of leaders in 1 Cor. 16:15–16. The Corinthians are urged to submit to the household of Stephanas and every co-worker and laborer in the gospel.[218] This text is like 1 Thessalonians in that the specific tasks carried out by leaders are vague. To be told that they work, labor, and minister (*diakonia* [1 Cor. 16:15]) gives us little idea of what leaders did. A bit more specific is 1 Thess. 5:12–13, for besides the word "labor," it is said that some "had charge of" and "admonished" (NRSV). It is impossible to derive any detailed picture of the function

---

215. Rightly Campbell 1994.

216. Contra Käsemann (1964a) and Dunn (1977: 109–16), who exalt the charismatic Paul over against the more structured expressions in the Pastoral Epistles, see Campbell 1994.

217. See Wanamaker 1990: 191–94; Best 1972: 234–35, though I differ from them in interpreting *proistamenous* as referring to those who rule rather than to those who are patrons (rightly Morris 1959: 165–66; Beale 2003: 160). Others think that both meanings are in view here (Bruce 1982b: 119; Marshall 1983: 148).

218. Those mentioned in 1 Cor. 16:15–16 probably functioned as leaders, but Garland (2003: 168–70) rightly emphasizes that their leadership was not to be self-seeking but rather designed to strengthen others. See also Thiselton 2000: 1338–39.

of leaders from these texts. The Corinthian congregation is summoned to "be subject" (*hypotassō*) to such leaders. The call to submission is not an example of authority being enforced from above. Paul does not say that the leaders are to compel the congregation to submit. He urges the congregation to submit voluntarily and gladly to leadership.

Galatians 6:6 indicates that there were teachers in the earliest churches.[219] Those who are instructed in the word are to provide financial support for those who do the teaching. Financial support for teachers suggests a regular teaching ministry that is supported by the community (cf. 1 Cor. 9:14). Those teaching presumably also exercised a leadership role in the congregation. One of the most interesting texts with reference to leadership is Phil. 1:1, where Paul addresses "the overseers and deacons" (*episkopois kai diakonois*).[220] Nowhere else does Paul identify leaders by title in the introduction to his letters, and even in Philippians those who bear such titles do not appear in any explicit way elsewhere. Perhaps the leaders are addressed because they are being summoned to live lives of humility and service, following the example of Paul (Phil. 1:12–26), Christ (Phil. 2:5–11), Timothy (Phil. 2:19–24), and Epaphroditus (Phil. 2:25–30). Scholars have often labeled such "offices" as early catholic, which means that the church is beginning to take on an institutional form that culminated in and found its full expression in Roman Catholicism. It is unpersuasive to argue that Philippians is early catholic, for the letter contains no other evidence of such a trend, and merely listing offices does not certify the presence of early catholicism. The reference to leaders is almost casual, and no definite instruction regarding their functions is communicated. What is striking is that leaders with specific offices existed, and presumably they exercised definite roles in guiding the community.

The Pastoral Epistles say more about leaders than do all the other Pauline letters. Titus is instructed to appoint "elders" in every city (Titus 1:5),[221] but two verses later the term "overseer" appears (Titus 1:7). The singular "overseer" is sometimes seen as distinct from the plural "elders," but it is more likely that "overseer" is a generic term here.[222] The term

219. For a helpful discussion of what can be gleaned about these teachers, see Longenecker 1990: 278–79.

220. O'Brien (1991: 46–50) rightly argues that two distinct offices are in view here. See also the helpful discussion in Fee 1995: 66–69, though he is mistaken in thinking that the term "elders" embraces both overseers and deacons.

221. As Fitzmyer (2004: 584) points out, neither Timothy nor Titus is called "bishop" or "overseer" (so also W. Mounce 2000: 387). Further, even though Timothy is called "minister" (*diakonos* [1 Tim. 4:6]), the term is clearly generic here and does not apply to any particular office (so Fitzmyer 2004: 587).

222. Rightly W. Mounce 2000: 387, 390; Knight 1992: 290–91, 175–77; Fitzmyer 2004: 587; cf. Marshall 1999: 149, 160. Contra Campbell 1994: 182–205; F. Young 1994, though

"elder" (*presbyteros*) derives especially from the Jewish background, designating those who were respected leaders in the community. Discerning their precise role in both the OT and later Jewish literature is difficult. The background to the term "overseer" (*episkopos*) is more difficult. Some have emphasized a Greco-Roman background, and others have seen parallels or influence in the Dead Sea Scrolls.[223] In any case, the term seems to stress function, the task of superintending and watching over the health of early Christian congregations.

The parallel between Philippians and 1 Timothy is especially interesting because both refer to overseers and deacons (*diakonoi* [Phil. 1:1; 1 Tim. 3:1–13]). Often the term *diakonos* is used in a general way to refer to the ministry in which Paul and others are engaged (1 Cor. 3:5; 2 Cor. 3:6; 6:4; 11:23; Eph. 3:7; 6:21; Col. 1:7, 23, 25; 4:7; 1 Tim. 4:6). In these texts no specific office is designated by the term. An office does seem to be intended, though, in some texts (Rom. 16:1; Phil. 1:1; 1 Tim. 3:8, 12). It is likely, for instance, that Phoebe was a deacon of the church at Cenchrea (Rom. 16:1).[224] Delineating the distinction between overseers/ elders and deacons is not easy, but two requirements for overseers are not repeated for deacons.[225] Overseers and elders must have an ability to teach, and they must also possess leadership abilities (1 Tim. 3:2, 4–5; 5:17; Titus 1:9).[226] These requirements are never stated for deacons, suggesting that deacons engaged in a ministry of assistance and service rather than teaching and ruling.[227]

Many scholars are persuaded that the Pastoral Epistles are later documents, even dating to the second century, since attention is focused on the structure of the church and leaders. Evidence exists, however, to distinguish the Pastorals from the structures found in the second century. For example, in the letters of Ignatius the monarchial episcopate takes center stage, and exhortations to submit to the bishop percolate throughout his letters. No monarchial episcopate is found in the Pastorals. The leaders function in a collegial fashion as a group, and no one

---

Fitzmyer (2004: 591) thinks that the functions of the elders and overseers were distinct in Ephesus. For a convincing treatment, see Merkle 2003.

223. For a survey of backgrounds, see Beyer, *TDNT* 2:608–20.

224. In support of Phoebe being a deacon, see Schreiner 1998: 786–88.

225. In a major study J. N. Collins (1990) suggests that the *diakonia* word group designates authoritative emissary and mediator and go-between rather than lowly service. Clarke (2000: 233–45) shows, however, that Collins's interpretation is questionable, and that the notion of service is most likely.

226. Rightly W. Mounce 2000: 174; Fitzmyer (2004: 589) probably is wrong in saying that "the most important" qualification is the ability to teach, for Paul emphasizes character qualities, but it is true that teaching does distinguish overseers from deacons.

227. Much remains unsaid, suggesting some freedom for each congregation to work matters out in accord with what is needed (so Schlatter 1999: 314).

has an office above another. The leaders certainly have a significant role in the Pastorals, but constant appeals to their authority by virtue of their office is lacking. Paul emphasizes the authoritative teaching, not the authoritative person.

We have noted that two distinct functions are prescribed for the overseers/elders. They are to teach and lead. These two functions are, of course, rather general. Still, they provide the superstructure under which overseers/elders do their work. Their primary calling is to pass on the tradition and truth of the gospel. In other words, their leadership, unlike in many denominations today, is not primarily bureaucratic. Overseers/elders exert their leadership through their teaching ministry, by their adherence to the gospel (1 Tim. 5:17). The importance of tradition and teaching in the Pastoral Epistles is undeniable. Paul often contrasts unhealthy teaching with that which is sound (1 Tim. 1:10; 6:3; 2 Tim. 1:13; 4:3; Titus 1:9, 13; 2:1–2). The truth that must be safeguarded is the gospel (1 Tim. 3:16). False teachers veer away from the truth (1 Tim. 1:3–11; 4:1–5), and so teaching centered upon the faithful word is crucial (1 Tim. 1:15; 3:9; 4:9; 2 Tim. 2:11; Titus 3:8). It seems that in every case the faithful saying has to do with "salvation," indicating again that the saving message is the focus, not the leaders themselves.

Church Discipline

Discipline and correction permeate the Pauline letters, and in some instances severe measures were required. The case in 1 Cor. 5 of the man committing incest is instructive. Probably he was having sexual relations with his stepmother, since Paul says that "he has his father's wife," not "he has his mother" (1 Cor. 5:1).[228] Paul mandates the eviction of this man from the church, and once he is severed from the church, he enters Satan's sphere (1 Cor. 5:3–5). The motive behind such discipline is love, so that the man's "spirit may be saved in the day of the Lord" (1 Cor. 5:5). Such salvation will not occur without "the destruction of the flesh" (1 Cor. 5:5). What incenses Paul about such laxity in the church is that "a little leaven leavens the whole lump" (1 Cor. 5:6). In other words, tolerating such sin inevitably means that sin will spread further in the church. The purity of the church is at stake, for once a sin of such magnitude is tolerated, other sins will seep into and be accepted by the church.

Paul's advice in 2 Thessalonians matches the text in 1 Cor. 5. Those who ignore the instructions in the letter are to be isolated so that they will be shamed into repentance (2 Thess. 3:14–15). Refusing fellowship with the recalcitrant must flow from love. There is a kind of admonition

---

228. So Conzelmann 1975: 96; Garland 2003: 158.

that is fraternal and family oriented, which is not rooted in enmity and hatred, and yet discipline is still administered.

Once we comprehend this paradigm, Paul's instructions regarding those who have ceased to work are clear (2 Thess. 3:6–13).[229] Paul explained in the first letter that laziness must be avoided, especially because it is a poor recommendation of the Christian faith to unbelievers (1 Thess. 4:11–12; 5:14). Paul's own labor to support himself financially (2 Thess. 3:7–9) functions as an example of the kind of diligence that the Lord requires, even though Paul himself, strictly speaking, deserves financial support. In order to rouse the lazy, their food should be withheld until they are willing to work (2 Thess. 3:10).

Discipline is especially directed toward the recalcitrant who refuse to repent. Apparently, this is the case with the man committing incest (1 Cor. 5). The argumentative person who ferociously enters debates and rejects correction falls into the same category (Titus 3:9–11). Even in this case a first and a second warning are to be given, but if resistance continues, then the stubborn are to be left to their own devices. Paul warns the Corinthians that he will be forced to exercise discipline if they do not respond suitably (2 Cor. 12:19–13:3; cf. 1 Cor. 4:18–21). Church expulsion is limited to cases of unrepentant sinful behavior or to deviant teaching that transgresses the standard of the gospel. It is the gospel itself that is the norm for discipline, and those who are being transformed by the gospel long to love, encourage, and strengthen others. Part of this strengthening occurs in mutual admonition and correction, which occasionally even reaches the point of having to expel an unrepentant member.

The General Epistles and Revelation

The General Epistles and Revelation do not contain a detailed discussion on the church. All of these texts are addressed, of course, to churches, speaking to the corporate life of the various communities. Since each piece of literature responds to specific circumstances in the churches, the space given to the topic of the church varies. We need to remind ourselves again of the occasional nature of the writings. The failure to say more about the church does not lead to the conclusion that the authors had little interest in the church. For instance, none of the authors

---

229. Wanamaker (1990: 279–88) rightly argues that the issue in this text is indolence (cf. Marshall 1983: 220; Best 1972: 331–35). Donfried (2002: 221–31) argues that the term *ataktōs* in this text means "disorderly," in the sense that they violate Pauline commands more generally, but such a view does not account as well for the context in which the term is found.

mentions the Lord's Supper, but it would be rash to conclude from this that the Lord's Supper was not practiced or that it was rejected. The authors included only what was most pressing in response to situations that arose in the churches.

Hebrews

In Hebrews the people of God are considered to be children of one Father (Heb. 2:10–11).[230] Jesus is enthroned as Lord (Heb. 1:3), but he is also the brother of all believers, so that they form one assembly or congregation (Heb. 2:11–12). All believers are gathered together to give praise to God for his saving goodness (Heb. 2:12). The sacrifice that pleases God is one of praise (Heb. 13:15). The church is also conceived of as a house (Heb. 3:6), and Jesus as the faithful Son (Heb. 3:1–6). The term "house" (*oikos*) indicates that the church is the new people of God, the true dwelling place of God.[231] The church of Jesus Christ is conceived of as "the assembly of the firstborn who are enrolled in heaven" (Heb. 12:23).[232] The people of God are, so to speak, a heavenly people, just as the true city of God is in heaven rather than on earth; it is "the heavenly Jerusalem" rather than the earthly Jerusalem (Heb. 12:22).[233] The church as a community faced persecution in Hebrews (Heb. 10:32–34), and thus it was tempting to neglect regular meeting with other believers (Heb. 10:25). Therefore, the author admonishes believers to meet together consistently, for such meetings are the context in which regular encouragement of one another occurs, so that believers receive strength "to stir up one another to love and good works" (Heb. 10:24). The author briefly sketches some features of community life in Heb. 13:1–6. Apostasy is prevented by the daily encouragement and exhortation from fellow believers (Heb. 3:13), and such exhortation cannot be gained apart from community. Hebrews allows no room for a Christian faith that operates only in the individual and private sphere. Faith and obedience can be cultivated and grow only in concert with other believers. The author is concerned that a poisonous, bitter spirit does not sprout in the community and defile many (Heb. 12:14–17). Peace and holiness must be sought with diligence lest the church lose its cohesion and purpose for existence.

230. For the church in Hebrews, see Rissi 1987: 117–24.

231. In Num. 12:7 the house also signified the people of God over whom Moses functioned as a leader (so Lane 1991a: 78).

232. Some understand this heavenly assembly to refer to angels, but probably it refers to the heavenly assembly of God's people (so Attridge 1989: 375; Bruce 1964: 376–77; Lane 1991b: 468–69).

233. See Peterson 1982: 161–62.

Hebrews refers to the leaders of the church in light of its central purpose: believers must persevere in faith. Hence, they are exhorted to remember their former leaders because their lives testified to the vitality of their faith (Heb. 13:7). Clearly, the author wants them to recall their love and admiration for those who led them, so that they would pattern their lives after such leaders. The love that flowed from leaders to the congregation, the author is convinced, would leave its stamp upon the readers. The influence of leaders is not confined to their example, for they shaped the community through their proclamation of "the word of God" (Heb. 13:7). The leaders called attention not to themselves but rather to the work of God in Christ. They summoned the church to the gospel, the work of Christ on the cross as the basis for salvation.

When we compare the reference to leaders in Heb. 13:7 with the second reference in Heb. 13:17, it appears that the leaders in view in Heb. 13:7 may have already died.[234] They are to remember them and "the outcome of their way of life" (Heb. 13:7). On the other hand, they are to "obey" and "submit to" the leaders that they have now (Heb. 13:17). Again such obedience must be construed in light of the letter as a whole. Obedience is profitable and not harmful to the church, for such obedience to the leaders means that the readers continue in the faith and avoid apostasy. The author writes, in other words, about obeying leaders who are themselves obedient to the gospel that they proclaim. He is commending not a blind submission to authority but rather a humble acceptance of those who are appointed to watch over the lives of believers. Leaders themselves, he reminds his readers, will give an account of their work, and so they must not use their positions for selfish purposes. The author of Hebrews is not interested in the titles that leaders bore, for he simply calls them "leaders" (*hēgoumenoi*). This does not mean, of course, that the leaders lacked titles, but only that it was not part of the author's purpose to communicate whether they had titles. It seems that the focus of their work involved the proclamation of the word and the nurturing of believers. We could scarcely gain a clear profile of spiritual gifts from Hebrews, but the author does mention them in passing in Heb. 2:4. Here the gifts of the Spirit are associated with the signs, wonders, and miracles that attest the validity of the gospel.[235] The gifts granted by God were distributed in accordance with his will. Hebrews does not address the responsibility of the church to evangelize, presumably because the danger of apostasy took center stage. A church that maintains the faith in the midst of suffering proclaims to the world

---

234. The leaders who spoke the word were deceased when the letter was written (so Lane 1991b: 527; Attridge 1989: 392 [probably]).

235. See Attridge 1989: 67; Lane 1991a: 39–40.

the preciousness of Christ's sacrifice and the beauty of the gospel, but Hebrews does not focus on this theme.

James

The parenetic and practical character of James precludes any detailed discussion of the church. Nevertheless, some fascinating hints about the nature of the church are communicated here and there. The first verse refers to the readers as "the twelve tribes in the Dispersion" (James 1:1). Scholars debate whether this refers to Jewish or Gentile believers,[236] but the issue is not vital for the discussion here. In either case, the church of Jesus Christ is now viewed as the true people of God, just as the twelve tribes were counted as God's people in the OT. That the church is an assembly of believers is indicated by James 5:14, which speaks of "the elders of the church." The Jewish character of the assembly is suggested by the word "synagogue" in James 2:2. The letter of James as a whole emphasizes the love and nurture that should mark the life of the community. Widows and orphans should receive care in their financial distress (James 1:27). Believers should be treated with equal dignity and honor, and discrimination against any social group must not be tolerated (James 2:1–13). Evil and bitter speech tears down others and releases a poisonous spirit, and thus believers are to show tenderness and kindness to one another and to all (James 3:1–12; 4:11–12). The community life of believers is reflected in James 5:13–20. Believers should praise God in song to express their joy. In their communal life believers should confess their sins to one another and pray for one another. Fellow believers are to extend care for one another so that one who is wandering should be sought out and brought back to the community if possible. An individualistic faith that exists apart from others contradicts the nature of life together as the people of God. The incidental way in which James refers to elders in the church indicates that he does not intend to provide teaching on leaders in the church (James 5:14).[237] The Jewish background of James probably provides the context for elders because elders held positions of authority in Jewish communities. Apparently, a number of elders together functioned as

236. Davids (1982: 64) thinks that the book is addressed to Jewish Christians who live outside Palestine in Syria and Asia Minor (cf. Moo 2000: 49–50). Laws (1980: 47–49) maintains that the significance of the designation lies mainly in its claim that the people of God are now the true Israel, so that the ethnic composition of the community cannot be determined by what is said here (so also Dibelius 1975: 66–67).

237. See L. Johnson 1995: 330. Contra the suggestion of Laws (1980: 226), the reference here is to leaders, not merely older members of the congregation. Davids (1982: 192–93) notes here that the elders are officials and plural leaders of a local assembly. See also Dibelius 1975: 252–53.

leaders in the church, for James speaks of "the elders of the church" (James 5:14). In this instance he focuses on their role in praying for the sick in the congregation. We see here that pastoral oversight involves not only the proclamation of the word but also prayer for those who are suffering. The reference to elders, which we have noted in a number of other instances in the NT, suggests that "elders" was a common designation for leaders in the early church.

James does not exhort his readers to evangelize others; rather, he focuses on their life together as believers. Still, if believers lived as James instructed, the righteousness and love present in their lives would surely stand out in their communities. In our modern world we are able to shut ourselves off from outsiders, but in the world that James addressed people lived more communal lives. Hence, if believers did not discriminate against others (James 2:1–13), if their speech was marked by joyous love instead of quarrels (3:1–12; 4:1–6), if they persevered when facing difficulty (1:2–18), if they showed concern for the socially marginalized (1:27), and if they displayed their wisdom in righteous living, unbelievers would recognize and be provoked to ask what caused such a transformation.

1 Peter

In 1 Peter the church of Jesus Christ is conceived of as the true Israel, the genuine remnant of God's people. Just as Israel was God's elect people in the OT, now the church constitutes God's elect ones (1 Pet. 1:2). This letter almost certainly is addressed to Gentiles (1 Pet. 1:18; 4:3), but now they have become part of the true Israel. They are God's exiles dispersed throughout the world (1 Pet. 1:1; 2:11). As God's people, the church is discriminated against and persecuted for their faith. Hence, they are God's dispersed ones who live as sojourners in this world as they await their final inheritance. The theme that the church is the true Israel continues in 1 Pet. 2:9–10. The church is God's "chosen race" (*eklekton genos*). The nearest parallel to the expression used here derives from Isa. 43:20, where the Lord promises to deliver Israel in a second exodus. The second exodus is ultimately fulfilled in the salvation accomplished in Jesus Christ and in the new people of God, composed of both Jews and Gentiles. Peter also draws on one of the charter statements of Israel, Exod. 19:6, in designating the church as "a royal priesthood" (*basileion hierteuma*)[238] and "a holy nation" (*ethnos hagion*). Israel was to serve

238. For this reading, see Achtemeier 1996: 164; Goppelt 1993: 149n65. J. Elliott (1966: 196) understands the text in a remarkably different way, with the result that the church is the house of God as king (see also Dryden 2006: 121–22). For further discussion, see Schreiner 2003: 114–15.

as God's priest, communicating his glory to the surrounding nations.[239] Now the church of Jesus Christ, the true Israel, is to mediate God's blessings to the world (cf. 1 Pet. 2:5). The church of Jesus Christ is set apart as God's special and holy people. That the church functions as the true Israel is also communicated in 1 Pet. 2:10. Peter alludes to Hosea 2:23, and interestingly Paul alludes to the same text and employs it in a remarkably similar way in Rom. 9:25–26. In Hosea God rejects Israel as his people because of their sin, but he promises to have mercy on them and to restore them again as his people. Peter sees this promise fulfilled in the church of Jesus Christ, made up of both Jews and Gentiles. They are the true Israel of God; they are those who were not a people but are now included within the circle of God's blessing.

Not only is the church the true Israel, but also it constitutes the true temple. Jesus is both the living stone and the cornerstone of God's temple (1 Pet. 2:4–8). All those who belong to Jesus are also living stones and are being built up as God's spiritual house. The temple in Jerusalem is no longer the center of God's purposes; rather, the church of Jesus Christ, composed of believers from every ethnic background and social class, constitutes the temple of God.[240] As God's spiritual household (1 Pet. 4:17), it faces the purifying and discriminating work of persecution, so that its trust in God in the midst of suffering will bring him glory on the last day (1 Pet. 4:19).

In the past 1 Peter was often seen as a baptismal document, but such a view is not often held today.[241] In fact, baptism is mentioned in only one verse in 1 Peter, though the meaning of that verse is keenly debated.[242] The water that deluged the world in Noah's day, and through which Noah was saved, functions as a model or pattern for Christian believers. But to what is the water related in the new covenant? The answer is baptism. In fact, we have the surprising statement that "baptism . . . now saves you" (1 Pet. 3:21). Before examining that statement, we must consider in what way the flood waters prefigured or corresponded to baptism. The waters of the flood deluged the ancient world and were the agent of death. Similarly, baptism, which was done by immersion during the time of the NT, occurs when one is plunged under the water. Anyone who is submerged under water dies. Just as the chaotic waters of the flood were the agent of destruction, so too the waters of baptism are waters of destruction. In NT theology, however (cf. Matt. 3:16; Mark

239. The emphasis, then, is on the church serving as God's priests corporately, not individualistically. For this point, see Best 1969: 287.

240. In support of this view, see Beale 2004: 331–33.

241. See Schreiner 2003: 42–43.

242. The discussion that follows is largely drawn from Schreiner 2003: 193–96, but with some alterations.

10:38–39; Rom. 6:3–5), believers survive the death-dealing baptismal waters because they are baptized with Christ. They are rescued from death through his death and resurrection (Rom. 6:3–5; Col. 2:12). Hence, we are not surprised to read in 1 Pet. 3:21 that baptism saves "through the resurrection of Jesus Christ." The waters of baptism, like the waters of the flood, demonstrate that destruction is at hand, but believers are rescued from these waters in that they are baptized with Christ, who has also emerged from the waters of death through his resurrection. Just as Noah was delivered through the stormy waters of the flood, so too believers have been saved through the stormy waters of baptism by virtue of Christ's triumph over death. The word "now" refers to the present eschatological age of fulfillment. With the coming of Jesus Christ, the age of salvation has arrived.[243]

It is clear, then, that Peter does not succumb to a mechanical view of baptism, as if the rite itself contains an inherent saving power. Such a sacramental view is far from his mind. The saving power of baptism is rooted in the resurrection of Jesus Christ.[244] Peter remarks that baptism is "not the removal of dirt from the flesh" (1 Pet. 3:21 NASB). Any notion that baptism is inherently saving is ruled out, for the point is not that the water itself somehow cleanses.[245] Water removes dirt from the skin, but baptism does not save simply because someone has been submerged in the water.

The meaning of baptism is explained in the contrasting clause. It is not removing dirt from the flesh but rather "the pledge of a good conscience" (1 Pet. 3:21 NIV). The NIV translation represents one interpretation of the phrase. The word translated "pledge" (eperōtēma) occurs only here in the NT. On the other hand, the meaning of the noun may be derived from the verb (eperōtaō), which often has the meaning of "ask" or "request" in the NT, occurring fifty-six times there (e.g., Matt. 12:10; 16:1; 27:11; Mark 7:5; 9:21; Luke 2:46; John 18:7; 1 Cor. 14:35).[246] If the meaning is derived from the verb (eperōtaō), then the translation "ask, request, appeal" fits. We see this interpretation in the ESV: "an appeal to God for a good conscience." The interpretation reflected in the NIV can be supported by the usage of the word in the papyri. In these instances the term can be used of stipulations found in contracts. One pledges or promises to abide by the terms of the contract and the stipulations found therein. Similarly, one can understand the text to refer to the promise

---

243. So also J. Elliott 2000: 674; Brox 1986: 177.
244. Achtemeier 1996: 267–68.
245. So Selwyn 1981: 204; J. Elliott 2000: 679.
246. So Grudem 1988b: 163–64; Beare 1947: 149; Michaels 1988: 217; Greeven, *TDNT* 2:688–89.

or pledge made at baptism.[247] This interpretation certainly is possible on lexical grounds and does not contradict Petrine theology. It seems more likely, however, that the meaning of the noun is derived from the verb. Both interpretations of the word *eperōtēma* are possible lexically. In context, however, it seems more likely that baptism is associated with an appeal or request to God for a good conscience. The genitive in the phrase is probably objective. Believers in baptism ask God, on the basis of the death and resurrection of Christ, to cleanse their consciences and forgive their sins.[248] The idea, then, is quite similar to Heb. 10:22, where believers may draw near to God confidently because their "hearts" have been "sprinkled clean from an evil conscience" (cf. Heb. 10:2).[249] In Hebrews there is no doubt that a cleansed conscience is due to the cross of Christ. So too Peter emphasizes in 1 Pet. 3:18–22 Christ's death as the means by which believers are brought into God's presence. He died for believers, the righteous for the unrighteous, and thus believers enter God's presence on the basis of God's grace alone. Peter focuses not on promises that believers make when baptized but rather on the saving work of Christ and his resurrection. Believers in baptism can be confident, on the basis of the work of the crucified and risen Lord, that their appeal for good consciences will be answered.

Peter stresses in particular the love and joy that bind the church together. The church in Babylon, almost certainly meaning Rome, sends greetings to believers in a sister church (1 Pet. 5:13). Believers are to greet one another with a holy kiss of love and affection (1 Pet. 5:14). Peter returns repeatedly to the need to extend love to one another (1 Pet. 1:22; 3:8; 4:8). Such love means that ill-will, deception, jealousy, and gossip are to be avoided (1 Pet. 2:1; 3:10). Humility, tenderness, and forgiveness are to distinguish the people of God (1 Pet. 3:8–9). Peace and goodness are to be sought for with diligence (1 Pet. 3:11). Unbelievers must be given no objective grounds for criticizing believers, and thus the church must retain a godly character (1 Pet. 3:13–17; 4:15). The good "conduct" (*anastrophē*) of believers sets them apart from the world in which they live.[250]

Peter also addresses the leaders in the community, and he calls them "elders" (1 Pet. 5:1–4).[251] Apparently, elders served as leaders

247. So Angel, *NIDNTT* 2:880–81; J. Elliott 2000: 679–80; Brox 1986: 178; Hartman 1997: 119.

248. In support of this interpretation, see Achtemeier 1996: 271–72; Goppelt 1993: 268–69; Schelke 1980: 109.

249. Many scholars see a reference to baptism in Heb. 10:22. See Hartman 1997: 124; Attridge 1989: 289; Lane 1991a: 287; Bruce 1964: 250–51.

250. *Anastrophē* is one of Peter's favorite words (1 Pet. 1:15, 18; 2:12; 3:1, 2, 16).

251. An official use of the term "elder" is likely here, as most commentators affirm (e.g., Selwyn 1981: 228; Goppelt 1993: 340; Achtemeier 1996: 321–22).

in all the churches that Peter addressed: Pontus, Galatia, Cappadocia, Asia, and Bithynia (1 Pet. 1:1). If elders were in place in all the churches in such regions, then presumably they were quite common in early Christianity. We have already seen that leaders were also called elders in the churches that James addressed, in Acts, and in the Pauline letters. Elders were appointed on Paul's first missionary journey in Pisidian Antioch, Iconium, Lystra, and Derbe (Acts 14:23). The churches in Jerusalem also had elders (Acts 15:2). We see elders also in the Ephesian churches (Acts 20:17; 1 Tim. 5:17). Apparently, elders were appointed also on the island of Crete (Titus 1:5). If "elder" and "overseer" refer to the same office, then there were elders also in Philippi (Phil. 1:1). The Epistle of James may have been written to Palestinian churches, and if so, then we see elders in the general area of Palestine (James 5:14).

Peter emphasizes the ministry of the elders. They are to shepherd and pastor the flock that God has given them, and such shepherding involves "oversight" (*episkopountes*) and leadership over the church (1 Pet. 5:2).[252] Presumably, their leadership consisted particularly in their teaching of the word of God. Nevertheless, Peter places the emphasis on the kind of leadership carried out by the elders with three contrasts (1 Pet. 5:2–4). They are to serve not out of compulsion but rather from eagerness to fulfill the will of God. Nor should their motive be financial gain; rather, they should be moved by eagerness to help the people of God. Finally, leaders face the danger of using their leadership to manipulate and coerce others. Leaders must not use their personalities or gifts to force others to conform. They rule by virtue of the gospel, not the force of their own personalities. Hence, they should serve as examples for the flock rather than trying to compel the church to do what they wish. Peter assures elders that they will be rewarded for their service on the last day.

The identity of the young who are to submit to the elders is difficult to discern (1 Pet. 5:5).[253] The commentaries discuss a number of possibilities. Perhaps Peter thinks especially of the young because they are more prone to be headstrong and resistant to leadership. In any case, the whole community is to live humbly and graciously with one another, for that is the oil that lubricates a truly Christian community.

---

252. The participle *episkopountes* is absent in some texts, but most likely it is original because it is present in the majority of witnesses and in the corrector of Codex Sinaiticus. Perhaps some scribes omitted it because later church tradition distinguished the offices of elder and overseer (bishop).

253. For further discussion on this matter, see Schreiner 2003: 236–38.

Peter briefly mentions spiritual gifts, dividing them into gifts of speech and of service and stressing that they spring from God's grace (1 Pet. 4:10–11). The gifts reflect God's goodness to his church. Since gifts are received by God, users must administer them as stewards, not advertise them like performers. They are given to strengthen others, and those using them should not call attention to themselves. Those who speak, then, must labor to be faithful and speak God's words. Those who serve must rely on God's strength, not their own. Thereby the church will be helped and God glorified.

Most NT letters do not give specific admonitions to engage in evangelism. Such an omission could be interpreted in various ways. Perhaps when churches live out the gospel in accord with the admonitions in the various letters, the gospel will naturally become attractive to outsiders. Peter is quite concerned that believers behave in such a way that unbelievers will be compelled to admit (either now or eschatologically) that God is in the midst of the church (1 Pet. 2:11–12, 15, 20; 3:14, 16; 4:14–16). Insults rained upon their heads must be undeserved, so that opposition to Christians is not based on their failure to live in a way that conforms with goodness. It seems also that such godly behavior is intended to have an evangelistic impact as well. Peter specifically remarks that wives are to live godly lives in the hope that husbands will be converted (1 Pet. 3:1–6). By extension, it seems that the same could be true of the relationship between slaves and masters, though nothing explicit is said in this regard (1 Pet. 2:18–25). Indeed, the admonition to do "good deeds" so that unbelievers will "glorify God on the day of visitation" (1 Pet. 2:12) most likely refers to the salvific effect of the lives of believers, though commentators are divided over whether Peter here thinks of the final judgment or of salvation.[254] If salvation is in view, then the ethical exhortations given to believers, which often have in view the impact of Christian behavior on unbelievers, are implicitly suffused with an evangelistic import.

2 Peter and Jude

Nothing specific about the church is said in 2 Peter and Jude. The letters are addressed to churches threatened by false teachers. It is clear from these letters that the purity of the churches concerns both authors. Believers must not be corrupted by false teachings. Both letters reflect that the churches are in danger from libertinism, which throws off all moral restraints. The libertinism probably arose from a distortion of Pauline teaching (2 Pet. 3:15–16). The community that God has called

---

254. See Schreiner 2003: 123–24.

out for himself needs to evidence a moral goodness that is beautiful and lovely, so as to bear witness to his saving love. The call for churches to be holy, then, is the main contribution of these two letters in terms of ecclesiology.

Revelation

Revelation is addressed to churches in first-century Asia Minor that faced persecution and suffering. The people of God are exhorted to hold firm and to resist the enticement to compromise with Rome by honoring the emperor as Lord. The church is marked by suffering (e.g., Rev. 6:9–11; 11:8), but in the midst of such suffering they are to acknowledge God's rule and reign in history and worship him as the only Lord and sovereign (e.g., Rev. 4:1–5:13; 7:12, 15; 15:3–4). One of the striking characteristics of Revelation is that the book is addressed to churches (Rev. 1:4, 11; 2:1–3:22). Each church in particular is named in the introduction to the various letters (Rev. 2:1, 8, 12, 18; 3:1, 7, 14), and yet the letters intended for a specific church are also specifically said to be for all the churches (Rev. 2:7, 11, 17, 29; 3:6, 13, 22). Revelation is not a timeless apocalypse that charts out the course of world history in an abstract fashion; rather, it is addressed to churches facing the threat of Roman imperialism in the first century. The churches are described as "lampstands" (Rev. 1:12, 20; 2:1, 5).[255] The two witnesses, which probably refer to the church, are also designated as two lampstands (Rev. 11:4).[256] As lampstands, the churches are to manifest the light of God's goodness and supremacy to the world. They shine in all their brightness when they refuse compromise with Rome and endure discrimination and persecution for Christ's sake. As witnesses, they proclaim God's lordship over the idolatry of Rome that demands total allegiance. The church calls on all peoples everywhere to be saved from the coming judgment.[257] Their faithfulness to Christ in

255. See Beale 1999b: 206–8, where he also emphasizes that the lampstands denote God's presence with his people.

256. The two witnesses represent the prophetic witness of the whole community, Jew and Gentile (Schnabel 2002b: 247). The lampstands depict their witness-bearing function, for they call for repentance, and the number "two" derives from the OT requirement for two witnesses (Deut. 17:6; 19:5) (Schnabel 2002b: 248).

257. Rissi (1966: 80–83) argues that Revelation promises universal salvation. The view of Bauckham (1993a: 84–108; 1993b: 238–337) is rather complex. He suggests that the opening of the scroll in Rev. 5 and Rev. 10 is linked with the missionary witness of the church, so that the suffering of the church and the death of faithful believers lead to the repentance of the nations (Rev. 11:13). Bauckham (1993b: 12–13, 310–13) interprets Rev. 11:3–13; 14:14–16; 15:2–4 as forecasting a kind of universalist hope, for in Rev. 21:3–4; 22:2–3 we see all nations, not just the covenant people, included in God's saving promises. The open gates of the new Jerusalem point to the salvation of the nations. But contrary to Rissi, Bauckham (1993b: 313n100) rejects universalism in Rev. 21:8, 27; 22:15. Schnabel (2002b: 251–53),

the midst of opposition communicates to the world that Christ is to be esteemed above the emperor.

One of the fundamental themes in Revelation is that the church is the true Israel. This truth is communicated in a variety of ways. In the OT Israel was a priestly kingdom (Exod. 19:6), intended to mediate God's blessing to the world. Now, however, God's priestly kingdom is the church of Jesus Christ (Rev. 1:6). God's kingdom cannot be identified with Rome, nor are the Roman priests the mediators of his blessing. Believers in Jesus Christ, the small communities scattered throughout the Greco-Roman world, represent God's outpost in the world. Twice in Revelation Jewish synagogues are called a "synagogue of Satan" (Rev. 2:9; 3:9).[258] In our social context we blanch at reading such a strong denunciation, especially because of the anti-Semitism that has stained Christian history. We must locate John's words, however, in their own historical context. The church was small and politically powerless, lacking any legal rights in contrast to Judaism, which was recognized as a legal religion in the Greco-Roman world. Furthermore, the tables were turned in early Christian history so that the Jews occasionally persecuted the new Christian sect. John never intended his words to provide a platform for discriminating against or putting Jews to death. He does not identify the synagogues as satanic in order to foment hatred against Jews. The shocking designation is intended to prevent Christians from committing apostasy and from joining the wrong side. Surprisingly enough, says John, the Jews are not the people of God. The small community that is loyal to Jesus Christ represents the true people of God. The stunning reversal is communicated in the words of Rev. 3:9. Jewish

---

on the other hand, questions the plausibility of Bauckham's construal. Schnabel rightly argues that the visions in Rev. 10–11 focus on judgment rather than salvation. The fear in view in Rev. 11:13 points to judgment, and "the rest" (*hoi loipoi*) are unbelievers, as in Rev. 9:20; 19:21; 20:5. Even though giving God glory might suggest salvation, we know that God is also glorified in judgment (cf. Ps. 97:7–9; Isa. 42:12–13). Judgment instead of salvation is also supported by the context of Revelation, where the theme of judgment predominates. Not all giving of glory to God is salvific, as the example of Nebuchadnezzar giving God glory reveals (Dan. 4:34). Moreover, the seven thousand who give glory to God in Rev. 11:13 may refer to the complete judgment of unbelievers or the salvation of the faithful remnant without implying the conversion of the nations, for the focus of Rev. 11:13 is the fate of the two witnesses, not the salvation of the nations (see Schnabel 2002b: 253–55). Bauckham (1993b: 283–96) also argues with reference to the two harvests in Revelation (Rev. 14:14–20) that the grain harvest is salvific and the vintage represents judgment. But again it seems that both refer to judgment (Schnabel 2002b: 257–62). For further discussion, see Bauckham 1993b: 306–18; Schnabel 2002b: 262–70.

258. See Aune (1997: 164–65), who helpfully points out that similar expressions were used in intra-Jewish disputes at Qumran and in the testamentary literature. And conversely, the expression indicates that the church of Jesus Christ is now the true Israel (Beale 1999b: 241).

unbelievers will come and bow down before believers in Christ Jesus. According to Ps. 86:9, it is the Gentile nations that will bow in the future before Yahweh the God of Israel. Israel's enemies in the OT will bow at Israel's feet when the Lord vindicates his people (Isa. 60:14). They shall even "lick the dust" at the feet of Israel (Isa. 49:23). John, alluding to the same text, maintains that the Jews who oppose the Christian church will actually bow before believers at the eschaton and acknowledge that God is with them.[259]

That the church is the new Israel is also communicated in Rev. 7:1–8; 14:1–5.[260] Some interpreters, of course, understand the 144,000 as literally referring to Israel. The arguments presented previously suggest that John uses "Israel" symbolically to refer to the new people of God. The twelve tribes of Israel point now to a greater fulfillment: the church of Jesus Christ. The 144,000 is symbolic in that it is twelve squared and multiplied by one thousand. It represents, then, the totality of God's people and the fulfillment of God's promises to Abraham.[261] It also represents God's army in that it is comparable to the census of Israel as God's army in the OT. God's warriors are those who suffer for the sake of the Lamb. The church of Jesus Christ is, then, the true synagogue of God, the place where his people gather together.[262] The church does not cancel out ethnic Israel, for the names of the twelve tribes are on the gates of the heavenly city (Rev. 21:12). But the true Israel, composed of both Jews and Gentiles, finds its fulfillment in the church of Jesus Christ. The apostles' names are inscribed on the foundations of the city wall (Rev. 21:14). No one who is not built upon the apostolic foundation of the gospel of Jesus Christ will be included in the city. Just as the people of God can be described as the true Israel, they can also be depicted as an uncountable multitude (Rev. 7:9–17). Placing the 144,000 (Rev. 7:1–8) next to an innumerable multitude (Rev. 7:9–17) is no contradiction. John portrays the church with two different pictures so as to teach that the church is the true Israel, fulfilling Israel's purpose, and also that it is an innumerable host from every tribe, tongue, people, and nation, fulfilling the promise to Abraham that the whole world would be blessed through him (cf. Gen. 12:3). Revelation emphasizes the universality of the people of God. Christ ransomed some from every cultural background (Rev. 5:9). John emphasizes that in the heavenly city God resides with human beings

259. Rightly Osborne 2002: 190–91; contra Beale (1999b: 287–88), who sees a reference to the eschatological salvation of the Jews here.

260. Bauckham 1993a: 77; 1993b: 180; Beale 1999b: 416–23.

261. Bauckham 1993a: 77. For Beale's construal of this promise in Rev. 7:9, see Beale 1999b: 429–30.

262. Smith (1990; 1995) argues that the listing of the twelve tribes is a Christian interpretation, whereas Bauckham (1991) sees it as a traditional Jewish image.

so that "they will be his peoples" (Rev. 21:3 NRSV). The plural "peoples" (*laoi*) celebrates the diversity of God's saving work, which includes human beings from every cultural and linguistic background.[263]

The people of God are also described as the true temple—the dwelling place of God. When John is instructed to measure the temple, a literal temple in Jerusalem is not in view (Rev. 11:1–2).[264] This is confirmed by the admonition to measure "those who worship there" (Rev. 11:1). No literal measurement is needed of those who worship in the temple. Those measured represent those who are protected from God's wrath when he begins to mete out judgment from his temple—that is, heaven (Rev. 11:19; 14:15, 17; 16:1, 17). Conversely, the outer court of the temple, which is unmeasured, represents the persecution inflicted by unbelievers before God's reign is complete (Rev. 11:2).[265] During the time of imperfection and evil—the forty-two months—God's people will be subjected to persecution. Still, God promises to make his own a pillar in his temple (Rev. 3:12). No literal temple exists in the new Jerusalem (Rev. 21:22), and thus the image of being a pillar in the temple promises that believers will be in God's presence forever. They will worship him in his temple (which does not literally exist!) with rapturous joy all their days (Rev. 7:15). The beast reviles God's name and his "dwelling" (Rev. 13:6), but God's dwelling is defined not in terms of a building but rather as his people, as "those who dwell in heaven."

The people of God in Revelation are also depicted as a woman. The OT antecedents are clear, for often in the OT Israel is portrayed as the bride of Yahweh (e.g., Hosea 1:1–3:5; Jer. 2:2, 20, 24, 32–34; 3:1–2, 6–11, 20). The Messiah came from God's people (Rev. 12:1–5). To the people of God is promised the rule over the world, symbolized in her wearing a crown of twelve stars, being adorned with the sun, and having the moon placed under her feet (Rev. 12:1).[266] God's people presently live in the wilderness of difficulty, where Satan tempts her during the 1,260 days of Satan's rule (Rev. 12:6). This represents the period from Christ's death and resurrection until his return. But just as God delivered Israel from Egypt on eagles' wings (Exod. 19:4), so too he will preserve his people in the wilderness from Satan's attacks, so that Satan (under the guise of the Roman Empire) will not triumph over them (Rev. 12:14). Here the time period is described as forty-two months, but that is simply another

263. See Osborne 2002: 734; Beale 1999b: 1047.
264. So R. Mounce 1977: 219–20; Beale 1999b: 557–65; Osborne 2002: 409–11; Aune (1998: 598, 604) mistakenly sees a reference to physical protection as well.
265. R. Mounce 1977: 220–21; Caird 1966: 132; Osborne 2002: 412–13; Beale 1999b: 565–71.
266. For a survey of possibilities, see Aune 1998: 680–81. Cf. R. Mounce 1977: 236; Caird 1966: 149; Beale 1999b: 626–27; Osborne 2002: 456.

way of saying 1,260 days. The woman is also said to have children, and some have attempted to distinguish the identity of the woman and her children (Rev. 12:17). But as we have already seen in 2 John, such a move misreads the text. The woman represents the church as a whole, and the children the individual members of the church.[267] Revelation 12 emphasizes that God will fortify and sustain the church so that it is able to withstand the attacks of the dragon.

That the church is portrayed as a woman is confirmed by the conclusion of Revelation. The church is the bride of Christ (Rev. 19:7; 22:17), and she will enjoy the marriage supper of the Lamb (Rev. 19:7, 9). The day of consummation is coming, and the bride, Christ's church, will be radiant on that day because she has refused to defile herself, so that her garments are dazzling and pure for the coming wedding (Rev. 19:8).

We see in Revelation that the church represents the true Israel. The church faces a great conflict and temptation, for compromising with Roman imperialism would entail entering the mainstream of society and obtaining economic security. John calls the church to a countercultural stance and to endurance in the midst of a society that persecutes and even kills those who refuse to bow the knee to Rome. Temporary pain will give way to everlasting joy as the church anticipates the marriage supper of the Lamb. The church witnesses to the world in its refusal to capitulate to Rome and in its allegiance to Jesus Christ. Unbelievers are summoned through the church's witness to flee the economic and political security offered by Rome. They are to find refuge in Jesus Christ, knowing that a promise of a new heaven and a new earth awaits those who are faithful.

Conclusion

The most striking thing about the church in the NT is that the people of God are defined by their relationship to Jesus. The true Israel consists not of ethnic Jews but rather of those who confess Jesus Christ as Savior and Lord. Hence, the focus on the church as the true Israel fits with the Christ-centered and God-focused thesis of this book. Most often the church is called upon to live in accord with its calling, so that Christ is glorified in the way they love one another and by the moral beauty of their lives. The distinctiveness of the church is marked by baptism, which symbolizes the leaving behind of the old life and one's newfound devotion to Jesus Christ. So too, the church regularly observed the Lord's Supper, reminding themselves that their new life, which commenced in

---

267. See R. Mounce 1977: 247; Osborne 2002: 484–85; Beale 1999b: 676–78.

baptism, was based on the death of Jesus Christ. We see, then, that the church in the NT represents those who belong to Jesus Christ. Sometimes it is called the people of God, or the body of Christ, or the true Israel, or the temple of God, or God's "assembly" (church) or synagogue. In every instance the church represents those who have experienced God's saving promises, who have repented of their sin and put their faith in Jesus Christ.

Like any organization, the church had leaders, and typically they are described as elders or overseers, which is the same office. Some evidence exists for a second office of deacons, who functioned as assistants or helpers of the elders. Such leaders were servants of the church who were to guide the church in accord with the teaching of the gospel and were by no means to wield their authority tyrannically. Indeed, the whole congregation is blessed with spiritual gifts, so that all minister to one another when the church is gathered. Every member of the body has received the Spirit. Those within the community who teach or live in a way that is contrary to the gospel and refuse to turn from evil are to be disciplined, but such discipline is to be carried out in a spirit of love and with the desire that the one who has succumbed to evil will repent and be restored to the community. The community, after all, is called upon to live in such a way that God is glorified through Jesus Christ. Such a lifestyle is possible only through the power of the Spirit. The church of Jesus Christ represents God's people on earth, and they reflect his glory by living in a way that pleases him in a world that has veered away from the living God.

We also have indications that the church is to proclaim the gospel to the ends of the earth. The message of Jesus as the crucified and risen Lord should not be restricted to a certain people or geographical region. All people everywhere are called upon to repent and put their faith in Jesus Christ as Lord and Savior. The mandate to proclaim the gospel is clearer in the Gospels and Acts and, curiously, is not emphasized to the same extent in the Epistles. Still, we saw some indications in the Epistles that the churches were to herald the good news as well. Certainly, the Epistles emphasize that the fragrance of the gospel is wafted abroad when churches live in love and thereby bring glory to God.

18

✿ ✿ ✿ ✿ ✿ ✿ ✿ ✿ ✿ ✿ ✿ ✿ ✿ ✿ ✿ ✿ ✿ ✿

The Social World
of God's People

What does the NT say about the interaction of believers with the world in which they live? What is their relationship to the social world and environment in which they live out their faith day by day? We must note at the outset that eschatology colors everything for believers in Jesus Christ. The fulfillment of God's promised salvation indicates that the new era has dawned, even though believers await the consummation of all that God has promised. The relationship of believers to the world is poised in the tension between the already and the not yet. On the one hand, God's promises are fulfilled so that believers are even now children of God; on the other hand, they await the completion of God's work in their lives. Both they and the world are not all that they should be and all that they will be. Hence, believers can face the world with both unblinking reality and unfazed optimism. They estimate the world with unblinking reality in identifying and proclaiming the evil that still inhabits the created order. They do not paper over the wickedness of the world or even the evil that still inhabits their lives, as if they were out of touch with the world as it really is. However, believers also are animated by unfazed optimism. They know that God will fulfill his purpose and bring in a new creation—a new heaven and a new earth, where righteousness dwells. The evil that stains the world now cannot last and will not triumph. The hope of the gospel promises that righteousness will conquer and evil will be defeated. Therefore, everything that believers face in the world must be assessed in light of the future, for the future world of righteousness represents ultimate reality. Evil's reign will be short-lived. Hence, believers can face the world without falling prey to cynicism, despair, or misrepresentation. They encounter the world knowing its destiny and with the certainty that a new creation will dawn.

It will be helpful to begin this chapter with a brief introduction in which the eschatological worldview of the NT writers is considered. I start with the eschatological standpoint of Paul, which is summarized by 1 Cor. 7:29–31: "This is what I mean, brothers: the appointed time has grown very short. From now on, let those who have wives live as though they had none, and those who mourn as though they were not mourning, and those who rejoice as though they were not rejoicing, and those who buy as though they had no goods, and those who deal with the world as though they had no dealings with it. For the present form of this world is passing away." We should not interpret these words as if Paul is world-denying or as a form of Stoicism.[1] He does not espouse an asceticism that distances itself from marriage and possessions. Paul does not reject the joys and sorrows of this world and prize a monastic life. Marriage and possessions are not repudiated but rather are qualified by Paul's eschatological standpoint. They must be considered in light of the impermanence of this present evil age. Marriage or riches should not be treasured as the highest good, for they too are destined to pass away. Those who attach themselves unreservedly to their spouses or to their possessions have forgotten, perhaps unconsciously, that the world is short-lived. Paul does not call for living an artificial life, so that joys and sorrows are viewed mechanically and impersonally. One could interpret Paul as supporting an almost Stoic view of life, so that no joys or sorrows ever touch believers deeply. Such an interpretation badly misunderstands Paul. His purpose is to avoid the view that heaven can be realized on earth. Given the eschatological future, believers must grasp that all joy and sorrows are fleeting. No human relationship or human emotion should be embraced as if it represents ultimate or final reality. Life in this world must be faced realistically, which means facing it provisionally.

Paul's eschatological stance manifests itself in his estimation of circumcision. If circumcision is required for salvation, then Paul rejects it utterly (Rom. 4:9–12; Gal. 2:3–5; 5:2–4; Phil. 3:2–11). But in and of itself, circumcision is completely irrelevant and insignificant to Paul (Gal.

---

1. See the convincing exegesis in Fee 1987: 337–42; Hays 1997: 127–28.

5:6; 6:15; 1 Cor. 7:19). What matters for Paul is the new creation—the end-time work of God inaugurated in Christ Jesus (Gal. 6:15). Accepting circumcision for cultural reasons is acceptable and legitimate, as long as one does not estimate such a practice as pleasing to God. Similarly, food and drink do not commend anyone to God (1 Cor. 8:8). Believers are free to eat whatever they wish, provided that they are not mastered by their bodily appetites (1 Cor. 6:12–13).[2] If people begin to dictate to others what they must eat in order to be pleasing to God (Col. 2:16–23), such impositions must be rejected as contrary to the gospel. Food is eliminated through the body in natural processes and possesses no inherent value. If the food that one eats scandalizes brothers or sisters, then believers should refrain out of love for the sake of fellow believers (Rom. 14:1–15:7; 1 Cor. 8:1–11:1). Such abstinence, however, cannot be explained in terms of the foods themselves. Food is not inherently defiled; it represents one of God's good gifts (1 Cor. 10:25–26). Further, those who prohibit marriage and the consumption of certain foods categorically deny God's good creation (1 Tim. 4:1–5). Paul does not commend asceticism, nor does he proscribe any foods or marriage. Nevertheless, all of these gifts must be assessed in light of God's new-creation work and the future realization of God's promises. Given their temporary nature, they must not be embraced as the highest good, but neither should they be rejected. Believers enjoy the gifts that God has given (1 Tim. 6:17), but they do not grasp them selfishly. They are always ready to give generously to those in need (1 Tim. 6:17–19).

The stance of believers vis-à-vis the world can be gleaned by noting briefly a few other themes in the NT. The apostle John admonishes believers not to love the world, for the world and all its joys are temporary, whereas the joy that comes from God never ends. Both 1 Peter and Hebrews remind believers that they are exiles and sojourners in this world (1 Pet. 1:1; 2:11; Heb. 11:13; cf. 1 Pet. 1:17). Despite the contrary view of some, Peter does not refer to a literal exile in his letter but rather uses the term "exile" metaphorically.[3] The readers look forward to the day when suffering will cease, and they will enjoy eschatological salvation. In the same way, the author of Hebrews reminds his readers that they, like Abraham, Isaac,

2. Some church members in Corinth may have frequented prostitutes to satisfy their bodily lusts (Rosner 1994: 127–28). Hays (1997: 101–2) argues that the Corinthian stance here reflects a common Hellenistic view regarding sex with prostitutes in a patriarchal society.

3. J. Elliott (1981: 37–49, 129–32; 2000: 100–102) understands the term literally and metaphorically, but a metaphorical reading is more likely (so Chin 1991; Feldmeier 1992: 203–10; Bechtler 1998: 78–81). See the helpful discussion by Dryden (2006: 126–32), who sees a social component to living as exiles but does not understand the term literally, as Elliott does.

and Jacob, are exiles in this world. They anticipate the heavenly city and the city to come (Heb. 11:10–16; 13:14). We think of Revelation, where the beast currently rules the world, but a new heavens and new earth are promised where God will be all in all (Rev. 21:1). Eschatological reservation and anticipation characterize the NT witness and are fundamental for grasping the stance of the NT toward life in this world.

The social world of the NT is approached in this chapter topically. Here we consider five issues in the social world of the NT: (1) riches and poverty; (2) the role of women; (3) marriage, divorce, and children; (4) the relationship to governing authorities; and (5) slavery. Since I am taking a topical approach in this chapter, we will consider each NT writer on the topic at hand.

Riches and Poverty

Luke-Acts

The radical reevaluation of life in the world is evident in the Lukan teaching about riches and poverty. Instead of consulting all three Synoptic Gospels on the theme of riches and poverty, I will confine this discussion to Luke-Acts because Luke focuses particularly on this theme and parallels most of the relevant texts in Matthew and Mark.

Jesus pronounces a blessing for the poor, the hungry, the sorrowful, and persecuted while announcing judgment on those who are rich, full, laughing, and esteemed by their peers (Luke 6:20–26).[4] The sayings here cannot be interpreted as literal statements, as if every single person in the world suffering from poverty receives blessing from God.[5] Those suffering physical deprivation represent those trusting in the God of Israel for their every need.[6] The reference to persecution reveals that it is their allegiance to "the Son of Man" (Luke 6:22) that draws the ire of others. The blessing does not belong to all people everywhere who face discrimination for a multitude of reasons; the blessing is reserved for those mistreated because of their commitment to Jesus. Hence, the

---

4. For this theme in Luke-Acts, see L. Johnson 1977; Seccombe 1982.

5. See Seccombe 1982: 23–96; Meier 1994: 384–86n157.

6. Heard (1988: 47–58) argues that the poor are the faithful remnant in Israel, and that Isa. 56–66 functions as the background for identifying the poor. But contra Heard (1988: 57), the poor should not necessarily be identified with those who are faithful to Torah but rather those who are disciples of Jesus. Hence, the poor represent Jesus' persecuted disciples (Esser, *NIDNTT* 2:824–25; cf. Seccombe 1982: 88–91). Those who emphasize literal poverty, then, are mistaken (rightly, Fitzmyer 1981a: 532; Merklein, *EDNT* 3:194; Tannehill 1986: 127–32). R. Brown (1977: 363–64) argues that the emphasis is on spiritual poverty, although physical deprivation is not absent. See also L. Johnson 1977: 140. Green (1995: 79–84) maintains that "poor" denotes the idea of lower social status and not merely poverty.

Matthean "poor in spirit" (Matt. 5:3) is not distant from the Lukan meaning.[7] Still, we cannot wash out of the Lukan sayings any reference to literal poverty. Jesus speaks of those who have placed their lives in the hands of God and suffer poverty, hunger, sorrow, and persecution.

Jesus' blessings and woes are shocking because they turn the values of the world upside down. Such words can be spoken only because one's status in this world must be assessed in light of the eschaton. Those who are poor and mistreated for Jesus' sake enjoy the power of the kingdom now and the promise of eschatological satisfaction and joy. On the other hand, those who are rich and respected now will weep and suffer hunger on the last day. The pleasures of earthly life are relativized in light of the future kingdom.

Mary's song celebrates the same message, for she looks forward to a day, now that Jesus has been conceived, when God will display his strength (Luke 1:51–53). The arrogant will be dispersed, those with political power deposed, and the wealthy will suffer loss. Conversely, the humble will be raised up, and the hungry provided with food.[8] The poor should not be equated with all those lacking material possessions, for they are limited to the people of God mistreated by unbelieving nations.[9] If the eschaton were merely a pious dream, then pursuing power and wealth would be sensible. Jesus' distinctive mission is to preach good news—that is, the fulfillment of God's saving promises to the poor (Luke 4:18). The significance of Jesus' announcement is evident, for he promises such fulfillment in his programmatic speech in Nazareth, which represents the inauguration of Jesus' ministry in Luke. The good news for the poor cannot be equated with a romantic acceptance of poverty. The coming of the kingdom signals that those who are downtrodden and poor will not be in such a position forever. God's saving promises are about to become a reality, so that the poor will experience God's favor. Once again the word "poor" must not be stripped of its literal meaning.

7. Esser (*NIDNTT* 2:824) argues that Matt. 5:3 "brings out the OT and Jewish background of those who in affliction have confidence only in God." For a view of riches and poverty compatible with what is being argued here, see Marshall 1970: 141–44.

8. The aorist tense could refer to the past, but given the eschatological cast of Luke's Gospel and the fact that what Mary promises here had not happened in Israel's history, it seems that the promises related to the future. R. Brown (1977: 363) takes them as being fulfilled in the death and resurrection of Christ, arguing that these verses are postresurrection perspectives on what has been accomplished salvifically through Jesus. Fitzmyer (1981a: 360–61) rejects the notion that they are prophetic perfects or relate to the victories of the Maccabees. He thinks that they figuratively relate to the life and ministry of Jesus. Marshall (1978b: 83–84) suggests that they could be prophetic perfects that are realized in part even now. Marshall's view is the most satisfactory (see also Seccombe 1982: 76–77). A helpful survey and explanation of the text is found in Bock 1994: 153–56.

9. So Seccombe 1982: 82.

On the other hand, there is almost certainly a spiritual dimension to the term. The liberty promised to captives refers not to those liberated from prisons in Palestine but rather to those who are freed from captivity to sin by Jesus. The sight promised to the blind is both literal and spiritual.[10] Jesus opened the eyes of the blind, but such healings pointed to the spiritual opening of eyes that occurred in his ministry. Similarly, the good news promised to the poor includes the spiritual riches given to those who put their trust in Jesus (cf. Luke 7:22–23).

Those who heed Jesus' message about the coming of the kingdom cannot view money and property in the same way. The message of the Baptist, in this respect, was the same as that taught by Jesus (Luke 3:11–14). Genuine repentance displays itself in a willingness to share food and clothing with those in need. Given John's ascetic way of life, we might expect him to advocate radical social change.[11] But we find nothing of the kind. Tax collectors are not encouraged to resign their position in order to pursue another way of life; rather, they are mandated to be just and honest as tax collectors, taking no more than is lawful. Similarly, John does not demand that soldiers forsake the military for a civilian calling. He exhorts them to be satisfied with their wages and to avoid using their positions as a means of extorting money from those under their authority.

Jesus constantly warns about the danger of riches, because they can turn people away from the kingdom. In the parable of the soils the word of God can be choked out by riches and the desire for pleasure (Luke 8:14). A man pleads with Jesus to intervene in a family financial dispute and serve as the arbiter in the case (Luke 12:13–15). Jesus refuses to become entangled in a family debate over how an inheritance should be divided, but he warns the man about the peril of covetousness, reminding him that life cannot be defined by one's riches. Jesus' admonition to this man leads into the parable of the rich fool (Luke 12:16–21). The rich man is a fool because he fails to think eschatologically. He has forgotten that death is impending and could occur at any moment, so that he spends his life thinking about his investments. The rich man is convinced that his retirement will last for many years, and that he can spend them eating, drinking, and rejoicing. Jesus does not condemn the man because his crops were bountiful, for the latter represent God's blessing. Nor should the parable be read to say that all capital investment is wrong.[12] The rich man is foolish because he fails to reckon with God.[13] He betrays

10. See the careful discussion in Bock 1994: 408–9.
11. As Fitzmyer (1981a: 465) notes, John does not call for an overturning of the social structures of his day.
12. Contra Seccombe (1982: 144), his sin was not "stockpiling" per se. For a more convincing reading, see Hultgren 2000: 109.
13. See Marshall 1978b: 524; Fitzmyer 1985: 972.

what can almost be called a deistic view of life that forgets about God's intervention in the world, so that he faces the sudden shock of death at the inception of his retirement. Fundamentally, he has lived as a practical atheist. He has padded his retirement account but did not find God to be his treasure and pleasure.[14]

Jesus' warnings about riches are not reserved for unbelievers. His own disciples need to be on guard constantly, for they too are prone to being subverted by wealth (Luke 12:22–34).[15] Worrying about wealth uncovers a lack of trust in God's fatherly care, and even more fundamentally a desire to live for oneself rather than for the kingdom of God.[16] Jesus was not an ascetic who demanded renunciation of the world. He warned about the danger of riches because they so easily separate people from God.[17] Those who give generously and who refuse to cave in to worry demonstrate that their treasure is found in God rather than in possessions. The Pharisees ridicule Jesus' teaching because they cannot tolerate anyone who criticizes their love affair with money (Luke 16:14–15). One of the reasons why Jesus cleanses the temple is that it has become a place of financial profit instead of a place for prayer and worship (Luke 19:45–46). Inviting the poor and the physically impaired for meals is a mark of living for God's kingdom, and those who do so will receive the reward of the kingdom on the final day (Luke 14:12–14).

Jesus often emphasizes in Luke that only those who repudiate riches as their god will enter the kingdom. The rich ruler desired to obtain eternal life on the last day (Luke 18:18). In other words, he desired to be saved (Luke 18:26) and to enter the kingdom of God (Luke 18:24). Jesus demanded that he surrender all his possessions and follow in discipleship in order to receive salvation and enjoy treasure in heaven (Luke 18:22).[18] The rich ruler could not bring himself to part with his wealth, and so he departed from Jesus. Freedom from the tyranny of money belongs only to those who have experienced the miracle of God's saving power (Luke 18:27). Peter and the disciples enjoyed the power of grace, for they abandoned all that they owned to follow Jesus (Luke 18:28–30).

14. Heard (1988: 61) remarks, "The rich man's sin was hoarding; he was trying to keep all of God's blessings for himself."

15. Luke 12:33 does not literally mean that all of Jesus' disciples should surrender all their goods; however, they must be willing to use their money for the sake of the kingdom (so Bock 1996: 1167; see also Seccombe 1982: 153–55). Heard (1988: 62) views the text as an injunction against hoarding their goods.

16. Seccombe (1982: 150–52) argues that the anxiety that accompanies discipleship is prohibited here, not merely anxiety in general.

17. See Schlatter 1997: 166–74.

18. Bock points out the example of Zacchaeus (Luke 19:8), who gave away half of his possessions. He rightly notes that the issue is God's supremacy, and the particulars of what Jesus demands are not imposed on all (Bock 1996: 1482–83). See also Seccombe 1982: 118–32.

Luke does not imply that every believer is required literally to surrender all wealth in order to receive eternal life.[19] Such was demanded of the rich ruler. However, salvation came to the household of Zacchaeus when he gave half of his possessions to the poor and repaid fourfold those whom he had swindled (Luke 19:1–10).[20] No formula should be read out of Luke's teaching, as if we can calculate precisely how much should be relinquished in order to gain life eternal.[21] Jesus did not specify how much someone should give, for he was concerned not with quantity but rather with repentance that manifested itself in devotion to God.[22] Presumably, Mary the mother of John Mark enjoyed significant wealth, for she was able to accommodate the church meeting at her house (Acts 12:12).[23] Apparently, it was not demanded of her that she sell her house and give all her wealth to the poor. Still, we must avoid going to the other extreme. Zacchaeus's salvation should not be disentangled from his wealth, for the saving power of the kingdom revealed itself in his newly found generosity and in his willingness to right past wrongs. The mother of John Mark did not hoard her wealth; she used her house for the church. The issue for Luke is what possesses human beings, for those who are captivated by money serve it as their god. The radical demand of the kingdom manifests itself in the account of the poor widow who gave so little and yet gave all that she had (Luke 21:1–4).

The parable of the dishonest manager is one of the most disputed accounts in the Lukan Gospel (Luke 16:1–9).[24] The manager did not work honestly, and therefore his master fired him. In order to secure his future comfort, the manager dramatically reduced the debts of those who owed the master money, reducing the debt by 50 percent for some, 20 percent for others. Such behavior was not an example of social justice.[25] The manager acted selfishly to secure his own future, for he was incapable of manual labor and ashamed to beg. What does this parable say to a follower of Jesus, especially since the manager is commended as one who is dishonest? The parable works by way of contrast and compari-

19. Heard (1988: 68) maintains that disciples must be willing "to abandon all, if called upon to do so."

20. We see here the generosity of Zacchaeus (so Bock 1996: 1520). Heard (1988: 73) notes that Zacchaeus "remained a man of considerable substance."

21. Rightly Juel 1983: 91; Heard 1988: 73.

22. So Schlatter 1997: 172.

23. Heard 1988: 68. Polhill (1992: 281n153) remarks that Mary's home functions as evidence that private property was retained in the early church, and possessions were shared freely.

24. Space is lacking here to examine the parable in any detail. For a helpful exposition, see Bailey 1976: 86–110. See also Seccombe 1982: 160–69.

25. Contra Fitzmyer (1985: 1101), it is unclear that the reduction of the bill is related to the manager's commission (cf. Bock 1996: 1329–30).

son.[26] In contrast to the dishonest manager, believers should not conduct themselves unethically in the use of their possessions; but like him, they should use their money to secure their future. Indeed, they should use their wealth in such a way that they will be welcomed into "eternal dwellings" (Luke 16:9).[27] The use of possessions will play a role in the final judgment.[28] Jesus' commentary subsequent to the parable supports the interpretation offered here (Luke 16:10–13). True riches will be granted eschatologically only to those who use their wealth for the sake of the kingdom. The way people use their money will reveal whether they are devoted to God or to wealth, whether they serve God or money.

The parable of the rich man and Lazarus demonstrates a reversal of roles in the future (Luke 16:19–31). The rich man lives in luxury but blissfully ignores the needs of the poor, and therefore he will face judgment and torment (cf. Isa. 58:7).[29] Johnson argues that in context the rich man represents the Pharisees (cf. Luke 16:14–15) who ignore the message of the law and the prophets, which demand generosity to the poor.[30] The opulent lifestyle of the rich man reveals what he worships. We should note that the parable includes the message that repentance is possible, but repentance cannot be restricted to an internal change of mind that lacks an accompanying concrete change in everyday living. Genuine repentance involves the kind of change that we see in the life of Zacchaeus, where love for the needy manifests itself practically.[31] Similarly, the communal life of the early church, in which the needs of the poor believers were met, functions as a paradigm of generosity for Luke (Acts 2:44–45; 4:32–37).[32] Luke does not mandate the surrender of private property, nor does he advocate any particular social arrangement.[33] The deaths of Ananias and Sapphira cannot be attributed to their failure to give all their wealth to the church (Acts 5:1–11). Peter specifically remarked that their possessions belonged to them, and that they were

26. See Jeremias 1972: 182.

27. Fitzmyer (1985: 1098) maintains that the manager is commended for his prudence, not his dishonesty.

28. See Bock 1996: 1334–35; L. Johnson 1977: 157.

29. Contra Jeremias (1972: 186), who separates Jesus' message from the Lukan context.

30. L. Johnson 1977: 140–44; cf. Seccombe 1982: 176–79.

31. Marshall 1970: 242; Heard 1988: 65.

32. For more detailed discussion of these texts, where they are placed in their literary context, see L. Johnson 1977: 183–204. For parallels and a discussion of the Lukan context, see Seccombe 1982: 200–209. L. Johnson (1977: 161) also notes that Luke 15:31 functions as an interesting parallel, demonstrating that when people are alienated from one another, they do not share all things in common. In addition, laying one's possessions at the feet of the apostles signifies submission to the authority of the twelve (L. Johnson 1977: 201–4).

33. Rightly Seccombe 1982: 207–9; Capper 1998: 512.

free to do what they wished with the proceeds from the land that they sold (Acts 5:4). The sin of Ananias and Sapphira was lying, in that they colluded together to promote the view that they were exceedingly generous in giving up all the money from the land that they sold for the sake of the church.[34] Remarkable generosity and providing for the needy are commended by Luke, but this should not be read to demand the surrender of one's possessions into a common purse.

Concern for those in need animates Luke. Cornelius is commended because he gives alms for the poor (Acts 10:2). The failure to provide for the physical needs of the Hellenistic widows is no light matter (Acts 6:1–6), for the witness of the church is severely compromised if some are lacking food and care. Hence, the apostles took pains to remedy the situation immediately and fairly. The predicted famine in Jerusalem could not be shrugged off by the church in Antioch as a plight that was far away (Acts 11:27–30). The church immediately took action and sent gifts to needy brothers and sisters in Jerusalem. Paul commended his ministry by reminding the Ephesian elders that he worked to support himself and did not use his ministry as a pretext for financial advantage (Acts 20:33–34). Perhaps the Lukan message on money can be summed up in the words of Jesus recited by Paul: "It is more blessed to give than to receive" (Acts 20:35). Luke does not conceive of giving as something onerous and painful. To supply the needs of others does not dampen joy but rather enhances it. Joy is amplified and expanded when believers demonstrate by giving to others that God is their portion.

The Pauline Literature

Paul, like Luke, often speaks of the financial responsibility belonging to believers. False teachers can be discerned in part by their desire to take advantage of believers financially. They are "peddlers of God's word" (2 Cor. 2:17). Their desire to spread the gospel is stained with impure motives and a yearning for financial advantage (1 Tim. 6:5). Paul, on the other hand, refused to accept payment so that he would serve as an example for his hearers (1 Cor. 9:1–23; 1 Thess. 2:5). In 2 Corinthians he contrasts himself with the false teachers, emphasizing the purity of his motives and his financial integrity (2 Cor. 2:17; 4:2). In 2 Corinthians he would in no circumstances accept support from the church, thereby demonstrating that he was distinct from the false apostles (2 Cor. 11:7–15). Unbelievers display their spiritual state by their love for money rather than God (2 Tim. 3:2).

The new life of believers is marked by giving and generosity rather than greed and coveting. New life in Christ does not fit with stealing (Rom.

---

34. The sin in this case was lying, not the failure to give all that they owned (so Barrett 1994: 262; Heard 1988: 68; L. Johnson 1977: 208; Seccombe 1982: 212).

13:9; Eph. 4:28). Believers should work industriously so that they have the ability to share with those who are in need. In 1–2 Thessalonians Paul warns believers about laziness, presumably because some had ceased working in light of the nearness of the Lord's coming (1 Thess. 4:11–12; 5:14; 2 Thess. 3:6–12). The failure to work would bring disrepute to the gospel among unbelievers, and when believers become idle and bored, they open themselves up to evil. They should imitate Paul's example of hard work and thus cease to be a financial burden to anyone (2 Thess. 3:7–9). Believers should be eager to assist those in financial need, but it is unloving to provide money for those who are able to work but refuse to do so, for believers thereby promote a life of lassitude (2 Thess. 3:10).

Believers are not criticized for being rich (1 Tim. 6:17–19), nor is the pleasure that comes from wealth despised. God is the creator of the world and the gifts in it (1 Tim. 4:3–5; cf. 1 Cor. 10:23–25). Still, those who acquire wealth are disposed to arrogance and pride, so that their lives center on money rather than God. Those with riches are in danger of placing God at the periphery rather than the center of their lives. Greed, according to Paul, is tantamount to idolatry (Eph. 5:3; Col. 3:5). Moreover, God grants wealth so that the rich will share with those in need and live generously. Only those who turn away from wealth as their god will truly enjoy life on the last day (1 Tim. 6:19). Generosity and a willingness to help those in need should be the signature of those who belong to God (Rom. 12:8). Such generosity manifests itself in willingness to provide hospitality (Rom. 12:13; 1 Tim. 5:10). The church should provide support for teachers and leaders in its midst so that they can devote themselves to the gospel (1 Cor. 9:1–14; Gal. 6:6–8; 1 Tim. 5:17–18).

Generosity and a desire to help those in need should be the hallmark of God's people. Widows who have lived godly lives and are past the age of sixty should be supported by the church if they are bereft of family who could assist them (1 Tim. 5:3–16).[35] Paul commends the Philippian church for their support in his proclamation of the gospel (Phil. 1:3–6; 4:10–19). He is grateful for their generosity, but he avoids any sense of desperation or panic. He has learned the lesson of contentment even when he has very little. The generosity of the Philippians represents God's work in their hearts, but any notion that they are the ultimate providers must be rejected. God is the one who supplies all their needs in Christ Jesus. Those who give to assist others could be filled with pride instead of giving glory to God, and giving that puts the spotlight on the generosity of the giver rather than God is actually contrary to love (1 Cor. 13:3).

---

35. Against seeing an order of widows, see L. Johnson 1996: 179–83. In favor of such, see Kidd 1990: 104–6.

One of Paul's concerns that surfaces on several occasions in his letters is the collection for the poor saints in Jerusalem (Rom. 15:22–29; 1 Cor. 16:1–4; 2 Cor. 8:1–9:15; Gal. 2:10).[36] The collection should not be viewed as a tax or levy owed by Gentiles. Paul encourages Gentiles to give to the Jerusalem poor because the message of salvation that Gentiles enjoyed originally came from the Jews, and thus the Gentiles were indebted to them spiritually. By giving, Gentiles demonstrated their solidarity with believers in Jerusalem and testified to the unity of the people of God. Moreover, those who give indicate that they have been grasped by grace, for they imitate Christ, who gave up his riches and became poor for the benefit of others (2 Cor. 8:9; 9:15). Paul also emphasizes in 2 Cor. 8–9 that giving is the pathway to blessing and joy.[37]

Other New Testament Witnesses

The remainder of the NT touches on riches and poverty here and there, confirming what we have seen elsewhere. Hospitality played a crucial role in the Greco-Roman world, especially among believers who needed to stay in someone else's home in order to afford travel. Hence, we are not surprised to find admonitions to show hospitality (Heb. 13:2; 1 Pet. 4:9). On the other hand, to show hospitality to those who taught a deficient Christology would be to support and thereby participate in a false gospel (2 John 7–11). Conversely, those who traveled for the sake of the name of Christ in order to bring the good news to others should be financially supported by other believers (3 John 5–8). False teachers are motivated by greed (2 Pet. 2:3, 14), and, like Balaam, they propagate their message for financial advantage (2 Pet. 2:15–16; Jude 11). Those who love the things of this world will not enjoy the blessings of the age to come (1 John 2:15–17). True love responds to the practical needs of those who lack food and clothing (1 John 3:17; cf. Heb. 13:16; James 2:15–16).

Believers face the temptation of compromising their faith for the sake of the comfort and joys of this world. One of the allures of the whore of Babylon is the glittering wealth and beauty that adorns her (Rev. 17:4). The luxuries and delights of the world are available for those who cast their lot with Babylon (Rome) and worship the beast (Rev. 13:16–17; 18:7). The goods imported into Rome dazzled and delighted (Rev. 18:11–16), but those who aligned themselves with Rome were destined to suffer judgment along with her. They did not reckon with God and the coming eschatological judgment. Believers should not capitulate to Babylon,

36. For a useful study of the Pauline collection, see Nickle 1966.
37. Some argue that 2 Cor. 8–9 represents two different letters (e.g., H. Betz 1985), but there are good reasons to think that they were written at the same time (so Carson, Moo, and Morris 1992: 275–77; Harris 2005: 27–29).

for the joys of belonging to that city are fleeting, and Babylon will be utterly destroyed. Believers triumph over the love of money by trusting that God will supply all their needs, that he will never forsake them (Heb. 13:5–6). The confidence that God will supply every financial need provides strength for believers not to compromise with Babylon.

The letter of James often addresses riches and poverty. Attention to this theme is due in part to the circumstances of the readers, who were suffering from the pressures of life (James 1:2–4, 12–15).[38] These difficulties likely included financial troubles (James 1:9). James's interest in the theme also reflects dependence on the Jesus tradition, where the danger of wealth is also addressed often.[39] It seems that James never uses the term "rich" (*plousios*) to refer to believers. The poor, according to James 1:9, will experience eschatological vindication on the last day. James describes the poor person as a "brother" (*adelphos*), indicating a member of the people of God. By way of contrast, the word "brother" is dropped when James refers to the rich, and the rich will face eschatological humiliation and pass away (James 1:10).[40] In James 1:11 he does not merely say that the wealth of the rich will pass away, but that the rich themselves "will fade away" (James 1:11). The polemic against the rich continues in James 2:6–7. The rich are described as those who oppress believers, bring them to court, and revile the name of Christ. Clearly, those who speak against Christ do not belong to the people of God. In James 5 the future judgment of the rich is portrayed (James 5:1–6). James prophesies that eschatological judgment is coming, and the accumulated riches of the wealthy will be worthless to fend off judgment in that day. The rich have lived sumptuously and luxuriously on their large estate farms while depriving laborers of wages.

James does not directly identify those who have wealth in James 4:13–16 as unbelievers.[41] He severely admonishes the wealthy not to fall prey to arrogance, as if their own ingenuity could account for future profits. Such pride fails to see that life is a wisp of air that could float away at any time. Any success in business is due to God's will and cannot be ascribed ultimately to the ability of the businessperson.

It is important to recall that James does not address unbelievers in his letter. He directs his remarks to believers who are tempted to fawn

---

38. Bauckham (1999b: 188–91) argues that the rich and the poor are societal extremes, and the majority of the readers are neither.

39. See Davids 1982: 44–47.

40. See Davids 1982: 76–77; Laws 1980: 62–64; L. Johnson 1995: 190–91; Edgar 2001: 148–49; L. Cheung 2003: 256, 261. Contra Moo 2000: 66–67.

41. Penner (1996: 172–77) argues that James 4:13–5:6 contains a denunciation of the rich that resonates with Jer. 12:1–4, and thus the object of James's words are arrogant unbelievers.

over the rich. Believers may show partiality to the rich and ignore the poor when the former join them in worship (James 2:1–13). If believers smuggle themselves into the good graces of the rich, they enhance their own lives. In effect, believers have become "adulteresses" in that they have traded their devotion to God for love of the world and its approval and comfort (James 4:1–4). They use prayer as a means to try to acquire what they desire. So too they grovel before the rich because of the advantage that the rich can bestow upon them. James reminds them that God has chosen the poor to be members of his kingdom (James 2:5). Furthermore, it is only those who show mercy to the needy who will experience God's mercy on the last day (James 2:13).

Those who trust that God will provide for their needs are liberated to serve and help others. James has no use for religion that is limited to hearing about the needs of others and does not reach the heart and extend to one's hands. Hence, widows and orphans are supported and cared for, not forgotten (James 1:27). The poor person who enters the community is treated with the same dignity and respect as the rich (James 2:1–13). Faith works in providing for the needs of one who lacks food and clothing (James 2:14–16); it does not merely mouth pious platitudes invoking God's blessing on those who are hungry and ill-clad. According to James, genuine faith must lead to practical and observable works, or it is not genuine faith at all.

Conclusion

The NT teaching on riches fits with the central themes of this book. Riches and poverty must be considered in light of the eschatology of the NT. To become consumed with riches is folly because the present world is passing away, and the new creation has been inaugurated and most certainly will be consummated. In addition, those who are entranced with riches demonstrate that their treasure is money rather than God. The God-centered vision of the NT summons readers to find their joy in the Father, the Son, and the Spirit.

Women

Luke-Acts

Women were often denigrated in the ancient world and clearly did not have the same status as men.[42] The Lukan account of women should be

---

42. For a helpful survey of the status of women and wives in the Greco-Roman world, see J. Elliott 2000: 553–58, 585–99.

interpreted in light of the fulfillment of God's saving purposes in Christ.[43] The new people of God are marked by inclusion and equality. Gentiles are not required to observe the law in order to enter God's people, and women have the same access to the promise of salvation as do men. In the Lukan birth narratives women play a prominent role (Luke 1–2). Elizabeth and Mary are featured as godly women who trusted in Yahweh and kept his commandments. Elizabeth, along with her husband, Zechariah, was blameless in her devotion to God's commands (Luke 1:6). Mary functions as the model disciple in her willingness to be the Lord's servant and to do his will (Luke 1:38). The Holy Spirit descended upon Elizabeth so that she spoke God's word, prophesying to Mary about the birth of the Christ (Luke 1:41–45). Similarly, Mary also spoke the word of the Lord, and she dwelled not upon the blessings bestowed upon her but rather on the fulfillment of God's covenant promises (Luke 1:46–55). Anna is designated as a prophetess and declares the word of the Lord (Luke 2:36–38). Each of the women speaks of God fulfilling his covenant in history, and Elizabeth and Mary fill vital roles in the accomplishment of God's saving purpose.

Luke often focuses on Jesus' compassion for women, showing that God's saving purpose includes women as well as men. Jesus healed Simon's mother-in-law from her fever (Luke 4:38–39), raised the widow of Nain's son from the dead (Luke 7:11–17), showed forgiving mercy to the sinful woman who demonstrated her love for him while he was eating in the home of a Pharisee (Luke 7:36–50), and healed the woman with a hemorrhage and raised Jairus's daughter from the dead (Luke 8:40–56). The miracles that Jesus performed point to his saving power, to the truth that "God has visited his people" (Luke 7:16). They also testify that salvation is obtained by trusting God. Hence, Jesus said to the sinful woman, "Your faith has saved you; go in peace" (Luke 7:50). The same words are uttered to the woman saved from her hemorrhage (Luke 8:48), indicating that physical healing functions as a pointer to eschatological salvation.[44]

The same practical concern for women surfaces in Acts. The witness of the church was compromised by the failure to care for the Hellenistic widows (Acts 6:1–6), for if the church did not attend to the everyday needs of those in the community, then the truth of its message of salvation for the world was called into question. Peter raised Dorcas from the dead, a woman whose love for believers was manifested in a variety of practical ways (Acts 9:36–41). The expulsion of a demon from a girl

43. For a survey of Luke's view on women, see Tannehill 1986: 132–39; see also Green 1995: 91–94.

44. Here the ESV obscures the parallel by giving different English translations to identical Greek phrases in Luke 7:50; 8:48.

who practiced fortune-telling rescued her from men who exploited her for their own financial advantage, so that she now experienced the saving work of God in Christ (Acts 16:16–18).

The Lukan concern for women displays itself in diverse ways. In the parables about God's seeking of the lost, he includes parables about the lost sheep (Luke 15:3–7) and the lost coin (Luke 15:8–10). The former centers on the world of men, but the latter identifies with the world of women (cf. Luke 17:35). We should note that both stories belong to the center of the Lukan Gospel, featuring God's desire to save all. The parable of the widow and the unjust judge (Luke 18:1–8) recognizes and identifies with the plight of women in the ancient Near East. Hence, the sacrifice of the widow in giving all her money is remarkable (Luke 21:1–4). Women who were followers of Jesus express their love for him by attending to him at his death (Luke 23:49, 55–56). Luke also notes the conversion of specific women, such as Lydia (Acts 16:14–15) and Damaris (Acts 17:34), and in other texts he comments that women were saved (Acts 5:14; 8:12; 17:4, 12), or that both men and women were arrested (Acts 8:3; 9:2; 22:4), showing the inclusion of women among the people of God. Luke never collapses into sentimentality, and so we see Jesus correcting a woman who pronounced a blessing upon Mary, who bore and nursed him, reminding her that obedience to God is the only pathway to true blessing (Luke 11:27–28).

Luke also emphasizes the role of women in ministry. Not only men followed Jesus; women also were his disciples and supported his ministry financially (Luke 8:1–3).[45] Often in Judaism and in the Greco-Roman world women were discouraged from receiving an education. Jesus, on the contrary, commended Mary, who chose to listen to the word of the Lord, rather than following the custom of Martha, who was troubled by the preparations for Jesus' meal (Luke 10:38–42).[46] When Jesus was raised from the dead, he appeared first to women, even though they were not accepted as valid witnesses in Israel, and proclaimed to them his victory over death (Luke 24:1–12). They in turn shared the good news with the male disciples. Jesus' disciples persevered in prayer for many days before the day of Pentecost, and Luke notes that women were included in that number (Acts 1:14). The gift of prophecy did not belong to men alone, for the fulfillment of Joel's prophecy regarding the coming of the Spirit and the fulfillment of God's saving promises occurred when the

45. So also Tannehill 1986: 138. Jervell (1984: 153) rightly says that the women described here were not missionaries but rather were engaged in "diaconal tasks," although Jervell (1984: 146–57) wrongly places the emphasis on women being Jews and daughters of Abraham and suggests that this is the reason they are more prominent in Luke than in Acts.

46. Tannehill (1986: 137) notes that Mary was functioning as a disciple here. So also Witherington 1984: 101.

Spirit was poured out on both men and women (Acts 2:18). That women functioned as prophets is confirmed by Philip's four daughters, who were known for their prophetic activity (Acts 21:9). Nor is it the case that men are exempted from learning from women, for both Priscilla and Aquila took Apollos aside and gave him more accurate instruction in the truth of the gospel (Acts 18:26). We see, then, that women also play a role in spreading and instilling the good news of salvation.

Matthew and Mark

Just as Luke focuses upon women, we find in both Matthew and Mark the same concern for women.[47] It is unusual in a genealogy for women to be named at all, but Matthew calls attention to four women in his genealogy (Matt. 1:3, 5–6), perhaps in part because they anticipate the role that Mary played in the birth of Jesus (Matt. 1:18–25). Both Matthew and Mark include the account of the healing of the woman with the hemorrhage and the raising of Jairus's daughter (Matt. 9:18–25; Mark 5:22–43). The parable of the leaven in the dough hails from the world of women (Matt. 13:33), as do his illustrations from a common occupation for women (Matt. 24:41) and the parable of the ten virgins (Matt. 25:1–13). Jesus showed compassion by healing the daughter of the Canaanite woman (Matt. 15:22–28; Mark 7:25–30). Jesus' teaching on divorce also protects women from being mistreated by husbands (Matt. 5:31–32; 19:1–12; Mark 10:2–12). Both Matthew and Mark record that Mary prepared Jesus for his burial with ointment (Matt. 26:6–13; Mark 14:3–9). Women were present at Jesus' death, desired to attend to him at his burial, and were the first witnesses of the resurrection (Matt. 27:55–56, 61; 28:1–10; Mark 15:40–41, 47; 16:1–8).

John's Gospel

Women also play a surprisingly prominent role in John's Gospel. In John 2:1–11 a fascinating interaction takes place between Jesus and his mother. When she tried to persuade Jesus to intervene and to provide wine for a wedding feast, he made it clear that he followed the mandate of his Father instead of his mother. Still, she was confident that Jesus would do something to help and instructed the servants to do whatever he requested. The encounter with the Samaritan woman demonstrated Jesus' compassion and love for a woman who was an outcast (John 4:4–42). Jesus reveals that women and Samaritans are not outside his saving purposes, even if the disciples were scandalized that

47. The discussion is abbreviated here to avoid undue repetition of what was said regarding Luke.

Jesus conversed with a woman. She became the means by which the rest of the Samaritans in the village heard the good news about Jesus. Near the end of his ministry, Jesus raised Lazarus from the dead. Jesus' encounter with Lazarus's sisters, Martha and Mary, is sketched in by John in some detail (John 11:1–44). Both of these women function as model disciples; Martha recognized Jesus as the Messiah and the Son of God. John also includes the account of Mary anointing Jesus before his death (John 12:1–8). The women who were faithful to Jesus, standing near the cross, are named (John 19:25). John also includes the account in which John took Mary as his mother (John 19:26–27). John also focuses on the role of Mary Magdalene in his resurrection account (John 20:1–2), and Jesus appeared first to Mary (John 20:11–18), who recounted the good news to others.

The Pauline Literature

According to the Pauline letters, women were involved in the ministry of the church in remarkable ways. A number of women are identified as those who "labor" (*kopiaō*) for the Lord, including Mary, Tryphaena, Tryphosa, and Persis (Rom. 16:6, 12). Elsewhere Paul uses the term "labor" of his own ministry (1 Cor. 4:12; 15:10; Gal. 4:11; Phil. 2:16; Col. 1:29; 1 Tim. 4:10) and that of other leaders (1 Cor. 16:16; 1 Thess. 5:12; 1 Tim. 5:17). Other women are singled out as co-workers (*synergos*) in the gospel, such as Prisca (Rom. 16:3) and Euodia and Syntyche (Phil. 4:2–3), and this term is used also of Timothy (Rom. 16:21; 1 Thess. 3:2), Titus (2 Cor. 8:23), and other co-workers (2 Cor. 8:23; Phil. 2:25; Col. 4:11; Philem. 1, 24), and of Paul and Apollos as co-workers with God (1 Cor. 3:9). It seems in the case of Euodia and Syntyche that they functioned as missionaries, for Paul refers to their efforts in spreading the gospel (Phil. 4:3). Prisca and Aquila also established house churches as they traveled (Rom. 16:3–5; 1 Cor. 16:19; 2 Tim. 4:19). It has now been established by scholarship that Junia in Rom. 16:7 is a woman.[48] It is possible that the text describes her and Andronicus (quite possibly her husband) as "well known to the apostles" (ESV), but more likely the phrase should be rendered "prominent among the apostles" (NRSV). In this latter instance the term "apostle" refers to one who is a missionary.[49] Junia probably worked particularly with other women in propagating the gospel.

It is also quite likely that women served as deacons in the early church. The NRSV reflects this view in identifying Phoebe as "a deacon of the

---

48. This is almost universally supported now. See Schreiner 1998: 795–96.
49. So Schnackenburg 1970: 294; Käsemann 1980: 413–14; Stuhlmacher 1994: 249. Contra Dunn 1988b: 895; Byrne 1996: 453.

church at Cenchreae" (Rom. 16:1 NRSV).[50] The reference to a particular church after the term "deacon" suggests that an office is in view. Some have even contended that the word *prostatis* in Rom. 16:2 demonstrates that Phoebe held a prominent office, but this term dos not designate leadership and is aptly translated by the NRSV as "benefactor." Phoebe was a patron of the church and evidently assisted Paul financially as well. Whether women are identified as deacons in 1 Tim. 3:11 is disputed, but there are a number of reasons to answer in the affirmative. First, the word "likewise" suggests that Paul continues to speak of deacons. Second, the qualifications listed are remarkably similar to what is required for male deacons (1 Tim. 3:8). Third, a reference to wives is improbable, for then Paul would be addressing the wives of deacons and saying nothing about the wives of elders, which is quite unlikely because elders had greater responsibility than deacons. Fourth, it is evident from an early period in church history that there were female deacons.[51]

Some arguments supporting women in leadership are quite unconvincing.[52] Even though the church met in Chloe's house (1 Cor. 1:11), it does not follow that she was the leader, for when the church met in the house of John Mark's mother, she was not a leader in the Jerusalem church (Acts 12:12). Whether Paul placed any restrictions on women in ministry is controversial today. It seems that women functioned as deacons, but they did not serve as pastors, overseers, or elders. These latter three functions likely represent the same office (cf. Acts 20:17, 28; Titus 1:5, 7; 1 Pet. 5:1–2). In 1 Tim. 2:12 Paul prohibits women from teaching or exercising authority over men.[53] Some have maintained that the admonition here should be understood as a temporary restriction inasmuch as the women were propagating false teaching or lacked the necessary education to serve as teachers. Such a view should be rejected, for Paul grounds his directive in the created order—in Adam being formed before Eve (1 Tim. 2:13). Paul easily could have stated that the command was due to women spreading or being duped by false teaching, but instead he grounds his command on God's good creation. The difficult verse that follows (1 Tim. 2:14) likely refers to Eve's being deceived first, so that in the process Satan subverted God's created intention by approaching Eve rather than Adam. According to Paul, women can serve as deacons because a diaconal ministry is supportive and does not involve teaching

---

50. In support of Phoebe as a deacon, see Wilckens 1982: 131; Moo 1996: 914; Byrne 1996: 447.

51. See Pliny, *Letters* 10.96.

52. For a representative expression of this view, see Payne 1981: 173–75, 183–85, 190–97.

53. For an intensive discussion of this text, including extensive interaction with the alternative interpretations, see Schreiner 2005.

or exercising authority over men. The office of elder or overseer is restricted to men, for qualifications for pastoral ministry include being able to teach and to lead (1 Tim. 3:2; 5:17; Titus 1:9)—the very two activities prohibited for women, according to 1 Tim. 2:12.

Paul's instructions in 1 Cor. 11:2–16 on the adornment of women are quite controversial and difficult to grasp. Scholars differ on whether the adornment in question relates to hairstyle or to the wearing of a veil or a shawl.[54] While 1 Cor. 11:15 seems to support a reference to hairstyle, the remaining verses slightly support a reference to a shawl or veil on the head. Paul desires that women wear such a shawl because of the headship of men (1 Cor. 11:3). Some scholars maintain that Paul refers to wives in this text, but the context does not provide any clear evidence supporting a reference to wives such as we find in other texts where wives are admonished.[55] Debate also exists over whether the word "head" (*kephalē*) here means "authority over" or "source." Careful studies of the term indicate that the word regularly designates authority when used metaphorically.[56] Even if the term should be translated "source" here, the meaning of the text does not change significantly, for then women would be required to wear a shawl on their heads because men are their source. Once again Paul draws on the created order to justify a difference between men and women (1 Cor. 11:8–9).[57] The Pauline instructions are not restricted to the Corinthian situation but rather represent the practice in all the churches (1 Cor. 11:2, 16). Women are permitted and even encouraged to prophesy and pray in church (1 Cor. 11:5), but they are to do so in a manner and with a demeanor that support the created order. A difference in role between men and women does not cancel out the fundamental equality of men and women in Christ (1 Cor. 11:11–12).[58] We are reminded of Gal. 3:28, where men and women are one in Christ and have equal access to the promise of salvation. Certainly, there are

54. In support of a shawl or veil, see Fee 1987: 506–12; Keener 1992: 22–31; C. Thompson 1988; in support of hairstyle, see Hurley 1981: 254–71; Blattenberger 1997; Hays 1997: 185–86.

55. Rightly Hays 1997: 185.

56. For the meaning "authority" in the term "head," see Fitzmyer 1993a; Grudem 1985; 1991; 2001; Arnold 1994; in support of "source," see Mickelsen and Mickelsen 1986; Kroeger 1987. Cervin (1989) argues that the term means "preeminent," but even if this is correct, preeminence cannot be separated from authority in the ancient world. Hays (1997: 184) endorses egalitarianism but agrees that "head" denotes authority in this text.

57. Fee (1987: 491–530) agrees that distinctions between the sexes are enforced, but he seems to limit the differences to homosexuality. Hays (1997: 186–87, 190–92) distances himself from Paul's teaching here but warns against explaining away what is said.

58. Keenly debated is 1 Cor. 11:10. It may mean that women should wear a symbol of authority on their head, or that they should wear their hair properly and take control of their own head (Hays 1997: 187–88), or that they have authority to prophesy and pray. The last option does not fit well in the context, and the first one is the most likely.

social ramifications to the equality enjoyed by men and women in Christ. According to Paul's own writings, however, the equality between men and women does not cancel out a difference in function or role. In the same way, God is the head of Christ (1 Cor. 11:3), and Christ submits to the Father (1 Cor. 15:28), without compromising the truth that Christ is God (Rom. 9:5; Titus 2:13; cf. Phil. 2:6; Col. 1:15) and is also equal to the Father. The cultural expression in the first century of the role difference between men and women manifested itself in the wearing of a shawl.

Another much debated text regarding women is 1 Cor. 14:33b–36.[59] Paul insists that women must be silent in church. In this case he probably addresses wives, for they are instructed to ask questions of their husbands at home instead of at the private meeting. Some have argued that 1 Cor. 14:34–35 represents a later interpolation because these verses are placed after 1 Cor. 14:40 in a few Western manuscripts.[60] The interpolation theory is unpersuasive, for we can see why scribes might move the discussion of women to the end of the chapter so that Paul's words on prophecy are uninterrupted. Furthermore, there is no manuscript evidence for the omission of these verses. The command to be silent is not absolute, for Paul has already said that women can pray and prophesy if they are adorned properly (1 Cor. 11:5). Paul would scarcely go into such detail about proper adornment for prayer and prophecy if speaking in the assembly is absolutely forbidden. Nor is it compelling to say that the meetings envisioned in 1 Cor. 11:2–16 are private or home meetings rather than formal meetings of the church, for such a view is anachronistic because there is no evidence that some meetings in the early church were unofficial. Others maintain that Paul prohibits women from speaking in tongues. However, contextual evidence is lacking to narrow the prohibited speech to tongue-speaking. A more credible view is that women are banned from passing judgment on prophecy because such an activity would constitute leadership over men, which Paul rules out in 1 Tim. 2:12.[61] Although this view could be correct and fits with Paul's larger view on the relationship between men and women, the prohibition is again rather general, and evidence is again lacking for this specific reading.

It seems that the most natural reading of this text is that the women were disrupting the worship service of the church by asking questions.

59. For a discussion of the interpretive options, see Fee 1987: 699–705; Carson 1991a: 141–45; Keener 1992: 70–100; Hays 1997: 245–49; Thiselton 2000: 1150–61.

60. Payne (1995) argues that evidence from Codex Fuldensis and a "bar-umlaut" siglum in Vaticanus indicate that 1 Cor. 14:34–35 is a later interpolation. Niccum (1997) demonstrates, however, that the evidence adduced by Payne does not really support an interpolation. An interpolation is also supported by Fee (1987: 699–702), but he is successfully refuted by Thiselton (2000: 1148–49).

61. So Carson 1991a.

It is unnecessary to say that the women were sitting apart from their husbands and creating a clamor by shouting questions across the room. Apparently, the questions were voiced in a way that was challenging and abrasive. Therefore, Paul reminds the congregation of the scriptural principle that wives are to submit to their husbands. The reference to the law, then, probably is to Gen. 1–2, where the role relationship between men and women is sketched in. Paul does not demand that women be silent in the assembly in every conceivable situation. He mandates their silence in this case because their speaking issues from recalcitrant spirits that refuse to uphold order in the church.

Remaining Witnesses

In the remainder of the NT we have a few references to women. Hebrews lifts up Sarah, Rahab, and other women as exemplars of faith (Heb. 11:11, 31, 35). Sarah is commended by Peter as the model of a godly and obedient wife (1 Pet. 3:6). A false prophet, who is called Jezebel, is condemned for her deleterious teaching (Rev. 2:20–23). John takes umbrage not at this woman serving as a prophet but rather at the content of her prophecies. The "elect lady" (2 John 1) and "elect sister" (2 John 13) probably do not refer to individual women or even leaders of churches. Most scholars agree that here we have references to the church.[62]

Conclusion

The new age inaugurated by Jesus Christ clarifies that men and women are equal in Christ, that women become Abraham's children in the same way as do men: through faith in Christ Jesus (Gal. 3:26–29). Jesus treated women with remarkable dignity and encouraged women to learn his word and to become his disciples. Women were gifted as prophets, deacons, and missionaries. They labored in ministry along with men. Still, the new age in Christ did not signal an abolition of all role distinctions between men and women. Women did not function as pastors, elders, and overseers. Women and men were considered to be equal, and yet men maintained the particular responsibility of ruling in the church.

Marriage, Divorce, and Children

The Synoptic Gospels on Marriage and Divorce

The Synoptic Gospels address marriage and divorce, but the subject is omitted in John's Gospel. One longer text exists (Matt. 19:3–12; Mark

---

62. See chapter 17, note 132.

10:2–12), and then two brief sayings (Matt. 5:31–32; Luke 16:18). In the longer text the Pharisees query Jesus about divorce, and his view must be placed into the context of Jewish debates. The school of Hillel advocated a rather lax policy, interpreting Deut. 24:1–4 to permit divorce for almost any reason. We see in the life of Josephus such a policy carried out. The school of Shammai prescribed a stricter interpretation, arguing that divorce was acceptable only for serious sexual sin such as adultery. Interestingly, the Qumran community seems to have banned divorce altogether.[63]

Jesus refused to focus on when divorce is permitted and emphasizes instead the permanence of marriage. He appealed to Gen. 1:27; 2:24 to impress on his hearers that marriage is rooted in creation as part of God's good intention for human beings. The presence of a single male and a single female is significant, for it indicates that marriage is constituted by the union of one man and one woman. God did not intend marriage to be polygamous, for there was only one man and one woman in the beginning. The essence of marriage is explicated in the three elements found in Gen. 2:24: marriage involves leaving, cleaving, and one flesh. First, marriage demands leaving one's current family, so that one's family of origin is no longer primary. Second, marriage is covenantal, for the word "cleave" has covenantal associations. One cleaves to one's husband or wife, just as Israel is to cleave to the Lord and the Lord alone. One leaves one's family of origin and attaches oneself to a new covenantal bond. Third, marriage is consummated in a one-flesh union. A husband and wife become one flesh at sexual consummation, though the one-flesh union is deeper than sexual union. All three elements must exist for marriage. A man and a woman are not married merely by having sexual relations; a covenant commitment must also be included.

Jesus emphasizes that the covenant commitment of marriage is fundamental, and that such unions are not to be broken by divorce. God has joined together those who pledge themselves to one another in marriage. To break that bond is to sever what God has united, and thus it is forbidden. The divorce sayings in the teaching of Jesus emphasize, therefore, that divorce and remarriage are adulterous. Jesus did not engage in a detailed rabbinic debate in which he considered whether divorce was justified in any given case. He emblazons on the conscience the general principle that marriage is inviolable and that divorce and remarriage constitute adultery.

Nevertheless, an exception clause is found in both Matthean texts, and this clause has, of course, engendered much discussion.[64] Some have

---

63. For detailed treatments on divorce and remarriage, see Hugenberger 1998; Instone-Brewer 2002.

64. For a survey of the options and a view similar to the one argued for here, see Hays 1996: 352–56.

maintained that since the exception clause is found only in Matthew, it is Matthean rather than authentic.[65] Such a view is unlikely, for when we examine Matthew as a whole, we see that Matthean composition is marked by severity, not looseness. Others have argued that the exception relates to sexual sin in the betrothal period, and this would explain why the exception is restricted to Matthew's Gospel, for in Jewish culture to break an engagement was considered to be almost as serious as dissolving a marriage.[66] Moreover, Joseph's reaction to Mary's alleged sin in Matt. 1:18–20 could function as an illustration of an engagement being severed because of sexual sin during the betrothal period. Despite the grounding of the betrothal view in the Matthean context, the solution proposed fails to satisfy, for it is scarcely clear that the word *porneia* can be restricted to sin during the engagement period. The word *porneia* is a broad term that refers to sexual sin generally, and thus clear contextual clues would be needed in Matt. 5:31–32 or 19:3–12 if the word were to be narrowed to sexual infidelity during engagement.

The word *porneia* in the exception clauses could be defined as "incest." In that case, marriages should be dissolved if it is discovered that the consummated relationship is incestuous. The word *porneia* clearly refers to incest in 1 Cor. 5:1, and a good case can be made for such a definition in Acts 15:20, 29. Such a definition, however, is not at all persuasive in the Matthean exception clauses. We have already noted that the word *porneia* is a broad term referring to sexual immorality in general. Therefore, convincing contextual evidence is necessary in order to narrow the term to the meaning "incest." The context in 1 Cor. 5:1 provides such information, so that it is quite clear that incest is in view. Acts 15:20, 29 are more debatable, precisely because the context does not resolve the matter decisively. We have no contextual evidence, however, in Matthew that the word *porneia* should be restricted in such a way. Perhaps even more important is the fact that incestuous marriages were declared to be illegitimate. The couple did not divorce. The marriage was simply cancelled. Finally, what evidence we have suggests that incestuous marriages were quite rare in Israel, and thus it seems unlikely that Jesus would speak to a situation that was uncommon.

Another solution is proposed by Heth and Wenham. They argue that the word *porneia* is a broad term, but the exception applies syntactically to divorce but not to remarriage.[67] This means that a person may legitimately divorce for sexual immorality, but even if divorce is permis-

65. For example, Stein, *DJG* 197.

66. For a survey of the various positions regarding divorce and remarriage along with a penetrating evaluation, see Köstenberger 2004: 227–58. For further helpful discussion, see Blomberg 1990b.

67. Heth and G. Wenham 1984; so also Luz 2001: 492–94.

sible, remarriage is always excluded. The exception allows for divorce but never remarriage. Heth and Wenham appeal to the practice of the early church fathers in the first centuries to support their view. Recently Heth has abandoned this view, but Wenham stands by his initial conclusions.[68] Once again the view fails to persuade, for it is not clear syntactically that the exception clause relates to divorce but excludes remarriage. The exception clause reads more naturally if both divorce and remarriage are included.

It seems, then, that Matthew argues that marriage is indissoluble unless sexual sin occurs.[69] If there is sexual sin, then divorce is permissible. Some object that such a solution is implausible, for then Jesus' view becomes indistinguishable from that of the school of Shammai, and how then can we account for the astonishment of the disciples (Matt. 19:10–12) if Jesus' view is similar to that of Shammai? Jesus' view, however, still stands in contrast with the school of Shammai, for the latter *required* divorce for sexual sin. Jesus does not require divorce but *permits* it, and he emphasizes the indissolubility of marriage.[70] Others object that such a view contradicts Mark (Mark 10:2–12) and Luke (Luke 16:18), where any remarriage after divorce is identified as adultery. This objection fails to see that both Mark and Luke summarize Jesus' general teaching on marriage. What Jesus focuses on is the permanence of marriage. Failure to include an exception is hardly surprising, for they communicate the main point of Jesus' teaching: marriage is indissoluble. We have a helpful example that clarifies the difference between Matthew and Mark when the Pharisees and Sadducees approach Jesus and ask for a sign. In Matthew Jesus says, "An evil and adulterous generation asks for a sign, but no sign will be given to it except the sign of Jonah" (Matt. 16:4). In Mark he replies, "Truly, I say to you, no sign will be given to this generation" (Mark 8:12). Notice that the exception is omitted in Mark but is specified in Matthew. Mark relays the general principle—no sign will be given—but Matthew adds that there will be an exception. We see precisely the same pattern in the saying on divorce. Mark communicates Jesus' general teaching: marriage and divorce constitute adultery. Matthew concurs with this view but adds the exception relating to sexual infidelity.

Paul on Marriage and Divorce

Paul's view of marriage finds its roots in the OT. Those who reject marriage subscribe to demonic teaching, for marriage is part of the created

---

68. Heth 2002; G. Wenham 2002.
69. See Davies and Allison 1997: 16–17.
70. See Bockmuehl 1989.

order and represents one of God's good gifts to human beings (1 Tim. 4:1–5). Here Paul almost certainly reflects on the creation account, in which God formed Adam and Eve for one another and instituted marriage. In 1 Timothy younger women whose husbands have died are encouraged to remarry and bear children (1 Tim. 5:11–15). Apparently, some of these women had pledged themselves to a single life after the death of their husbands, but they now longed to marry and too often spent their time in gossip and unfruitful activities. One of the benefits of marriage is that it will secure these women to a productive use of their time, so that they can concentrate on raising their children and managing their households. We find a similar perspective in Titus 2:3–5. The older women are to instruct the younger women so that the latter live lives that are pleasing to God. The younger women are to love and submit to their husbands, love their children, and manage their homes in an appropriate way. They are to live morally upright lives, and in all that they do they must conduct themselves in such a way that the gospel is not vilified.

What Paul says in 1 Cor. 7 seems to contradict his advice in 1 Tim. 5, for in 1 Cor. 7 he recommends the single life, whereas in 1 Tim. 5 he advises young widows to marry. The contradiction is only apparent. Paul recommends a single life if one can be wholly devoted to the Lord and serve him in a wholehearted way (1 Cor. 7:32–35). Paul recognizes that all do not possess the gift to be single (1 Cor. 7:7, 36–40), and the widows in 1 Tim. 5 were behaving in a manner that clarified for Paul their need to remarry. What Paul says about singleness in 1 Cor. 7 is remarkable because the standard Jewish view was that all *should* marry. Paul's eschatological reservation leads to a reevaluation of the importance of marriage. Even though marriage is good because it is part of the created order, it should not be identified with the highest good. It is one of the goods of the present age that is destined to pass away. Hence, those who have the strength to remain single for the sake of the kingdom are commended and encouraged. Still, the single life is not mandated, and each person must seek the gift that God has given. A strong sexual desire may indicate that one should marry (1 Cor. 7:9, 36). In this vein, 1 Cor. 7:1–5 has often been misunderstood. Paul does not reluctantly concede that sexual relations must occur from time to time in marriage; rather, he responds to some ascetic Corinthians who believed that abstinence from sexual relations in marriage represented a higher level of spirituality.[71] Paul emphatically rejects such a view, contending that both husbands and wives belong to each other, and that their bodies are no longer their own. They have an obligation to be available for sexual relations and

---

71. So Fee 1987: 273–84; Hays 1997: 113–14.

cannot justify lifelong abstinence by trumpeting their spiritual devotion. The Pauline concession is not, therefore, that husbands and wives may have sexual relations; rather, he concedes that a couple may choose to abstain from sexual relations for a limited period of time in order to devote themselves to prayer.[72] Paul does not endorse such abstinence for short periods of time, but he does permit it. We should also observe the mutuality of the husband-wife relationship in 1 Cor. 7:3–5. We will note shortly that Paul also counsels a wife to submit to her husband. We must beware, however, of restricting Paul's understanding of the husband-wife relationship so that it becomes one-dimensional. It is evident that he also understood that husbands and wives are to relate to one another as equals and co-heirs in the gospel (cf. Gal. 3:28).

The Pauline teaching on equality and mutuality between husbands and wives does not cancel out the particular responsibilities to which husbands and wives are called. Husbands are enjoined to love their wives, and wives are called upon to submit to their husbands (Eph. 5:22–33; Col. 3:18–19). Paul's teaching on husbands and wives, parents and children, and masters and slaves forms part of what has been identified as the household code. Scholars have investigated carefully the origin of the code, and various theories have been propounded. Probably the most common view now is that the codes are modeled after Aristotelian teaching, though even in this case they are transformed by the gospel of Christ.[73] The nearest parallels, then, derive from Hellenistic Judaism (Philo, *Decalogue* 165–167; *Hypothetica* 7.14; *Spec. Laws* 2.226–227; Josephus, *Ag. Ap.* 2.190–219; Ps.-Phoc. 175–227).

The love that husbands are to have for their wives is sacrificial, modeled after Christ's love for the church (Eph. 5:25). Severity and harshness are to be excluded (Col. 3:19). Genuine love means that wives are nourished and cherished, just as one cherishes and nourishes one's own body (Eph. 5:28–30, 33). Husbands are to love their wives as their "head" (*kephalē* [Eph. 5:23]). The word "head" has stirred much discussion, and many argue that the word means "source" rather than "authority over." It is possible that the word may designate "source" in some texts (Eph. 4:15; Col. 2:19).[74] In other texts, however, it is quite clear that the term refers to the authority that one has over others (cf. Eph. 1:22; Col. 1:18; 2:10).[75] The notion of authority is also clear in Eph. 5:23, for wives are called

---

72. So Fee 1987: 283–84; Thiselton 2000: 510–11. Contra Conzelmann 1975: 118.

73. For a helpful survey of research, see O'Brien 1982: 214–19; Goppelt 1993: 162–79; Dunn 1996b: 242–46; Lincoln 1999. For an Aristotelian background, see Balch 1981; J. Elliott 2000: 504–7. Crouch (1972) argues that the household code in Colossians was intended to restrain women and slaves whose understanding of Gal. 3:28 led to social unrest.

74. So Arnold 1994.

75. See note 56 above.

upon to subject themselves "because" (*hoti*) husbands are the head. The collocation of submission and headship indicates that authority is in view. Furthermore, it is difficult to grasp in what sense husbands could be conceived of as the source of their wives, for they are not the source of their wives either physically or spiritually. Of course, this headship is not to be exercised tyrannically or abusively, since husbands are to nourish and cherish their wives. Nor do the different functions of husbands and wives signal that wives are inferior, for Christ will submit to the Father at the conclusion of history but remains equal to him in essence and dignity (1 Cor. 15:28). Nor can the relationship between husbands and wives be relegated to the culture of the first century. Paul cites the same verse about marriage from Gen. 2:24 that was quoted by Jesus in his controversy with the Pharisees (Eph. 5:31). Paul argues from this text that the relationship between husbands and wives is a mystery in that it reflects the relationship between Christ and the church. Since marriage mirrors Christ's relationship to the church, the call to the husband to love his wife and the wife to subject herself to the husband cannot be dismissed as a cultural accretion.[76]

The Pauline view of divorce is explicated in Rom. 7:2–3; 1 Cor. 7:10–16. The text in Romans does not directly address the matter of divorce. Paul uses an illustration from marriage and divorce to explain his view of the law. Even though divorce is not the main topic, Paul's use of the illustration is instructive. Marriage is binding as long as a person lives (so 1 Cor. 7:39). To remarry while one's spouse is alive constitutes adultery. Only after a spouse has died is remarriage permissible. Paul's comments in 1 Cor. 7:10–11 fit with the scenario painted in Romans. Divorce and remarriage are not options for Christians. Anyone who separates from a spouse should either remain single or seek reconciliation. The Pauline reflections on divorce could be interpreted to rule out divorce in any and every circumstance. On the other hand, it is possible that his statements could be interpreted as generalizations that allow exceptions. Paul's advice concerning those who are married to unbelievers suggests that the latter is correct (1 Cor. 7:12–16). If a believer is married to an unbeliever, the believer should not initiate the divorce. Nor should the believer worry that marriage to an unbeliever causes defilement, for the unbelieving partner is sanctified through marriage to a believer. If, however, the unbeliever forsakes the marriage, then the believer need not be troubled and feel compelled to go to extraordinary lengths to continue the marriage. The believer is called not to bondage but rather to peace. Paul clearly grants believers freedom to divorce when the unbeliever desires it. Does this freedom from the previous marriage also involve

76. So O'Brien 1999: 430–35; see also Köstenberger 1991.

permission to remarry? The language that Paul uses is unclear, and thus controversy over this matter persists. It seems most likely, however, that the dissolution of the previous marriage would also grant freedom to remarry.[77] The typical Jewish view was that divorce opened the door to a new marriage. If Paul departed from the standard view, then further clarification would have been necessary to ensure that the readers understood that remarriage was prohibited. To say in 1 Cor. 7:15 that readers are not bound to a marriage (*douloō*) falls in the same semantic range with the verb "bound" (*deō*) in 1 Cor. 7:39, suggesting that freedom from bondage also involves freedom to remarry.

Paul also requires that an overseer be "a man of one woman" (1 Tim. 3:2 my translation). The same construction in reference to women is used in 1 Tim. 5:9: "a woman of one man." Only women who fulfill this qualification are eligible for financial compensation as widows. The construction is difficult to interpret because it occurs in a listing of qualifications and without any further elaboration. Several options are possible.[78] (1) Any remarriage disqualifies one from serving as an overseer or from receiving financial compensation as a widow. The NRSV appears to endorse this view, translating the phrase in 1 Tim. 3:2; 5:9 as "married only once." Such a view is unlikely, for elsewhere Paul allows remarriage after the death of one's spouse (Rom. 7:3; 1 Cor. 7:39). It seems improbable that Paul would prohibit widows from receiving assistance if they conformed to his instructions on remarriage elsewhere. (2) What Paul forbids in 1 Tim. 3:2 is polygamy. This view fails because it does not account for the parallel expression in 1 Tim. 5:9, where Paul cannot be prohibiting polyandry, for marriage to more than one husband was unheard of in the Greco-Roman world. In addition, polygamy was quite rare in any case, and thus it is unlikely that this is what Paul precludes. (3) Those who divorce and remarry are forbidden from serving as bishops or from receiving funds as widows. This view is more plausible than the first two and quite possibly is correct. However, the exclusion of drunkards in 1 Tim. 3:3 suggests that a fourth view is correct. (4) The overseer must have a significant history of being a faithful and loving spouse, so that his marriage is respected in the community and no reproach is brought upon the church for appointing the person in question as an overseer. The requirement that an overseer not be a drunkard supports the view maintained here. When Paul says that an overseer cannot be a drunkard, he is not suggesting that the overseer could never have been a drunkard at any time in his life. His point is that the overseer must now have a long

77. So also Hays 1996: 361. Contra Fee (1987: 302–5), who thinks that remarriage is not within the purview of Paul's thinking here.

78. For a survey of options and a defense of the view suggested here, see Page 1993; Köstenberger with Jones 2004: 259–66.

and settled reputation in the community as a person of sensibility and sobriety. So too those who have demonstrated for a significant number of years that they are faithful husbands may serve as overseers.

The Petrine View of Marriage

The Petrine view on marriage seems remarkably similar to Paul's (1 Pet. 3:1–7), and thus some have believed in a shared tradition. Peter focuses on the responsibility of wives to subject themselves to husbands, perhaps because Peter particularly focuses on those who are in subordinate positions, for he addresses churches facing persecution.[79] Hence, the response of wives is paradigmatic for all believers.[80]

We should also note that Peter's focus is on wives whose husbands are unbelievers. Such husbands will not be won over to the faith by wives badgering them to believe. Wives are to influence husbands by their gentle spirits and godly behavior. In the Greco-Roman world, as today, there was a tendency to focus on outward adornment rather than moral character. Greco-Roman moralists exhorted women on this matter, such as Seneca, Dio Chrysostom, Juvenal, Plutarch, Epictetus, Pliny, Tacitus, and Ovid.[81] Peter, therefore, exhorts his readers to focus on inner beauty rather than on braided hair, flashy jewelry, and stunning clothing.[82] Like the holy women of old, they are to put their hope and trust in God and subject themselves to their husbands. This submission should flow from hope in God rather than from fear. We must keep in mind that for a wife to worship any god other than those of her husband was countercultural in the Greco-Roman world. Plutarch remarked, "The gods are the first and most significant friends. For this reason, it is proper for a wife to recognize only those gods whom her husband worships and to shut the door to superstitious cults and strange superstitions."[83] It follows, therefore, that the wife's submission cannot be absolute and without exceptions. Obviously, these wives, in devoting themselves to the Christian God, were not following their husbands in the most important arena of life. Nor does

---

79. Peter, like Paul, has in mind voluntary submission of wives, not an enforced submission by husbands (A. Spencer 2000: 109).

80. Goppelt (1993: 218–19) contends that the call to submission contradicts the fundamental equality of women. But Peter himself did not see it that way, for he identified wives as co-heirs. J. Kelly (1981: 127) rightly argues that the command derives from the creation order (see also Schelke 1980: 88).

81. Seneca, *Helv.* 16.3–4; *Ben.* 1.10.2; 7.9.4–5; Dio Chrysostom, *Ven.* 7.117; Juvenal, *Sat.* 6.457–463; 490–511; Plutarch, *Conj. praec.* 141E; Epictetus, *Ench.* 40; Tacitus, *Ann.* 3.53; Ovid, *Am.* 3.130–149.

82. Rightly Balch 1981: 101–2; Achtemeier 1996: 212; Michaels 1988: 160.

83. Plutarch, *Conj. praec.* 140D (translation from J. Elliott 2000: 557–58).

the submission demanded imply inequality, for wives are also heirs together with their husbands. They share the same eschatological destiny. Husbands are to treat their wives with generosity and tenderness, particularly because they are weaker physically, and husbands could use their physical strength to abuse, intimidate, or coerce their wives. Husbands who fail to honor their wives will find that their prayers are hindered.[84]

Parents and Children

The NT does not dwell on the relationship between parents and children.[85] Once again the understanding of the nature of the relationship is rooted in the OT Scriptures. Parents are required to love and to provide for their children (1 Thess. 2:11; Titus 2:4; cf. 2 Cor. 12:14). A good parent longs to bless children with good gifts (Matt. 7:9–11). Children often were disparaged and looked down upon in the ancient world (cf. Matt. 18:4; 19:13–14), but instead they should be valued as those whom God loves. Children are under the authority of their parents and thus are required to obey them (Eph. 6:1; Col. 3:20). Paul introduces the fifth commandment to say that children should honor their parents (Eph. 6:2). Children are undeveloped in their thinking, and so they need to mature (cf. 1 Cor. 13:11; 14:20; Eph. 4:14; cf. Luke 7:32). Hence, they must be managed and disciplined so that they will grow in godly character (1 Tim. 3:12). Parents who love their children will discipline them to the best of their ability so that children will grow in moral stature (Heb. 12:7–11). The author of Hebrews remarks that the failure to discipline a child suggests that the child is illegitimate, and thus all parents who care for their children will attend to their character. Conversely, children should respect and honor their parents, who administer discipline. Fathers need to beware of exasperating and provoking their children with relentless correction (Eph. 6:4; Col. 3:21). Otherwise, children might despair of improving and give up trying to change. The NT, then, does not recommend discipline alone, but rather discipline administered in a context of nurture, love, and instruction.

84. We should add that Hebrews contains a very brief admonition regarding marriage, enjoining the readers to honor marriage and to avoid fornication and adultery (Heb. 13:4).

85. For a thorough study of this theme that explores the NT teaching on children and considers such teaching in light of the Greco-Roman world, see Balla 2003. Balla shows that in both the Jewish and the Greco-Roman worlds the duty of children to honor their parents was expected. Nor do the so-called radical sayings of Jesus cancel out this duty, though they do reflect the view that the claims of God take precedence over what parents require.

Conclusion

Marriage, parenting, and children are part of the created order and thus will not persist in the new creation. Believers must not give their primary attachment to such relationships so that they take precedence over God himself. Still, all these relationships are good gifts of God and are not to be rejected. NT writers specify how one can please God in these various relationships.

Government

Luke-Acts

God's people are called to live in society in the interval between the coming of Jesus, with its fulfillment of God's covenantal promises in him, and the consummation of the kingdom, with its destruction of God's enemies. In this in-between time human governments impose their structure and form of rule over human beings. Luke's two-volume work reveals the stances and convictions of early Christians vis-à-vis the government.[86] It is evident that current governmental structures do not reflect the future kingdom of God. Believers await the day when evil rulers will be deposed and God will fulfill his covenant with his people (Luke 1:50–55, 68–75). Even with the fulfillment of God's covenant in the person of the Christ, the deposition of evil rulers has not been realized. The cross and resurrection precede the day when Jesus will return and subjugate all of his enemies. In the meantime government, since it is distorted by selfish ambition, continues to inflict misery upon human beings.[87] Pilate slaughtered some Galileans who had come to offer sacrifices in Jerusalem (Luke 13:1), perhaps because of their nationalistic ambitions. Herod Antipas imprisoned and eventually beheaded the Baptist for having publicly denounced Herod's sin in marrying the wife of his brother Philip (Luke 3:19–20). The Pharisees warned Jesus to flee because Herod Antipas wanted to put him to death (Luke 13:31–33). Jesus did not gloss over the venality of Antipas but rather identified him as a shrewd and calculating political operative. Jesus did not fear Herod, for Herod could not thwart the plan of God in which Jesus would die in Jerusalem. Luke implies here that God reigns and rules over the kingdoms

86. Brent (1999: 73–139) argues that Luke-Acts interacts significantly with the imperial cult, but his thesis depends on a later date for Luke-Acts (ca. AD 85) than I think is probable, and it also seems to me that he reads his thesis into Luke-Acts unsuccessfully. For the view that the imperial cult played a significant role even under Augustus, see Brent 1999: 17–72.

87. It has often been argued that Luke wrote both his Gospel and Acts as a political apology for the Christian movement, but this is unlikely (see Maddox 1982: 91–99).

of the world, even when their intentions are malicious. A similar note is sounded in Acts 4:24–28, where Ps. 2 is quoted. The governmental and religious leaders, in fulfillment of prophecy, have conspired against the Lord and his Christ. Those in power think that their evil machinations will succeed, but unwittingly they fulfill God's predestined plan, for God's saving purposes were realized in the cross of Christ, contrary to the expectations of those wielding influence. Herod Antipas put James the brother of John to death and imprisoned Peter (Acts 12:1–24). The same hatred that animated the execution of Jesus had flared up again. Nevertheless, Luke structures the chapter so that believers will take comfort in God's sovereignty and ultimate victory. When God chooses, he can free Peter from imprisonment, no matter how securely he is guarded. Most important, at the end of the day rulers such as Herod will be judged and removed. Herod arrogated to himself divine prerogatives, and so God struck him dead, demonstrating that those who slay believers will face their own day of judgment.

We noted earlier how the wickedness of Pilate revealed itself in his unwillingness to vindicate Jesus at this trial, even though he declared repeatedly that Jesus was innocent (Luke 23:4, 14, 20, 22; Acts 3:13). The Jewish leaders are also indicted for conspiring to arrest Jesus so that they could have him killed. The same pattern continues in Acts. Peter and John were inexplicably arrested and interrogated after they healed a man who was lame (Acts 4:8–12). The Sanhedrin wanted to punish the apostles, but they themselves admitted that they had no rational grounds for inflicting punishment on them (Acts 4:13–22). Similarly, the flogging of the apostles, which was a reaction to apostolic preaching on the resurrected Jesus, could not be supported on any legal basis (Acts 5:17–42). The charges against Stephen were distorted and false, and he was murdered when the Sanhedrin was seized with irrational fury (Acts 6:8–7:60).

Often in Acts the Jews incited (or attempted to incite) the townspeople or legal authorities against Paul (Acts 13:45; 14:2, 19; 17:1–9, 13; 18:12–17). In Philippi the Roman authorities had Paul and Silas flogged (Acts 16:19–40). Upon discovering that justice has been miscarried because they had flogged Roman citizens, the magistrates entreated Paul and Silas to leave the city. Paul insisted, however, that the magistrates apologize and admit that they had acted illegally. Paul was not motivated by revenge; he demanded that the magistrates apologize so that no precedent would be established whereby governing authorities would feel justified in flogging preachers of the gospel.[88] Thereby Paul would still have opportunity to proclaim the good news to the

---

88. Barrett (1998: 802) observes that the story serves "as a warning to magistrates."

ends of the earth. When Paul was pounced upon and beaten in the temple, the alleged reason for the attack lacked basis, for Paul had not brought a Gentile into the temple (Acts 21:29). The tribune acknowledged that the charges against Paul did not warrant imprisonment or death (Acts 23:29).[89] Paul proceeded to defend his good behavior before the procurator Felix, who obviously believed that the charges against Paul were baseless (Acts 24:10–27). Similarly, when Festus explained Paul's situation to King Agrippa, he conceded that Paul had done nothing deserving death and even admitted that he could not think of any charges to send on to Caesar (Acts 25:22–27). The injustice of Paul's incarceration is blatant if civil authorities could not provide a reason for his trial. After Paul presented his case before Agrippa, Festus, and others, the consensus was that he had done nothing justifying death or imprisonment (Acts 26:31). Indeed, the political authorities conceded that had Paul not appealed to Caesar, he would have been freed (Acts 26:32; cf. 28:17–20).

What we see in Luke and Acts is that civil authorities often acted contrary to justice in their treatment of Jesus and his disciples. The governing authorities certainly are not portrayed as paragons of virtue. We also see, at the same time, that Christians do not constitute a political threat to the empire.[90] Believers were not engaging in illegal activity, and the charges against them were trumped up or lacked a credible foundation.

Not every text paints governing authorities in a bad light. Luke recognizes the goodness of the centurion whose slave was healed by Jesus (Luke 7:1–10). The centurion Cornelius was a righteous and good man, and he received the gift of salvation (Acts 10:1–11:18). The proconsul Sergius Paulus responded positively to the gospel (Acts 13:5–12). Similarly, there are instances in which the government recognizes what is just and acts accordingly. When the Jews brought charges against Paul, inciting the proconsul Gallio so that he might take action against Paul, Gallio dismissed the charges and scolded the Jews for bringing internecine religious disputes into the political realm (Acts 18:12–17). Demetrius, a silversmith who made shrines for Artemis, precipitated a riot against Paul and his co-workers in Ephesus (Acts 19:23–41). Officials from the province were friendly to Paul and entreated him not to make an appearance before the out-of-control crowd (Acts 19:31). Luke somewhat humorously informs the reader that most members of this crowd had no idea what all the screaming and shouting was about (Acts 19:32). The town clerk defended Paul and his companions, noting that no evidence

89. Rightly Fitzmyer 1998: 728; Barrett 1998: 1084.
90. But as Barrett (1998: 1) notes, this can hardly function as the purpose of the book.

of wrongdoing had been produced, and that normal legal means existed to resolve any dispute (Acts 19:37–39). The riot might bring the wrath of Rome upon Ephesus because no basis existed for the activity (Acts 19:40). The reasoned discourse of the town clerk restored order, demonstrating that governing authorities exist to prevent anarchy.

Despite the injustice of ruling authorities, Luke gives no indication that Christians should induce violent revolt. Joseph and Mary obeyed the census and returned to Joseph's hometown to register in accordance with the decree promulgated (Luke 2:1–7). We also see in this text the working out of God's purposes, for the census functions as the means by which the prophecy was fulfilled that Jesus would be born in Bethlehem (cf. Mic. 5:2). Most significantly, Jesus counseled his followers to pay taxes to Caesar (Luke 20:20–26).[91] Therefore, Jesus did not side with some who argued that paying taxes to Caesar compromised God's lordship and was tantamount to idolatry.[92] Nor did Jesus deify Caesar, for he taught that people must give God his due. Surely this means that God demands supreme allegiance and devotion, so that if a decision comes between obeying God and human authorities, God must be obeyed (Acts 5:29).[93]

We will not revisit texts in the other Gospels that substantially echo what we have found in Luke-Acts. Luke-Acts gives us the fullest portrait, but the other Gospels do not stand in tension with what we find in Luke-Acts. The wickedness of rulers is apparent in Matthew. Herod tried to discern from the magi where and when Jesus was born so that he could put to death the promised heir (Matt. 2:1–19). When the magi failed to return, Herod slaughtered all infants aged two years and younger in the environs of Bethlehem. Although this event is not documented elsewhere, it fits perfectly with Herod's character, for he was well known for executing some of his children and his wife, Mariamne. The sovereignty of God also shines in this situation, for even though Herod the Great schemed to destroy the Messiah, his plot failed and God's purposes were accomplished. Herod's sons were not a remarkable improvement. When Joseph learned that Archelaus was the ruler of Judea, he relocated to Galilee instead (Matt. 2:22). The other son, Herod Antipas, displayed his character in imprisoning and killing John the Baptist (Matt. 14:1–12; Mark 6:14–29).

---

91. For a clear survey of the interpretive options, see Fitzmyer 1985: 1292–94. Jesus bested his adversaries in the argument, for he showed that they carried and used the coin with Caesar's image, while he himself did not have it (so Fitzmyer 1985: 1291).

92. See Josephus, *J.W.* 2:118.

93. See Marshall (1978b: 736), who argues that Jesus grounds "obedience to the earthly ruler in obedience to God—the law of God requires that men obey his delegated authority on earth."

The Pauline Literature

Pride of place in the Pauline view of government belongs to Rom. 13:1–7. Even if Titus 3:1 were judged to be post-Pauline, the sentiment expressed there fits with Rom. 13:1–7.[94] Believers are enjoined to submit to governing authorities.[95] Despite the protests of a few scholars, the authorities here do not include angelic powers.[96] Submission to demonic powers is unthinkable for Paul (cf. Col. 2:8–15), and obviously taxes are paid to civil authorities, not angels. Paul emphasizes that rulers have been appointed and instituted by God. Seeing God as the one who ordains rulers is hardly a novel insight. Paul reaches back here to the OT, where God's sovereignty over rulers is regularly taught (2 Sam. 12:8; Prov. 8:15–16; Isa. 45:1; Jer. 27:5–6; Dan. 2:21, 37; 4:17, 25, 32; 5:21; cf. Wis. 6:1–3; Sir. 17:17; *Let. Aris.* 219, 224; Josephus, *J.W.* 2.140).

God's sovereignty is illustrated in the raising up of Pharaoh (Rom. 9:17).[97] We see the same truth in 2 Thessalonians. The man of lawlessness will arrive, deifying himself and opposing the one true God (2 Thess. 2:3–8). Nonetheless, he will not appear until the restrainer is removed (2 Thess. 2:6–7).[98] The restraint upon evil is imposed by God himself, and thus in this text we are informed that the evil ruler will arrive at a time that God ordains. Even though Paul locates the raising up of Pharaoh and the arrival of the man of lawlessness in the will of God, he does not conclude from this that God is responsible for evil, nor does he exempt Pharaoh or the man of lawlessness from responsibility for their evil actions. God sovereignly ordains what occurs, and yet he is not stained by any evil. Moreover, the man of lawlessness and Pharaoh are held responsible for their evil behavior.

Believers are called upon to submit to authorities (cf. Titus 3:1) because they sustain order in society by punishing evil and commending what is good. Rulers have the right and duty to use the sword to enforce justice against those who practice evil (Rom. 13:4). It is likely that the

94. Occasionally scholars have argued that Rom. 13:1–7 represents a later interpolation (e.g., Kallas 1965; Schmithals 1975: 175–87), but such a view has not gained currency in NT scholarship.

95. The word "submit" cannot be diluted to mean "deference," "respect," or "respectful cooperation with others" (contra Achtemeier 1996: 182; Michaels 1988: 124; A. Spencer 2000: 110). Note how the verb "obey" is in the same semantic range as "submit" in 1 Pet. 3:5–6. Rightly Grudem 1988b: 135–37; Goppelt 1993: 224n44. See also Kamlah 1970: 240–41.

96. Contra Cullmann 1956: 95–114; Wink 1984: 46–47.

97. This paragraph follows Schreiner 2001: 449.

98. Wanamaker (1990: 254–57) argues that the verb *katechō* should be rendered "prevail," and that the one who prevails until removed from the scene is the Roman emperor. For a survey of options, see Morris 1959: 224–27; Marshall 1983: 193–200; Beale 1999b: 213–18.

reference to the sword refers to capital punishment, which is enacted upon those who kill with malice aforethought.[99] Again Paul draws upon OT tradition, especially Gen. 9:6. The reference to taxes in Rom. 13 may be accounted for by high taxes that provoked controversy during Nero's reign,[100] but in any case Paul addresses the issue generally instead of dwelling upon circumstances in Rome.

Occasionally Rom. 13:1–7 has almost been accepted as a treatise, as if Paul comprehensively speaks of the relationship that believers should have with ruling authorities. However, we must recall that the admonition is quite brief and was originally written to the Roman churches. Paul did not intend to examine the role of government in any detail. Hence, the exhortations in this text cannot support the claim that in every possible situation the government must be obeyed. The call to submit represents the normal way that believers should respond to civil rulers. Believers should not be inclined to take umbrage and resist those in authority; rather, they are to respond deferentially and submissively to what is mandated. Paul was well aware from his own experience as a missionary that those in power could act unjustly and thereby promote evil rather than good. The story of Jesus' trial and execution itself represented a miscarriage of justice. Furthermore, the text is forced to say more than it intends if unrestricted authority is assigned to governments. It was simply not Paul's purpose to specify the cases in which faithfulness to God would demand contravention of what the government ordained.

1 Peter

The perspective on government in 1 Pet. 2:13–17 is quite similar to what we find in Romans, which explains why some scholars think that the author draws on Pauline traditions or that Romans and 1 Peter share a common tradition. Peter does not say that rulers are ordained by God; instead, he emphasizes that believers should submit to governing authorities. As in Rom. 13, the government exists to punish evildoers and praise those who practice goodness. Hence, the government exists to prevent anarchy and lawlessness from overwhelming society. Even the worst governments provide some restraint upon evildoers. In his first letter Peter addresses a church facing criticism and persecution, and he does not want believers to exacerbate the situation by rebelling against the current government. Believers should be known for their good behavior and exemplary citizenship. Their obedience does not stem from servility or obsequiousness, for believers are free in Christ. Such freedom, however, should not become a platform for evil and licentiousness but

---

99. In support of a reference to capital punishment, see Schreiner 1998: 684–85.
100. See Schreiner 1998: 686.

rather should be used for good. Believers should honor the emperor and all people. Once again Peter does not raise the question of exceptions but rather conveys the ordinary response of believers to political power.

Revelation

John, in Revelation, looks at government from another perspective.[101] The city of Rome represents Babylon with all its greed, love of luxury, and immorality (Rev. 17:1–19:10). Most significantly, Babylon spills the blood of the saints (Rev. 17:6; 18:24; 19:2). Believers lived in a context in which the governing authority oppressed them and even put them to death (Rev. 2:13; 6:9–11; 20:4; cf. 3:10). Satan likely finds a home in Pergamum because the emperor cult was practiced there (Rev. 2:13).[102] The Roman Empire is presented not as a model of justice and righteousness but rather as a rapacious and inhuman beast that tramples upon and mistreats God's people (Rev. 13:1–18). The image of the beast hails from Dan. 7, where the kingdoms of the world are portrayed as inhuman beasts that wreak havoc upon their subjects. The beast of Revelation combines the evil characteristics of all the beasts of Dan. 7, so that the Roman Empire is viewed as the culmination and climax of the evil rule of human beings.[103] What stands out particularly is that the beast of Revelation demands supremacy and worship, so that it stands as an apparent rival to Almighty God and the Lamb. The beast has its own prophet speaking on its behalf (Rev. 13:11–18), and it lays claim to its own resurrection (Rev. 13:3).[104] As Bauckham observes, we have the unholy trinity of the dragon, the first beast, and the second beast, with the dragon giving his authority to the first beast (as the Father grants his authority to Christ), and the second beast summoning all to worship the first (as the Spirit glorifies Christ).[105] The beast wields its power over believers, persecuting and slaying those who oppose it (Rev. 13:7).

101. See Cullmann 1956: 71–85.

102. The influence of the emperor cult in the NT is disputed. For a helpful introduction, see Cuss 1974. For the role of the cult in Asia Minor, see Price 1984. For the view that the cult played a major role in Revelation, see Brent 1999: 164–209.

103. Most scholars argue that the number 666 in Rev. 13:18 refers to Nero. Bauckham (1993b: 384–452) argues that John historicizes the apocalyptic traditions regarding the return of Nero.

104. The second beast, or the prophet, may here refer to the priesthood of the emperor cult (so Price 1984: 197). So also Caird 1966: 17; Bauckham 1993b: 446. R. Mounce (1977: 259) thinks that the reference is either to the priesthood for the emperor cult or "the provincial council responsible for enforcing emperor worship throughout Asia" (so also Beale 1999b: 717). Osborne (2002: 510) argues that the reference transcends the priesthood promoting the imperial cult.

105. Bauckham 1993b: 434. The entire discussion by Bauckham (1993b: 431–41) on christological parody here is remarkably insightful.

Whereas Paul focuses on government as an entity that restrains evil, John emphasizes the satanic and demonic character of government. The problem with Rome and every government is the desire for totalitarian rule. Lurking behind the government's demand for absolute commitment and submission is Satan himself, who uses government to advance his own ends in order to procure worship of himself.

It might appear that Revelation represents government run riot as it exercises its insatiable appetite over the lives of others. Indeed, Rome's power comes from Satan himself (Rev. 13:4). Nevertheless, God reigns sovereignly over all the beast does, so that the beast accomplishes nothing apart from God's will. Revelation often refers to God's throne, highlighting the truth that he rules over all (e.g., Rev. 1:4; 3:21). The entirety of Rev. 4 focuses on God as creator and thus as the sovereign one. So too Jesus is the ruler of the kings of the earth (Rev. 1:5). Even in Rev. 13, which features the beast's rule on earth, John repeatedly remarks that the authority that belongs to the beast "was given" (*edothē*) to him. Most likely, this verbal form is a divine passive, emphasizing that whatever limited authority the beast has was granted by God himself.[106] Hence, God allowed him to blaspheme (Rev. 13:5), to rule for forty-two months over the entire world (Rev. 13:5, 7), and to conquer the saints and put them to death (Rev. 13:7). Even the abilities and miracles of the false prophet were given to him (Rev. 13:14–15). But although God rules over all, evil cannot be ascribed to him. The intentions and motives of Satan and the beast are malicious, but God's intentions and motives are perfect, even though he ultimately reigns and rules over all that happens. John attempts no philosophical defense of how God can rule over all things while remaining untainted by evil. He simply assumes that God rules over all and yet at the same time affirms that the evil inflicted by Satan and the beast is horrific and deserving of judgment by God.

Conclusion

Believers await the day when God's reign over the world will be consummated. In the meantime God has ordained governing authorities to prevent anarchy and to regulate lawlessness, so that a measure of peace and order exists in the world. Believers are called upon to submit to these authorities unless the authorities mandate something that God forbids. NT writers are not naïve about the venality and evil of governing powers. In both Luke-Acts and Revelation the profound evil and even demonic character of the state is unmasked. The *pax Romana* certainly was not the whole story behind Roman rule! Nevertheless, believers are

---

106. So R. Mounce 1977: 254; Beale 1999b: 695; Osborne 2002: 499; Caird 1966: 167.

not encouraged to adopt a revolutionary mind-set, as if they could usher in the kingdom of God through political change. They are to pay taxes and ordinarily subordinate themselves to authority. Still, their ultimate devotion is to God himself and Jesus as Lord, and thus any governmental demand for unconditional loyalty must be resisted.

Slavery[107]

Slavery was quite common in the Greco-Roman world.[108] It has been estimated that the ratio of slave to free in the Roman Empire was 1:5. If the population during the time of Augustus was fifty to sixty million, then ten to twelve million were slaves. People did not become slaves only through being captured in war, though being defeated in war was one of the primary paths to slavery. Slavery was also forced on people through kidnapping, or many were born into a household of slaves. In some instances those suffering economic difficulties would sell themselves into slavery.[109] Others were purchased as slaves or were enslaved because of their crimes. Many slaves lived miserably, particularly those who toiled in mines. Other slaves, however, served as doctors, teachers, managers, musicians, artisans, barbers, cooks, shopkeepers, and they could even own other slaves.[110] In some instances slaves were better educated than their masters. Those who are familiar with slavery from the history of the United States must beware of imposing that historical experience on NT times, for slavery in the Greco-Roman world was not based on race, and American slaveholders discouraged the education of slaves. Still, slaves in the Greco-Roman world were under the control of their masters and thus had no independent existence.[111] They could suffer brutal mistreatment at the hands of their owners, and children born in slavery belonged to masters rather than the parents who gave them birth. Slaves had no legal rights, and masters could beat them, brand them, and abuse them physically and sexually. Harrill remarks, "Despite claims by some NT scholars, ancient slavery was not more humane than modern slavery."[112] Seneca's observation exposes the evil of slavery: "You may take [a slave] in chains and at your pleasure expose

107. On slavery in the ancient world, see Bartchy 1973: 37–120; *DLNT* 1098–1102; D. Martin 1990: 1–49; Harrill 1995: 11–67. The following material on slavery represents minor revisions of Schreiner 2003: 135–36; 2001: 435.

108. The statistics that follow are from Harris 1999: 34. For his survey of slavery in the Roman Empire, see Harris 1999: 25–45.

109. See Harrill 1995: 30–42.

110. See Harrill 1995: 47.

111. See Bartchy, *ABD* 6:66.

112. Harrill (1995: 95–99) criticizes in particular the work of Bartchy here.

him to every test of endurance; but too great violence in the striker has often dislocated a joint, or left a sinew fastened in the very teeth it has broken. Anger has left many a man crippled, many disabled, even when it found its victim submissive" (*Ira* 3.27.3).[113] Ancient slavery was doubtless cruel and often oppressive, but it does not follow that all masters were cruel.[114] Slaves could purchase their freedom in the Greco-Roman world with the help of their masters, a procedure called manumission. Manumission, according to Harrill, was available mainly for urban slaves, but most slaves had no prospect for it. Harris, on the other hand, provides convincing evidence that manumission was quite common, even if manumission did not bring complete freedom from one's master.[115]

The two writers in the NT who give admonitions relative to slavery are Peter (1 Pet. 2:18–25) and Paul. Peter admonishes slaves to submit to their masters, even if their masters are cruel and unjust. Those who suffer evil as slaves, though living lives that are morally commendable, will be rewarded by God. Slaves who live in such a way imitate Christ, who also suffered unjustly and entrusted his life to the God who will pronounce final judgment. Even though Peter addresses slaves, it is likely that the exhortation given to slaves applies analogously to all the members of the churches, for the theme of the letter is the proper response to suffering.[116] The words to slaves, then, function as a model for how to respond to a situation in which one is mistreated. Peter does not consider whether the institution of slavery is fitting in society, but he does not write as a powerful member of society addressing the responsibility of social inferiors. He writes as a fellow believer and one who also suffers for the gospel (1 Pet. 5:1). He writes as one who has no political or social influence. The churches addressed represent tiny outposts of believers dwarfed by the larger society. The social situation inhabited by Peter and the church in the first century precluded any political critique of the institution. Interestingly, however, Revelation's indictment of Rome for its materialism and licentiousness includes the practice of buying and selling human beings (Rev. 18:13), suggesting that such a practice is dehumanizing.[117]

113. I owe this reference to J. Elliott 2000: 521.

114. See the balanced survey in Harris 1999: 41–44.

115. Harris 1999: 40–41; cf. Harrill 1995: 53–56. Harrill (1995: 75) remarks, "Urban manumission under Roman rule was a regular and frequent occurrence." Harrill (1995: 94, 100) criticizes Bartchy for saying that slaves could not refuse manumission. But Harris (1999: 60–61) argues that Bartchy rightly says that masters decided whether slaves would be free.

116. So Achtemeier 1996: 196–97; Michaels 1988: 135.

117. See Osborne 2002: 650; Beale 1999b: 910.

Paul's eschatological reserve is central in discerning his view on slavery. Hence, one's social standing or class was rather insignificant. The present age is temporary and soon passing away, and thus whether one is slave or free is of little importance (1 Cor. 7:29–31). Indeed, Paul believes that God has "assigned" (*emerisen* [1 Cor. 7:17]) the calling (1 Cor. 7:17, 20, 24) for each person. Therefore slaves should not worry about their status as slaves (1 Cor. 7:21). What really matters is that slaves are free in Christ;[118] conversely, citizens who are free need to remember that they are slaves of Christ (1 Cor. 7:22). Social status is not to be prized; what is crucial is that believers live out their redemption in Christ (1 Cor. 7:23).[119] Believers are not to become slaves to the people of this world. As Rom. 6:15–23 emphasizes, they are to be slaves of righteousness instead of slaves of wickedness.

When Paul asserts in Gal. 3:28 that there is neither slave nor free, he is not denying the social realities of the Greco-Roman world. His instructions to slaves in Ephesians (Eph. 6:5–9), Colossians (Col. 3:22–4:1), and Philemon reveal that he was no revolutionary; the social pattern of Greco-Roman society is maintained. At the same time the Pauline gospel transforms the social world in that slavery was viewed in a new way. Paul treats slaves as human beings and exhorts them as believers to live in a way that is pleasing to God. He addresses them not as chattel or property but rather as individuals who are to respond to the gospel of Jesus Christ. In Christ Jesus it is irrelevant whether one is slave or free. Belonging to Christ is the fundamental and decisive reality. We should not conclude that Paul's view of slavery was bereft of concrete social consequences. Recognizing that a slave is a brother or sister in Christ would certainly transform how that individual was treated. The social stratification of this world is only temporary. Hence, believers should not live as if it were ultimate, as if it says anything of great significance about a fellow believer. If believers disdained and scorned slaves because of their social standing, they would thereby reveal that they had capitulated to the present evil age instead of setting their hopes on the age to come. Christ has immersed both slaves and free in the Spirit (1 Cor. 12:13). In the new Adam whether one is a Gentile or a Jew, circumcised or uncircumcised, a member of the lower social classes like barbarians, or part of the despised Scythians, or even slave or free is irrelevant (Col.

---

118. The themes touched on below are beautifully worked out in Harris 1999.

119. Contra D. Martin (1990: 51–68), who maintains that slavery to Christ is used to designate leadership and status improvement. Harris (1999: 128–31) rightly commends Martin for his research and for seeing that the term *doulos* could be used with a positive nuance. But the notion that in Paul's view slavery signifies the improvement of status is unconvincing, and Martin downplays the servility associated with slavery, a servility that most readers would hear in the word *doulos*.

3:11). The new Adam, Christ, encompasses all. Both masters and slaves are brothers and sisters in the Lord. In the believing community there are two defective ways of thinking, and both flow from the same mistaken mind-set. Some might think highly of themselves because of their distinguished social class, while others might rue their fate because they were slaves. Paul rejects both conclusions. What matters is the gift of the Spirit and belonging to Christ as the second Adam. Those who belong to Christ are members of the new humanity, the new man—Christ. The old humanity is part and parcel of the evil age that is passing away.

It does not follow from this that life in this world is irrelevant or a mirage. Paul encourages slaves to avail themselves of freedom if this is possible (1 Cor. 7:21).[120] We have specific evidence, it seems, that Paul does not commend slavery. If believers can free themselves from servitude, they should do so.[121] Nevertheless, what Paul emphasizes is the insignificance of one's social position before God. Paul reminds the Corinthians that God typically bypasses intellectuals, the powerful, and the elite (1 Cor. 1:26–28). God has chosen those who are intellectually inferior in the eyes of the world, those who are socially powerless, and those who are from the lower classes.

In Paul's letter to Philemon we see how he works out the relationship between a master and his slave. The exhortation to receive Onesimus back "no longer as a slave but more than a slave, a beloved brother" (Philem. 16) suggests that Onesimus was Philemon's slave. That Philemon exercised authority over Onesimus is apparent from a number of other clues: the latter was formerly "useless" to Philemon, but now a change is envisioned (Philem. 11); Paul needs Philemon's consent regarding the future of Onesimus (Philem. 14); and Paul promises to repay any debt incurred because of Onesimus (Philem. 18–19). What is more difficult, probably impossible, to resolve are the circumstances that brought Onesimus to Paul.[122] Was he a fugitive running from Philemon, and did he accidentally run into Paul? Or, was he fleeing from Philemon

120. For a detailed examination of the history of interpretation, along with a fresh investigation of the syntax and context of 1 Cor. 7:21, see Harrill 1995: 68–128. His results demonstrate that Paul calls upon slaves to avail themselves of freedom if the opportunity arises (see also Fee 1987: 315–18; Harris 1999: 60–61). Harrill (1995: 194) translates the verse, "You were called as a slave. Do not worry about it. But if you can indeed become free, *use instead* freedom." Bartchy (1973: 155–59) maintains, on the other hand (but unconvincingly), that the verse teaches that manumitted slaves should live as freedmen in harmony with God's calling. See also the lengthy discussion by Thiselton (2000: 553–59), who says the point is that one must use one's present situation.

121. This is contrary to the view of some commentators who argue that in 1 Cor. 7:21 Paul exhorts slaves to remain in their slavery (so Barrett 1968: 170–71; Conzelmann 1975: 127).

122. For the view that Onesimus was not a fugitive, see Dunn 1996b: 301–7.

and intentionally going to Paul for help? Some think that Philemon sent him to Paul, but if this is the case, he apparently was reluctant to return home. As is so often the case in Pauline letters, we must admit that we do not, and ultimately cannot, know the answers to these questions. Paul and Philemon were well aware of the situation, and thus no elaboration is provided in the letter itself. We do know that Onesimus was Philemon's slave, that he encountered Paul, that he was converted under Paul's ministry (suggesting at the least that he sought out Paul [Philem. 10]), that he ministered to Paul in prison, and that Paul felt obligated to send him back to Philemon.

What leaps out to a modern-day reader is that Paul nowhere explicitly asks Philemon to liberate Onesimus, though some see this as implied in the letter. Similarly, 1 Tim. 6:2 is most plausibly read as an injunction for slaves to obey believing masters precisely because such masters are part of the family of God.[123] Nor did Paul advise Christian masters to free their Christian slaves. He exhorts masters and slaves to comport themselves well as Christians in their respective stations of life. We must keep in mind that Paul was not nurtured in the political traditions of the modern Western world. Ending an institution such as slavery, even in the Christian community, probably never entered Paul's mind, for evidence is lacking that people in Paul's day considered ending slavery. In any case, a public campaign by the fledgling Christian movement to eradicate slavery would have been futile. The political wherewithal to accomplish such an aim was totally lacking. On the other hand, we must also emphasize that the Christian movement did not institute or create slavery.[124] Slavery was an accepted social institution in the Greco-Roman world, and believers had to interact with the world as it was and could not construct a dreamy utopia of a new social system in the midst of the hard realities of life in the ancient world. Indeed, many slaves presumably would have lost the only means available to them for financial survival if they had repudiated slavery as a system.[125]

We have already noted that 1 Cor. 7:21 indicates that Paul prefers freedom for believers, implying that he did not endorse slavery as a social system. The Pauline view may be traced back to the OT, where enslaving a fellow Hebrew is frowned upon (Exod. 21:2–11; Neh. 5:5). Contrasting Paul's perspective on slavery with his view of marriage and the family is

---

123. So Dibelius and Conzelmann 1972: 82; Knight 1992: 246–47; Marshall 1999: 630–33; W. Mounce 2000: 328–29.

124. Rightly Harris 1999: 61–62. Harris goes on to say that even slaves in the Greco-Roman world never imagined a world in which slavery would cease to exist.

125. Harris (1999: 67) speaks of "a vast mass of persons suddenly unemployed and without the means of self-support."

instructive. Paul locates the role differences between men and women in the created order, in the good world that God initiated before the fall into sin. The different functions of men and women are not ascribed to sin. He traces back their different functions to God's intention in creation, just as he rejects homosexuality because it violates the created order. Similarly, the relationship between parents and children is rooted in creation. God intended Adam and Eve to be fruitful and multiply (Gen. 1:28), and thus from the inception of the world the responsibility of parents to nurture children is enforced. The entrance of sin, of course, impinges upon the relationship between men and women and between parents and children. Abuses and distortions are now introduced that did not exist in the world before the fall into sin. When Paul addresses husbands and wives and parents and children, he particularly warns those with "more power" to beware of abusing their leadership responsibilities, for he is keenly aware of how easily those with power are liable to mistreat those under their responsibility. Nevertheless, nowhere does Paul suggest that marriage or the family as institutions are inherently defective. He grounds them in the created order, seeing them as a fitting and good part of life in this world.

Paul nowhere locates, on the other hand, the institution of slavery in the created order. Nothing in Gen. 1–2 suggests that slavery is God's intention for some human beings. Indeed, if one were to argue from Gen. 1–2, the contrary conclusion should be drawn. Paul never criticizes slavery directly, but neither does he ground it in creation as he does the relationship between men and women and the institutions of marriage and the family. The kidnapping and selling of slaves is considered to be a heinous crime and contrary to the gospel (1 Tim. 1:9–11; cf. Deut. 24:7).[126] He does not specifically recommend the elimination of slavery, but neither does he endorse it. As Harris says, "Toleration is not the same as approval. Apostolic directives about the conditions of slavery should not be read as approval of slavery as an institution."[127]

We have no direct word in Philemon regarding Paul's oral instructions to Onesimus, but we can conclude from the letter that he exhorted

126. See Harris 1999: 53–54.
127. Harris 1999: 62. Harris (1999: 62) proceeds to say that the "distinction between acceptance and endorsement, between toleration and approval, is not a case of scholastic casuistry or semantic gymnastics." Harris (1999: 62–65) supports his argument with three reasons. First, we have other instances where a practice is tolerated but not commended. For instance, divorce is permitted in some instances but is never recommended or conceived of as the ideal. Second, the NT writings did not approve of slavery but rather addressed slaves as human beings responsible to the Lord and warned masters of abusing their power. Third, the oneness of all believers in Christ undercuts the institution of slavery at its heart.

him to return to Philemon, to submit to the latter's authority, and to be a useful and helpful slave. These instructions fit with the exhortations given to slaves elsewhere. The exhortations for slaves in Ephesians and Colossians are remarkably similar (Eph. 6:5–8; Col. 3:22–25). Slaves are called upon to obey their masters. Not only are slaves to submit to masters (cf. Titus 2:9), but also they are to do their work in a wholehearted way, doing the best job that they can. Titus fills out what doing a good job entails (Titus 2:9–10). They should not contradict their masters, nor should they misappropriate funds from them; they should be slaves whom their masters can trust. By doing so they would show unbelieving masters the beauty of the gospel. Similarly in 1 Tim. 6:1 slaves are summoned to honor their unbelieving masters so that God's name and the gospel will not be besmirched in the eyes of the world.

In Ephesians and Colossians slaves are commanded to obey their masters out of fear of the Lord, for the former should have a wholehearted desire to please and honor him in whatever they do (Eph. 6:5–8; Col. 3:22–25). We see that a central theme of Paul's theology emerges in his admonition to slaves. They are to glorify and honor God in all that they do. Slaves who obey their masters are promised an eternal inheritance (Col. 3:24; cf. Eph. 6:8).

Admonitions for masters are notable for their brevity (Eph. 6:9; Col. 4:1), presumably because fewer masters than slaves existed in the early Christian community. Paul warns masters against abusing their authority. He is well aware that those who possess authority are prone to use their social position to oppress those beneath them. Masters must desist from threatening in a domineering and imperious way, as if they are the ultimate authority in the lives of slaves. For masters too have the same Lord in heaven, and he is impartial and will judge them if they mistreat their slaves. Thus masters must do what is right and grant what is fair to their slaves, and, like slaves, they are to conduct their work as masters out of reverence for Christ.

In summary, slavery is never commended as an institution, for it is not rooted in the created order or God's intention for human beings. Still, early Christians did not criticize the institution per se, nor did they advocate overthrowing it. Slavery exists in the present evil world before the consummation of the end, but a new creation is coming in which slavery and all other evils will vanish. In the meantime, believing slaves are to submit to their masters and thereby commend the gospel in the social situation in which they resided. If they are able to gain their freedom, they should do so, but one's social status should not be prized or despised, for the present scheme of the world is passing away.

Conclusion

What stands out when we consider the social world of first-century Christians is the eschatological perspective on the reality of everyday life. No gift or pleasure in this world, whether it relates to riches or marriage, is to be elevated as supreme, for the present evil age will not last forever. Believers look forward to the age to come, to the new creation, and to the heavenly city where righteousness dwells. They realize that they are exiles and sojourners on this earth. Hence, no human government, even one as powerful as Rome, will last forever. When we consider the status of women and slaves, we note that the NT writers did not advocate toppling the social system of the day. Still, both women and slaves were prized as human beings made in the image of God. The social hierarchy that exists during the present age will not endure. A new world is coming in which the old things will have passed away. The eschatological perspective on social issues, then, fits with the God-centeredness of the NT vision. What matters during one's temporary earthly sojourn is not one's social position but rather one's relationship to God. The supremacy of God and the centrality of Christ should manifest themselves in the way Christians live in the warp and woof of their everyday lives. Thereby others would see that there is something greater than sexual pleasure, political power, or earthly comfort. The kingdoms of the world will fade, and the kingdom of the Lord and his Christ will remain.

19

❀ ❀ ❀ ❀ ❀ ❀ ❀ ❀ ❀ ❀ ❀ ❀ ❀ ❀ ❀ ❀ ❀ ❀

The Consummation of God's Promises

Introduction

We have seen in this book that the already–not yet pervades the NT and is crucial for understanding NT theology. God's promises have been fulfilled with the coming of Jesus Christ, in his ministry, death, and resurrection. The resurrection of Jesus Christ and the pouring out of the Spirit signal the arrival of the age to come. Even though the new creation, the new exodus, and the coming age have arrived, they have not been consummated. Death has not yet been extinguished as the last enemy. Satan still afflicts the people of God, and suffering still characterizes the existence of God's people. Not only so, but Christians still struggle against sin and are not yet free from it entirely. Indeed, the old creation persists, so that it too groans as it awaits liberation from the tentacles of sin and death (Rom. 8:18–25). Hence, the final fulfillment of God's promises is essential so that the universe will reach its intended goal. The in-between times will end, and the glory of God as Father, Son, and Spirit will shine forever.

In the NT the coming of Jesus, the future salvation and reward of his people, and the final judgment are closely linked. For the sake of clarity I will separate them into distinct topics. Nevertheless, we must keep in mind that ultimately the three are interrelated, and thus there inevitably will be some overlap in the discussion. When Jesus returns, the consummation and fulfillment of all of God's saving promises will be realized. The promised reward for believers will be given, and the judgment threatened for those who refuse to believe and obey will be executed. Both God and the Lamb will be worshiped forever by the saints, and the sufferings and groanings of the old creation will pass away.

The Coming of Jesus

The Synoptic Gospels and Acts

In considering the coming of Jesus, we will consider the Synoptic Gospels together because their teachings overlap considerably, and I will insert what Acts says with the Synoptics because Luke and Acts were written by the same author. From there, John's Gospel and the Johannine Epistles along with Revelation will be examined, then the Pauline literature, and the General Epistles.

The Synoptics warn readers that they stand in danger of being deceived about Christ's coming. False messianic claimants will arise, and those who identify themselves as the Messiah are charlatans (Matt. 24:4–5 par.).[1] The outbreak of wars and the onset of famines or earthquakes do not signal that the end has arrived, for these things are simply the beginning of birth pangs (Matt. 24:6–8 par.).[2] The assertion that the Messiah has appeared at this or that location should be rejected, for when Jesus comes again, his arrival will be as clear as lightning that illumines the entire sky (Luke 17:23–24).

In the eschatological discourse in the Synoptics (Matt. 24; Mark 13; Luke 21) the coming of Jesus is closely linked with the destruction of Jerusalem.[3] The destruction of Jerusalem and its temple, of course, functions as a judgment upon Israel for its failure to repent after hearing the kingdom message of Jesus or to recognize him as the Messiah. Israel's defeat at the hands of the Romans in AD 70 verified the truth of Jesus' message and his self-claims. Jesus did not merely predict that Jerusalem would be taken (cf. Luke 21:20–24 par.); he also emphasized

---

1. As Hagner (1995: 690–91) points out, Theudas (Acts 5:36), Judas the Galilean (Acts 5:37), and the Egyptian (Acts 21:38) qualify as messianic claimants, as did Simon bar Kosiba in AD 135.

2. The metaphor of birth pangs could be used in a variety of ways (see France 2002: 512–13). As Hagner (1995: 684) says, "The time is deliberately left indeterminate, thus focusing on the need to be ready at any time."

3. The literature on these chapters is immense. For a brief and clear survey of interpretation, see Carson 1984: 488–95; Davies and Allison 1997: 328–31; Luz 2005: 184–89.

that his followers would face intense opposition (see esp. Luke 21:12–19), leading in some instances to opposition from friends and even family, and in some instances to arrest and even death. The judgment to come and the promise of vindication are inseparable from the call to endure to the end to receive the final reward (Luke 21:19 par.).

The more that one emphasizes the promised judgment on Jerusalem in the eschatological discourse, the more the promised coming of Jesus in the discourse becomes a puzzle. Matthew and Mark predict that after the distress inflicted upon Jerusalem the sun will be darkened, the moon will cease giving light, stars will fall from the sky, and the powers of heaven will tremble (Matt. 24:29; Mark 13:24–25). Luke's language is similar, though he emphasizes not only the signs in the heavens but also the stirring up of the seas and the fear that grips human beings (Luke 21:25–26). After these events the Son of Man will return on the clouds of heaven (Mark 13:26; Luke 21:27), and Matthew adds that they will see "the sign of the Son of Man" (Matt. 24:30). Many scholars have argued that Jesus was mistaken.[4] He promised that he would come after Jerusalem was destroyed, but he failed to do so. The notion that Jesus erred is also confirmed for many by Matt. 10:23.[5] Jesus pledged that he would come before the disciples finished proclaiming the gospel in Israel, but two thousand years have now passed, and Jesus clearly did not come during the days when his disciples preached the message of the kingdom in Israel.[6] Jesus also assured some of his disciples that they would not die before they saw "the Son of Man coming in his kingdom" (Matt. 16:28). But all the disciples died without Jesus coming, and thus some argue that Jesus was mistaken. Jesus promised to come soon (cf. Luke 18:8), but the passing of two thousand years calls into question the legitimacy of his word.

Others have maintained that Jesus was not actually mistaken, for he did not promise that he would personally come on the clouds of heaven. Wright says that many have misunderstood the sayings about the coming of the Son of Man as referring to a literal return of Jesus to earth flying on the clouds.[7] Wright maintains that people have failed to see that what we

4. For example, Schweitzer 1968: 223–69, 330–97; Kümmel 1974: 149. Hagner (1995: 711–13) argues that the evangelist understood the message of Jesus in terms of an immediate coming, though Jesus himself did not intend such an interpretation.

5. Schweitzer (1968: 358–60, 370–77, 386, 389) argued that Jesus predicted the end before the disciples finished their missionary work in Israel. When the disciples returned, thereby proving Jesus incorrect, he determined to go to Jerusalem to compel the coming of the kingdom.

6. For a survey of discussion on this verse, see Beasley-Murray 1987: 283–91. Contrary to the view maintained here, Meier (1994: 339–48) argues that Matt. 10:23; Mark 9:1 (and par.); Mark 13:30 (and par.) are inauthentic.

7. Wright 1996: 339–68.

have in these texts is apocalyptic imagery that should not be interpreted literally. The coming of Jesus predicted in the eschatological discourse, then, is fulfilled in the destruction of Jerusalem.[8] "The sign of the Son of Man" (Matt. 24:30) did not come to pass by Jesus literally flying down to the earth on clouds. The Son of Man came with power and glory when his prophecy about the destruction of Jerusalem came to pass. Those who think that Jesus was mistaken have themselves fallen into error, for they read the Gospels literally and fail to interpret apocalyptic language properly. The saying about not finishing the evangelization of the cities of Israel before the Son of Man comes should be understood similarly (Matt. 10:23), for Jesus returns in the destruction of Jerusalem in AD 70 and thereby judges Israel and vindicates his disciples.[9] The saying about some of Jesus' disciples not dying before he comes in his kingdom could be understood in the same way (Matt. 16:28 par.), though this word of Jesus has also been applied to the transfiguration, Jesus' resurrection, and Pentecost, and thus it need not refer to a literal coming of Jesus.

Unraveling the meaning of Jesus' words when he refers to the coming of the Son of Man is not easy, particularly since they are embedded in a discourse on the destruction of Jerusalem and its temple—a judgment that was fulfilled in AD 70. Even though we can understand on a simple reading why some think that Jesus was mistaken, this view suffers from some serious weaknesses. First, it is difficult to believe that the Synoptics would have continued to be used as authoritative documents after AD 70 if they were understood to contain such an egregious error. Jesus guaranteed, in speaking about this very matter, that his words would never pass away (Matt. 24:35 par.), but if he got it wrong about his return, then he made an error on a matter that was fundamental to his message.[10] Surely the early church would have recognized the same flaw that is apparent to scholars and questioned the use of the Synoptics as Scripture. The continued use of the Synoptics and the persistent hope for a return of Jesus in the life of the early church suggest that from the beginning the words of Jesus were interpreted as not being in error. Second, if the Gospels were actually written after AD 70, then the Synoptic writers included words of Jesus that clearly did not come true. He pledged that he would return when the temple was destroyed, but he did not do so.

8. France (2002: 500–503, 530–40) argues that Mark 13 and Matt. 24 relate to the destruction of the temple until Mark 13:32 and Matt. 24:36, where the reference shifts to the parousia.

9. See Wright 1996: 365.

10. The early Christians who preserved the Gospels as authoritative understood the Gospel writers to have preserved the words of Jesus reliably. Hence, it is not satisfying to segregate the view of Jesus from the alleged errors of the Gospel authors.

But it is much more plausible that the Gospel writers did not think that Jesus' failure to come in AD 70 violated his words.

A fascinating word about the nearness of Jesus' coming is found in Acts 3:19–21. Peter calls upon his Jewish hearers to repent and experience forgiveness of sins through Jesus. If they do so, "times of refreshing" will come, and God will "send the Christ," which is Jesus, to them.[11] Some maintain that Peter teaches here that if all the Jews repent, Jesus will return immediately.[12] Other Jewish writings reflect a similar viewpoint. For instance, Satan realized "that on the day in which Israel trusts, the enemy's kingdom will be brought to an end" (*T. Dan* 6:4). We also read that God will consummate history (*T. Sim.* 6:2–7) "if you divest yourselves of envy and every hardness of heart" (*T. Sim.* 6:2 [see also *4 Ezra* 4:39; *2 Bar.* 78:6–7]). Polhill, however, probably is correct in saying that the verses teach that Jesus has already come as the Messiah, and whether Israel will be refreshed at his return depends on Israel's repentance.[13] If this is correct, then the times of refreshing, in dependence upon Isa. 32:15, may refer to the gift of the Spirit.[14] Acts 3:21 clarifies that Jesus will return from heaven only when everything that the prophets promised has come to pass, so that the entire universe is restored to what God intended from the beginning. The coming of Jesus, then, represents the fulfillment of salvation history—the completion and fulfillment of all of God's saving promises. We have, then, the typical already–not yet feature of NT eschatology. The Spirit represents the inauguration of the fulfillment of God's promises, which will be consummated when Jesus returns and all things are restored.

It is also possible that some of the statements that refer to the coming of Jesus do not refer to his personal coming in the future. The promise that some of the disciples would not die before seeing Jesus as the Son of Man coming in his kingdom (Matt. 16:28 par.) has been interpreted variously as noted earlier. Some have contended that Jesus was mistaken, but it is also possible that Jesus referred to his transfiguration, his resurrection-exaltation, or Pentecost.[15] Many scholars dismiss a reference

---

11. Barrett (1994: 205) argues that the plural *kairoi* shows that the parousia is not in view in Acts 3:20 but rather points to periodic realizations of refreshing throughout history.

12. See Haenchen 1971: 208. Against this view, see Fitzmyer 1998: 288.

13. Polhill 1992: 134–35.

14. So Pao 2000: 132–33.

15. For a survey of interpretations, see Carson 1984: 380–81; Hagner 1995: 486–87; Bock 1996: 858–59; Luz 2001: 386–87. We can add to the list above the view that the saying was fulfilled in the destruction of Jerusalem. In support of a reference to the transfiguration, see Cranfield 1963: 285–88; Blomberg 1992: 261; Fitzmyer 1985: 786 (partially); in support of the resurrection-exaltation of the Son of Man, see France 2002: 342–43. Marshall (1978b: 378–79) thinks that all three may be in view (cf. the anticipatory view of Nolland

to the transfiguration because it does not represent an actual coming of Jesus in his kingdom. It seems, nevertheless, that a good case can be made for a reference to the transfiguration. In each of the Synoptics the words about Jesus' coming are immediately followed by the account of the transfiguration (Matt. 17:1–13; Mark 9:2–13; Luke 9:28–36), suggesting that the transfiguration represents the fulfillment of Jesus' words about his coming. We should also observe that Jesus said that only some of the disciples would not die before seeing him come in power (Matt. 16:28 par.), and this fits with Jesus bringing only Peter, James, and John with him onto the mountain. It is also instructive to introduce a canonical perspective at this juncture. Apparently 2 Pet. 1:16–18 construes the transfiguration as a prelude to the second coming of Jesus, functioning as an anticipation of his coming on the last day.[16] It seems, then, that not every reference to the coming of Jesus should necessarily be understood as referring to his coming in the future.

In the eschatological discourse (Matt. 24 par.), as discussed previously, the coming of Jesus is closely related to the destruction of Jerusalem. Hence, some have maintained that Jesus does not refer to a personal coming here but rather uses apocalyptic language to speak of his coming as the judgment on Jerusalem and the vindication of his people. Although this proposal spares Jesus from error, it is not the most natural way of understanding the language of the text. The text speaks of "the Son of Man coming on the clouds of heaven with power and great glory" (Matt. 24:30; cf. Mark 13:26; Luke 21:27). The reference to clouds suggests his personal presence when he comes, for all three parallel passages say that he will be *seen* when he comes. To say that Jesus is *seen* in the destruction of the temple and Jerusalem stretches the language, even in an apocalyptic context, beyond what is credible.[17] Acts 1:9–11 confirms that Luke understood the coming to be a physical and personal appearance of Jesus. The disciples saw Jesus depart from earth on a cloud, and they are told that just as he was "taken up . . . into heaven," so he "will

---

2005: 695–96). Bock (1996: 859–60) sees a reference to both the transfiguration and the resurrection. Davies and Allison (1991: 677–79) claim that the resurrection is a foreshadowing of the second coming. Kümmel (1957: 25–29) thinks that we have an example here of a mistake in Jesus' teaching (cf. Luz 2001: 387). Hagner (1995: 485–87) contends that the evangelist misapplied what Jesus said here, thinking that Jesus intended to refer to his parousia, whereas the reference probably was to the destruction of Jerusalem and the temple. Against this view, as Bock (1994: 858) notes, is the claim here that only "some" would see the coming of the kingdom.

16. See the more detailed discussion in Schreiner 2003: 312–18.

17. See Stein 2001: 213; Bock 1996: 1686; Fitzmyer 1985: 1349–50; Carson 1984: 505–6; Marshall 1978b: 776–77.

come in the same way as you saw him go into heaven" (Acts 1:11).[18] Since his departure was seen as he was lifted on a cloud, it follows that his coming will also be seen as he arrives on a cloud.

Jesus' coming with glory also suggests a coming that is visible and evident to all, and the destruction of Jerusalem, although it represented a significant confirmation of Jesus' words, did not function as indisputable evidence that Jesus was Israel's Messiah. Indeed, Matthew says that "all the tribes of the earth will mourn" (Matt. 24:30) when Jesus comes. France reads this to say that all the Jewish tribes of the land will mourn when Jerusalem falls.[19] Such a reading is possible, but the allusion to Zech. 12:10–12, which elsewhere in the NT refers to the parousia (cf. Rev. 1:7), suggests that the phrase encompasses all peoples and should not be limited to the Jewish people.[20] Further, the gathering of the angels most likely occurs at the end of history and cannot be explained as the success of the gospel after AD 70 (Matt. 24:31 par.).[21] We see elsewhere in Matthew that angels collect people for the final judgment (Matt. 13:39, 41, 49). Another argument supporting a reference to Jesus' personal and visible coming is found in Luke 21:28, where the coming of the Son of Man is linked to the nearness of redemption for God's people. Obviously, redemption here cannot refer to conversion or initiation into the people of God, for the redemption is future and belongs to those who are already members of the people of God. Nor could the destruction of Jerusalem qualify as the disciples' future redemption, for the razing of that city, although it vindicated Jesus' words, did not redeem anyone. Therefore Luke must be referring to eschatological redemption that occurs when Jesus returns visibly and physically and ushers in the day of judgment.

The personal and visible character of Jesus' coming is also suggested by the analogy drawn between his coming and lightning flashing over the entire sky (Matt. 24:26–27 par.).[22] The illustration is intended to dispel any idea that the Messiah was hidden in the wilderness or secreted away in some town. The coming of the Messiah, on the contrary, would

18. Wright (1996: 635) argues that Acts 1:11 does not come from the historical Jesus and thus is "a post-Easter innovation." There is no reason to doubt authenticity here, for Wright seems to be moved to adopt this interpretation to sustain his view of Christ's return. Further, even if the saying were inauthentic, it would constitute early evidence for a view of Christ's return contrary to Wright's view. For a clear explanation of what will take place, see Barrett 1994: 84.

19. France 1971: 236–38.

20. For a defense of the reading adopted here, see Carson 1984: 493–94, 505; cf. Nolland 2005: 984; Luz 2005: 201.

21. See especially Carson 1984: 506–7; Hagner 1995: 714–15; Luz 2005: 202–3.

22. See Carson 1984: 503; Hagner 1995: 707.

be as clear and unmistakable as lightning that illumines the entire sky.[23] It is doubtful that this image fits with the destruction of Jerusalem in AD 70, for the issue at stake is the personal location of the Messiah. The razing of Jerusalem does not answer that particular question, for some will declare that the Messiah is in the wilderness or some other locality. The rebuttal to such claims is that the return of the Messiah will be a public event accessible to all.

Jesus' declaration before the Sanhedrin that he was the Son of Man and would return seated at God's right hand with the clouds of heaven refers to a personal and visible coming in the future (Matt. 26:64 par.).[24] The Synoptic parallels make it even clearer than Matthew that a future physical coming is envisioned (Mark 14:62; Luke 21:27). Jesus' saying cannot be limited to the destruction of Jerusalem, for when Jerusalem was destroyed, it was not clear to Jewish authorities that Jesus was vindicated. There is no evidence that they perceived Jesus' vindication in the events that transpired. The text is interpreted more naturally as saying that the Sanhedrin would actually see Jesus at God's right hand, and that they would see him returning to earth.

When Jesus says that his disciples will not finish evangelizing the towns of Israel before the Son of Man comes (Matt. 10:23), the reference possibly is to the destruction of Jerusalem.[25] In this verse nothing is said about seeing the Son of Man or of his coming with power and glory. In any case, Jewish evangelism is to be continued until Jesus returns (cf. Matt. 28:18–20). The task of proclaiming the good news to the Jews in Israel will not be completed *before* Jesus comes in judgment.

The issue of the accuracy of what Jesus said also arises, as we have seen, in the eschatological discourse. The coming of Jesus is linked with the destruction of Jerusalem, but it is obvious that Jesus did not return when Jerusalem was destroyed. What we must recognize here is the nature of biblical prophecy. Often an act of judgment or salvation functions as a type or correspondence of a future judgment or salvation.[26] The judgment of Jerusalem, then, functions as a prelude to and anticipation of the final judgment. It is at the time of the final judgment that Jesus will come again. It could be objected that this is special pleading to

23. So Nolland 2005: 980; Davies and Allison 1997: 354; Luz 2005: 199.

24. Luke (Luke 22:69) emphasizes Jesus' vindication at his resurrection-ascension (Bock 1996: 1797). Some argue that the "coming" element of the saying in Matthew and Mark refers not to the parousia but rather to a coming in history (resurrection-ascension) to receive divine authority (e.g., France 2002: 611–13; Hooker 1967: 167–71). Against this view, see Bock 1987: 141–42.

25. See Hagner 1993b: 278–80.

26. In support of a typological view here, see the interpretation of the chapter in Carson 1984: 488–511.

salvage the accuracy of Jesus' words. We should recall again that Jesus himself said in this very discourse that his words would not pass away (Matt. 24:35 par.). Still, this objection must be seriously contemplated. We have evidence from the OT itself that biblical prophecy functions the way being proposed here. If we consider the promise of the new exodus in Isaiah (Isa. 40:3–11; 42:16; 43:2, 5–7, 16–19; 48:20–21; 49:8–11; 51:10–11), the point being made will be clarified. Isaiah promises in these texts that Israel will return from Babylon to the land of promise, and this prophecy became a reality in 536 BC. Even though Israel returned to Zion, the whole of what was prophesied in Isa. 40–66 did not become a reality. Isaiah promises a new creation (Isa. 43:18–21), even a new heavens and earth (Isa. 65:17–22; 66:22) that would inaugurate an era of peace, joy, and long life. Isaiah predicts that Israel will never be confounded or defeated again (Isa. 45:17), and that all nations will bow and acknowledge that Yahweh is Lord (Isa. 45:23–24; 49:22–23). The Lord's salvation will reach the very ends of the earth (Isa. 49:6; 55:5), and Israel's boundaries will expand so that the nations are under their rule (Isa. 54:2–3; 61:5; 66:23). The nations will come to Zion and bring their wealth to Jerusalem (Isa. 60). Clearly, the promises of Isa. 40–66 were not fulfilled in their entirety when Israel returned from Babylon. Nevertheless, neither the Jews nor the early Christian movement argued that Isaiah was mistaken.

Early Christians believed that the fullness of what Isaiah prophesied would be fulfilled in the future. Indeed, they believed that many of the prophecies uttered by Isaiah were beginning to be fulfilled in the ministry of Jesus of Nazareth.[27] The main point being made here is that what we see in the eschatological discourse of Jesus replicates the character of Isa. 40–66. Just as the prophecy of Isaiah was fulfilled in part (Israel did return from Babylon, but the whole of creation was not transformed), so too Jesus' prophecy was fulfilled in part (Jerusalem was destroyed, but Jesus did not return). The fact that Isaiah's prophecy, though only partially fulfilled, was not considered wrong functions as a paradigm for the eschatological discourse. The people of God had often seen from the OT that prophecies were partially realized, and hence they anticipated the complete fulfillment in the future. Such a perspective helps explain why the early church was neither scandalized nor plunged into a crisis of confidence by the fact that Jesus did not come in AD 70 when Jerusalem was destroyed. The judgment of Jerusalem also functions as a pattern of the future judgment still to come.

Even though it has often been emphasized that Jesus would return immediately, and surely he encourages his disciples to be prepared for

27. This view is worked out in the Gospel of Mark in Watts 2000.

his coming, there are some indications of delay before his return. Jesus announced that the gospel would be proclaimed to all nations before his return (Matt. 24:14).[28] We must beware of imposing a rigid definition of "all nations" upon the gospels, as if we can engage in eschatological calculation from Jesus' words here. The word "all" is not invariably used in a comprehensive sense. To say that "all Judea" (Matt. 3:5) or "all Jerusalem" (Mark 1:5) came out to hear the Baptist does not mean that every single person from Jerusalem and Judea heard John's preaching. The phrase "all nations" (Matt. 24:14) indicates the extensive scope of the gospel without giving us a mathematical formula for determining when the end will arrive. Nevertheless, the declaration that the gospel must be preached to all nations implies an interval of time before the return of Jesus.

Some of Jesus' parables also suggest a period of some delay. Wicked slaves will fall prey to sin when they begin to think that the return of the master is delayed (Matt. 24:48; Luke 12:45).[29] In the parable of the virgins the bridegroom delays before coming (Matt. 25:5). The time before the return of Jesus is portrayed in terms of a journey by a master (Matt. 25:14).[30]

On the one hand, Jesus' coming is relatively soon, for it seems at first glance that he will come at the destruction of Jerusalem, as noted above (see also Matt. 23:37–39 par.);[31] on the other hand, it is also stressed that no one can predict or calculate the day of the Son of Man's return. Even the angels and, shockingly, Jesus himself do not know the time of his return (Matt. 24:36 par.).[32] Knowledge of the exact time is reserved to the Father alone; only he knows when Jesus will return. The coming

28. See the cautions in Hagner 1995: 696. France (2002: 516) argues that the gospel will be proclaimed to all nations before the temple is destroyed. France (2002: 517) wisely comments that if the reference here is to the parousia (which I think it is), we must beware of overliteralizing the verse and saying that the parousia will be delayed until the very last people group on earth has been reached, for clarity is lacking on the exact parameters of what constitutes an *ethnos*, on the meaning of the term "all," and on what it means to say the gospel has been proclaimed.

29. Marshall (1978b: 533–34) argues in the Lukan context that there are good reasons to think that the teaching on delay hearkens back to the historical Jesus (see also Bock 1996: 1171–72).

30. For indications of delay in the teaching of Jesus, see Carson 1984: 490.

31. It has been customary in Lukan scholarship since the work of Conzelmann (1960) to argue that Luke emphasized the delay of the parousia. But Conzelmann overemphasized this theme, and there are actually indications of imminence and delay (see Maddox 1982: 100–157).

32. The significance of the claim to ignorance in context is explained effectively by Lane (1974: 482), who argues that the emphasis here is pastoral. If even the Son and angels do not and cannot know the time of the parousia, then the church must be vigilant and continue to live by faith until the end. Not knowing the day does not mean that the

of the Son is compared to the days of Noah (Matt. 24:37–44 par.). Life was proceeding in its usual fashion when the flood arrived suddenly. No one was able to gauge that the judgment was at hand. Because the day of Jesus' coming is incalculable, all are warned to be ready.

If any theme is emphasized relative to Jesus' coming, it is that his disciples must be prepared for his return. On the one hand, as noted above, the timing of Jesus' return is unknown; on the other hand, other sayings suggest that certain signs precede his coming that forecast his near appearance. Just as the leaves of the fig tree sprout when the fruit is about to appear, so too certain signs will precede Jesus' coming (Matt. 24:32–33 par.). We must recognize again, however, that many of the signs (Matt. 24:4–28) listed relate specifically to the destruction of Jerusalem, and determining if they have some correspondence to Jesus' future return is quite difficult. The disciples must respond by being prepared. They are to be like slaves faithfully working for their master until he returns (Matt. 24:45–51 par.). They are to be like wise virgins who anticipate the return of the bridegroom and have oil in their lamps (Matt. 25:1–13). They are to use their talents faithfully so that they receive the reward of eternal life when he comes (Matt. 25:14–30 par.). The readiness demanded, therefore, does not relate to eschatological calculation, as if faithful disciples could forecast the time when Jesus would return.[33] The disciples demonstrate that they are ready for his return by doing God's will. Hence, when the Son of Man returns in glory, the sheep will be rewarded for their godly and faithful behavior with an eternal reward, while the wicked will be punished forever because they have failed to practice goodness (Matt. 25:31–46). The parable of the unjust judge concludes on a somber note, asking whether human beings will persist in faith until the coming of the Son of Man (Luke 18:8).

The disciples must steel themselves for difficult times ahead. They will be tempted to apostatize because of the intensity of the persecution and the hatred that corrupts the community (Matt. 24:9–13 par.). False prophets will rise up and win over some disciples to their insight. Therefore, Jesus' followers must endure to the end in order to receive salvation, for the final reward belongs only to those who continue to put their faith in Jesus as the Messiah.

In summary, the Synoptics and Acts clearly teach a future coming of Jesus, though they warn against a kind of eschatological speculation that would try to ascertain the precise time of his arrival. Most important,

---

month or year can be calculated (rightly Carson 1984: 508; Hagner 1995: 716). For the history of interpretation, see Luz 2005: 213–14.

33. Readiness does not mean that one calculates the time of the end; rather, it involves living in a godly way that demonstrates preparedness (so Hagner 1995: 730, 737, 746; Carson 1984: 518; Lane 1974: 483–84).

Jesus' future coming should function as an encouragement and warning for his disciples to be ready.

The Johannine Literature

Scholars have long recognized that the Gospel of John focuses on realized eschatology, and therefore few sayings exist on the return of Jesus. Despite the emphasis on realized eschatology, John does not abandon future eschatology. In his farewell discourse Jesus comforts his disciples, who are grieved because he will soon depart from them. He promises the disciples that his Father's home consists of "many rooms" (John 14:2), and that he departs to prepare a place for them. He then pledges that he will return and take his disciples to himself so that in the future they will be with him forever. Some have understood Jesus to be speaking of the coming of the Spirit here and not his second coming, but the context clearly indicates that the return of Jesus is intended.[34] (1) Jesus refers to the Father's house that has dwelling places, and this house is not on earth. (2) Jesus goes to prepare a dwelling for his disciples in the house of his Father, which is inaccessible to the disciples on earth. (3) Jesus does not come, in this context, to reside in the disciples; rather, he comes to take the disciples so that they might be with him. Jesus said, "I . . . will take you to myself, that where I am you may be also" (John 14:3). Clearly, the disciples will be transported to a new locality when Jesus comes. The coming of Jesus is the hope of believers because it represents the realization in full of the fellowship that the disciples enjoyed with Jesus while he was on earth. When he returns, their fellowship will be deeper and richer and unbroken, and they will dwell with the Father and the Son forever.

The only other reference to Jesus' coming in John's Gospel is incidental (John 21:18–23), but the fact that it is incidental reveals that it was a part of the worldview of the writer.[35] We are reminded again that none of the NT writings were intended to be comprehensive expositions of the Christian faith. This commonsense observation has often been made in this book, but it bears repeating because anyone who has read widely in NT scholarship knows that the partial nature of NT documents has

---

34. The meaning of the text is disputed. Some take it to refer to the parousia or the death of disciples (e.g., Barrett 1978: 457). Others argue that the reference is to Jesus' parousia or the resurrection (Lindars 1972: 471). Gundry (1967a) argues that it refers to the coming of the Spirit and the parousia. Bultmann (1971: 602) thinks that it is the coming that occurs at death. But the most likely view is that we have a reference here exclusively to Jesus' future coming (so Beasley-Murray 1987: 250–51; Carson 1991b: 488–89; Ridderbos 1997: 489–92; Köstenberger 2004: 426–27).

35. Many scholars, however, see John 21 as an appendix added to the Gospel. For arguments supporting the originality of the chapter, see Carson 1991b: 665–68.

been repeatedly ignored or forgotten. The text in question here occurs in the final chapter of John's Gospel. Jesus summoned Peter to follow him and symbolically indicates the manner in which Peter will die (John 21:18–23). Peter then inquired about the fate of the Beloved Disciple, and Jesus replied that if it is his will that the Beloved Disciple lives "until I come" (John 21:22–23), this is Jesus' prerogative as Master and Lord. Apparently, death and sorrow will continue in this world, even after the coming of the Spirit, but a new world will dawn when Jesus comes. Those who are alive when he comes will not experience death. The last chapter of John's Gospel corrects any notion that Jesus promised to come before the Beloved Disciple died. It seems even from this text that the themes of imminence and the uncertainty of Jesus' coming are preserved. His coming is imminent in that it could occur during John's lifetime, but it is also uncertain, for there is no guarantee that he would come before John's death.

Earlier we examined the eschatological character of 1 John. John declares that this world and the age of darkness are passing away (1 John 2:8, 17). The presence of antichrists reveals that the last hour has dawned (1 John 2:18). The last hour will come to an end when Jesus is revealed (1 John 2:28), and John immediately defines this manifestation of Jesus as his "coming." His coming is the day of judgment in which those who did not remain in him will experience the shame of judgment. The day of his revelation will also be the day when believers "see him as he is" (1 John 3:2).[36] Then they will be transformed into Jesus' likeness and will experience the fullness of salvation. The day of Jesus' coming promises transformation for believers so that they will be like Jesus, or a day of judgment for those who do not belong to Jesus.

If we consider Revelation to be part of the Johannine corpus, and there are good reasons to do so, we see that future eschatology plays a significant role in John's thought, reminding us again of the limited nature of the various canonical documents. John often refers to the forthcoming judgment and reward associated with the end in Revelation, and these will be examined in due course. The final judgment and reward are inseparable from Jesus' coming and occur when Jesus comes again (cf. Rev. 2:25). Here we attend to the texts that refer to the coming of Jesus in Revelation. The book commences with the claim that it relates to what "must soon take place" (Rev. 1:1) and indicates that "the time is near" (Rev. 1:3).[37] It closes with the assurance that the

36. The consequence of seeing Jesus is that believers are made like him (Marshall 1978a: 172–73). For further defense of this view, see Smalley 1984: 146–47. R. Brown (1982: 395–96) thinks that the text is too vague to come to a clear conclusion.

37. Caird (1966: 12) thinks that the nearness refers not to the coming of Christ and the consummation of history but rather the imminent persecution of the church. But

end "must soon take place" (Rev. 22:6) and that "the time is near" (Rev. 22:10). John refers to the entirety of his prophecy with these words and not exclusively to the coming of Jesus. Nonetheless, the coming of Jesus is one of the events that will take place soon. This is confirmed by the concluding words in Revelation. Immediately after saying that the prophesied events will be fulfilled soon, Jesus twice declares, "Behold, I am coming soon" (Rev. 22:7, 12). The book closes with a third promise, "Surely I am coming soon," and John immediately adds, "Amen. Come, Lord Jesus!" (Rev. 22:20). The promise that Jesus is coming soon occurs elsewhere in the book (Rev. 3:11) and can justly be said to pervade the message of Revelation as a whole (Rev. 1:7). Sometimes the coming one is said to be the Father (Rev. 1:4, 8; 4:8). In some contexts the coming of Jesus may refer not to the coming that inaugurates the new heavens and new earth but rather one that refers to a judgment in history, but it is more likely that all of these texts also refer to the parousia as well (cf. Rev. 2:5, 16; 3:3; 16:15).[38]

The most extended description of Jesus' coming is in Rev. 19:11–21. Jesus will ride on a white horse when he comes to judge and make war on those who oppose him. His robe being dipped in blood echoes Isa. 63:1–6, where Yahweh's garments are spattered and stained with blood in his judgment of Edom. The OT background indicates that the blood on Jesus' robe symbolizes not his redeeming work but rather the inflicting of wrath on his enemies. A reference to judgment fits the context of Rev. 19:11–21 as well. Jesus comes with heaven's armies and a sharp sword to defeat his enemies and to rule them with an iron rod. The iron rod alludes to Ps. 2, where Yahweh promises that his anointed one will triumph over the nations that resist his rule and the rule of his Messiah. Furthermore, in Rev. 19 Jesus comes to tread the winepress of God's wrath so that God's enemies receive their just deserts. The judgment scene fits with the last verses of the chapter (Rev. 19:17–21). Here John echoes Ezek. 39 and anticipates the birds gorging themselves on the flesh of Jesus' enemies. The beast and the false prophet are captured and flung into the lake of fire, and Jesus' remaining enemies are slain by his word (i.e., the sword coming from his mouth). Hence, Rev. 19:11–21 emphasizes that the coming of Jesus represents the day of judgment for those who oppose him and do not submit to his rule.

In summary, only Revelation in the Johannine literature emphasizes the day of Jesus' coming in which he will judge his enemies and reward

---

most see a reference to the parousia and the end of history (see Aune 1997: 21; Osborne 2002: 59). Beale (1999b: 185) claims there are provisional fulfillments before the final fulfillment at the end.

38. For the former view, see Caird 1966: 32; R. Mounce 1977: 89; Beale 1999b: 232–33; for the latter view, see Osborne 2002: 118.

the righteous. On that day God will fulfill his saving promises and the new heavens and new earth—the new creation—will commence. Even though it is not emphasized, Jesus' coming is not entirely absent from John's Gospel or 1 John. Jesus will return and take the disciples to the place where he resides, and thus they have nothing to fear and should persist in faith. Indeed, at Jesus' coming believers can be full of confidence, for they will be transformed into his likeness upon seeing him.

The Pauline Literature

The future coming of Christ in Paul's writings, as is typically the case in the rest of the NT, is linked with the day of judgment and reward.[39] It indicates an eschatological proviso or reservation in Paul's theology, for even though God's saving promises have received their "yes" in Christ (2 Cor. 1:20), the full realization of those promises has not yet been obtained. Overrealized eschatology, which posits the attainment of a heavenly existence in the here and now, is categorically rejected by Paul. Contrary to the view of certain false teachers, the physical resurrection of believers has not yet occurred (2 Tim. 2:18). The resurrection of Christ is separated by an interval from the physical resurrection of believers, so that the resurrection of believers will take place only when Jesus comes again (1 Cor. 15:23).

Paul uses three different terms to describe the coming of Jesus: his coming (*parousia*), appearance (*epiphaneia*), and revelation (*apokalypsis*). The word "coming" denotes Stephanas's arrival to meet with Paul (1 Cor. 16:17) and Titus's meeting with the Corinthians (2 Cor. 7:6–7). The word "coming" in the NT always conveys the notion that a person is physically present with someone (cf. 2 Cor. 10:10; Phil. 1:26; 2:12). When Paul speaks of the "coming" (*parousia*) of Jesus, then, he refers to a future event in which he will return personally and bodily (cf. 1 Cor. 15:23; 1 Thess. 2:19; 3:13; 4:15; 5:23; 2 Thess. 2:1, 8). The word "appearance" (*epiphaneia* [2 Thess. 2:8; 1 Tim. 6:14; 2 Tim. 1:10; 4:1, 8; Titus 2:13]) is used especially in the Pastoral Epistles. In Hellenistic thought the term was used for the manifestation of a hidden deity in which the deity intervenes to help the people.[40] In one instance Paul uses it to refer to Christ's first coming (2 Tim. 1:10), but the aforementioned texts indicate that most often the term denotes Christ's second coming. A verbal form

---

39. For a thorough study of the future coming of Jesus in Pauline theology, see Plevnik 1997.

40. In a thorough study of *epiphaneia* Lau (1996: 179–225) demonstrates that the word normally has the idea of both manifestation of what is hidden and intervention to help those in need. See also Stettler 1998: 139–49. For a summary of research, along with his own evaluation, see Marshall 1999: 287–96.

of the word occurs in Col. 3:4, which speaks of Christ's future manifestation. Even now Jesus is present with his people, but the fullness of his glory and divinity is hidden, but it will be manifested. Finally, the word "revelation" (*apokalypsis*) is used twice to refer to Jesus' coming (1 Cor. 1:7; 2 Thess. 1:7). The word "revelation" implies that Jesus is now hidden from his people, but he will be unveiled to all on the last day.

If we can speak of the hope of Jesus' coming as the primitive hope of the church, it is evident that this hope permeates Pauline theology. We see this clearly in the use of the Aramaic phrase *marana tha*, which is translated "Our Lord, come!" (1 Cor. 16:22). Paul almost certainly draws upon the wording of the early Palestinian church by which they expressed their longing for Jesus' return.[41] In the Pauline writings the coming of Jesus Christ is associated with "the day," whether it is called "the day of the Lord" or just "the day," or "the day of the Lord Jesus Christ," or even "that day" (cf. Rom. 2:5, 16; 1 Cor. 1:8; 3:13; 5:5; 2 Cor. 1:14; 1 Thess. 5:2; 2 Thess. 1:10; 2:2; 2 Tim. 1:18; 4:8). The Pauline language here clearly hearkens back to and finds its antecedent in the day of the Lord so often spoken of in the OT (e.g., Isa. 13:6, 9; Joel 1:15; 2:1; Amos 5:18; Obad. 15; Zeph. 1:7, 14).[42] In the OT there are days of the Lord that precede the final and great day of the Lord. The day of the Lord is the day when the Lord will judge his adversaries and save his people, but the Lord will save his people only if they truly trust in him and obey his word (Amos 5:18). In the same way, Paul envisions the day of the Lord as the day when the Lord Jesus will return.[43] On this day those who belong to the people of God will be rewarded and experience the consummation of their salvation, whereas those who disobey God and refuse to heed the gospel will be judged.

The coming of Jesus represents the hope of believers and thus is eagerly anticipated. It is often said that in Colossians we see realized eschatology; however, eschatological reservation also exists in the letter. Only when Jesus is manifested will the glory of saints be manifested as well (Col. 3:4).[44] Presumably, the saints will be glorified because what is hidden now will be revealed: the stunning glory of Jesus (Titus 2:13). The glory and joy will be so great that the coming of Jesus is designated as the "blessed hope" of believers (Titus 2:13). The saints will marvel and be full of joy when Jesus returns (2 Thess. 1:10). Not only will they

41. For the imperative sense of this verse, compare Rev. 22:20; *Did.* 10:6. Rightly Hofius 1993: 11n213; Hays 1997: 292–93.

42. For a brief survey on the day of the Lord, see Hiers, *ABD* 2:82–83. More recently, see House 2007: 179–224.

43. The day of the Lord is interpreted as the day of Christ in Pauline theology (see Kreitzer 1987: 112–29).

44. See O'Brien 1982: 167–68.

rejoice in God, but also they will find pleasure in what God has done in and through other believers (2 Cor. 1:14; 1 Thess. 2:19). When Jesus comes, salvation will be consummated, for he will rescue believers on that day from God's eschatological wrath (1 Thess. 1:10). The body that is now marred by sin will be transformed and changed so that it is like the glorious and powerful body of the risen Christ (Phil. 3:20–21).[45] Believers are keenly aware that the fullness of God's saving work has not been completed in them, and thus they await the coming of the Lord (1 Cor. 1:7). Still, they live in confidence because they are assured that God will finish the sanctifying work that he has begun (1 Cor. 1:8; Phil. 1:6; 1 Thess. 5:23–24). The promise of future holiness does not preclude exhortations and prayers for believers to live holy lives until the coming of Jesus Christ (1 Thess. 3:13). Believers must cling to the gospel until Jesus' coming (1 Tim. 6:14; 2 Tim. 1:18). Since the day is near, they must reject the weapons of wickedness and clothe themselves with Jesus Christ (Rom. 13:14). Those who have longed for Jesus' coming may be confident that they will receive "the crown of righteousness" (2 Tim. 4:8). It seems that Paul also promises that at the coming of the Lord Jesus Israel will be saved (Rom. 11:26–27), for at or near his coming he will remove ungodliness from Israel and forgive their sins.[46]

The coming of Jesus Christ is also a day of judgment. On that day God's wrath and righteous judgment will be revealed (Rom. 2:5). He will judge the secret things that people have hidden and bring them to light for all to see (Rom. 2:16). The day of the Lord will reveal whether ministers have faithfully built on the foundation of Christ (1 Cor. 3:13).[47] Only those who turn from evil will be saved from punishment on that day (1 Cor. 5:5). Believers are to proclaim the word with earnestness, for Jesus is coming to establish his kingdom and to pronounce judgment upon all (2 Tim. 4:1–2).

Jesus' coming is addressed particularly in the Thessalonian letters, for clearly the Thessalonians were confused about Jesus' coming and its implications.[48] In 1 Thess. 4:13–18 the Thessalonians are confused about the fate of the believing dead. They apparently were convinced that the believing dead would suffer from some disadvantage when Jesus re-

45. So O'Brien 1991: 463–65; Fee 1995: 380–84.

46. Munck (1959: 297–308) contends that Paul believed that the collection of money that he was gathering for the saints in Jerusalem would play a vital role in the conversion of Israel. Such a view does not seem to be supported by Paul's argument in Rom. 9–11, for in these chapters he makes no mention of the collection.

47. Hays (1997: 55–56) rightly argues that here Paul discusses the ministries not of individual believers but rather of church leaders. So also Schnabel 2004a: 952.

48. Longenecker (1985), however, rightly observes that in 1–2 Thessalonians Christology is more fundamental than eschatology.

turned.[49] Given our separation from the historical situation addressed, it is difficult to reconstruct precisely what they were thinking. Paul assures the Thessalonians that the believing dead would not be left behind when Jesus returns.[50] In fact, they will be raised first, and then those who are living will be snatched up. Paul's main purpose in this text, then, is to provide comfort for those who were grieving over the believing dead (cf. 1 Thess. 4:13, 18). Some details about the Lord's coming are given in 1 Thess. 4:16: "For the Lord himself will descend from heaven with a cry of command, with the voice of an archangel, and with the sound of the trumpet of God." It is clear from this text that Jesus will return with fanfare, rendering improbable the popular notion that "a secret rapture" precedes the coming of Jesus by seven years.

In 1 Thess. 5:1–11 Paul echoes the Jesus tradition, asserting that the day of the Lord will arrive like a thief. No definite eschatological calculation can determine when he will come. Indeed, he will come at the very time when the world thinks that peace and safety are at hand. For believers, then, the coming of the Lord is a call to spiritual vigilance and alertness. The judgment associated with Jesus' coming is emphasized in 2 Thess. 1:5–10. Jesus will return with a multitude of angels and "in flaming fire" (2 Thess. 1:8). He will pour out his vengeance on the disobedient and on those who have no knowledge of God. Paul writes these words to the Thessalonians in order to encourage them to persevere, assuring them that those who oppose and persecute them will be repaid for their conduct and their mistreatment of believers.

When Paul writes 2 Thessalonians, the Thessalonians are still confused about Jesus' coming. They appear to think either that the second coming and final resurrection have already occurred in the spiritual realm or that Christ's coming will occur any second, presumably because of the intensity of affliction that they endured (2 Thess. 1:4–7; 2:1–3).[51] Paul is

49. Wanamaker (1990: 172) surveys the options and argues that the Thessalonians "feared that their dead would lose out on the chance to be assumed to heaven at the time of the parousia" (see also Wanamaker 1990: 164–66). Beale (2003: 131–33) suggests that the Thessalonians were beginning to doubt the physical resurrection of dead believers.

50. Mearns (1981) argues that Paul changed his eschatology in 1–2 Thessalonians, and the first change was precipitated by the death of a number of believers in Thessalonica. Before their deaths Paul largely held to a realized eschatology. Responding to Mearns would require more space than is available. Still, the notion that the death of Christians, in any number, surprised Paul is quite improbable, given the death of Stephen (Acts 8:1), and surely many other believers died during the fifteen to twenty years Paul served as a missionary before writing 1 Thessalonians.

51. Beale (2003: 199–201) argues that the situation was one in which some were arguing for an already accomplished spiritual resurrection and an already realized coming of Christ. In a fascinating article Stephenson (1968: 442–51) argues that the notion that the day of the Lord is already present, though it has ample support lexically, cannot be the literal meaning of 2 Thess. 2:2. Such a view does not make sense, he claims, for if

concerned that the Thessalonians might be deluded and instructs them not to lose their heads in eschatological enthusiasm (2 Thess. 2:2–7). The Lord will not come before the man of lawlessness appears and a great apostasy occurs.[52] Paul is convinced that neither of these events has yet transpired, and thus the Lord's coming cannot have already occurred nor can it take place any second. The lawless one is being restrained by something or someone, and he will not appear on the scene until such restraint is removed. Scholars have long puzzled over the identity of the restrainer, and that discussion need not detain us here. To say that the lawless one will take a seat in God's temple and proclaim himself as God may be a reference to the Jerusalem temple. But elsewhere in Paul the temple of God or of the Lord refers to the church (cf. 1 Cor. 3:16–17; 2 Cor. 6:16; Eph. 2:21), and so it is more likely that the lawless one engenders apostasy in the church and identifies himself as God.[53] The time of triumph for the lawless one will be short-lived, for the Lord Jesus will destroy him by his word (2 Thess. 2:8).

In 1 Thess. 5 Paul teaches that the Lord will come suddenly and surprisingly like a thief, but in 2 Thess. 2 certain signs must take place before the Lord comes. Does 2 Thessalonians sacrifice the imminence of Jesus' coming, and does it lead to eschatological calculation? Some have argued that the eschatological differences here indicate that 2 Thessalonians is

---

the Thessalonians believed that the rapture had come, they could not have believed that Paul was left out. They could not be arguing for an already realized resurrection along the lines of 2 Tim. 2:18, for if they were advocating such a view, Paul would have responded to them with the kind of discussion found in 1 Cor. 15. Nor will it do to say that the day of the Lord is an extended period of time, for the day of the Lord is matched with the parousia in 1–2 Thessalonians. Hence, Stephenson (1968: 451) concludes that Paul speaks hyperbolically and rejects the notion that the day of the Lord is "immediately round the corner." The difficulty with Stephenson's view is that it does not accord with the typical understanding of the verb *enistēmi*. For a more general discussion, see Wanamaker 1990: 237–41.

52. The apostasy here does not refer specifically to apostasy in Israel (so Best 1972: 282–83) or among unbelievers; rather, it points to apostasy in the church of Jesus Christ generally (so Beale 2004: 274–75). The apostasy in view means that a large number in the church, perhaps the majority, will fall away (Beale 2004: 280–81). As Beale notes, such a falling away does not preclude unbelievers from intensifying their unbelief as well as their persecution of genuine believers.

53. Beale (2004: 269–92) rightly argues that the temple of God in 2 Thess. 2:4 refers to the church of Jesus Christ and not a literal temple in Jerusalem. Contra Wanamaker 1990: 246; Bruce 1982b: 168–69, though Bruce still takes the statement metaphorically to refer to one who usurps God's place. For a view similar to Bruce's, see Marshall 1983: 190–92. Beale (2004: 275) observes that the phrase occurs on ten occasions in the NT, and in every instance except Matt. 26:61 refers to the church. Further, Beale (2004: 279) finds it unlikely that believers would be tempted to apostatize by the man of lawlessness using the literal temple as his base of operations, for Christians no longer believed in the centrality of that temple.

not authentic, and that it fundamentally contradicts 1 Thessalonians.[54] The two letters indeed have different emphases, but it is unclear that they contradict one another. We have already seen in the teaching of Jesus that a tension existed between sayings that emphasize imminence and sayings that emphasize delay. The same tension seems to exist in Paul. The two signs that will precede the coming of the Lord in 2 Thess. 2 are not definitive enough to allow people to precisely calculate the time of the Lord's coming. Nor do they necessarily rule out the imminence of Christ's coming, for presumably the signs could come to pass rather quickly. Wanamaker rightly says that "first-century Christians clearly had no trouble holding together the ideas of the imminence of the coming of Christ with a series of events portending its coming, as Mark 13 shows."[55] In any case, 1 Thess. 5 emphasizes that the Lord's coming will be surprising and unexpected to unbelievers. Moreover, those who disobey the gospel will lack the discernment to identify the arrival of the lawless one and the apostasy.

In summary, Paul reiterates what we have seen elsewhere in the NT. Jesus' future coming will bring comfort and relief to saints and will portend the judgment of the ungodly. Hence, believers are encouraged to endure difficulties and persecution, knowing that the opposition that they face will be short-lived.

Hebrews

Hebrews rarely refers to Jesus coming in the future, but the paucity of references to the second coming may be misleading because the author often speaks of the future hope and coming judgment. The coming of Jesus must not be divorced from the judgment and reward, but the author focuses on the punishment or joy awaiting human beings in order to motivate his readers to persevere and to avoid apostasy. The meaning of Heb. 1:6 is debated, but it may refer to Jesus' return, when the angels would recognize his lordship over the world and worship him.[56] The word "again" (*palin*) may modify the verb "brings" (*eisagagē*), and if so, then we have a reference to Jesus' return. This interpretation may be supported by Heb. 2:5, which says that the "world" (*oikoumenē*) over which Jesus will rule is the future one, and that angels will not rule in the future. The same word "world" (*oikoumenē*) occurs in Heb. 1:6, and thus a link may be established between the two texts. We cannot be certain about the meaning of Heb. 1:6, and the author may have the first

54. On this matter, see Marshall 1983: 36–38.
55. Wanamaker 1990: 178.
56. So, for example, Käsemann 1984: 101.

coming of Jesus in mind, though on balance a reference to the second coming is slightly preferred.

We have two clear references to the second coming in Hebrews. The author emphasizes in Heb. 9:11–28 the definitive and effective nature of Jesus' sacrifice on the cross. His one sacrifice is effective forever and needs no supplementation by further sacrifices. In Heb. 9:23–28 the death of Jesus delivers those who belong to him from judgment on the last day. The day of final judgment and salvation approaches, and it will come, Hebrews declares, when Jesus "appear[s] a second time" (Heb. 9:28). On this occasion those who are already cleansed by his once-for-all sacrifice will experience the completion of their salvation.

In Heb. 10:35–39 the second coming of Jesus is again tied to future reward and the coming judgment. The readers are exhorted to persevere in faith and not to abandon their confidence. Those who endure in faith until the end will receive the promised reward, but those who shrink back will face destruction. The author of Hebrews cites Hab. 2:3–4 in the midst of his argument and understands it to refer to Jesus' coming. Since Jesus will come and not postpone his arrival, believers must endure in faith so as to receive the promised reward. We are not surprised to find in Hebrews that the coming of Jesus is intertwined with the day of judgment and salvation.

1 Peter

The coming of Jesus in 1 Peter must be understood in light of the situation addressed in the letter. The readers were suffering, and Peter reminds them often of their future inheritance, warning them at the same time about the judgment that will be inflicted upon those who do not continue in faith. The suffering faced by believers in the present time produces joy because the authenticity of their faith will lead to a great reward "at the revelation of Jesus Christ" (1 Pet. 1:7). The same connection between suffering and future reward is confirmed in 1 Pet. 4:13. Believers are to rejoice in their sufferings in the present, for when Christ's "glory is revealed," they will exult and rejoice in a way that transcends and completes the joy they experience now. Peter is full of confidence because just as he has participated in Christ's sufferings, so too he will share in the glory that will be revealed at Christ's coming (1 Pet. 5:1). In the same way, elders who carry out their responsibilities in a godly fashion will receive a reward "when the chief Shepherd appears" (1 Pet. 5:4). The future-oriented character of the letter is confirmed by 1 Pet. 1:13, where the readers are exhorted to place their hope entirely "on the grace that will be brought to you at the revelation of Jesus Christ." The consummation of God's gracious purposes will be realized when

Jesus returns and vindicates his people. Peter uses the noun "revelation" (*apokalypsis*) most often (1 Pet. 1:7, 13; 4:13). Elsewhere he uses the verb "reveal" (*apokalyptō* [1 Pet. 5:1]) and the verb "manifest" (*phaneroō* [1 Pet. 5:4 my translation]). The noun and verbs relating to revelation suggest that the curtain will be pulled back when Jesus returns, and God's people will see what has been hidden: the glorious future reserved for them. The word "manifest" similarly implies that Jesus is present even during the current age, but a day is coming when his presence will be evident and clear to all. Believers are to endure suffering, knowing that what is now hidden and obscure will soon become visible.

James

The letter of James is known for its practical and admonitory character, and it contains only two explicit references to Jesus Christ (James 1:1; 2:1). The necessity of good works for receiving a final reward is often taught in the letter. Furthermore, a day of judgment is impending upon those who give way to evil (James 5:1–6). James follows these words with his only reference to the Lord's coming (James 5:7–9). The readers are exhorted to patience until the Lord's coming. The need for patience is compared to farmers who wait for the early and latter rain before harvesting a crop. The Lord's nearness almost certainly refers, given the context, to his promise to come soon. Accordingly, the readers should fortify their hearts and endure to the end. In addition, they should not allow the tension and pressures of their current lives to lead to complaining about others. Otherwise, they themselves will face judgment. James here seems to draw on the Jesus tradition (cf. Matt. 7:1–5 par.). Criticizing others is precluded because Jesus, as the coming one, stands at the door, ready to pronounce final judgment on the last day.

2 Peter and Jude

In 2 Peter the second coming of Jesus is clearly one of the most important themes in the letter. The false teachers denied that Jesus would return, arguing perhaps that OT texts predicting his return were improperly interpreted (2 Pet. 1:20).[57] If Jesus does not return, then neither would there be a future judgment, and thus the denial of Jesus' coming opened the door to libertinism and ethical anarchy. The false teachers insisted that it was ludicrous to expect Jesus to return, for the world was marked by uniformity, and life on earth has remained the same since the creation of the world (2 Pet. 3:4). They probably also pointed to the long interval between the so-called promise to return

57. For this view, see Bigg 1901: 269–70; J. Kelly 1981: 323–24.

and present experience (2 Pet. 3:9). The "delay" demonstrated that the alleged coming of Jesus was a fantasy.

Peter does not consider the denial of the second coming to be a minor error, but instead argues in 2 Pet. 2 that the view of the "teachers" demonstrates that they are false teachers (2 Pet. 2:1) and do not belong to the people of God. The transfiguration functions as an anticipation of and prelude to Jesus' second coming because Jesus' majesty was evident, and he received honor and glory from the Father on that occasion (2 Pet. 1:16–18).[58] The glory that Jesus received cannot be dismissed as unhistorical, for Peter was an eyewitness to what occurred. The transfiguration confirms and strengthens the interpretation of prophecy (2 Pet. 1:19) because it clarifies that OT prophecy points to the return of Jesus. Hence, prophecy illumines the future, revealing that Jesus will come again.[59] The new day promised in Scripture will dawn, and Jesus as the morning star will rise in the hearts of believers. Anyone who interprets prophecy as if there is not a return of Jesus distorts the meaning of such prophecies, for prophecy and its interpretation derive from the Holy Spirit (2 Pet. 1:20–21).

In 2 Pet. 3 Peter responds to the objections of the false teachers by which they allegedly refute the second coming. The adversaries pointed to the fact that everything had remained the same since "the fathers fell asleep" (2 Pet. 3:4). Here "the fathers" does not refer to the first apostolic generation. The word "fathers" (*pateres*) in the NT often refers to the OT patriarchs, but it never refers to the first apostolic generation (e.g., Matt. 23:30, 32; Luke 1:55, 72; 11:47; John 4:20; Acts 3:13, 25; 15:10; 28:25; Rom. 11:28; 15:8; 1 Cor. 10:1; Heb. 1:1; 3:9; 8:9).[60] Moreover, there are scores of verses in the OT where the word "fathers" denotes the patriarchs. In addition, the verse itself supplies compelling evidence that "the fathers" refers to the OT patriarchs, for what Peter says about them is paralleled by the phrase "from the beginning of creation." Peter refers, then, to the view of the false teachers that life on earth has continued without interruption from the creation of the world.

Peter uses three arguments to rebut the uniformitarian perspective of the false teachers. First, they have failed to perceive the implications of God's creation of the world (2 Pet. 3:5). The creation of the world demonstrates that life on earth is not uniform; it had a beginning that constituted a massive break with what preceded. Second, life on earth has not proceeded without intervention since creation, for a flood overwhelmed and destroyed the world during the time of Noah (2 Pet. 3:6).

58. So Fornberg 1977: 80.

59. For further support of this view, see Schreiner 2003: 318–21.

60. Contrary to the view of many commentators (e.g., Bauckham 1983: 291–92; J. Kelly 1981: 355–56).

Any claim to uniformity is contradicted by the biblical account of God's judgment of the world (cf. 2 Pet. 2:5). Third, in the future the world will face judgment by fire, and on that day the unrighteous will face judgment and destruction (2 Pet. 3:7). Peter, drawing on the Jesus tradition, warns that the day of the Lord will arrive like a thief, and thus no one can decipher the timing of its arrival by observing the current world (2 Pet. 3:10). The current world will be consumed with fire, and a new heavens and new earth will dawn (2 Pet. 3:12–13).[61]

Peter gives two further explanations for the apparent delay in the Lord's coming.[62] First, what seems like a delay from the human perspective is not a delay from God's standpoint, for a thousand years for human beings is, so to speak, only a day for God (2 Pet. 3:8). God does not experience temporal reality in the same way that human beings do, so that what is an excruciatingly long time for human beings is not so for God. Second, the promised coming is longer from the human perspective than might be expected, but the delay affords human beings the opportunity to repent and be saved (2 Pet. 3:9, 15). Hence, the apparent delay serves a merciful purpose and cannot be assigned to a failure of God to keep his promise.

The second coming does not loom as largely in Jude as in 2 Peter, though much of the content of the two letters is the same, and though Jude also faces antinomians. Jude appeals to a prophecy of *1 Enoch* to substantiate the future coming of the Lord (Jude 14–15). The Lord is coming to execute judgment on all the ungodly so that the Lord's triumph over evil will be completed. Thereby Jude assures his readers that victory belongs to the Lord, and the impact of those who pursue wickedness will be short-lived.

Conclusion

The second coming of Jesus is standard fare in NT theology and is indissolubly linked with the future judgment and the reward of God's people. Jesus' coming represents the consummation and fulfillment of God's promises and the dawn of the new creation. In light of the certainty of his coming, believers are exhorted to perseverance, faith, and godly living.

61. Scholars debate the significance of Peter's statement here. Some think that he predicts the annihilation of the present world and the creation of a completely new world (e.g., Overstreet 1980: 362–65). It seems more likely, although certainty is impossible, that God will purify the old world by fire and create out of the same elements a new world (Wolters 1987).

62. Fornberg (1977: 69) maintains that many scholars have overemphasized the problem of the delay of the parousia, noting that many passages in the Gospels indicate that a temporal interval will obtain before Christ returns.

Judgment

The Synoptic Gospels and Acts

We begin by tracing the theme of judgment in the Synoptic Gospels and Acts. The threat of a future judgment for those who disobey and disbelieve cannot be swept aside as a minor theme, for it is pervasive in the Synoptics and Acts. We are again justified in integrating the Synoptics on this matter because the differences among them are minimal. John the Baptist warned his audiences about the danger of listening to his proclamation while not truly repenting, for God's future wrath would be poured out on the disobedient (Matt. 3:7–10 par.). Those trees that do not yield fruit will be cut down and cast into the fire.

In the teaching of Jesus the future judgment is expressed in a variety of ways. Those who do not repent will perish (Luke 13:1–5). Israel, which is represented by the fig tree, will be cut down if it does not produce fruit (Luke 13:6–9). Those who censoriously judge others will find themselves on the last day face-to-face with the judgment of God (Matt. 7:1–2 par.). Similarly, those who refuse to forgive others who injure them will not receive forgiveness from God (Matt. 6:12, 14–15; 18:34–35). Their implacable fierceness toward others will redound on their own heads because the failure to forgive reveals that they have never truly enjoyed God's forgiveness. Those who refuse to seek forgiveness from those whom they have wronged will be, so to speak, cast into an eternal prison from which they will never escape (Matt. 5:21–26; cf. Luke 12:57–59). Even though the road to life is open to all, few will find it, and most will travel the broad road to destruction instead (Matt. 7:13–14 par.). Indeed, many Jews, whom one would expect to respond positively to the kingdom message of Jesus as the chosen people, will refuse to do so, and so they will be excluded from the end-time banquet (Matt. 8:11–12 par.). God will consign them to darkness, and they will suffer in agony from "weeping and gnashing of teeth" (Matt. 8:12).

The phrase "weeping and gnashing of teeth" occurs often in Matthew to express the anguish of future judgment. In the parable of the weeds those who practice evil will "at the close of the age" be hurled into a fiery furnace and weep and gnash their teeth (Matt. 13:40–42). The furnace metaphorically portrays the suffering destined for those whom God will judge. So too in the parable of the dragnet the angels "at the close of the age" will "separate the evil from the righteous" (Matt. 13:49). On the final day of judgment those who practiced evil will be cast into a fiery furnace and will weep and gnash their teeth (Matt. 13:50). Those who try to enter the wedding party, which symbolizes the messianic banquet of the last days, without appropriate clothing will be evicted from the feast and cast into the darkness, and they will weep and gnash their teeth (Matt. 22:11–13). Those slaves who do not live to please the master but rather indulge in evil while he is absent will find that he will return suddenly (Matt. 24:44–51 par.). The master will not spare such a slave and will "cut him in pieces" (Luke 12:46) and exclude him from any reward. The person who squandered his talent (Matt. 25:14–30 par.), which refers to the failure to pursue a life of goodness, will be cast "into the outer darkness. In that place there will be weeping and gnashing of teeth" (Matt. 25:30). In the Lukan version the enemies who did not want the nobleman to rule over them are slaughtered when the nobleman returns as a king (Luke 19:27).

Jesus threatens his contemporaries with judgment in a variety of colorful ways. For those who turn others away from the righteous way, it would be preferable for a millstone to be tied around the neck and for them to be drowned in the sea (Matt. 18:6 par.). Those who seek for their lives and find them in the present era will lose them in God's sight on the last day (Matt. 10:39; 16:25 par.). Those who deny Jesus when facing pressure and ostracism from human beings will be denied by Jesus on the last day before his Father (Matt. 10:33 par.). Those who blaspheme against the Holy Spirit will never find forgiveness (Matt. 12:32 par.). Every plant that was not planted by the Father will be uprooted on the day of judgment (Matt. 15:13). On the last day some will be taken in judgment, while others will be spared (Matt. 24:40–41). People will be condemned on the day of judgment for the evil words that they have uttered (Matt. 12:36). The people of Nineveh and the Queen of the South will confirm the rightness of the judgment that will be meted out to Jesus' generation (Matt. 12:41–42 par.). Merely calling Jesus "Lord" will not exempt people from judgment (Matt. 7:21–23), nor will the performing of miracles, the uttering of prophecies, and the casting out of demons. Only those who do the will of God will be spared from judgment. Similarly, the building of a house—that is, verbal profession of faith and commitment—is insufficient for eschatological salvation (Matt. 7:24–27 par.). Only those who withstand the storms of life and persevere in obedience will receive a final reward. Those who practice disobedience will be judged. Those who stubbornly resist the message of the kingdom will experience a judgment greater than Sodom's (Matt. 10:15), so that the Galilean cities that heard the preaching of Jesus and did not repent will perish on judgment day (Matt. 11:20–24 par.).

Jesus often used the image of fire or hell (*geenna*) for the last judgment, alluding to the valley of Hinnom south of Jerusalem (Josh. 15:8; 18:16).[63] Children were sacrificed to idols at this locality (2 Chron. 28:3; 33:6; Jer. 7:31; 32:35), and Josiah defiled the valley so that it was rendered

---

63. See Böcher, *EDNT* 1:239–40.

unclean (2 Kings 23:10). Jeremiah prophesied that the valley of Hinnom would be a place of future slaughter (Jer. 7:32; 19:6; see also *1 En.* 27:1–3; 54:1–6; 90:25–27; *Sib. Or.* 1:103; 2:292; *2 Bar.* 59:10; 85:13; *4 Ezra* 7:36). It is likely that the references to fiery judgment also reflect the same circle of ideas (cf. Isa. 66:24). Jesus likely picked up this tradition in his references to hell. Those who allow lust to gain sway in their hearts and do not perform radical surgery, here portrayed as gouging out one's eye or cutting off part of one's hands or feet, will suffer in hell (Matt. 5:27–30; see also 18:8–9; Mark 9:43–47). The same threat of hell is directed against those whose anger leads them to insult and demean others (Matt. 5:22). People should tremble and fear the one who can cast both body and soul into hell (Matt. 10:28 par.). The scribes and Pharisees in winning a convert make the person "twice as much a child of hell as yourselves" (Matt. 23:15). Those who are snakes and live as the offspring of the evil one will not escape the judgment of hell (Matt. 23:33 par.). The references to a fiery judgment should be placed with the threat of hell (Matt. 3:10, 12 par.; 7:19; 13:40, 42, 50). In the parable of the sheep and the goats those who have failed to pursue the good and lived evil lives will be consigned to "the eternal fire" (Matt. 25:41), a judgment described as "eternal punishment" over against "eternal life" (Matt. 25:46). Perhaps we can include here the parable of the rich man and Lazarus, though it is difficult to determine how far we should apply the details of the parable (Luke 16:19–31). In any case, the parable clearly teaches that the rich man will experience judgment because of his lack of concern for the poor. The punishment is described as torment, and he suffers in agony from fire, longing for even a drop of water on his tongue.

The judgment in Acts is expressed, as we might expect, particularly in the speeches in which the gospel is proclaimed. Peter urges his hearers to save themselves from their wicked generation (Acts 2:40). The notion of saving themselves suggests that they would spare themselves from a future judgment. Jesus, as the resurrected one, has been "appointed by God to be the judge of the living and the dead" (Acts 10:42). In Paul's speech to the Athenians Jesus' resurrection serves as confirmation of the claim that he would judge the world on the appointed day (Acts 17:31). Felix becomes spooked in personal conversation with Paul when the latter teaches him about the judgment to come (Acts 24:25). More vaguely, Paul threatens those who refuse to perceive the saving work that God has done in and through the ministry of Jesus (Acts 13:40–41). A day is coming when all God's enemies will be placed under Christ's feet (Acts 2:35), and this day is nothing less than the day of the Lord prophesied in the OT (Acts 2:20).

In summary, a future judgment is taught often in the Synoptics and regularly appears in Acts. Such a judgment indicates that the decisions made in life are momentous, that human beings are responsible moral agents who must choose goodness over evil, life over death. God is a just judge who will recompense those who sin and fail to repent. Such teaching also provides encouragement to the righteous to persevere in trusting the Lord until the final day.

The Johannine Literature

As we noted earlier, the Gospel of John fixes its attention on realized eschatology. Nonetheless, the judgment that rests even now on those who refuse to believe in Jesus as the Messiah has a future dimension. God's wrath remains now on those who disbelieve in the Son, and so they "shall not see life" (John 3:36; cf. 9:39–41). The verb *opsetai* ("will [not] see") is in the future tense, suggesting that judgment cannot be limited to the present time. This is confirmed by John 5:27–29, where Jesus asserts a future resurrection of the righteous and wicked in which the former will enjoy life and the latter will suffer condemnation. Similarly, in the midst of one of his dialogues with the religious leaders Jesus prophesies that they will die in their sins unless they believe (John 8:24). Again, the relevant verb is in the future tense, *apothaneisthe* ("will die"), indicating that the death in view has not been fully realized. Conversely, Jesus promises that those who obey his word "will never see death" (John 8:51), which implies that those who refuse to keep it will experience death. The context of the discourse discloses that the death in view is not merely physical death. The word that Jesus has spoken during his ministry in the present age will serve as the vehicle of judgment on the last day (John 12:48).

The Johannine Epistles, like John's Gospel, center on present eschatology. Still, the present world "is passing away" (1 John 2:8, 17), and only those who do God's will remain forever, which implies a future judgment. When Jesus is revealed, the day of judgment will be at hand (1 John 2:28). Only those who practice love will enjoy confidence before God when the judgment arrives (1 John 4:17). There is sin that leads to death (1 John 5:16), and given the context of 1 John as a whole, the death in view should be identified not as physical death but rather as final judgment.[64] This fits with the threat posed by the secessionists (1 John 2:19). They claim fellowship with God and Christ but do not truly belong to the people of God (1 John 1:6–10; cf. 2:3–6; 4:1–6). This also accords with 2 John 8, where believers are exhorted not to forfeit their reward by paying heed to the docetic teaching about Jesus (2 John

---

64. Rightly Marshall 1978a: 247–49; Smalley 1984: 297–98.

7), and those who succumb to such teaching do not belong to the Father and the Son (2 John 9).

If the Gospel of John and the Johannine Epistles are characterized by realized eschatology, Revelation is notable for its future eschatology and its emphasis on a future judgment and a future salvation. This dramatic difference confirms for many the impossibility of the apostle John being the author of Revelation. We need to recognize, however, that there are texts that refer to future judgment and salvation in John's Gospel and the Johannine Epistles. Hence, the differences may be accounted for by the circumstances that called forth the various writings. NT scholars have all too often isolated NT documents from their origin and forgotten their own dictum that the writings are occasional. As a result, they have read the NT writings as if they contained the comprehensive theology of the writer in question. When we recall the purposes of each writing, the increased emphasis on the future in Revelation can be accounted for by the situation that evoked its writing and the genre that John chose to adopt.

The theme of judgment pervades Revelation.[65] Not every judgment prophesied relates to the final reckoning, though the judgments in history serve as a prelude and an anticipation of the final judgment. In Revelation judgment is portrayed in the opening of seven seals (Rev. 6:1–17; 8:1), the sounding of seven trumpets (Rev. 8:2–9:21; 11:15–19), and the pouring out of seven bowls (Rev. 15:5–16:21). The number "seven" designates the completeness and the finality of God's judgment. The seals, trumpets, and bowls increase in severity, so that the judgment of the bowls brings devastation upon the whole earth. The first five seal judgments characterize human history from the time of Christ's cross and resurrection until the time of the end (Rev. 6:1–11). During this period of time there are wars, famines, death, and the persecution and martyrdom of the people of God. Interestingly, the same features mark the time of the end according to the Synoptic Gospels, for Jesus predicts wars (Matt. 24:6–7), famines (Matt. 24:7), and persecution (Matt. 24:9–13). The first six trumpet judgments serve as a prelude to the end and may also designate all of history between the cross and resurrection. Given the apocalyptic language used, it is difficult to specify the nature of the judgments.[66] The first four trumpets bring devastation to one-third of the world: to greenery, life in and on the sea, fresh waters, and the sun

---

65. Revelation is profoundly shaped by the OT. On the use of the OT in Revelation, see Moyise 1995; Beale 1984. Moyise focuses on intertextuality, and Beale emphasizes the formative nature of Daniel in John's use of the OT. Moyise rightly claims that Beale outruns the evidence in seeing the entire book as having been modeled on Daniel.

66. Bauckham (1993a: 20) maintains that the images of judgment in Revelation must not be taken literally: "John has taken some of his contemporaries' worst experiences and

and moon (Rev. 8:6–12). Demonic locusts also so torment human beings that they long to die (Rev. 9:1–11), and one-third of human beings are killed by a demonic cavalry (Rev. 9:13–19). The first six bowl judgments are much more severe and seem to represent the final judgment or judgments that indicate that the end is imminent (Rev. 16:2–16). Those who worship the beast receive an evil sore, the sea turns to blood and everything in the seas perishes, all fresh water becomes blood, the wicked are scorched with heat, the world is plunged into darkness, and the final battle of Armageddon is at hand.

The seals, trumpets, and bowls increase in intensity, and yet it also seems that they overlap, for in every case the judgments culminate in the end. The seals and trumpets appear to characterize the time from Christ's death and resurrection until the time of the end, whereas the bowls seem to include events that immediately precede the end. Still, the sixth seal, the seventh trumpet, and the seventh bowl all signal the coming of the end. One curious feature is that the end appears to commence with the sixth seal instead of the seventh. It seems, however, that the seventh seal is a literary device that is designed to introduce the seven trumpets (Rev. 8:1–5), and the literary connection between the seals and trumpets would explain why the end is conveyed by the sixth seal.[67] There is no doubt that the seventh trumpet introduces the end, for John specifically indicates that the kingdoms of the world are now under the reign of the Lord Messiah, and that he will reign forever (Rev. 11:15). God has taken his power and begun to reign (Rev. 11:17). Similarly, the seventh bowl is introduced with the words "It is done!" (Rev. 16:17). History has reached its climax. One of the noteworthy features of Revelation is its cyclical nature, so that the end of history is conveyed repeatedly in the book. Hence, Revelation does not represent a continuous story line from start to finish; rather, history is schematized in a number of different ways, and John brings the reader to the end of all things and then starts the story over again. The entirety of history and the end thereof is portrayed, therefore, in a diversity of ways. By covering the same ground several times, John provides his readers with a diversity of perspectives on history and the coming judgment and salvation.

When we examine the sixth seal (Rev. 6:12–17), it is evident from the remainder of the book and the language used in the seal itself that this seal portrays the final judgment.[68] The sixth seal commences with an earthquake (Rev. 6:12). Elsewhere in Revelation an earthquake symbol-

---

worst fears of wars and natural disasters, blown them up to apocalyptic proportions and cast them in biblically allusive terms."

67. See Beale 1999b: 445–46.

68. Rightly Beale 1999b: 396–401.

izes that the end of history has arrived.[69] When the angel casts the cen-
ser to the earth that will inaugurate the blowing of the seven trumpets,
an earthquake occurs, for the seven trumpets herald the coming of the
end (Rev. 8:5). The fall of the city of man and the vindication of God's
people are coincident with an earthquake (Rev. 11:13). When the seventh trumpet has sounded and the kingdoms of the world have become
the kingdoms of the Christ, an earthquake occurs (Rev. 11:19). So too,
when the seventh bowl is poured out, a massive earthquake shakes the
city of Babylon (Rev. 16:18). The end is also accompanied by thunder
and lightning (Rev. 8:5; 11:19; 16:18) and a great hailstorm (Rev. 11:19;
16:21). God's temple is opened, and the ark of the covenant, missing
since the days of Jeremiah, appears (Rev. 11:19). We are told that the
tabernacle of testimony is opened before the seven bowls are poured out
(Rev. 15:5). The thunder, lightning, and hailstorm indicate that the day
of God's judgment is at hand—a judgment that is awesome and terrible.
The opening of the temple and the manifestation of the ark suggest that
God is about to reveal himself to his people in a new, dramatic, and
culminating fashion.

We return to the sixth seal and note that it has all the features of the
final judgment. The language of the sixth seal recalls the day of the Lord
in the OT (cf. Isa. 13:10; 34:4; Joel 2:10). The sun turns black and the
moon becomes red as blood, the stars hurtle to the earth, and the sky is
rolled up like a scroll (Rev. 6:12–14). The end is at hand, and the cosmos
is reeling and falling apart. The dissolution of the world is confirmed
by the displacement of mountains and islands (Rev. 6:14). Similarly, the
final judgment and the end are indicated by the fleeing of the islands and
the absence of the mountains in the seventh trumpet (Rev. 16:20).[70] The
"great white throne" judgment of Revelation depicts the same event, for
at the time of the judgment earth and heaven flee from God's presence
(Rev. 20:11). The world as humans know it is no more. The consummation of all things is also portrayed when all human beings hide in
caves and in the mountains, pleading for the rocks and mountains to
fall on them so that they will be spared from the wrath of God and the
Lamb (Rev. 6:15–16). Once again the imagery of hiding hearkens back
to the day of the Lord in the OT (Isa. 2:10, 19), and the entreaty to the
mountains to fall on them alludes to the judgment proclaimed in Hosea
(Hosea 10:8).

The judgments in the seals, trumpets, and bowls represent the wrath
of God and the Lamb (Rev. 6:16–17; 11:18; 15:1, 7; 16:1, 19). When God
pours out his wrath, he will complete his righteous judgment and destroy

69. See Bauckham 1977.
70. See R. Mounce 1977: 304; Beale 1999b: 844.

those who have devastated the earth (Rev. 11:18; 15:1). The imagery of Rev. 8:1–5 indicates that the judgments poured out are also a result of the saints' prayers.[71] God responds to his people by vindicating them and thereby demonstrating that he is righteous (Rev. 6:9–11). God's judgments leading up to and anticipating the final judgment are designed to provoke human beings to repent and turn from their sins (Rev. 9:20–21; 16:9, 11). Unfortunately, most will not turn from their sin and idolatry when they are judged; instead of repenting, they will become embittered with God and curse him because of the pain inflicted on them. John particularly emphasizes that God's judgments are righteous (Rev. 15:3–4; 16:5–7; 19:2). Unlike the acts of a crazed deity drunk with fury, God's judgments are not arbitrary and capricious. His judgments demonstrate that he is holy, true, and just. They do not call into question his goodness but rather verify it. The wicked deserve God's judgments because they have wantonly and maliciously shed the blood of God's people (Rev. 16:6; 19:2). God's judgments represent his fair and just compensation for the evil that the wicked have inflicted on others.

The judgment in Revelation is not exhausted by the seals, trumpets, and bowls. The phrase "those who dwell on the earth" becomes a technical term for unbelievers (Rev. 3:10; 6:10; 8:13; 11:10; 13:8, 12; 17:2, 8; cf. 13:14). Their names are not inscribed in the book of life, and they worship the beast rather than the true and living God (Rev. 13:8, 12; 17:8). They are dazzled by the signs and wonders that the false prophet does to enhance the stature of the beast (Rev. 13:14), and they drink deeply from the wine of Babylon's harlotry (Rev. 17:2). They rejoice over the death of God's people (Rev. 11:10). Therefore, they will face the impending hour of testing and woe (Rev. 3:10; 8:13).

The last judgment is also portrayed in the impending fall of Babylon (Rev. 14:8; 16:19; 17:1–19:5). Babylon is described as a whore (Rev. 17:1, 15–16; 19:2) who has corrupted the world. The use of the term "Babylon" to describe God's enemy draws on the OT, where Babylon is the great city that opposes the things of God (e.g., Isa. 13:1–14:23; 21:9; 47; Jer. 50:1–51:64). Babylon, according to John, is clearly the city of Rome (Rev. 17:1, 18). Rome will be judged because of its harlotry (Rev. 17:2). The city enjoyed glittering luxury (Rev. 17:4), and an incredible array of merchandise flowed into the city, so that kings and merchants will lament at its downfall (18:3, 9–19). Rome will fall because of its blasphemy and persecution of God's people (Rev. 17:3, 6; 18:24; 19:2). John emphasizes that the judgment of Rome means that the city receives what it deserves (Rev. 18:4–8), and it reveals God's might, strength, and

71. So Caird 1966: 107; R. Mounce 1977: 182–83; Beale 1999b: 454–57.

sovereignty over all.[72] God has vindicated his people by judging Rome, and therefore the saints will rejoice (Rev. 18:20). All of heaven will resound with praise and honor and will worship God for his salvation, glory, and power (Rev. 19:1–5). They will be filled with praise because of God's righteous judgments and the vindication of his people whose blood Babylon has spilled.

The judgment over the earth is ultimately the work of the Son of Man, and it is represented, as in the OT, as a reaping and harvesting of the earth (Rev. 14:14–16; cf. Joel 3:12–13; Jer. 51:33).[73] The judgment is also portrayed as the gathering of the grape harvest and the trampling of grapes in which the blood of grapes flows everywhere (Rev. 14:17–20). We noted earlier that when Jesus comes, he comes as judge to destroy the wicked (Rev. 19:11–21). The image of the winepress again denotes the outpouring of his wrath (Rev. 19:15), and the robe dipped in blood (Rev. 19:13) designates not redemption but rather the blood that is spilled in judgment (cf. Isa. 63:1–7). Both the false prophet and the beast are judged and cast into the lake of fire (Rev. 19:20). The sword that proceeds from Jesus' mouth slays the rest (cf. Ezek. 38:20–23), and the birds that Ezekiel prophesied would consume human beings (Ezek. 39:4, 17–20) will gorge themselves on human flesh (Rev. 19:17–21).

The final judgment is also described in the "great white throne" judgment (Rev. 20:11–15). Those whose names are inscribed in the book of life will be spared from judgment. All people everywhere will be assessed according to their works, and those who have practiced evil will be cast into the lake of fire. John affirms elsewhere that the final judgment will be according to people's works (Rev. 22:12). No unclean person will enter the new Jerusalem, nor will those who do what is abominable or practice lying (Rev. 21:27). The same message is affirmed when Jesus speaks of those who are not part of the new Jerusalem: "Outside are the dogs and sorcerers and sexually immoral and murderers and idolaters, and everyone who loves and practices falsehood" (Rev. 22:15). Similarly, those who supplement or detract from John's prophetic words will experience

---

72. Bauckham (1993a: 20–21) rightly observes that the pictures of the judgment of Babylon should not be pressed so as to depict the literal judgment of Rome. On the one hand, Babylon perishes in an earthquake (Rev. 16:17–21); on the other hand, the city is treated like a harlot who "is stripped, devoured and burned by the beast and the ten kings" (Bauckham 1993a: 21). Finally, the city becomes the dwelling place of "desert creatures," and yet the smoke of the city ascends forever (Rev. 18:2; 19:3). John does not expect readers to do the mental gymnastics of trying to explain how each of these judgments coheres literally.

73. Some scholars argue that both the grain and vintage harvests symbolize judgment (R. Mounce 1977: 279–83; Aune 1998: 801–3; Beale 1999b: 770–84), whereas others think that the grain harvest represents salvation, and the vintage harvest judgment (Bauckham 1993b: 290–96; Osborne 2002: 549–56). The OT background from Joel 3 suggests that judgment is in view. See also the convincing arguments of Beale and Aune.

the threatened plagues and will neither eat of the tree of life nor enter the holy city (Rev. 22:18–19).

We have noted in several texts that the final judgment is described as "the lake of fire" (Rev. 19:20; 20:10, 14–15).[74] The lake of fire is the final habitation of the beast and false prophet (Rev. 19:20), the devil (Rev. 20:10), death and Hades (Rev. 20:14–15), and those whose names are not written in the book of life.[75] The punishment of the lake of fire, as the image of fire suggests, involves eternal torment (Rev. 20:10). Further, the lake of fire is identified as the second death (Rev. 20:14), and the expression "second death" suggests a definitive and final death from which there is no return. Those who fail to overcome will be destroyed by the second death (Rev. 2:11), while those who enjoy the first resurrection will never experience the second death (Rev. 20:6). Conversely, those who practice evil will not escape the second death; they will be removed from the book of life (Rev. 3:5). This is clear from Rev. 21:8: "But as for the cowardly, the detestable . . . murderers, the sexually immoral, sorcerers, idolaters, and all liars, their portion will be in the lake that burns with fire and sulfur, which is the second death." Physical death does not represent the final punishment, for believers who experience physical death because of their allegiance to Jesus will not be harmed by the second death (Rev. 2:10–11; 12:11). Jesus possesses the keys to death and Hades (Rev. 1:18) and will triumph over them forever (Rev. 20:14; 21:4). We noted above that those in the lake of fire experience eternal torment (Rev. 20:10).[76] The future punishment of those who worship the beast is defined in terms of agonizing torment (Rev. 14:9–11). The torment never ceases, and those who experience God's wrath will "have no rest, day or night" (Rev. 14:11).[77] That the future judgment brings torment is confirmed in the case of Babylon, which will face torment for her whoredom (Rev. 18:7, 10, 15).

In summary, the Gospel of John and 1 John, with their realized eschatology, focus on the judgment that is actualized by the unbelief and disobedience of human beings. Yet even in these writings there is also the message of a final judgment that brings to completion what has begun in the present age. John in Revelation, on the other hand, focuses on the last judgment, and he expresses its reality in a variety of ways and with fiery intensity. John assures the righteous that wickedness will

74. For background, see Osborne 2002: 690–91; Beale 1999b: 970.

75. Contra Rissi 1966: 73–74, the open gates in Revelation do not signify that the lake of fire is not a permanent resting place.

76. Hence, annihilation is not contemplated (so Osborne 2002: 715–16; Beale 1999b: 1028–30).

77. The torment lasts forever, and the wicked are not obliterated (rightly Beale 1999b: 762–63; Osborne 2002: 541–43).

be punished and that everyone who has embraced evil will be repaid. Further, the message of final judgment also functions to encourage the righteous to persevere. They must remain faithful to the end, for they do not want to face the destiny of the disobedient.

The Pauline Literature

The final judgment in Paul's writings is expressed in a variety of ways. Often it is depicted as the outpouring of God's wrath (*orgē*). Normally for Paul, God's wrath is eschatological, denoting his final judgment, though we see in Rom. 1:18–32 that the wrath of God operates even now in that God remands people to the consequences of their sin even in the present era (cf. Rom. 4:15; Eph. 2:3).[78] The culmination and final expression of God's wrath are reserved for the day of judgment (Rom. 5:9; 1 Thess. 1:10; 5:9). Those who fail to repent are storing up wrath against themselves in the day to come (Rom. 2:5), and they will experience God's righteous fury (Rom. 2:8). God's wrath is not arbitrary; it is destined for those who continue in disobedience (Eph. 5:6; Col. 3:6). Christians should refrain from vengeance and wait for God's wrath, which will put all things right in the end (Rom. 12:19). Some scholars have depersonalized Paul's view of God's wrath, maintaining that it should be understood as the natural consequence of sin.[79] Such a view reads Paul through the lenses of Western culture and predispositions, for Paul was nurtured in the OT, where it is clear that God's wrath is personal. Detaching God's wrath from his character reflects a deism that comports with modern sensibilities but deviates from a proper understanding of Paul.

We have seen in our discussion that wrath is closely related to God's judgment. As we noted in terms of God's wrath, his judgment is mainly eschatological. All persons will stand before God at the final judgment (Rom. 3:5; 14:10). He will assess all according to their works (Rom. 2:6; 2 Cor. 5:10; 11:15; cf. 2 Tim. 4:14). Since everything that a person has done will be disclosed accurately and fully (1 Cor. 4:5), God's judgment will accord with the truth (Rom. 2:2); that is, it will fit with the way things really are. Therefore, no one will be able to complain that the judgment is unfair, for God's judgment is "righteous" (Rom. 2:5). He will impartially judge all in accordance with their behavior (Rom. 2:6–11). Those who have the law will be appraised by whether they have kept the law, and those who lack the law by whether they have lived according to the law written on their hearts (Rom. 2:12–13). God's judgment of behavior will not fall prey to superficiality, for he evaluates all people

78. Contra Eckstein (1987), who sees a future outpouring of God's wrath even in Rom. 1:18–32.
79. So Dodd 1932: 21–24; Green and Baker 2000: 51–56.

in accord with their "secrets" (Rom. 2:16), so that his final assessment will be indisputable.

In 2 Thessalonians Paul emphasizes God's justice in judging. God does not judge arbitrarily; rather, he inflicts punishment on those who hate the truth and delight in wickedness (2 Thess. 2:10–12). The punishment that the ungodly receive is just, because it is fair compensation for their mistreatment of believers (2 Thess. 1:6).[80] Paul here reflects the *lex talionis* view found in the OT, whereby the punishment is proportional to the crime. The judgment in 2 Thess. 1 occurs at the second coming, when Jesus arrives with his powerful angels (2 Thess. 1:7–10). Here we have language that is reminiscent of Jesus' words on hell as given in the Synoptics. Jesus will come with fire and avenge those who do not know God and those who have refused to obey the gospel. The destruction contemplated is likely one that lasts forever (2 Thess. 1:9).[81] Those who are penalized are separated from the Lord's gracious presence forever.

The metaphor of fire is used elsewhere to designate the winnowing process of the judgment (1 Cor. 3:13–15). Often the final consequence of the judgment is designated as "perishing" or "destruction" (*apollymi*, *apōleia* or *olethron*). We already noted in 2 Thess. 1:9 that those who are unsaved will face "eternal destruction" when Jesus comes. This destruction will come suddenly and without warning (1 Thess. 5:3). Those who make riches their god will end up being destroyed (1 Tim. 6:9). Similarly, those who oppose believers indicate from their opposition that they are headed to destruction (Phil. 1:28). The enemies of the cross who serve their own bellies and live for earthly things will be destroyed (Phil. 3:19). The "man of lawlessness" will flourish for a time, but ultimately he is destined for "destruction" (2 Thess. 2:3). God has even ordained who will experience eschatological destruction (Rom. 9:22). Such a statement, however, can never be abstracted from the remainder of what Paul teaches, for destruction comes because people have sinned (Rom. 2:12) and because they have rejected the message of the cross (1 Cor. 1:18). Those who perish do not find the message of the cross attractive; they are repelled by it and find it redolent of death (2 Cor. 2:16). So too Paul can say that those who are perishing do so because they are blinded by Satan (2 Cor. 4:4), but the blinding work of Satan again does not exempt people from personal responsibility. Paul clearly thinks that those who did not receive the gospel should do so and are rightly held guilty for not doing so.

80. See Wanamaker 1990: 224.
81. So Wanamaker 1990: 228–29; Morris 1959: 205–6; Best 1972: 261–62; Beale 2003: 188–89; cf. Marshall 1983: 178–80.

The consequence of sin is also described as death (Rom. 6:16, 21, 23; 8:6). Death has entered the world and rules over all people because of Adam's sin (Rom. 5:12–19; 1 Cor. 15:21). The death in view here cannot be limited to either physical death or separation from God, for it entails both. The Mosaic law, even though it comes from God, did not conquer death but rather became a tool of sin and thus also brought about death (Rom. 7:5, 10, 13; 2 Cor. 3:7). Paul also describes the final judgment as eschatological humiliation or shame (Rom. 9:33; 10:11; 1 Cor. 1:27; cf. Phil. 1:20). Psychologically, the future punishment of the wicked involves anguish (Rom. 2:9; 2 Thess. 1:6) and distress (Rom. 2:9).

In summary, in Paul's writings the final judgment is the result of God's wrath and is often described in terms of destruction and death. It represents Gods' just reprisal on those who fail to believe the gospel and on those who refuse to do his will. We should note that one of Paul's purposes in emphasizing the final judgment is to encourage his readers to persevere, reminding them that they do not want to face the fate of the wicked.

Hebrews

The sermonic character of Hebrews, in which the author exhorts his readers not to apostatize, sets the parameters for the letter as a whole. The exhortations given and the judgments threatened are set within the framework of encouraging and warning his readers not to fall away from the living God. The author attempts to motivate his readers by using the image of escaping from judgment. Those who abandon the faith will not escape the one who has accomplished such a great salvation and who has warned them from heaven (Heb. 2:3; 12:25). The future reward is designated as rest, and those who harden their hearts and continue in disbelief and disobedience will not enjoy God's rest (Heb. 3:11, 18–19; 4:3, 5). Instead of having rest, they will suffer, so to speak, from eschatological exhaustion and weariness. In Heb. 6:7–8 the author provides an illustration from the world of agriculture. Those who commit apostasy are likened to those who have received refreshing rains from God and yet have produced not fruit but only thorns and thistles instead. Vegetation that produces no fruit will be cursed and end up being burned. The author uses the image of burning to depict the final judgment and suggests that those who turn away will be cursed by God.[82]

Similarly, in the severe warning contained in Heb. 10:26–31 the author admonishes the readers of the consequence of deliberately forsaking the sacrifice of Christ. The punishment is worse than the death sen-

---

82. Rightly Attridge 1989: 173.

tence imposed under the Mosaic covenant. Sinners will experience God's judgment and his consuming fire (Heb. 10:27; 12:29). Physical death is clearly a result of sin, for Satan holds people in bondage because of the fear of death (Heb. 2:14–15). But the author of Hebrews contemplates the judgment that follows death (Heb. 9:27), which suggests an even more terrible sentence than physical death awaiting those who do not obey the Lord. God will pour his vengeance and judgment on those who abandon the sacrifice of Christ (Heb. 10:30). They face the terrifying prospect of falling into the hands of the living God (Heb. 10:31). Those who fall into God's judging hands will find that he shows no delight or tenderness toward those who have been too timid to persevere (Heb. 10:38). Those who shrink back will ultimately experience destruction (*apōleia* [Heb. 10:39]).

James

The future judgment in James is inseparable from the parenetic character of the letter. For instance, the consequence of sin is death (James 1:15).[83] Similarly, if a person in sin does not turn away from evil, death will be the final result (James 5:20). The rich will experience eschatological humiliation instead of exaltation (James 1:10). The judgment of the rich is compared to a beautiful flower. When a flower blossoms and stands forth in the richness of its beauty, it seems that it will never fade (James 1:11). But God's judgment is like the sun, for just as the sun's steady beating day after day causes a flower to wither and fall from the stem so that its beauty is lost, so also the rich will disappear on the day of judgment. We see in another prophecy that the rich will be judged (James 5:1–6). The rich are those who have exploited the poor and held back their wages. On the last day, however, the rich will wail in sorrow because of their impending misery. The riches in which they place their trust will vanish. Their treasure in the last day will be punishment, not wealth. The subsequent paragraph indicates that this judgment will be unleashed on the day when the Lord returns (James 5:7–9). Jesus is the judge who stands at the door. Those who do not show mercy to others will be deprived of mercy on the last day (James 2:13), for God alone is the judge of all (James 4:12).

1 Peter

Peter, in his first letter, refers to the reward that believers will receive far more than he speaks of judgment, perhaps because he seeks to focus on the future blessing promised to suffering believers. Still, some

83. For the eschatology of James, see Chester 1994: 16–20.

statements about God's judgment do exist. God is an impartial judge who assesses people according to their deeds (1 Pet. 1:17). Jesus did not resort to threats and vengeance, for he was persuaded that God would judge justly on the last day those who mistreated him (1 Pet. 2:23). God shows his favor to the righteous, but on the day of judgment he turns his face away from those who practice evil (1 Pet. 3:12). Those who ridicule and persecute believers may currently enjoy social approbation, but they will have to give a final account to God as judge on the last day (1 Pet. 4:5).[84] Even now believers face a purifying judgment through suffering, and thus it follows that the recompense for unbelievers will be far worse (1 Pet. 4:17–18).

2 Peter and Jude

The theme of judgment pervades the short letters of 2 Peter and Jude. In both letters false teachers have threatened the church, and the authors promise that these teachers will experience adverse consequences for their actions. It seems that in both 2 Peter and Jude the false teachers propounded libertinism (2 Pet. 2:1–3; Jude 4). These teachers were brimming with confidence and authoritatively commanded others (2 Pet. 2:10–12; Jude 8–10), but both authors respond by emphasizing that judgment on those who indulge in evil will be sure. Both Peter and Jude remind their readers of judgments that God carried out in history:[85] the flood (2 Pet. 2:5; 3:6); the angels who violated their proper domain at the time preceding the flood (2 Pet. 2:4; Jude 6); the judgment upon the Israelites who sinned in the wilderness (Jude 5); the destruction of Sodom and Gomorrah (2 Pet. 2:6; Jude 7). The punishment of angels in history anticipates the final reckoning that they will receive on the day of judgment (2 Pet. 2:4; Jude 6). The fiery destruction of Sodom and Gomorrah functions as a type of the "eternal fire" (Jude 7; cf. 2 Pet. 2:6).

84. In 1 Pet. 4:6 Peter does not indicate that the gospel will be proclaimed to the physically dead; rather, he warns that the disobedient will be judged by God. Therefore, the church should endure persecution, for if they join the ranks of the wicked, they too will be judged. Peter's warning to the righteous here would be deprived of its power if he immediately added that those who disobey will have another occasion after physical death to hear the gospel and be spared from judgment. Why would it be so crucial for the righteous to persist in faith if they, along with their persecutors, will receive a second chance later? The most likely interpretation of the verse, therefore, is that Peter refers to believers who heard and believed the gospel when they were alive but who had since died. For this view, see Achtemeier 1996: 290–91; J. Elliott 2000: 733–34. For further discussion of the text, see Schreiner 2003: 205–10.

85. The details of both of these texts are the subject of debate. See Schreiner 2003: 335–41, 441–54.

God's judgments in history, therefore, serve as a prelude to and anticipation of the final judgment. They guarantee that God will condemn the ungodly, for God has prescripted their judgment from the beginning (Jude 4). These examples also demonstrate that even though God's judgments are not immediate, they are certain (2 Pet. 2:9). The delay will not last forever (2 Pet. 2:3). God has reserved the present heavens and earth for a fiery judgment that will spell the "destruction of the ungodly" (2 Pet. 3:7). Peter uses the language of the day of the Lord to sketch in the judgment, summoning up a common OT motif (2 Pet. 3:10). He may also allude to the words of Jesus, for he says that the day of judgment will surprise the wicked and come like a thief. The current heavens and earth will pass away, and the elements of the world will be dissolved (2 Pet. 3:10–12). The false teachers distort both Paul's writings and the OT Scriptures, and hence they will face eschatological destruction (2 Pet. 3:16; cf. 2:1). Their destruction is compared to the corruption and dissolution of animals (2 Pet. 2:12). Jude pronounces a woe oracle of judgment on those who imitate Cain, Balaam, and Korah (Jude 11). The image of "the gloom of utter darkness" is introduced to describe the impending judgment (Jude 13). Interestingly, Jude cites a prophecy from *1 En.* 1:9 in support of the coming judgment (Jude 14–15). This prophecy focuses on Christ's coming and emphasizes that all the godless will be judged for their ungodly lives.

Conclusion

The NT writers frequently teach that there will be a future and definitive judgment on the wicked. God will manifest his judgment by punishing those who refuse to believe in the gospel and those who have disobeyed his will. Such a judgment is described in a variety of ways, but clearly it will involve both physical and psychological torment and will last forever. Such a judgment testifies to God's justice, assuring believers that those who practice evil will receive just recompense for their actions. Further, the judgment functions as a motivation for the righteous to persevere, for if they join the wicked, they will face the same destiny that awaits those who have rejected the gospel.

Reward

The Synoptic Gospels and Acts

We saw in the Synoptic Gospels that those who refuse to repent when the message of the kingdom is proclaimed will face judgment, and it follows as a corollary that those who believe and obey will receive a final reward. Many of the Beatitudes promise an eschatological benefit for those who are Jesus' disciples. The mournful will receive comfort; the meek will inherit the earth; those hungry for righteousness will be satisfied; the merciful will know God's mercy; the pure in heart will see God; peacemakers will be God's children (Matt. 5:4–9; cf. Luke 6:21). Each of the Beatitudes conveys different aspects of the end-time reward promised to Jesus' followers. Perhaps the recompense of the disciples is best captured by the promise that they will see God (Matt. 5:8). Another way of putting this is that they will realize fully what it is to be God's children, or that the righteousness that they long for will be their possession. The wicked will no longer oppress the righteous and rule the world; a day is coming when peace will reign and the humble will enjoy a new creation. Those who are persecuted now are guaranteed an astonishing reward in heaven (Matt. 5:12 par.).

Jesus did not teach a disinterested Kantian ethic. He promised his disciples remarkable rewards if they followed him.[86] Practicing religion to impress people should be avoided because those whose piety is designed to win accolades from human beings will not receive a final reward from God (Matt. 6:1). Three examples of this principle are unfolded to illustrate Jesus' teaching in the areas of almsgiving, prayer, and fasting (Matt. 6:2–18). Jesus uses colorful examples to convey the intense desire of the human heart to gain praise from others. Only those who practice piety with authenticity and apart from the gaze of others will receive an eschatological recompense. Clearly, Jesus does not disavow the desire to receive such a reward but rather appeals to it, for he consistently teaches that those who pander to human beings will lose their reward, whereas those who live to honor God will benefit. Similarly, Jesus' disciples should not hoard wealth on this earth, for such treasures will perish (Matt. 6:19–29 par.). Instead, they should use money in such a way that they amass treasures in heaven. Those who are freed from worry and give to assist others will enjoy "a treasure in the heavens that does not fail" (Luke 12:33). The rich ruler is assured that he will have such treasure in the future as well if he sells his possessions and becomes Jesus' disciple (Matt. 19:21 par.).

As we would expect, the promised reward is conveyed with a number of different images. Those who acknowledge Jesus before other human beings will be acknowledged by Jesus in the Father's presence on the day of judgment (Matt. 10:32 par.). Giving up one's life for Jesus' sake is a frightening prospect, but ultimately it is worth it because those who surrender their lives will end up finding them (Matt. 10:39 par.; 16:25 par.). Those who welcome and support prophets, righteous persons,

---

86. On this theme, see Piper 1979.

and disciples who trust in Jesus will be recompensed (Matt. 10:41–42 par.). So too, those who love their enemies will receive a stunning reward in heaven (Matt. 5:44–48 par.). One of the most striking images of the benefit that believers will receive appears in Jesus' parable about watchful slaves (Luke 12:35–40). Those slaves who do the will of the master will receive a blessing when Jesus returns. The master will adorn himself as a slave and serve them when he returns so that they enjoy the eschatological banquet (cf. Matt. 26:29 par.). The disciples are promised a special role in judging the twelve tribes of Israel (Matt. 19:28 par.), and those who have risked all for Jesus' sake will receive a reward far beyond anything they imagined and will receive "eternal life" (Matt. 19:29 par.). The Synoptics do not often speak of the future reward in terms of "eternal life," but the term does occur in the account of the rich ruler (Matt. 19:16 par.), and it is the reward received by the righteous in the parable of the sheep and the goats (Matt. 25:46). The future reward for disciples can also be described as the reception of the kingdom, with the promise that the Father finds joy in granting the kingdom to his own (Luke 12:32). Jesus speaks of those who are justified or vindicated before God by their words (Matt. 12:37). Matthew also picks up the language of Daniel (Dan. 12:3), assuring those who do God's will that "they will shine like the sun" in the Father's kingdom (Matt. 13:43). The evil and righteous will not coexist together forever, for at the consummation of the age they will be separated from one another (Matt. 13:49). Those who have given up their lives for Jesus' sake will find their lives (Matt. 16:24–27 par.). Those who have faithfully done what God commanded will be spared on the day of judgment (Matt. 24:40–41 par.). The faithful slaves will receive positions of responsibility in the coming kingdom (Matt. 24:47 par.). Those who have used their talents faithfully will be rewarded (Matt. 25:14–30 par.). Those who have cared for fellow Christians who were hungry, sick, cold, or imprisoned will be rewarded with the future kingdom and eternal life (Matt. 25:31–46).

The Synoptics rarely speak of the future reward in terms of the resurrection of believers; they focus instead on the resurrection of Jesus from the dead. Jesus' debate with the Sadducees makes it clear that the resurrection of the dead was part of the eschatological hope for believers (Matt. 22:23–33 par.). Jesus argues from texts such as Exod. 3:6 that a future resurrection will be the portion of Abraham, Isaac, and Jacob (Matt. 22:32 par.). "I am the God" of these patriarchs indicates that they are alive now in a disembodied state and will receive their resurrection in the future.[87] The only other clear reference to the resurrection of be-

---

87. This is convincingly explicated in Wright 2003: 423–26.

lievers occurs in Luke 14:14: those who show material kindness to the needy "will be repaid at the resurrection of the just."

The missionary preaching of Acts naturally concentrates upon the resurrection of Jesus from the dead, demonstrating that his resurrection was rooted in OT prophecy and eyewitness testimony (Acts 1:22; 2:24–32; 3:15, 26; 4:2, 10, 33; 5:30; 10:40–41; 13:30–37; 17:3, 18, 31). We noted previously, however, that the resurrection of Jesus represents the inauguration of the end, and thus his resurrection guarantees the resurrection of God's people (Acts 4:2). Hence, the resurrection of Jesus animates the ministry of Paul and grants him hope of a future resurrection (Acts 23:6). The hope of the resurrection, however, does not exclude the resurrection of the unrighteous, as Acts 24:15 clarifies. The future resurrection will consummate the expectation of the righteous and introduce the day of judgment for those who have given themselves to evil.

In summary, reward for the righteous is communicated in a variety of colorful ways in the Synoptic Gospels and is confirmed in Acts as well. The reward is nothing other than eternal life, but it is described in terms of receiving mercy, inheriting the earth, being satisfied, enjoying the messianic banquet, being raised from the dead, and seeing God. Believers are motivated to continue to believe and obey by the wondrous future that is promised to them.

The Johannine Literature

We noted in chapter 2 that John emphasizes realized eschatology, promising that believers have eternal life even now. Nevertheless, the expression "eternal life" also refers to the reward that believers will enjoy forever, for the word "eternal" intimates that the life given never comes to an end. This is suggested by the contrast between having eternal life and perishing (John 3:16; 10:28), for just as perishing suggests a future judgment on the ungodly, so also eternal life points to a life that extends forever.[88] The one who possesses eternal life now will be spared the coming judgment (John 5:24). Those who look out for themselves and cling to their lives will lose them, whereas those who hate their lives will gain eternal life (John 12:25). The very nature of eternal life is that it endures and persists (John 6:27), and thus it cannot be limited to the present age.

The future character of eternal life is confirmed by its collocation with the future resurrection. Jesus is "the resurrection and the life" (John 11:25). Nor can this resurrection be defined only in terms of realized eschatology, for on several occasions in John's Gospel eternal life is linked

---

88. Note the future tense of the verb *apolōntai* in John 10:28.

with the future resurrection. Those who have eternal life will be raised by the Son from the dead on the final day (John 6:40). All those given by the Father to the Son will be raised on the last day, and not a single one of them will be lost (John 6:39; cf. 10:28–29). Only those drawn by the Father will come to the Son, and they are promised that they will enjoy the saving resurrection on the last day (John 6:44). Similarly, those who eat Jesus' flesh and drink his blood have eternal life now and will be raised by Jesus on the last day (John 6:54). It is difficult to determine whether the raising of the dead accomplished by the Father in John 5:21 is spiritual or designates the final physical resurrection. We have no doubt, however, that John 5:28–29 refers to a future physical resurrection. John refers specifically to those who will come out of their tombs. This text must be distinguished from John 6 because the resurrection here includes the righteous and the unrighteous. The unrighteous will be raised from the dead but will end up condemned, whereas those who practiced goodness will enjoy a resurrection of life. Some scholars have excised John's statements on future resurrection, arguing that they are interpolations that conflict with John's realized eschatology. Those who resort to interpolations, however, fall prey to their own conceptions of Johannine theology and flatten it out instead of perceiving its fullness and complexity. By insisting that these verses are interpolations, they force John into a one-dimensional perspective. Such a judgment forces Johannine theology into a predetermined grid instead of acknowledging what we actually have in the text.

The Johannine Epistles, given their limitations, do not refer often to the end-time reward of believers. John does recognize the eschatological transition, so that the true light is now shining and the darkness is fading away (1 John 2:8, 17). Hence, those who do the will of God will remain forever (1 John 2:17).[89] Those who remain in the Son and the Father will receive eternal life as promised (1 John 2:25). Eternal life is prominent in John's Gospel, and so the promise of eternal life in 1 John links the two documents (1 John 1:2; 3:15; 5:11, 13, 20; cf. 5:12). What believers will be when Jesus returns has not been disclosed fully, but moral transformation is promised to them so that they will be like Jesus when he is revealed, and they will see his face (1 John 3:2–3). The struggle with evil that marks this present age will cease, and a new era will dawn. Nor are believers paralyzed by fear as the day of judgment approaches. As love is perfected in them, they look forward to the day of judgment with confidence and boldness, convinced by the love that floods their hearts that they will not be punished on the day judgment

89. Marshall (1978a: 146) says, "He will remain standing amid the storms of judgment." Cf. Smalley 1984: 88–89.

arrives (1 John 4:17–18).[90] Believers are full of assurance, knowing that they now enjoy eternal life because the Son of God resides in them (1 John 5:12–13; cf. 2:12–14). The same assurance is found in 2 John. Those who have the truth residing in them will never lose it; they have the truth as a permanent possession (2 John 2). Still, in order to "receive a full reward" (2 John 8 NRSV) believers must resist the docetic Christology advocated by the deceivers. This reward is not an optional extra but rather is necessary for salvation, for those who pay heed to the false Christology do not belong to God (2 John 9).[91]

Just as Revelation dwells upon future judgment, so too the future reward of believers occupies much of John's attention. Suffering believers are reminded of the consequence of failing to endure and of the great blessing that will be theirs if they remain faithful. Indeed, the book begins with the promise of blessing for those who read, hear, and keep the message contained therein (Rev. 1:3). The book closes with the same promise of blessing for those who obey the book's message (Rev. 22:7). The blessing is almost certainly the eschatological reward, as the remaining texts about blessing in the book indicate.[92] Those who "die in the Lord" will receive blessing and eschatological rest because their deeds demonstrate that they truly belong to God (Rev. 14:13). So too those who are vigilant and stay awake and are clothed with goodness will be rewarded with blessing when Jesus returns (Rev. 16:15). The end-time blessing is reserved for those invited to the Lamb's marriage supper (Rev. 19:17; cf. 3:20). Those who enjoy the first resurrection are blessed (Rev. 20:6), for they have been faithful to Jesus and have refused to worship the beast (Rev. 20:4). Those who have washed their robes are blessed, in contrast to those who practice evil and are banished from the holy city (Rev. 20:14–15; 21:27). If John describes physical resurrection, it is in his description of the first resurrection, but whether the first resurrection is literal or spiritual is a subject of intense debate and need not detain us here.[93]

Those who belong to Jesus enjoy the kingdom now and will reign with him in the future (Rev. 1:6, 9; 5:10). Just as Jesus will rule over the nations with an iron rod, so too will Jesus' followers because they have conquered (Rev. 2:26–27; 3:21). Those who participate in the first resurrection will

90. See Smalley 1984: 258–60.

91. R. Brown 1982: 686–87; Smalley 1984: 330–32. Marshall (1978a: 72–73) is ambivalent on this point.

92. Beale (1999b: 1127) rightly sees that the blessing is eschatological reward.

93. For a helpful discussion of the various views, see Grenz 1992. For support of premillennialism, see Ladd 1977: 17–40; Blaising 1999: 157–227; Osborne 2002: 699–719; amillennialism, Kline 1975; 1976; Hoekema 1979: 223–38; Beale 1999b: 972–1031; postmillennialism, Chilton 1987: 493–529.

reign with Christ for a thousand years (Rev. 20:6), although the nature of this reign is intensely debated, and scholars differ on whether it refers to the reign of saints in heaven during the time between the resurrection and return of Christ or to a reign of the saints on earth before the inauguration of the new heavens and new earth.

The Roman Empire, as the beast, threatened the church of God with death, but John assures his readers that they will triumph over death.[94] Those who conquer will receive the blessing that Adam never received, for they will eat of the tree of life in paradise and therefore will never die (Rev. 2:7). John figuratively describes the tree of life as having healing properties (Rev. 22:2), and it seems likely that the healing refers to final salvation (cf. Rev. 22:18–19).[95] Only those whose robes are washed can partake of the tree (Rev. 22:14), and the washing likely refers to those cleansed by Jesus' death. Those who are faithful to Jesus until death will be granted a crown that is eternal life (Rev. 2:10). They may suffer from physical death, but the second death will not injure them (Rev. 2:11), and they will never be erased from the book of life (Rev. 3:5).

The joy and gladness of the future reward are described in a variety of ways in Revelation. The redeemed stand on Mount Zion, which symbolizes heaven, and play harps and sing a new song for joy (Rev. 14:1–3).[96] Those who belong to God and the Lamb will never suffer from hunger, thirst, and intense heat (Rev. 7:16). Every tear will be wiped from their eyes (Rev. 7:17; 21:4). Mourning, crying, and pain will be only a memory (Rev. 21:4). The Lamb will satisfy his thirsty people with the springs of the water of life (Rev. 7:17; 21:6; 22:1, 17). The glory and beauty of the future prepared for God's people are symbolized in the white robes and fine linen that will be worn (Rev. 3:4–5, 18; 6:11; 7:9, 13–14; 19:8, 14), representing the purity and wholeness that the saints will enjoy. Those rewarded will partake of hidden manna (Rev. 2:17), which is reserved for those who specially belong to the Lord. The white stone probably refers to stones that served as admission tokens that permitted one to enter a city, thereby signifying entrance into the holy city (Rev. 2:17). Those who conquer will be pillars in God's temple, and God's name and the name of the new Jerusalem will be inscribed on them (Rev. 3:12). In other words, they will be part of the new community, the new heavens and earth.

All the blessings promised to believers can be summed up in the promise that God himself will dwell with his people (Rev. 21:3).[97] God's

---

94. On the relationship of the beast to Nero, see Bauckham 1993b: 384–452.

95. See Beale 1999b: 1108; Osborne 2002: 772.

96. Perhaps we have an already–not yet schema here (so Beale 1999b: 732; Osborne 2002: 525).

97. Beale (2004: 313–34) argues that in Revelation we have the consummation of redemptive history in the coming of the new temple.

abiding presence with his people represents the fulfillment of all his covenantal and saving promises and is the climax of all of redemptive history. The fulfillment of God's promises cannot be restricted to the consummation of God's relationship with human beings. God fulfills his promises in a new creation when he creates a new heaven and new earth (Rev. 21:1).[98] The promise of a new heaven and new earth is rooted in the OT. We see in Isaiah that the creation of the new heaven and new earth will transform Jerusalem and introduce a joy and prosperity that will never end (Isa. 65:17–25). In this new world the wolf and the lamb will abide together. The lion will no longer be carnivorous, and the serpent (with allusions to the triumph promised in Gen. 3:15) will feed on dust. Those who inhabit the new Jerusalem will worship God forever. The new creation is inseparable from the creation of the new Jerusalem (Rev. 21:1–2), just as we saw in Isa. 65:17–25.

Is the new Jerusalem a place or a people? We read about the new Jerusalem as a city descending from heaven, and also it is likened to God's people as his bride (Rev. 21:2). So too, when the angel tells John that he will show him the Lamb's wife, his bride, John sees the new Jerusalem descending from heaven (Rev. 21:9–10). It is probably best not to opt for an "either-or" answer here, as if we must choose between the new Jerusalem as a place or a people.[99] John is likely conveying the truth that the new creation introduces a new world and a new, or consummated, people. It is both a people and a place, a stunningly beautiful bride and a magnificently luminous new world.[100] Such a reading fits with what John does elsewhere—for example, Jesus is both the Lion and the Lamb (Rev. 5:5–6). John is told that Jesus is a lion, but when John looks, he sees a lamb; his seeing a lamb does not rule out the truth that Jesus is also a lion. Further support for a "both-and" option comes in the description of the city with its gates and foundations (Rev. 21:12–14). The reference to gates and foundations and a high wall supports a reference to a place, but we also see that the city contains the people of God from all the ages, for the names of the twelve tribes are inscribed on the gates, and the twelve apostles on the foundations (Rev. 21:12–14).

John devotes his energy to describing the new Jerusalem, and the language employed indicates that he writes symbolically, for he is attempting to describe the indescribable, to capture a coming world beyond human imagination. Probably the most important thing about the city is that it

98. See Rissi 1966: 55–56.
99. Gundry (1987) falls into this error in asserting that the new Jerusalem is a people and therefore excludes any notion of place.
100. So also Bauckham 1993a: 132–40; Osborne 2002: 733.

redounds with God's glory (Rev. 21:11).[101] Those who inhabit it and gaze upon it behold God's beauty, loveliness, power, and might. The beauty of the city is compared to a precious jewel that dazzles (Rev. 21:11). The indescribable beauty of the city is conveyed by its wall being made of jasper, the city itself of translucent gold, the foundations of the wall with stunning jewels, and the gates with dazzling pearls (Rev. 21:18–21). The stones represent paradise restored (Gen. 2:11–12; Ezek. 28:13) and fulfill the prophecy regarding the new Jerusalem (Isa. 54:11–12).[102]

The high wall of the city symbolizes its impregnability and safety from all evil influences (Rev. 21:12).[103] In the ancient world cities were fortified by walls in order to deny enemies easy access. This wall is measured at 144 cubits (Rev. 21:17), a number that results from multiplying twelve by twelve. The number symbolizes, then, the perfection of this wall. In the old creation no wall was ever perfect. All were subject to the sands of time and the vicissitudes of history. But this wall will never be scaled and will never crumble. John proceeds to say that the measure of 144 cubits is not merely a human measurement but also is angelic. Of course, no one knows what an angelic measurement is; by referring to angels, John conveys to readers that he writes symbolically.[104]

Those who are evil can never enter the gates of the city or defile it, for the city is reserved for those who have washed their robes and eaten of the tree of life (Rev. 22:14–15; cf. 21:27). The city is a perfect cube, and its length, width, and height are twelve thousand stadia (Rev. 21:16). So too, in the OT the holy of holies was a perfect square (1 Kings 6:20),[105] and John's allusion here to the holy of holies highlights the main significance of the city, for just as God specially dwelled in the holy of holies in all his awesome and fearsome majesty, so also he will dwell graciously and majestically in the new creation, the new Jerusalem. English versions that translate *stadiōn dōdeka chiliadōn* as "fifteen hundred miles" miss the point entirely (e.g., NASB), robbing the English reader of the symbolic significance of the number "twelve" being multiplied by one thousand. The symbolism of John's language is also evident when he says that the gates of the city will never be closed (Rev. 21:25). A high wall is useless if the citizens do not protect the city by closing its gates;

101. Bauckham (1993a: 132–33) argues that it also represents the cosmic mountain, the place where heaven and earth meet.

102. Bauckham 1993a: 134. Rissi (1966: 72) sees a link to Ezek. 28 and thinks that it indicates "a priestly function on behalf of the people of the twelve tribes." For fuller discussion, see Osborne 2002: 754–59; Beale 1999b: 1079–88.

103. Also, those who are evil are outside the walls (Rev. 22:15) (see Rissi 1966: 67–68).

104. Rightly Beale 1999b: 1077; contra Osborne (2002: 754), who says that the angel used what was typical or standard for human measurements.

105. Rightly Rissi 1966: 62.

the impregnability of a massive wall is compromised by leaving the gates of the city constantly open (cf. Isa. 60:11). However, the gates remaining open communicates another dimension of life in the new Jerusalem. The city is so safe and secure that the gates never need to be closed.[106] No enemy will ever threaten the serene peace that its citizens enjoy. At first glance, the nations bringing their honor and glory into the new Jerusalem might suggest its imperfection (Rev. 21:24, 26). But here John alludes to Isa. 60, where the Lord arises and shines his light on Israel and Jerusalem. The nations will see the favor that the Lord has bestowed on Israel, and they will travel to the nation bringing their goods from afar. Once again, then, the language employed should be construed symbolically, not literally. The nations do not literally bring their merchandise into the new Jerusalem. This is simply John's way of saying that every good gift of the old creation finds its completion and fulfillment in the new creation.[107]

The temple of the old creation always pointed to the fulfillment in the new creation. In the new Jerusalem there is no need for a physical temple, for its temple is the Lord and the Lamb (Rev. 21:22). The temple stood for the Lord's presence with his people, but the presence of the Lord and the Lamb with his people represents the culmination of what God has promised. When God promises, then, that his people will be pillars in his temple (Rev. 3:12) or that they will serve him constantly in his temple (Rev. 7:15), it is clear from the conclusion of Revelation that the reference to the temple is symbolic. Those who conquer will dwell with God forever.

In the old creation the sun provided illumination and warmth for human beings, but in the new creation the sun and moon are superfluous, as Isa. 60:19–20 prophesied. God's glory and the Lamb provide the city with its warmth and illumination (Rev. 21:23). No night exists in the city, and thus no danger of evil or corruption exists (Rev. 21:25; 22:5). Nothing cursed exists in the city; rather, it is filled with God's throne and the presence of the Lamb (Rev. 22:3). The new Jerusalem will pulsate with joy as the saints worship God forever. The consummation of all that God has promised will be theirs, for they will behold God's face, and his name will be on their foreheads (Rev. 22:4).[108]

In summary, in the Gospel of John and 1 John the reward of believers is described in terms of eternal life, and this life eternal that believers

---

106. See Osborne 2002: 764.

107. Bauckham (1993a: 135) says, "It consummates human history and culture insofar as these have been dedicated to God." For support of the view that John does not speak literally here, see Beale 1999b: 1094–96.

108. Bauckham (1993a: 142) remarks about seeing God's face, "This will be the heart of humanity's eternal joy in their eternal worship of God."

have now will culminate in the resurrection. In the book of Revelation the future reward of believers is described with a kaleidoscope of images. John calls his readers' attention to the astonishing reward that awaits believers who persevere until the end, encouraging them thereby to continue to endure persecution. The sum and substance of the reward, however, is the presence of God with his people—seeing God's face. And yet it is not only God who takes center stage, but also the Lamb. Hence, one of the major themes of this book is evident in the final reward of believers, for the joy that awaits saints is the luminous presence of God and the Lamb forever.

The Pauline Literature

The final reward of believers is described by Paul in a variety of ways. Furthermore, what believers will receive on the day of judgment is tied together with the Pauline conception of salvation, the already–not yet, as noted previously. Hence, I will not review what was said earlier about how salvation both has been inaugurated and will be consummated. Instead, I will briefly sketch in the various ways in which Paul conceives of the reward awaiting believers.

The final reward for believers is inseparable from the second coming of Christ, and when he comes, believers will see him personally and face-to-face (1 Cor. 13:12). Paul does not elaborate on this future encounter with Jesus Christ, though he does remark elsewhere that believers will be astonished and marvel when Christ returns (2 Thess. 1:10). The joy awaiting believers is comparable to a wedding in which a betrothed woman is finally united with the one she loves (2 Cor. 11:2). Since Christ will appear in glory, it follows that those who belong to him will be manifested in glory when he comes (Col. 3:4). Death is not the end for believers, nor is it the portal into nonexistence. Instead, those who belong to Christ will continue to be the Lord's (Rom. 14:8), though in a deeper and richer way than can be comprehended now. They will enjoy relief and freedom from the sufferings and afflictions that characterize this present evil age (2 Thess. 1:7; cf. Gal. 1:4). They will rest in the comfort that God reserves for his own (2 Cor. 1:3–7). When Christ comes, believers will be full of joy and gladness; they will rejoice in the Lord and in other believers whom they helped obtain final salvation (Phil. 4:1; 1 Thess. 2:19–20; 3:9).

I argued earlier that justification is God's eschatological pronouncement that has been declared in advance of the final judgment. On the last day God's declaration that those who believe in Christ are exempt from judgment will be broadcast to the world (e.g., Rom. 2:13; Gal. 2:17). The final reward of believers is often designated as "salvation" because believers are rescued from God's wrath, which will be poured out on the last day (Rom. 5:9–10; 1 Thess. 1:10; 5:9; cf. Rom. 13:11; 1 Tim. 2:15; 4:16; 2 Tim. 2:10; 4:18). It is on that day that believers will receive the final reward, and they will be praised (*epainos*) before all by God (Rom. 2:29; 1 Cor. 4:5), and those who are truly the Lord's will stand before him (Rom. 14:4; 1 Cor. 10:12). The praise in view here should not be interpreted vaguely; it refers to the eternal life that God will grant to believers. Eternal life is granted only to those who do what is good, and it will not be the portion of those who practice evil (Rom. 2:7; 6:22–23; 8:6; Gal. 6:8; 1 Tim. 6:19). On the other hand, eternal life is God's gift and is not earned by anyone. Some claim that Paul failed to notice or resolve this tension in his thinking, but such a conclusion is unpersuasive because the notion that eternal life is a result of works and is God's free gift stands in the very same context (Rom. 6:22–23). Eternal life is the result of God's mercy and is granted only to those who put their trust in Christ (1 Tim. 1:16). Those who enjoy life and immortality do so not on the basis of works but rather because of God's grace that was given to them before the world began (2 Tim. 1:9–10; Titus 3:5–7). Hence, God will see to it that believers are holy and blameless on the day he assesses all people (1 Cor. 1:8; Eph. 1:4; 5:27; Col. 1:22; 1 Thess. 3:13; 5:23).

God's judgment on that day will be *according* to works but not on the *basis* of works (Rom. 2:6–10; 2 Cor. 5:10).[109] Romans 2:26–29 clarifies that these works are the result of the Spirit's transforming energy in believers. The final reward often is described in terms of inheritance, and Paul often links the inheritance of believers with entrance into the kingdom of God. Those who practice evil and give themselves over to wickedness will not inherit God's kingdom (1 Cor. 6:9–10; Gal. 5:21; Eph. 5:5). The eschatological prize is reserved for those who run the race to the end (1 Cor. 9:24–27; Phil. 3:12–14). The kingdom is reserved for those whom God calls into it (1 Thess. 2:12), and God pledges to save those who belong to him so that they will inherit his promises (Gal. 3:29; 4:7; Titus 3:7). Indeed, these texts from Galatians and Titus are most emphatic in asserting that the inheritance cannot be gained by works; it is obtained only by faith and God's grace.

Paul's contention that only those who do good works will inherit the kingdom needs careful explication. These good works are the fruit of faith and a result of the Spirit's works. They do not, in and of themselves, achieve salvation.[110] Paul does speak of justification by works (Rom. 2:13). Gaffin rightly notes that there are not two justifications: "one present, by

---

109. Gaffin (2006: 97) rightly argues that Paul refers here to the good works that are necessary to obtain eternal life, not to a separate reward that is distinct from eternal life.

110. For further discussion of this theme, see Schreiner 1993b.

faith and one future, by works; or, present justification by faith alone, future justification by faith plus works, the former based on Christ's work, the latter based on our works, even if seen as Spirit-empowered; or, yet again, present justification based on faith in anticipation of future justification on the basis of a lifetime of faithfulness."[111] Instead, Gaffin finds the solution in the already–not yet character of Paul's theology, in the truth that faith works through love (Gal. 5:6). Future justification, then, is the manifestation of present justification. It is not as if present and future justification operate on different principles. Works "are not the ground or basis. Nor are they (co-)instrumental, a coordinate instrument for appropriating divine approbation as they supplement faith. Rather, they are the essential and manifest criterion of that faith, the integral 'fruits and evidences of a true and living faith.'"[112]

Believers will be glorified (Rom. 8:17, 30; Col. 3:4) on the day Christ returns. Paul often uses the word "glory" (*doxa*) to capture the future joy of believers.[113] Future glory is the hope that animates believers in the midst of trials and difficulties (Rom. 5:2; 8:18, 21), and this hope is based on Christ indwelling them even now (Col. 1:27). The glory awaiting believers is not perceived now, but although it is hidden, the glory will be exceedingly great when it is revealed (2 Cor. 4:17–18; 2 Tim. 2:10). Therefore, believers will be astonished and seized with joy when they finally receive the glory that God has promised and reserved for them from the beginning (Rom. 9:23; 1 Cor. 2:7; 1 Thess. 2:12; 2 Thess. 2:14). Different terms are used to convey the same reality, for a single word cannot capture the fullness of the joy awaiting believers. Not only will believers enjoy glory but also they will find peace from all that troubles them now (Rom. 2:10; 8:6). Instead of the shame and obloquy that comes from the world, honor will be given to them by God (Rom. 9:21; cf. 2 Tim. 2:20–21).

Paul promises those in Christ that they will obtain immortality or incorruption (Rom. 2:7; 1 Cor. 15:42, 50, 53–54; 2 Tim. 1:10).[114] The promise of immortality, however, is rooted in the Pauline conception of the resurrection. In Jewish thought the resurrection spelled the coming of the eschaton, the inauguration of the age to come, and therefore the passing away of this present evil age. In Paul's theology the age to come has arrived with the resurrection of Christ (Rom. 1:4; 2 Tim. 2:8). Christ's resurrection is a historical event and can be verified by witnesses (1 Cor. 15:1–11).[115] What must be recognized, however, is that the resurrection

---

111. Gaffin 2006: 98.
112. Gaffin 2006: 98. See also Gaffin 2006: 102–3.
113. On glory in Paul's writings, see Hegermann, *EDNT* 1:346–47.
114. See Harris 1983: 189–205.
115. On 1 Cor. 15:1–11, see Wright 2003: 317–29.

of believers does not take place immediately when they believe. The resurrection of Christ signaled the inauguration of the age to come, but an unexpected interval intervenes between Christ's resurrection and the resurrection of believers. Christ is the firstfruits, and the resurrection of believers will not take place until Jesus Christ comes again (1 Cor. 15:20–28).[116] The interval between Christ's resurrection and the resurrection of believers does not play a minor role in Pauline theology. Those who teach that the resurrection has already occurred have abandoned the faith (2 Tim. 2:18). The resurrection of believers is a future event and promise based on the resurrection of Jesus Christ (Rom. 8:10–11; 1 Cor. 6:14; 2 Cor. 4:14; 5:1–10).

One of the most fascinating texts on the resurrection is 1 Thess. 4:13–18. Paul assures the Thessalonians that the believing dead are at no disadvantage and will be raised before living believers are snatched up. He comforts believers with the truth that they will be with one another and the Lord forever. In 1 Thessalonians Paul teaches that living believers will be snatched up by the Lord, while in 1 Corinthians he adds the idea that the living will be instantaneously transformed when the Lord returns (1 Cor. 15:51–53). Their mortal bodies will be changed so that they become immortal, for believers cannot enter God's presence with their corruptible bodies (1 Cor. 15:50).[117]

We should pause here to emphasize that for Paul, the resurrection is not ethereal but rather involves the physical raising of bodies from the dead. The Corinthians apparently found the notion of a physical resurrection repugnant, maintaining perhaps that a spiritual resurrection with Christ constitutes the hope of believers. Paul affirms most emphatically the physicality of the resurrection hope, arguing that Christ was raised from the dead and appeared to many witnesses (1 Cor. 15:1–11), and that the refusal to accept the physical resurrection of believers amounted to a denial of Christ's resurrection (1 Cor. 15:20–28). Paul identifies as fools those who reject a physical resurrection because they cannot conceive of how bodies could be transformed,[118] and he presents a long argument in support of the physical resurrection of believers (1 Cor. 15:35–58). He argues for both continuity and discontinuity between the corruptible earthly body and the resurrection body, comparing the promise of the resurrection to a seed that seems lifeless but sprouts wheat or grain. The variety of "bodies" in the created world, both earthly and heavenly, demonstrates that the resurrection will become a reality. Currently, the human body is plagued by weakness and dishonor, sharing the perishable

---

116. It is likely that Paul does not intend to specify an interval in 1 Cor. 15:24, so it is difficult to see a millennial reign taught here (so Fee 1987: 752–54).

117. See Fee 1987: 799–802; Thiselton 2000: 1292–96.

118. See Wright 2003: 342–60.

character of the body inherited from Adam. In the future, however, the body will be glorious and strong, sharing in the body of the glorified and resurrected Christ. One might think that in Paul's view the resurrection body is not physical, for he refers to "a spiritual body" (1 Cor. 15:44). Identifying the body as spiritual does not mean, however, a nonphysical body, for the whole of 1 Cor. 15 emphasizes the bodily character of the resurrection.[119] Here "spiritual" refers to the Holy Spirit, the gift of the new age, and thus the point here is that the body will be animated and empowered by the Holy Spirit. The weakness and death of the natural body will be relegated to the past, and the new body will be incorruptible and imperishable because of the work of the Spirit. Therefore, when Paul asserts that "flesh and blood cannot inherit the kingdom of God" (1 Cor. 15:50), he does not exclude resurrected bodies from the future kingdom; rather, the corruptible and mortal bodies inherited from Adam cannot enter God's kingdom. Only those transformed by the Holy Spirit will enjoy God's presence.[120] Believers live in the interval before the completion of such a promise, but the promise of the future resurrection guarantees their final victory over death. The promise of the Pauline gospel will reach its fruition with the redemption of the body (Rom. 8:23; Eph. 1:14)—the leaving of the old creation and the dawning of the new creation.

Some have argued that Paul altered his view of the timing of the resurrection. When he wrote 1 Corinthians, he clearly believed that the resurrection of believers would coincide with Christ's coming (1 Cor. 15:23–24, 52). Did the traumatic experience related in 2 Cor. 1:8–11, among other things, jolt Paul out of his former view so that he now anticipated the resurrection to occur immediately upon death?[121] Those supporting this view usually point to 2 Cor. 5:1–10 as evidence of such a change. This text, however, is too ambiguous to signal such a change.[122] Since Paul addresses the same church, he would have needed to make it much clearer that he was proposing a different time for the resurrection. He emphasizes instead in 2 Cor. 5:1–10 what we have already seen in 1 Cor. 15. The groaning and burden associated with the present body will give way to the stability and delight of being clothed with a new body. The old body is as temporary and weak as a tent and is destined to die, whereas the new body that awaits believers is as solid and sturdy and permanent as a house. Paul could be understood to say that

---

119. Rightly Lincoln 1981: 42; Wright 2003: 348–56.

120. Rightly Wright 2003: 358–59; Hays 1997: 272.

121. So, for example, Moule 1966b; W. Davies 1948: 309–19. See also Harris 2005: 174–82.

122. Rightly Lincoln 1981: 59–71; Witherington 1992: 204–8; Wright 2003: 361–72. For a significant older work that demonstrates the weakness of the development theory relative to Paul's eschatology, see Lowe 1941.

the resurrection body is received at death, for he says that when our earthly tent is dismantled, "we have a building from God" (2 Cor. 5:1). The present tense "we have" (*echomen*) could be construed to say that the resurrection body becomes the possession of believers immediately upon death, but it is more likely that the present tense is used to denote the confidence and certainty of the reception of the resurrection body.[123] The notion that the present tense denotes present time is a fallacy, for the temporal significance of the tense must be discerned in context. Hence, the present tense does not clearly convey a change in the time of the resurrection.[124] This seems to be confirmed by Phil. 3:20–21, which likely was written after 2 Corinthians. Here Paul expects the present body, with all its attendant difficulties, to be transformed when Jesus Christ appears.

Believers are not merely promised resurrected bodies, for God also has promised his people a new creation (Rom. 8:18–25). Presently the creation labors under the burden of sin, so that the created order groans and strains because of the impact of human sin. God's promises will be fulfilled in their entirety when the new creation dawns and the limitations of the present created order are transcended. The new creation will be a perfect world of freedom and joy in which the sadness and sighing of the present world flee away. Death and every demonic power will be defeated so that every enemy will be subjected to Christ, who will hand the kingdom over to God so that God will be all in all forever and ever (1 Cor. 15:24–28).[125] It is this new world that Paul has in mind when he says that Abraham and his heirs will inherit the world (Rom. 4:13). All those who are children of Abraham will enjoy the new world that God has planned for them. Not only will they enjoy this new world, but also they will reign over it. Believers will judge the world and judge angels (1 Cor. 6:2–3). Details on what is involved here are scanty, but it is clear that believers will reign with Christ (2 Tim. 2:12; cf. Rom. 5:17) and will inherit God's kingdom (1 Cor. 6:9–10; 15:50; Gal. 5:21; Eph. 5:5).

123. So Lincoln 1981: 63–65; Osei-Bonsu 1986. For a thorough discussion of the options, see Harris 2005: 374–80. Harris (2005: 380) argues that Paul speaks of an "ideal possession of the spiritual body at death with real possession at the parousia." This seems less likely than the view proposed above, for Paul probably does not argue so abstractly here, and it is difficult to grasp how this view can be differentiated *practically* from the view proposed here, since the believer does not yet possess the resurrected body upon death.

124. In fact, it seems that Paul believes in an intermediate state according to 2 Cor. 5:1–10; Phil. 1:21–23 (so Lincoln 1981: 70–71, 104–6; Barrett 1973: 153–55, 159). Against this view, see Garland (1999: 251–52), who rejects any notion of an intermediate state here. For a wider defense of such an intermediate state, see Esler 2005: 199–208, 234–51.

125. Does Paul envision a temporary kingdom ruled by Christ before the coming of the end? For a discussion of the history of scholarship on the topic, along with some arguments supporting such a notion, see Kreitzer 1987: 131–64.

In summary, Paul gives sustained attention to the future reward of believers. Those who put their faith in Jesus Christ and manifest their faith by good works will receive eternal life. They will be saved from God's wrath on the final day. They will find peace and joy forevermore. They will marvel and be astonished with joy when Christ appears, and they will shine with glory when Christ appears. Believers will be raised from the dead and will inhabit the new creation that God has promised. In a variety of ways Paul traces out the joy set before believers, inspiring them to continue to believe and obey until the day of redemption.

Excursus: The Future of Israel

Most writers in the NT say nothing about the future of Israel. Paul stands out in this regard, for in Rom. 9–11 he devotes extensive discussion to Israel's future. Paul's view of Israel, of course, must be set against the backdrop of what he says elsewhere.[126] The fundamental question addressed in Galatians is the identity of the children of Abraham. Is it limited to those who have received circumcision? Should the people of God be defined in ethnic and Jewish terms? Paul's answer is clear and emphatic. The children of Abraham cannot be identified merely with those who are Jewish and receive circumcision. Those who believe in Christ Jesus are the genuine children of Abraham (Gal. 3:6–9). True circumcision has nothing to do with the physical operation; rather, it is a spiritual reality that belongs to those who have been the beneficiaries of the work of the Holy Spirit (Rom. 2:28–29; Phil. 3:3; Col. 2:11–12). The "Israel of God" (Gal. 6:16) finds its locus in God's work of new creation (Gal. 6:15), which is inseparable from the new life that belongs to those who are crucified to the world (Gal. 6:14).

Paul expresses the same truth in a different way in Eph. 2:11–3:13. The new people of Christ center on the "one new man" (Eph. 2:15), the church of Jesus Christ. The "dividing wall" that segregated Jews from Gentiles has been broken down (Eph. 2:14). Through the death of Jesus Christ both Jews and Gentiles have been brought near to God, and they are one people of God through Jesus Christ. Gentiles no longer stand on the outside as strangers to God's covenants and promises. They are now integrated as full citizens into the people of God and are co-heirs with the Jews and members of the same body (Eph. 2:19; 3:6). The new people of God is not fundamentally Jewish or Gentile but rather is Christ-centered.

Romans 9:6–13 stands in basic agreement with this perspective, for God never promised that every biological descendant of Abraham would

---

126. Some scholars conclude that Paul ends up contradicting himself. E. Sanders 1983: 193, 197–99; Hübner 1984b: 122; Räisänen 1988: 192–96.

receive blessing. There has always been a true Israel within the confines of ethnic Israel. In this context Paul probably restricts Israel to ethnic Israel, in contrast to Gal. 6:16,[127] for there is no clear evidence anywhere in Rom. 9–11 that the term "Israel" is broadened to include a reference to Gentile believers. Paul teaches here, in continuity with the prophetic tradition, that there has always been a remnant within Israel (Rom. 9:24–29; 11:1–10).

It might seem that the salvation of a remnant is Paul's answer regarding the future of Israel as an ethnic people. God is fulfilling his promise in saving a segment of ethnic Israel throughout history. The claim that "all Israel will be saved" (Rom. 11:26) is interpreted along these lines by some scholars, so that Paul teaches here that throughout history God will save a remnant of ethnic Israel.[128] Others have maintained that "Israel" here refers to the church of Jesus Christ, composed of both Jews and Gentiles.[129] This latter view, though rightly seeing that for Paul "Israel" does not exclusively refer to ethnic Israel, suffers from serious problems and should be rejected. First, it is nowhere clear that the term "Israel" in Rom. 9–11 refers to the church of Jesus Christ. It consistently refers to ethnic Israel.[130] Second, in the immediately preceding verse, Rom. 11:25, "Israel" denotes ethnic Israel over against the Gentiles. The hardening of Israel will last during the time that the Gentiles are streaming into the people of God. Paul then asserts in Rom. 11:26 that "all Israel will be saved." It seems clear that "Israel" must refer to the same entity just noted in Rom. 11:25, especially when we add to this the temporary hardening of Israel in that verse that gives way to their inclusion in Rom. 11:26. Third, Rom. 11:28 confirms that Paul continues to speak of ethnic Israel as a distinct entity.

The notion that the salvation of all Israel refers to the salvation of a remnant, noted above, is unpersuasive as well. Such a view fails to see that the preservation of a remnant never exhausts the promises of God. Instead, the remnant testifies that God will fulfill his promises in all their richness and fullness.[131] Paul speaks not of the salvation of merely a remnant but rather of "all Israel." Moreover, the term "mystery" in

---

127. Whether Gal. 6:16 refers to the church of Jesus Christ as the Israel of God is disputed. It is most likely that we have a reference to the church. Contra Richardson 1969: 70–84. Rightly H. Betz 1979: 322–23; Longenecker 1990: 298–99; Weima 1993: 105; Martyn 1997: 574–77; Beale 1999a. Beale argues that Isa. 54:10 and the new-creation background of Isa. 32–66 function as the background of the Pauline usage. Other scholars maintain that Paul speaks of Jewish Christians (e.g., Richardson 1969: 74–84).

128. So Ridderbos 1975: 358–59; D. Robinson 1967: 94–95; Merkle 2000; Schnabel 2004b: 1317–19.

129. R. Martin 1989: 134–35; Wright 1992b: 236–46; Calvin 1961: 255.

130. Rightly Das 2003: 106–7.

131. Rightly Das 2003: 108.

Rom. 11:25 suggests a unique and climactic disclosure in the course of Paul's argument. It is scarcely a mystery to say that God would continue to save a remnant of Israel all throughout history.[132] This latter observation is strengthened when we observe the temporal character of Paul's argument. Most scholars have argued that the phrase "and in this way" (*kai houtōs*) designates manner rather than time, though some have maintained that the phrase has temporal dimensions.[133] Even if the phrase denotes manner, temporal ideas are woven into the context. Israel will be hardened "until the fullness of the Gentiles has come in" (Rom. 11:25). Paul looks forward to the day when Israel will be grafted again onto the olive tree (Rom. 11:23–24), anticipating a future when the transgression and hardening that afflicts Israel now will be replaced by their "full inclusion" (*plērōma* [Rom. 11:12]). Presently the majority of Israel is rejected (*apobolē*) by God, but Paul looks forward to their future "acceptance" (*proslēmpsis* [Rom. 11:15]). The acceptance and conversion of Israel is the last event in salvation history before the resurrection—what Paul identifies as "life from the dead" (Rom. 11:15). A future salvation also seems likely from Rom. 11:26, where the deliverer coming from Zion is likely a reference to Christ's future coming, suggesting that Israel will be saved at or near the second coming of Christ.[134]

It seems, then, that the salvation of Israel refers to an end-time event near or at the second coming of Christ when ethnic Israel will be saved.[135] To say that "all Israel will be saved" does not mean that every single Israelite throughout history will be saved, for Paul refers to an eschatological

132. So Das 2003: 108.

133. See van der Horst 2000.

134. Das (2003: 110) argues that the reference here is to Christ's first coming, but the future tense suggests otherwise.

135. Paul's harsh words against Israel in 1 Thess. 2:14–16 seem to contradict the hope expressed in Rom. 11:26, and scholars have responded in a variety of ways to the former text. Some have maintained that the passage is a later interpolation (Pearson 1971; D. Schmidt 1983). However, the arguments and evidence for this are not compelling (so Hagner 1993a). Others argue that we must accept the fact that Paul contradicts what he teaches in Rom. 9–11 (so Okeke 1981; Simpson 1990). The latter view exaggerates the significance of the text, for Paul speaks not of all Jews but rather only of those who persecute the church and oppose the gospel. Furthermore, the text does not preclude the future repentance or conversion of even some of the Jewish persecutors. Otherwise, what Paul writes here would preclude the possibility of his own conversion, for he once persecuted the church. The reference in 1 Thess. 2:16 to the coming of God's wrath, even though stated with an aorist verb (*ephthasen*), should be interpreted to refer to a future event—God's final judgment. The use of the aorist is not surprising here, for it designates the certainty of final judgment, just as the aorist *edoxasen* in Rom. 8:30 refers to the certain promise of glorification. Das (2003: 128–39) proposes another solution. He accepts the passage as authentic but argues that the pronouncement of wrath is not a final one, so that the Jews referred to here may still be saved. Donfried (2002: 195–208) says that God's wrath is directed against Israel until the end, and then they will be saved.

event. Nor does it mean that every single ethnic Israelite alive at the time of Israel's salvation will necessarily be included. The promise is for the majority of the nation. Thus, God fulfills his saving promises to his people (Rom. 9:6) and confirms the validity of his word. Paul brings up the issue of Israel's salvation because it pertains to God's faithfulness to his covenantal promises, showing that God is true to his word.[136]

It has become increasingly popular to argue that Rom. 9–11 promises salvation for Israel, but Israel's salvation is obtained without faith in Jesus Christ.[137] The two-covenant theory maintains that Gentiles are saved through faith in Christ, whereas Israel finds salvation by observing its unique covenant with God through devotion to Torah. Israel errs when it imposes the Torah upon the Gentiles, for then it does not recognize that the Gentiles are saved in a different way from the Jews. The notion that Israel is saved apart from faith in Christ badly misreads Rom. 9–11.[138] We must keep in mind that Rom. 9–11 is a unit, and therefore any single part of this unit must be read with a view to the whole. That faith in Christ is required for Israel's salvation is clear from several pieces of evidence. (1) Paul grieves because Israel is separated from Christ, and he is almost willing to be cursed forever by God for the sake of his kinfolk (Rom. 9:3). The reason why Paul grieves for Israel is that as long as they are separated from Christ, they remain unsaved (Rom. 10:1). (2) The whole of Rom. 9:30–10:21 indicts Israel for failing to believe in the gospel and to trust in Christ for salvation. (3) Related to this, Rom. 9:30–10:21 specifically excludes the Torah as the way to salvation. Paul does not suggest that the Torah constitutes a different way of salvation for Jews. He sees Torah-righteousness as a false path that stands in contrast to faith in Christ. (4) The deliverer from Zion who will rescue Israel from its sins is Jesus himself (Rom. 11:26). Hence, Israel will be saved only when they put their faith in Jesus.[139] (5) Paul specifically remarks in Rom. 11:23 that Israel's unbelief is what prevents them from being grafted onto the olive tree.

I conclude, then, with the observation that Paul identifies the church of Jesus Christ as the true Israel (e.g., in Galatians), and at the same time he posits a future salvation for ethnic Israel (Rom. 9–11). However, this

136. This view does not suggest that the Jews are saved at the parousia on the basis of their ethnic prerogatives (as Schnabel [2002a: 56] seems to suggest); rather, they are saved solely because of God's stunning mercy.

137. For example, Stendahl 1976: 3; Gaston 1987: 92–99; Gager 1983: 252, 261.

138. For criticisms of this view, see E. Sanders 1978; Hafemann 1988; Hvalvik 1990; Das 2003: 97–106.

139. Hofius (1990: 37) says that Israel is not saved through "the evangelistic preaching of the church. Instead 'all Israel' is saved directly by the Kyrios himself. But that means that it is *not* saved without Christ, *not* without the gospel, and *not* without faith in Christ."

future salvation for ethnic Israel is obtained only through faith in Jesus Christ. In other words, those ethnic Jews who believe become part of the true Israel—the church of Jesus Christ. By reversing the expected order and saving the Gentiles first and then Israel, God showers unexpected mercy upon human beings, so that no one can claim that salvation is a right to be grasped.[140]

Hebrews

One way that the author of Hebrews dissuades his readers from committing apostasy is to remind them of the reward that will be theirs if they persevere in faithfulness. Indeed, the theology of reward figures largely in Hebrews. The author asserts that one cannot even please God unless one is convinced that God "rewards those who seek him" (Heb. 11:6). If they do not forsake their allegiance to Christ, they will receive "a great reward" (Heb. 10:35). Since God is faithful, those who persist in believing will receive what he has promised (Heb. 10:36). The promise, as Heb. 10:39 makes plain, is nothing less than salvation, for it is contrasted with eschatological destruction. The author of Hebrews does not contemplate a reward beyond eternal life; for him, the reward *is* eternal life or salvation. Salvation is the eschatological gift that believers will inherit (Heb. 1:14). This salvation is reserved for those who respond to the warnings in the letter (Heb. 6:9). They will inherit God's saving promises for his people (Heb. 6:12). The blessing that God has for his people is the hope of inheriting all that he has promised (Heb. 6:7, 18). The future reward is also described as an unshakable kingdom (Heb. 12:28), signifying the inviolability of God's promise. God will bring his children to glory, so that the corruption and imperfection of the present world will vanish (Heb. 2:10). The future blessing is also designated as "rest" (Heb. 3:11, 18; 4:1, 3, 5, 8–11). The author explains that the rest was not fully obtained under Joshua or in the days of David, and it still remains for the readers. The rest culminates when life ends, when human beings cease from their works on earth (Heb. 4:10), when the Sabbath rest of the OT finds its fulfillment in the heavenly rest.[141]

Hebrews does not emphasize that the reward obtained will involve the resurrection from the dead. Still, the author implies that he holds to the hope of the resurrection (Heb. 6:2; 11:35) and concentrates instead on the motivation for endurance provided by the hope that believers have. This is especially prominent in Heb. 11, where, as we noted previously, the believers of old relied not on present circumstances or what their eyes could see but rather on the promise of God. Moses surrendered all

---

140. This is beautifully captured in Thielman 1994a.
141. So Lincoln 1982: 205–14.

the advantages of belonging to Pharaoh's household for the sake of the future reward (Heb. 11:24–26). Believers under the old covenant will not obtain the perfection God pledged apart from the work of Christ and the company of new-covenant believers (Heb. 11:39–40).

The reward of believers is also described in terms of the heavenly city to come.[142] That city exists even now as the heavenly city, the new Jerusalem, and believers belong to this heavenly city here and now (Heb. 12:22–23). Still, what is now invisible to the saints—participation in the heavenly city—will become visible to all and will be fully realized in the future. Like Abraham, believers anticipate the city to come (Heb. 11:10), for since God is its builder and designer, that city will never perish. The homeland for believers is not this present earth as it is now; God has prepared a better country and city for his own—a heavenly city (Heb. 11:13–16). Here the promises made to Abraham, Isaac, and Jacob will find their ultimate fulfillment. Hebrews 13:13–14 confirms that longing for the heavenly city should not be restricted to Abraham, Isaac, and Jacob. Believers are now exiles outside the circle of those who are accepted in earthly society. The city of this world does not and will not endure. However, the city to come, the heavenly one, will never pass away. It remains the sure hope and great expectation of believers.

The promise of the heavenly city is not as detailed as we find in Revelation, but Hebrews clearly travels in the same circle of ideas. The present created order will be shaken (Heb. 12:25–29), and a new, unshakable order will be introduced. This thought seems quite similar to Revelation's promise of a new heaven and a new earth. The old creation will give way to the new creation, the city of man to the city of God. Hebrews, then, encourages believers to persevere, knowing that a great reward lies before them, so that they, like Jesus, should endure because of the joy set before them (Heb. 12:2).

James

James only glances at and does not dwell on the future reward of believers. Those who respond to trials in a godly way will be perfected morally (James 1:4). This is quite similar to John's promise that God's children will be like Jesus (1 John 3:2). Those who endure trials will be given "the crown of life" (James 1:12), and here the crown refers to the promise of eternal life that will belong to those who are truly the Lord's. In the same way, believers are inheritors of God's kingdom (James 2:5). James does not elaborate on what is involved in being an heir of the kingdom, but it seems to fit with the promises that we find elsewhere

142. See Attridge 1989: 332, 374, 399.

of enjoying the new creation. God also promises that those who are humble will receive eschatological vindication (James 1:9). A day of reversal is coming in which the humble will be rewarded for their faith and obedience.

1 Peter

The future reward of believers looms large in 1 Peter, presumably because Peter desired to comfort persecuted believers with the certain hope of final reward, for such a hope encourages them to persevere in the midst of difficulties. Hence, from the outset of the letter Peter reminds believers of the "living hope" that is theirs "through the resurrection of Jesus Christ" (1 Pet. 1:3). The resurrection of Jesus Christ is the inauguration of the age to come and functions as the promise, by implication, of the final resurrection of believers. The end-time reward of believers is designated an inheritance (1 Pet. 1:4; 3:9), and it is emphasized that the inheritance cannot be defiled or stained, so that nothing can diminish the joy that awaits believers. The reward of believers is also described as grace that will be received on the final day (1 Pet. 1:13; 2:20). The life of the future is one of remarkable joy and gladness (1 Pet. 4:13), when believers will be exalted instead of humiliated (1 Pet. 5:6). They will then enjoy eschatological salvation (1 Pet. 1:5, 9), and praise, glory, and honor will redound in their lives (1 Pet. 1:7; 2:7). The good days that all humans long for will be theirs forever (1 Pet. 3:10).

2 Peter and Jude

We noted earlier that 2 Peter and Jude concentrate upon the judgment to be inflicted upon the false teachers. Still, the future reward of believers is also included in both letters. The participation in the divine nature, which belongs to believers even now, will consummate in the fulfillment of all of God's promises to his people (2 Pet. 1:4). Just as the Lord saved Lot and Noah in the midst of wicked generations, so too will he preserve his people so that they will receive what is promised on the last day (2 Pet. 2:5, 7, 9). Those who practice godly qualities and truly live out their faith will not fall short of receiving what is promised; they will receive the reward of entering in the kingdom of Jesus Christ (2 Pet. 1:10–11).[143] They will be found in him as blameless on the last day and inherit salvation (2 Pet. 3:14–15). In other words, they will enjoy the new heavens and new earth that God has promised (2 Pet. 3:13). The brevity of Peter's letter is such that he does not elaborate on the nature of the new heavens and new earth. Righteousness will reign supreme

---

143. For further support of the view offered here, see Schreiner 2003: 304–6.

in the new world or new creation. The present heavens and earth will be burned up with fire (2 Pet. 3:10, 12). What is unclear is whether the present heavens and earth are destroyed and then God creates a new heavens and new earth, or whether the burning of the present heavens and earth constitutes a transformation and purification of the present world, so that the new heavens and new earth stand in continuity with the current universe but are completely transformed. Certainty on this matter is impossible, but it seems more likely that Peter refers to a purging and transformation of the old creation so that it becomes a new creation. In the same way, Hebrews looks forward to the heavenly city to come, and Revelation to the descent of the heavenly city, which is nothing other than the new heavens and new earth. Peter promises not merely an individual reward for believers but rather a new creation.

Jude looks forward to the coming of Jesus Christ, who will show mercy to his own and grant believers the gift of eternal life (Jude 21). In the last day they will stand, unblemished, with inexpressible joy before God (Jude 24). The perfection that believers long for will then be a reality.

Conclusion

The promised new creation will become a reality at the coming of Jesus Christ. God's covenantal promises will then be fulfilled, and the groaning of the old creation will end when the new world dawns with all its stunning beauty. What will make the new creation so ravishing is a vision of God and his dwelling with his people. Believers will enter the new creation with the resurrected bodies that they have been awaiting eagerly in the interval between the already and the not yet. They will receive the reward of eternal life and the kingdom promises that they grasped by faith while on this earth. The final inheritance and salvation that were longed for will then become a reality. Conversely, those who refused to believe in Christ and to obey his word will face a final judgment. Their destruction will be concomitant with the destruction of Satan. The arrival of God's kingdom in its fullness will involve not only reward for believers but also punishment for the wicked who resisted the gospel and mistreated believers. The new world and new universe will have arrived, and God will be all in all. Believers will worship and enjoy the Father, the Son, and the Spirit forever.

Epilogue

My intention in the epilogue is to sum up with brevity where we have been in this book. I have argued that the NT focuses on the fulfillment of the saving promises of God given in the OT. The NT represents the climax of the story begun in the OT, but it is a bit like a mystery novel because the story is fulfilled in an astonishing way. God's promises are fulfilled in Christ through the Spirit, and yet we still await the fullness of what was promised. There is an already–not yet character to the fulfillment. The promises are inaugurated but not consummated.

We must also see the main characters in the story. The promises that are coming to pass are the promises of God, who, as the Lord of history, is working out his plan. In particular, he has sent his Son, Jesus Christ, as the one who fulfills the promises made to Abraham, Moses, David, and the prophets. Jesus is the son of Abraham, the prophet greater than Moses, the true David (the Messiah), the Son of Man, the Lord, and the Son of God. Indeed, he is divine. It is through him that God's promises have become a reality. He is the one sent by the Father, the one who has come to do his Father's will. But also, the promises were brought to fruition through Jesus in a way that subverted human expectations. Jesus conquered sin and death by taking on the role of the Servant of the Lord. He conquered evil by submitting to suffering and taking at the cross the punishment due his people. The NT writers, using words such as "salvation," "reconciliation," "justification," "redemption," and "adoption," burst at the seams trying to express what Jesus the Christ did at the cross. Further, the NT fulfills the OT because the salvation that God promised has been effected by the Spirit who was promised in the OT. Jesus was both the bearer of the Spirit and the one who poured out his Spirit on God's people. He carried out his ministry in the power of the Spirit, and after his resurrection and exaltation Jesus gave that same Spirit to those who belong to him.

The rest of the NT explains how the story of God's promise works itself out in the lives of human beings. Human beings need God's liberating work because of the power of sin and death. Sin and death are the two towers of evil that devastate human beings, and human beings are not merely pawns of sin but rather have actively given themselves over to it. Hence, to enjoy the victory won by Jesus over evil, they must repent of their evil and put their trust in Jesus Christ as Savior, Redeemer, and Lord. This repenting faith is a persevering faith, a radical faith, a faith that honors God and Christ in the giving of one's entire being to God and Jesus Christ. Hence, those who live under the reign of God and Christ live a new kind of life. Indeed, the church of Jesus Christ is a new community in which the love of Christ is displayed. They are now the true Israel, and they are to display God's beauty in how they relate to one another and to the world as they proclaim the good news of Christ's salvation to the world.

Finally, the story is not over yet. Believers still await the consummation. They await the new creation, the completion of the new exodus, and the final fulfillment of the new covenant. Jesus will come again and transform the universe. There is a new world coming, a new creation, a new heavens and a new earth. In that coming world God will be all in all, and Jesus Christ will be honored forever and ever. And the paradise that was lost will be regained—and more than regained, it will be surpassed. And we will see his face (Rev. 22:4), and his glory will be magnified through Christ forever and ever.

APPENDIX

 ✿ ✿ ✿ ✿ ✿ ✿ ✿ ✿ ✿ ✿ ✿ ✿ ✿ ✿

Reflections on New Testament Theology

Introduction

In one sense, the discipline of biblical theology[1] is as old as the history of the church.[2] For instance, the early church fathers articulated "the rule of faith" (*regula fidei*) to summarize the message of the Scriptures. Irenaeus, in his criticism of Gnosticism, worked from a certain conception of salvation history. Certainly, the Reformers did biblical theology, even if they did not always distinguish it sharply from systematic theology. In the post-Reformation period Cocceius (1603–1669) realized the centrality of the covenant in the Scriptures, and subsequently covenant theology has played a major role in the Reformed tradition. We should not underestimate the importance of the covenant in biblical theology, for covenant theology understands the Scriptures along a historical timeline focusing on God's fulfillment of his saving promises.[3] The redemptive-historical character of the Bible is recognized in covenant theology, for

---

1. This chapter does not intend to explain or resolve the issues involved in doing biblical or NT theology. The issues are too complex to be negotiated in the sketchy survey found here. My intention is to acquaint the reader at the introductory level with some of the issues and to indicate my own approach to biblical theology.

2. On the importance of continuing to pursue biblical theology, see Hengel 1994: 329.

3. For an excellent and insightful discussion of the role of covenant and eschatology in the doing of theology, see Horton 2002.

God's saving program is understood to be covenantal, and it is also discerned that God fulfills his promises in stages. An emphasis on biblical theology is also found in Pietism. P. J. Spener (1635–1705) and A. H. Francke (1663–1727) returned to the Scriptures afresh to distinguish the message of the Bible from the Protestant orthodoxy of their day, even if they did not produce full-fledged biblical theologies.

Johann Philip Gabler

Most scholars locate the beginning of biblical theology in an address given by Johann Philip Gabler (1753–1826) in 1787, titled "An Oration on the Proper Distinction between Biblical and Dogmatic Theology and the Specific Objectives of Each."[4] It is entirely too neat, of course, to specify a date when biblical theology began to be practiced formally. J. S. Semler (1725–1791) was part of a movement that attempted to discover timeless truths in the Scriptures and to discern the word of God in the Bible. Such an enterprise meant that Semler baptized his own ability to declare what constituted God's word, and that a rational process existed by which the word of God could be extracted from Scripture.

Others were thinking, then, about doing biblical theology before Gabler. Still, Gabler's address is a helpful starting point for biblical theology. Gabler worried that dogmatic theology was sundered from Scripture, and he hoped that biblical theology would open fresh windows on old problems and inform dogmatic theology so that greater agreement about the teaching of the Scriptures could be attained. The frustrating diversity present in systematic theology could be remedied, Gabler hoped, by biblical theology.[5] On the one hand, Gabler certainly was correct. Systematic theology should be informed by biblical theology. Too often systematic theology has been captured by ideological or philosophical agendas that have domesticated biblical teaching. On the other hand, Gabler's naïveté is striking. Biblical theology and critical study have not led to any more of a consensus than has systematic theology.[6] Scholars disagree just as sharply about biblical theology as they do about systematic theology. We now understand that biblical theology cannot claim pride of place in the sense that it will objectively and clearly resolve the disputes in the systematic realm. Still, such was the hope of Gabler in his oration.

4. For an English translation, see Sandys-Wunsch and Eldredge 1980: 134–44.
5. Boers (1979: 24) remarks that Gabler wanted "to insure that the Bible was reestablished as the basis of all theology, with a biblically based dogmatic theology as its crown and final achievement." See also Sandys-Wunsch and Eldredge 1980: 145, 148–49.
6. Baird (1992: 399), after reviewing the period from Deism to Tübingen in NT studies, observes that "final answers may be illusory."

It has also often been said that Gabler argued for a historical and objective approach to biblical theology.[7] Such a historical approach would differentiate biblical from systematic theology. Scholars have recently and rightly argued, however, that Gabler's approach was not merely historical. He also believed that biblical theology was to have an interpretive function.[8] History was to be the foundation for biblical theology for Gabler, but the task would not be carried out correctly if scholars contented themselves merely with history or description.[9]

Gabler identified three steps in doing biblical theology. First, we must study the biblical texts in their historical context and collect all the material in the canon, both that which is contingent and that which is unchanging. For Gabler, such a task comprises "true" biblical theology. "'True [*wahre*] biblical theology' is the historical study of the OT and the NT, their authors and the contexts in which they were written."[10] This stage comprises the historical and descriptive work of biblical theology, but it is merely the first step in Gabler's program. He did not believe that biblical theology consisted merely in describing what the Scriptures said. Second, we must classify the material that arises above historical particulars and is not contingent. What is normative now functions as the filter for studying the material collected in the first stage. Clearly, in this second step Gabler has transcended mere description. The biblical theologian is now determining what is contingent and what is transcendent.[11] The worldview and philosophy of the interpreter clearly play a decisive role in the second stage. Third, we must arrive at common ideas that are divine and that transcend what are merely human thoughts.[12] These are universal ideas that are identified with ahistorical and unconditioned concepts and precepts.[13] These universal ideas are foundations for a "pure" (*reine*) biblical theology: "The genuine agreements among the authors are then to be checked for their consistency with what is universal."[14] Biblical theology, then, for Gabler is timeless to the extent that it matches universal ideas. Indeed, Gabler already claimed to know from his own philosophy what notions are universal, and so it seems

---

7. For example, Hasel 1984: 115–17. For a nuanced and thoughtful approach to doing biblical theology that advocates a historical approach, see Barr 1999.

8. Scobie, 1991a: 51.

9. So Scobie, *NDBT* 13.

10. Scobie, *NDBT* 13.

11. Sandys-Wunsch and Eldredge (1980: 147) remark that in Gabler's scheme one of the purposes of biblical theology is to identify the "purely historical characteristics in order to eliminate them and leave the truth exposed."

12. Stuckenbruck 1999: 145.

13. Stuckenbruck 1999: 145.

14. Stuckenbruck 1999: 146.

that the truths that emerge unscathed in his biblical theology are those that accord with his preexisting philosophical conceptions.

"Pure" biblical theology, according to Gabler, seeks to differentiate "what is merely time-conditioned and what is eternal Christian truth; it is the latter that becomes the subject-matter of dogmatic theology. On this view, biblical theology is not merely descriptive but is also part of the hermeneutical process."[15] Indeed, we could say that "pure" biblical theology for Gabler is inextricably linked to his worldview. Stuckenbruck rightly concludes that the historical check in Gabler's system is abandoned once one reaches the later stages of analysis.[16] Gabler did not escape dogmatic preconceptions after all, for universal ideas are the foundation for dogmatics.

Gabler hoped that theological unity could be achieved, believed in a coherent biblical theology, and thought that biblical texts have one meaning.[17] And yet he followed Semler by distinguishing between the word of God and Scripture.[18] Such a move has massive consequences, for now the interpreter determines the transcendent word in doing biblical theology. Inevitably, one's philosophy or worldview dictates what is accepted as God's word. Gabler failed to see clearly that his view of biblical theology was biased from the outset, so that "pure" biblical theology was domesticated by so-called universal ideas.[19] Historical exegesis, then, was not as decisive in Gabler's view of biblical theology as many claim. Indeed, it played a largely negative role for Gabler—by means of it we determine the time-conditioned elements of the Scriptures and separate them from the universal notions in the text.[20] For example, Gabler looked for truths behind miracles while rejecting their historicity. In this respect he differed from those who said that the Bible falsified history and contained no truth claim.[21] One needed, then, to excise the myth to see the text's real meaning, for a "'pure' biblical theology can

15. Scobie, *NDBT* 13.
16. Stuckenbruck 1999: 147.
17. Stuckenbruck 1999: 147.
18. Stuckenbruck 1999: 148.
19. Some contemporaries argue from the partiality of our worldview for postmodernism. Green (2002: 8), for example, essentially opts for a postmodern approach to biblical theology so that readings are "valid," "depending on who is doing the reading." In my view, such an approach endorses hermeneutical nihilism. Green (2002: 9–10) ends up endorsing the view that Scripture does not speak harmoniously, or at least the notion that we can never express what that harmony is. Hence, Green (2002: 20) posits a disjunction between God's creative and redemptive work and "an objective reading of biblical texts." Clearly, texts are read within the context of a worldview, but such worldviews must be defended. Otherwise, we seem to be left to the arbitrary task of reading the Bible in our community without the benefit of outside checks and balances.
20. Stuckenbruck 1999: 148–49.
21. Stuckenbruck 1999: 152.

only consist of that which transcends the particular."[22] We see here the impact of Gabler's worldview in doing biblical theology, for he assumes that miracles cannot be historical, and that the truth lies in the myth taught behind or within the husk of the story.

It is interesting to compare Gabler to a more recent proposal on biblical theology, the work of Krister Stendahl (b. 1921).[23] Stendahl moves in a different direction from Gabler when he says that biblical theology seeks to understand only what a text meant, and systematic theology what a text means. Stendahl neatly segregates biblical from systematic theology, so that the former is historical and the latter enters the realm of philosophy. Gabler held to a similar distinction, but he did not leave the task of "what it means" to systematic theology. Isolating that which is normative is *part* of biblical theology for Gabler. Hence, he has a larger sphere for biblical theology than does Stendahl. Gabler wanted to provide ideas that were normative for dogmatics. Stendahl limits biblical theology to mere description. We have noted some weaknesses in Gabler's approach, but the problem with Stendahl's approach is captured by Vanhoozer. "Stendahl appears to have translated Kant's distinction between public fact and private values into the practice of biblical interpretation with fateful results. . . . it is not at all clear how one can move from description of the past to present or future application."[24] On the other hand, Gabler's rationalism reduced the Bible to timeless truths, swept up history into his philosophical approach, and eliminated biblical truths that modern believers could not accept. This brief examination of the person who set forth the program for biblical theology leads us to the question of how we should approach biblical theology.

Approaches to New Testament Theology

The goal in this section is not to examine comprehensively the history of or approaches to NT theology. I will simply take some soundings of particular persons or movements that will provide some background

22. Stuckenbruck 1999: 152. For the importance of myth in Gabler's thinking, see Baird 1992: 186. Baird quotes from Gabler's introduction, where Gabler says, "Myths are generally legends of the ancient world expressed in the sensual way of thinking and speaking of that time. In these myths, one should not expect an event to be explained as it actually happened; but only as it had to be presented in that age according to the sensual way of thinking and judging, and in pictorial, visual, and dramatic speech and expression in which an event could be represented in that time." So, for example, Jesus' temptation was actually an inner experience of conflict perhaps caused by a vision, but the evangelists, being limited to their time period, portrayed it as if Satan tempted him (Baird 1992: 187).

23. Stendahl, *IDB* 1:418–32.

24. Vanhoozer, *NDBT* 53–54.

to the task of NT theology. Shortly after Gabler, biblical and systematic theology were effectively divorced from one another. Biblical theology played virtually no role in informing the task of dogmatics. One reason for this is that those doing biblical theology worked from naturalistic presuppositions. Biblical theology was not explored from a neutral standpoint. The worldview of contributors colored their work significantly.

In the 1800s the work of F. C. Baur (1792–1860) and D. F. Strauss (1808–1874) had a massive impact on biblical studies. Their work was characterized by a historical approach in which they sought to reconstruct the actual history of the NT era. Their conclusions flowed from their critical formulation of the events recorded in the NT. In Baur's work we perceive the impact of Hegelian philosophy, and in particular the Hegelian dialectic. He posited a struggle between Jewish Christianity (Petrine materials, Matthew, Revelation) and Gentile Christianity (Galatians, 1–2 Corinthians, Romans). We have the classic case here of a thesis and antithesis. Baur argued that the conflict led to a synthesis identified as early catholicism (Mark, John, Acts). Baur's reconstruction, though eventually rejected in terms of its specific proposal, had an enormous impact upon NT studies and continues to influence scholars to this day. Strauss argued that the life of Jesus, as portrayed by the evangelists, should be understood mythically, and he vigorously rejected the rationalistic explanations of the miracles of Jesus that were typical of the scholarship of his day. Strauss saw the whole of what the evangelists wrote as mythical, but his work engendered immense controversy because he also identified as myths any account that contained the miraculous—for example, the virgin birth, the feeding of the five thousand, and Jesus' resurrection from the dead.[25] Miracles cannot be accepted, for they contradict the laws of nature.[26] Strauss insisted that Jesus must be studied on historical grounds, and that such study rules out an appeal to the supernatural because what is historical by definition excludes the miraculous.

The work of Baur and Strauss and others (what is called the Tübingen school) has at least two strengths. They recognized the diversity of Scripture. Matthew and James certainly have an emphasis different from that of Paul. We need to beware of homogenizing the NT witness into a bland unity that fails to recognize the multiple perspectives found in the various authors. Furthermore, they also understood the historical

25. For support of this point, see Baird 1992: 251–53.
26. D. Strauss says that "the critic . . . is doing a good and necessary work, when he sweeps away all that makes Jesus a supernatural Being . . . but refers mankind for salvation to the ideal Christ, to that moral pattern in which the historical Jesus did indeed first bring to light many principal features" (cited in Baird 1992: 256–57).

nature of biblical revelation. Biblical theology differs from systematic theology in that it concentrates on the historical timeline of Scripture, attending particularly to progress of revelation. Even though the work of the Tübingen school applies this principle in defective ways, the historical nature of biblical revelation was grasped.

The defects in the Tübingen school outweigh its insights. First, the Hegelian approach of Baur is inherently distorting, demonstrating that a particular philosophical worldview was applied to the NT. The schema of thesis, antithesis, synthesis attracts because of its simplicity, but ultimately it fails to do justice to the nature of the documents in question because the pattern is read into the NT. The second problem is related to the first. The Tübingen school reconstructed NT history in accord with its own philosophical conception of reality and thereby departed from the NT itself. Arbitrary historical reconstructions became the basis for NT study. Finally, the legacy of the Enlightenment cast its shadow on the work of Baur and others. The possibility of miracles was denied fundamentally, betraying an antisupernatural worldview, an atheistic conception of NT theology. To say that history by definition excludes the miraculous is to determine in advance that miracles cannot and will not occur. Such a stance reveals the philosophical commitment of scholars who advocate this view rather than opening oneself up to the possibility of divine action in history.[27]

It is interesting to observe that by the 1850s scholars had ceased trying to write a theology of the entire Bible. Instead, we find separate theologies of the NT and the OT. One will scarcely attempt to write a theology of the whole Bible if the documents do not present a coherent message at least at some level. By the latter part of the nineteenth century histories of religion were increasingly popular. A history of religion merely describes the religion found in the OT or the NT. A NT theology suggests some kind of overarching unity to the message of the NT. A history of religion merely presents the worldview and religious life of Israel or the church from an allegedly detached and objective standpoint. The different standpoints toward NT theology are illustrated by contrasting the work of William Wrede and Wilhelm Bousset with that of Adolf Schlatter.[28]

Boers rightly argues that William Wrede (1859–1906), to use Gabler's terms, practiced "true" biblical theology but not "pure" biblical theology.[29] Wrede believed that biblical theology was limited to the historical

27. By contrast, see Stuhlmacher (1977), who is open to transcendence in doing biblical theology.

28. For an evaluation of Wrede and Schlatter with a consideration of NT theology generally, especially the contribution of Bultmann, see Morgan 1973: 1–67.

29. Boers 1979: 46.

task, and so he went no further than the first step in Gabler's scheme of biblical theology. Scholars, according to Wrede, should attempt to describe the religion contained in the NT. Wrede's program for biblical theology is enunciated in his essay "On the Task and Method of So-Called New Testament Theology," written in 1897.[30] We immediately notice that he speaks of "so-called" (*sogennanten*) NT theology. Wrede doubted that NT theology could be done. He adopted a historical approach, arguing that the only task in NT theology is descriptive. Wrede was part of the "history of religions" school (*Religionsgeschichtliche Schule*). He repudiated the idea that one could write a NT theology, for such an endeavor accepts a divine coherence in the NT. Instead, if we are to function truly as historians, we will confine ourselves to a history of religion, whether of Israel or of the early church. He was convinced that a believing stance toward the documents biased historical work from the outset and disqualified one from serving as a historian. One must exclude any notion of inspiration or the idea that the documents are authoritative if one engages in scholarly work. It follows, then, that one must go beyond the canon to write a genuine history of religion. The very notion of the canon privileges certain writings and accepts them as authoritative, but, according to Wrede, such a judgment disqualifies one as a historian. The very nature of history means that all the sources must be consulted, and no history of the early church can be written that includes Revelation but excludes, say, *1 Clement* or the *Didache*. At the end of the day, then, Wrede rejected any notion of NT theology. He argued instead that one should engage in writing a history of religion.

The program of Wrede is carried out, at least in part, by Wilhelm Bousset (1865–1920) in his work *Kyrios Christos*, published in 1913.[31] Bousset attempted to understand Pauline theology on historical grounds, trying to discern the shift from Palestinian to Hellenistic Christianity. Bousset maintained that Hellenistic Christians were mystery worshipers before their conversion. Not surprisingly, they transferred their concepts of the mystery gods to the Christian faith. The person largely responsible for this shift was the apostle Paul, and hence, in effect, Paul turned the Christian faith into a mystery cult. Bousset attempted to account for the rise of Pauline theology on the basis of history. He located its genesis in a historical movement from which Pauline communities derived their theology.

A radically different approach to NT theology was suggested by Adolf Schlatter (1852–1938) in the late nineteenth and the early twentieth

---

30. Wrede's essay is translated in Morgan 1973: 68–116.
31. The English translation was published in 1970. See Bousset 1970.

centuries.[32] Boers thinks that Schlatter allowed dogmatic theology to preempt biblical theology,[33] but it appears that Schlatter rightly grasped that biblical theology could not be performed in a philosophical vacuum. Scholars in the history of religions school adopted atheistic presuppositions in doing NT theology. They assumed that the ground of NT theology was immanent instead of transcendent. Schlatter, on the other hand, maintains that absolute historical objectivity is an illusion. Those who think that they are neutral actually oppose the NT proclamation. Schlatter is not arguing that history should be ignored or swept under the table. He warns that one who engages in theological work apart from observing and perceiving what happened historically "is at best a poet and at worst a dreamer."[34] Biblical theologians are called upon to observe carefully what the texts actually say and not blind themselves to the text because of preconceived notions.[35] Genuine NT theology is an exercise in humility, for we must acknowledge that much is hidden from us, that we do not have a "God's-eye view" of all that was accomplished.[36] Hence, presuppositions play a vital role in doing NT theology: "We have to be clear that historical criticism is never based on historical fact alone, but always has roots in the critic's dogma, too."[37] Furthermore, if we are going to do historical study legitimately, the OT documents are fundamental for understanding the NT. Nor does Schlatter agree with Wrede on the canon. He maintains that the distinctiveness of the canon is rooted in history.[38] The early Christians, after the time of the NT, assigned a unique role to the canonical writings. Hence, the uniqueness of the canon is not merely an arbitrary construct but rather finds its validity in the history of the church. Schlatter wrote his NT theology in a two-volume work during the first part of the twentieth century. The enduring quality of his work is evident, for it was translated into English in the latter part of the 1990s.[39] Schlatter's work differs from virtually all other NT theologies in that he consistently emphasizes the impact that the message of Jesus had on the lives of hearers. Schlatter's work does not merely dabble in ideas; he brings readers face-to-face with the call to repent.

32. Schlatter's essay "The Theology of the New Testament and Dogmatics" is translated in Morgan 1973: 117–66.
33. Boers 1979: 75.
34. Schlatter 1973: 121.
35. "It is clear that without the honest attempt to lay aside all personal concerns and opinions of one's school or party, and seriously to *see*, academic work degenerates into hypocrisy" (Schlatter 1973: 122).
36. Schlatter 1973: 143, 149–50.
37. Schlatter 1973: 155.
38. Schlatter 1973: 146–47.
39. Schlatter 1997; 1999.

During the same time period that Schlatter was writing, Geerhardus Vos (1862–1949) was quietly but consistently doing significant work in biblical theology.[40] Vos grasped the eschatological character of biblical theology and explored this theme in many of his books and essays. The impact of Vos's thinking is evident in the more recent work of George Ladd, where redemptive history is featured.[41] Vos was working unobtrusively, but he recognized the historical character of biblical revelation, and at the same time he sifted carefully the work of historical critical scholars, learning from them where their work was useful but rejecting what was unpersuasive. Whereas Vos's work is relatively unknown, Karl Barth (1886–1968) had a remarkable effect in creating an interest in biblical theology. During and after World War I people were losing faith in evolutionary naturalism and the inherent goodness of human beings. The twentieth century verified that there was something terribly wrong with the human condition. Many began to doubt that historical truth could be gleaned through pure objectivity. Barth reminded many of the primacy of revelation, and he reenergized an interest in theology. Barth's influence appears in the work of Walther Eichrodt and the latter's massive OT theology in the 1930s.[42]

Rudolf Bultmann (1884–1976) at one level appeared to complement Barth in the area of NT theology, but Bultmann, probably the most influential NT scholar of the twentieth century, had several different strands to his thought. Boers maintains that Bultmann tried to produce the "pure" biblical theology advocated by Gabler, though Boers does not think that Bultmann succeeded. Bultmann is a fascinating study because in part he accepted the program of Wrede and the history of religions school. He accepted the naturalism of Wrede and eliminated the possibility of any supernatural intervention of God via miracles. The emphasis on history of religions in his work manifested itself in his conclusions regarding the influence of pre-Christian Gnosticism on the NT. Bultmann, however, was not content with a mere historical description of the NT message. He went beyond Wrede (and Stendahl) in demythologizing the text to discover the unchanging message for his contemporaries. Unlike Wrede, he wrote a NT theology, and hence he did not limit himself with "true" biblical theology but also attempted to write a "pure" biblical theology. Bultmann located the kerygma in the theology of Paul and John and maintained that the message of Jesus was merely a presupposition for NT theology, not part of NT theology itself. He utilized Heideggerian existentialism to uncover the core of the

40. Vos 1930; 1953; 1980; 2001.
41. See Ladd 1993.
42. Eichrodt 1961; 1967. For a helpful summary of major OT theologies, see Barr 1999: 27–51, 286–344, 439–67, 497–529, 541–62.

kerygma, focusing on anthropology. Existentialism, then, became the presupposition by which the NT message was assessed. For instance, the coming of God's kingdom does not indicate a real event in space-time history; rather, it indicates that human beings ought to make a decision for God before it is too late. There is scarcely space here to examine Bultmann's theology in detail, but it appears that alien categories and assumptions dictate the contours of his NT theology.

The biblical theology movement arose in the 1940s and 1950s, and it can be traced to the influence of Karl Barth. Several features characterize the biblical theology movement. First, proponents of this movement were opposed to philosophical systems. They desired the Bible to speak for itself with pristine freshness instead of subordinating it to philosophical worldviews. Second, they contrasted Greek thought with Hebrew thought. The latter was conceived to be experiential, concrete, and temporal, whereas the former was abstract, philosophical, and atemporal. Third, they emphasized unity between the two Testaments. Fourth, they featured the uniqueness of the Bible over against its environment. When one compared the cultures and religions of the day, the Bible stood out. Fifth, those in the biblical theology movement reacted, as did Barth, against the older liberal theology. Sixth, they stressed the revelation of God in history. The mighty acts of God in history revealed his lordship and uniqueness.

The biblical theology movement had many strengths, but it was also criticized sharply. James Barr, in particular, demonstrated that the alleged contrast between Greek thought and Hebrew thought could not be substantiated.[43] The biblical theology movement overemphasized the simplicity and concrete nature of Hebrew thought, as if it could be separated completely from any philosophical worldview. Nor was it clear how the Bible could be segregated from its environment if the critical view of the Bible, which was not repudiated entirely by the biblical theology movement, is embraced.[44] Finally, the acts of God cannot be separated from the word of God. God's deeds must be interpreted, and hence actions without words are not revelatory. The biblical pattern of revelation contains both work and word, both event and explanation.

Brevard Childs criticized the biblical theology movement and proposed his own alternative, the canonical approach. The final form of the text becomes the basis for biblical theology. According to Childs, the historical and descriptive task is not neutral, and the final form of the text must be seen as a witness to a greater reality. The two Testaments must be

43. See especially Barr 1961: 14–88.
44. See Childs 1970. For his theology embracing both the OT and the NT, see Childs 1992.

interpreted intertextually. In other words, Childs acknowledged the reality of the living God in his canonical approach. He saw the entire canon as pointing to God's word and his work in the world. Childs repudiated the approach of Stendahl, in which the goal of biblical theology is limited to what the Bible meant, for in the canonical approach what it meant and what it means are linked together. Childs rightly established the importance of doing theology from the whole Bible, and he correctly saw a unity in the canon. Still, one wonders about the intellectual coherence of Childs's proposal. By a leap of faith he divorced the final canonical form from historical-critical judgments, but he embraced historical critical conclusions in his analysis of the history of the text.[45] How does one legitimately posit a canonical text that is a theological unity if the basis by which one arrives at the text is a historical method that splits the text into a thousand pieces?[46] What if the previous redaction of the text contradicts the final redaction? Carson rightly says, "Childs emerges with a unity of result, but it is less than clear how he gets there as long as the unity of the foundation documents is affirmed by little more than the results, and is more or less adopted by assuming ecclesiastical tradition regarding the boundary of the canon."[47]

A remarkably different method of doing biblical theology is proposed and worked out by Donald Guthrie.[48] Guthrie's way of doing biblical theology has many affinities with the way systematic theology typically has been done. Scholars are apt to dismiss Guthrie's work as biased, but there is something to be said on behalf of his work. The central categories of systematic theology, after all, derive from Scripture. They have been included for hundreds of years because of their interest to the people of God. Some biblical theologies may be prone to avoid them because they want to avoid any impression that they are doing systematic theology. Guthrie also addressed questions that people have in approaching biblical theology with a simple and clear approach. Still, there are deficiencies in Guthrie's work. First, the focus on systematics may lead to the imposition of categories that are alien to biblical thought. Second, if one adopts systematic categories, themes actually featured by biblical writers may be neglected because they do not fit the presupposed categories. Finally, and most important, a systematic approach does not concentrate sufficiently on the historical timeline of Scripture. The genius of biblical

45. For an insightful critical interaction with Childs's program, see Noble 1995. For a sharply critical response to Childs, see Barr 1999: 378–438.
46. For the notion that the preliminary stages of the text were also inspired, see Grisanti 2001.
47. Carson, *NDBT* 97.
48. Guthrie 1981.

theology is that it unfolds the theology of the Scriptures historically, paying attention to where we are in redemptive history.

It is not my purpose here to comment on the various proposals for biblical theology in an exhaustive way.[49] It is instructive, however, to note some of the all-embracing themes or centers that have been proposed. Walther Eichrodt suggested covenant for the OT;[50] Gerhard von Rad, tradition history;[51] Walter Kaiser, God's promise;[52] Samuel Terrien, the Lord's elusive presence;[53] Graeme Goldsworthy, the kingdom.[54] A number of scholars have maintained that the central theme of the Scriptures is justification.[55] Salvation history has been defended by others.[56] Alternatively, William Dumbrell, in his work on Rev. 21–22, suggests the new Jerusalem, new temple, new covenant, new Israel, and new creation.[57] Both I. Howard Marshall and Frank Thielman have recently explicated the theology of the NT by examining the theology of each of its books in order while at the same time maintaining the unity of the canonical witness.[58] We see a more standard critical approach in the work of Georg Strecker.[59] Harmut Gese and Peter Stuhlmacher have worked out in some detail a history of traditions approach.[60] The multiplicity of approaches and themes reveals the complexity of biblical theology, and it also demonstrates that there will never be agreement on a single center. On the other hand, G. B. Caird, in a work completed by L. D. Hurst, offered a thematic approach with salvation functioning as the theme. Caird imagined a conference table, akin to the apostolic conference, where Paul, Peter, James, and others presented and debated

49. Continuing interest in biblical theology is evident in the essays in Rowland and Tuckett 2006, where the nature of biblical theology is discussed. What is striking, but unsurprising in our modern era, is the sheer diversity of suggested approaches.

50. Eichrodt 1961; 1967.

51. Von Rad 1962; 1965.

52. Kaiser 1978.

53. Terrien 1983.

54. Goldsworthy 1981.

55. Many scholars have proposed this view, but the fountainhead is Martin Luther.

56. For example, Cullmann 1967; Kümmel 1973; Goppelt 1981; 1982b; Ladd 1993. See also, on the work of Paul, Ridderbos 1975. See the significant work by Yarbrough (2004). Yarbrough shows the enduring legacy of salvation historical approaches and criticizes scholars who reject the legitimacy of redemptive history.

57. Dumbrell 1985.

58. Marshall 2004; Thielman 2005.

59. Strecker 2000.

60. Gese 1981; Stuhlmacher 1992; 1999. For a summary and evaluation of Gese, see Barr 1999: 362–77. Note also the remarkable six-volume project by Wilckens, now in progress (Wilckens 2003; 2005a; 2005b; 2005c; forthcoming). Other German NT theologies have been written by Hübner 1990; 1993; 1995; Weiser 1993; Gnilka 1994; Schmithals 1997; Hahn 2002a; 2002b. For a French contribution, see Vouga 2001. For a useful survey of NT theologies in the 1990s, see Matera 2005: 6–15.

their understanding of God's saving action in Christ.[61] Many scholars now agree that the language of one single center is reductionistic and should be avoided. Hasel says that a multithematic approach does most justice to the biblical materials, though he also remarks that any central theme would almost certainly focus on God.[62] Lemcio proposes a sixfold emphasis: (1) God (2) sent or raised (3) Jesus; human beings (4) must respond in repentance and faith (5) to God, and therefore (6) they will receive benefits.[63] Scobie agrees that a single center should not be sought and instead several interlocking themes should be woven together.[64] I argue in this book that magnifying God in Christ is the foundation or goal of NT theology, and God works out his purpose in salvation history to reach that goal.[65]

It may be instructive to compare two recent and remarkably different proposals for doing NT theology, those of Heikki Räisänen and Peter Balla. Räisänen's scheme for biblical theology is explicated in his 1990 work, *Beyond New Testament Theology*.[66] The title tells all, and the book hearkens back to the work of Wrede.[67] According to Räisänen, the goal of NT theology is to clarify the role of religion in society rather than to serve the church. Räisänen rues the influence of Barth, maintaining that a fatal mistake was made when scholars abandoned the history of religions school and adopted dialectical theology. In many ways Räisänen is a reincarnation of Wrede, arguing that the latter correctly distinguished theology from religion. Unfortunately, according to Räisänen, the vision sketched in by Wrede was not followed, and religion and theology have been improperly amalgamated when they should be kept distinct.

Räisänen, then, proposes a modified form of Wrede's program. He identifies six principles for biblical theology. First, the intended audience must be the secular community rather than the church. If the focus shifts to the latter, then the scientific character of the enterprise is undermined.

61. Caird 1994. Recently, Esler (2005) has advocated an interpersonal and dialogical approach. The book advocates a method and approach and does not constitute a NT theology itself. One of many fascinating elements in the book is the vigorous defense of authorial intent in interpretation.

62. Hasel 1978: 204–20.

63. Lemcio 1988. Note how Lemcio's proposal fits in many respects with the outline of this book.

64. Scobie 1991b: 178.

65. Green (2002: 15) worries that a center betrays "Enlightenment idealism" and replaces "the story of God" with a "theological abstraction." Those who contend for a supernatural worldview and a truthful scriptural word can hardly be identified as Enlightenment idealists, unless one were to anachronistically place Augustine in that category. Furthermore, Green's story itself becomes an abstraction if the story floats apart from all truth claims.

66. Räisänen 1990.

67. Ten years later a revised edition appeared (Räisänen 2000). For a more positive assessment of Räisänen, see Barr 1999: 530–40.

Second, NT theology should be concerned with information rather than proclamation. Bultmann and Conzelmann both went astray at this very point. When NT theologians try to speak a prophetic word, they lose an objective basis. The theologian can present results without fear if addressing the academy instead of cautiously checking to see if the church approves of the results. In a post-Christian world Christian documents cannot be normative for society. Our task is merely to explain what they say. Third, NT theology, according to Räisänen, encompasses early Christian thought and not just the canon. Limiting the task to the canon makes sense if the goal is proclamation, but such a decision does not fit with historical work. Those who ground NT theology on the canon of Scripture are allowing their personal faith and bias to intrude upon the work of doing NT theology. Räisänen insists that no unity can be derived from canonical documents anyway, and thus the canon provides little assistance. Fourth, NT theology should be purely historical. Historical research does not have the aim of doing theology. What Räisänen calls "actualizing concerns" (i.e., the relevance of the literature for today) should not affect historical research. We must be honest with the data and approach it as we would any other piece of literature. Fifth, faith should not be required for someone to do historical work. In fact, the scholar must maintain distance from the subject matter and from personal values. Otherwise, the scholar is liable to read personal convictions into the NT. Finally, a NT theology is interested not in reconstructing the historical Jesus but rather in the faith image of Jesus as he is portrayed in the NT. The historical Jesus is lost in the sands of history. We can only know Jesus as he is presented in the Gospels.[68]

Peter Balla offered remarkably different conclusions in his 1997 monograph, *Challenges to New Testament Theology: An Attempt to Justify the Enterprise.*[69] In one sense, Balla is in agreement with Räisänen. He maintains that NT theology is justified as a historical enterprise. Balla defines theology as "all affirmations and actions which are in relationship with God."[70] Nevertheless, he thinks that one can limit NT theology to the canon, even if one does not grant unique status to the NT. NT theology may function as a purely historical enterprise in an academic context. We do not need to presuppose the uniqueness of the NT canon or an underlying unity in its message.

Balla effectively contests Walter Bauer's thesis that heresy preceded orthodoxy in a number of locales in the early history of the church. Bauer concluded that political factors determined what was labeled as heresy

---

68. For a proposal that focuses on the diversity of the NT, see Dunn 1977. Unfortunately, Dunn sees so much diversity that there is very little unity (rightly Lemcio 1988: 4–5).

69. Balla 1997.

70. Balla 1997: 21.

and what was accepted as orthodoxy.[71] Balla maintains that Bauer often argued from silence and misinterpreted the evidence.[72]

Balla defends limiting NT theology to the canon because history shows that early Christians made distinctions in recognizing which writings were authoritative.[73] Hence, limiting one's study to the canon is justified on historical grounds. Marcion's heresy, according to Balla, did not lead to establishment of canon but rather strengthened the process of elevating certain writings to the same status as the OT.[74] The apostles likely saw themselves as successors to OT prophets (cf. 2 Pet. 3:16) and were conscious of their unique authority. Moreover, there are good grounds for defending a theological unity in studying the NT. We cannot prove the notion of theological development in NT documents, nor is it evident that the theology of Jesus and Paul diverge. What we have in the NT is a basic creed shared by all believers.

Balla draws a clear line between dogmatic and biblical theology, for applying the text and systematizing it belong to the former, whereas biblical theology is historical in nature. It follows, therefore, that both believers and unbelievers can do NT theology. In this respect it seems that Balla has adopted Stendahl's program. Balla insists that no presuppositions should be adopted; we can study the documents historically whatever our faith stance. We do not demand that people become believers to do NT theology, though all should be open to what the documents say. The goal in NT theology is to describe the content of the NT, not to advocate its truth.[75] The enterprise, then, is historical, though a historical approach does not eliminate the theological dimension of the task. Still, theological presuppositions should not presuppose any particular results. The task should be restricted to the canon, but we should avoid any canon within the canon.

Method in New Testament Theology

How should we approach doing a NT theology? Here I will draw on definitions from several scholars.[76] Systematic theology has an atemporal focus, whereas biblical theology emphasizes the biblical timeline, the development of redemptive history. Any competent systematic

71. Bauer 1971 (German original, 1934).
72. Balla 1997: 50–56.
73. Hengel (1994: 332) also argues that study can be limited to the canon on historical grounds.
74. Balla 1997: 145.
75. Balla 1997: 217.
76. In this section I am particularly influenced by Carson and by Scobie.

theology is informed, of course, by biblical theology and takes into account constantly the progress of revelation in Scripture. Still, biblical theology more specifically explicates the redemptive-historical time line of Scripture and does not move beyond it in applying the Scriptures to today's world. Systematic theology, on the other hand, applies the theology of the Bible to today. Hence, Frame correctly says that systematic theology is theology in application.[77] Carson defines biblical theology this way: "Biblical theology is the theology of the whole Bible, descriptively and historically considered."[78] Scobie offers this definition: "Biblical Theology may be defined as the ordered study of the understanding of the revelation of God contained in the canonical scriptures of the Old and New Testaments."[79] Both definitions emphasize that biblical theology comprises the whole Bible, and that history is fundamental to biblical theology. Biblical theology recognizes the stages of growth and development in God's revelation and unfolds God's revelation genetically. Another way of putting it is to say that biblical theology "lets the biblical text set the agenda."[80] The task of biblical theology is captured well by Vanhoozer: "'Biblical theology' is the name of an interpretive approach to the Bible which assumes that the word of God is textually mediated through the diverse literary, and historically conditioned, words of human beings."[81] He goes on to say, "To state the claim more positively, biblical theology corresponds to the interests of the texts themselves."[82]

The focus on the explicit concern of the biblical text distinguishes biblical theology from systematic theology. Carson says that biblical theology "stands closer to the text than systematic theology, aims to achieve genuine sensitivity with respect to the distinctiveness of each corpus, and seeks to connect the diverse corpora using their own categories. Ideally, therefore, biblical theology stands as a kind of bridge discipline between responsible exegesis and responsible systematic theology (even though each of these inevitably influences the other two)."[83] The dream of Gabler, though carried out very imperfectly in history (even by Gabler himself), that biblical theology inform systematic theology should be one of the primary goals of biblical theology. Still, the two disciplines should not be fused together, and the distinctions between biblical and systematic theology need to be maintained. For

77. Frame 1987: 97–98.
78. Carson 1995: 20.
79. Scobie 1991a: 36.
80. Rosner, *NDBT* 5.
81. Vanhoozer, *NDBT* 56.
82. Vanhoozer, *NDBT* 56.
83. Carson, *NDBT* 94.

instance, systematic theology, contrary to biblical theology, takes into consideration historical theology.[84] The Scriptures cannot be applied effectively to today's world if the systematic theologian does not reflect upon how it has been applied throughout two thousand years of church history. We have already noted that systematic theology consists of application of the theology of the Bible to its readers. Historical theology, however, is not part of the database of biblical theology.[85] Certainly, all of us are influenced by the history of the church, but in doing biblical theology we do not explicitly consider the doctrinal formulations of church history. Carson expresses well the difference between systematic and biblical theologies, remarking that biblical theology is a "mediating discipline," whereas systematic theology is a "culminating discipline." It follows, then, that the inductive work of biblical theology should be the basis of all systematic theology. Systematic theology expresses one's worldview and how it applies to the contemporary society; biblical theology contains fundamental building blocks in that worldview. Hence, systematic theology can speak to contemporaries with authenticity only if it is grounded in biblical theology. The ultimate goal of studying the Bible, then, is to form a systematic theology, for applying the Bible to today is where the rubber meets the road. Biblical theology, however, keeps systematic theology from imposing alien thought forms upon the system.

Biblical theology will have the greatest impact on systematics if it encompasses the whole Bible. Carson rightly observes, "But ideally, biblical theology, as its name implies, even as it works inductively from the diverse texts of the Bible, seeks to uncover and articulate the unity of *all* the biblical texts taken together, resorting primarily to the categories of those texts themselves. In this sense it is canonical biblical theology, 'whole-Bible' biblical theology."[86] In other words, biblical theology "must presuppose a coherent and agreed canon."[87] Matera rightly says that NT theology is not merely a history of religion but rather "has a specifically theological task."[88] Hence, he argues that we should be bold enough to say that there is "inner coherence."[89]

It follows, then, that the matter of presuppositions is crucial in doing biblical theology. Virtually all would agree that fundamental to any biblical

84. For the following points, see Carson, *NDBT* 101–2.
85. Goldsworthy (2003), however, is also correct in maintaining that biblical theology, to be fruitful, must interact with and be conversant with both historical and dogmatic theology, for we do not do our work in a vacuum.
86. Carson, *NDBT* 100.
87. Carson 1995: 27.
88. Matera 2005: 15.
89. Matera 2005: 16.

theology is the studying of the text in its historical context.[90] Nor am I denying that careful attention must be given to texts in their historical contexts. The raw data of the text must not be squeezed into some preformed mold. Indeed, some scholars (e.g., Stendahl, Räisänen, Balla) maintain that we can function as objective historians in doing biblical theology. They claim that both believers and unbelievers can approach biblical theology as a historical discipline. Certainly, the historic rootedness of the text must be respected, and we can learn from those who adopt worldviews opposed to our own. Nevertheless, those who maintain that biblical theology can be studied from a neutral standpoint are mistaken. Everyone approaches the text with a worldview, a philosophy that influences how he or she reads the text. No neutral Archimedean standpoint from which to assess the biblical text exists. No human being has a "God's-eye view" by which to assess all of reality. Balla rightly says that there are historical grounds for limiting biblical theology to the canon. Still, such a position must not rest solely on historical grounds. One must also presuppose that the canon is the limit for biblical theology because it is the word of God. This is not to say that one arbitrarily presupposes the truth of God's word, for no other worldview makes sense of all reality as the biblical worldview does, and all other worldviews can survive only by borrowing from the biblical worldview at some point. Still, the divine character and authority of the Scriptures cannot be proved definitively; it is not as if we can demonstrate conclusively to others that the Scriptures are true. The starting point for grasping all of reality must be presupposed in any philosophical worldview, though it can be demonstrated that no other worldview makes sense of the world except the worldview generated by the canon of the entire Bible.

Vanhoozer rightly perceives that theological commitments are entailed in doing biblical theology. He remarks, "*Contra* Gabler, one does not first do one's historical homework and only then begin to do theology. On the contrary, one's exegesis is already affected by one's dogmatic beliefs. The relationship between exegesis and theology is more a dialogical conversation than it is a linear or unidirectional process. Hermeneutics, in calling attention to the assumptions readers bring to the text, reminds us that theology is involved in the task of exegesis from the outset."[91] We think again of Balla at this point. Balla's emphasis on history should be maintained. Still, he appears to think that a neutral and historical approach can demonstrate that Paul and James do not contradict each other on

---

90. Though it should be observed that too often speculation replaces sober historical study (rightly Hengel 1994: 334–37). In particular, Hengel (1994: 337) warns scholars against the lust for new results and new insights.

91. Vanhoozer, *NDBT* 55. Green (2002: 16) rightly sees as well that "the relationship between scripture and doctrine" is "mutually informing and influencing."

the issue of justification. In one sense, Balla is correct. Careful exegesis of the text indicates that James and Paul are not polar to one another. Hence we must argue from the data of the text to show that James and Paul cohere. On the other hand, I suspect that Balla favors arguments that resolve the alleged contradiction between Paul and James because of his worldview. Others perceive the data differently precisely because of their belief that the Scriptures do not contain a noncontradictory word. Indeed, many modern scholars believe that scientific, rational, and reasonable criticism must acknowledge errors in the Bible, and that any other stance is precritical and anti-intellectual. In other words, they approach the Bible with an Enlightenment worldview from the outset. They are mistaken, however, in thinking that their own worldview is neutral. Vanhoozer remarks, "Modern biblical criticism, while professing to study the text scientifically, in fact approached the text with the anti-theological presuppositions of secular reason and hence with a bias against the unity of the text and an anti-narrative hermeneutic."[92] Many scholars would not recognize themselves in Vanhoozer's indictment and would claim that they are guided simply by the phenomena of the text. They fail to see clearly, however, that even their perception of phenomena is informed by their worldviews—their philosophical presuppositions. Scobie also insists that biblical theology is not purely neutral: "Its presuppositions, based on a Christian faith commitment, include belief that the Bible conveys a divine revelation, that the Word of God in Scripture constitutes the norm of Christian faith and life, and that all the varied material in both Old and New Testaments can in some way be related to the plan and purpose of the one God of the whole Bible. Such a Biblical Theology stands somewhere between what the Bible 'meant' and what it 'means.'"[93]

When we do biblical theology, we must not think that it can be approached from a putative objective standpoint. Vanhoozer says, "Reading the Testaments together involves taking hermeneutical as well as theological positions. . . . To read the Bible typologically or intertextually is to let Christian theology transform the presuppositions one brings to the text."[94] One of the crucial matters in this whole endeavor is whether we pay attention to the divine intention in reading Scripture.[95] I am not suggesting that the divine intention is accessed in some mystical

92. Vanhoozer, *NDBT* 58.
93. Scobie 1991a: 50–51.
94. Vanhoozer, *NDBT* 60.
95. Plantinga (2003: 25) states the assumption that undergirds this work: "Second, an assumption of the enterprise is that the principal author of the Bible—the entire Bible—is God himself. Of course, each of the books of the Bible has a human author or authors as well; but the principal author is God. This impels us to treat the whole more like a unified

way apart from the words of the text. The divine meaning of the text is not granted via dreams or private revelations. Nor am I jettisoning the importance of historical study. Understanding the meaning of human authors is fundamental to biblical theology and foundational to grasping God's meaning. Focusing on presuppositions does not mean that historical evidence is ignored. Schlatter (1973: 136) rightly reminds us that we must see what the text says. Still, when we consider the many authors of Scripture and their various intentions, we realize that God was superintending the whole process, and that there is a divine intention that is realized through the historical process.[96] For example, the writer of Ps. 2 certainly was speaking of a king in Israel's history. But when we read the whole of Scripture, it is clear that this psalm ultimately refers to Jesus Christ. So Vanhoozer rightly says that we must read the Bible "according to its truest, fullest, *divine* intention."[97] The divine meaning is not contrary to the human meaning, but it may transcend it in ways the original author did not grasp. Vanhoozer says, "Only the final form of the text displays the divine communicative act in its completeness; hence the final form is the best evidence for determining what the authors, human and divine, are ultimately doing."[98] Biblical scholars, however, simply will not read the text in this way if they do not accept the notion that Scripture is God's inspired word without contradictions.

Many who see the Scriptures merely as the word of human authors naturally conclude that these human authors disagree with one another, that there is no unified word. Hence, there is no possibility of doing a biblical theology of the whole Bible, for the Bible contains competing theologies.[99] Vanhoozer rightly observes, "To limit biblical theology to historical description is to abandon the attempt to read the Bible as theologically normative for the church and to reject the notion of divine inspiration and divine authorship, and thus to refuse to read the Bible as the word of God."[100] He concludes, "The suggestion of the present article

---

communication than a miscellany of ancient books. Scripture is not so much a library of independent books as itself a book with many subdivisions but a central theme."

96. Plantinga (2003: 19–57) argues that those who accept the inspiration of Scripture and God's intervention in the world have solid grounds for thinking that Scripture is the word of God and represents God's perspective on reality. This stands in contrast to the way historical criticism is often practiced whereby God's intervention in the world is excluded a priori.

97. Vanhoozer, *NDBT* 61.

98. Vanhoozer, *NDBT* 62.

99. Green (2002: 11) follows Goldingay in saying that Scripture is inspired in the sense that it continues to bear significance and meaning beyond its original readers. Such a definition of inspiration is quite attenuated and is difficult to distinguish from one that applies to literary classics prized throughout history.

100. Vanhoozer, *NDBT* 63.

is that having a theological interest, far from being arbitrary, is rather required if one is to do justice to the nature of the Bible itself, taken not only as a collection of human speech acts but also as a unified divine *canonical* act."[101] In this book I have assumed that the NT theology is rooted in the word of God that is unified and coherent. At the same time, I would argue that there is substantial evidence to buttress such a claim. For example, there are good grounds for thinking John's Gospel is not merely interested in theology but is also based on accurate history.

The matter of presuppositions is crucial in how biblical theology works out, for those who do not perceive the entire canon as God's authoritative word inevitably opt for some form of a canon within the canon. Biblical theology must be canonical and concerned with both Testaments together.[102] Hence, it "inevitably involves Christian presuppositions."[103] Marcion established his own canon by excluding a number of books that were generally accepted. Luther seemed to fall into the mistake of a canon within the canon when he denigrated James and exalted that which presented Christ. Liberals gave pride of place to their own reconstruction of the historical Jesus. Bultmann favored Paul and John over against the rest of the NT. Stuhlmacher represented a genuine advance with his hermeneutics of consent. He argued that we must accept the inherent power of the scriptural word, that we must be open to transcendence and to faith.[104] Faith and the miraculous cannot be excluded in doing biblical theology. These are remarkable positions coming from someone who studied under Ernst Käsemann. Still, Stuhlmacher argues that Paul and James contradict one another. It is difficult to know where God's word is according to Stuhlmacher's scheme. Should we prefer Paul or James, and on what basis should we prefer one over the other apart from our subjective preferences? Any canon within the canon fails to recognize that the whole of Scripture is the word of God. Hasel rightly remarks that we need to do biblical theology in a way "that seeks to do justice to all dimensions of reality to which the biblical texts testify."[105]

The goal of my NT theology is to acknowledge that the NT claims to be a word from God. As such, the NT is authoritative and consistent. Hence, it really is possible to write a NT theology, even though no NT theology can ever plumb the depths of the message contained therein.

101. Vanhoozer, *NDBT* 62.
102. Scobie 1991a: 52.
103. Scobie 1991a: 55.
104. Stuhlmacher 1977.
105. Hasel 1982: 66.

Bibliography

Aalen, S. "δόξα." *NIDNTT* 2:44–48.

Abasciano, Brian J. 2006. "Corporate Election in Romans 9: A Reply to Thomas Schreiner." *JETS* 49:351–71.

Achtemeier, Paul J. 1996. *First Peter*. Hermeneia. Minneapolis: Fortress.

Adamson, James B. 1989. *James: The Man and His Message*. Grand Rapids: Eerdmans.

Ådna, Jostein. 2006. "The Servant of Isaiah 53 as Triumphant and Interceding Messiah: The Reception of Isaiah 52:13–53:12 in the Targum of Isaiah with Special Attention to the Concept of the Messiah." Pages 189–224 in *The Suffering Servant: Isaiah 53 in Jewish and Christian Sources*. Edited by B. Janowski and P. Stuhlmacher. Translated by D. P. Bailey. Grand Rapids: Eerdmans.

Agersnap, Søren. 1999. *Baptism and the New Life: A Study of Romans 6.1–14*. Aarhus, Denmark: Aarhus University Press.

Alexander, T. D. 2002. *From Paradise to Promised Land: An Introduction to the Pentateuch*. 2nd ed. Grand Rapids: Baker Academic.

Allan, John A. 1963. "The 'in Christ' Formula in the Pastoral Epistles." *NTS* 10:115–21.

Allison, Dale. 1982. "The Pauline Epistles and the Synoptic Gospels: The Pattern of the Parallels." *NTS* 28:1–32.

———. 1993. *The New Moses: A Matthean Typology*. Minneapolis: Fortress.

Anderson, A. A. 1972. *Psalms 73–50*. Vol. 2 of *The Book of Psalms*. NCB. Grand Rapids: Eerdmans.

Anderson, Paul N. 1996. *The Christology of the Fourth Gospel: Its Unity and Disunity in the Light of John 6*. WUNT 2/78. Tübingen: Mohr Siebeck.

Angel, G. T. D. "ἐρωτάω." *NIDNTT* 2:879–81.

Arnold, Clinton E. 1994. "Jesus Christ: 'Head' of the Church (Colossians and Ephesians)." Pages 346–66 in *Jesus of Nazareth: Lord and Christ; Essays on the Historical Jesus and New Testament Christology*. Edited by J. B. Green and M. Turner. Grand Rapids: Eerdmans.

———. 1996. "Returning to the Domain of the Powers: *Stoicheia* as Evil Spirits in Galatians 4:3, 9." *NovT* 38:55–76.

Attridge, Harold W. 1989. *The Epistle to the Hebrews*. Hermeneia. Philadelphia: Fortress.

Aune, David E. 1969. "The Problem of the Messianic Secret." *NovT* 11:1–31.

———. 1983. *Prophecy in Early Christianity and the Ancient Mediterranean World*. Grand Rapids: Eerdmans.

———. 1997. *Revelation 1–5*. WBC 52A. Dallas: Word.

———. 1998. *Revelation 6–16*. WBC 52B. Nashville: Thomas Nelson.

Avemarie, Friedrich. 1996. *Tora und Leben: Untersuchungen zur Heilsbedeutung der Tora in der frühen rabbinischen Literatur*. TSAJ 55. Tübingen: Mohr Siebeck.

———. 1999. "Erwählung und Vergeltung: Zur optionalen Struktur rabbinischer Soteriologie." *NTS* 45:108–26.

Badenas, Robert. 1985. *Christ, the End of the Law: Romans 10.4 in Pauline Perspective*. JSNTSup 10. Sheffield: JSOT Press.

Bailey, Kenneth E. 1976. *Poet and Peasant: A Literary-Cultural Approach to the Parables in Luke*. Grand Rapids: Eerdmans.

———. 1980. *Through Peasant Eyes: More Lucan Parables, Their Culture and Style*. Grand Rapids: Eerdmans.

Baird, William. 1992. *From Deism to Tübingen*. Vol. 1 of *History of New Testament Research*. Minneapolis: Fortress.

———. 2003. *From Jonathan Edwards to Rudolph Bultmann*. Vol. 2 of *History of New Testament Research*. Minneapolis: Fortress.

Balch, David L. 1981. *Let Wives Be Submissive: The Domestic Code in 1 Peter*. SBLMS 26. Chico, CA: Scholars Press.

Baldwin, Joyce G. 1978. *Daniel*. TOTC. Leicester, UK: Inter-Varsity Press.

Ball, David Mark. 1996. *"I Am" in John's Gospel: Literary Function, Background and Theological Implications*. JSNTSup 124. Sheffield: Sheffield Academic Press.

Balla, Peter. 1997. *Challenges to New Testament Theology: An Attempt to Justify the Enterprise*. WUNT 2/95. Tübingen: Mohr Siebeck.

———. 2003. *The Child-Parent Relationship in the New Testament and Its Environment*. WUNT 155. Tübingen: Mohr Siebeck.

Balz, H. "κόσμος." *EDNT* 2:309–13.

Banks, Robert. 1975. *Jesus and the Law in the Synoptic Tradition*. SNTSMS 28. Cambridge: Cambridge University Press.

Barclay, John M. G. 1988. *Obeying the Truth: A Study of Paul's Ethics in Galatians*. Edinburgh: T & T Clark.

———. 1996. "'Do We Undermine the Law?' A Study of Romans 14.1–15.6." Pages 287–308 in *Paul and the Mosaic Law*. Edited by J. D. G. Dunn. WUNT 89. Tübingen: Mohr Siebeck.

Barnett, Paul. 1999. *Jesus and the Rise of Early Christianity: A History of New Testament Times*. Downers Grove, IL: InterVarsity Press.

Barr, James. 1961. *The Semantics of Biblical Language*. Oxford: Oxford University Press.

———. 1988. "'*Abbā*' Isn't 'Daddy.'" *JTS* 39:28–47.

———. 1999. *The Concept of Biblical Theology*. Minneapolis: Fortress.

Barrett, C. K. 1954. "The Eschatology of the Epistle to the Hebrews." Pages 363–93 in *The Background to the New Testament and Its Eschatology*. Edited by W. D. Davies and D. Daube. Cambridge: Cambridge University Press.

———. 1968. *A Commentary on the First Epistle to the Corinthians*. HNTC. New York: Harper & Row.

———. 1970. *Luke the Historian in Recent Study*. Philadelphia: Fortress.

———. 1973. *A Commentary on the Second Epistle to the Corinthians*. HNTC. New York: Harper & Row.

———. 1978. *The Gospel According to St. John: An Introduction with Commentary and Notes on the Greek Text*. 2nd ed. London: SPCK.

———. 1982. *Essays on John*. Philadelphia: Westminster.

———. 1994. *Acts 1–14*. ICC. Edinburgh: T & T Clark.

———. 1998. *Acts 15–28*. ICC. Edinburgh: T & T Clark.

Bartchy, S. Scott. 1973. *Mallon Chresai: First-Century Slavery and the Interpretation of 1 Corinthians 7:21*. SBLDS 11. Missoula, MT: Society of Biblical Literature.

———. "Slave, Slavery." *DLNT* 1098–1102.

———. "Slavery: New Testament." *ABD* 6:65–73.

Barth, G. 1963. "Matthew's Understanding of the Law." Pages 58–164 in *Tradition and Interpretation in Matthew*. Edited by G. Bornkamm, G. Barth, and J. H. Held. Philadelphia: Westminster.

———. "πίστις." *EDNT* 3:91–97.

Bassler, Jouette M. 1982. *Divine Impartiality: Paul and a Theological Axiom*. SBLDS 59. Chico, CA: Scholars Press.

Bauckham, Richard J. 1977. "The Eschatological Earthquake in the Apocalypse of John." *NovT* 19:224–33.

———. 1983. *Jude, 2 Peter*. WBC 50. Waco: Word.

———. 1985. "The Son of Man: 'A Man in My Position' or 'Someone'?" *JSNT* 23:23–33.

———. 1990. *Jude and the Relatives of Jesus in the Early Church*. Edinburgh: T & T Clark.

———. 1991. "The List of the Tribes in Revelation 7 Again." *JSNT* 42:99–115.

———. 1993a. *The Theology of the Book of Revelation*. NTT. Cambridge: Cambridge University Press.

———. 1993b. *The Climax of Prophecy: Studies on the Book of Revelation*. London: T & T Clark.

———. 1995. "James and the Jerusalem Church." Pages 415–80 in *The Book of Acts in Its Palestinian Setting*. Vol. 4 of *The Book of Acts in Its First Century Setting*. Edited by R. Bauckham. Grand Rapids: Eerdmans.

———, ed. 1998. *The Gospels for All Christians: Rethinking the Gospel Audiences*. Grand Rapids: Eerdmans.

———. 1999a. *God Crucified: Monotheism and Christology in the New Testament*. Grand Rapids: Eerdmans.

———. 1999b. *James: Wisdom of James, Disciple of Jesus the Sage*. New York: Routledge.

———. 2001. "The Restoration of Israel in Luke-Acts." Pages 435–87 in *Restoration: Old Testament, Jewish, and Christian Perspectives*. Edited by J. M. Scott. JSJSup 72. Leiden: Brill.

———. 2006. *Jesus and the Eyewitnesses: The Gospels as Eyewitness Testimony*. Grand Rapids: Eerdmans.

———. 2007. "Historiographical Characteristics of the Gospel of John." *NTS* 53:17–36.

Bauer, Walter. 1971. *Orthodoxy and Heresy in Earliest Christianity*. Translated by the Philadelphia Seminar on Christian Origins. Edited by R. A. Kraft and G. Krodel. Philadelphia: Fortress.

Baugh, Steven M. 1992. "'Savior of All People': 1 Tim. 4:10 in Context." *WTJ* 54:331–40.

———. 2000. "The Meaning of Foreknowledge." Pages 183–200 in *Still Sovereign: Contemporary Perspectives on Election, Foreknowledge, and Grace.* Edited by T. R. Schreiner and B. A. Ware. Grand Rapids: Baker Academic.

Beale, G. K. 1984. *The Use of Daniel in Jewish Apocalyptic Literature and in the Revelation of St. John.* Lanham, MD: University Press of America.

———. 1999a. "Peace and Mercy upon the Israel of God: The Old Testament Background of Galatians 6,16b." *Bib* 80:204–23.

———. 1999b. *The Book of Revelation.* NIGTC. Grand Rapids: Eerdmans.

———. 2003. *1–2 Thessalonians.* IVPNTC 13. Downers Grove, IL: InterVarsity Press.

———. 2004. *The Temple and the Church's Mission: A Biblical Theology of the Dwelling Place of God.* Downers Grove, IL: InterVarsity Press.

Beare, F. W. 1947. *The First Epistle of Peter: The Greek Text with Introduction and Notes.* Oxford: Blackwell.

Beasley-Murray, G. R. 1962. *Baptism in the New Testament.* Grand Rapids: Eerdmans.

———. 1986. *Jesus and the Kingdom of God.* Grand Rapids: Eerdmans.

———. 1987. *John.* WBC. Waco: Word.

Bechtler, S. R. 1998. *Following in His Steps: Suffering, Community, and Christology in 1 Peter.* SBLDS 162. Atlanta: Scholars Press.

Beckwith, Roger T. 1995. "Sacrifice in the World of the New Testament." Pages 105–10 in *Sacrifice in the Bible.* Edited by R. T. Beckwith and M. J. Selman. Grand Rapids: Baker Academic.

Beker, J. Christiaan. 1980. *Paul the Apostle: The Triumph of God in Life and Thought.* Philadelphia: Fortress.

Bell, Richard H. 2002. "Sacrifice and Christology in Paul." *JTS* 53:1–27.

Bellefontaine, Elizabeth. 1993. "The Curses of Deuteronomy 27: Their Relationship to the Prohibitives." Pages 258–68 in *A Song of Power and the Power of Song: Essays on the Book of Deuteronomy.* Edited by D. L. Christensen. SBTS 3. Winona Lake, IN: Eisenbrauns.

Belleville, Linda L. 1980. "'Born of Water and Spirit': John 3:5." *TJ* 1:125–41.

———. 1986. "'Under Law': Structural Analysis and the Pauline Concept of Law in Galatians 3:21–4:11." *JSNT* 26:53–78.

———. 1991. *Reflections of Glory: Paul's Polemical Use of the Moses-Doxa Tradition in 2 Corinthians 3:1–18.* JSNTSup 52. Sheffield: Sheffield Academic Press.

Bennema, Cornelis. 2003. "Spirit-Baptism in the Fourth Gospel: A Messianic Reading of John 1,33." *Bib* 84:35–60.

Berger, K. "χάρις." *EDNT* 3:457–60.

Best, Ernest. 1969. "1 Pet. 2:4–10: A Reconsideration." *NovT* 11:270–93.

———. 1970a. "Discipleship in Mark: Mark 8:22–10:52." *SJT* 23:323–37.

———. 1970b. "1 Peter and the Gospel Tradition." *NTS* 16:95–113.

———. 1971. *1 Peter.* NCB. Grand Rapids: Eerdmans.

———. 1972. *A Commentary on the First and Second Epistles to the Thessalonians.* HNTC. New York: Harper & Row.

———. 1981. "'Dead in Trespasses and Sins' (Eph. 2.1)." *JSNT* 13:9–25.

———. 1998. *Ephesians.* ICC. Edinburgh: T & T Clark.

Betz, Hans Dieter. 1979. *Galatians.* Hermeneia. Philadelphia: Fortress.

———. 1985. *2 Corinthians 8 and 9: A Commentary on Two Administrative Letters of the Apostle Paul*. Hermeneia. Philadelphia: Fortress.

Betz, Otto. 1998. "Jesus and Isaiah 53." Pages 70–87 in *Jesus and the Suffering Servant: Isaiah 53 and Christian Origins*. Edited by W. H. Bellinger Jr. and W. R. Farmer. Harrisburg, PA: Trinity Press International.

Beyer, Hermann W. "ἐπισκέπτομαι." *TDNT* 2:599–622.

Bietenhard, H. "ὄνομα." *NIDNTT* 2:648–56.

Bigg, Charles. 1901. *The Epistles of St. Peter and St. Jude*. ICC. Edinburgh: T & T Clark.

Black, Matthew. 1992. "The Messianism of the Parables of Enoch: Their Date and Contribution to Christological Origins." Pages 145–68 in *The Messiah: Developments in Earliest Judaism and Christianity*. Edited by J. H. Charlesworth. Minneapolis: Fortress.

Blackburn, Barry. 1991. *Theios Anēr and the Markan Miracle Traditions: A Critique of the Theios Anēr Concept as an Interpretative Background of the Miracle Traditions Used by Mark*. WUNT 2/40. Tübingen: Mohr Siebeck.

Blaising, Craig. 1999. "Premillennialism." Pages 157–227 in *Three Views on the Millennium and Beyond*. Edited by D. Bock. Grand Rapids: Zondervan.

Blattenberger, David E., III. 1997. *Rethinking 1 Corinthians 11:2–16 through Archaeological and Moral-Rhetorical Analysis*. SBEC 36. Lewiston, NY: Mellen.

Block, Daniel I. 1995. "Bringing Back David: Ezekiel's Messianic Hope." Pages 167–88 in *The Lord's Anointed: Interpretation of Old Testament Messianic Text*. Edited by P. E. Satterthwaite, R. S. Hess, and G. J. Wenham. Grand Rapids: Baker Academic.

———. 1997. *The Book of Ezekiel: Chapters 1–24*. NICOT. Grand Rapids: Eerdmans.

———. 1998. *The Book of Ezekiel: Chapters 25–48*. NICOT. Grand Rapids: Eerdmans.

Blomberg, Craig L. 1984. "The Law in Luke-Acts." *JSNT* 22:53–80.

———. 1990a. *Interpreting the Parables*. Downers Grove, IL: InterVarsity Press.

———. 1990b. "Marriage, Divorce, Remarriage, and Celibacy: An Exegesis of Matthew 19:3–12." *TJ* 11:161–96.

———. 1992. *Matthew*. NAC. Nashville: Broadman.

———. 1998. "The Christian and the Law of Moses." Pages 397–416 in *Witness to the Gospel: The Theology of Acts*. Edited by I. H. Marshall and D. Peterson. Grand Rapids: Eerdmans.

———. 2001. *The Historical Reliability of John's Gospel: Issues and Commentary*. Downers Grove, IL: InterVarsity Press.

Böcher, O. "γέεννα." *EDNT* 1:239–40.

Bock, Darrell. 1987. *Proclamation from Prophecy and Pattern: Lucan Old Testament Christology*. JSNTSup 12. Sheffield: JSOT Press.

———. 1994. *Luke 1:1–9:50*. BECNT. Grand Rapids: Baker Academic.

———. 1996. *Luke 9:51–24:53*. BECNT. Grand Rapids: Baker Academic.

———. 1998. "Scripture and the Realization of God's Promises." Pages 41–62 in *Witness to the Gospel: The Theology of Acts*. Edited by I. H. Marshall and D. Peterson. Grand Rapids: Eerdmans.

———. 2000. *Blasphemy and Exaltation in Judaism and the Final Examination of Jesus: A Philological-Historical Study of the Key Jewish Themes Impacting Mark 14:61–64*. Grand Rapids: Baker Academic.

Bockmuehl, Markus. 1989. "Matthew 5.32; 19.9 in the Light of Pre-Rabbinic Halakah." *NTS* 35:291–95.

————. 2000. *Jewish Law in Gentile Churches: Halakhah and the Beginning of Christian Public Ethics*. Grand Rapids: Eerdmans.

Boers, Hendrikus. 1979. *What Is New Testament Theology? The Rise of Criticism and the Problem of a Theology of the New Testament*. Philadelphia: Fortress.

Bolt, Peter G. 2004. *The Cross from a Distance: Atonement in Mark's Gospel*. Downers Grove, IL: InterVarsity Press.

Borgen, Peder. 1980. "Observations on the Theme 'Paul and Philo': Paul's Preaching of Circumcision in Galatia (Gal. 5:11) and Debates on Circumcision in Philo." Pages 85–102 in *The Pauline Literature and Theology: Scandinavian Contributions* [= *Die Paulinische Literatur und Theologie: Skandinavische Beiträge; Anlässlich der 50. Jährigen Gründungs-Feier der Universität von Århus*]. Edited by S. Pedersen. Teologiske Studier (Forlaget Aros) 7. Aarhus, Denmark: Aros; Göttingen: Vandenhoeck & Ruprecht.

————. 1982. "Paul Preaches Circumcision and Pleases Men." Pages 37–46 in *Paul and Paulinism: Essays in Honor of C. K. Barrett*. Edited by M. D. Hooker and S. G. Wilson. London: SPC.

————. 1988. "Catalogues of Vices: The Apostolic Decree, and the Jerusalem Meeting." Pages 126–41 in *The Social World of Formative Christianity and Judaism: Essays in Tribute to Howard Clark Kee*. Edited by J. Neusner et al. Philadelphia: Fortress.

————. 1992. "There Shall Come Forth a Man: Reflections on Messianic Ideas in Philo." Pages 341–61 in *The Messiah: Developments in Earliest Judaism and Christianity*. Edited by J. H. Charlesworth. Minneapolis: Fortress.

Boring, M. Eugene. 1990. "Mark 1:1–15 and the Beginning of the Gospel." *Semeia* 52:43–81.

Borsch, F. H. 1992. "Further Reflections on 'The Son of Man': The Origins and Development of the Title." Pages 130–44 in *The Messiah: Developments in Earliest Judaism and Christianity*. Edited by J. H. Charlesworth. Minneapolis: Fortress.

Bosch, David J. 1991. *Transforming Mission: Paradigm Shifts in Theology of Mission*. Maryknoll, NY: Orbis Books.

Bousset, Wilhelm. 1970. *Kyrios Christos: A History of Belief in Christ from the Beginnings of Christianity to Irenaeus*. Translated by J. E. Steely. 5th ed. Nashville: Abingdon.

Bowers, Paul. 1991. "Church and Mission in Paul." *JSNT* 44:89–111.

Brady, James R. 1992. *Jesus Christ: Divine Man or Son of God?* Lanham, MD: University Press of America.

Brandon, S. G. F. 1967. *Jesus and the Zealots: A Study of the Political Factor in Primitive Christianity*. New York: Scribner.

Braswell, J. P. 1991. "'The Blessing of Abraham' versus 'The Curse of the Law': Another Look at Gal. 3:10–13." *WTJ* 53:73–91.

Brauch, M. T. 1977. "Appendix: Perspectives on 'God's Righteousness' in Recent German Discussion." Pages 523–42 in *Paul and Palestinian Judaism: A Comparison of Patterns of Religion* by E. P. Sanders. Philadelphia: Fortress.

Brent, Allen. 1999. *The Imperial Cult and the Development of Church Order: Concepts and Images of Authority in Paganism and Early Christianity before the Age of Cyprian*. VCSup 45. Leiden: Brill.

Breytenbach, Cilliers. 1989. *Versöhnung: Eine Studie zur paulinischen Soteriologie*. WMANT 60. Neukirchen-Vluyn: Neukirchener Verlag.

Broer, I. 1986. "Anmerkungen zum Gesetzesverständnis des Matthäus." Pages 128–45 in *Das Gesetz im Neuen Testament*. Edited by K. Kertelge. QD 108. Freiburg: Herder.

Brown, Colin. 1984. *Miracles and the Critical Mind*. Grand Rapids: Eerdmans.

Brown, Raymond E. 1966. *The Gospel According to John I–XII*. AB 29. Garden City, NY: Doubleday.

———. 1970. *The Gospel According to John XIII–XXI*. AB 29A. Garden City, NY: Doubleday.

———. 1977. *The Birth of the Messiah: A Commentary on the Infancy Narratives in Matthew and Luke*. Garden City, NY: Doubleday.

———. 1982. *The Epistles of John*. AB 30. Garden City, NY: Doubleday.

———. 1994. *The Death of the Messiah: From Gethsemane to the Grave; A Commentary on the Passion Narratives in the Four Gospels*. 2 vols. ABRL. New York: Doubleday.

Brox, N. 1986. *Der erste Petrusbrief*. 2nd ed. EKKNT. Neukirchen-Vluyn: Neukirchener Verlag.

Bruce, F. F. 1951. *The Acts of the Apostles: The Greek Text with Introduction and Commentary*. London: Tyndale.

———. 1954. *Commentary on the Book of Acts*. NICNT. Grand Rapids: Eerdmans.

———. 1964. *The Epistle to the Hebrews*. NICNT. Grand Rapids: Eerdmans.

———. 1975. "Paul and the Law of Moses." *BJRL* 57:259–79.

———. 1982a. *The Epistle to the Galatians*. NIGTC. Grand Rapids: Eerdmans.

———. 1982b. *1 & 2 Thessalonians*. WBC 45. Waco: Word.

———. 1984. *The Epistles to the Colossians to Philemon and to the Ephesians*. NICNT. Grand Rapids: Eerdmans.

Bryan, Steven M. 2002. *Jesus and Israel's Traditions of Judgement and Restoration*. SNTSMS 117. Cambridge: Cambridge University Press.

Büchsel, F. "ἱλάσκομαι." *TDNT* 3:310–18.

———. "μονογενής." *TDNT* 4:737–41.

Buckwalter, H. Douglas. 1996. *The Character and Purpose of Luke's Christology*. SNTSMS 89. Cambridge: Cambridge University Press.

———. 1998. "The Divine Saviour." Pages 107–23 in *Witness to the Gospel: The Theology of Acts*. Edited by I. H. Marshall and D. Peterson. Grand Rapids: Eerdmans.

Bühner, J. A. "παῖς." *EDNT* 3:5–6.

Bultmann, Rudolf K. 1951. *Theology of the New Testament*. Vol. 1. Translated by K. Grobel. New York: Scribner.

———. 1955. *Theology of the New Testament*. Vol. 2. Translated by K. Grobel. New York: Scribner.

———. 1960. "Romans 7 and the Anthropology of Paul." Pages 147–57 in *Existence and Faith*. New York: Meridian.

———. 1962. *Jesus and the Word*. Translated by L. P. Smith and E. H. Lantero. New York: Scribner.

———. 1963. *The History of the Synoptic Tradition*. Translated by J. Marsh. Rev. ed. New York: Harper & Row.

———. 1964. "*Dikaiosynē Theou*." *JBL* 83:12–16.

———. 1971. *The Gospel of John: A Commentary*. Translated by G. R. Beasley-Murray. Philadelphia: Westminster.

———. 1995. "The Problem of Ethics in Paul." Pages 195–216 in *Understanding Paul's Ethics: Twentieth Century Approaches*. Edited by B. S. Rosner. Grand Rapids: Eerdmans.

———. "πιστεύω." *TDNT* 6:174–228.

Burge, Gary M. 1987. *The Anointed Community: The Holy Spirit in the Johannine Tradition.* Grand Rapids: Eerdmans.

Burkett, Delbert. 1994. "The Nontitular Son of Man: A History and Critique." *NTS* 40:504–21.

———. 1999. *The Son of Man Debate: A History and Evaluation.* SNTSMS 107. Cambridge: Cambridge University Press.

Byrne, B. 1996. *Romans.* SP 6. Collegeville, MN: Liturgical Press.

Cadbury, Henry J. 1927. *The Making of Luke-Acts.* New York: Macmillan.

———. 1933. "The Titles of Jesus in Acts." Pages 354–75 in *The Acts of the Apostles: Additional Notes to the Commentary.* Part 1, vol. 5 of *The Beginnings of Christianity.* Edited by F. J. Foakes-Jackson and K. Lake. London: Macmillan.

Caird, G. B. 1966. *A Commentary on the Revelation of St. John the Divine.* New York: Harper & Row.

———. 1994. *New Testament Theology.* Completed and edited by L. D. Hurst. Oxford: Clarendon Press.

Callan, Terrance. 2001. "The Christology of the Second Letter of Peter." *Bib* 82:253–63.

———. 2003. "The Style of the Second Letter of Peter." *Bib* 84:202–24.

Calvin, John. 1961. *The Epistles of Paul the Apostle to the Romans and to the Thessalonians.* Translated by R. MacKenzie. Calvin's Commentaries 8. Edited by D. W. Torrance and T. F. Torrance. Repr., Grand Rapids: Eerdmans.

Campbell, R. Alastair. 1994. *The Elders: Seniority within Earliest Christianity.* Edinburgh: T & T Clark.

———. 1996. "Jesus and His Baptism." *TynBul* 47:191–214.

Capes, David B. 1992. *Old Testament Yahweh Texts in Paul's Christology.* WUNT 2/47. Tübingen: Mohr Siebeck.

Capper, Brian. 1998. "Reciprocity and the Ethic of Acts." Pages 499–518 in *Witness to the Gospel: The Theology of Acts.* Edited by I. H. Marshall and D. Peterson. Grand Rapids: Eerdmans.

Caragounis, Chrys C. 1986. *The Son of Man: Vision and Interpretation.* WUNT 38. Tübingen: Mohr Siebeck.

Carey, George L. 1981. "The Lamb of God and Atonement Theories." *TynBul* 32:97–122.

Carras, George P. 1992. "Romans 2,1–29: A Dialogue on Jewish Ideals." *Bib* 73:183–207.

Carson, D. A. 1979. "The Function of the Paraklete in John 16:7–11." *JBL* 98:547–66.

———. 1981a. *Divine Sovereignty and Human Responsibility: Biblical Perspectives in Tension.* Atlanta: John Knox.

———. 1981b. "Historical Tradition in the Fourth Gospel: After Dodd, What?" Pages 83–145 in *Studies of History and Tradition in the Four Gospels.* Vol. 2 of *Gospel Perspectives.* Edited by R. T. France and D. Wenham. Sheffield: JSOT Press.

———. 1982. "Understanding Misunderstandings in the Fourth Gospel." *TynBul* 33:59–91.

———. 1984. "Matthew." Pages 3–599 in *The Expositor's Bible Commentary.* Edited by F. E. Gaebelein. Grand Rapids: Zondervan.

———. 1987a. "The Purpose of the Fourth Gospel: John 20:31 Reconsidered." *JBL* 106:639–51.

———. 1987b. *Showing the Spirit: A Theological Exposition of 1 Corinthians 12–14.* Grand Rapids: Baker Academic.

———. 1988. "John and the Johannine Epistles." Pages 245–64 in *It Is Written: Scripture Citing Scripture; Essays in Honour of Barnabas Lindars, SSF*. Edited by D. A. Carson and H. G. M. Williamson. Cambridge: Cambridge University Press.

———. 1991a. "'Silent in the Churches': On the Role of Women in 1 Corinthians 14:33b–36." Pages 140–53 in *Recovering Biblical Manhood and Womanhood: A Response to Evangelical Feminism*. Edited by J. Piper and W. Grudem. Wheaton: Crossway.

———. 1991b. *The Gospel According to John*. PNTC. Grand Rapids: Eerdmans.

———. 1995. "Current Issues in Biblical Theology: A New Testament Perspective." *BBR* 5:17–41.

———. 2005. "Syntactical and Text-Critical Observations on John 20:31: One More Round on the Purpose of the Fourth Gospel." *JBL* 124:693–714.

———. "Systematic Theology and Biblical Theology." *NDBT* 89–104.

Carson, D. A., Douglas J. Moo, and Leon Morris. 1992. *An Introduction to the New Testament*. Grand Rapids: Zondervan.

Carson, D. A., Peter T. O'Brien, and Mark A. Seifrid, eds. 2001. *The Complexities of Second Temple Judaism*. Vol. 1 of *Justification and Variegated Nomism: A Fresh Appraisal of Paul and Second Temple Judaism*. WUNT 2/140. Tübingen: Mohr Siebeck; Grand Rapids: Baker Academic.

Casey, P. M. 1979. *The Son of Man: The Interpretation and Influence of Daniel 7*. London: SPCK.

———. 1985. "The Jackals and the Son of Man (Matt. 8:20//Luke 9:58)." *JSNT* 23:3–22.

———. 1987. "General, Generic, and Indefinite: The Use of the Term 'Son of Man' in Aramaic Sources and in the Teaching of Jesus." *JSNT* 29:21–56.

Catchpole, David R. 1977. "Paul, James and the Apostolic Decree." *NTS* 23:428–44.

Caulley, T. S. 1982. "The Idea of 'Inspiration' in 2 Peter 1:16–21." ThD diss., University of Tübingen.

Cervin, Richard S. 1989. "Does *Kephalē* Mean 'Source' or 'Authority Over' in Greek Literature? A Rebuttal." *TJ* 10:85–112.

Charles, J. D. 1990. "'Those' and 'These': The Use of the Old Testament in Jude." *JSNT* 38:109–24.

———. 1997. *Virtue amidst Vice: The Catalog of Virtues in 2 Peter 1*. JSNTSup 150. Sheffield: Sheffield Academic Press.

Charlesworth, James H., ed. 1983–1985. *The Old Testament Pseudepigrapha*. 2 vols. Garden City, NY: Doubleday.

———. 1992. "From Messianology to Christology: Problems and Prospects." Pages 3–35 in *The Messiah: Developments in Earliest Judaism and Christianity*. Edited by J. H. Charlesworth. Minneapolis: Fortress.

Chester, Andrew. 1994. *The Theology of the Letters of James, Peter, and Jude*. NTT. Cambridge: Cambridge University Press. [See below, Ralph P. Martin, who wrote the sections on Peter and Jude.]

Cheung, Alex T. 1999. *Idol Food in Corinth: Jewish Background and Pauline Legacy*. JSNTSup 76. Sheffield: Sheffield Academic Press.

Cheung, Luke L. 2003. *The Genre, Composition and Hermeneutics of James*. PBTM. Carlisle: Paternoster.

Childs, Brevard S. 1970. *Biblical Theology in Crisis*. Philadelphia: Westminster.

———. 1974. *The Book of Exodus: A Critical, Theological Commentary*. OTL. Philadelphia: Westminster.

———. 1992. *Biblical Theology of the Old and New Testaments: Theological Reflection on the Christian Bible*. Minneapolis: Fortress.

———. 2001. *Isaiah*. OTL. Louisville: Westminster John Knox.

Chilton, David. 1987. *The Days of Vengeance: An Exposition of the Book of Revelation*. Fort Worth: Dominion Press.

Chin, M. 1991. "A Heavenly Home for the Homeless: Aliens and Strangers in 1 Peter." *TynBul* 42:96–112.

Clark, Andrew C. 1998. "The Role of the Apostles." Pages 169–90 in *Witness to the Gospel: The Theology of Acts*. Edited by I. H. Marshall and D. Peterson. Grand Rapids: Eerdmans.

Clarke, Andrew D. 2000. *Serve the Community of the Church: Christians as Leaders and Ministers*. Grand Rapids: Eerdmans.

Clements, R. E. 1998. "Isaiah 53 and the Restoration of Israel." Pages 39–54 in *Jesus and the Suffering Servant: Isaiah 53 and Christian Origins*. Edited by W. H. Bellinger Jr. and W. R. Farmer. Harrisburg, PA: Trinity Press International.

Cohn-Sherbok, Dan. 1997. *The Jewish Messiah*. Edinburgh: T & T Clark.

Collins, Adela Yarbro. 2004. "The Charge of Blasphemy in Mark 14.64." *JSNT* 26:379–401.

Collins, John C. 2003. "Galatians 3:16: What Kind of Exegete Was Paul?" *TynBul* 54:75–86.

Collins, John J. 1993. *A Commentary on the Book of Daniel*. Hermeneia. Minneapolis: Fortress.

———. 1995. *The Scepter and the Star: The Messiahs of the Dead Sea Scrolls and Other Ancient Literature*. ABRL. New York: Doubleday.

Collins, John N. 1990. *Diakonia: Re-interpreting the Ancient Sources*. New York: Oxford University Press.

Conzelmann, Hans. 1960. *Theology of Luke*. Translated by G. Buswell. London: Faber & Faber.

———. 1969. *An Outline of the Theology of the New Testament*. Translated by J. Bowden. New York: Harper & Row.

———. 1975. *1 Corinthians*. Hermeneia. Philadelphia: Fortress.

———. 1987. *Acts of the Apostles*. Translated by J. Limburg, A. T. Kraabel, and D. H. Juel. Edited by E. J. Epp with C. R. Matthews. Hermeneia. Philadelphia: Fortress.

Conzelmann, Hans, and Andreas Lindemann. 1988. *Interpreting the New Testament: An Introduction to the Principles and Methods of New Testament Exegesis*. Peabody, MA: Hendrickson.

Cosgrove, Charles. 1984. "The Divine *Dei* in Luke-Acts: Investigations into the Understanding of God's Providence." *NovT* 26:168–90.

Couser, Greg A. 2000. "God and Christian Existence in the Pastoral Epistles: Toward Theological Method and Meaning." *NovT* 42:262–83.

Cranfield, C. E. B. 1963. *The Gospel According to Saint Mark: An Introduction and Commentary*. Cambridge: Cambridge University Press.

———. 1975. *A Critical and Exegetical Commentary on the Epistle to the Romans: Introduction and Commentary on Romans I–VIII*. ICC. Edinburgh: T & T Clark.

———. 1979. *A Critical and Exegetical Commentary on the Epistle to the Romans: Commentary on Romans IX–XVI and Essays*. ICC. Edinburgh: T & T Clark.

————. 1990. "Giving a Dog a Bad Name: A Note on Heikki Räisänen's *Paul and the Law*." *JSNT* 38:77–85.

————. 1991. "The Works of the Law in the Epistle to the Romans." *JSNT* 43:89–101.

Creed, John Martin. 1930. *The Gospel According to St. Luke: The Greek Text with Introduction, Notes, and Indices*. London: Macmillan.

Cross, Anthony R. 1999. "'One Baptism' (Ephesians 4.5): A Challenge to the Church." Pages 173–209 in *Baptism, the New Testament and the Church: Historical and Contemporary Studies in Honour of R. E. O. White*. Edited by S. E. Porter and A. R. Cross. JSNTSup 171. Sheffield: Sheffield Academic Press.

————. 2002. "Spirit- and Water-Baptism in 1 Corinthians 12.13." Pages 120–48 in *Dimensions of Baptism: Biblical and Theological Studies*. Edited by S. E. Porter and A. R. Cross. JSNTSup 234. London: Sheffield Academic Press.

Crouch, J. E. 1972. *The Origin and the Intention of the Colossian Haustafel*. FRLANT 109. Göttingen: Vandenhoeck & Ruprecht.

Croy, N. Clayton. 1998. *Endurance in Suffering: Hebrews 12:1–13 in Its Rhetorical, Religious, and Philosophical Context*. SNTSMS 98. Cambridge: Cambridge University Press.

Crump, David Michael. 1992. *Jesus the Intercessor: Prayer and Christology in Luke-Acts*. WUNT 2/49. Tübingen: Mohr Siebeck.

————. 2006. *Knocking on Heaven's Door: A New Testament Theology of Petitionary Prayer*. Grand Rapids: Baker Academic.

Cullmann, Oscar. 1956. *The State in the New Testament*. New York: Scribner.

————. 1963. *The Christology of the New Testament*. Translated by S. C. Guthrie and C. A. M. Hall. Rev. ed. Philadelphia: Westminster.

————. 1964. *Christ and Time: The Primitive Christian Conception of Time and History*. Translated by F. Filson. Rev. ed. Philadelphia: Westminster.

————. 1967. *Salvation in History*. Translated by S. G. Sowers. New York: Harper.

————. 1995. *Prayer in the New Testament: With Answers from the New Testament to Today's Questions*. Translated by J. Bowden. Fortress: Minneapolis.

Culpepper, R. Alan. 1983. *Anatomy of the Fourth Gospel: A Study in Literary Design*. FFNT. Philadelphia: Fortress.

Cuss, Dominique. 1974. *Imperial Cult and Honorary Terms in the New Testament*. Paradosis 23. Fribourg: University Press.

Dahl, Nils Alstrup. 1986. "Gentiles, Christians, and Israelites in the Epistle to the Ephesians." *HTR* 79:31–39.

Danby, Herbert, ed. 1933. *The Mishnah*. New York: Oxford University Press.

Danker, Frederick William, and William Arndt, eds. 2000. *A Greek-English Lexicon of the New Testament and Other Early Christian Literature*. 4th ed. Chicago: University of Chicago Press.

Das, A. Andrew. 2001. *Paul, the Law, and the Covenant*. Peabody, MA: Hendrickson.

————. 2003. *Paul and the Jews*. Peabody, MA: Hendrickson.

Davids, Peter H. 1982. *The Epistle of James*. NIGTC. Grand Rapids: Eerdmans.

Davidson, Richard M. 1981. *Typology in Scripture: A Study of Hermeneutical Typos Structures*. AUSDDS 2. Berrien Springs, MI: Andrews University Press.

Davies, Glenn N. 1990. *Faith and Obedience in Romans: A Study in Romans 1–4*. JSNTSup 39. Sheffield: JSOT Press.

Davies, W. D. 1948. *Paul and Rabbinic Judaism: Some Rabbinic Elements in Pauline Theology*. London: SPCK.

———. 1952. *Torah in the Messianic Age and/or the Age to Come.* JBLMS 7. Philadelphia: Society of Biblical Literature.

———. 1964. *The Setting of the Sermon on the Mount.* Cambridge: Cambridge University Press.

Davies, W. D., and Dale C. Allison. 1988. *Introduction and Commentary on Matthew I–VII.* Vol. 1 of *A Critical and Exegetical Commentary on the Gospel According to Saint Matthew.* ICC. Edinburgh: T & T Clark.

———. 1991. *Commentary on Matthew VIII–XVIII.* Vol. 2 of *A Critical and Exegetical Commentary on the Gospel According to Saint Matthew.* ICC. Edinburgh: T & T Clark.

———. 1997. *Introduction and Commentary on Matthew XIX–XXVIII.* Vol. 3 of *A Critical and Exegetical Commentary on the Gospel According to Saint Matthew.* ICC. Edinburgh: T & T Clark.

Deidun, Thomas J. 1981. *New Covenant Morality in Paul.* AnBib 89. Rome: Biblical Institute Press.

Deines, Roland. 1997. *Die Pharisäer: Ihr Verständnis im Spiegel der christlichen und jüdischen Forschung seit Wellhausen und Graetz.* WUNT 101. Tübingen: Mohr Siebeck.

———. 2001. "The Pharisees between 'Judaisms' and 'Common Judaism.'" Pages 443–504 in *The Complexities of Second Temple Judaism.* Vol. 1 of *Justification and Variegated Nomism: A Fresh Appraisal of Paul and Second Temple Judaism.* Edited by D. A. Carson, P. T. O'Brien, and M. A. Seifrid. WUNT 2/140. Tübingen: Mohr Siebeck; Grand Rapids: Baker Academic.

Deissmann, Adolf. 1927. *Paul: A Study in Social and Religious History.* Translated by W. E. Wilson. 2nd ed. New York: George H. Doran.

Delling, G. "τελειωτής." *TDNT* 8:86–87.

Demarest, Bruce. 1976. *A History of Interpretation of Hebrews 7,1–10 from the Reformation to the Present.* BGBE 19. Tübingen: Mohr Siebeck.

Dempster, Stephen G. 2003. *Dominion and Dynasty: A Biblical Theology of the Hebrew Bible.* Downers Grove, IL: InterVarsity Press.

———. 2007. "The Servant of the Lord." Pages 128–78 in *Central Themes in Biblical Theology: Mapping Unity in Diversity.* Edited by S. J. Hafemann and P. R. House. Nottingham, UK: Inter-Varsity Press.

deSilva, David A. 1995. *Despising Shame: Honor Discourse and Community Maintenance in the Epistle to the Hebrews.* SBLDS 152. Atlanta: Scholars Press.

Dibelius, Martin. 1934. *From Tradition to Gospel.* Translated by B. L. Woolf. 2nd ed. London: Nicholson & Watson.

———. 1975. *A Commentary on the Epistle of James.* Revised by H. Greeven. Translated by M. A. Williams. Edited by H. Koester. Hermeneia. Philadelphia: Fortress.

Dibelius, Martin, and Hans Conzelmann. 1972. *The Pastoral Epistles.* Translated by P. Buttolph and A. Yarbro. Edited by H. Koester. Hermeneia. Philadelphia: Fortress.

Doble, Peter. 1996. *The Paradox of Salvation: Luke's Theology of the Cross.* SNTSMS 87. Cambridge: Cambridge University Press.

Dodd, C. H. 1932. *The Epistle of Paul to the Romans.* MNTC. London: Hodder & Stoughton.

———. 1935. *The Bible and the Greeks.* London: Hodder & Stoughton.

———. 1936. *The Parables of the Kingdom.* London: Nisbet.

———. 1953. *The Interpretation of the Fourth Gospel.* Cambridge: Cambridge University Press.

Donfried, Karl Paul. 2002. *Paul, Thessalonica, and Early Christianity*. Grand Rapids: Eerdmans.

Drane, John W. 1975. *Paul: Libertine or Legalist? A Study in the Theology of the Major Pauline Epistles*. London: SPCK.

Dryden, J. de Waal. 2006. *Theology and Ethics in 1 Peter: Paraenetic Strategies for Christian Character Formation*. WUNT 2/209. Tübingen: Mohr Siebeck.

Dumbrell, William J. 1985. *The End of the Beginning: Revelation 21–22 and the Old Testament*. Homebush West, NSW: Lance.

———. 1986. "Law and Grace: The Nature of the Contrast in John 1:17." *EvQ* 58:25–37.

Dunn, James D. G. 1970a. *Baptism in the Holy Spirit: A Re-examination of the New Testament Teaching on the Gift of the Spirit in Relation to Pentecostalism Today*. Philadelphia: Westminster.

———. 1970b. "The Messianic Secret in Mark." *TynBul* 21:92–117.

———. 1970c. "2 Corinthians III.17—'The Lord Is the Spirit.'" *JTS* 21:309–20.

———. 1971. "John 6: A Eucharistic Discourse?" *NTS* 17:328–38.

———. 1975a. "Rom. 7,14–25 in the Theology of Paul." *TZ* 31:257–73.

———. 1975b. *Jesus and Spirit: A Study of the Religious and Charismatic Experience of Jesus and the First Christians as Reflected in the New Testament*. London: SCM Press.

———. 1977. *Unity and Diversity in the New Testament: An Inquiry into the Character of Earliest Christianity*. Westminster: Philadelphia.

———. 1983. "The New Perspective on Paul." *BJRL* 65:95–122.

———. 1985. "Works of the Law and the Curse of the Law (Galatians 3:10–14)." *NTS* 31:523–42.

———. 1988a. *Romans 1–8*. WBC 38A. Dallas: Word.

———. 1988b. *Romans 9–16*. WBC 38B. Dallas: Word.

———. 1990. *Jesus, Paul, and the Law: Studies in Mark and Galatians*. Louisville: Westminster John Knox.

———. 1991. "Once More *Pistis Christou*." Pages 730–44 in *SBL Seminar Papers, 1991*. Edited by E. H. Lovering Jr. Atlanta: Scholars Press.

———. 1992a. "Yet Once More—'The Works of the Law': A Response." *JSNT* 46:99–117.

———. 1992b. "The Justice of God: A Renewed Perspective on Justification by Faith." *JTS* 43:1–22.

———. 1993. *A Commentary on the Epistle to the Galatians*. BNTC. Peabody, MA: Hendrickson.

———. 1996a. *Christology in the Making: A New Testament Inquiry into the Origins of the Doctrine of the Incarnation*. 2nd ed. Grand Rapids: Eerdmans.

———. 1996b. *The Epistles to the Colossians and to Philemon*. NIGTC. Grand Rapids: Eerdmans.

———. 1997. "4QMMT and Galatians." *NTS* 43:147–53.

———. 1998. *The Theology of Paul the Apostle*. Grand Rapids: Eerdmans.

Du Plessis, I. J. 1994. "The Saving Significance of Jesus and His Death on the Cross in Luke's Gospel—Focusing on Luke 22:19b–20." *Neot* 28:523–40.

Easton, B. S. 1932. "New Testament Ethical Lists." *JBL* 51:1–12.

Eckert, J. "καλέω." *EDNT* 2:240–44.

Eckstein, H. J. 1987. "'Denn Gottes Zorn wird von Himmel her offenbar werden': Exegetische Erwägungen zu Röm 1:18." *ZNW* 78:74–89.

Edgar, David Hutchinson. 2001. *Has God Not Chosen the Poor? The Social Setting of the Epistle of James*. JSNTSup 206. Sheffield: Sheffield Academic Press.

Edwards, Ruth B. 1988. *"Charin anti Charitos* (John 1:16): Grace and Law in the Johannine Prologue." *JSNT* 32:3–15.

Ehrman, Bart D. 1991. "The Cup, the Bread, and the Salvific Effect of Jesus' Death in Luke-Acts." Pages 576–91 in *SBL Seminar Papers, 1991*. Edited by E. H. Lovering Jr. Atlanta: Scholars Press.

Eichrodt, Walther. 1961. *Theology of the Old Testament*. Vol. 1. Translated by J. A. Baker. Philadelphia: Westminster.

———. 1967. *Theology of the Old Testament*. Vol. 2. Translated by J. A. Baker. Philadelphia: Westminster.

Elliott, J. H. 1966. *The Elect and the Holy: An Exegetical Examination of 1 Peter 2:4–10 and the Phrase "basileion hierateuma."* NovTSup 12. Leiden: Brill.

———. 1981. *Home for the Homeless: A Sociological Exegesis of 1 Peter, Its Situation and Strategy*. Philadelphia: Fortress.

———. 2000. *1 Peter*. AB 37B. New York: Doubleday.

Elliott, Mark A. 2000. *The Survivors of Israel: A Reconsideration of the Theology of Pre-Christian Judaism*. Grand Rapids: Eerdmans.

Elliott-Binns, L. E. 1956. "James 1:18: Creation or Redemption?" *NTS* 3:148–61.

Ellis, E. Earle. 1957. *Paul's Use of the Old Testament*. Grand Rapids: Eerdmans.

———. 1992. "Pseudonymity and Canonicity of New Testament Documents." Pages 212–24 in *Worship, Theology and Ministry in the Early Church: Essays in Honor of Ralph P. Martin*. Edited by M. J. Wilkins and T. Paige. JSNTSup 87. Sheffield: JSOT Press.

Emmrich, Martin. 2003. "Hebrews 6:4–6—Again! (A Pneumatological Inquiry)." *WTJ* 65:83–95.

Ervin, Howard M. 1984. *Conversion-Initiation and the Baptism in the Holy Spirit: A Critique of James D. G. Dunn, Baptism in the Holy Spirit*. Peabody, MA: Hendrickson.

Esler, F. S. 2005. *New Testament Theology: Communion and Community*. Minneapolis: Fortress.

Espy, John M. 1985. "Paul's 'Robust Conscience' Re-examined." *NTS* 31:161–88.

Esser, H. H. "πτωχός." *NIDNTT* 2:820–25.

Evans, Craig A. 1988. *To See and Not Perceive: Isaiah 6.9–10 in Early Jewish and Christian Interpretation*. JSOTSup 64. Sheffield: JSOT Press.

———. 1989. "Jesus' Action in the Temple: Cleansing or Portent of Destruction?" *CBQ* 51:237–70.

———. 1993. *Word and Glory: On the Exegetical and Theological Background of John's Prologue*. JSNTSup 89. Sheffield: JSOT Press.

———. 1998. "Are the 'Son' Texts at Qumran Messianic? Reflections on 4Q369 and Related Scrolls." Pages 135–53 in *Qumran-Messianism: Studies on the Messianic Expectations in the Dead Sea Scrolls*. Edited by J. H. Charlesworth, H. Lichtenberger, and G. S. Oegema. Tübingen: Mohr Siebeck.

———. 2001. *Mark 8:28–16:20*. WBC 34B. Nashville: Thomas Nelson.

———. 2002. "The Baptism of John in a Typological Context." Pages 45–71 in *Dimensions of Baptism: Biblical and Theological Studies*. Edited by S. E. Porter and A. R. Cross. JSNTSup 234. Sheffield: Sheffield Academic Press.

Evans, Craig A., and Donald A. Hagner. 1993. *Anti-Semitism and Early Christianity: Issues of Polemic and Faith*. Minneapolis: Fortress.

Farmer, W. R. 1957–1958. "Judas, Simon, and Athronges." *NTS* 4:147–55.

———. 1998. "Reflections on Isaiah 53 and Christian Origins." Pages 260–80 in *Jesus and the Suffering Servant: Isaiah 53 and Christian Origins.* Edited by W. H. Bellinger Jr. and W. R. Farmer. Harrisburg, PA: Trinity Press International.

Fee, Gordon D. 1980. "*Eidōlothyta* Once Again: An Interpretation of 1 Corinthians 8–10." *Bib* 61:172–97.

———. 1987. *The First Epistle to the Corinthians.* NICNT. Grand Rapids: Eerdmans.

———. 1988. *1 and 2 Timothy, Titus.* NIBCNT 13. Peabody, MA: Hendrickson.

———. 1992. "Philippians 2:5–11: Hymn or Exalted Pauline Prose?" *BBR* 2:29–46.

———. 1994. *God's Empowering Presence: The Holy Spirit in the Letters of Paul.* Peabody, MA: Hendrickson.

———. 1995. *Paul's Letter to the Philippians.* NICNT. Grand Rapids: Eerdmans.

Feldmeier, R. 1992. *Die Christen als Fremde: Die Metapher der Fremde in der antiken Welt, im Urchristentum und im 1. Petrusbrief.* WUNT 64. Tübingen: Mohr Siebeck.

Fisk, Bruce N. 1989. "Eating Meat Offered to Idols: Corinthian Response and Pauline Response in 1 Corinthians 8–10 (A Response to Gordon Fee)." *TJ* 10:49–70.

Fitzmyer, J. A. 1967. "Further Light on Melchizedek from Qumran Cave 11." *JBL* 86:25–41.

———. 1979. *A Wandering Aramean: Collected Aramaic Essays.* SBLMS 25. Chico, CA: Scholars Press.

———. 1981a. *The Gospel According to Luke I–IX.* 2nd ed. AB 28. New York: Doubleday.

———. 1981b. *To Advance the Gospel: New Testament Studies.* New York: Crossroad.

———. 1985. *The Gospel According to Luke X–XXIV.* 2nd ed. AB 28A. New York: Doubleday.

———. 1989. *Paul and His Theology: A Brief Sketch.* Englewood Cliffs, NJ: Prentice Hall.

———. 1993a. "*Kephalē* in I Corinthians 11:3." *Int* 47:52–59.

———. 1993b. *According to Paul: Studies in the Theology of the Apostle.* New York: Paulist Press.

———. 1993c. "The Consecutive Meaning of *eph' hō* in Romans 5:12." *NTS* 39:321–39.

———. 1993d. *Romans.* AB 33. New York: Doubleday.

———. 1998. *The Acts of the Apostles.* AB 31. New York: Doubleday.

———. 2000. "Melchizedek in the MT, LXX, and NT." *Bib* 81:63–69.

———. 2002. "The Savior God: The Pastoral Epistles." Pages 181–96 in *The Forgotten God: Perspectives in Biblical Theology.* Edited by A. A. Das and F. J. Matera. Louisville: Westminster John Knox.

———. 2004. "The Structured Ministry of the Church in the Pastoral Epistles." *CBQ* 66:582–96.

———. "κύριος." *EDNT* 2:328–31.

Fletcher-Louis, Crispin H. T. 2003. "'Leave the Dead to Bury Their Own Dead': Q 9.60 and the Redefinition of the People of God." *JSNT* 26:39–68.

Fohrer, G., and W. Foerster. "σωτήρ." *TDNT* 7:1004–24.

Forbes, Christopher. 1995. *Prophecy and Inspired Speech in Early Christianity and Its Hellenistic Environment.* WUNT 2/75. Tübingen: Mohr Siebeck.

Fornberg, T. 1977. *An Early Church in a Pluralistic Society: A Study of 2 Peter.* ConBNT 9. Lund: Gleerup.

Fossum, Jarl. 1987. "Kyrios Jesus as the Angel of the Lord in Jude 5–7." *NTS* 33:226–43.

———. 1995. *The Image of the Invisible God: Essays on the Influence of Jewish Mysticism on Early Christianity*. NTOA 30. Göttingen: Vandenhoeck & Ruprecht.

Frame, John M. 1987. *The Doctrine of the Knowledge of God: A Theology of Lordship*. Phillipsburg, NJ: Presbyterian & Reformed Publishing.

———. 2002. *The Doctrine of God*. Phillipsburg, NJ: Presbyterian & Reformed Publishing.

France, R. T. 1971. *Jesus and the Old Testament: His Application of Old Testament Passages to Himself and His Mission*. Downers Grove, IL: InterVarsity Press.

———. 1989. *Matthew: Evangelist and Teacher*. Grand Rapids: Academie Books.

———. 1996. "The Writer of Hebrews as a Biblical Expositor." *TynBul* 47:245–76.

———. 2002. *The Gospel of Mark*. NIGTC. Grand Rapids: Eerdmans.

Frankemölle, H. 1986. "Gesetz im Jakobusbrief: Zur Tradition, kontextuellen Verwendung und Rezeption eines belaseten Begriffes." Pages 175–221 in *Das Gesetz im Neuen Testament*. Edited by K. Kertelge. QD 108. Freiburg: Herder.

Franklin, Eric. 1975. *Christ the Lord: A Study in the Purpose and Theology of Luke-Acts*. Philadelphia: Westminster.

Friedrich, Gerhard. 1954. "Das Gesetz des Glaubens Röm. 3,27." *TZ* 10:401–17.

Fuchs, E., and P. Reymond. 1980. *La deuxième épître de Saint Pierre; L'épître de Saint Jude*. CNT 2/136. Lausanne: Delachaux & Niestlé.

Fuller, Daniel P. 1975. "Paul and 'The Works of the Law.'" *WTJ* 38:28–42.

———. 1980. *Gospel and Law: Contrast or Continuum?* Grand Rapids: Eerdmans.

Fung, Ronald Y. K. 1981. "The Status of Justification by Faith in Paul's Thought: A Brief Survey of a Modern Debate." *Themelios* 6:4–11.

Furnish, Victor Paul. 1984. *II Corinthians*. AB 32A. New York: Doubleday.

Gaffin, Richard B., Jr. 1988. "'Life-Giving Spirit': Probing the Center of Paul's Pneumatology." *JETS* 41:573–89.

———. 2006. *"By Faith, Not By Sight": Paul and the Order of Salvation*. Waynesboro, GA: Paternoster.

Gager, John G. 1983. *The Origins of Anti-Semitism: Attitudes toward Judaism in Pagan and Christian Antiquity*. New York: Oxford University Press.

Gagnon, Robert A. J. 2001. *The Bible and Homosexual Practice: Texts and Hermeneutics*. Nashville: Abingdon.

Gardner-Smith, P. 1938. *Saint John and the Synoptic Gospels*. Cambridge: Cambridge University Press.

Garland, David E. 1979. *The Intention of Matthew 23*. NovTSup 52. Leiden: Brill.

———. 1999. *2 Corinthians*. NAC. Nashville: Broadman & Holman.

———. 2003. *1 Corinthians*. BECNT. Grand Rapids: Baker Academic.

Garlington, Don B. 1994. *Faith, Obedience, and Perseverance: Aspects of Paul's Letter to the Romans*. WUNT 79. Tübingen: Mohr Siebeck.

Garrett, Duane A. 1997. *Hosea, Joel*. NAC. Nashville: Broadman & Holman.

Gasque, W. Ward. 1989. *A History of the Interpretation of the Acts of the Apostles*. Peabody, MA: Hendrickson.

Gaston, Lloyd. 1987. *Paul and the Torah*. Vancouver: University of British Columbia Press.

Gathercole, Simon J. 2003. *Where Is Boasting? Early Jewish Soteriology and Paul's Response in Romans 1–5*. Grand Rapids: Eerdmans.

———. 2006. *The Pre-existent Son: Recovering the Christologies of Matthew, Mark, and Luke*. Grand Rapids: Eerdmans.

Gempf, Conrad. 1993. "Public Speaking and Published Accounts." Pages 259–303 in *The Book of Acts in Its Ancient Literary Setting*. Vol. 1 of *The Book of Acts in Its First Century Setting*. Edited by B. W. Winter. Grand Rapids: Eerdmans.

Gentry, Peter. 2003. "The Son of Man in Daniel 7: Individual or Corporate?" Pages 59–75 in *Acorns to Oaks: The Primacy and Practice of Biblical Theology; A Festschrift for Dr. Geoff Adams*. Edited by M. A. G. Haykin. Dundas, ON: Joshua Press.

Gese, Hartmut. 1981. *Essays on Biblical Theology*. Translated by K. Crim. Minneapolis: Augsburg.

Gleason, Randall C. 2002. "The Eschatology of the Warning in Hebrews 10:26–31." *TynBul* 53:97–120.

Gnilka, Joachim. 1994. *Theologie des Neuen Testaments*. HTKNT. Freiburg: Herder.

Goldsworthy, Graeme. 1981. *Gospel and Kingdom: A Christian Interpretation of the Old Testament*. Exeter: Paternoster.

———. 2003. "The Ontological and Systematic Roots of Biblical Theology." *RTR* 62:152–64.

———. "Kingdom of God." *NDBT* 615–20.

Gombis, Timothy G. 2002. "Being the Fullness of God in Christ by the Spirit: Ephesians 5:18 in Its Epistolary Setting." *TynBul* 53:259–71.

Gooch, Peter D. 1993. *Dangerous Food: 1 Corinthians 8–10 in Its Context*. Waterloo, ON: Wilfrid Laurier University Press.

Goppelt, Leonhard. 1981. *The Ministry of Jesus in Its Theological Significance*. Vol. 1 of *Theology of the New Testament*. Translated by J. E. Alsup. Edited by J. Roloff. Grand Rapids: Eerdmans.

———. 1982a. *Typos: The Typological Interpretation of the Old Testament in the New*. Translated by D. H. Madvig. Grand Rapids: Eerdmans.

———. 1982b. *The Variety and Unity of the Apostolic Witness to Christ*. Vol. 2 of *Theology of the New Testament*. Translated by J. E. Alsup. Edited by J. Roloff. Grand Rapids: Eerdmans.

———. 1993. *A Commentary on 1 Peter*. Grand Rapids: Eerdmans.

Gordon, T. David. 1989. "A Note on *Paidagōgos* in Galatians 3.24–25." *NTS* 35:150–54.

Green, Joel B. 1988. *The Death of Jesus: Tradition and Interpretation in the Passion Narrative*. WUNT 2/33. Tübingen: Mohr Siebeck.

———. 1990. "The Death of Jesus, God's Servant." Pages 1–28 in *Reimaging the Death of the Lukan Jesus*. BBB 73. Edited by D. D. Sylva. Frankfurt: Hahn.

———. 1995. *The Theology of the Gospel of Luke*. Cambridge: Cambridge University Press.

———. 1997. *The Gospel of Luke*. NICNT. Grand Rapids: Eerdmans.

———. 1998. "'Salvation to the End of the Earth' (Acts 13:47): God as the Saviour in the Acts of the Apostles." Pages 83–106 in *Witness to the Gospel: The Theology of Acts*. Edited by I. H. Marshall and D. Peterson. Grand Rapids: Eerdmans.

———. 2002. "Scripture and Theology: Failed Experiments, Fresh Perspectives." *Int* 56:5–20.

Green, Joel B., and Mark D. Baker. 2000. *Recovering the Scandal of the Cross: Atonement in New Testament and Contemporary Contexts*. Downers Grove, IL: InterVarsity Press.

Greeven, Heinrich. 1952–1953. "Propheten, Lehre, Vorsteher bei Paulus: Zur Frage der 'Ämter' im Urchristentum." *ZNW* 44:1–43.

———. "ἐπερωτάω, ἐπερώτημα." *TDNT* 2:687–89.

Grenz, Stanley J. 1992. *The Millennial Maze: Sorting Out Evangelical Options.* Downers Grove, IL: InterVarsity Press.

Grigsby, Bruce H. 1982. "The Cross as an Expiatory Sacrifice in the Fourth Gospel." *JSNT* 15:51–80.

Grindheim, Sigurd. 2003. "What the OT Prophets Did Not Know: The Mystery of the Church in Eph. 3,2–13." *Bib* 84:531–53.

———. 2005. *The Crux of Election: Paul's Critique of the Jewish Confidence in the Election of Israel.* WUNT 2/202. Tübingen: Mohr Siebeck.

Grisanti, Michael A. 2001. "Inspiration, Inerrancy, and the OT Canon: The Place of Textual Updating in Inerrant View of Scripture." *JETS* 44:577–98.

Grudem, Wayne A. 1982. *The Gift of Prophecy in 1 Corinthians.* Washington, DC: University Press of America.

———. 1985. "Does *Kephalē* ('Head') Mean 'Source' or 'Authority Over' in Greek Literature? A Survey of 2,336 Examples." *TJ* 6:38–59.

———. 1988a. *The Gift of Prophecy in the New Testament and Today.* Westchester, IL: Crossway.

———. 1988b. *The First Epistle of Peter.* TNTC. Grand Rapids: Eerdmans.

———. 1991. "The Meaning of *Kephalē* ('Head'): A Response to Recent Studies." Pages 452–68, 534–41 in *Recovering Biblical Manhood and Womanhood: A Response to Evangelical Feminism.* Edited by J. Piper and W. Grudem. Wheaton: Crossway.

———. 2000. "Perseverance of the Saints: A Case Study from Hebrews 6:4–6 and the Other Warning Passages in Hebrews." Pages 133–82 in *Still Sovereign: Contemporary Perspectives on Election, Foreknowledge, and Grace.* Edited by T. R. Schreiner and B. A. Ware. Grand Rapids: Baker Academic.

———. 2001. "The Meaning of *Kephalē* ('Head'): An Evaluation of New Evidence, Real and Alleged." *JETS* 44:25–65.

Grundmann, Walter. 1933. "Gesetz, Rechtfertigung und Mystik bei Paulus: Zum Problem der Einheitlichkeit der paulinischen Verkündigung." *ZNW* 32:52–65.

———. "ταπεινός." *TDNT* 8:1–26.

Gundry, R. H. 1966. "Ecstatic Utterance (N.E.B.)?" *JTS* 17:299–307.

———. 1967a. "In My Father's House Are Many *Monai* (John 14:2)." *ZNW* 58:68–72.

———. 1967b. "'*Verba Christi*' in I Peter: Their Implications concerning the Authorship of I Peter and the Authenticity of the Gospel Tradition." *NTS* 13:336–50.

———. 1974. "Further *Verba* on *Verba Christi* in I Peter." *Bib* 55:211–32.

———. 1980. "The Moral Frustration of Paul before His Conversion: Sexual Lust in Romans 7:7–25." Pages 228–45 in *Pauline Studies: Essays Presented to Professor F. F. Bruce on His Seventieth Birthday.* Edited by D. A. Hagner and M. J. Harris. Grand Rapids: Eerdmans.

———. 1985. "Grace, Works, and Staying Saved in Paul." *Bib* 66:1–38.

———. 1987. "The New Jerusalem: People as Place, not Place for People." *NovT* 29:254–64.

———. 1994. *Matthew: A Commentary on His Handbook for a Mixed Church under Persecution.* 2nd ed. Grand Rapids: Eerdmans.

Gundry Volf, Judith M. 1990. *Paul and Perseverance: Staying In and Falling Away*. WUNT 2/37. Tübingen: Mohr Siebeck.

Guthrie, Donald. 1981. *New Testament Theology*. Downers Grove, IL: InterVarsity Press.

Guy, Laurie. 1997. "The Interplay of the Present and the Future in the Kingdom of God (Luke 19:11–44)." *TynBul* 48:119–37.

Haenchen, Ernst. 1971. *The Acts of the Apostles*. Translated by B. Noble and G. Shinn, under the supervision of H. Anderson, and with the translation revised by R. McL. Wilson. Philadelphia: Westminster.

Hafemann, Scott J. 1986. *Suffering and Spirit: An Exegetical Study of II Cor. 2:14–3:3 within the Context of the Corinthian Correspondence*. WUNT 2/19. Tübingen: Mohr Siebeck.

———. 1988. "The Salvation of Israel in Romans 11:25–32: A Response to Krister Stendahl." *ExAud* 4:38–58.

———. 1995. *Paul, Moses, and the History of Israel: The Letter/Spirit Contrast and the Argument from Scripture in 2 Corinthians 3*. WUNT 81. Tübingen: Mohr Siebeck.

———. 2000. *2 Corinthians*. NIVAC. Grand Rapids: Zondervan.

Hagner, Donald A. 1993a. "Paul's Quarrel with Judaism." Pages 128–50 in *Anti-Semitism and Early Christianity: Issues of Polemic and Faith*. Edited by C. A. Evans and D. A. Hagner. Minneapolis: Fortress.

———. 1993b. *Matthew 1–13*. WBC 33a. Dallas: Word.

———. 1995. *Matthew 14–28*. WBC 33b. Dallas: Word.

Hahn, Ferdinand. 2002a. *Die Vielfalt des Neuen Testaments: Theologiegeschichte des Urchristentums*. Vol. 1 of *Theologie des Neuen Testaments*. Tübingen: Mohr Siebeck.

———. 2002b. *Die Einheit des Neuen Testaments: Thematische Darstellung*. Vol. 2 of *Theologie des Neuen Testaments*. Tübingen: Mohr Siebeck.

Hamilton, James M., Jr. 2006a. "The Glory of God in Salvation through Judgment: The Centre of Biblical Theology?" *TynBul* 57:57–84.

———. 2006b. *God's Indwelling Presence: The Holy Spirit in the Old and New Testaments*. NACSBT. Nashville: Broadman & Holman.

Hanson, Paul. 1998. "The World of the Servant of the Lord in Isaiah 40–55." Pages 9–22 in *Jesus and the Suffering Servant: Isaiah 53 and Christian Origins*. Edited by W. H. Bellinger Jr. and W. R. Farmer. Harrisburg, PA: Trinity Press International.

Hare, D. R. A., and D. J. Harrington. 1975. "'Make Disciples of All the Gentiles' (Mt 28:19)." *CBQ* 37:359–69.

Harnack, Adolf von. 1957. *What Is Christianity?* Translated by T. B. Saunders. New York: Harper.

———. 1995. "The Old Testament in the Pauline Letters and in the Pauline Churches." Pages 27–49 in *Understanding Ethics: Twentieth Century Approaches*. Edited by B. S. Rosner. Grand Rapids: Eerdmans.

Harner, Philip B. 1970. *The "I Am" of the Fourth Gospel: A Study in Johannine Usage and Thought*. Philadelphia: Fortress.

Harrill, J. Albert. 1995. *The Manumission of Slaves in Early Christianity*. HUT 32. Tübingen: Mohr Siebeck.

Harris, Murray J. 1983. *Raised Immortal: Resurrection and Immortality in the New Testament*. Grand Rapids: Eerdmans.

———. 1992. *Jesus as God: The New Testament Use of Theos in Reference to Jesus*. Grand Rapids: Baker Academic.

———. 1999. *Slave of Christ: A New Testament Metaphor for Total Devotion to Christ*. Downers Grove, IL: InterVarsity Press.

———. 2005. *The Second Epistle to the Corinthians*. NIGTC. Grand Rapids: Eerdmans.

Hartman, Lars. 1995. "Code and Context: A Few Reflections on the Parenesis of Colossians 3:6–4:1." Pages 177–91 in *Understanding Paul's Ethics: Twentieth Century Approaches*. Edited by B. S. Rosner. Grand Rapids: Eerdmans.

———. 1997. *"Into the Name of the Lord Jesus": Baptism in the Early Church*. SNTW. Edinburgh: T & T Clark.

———. "Baptism." *ABD* 1:583–94.

———. "ὄνομα." *EDNT* 2:519–22.

Hasel, Gerhard F. 1978. *New Testament Theology: Basic Issues in the Current Debate*. Grand Rapids: Eerdmans.

———. 1982. "Biblical Theology: Then, Now, and Tomorrow." *HBT* 4:61–93.

———. 1984. "The Relationship between Biblical Theology and Systematic Theology." *TJ* 5:113–27.

Hawkin, David J. 1972. "The Incomprehension of the Disciples in the Markan Redaction." *JBL* 91:491–500.

Hay, David M. 1973. *Glory at the Right Hand: Psalm 110 in Early Christianity*. SBLMS 18. Nashville: Abingdon.

Hays, Richard B. 1987. "Christology and Ethics in Galatians: The Law of Christ." *CBQ* 49:268–90.

———. 1989. *Echoes of Scripture in the Letters of Paul*. New Haven: Yale University Press.

———. 1991. *"Pistis* and Pauline Christology: What Is at Stake?" Pages 714–29 in *SBL Seminar Papers, 1991*. Edited by E. H. Lovering Jr. Atlanta: Scholars Press.

———. 1996. *The Moral Vision of the New Testament: Community, Cross, New Creation; A Contemporary Introduction to New Testament Ethics*. San Francisco: HarperSanFrancisco.

———. 1997. *First Corinthians*. IBC. Louisville: John Knox.

———. 2001. *The Faith of Jesus Christ: An Investigation of the Narrative Substructure of Galatians 3:1–4:11*. 2nd ed. SBLDS 56. Chico, CA: Scholars Press.

Head, Peter M. 1995. "The Self-Offering and Death of Christ as a Sacrifice in the Gospels and the Acts of the Apostles." Pages 111–29 in *Sacrifice in the Bible*. Edited by R. T. Beckwith and M. J. Selman. Grand Rapids: Baker Academic.

Heard, Warren. 1988. "Luke's Attitude toward the Rich and Poor." *TJ* 9:47–80.

Hegermann, H. "δόξα." *EDNT* 1:344–48.

Hemer, Colin J. 1989. *The Book of Acts in the Setting of Hellenistic History*. Edited by C. H. Gempf. WUNT 49. Tübingen: Mohr Siebeck.

Hengel, Martin. 1971. *Was Jesus a Revolutionist?* Translated by W. Klassen. Philadelphia: Fortress.

———. 1974. *Judaism and Hellenism: Studies in Their Encounter in Palestine during the Early Hellenistic Period*. London: SCM Press.

———. 1976. *The Son of God: The Origin of Christology and the History of Jewish-Hellenistic Religion*. Translated by J. Bowden. Philadelphia: Fortress.

———. 1977. *Crucifixion in the Ancient World and the Folly of the Message of the Cross*. Philadelphia: Fortress.

———. 1980. *Acts and the History of Earliest Christianity*. Translated by J. Bowden. Philadelphia: Fortress.

———. 1981. *The Atonement: The Origins of the Doctrine in the New Testament*. Translated by J. Bowden. Philadelphia: Fortress.

———. 1983. *Between Jesus and Paul: Studies in the Earliest History of Christianity*. Philadelphia: Fortress.

———. 1987. "Der Jakobusbrief als antipaulinische Polemik." Pages 248–65 in *Tradition and Interpretation in the New Testament: Essays in Honor of E. Earle Ellis for His 60th Birthday*. Edited by G. F. Hawthorne with O. Betz. Grand Rapids: Eerdmans.

———. 1989a. *The Johannine Question*. Philadelphia: Trinity Press International.

———. 1989b. *The Zealots: Investigations into the Jewish Movement in the Period from Herod I until 70 A.D.* Translated by D. Smith. Edinburgh: T & T Clark.

———. 1991. In collaboration with Roland Deines. *The Pre-Christian Paul*. Philadelphia: Trinity Press International.

———. 1994. "Aufgaben der neutestamentlichen Wissenschaft." *NTS* 40:321–57.

———. 1996. *The Charismatic Leader and His Followers*. Translated by J. C. G. Greig. Edited by J. Riches. SNTW. Edinburgh: T & T Clark.

———. 1997. "Präexistenz bei Paulus?" Pages 479–518 in *Jesus Christus als der Mitte der Schrift: Studien zur Hermeneutik des Evangeliums*. Edited by H.-J. Eckstein and H. Lichtenberger. BZNW 86. Berlin: de Gruyter.

———. 2000. *The Four Gospels and the One Gospel of Jesus Christ: An Investigation of the Collection and Origin of the Canonical Gospels*. Harrisburg, PA: Trinity Press International.

———. 2006. In collaboration with Daniel P. Bailey. "The Effective History of Isaiah 53 in the Pre-Christian Period." Pages 75–146 in *The Suffering Servant: Isaiah 53 in Jewish and Christian Sources*. Edited by B. Janowski and P. Stuhlmacher. Translated by D. P. Bailey. Grand Rapids: Eerdmans.

Hengel, Martin, and Anna Maria Schwemer. 1997. *Paul between Damascus and Antioch: The Unknown Years*. Louisville: Westminster John Knox.

Hermisson, Hans-Jürgen. 2006. "The Fourth Servant Song in the Context of Second Isaiah." Pages 16–47 in *The Suffering Servant: Isaiah 53 in Jewish and Christian Sources*. Edited by B. Janowski and P. Stuhlmacher. Translated by D. P. Bailey. Grand Rapids: Eerdmans.

Herrick, Gregg. 1997. "The Atonement in Lucan Theology in Recent Discussion." http://www.bible.org/page.php?page_id=999 (accessed April 11, 2007).

Hester, James D. 1968. *Paul's Concept of Inheritance: A Contribution to the Understanding of Heilsgeschichte*. SJTOP 14. Edinburgh: Oliver & Boyd.

Heth, William A. 2002. "Jesus on Divorce: How My Mind Has Changed." *SBJT* 6:4–29.

Heth, William A., and Gordon J. Wenham. 1984. *Jesus and Divorce: The Problem with the Evangelical Consensus*. Nashville: Thomas Nelson.

Hiers, R. "Day of the Lord." *ABD* 2:82–83.

Higgins, A. J. B. 1964. *Jesus and the Son of Man*. London: Lutterworth.

Hill, Craig C. 1992. *Hellenists and Hebrews: Reappraising Division within the Earliest Church*. Minneapolis: Fortress.

Hill, David. 1967. *Greek Words and Hebrew Meanings: Studies in the Semantics of Soteriological Terms*. SNTSMS 5. Cambridge: Cambridge University Press.

Hoehner, Harold W. 2002. *Ephesians: An Exegetical Commentary.* Grand Rapids: Baker Academic.

Hoekema, Anthony A. 1979. *The Bible and the Future.* Grand Rapids: Eerdmans.

Hofius, Otfried. 1987. "Struktur und Gedankengang des Logos-Hymnus." *ZNW* 78:1–25.

———. 1989. *Paulusstudien I.* WUNT 51. Tübingen: Mohr Siebeck.

———. 1990. "'All Israel Will Be Saved': Divine Salvation and Israel's Deliverance in Romans 9–11." *PSB* 1:19–39.

———. 1993. "The Lord's Supper and the Lord's Supper Tradition: Reflections on 1 Corinthians 11:23b–25." Pages 75–115 in *One Loaf, One Cup: Ecumenical Studies of 1 Cor. 11 and Other Eucharistic Texts.* Edited by B. F. Meyer. Macon, GA: Mercer University Press.

———. 2000. *Neutestamentliche Studien.* WUNT 132. Tübingen: Mohr Siebeck.

———. 2001. "The Adam-Christ Antithesis and the Law: Reflections on Romans 5:12–21." Pages 165–205 in *Paul and the Mosaic Law.* Edited by J. D. G. Dunn. Grand Rapids: Eerdmans.

———. 2002. *Paulusstudien II.* WUNT 143. Tübingen: Mohr Siebeck.

———. 2006. "The Fourth Servant Song in the New Testament Letters." Pages 163–88 in *The Suffering Servant: Isaiah 53 in Jewish and Christian Sources.* Edited by B. Janowski and P. Stuhlmacher. Translated by D. P. Bailey. Grand Rapids: Eerdmans.

Holladay, Carl R. 1977. *Theios Aner in Hellenistic-Judaism: A Critique of the Use of This Category in New Testament Christology.* SBLDS 40. Missoula, MT: Scholars Press.

Holtz, Traugott. 1995. "The Question of the Content of Paul's Instructions." Pages 51–71 in *Understanding Paul's Ethics: Twentieth Century Approaches.* Edited by B. S. Rosner. Grand Rapids: Eerdmans.

Hooker, Morna D. 1959. *Jesus and the Servant: The Influence of the Servant Concept of Deutero-Isaiah in the New Testament.* London: SPCK.

———. 1967. *The Son of Man in Mark: A Study of the Background of the Term "Son of Man" and Its Use in St. Mark's Gospel.* Montreal: McGill University Press.

———. 1991. *A Commentary on the Gospel According to St. Mark.* London: A & C Black.

———. 1998. "Response to Mikeal Parsons." Pages 120–24 in *Jesus and the Suffering Servant: Isaiah 53 and Christian Origins.* Edited by W. H. Bellinger Jr. and W. R. Farmer. Harrisburg, PA: Trinity Press International.

———. 2006. "The Nature of New Testament Theology." Pages 75–92 in *The Nature of New Testament Theology: Essays in Honour of Robert Morgan.* Edited by C. Rowland and C. Tuckett. Malden, MA: Blackwell.

Hoover, Roy W. 1971. "The *Harpagmos* Enigma: A Philological Solution." *HTR* 64:95–119.

Horbury, William. 1998. *Jewish Messianism and the Cult of Christ.* London: SCM Press.

Horrell, David. 1997. "Theological Principle or Christological Praxis? Pauline Ethics in 1 Corinthians 8.1–11.1." *JSNT* 67:83–114.

———. 2002. "The Product of a Petrine Circle? A Reassessment of the Origin and Character of 1 Peter." *JSNT* 86:29–60.

Horsley, R. A. 1992. "Messianic Figures and Movements in First-Century Palestine." Pages 276–95 in *The Messiah: Developments in Earliest Judaism and Christianity.* Edited by J. H. Charlesworth. Minneapolis: Fortress.

Horsley, Richard A., and John A. Hanson. 1985. *Bandits, Prophets, and Messiahs: Popular Movements in the Time of Jesus.* Minneapolis: Winston.

Horst, Pieter W. van der. 2000. "'Only Then Will All Israel Be Saved': A Short Note on the Meaning of *kai houtōs* in Romans 11:26." *JBL* 119:521–25.

Horton, Michael S. 2002. *Covenant and Eschatology: The Divine Drama*. Louisville: Westminster John Knox.

House, Paul R. 1998. *Old Testament Theology*. Downers Grove, IL: InterVarsity Press.

———. 2007. "The Day of the Lord." Pages 179–224 in *Central Themes in Biblical Theology: Mapping Unity in Diversity*. Edited by S. J. Hafemann and P. R. House. Nottingham, UK: Inter-Varsity Press.

Howard, David M., Jr. 1990. "Review Article: The Case for Kingship in Deuteronomy and the Former Prophets." *WTJ* 52:101–15.

Howard, George. 1979. *Paul: Crisis in Galatia; A Study in Early Christian Theology*. SNTSMS 35. Cambridge: Cambridge University Press.

Hubbard, Moyer V. 2002. *New Creation in Paul's Letters and Thought*. SNTSMS 119. Cambridge: Cambridge University Press.

Hübner, Hans. 1973. *Das Gesetz in der synoptischen Tradition: Studien zur These einer progressiven Qumranisierung und Judaisierung innerhalb der synoptischen Tradition*. Witten: Luther-Verlag.

———. 1984a. *Law in Paul's Thought*. Edinburgh: T & T Clark.

———. 1984b. *Gottes Ich und Israel: Zum Schriftgebrauch des Paulus in Römer 9–11*. FRLANT 136. Göttingen: Vandenhoeck & Ruprecht.

———. 1990. *Prolegomena*. Vol. 1 of *Biblische Theologie des Neuen Testaments*. Göttingen: Vandenhoeck & Ruprecht.

———. 1993. *Die Theologie des Paulus und ihre neutestamentliche Wirkungsgeschichte*. Vol. 2 of *Biblische Theologie des Neuen Testaments*. Göttingen: Vandenhoeck & Ruprecht.

———. 1995. *Hebräerbrief, Evangelien und Offenbarung, Epilegomena*. Vol. 3 of *Biblische Theologie des Neuen Testaments*. Göttingen: Vandenhoeck & Ruprecht.

———. "μένω." *EDNT* 2:407–8.

Hugenberger, Gordon. 1995. "The Servant of the Lord in the 'Servant Songs' of Isaiah: A Second Moses Figure." Pages 105–40 in *The Lord's Anointed: Interpretation of Old Testament Messianic Texts*. Edited by P. E. Satterthwaite, R. S. Hess, and G. J. Wenham. Grand Rapids: Baker Academic.

———. 1998. *Marriage as a Covenant: Biblical Law and Ethics as Developed from Malachi*. Grand Rapids: Baker Academic.

Hughes, J. J. 1979. "Hebrews ix 15ff. and Galatians iii 15ff.: A Study in Covenant Practice and Procedure." *NovT* 21:27–96.

Hughes, Philip E. 1977. *A Commentary on the Epistle to the Hebrews*. Grand Rapids: Eerdmans.

Hultgren, Arland J. 2000. *The Parables of Jesus: A Commentary*. Grand Rapids: Eerdmans.

Hurley, James B. 1981. *Man and Woman in Biblical Perspective*. Grand Rapids: Zondervan.

Hurst, L. D. 1987. "The Christology of Hebrews 1 and 2." Pages 151–64 in *The Glory of Christ in the New Testament: Studies in Christology*. Edited by L. D. Hurst and N. T. Wright. Oxford: Clarendon Press.

———. 1990. *The Epistle to the Hebrews: Its Background of Thought*. SNTSMS 65. Cambridge: Cambridge University Press.

Hurtado, Larry. 1988. *One God, One Lord: Early Christian Devotion and Ancient Jewish Monotheism*. Philadelphia: Fortress.

———. 2003. *Lord Jesus Christ: Devotion to Jesus in Earliest Christianity*. Grand Rapids: Eerdmans.

Hvalvik, Reidar. 1990. "A 'Sonderweg' for Israel: A Critical Examination of a Current Interpretation of Romans 11.25–27." *JSNT* 38:87–107.

Instone-Brewer, David. 2002. *Divorce and Remarriage in the Bible: The Social and Literary Context*. Grand Rapids: Eerdmans.

Jackson-McCabe, Matt A. 2001. *Logos and Law in the Letter of James: The Law of Nature, the Law of Moses, and the Law of Freedom*. NovTSup 100. Leiden: Brill.

Jenson, Philip P. 1995. "Models of Prophetic Prediction and Matthew's Quotation of Micah 5:2." Pages 189–211 in *The Lord's Anointed: Interpretation of Old Testament Messianic Texts*. Edited by P. E. Satterthwaite, R. S. Hess, and G. J. Wenham. Grand Rapids: Baker Academic.

Jeremias, Joachim. 1954–1955. "Paul and James." *ExpTim* 66:368–71.

———. 1967. *The Prayers of Jesus*. SBT 2/6. London: SCM Press.

———. 1971. *New Testament Theology: The Proclamation of Jesus*. Translated by J. Bowden. New York: Scribner.

———. 1972. *The Parables of Jesus*. 2nd ed. New York: Scribner.

Jervell, Jacob. 1972. *Luke and the People of God: A New Look at Luke-Acts*. Minneapolis: Augsburg.

———. 1984. *The Unknown Paul: Essays on Luke-Acts and Early Christian History*. Minneapolis: Augsburg.

———. 1996. *The Theology of the Acts of the Apostles*. Cambridge: Cambridge University Press.

Johnson, Luke T. 1977. *The Literary Function of Possessions in Luke-Acts*. SBLDS 39. Missoula, MT: Scholars Press.

———. 1982a. "Rom. 3:21–26 and the Faith of Jesus." *CBQ* 44:77–90.

———. 1982b. "The Use of Leviticus 19 in the Letter of James." *JBL* 101:391–401.

———. 1995. *The Letter of James*. AB 37A. New York: Doubleday.

———. 1996. *Letters to Paul's Delegates: 1 Timothy, 2 Timothy, Titus*. Valley Forge, PA: Trinity Press International.

———. 2002. "God Ever New, Ever the Same: The Witness of James and Peter." Pages 211–27 in *The Forgotten God: Perspectives in Biblical Theology*. Edited by A. A. Das and F. J. Matera. Louisville: Westminster John Knox.

———. 2006. "Does a Theology of the Canonical Gospels Make Sense?" Pages 93–122 in *The Nature of New Testament Theology: Essays in Honour of Robert Morgan*. Edited by C. Rowland and C. Tuckett. Malden, MA: Blackwell.

Johnson, S. Lewis, Jr. 1980. *Old Testament in the New: An Argument for Biblical Inspiration*. Grand Rapids: Zondervan.

Johnston, George. 1970. *The Spirit-Paraclete in the Gospel of John*. SNTSMS 12. Cambridge: Cambridge University Press.

Jones, Donald L. 1974. "The Title *Kyrios* in Luke-Acts." Pages 85–101 in vol. 2 of *SBL Seminar Papers, 1974*. Edited by G. MacRae. Cambridge, MA: Society of Biblical Literature.

Joubert, S. J. 1998. "Facing the Past: Transtextual Relationships and Historical Understanding of the Letter of Jude." *BZ* 42:56–70.

Juel, Donald. 1983. *Luke-Acts: The Promise of History*. Atlanta: John Knox.

Kaiser, Walter C., Jr. 1978. *Toward an Old Testament Theology*. Grand Rapids: Zondervan.

Kallas, James. 1961. *The Significance of the Synoptic Miracles*. London: SPCK.

———. 1965. "Romans xiii.1–7: An Interpolation." *NTS* 11:365–74.

Kamlah, E. 1970. "*'Hypotassesthai'* in den neutestamentlichen 'Haustafeln.'" Pages 237–43 in *Verborum Veritas: Festschrift für Gustav Stählin zum 70. Geburtstag*. Wuppertal: Brockhaus.

Kammler, Hans-Christian. 2003. "Die Prädikation Jesu Christi als 'Gott' and die paulinische Christologie: Erwägungen zur Exegese von Röm 9,5b." *ZNW* 92:164–80.

Karris, R. J. 1985. *Luke: Artist and Theologian; Luke's Passion Account as Literature*. New York: Paulist Press.

Käsemann, Ernst. 1964a. "Ministry and Community in the New Testament." Pages 63–94 in *Essays on New Testament Themes*. Translated by W. J. Montague. Philadelphia: Fortress.

———. 1964b. *Essays on New Testament Themes*. Translated by W. J. Montague. Philadelphia: Fortress.

———. 1968. *The Testament of Jesus: A Study of the Gospel of John in the Light of Chapter 17*. Translated by G. Krodel. Philadelphia: Fortress.

———. 1969. "'The Righteousness of God' in Paul." Pages 168–82 in *New Testament Questions of Today*. Translated by W. J. Montague. Philadelphia: Fortress.

———. 1980. *Commentary on Romans*. Translated and edited by G. W. Bromiley. Grand Rapids: Eerdmans.

———. 1984. *The Wandering People of God: An Investigation of the Letter to the Hebrews*. Translated by R. A. Harrisville and I. L. Sandberg. Minneapolis: Augsburg.

Keck, Leander E. 1986. "Toward the Renewal of New Testament Christology." *NTS* 32:362–77.

———. 2006. "Paul in New Testament Theology: Some Preliminary Remarks." Pages 109–22 in *The Nature of New Testament Theology: Essays in Honour of Robert Morgan*. Edited by C. Rowland and C. Tuckett. Malden, MA: Blackwell.

Kee, Howard Clark. 1990. *Good News to the Ends of the Earth: The Theology of Acts*. Philadelphia: Trinity Press International.

Keener, Craig S. 1992. *Paul, Women and Wives: Marriage and Women's Ministry in the Letters of Paul*. Peabody, MA: Hendrickson.

———. 2003. *The Gospel of John: A Commentary*. Vol. 1. Peabody, MA: Hendrickson.

Kelly, Brian. 1995. "Messianic Elements in the Chronicler's Work." Pages 249–64 in *The Lord's Anointed: Interpretation of Old Testament Messianic Texts*. Edited by P. E. Satterthwaite, R. S. Hess, and G. J. Wenham. Grand Rapids: Baker Academic.

Kelly, J. N. D. 1981. *A Commentary on the Epistles of Peter and Jude*. Grand Rapids: Baker Academic.

Kertelge, Karl. 1967. *"Rechtfertigung" bei Paulus: Studien zur Struktur und zum Bedeutungsgehalt des paulinischen Rechtfertigungsbegriffs*. NTAbh 3. Münster: Aschendorff.

Kidd, Reggie. 1990. *Wealth and Beneficence in the Pastoral Epistles: A "Bourgeois" Form of Early Christianity?* SBLDS 122. Atlanta: Scholars Press.

Kidner, Derek. 1975. *Psalms 73–150: A Commentary on Books III–V of the Psalms*. Downers Grove, IL: InterVarsity Press.

Kilgallen, J. 1976. *The Stephen Speech: A Literary and Redactional Study of Acts 7,2–53*. AnBib 67. Rome: Biblical Institute Press.

———. 1988. "Acts 13,38–39: Culmination of Paul's Speech in Pisidia." *Bib* 69:480–506.

Kim, Seyoon. 1982. *The Origins of Paul's Gospel.* Grand Rapids: Eerdmans.

———. 1983. *The Son of Man as the Son of God.* Grand Rapids: Eerdmans.

———. 2002. *Paul and the New Perspective: Second Thoughts on the Origin of Paul's Gospel.* Grand Rapids: Eerdmans.

Kingsbury, Jack Dean. 1975. *Matthew: Structure, Christology, Kingdom.* Philadelphia: Fortress.

———. 1983. *The Christology of Mark's Gospel.* Philadelphia: Fortress.

———. 1986. *Matthew as Story.* Philadelphia: Fortress.

Klappert, B., and G. Fries. "λόγος." *NIDNTT* 3:1081–1117.

Klausner, Joseph. 1929. *Jesus of Nazareth: His Life, Times, and Teaching.* Translated by H. Danby. New York: Macmillan.

Klein, William W. 1990. *The New Chosen People: A Corporate View of Election.* Grand Rapids: Academie Books.

Kleinknecht, H. "λόγος." *TDNT* 4:77–91.

Kline, Meredith. 1975. "First Resurrection." *WTJ* 37:366–75.

———. 1976. "First Resurrection: A Reaffirmation." *WTJ* 39:110–19.

Knight, George W., III. 1992. *The Pastoral Epistles.* NIGTC. Grand Rapids: Eerdmans.

Koester, Craig R. 2003. *Symbolism in the Fourth Gospel: Meaning, Mystery, Community.* 2nd ed. Minneapolis: Fortress.

Köstenberger, Andreas. 1991. "The Mystery of Christ and the Church: Head and Body, 'One Flesh.'" *TJ* 12:79–94.

———. 1998. *The Missions of Jesus and the Disciples according to the Fourth Gospel: With Implications for the Fourth Gospel's Purpose and the Mission of the Contemporary Church.* Grand Rapids: Eerdmans.

———. 2002. "John." Pages 2–216 in *John, Acts.* Vol. 2 of *Zondervan Illustrated Bible Backgrounds Commentary.* Edited by C. E. Arnold. Grand Rapids: Zondervan.

———. 2004. *John.* BECNT. Grand Rapids: Baker Academic.

———. 2007. "Baptism in the Gospels." Pages 11–34 in *Believer's Baptism: Sign of the New Covenant in Christ.* Edited by T. R. Schreiner and S. D. Wright. Nashville: Broadman & Holman.

Köstenberger, Andreas J., with David W. Jones. 2004. *God, Marriage, and Family: Rebuilding the Biblical Foundation.* Wheaton: Crossway.

Köstenberger, Andreas J., and Peter O'Brien. 2001. *Salvation to the Ends of the Earth: A Biblical Theology of Mission.* Downers Grove, IL: InterVarsity Press.

Kreitzer, L. Joseph. 1987. *Jesus and God in Paul's Eschatology.* JSNTSup 19. Sheffield: JSOT Press.

Kroeger, Catherine Clark. 1987. "The Classical Concept of Head as Source." Pages 267–83 in *Equal to Serve: Women and Men in the Church and Home.* Edited by G. G. Hull. Old Tappan, NJ: Revell.

Kruse, Colin. "Virtues and Vices." *DPL* 962–63.

Kümmel, Werner G. 1957. *Promise and Fulfillment: The Eschatological Message of Jesus.* SBT. London: SCM Press.

———. 1973. *The Theology of the New Testament according to Its Major Witnesses: Jesus— Paul—John.* Translated by J. E. Steely. Nashville: Abingdon.

———. 1974. *Römer 7 und das Bild des Menschen im Neuen Testament: Zwei Studien*. TB 53. Munich: Kaiser.

Laato, Timo. 1991. *Paulus und das Judentum: Anthropologische Erwägungen*. Åbo: Åbo Akademis Förlag.

———. 1997. "Justification according to James: A Comparison with Paul." *TJ* 18:43–84.

Ladd, George E. 1957. "Why Not Prophetic-Apocalyptic?" *JBL* 76:192–200.

———. 1972. *A Commentary on the Revelation of John*. Grand Rapids: Eerdmans.

———. 1977. "Historic Premillennialism." Pages 17–40 in *The Meaning of the Millennium: Four Views*. Edited by R. G. Clouse. Downers Grove, IL: InterVarsity Press.

———. 1993. *A Theology of the New Testament*. Edited by D. A. Hagner. Rev. ed. Grand Rapids: Eerdmans.

Lake, Kirsopp, and Henry J. Cadbury. 1979. *The Acts of the Apostles: English Translation and Commentary*. Part I, vol. 4 of *The Beginnings of Christianity*. London: Macmillan.

Lane, William L. 1974. *The Gospel According to Mark*. NICNT. Grand Rapids: Eerdmans.

———. 1991a. *Hebrews 1–8*. WBC 47A. Dallas: Word.

———. 1991b. *Hebrews 9–13*. WBC 47B. Dallas: Word.

Lau, Andrew Y. 1996. *Manifest in the Flesh: The Epiphany Christology of the Pastoral Epistles*. WUNT 2/86. Tübingen: Mohr Siebeck.

Laws, Sophie. 1980. *A Commentary on the Epistle of James*. HNTC. San Francisco: Harper & Row.

Lee, Aquila H. I. 2005. *From Messiah to Preexistent Son: Jesus' Self-Consciousness and Early Christian Exegesis of Messianic Psalms*. WUNT 2/192. Tübingen: Mohr Siebeck.

Lehne, Susanne. 1990. *The New Covenant in Hebrews*. JSNTSup 44. Sheffield: JSOT Press.

Lemcio, Eugene E. 1988. "The Unifying Kerygma of the New Testament." *JSNT* 33:3–17.

Liebers, Reinhold. 1989. *Das Gesetz als Evangelium: Untersuchungen zur Gesetzeskritik des Paulus*. ATANT 75. Zürich: Theologischer Verlag.

Lightfoot, J. B. 1953. *St. Paul's Epistle to the Philippians*. Grand Rapids: Zondervan.

Lincoln, Andrew T. 1981. *Paradise Now and Not Yet: Studies in the Role of the Heavenly Dimension in Paul's Thought with Special Reference to His Eschatology*. SNTSMS 43. Cambridge: Cambridge University Press.

———. 1982. "Sabbath, Rest, and Eschatology in the New Testament." Pages 197–220 in *From Sabbath to Lord's Day: A Biblical, Historical, and Theological Investigation*. Edited by D. A. Carson. Grand Rapids: Zondervan.

———. 1987. "The Church and Israel in Ephesians 2." *CBQ* 49:605–24.

———. 1990. *Ephesians*. WBC 42. Dallas: Word.

———. 1999. "The Household Code and Wisdom Mode of Colossians." *JSNT* 74:93–112.

———. 2000. *Truth on Trial: The Lawsuit Motif in the Fourth Gospel*. Peabody, MA: Hendrickson.

Lindars, Barnabas. 1972. *The Gospel of John*. NCB. Grand Rapids: Eerdmans.

———. 1983. *Jesus Son of Man: A Fresh Examination of the Son of Man Sayings in the Gospels in the Light of Recent Research*. London: SPCK.

———. 1991. *The Theology of the Letter to the Hebrews*. Cambridge: Cambridge University Press.

Litfin, Duane. 1994. *St. Paul's Theology of Proclamation: 1 Corinthians 1–4 and Greco-Roman Rhetoric*. SNTSMS 79. Cambridge: Cambridge University Press.

Lohse, Eduard. 1971. *Colossians and Philemon*. Hermeneia. Philadelphia: Fortress.

Longenecker, Richard N. 1970. *The Christology of Early Jewish Christianity*. SBT 2/17. Naperville, IL: Allenson.

———. 1978. "The Melchizedek Argument of Hebrews: A Study in the Development and Circumstantial Expression of New Testament Thought." Pages 161–85 in *Unity and Diversity in New Testament Theology: Essays in Honor of George E. Ladd*. Edited by R. A. Guelich. Grand Rapids: Eerdmans.

———. 1982. "The Pedagogical Nature of the Law in Galatians 3:19–4:7." *JETS* 25:53–61.

———. 1985. "The Nature of Paul's Early Eschatology." *NTS* 31:85–95.

———. 1990. *Galatians*. WBC 41. Dallas: Word.

Longman, Tremper, III, and Daniel G. Reid. 1995. *God Is a Warrior*. SOTBT. Grand Rapids: Zondervan.

Lowe, J. 1941. "An Examination of Attempts to Detect Developments in St. Paul's Theology." *JTS* 42:129–42.

Lull, David. 1986. "'The Law Was Our Pedagogue': A Study in Galatians 3:19–25." *JBL* 105:481–98.

Luz, Ulrich. 1968. *Das Geschichtsverständnis des Paulus*. BEvT 49. Munich: Kaiser.

———. 1989. *Matthew 1–7*. Translated by W. C. Linss. Minneapolis: Augsburg.

———. 1995. *The Theology of the Gospel of Matthew*. Translated by J. B. Robinson. Cambridge: Cambridge University Press.

———. 2001. *Matthew 8–20*. Translated by J. E. Crouch. Hermeneia. Minneapolis: Fortress.

———. 2005. *Matthew 21–28*. Translated by J. E. Crouch. Hermeneia. Minneapolis: Fortress.

Machen, J. Gresham. 1965. *The Virgin Birth of Christ*. Grand Rapids: Baker Books.

Maddox, Robert. 1982. *The Purpose of Luke-Acts*. FRLANT 126. Göttingen: Vandenhoeck & Ruprecht.

Maier, G. 1984. "Jesustradition im 1. Petrusbrief." Pages 85–128 in *The Jesus Tradition Outside the Gospels*. Vol. 5 of *Gospel Perspectives*. Edited by D. Wenham. Sheffield: JSOT Press.

Marcus, Joel. 2000. *Mark 1–8*. AB 27A. New York: Doubleday.

Marshall, I. H. 1970. *Luke: Historian and Theologian*. Grand Rapids: Zondervan.

———. 1974. "The Development of the Concept of Redemption in the New Testament." Pages 153–69 in *Reconciliation and Hope: New Testament Essays on Atonement and Eschatology Presented to L. L. Morris on His Sixtieth Birthday*. Edited by R. Banks. Grand Rapids: Eerdmans.

———. 1976. *The Origins of New Testament Christology*. Downers Grove, IL: InterVarsity Press.

———. 1978a. *The Epistles of John*. NICNT. Grand Rapids: Eerdmans.

———. 1978b. *The Gospel of Luke*. NIGTC. Grand Rapids: Eerdmans.

———. 1980a. *Last Supper and Lord's Supper*. Grand Rapids: Eerdmans.

———. 1980b. *The Acts of the Apostles*. TNTC. Grand Rapids: Eerdmans.

———. 1983. *1 and 2 Thessalonians: Based on the Revised Standard Version*. Grand Rapids: Eerdmans.

———. 1996. "Salvation, Grace and Works in the Later Writings in the Pauline Corpus." *NTS* 42:339–58.

———. 1999. In collaboration with Philip H. Towner. *The Pastoral Epistles*. ICC. Edinburgh: T & T Clark.

———. 2002. "The Meaning of the Verb 'Baptize.'" Pages 8–24 in *Dimensions of Baptism: Biblical and Theological Studies*. Edited by S. E. Porter and A. R. Cross. JSNTSup 234. London: Sheffield Academic Press.

———. 2004. *New Testament Theology: Many Witnesses, One Gospel*. Downers Grove, IL: InterVarsity Press.

———. 2005. "Political and Eschatological Language in Luke." Pages 157–77 in *Reading Luke: Interpretation, Reflection, Formation*. Edited by C. G. Bartholomew, J. B. Green, and A. C. Thiselton. SHS 6. Grand Rapids: Zondervan.

Martin, Dale B. 1990. *Slavery as Salvation: The Metaphor of Slavery in Pauline Christianity*. New Haven: Yale University Press.

Martin, Ralph P. 1986. *2 Corinthians*. WBC 40. Waco: Word.

———. 1988. *James*. WBC 48. Waco: Word.

———. 1989. *Reconciliation: A Study of Paul's Theology*. Rev. ed. Grand Rapids: Zondervan.

———. 1994. *The Theology of the Letters of James, Peter, and Jude*. NTT. Cambridge: Cambridge University Press. [See above, Andrew Chester, who wrote the section on James.]

———. 1997. *A Hymn of Christ: Philippians 2:5–11 in Recent Interpretation and the Setting of Early Christian Worship*. Rev. ed. Downers Grove, IL: InterVarsity Press.

Martyn, J. Louis. 1979. *History and Theology in the Fourth Gospel*. Rev. ed. Nashville: Abingdon.

———. 1985. "Apocalyptic Antinomies in Paul's Letter to the Galatians." *NTS* 31:410–24.

———. 1997. *Galatians*. AB 33A. New York: Doubleday.

Matera, Frank J. 1992. *Galatians*. SP. Collegeville, MN: Liturgical Press.

———. 2005. "New Testament Theology: History, Method, and Identity." *CBQ* 67:1–21.

Mathewson, Dave. 1999. "Reading Heb. 6:4–6 in Light of the Old Testament." *WTJ* 61:209–25.

Matlock, Barry. 2000. "Detheologizing the *Pistis Christou* Debate: Cautionary Remarks from a Lexical Semantic Perspective." *NovT* 42:1–23.

McCartney, D. G. 1989. "The Use of the Old Testament in the First Epistle of Peter." PhD diss., Westminster Theological Seminary.

McConnell, R. S. 1969. *Law and Prophecy in Matthew's Gospel: The Authority and Use of the Old Testament in the Gospel of St. Matthew*. Basel: Reinhardt.

McEleney, N. J. 1974. "The Vice Lists of the Pastoral Epistles." *CBQ* 36:203–19.

McKelvey, R. J. 1961–1962. "Christ the Cornerstone." *NTS* 8:352–59.

———. 2003. "Jews in the Book of Revelation." *IBS* 25:175–94.

McKnight, Scot. 1991. *A Light among the Gentiles: Jewish Missionary Activity in the Second Temple Period*. Minneapolis: Fortress.

———. 1992. "The Warning Passages in Hebrews: A Formal Analysis and Theological Conclusions." *TJ* 13:21–59.

Mearns, C. L. 1981. "Early Eschatological Development in Paul: The Evidence of I and II Thessalonians." *NTS* 27:137–57.

Meier, John P. 1976. *Law and History in Matthew's Gospel: A Redactional Study of Mt. 5:17–48*. AnBib 71. Rome: Biblical Institute Press.

———. 1977. "Nations or Gentiles in Matthew 28:19?" *CBQ* 39:94–102.

———. 1985a. "Structure and Theology in Heb. 1,1–14." *Bib* 66:168–89.

———. 1985b. "Symmetry and Theology in the Old Testament Citations of Heb. 1,5–14." *Bib* 66:504–33.

———. 1991. *The Roots of the Problem and the Person*. Vol. 1 of *A Marginal Jew: Rethinking the Historical Jesus*. New York: Doubleday.

———. 1994. *Mentor, Message and Miracles*. Vol. 2 of *A Marginal Jew: Rethinking the Historical Jesus*. New York: Doubleday.

———. 2001. *Companions and Competitors*. Vol. 3 of *A Marginal Jew: Rethinking the Historical Jesus*. New York: Doubleday.

Menzies, Robert P. 1994. *Empowered for Witness: The Spirit in Luke-Acts*. JPTSup 6. Sheffield: Sheffield Academic Press.

Merkle, Benjamin L. 2000. "Romans 11 and the Future of Ethnic Israel." *JETS* 43:709–21.

———. 2003. *The Elder and Overseer: One Office in the Early Church*. New York: Peter Lang.

Merklein, H. "πτωχός." *EDNT* 3:193–95.

Metzger, Bruce M. 1983. "The Fourth Book of Ezra: A New Translation and Introduction." Pages 517–59 in *The Old Testament Pseudepigrapha*. Vol. 1 of *Apocalyptic Literature and Testaments*. Edited by J. H. Charlesworth. Garden City, NY: Doubleday.

———. 1994. *A Textual Commentary on the Greek New Testament: A Companion Volume to the United Bible Societies' Greek New Testament*. 2nd ed. London: United Bible Societies.

Meyer, B. F. 1979. *The Aims of Jesus*. London: SCM Press.

Michaels, J. Ramsey. 1988. *1 Peter*. WBC 49. Waco: Word.

Michel, Otto. 1966. *Der Brief an die Hebräer*. 12th ed. KEK. Göttingen: Vandenhoeck & Ruprecht.

———. "παῖς θεοῦ." *NIDNTT* 3:607–13.

Mickelsen, Berkeley, and Alvera Mickelsen. 1986. "What Does *Kephalē* Mean in the New Testament?" Pages 97–110 in *Women, Authority and the Bible*. Edited by A. Mickelsen. Downers Grove, IL: InterVarsity Press.

Mitton, C. Leslie. 1966. *The Epistle of James*. Grand Rapids: Eerdmans.

Moessner, David P. 1990. "'The Christ Must Suffer,' the Church Must Suffer: Rethinking the Theology of the Cross in Luke-Acts." Pages 165–95 in *SBL Seminar Papers, 1990*. Edited by D. J. Lull. Atlanta: Scholars Press.

———. 1996. "The 'Script' of the Scriptures in Acts: Suffering as God's 'Plan' (*Boulē*) for the World, for the 'Release of Sins.'" Pages 218–50 in *History, Literature and Society in the Book of Acts*. Edited by B. Witherington III. Cambridge: Cambridge University Press.

———. 2005. "Reading Luke's Gospel as Ancient Hellenistic Narrative: Luke's Narrative Plan of Israel's Suffering Messiah as God's Saving 'Plan' for the World." Pages 125–51 in *Reading Luke: Interpretation, Reflection, Formation*. Edited by C. G. Bartholomew, J. B. Green, and A. C. Thiselton. SHS 6. Grand Rapids: Zondervan.

Mohrlang, Roger. 1984. *Matthew and Paul: A Comparison of Ethical Perspectives*. SNTSMS 48. Cambridge: Cambridge University Press.

Moloney, Francis J. 2002. "Telling God's Story: The Fourth Gospel." Pages 107–22 in *The Forgotten God: Perspectives in Biblical Theology*. Edited by A. A. Das and F. J. Matera. Louisville: Westminster John Knox.

Montefiore, Claude G. 1914. *Judaism and St. Paul: Two Essays*. London: Goschen.

Montefiore, Claude G., and H. Loewe. 1974. *A Rabbinic Anthology*. New York: Schocken.

Moo, Douglas J. 1983. "'Law,' 'Works of the Law,' and Legalism in Paul." *WTJ* 45:73–100.

———. 1984. "Jesus and the Authority of the Mosaic Law." *JSNT* 20:3–49.

———. 1991. *Romans 1–8*. WEC. Chicago: Moody.

———. 1996. *Romans*. NICNT. Grand Rapids: Eerdmans.

———. 2000. *The Letter of James*. PNTC. Grand Rapids: Eerdmans.

Moore, George Foote. 1921. "Christian Writers on Judaism." *HTR* 14:197–254.

Morgan, Robert. 1973. *The Nature of New Testament Theology: The Contributions of William Wrede and Adolf Schlatter*. SBT 25. Naperville, IL: Allenson.

Morris, Leon. 1959. *The First and Second Epistles to the Thessalonians*. NICNT. Grand Rapids: Eerdmans.

———. 1965. *The Apostolic Preaching of the Cross*. 3rd ed. Grand Rapids: Eerdmans.

———. 1969a. *Studies in the Fourth Gospel*. Grand Rapids: Eerdmans.

———. 1969b. *The Revelation of St. John*. TNTC. Grand Rapids: Eerdmans.

———. 1971. *The Gospel According to John*. NICNT. Grand Rapids: Eerdmans.

Motyer, J. Alec. 1993. *The Prophecy of Isaiah: An Introduction and Commentary*. Downers Grove, IL: InterVarsity Press.

Moule, C. F. D. 1966a. "The Christology of Acts." Pages 159–85 in *Studies in Luke-Acts: Essays Presented in Honor of Paul Schubert*. Edited by L. Keck and J. L. Martyn. Nashville: Abingdon.

———. 1966b. "St. Paul and Dualism: The Pauline Conception of the Resurrection." *NTS* 12:106–23.

———. 1977. *The Origin of Christology*. Cambridge: Cambridge University Press.

———. 1995. "'The Son of Man': Some of the Facts." *NTS* 41:277–79.

Mounce, Robert H. 1977. *The Book of Revelation*. NICNT. Grand Rapids: Eerdmans.

Mounce, William D. 2000. *Pastoral Epistles*. WBC 46. Nashville: Thomas Nelson.

Moxnes, H. 1988. "Honor, Shame, and the Outside World in Paul's Letter to the Romans." Pages 207–18 in *The Social World of Formative Christianity and Judaism: Essays in Tribute to Howard Clark Kee*. Edited by J. Neusner et al. Philadelphia: Fortress.

Moyise, Steve. 1995. *The Old Testament in the Book of Revelation*. JSNTSup 115. Sheffield: Sheffield Academic Press.

Müller, Christian. 1964. *Gottes Gerechtigkeit und Gottes Volk: Eine Untersuchung zu Römer 9–11*. FRLANT 86. Göttingen: Vandenhoeck & Ruprecht.

Müller, P.-G. "ἀρχηγός." *EDNT* 1:163–64.

Munck, Johannes. 1959. *Paul and the Salvation of Mankind*. Translated by F. Clarke. Richmond: John Knox.

Murphy O'Connor, Jerome. 1976. "Christological Anthropology in Phil. II, 6–11." *RB* 83:25–50.

Murray, John. 1959. *The Epistle to the Romans*. Vol. 1. NICNT. Grand Rapids: Eerdmans.

Mussner, F. 1964. *Der Jakobusbrief*. 4th ed. HTKNT 13. Freiburg: Herder.

Neirynck, F. 1986. "Paul and the Sayings of Jesus." Pages 265–321 in *L'Apôtre Paul: Personnalité, style et conception du ministère*. Edited by A. Vanhoye. BETL 73. Leuven: Leuven University Press.

Neusner, Jacob. 1971. *The Rabbinic Traditions about the Pharisees before 70*. 3 vols. Leiden: Brill.

———. 1984. *Messiah in Context: Israel's History and Destiny in Formative Judaism*. Philadelphia: Fortress.

———. 1991. "Mr. Sanders' Pharisees and Mine: A Response to E. P. Sanders, *Jewish Law from Jesus to the Mishnah*." *SJT* 44:73–95.

Niccum, Curt. 1997. "The Voice of the Manuscripts on the Silence of Women: The External Evidence for 1 Corinthians 14.34–35." *NTS* 43:242–55.

Nickle, Keith F. 1966. *The Collection: A Study in Paul's Strategy*. SBT 48. Naperville, IL: Allenson.

Nicole, Roger R. 1955. "C. H. Dodd and the Doctrine of Propitiation." *WTJ* 17:117–57.

———. 1975. "Some Comments on Hebrews 6:4–6 and the Doctrine of the Perseverance of God with the Saints." Pages 355–64 in *Current Issues in Biblical and Patristic Interpretation*. Edited by G. Hawthorne. Grand Rapids: Eerdmans.

Noble, Paul R. 1995. *The Canonical Approach: A Critical Reconstruction of the Hermeneutics of Brevard S. Childs*. BIS 16. Leiden: Brill.

Nolland, John. 1980. "A Fresh Look at Acts 15.10." *NTS* 27:105–15.

———. 1986. "Grace as Power." *NovT* 28:26–31.

———. 1998. "Salvation-History and Eschatology." Pages 63–81 in *Witness to the Gospel: The Theology of Acts*. Edited by I. H. Marshall and D. Peterson. Grand Rapids: Eerdmans.

———. 2005. *The Gospel of Matthew*. NIGTC. Grand Rapids: Eerdmans.

O'Brien, Peter T. 1977. *Introductory Thanksgivings in the Letters of Paul*. NovTSup 49. Leiden: Brill.

———. 1982. *Colossians, Philemon*. WBC 44. Waco: Word.

———. 1987a. "The Church as a Heavenly and Eschatological Entity." Pages 88–119 in *The Church in the Bible and the World: An International Study*. Edited by D. A. Carson. Grand Rapids: Baker Academic.

———. 1987b. "Romans 8:26, 27: A Revolutionary Approach to Prayer?" *RTR* 46:65–73.

———. 1991. *The Epistle to the Philippians*. NIGTC. Grand Rapids: Eerdmans.

———. 1992. "Justification in Paul and Some Crucial Issues of the Last Two Decades." Pages 69–95 in *Right with God: Justification in the Bible and the World*. Edited by D. A. Carson. Grand Rapids: Eerdmans.

———. 1999. *The Letter to the Ephesians*. PNTC. Grand Rapids: Eerdmans.

———. 2004. "Was Paul Converted?" Pages 361–91 in *The Paradoxes of Paul*. Vol. 2 of *Justification and Variegated Nomism: A Fresh Appraisal of Paul and Second Temple Judaism*. Edited by D. A. Carson, P. T. O'Brien, and M. A. Seifrid. WUNT 2/140. Tübingen: Mohr Siebeck; Grand Rapids: Baker Academic.

O'Donnell, Matthew Brook. 1999. "Two Opposing Views on Baptism with/by the Holy Spirit and of 1 Corinthians 12:13: Can Grammatical Investigation Bring Clarity?" Pages 311–36 in *Baptism, the New Testament and the Church: Historical and Contemporary Studies in Honour of R. E. O. White*. Edited by S. E. Porter and A. R. Cross. JSNTSup 171. Sheffield: Sheffield Academic Press.

Oegema, Gerbern S. 1998. "Messianic Expectations in the Qumran Writings: Theses on Their Development." Pages 53–82 in *Qumran-Messianism: Studies on the Messianic Expectations in the Dead Sea Scrolls*. Edited by J. H. Charlesworth, H. Lichtenberger, and G. S. Oegema. Tübingen: Mohr Siebeck.

Oepke, A. "λούω." *TDNT* 4:295–307.

Okeke, G. E. 1981. "1 Thessalonians 2:13–16: The Fate of the Unbelieving Jews." *NTS* 27:127–36.

Oropeza, B. J. 2000. *Paul and Apostasy: Eschatology, Perseverance, and Falling Away in the Corinthian Congregation*. WUNT 2/115. Tübingen: Mohr Siebeck.

Ortlund, Raymond C., Jr. 2002. *God's Unfaithful Wife: A Biblical Theology of Spiritual Adultery*. Downers Grove, IL: InterVarsity Press.

Osborne, Grant R. 2002. *Revelation*. BECNT. Grand Rapids: Baker Academic.

Osei-Bonsu, Joseph. 1986. "Does 2 Corinthians 5:1–10 Teach the Reception of the Resurrection Body at the Moment of Death?" *JSNT* 28:81–101.

Oswalt, John N. 1986. *The Book of Isaiah: Chapters 1–39*. NICOT. Grand Rapids: Eerdmans.

O'Toole, Robert F. 2000. "How Does Luke Portray Jesus as Servant of YHWH?" *Bib* 81:328–46.

Overstreet, R. Larry. 1980. "A Study of 2 Peter 3:10–13." *BSac* 137:354–71.

Owen, Paul, and David Shepherd. 2001. "Speaking Up for Qumran, Dalman and the Son of Man: Was *Bar Enasha* a Common Term for 'Man' in the Time of Jesus?" *JSNT* 81:81–122.

Page, Sidney. 1993. "Marital Expectations of Church Leaders in the Pastoral Epistles." *JSNT* 50:105–20.

Palmer, Darryl W. 1993. "Acts and the Ancient Historical Monograph." Pages 1–29 in *The Book of Acts in Its Ancient Literary Setting*. Vol. 1 of *The Book of Acts in Its First Century Setting*. Edited by B. W. Winter. Grand Rapids: Eerdmans.

Pamment, Margaret. 1981. "The Kingdom of Heaven according to the First Gospel." *NTS* 27:211–32.

Pancaro, S. 1975. *The Law in the Fourth Gospel: The Torah and the Gospel, Moses and Jesus, Judaism and Christianity according to John*. NovTSup 42. Leiden: Brill.

Pao, David W. 2000. *Acts and the Isaianic New Exodus*. Grand Rapids: Baker Academic.

———. 2002. *Thanksgiving: An Investigation of a Pauline Theme*. Downers Grove, IL: InterVarsity Press.

Parsons, Michael. 1995. "Being Precedes Act: Indicative and Imperative in Paul's Writing." Pages 217–47 in *Understanding Paul's Ethics: Twentieth Century Approaches*. Edited by B. S. Rosner. Grand Rapids: Eerdmans.

Pate, C. Marvin. 1995. *The End of the Age Has Come: The Theology of Paul*. Grand Rapids: Zondervan.

Paulsen, H. 1992. *Der Zweite Petrusbrief und der Judasbrief*. KEK. Göttingen: Vandenhoeck & Ruprecht.

Payne, Philip B. 1981. "Libertarian Women in Ephesus: A Response to Douglas J. Moo's Article, '1 Timothy 2:11–15: Meaning and Significance.'" *TJ* 2:169–97.

———. 1995. "Fuldensis, Sigla for Variants in Vaticanus, and 1 Corinthians 14.34–5." *NTS* 41:240–62.

Pearson, Birger. 1971. "I Thessalonians 2:13–16: A Deutero-Pauline Interpolation." *HTR* 64:79–91.

Peisker, C. H. "προφήτης." *NIDNTT* 3:74–92.

Penner, Todd C. 1996. *The Epistle of James and Eschatology: Re-reading an Ancient Christian Letter.* JSNTSup 121. Sheffield: Sheffield Academic Press.

Penney, John Michael. 1997. *The Missionary Emphasis of Lukan Pneumatology.* JPTSup 12. Sheffield: Sheffield Academic Press.

Pennington, Jonathan. 2007. *Heaven and Earth in the Gospel of Matthew.* NovTSup 126. Leiden: Brill.

Perrin, Norman. 1967. *Rediscovering the Teaching of Jesus.* New York: Harper & Row.

Pervo, Richard I. 1987. *Profit with Delight: The Literary Genre of the Acts of the Apostles.* Philadelphia: Fortress.

Peterlin, Davorin. 1995. *Paul's Letter to the Philippians in Light of Disunity in the Church.* NovTSup 79. Leiden: E. J. Brill.

Peterson, David. 1982. *Hebrews and Perfection: An Examination of the Concept of Perfection in the "Epistle to the Hebrews."* SNTSMS 47. Cambridge: Cambridge University Press.

———. 1993. "The Motif of Fulfillment and the Purpose of Luke-Acts." Pages 83–104 in *The Book of Acts in Its Ancient Literary Setting.* Vol. 1 of *The Book of Acts in Its First Century Setting.* Edited by B. W. Winter. Grand Rapids: Eerdmans.

———. 1995. *Possessed by God: A New Testament Theology of Sanctification and Holiness.* Grand Rapids: Eerdmans.

———. 1998. "The Worship of the New Community." Pages 373–95 in *Witness to the Gospel: The Theology of Acts.* Edited by I. H. Marshall and D. Peterson. Grand Rapids: Eerdmans.

Petzer, J. H. 1984. "Luke 22:19b–20 and the Structure of the Passage." *NovT* 26:249–52.

Petzer, Kobus. 1991. "Style and Text in the Lucan Narrative of the Institution of the Lord's Supper (Luke 22:19b–20)." *NTS* 37:113–29.

Picirilli, Robert E. 1975. "Meaning of Epignosis." *EvQ* 47:85–93.

Piper, John. 1979. *"Love Your Enemies": Jesus' Love Command in the Synoptic Gospels and in the Early Christian Paranaesis; A History of the Tradition and Interpretation of Its Uses.* SNTSMS 38. Cambridge: Cambridge University Press.

———. 1980. "Hope as the Motivation of Love: 1 Peter 3:9–12." *NTS* 26:212–31.

———. 1993. *The Justification of God: An Exegetical and Theological Study of Romans 9:1–23.* 2nd ed. Grand Rapids: Baker Academic.

———. 2002. *Counted Righteous in Christ: Should We Abandon the Imputation of Christ's Righteousness?* Wheaton: Crossway.

Plantinga, Alvin. 2003. "Two (or More) Kinds of Scripture Scholarship." Pages 19–57 in *"Behind" the Text: History and Biblical Interpretation.* SHS 4. Edited by C. Bartholomew et al. Grand Rapids: Zondervan.

Plevnik, Joseph. 1986. "Recent Developments in the Discussion concerning Justification by Faith." *TJT* 2:47–62.

———. 1989. "The Center of Pauline Theology." *CBQ* 51:461–78.

———. 1997. *Paul and the Parousia: An Exegetical and Theological Investigation.* Peabody, MA: Hendrickson.

———. 2003. "The Understanding of God as the Basis of Pauline Theology." *CBQ* 65:554–67.

Plummer, Robert L. 2006. *Paul's Understanding of the Church's Mission: Did the Apostle Paul Expect the Early Christian Communities to Evangelize?* PBM. Waynesboro, GA: Paternoster.

Pokorný, Petr. 1991. *Colossians.* Translated by S. S. Schatzmann. Peabody, MA: Hendrickson.

Polhill, John B. 1992. *Acts.* NAC. Nashville: Broadman & Holman.

Porter, Stanley E. 1989. *Verbal Aspect in the Greek of the New Testament, with Reference to Tense and Mood.* New York: Peter Lang.

———. 1990. "Two Myths: Corporate Personality and Language/Mentality Determinism." *SJT* 43:289–307.

———. 1994. *Idioms of the Greek New Testament.* 2nd ed. Sheffield: JSOT Press.

Price, S. R. F. 1984. *Rituals and Power: The Roman Imperial Cult in Asia Minor.* Cambridge: Cambridge University Press.

Procksch, O. "ἁγιάζω, ἁγιασμός." *TDNT* 1:111–13.

Provan, Iain W. 1995. "The Messiah in the Book of Kings." Pages 67–85 in *The Lord's Anointed: Interpretation of Old Testament Messianic Texts.* Edited by P. E. Satterthwaite, R. S. Hess, and G. J. Wenham. Grand Rapids: Baker Academic.

Przybylski, Benno. 1980. *Righteousness in Matthew and His World of Thought.* SNTSMS 41. Cambridge: Cambridge University Press.

Radl, W. "προορίζω." *EDNT* 3:159.

———. "σῴζω." *EDNT* 3:319–21.

Radmacher, Earl D. 1990. "First Response to 'Faith According to the Apostle James' by John F. MacArthur Jr." *JETS* 33:35–41.

Rainbow, Paul A. 2005. *The Way of Salvation: The Role of Christian Obedience in Justification.* Waynesboro, GA: Paternoster.

Räisänen, Heikki. 1983. *Paul and the Law.* Philadelphia: Fortress.

———. 1986. *The Torah and Christ: Essays in German and English on the Problem of the Law in Early Christianity.* SESJ 45. Helsinki: Finnish Exegetical Society.

———. 1988. "Paul, God, and Israel: Romans 9–11 in Recent Research." Pages 178–206 in *The Social World of Formative Christianity and Judaism: Essays in Tribute to Howard Clark Kee.* Edited by J. Neusner et al. Philadelphia: Fortress.

———. 1990. *Beyond New Testament Theology: A Story and a Progamme.* Philadelphia: Trinity Press International.

———. 1992. *Jesus, Paul, and Torah: Collected Essays.* Translated by D. E. Orton. JSNTSup 43. Sheffield: JSOT Press.

———. 2000. *Beyond New Testament Theology: A Story and a Progamme.* 2nd ed. London: SCM Press.

Reasoner, Mark. 1999. "The Theme of Acts: Institutional History or Divine Necessity in History?" *JBL* 118:635–59.

Reitzenstein, Richard. 1978. *Hellenistic Mystery-Religions: Their Basic Ideas and Significance.* Pittsburgh: Pickwick.

Rengstorf, Karl H. "διδάσκω." *TDNT* 2:135–65.

Reumann, John H. P. 1982. *Righteousness in the New Testament: Justification in the United States Lutheran-Roman Catholic Dialogue, with Responses by Joseph A. Fitzmyer and Jerome D. Quinn.* Philadelphia: Fortress.

Rhee, Victor (Sung-Yul). 2001. *Faith in Hebrews: Analysis within the Context of Christology, Eschatology, and Ethics.* StBL 19. New York: Peter Lang.

Rhyne, C. T. 1981. *Faith Establishes the Law*. SBLDS 55. Chico, CA: Scholars Press.

Richardson, Peter. 1969. *Israel in the Apostolic Church*. SNTSMS 10. Cambridge: Cambridge University Press.

Ridderbos, Herman. 1975. *Paul: An Outline of His Theology*. Grand Rapids: Eerdmans.

———. 1997. *The Gospel According to John: A Theological Commentary*. Translated by J. Vriend. Grand Rapids: Eerdmans.

Rissi, Mathias. 1966. *The Future of the World: An Exegetical Study of Revelation 19.11–22.15*. SBT 23. Naperville, IL: Allenson.

———. 1987. *Die Theologie des Hebräerbriefs: Ihre Verankerung in der Situation des Verfassers und seiner Leser*. WUNT 41. Tübingen: Mohr Siebeck.

Rivkin, Ellis. 1978. *A Hidden Revolution: The Pharisees' Search for the Kingdom Within*. Nashville: Abingdon.

Robinson, D. W. B. 1967. "The Salvation of Israel in Romans 9–11." *RTR* 26:81–96.

Robinson, J. A. T. 1962. *Twelve New Testament Studies*. Naperville, IL: Allenson.

Rodriguez, Angel Manuel. 1979. "Substitution in the Hebrew Cultus and in Cultic-Related Texts." ThD diss., Andrews University Theological Seminary.

Rogerson, John W. 1970. "The Hebrew Conception of Corporate Personality: A Re-examination." *JTS* 21:1–16.

Roloff, J. "ἐκκλησία." *EDNT* 1:410–15.

Rooke, Deborah W. 2000. "Jesus as Royal Priest: Reflections on the Interpretation of the Melchizedek Tradition in Heb. 7." *Bib* 81:81–94.

Rosner, Brian S. 1994. *Paul, Scripture, and Ethics: A Study of 1 Corinthians 5–7*. AGJU 22. Leiden: Brill.

———. 1995. *Understanding Paul's Ethics: Twentieth Century Approaches*. Grand Rapids: Eerdmans.

———. 1998. "The Progress of the Word." Pages 215–33 in *Witness to the Gospel: The Theology of Acts*. Edited by I. H. Marshall and D. Peterson. Grand Rapids: Eerdmans.

———. "Biblical Theology." *NDBT* 3–11.

Rowe, C. Kavin. 2003. "Luke and the Trinity: An Essay in Ecclesial Biblical Theology." *SJT* 56:1–26.

Rowland, Christopher, and Christopher Tuckett, eds. 2006. *The Nature of New Testament Theology: Essays in Honour of Robert Morgan*. Malden, MA: Blackwell.

Russell, Walter B. 1993. "Does the Christian Have 'Flesh' in Gal. 5:13–26?" *JETS* 36:179–87.

———. 1995. "The Apostle Paul's Redemptive-Historical Argumentation in Galatians 5:13–26." *WTJ* 57:333–57.

Sanders, E. P. 1977. *Paul and Palestinian Judaism: A Comparison of Patterns of Religion*. Philadelphia: Fortress.

———. 1978. "Paul's Attitude toward the Jewish People." *USQR* 33:175–87.

———. 1983. *Paul, the Law, and the Jewish People*. Philadelphia: Fortress.

———. 1985. *Jesus and Judaism*. Philadelphia: Fortress.

———. 1990. *Jewish Law from Jesus to the Mishnah: Five Studies*. Philadelphia: Trinity Press International.

———. 1992. *Judaism: Practice and Belief, 63 BCE–66 CE*. Philadelphia: Trinity Press International.

Sanders, Jack T. 1987. *The Jews in Luke-Acts*. Philadelphia: Fortress.

Sandys-Wunsch, John, and Laurence Eldredge. 1980. "J. P. Gabler and the Distinction between Biblical and Dogmatic Theology: Translation, Commentary, and Discussion of His Originality." *SJT* 33:133–58.

Sapp, David A. 1998. "The LXX, 1QIsa, and MT Versions of Isaiah 53 and the Christian Doctrine of Atonement." Pages 170–92 in *Jesus and the Suffering Servant: Isaiah 53 and Christian Origins*. Edited by W. H. Bellinger Jr. and W. R. Farmer. Harrisburg, PA: Trinity Press International.

Satterthwaite, Philip E. 1995. "David in the Books of Samuel: A Messianic Hope?" Pages 41–65 in *The Lord's Anointed: Interpretation of Old Testament Messianic Texts*. Edited by P. E. Satterthwaite, R. S. Hess, and G. J. Wenham. Grand Rapids: Baker Academic.

Schäfer, Peter. 1974. "Die Torah der messianischen Zeit." *ZNW* 65:27–42.

Schelke, K. H. 1980. *Die Petrusbriefe; der Judasbrief*. HTKNT. Freiberg: Herder.

Schibler, Daniel. 1995. "Messianism and Messianic Prophecy in Isaiah 1–12 and 28–33." Pages 87–104 in *The Lord's Anointed: Interpretation of Old Testament Messianic Texts*. Edited by P. E. Satterthwaite, R. S. Hess, and G. J. Wenham. Grand Rapids: Baker Academic.

Schlatter, Adolf. 1973. "The Theology of the New Testament and Dogmatics." Pages 117–66 in *The Nature of New Testament Theology: The Contributions of William Wrede and Adolf Schlatter*. Edited and translated by R. Morgan. SBT 25. Naperville, IL: Allenson.

———. 1997. *The History of the Christ: The Foundation for New Testament Theology*. Translated by A. J. Köstenberger. Grand Rapids: Baker Academic.

———. 1999. *The Theology of the Apostles: The Development of New Testament Theology*. Translated by A. J. Köstenberger. Grand Rapids: Baker Academic.

Schmidt, D. 1983. "I Thess 2:13–16: Linguistic Evidence for an Interpolation." *JBL* 102:269–79.

Schmidt, K. L. "καλέω." *TDNT* 3:487–500.

Schmithals, Walter. 1975. *Der Römerbrief als historisches Problem*. SNT 9. Gütersloh: Mohn.

———. 1997. *The Theology of the First Christians*. Louisville: Westminster John Knox.

Schnabel, Eckhard J. 1995. "How Paul Developed His Ethics." Pages 267–97 in *Understanding Paul's Ethics: Twentieth Century Approaches*. Edited by B. S. Rosner. Grand Rapids: Eerdmans.

———. 2002a. "Israel, the People of God, and the Nations." *JETS* 45:35–57.

———. 2002b. "John and the Future of the Nations." *BBR* 12:243–71.

———. 2004a. *Jesus and the Twelve*. Vol. 1 of *Early Christian Mission*. Downers Grove, IL: InterVarsity Press.

———. 2004b. *Paul and the Early Church*. Vol. 2 of *Early Christian Mission*. Downers Grove, IL: InterVarsity Press.

Schnackenburg, Rudolf. 1964. *Baptism in the Thought of St. Paul: A Study in Pauline Theology*. Translated by G. R. Beasley-Murray. Oxford: Blackwell.

———. 1970. "Apostles before and during Paul's Time." Pages 287–303 in *Apostolic History and the Gospel: Biblical and Historical Essays Presented to F. F. Bruce on His Sixtieth Birthday*. Edited by W. W. Gasque and R. P. Martin. Translated by M. Kwiran and W. W. Gasque. Grand Rapids: Eerdmans.

Schneider, G. "παιδαγωγός." *EDNT* 3:2–3.

Schnider, F. "προφήτης." *EDNT* 3:183–86.

Schoeps, H. J. 1961. *Paul: The Theology of the Apostle in the Light of Jewish Religious History*. Translated by H. Knight. Philadelphia: Westminster.

Scholer, John M. 1991. *Proleptic Priests: Priesthood in the Epistle to the Hebrews*. JSNTSup 49. Sheffield: Sheffield Academic Press.

Schrage, Wolfgang. 1981. *Die konkreten Einzelgebote in paulinischen Paränese: Ein Beitrag zur neutestamentlichen Ethik*. Gütersloh: Mohn.

———. 1995. "The Formal Ethical Interpretation of Pauline Paraenesis." Pages 301–35 in *Understanding Paul's Ethics: Twentieth Century Approaches*. Edited by B. S. Rosner. Grand Rapids: Eerdmans.

Schreiner, Thomas R. 1991. "'Works of the Law' in Paul." *NovT* 33:217–44.

———. 1993a. *The Law and Its Fulfillment: A Pauline Theology of Law*. Grand Rapids: Baker Academic.

———. 1993b. "Did Paul Believe in Justification by Works? Another Look at Romans 2." *BBR* 3:131–58.

———. 1998. *Romans*. BECNT. Grand Rapids: Baker Academic.

———. 2000. "Does Romans 9 Teach Individual Election unto Salvation?" Pages 89–106 in *Still Sovereign: Contemporary Perspectives on Election, Foreknowledge, and Grace*. Edited by T. R. Schreiner and B. A. Ware. Grand Rapids: Baker Academic.

———. 2001. *Paul, Apostle of God's Glory in Christ: A Pauline Theology*. Downers Grove, IL: InterVarsity Press.

———. 2003. *1, 2 Peter, Jude*. NAC. Nashville: Broadman & Holman.

———. 2005. "An Interpretation of 1 Timothy 2:9–15: A Dialogue with Scholarship." Pages 85–120, 207–29 in *Women in the Church: An Analysis and Application of 1 Timothy 2:9–15*. Edited by A. J. Köstenberger and T. R. Schreiner. 2nd ed. Grand Rapids: Baker Academic.

———. 2006a. "A New Testament Perspective on Homosexuality." *Themelios* 31:62–75.

———. 2006b. "The Penal Substitution View." Pages 67–98 in *The Nature of the Atonement: Four Views*. Edited by J. Beilby and P. R. Eddy. Downers Grove, IL: InterVarsity Press.

———. 2006c. "Corporate and Individual Election in Romans 9: A Response to Brian Abasciano." *JETS* 49:373–86.

———. 2007. "The Commands of God." Pages 66–101 in *Central Themes in Biblical Theology: Mapping Unity in Diversity*. Edited by S. J. Hafemann and P. R. House. Nottingham, UK: Inter-Varsity Press.

———. "Circumcision." *DPL* 137–39.

Schreiner, Thomas R., and Ardel Caneday. 2001. *The Race Set before Us: A Biblical Theology of Perseverance and Assurance*. Downers Grove, IL: InterVarsity Press.

Schrenk, G. "δικαιοσύνη." *TDNT* 2:192–210.

Schultz, Richard. 1995. "The King in the Book of Isaiah." Pages 141–65 in *The Lord's Anointed: Interpretation of Old Testament Messianic Texts*. Edited by P. E. Satterthwaite, R. S. Hess, and G. J. Wenham. Grand Rapids: Baker Academic.

Schürmann, Heinz. 1974. "'Das Gesetz des Christus' (Gal. 6, 2): Jesu Verhalten und Wort als letzgültige sittliche Norm nach Paulus." Pages 282–300 in *Neues Testament und Kirche: Für Rudolf Schnackenburg*. Edited by J. Gnilka. Freiburg: Herder.

Schweitzer, Albert. 1931. *The Mysticism of Paul the Apostle*. New York: Henry Holt.

———. 1968. *The Quest of the Historical Jesus: A Critical Study of Its Progress from Reimarus to Wrede*. Translated by W. Montgomery. Repr., New York: Macmillan.

Schweizer, Eduard. 1970. *The Good News According to Mark*. Translated by D. H. Madvig. Atlanta: John Knox.

———. 1979. "Traditional Ethical Patterns in the Pauline and post-Pauline Letters and Their Development (Lists of Vices and House Tables)." Pages 195–209 in *Text and Interpretation: Studies in the New Testament Presented to Matthew Black*. Edited by E. Best and R. McL. Wilson. Cambridge: Cambridge University Press.

———. 1982. *The Letter to the Colossians*. London: SPCK.

Scobie, Charles H. H. 1991a. "The Challenge of Biblical Theology." *TynBul* 42:31–61.

———. 1991b. "The Challenge of Biblical Theology." *TynBul* 42:163–94.

———. "Biblical Theology." *NDBT* 3–20.

Scott, James M. 1992. *Adoption as Sons of God: An Exegetical Investigation into the Background of Huiothesia in the Pauline Corpus*. WUNT 2/48. Tübingen: Mohr Siebeck.

———. 1993a. "Paul's Use of Deuteronomic Tradition." *JBL* 112:645–65.

———. 1993b. "'For as Many as Are of the Works of the Law Are under a Curse' (Galatians 3:10)." Pages 187–221 in *Paul and the Scriptures of Israel*. Edited by C. A. Evans and J. A. Sanders. JSNTSup 83. Sheffield: JSOT Press.

———. 1995. *Paul and the Nations: The Old Testament and Jewish Background of Paul's Mission to the Nations with Special Reference to the Destination of Galatians*. WUNT 84. Tübingen: Mohr Siebeck.

———. 1997. *Exile: Old Testament, Jewish, and Christian Conceptions*. Edited by J. M. Scott. JSJSup 56. Leiden: Brill.

Scroggs, R. 1983. *The New Testament and Homosexuality: Background for Contemporary Debate*. Philadelphia: Fortress.

Seccombe, David Peter. 1982. *Possessions and the Poor in Luke-Acts*. SNTSU B/6. Linz: Fuchs.

———. 1998. "The New People of God." Pages 349–72 in *Witness to the Gospel: The Theology of Acts*. Edited by I. H. Marshall and D. Peterson. Grand Rapids: Eerdmans.

Segal, Alan F. 1977. *Two Powers in Heaven: Early Rabbinic Reports about Christianity and Gnosticism*. SJLA 25. Leiden: Brill.

———. 1990. *Paul the Convert: The Apostolate and Apostasy of Saul the Pharisee*. New Haven: Yale University Press.

Seifrid, Mark A. 1985. "Paul's Approach to the Old Testament in Rom. 10:6–8." *TJ* 6:3–37.

———. 1987. "Jesus and the Law in Acts." *JSNT* 30:39–57.

———. 1989. "Messiah and Mission in Acts: A Brief Response to J. B. Tyson." *JSNT* 36:47–50.

———. 1994. "Blind Alleys in the Controversy over the Paul of History." *TynBul* 45:73–95.

———. 2000a. "The 'New Perspective on Paul' and Its Problems." *Themelios* 25:8–12.

———. 2000b. *Christ, Our Righteousness: Paul's Theology of Justification*. Downers Grove, IL: InterVarsity Press.

———. 2001. "Righteousness Language in the Hebrew Scriptures and Early Judaism." Pages 415–42 in *The Complexities of Second Temple Judaism*. Vol. 1 of *Justification and Variegated Nomism: A Fresh Appraisal of Paul and Second Temple Judaism*. Edited by D. A. Carson, P. T. O'Brien, and M. A. Seifrid. WUNT 2/140. Tübingen: Mohr Siebeck; Grand Rapids: Baker Academic.

———. 2005. "The Knowledge of the Creator and the Experience of Exile: The Contours of Paul's Theo-logy." Paper presented at the Society for New Testament Studies Seminar "Inhalte und Probleme einer neutestamentlichen Theologie," Martin-Luther-Universität, Halle-Wittenberg, 2–7 August 2005.

———. "In Christ." *DPL* 433–36.

Selwyn, E. G. 1981. *The First Epistle of St. Peter*. 2nd ed. Grand Rapids: Baker Academic.

Senior, Donald. 1984. *The Passion of Jesus in the Gospel of Mark*. Wilmington, DE: Michael Glazier.

———. 1985. *The Passion of Jesus in the Gospel of Matthew*. Wilmington, DE: Michael Glazier.

———. 1989. *The Passion of Jesus in the Gospel of Luke*. Wilmington, DE: Michael Glazier.

Shelton, James B. 1991. *Mighty in Word and Deed: The Role of the Holy Spirit in Luke-Acts*. Peabody, MA: Hendrickson.

Sherwin-White, A. N. 1963. *Roman Society and Roman Law in the New Testament*. Oxford: Clarendon Press.

Silva, Moisés. 1976. "Perfection and Eschatology in Hebrews." *WTJ* 39:60–71.

———. 1986. "The Place of Historical Reconstruction in New Testament Criticism." Pages 109–33 in *Hermeneutics, Authority, and Canon*. Edited by D. A. Carson and J. D. Woodbridge. Grand Rapids: Zondervan.

———. 1990. "Is the Law against the Promises? The Significance of Galatians 3:21 for Covenant Continuity." Pages 153–66 in *Theonomy: A Reformed Critique*. Edited by W. S. Barker and W. R. Godfrey. Grand Rapids: Zondervan.

———. 2004. "Faith versus Works of Law in Galatians." Pages 217–48 in *The Paradoxes of Paul*. Vol. 2 of *Justification and Variegated Nomism: A Fresh Appraisal of Paul and Second Temple Judaism*. Edited by D. A. Carson, P. T. O'Brien, and M. A. Seifrid. WUNT 2/140. Tübingen: Mohr Siebeck; Grand Rapids: Baker Academic.

———. 2005. *Philippians*. 2nd ed. BECNT. Grand Rapids: Baker Academic.

Simpson, John W., Jr. 1990. "The Problems Posed by 1 Thessalonians 2:15–16 and a Solution." *HBT* 12:42–72.

Smalley, Stephen S. 1973. "Spirit, Kingdom and Prayer in Luke-Acts." *NovT* 15:59–71.

———. 1978. *John: Evangelist and Interpreter*. Nashville: Thomas Nelson.

———. 1984. *1, 2, 3 John*. WBC 51. Waco: Word.

Smith, Christopher R. 1990. "The Portrayal of the Church as the New Israel in the Names and Order of the Tribes in Revelation 7.5–8." *JSNT* 39:111–18.

———. 1995. "The Tribes of Revelation 7 and the Literary Competence of John the Seer." *JETS* 38:213–18.

Snodgrass, Klyne R. 1988. "Matthew and the Law." Pages 536–54 in *SBL Seminar Papers, 1988*. Edited by D. J. Lull. Atlanta: Scholars Press.

Soards, Marion L. 1987. "Käsemann's 'Righteousness' Reexamined." *CBQ* 49:264–67.

Spencer, A. B. 2000. "Peter's Pedagogical Method in 1 Peter 3:6." *BBR* 10:107–19.

Spencer, F. Scott. 2005. "Preparing the Way of the Lord: Introducing and Interpreting Luke's Narrative; A Response to David Wenham." Pages 104–24 in *Reading Luke: Interpretation, Reflection, Formation*. Edited by C. G. Bartholomew, J. B. Green, A. C. Thiselton. SHS 6. Grand Rapids: Zondervan.

Spicq, Ceslas. 1952–1953. *L'Épître aux Hébreux*. 2 vols. EBib. Paris: Gabalda.

Sproul, R. C. 1995. *Faith Alone: The Evangelical Doctrine of Justification*. Grand Rapids: Baker Academic.

Squires, John T. 1993. *The Plan of God in Luke-Acts*. SNTSMS 76. Cambridge: Cambridge University Press.

Stanley, Christopher D. 1990. "'Under a Curse': A Fresh Reading of Galatians 3:10–14." *NTS* 36:481–511.

Stanton, Graham. 1988. "Matthew." Pages 205–19 in *It Is Written: Scripture Citing Scripture; Essays in Honour of Barnabas Lindars*. Edited by D. A. Carson and H. G. M. Williamson. Cambridge: Cambridge University Press.

Starr, J. M. 2000. *Sharers in Divine Nature: 2 Peter 1:4 in Its Hellenistic Context*. ConBNT 33. Stockholm: Almqvist & Wiksell.

Stein, Robert H. 1981. *An Introduction to the Parables of Jesus*. Philadelphia: Westminster.

———. 1988. *Difficult Passages in the Epistles*. Grand Rapids: Baker Academic.

———. 2001. "N. T. Wright's *Jesus and the Victory of God:* A Review Article." *JETS* 44:207–18.

———. 2007. "Baptism in Luke-Acts." Pages 35–66 in *Believer's Baptism: Sign of the New Covenant in Christ*. Edited by T. R. Schreiner and S. D. Wright. Nashville: Broadman & Holman.

———. "Divorce." *DJG* 192–99.

Stendahl, Krister. 1976. *Paul among Jews and Gentiles, and Other Essays*. Philadelphia: Fortress.

———. "Biblical Theology, Contemporary." *IDB* 1:418–32.

Stenschke, Christoph. 1998. "The Need for Salvation." Pages 125–44 in *Witness to the Gospel: The Theology of Acts*. Edited by I. H. Marshall and D. Peterson. Grand Rapids: Eerdmans.

———. 1999. *Luke's Portrait of Gentiles Prior to Their Coming to Faith*. WUNT 2/108. Tübingen: Mohr Siebeck.

Stephenson, A. M. G. 1968. "On the Meaning of *enestēken hē hēmera tou kyriou* in 2 Thessalonians 2,2." Pages 442–51 in *Studia Evangelica: Papers Presented to the Third International Congress on New Testament Studies Held at Christ Church, Oxford, 1965*. Vol. 1. Edited by F. L. Cross. TUGAL 102. Berlin: Akademie-Verlag.

Stettler, Hanna. 1998. *Die Christologie der Pastoralbriefe*. WUNT 2/105. Tübingen: Mohr Siebeck.

———. 2004. "Sanctification in the Jesus Tradition." *Bib* 85:153–78.

Stockhausen, Carol Kern. 1989. *Moses' Veil and the Glory of the New Covenant: The Exegetical Structure of II Cor. 3, 1–4, 6*. AnBib 116. Rome: Pontifical Biblical Institute.

Stott, John. 1964. *The Epistles of John*. TNTC. Grand Rapids: Eerdmans.

Strauss, Mark L. 1995. *The Davidic Messiah in Luke-Acts: The Promise and Its Fulfillment in Lukan Christology*. JSNTSup 110. Sheffield: Sheffield Academic Press.

Strecker, Georg. 2000. *Theology of the New Testament*. Translated by M. E. Boring. Louisville: Westminster John Knox.

Stronstad, Roger. 1984. *The Charismatic Theology of St. Luke*. Peabody, MA: Hendrickson.

Stuckenbruck, Loren T. 1995. *Angel Veneration and Christology: A Study in Early Judaism and in the Christology of the Apocalypse of John*. WUNT 2/70. Tübingen: Mohr Siebeck.

———. 1999. "Johann Philipp Gabler and the Delineation of Biblical Theology." *SJT* 52:139–57.

Stuhlmacher, Peter. 1966. *Gerechtigkeit Gottes bei Paulus*. 2nd ed. FRLANT 87. Göttingen: Vandenhoeck & Ruprecht.

———. 1977. *Historical Criticism and Theological Interpretation of Scripture: Towards a Hermeneutics of Consent*. Translated by R. A. Harrisville. Philadelphia: Fortress.

———. 1983. "Jesustradition im Römerbrief: Eine Skizze." *TBei* 14:240–50.

———. 1986. *Reconciliation, Law, and Righteousness: Essays in Biblical Theology*. Philadelphia: Fortress.

———. 1987. "The Hermeneutical Significance of 1 Cor. 2:6–16." Pages 328–47 in *Tradition and Interpretation in the New Testament: Essays in Honor of E. Earle Ellis for His 60th Birthday*. Translated by C. Brown. Edited by G. F. Hawthorne and O. Betz. Grand Rapids: Eerdmans.

———. 1992. *Grundlegung: Von Jesus zu Paulus*. Vol. 1 of *Biblische Theologie des Neuen Testaments*. Göttingen: Vandenhoeck & Ruprecht.

———. 1993. *Jesus of Nazareth, Christ of Faith*. Translated by S. S. Schatzmann. Peabody, MA: Hendrickson.

———. 1994. *Paul's Letter to the Romans*. Translated by S. Hafemann. Louisville: Westminster John Knox.

———. 1999. *Von der Paulusschule bis zur Johannesoffenbarung: Der Kanon und seine Auslegung*. Vol. 2 of *Biblische Theologie des Neuen Testaments*. Göttingen: Vandenhoeck & Ruprecht.

———. 2006. "Isaiah 53 in the Gospel and Acts." Pages 147–62 in *The Suffering Servant: Isaiah 53 in Jewish and Christian Sources*. Edited by B. Janowski and P. Stuhlmacher. Translated by D. P. Bailey. Grand Rapids: Eerdmans.

Suggs, M. J. 1970. *Wisdom, Christology, and Law in Matthew's Gospel*. Cambridge: Harvard University Press.

Talbert, C. H. 1976. "Shifting Sands: The Recent Study of the Gospel of Luke." *Int* 30:381–95.

Talmon, S. 1992. "The Concepts of Mašiaḥ and Messianism in Early Judaism." Pages 79–115 in *The Messiah: Developments in Earliest Judaism and Christianity*. Edited by J. H. Charlesworth. Minneapolis: Fortress.

Tannehill, Robert C. 1986. *The Gospel according to Luke*. Vol. 1 of *The Narrative Unity of Luke-Acts: A Literary Interpretation*. Philadelphia: Fortress.

Terrien, Samuel L. 1983. *The Elusive Presence: The Heart of Biblical Theology*. San Francisco: Harper & Row.

Thielman, Frank. 1994a. "Unexpected Mercy: Echoes of a Biblical Motif in Romans 9–11." *SJT* 47:169–81.

———. 1994b. *Paul and the Law: A Contextual Approach*. Downers Grove, IL: InterVarsity Press.

———. 1995. "Law and Liberty in the Ethics of Paul." *ExAud* 11:63–75.

———. 1999. *The Law and the New Testament: The Question of Continuity*. New York: Crossroad.

———. 2005. *Theology of the New Testament: A Canonical and Synthetic Approach*. Grand Rapids: Zondervan.

Thiselton, Anthony C. 1977–1978. "Realized Eschatology at Corinth." *NTS* 24:510–26.

———. 1979. "The 'Interpretation' of Tongues: A New Suggestion in the Light of Greek Usage in Philo and Josephus." *JTS* 30:15–36.

———. 2000. *The First Epistle to the Corinthians.* NIGTC. Grand Rapids: Eerdmans.

Thompson, Cynthia L. 1988. "Hairstyles, Head-Coverings, and St. Paul: Portraits from Roman Corinth." *BA* 51:99–115.

Thompson, Marianne Meye. 1988. *The Humanity of Jesus in the Fourth Gospel.* Philadelphia: Fortress.

———. 2000. *The Promise of the Father: Jesus and God in the New Testament.* Louisville: Westminster John Knox.

———. 2001. *The God of the Gospel of John.* Grand Rapids: Eerdmans.

Thompson, Michael. 1991. *Clothed with Christ: The Example and Teaching of Jesus in Romans 12.1–15.13.* JSNTSup 59. Sheffield: JSOT Press.

Thompson, R. W. 1986. "How Is the Law Fulfilled in Us? An Interpretation of Rom. 8:4." *LS* 11:31–40.

Thurén, L. 1995. *Argument and Theology in 1 Peter: The Origins of Christian Paraenesis.* JSNTSup 114. Sheffield: Academic Press.

Tiede, David L. 1980. *Prophecy and History in Luke-Acts.* Philadelphia: Fortress.

———. 1993. "'Fighting against God': Luke's Interpretation of Jewish Rejection of the Messiah Jesus." Pages 102–12 in *Anti-Semitism and Early Christianity: Issues of Polemic and Faith.* Edited by C. A. Evans and D. A. Hagner. Minneapolis: Fortress.

Turner, Max M. B. 1982. "The Sabbath, Sunday, and the Law in Luke/Acts." Pages 100–157 in *From Sabbath to Lord's Day: A Biblical, Historical and Theological Investigation.* Edited by D. A. Carson. Grand Rapids: Zondervan.

———. 1996. *Power from on High: The Spirit in Israel's Restoration and Witness in Luke-Acts.* JPTSup 9. Sheffield: Sheffield Academic Press.

———. 1998. "The 'Spirit of Prophecy' as the Power of Israel's Restoration and Witness." Pages 327–48 in *Witness to the Gospel: The Theology of Acts.* Edited by I. H. Marshall and D. Peterson. Grand Rapids: Eerdmans.

———. 2005. "Luke and the Spirit: Renewing Theological Interpretation of Biblical Pneumatology." Pages 267–93 in *Reading Luke: Interpretation, Reflection, Formation.* Edited by C. G. Bartholomew, J. B. Green, and A. C. Thiselton. SHS 6. Grand Rapids: Zondervan.

Twelftree, Graham H. 1993. *Jesus the Exorcist: A Contribution to the Study of the Historical Jesus.* WUNT 2/54. Tübingen: Mohr Siebeck.

———. 1999. *Jesus the Miracle Worker: A Historical and Theological Study.* Downers Grove, IL: InterVarsity Press.

Tyson, Joseph B. 1986. *The Death of Jesus in Luke-Acts.* Columbia: University of South Carolina Press.

Unnik, W. C. van. 1969. "The Critique of Paganism in I Peter 1:18." Pages 129–42 in *Neotestamentica et Semitica: Studies in Honour of Matthew Black.* Edinburgh: T & T Clark.

VanderKam, J. C. 1973. "The Theophany of Enoch 1:3b-7,9." *VT* 23:129–50.

———. 1992. "Righteous One, Messiah, Chosen One, and Son of Man in 1 Enoch 37–71." Pages 169–91 in *The Messiah: Developments in Earliest Judaism and Christianity.* Edited by J. H. Charlesworth. Minneapolis: Fortress.

Vanhoozer, Kevin J. "Exegesis and Hermeneutics." *NDBT* 52–64.

Vermes, Geza. 1973. *Jesus the Jew: A Historian's Reading of the Gospels.* London: William Collins.

———. 1983. *Jesus and the World of Judaism*. Philadelphia: Fortress.

———. 1993. *The Religion of Jesus the Jew*. Minneapolis: Fortress.

Verseput, Donald J. 1987. "The Role and Meaning of the 'Son of God' Title in Matthew's Gospel." *NTS* 33:532–56.

Vickers, Brian. 2004. "The Kingdom of God in Mark." *SBJT* 8:12–35.

———. 2006. *Jesus' Blood and Righteousness: Paul's Theology of Imputation*. Wheaton: Crossway.

Vielhauer, Phillip. 1963. "Jesus and der Menschensohn: Zur Diskussion mit Heinz Eduard Tödt und Eduard Schweizer." *ZTK* 60:133–77.

———. 1966. "On the 'Paulinism' of Acts." Pages 33–50 in *Studies in Luke-Acts: Essays Presented in Honor of Paul Schubert*. Edited by L. Keck and J. L. Martyn. Nashville: Abingdon.

Von Rad, Gerhard. 1962. *The Theology of Israel's Historical Traditions*. Vol. 1 of *Old Testament Theology*. Translated by D. M. G. Stalker. New York: Harper & Row.

———. 1965. *The Theology of Israel's Prophetic Traditions*. Vol. 2 of *Old Testament Theology*. Translated by D. M. G. Stalker. New York: Harper & Row.

Vos, Geerhardus. 1930. *The Pauline Eschatology*. Phillipsburg, NJ: Presbyterian & Reformed Publishing.

———. 1953. *The Self-Disclosure of Jesus: The Modern Debate about the Messianic Consciousness*. Edited by J. G. Vos. 2nd ed. Phillipsburg, NJ: Presbyterian & Reformed Publishing.

———. 1980. *Redemptive History and Biblical Interpretation: The Shorter Writings of Geerhardus Vos*. Edited by R. B. Gaffin Jr. Phillipsburg, NJ: Presbyterian & Reformed Publishing.

———. 2001. *The Eschatology of the Old Testament*. Edited by J. T. Dennison Jr. Phillipsburg, NJ: Presbyterian & Reformed Publishing.

Vouga, François. 2001. *Une théologie du Nouveau Testament*. MdB 43. Geneva: Labor et Fides.

Wagner, Günter. 1967. *Pauline Baptism and the Pagan Mysteries: The Problem of the Pauline Doctrine of Baptism in Romans VI.1–11 in the Light of Its Religio-Historical 'Parallels.'* Edinburgh: Oliver & Boyd.

Wagner, J. Ross. 2002. *Heralds of the Good News: Isaiah and Paul "in Concert" in the Letter to the Romans*. NovTSup 101. Leiden: Brill.

Wallace, Daniel B. 1996. *Greek Grammar Beyond the Basics: An Exegetical Syntax of the New Testament*. Grand Rapids: Zondervan.

Wallis, Ian G. 1995. *The Faith of Jesus Christ in Early Christian Traditions*. SNTSMS 84. Cambridge: Cambridge University Press.

Walton, Steve. 2000. *Leadership and Lifestyle: The Portrait of Paul in the Miletus Speech and 1 Thessalonians*. SNTSMS 108. Cambridge: Cambridge University Press.

Walvoord, John F. 1966. *The Revelation of Jesus Christ*. Chicago: Moody.

Wanamaker, C. A. 1990. *The Epistles to the Thessalonians*. NIGTC. Grand Rapids: Eerdmans.

Warfield, B. B. 1950. *The Person and Work of Christ*. Grand Rapids: Baker Academic.

Watson, Francis. 2004. *Paul and the Hermeneutics of Faith*. London: T & T Clark.

Watts, Rikki E. 1998. "Jesus' Death, Isaiah 53, and Mark 10:45: A Crux Revisited." Pages 125–51 in *Jesus and the Suffering Servant: Isaiah 53 and Christian Origins*. Edited by W. H. Bellinger Jr. and W. R. Farmer. Harrisburg, PA: Trinity Press International.

———. 2000. *Isaiah's New Exodus in Mark*. Grand Rapids: Baker Academic.

Webb, Robert L. 1991. *John the Baptizer and Prophet: A Socio-historical Study*. JSNTSup 62. Sheffield: Sheffield Academic Press.

Webb, W. J. 1993. *Returning Home: New Covenant and Second Exodus as the Context for 2 Corinthians 6:14–7:1*. JSNTSup 85. Sheffield: JSOT Press.

Wedderburn, A. J. M. 1987. *Baptism and Resurrection: Studies in Pauline Theology against Its Graeco-Roman Background*. WUNT 44. Tübingen: Mohr Siebeck.

Weima, Jeffrey A. D. 1990. "The Function of the Law in Relation to Sin: An Evaluation of the View of H. Räisänen." *NovT* 32:219–35.

———. 1993. "Gal. 6:11–18: A Hermeneutical Key to the Galatian Letter." *CTJ* 28:90–107.

———. 1994. *Neglected Endings: The Significance of the Pauline Letter Closings*. JSNTSup 101. Sheffield: JSOT Press.

Weinfeld, Moshe. 1972. *Deuteronomy and the Deuteronomic School*. Oxford: Clarendon Press.

Weiser, Alfons. 1993. *Theologie des Neuen Testaments II: Die Theologie des Evangelien*. KSt 8. Stuttgart: Kohlhammer.

Weiss, Johannes. 1971. *Jesus' Proclamation of the Kingdom of God*. Philadelphia: Fortress.

Wendland, E. R. 2000. "'Stand Fast in the True Grace of God!' A Study of 1 Peter." *JTT* 13:25–102.

Wenham, David. 1987. "Being 'Found' on the Last Day: New Light on 2 Peter 3:10 and 2 Corinthians 5:3." *NTS* 33:477–79.

———. 1995. *Paul: Follower of Jesus or Founder of Christianity?* Grand Rapids: Eerdmans.

———. 2005. "The Purpose of Luke-Acts: Israel's Story in the Context of the Roman Empire." Pages 79–103 in *Reading Luke: Interpretation, Reflection, Formation*. Edited by C. G. Bartholomew, J. B. Green, and A. C. Thiselton. SHS 6. Grand Rapids: Zondervan.

Wenham, Gordon J. 1995. "The Theology of Old Testament Sacrifice." Pages 75–87 in *Sacrifice in the Bible*. Edited by R. T. Beckwith and M. J. Selman. Grand Rapids: Baker Academic.

———. 2002. "Does the New Testament Approve Remarriage after Divorce?" *SBJT* 6:30–45.

Westerholm, Stephen. 1978. *Jesus and Scribal Authority*. ConBNT 10. Lund: Gleerup.

———. 1986. "Torah, *nomos*, and Law: A Question of 'Meaning.'" *SR* 15:327–36.

———. 1988. *Israel's Law and the Church's Faith: Paul and His Recent Interpreters*. Grand Rapids: Eerdmans.

———. 2004. *Perspectives Old and New on Paul: The "Lutheran" Paul and His Critics*. Grand Rapids: Eerdmans.

———. 2006. "Justification by Faith Is the Answer: What Is the Question?" http://www.ctsfw.edu/events/symposia/papers/sym2006westerholm.pdf (accessed May 23, 2006).

Whybray, R. N. 1978. *Thanksgiving for a Liberated Prophet: An Interpretation of Isaiah Chapter 53*. JSOTSup 4. Sheffield: Department of Biblical Studies, University of Sheffield.

Wilckens, Ulrich. 1980. *Der Brief an die Römer*. Vol. 2. EKKNT. Zürich: Neukirchener Verlag.

———. 1982. "Zur Entwicklung des paulinischen Gesetzesverständnisses." *NTS* 28:154–90.

———. 2003. *Jesu Tod und Auferstehung und die Entstehung der Kirche aus Juden und Heiden.* Part 2 of *Geschichte der urchristlichen Theologie,* vol. 1 of *Theologie des Neuen Testaments.* Neukirchen-Vluyn: Neukirchener Verlag.

———. 2005a. *Geschichte des Wirkens Jesu in Galiläa.* Part 1 of *Geschichte der urchristlichen Theologie,* vol. 1 of *Theologie des Neuen Testaments.* 2nd ed. Neukirchen-Vluyn: Neukirchener Verlag.

———. 2005b. *Die Briefe des Urchristentums: Paulus und seine Schüler, Theologen aus dem Bereich judenchristlicher Heidenmission.* Part 3 of *Geschichte der urchristlichen Theologie,* vol. 1 of *Theologie des Neuen Testaments.* Neukirchen-Vluyn: Neukirchener Verlag.

———. 2005c. *Die Evangelien, die Apostelgeschichte, die Johannesbriefe, die Offenbarung und die Entstehung des Kanons.* Part 4 of *Geschichte der urchristlichen Theologie,* vol. 1 of *Theologie des Neuen Testaments.* Neukirchen-Vluyn: Neukirchener Verlag.

———. Forthcoming. *Kritik der historischen Bibelkritik.* Vol. 3 of *Theologie des Neuen Testaments.* Neukirchen-Vluyn: Neukirchener Verlag.

Wilkins, Michael J. 1995. *Discipleship in the Ancient World and Matthew's Gospel.* 2nd ed. Grand Rapids: Baker Academic.

Williams, Catrin H. 2000. *I Am He: The Interpretation of "Anî Hû" in Jewish and Early Christian Literature.* WUNT 2/113. Tübingen: Mohr Siebeck.

Williams, Sam K. 1975. *Jesus' Death as Saving Event: The Background and Origin of a Concept.* HDR 2. Missoula, MT: Scholars Press.

———. 1980. "The 'Righteousness of God' in Romans." *JBL* 49:241–90.

———. 1987. "Again *Pistis Christou.*" *JBL* 49:431–47.

Williamson, Ronald H. 1970. *Philo and the Epistle to the Hebrews.* ALGHJ 4. Leiden: Brill.

Wilson, Stephen G. 1983. *Luke and the Law.* SNTSMS 50. Cambridge: Cambridge University Press.

Wink, Walter. 1984. *Naming the Powers: The Language of Power in the New Testament.* Philadephia: Fortress.

Winter, Bruce W. 1997. *Philo and Paul among the Sophists.* SNTSMS 96. Cambridge: Cambridge University Press.

Wisdom, Jeffrey R. 2001. *Blessing for the Nations and the Curse of the Law: Paul's Citation of Genesis and Deuteronomy in Gal. 3.8–10.* WUNT 2/133. Tübingen: Mohr Siebeck.

Witherington, Ben, III. 1984. *Women in the Ministry of Jesus: A Study of Jesus' Attitudes to Women and Their Roles as Reflected in His Earthly Life.* SNTSMS 51. Cambridge: Cambridge University Press.

———. 1990. *The Christology of Jesus.* Minneapolis: Fortress.

———. 1992. *Jesus, Paul and the End of the World.* Downers Grove, IL: InterVarsity Press.

———. 1994. *Jesus the Sage: The Pilgrimage of Wisdom.* Minneapolis: Fortress.

———. 1998. "Salvation and Health in Christian Antiquity: The Soteriology of Luke-Acts in Its First Century Setting." Pages 145–66 in *Witness to the Gospel: The Theology of Acts.* Edited by I. H. Marshall and D. Peterson. Grand Rapids: Eerdmans.

Witmer, Stephen E. 2006. "*Theodidaktoi* in 1 Thessalonians 4:9: A Pauline Neologism." *NTS* 52:239–50.

Wolters, A. 1987. "Worldview and Textual Criticism in 2 Peter 3:10." *CTJ* 25:28–44.

Wrede, William. 1962. *Paul.* Repr., Lexington: American Theological Library Association.

———. 1971. *The Messianic Secret*. Translated by J. C. G. Greig. Greenwood, SC: Attic.

Wright, N. T. 1980. "The Meaning of περὶ ἁμαρτίας in Romans 8:3." Pages 453–59 in *Papers on Paul and Other New Testament Authors*. Vol. 3 of *Studia Biblica 1978: Sixth International Congress on Biblical Studies, Oxford, 30 April 1978*. Edited by E. A. Livingstone. JSNTSup 3. Sheffield: JSOT Press.

———. 1992a. *The Climax of the Covenant: Christ and the Law in Pauline Theology*. Minneapolis: Fortress.

———. 1992b. *The New Testament and the People of God*. Vol. 1 of *Christian Origins and the Question of God*. Minneapolis: Fortress.

———. 1995. "Romans and the Theology of Paul." Pages 3–67 in *Romans*. Vol. 3 of *Pauline Theology*. Edited by D. M. Hay and E. E. Johnson. Minneapolis: Fortress.

———. 1996. *Jesus and the Victory of God*. Vol. 2 of *Christian Origins and the Question of God*. Minneapolis: Fortress.

———. 1997. *What St. Paul Really Said: Was Paul of Tarsus the Real Founder of Christianity?* Grand Rapids: Eerdmans.

———. 1998. "The Servant and Jesus: The Relevance of the Colloquy for the Current Quest for Jesus." Pages 281–97 in *Jesus and the Suffering Servant: Isaiah 53 and Christian Origins*. Edited by W. H. Bellinger Jr. and W. R. Farmer. Harrisburg, PA: Trinity Press International.

———. 2003. *The Resurrection of the Son of God*. Vol. 3 of *Christian Origins and the Question of God*. Minneapolis: Fortress.

Yamauchi, E. 1973. *Pre-Christian Gnosticism: A Survey of the Proposed Evidences*. Grand Rapids: Eerdmans.

Yarbrough, Robert W. 2004. *The Salvation Historical Fallacy? Reassessing the History of New Testament Theology*. History of Biblical Interpretation 2. Leiden: Deo.

Yeung, Maureen W. 2002. *Faith in Jesus and Paul: A Comparison with Special Reference to 'Faith That Can Remove Mountains' and 'Your Faith Has Healed/Saved You.'* WUNT 2/147. Tübingen: Mohr Siebeck.

Yinger, Kent L. 1999. *Paul, Judaism, and Judgment according to Deeds*. SNTSMS 105. Cambridge: Cambridge University Press.

Young, Frances M. 1994. "On *Episkopos* and *Presbyteros*." *JTS* 45:142–49.

———. 1998. "Who's Cursed—and Why? (Galatians 3:10–14)." *JBL* 117:79–92.

Young, Norman H. 1987. "Paidagogos: The Social Setting of a Pauline Metaphor." *NovT* 29:150–76.

Zehnle, Richard. 1969. "The Salvific Character of Jesus' Death in Lucan Soteriology." *TS* 30:420–44.

Ziesler, J. A. 1972. *The Meaning of Righteousness in Paul: A Linguistic and Theological Enquiry*. SNTSMS 20. Cambridge: Cambridge University Press.

———. 1988. "The Role of the Tenth Commandment in Romans 7." *JSNT* 33:31–56.

———. 1989. *Paul's Letter to the Romans*. TPINTC. Philadelphia: Trinity Press International.

Zimmerli, W., and J. Jeremias. 1957. *The Servant of God*. London: SCM Press.

Name Index

Scripture Index

Romans

Subject Index